WEST LEGAL STUDIES IN BUSINESS
ACADEMIC SERIES

REAL ESTATE LAW

EIGHTH EDITION

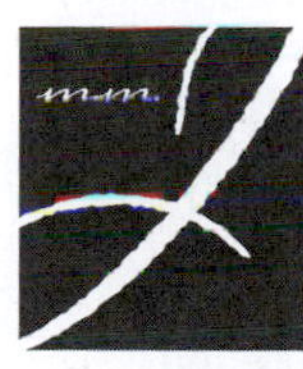

MARIANNE M. JENNINGS
Professor of Legal and Ethical Studies
W.P. Carey School of Business
Arizona State University
Member of the Arizona State Bar

Australia · Brazil · Canada · Mexico · Singapore · Spain · United Kingdom · United States

Real Estate Law
Marianne M. Jennings

VP/Editorial Director:
Jack W. Calhoun

Editor-in-Chief:
Rob Dewey

Acquisitions and Developmental Editor:
Steve Silverstein

Marketing Manager:
Jennifer Garamy

Associate Content Project Manager:
Scott Dillon

Managing Technology Project Manager:
Pam Wallace

Associate Technology Project Manager:
Rob Ellington

Manufacturing Coordinator:
Kevin Kluck

Senior Art Director:
Michelle Kunkler

Cover and Internal Designer:
Ke Design, Cincinnati

Cover Image:
© Joe Sohm/Getty Images, Inc.

Production House:
Integra Software Services (P) Ltd.

Printer:
Thomson West
Eagan, MN

Printed in the United States of America
1 2 3 4 5 10 09 08 07

ISBN 13: 978-0-324-65020-4
ISBN 10: 0-324-65020-5

Library of Congress Control Number: 2007925969

For more information about our products, contact us at:
Thomson Learning Academic Resource Center
1-800-423-0563

Thomson Higher Education
5191 Natorp Boulevard
Mason, OH 45040
USA

BRIEF CONTENTS

CONTENTS

Part 1: The Nature of Real Estate and Ownership of Real Estate Interests

Part 2: Real Estate Ownership

PREFACE

Since the time that the 7th edition of *Real Estate Law* was published, the dull, old area of real estate law has suddenly catapulted to the front page of newspapers and become a topic of heated debate. The housing market exploded around the country, and economic development, coupled with the taking of property, caught the eye of even the U.S. Supreme Court. NIMBYs (not in my backyard) caught our attention for their vocal objections and lawsuits. NoWIMPs (not with my property) were challenging takings and gaining ballot propositions to control eminent domain. Housing prices skyrocketed, but low interest rates still brought record numbers of buyers into the home markets. Many of those buyers took on sizeable mortgages that have left them and us with questions, yet again, about adjustable rate mortgages. And then came the subprime lenders. Real estate value has attracted investors interested in its infamous profits from a "flip," or quick sale. And then we have experienced the tyranny and benefits of homeowners' associations. They control everything from the color of houses to the monthly fees to whether owners can fly flags.

It feels as if muddling old real estate law has become the topic on the tip of everyone's tongues since the time of the 7th edition. The conversations bring questions: How much power does this homeowners' association have? Can the city really take my property to put in a Bass Pro Shop? And this ARM is still a hefty mortgage, can I get out of it? There are market pressures, fast-moving transactions, and even some who would take advantage of a thriving market and high demand. As a result, there are new laws and regulations affecting everything from listing agreements to homeowners' associations to economic development and takings. The events of September 11, 2001, continue to affect real estate transactions via the Patriot Act and required disclosures on the transfer of property via escrow agents (see Chapter 16 for more information).

Real Estate Law has been a practical and hands-on study of the laws affecting real property since the time of the first edition in 1984. However, now in its 23rd year and 8th edition, *Real Estate Law* charts new territory with its clear and cutting-edge coverage of everything from the basics to the new issues and laws that affect real property.

This edition continues its focus on the three-step approach to understanding the laws that affect real estate:

1. A clear explanation of the applicable laws
2. An example, a case, or a Consider question to help the reader see the application of the law in a particular circumstance.
3. Review materials for self-testing on the concepts presented, such as more Considers and the chapter problems.

You find no feudal land systems or archaic terms as a focus of this text. Brokers faced with dual-representation issues need clear discussions of the law and how to apply it. Partners, couples, and putative spouses continue to have their disputes over property with new categories of rights in those relationships. Home buyers faced with questions about their homeowners' association need simple explanations of their rights (see Chapter 11). What the 8th edition continues to offer is a format for learning and understanding.

Most real estate books favor a black-letter law approach in which the laws, rules, and terms are presented, but few or no cases and examples help students and professionals grasp the concept and understand how it affects their decisions, rights, and planning.

This is a book that continues to address the real-life situations that those involved in real property transactions encounter. The problems and cases in this and previous editions have been developed through classroom use and experience from my 30 years of teaching. This teaching approach allows the students to really understand and grasp the material, and they are able to use their problem-solving skills in their professional and personal real estate transactions. If there were ever a remark I dreaded to hear from a student, it was, "I'll never use this." Each chapter shows students how they will use the material.

Real Estate Law has long been an innovative book that showed that the law of real property need not be a boring subject. Within the pages of the 8th edition the reader will find a judicial decision on the validity of Barry Bonds' prenuptial agreement; the *Kelo* case that changed eminent domain forever; several NIMBY cases; a case on whether drug use should preclude an individual from being a licensed real estate agent; a decision that explains when emotional issues related to a property's use must be disclosed; and an update on the legislative activity in this highly emotional area! Readers can study what happens when buyers try to avoid a real estate agent in order to escape paying the agent's commission. They can also learn when minimum-age requirements for housing are valid and what a landlord can do when a tenant is using or selling drugs in the rented property. And what happens when a homeowners' association tries to foreclose on your property for not paying your fines?

This book does not turn its readers into real estate lawyers; however, it does train the lay person to spot legal issues and important areas in which extra caution, and perhaps legal advice, is warranted. The reader will understand the material, but the ghosts, the baseball players, and the eccentric nude tenant will help make the principles learned endure.

The Revised Edition

As the saying goes, "If it ain't broke, don't fix it." The 1st through 7th editions of *Real Estate Law* were well received by students and instructors. Indeed, many brokers, agents, developers, and lawyers have found it to be a useful handbook. It has proved to be a successful textbook as well as a practical guide for those in the industry. The 8th edition continues the successful and unique features of previous editions.

However, we do listen when feedback comes, and the complexion of the real estate industry has changed over the 23 years of this book's publication. This edition brings a few organizational changes and a number of expanded topics. The chapter on multiunit housing has been renamed to reflect increased coverage of homeowners' associations in all types of home ownership. The chapter on land development has been reorganized and revamped to reflect the dramatic increase in issues related to economic development. This edition continues its coverage of the social issues related to real estate ownership, including group homes, social-issue zoning, issues related to the Americans with Disabilities Act, Section 8 housing, environmental issues, and the evolving law on disclosures on so-called meth houses and other property use and location issues.

Real Estate Law, 8th edition, has new materials, updated materials, and some reorganization, but the color, excitement, and interest levels of the first seven editions have only increased. There has, yet again, been substantial rewriting to rid us of the passive voice, which has been reduced slowly but surely through each edition. The reworking brings yet more life to real property. Activism in real estate law issues has brought even more real life to this edition.

Organization

The 8th edition carries through the four-part organization. Part 1 covers the basics of real estate law: the nature of real estate and real estate interests, included to provide the students with a richer backdrop earlier in the text. "Land Interests: Present and Future" remains as Chapter 2 so that students have the big picture of the types of ownership and land interests before delving into specific issues related to land ownership, such as easements and liens. New to this edition is the restructuring of Chapter 11 on multiunit interests to expand the coverage of the dynamic area of association law and the rights of owners.

Part 2 focuses exclusively on legal issues related to the types of land ownership. Part 3 remains a collection of all the legal issues involved in all types of transfers of title to property. Part 3 takes the transfer of property from listing agreement to financing to closing of escrow.

Part 4 continues to cover the issues related to land use and development such as zoning, environmental concerns, and constitutional rights and constraints with regard to land use and transfer, with the order of the chapters varied slightly to strengthen the flow of the material. The combined chapter on real estate development, first introduced in the 6th edition, has changed substantially in this edition to reflect the critical role of economic development projects and local governments in the land development process. This chapter, because of its topics of significance, has been moved ahead of the final chapter on tax issues.

The structure of the 8th edition still allows instructors to cover chapters as they see fit and even reorder the coverage. Cross-references in all chapters help with such restructuring and can show students how the chapter pieces fit together to supply them with an understanding of all the laws and regulations affecting real property.

Text Features

Cases

Very few real estate law books have the benefit of reported cases. The cases used are colorful illustrations of points covered in the descriptive materials. I have rewritten the facts of the cases in order to simplify the court's language and help students attain a clear grasp of the facts before they begin to read and understand the judicial opinion. After the judge's name is listed, the language of the court begins. However, I have also carefully edited the opinions chosen and reduced their length in order to be sure students grasp the point and the court's analysis. There are new cases throughout the 8th edition, many of them with 2006 dates.

Case Questions

The restatement of case facts and significant editing help students grasp even the most complex judicial decisions on real property law. However, to be sure that the students understand the case decisions, each case is followed by Case Questions to review facts and findings and to help the students think about what they have read and how to apply it. The case questions ensure that the readers understand both the facts of the case and the conclusion of the court.

Practical Tips

Highlighted suggestions for avoiding legal problems and litigation in real estate, called Practical Tips, have been updated and appear in each chapter. These tips include lists, questions, and ways to avoid the problems that caused the litigation in the chapter cases and Considers. The tips provide yet another practical component to the text and increase its value as a handbook.

Consider Questions

Numbered Consider questions, appearing immediately after their applicable text material, help readers grasp the segments of each chapter as they read along. These questions refine reading habits as well as improve comprehension.

Ethical Issues

Continuing this popular feature, this edition includes updated Ethical Issues for each chapter. These real and hypothetical problems allow students to discuss and debate real-world dilemmas that real estate professionals face regularly.

Web Exhibits

First introduced in the 6th edition, the forms that took up great amounts of text space have been omitted from the text and noted with a Web Exhibit designation. These exhibits are found on the text website; this process enables students and instructors to see the most up-to-date forms that are discussed in the text and frees up the text for coverage of more material. Simply go to the website at **www.thomsonedu.com/westbuslaw/jennings**, click on the title of this edition, and then, on the menu to the left, choose Internet Applications to select the correct chapter and exhibit.

Charts, Diagrams, and Illustrations

Throughout the book, charts, diagrams, and illustrations aid readers' understanding of the lengthy and complex topics. For example, there are charts and diagrams depicting the relationships of land interests, Article 9 security interests, easements, and the relationships between and among contractors and subcontractors. This edition offers PowerPoint slides for instructors to use that include the figures from the chapters as well as additional diagrams, problems, illustrations, and charts to help with teaching.

Cautions and Conclusions

Each chapter concludes with Cautions and Conclusions, a feature that wraps up the issues addressed in the chapter. In some chapters, there are precautions, recommendations, or points critical for real estate transactions and professionals in the real world. In other chapters, these are conclusions to be drawn from reading the material covered.

Chapter Problems

Most of the end-of-chapter problems are actual cases, with the case citations. Answers are provided in the *Instructor's Manual/Test Bank.* The cases are short enough to spark interest and yet detailed enough to allow discussion and review of the chapter concepts. Many chapter problems were once cases in the 1st through 7th editions and have become end-of-chapter review problems as new cases replaced them. Some of the previous cases are found in full in the *Instructor's Manual/Test Bank* so that an instructor could copy and distribute the case to have the students read for purposes of determining the answer to the chapter problems.

Glossary

The glossary of key terms appears at the end of the text and provides short definitions of the terms that are bold-faced in the text.

Supplemental Items

Instructor's Manual/Test Bank (ISBN: 0-324-26995-1)

The *Instructor's Manual/Test Bank* was designed to help in lecture preparation. Each chapter is outlined in detail, with examples and illustrations of each of the chapter points. The cases are briefed within the outline as they appear in the text. Answers to all of the Case Questions, Consider questions, and Chapter Problems are provided in the *Instructor's Manual/Test Bank.* Also included are discussion suggestions and resolution for the Ethical Issues.

Each chapter in the Instructor's Manual has a list of books and law review articles called Resources. These materials can be used to enhance the instructor's understanding of a topic. They have been updated for this edition.

Some cases that were eliminated from the 1st through 7th editions to make way for new ones have been added to the *Instructor's Manual/Test Bank* to provide supplemental readings for class use. Interactive learning exercises for each chapter, called In-Class Exercises, are again provided in this edition.

Also included in the manual are sample examination questions. There are true/false, multiple-choice, and essay questions for each chapter. The true/false questions are easier and can be used for a quick review quiz. The multiple-choice and essay questions require the students not only to know the laws and materials covered but to think and apply them to various scenarios that differ from any presented in the cases, Considers, and problems in the chapter. This edition offers a still larger menu from which instructors can select questions.

Real Estate Law Website

The website for *Real Estate Law,* at **www.thomsonedu.com/westbuslaw/jennings**, contains supplements, Internet materials from the text, Web Exhibits, case updates, and links to other useful West Legal Studies sites, including West's Legal Resources Center. The Resources Center provides course support for students and instructors.

eCoursepacks

eCoursepacks provide a tailor-fit, easy to use, and online companion for your course. eCoursepacks give educators access to content from thousands of current popular, professional, and academic periodicals; business and industry information from Gale; and the ability to easily add your own material. Permissions for all eCoursepack content are already secured, saving you the time and worry of securing rights.

eCoursepacks' online publishing tools also save you time, allowing you to quickly search the databases and make selections, organize all your content, and publish the final online product in a clean, uniform, and full-color format. eCoursepacks are the best way to provide your audience with current information easily, quickly, and inexpensively. To learn more, visit **http://ecoursepacks.swlearning.com**.

Videos

Videos are available to qualified adopters using this text. You may be eligible to access the entire library of West videos, a vast selection covering most business law issues. There are some restrictions, and if you have questions, please contact your local Thomson Learning/West Legal Studies Sales Representative or visit **http://www.westbuslaw.com/video_library.html**.

Debts of Gratitude

Although only my name appears on this book, I cannot claim it as my book alone. As with all achievements in my life, my finished work is the result of the cooperation, work, and sacrifice of many. I cannot name everyone who has helped me in my continuing evolution as an author, but there are those who warrant special note for their efforts in bringing this work to publication:

- Dick Crews, my original editor, who had the educational foresight to see the need for this book and who has been proven correct through the success of seven editions. In 1983 Dick said, "Your book will be around for a long time." Twenty years and counting.
- James Moody, my dad, a never-ending source of stories, fodder, and the right thing to do when buying and selling real estate.
- Steve Silverstein, the acquisitions editor who stepped in to take over as Developmental Editor
- My patient and tolerant Production Editor Scott Dillon, whose job it was to be patient as I slipped on sending things in.
- My students who continue to teach me how to improve *Real Estate Law*
- Kris Tabor, my long-suffering friend and assistant, who handles the unenviable tasks of word processing my scribbles into a polished instructor's manual
- The instructors who use *Real Estate Law* and communicate with me via e-mail to update me, correct me, and offer their insights on teaching
- The reviewers for this edition for their work in offering improvements and suggestions. My thanks to the following reviewers:
  - Hakim Ben Adjoua, Columbus State Community College
  - Dr. Ronald C. Goldfarb, Middlesex County College
  - Karen A. Holmes, Hudson Valley Community College
  - Ann Morales Olazábal, University of Miami
  - William C. Weaver, University of Central Florida
- All of the Realtors, developers, lenders, lawyers, and companies that have consented to have their forms and works reproduced in this text in order to make the experience of learning hands-on for the students. Their dedication to education is evidenced by their complete cooperation in granting permission for these items to be used.
- Last, but certainly not least, I am grateful to my husband, Terry, and my children, Sarah, Sam, and John, who sacrifice some of their quality time with me as I hover over the computer. Their "How many chapters do you have left?" keeps me going. I am grateful that they care and are involved. Their presence with me

in my office, lying on the floor doing their homework as I worked, is something I cherish. During the production of this edition, our darling daughter Claire passed away after nearly 20 years of a life with profound disabilities. Her stamina, her patience, her cheerfulness, and her willingness to endure remain with me as reminders of what we can do if we but forge onward. And so we do, but always with her example as the goal.

A Word for Students

In using this book, read the material that describes the law first. Follow that by reading the cases that appear in each section. Answer the case questions after each case to make sure that you understood the case and that you grasped the issues and principles of law. Try to solve the Consider questions and Chapter Problems on your own before the instructor gives you the answers. If you can solve all the Consider and Chapter Problems, you understand the chapter material. The figures in chart form are designed to streamline ideas and summarize lengthy topics so that you can commit the concepts to memory. The charts are an excellent form of review for examinations and quizzes. Also visit the text's website for important case updates and other useful links.

If you would like to consult the Uniform Commercial Code, especially Article 9 on secured transactions, you can go to http://www.nccusl.org. or to http://www.law.cornell.edu/ucc/ucc.table.html.

Finally, remember to apply what you have learned when your course is over. Application is the true test of learning. Good luck with the book and its application. Enjoy the color and flavor of real estate law—it is abundant in this book. And I am always happy to hear from you, at marianne.jennings@asu.edu

Marianne M. Jennings

Introduction and Sources of Real Estate Law

CHAPTER 1

Possession is nine points of the law.

Source unknown

The above quote is but one example of an old adage on the laws that govern property ownership. In some areas of real estate law, this old adage is the guiding principle. While the source of this particular principle of real estate law may be unknown, there are a significant number of well-known and detailed sources of real estate law, and this chapter answers the question, Where can real estate law be found? One distinguishing feature of real estate law is that its problems are not solved by turning to a single statute or ordinance: A zoning issue cannot be resolved by examining only city ordinances, and a question on adverse possession is not always answered by turning to a statute.

Real estate law is not one simple body of law, as its name implies. Rather, it is made up of many different types of laws that have been passed by many different bodies at varying levels of government. No single governmental body issues laws that are complete or exclusive sources of real estate law. Those who are involved with real estate should be familiar with the laws that affect real estate ownership, use, and transactions and the sources of those laws. A familiarity with who and what are involved in the making of real estate law helps to ensure that those included in real estate transactions do not overlook legal issues, rights, or processes. Knowing which sources to check to determine legal concerns helps prevent major problems, dissatisfaction, and perhaps even litigation.

Sources of Real Estate Law

If all the sources of real estate law were diagrammed in a scheme depicting their relationships, such a scheme would probably take the pyramidal form depicted in Figure 1.1.

Figure 1.1 Sources of Real Estate Law

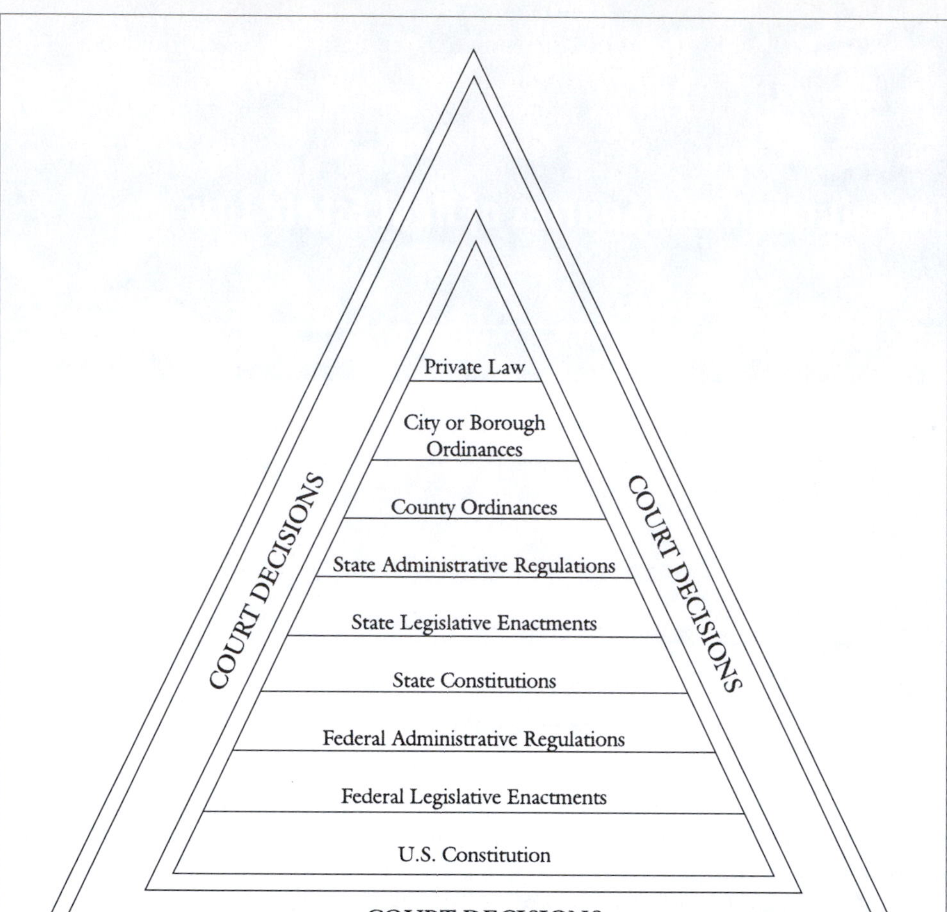

The discussion of these sources of law will begin at the bottom of the pyramid with the United States Constitution. All other sources of real estate law must be consistent with the constitutional rights that are shown as the foundation of this pyramid. Court decisions, the final area of discussion, have their position in the pyramid and discussion because these decisions can deal with laws in any of the other pyramid sources.

The United States Constitution

The **United States Constitution** has several provisions that affect real estate transfers and ownership. The Fourth Amendment affords property owners the right to be secure in their "houses," and from this language has sprung a long series of cases on property owners' rights regarding searches and seizures on their property, as well as the proper issuance and execution of search warrants.

The provisions of the Constitution most relevant to real estate law are two similar clauses found in the Fifth and Fourteenth Amendments. The **Fifth Amendment** prohibits the federal government from depriving any person of "property without due process of law" and from taking private property for public use "without just compensation." The due process provisions have resulted in many cases that deal with obtaining judgments against a person's property and foreclosing on a security interest or mortgage in real property. (See Chapters 5, 15, and 19.) The just-compensation provision offers protection for landowners when their property is to be taken by the government. This practice, referred to as **eminent domain**, has resulted in a long series of litigated cases (Chapter 19) involving questions such as, When is the government actually taking property? and What constitutes just compensation? For example, one issue that the U.S. Supreme Court recently addressed is whether a local government has a sufficient public purpose for taking private land when the reason for the taking is economic development. The court issued a decision in a controversial and emotional area: When can local governments take private property to allow a different use?

The **Fourteenth Amendment's** language is almost identical to the Fifth Amendment, but applies to state governments. The Fourteenth Amendment provides that no state may "deprive any person of... property, without due process of law." The amendment puts further restrictions on state laws by making it unconstitutional for any state law to interfere with any rights given to citizens in the U.S. Constitution. The Fourteenth Amendment also requires the states to apply the law equally to all citizens so that all citizens enjoy the same protections, the same forms of relief, and equal opportunities for land ownership. Many of the racial discrimination cases on land purchases and sales have been based on this portion of the Fourteenth Amendment, which is referred to as the **Equal Protection Clause**.

These constitutional provisions set the parameters or establish the minimum rights that cannot be violated by the other governmental bodies that make laws. Constitutional provisions seem broad and general, but they protect fundamental rights in real estate ownership, transactions, and processes.

Federal Legislative Enactments

The Constitution establishes a legislative branch of the federal government, which is authorized to enact laws to carry out the objectives of the Constitution and for the operation of the federal government. Congress, as the legislative branch created in the Constitution, can pass legislation, as part of its jurisdiction, that regulates real estate transactions. All Congressional enactments are printed in a series of volumes called the **United States Code (U.S.C.)**. The major Congressional enactments affecting real estate transactions are discussed in great detail in subsequent chapters, but the following examples illustrate the types of laws found in the United States Code following their Congressional passage:

- The **Interstate Land Sales Full Disclosure Act (ILSFDA)** deals with the sale of undeveloped land to out-of-state residents. 15 U.S.C. §§ 1701 *et seq.* (discussed in Chapter 14).
- The **Real Estate Settlement Procedures Act (RESPA)** deals with maximum closing costs and good-faith estimates of closing costs. 12 U.S.C. §§ 2601 *et seq.* (discussed in Chapter 16).
- The **Internal Revenue Code (IRC)** deals with the income tax and depreciation aspects of real estate transactions. 26 U.S.C. §§ 1 *et seq.* (discussed in Chapter 22).
- The **Comprehensive Environmental Response, Compensation, and Liability Act (CERCLA)** is a federal act that authorizes the cleanup of disposal sites for hazardous waste and permits the government to collect cleanup costs from current and former property owners. 42 U.S.C. §§ 9601 *et seq.* (discussed in Chapter 20).

Notice that each of the statutes includes an abbreviation such as "26 U.S.C. § 1" after its name. This abbreviation is referred to as a **citation** or **cite** and represents the location of the statute in the series of volumes that make up the U.S.C. The number preceding "U.S.C." is the title or volume number of the United States Code where the statute may be found. The symbol § (or §§ for multiple sections) after "U.S.C." means "section;" it is followed by the section number, which represents the location of the statute within the particular volume. For example, "26 U.S.C. § 305" would be a cite for a statute that could be found in the 26th volume of the U.S.C., where Section 305 appears. This particular section describes the proper depreciation methods for property. When a cite is furnished, you know that a federal law affects the issue, transaction, or property and, using the citation system, you would be able to find the exact language of the statute.

Federal Administrative Regulations

For each federal legislative enactment passed by Congress, a new agency is created or an existing agency assigned to implement and enforce the law. For example, the ILSFDA is enforced by a federal agency, the Department of Housing and Urban Development (HUD). HUD has been designated (it was an existing agency at the time the ILSFDA was passed) as the agency responsible for carrying out the general provisions and purposes of ILSFDA. To accomplish that task, HUD developed procedures and forms for compliance with and enforcement of the law. Agencies fill in the details to carry out general statutory provisions with their procedures and compliance and enforcement roles.

For example, the ILSFDA was passed by Congress in a general form and was intended to protect those who purchased undeveloped property without first having the opportunity to visually inspect it. The general provision established in the statute was for each buyer to be furnished with a full report disclosing critical information about the property, such as whether water is available and whether the property is accessible by road (see Chapter 14).

Given the responsibility of enforcement under the act, HUD then passed regulations establishing the details for disclosing the information Congress had required. HUD has since passed regulations that establish how to disclose the required information, what information must be on file with HUD, the forms the disclosures are made on, and penalties for the failure to make the required disclosures and filings. The regulations of an administrative agency fill in the details on the Congressional statute's skeletal purpose.

Another example of a federal regulatory scheme is that created by the Environmental Protection Agency (EPA) under authority granted by Congress in CERCLA. CERCLA authorized the EPA to clean up sites contaminated by toxic wastes (42 U.S.C. §§ 9601 *et seq.*; see Chapter 20). The federal regulations for this environmental cleanup statute list 700 substances that are considered toxic wastes that require cleanup and result in application of liability provisions for the failure to do the necessary cleanup on land contaminated with any of the toxic substances (40 C.F.R. § 302). Congress established the statutory authority for cleaning up "toxic wastes," and the regulations define what is waste and provide for EPA enforcement steps.

All federal regulations appear in a series of volumes referred to as the **Code of Federal Regulations (CFR)**. When an abbreviation, citation, or cite such as "12 C.F.R. § 226" appears in a book or a real estate document, you know that a federal regulation applies and, using the cite, you could find the regulation. In the example, 12 is the volume number within the CFR, and 226 is the section number of the regulation within that particular volume.

The CFR is a series of paperback volumes that is reprinted every year because of the many changes in administrative agency regulations. In addition, a daily update to the CFR, called the *Federal Register*, is published each working day and includes changes and proposed changes in existing regulations.

State Constitutions

State constitutions are similar to the U.S. Constitution in that they too provide a framework for state legislative bodies and agencies and their authority and limits. However, most state constitutions tend to be more detailed than the basic structure and language of the U.S. Constitution, which emphasizes government structure and powers. For example, California's state constitution has a provision covering *usury*, or charging in excess of a certain maximum interest rate in a credit transaction (Cal. Const. Art. 15, § 1) (see Chapter 15). Five additional examples of provisions from state constitutions are as follows:

1. California—has several sections that provide exemption of certain types of property from taxation, including property used for religious worship or higher education (Cal. Const. Art. 13, § 3).
2. Arizona—allows any person who holds a real estate broker's or salesman's license to draft and fill out any forms related to the sale or leasing of real property, including earnest money receipts, purchase agreements, deeds, mortgages, leases, bills of sale, and other necessary documents (Ariz. Const. Art. 26, §§ 1–3).
3. New Jersey—exempts the real property used exclusively for religious, educational, charitable, or cemetery purposes from taxation (N.J. Const. Art. VIII, § 1, Paragraph 2).
4. New York—has several sections that create preserves, recreational areas, reservoirs, and wildlife conservation policies (N.Y. Const. Art. XIV, §§ 1–3).
5. Texas—covers the requirements for homestead exemptions (Tex. Const. Art. 16, § 51).

As these examples illustrate, state constitutions tend to be more specific than the U.S. Constitution and are viable sources for relevant real estate law.

State Legislative Enactments

Just as at the federal level, the legislative bodies in each state enact laws that affect property rights and transactions. State statutes include procedures for obtaining licenses for selling real estate, methods of financing real estate purchases, time periods for adverse possession, and provisions for creating a will or probating an estate. A great amount of the detail of real estate law is found within the state legislative enactments.

State legislative enactments contain the so-called uniform laws, a great many of which apply in real estate transactions. Uniform laws are drafted by representatives of industry, academe, and the legal professions after comments and input by members of all three groups. Examples of uniform laws adopted by states that affect real estate transactions include the Uniform Marital Property Act, the Uniform Probate Code, the Uniform Commercial Code, the Uniform Partnership Act, and the Model Residential Landlord/Tenant Act.

These state legislative enactments are found in varying volumes and sources. In Texas, the legislative enactments are found in *Vernon's Texas Codes, Annotated* (for example, V.T.C.A., *Water Code*, § 1.001). In Illinois, the state statutes are found in *Smith-Hurd's Annotated Illinois Statutes* (for example, S.H.A. Ch. 96, § 4601). Oregon's Statutes are called *Oregon Revised Statutes* (for example, O.R.S. § 79.1090).

State Administrative Regulations

Again, as at the federal level, state legislative bodies also create or assign administrative agencies to enforce their enacted legislation. These state agencies perform the same functions as the federal agencies in that they provide details, forms, and procedures necessary for compliance with state laws. For example, all states have laws regarding the licensing of real estate agents and brokers. In each state an agency is responsible for the collection of licensing fees, administration of exams, enforcement of state laws, and the discipline of those with licenses who have violated the laws and regulations on brokers and agents.

County, City, and Borough Ordinances

A great amount of real estate law can be found in the smallest and most local entity, such as a county, city, or borough. For example, most of the laws relating to zoning can be found in the laws passed by local entities and are referred to as **ordinances**. Other topics covered by ordinances on a local level include building permits, building inspections, fire codes, building-height restrictions, noise regulations, and curfews. Many of the battles over economic development, the location of power plants, and even whether a new Wal-Mart store can be built are grounded in the application and interpretation of these local laws. (The zoning discussion appears in Chapter 18. Chapter 21 includes a discussion of economic development issues.)

Private Law

One type of law in the pyramid comes from individuals and landowners: **private law**. Private law consists of those rules and regulations created by landowners for their protection in the use of their land by others. For example, landlords can create and post regulations on the use of common facilities by tenants, such as pools, laundry areas, parking lots, and walkways. (Chapter 9 includes a complete discussion of residential landlord–tenant relationships.) In some instances, private developers have placed added restrictions and covenants on the use of property in their developments. Some residential developments permit only those above the age of 18 years to live as residents in the area. (See Chapter 19 for a complete discussion.) One area of private law that has increased significantly over the past decade is that of homeowner associations. Litigation over private homeowner association rules almost always involves a question of whether the private rules of the association violate rights given by laws and the constitutions in other areas of the pyramid (see Chapter 11 for more discussion).

Private law is also created through contracts for the purchase, sale, lease, or mortgage of real estate. The parties who validly and voluntarily enter into contractual obligations are bound by the terms of the contract as a form of private law, and such obligations can be enforced, like public laws, through the courts.

Private transactions in real estate have unique standing in that substantial public records and filings are maintained on private transactions in parcels of land. For example, the typical recorder's office will contain all the filings on the transfer and pledge of a parcel of land, as well as information about methods of financing and any back-due taxes.

> **Practical Tip**
>
> *Know how and where to find your state statutes and regulations along with your city and county ordinances. Learn the names of your statutes, regulations, and ordinances, and how they are organized. Request to be placed on mailing lists of state administrative agencies so that you will know of enforcement actions, proposed rule changes, and compliance information. Check the agendas for the meetings of city councils. When they will consider zoning issues, you can attend and provide input. Follow legislative sessions and proposed laws through the media or through professional organizations such as the National Association of Realtors.*

The information in public records controls the rights of the parties, both present and future, with regard to that land. These recorded documents (see Chapters 13–15) of private transactions provide public notice with respect to that land, and rights of parties are determined by the presence or absence of these documented private transactions.

All private law is still subject to the boundaries and rights established in the previously discussed constitutional and statutory sources. A private law related to real estate may not abridge constitutional rights and freedoms. (See Chapter 19 for a full discussion of constitutional rights.)

Court Decisions

The prior discussions of the various sources of law seem complete, and it would be difficult to imagine that much more detail could exist in real estate law. However, the constitutions, statutes, and ordinances are only general statements of the law that leave many terms undefined and also result in questions of application and interpretation. To whom does the law apply? When does the law apply and how is it to be applied? Finding the answers to these questions requires interpretation of law from all levels, a process that is carried out by the various courts in the state and federal judicial systems. The role of the courts is to answer the questions of application and to clarify ambiguities in statutes, ordinances, and contracts.

For example, suppose that a state statute requires "good faith" by all parties in performing their contract obligations. The meaning of "good faith" will be established through court cases and judicial interpretation. Is a party acting in good faith when she is unable to obtain financing from one lender and refuses to apply with another lender? Is a broker acting in good faith when he lists a property and then does not advertise or promote its sale? Without case examples and judicial opinions on the definition of "good faith," the statute would be meaningless.

Permanent records of courts' decisions can be found in opinions published in books that far exceed in number the volumes devoted to statutes. These opinions must be consulted in discerning the complete meaning of a statute or ordinance.

In addition to their interpretive function, the courts also have the responsibility of making, applying, and analyzing the **common law**. Common law is law that is recognized as being law but is not in any code or statute. The concept of nuisance (see Chapter 4) was developed by the courts to prevent others from interfering with your use and enjoyment of your property. Nuisance examples and the requirements for establishing a nuisance as well as appropriate remedies are found in case law. The law on nuisance comes largely from the courts, not from statutes.

Common law originated in England and continues to exist within case law, changing and growing on a case-by-case basis. Because most American real property concepts can be traced to the English rules on real estate ownership and transfer, common law remains an important source of real estate law.

Reliance on common law or prior court opinions in developing interpretations or resolutions to factually similar problems is also called following **case precedent**. Precedent can be used as a guideline for contracts and transactions that occur after the judicial decision. Once a court has interpreted a particular statute or contract, other parties can use and rely upon the court's interpretation.

For example, a statute from the state of New York (see box below) gives tenants the right to habitable premises when they lease residential property.

Real Property Law § 235-b Warranty of Habitability

In every written or oral lease or rental agreement for residential premises the landlord or lessor shall be deemed to covenant and warrant that the premises so leased or rented and all areas used in connection therewith in common with other tenants or residents are fit for human habitation and for the uses reasonably intended by the parties and that the occupants of such premises shall not be subjected to any conditions which would be dangerous, hazardous or detrimental to their life, health or safety. When any such condition has been caused by the misconduct of the tenant or lessee or persons under his direction or control, it shall not constitute a breach of such covenants and warranties.

Any agreement by a lessee or tenant of a dwelling waiving or modifying his rights as set forth in this section shall be void as contrary to public policy. In determining the amount of damages sustained by a tenant as a result of a breach of warranty set forth in the section, the court; [*sic*]

a. need not require any expert testimony; and
b. shall, to the extent the warranty is breached or cannot be cured by reason of a strike or other labor dispute which is not caused primarily by the individual landlord or lessor and such damages are attributable to such strike, exclude recovery to such extent, except to the extent of the net savings, if any, to the landlord or lessor by reason of such strike or labor dispute allocable to the tenant's premises, provided, however, that the landlord or lesser [*sic*] has made a good faith attempt, where practicable, to cure the breach.

Notice that the statute uses very general terms in defining what is required for premises to be habitable. What does "habitable" mean? The courts through resolution of landlord–tenant disputes will provide that definition through judicial opinions issued in litigated cases.

While the rights of landlords and tenants are discussed at length in Chapters 9 and 10, the following landlord–tenant cases illustrate the role of the judiciary in applying the general standards of the statute on habitability to different sets of facts.

Solow v. Wellner

658 N.E.2d 1005 (N.Y. 1995)

FACTS

Sheldon Solow (landlord/petitioner) is the manager of a 300-unit luxury apartment building on the Upper East Side of Manhattan. Rents in the building ranged from $1,064.89 per month for a studio apartment on the fourth floor to $5,379.92 per month for a two-bedroom apartment on the 44th floor. Prior to signing a lease, each tenant was given a brochure that contained the following descriptions of the building and its amenities:

Panoramic views of New York City, its rivers and bridges; Long Island Sound and the Palisades. Solar glass thermopane windows. Private membership, rooftop, year-round Pool Club. 24-hour attended lobby.

Video-monitored service and garage entrances. Four pipe central air-conditioning system providing a choice of cooling and/or heating during transitional seasons. Air-conditioned lobby and corridors.

Kitchens:
Ceramic tile floors
Formica counter tops and cabinet areas
G.E. 4-cycle dishwasher
G.E. 2-door frost-free refrigerator and Automatic Icemaker
Tappan range with 2 continuous cleaning ovens, digital clock and automatic timer
Charcoal filtered range hood
Stainless steel sink

Bathrooms with Dupont "Corian" molded sinks and counter tops; quarry tile floors

Sprinkler and smoke alarm systems in all public corridors

Oak parquet floors

4 high speed Otis elevators equipped with intercom phone

Master T.V. antenna system; Cable T.V. available

Direct access to underground garage

46th floor laundry room with spectacular city views

Smoke alarms in each apartment

The brochure listed many other amenities. Despite the promises and brochures, the tenants grappled with dysfunctional systems and the resulting inconvenience. The elevator did not work consistently and tenants waited interminable lengths of time for elevators, particularly during the morning and evening rush hours. Tenants were frequently late to work and other appointments and found themselves hoofing it on the stairs to and from their apartments. The elevators also skipped floors and opened on the wrong floors. Although there were four cars serving the building, one is a service car used primarily by building staff and all to service a 301-apartment, 46-story building.

Tenants complained about the stench emanating from garbage stored between the package room and the garage. Tenants spotted mice in that area. The door separating the garage from the building was always unlocked, creating a security problem. Fixtures were removed in the public areas, leaving exposed wiring. In February and March of 1988, there were two floods at the front entrance that turned egress and entry into an obstacle course. In October 1988 water cascaded down the front of the building, barring entrance and seeping into the mailboxes and their contents. The package-room service began deteriorating in 1985 and remained at a low level, resulting in delivery delays of one to two weeks.

The air conditioning in the lobby was frequently inoperative. The lobby carpets were often left dirty. The hallway fire alarms did not function on several occasions. The laundry room on the 46th floor was dirty, had overflowing sinks, had sections of acoustical tile missing, and suffered from roach infestation. There were often 60 to 70 bags of garbage piled inside the main entrance inside the building. The compactor room on the ground floor had garbage all over the floor and was heavily infested with mice and roaches. The electronically operated security door at the valet station had an inoperative lock, thereby allowing anyone to walk into the building. The boiler room in the sub-basement had four to five inches of standing water.

There were no sign-up sheets for tenants to request an exterminator. To get extermination services, they had to leave a note with the concierge. An exterminator did not come to the building on a regular basis.

The air conditioner that serviced the individual apartments leaked. The galvanized pipes that provided the runoff of drainage were placed at an angle that prevented them from carrying the water into the building's drainage system and ultimately into the city sewer system. Apartments had buckling floors from the poor drainage. As a result, approximately 10,000 and 11,000 square feet of parquet floors were replaced.

There were soiled carpets in the public hallways, trash in the rear stairwells, unemptied ashtrays, and graffiti on some walls caused by a lack of cleaning supplies or equipment (one operable vacuum cleaner for the entire building!).

From October 1987 through May 1988, many of the tenants in the building stopped paying rent on the grounds that the landlord had breached the implied warranty of habitability as provided under Section 235-b of Real Property Law. Solow brought suit seeking payment of rent. The tenants counterclaimed for breach of the implied warranty of habitability. Following a 21-month trial, 12,000 pages of transcript, and frequent acrimony, the trial court held that the landlord had breached the warranty of habitability and awarded attorney fees. The appellate court modified the finding by limiting the breach of warranty of habitability only to the lack of elevator service, reversed and remanded, and the tenants then appealed.

JUDICIAL OPINION

Levine, Judge. Pursuant to Real Property Law Section 235-b, every residential lease contains an implied warranty of habitability which is limited by its terms to three covenants: (1) that the premises are "fit for human habitation," (2) that the premises are fit for "the uses reasonably intended by the parties," and (3) that the occupants will not be subjected to conditions that are "dangerous, hazardous or detrimental to their life, health or safety." In *Park W. Mgt. Corp. v. Mitchell,* 391 N.E.2d 1288, *cert. denied* 444 U.S. 992, this Court described the statutory warranty as creating an implied promise by the landlord that the demised premises are fit for human occupancy. We specifically rejected the contention that the warranty was intended to make the landlord "a guarantor of every amenity customarily rendered in the landlord-tenant relationship" and held that the implied warranty protects only against conditions that materially affect the health and safety of tenants or deficiencies that "in the eyes of a *reasonable person*... deprive the tenant of the *essential functions* which a residence is expected to provide."

While Civil Court based its finding of a breach of warranty of habitability in part on conditions reasonably related to health and safety and essential functions, it did not limit the implied warranty to such matters. Instead, the court interpreted the second prong of the statutory covenant—that the premises are fit "for the uses reasonably intended by the parties"—as encompassing the level of services and amenities that tenants reasonably expect to be provided under the financial and other terms of their individual leases.

We reject Civil Court's interpretation of the statute. As discussed, the implied warranty of habitability sets forth a minimum standard to protect tenants against conditions that render residential premises uninhabitable or unusable. Thus, the statutory references to "uses reasonably intended by the parties", rather than referring to a broad spectrum of expectations arising out of the parties' specific contractual arrangement, reflects the Legislature's concern that tenants be provided with premises suitable for residential habitation, in other words, living quarters having "those essential functions which a resident is expected to provide." This prong of the warranty therefore protects against conditions that, while they do not render an apartment unsafe or uninhabitable, constitute deficiencies that prevent the premises from serving their intended function of residential occupation. Thus, for example, Appellate Term correctly concluded that operable elevator service is an essential attribute of a high-rise residential apartment building because a reasonable person could find that it is indispensable to the use of the demised premises.

The trial court's contrary interpretation based on expectations arising from the terms of the lease, would make the statutory implied warranty of habitability coextensive with the parties' lease agreement. However, the statute's nonwaiver clause indicates a legislative intent to insure the independence of the warranty of habitability from the specific terms of a lease. Moreover, section 235-b was intended to provide an objective, uniform standard for essential functions, while the trial court's standard creates an individualized subjective standard dependent on the specific terms of each lease. Furthermore, grafting the tenant's contractual rights onto the implied warranty would unnecessarily duplicate other legal and equitable remedies of the tenant.

Affirmed.

CASE QUESTIONS

1. Describe the type of building and apartments the tenants were led to expect.
2. Describe the problems in the building.
3. Did the problems reach the level of threats to life, health, and safety?
4. Is the warranty of habitability one that varies according to lease agreements and the nature of property?
5. Is the information in the brochure relevant for the case?
6. If you had been a tenant, would you have withheld your rent?

Aftermath

Finally, after what the court referred to as "protracted litigation," the court awarded the landlord $326,842.13, 766 N.Y.S.2d 559 (2003).

Ethical Issue

In a case related to *Solow v. Wellner*, a motion for sanctions against the attorney for the tenants was heard by the civil and supreme courts of New York. As a result, the attorney for the plaintiffs/tenants was sanctioned $1,000 for each plaintiff for a total of $62,000 for "frivolous conduct." The courts held that Ray L. LeFlore had engaged in that conduct "primarily to delay or prolong the resolution of litigation, or to harass or maliciously injure another."

Was it ethical of the lawyer to prolong the litigation? Should the landlord have settled the case? Why do you think the landlord's case was in litigation for so many years? Do you think the tenants should have been permitted to rely on the brochure? *Solow v. Wellner*, 618 N.Y.S.2d 845 (1994).

Poyck v. Bryant

820 N.Y.S.2d 774 (2006)

FACTS

Stan Bryant and Michelle Bryant ("defendants," "tenants," or "the Bryants") leased a unit in a condominium project from Peter Poyck ("plaintiff," "landlord," or "Poyck").

After living in the apartment for approximately three years, in March, 2001, new neighbors moved next door to the Bryants. The new neighbors constantly smoked in the common fifth floor hallway and in apartment 5-C. The tobacco smoke or secondhand smoke penetrated into the Bryants' apartment. At that time, the Bryants complained to the building superintendent, Frank Baldanza ("Super") about the hazardous secondhand smoke condition. The super spoke to the neighbors to no avail. The incessant smoke continued unabated.

When the super's efforts failed, Stanley Bryant wrote a letter dated June 29, 2001 to the super and to Peter Poyck as well as to Poyck's attorney, Charles Corso ("Corso") seeking a solution to the hazardous smoking problem:

To date, their [next door neighbors in apartment 5-C] tobacco smoke continues to permeate this end of the fifth floor hallway and my home. This is not simply a matter of unpleasant odors; it represents an ongoing health hazard for my wife who is recovering from her second cancer surgery and who is extremely allergic to tobacco smoke. Prior to the current tenant moving into 5-C, this problem did not exist on the fifth floor.

To try to remedy the situation, I have sealed my apartment entry door with weather stripping and a draft barrier. I operate two hepa air filters round the clock, incurring additional electric charges. Despite these efforts, we can still smell the smoke from 5-C in our apartment.

If you can help in any way to remedy this problem, we would be extremely appreciative. Failing that, we must consider finding a healthier living situation.

The landlord took no action to curtail their neighbors' smoking that was invading the Bryants' home. About thirty days later, the Bryants left their apartment and wrote a letter to their landlord dated August 1, 2001, notifying him of their decision as follows:

Due to my wife's continuing health concerns and our most recent and apparently ongoing smoking' issue with our next door neighbor (please refer to our letter to Frank Baldanza dated June 29th) we have found it necessary to look elsewhere for more appropriate living quarters. Please note that we will be vacating this apartment by the end of August, 2001.

Poyck brought suit to collect rent and late charges for the months of August, 2001 through December, 2001, at $2,597 per month against the Bryants. The Bryants alleged a defense of breach of the implied warranty of habitability and constructive eviction due to secondhand smoke. Poyck moved for summary judgment.

JUDICIAL OPINION

Hagler, Judge. The novel issue to be determined herein is whether secondhand smoke emanating from a neighbor gives rise to a breach of the implied warranty of habitability and a constructive eviction under the realities of modern urban dwelling. Most urban dwelling in New York City comprises "vertical living" in high-rise apartment buildings with possibly multiple neighbors in all directions. With multiple neighbors living beside each other comes basic duties and responsibilities. There is a duty to protect each other's right to privacy and a responsibility not to invade a neighbor's privacy. The unwanted invasion of privacy comes in many guises such as noise, smells, odors, fumes, dust, water and even secondhand smoke.

The key to avoiding such unneighborly behavior is for the neighbor to follow the often forgotten "Golden Rule" You shall love your fellow or neighbor as yourself. The Golden Rule is a general principle of ethics which essentially admonishes neighbors as follows: What is hateful to you, do not do to your neighbor. The landlord also has an obligation to ensure that the conditions do not render the apartment "unsafe and uninhabitable" or prevents the premises from serving their intended function of residential occupation. When neighbors fail to respect each other and the landlord does not act, the law imposes its will on landlords and tenants through the statutory enacted implied warranty of habitability pursuant to Real Property Law ("RPL") § 235-b.

In the landmark case of *Park West Management Corp. v. Mitchell*, 47 N.Y.2d 316, 418 N.Y.S.2d 310, 391 N.E.2d 1288 (1979), the Court of Appeals defined the history and parameters of RPL § 235-b or the implied warranty of habitability. RPL § 235-b was enacted in August, 1975, to provide modern urban dwellers with much needed protections and rights to compel landlords to make necessary repairs and essential services. In other words, RPL § 235-b placed "the tenant in parity legally with the landlord." For more than thirty years, this powerful law continues to impose a warranty of habitability in every landlord–tenant relationship where the landlord impliedly warrants as follows:

first, that the premises are fit for human habitation;
second, that the condition of the premises is in accord with the uses reasonably intended by the parties; and,
third, that the tenants are not subjected to any conditions endangering or detrimental to their life, health or safety.

The scope and breadth of RPL § 235-b is far-reaching. Landlords must warrant against "latent" and "patent" conditions throughout the entire tenancy "occasioned by ordinary deterioration, work stoppage by employees, ***acts of third parties*** or natural disaster . . ." The standard for a breach of the implied warranty of habitability is measured "in the eyes of a reasonable person" not in a vacuum which ignores the "essence of the modern dwelling unit." RPL § 235-b was intended to provide an objective standard for "**those essential functions which a residence is expected to provide**." *Solow v. Wellner*, 86 N.Y.2d 582, 589, 635 N.Y.S.2d 132, 658 N.E.2d 1005 (1995).

While there appears *[sic]* to be no reported cases dealing with secondhand smoke in the context of implied warranty of habitability, secondhand smoke is just as insidious and invasive as the more common conditions such as noxious odors, smoke odors, chemical fumes, excessive noise, and water leaks and extreme dust penetration. Indeed, the U.S. Surgeon General, the New York State Legislature and the City of New York City Counsel declared that there is a substantial body of scientific research that breathing secondhand smoke poses a significant health hazard. U.S. Surgeon General's report on *The Health Consequences of Involuntary Smoking* (December, 1986). Therefore, this Court holds as a matter of law that secondhand smoke qualifies as a condition that invokes the protections of RPL § 235-b under the proper circumstances. As such, it is axiomatic that secondhand smoke can be grounds for a constructive eviction.

The gravamen of plaintiff's motion is that he cannot be held liable for the actions of third parties beyond his control such as the neighbors in unit 5-C. This argument is misplaced as the Court of Appeals since 1979 has clearly stated that the acts of third parties are within the scope of a landlord's responsibility pursuant to RPL § 235-b. *Park West Management Corp.*, 47 N.Y.2d at 326, 418 N.Y.S.2d 310, 391 N.E.2d 1288. The courts have continuously held that the implied warranty of habitability can apply to conditions beyond a landlord's control. *Elkman v. Southgate Owners Corp.*, 233 A.D.2d 104, 649 N.Y.S.2d 138 (1st Dept. 1996) (an alleged noxious odor emanating from a retail fish store in an adjacent building neither owned nor controlled by the landlord cooperative corporation may be a breach of the implied warranty of habitability); *Sargent Realty Corp. v. Vizzini*, 101 Misc.2d 763, 421 N.Y.S.2d 963 (Civ. Ct. N.Y. County 1979) (floods caused by upstairs tenant on four occasions which landlord allowed to persist resulted in substantial abatement); *Quasha v. Third Colony Corp.*, October 10, 1990, N.Y.L.J., p. 22, col. 2 (Sup. Ct. N.Y. County) (noise emanating from neighbor stated a claim for breach of implied warranty of habitability); *Solomon v. Brandy*, September 7, 1994, N.Y.L.J., p. 22, col. 6 (Civ. Ct. Bronx County) (evicted neighboring tenant who caused nuisance resulting in lack of water supply to tenant did not constitute a good faith defense to the implied warranty of habitability).

While the landlord contends that he had no control over the neighbors in apartment 5-C, he failed to offer any evidence that he took any action to eliminate or alleviate the hazardous condition. The landlord could have asked the board of managers of the condominium to stop the neighbors from smoking in the hallway and elevator as well as to take preventive care to properly ventilate unit 5-C so that the secondhand smoke did not seep into the Bryants' apartment. Specifically, Real Property Law § 339-v(1)(i) mandates that condominium by-laws restrict the use and maintenance of both the units and common elements such as the hallways and elevators so as to "prevent unreasonable interference with the use of respective units and of the common elements by several unit owners." The board of managers and even the landlord could have commenced an action for damages or injunctive relief for non-compliance with the by-laws and decisions of the board of managers pursuant to the Condominium Act.

Inasmuch as there are triable issues of fact as to whether the secondhand smoke breached the implied warranty of habitability and caused a constructive eviction, plaintiff's motion to strike and/or dismiss the defendants' third and fourth affirmative defenses and first and second counterclaims must be denied.

CASE QUESTIONS

1. Describe the extent of the secondhand smoke problem and what the tenants and landlord did to abate the problem.

2. Does it matter that the landlord is not the cause of the problem?

3. Does secondhand smoke qualify as grounds for a breach of the implied warranty of habitability?

CONSIDER 1.1

Applying both the law and the case precedent on a landlord's warranty of habitability, discuss the following issues and questions.

a. Suppose a landlord included the following clause in a lease.

Landlord ... shall not be liable for any damages to ... property resulting from falling ... water which may leak from any part of said building or from the pipes, appliances or plumbing works unless caused by or due to the negligence of Landlord ... nor shall Landlord be liable for any such damage caused by other tenants.

Is the clause enforceable? Does it eliminate the warranty of habitability? *Spatz v. Axelrod Management Co., Inc.*, 630 N.Y.S.2d 461 (City Civ. Ct. 1995).

b. Several tenants complain to their landlord that the doorbells and buzzers for their apartments do not work and that there are no mailboxes. Has the landlord breached the warranty of habitability? *Kachian v. Aronson*, 475 N.Y.S.2d 215 (1984).

CONSIDER 1.1

(continued)

c. Would the warranty of habitability apply to a restaurant tenant experiencing water leaks onto its grill? *Manhattan Mansions v. Moe's Pizza*, 561 N.Y.S.2d 331 (1990).

d. Would the warranty of habitability protect a condominium owner who experiences defects in the common areas? *Matter of Abbady*, 629 N.Y.S.2d 6 (1995).

e. Janet L. Benitez is a tenant in a basement apartment in Yonkers, New York. Sebastino Restifo is the landlord. On August 10, 1995, a large quantity of water cascaded from the ceiling of the Benitez apartment, causing severe water damage to a carpet, bed, bureau, clothing, phone, and compact disc player. Benitez replaced the carpet, bureau, mattress, and some clothing.

The water had come from the third floor apartment of Mrs. Alamar. The Benitez apartment had been flooded previously by Mrs. Alamar because she was a problem tenant who filled her kitchen sink so that the water would overflow onto the kitchen floor and eventually down to the apartments below, including Benitez's. Benitez filed suit seeking to recover the cost of replacing her property on the grounds of breach of the implied warranty of habitability as provided in Section 235-b. *Benitez v. Restifo*, 641 N.Y.S.2d 523 (City Civ. Ct. 1996). Should she recover for her property damage under 235-b?

Justification for Studying Real Estate Law: Some Cautions and Conclusions

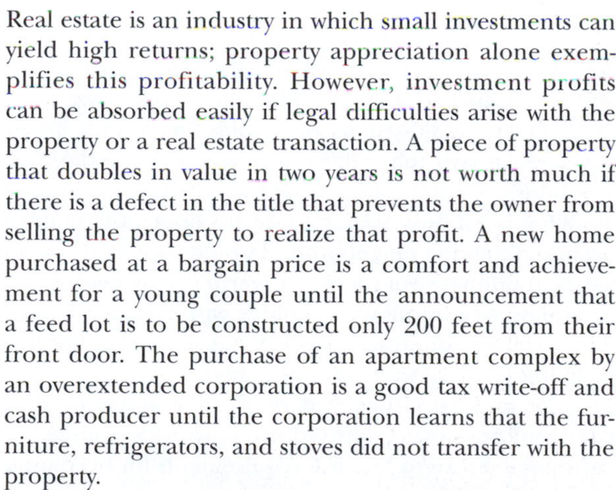

Real estate is an industry in which small investments can yield high returns; property appreciation alone exemplifies this profitability. However, investment profits can be absorbed easily if legal difficulties arise with the property or a real estate transaction. A piece of property that doubles in value in two years is not worth much if there is a defect in the title that prevents the owner from selling the property to realize that profit. A new home purchased at a bargain price is a comfort and achievement for a young couple until the announcement that a feed lot is to be constructed only 200 feet from their front door. The purchase of an apartment complex by an overextended corporation is a good tax write-off and cash producer until the corporation learns that the furniture, refrigerators, and stoves did not transfer with the property.

All of the errors made in these transactions involve legal issues that could have been avoided if the parties had a basic knowledge of real estate law. The remainder of this book is devoted to providing such knowledge.

As you proceed through the book, think about the questions in the following section which the author uses to introduce the notion of "real estate law." Pay close attention to the Cautions and Conclusions sections in each chapter as you look for answers.

The Most Frequently Asked Real Estate Questions

1. If I move out of my apartment before the lease expires, do I still owe the rent? What if the landlord re-rents the apartment? Will I still owe rent?
2. If a seller backs out of the sale of property, does she still owe the broker the commission?
3. If a buyer backs out of the purchase of property, does the broker still get his commission? What happens to the earnest money deposit?
4. Do all real estate contracts have to be in writing?
5. What if I buy a home and the general contractor has not paid all the subcontractors? Will I have to pay them?
6. If I die without a will, does my property go to the state?
7. If I own a house before I am married, does my spouse own it after we are married?
8. Who is the mortgagor? Who is the mortgagee?
9. How long does it take to foreclose on a property mortgage?
10. If people cut across my property for a path, am I liable if they are hurt? Can they claim any interest in my property?

11. If the fence on my property is in the wrong place, do I own the property that was accidentally included?
12. Can the EPA require me to clean up or pay for the cleanup of toxic waste on land that I just bought?
13. Is my broker working for me or for the buyer?
14. What happens if my property deed is not recorded?
15. If a property has two mortgages, which mortgage has priority?

CONSIDER 1.2

For each of the frequently asked questions, list the sources of law from the pyramid shown in Figure 1.1 that would be consulted for answers.

Key Terms

United States Constitution, 2
Fifth Amendment, 2
eminent domain, 3
Fourteenth Amendment, 3
Equal Protection Clause, 3
United States Code (U.S.C.), 3
Interstate Land Sales Full Disclosure Act (ILSFDA), 3
Real Estate Settlement Procedures Act (RESPA), 3
Internal Revenue Code (IRC), 3
Comprehensive Environmental Response, Compensation, and Liability Act (CERCLA), 3
citation, 3
cite, 3
Code of Federal Regulations (CFR), 4
ordinances, 6
private law, 6
common law, 7
case precedent, 7

Chapter Problems

1. Jean Vollenweider (defendant) is a tenant in a condominium apartment owned by Palais Partners. Vollenweider refused to pay rent (the rent is $3,870 per month) during the months of March and April, 1995, because Palais did nothing in response to Vollenweider's complaints about the conduct of a neighbor. The neighbor, who did not have coverings on his windows, would walk about nude in his apartment and occasionally engage in behavior related to his nudity. Vollenweider's apartment faces the nude neighbor's and the scenes were unavoidable when Vollenweider was at home. Palais brought suit for nonpayment of rent and Vollenweider defended on the grounds of constructive eviction and breach of the warranty of habitability. Is there a constructive eviction? Is there a breach of the warranty of habitability? *Palais Partners v. Vollenweider*, 640 N.Y.S.2d 272 (City Civ. Ct. 1997).

2. Mr. and Mrs. Ralph Williams of Montana purchased an acre of land in a new Florida development called Sunnydale. When the Williamses arrived at Sunnydale they did not find the green, lush parcels they were told of, but instead found property resembling the moon's surface. In determining their rights, to which sources of law should Mr. and Mrs. Williams turn?

3. "Wait a minute," Ella objected, "How can the city take my property to build a Bass Pro Shop? I was here first!" Discuss Ella's rights by helping her with a list of the types of laws that will be involved in answering her questions.

4. When Tom Buttom purchased his home, the builder promised that the neighborhood would consist of single-family dwellings. Tom has just learned that because of economic conditions, the builder will be constructing duplex houses on Tom's street. What sources of law will be helpful to Tom in determining his rights?

5. Jane Jenkins, a licensed real estate agent in New York, will be moving to California. To what sources of law can Jane turn to find the requirements for becoming licensed in California?

6. A deed restriction requires every house in a subdivision to have a "minimum of 2,000 square feet of living space." Although the restriction seems clear, consider the following interpretive problems:

a. Is a garage part of the 2,000 square feet?
b. Are porches part of the 2,000 square feet?

What sources of law would be helpful in determining what is considered to be included in the term "living space"?

7. Ralph and Lillian Palmer owned a dump site in a wooded area in the northern part of Arizona. Cabin owners in the area used the dump site for their trash, and commercial trucks often would bring their loads of trash to the site for a fee. The site has had old batteries, medical refuse, and oil discarded from auto repair shops. The EPA maintains that substances from the site are leaking into the surrounding soil and water supply. What sources of law provide the EPA with its authority?

8. Some isolated parcels within national forests are privately owned. Often, the United States Forest Service will try to arrange exchanges with landowners. With an exchange, the Forest Service will then have a clean parcel and the landowner is given property in an area with development potential near a city or small town. Discuss the types of laws and government agencies that would be involved in such an exchange.

9. Susan Hewitt is a licensed broker in Arizona. She is confused and concerned about her role as an agent for sellers when she lists properties. For example, often prospective buyers will ask her questions about the sellers, their cash needs, their reasons for selling their property, and whether their circumstances require them to sell quickly. What sources of law would help Susan clarify her role with both sellers and buyers?

10. Mr. Fred Saddy leased the premises known as 61 George Street, Manhasset, New York, from John and Helen Kekllas for the period from September 6, 1976, to May 7, 1977, for a monthly rent of $575.00.

The Kekllases had just purchased the premises, which were in disrepair. There were strong odors of cats and cat urine in the garage, the basement of the premises, and in and about a dinette area in the kitchen. During the summer of 1976, the Kekllases had made substantial repairs to the premises, including painting and wallpapering. This work was done after the Kekllases had contracted with Checkmate Exterminators to treat the premises for the odor of cat urine. Checkmate gave a three-month guarantee on its odor treatment.

Mr. and Mrs. Saddy moved in on September 8, and by September 10, Mrs. Saddy was complaining of nausea and watery eyes due to the smell of cat urine. The house had been previously occupied by a mother, age 75, and her daughter, who was in her mid-1950s, who housed two to four cats during their residency there. One was kept in the basement, one in the garage, and the others in the house. Mr. Saddy refused to pay rent on the grounds that the odor breached the warranty of habitability, and Mr. Kekllas filed suit to have the Saddys evicted. Has the warranty of habitability been breached? Refer to the cases and problems in the text to determine your answer. *Kekllas v. Saddy*, 389 N.Y.S.2d 756 (Dist. Ct. 1976).

For research activities related to this chapter, go to our text companion website at www.thomsonedu.com/westbuslaw/jennings.

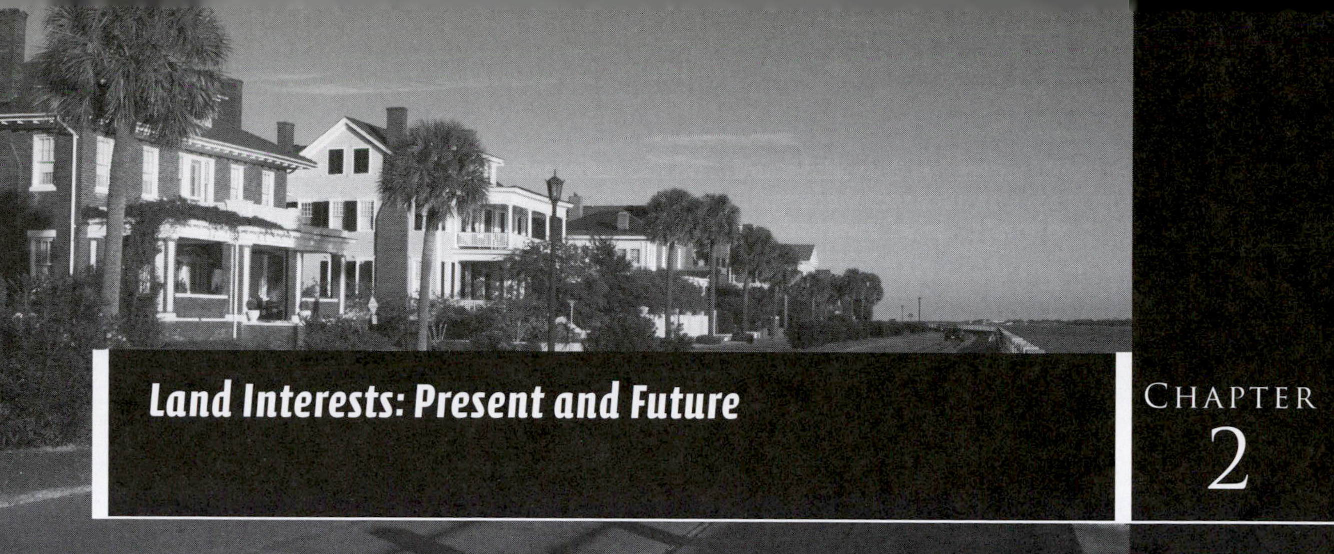

Chapter 2

Land Interests: Present and Future

Those hours when happy hours were my estate,—Entailed, as proper, for the next in line, Yet mine the harvest, and the title mine—. . . .

Edna St. Vincent Millay, *Mine the Harvest: A Collection of New Poems 121* (1954)

The late Senator Burton K. Wheeler of Montana, a leading isolationist of the World War II era, gave [the following answer] when asked in a University of Michigan Law School class in the early 1900s: What is the rule in Shelley's Case?
After a moment of thought, Wheeler is said to have responded, "Sir the Rule in Shelley's case is the same as the rule in any other man's case! The law brooks no favorites!"

Shelley's Tourist Attraction, *7 GREENBAG 175* (2004)

There is no knowing how estates will go when once they come to be entailed.

Jane Austen, *Pride and Prejudice*

Land has different levels and types of ownership or title. Because of its permanent nature, title to land can exist in the present or in the future. Title to land can also be for a partial interest in that land. Likewise, land possession can be transferred without an accompanying transfer of title. This chapter explains the various types and degrees of interests and title in land.

As the opening quotes of this chapter demonstrate, land interests vary and are complex. The major question answered in this chapter is, How can an owner hold title to property? Additional related questions are, How long can an interest be held? And, can interests be transferred? The degree and extent of ownership are the focus of this chapter's discussion. Figure 2.1 depicts the full extent and the interrelationships of land interests.

Figure 2.1 Land Interests

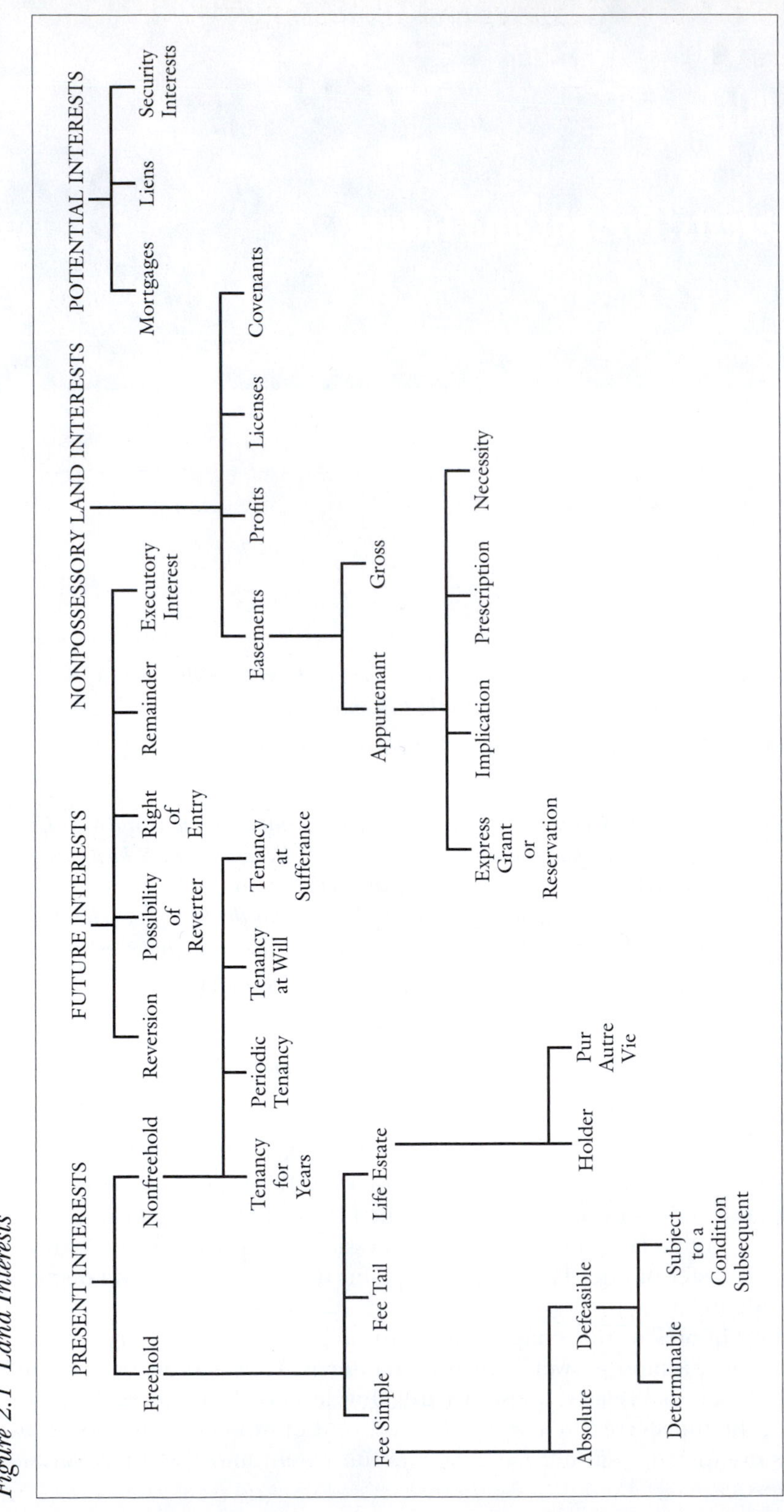

Land Interests—Freehold Estates and Accompanying Future Interests

Freehold Estates

The terms **freehold** and **fee**, adopted from English common law, hold significance for understanding the methods of land ownership. Freehold means that an interest in land is uncertain or unlimited in duration. Fee here means that an interest in land is inheritable. Fee freehold estates are both uncertain or unlimited in duration and inheritable by others upon the death of the interest holder.

Fee Simple Absolute Ownership

A **fee simple absolute**, often called simply a **fee simple**, is an interest in land representing the greatest extent of property ownership available. In lay terms, the fee simple absolute estate would be described as absolute ownership. The owners of fee simples are free to transfer their interests to others at any time, including upon death.

At common law, a fee simple estate was created when the transfer or grant made by the owner or grantor read, "To A and his heirs," with "and his heirs" used to indicate the inheritability of the interest. However, in most states, the language requirement of "and his heirs" has been eliminated so that a fee simple can be created simply by using "To A" language.

Fee Simple Defeasible

A **fee simple defeasible** is an interest in land that is uncertain or unlimited in duration and that has the potential of being terminated. There are two types of fee simple defeasible estates—the **fee simple determinable** and the **fee simple subject to a condition subsequent**.

Fee Simple Determinables and Possibility of Reverter

This land interest is uncertain and inheritable. In **fee simple determinable**, the grantor is giving the grantee full title and right to the property so long as the grantee complies with an attached restriction. An example of language creating a fee simple determinable is "To A so long as the premises are used for school purposes." The most important characteristic distinguishing a fee simple determinable from a fee simple absolute is that A's interest will terminate if the property is not used for school purposes. If A does not comply with the restriction, title to the property will revert to the grantor. When the interest reverts to the grantor, the grantor's future interest becomes a present interest.

Possibility of Reverter—The Fee Simple Determinable Future Interest

Suppose the grant is made "To A so long as the property is used for residential purposes." A builds a factory. What happens to the land interest? The rule for fee simple determinable, noted earlier, requires that upon A's violation of the restriction, A's interest terminates and title to the property reverts to the grantor. This potential loss of title is a future interest called the **possibility of reverter**. The possibility of reverter is an interest the grantor, along with his or her heirs, holds in the property that was conveyed as a fee simple determinable to another.

Possibilities of reverter have the characteristics of other land interests. Under common law, grantors are free to transfer their possibilities of reverter any time while alive (***inter vivos***), and their reverters pass upon their death (**testamentary**) to their heirs or devisees. Many states have now passed statutes regulating the possibility of reverter. In some states, this future interest cannot be transferred or inherited. In others, statutes have been enacted that restrict the possibility of reverter by placing a time limit on validity of the interest—in many states the maximum is 40 years.[1] Still other states require the grantor or holder of the interest to periodically rerecord a notice that the interest exists. All of these state-enacted statutes are notice systems, which are tremendous helps in land transactions because the future interests of others can be determined without having to examine the granting language in each deed transferring title to the property. The constitutionality of these statutes has been questioned in some court cases, but generally upheld.

Fee Simple Subject to a Condition Subsequent

A grantor can accomplish the same purposes as a fee simple determinable grant through the use of a grant of a **fee simple subject to a condition subsequent**. This interest is created with slightly different language such as, "To A on the condition that the land be used for school purposes and if the land is ever not used for school purposes, (the grantor) may reenter and repossess the land." The fee simple subject to a condition subsequent is similar to a fee simple determinable in that A will lose the interest if there is not compliance with the restriction. The difference between the two is that the violation of a fee simple determinable restriction terminates A's interest automatically and immediately, whereas violation of a condition subsequent grant requires some action on the part of the grantor (O) before the interest of A terminates. The grantor must take steps, generally through a quiet title action, to regain title to the property.

Right of Entry/Power of Termination

The following language creates a fee simple subject to a condition subsequent in the grantee but also reserves an interest for the grantor: "To my niece Sally on the condition that liquor never be served on the premises, and should liquor ever be served, I reserve the right to reenter and take possession of and title to the property." Sally holds the present interest of a fee simple subject to a condition subsequent, but the grantor/uncle holds a future interest called a **right of entry** or **power of termination**. As discussed earlier, the grantor's future interest does not become a present interest automatically. The grantor must take steps to, in effect, take title and possession of the property.

> ***Practical Tip***
>
> *Restrictions on land use are enforceable. If a restriction is to be imposed as part of a transfer, have it drafted carefully to reflect intent and all the constraints. If property is being sold, listed, or purchased, verify the existence of restrictions, compare property use, and clarify ambiguities.*

At common law, the right of entry could not be transferred *inter vivos* but could be transferred at death. Some states have passed statutes that vary these common law rules. However, at common law and in most states, the grantor is permitted to transfer the right of entry to the present interest holder of the

1. For a discussion of the types of state statutes and their validity (such as statutes that cancel, destroy, nullify, or limit enforcement of possibilities of reverter or rights of reentry), see 87 A.L.R.3d 1011. The Uniform Simplification of Land Transfers Act (1976) provides in § 3-409 that a possibility of reverter or right of entry for condition is extinguished 30 years after it or a notice of intent to preserve the interest was most recently recorded. A notice of intent is a statutorily imposed recording requirement for continuing the interest. Without that filing, or recording, as noted in the USLTA, the interest ends.

fee simple subject to a condition subsequent. If such a transfer is made, the present and future interests merge, and the present holder of the fee simple subject to a condition subsequent will then hold a fee simple interest. In the example, if Sally's uncle conveyed his interest to her, Sally would then have a fee simple. As with the fee simple determinable, many states have passed time limitations and recording requirements for the continuing validity of the future right of entry interest. The restrictions and recording requirements are similar or identical to those described for possibilities of reverter.

Sometimes it is difficult to distinguish between a possibility of reverter and a right of entry because the language used is so similar. When land interest granted includes a phrase such as, "grantor shall have the right to reenter and reclaim the property," the task of determining the type of future interest created is easy. However, without such clear language the distinction is a fine one, and several judicial rules for interpretation have developed. First, the courts will examine the entire document to determine the grantor's intent. They will also look for certain phrases and words that are used as keys in determining the type of interest created. For example, language such as "until," "so long as," or "for so long" indicates a possibility of reverter. Language such as "but," "provided that," or "on the condition that" indicates a right of entry. In many states, the issue of which type of interest is created is resolved by a presumption in favor of the right of entry, because this type of future interest requires some action on the part of the parties to affect title to the property and does not have the immediate effect on title that a possibility of reverter would have.

In the following case the court deals with a question about a fee simple defeasible interest in an easement.

AKG Real Estate, LLC v. Kosterman

691 N.W.2d 711 (Wis. App. 2004)

FACTS

Some time prior to 1960, Louis and Angeline Chvilicek bought roughly 80 acres of vacant land on Highway 31 in Caledonia, Wisconsin. On August 25, 1960, they deeded four acres of that property (the Homestead) to their son Edward Chvilicek and his wife Audrey. The deed included a 30-foot-wide easement of right-of-way over the retained parcel (the Vacant Land) for ingress and egress between the Homestead and Highway 31.

In 1961, the elder Chvilicek granted Edward and Audrey a second easement along the same path. This easement was 66 feet in width. They all intended the expansion to allow for conversion of the easement into a public road, if they ever wished to dedicate the land for such use. After Louis passed away in 1961, Angeline conveyed the Vacant Land to her children and their spouses as tenants in common. Edward and Audrey received a 50 percent interest in the property. Joyce and Vincent White, Edward's sister and brother-in-law (who also passed away), received the remaining 50 percent.

AKG Real Estate, LLC, purchased the Vacant Land, comprising some 79.736 acres, in 1998, subject to easements, one for sewer and another for access that was described in the two deeds AKG received from the Chvilicek and from White, with the following relevant language in both deeds:

Reserving therefrom a private road easement for the benefit of EDWARD T. CHVILICEK and AUDREY M. CHVILICEK, husband and wife, their heirs and assigns, or subsequent owners of 4213 Highway 31, Racine, Wisconsin 53405 [the Homestead], until such time as public road access is made available for said real estate upon the following described easement of right of way, to wit: [legal description of the 30-foot easement].

AKG formulated plans to turn the land into a subdivision, including a public road. On March 30, 2000, the Chvilicek sold their property to Patrick J. and Susan A. Kosterman.

AKG and the Department of Transportation developed and approved a 2002 plat map for the proposed subdivision of "Quarry Springs." Under the plan, the Kostermans' easement path was altered significantly due to state regulations on the location of the public road that AKG proposed.

The Kostermans did not like the AKG proposal because it did not make the easement path a public road, which is what the Kostermans believed they paid for when they bought the Homestead. The Kostermans also disapproved because they would have to reconfigure their driveway for access.

Because the house on the Homestead faces north, the Kostermans wanted any neighboring properties to face south and lie in a straight row. AKG's plan had the neighboring houses in a cul-de-sac that had the Kostermans' view obstructed by odd angles of houses. In addition to these aesthetics, the Kostermans opined that the value of their property would be impaired by the proposed orientation of AKG's houses. Susan testified that when the couple bought the Homestead, she understood the easement path to provide a buffer protecting it from eventually having neighbors because (1) the eastern half of the Homestead was designated as an environmental corridor, and the Kostermans would own it; (2) wetlands lie just to the west of the property, so a house would be too close to the road. Patrick also desired to keep his same address, something AKG's plan would change.

The Kostermans would not agree to the proposal and the county and city required their approval for the subdivision to proceed. AKG filed suit seeking to have its right to termination of the easement declared. The trial court found the easement was extinguished and the Kostermans appealed.

JUDICIAL OPINION

Brown, Judge. The Kostermans submit that the deed is unambiguous, renewing their contention below that the "upon" clause in the language necessarily modifies "public road" and not "private road easement," as AKG contends.

Any other interpretation, they assert, is grammatically unsound and renders the clause meaningless.

We agree with the Kostermans that the language contained within the four corners of the 1998 deeds is the primary source of what AKG, the Chvilicek s, and White intended the condition subsequent to be. We further agree that the terms of the 1998 deeds are unambiguous and their construction is therefore purely a question of law. We do not, however, agree that the unambiguous terms support the Kostermans' interpretation.

[t]he same rules of construction applicable to other instruments apply to interpretation of a deed. A cardinal rule of construction is that courts will favor a construction that is reasonable, fair, and practical over one that is unreasonable. However grammatically palatable the Kostermans' proposed construction may be, it is substantively preposterous. It contemplates that a right-of-way over the Vacant Land will exist into perpetuity, until the easement path becomes a public road. It does not by its terms terminate even if Highway 31 someday ceases to be a road. Such an interpretation would require AKG to continue to allow the Kostermans to drive over its land, even if they could not go anywhere, an absurd result.

The interpretation AKG advances does not suffer from the same flaw. Moreover, it does not, as the Kostermans assert, read the "upon" clause out of the deed. Rather, it construes the clause to describe the location of the easement. One could reasonably expect the parties to include a term about where to place the easement.

We hold AKG was entitled to judgment as a matter of law. Once it provides public access, the condition subsequent will have been fulfilled. The easement will terminate by its own express terms.

Affirmed as to this issue.

CASE QUESTIONS

1. Give the history of ownership of the properties and easement involved. Why is the history of transfer and language in the deed important?
2. What type of interest was given in the easement?
3. What does the existence of that type of easement mean for AKG? For the Kostermans?
4. Can AKG proceed without the Kostermans' approval?

CONSIDER 2.1

In May 1977, Herbert and Maxine Bird purchased a 113-acre farm. They conveyed one acre of the land to Rayford Blackburn and his daughter, Glenda Dennis (Rucks). The deed from the Birds to Blackburn and Dennis contained the following language:

It being hereby mutually covenanted and agreed by and between the parties hereto that in the event the parties of the second part, Rayford Blackburn and Glenda Dennis, cease to live upon the hereinabove described premises or are desirous of selling the same that the party of the first part, Herbert H. Bird, shall be given the first and prior option to purchase the same at the price of Four Hundred Dollars ($400.00).

CONSIDER 2.1

(continued)

Shortly after the conveyance, Rayford died and Glenda was declared incompetent and unable to live by herself on the property. Herbert Bird tendered a check to Charles Dennis and Jeanna Johnson, the administrators of the estate of Rayford and co-guardians for Glenda, and requested that title to the one-acre parcel be turned over to him. Dennis and Johnson refused and the Birds filed suit. The trial court granted the Birds summary judgment and Dennis and Johnson appealed. Who should win? In determining the answer to this question, you must determine what type of land interest exists. *Dennis v. Bird*, 941 S.W.2d 486 (Ky. 1997)

Fee Tail Ownership

The position of **fee tail** interest in Figure 2.1 establishes it as an uncertain or unlimited estate that is inheritable. However, the distinction between fee simple and fee tail is that fee tail is inheritable only by lineal descendants or direct descendants of the grantee. Lineal descendants are children, grandchildren, great-grandchildren, and so on.

Fee tail interests present substantial problems because of the transfer restrictions and because finding lineal heirs can be cumbersome and confusing. To alleviate the problems of fee tail, many states have passed statutes that convert fee tail grants into fee simple absolutes. Thomas Jefferson considered the abolition of the fee tail in Virginia one of his finest accomplishments, something that lessened the "proportion of idle proprietors."[2] Delaware, Maine, Massachusetts, and Rhode Island still recognize the fee tail. However, disentailing, the process of converting from a fee tail to a fee simple, is available in all four states. In most states, creditors are not subject to fee tail restrictions—they can treat the interest like a fee simple.[3] Some states retain the fee tail interest. Other states permit holders of fee tails to eliminate the fee tail restrictions through a series of transfer transactions. Still other states permit fee tail grantees to hold a **life estate** and then pass title to the land to their heirs at death. Fee tails created prior to legislative changes are still valid.

Life Estate Ownership

Creation

Another type of freehold estate is the life estate, which is an interest in land valid only for the life of the holder or for some other measured life. A life estate is uncertain because it terminates when the person whose life is used as the measure dies. The first type of life estate, a conventional life estate, is created with the language "To A for his life." A's interest will automatically terminate at death. A second type of life estate, measured by a life other than that of the holder, is created by language such as "To A for the life of B" and is called a **life estate *pur autre vie*.**

The life estate appears to be an odd method of land ownership, but it is used effectively as an estate planning tool so that estate taxes may be postponed or reduced. For example, a wife who predeceases her husband might have a will granting her husband a life estate in some property with the provision that the property be given to the children at the termination of the husband's life interest, "To my husband for his life, and then to my children in equal shares." The husband holds only

2. John F. Hart, "A Less Proportion of Idle Proprietors: Madison, Property Rights, and the Abolition of Fee Tail," 58 *Wash & Lee L. Rev.167 (2001).*

3. Marianne M. Jennings, "Real Property Could Use Some Updating," 24 *Real Est. L.J.* 103, 107 to 108 (1995).

a lesser interest for life and will be taxed less, if at all, on his inheritance of the life estate. The distribution will be taxed in full at the time of the children's receipt of the property, with the result being that the wife's estate is not taxed for two transfers to those in her family.

Some states provide for the automatic creation of legal life estates in certain instances. Dower and curtesy are marital property rights for surviving spouses that entitle them to some portion of their deceased spouse's property. In some states, these marital rights are given to the surviving spouse in the form of a life estate required by statute. (Chapter 8 discusses dower and curtesy rights more fully.)

CONSIDER 2.2

Determine what types of future and present interests are created by the following language:

a. "To A so long as the premises are used for church purposes."
b. "To A and his heirs provided that the premises never be used for commercial purposes."
c. "To Cal Trans so long as the land is used for the construction of an off-ramp for access to Harrah's Club Casino."
d. "To Wyndham Development so long as the property is never used for the construction or operation of a Wal-Mart store."

Rights of Life Tenants

Those who hold life estates, referred to as **life tenants**, have the right of undisturbed possession during the time of their estate. However, life tenants cannot commit waste or destroy the property interest so that the rights of future interest holders are diminished (noted below). For example, cutting timber on the life estate property for the purpose of building fences or for fuel is appropriate conduct for a life tenant; however, cutting timber for commercial sale would be inappropriate because there is a dissipation of the value of the property and the interests of the future holders of title.

While alive, life tenants can transfer their interests, but a transferee's interest lasts only as long as the tenant/transferor is alive. An attempt by a life tenant to convey an interest at death is invalid. Similarly, creditors of the life tenant can have security in the property only until the life tenant's death. States have differing rules for tax liability between and among life tenants and those granted the future interest upon termination of the measuring life.

Reversions

A **reversion** is a future interest in the grantor that is created when the grantor has given someone else a lesser estate. For example, when the grantor makes the grant "To A for life," the present life estate of A will terminate upon A's death. At that point, the land must be transferred to someone, and in this case it will transfer back or revert to the grantor. Throughout A's life estate, the grantor has a future interest called a reversion. Other types of conveyances that would give the grantor a reversion include fee tails and the nonfreehold estates. For example, at the termination of any type of tenancy, the land reverts to the grantor.

CONSIDER 2.3

In 1976, Ruth Hooks Donalson executed a will devising a life estate in her separate property (consisting of productive oil wells) to her husband, George Donalson III, with a "reversionary interest" to other specified relatives. The will provided as follows:

My separate real property, hereinabove referred to in III A., including fee, surface, minerals, royalties, and mixed, and hereby intending to include all the rest, remainder and residue of my estate, not heretofore disposed of, I hereby give, devise and bequeath to my beloved husband, George E. Donalson, III., a Life Estate. My said husband is to enjoy the use and benefits of said properties, including the income derived from said properties, said income to become his separate property as paid. As stated, my said husband is to enjoy the use and benefits of said properties and to do with as he sees fit for the rest of his life, with reversion of the corpus of said properties upon his death as follows:

A. To my beloved niece, Olga Prather Singleton, one fourth (1/4) of the reversionary interest from the life estate left to my husband. Should the said Olga Prather Singleton predecease George E. Donalson, III., then her one fourth (1/4) of said reversionary interest shall vest in the natural children of Olga Prather Singleton, living at the time of the death of George E. Donalson, III., share and share alike.

Ruth died in 1977, and her will was probated the same year. A dispute arose between George and the holders of the "reversionary" interests over certain royalties and bonuses from the oil and gas produced from the estate property. The reversionary heirs argued that the royalties and bonuses are corpus of the estate, and that the will does not grant George the power to consume or dispose of the oil and gas royalties from the productive land. The heirs sued George for waste of the estate's assets, conversion, breach of fiduciary duty, fraud, and debt. George argues that he simply used the income from the property and that the income belonged to him while he was alive. Who is correct? *Singleton v. Donalson*, 2003 WL 22213472 (Tex. App. 2003)

Remainders

A **remainder** is a future interest created in someone other than the grantor. A remainder also follows a life estate or a fee tail. An example of language creating a remainder would be "To A for life, then to B." B holds the remainder interest, which is a future interest, because the interest becomes possessory only upon the death of A. In this example, the grantor has given to another what would have been a reversion, thereby creating a remainder. There are two types of remainders: vested and contingent.

Vested Remainders

A **vested remainder** is one given to someone identified and in existence who has the immediate right to the land interest upon termination of the freehold estate. In the example "To A for life, then to B," B holds a vested remainder because (1) B is identified and alive at the time of the grant, and (2) B will have the immediate right to the estate upon A's death. B's remainder is an example of one that is absolutely vested.

Two other types of vested remainders that may be created are **vested remainder subject to partial divestment** and **vested remainder subject to complete divestment**. "To A for life, then to the children of B," is a sample grant that can be used to illustrate the types of remainders. This example is one of a vested remainder if

B is dead and has one child. However, if B is alive, there is the possibility that B will have additional children during A's life estate. B's child holds a vested interest but could be divested of one-half or two-thirds of the interest should B have one or two more children before A's death. If A dies when B has three children, each child would receive a one-third interest. If A dies when B has one child, that child would receive the full interest. The potential for loss of part of the interest is referred to as divestment. The vested remainder created in the example when B is still alive is a vested remainder subject to partial divestment because B stands to lose part of his or her interest.

"To A for life, then to B, but if B is not married, then to C," is an example of a vested remainder subject to complete divestment. At the termination of A's life interest, B, ascertained and in existence at the time of the grant, will have a possessory interest. However, B could lose the interest by not marrying prior to A's death. In this instance, B loses the entire interest if the marriage requirement is not fulfilled at the time of A's death. This type of remainder in B is a vested remainder subject to complete divestment.

Contingent Remainders

A **contingent remainder** is the opposite of a vested remainder. That is, a contingent remainder is one in which the taker of the interest is unascertained or the interest has a condition precedent to its existence and will not pass automatically. An example of a contingent remainder is "To A for life, remainder to the children of B [a bachelor with no children]." It is possible that B may have children at the time of A's death and the children would be entitled to their interest, but at the time of the grant the takers (nonexistent children) are unascertained.

"To A for life, then if B is married, to B," is an example of a contingent remainder because of a condition precedent. In this example, B's interest does not automatically follow A's death, because B must meet the condition precedent of marriage to obtain the interest. There is a fine distinction between a condition precedent contingent remainder and vested remainder subject to a complete divestment. That distinction is that a condition preceding the remainder makes the remainder contingent, whereas a condition following the remainder makes the remainder subject to complete divestment.

When a contingent remainder future interest is created, a reversion or interest in the grantor is also created. If a contingent remainder fails (B is not married or has no children), the interest would revert to the grantor.

All types of remainders are transferable both *inter vivos* and at death. Obviously, a conveyance at death would be invalid if a condition of survival were attached to the remainder.

CONSIDER 2.4

Determine what types of present and future interests are involved in the following grants. Be sure to classify remainders according to their type, vested (partial or complete divestment) or contingent:

a. "To A for life, then to B"
b. "To A for life, then to B and her heirs"
c. "To B for life, then if A is married, to A"
d. "To A for life, then to B's heirs" (B is alive.)
e. "To A for life, then to B, but if B does not survive A, to C"

Executory Interests

In example e, "To A for life, then to B, but if B does not survive A, to C," a third party, C, has an interest that does not fit into any of the categories of future interests discussed so far. C holds an **executory interest**, which is a future interest that is not a remainder but is created in one other than the grantor. An executory interest is not vested at the time the grantor makes the grant and is considered to be vested only when the grantee takes possession (in this example, C). An executory interest usually arises in one of three circumstances. The first occurs when a fee simple determinable or a fee simple subject to a condition subsequent is given to two parties at the same time. For example, a grant "To A, so long as the premises are never used for commercial purposes and if they are so used, then to B" creates a fee simple defeasible interest in A and an executory interest in B. B's interest does not follow a life estate and is not a remainder. Further, B's interest is similar to a right of reversion or right of entry, but B is not a grantor; B's interest must be an executory interest.

A second circumstance that results in an executory interest occurs when the grantor creates a gap between present and future interests. An example would be "To A for life, then one year after A's death, to B." B does not have a remainder because there is no immediate vesting of B's interest. The one-year gap means that B holds an executory interest.

The third circumstance occurs when the grantor creates some future freehold estate, for example, "To A in 10 years." No present interest is created, and the 10-year interest cannot be classified as a grantor's interest because A is not the grantor. The interest is not a remainder because it does not follow another estate. A holds an executory interest. Figure 2.2 summarizes the future interests and their interrelationships with the present interests.

CONSIDER 2.5

Viva Parker Lilliston died in 1969 and in her will provided as follows:

Item Twelve: I give and devise my farm situated on the Seaside from Locustville, in the county of Accomack, State of Virginia... to my daughter, Margaret Lilliston Edwards, upon the conditions, set out in Item Fourteen.... Item Fourteen: all gifts made to my daughter, Margaret L. Edwards, individually and personally, under Items Eleven and Twelve of the Will, whether personal estate or real estate, are conditioned upon the said Margaret L. Edwards keeping the gift or devise herein free from encumbrances of every description, and in the event the said Margaret L. Edwards shall attempt to encumber some or sell her interest, or in the event any creditor or creditors of Margaret L. Edwards shall attempt to subject her interest in the gift or devise herein made to the payment of the debts of the said Margaret L. Edwards, then and in that event the interest of said Margaret L. Edwards therein shall immediately cease and determine, and the gift or devise shall at once become vested in her children, viz: Betty Bell Branch, Beverly Bradley, John R. Edwards, Bruce C. Edwards, Jill A. Edwards, and Jackie L. Edwards, in equal shares in fee simple...

In 1979, Margaret tried to obtain the consent of her children to sell the farm. Beverly Bradley, one of the listed children of Margaret, refused to give such consent. Margaret died in 1980 and left $1.00 to Beverly and directed that the farm be sold and the proceeds distributed among her other children. Beverly challenged the will, claiming that her interest had vested and could not be taken away. She claims that Margaret had a life estate and she and the other children had a remainder. Margaret's lawyer claims

CONSIDER 2.5 (continued)

that Margaret held a fee simple subject to a condition subsequent that she could convey at her death in the manner that she did.

What types of interests did Margaret and her children hold? *Edwards v. Bradley*, 315 S.E.2d 196 (Va. 1984)

CONSIDER 2.6

Determine what types of estates are created by the following language and examples:

a. "To A for life"
b. "To A and his heirs"
c. "To A"
d. "To A and B"
e. "To A and his female bodily heirs"
f. "To A provided the premises are never used for the sale of liquor"
g. "To A on the condition that the premises are never used for a dance hall"
h. "To A so long as the premises are used for church purposes"
i. "To my husband, Ralph, for life"
j. "To the trustee for First County Church so long as the premises are never used for the playing of bingo"
k. "To my granddaughter, Alfreda, and all of Alfreda's female issue"
l. "To my daughter, Sara, for the life of my brother, Sam"
m. "To my granddaughter so long as the premises are used for a library for Whitman College"
n. "To my son, John, and his bodily heirs"
o. "To Jess S. Long, and the children of his body begotten, and their heirs and assigns forever"
p. "To A for the period the land is used for a golf course"

Figure 2.2 Interrelationship of Present and Future Interests

Present Interests	Creation Language of Future Interests	Future Interests Created in Grantor	Others' Future Interests
Fee simple absolute	"To A" "To A and his heirs"	None	None
Fee tail	"To A and the heirs of his body" "To A and the female heirs of her body" "To A and the heirs of his body and his wife J"	Reversion if no heirs	None
Fee simple determinable	"To A so long as the property is used for church purposes"	Possibility of reverter	Executory interest
Fee simple subject to a condition subsequent	"To A on the condition that the property is used for church purposes"	Right of entry/Power of termination	Executory interest
Life estate/holder	"To A for life"	Reversion	Executory interest Remainder

Special Rules Governing Interests in Land

Three rules or doctrines that relate to land interests developed as common law in England and still apply to the construction and use of future interests: the Rule in Shelley's Case, the Doctrine of Worthier Title, and the Rule Against Perpetuities.

Rule in Shelley's Case

The **Rule in Shelley's Case** applies to grants made with the language "To A for life, remainder to the heirs of A." If the common law rules were followed, A would have a life estate and A's heirs would have a contingent remainder since heirs are unascertainable until the death of A. The Rule in Shelley's Case requires the merger of the present and future interests. Under this rule, A will have a fee simple absolute. Some states have passed legislation eliminating the effect of the Rule in Shelley's Case so that the present and future interests are not merged. The following case illustrates how the Rule in Shelley's Case and the state statutes abolishing it work.

LUSK V. BROYLES

694 So.2d 4 (Ala. Civ. App. 1997)

FACTS

In 1949, Andy Lusk and Mary Eliza Lusk executed a deed conveying certain rights in 130 acres (Parcel One) to Howard Lusk, who was the direct lineal ancestor of Elizabeth Broyles, Charles Lusk, and Homer Lusk (plaintiffs). The deed from Andy and Mary contained the following language:

KNOW ALL MEN BY THESE PRESENTS: That we Andy Lusk and his wife Mary Eliza Lusk... have this day... given, and granted, and by this instrument do give, grant and convey to... Howard Lusk for and during his natural life and at his death to the heirs of his body per stirpes

[Parcel One]...

To have and to hold the foregoing described lands unto the said Howard Lusk for and during his natural life, and at his death, the right and title to said lands to vest in the heirs at law of said Howard Lusk....

In 1952, Andy and Eliza Lusk executed a deed conveying to Howard an interest in an additional 40 acres of land (Parcel Two). This instrument is a printed form with typewritten additions to render it complete, and reads as follows:

KNOW ALL MEN BY THESE PRESENTS, that we, Andy Lusk and his wife, Eliza Lusk, parties of the first part, in consideration of the sum of One Hundred Dollars and other valuable consideration to us in hand paid by R.H. Lusk during his natural life and then to his bodily heirs, party of the second part, the receipt of which is hereby acknowledged, do hereby grant, bargain, sell and convey unto the said party of the second part, the following described property—to-wit:

[Parcel Two]

It is the intention of the grantors to convey to said R.H. Lusk only a life estate in and to said lands herein described, with the remainder to his bodily heirs.

Together with all and singular tenements, hereditaments, rights, members, privileges, and appurtenances thereunto belonging, or in any way appertaining, to have and to hold the same unto the said party of the second part, and to his heirs and assigns, forever; and we hereby warrant the title to the same against all claims whatever.

In 1994, one year before his death, Howard executed a deed conveying a fee simple interest in Parcels One and Two to himself and Ruth Lusk, his wife (grantee), as joint tenants with right of survivorship.

Upon Howard's death, the heirs (plaintiffs) filed suit for title to the property. The court found for the descendants (plaintiffs), and Ruth Lusk appealed.

JUDICIAL OPINION

Robertson, Presiding Judge. In light of these facts, we must consider whether Howard, at the time he executed the 1994 deed to the grantee, possessed a fee simple title to Parcels One and Two or only a life estate, with remainders vested in his bodily descendants (which include the plaintiffs). The grantee contends that the

1949 and 1952 deeds from Andy and Eliza to Howard conveyed common law estates in fee tail, which by operation of statute are converted to estates in fee simple absolute. The plaintiff heirs argue that the deeds instead conveyed life estates to Howard and remainders in fee simple to the heirs of his body, and that Howard therefore could not have conveyed to the grantee anything more than his own life estates (which necessarily terminate upon his death).

At common law, when an ancestor by any gift or conveyance took an estate of freehold, and in the same gift or conveyance the estate was limited to his or her heirs in fee or in tail, the words "the heirs" were deemed as a matter of substantive law to be words of limitation and not of purchase. See *Wolfe v. Shelley*, 72 Eng. Rep. 490 (1581). This is the famous, or infamous, principle of property law known as the "Rule in Shelley's Case." However, this rule of the common law is not followed in Alabama because it has been superseded by statute. Section 35-4-230, Ala. Code 1975, provides as follows:

Where a remainder created by deed or will is limited to the heirs, issue or heirs of the body of a person to whom a life estate in the same property is given, the persons who, on termination of the life estate, are the heirs, issue or heirs of the body of such tenant for life are entitled to take as purchasers by virtue of the remainder so limited by them.

Thus, the Rule in Shelley's Case would have operated to convert automatically a conveyance of a life estate to a grantee with remainder in fee to the grantee's heirs into a conveyance of a fee in the grantee. However, 35-4-230 alters this arbitrary rule, requiring that a grantor's intent to sever a grantee's life estate interest from the grantee's heirs' remainder interest be honored according to the express terms of the conveyance.

We now turn to the precise language of the 1949 and 1952 deeds themselves to determine whether they may be classified as expressly giving Howard a life estate and his bodily heirs a remainder. The granting clause of the 1949 deed to Parcel One conveys Parcel One to Howard Lusk for and during his natural life. Moreover, the same clause specifically grants Parcel One "to the heirs of his body per stirpes" at Howard's death. This language expressly conveys both a life estate to Howard and a remainder interest in his bodily heirs. Similarly, the granting clause of the 1952 Parcel Two deed, while less artfully drafted, conveys Parcel Two to Howard during his natural life, and conveys a remainder interest to his bodily heirs. Indeed, the grantors' intent to do this is evidenced by their statement in the deed that it was their intention "to convey to said R.H. Lusk *only a life estate* in and to [Parcel Two], with remainder to his bodily heirs." Thus, as a matter of law, Howard, in 1994 could have conveyed only his life estates in Parcels One and Two to the grantee, which life estates necessarily terminated upon his subsequent death.

The trial court correctly concluded that the grantee held no interest in Parcels One and Two after Howard's death.

Affirmed.

CASE QUESTIONS

1. What type of interest was granted to Howard Lusk?
2. How does Ruth Lusk claim an interest?
3. What does the Rule in Shelley's Case do to a grant such as the one to Howard?
4. What does the Alabama statute do to the grant to Howard Lusk despite the Rule in Shelley's Case?

Doctrine of Worthier Title

The **Doctrine of Worthier Title** applies to grants with the language "To A for life, remainder to the heirs of the grantor." Following the general future interest rules, A would have a life estate and the heirs would have either a vested remainder or a contingent remainder (depending on whether the grant was *inter vivos* or testamentary). However, under the Doctrine of Worthier Title, A has a life estate, the heirs have no interest, and the grantor holds a reversion. Legislation in some states has eliminated this doctrine or has permitted courts to determine the grantor's true intent in making the grant.

> ***Practical Tip***
>
> *Verify rights of those who are in possession of property: How long have they been there? What are the terms of their presence? Are they there by lease rights or some other form of grant? What rights do they have for renewal or options?*

Rule Against Perpetuities

The basic idea of the **Rule Against Perpetuities** (**RAP**) is to limit the length of time during which grantors may control the transfer, conveyance, and vesting of land interests. The purpose is to ensure that property ownership and transferability is not tied to the grave. However, the rule is arbitrary and applies only to contingent remainders and executory interests.

Generally stated, the rule provides that an interest is good only if it vests no later than 21 years after the death of the last individual who is part of the group of measuring lives for the grant. As noted earlier, a measuring life is the lifetime of individuals named in the grant. Vesting is the absolute right to receive property without conditions. If the 21-year vesting rule is violated by a grant, the grant is lost and title reverts to the grantor or the grantor's estate to be distributed according to the grantor's desires or according to state law if no will exists.

To understand the application of the rule, it is best to explain each portion of it in the context of an example. Here we will use the grant, made in a will, "To my children for life, remainder to any and all of my grandchildren who reach age 21" as the example for working through the rule's application:

Step One—Determine the type of interest involved. The children have a life estate. The grandchildren are unascertained (more could be born during the children's life estate) and therefore hold a contingent remainder. Furthermore, because there is a potential gap between the life estate of the children and the grandchildren (who must be 21), the grandchildren's interest could be classified as an executory interest.

Step Two—Determine whether the RAP is applicable. Because the RAP applies to both contingent remainders and executory interests, the rule is applicable to the grandchildren's interests.

Step Three—Determine when the interest would vest. The interest would vest when the last grandchild reached age 21.

Step Four—Determine the measuring lives in being. At the time of the will's grant, the children are alive and thus would be the measuring lives for purposes of the 21-year rule for vesting.

Step Five—Determine whether all interests will vest within 21 years after the death of the last measuring life. Consider all possibilities of birth and survival. Upon the death of the last child, there can be no more grandchildren. Thus, the longest it can take for a grandchild's interest to vest is 21 years after the death of the last child. (Gestation periods are not included in the 21 years.)

Step Six—Determine if the RAP is violated. Because all grandchildren will have the interest vested within 21 years after the lives in being of the children, the RAP is not violated and the grant is valid.

Because this complex rule could present difficulties in wills and other transfers, some states have passed statutes eliminating the rule or restricting its harsh effects. A Uniform Statutory Rule Against Perpetuities has been adopted in 24 states, and this uniform rule reduces some of the more complicated provisions in the rule such as its application to nonvested interests. In addition, a number of states have abolished the RAP.[4] The RAP is used less frequently because of the generation-skipping tax imposed by federal tax code on estates.

Even in states without such legislation, the effect of the RAP can be avoided simply by placing a **saving clause** in the will or grant of property. A saving clause either provides an alternative for distribution should the grant violate the rule or provides that the grant is to be interpreted so as to avoid violation of the rule.

Figure 2.3 summarizes the future interests, their related present interests, their language of creation, and the rules that govern them.

4. Alaska Stat. §34.27.051 (2002) (RAP is 1,000 years long); Del. Code Ann. tit. 25, §503 (2003) (110 years); Idaho Code §55-1522 (2003) (eliminates); 765 Illinois Comp. Stat. Ann. 305/4 (West 2003) (eliminates); S.D. Codified Laws §43-5-8 (Michie 2003) (eliminates); Wis. Stat. Ann. §700.16 (2003) (30 years).

Figure 2.3 Summary of the Creation and Rules of Future Interests

Future Interest	Related Present Interest	Sample Language of Creation	Applicability of Rules
Possibility of reverter	Fee simple determinable	"To A so long as the property is used for church purposes"	Some state limitation and filing requirements
Right of entry/ power of termination	Fee simple subject to condition subsequent	"To A on the condition that the property is used for church purposes"	Some state limitation filing requirements
Reversion	Life estate/fee tail	"To A for life" "To A for the life of B"	Doctrine of Worthier Title
Vested remainder	Life estate	"To A for life, then to B"	Rule in Shelley's Case; Doctrine of Worthier Title
Vested subject to partial divestment	Life estate	"To A for life, then to B's children" (B is alive with two children)	Rule in Shelley's Case; Doctrine of Worthier Title
Vested subject to complete divestment	Life estate	"To A for life, then to B but if B is not married, to C"	
Contingent remainder	Life estate	"To A for life, then to B's children" (B is a bachelor) "To A for life, then if B is married, to B"	Rule Against Perpetuities
Executory interest	Life estate Fee simple defeasible Fee tail	"To A for life, then in 10 years to B" "To B in 10 years"	Rule Against Perpetuities

The RAP causes a great deal of confusion whenever long-term property interests arise. Violation of the RAP in drafting wills and trusts is the largest area of malpractice litigation for estate-planning attorneys. In the following case the court deals with the confusion of just the simple issue of whether the RAP applies to lease options.

Texaco Refining and Marketing, Inc. v. Samowitz

570 A.2d 170 (Conn. 1990)

FACTS

Sam Samowitz (plaintiff) leased property from Texaco Refining and Marketing (defendants) in 1964. The lease term was 15 years with three options to renew for periods of five years each. The lease gave Samowitz "*the exclusive right, at lessee's option, to purchase the demised premises … at any time during the term of this lease or an extension or renewal thereof, from and after the 14th year of the initial term for the sum of $125,000.*"

On August 14, 1987, Samowitz gave notice, via certified mail, to Texaco that he desired to exercise his right to purchase the property. Texaco refused to convey the property on the grounds that the RAP was violated, and Samowitz brought suit. The trial court found for Samowitz and Texaco appealed.

JUDICIAL OPINION

Peters, Chief Justice. The defendants rely on the common law rule against perpetuities as their second argument for the unenforceability of the plaintiff's option to purchase their property. The rule against perpetuities states that "[n]o interest is good unless it must vest, if at all, not later than 21 years after some life in being at the creation of the interest." J. Gray, *The Rule Against Perpetuities* (4th Ed., 1942) p. 191; *Connecticut Bank & Trust Co. v. Brody*, 174 Conn. 616, 623, 392 A.2d 445 (1978). The defendants maintain that the option in this case did not vest within the time span mandated by the rule. We disagree.

The trial court determined that the option in the lease agreement did not violate the rule against perpetuities by construing the lease agreement as a series of discrete undertakings, first for an initial fourteen year term, and thereafter for each renewal term. Because the option could be exercised only within one of these discrete terms, none of which exceeded twenty-one years in length, the court held that the interest in the option would necessarily vest within the time period specified by the Rule Against Perpetuities.

Whatever might be the merits of the trial court's construction of the lease agreement, we prefer to consider a more basic question: do options in long-term leases fall within the jurisdiction of the Rule Against Perpetuities? Our precedents indicate that the rule applies to an unrestricted option to purchase real property; *Neustadt v. Pearce*, 145 Conn. 403, 405, 143 A.2d 437 (1958); *H.J. Lewis Oyster Co. v. West*, 93 Conn. 518, 530, 107 A. 138 (1919); but not to an option to renew the term of a real property lease. *Lonergan v. Connecticut Food Store, Inc.*, 168 Conn. 122, 124, 357 A.2d 910 (1975). We have not, however, previously considered the relationship between the rule against perpetuities and an option to purchase contained in a long-term commercial lease of real property.

The defendants have offered no reason of policy why we should extend the ambit of the rule against perpetuities to cover an option to purchase contained in a commercial lease. "The underlying and fundamental purpose of the rule is founded on the public policy in favor of free alienability of property and against restricting its marketability over long periods of time by restraints on its alienation." *Connecticut Bank & Trust Co. v. Brody*, supra, 174 Conn. at 624, 392 A.2d 445; 4 Restatement, Property (1944) pp. 2129–33. An option coupled with a long-term commercial lease is consistent with these policy objectives because it stimulates improvement of the property and thus renders it more rather than less marketable. 3 L. Simes & A. Smith, *The Law of Future Interests* (2d Ed. 1956) p. 162. Any extension of the rule against perpetuities would, furthermore, be inconsistent with the legislative adoption of the "second look" doctrine, pursuant to which an interest subject to the rule may be validated, contrary to the common law, by the occurrence of events subsequent to the creation of the interest. See General Statutes §45–95; *Connecticut Bank & Trust Co. v. Brody*, supra, at 627–28, 392 A.2d 445.

We therefore conclude that an option to purchase contained in a commercial lease, at least if the option must be exercised within the leasehold term, is valid without regard to the rule against perpetuities. This position is consistent with the weight of authority in the United States.

The plaintiff's option in this case was, therefore, enforceable.

There is no error.

CASE QUESTIONS

1. What land interest did Samowitz have?
2. What was the maximum length of the Samowitz/Texaco lease?
3. Does the lease violate the Rule Against Perpetuities? Explain.
4. Does the option to purchase violate the Rule Against Perpetuities?
5. Who ends up with title and possession in the case?

CONSIDER 2.7

Determine whether the Rule Against Perpetuities is violated by the following grant made while the grantor is alive: "To my children for life, remainder to any and all of my grandchildren who reach age 21." Be sure to use the six steps in your analysis.

CONSIDER 2.8

Would a 97-year lease violate the Rule Against Perpetuities? *Matter of Ferguson*, 751 P.2d 1008 (Colo. 1987)

Land Interests–Nonfreehold Estates

Nonfreehold estates are limited in duration and noninheritable. Chapters 9 and 10 include detailed coverage of the nonfreehold estates. In lay terms, a nonfreehold estate is a lease.

Practical Tip

The complexities of real estate law and real estate ownership can be confusing, and mistakes about notions of title and interest can be costly. Be certain sellers, buyers, brokers, and lenders understand the implications of various interests in real estate. Legal advice is often necessary to create, clarify, and interpret the form of ownership.

Economics of Land Interests

To this point, the discussion of land interests has focused on the legal rights and responsibilities provided for each type of interest. These legal protections are central in the law of real property. However, the reason for these protections lies in the importance of property ownership in free-market systems. The boxed excerpt "An Economic Theory of Property Rights" by Richard Posner explains the economic rationale for real property rights and protections.

An Economic Theory of Property Rights

Imagine a society in which all property rights have been abolished. A farmer plants corn, fertilizes it, and erects scarecrows, but when the corn is ripe his neighbor reaps it and sells it. The farmer has no legal remedy against his neighbor's conduct since he owns neither the land that he sowed nor the crop. After a few such incidents the cultivation of land will be abandoned and the society will shift to methods of subsistence (such as hunting) that involve less preparatory investment.

This example suggests that the legal protection of property rights has an important economic function: to create incentives to use resources efficiently. Although the value of the crop in our example, as measured by consumer willingness to pay, may have greatly exceeded the cost in labor, materials, and foregone alternative uses of the land, without property rights there is no incentive to incur these costs because there is no reasonable assured reward for incurring them. The proper incentives are created by the parceling out among the members of society of mutually exclusive rights to the use of particular resources. If every piece of land is owned by someone in the sense that there is always an individual who can exclude all others from access to any given area, then individuals will endeavor by cultivation or other improvements to maximize the value of the land.

The creation of exclusive rights is a necessary rather than sufficient condition for the efficient use of resources. The rights must be transferable. Suppose the farmer in our example owns the land that he sows but is a bad farmer; his land would be more productive in someone else's hands. The maximization of value requires a mechanism by which the farmer can be induced to transfer rights in the property to someone who can work it more productively. A transferable right is such a mechanism.

An example will illustrate. Farmer A owns a piece of land that he anticipates will yield him $100 a year, in excess of labor and other costs, indefinitely. The value of the right to a stream of future earnings can be expressed as a present sum. Just as the price of a share of common stock expresses the present value of the anticipated earnings to which the shareholder will be entitled, so the present value of a parcel of land that yields an annual net income of $100 can be calculated and is the minimum price that A will accept in exchange for his property right. Farmer B thinks he could net more than $100 a year from working A's land. The present value of B's higher expected earnings stream will, of course, exceed the present value calculated by A. Assume the present value calculated by A is $1,000 and by B $1,500.

Then the sale of the property by A to B will yield benefits to both parties if the price is anywhere between $1,000 and $1,500. At a price of $1,250, for example, A receives $250 more than the land is worth to him and B pays $250 less than the land is worth to him. Thus, there are strong incentives for the parties voluntarily to exchange A's land for B's money, and if B is as he believes a better farmer than A, the transfer will result in an increase in the productivity of the land. Through a succession of such transfers, resources are shifted to their highest valued, most productive uses and efficiency in the use of economic resources is maximized.

The foregoing discussion suggests three criteria of an efficient system of property rights. The first is universality. Ideally, all resources should be owned, or ownable, by someone, except resources so plentiful that everybody can consume as much of them as he wants without reducing consumption by anyone else (sunlight is a good, but not perfect example—why?). No issue of efficient use arises in such a case.

The second criterion is exclusivity. We have assumed so far that either the farmer can exclude no one or he can exclude everyone, but of course there are intermediate stages: the farmer may be entitled to exclude private individuals from reaping his crop, but not the government in time of war. It might appear that the more exclusive the property right, the greater the incentive to invest the right amount of resources in the development of the property.

The third criterion of an efficient system of property rights is transferability. If a property right cannot be transferred, there is no way of shifting a resource from a less productive to a more productive use through voluntary exchange. The costs of transfer may be high to begin with; a legal prohibition against transferring may, depending on the penalties for violation, make the costs utterly prohibitive.

DISCUSSION QUESTIONS

1. How do property rights serve to protect and "incent" landowners?

2. Why is it sometimes more economically efficient for a property owner to transfer property?

3. What are the three criteria of an efficient system of property rights?

Note: For the answer to the question on the exclusivity of sunlight, see Chapter 3.

From Richard Posner, *An Economic Analysis of Law.* Little, Brown and Company, 1973. Assigned to Aspen Law and Business, a division of Aspen Publishers, Inc. Reprinted with permission of the author.

Cautions and Conclusions

Knowledge of this chapter will be most useful in situations where land titles are being transferred. In the case of a transfer, all parties (buyers, sellers, brokers, agents, and financiers) need to analyze the transfer by checking the following issues:

1. What type of interest does the seller hold?
2. What restrictions are on the transfer? Could the land title be lost?
3. Does the seller have the right and ability to transfer the property? Can the seller transfer full title or simply a lesser interest, such as a life estate?
4. What type of language is being used in the conveyance? Is the buyer getting a fee simple absolute or a life estate? Are restrictions being imposed upon the buyer?
5. What are the implications of other parties' interests in the property in the future?

Land records (discussed in Chapter 13) provide the parties with answers to most of the above questions. The answers must be researched before any land transaction is completed.

Key Terms

contingent remainder, 26
Doctrine of Worthier Title, 30
executory interest, 27
fee, 19
fee simple, 19
fee simple absolute, 19
fee simple defeasible, 19
fee simple determinable, 19
fee simple subject to a condition subsequent, 19
fee tail, 23
freehold, 19
inter vivos, 20
life estate, 23
life estate *pur autre vie,* 23
life tenants, 24
nonfreehold estates, 34
possibility of reverter, 19
power of termination, 20
remainder, 25
reversion, 24
right of entry, 20
Rule Against Perpetuities (RAP), 30
Rule in Shelley's Case, 29
saving clause, 31
testamentary, 20
vested remainder, 25
vested remainder subject to complete divestment, 25
vested remainder subject to partial divestment, 25

Chapter Problems

1. Tom and Doyle Proctor were deeded 20 lots of land in a Florida subdivision with the understanding that they would construct an incinerator on the property. The deed contained no specifics on the incinerator or the Proctors' responsibilities. The developer claims a right of reentry. The Proctors claim the land is theirs as a fee simple estate. Who is correct? *Proctor v. Inland Shores, Inc.*, 373 S.E.2d 268 (Ga. 1988)

2. What type of interest is created by the following language?

IN CONSIDERATION of Ten Dollars... Grantor hereby grants... to Grantee, its successors and assigns, the entire interests in the Property... reserving and excepting unto Grantor the Production Royalty and Ten Cent Wheelage Royalty, both described below; subject only to the production royalty reserved in the Delcarbon Deed, to Grantor's right of re-entry for condition broken, as described below...

If Grantee defaults in the payment of annual fees... then Grantor shall be entitled to a reconveyance of the Property and delivery of exclusive possession thereto. Jelen and Son v. Kaiser Steel, Inc., 807 P.2d 1241 (Colo. 1991)

3. Kinney Land and Cattle Company conveyed, by warranty deed, to the state of Kansas 790 acres of land for use as a state park. There was a paragraph in the deed called "Clause of Reversion," which required the state to build and maintain a lake of a minimum of 150 acres. The failure to maintain the lake caused title to "revert to the grantor, successors or assigns." From 1934 to 1970, the state maintained a lake on the property, but the lake was never 150 acres in size. Shareholders of Kinney Land and Cattle have brought suit to quiet title to them in the 790 acres. Will they be given title? *Kinney v. State of Kansas and Kansas Fish and Game Commission*, 710 P.2d 1290 (Kan. 1985)

4. In each of the following, determine what type of present and future interests are created, and also the applicability of any of the three rules: the Rule in Shelley's Case, the Doctrine of Worthier Title, and the Rule Against Perpetuities.

(G = grantor; L/E = life estate; rem = remainder)

a. G→L/E→ A
→L/E→ A's widow
Rem to A's children at the death of the widow

b. G→L/E→ A

c. G→ A and her heirs on the condition that liquor never be sold on the premises

d. G→L/E→ A→Rem to B and his heirs if B shall survive A

Suppose A (during her lifetime) gave D the right to use the land for 10 years. What type of estate would be created?

e. G→ A so long as liquor is not sold on the premises

Suppose G later left all his interest to A. What type of estate would be created?

f. G→ A when A reaches age 25

g. G→L/E→ A (80 years old)
→L/E→children for life
→ Rem to grandchildren

h. G→L/E→ A→B and his heirs but if B shall predecease A→C

i. G→L/E→ A→heirs of A

j. G→L/E→ A→B if B lives to attain the age of 30 years (B is 5 years old)

5. W. E. Collins executed and delivered to the Church of God of Prophecy a warranty deed with the following language:

This transfer or deed is made with the full understanding that should the property fail to be used for the Church of God, it is to be null and void and property to revert to W. E. Collins or heirs.

What type of interests were created in the deed? Do any of the interests violate the Rule Against Perpetuities? *Collins v. Church of God of Prophecy*, 800 S.W.2d 418 (Ark. 1990)

6. A deed and contract provided that Dempsey, Carter, and Burton Layne would all hold title to 375 acres of land in Pittsylvania County, Virginia. Under the terms of the agreement, when one brother died, the remaining brothers or their heirs had the opportunity to purchase the deceased brother's one-third interest through a right of first refusal. Does the right of first refusal here violate the Rule Against Perpetuities? *Layne v. Henderson*, 351 S.E.2d 18 (Va. 1986); What about an option to repurchase property reserved by the grantor? *Dennis v. Bird*, 941 S.W.2d 486 (Ct. App. Ky. 1997)

7. Richard J. Long and Mary Long, his wife, conveyed by warranty deed dated September 30, 1949, to the Pompey Fire Department a parcel of land (called P-1). The deed, which was properly recorded in the Onondaga County Clerk's Office on November 15, 1949, stated that the grant of the parcel was for the purpose of "erecting thereon a fire house." The deed also included the following language:

In the event that the said premises are no longer used to house a fire department, then and in that event the land and building erected thereon is to revert to Richard J. Long and Mary Long, or their heirs and assigns.

Shortly after the conveyance, a firehouse was erected on P-1. The building is a two-story structure with a cinder block first floor and a wood frame second floor. The first floor contains three large bays to house fire trucks and equipment. The building was used continuously from 1950 to 1985 to house the Fire Department. In 1984, the Fire Department acquired another parcel of land (P-2) located about 300 yards from P-1. P-2 had an elementary school that was remodeled to include vehicle bays and other features of a well-equipped firehouse. In November 1985, the Fire Department moved its essential equipment and the majority of its functions to the P-2 facility. Does the Fire Department still own the land conveyed by the Longs? *Long v. Pompey Hill Volunteer Fire Dept.*, 539 N.Y.S.2d 1014 (1989)

8. What types of interest are created by the following language?

To my daughter, Edna M. Arehart, to have and to hold same for and during her lifetime, and at her death to her issue in equal shares, or if she shall have no issue, then to the Odd Fellows Home at York, Nebraska, provided, if my said daughter, Edna M. Arehart, shall be left a widow, then upon her becoming a widow, I give and devise all my real estate to her, by absolute title, believing she may need the same for her maintenance. Dover v. Grand Lodge of Nebraska Ind. Order of Oddfellows, 206 N.W.2d 845 (Neb. 1973)

9. Hixon, by his will, made the following grant:

To my wife, Alice, for her life, the net income from my property and upon her death said property to be distributed equally among my heirs.

What interests were created? Are they valid? *Harris Trust & Saving Bank v. Beach*, 495 N.E.2d 1170 (Ill. 1986)

10. On June 11, 1986, Arlene M. Van Den Boom married Thomas J. Van Den Boom. Thomas's will was executed on December 5, 1986, and he died on October 11, 1992, survived by his wife and four children from his first marriage, one of whom is Gary F. Van Den Boom (Van Den Boom).

Thomas's will states in pertinent part:

Article I

I direct that all of my debts, expenses of last illness and funeral expenses be paid as soon as possible after my death.

Article II

After the payment of my just debts and expenses of last illness and funeral expenses, I give, devise and bequeath my estate as follows: To my wife, ARLENE M. VAN DEN BOOM, I give a life estate in our homestead located in Aitkin County, Minnesota, with the remainder interest in the homestead to my children, GARY VAN DEN BOOM, KAY SICHAK, WAYNE VAN DEN BOOM and BRUCE VAN DEN BOOM, in equal shares with the right of representation.

Robert Janzen was appointed personal representative of Thomas's estate. Janzen filed an inventory and appraisement with the court on December 1, 1993. In May 1995, decedent's widow moved to close the estate, which Van Den Boom contested. Decedent's widow was awarded a life estate in the real property, with the remainder interest in the children, as directed by the will. Janzen was to proceed with the closing of the estate, which he failed to do. Decedent's widow, upon a second motion to close, was reimbursed by the district court for funeral expenses, income taxes, real estate taxes, and property insurance premiums, and Janzen was commended for his discharge of duties. As a result of this litigation, Janzen incurred significant attorney fees and expenses, which he submitted to the court.

Janzen and decedent's widow requested that decedent's homestead be sold to pay the debts and obligations of the estate, which included decedent's funeral expenses, decedent's 1992 federal and state income tax liabilities, maintenance, and Janzen's attorney fees and compensation. The district court approved the request to place the homestead on the market for sale. Van Den Boom appealed the decision because the sale of the homestead violated his future interest property rights in it. Is Van Den Boom correct? *In re Estate of Van Den Boom*, 590 N.W.2d 350 (Minn. App. 1999).

For research activities related to this chapter, go to our text companion website at www.thomsonedu.com/westbuslaw/jennings.

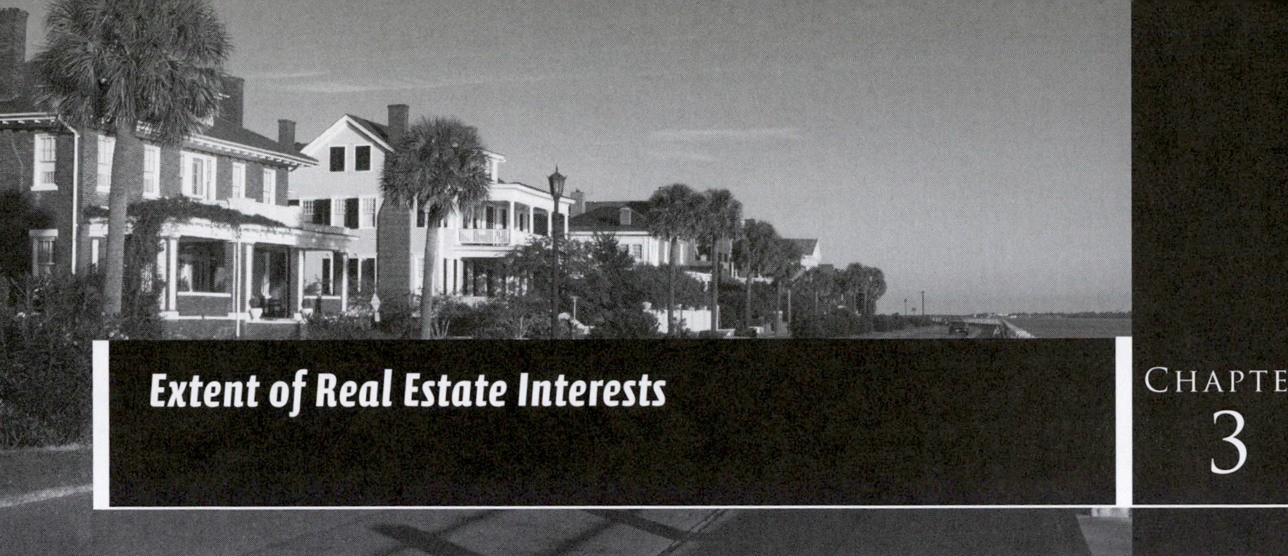

Extent of Real Estate Interests

CHAPTER 3

Broad acres are a patent of nobility; and no man but feels more of a man in the world if he have a bit of ground that he can call his own. However small it is on the surface, it is four thousand miles deep; and that is a very handsome property.

Charles Dudley Warner, *My Summer Is a Garden* (1871)

An old maxim in property law is "The owner of the soil owns also to the sky and to the depths." Land ownership involves so much more than surface rights. For example, the Trump Tower in New York City is built in the air rights once owned by Tiffany's. Tiffany's retained its surface rights but conveyed its air rights in its land to Donald Trump. This chapter answers the following questions: What do I own when I hold title to land? Where does my ownership interest start? Where does it end? Land ownership has been depicted as a wedge that runs from the core of the earth to the "heavens," as shown in Figure 3.1. Land interests include the surface, that which is below the surface, and the air that extends above the surface parcel.

Land Interests Above the Surface

Air Rights

The discussion of **air rights**, or the land interest above the surface, can be divided into two topics: (1) a determination of who can use the air and to what extent, and (2) a determination of what air interests can be transferred.

Who Can Use the Air?

The airspace of all property owners is used by others. In addition to constant air traffic in the airspace above property, manufacturers, processors, and auto drivers use the airspace in that their gases, smokes, and fumes invade the airspace in many pieces of property. Land owners enjoy limited protections in these types of uses

Figure 3.1 Extent of Land Ownership

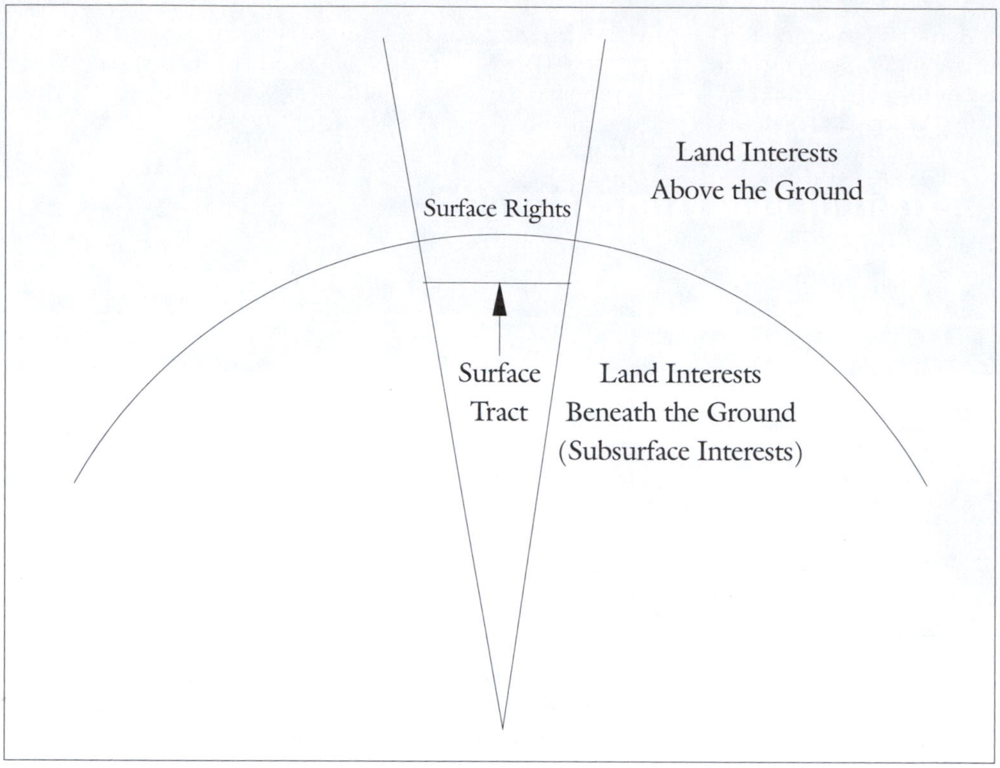

through environmental regulation (see Chapter 20), but specific relief for individual landowners often requires them to bring suits in nuisance or trespass. (Nuisance and trespass are discussed later in this chapter.) The following case is an example of how much the airspace of another can be used and deals with the rights of landowners in preventing and controlling the use of their airspace.

UNITED STATES V. CAUSBY

328 U.S. 256 (1946)

FACTS

Mr. and Mrs. Causby (respondents) owned 2.8 acres of land near an airport outside of Greensboro, North Carolina. On the property were a house where the Causbys resided and various outbuildings used for raising chickens. The end of the airport's northwest–southwest runway was 2,220 feet from the Causbys' barn and 2,275 feet from their house. The path of glide to the runway passed directly over their property at 67 feet above the house, 63 feet above the barn, and 18 feet above the highest tree. The U.S. government leased the airstrip in 1942, with the lease carrying renewal provisions until 1967. Bombers, transports, and fighters all used the airfield. At times, the airplanes came close enough to blow old leaves off trees, and the noise of the airplanes was startling. As a result of the noise, 6 to 10 of the Causbys' chickens were killed each day by "flying into the walls from fright." After losing 150 chickens, the Causbys gave up their business. They could no longer sleep well and became nervous and frightened.

The Causbys sued the U.S. government on the grounds that the United States was taking their airspace by eminent domain without compensating them. The lower court found for the Causbys, and the U.S. government appealed.

JUDICIAL OPINION

Douglas, Justice. The United States relies on the Air Commerce Act of 1926. Under those statutes the United States has "complete and exclusive national sovereignty in the air space" over this country. They grant any citizen of the United States "a public right of freedom of transit in air commerce through the navigable air space of the United States."

And "navigable air space" is defined as "airspace above the minimum safe altitudes of flight prescribed by the Civil Aeronautics Authority." And it is provided that "such navigable airspace shall be subject to a public right of freedom of interstate and foreign air navigation." It is, therefore, argued that since these flights were within the minimum safe altitudes of flight which had been prescribed, they were an exercise of the declared right of travel through the airspace. The United States concludes that when flights are made within the navigable airspace without any physical invasion of the property of the landowners, there has been no taking of property. It is ancient doctrine that at common law ownership of the land extended to the periphery of the universe—*Cujus est solum ejus est usque ad coelum.* But that doctrine has no place in the modern world. The air is a public highway, as Congress has declared. Were that not true, every transcontinental flight would subject the operator to countless trespass suits. Common sense revolts at the idea. To recognize such private claims to the airspace would clog these highways, seriously interfere with their control and development in the public interest, and transfer into private ownership that to which only the public has a just claim.

But the general principle does not control the present case. For the United States conceded on oral argument that if the flights over respondents' property rendered it uninhabitable, there would be a taking compensable under the Fifth Amendment. It is the owner's loss, not the taker's gain, which is the measure of the value of the property taken. Market value fairly determined is the normal measure of the recovery. And that value may reflect the use to which the land could readily be converted, as well as existing use. If, by reason of the frequency and altitude of the flights, respondents could not use this land for any purpose, their loss would be complete. It would be as complete as if the United States had entered upon the surface of the land and taken exclusive possession of it.

The path of glide for airplanes might reduce a valuable factory site to grazing land, an orchard to a vegetable patch, a residential section to a wheat field. Some value would remain. But the use of the airspace immediately above the land would limit the utility of the land and cause a diminution in its value.

We have said that the airspace is a public highway. Yet it is obvious that if the landowner is to have full enjoyment of the land, he must have exclusive control of the immediate reaches of the enveloping atmosphere. Otherwise buildings could not be erected, trees could not be planted, and even fences could not be run. The principle is recognized when the law gives a remedy in case overhanging structures are erected on adjoining lands. The landowner owns at least as much of the space above the ground as he can occupy or use in connection with the land. The fact that he does not occupy it in a physical sense—by the erection of buildings and the like—is not material. As we have said, the flight of airplanes, which skim the surface but do not touch it, is as much an appropriation of the use of the land as a more conventional entry upon it. We would not doubt that if the United States erected an elevated railway over respondents' land at the precise altitude where its planes now fly, there would be a partial taking even though none of the supports of the structure rested on the land. The reason is that there would be an intrusion so immediate and direct as to subtract from the owner's full enjoyment of the property and to limit his exploitation of it. While the owner does not in any physical manner occupy that stratum of airspace or make use of it in the conventional sense, he does use it in somewhat the same sense that space left between buildings for the purpose of light and air is used. The superadjacent airspace at this low altitude is so close to the land that continuous invasions of it affect the use of the surface of the land itself. We think that the landowner, as an incident to his ownership, has a claim to it and that invasions of it are in the same category as invasions of the surface.

The airplane is part of the modern environment of life, and the inconveniences which it causes are normally not compensable under the Fifth Amendment. The airspace, apart from the immediate reaches above the land, is part of the public domain. We need not determine at this time what those precise limits are. Flights over private land are not a taking, unless they are so low and so frequent as to be a direct and immediate interference with the enjoyment and use of the land. We need not speculate on that phase of the present case. For the findings of the Court of Claims plainly establish that there was a diminution in value of the property and that the frequent, low-level flights were the direct and immediate cause. We agree with the Court of Claims that a servitude has been imposed upon the land.

Affirmed.

CASE QUESTIONS

1. What type of business did the Causbys operate?
2. How close was the airstrip to the Causbys' home?
3. How close to the Causbys' land were the airplanes (in altitude) upon their runway approach?
4. What happened to the Causbys' chickens as a result of the airplanes?
5. What happened to the Causbys as a result of the airplanes?
6. Are the Causbys suing for nuisance?
7. What statute does the government say is controlling?
8. Can the use of airspace diminish the value of the surface of the land?
9. Do the Causbys win?

CONSIDER 3.1

Bergstrom Air Force Base, located in southeast Travis County, was closed in 1991 as a part of the federal government's military base closure policy. Under a 1942 agreement between the federal government and the City of Austin, the Bergstrom property reverted to the City. The City decided to develop a new municipal airport at the Bergstrom location. The airport began civilian operations in June 1997, and some military flights still operate from the airport. Travis County Landfill Company (TCLC) owns a 133-acre tract of land located about one-half mile south of the airport's main runway. TCLC had a Type IV landfill permit for this tract that would allow it to receive non-putrescible dry waste, such as construction rubble, tree clippings, and tires. The deed for the property conveys what is called an avigation easement, which allows 60,900 military aircraft unobstructed passage over TCLC's property each year. The deed also describes certain airspace above the property as approach-departure and transition zones, and conveys a "clearance" or "obstruction" easement that allows the City to prohibit or remove vegetation, buildings, and other structures that extend into those zones.

When civilian flights began operating from Bergstrom in 1997, TCLC sued the City alleging that the flights over its property constituted an unconstitutional taking of its property. TCLC sought a judgment declaring that the avigation easement does not grant the City civilian overflight rights. It also requested a temporary injunction preventing the City from directing civilian flights over its property until the City obtained overflight rights through condemnation proceedings or the purchase of an easement. TCLC further sought actual and exemplary damages for trespass and inverse condemnation, together with attorneys' fees, interest, and costs. *City of Austin v. Travis County Landfill Co., L.L.C.*, 73 S.W.3d 234 (Tex. 2002).

Should TCLC be compensated and awarded the injunction? How is this case the same or different from the *Causby* case?

The *Causby* case illustrates limitations on the use of airspace. The landowner is subject to use of the airspace by air traffic but is entitled to compensation in the event that the airspace is used in such a manner as to prevent use of the surface property. Other uses of airspace can interfere with the land of another. For example, when the eaves of a building or branches from a tree located on one parcel of land hang over onto another landowner's parcel of land, there is a taking of airspace. In the *Causby* case, the court mentioned that a remedy is available for overhang. The property owner affected by the overhang can bring suit for a court order requiring the removal of the eaves or branches, and in some states is even permitted to unilaterally end the invasion by clipping the tree branches.

> ***Practical Tip***
>
> *Check property for noise, air activity, and overhangs. Determine flight paths and plans for construction of airports, runways, and possible expansion of airport capacity and facilities.*

What Air Rights Can Be Transferred?

The second aspect of air rights deals with the ability of landowners to transfer interests in the air located above their property. The air above property is divided into two areas, the **column lot** and the **air lot.** The column lot comprises everything between the earth's surface and an imaginary plane 23 feet above the surface, and the air lot comprises everything above the 23-foot plane. It is possible for landowners to transfer some interest in their column or air lot.

For example, both the column lot and the air lot could be sold for the construction of a large building. Those constructing the building need only have title to or an easement (see Chapter 4) for small segments of the land surface for the placement of beams or the steel girder foundations of the building. In these types of transfers of column and air lots, landowners retain title to the surface but have conveyed their air rights or a portion thereof, as with Tiffany's and the Trump tower.

There are other examples of large buildings constructed through the use of airspace. In Chicago, the Prudential Mid-America building is built in both the air and column lots above the Illinois Central Terminal. The 52-story Prudential Tower is built in the column and air lots above a shopping mall and restaurants in Boston. In New York, the 59-story Met Life building is built in the column and air lots above Grand Central Station. These examples illustrate that dividing air and surface ownership enables maximum use of real property. Transfers of air rights have become so common that many states are reviewing the Model Airspace Act for possible adoption to govern these transfers.

The construction and sale of condominiums is another example of the use and transfer of airspace. When buyers purchase condominiums, they are actually purchasing the airspace located between the walls of their particular units. Ground or surface ownership is not conveyed as part of the title, but the condominium owners do hold real property interests. (See Chapter 11 for a complete discussion of condominiums.)

> ***Practical Tip***
>
> *The sale of air rights has become more popular in areas where upward construction is the only means for growth and expansion of existing facilities. Building height limitations in some areas, such as San Francisco, increase the value of limited air space. Creative solutions to the space problems businesses face include contacting current surface holders to determine their interest in the transfer of air rights.*

The Right to Light

Corresponding to the ownership of air as part of a real property interest is the ownership of light. In this era of energy-technology development, the issue of who owns the light is a critical one. Suppose the following hypothetical situation has occurred:

Anna and Beverly are neighbors. Anna has installed a series of solar collectors on the roof of her home. The collectors are positioned so that Anna obtains maximum efficiency in the use of the sun. However, Beverly has decided to plant several trees for backyard shade and within three years of planting, the now tall trees are interfering with the collection of sunlight by Anna's collectors.

In the absence of any statutory right and under common law, Anna has no legal rights against Beverly unless Anna can establish that Beverly's conduct was malicious and done with the intent of obstructing light from the collectors.

Many states have passed statutory protections for the right to light, and New Mexico (N.M.S.A. §§47-3-1 *et seq.*) and Wyoming (W.S.A. §§34-22-101 *et seq.*) both grant a statutory right to sunlight. Under the statutes, the first user of light for solar energy purposes acquires the right to unobstructed continued use. Other states have passed **solar easement laws** that permit the execution and recognition of easements for the protection of solar access.[1] These easement laws do not, however, create or protect solar rights. Some states have encouraged zoning as a tool to be used to incorporate solar access considerations.[2] Other states have enacted statutes that permit solar energy users to petition administrative review boards when adjoining landowners refuse to negotiate solar access easements.[3] Finally, California applies the law of easements to solar easements that meet the requirements of the statute (Cal. Civ. Code 801.5).

Also, in California, deed restrictions or covenants that prohibit or restrict the installation of solar energy systems are void and unenforceable (Cal. Civ. Code §714).[4] Presently, proposed uniform laws on solar rights and solar energy systems are being developed for use by state legislators in regulating this area of land ownership.

1. California, Colorado, Florida, Georgia, Idaho, Illinois (although *O'Neill v. Brown,* 609 N.E.2d 55 [Ill. 1995] held that Illinois was not a solar easement state despite its comprehensive solar energy act), Kansas, Kentucky, Maine, Maryland, Minnesota, New Jersey, North Dakota, and Virginia.
2. Connecticut, Massachusetts, Minnesota, Oregon, and Utah. Note: Oregon affords considerable authority to planning commissions in treating rights for solar systems.
3. Iowa and Wisconsin.
4. California also encourages installation of solar devices in new home construction. California Public Resources Code §25603.5.

CONSIDER 3.2

In 1979, the California Solar Shade Control Act took effect. In 1984–1985, John and Cecilia Zipperer built their solar home in Santa Clara with county permits. In 1991, the county of Santa Clara acquired the adjoining parcel of land, with the trees already on it, and it placed that land in a Parks Reserve. Since 1991, those trees have been growing at the rate of 10 to 15 feet per year. By 2004, the trees were about 100 feet taller than when the county acquired the land.

In 1997, the Zipperers' solar system began to malfunction because the trees on the county's land interfered with the sunlight reaching their solar panels. Despite numerous requests from the Zipperers, and notwithstanding verbal promises by "certain officials and certain individuals that this situation would be corrected," the county did not trim or remove the trees.

In 2002, Santa Clara county adopted an ordinance exempting itself from the Solar Shade Control Act. In 2004, the Zipperers filed suit against the county under the Solar Shade Control Act. Should the Zipperers win? What would they win? *Zipperer v. County of Santa Clara*, 133 Cal.App.4th 1013, 35 Cal.Rptr.3d 487 (Cal.App. 2005).

The courts have undertaken some protection for solar rights through the use of property theories. In *Prah v. Maretti*, 321 N.W.2d 182 (Wis. 1982), the court held, "The law of private nuisance is better suited to resolve landowners' disputes about property development in the 1980s than is a rigid rule which does not recognize a landowner's interest in access to sunlight."

At common law, the **Doctrine of Ancient Lights** provided protection for the use of light. Under the doctrine, anyone who used the light for an uninterrupted period of 20 years was entitled to protection for use of that light, and obstruction was prohibited. However, this doctrine has been rejected by the American courts, with most of them following the ruling set forth in the following landmark light-obstruction case.

FONTAINEBLEAU HOTEL CORP. V. FORTY-FIVE TWENTY-FIVE, INC.

114 So. 2d 357 (Fla. 1959)

FACTS

The Fontainebleau, a luxury hotel, was constructed in Miami facing the Atlantic Ocean in 1954. In 1955, the Eden Roc, another luxury hotel, was constructed adjoining the Fontainebleau and also facing the Atlantic Ocean. Shortly after the construction of the Eden Roc in 1955, the Fontainebleau undertook the construction of a 14-story addition to extend 160 feet in height and 416 feet in length running from east to west. During the winter months, from about two in the afternoon and for the remainder of the day, the shadow of the addition would extend over the cabana, swimming pool, and sunbathing areas of the Eden Roc.

The Eden Roc (Forty-Five Twenty-Five Corp., plaintiff/appellee) brought suit against the Fontainebleau Hotel Corp. (defendant/appellant) to stop construction of the addition after eight stories had been built. The Eden Roc alleged the construction would interfere with its sunlight, cast a shadow, and interfere with the guests' use and enjoyment of the property. The Eden Roc further alleged the construction of the addition was done with malice. The trial court found for Eden Roc. Fontainebleau appealed.

JUDICIAL OPINION

Per Curiam. It is well settled that a property owner may put his own property to any reasonable and lawful use, so long as he does not thereby deprive the adjoining landowner of any right of enjoyment of his property which is recognized and protected by law, and so long as his use is not such a one as the law will pronounce a nuisance.

No American decision has been cited, and independent research has revealed none, in which it has been held that—in the absence of some contractual or statutory obligation—a landowner has a legal right to the free flow of light and air across the adjoining land of his neighbor. Even at common law, the landowner had no legal right, in the absence of an easement or uninterrupted use and enjoyment for a period of 20 years, to unobstructed light and air from the adjoining land.

There being, then, no legal right to the free flow of light and air from the adjoining land, it is universally held that where a structure serves a useful and beneficial purpose, it does not give rise to a cause of action, either for damages or for an injunction even though it causes injury to another by cutting off the light and air and interfering with the view that would otherwise be available over adjoining land in its natural state, regardless of the fact that the structure may have been erected partly for spite.

We see no reason for departing from this universal rule. If, as contended on behalf of plaintiff, public policy demands that a landowner in the Miami Beach area are *[sic]* to refrain from constructing buildings on his premises that will cast a shadow on the adjoining premises, an amendment of its comprehensive planning and zoning ordinance, applicable to the public as a whole, is the means by which such purpose should be achieved.

The record affirmatively shows that no statutory basis for the right sought to be enforced by plaintiff exists. The so-called Shadow Ordinance enacted by the City of Miami Beach at plaintiff's behest was held invalid in *City of Miami Beach v. State ex rel. Fontainebleau Hotel Corp.* It also affirmatively appears that there is no possible basis for holding that plaintiff has an easement for light and air, either express or implied, across defendant's property, nor any prescriptive right thereto—even if it be assumed, *arguendo*, that the common-law right of prescription as to "ancient lights" is in effect in this state. And from what we have said heretofore in this opinion, it is perhaps superfluous to add that we have no desire to dissent from the unanimous holding in this country repudiating the English doctrine of ancient lights.

Reversed.

Aftermath: The Eden Roc solved its problem by building a second swimming pool that allowed guests to experience sun and swimming, without the Fontainebleau shadow. Interestingly, in an era in which skin cancer has become an issue, both pools, shaded and unshaded, enjoy guest use, the sunworshippers in the sunny pool and the sun precautionaries in the shaded one.

CASE QUESTIONS

1. Who owns the Eden Roc?
2. Who brought the original suit?
3. Why was the suit brought?
4. Will the court recognize the Doctrine of Ancient Lights?
5. Will the court recognize an easement?
6. What remedy does the court suggest?
7. Who wins on appeal?
8. Would it make any difference if the obstruction were at least partially motivated out of spite? See *Carlson v. Calusa Golf Inc.*, 498 So. 2d 461 (Fla. 1986).

Today, some courts have begun to use a theory of prescriptive easements (see Chapter 4) or one of nuisance (discussed later in this chapter) to afford some protection for a landowner's light.

However, there are still only limited statutory and judicial protections afforded for solar access, so parties who want to maintain rights to light should do so through private agreements with adjoining landowners who will give them easements for such rights. Some mortgage lenders that are lending for property with solar panels will require such easements to be obtained before the mortgage money will be advanced to the borrower. However, in spite of the need for such easements, many parties do not take the time to protect their rights. Recent surveys reveal that 95 percent of all owners of solar energy systems have not obtained easements for the protection of sunlight.

An easement for light should carefully specify the extent of the easement with the following information

Practical Tip

Before buying, selling, or listing property, ask the following questions and find answers:

1. *Does the home have solar reliance, passive or active?*
2. *Are the solar components in compliance with the CC&Rs?*
3. *Do the CC&Rs permit installation of solar devices?*
4. *Are there restrictions in the CC&Rs on expansion of solar units?*
5. *Are there obstructions or potential obstructions for the solar units (growing trees; possible construction)?*
6. *Does an easement for light exist?*
7. *Can I get an easement for light?*
8. *Are there statutory protections for light access?*
9. *Is there backup power for the solar panels and system?*

covered: State the purpose of the easement (for solar panels, windows, or a swimming pool) because the intent of the parties helps courts if interpretation is ever necessary; include the times of day when the sun is to be unobstructed so that rights are clear and the burden on the adjoining land is limited; and list the types of structures (height, width, and so on) that cannot be constructed. Before drafting the agreement, check for compliance with any statutory requirements and/or restrictions. Because light obstructions can come from larger structures located some distance away, a landowner may need easements from more than one adjoining or adjacent landowner.

Homeowners' associations and the covenants, conditions, and restrictions (CC&Rs) for subdivisions should address the issues of type, attachment, and aesthetics of solar units. The following language is an example of CC&R restrictions on solar devices upheld in California (*Palos Verdes Homes Ass'n. v. Rodman,* 182 Cal. App. 3d 324, 227 Cal. Rptr. 81 [1986]):

> *1. Solar Units not on the roof should be maintained a minimum of 5 ft from the property line and concealed from the neighboring view, and a fence or wall of sufficient height to accomplish same may be appropriate. 2. Solar Units on a roof should be within the wall line of the structure. However, the Art Jury may require more roof area between solar unit and roof edge if the roof overhang is minimal. . . . 3. Solar Units should be in or below the plane or roofing material. 4. Solar Units should be constructed of rigid materials . . . The Art Jury may ask for alternative combinations in smaller groupings when large areas of grouped solar panels are found not to be aesthetically satisfactory.*[5]

Ethical Issue

While case law makes it clear that in the absence of any private agreement or statutory protection there is no right to light, individuals and their property values are affected greatly when an adjoining landowner obstructs light. While the obstruction may not interfere with solar access, the obstruction nonetheless affects the character of the property and perhaps its value. What are the ethical issues in a situation in which a new landowner or current owner of a neighboring property undertakes a construction project that interferes with the light of surrounding property owners? How should the conflict between the right to use their property and the rights of adjoining landowners be resolved? Are the issues different when, as in the *Eden Roc* case, the effect will be a loss of business and strength for the competitor/adjoining landowner? How do you feel about the statement, "All landowners assume the risk of changes in the use of surrounding property?"

Right to a View

Several recent cases have raised the issue the right to a view. Many resort homes and homes in high-rises or located near mountains, oceans, or other scenic vistas carry a premium price because of the view from the home's interior. Do landowners in these premium properties have any rights when construction on adjoining properties results in obstruction of their view? In the following case, the court discusses the issue of "right to a view."

Practical Tip

There is no right to a view. If property is purchased or carries additional value because of location and view, the owner's only protection from obstruction is an easement, height restrictions, or other covenants placed on the adjoining properties. There are no legal guarantees that a view will always be preserved.

5. However, the California courts have not upheld restrictions on land use for view impairment. *Patterson v. Beuligmann.* Not Reported in Cal.Rptr.3d, 2004 WL 2294473, Cal.App. 4 Dist., 2004.

PIERCE V. NORTHEAST LAKE WASHINGTON SEWER AND WATER DISTRICT

870 P.2d 305 (Wash. 1994)

FACTS

Arthur and Patricia Pierce (petitioners) own property on a hillside near Seattle. The Northeast Lake Washington Sewer and Water District (District), a municipal corporation providing water and sewer services to 50,000 people, acquired 5.4 acres of residential property adjacent to the Pierces' land. The District applied for a permit to construct a 4.3-million-gallon water storage facility on the site. The District chose the location because the sloping hillside would enable it to obscure the sight of the tank from neighboring residences. The permit was granted with modifications in the tank's location.

However, the final position of the constructed tank blocked the panoramic view the Pierces had enjoyed of wooded terrain, Lake Washington, Mount Rainier, and the Cascades. The tank was visible from any window in the house.

After an appraiser issued his opinion that the construction of the tank resulted in a $30,000 reduction in value of the Pierces' property, the Pierces filed suit against the District for nuisance, trespass, negligence, and inverse condemnation. The trial court dismissed the suit for the failure to demonstrate compensable damages and the court of appeals affirmed. The Pierces appealed.

JUDICIAL OPINION

Smith, Justice. This is an action in inverse condemnation brought by Petitioners against Northeast Lake Washington Sewer and Water District, a municipal corporation. Inverse condemnation is an action to "recover the value of property which has been appropriated in fact, but with no exercise of the [condemnation] power." "Our constitution requires that just compensation be paid a landowner in the event of either a governmental 'taking' or 'damaging' of property."

Under a general takings analysis, the elements of an inverse condemnation action are not in dispute. However, the only Washington case which considered a property owner's right to a view is *State v. Calkins.* In that case the court stated

Clearly, there has been no specific declaration by our legislature of an intention to pay compensation for nonexistent property rights; i.e., access, air, view, and light; furthermore, absent such rights, the condemnation proceedings herein do not violate Art. I, Section 16, of our state constitution, which requires the payment of just compensation for the taking or damaging of property rights.

Although *Calkins* was not an action for inverse condemnation based upon interference with a property owner's right to a view, it is nevertheless somewhat indicative of this court's position on the matter. Because our own decisions have not squarely addressed this issue, we may look to decisions from other jurisdictions....

In *Pacifica Homeowners' Ass'n v. Wesley Palms Retirement Comm'ty*, 224 Cal. Rptr. 380 (1986), the California Court of Appeal concluded that "[a]s a general rule, a landowner has no natural right to air, light or an unobstructed view and the law is reluctant to imply such a right." However, "[s]uch a right may be created by private parties through the granting of an easement or through the adoption of conditions, covenants and restrictions by the Legislature."

In *Pacifica*, the Homeowners' Association (Association) attempted to enjoin the Wesley Palma Retirement Community from allowing trees on its property to grow higher than the Association's five-story building. The Association claimed a conditional use permit placed a limitation on tree height, which was "imposed particularly for the benefit of the uphill landowners including the Association." However, the court rejected the Association's arguments and stated that "[i]n the absence of any agreement, statute or governmentally imposed conditions on development creating a right to an unobstructed view, it cannot be said Wesley Palms . . . interfered with any right."

In *Gervasi v. Board of Comm'rs of Hicksville Water Dist.*, 256 N.Y.S.2d 910 (1965), the facts closely parallel those in this case. The plaintiffs in that case sought to enjoin the water district from completing construction of a water tank or to recover damages measured by the reduced value of their homes caused by construction of the water tank. In that case, the water district constructed a storage tank on its own property. The plaintiffs claimed construction and maintenance of the tank reduced the market value of their properties. The Court concluded that the plaintiffs had failed to state a cause of action because they had not been deprived of "property within the meaning of that provision as it ha[d] been construed by the courts." The court determined that the plaintiffs had no cause of action because the water district constructed the water tank on its own property. The court found no deprivation of property under the takings clause of the New York Constitution.

Similarly, in the case now before us, the District constructed a water tank on its own property. We conclude that Petitioners have not been deprived of any property rights because the District is acting only upon its property.

The court in Gervasi further concluded that "[d]amages cannot be recovered because of the unsightly character of a structure and aesthetic considerations are not compensable in the absence of a legislative provision."...we conclude that Petitioners are not entitled to compensation for damages solely because of the unsightly character and the unaesthetic appearance of the water tank.

Following the reasoning of...*Pacifica*...and *Gervasi,* we conclude that Petitioners do not have a cause of action for inverse condemnation based on their claimed "right to a view." The water tank was a permissible use constructed and maintained solely upon the property of the District.

Property value, or landowners' economic interest in their property, may be considered an essential element of ownership. In *Highline Sch. Dist. 401 v. Port of Seattle,* 548 P.2d 1085 (1976) this court concluded that "an inverse condemnation action for interference with the use and enjoyment of property *accrues when the landowner sustains any measurable loss of market value...*" Although *Highline* involved inverse condemnation based on aircraft noise and vibration, the premise that a measurable loss in a market constitutes interference with a landowner's use and enjoyment of property would be applicable in this case only if the decline in market value was caused by unlawful government interference.

In this case, based upon appraisal of Petitioners' property, there is no dispute that there was in fact a measurable loss in market value after construction of the water tank. David E. Hunnicutt conducted an appraisal and concluded that construction of the tank had caused an actual loss in value to Petitioners' property of at least $30,000.00. However, our prior decisions do not lead to the conclusion that loss in market value of Petitioners' property is of itself evidence of governmental interference with the use and enjoyment of property entitling them to compensation. If property, or a substantial portion of that property, is destroyed by the government for a public purpose, the landowner would unquestionably be entitled to compensation....That section, however, does not "authorize compensation merely for a depreciation in market value of property when caused by a legal act."

Petitioners claim they are entitled to compensation because the unaesthetic appearance of the unsightly water tank and the proximity of the tank to their property has caused a loss in market value. This court has not allowed compensation based merely upon proximity of a building or structure.

Petitioners further claim the overbearing presence of the water tank interferes with their use and enjoyment of their property and that they should therefore be compensated for damages. "Damages for which compensation is to be made is a damage to the property itself, and *does not include a mere infringement of the owner's personal pleasure or enjoyment.* Merely rendering private property less desirable for certain purposes, or even causing personal annoyance or discomfort in it use, will not constitute the damage contemplated...but the property itself must suffer some diminution in substance, or be rendered intrinsically less valuable by reason of the public use."

Petitioners are not entitled in this case to just compensation under the takings clause of the Washington Constitution. They cannot establish a property right or interest in their right to a view.[6]

Affirmed.

CASE QUESTIONS

1. Describe the problem with the placement of the tank and the impact on the Pierces' property.

2. What are the grounds the Pierces use for their claim?

3. Is there a right to a view for which the Pierces are entitled to compensation?

4. Is the right to a view a property interest?

ETHICAL ISSUE

In 1997, Donald Trump began construction of his Riverside South project in New York City on a railroad yard located between Lincoln Towers and the Hudson River. The first two towers (of 16 planned) blocked the views of the Lincoln Towers residences. One resident noted, "Can you imagine what this man is taking away? Can you imagine somebody taking away the moon?" Another said, "All of a sudden, here was this thing looming up against the sky. You couldn't see the sky. I felt anger—that someone could be allowed to

6. Some states have begun to classify interference with a view as a nuisance (see infra at page 46). There are also municipalities with ordinances that prevent interference with views. *Kucera v. Lizza,* 69 Cal. Rptr. 2d 582 (1997). However, the statutes are only for prospective actions and do not grant an easement for, or property rights in, a view.

take away your beauty for money." Those in the Lincoln Towers apartments with views of the Trump project have trouble selling their units and overall have fewer prospects view their units. The price difference between a Trump-facing apartment and one facing the river is $50,000. Evaluate the ethical issues in development projects like Trump's.

ETHICAL ISSUE

(continued)

CONSIDER 3.3

The *Boston Globe* describes it as follows: "It is the largest renewable-energy project ever proposed in the United States, 170 wind turbines able to churn out 420 megawatts of power—enough for a city of 200,000 people—and churn up controversy pitting one environmentalist against another."[7] The dispute over the placement of a wind farm six miles off Cape Cod, Massachusetts, has resulted in a battle among and between homeowners, environmentalists, technology companies, and even the Army Corps of Engineers. Homeowners oppose the wind farm because their view of the ocean changes dramatically. However, others note that the presence of the renewable energy source could help to wean the United States from oil dependence. Long-time researcher and author Wendy Williams has noted that the wind farms are a solution for those who are "actively seeking ways to meet their energy growth requirements without further polluting the atmosphere."[8] But former newscaster Walter Cronkite, a homeowner in the area, argues, "Our national treasures should be off limits to industrialization."[9] John Flicker, president of National Audubon Society, has said, "When you look at a wind turbine, you can find the bird carcasses and count them. With a coal-fired power plant, you can't count the carcasses, but it's going to kill a lot more birds."[10] What protections do the wind farm developers have? What protections do homeowners have? What ethical issues exist on both sides of the issue?[11]

Surface and Subsurface Rights

This section deals with the second part of this chapter's opening quote, which is the ownership of subsurface rights. Ordinarily, landowners own to the center of the earth, so that mineral rights are included in fee simple absolute ownership. However, landowners are free to convey their subsurface rights as liberally as their air rights. When subsurface rights are conveyed independently of surface rights, there are two different landowners. The owner of the surface rights cannot affect the ownership rights of the subsurface owner. Likewise, the subsurface owner cannot destroy the surface and thereby destroy the surface owner's interest.

7. Robert Preer, "Coastal Worries Fuel Local Support for Wind Farm." *Boston Globe*, January 6, 2005, http://www.boston.com
8. Energy collaborative argues for wind farm, Friday, February 14, 2003. http://www.capewind.org.
9. Mark Alan Lovewell, "Cronkite Withdraws Ad Against Turbines," http://www.mvgazette.com. August 28, 2003; Katharine Q. Seelye, "Windmills Sow Dissent For Environmentalists," *New York Times*, June 5, 2003, p. C1.
10. Carl Levesque, "For the Birds: Audubon Society Stands Up in Support of Wind Energy," December 14, 2006, American Wind Energy Association, http://www.awea.org; Greg Chang, "Bird lovers fighting killer windmills," *Arizona Republic*, November 13, 2005, p. A33.
11. Currently, the Massachusetts environmental agency has given the wind project the green light (http://www.boston.com "Cape wind project clears state hurdle," March 30, 2007).

Mineral Rights: Oil and Gas Ownership

Nature of Oil and Gas

Oil and gas are petroleum found in liquid and gaseous forms, respectively, beneath the earth's surface. Because oil and gas are not solid like other minerals and will flow from one location to another very readily, this type of property interest presents legal issues not encountered in connection with other subsurface mineral rights.

When oil was first discovered in 1859 at Titusville, Pennsylvania, the courts applied the standard Blackstone adage of he who owns the surface owns what is beneath the surface as well. However, when a well is drilled and oil and gas are brought to the surface, it is impossible to tell whether they came from directly beneath the landowner's surface or were drawn from another pool under adjoining land. Figure 3.2 illustrates the possible conflicting claims of oil and gas ownership between adjoining landowners.

Under Blackstone's rule of subsurface ownership, a landowner pumping oil and gas would be liable to other nearby landowners in the event the well drew oil from reservoirs that extended beneath property owned by others. Such a taking would constitute trespass and would discourage development of the resource. As a result, the courts developed a different rule of ownership for oil and gas rights called the **Rule of Capture.** Simply stated, the rule gives the owner of a tract of land title to all the oil and gas produced by wells located on his or her land even though some of the oil and gas may have migrated from adjoining lands or the well is actually taking oil and gas from a reservoir that stretches across a boundary line onto another's property. This form of ownership protects the driller from liability for trespass so long as the drilling is conducted from his or her property. However, drilling at an angle would be a physical trespass and is not protected under the Rule of Capture.

Two theories are followed under the Rule of Capture. So-called **ownership states** follow the Rule of Capture but provide that the landowner is the owner of the mineral rights that can be lost only if someone else first captures the oil and gas through drilling. The **nonownership states**—which include California, Louisiana, Oklahoma, and Wyoming—provide that no one owns the oil and gas until it has been captured.

Figure 3.2 Oil and Gas Ownership Issues

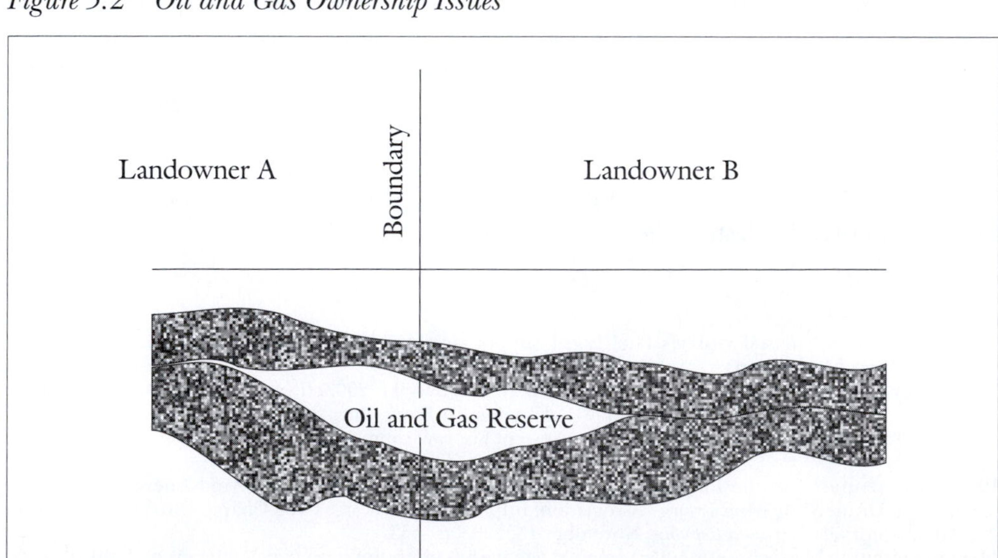

The difference between these two theories is simply the status of the rights prior to capture. Once capture has occurred, the rights are identical and vest at the same time under either theory.

The Rule of Capture has limits. For example, the rule does not apply after the gas is first captured by someone and stored in a subsurface or surface area. In other words, once the gas or oil has been captured, someone else cannot tap into the storage area and claim ownership under the Rule of Capture. The rule applies to drilling of oil and gas in their natural as opposed to stored states. Also, the Rule of Capture does not apply to what are referred to as "enhanced recovery operations," or sweeping. These types of processes involve, for example, using high-pressure water systems to drive oil reservoirs from beneath another's property to sweep them into reservoirs on your property so as to capture this oil and gas once it is beneath your land. Again, the Rule of Capture applies to oil and gas located naturally beneath your land or acquired through drilling from your land and not to recovery initiated by artificial shifting of the minerals. Some states permit recovery for trespass against those who use these "sweeping" techniques to recover oil and gas. Others will not permit a trespass action for "sweeping" if it can be shown that the adjoining landowner would not respond to a reasonable and fair proposal for recovery of the oil and gas. The idea behind this immunity for trespass is to encourage the development of the resource.

The **Doctrine of Correlative Rights** is another limitation on the Rule of Capture that imposes a good-faith requirement that no action will be taken that will cause the destruction of the oil and gas beneath the surface to prevent recovery by adjoining landowners. In other words, landowners cannot use the Rule of Capture to take action that prevents others from capturing the resources beneath their property. This type of action could occur if one landowner allowed a well to burn and drain the oil and gas from an adjoining landowner's subsurface reservoir.

A final limitation on the Rule of Capture is government regulation. Both state and federal governments have oil and gas conservation laws to both prevent waste of these resources and control the extent of drilling. For example, well-spacing regulations limit the number of wells that can be erected according to either a per-acre basis or the amount of space between wells. Also, particularly at the federal level, production limitations control the amount of drilling that can be done. Often referred to as **prorationing rules,** they establish limits on daily, weekly, or monthly production. Prorationing rules can be established either to prevent the early exhaustion of a well or to meet fluctuations in the price of oil and gas in the international markets.

Classification of Oil and Gas Interests

States vary in their positions as to whether oil and gas rights are real or personal property and what type of property interests they are. For example, some states treat oil and gas rights as a *profit a prendre,* or simply the right to enter the land of another and take a part or product of that land (see page 88). Other states have characterized these interests as fee simple determinables that end upon the Rule of Capture ownership by another. Other states have established a separate set of rules for oil and gas rights and the determination of issues such as trespass and suits to resolve title issues. The classification of oil and gas rights as real or personal property also varies and may largely be determined by taxation statutes that control whether the rights would be taxed as real or personal property under the state's revenue system.

Types of Oil and Gas Interests

Acquiring the right to drill for oil and gas can take several different forms. For example, many oil firms will refer to the fact that they own a **fee interest.** This form of ownership simply means that the company owns both the surface and subsurface rights. In other words, the firm has a fee simple in the property where it is drilling.

Other firms own the **mineral rights** or a **mineral interest.** This form of ownership simply means that the subsurface rights have been severed from the surface and air rights, and the company has the right to use the surface to capture the minerals but does not own the surface. This form of ownership grants only an easement on the surface to bring in the equipment necessary for drilling. In Louisiana, this form of ownership is called a **mineral servitude.**

A commonly used term, the **oil and gas lease,** is a form of ownership in which a portion of the mineral interest is assigned, usually in exchange for a royalty or share of the profits. A lease is the right to use the surface and remove the oil and gas. The lease could be an interest in perpetuity or one that ends when oil and gas are no longer produced. For example, suppose that farmer Adam has fee simple title to his farm and the subsurface rights. Farmer Adam could sell a mineral interest to ExxonMobil. ExxonMobil could then lease the interest to Xavier Oil Company in exchange for a share of the profits. Farmer Adam could also simply lease his mineral interest to ExxonMobil and ExxonMobil could use the surface to recover the oil and gas.

Practical Tip

Mineral rights are complex and require special details in the sale or lease agreement. The following are questions to be answered: Who owns the mineral rights? Will ownership be exclusive? Can the surface be used? What is included in the mineral rights? Oil? Gas? How and when is payment made? How much will the payments be? What happens upon default?

The oil and gas lease may also be used to create a **royalty interest,** which is a share of the oil produced from the land without any payment for the costs of its production. Royalty interests are usually stated in fraction form, such as one-eighth of production. Different amounts and names for royalty interests are used according to whether a landowner, lessee, or mineral interest is involved. Royalty interests are not real property interests. They are very similar to the personal property interest in the form of book royalties.

The various forms of ownership of oil and gas rights have many combinations, and the only limitations seem to be the creativity of those involved in the proposals. Any agreement for oil and gas rights should cover the issues of rights and responsibilities when land ownership is divided in this way between surface and subsurface interests. Damage to the surface by the owner of the subsurface rights is not unusual. But the lease or transfer of subsurface rights can include a provision that the subsurface owner either repair the surface or compensate the surface owner.

Creation of Oil and Gas Interests

Oil and gas interests are real property interests and under the **Statute of Frauds** these interests, regardless of type, must be in writing. The documents should specify the types of minerals that are included in the subsurface transfer if more than oil and gas are conveyed. For example, in *Western Nuclear, Inc. v. Andrus* (10th Cir. 1981), the parties were in a dispute about who owned the right to gravel on a piece of property, because it was unclear whether gravel was a mineral and the mineral rights had been severed from the surface rights.[12]

12. In a subsequent case, *Watt v. Western Nuclear, Inc.*, 462 U.S. 36 (1983), the U.S. Supreme Court reversed all prior gravel cases (pertaining to federal lands) and held that gravel is indeed a mineral. In another decision, *BedRoc Ltd., LLC v. U.S.* 541 U.S. 176 (2004), the court found that sand and gravel were not valuable minerals in applying state law in a particular interpretation of federal mineral rights.

Geothermal Energy

Geothermal resources present an interesting subsurface dilemma because of the difficulty of classifying these resources. **Geothermal energy** consists of steam in rock-surrounded pockets, so some states classify it as a water resource and use their water laws to determine ownership and other rights. Other states classify geothermal resource as an energy resource similar to oil or coal and treat it as a mineral. Some states (such as Idaho) have declared that geothermal resources are neither minerals nor a water resource and have developed a specialized scheme of regulation for this interest in real estate. The transfer of geothermal interests requires careful attention to state laws and exact detail in the conveyance.

The federal government also has statutes that affect geothermal energy. The Geothermal Steam Act of 1970 (30 U.S.C. §§1001 *et seq.*) regulates permits and use of this subsurface resource, and the Geothermal Energy Research, Development, and Demonstration Act (30 U.S.C. §§122 *et seq.*) encourages the development of this resource. Much of this resource is found on federal lands.

Water Rights

The rights to take water from and use water on land are real property interests. The rules of law on the nature and the extent of a landowner's right to use water vary depending on both the type of water source and the geographic region. The rules of law that developed in the Eastern jurisdictions where water is plentiful are quite different from the rules of law in the West, where water is scarce.

Water rights also vary according to the type of water body involved. The first type is surface or navigable waters, or those that flow. Ownership of navigable waters lies with the states as trustees for the public, subject to any federal rights and programs such as dams and water conservation systems built by the Army Corps of Engineers. Navigable water is defined as water that could be used for navigation regardless of whether it is so used, including natural and artificial lakes, rivers, and streams. Two theories of water rights are applicable to these bodies of waters: the **Riparian Doctrine** and **Prior Appropriation Doctrine.** Most states east of the Mississippi follow the Riparian Doctrine, and the arid Western states follow the Prior Appropriation Doctrine.[13] Some states follow a combination of the two theories.[14]

The Riparian Doctrine is based on sharing, and the Prior Appropriation Doctrine is based on "first in time is first in right," or the first to use the water has first claim to it. Figure 3.3 summarizes and compares the two doctrines. (The figure deals only with water use rights and not with the actual ownership of the land [riverbed] beneath the water.)

The title to the riverbeds or land beneath surface water is different from the water rights and may be with the state. Or the state may follow what is known as the **centerline rule,** which provides that the streambed is owned to the center by the abutting landowners.

Many landowners have private ponds that are within their property boundaries. These ponds are part of their real property interest, and they have all rights in them with the exception of any waters passing through them from upper to lower lands.

13. Alaska, Arizona, Montana, Nevada, Utah, and Wyoming.
14. California, Kansas, Mississippi, Nebraska, North Dakota, Oklahoma, Oregon, South Dakota, Texas, and Washington.

Figure 3.3 Water Rights

The Common Law Rules of Riparian Water Rights Compared with and Distinguished from the Doctrine of Prior Appropriation

Common Law Riparian Rules	Prior Appropriation Doctrine
1. THE DISTINGUISHING FEATURES OF THE COMMON LAW RIPARIAN RULES ARE EQUALITY OF RIGHTS AND REASONABLE USE—There is no priority of rights; the reasonable or permitted use by each is limited by a similar use in every other riparian.	1. THE DISTINGUISHING FEATURE OF THE PRIOR APPROPRIATION DOCTRINE IS FIRST IN TIME IS FIRST IN RIGHT—There is no equality of rights and no reasonable use limited by the rights of others.
2. To be a riparian, one needs only to be an owner of riparian land. Riparian land is land that abuts or touches the water of a lake or stream.	2. To be a prior appropriator, one must do four things: (a) have an intent to appropriate water, (b) divert the water from the source of supply, (c) put such water to a beneficial use, and (d) when applicable, follow the necessary administrative procedures.
3. No one can be a riparian who does not own riparian land.	3. One need not own land to be a prior appropriator. There is one exception—in some jurisdictions such as Arizona, if the appropriation is for irrigation purposes then the appropriator must own arable and irrigable land to which that water right is attached.
4. Riparian lands are lands bordering the stream and within the watershed. Under the natural flow theory, a riparian cannot use water on nonriparian lands. Under the reasonable use theory, a riparian may use water on water on nonriparian lands if such use is reasonable.	4. The prior appropriator may use the appropriated water on riparian and nonriparian lands alike. The character of the land is quite immaterial.
5. Under the common law riparian rules, the use of water for natural purposes is paramount and takes precedence over the use of water for artificial purposes. Natural uses include domestic purposes for the household and drinking, stock watering, and irrigating the garden. Artificial purposes include use for irrigation, power, mining, manufacturing, and industry.	5. The prior appropriation doctrine makes no distinction between use of water for natural wants and for artificial and industrial purposes.
6. The riparian owner, simply because he owns riparian land, has the right to have the stream of water flow to, by, through, or over his land under the riparian rights doctrine.	6. An owner of land, simply as such owner, has no right to have a stream of water flow to, by, through, or over his land under the prior appropriation doctrine.
7. The riparian has the right to have the water in its natural state free from unreasonable diminution in quantity and free from unreasonable pollution in quality.	7. The prior appropriator has the right to the exclusive use of the water free from interference by anyone, reasonable or unreasonable.
8. The rights of the riparians are equal.	8. The rights of the appropriators are never equal.
9. The basis, measure, and limit of the riparian's water right is that of reasonable use (unless natural flow states: limit use to not interrupting the natural flow).	9. The basis, measure, and limit of the water right of the prior appropriator is the beneficial use to which he has put the water. He has no right to waste water. If his needs are smaller than his means of diversion, usually a ditch, then his needs determine his right. If his ditch is smaller than his needs, then the capacity of his ditch determines his right.
10. The doctrine of riparian rights came to this country from the common law of England, although it seems to have had its origin in French law.	10. The doctrine of prior appropriation is statutory in our Western states, although its origin seems lost in antiquity.

Still another type of water is *percolating* or *groundwater*. This type of water includes all subsurface water other than water that flows in underground streams. The waters included in this group are Artesian waters, aquifers, underground lakes or pools, and waters that seep, ooze, or filter from an unknown source. Sometimes called groundwater rights or overlying rights, rights in these waters are governed by both the Riparian Doctrine and the Prior Appropriation Doctrine; however, the application of the rules differs because of the nature of the water source.

In the following case, the court discusses the rights of Riparian landowners v. government regulation of the use of bodies of water.

STUPAK-THRALL V. UNITED STATES

70 F.3d 881 (6th Cir. 1995); affirmed by an equally divided en banc court, 89 F.3d 1269 (6th Cir. 1996), cert. denied 519 U.S. 1090 (1997)[15]

FACTS

Kathy Stupak-Thrall and others (plaintiffs) own land on the northern shore of Crooked Lake in Michigan's Upper Peninsula near the Wisconsin border. Under Michigan law, these property owners are riparians and as such are given the right to use the surface of the lake including those uses "absolutely necessary for the existence of the riparian proprietor and his family, such as to quench thirst and for household purposes." Additional permissible riparian uses include "those which merely increase one's comfort and prosperity/...such as commercial profit and recreation."

The United States is also a riparian owner along Crooked Lake because about 95 percent of the lake's shoreline lies within the Sylvania Wilderness Area, a national wilderness administered by the Forest Service.

In 1992, the Forest Service adopted regulations (Amendment 1) that prohibit "sail-powered watercraft," "watercraft designed for or used as floating living quarters," and "nonburnable disposable food and beverage containers" on the lake. The regulations also discouraged use of electronic fish-finders, boom boxes, and any other mechanical or battery-operated devices.

Stupak-Thrall and other property owners filed suit challenging the authority of the federal government to regulate lake use on several grounds including their rights as riparians. The federal district court found for the Forest Service and the landowners appealed.

JUDICIAL OPINION

Moore, Circuit Judge.... [R]iparian rights are not absolute. Michigan law divides riparian uses into uses for "natural purposes," which are "those absolutely necessary for the existence of the riparian proprietor," and uses related to "artificial purposes," which are "those which merely increase one's comfort and prosperity." Each use for an artificial purpose must be for the benefit of the underlying land and reasonable in light of the correlative rights of the other proprietors. In other words, riparian uses such as sailing, waterskiing, and swimming are subject to "reasonable use" limitations and may not interfere materially with other riparian owners' similar rights. In *Thompson v. Enz*, 154 N.W.2d 473 (Mich. 1967), the court stated that a finding of reasonableness should center on three factors: (1) the "watercourse and its attributes," (2) the "use itself" and its effect on the water, and (3) the "consequential effects" on other riparian proprietors and the state.

We do not agree that the "reasonable use" doctrine governs the federal government's actions in this case. Although the *Thompson* decision is important here because it shows that the riparian rights of private citizens are not absolute under Michigan law, the "reasonable use" doctrine itself only makes sense when one riparian owner challenges another's use as unreasonable and the court makes a subsequent determination of reasonableness. It is inapplicable when one riparian proprietor unilaterally decides to ban certain uses of others, whether or not the uses themselves are unreasonable, and whether or not the banning proprietor actually has the power to do so. Indeed, the federal government's ability to impose restrictions does not stem from its status as a fellow riparian proprietor;

15. The case did not end at this point. The property owners continued their litigation, trying to establish that their land was not part of a federal reserve and that the federal regulations did not apply, *Stupak-Thrall v. Glickman*, 346 F.3d 579, (6th Cir. 2003). The court held that the claim was raised too late and after a determination of the issue by the lower courts.

it stems from its status as a sovereign. Its authority to regulate cannot come from a state law doctrine that merely balances the property rights of private owners vis-a-vis one another.

...[T]he Forest Service possesses a power delegated to it by Congress that is "analogous to the police power," and its exercise of this federal power does not violate Congress's express limitation deferring to "existing" state law rights in the wilderness act, so long as it does not exceed the bounds of permissible police power regulation under state law.

Amendment 1's purpose of preserving wilderness character is undoubtedly a proper aim under the Property Clause's police power and under Congress's delegation to the Forest Service, and the prohibition of certain forms of mechanical transport and certain types of food containers on Crooked Lake is certainly rationally related to achieving this goal.

Given the "minimal impact on plaintiffs' riparian uses of Crooked Lake," we conclude that the Forest Service's restrictions here are a valid exercise of the police power under state law, and they are therefore a valid exercise of the police power conferred on the Forest Service by the Property Clause and limited by Congress's express reservation for state law rights in the wilderness acts.

Affirmed.

CASE QUESTIONS

1. What regulations were considered objectionable?
2. What rights did riparians have under Michigan law?
3. Are riparian rights subject to government regulation?
4. What advice could you offer those who purchase property near government-controlled wilderness areas?

CONSIDER 3.4

Shanty Hollow Corporation was issued a permit by the New York State Department of Environmental Conservation to withdraw water from Schoharie Creek for purposes of its snowmaking equipment. Shanty Hollow operates a winter sport recreational area. The Catskill Center for Conservation and Development, property owners along the creek, and anglers brought suit against both the state and Shanty Hollow for excessive withdrawal of water from the creek. What is the result under the Riparian Doctrine? In contrast, what would be the result under the Prior Appropriation Doctrine? Like the *Stupak-Thrall* case, could there be a justification on the grounds that water use needs to be regulated? *Catskill Center v. NY Dept. of Environ.*, 642 N.Y.S.2d 986 (1996)

Water Rights at the Crossroads

The water rights area of real estate law has proven to be a dynamic one over the past few years because of the role of environmental regulation (see Chapter 20 for more information on environmental regulations on water use). Some scholars have written that the prior appropriation doctrine is often at odds with environmental goals and has encouraged government intervention regardless of water rights. Many state and local authorities have intervened in water-use and water-level issues because of public safety or issues surrounding the flora and fauna in or around the water. For example, in *Wortelboer v. Benzie County*, 537 N.W.2d 603 (Mich. App. 1995), the court upheld the right of the state to maintain lake levels to avoid the death of fish and the resulting smell. Likewise, property owners along a lake have been held to have standing to bring actions to require that lake levels be modified (*Glen Lake-Crystal River Watershed Riparians v. Glen Lake Ass'n*, 695 N.W.2d 508 [Mich.App., 2004]). In these cases, courts are balancing environmental interests with those of adjoining landowners concerned about drought effects due to too low levels and erosion damage due to levels that are too high.

Development projects that involve water (see Chapter 21 for more information on development) have been subjected to municipal and county reviews for project approval. California courts have noted that the traditional lines of legal reasoning on water rights and use have been changed to broader ones that are based primarily on whether the water use is "reasonable or wasteful" (*Imperial Irrigation District v. State Water Resources Control Board*, 225 Cal. App. 3d 548 (1990)). In issuing permits for use of public waters, states, particularly in the West, follow either a best possible use or maximum benefit doctrine in making decisions on who will gain access to these waters. Both doctrines require state officials to weigh the economic interests of parties with conflicting interests in land and water use. In many situations, there are emotional issues as developers seek water rights as adjoining landowners oppose their development projects (see Chapter 21 for more discussion of economic development issues and interests).

Thompson on Real Property summarizes the changes in water rights and their relationship to real property as follows: "Although the general rule is that water rights are a species of real property, that designation refers to the right of access to the water while it is in its natural state. Once the right is exercised and water is reduced to possession, it may be considered personal property of the water-right holder. As such, it may become an article of commerce." So the distinction between the traditional laws of real property and the new trends is that the proposed commercial use of water once it is captured pursuant to the legal rights can be regulated by various government entities. These entities now grapple with those who sell their riparian rights, for example, to nonriparians. The issue becomes one of deciding whether to honor the real property origins of water rights and the reliance land owners have placed on that system or to intervene for the sake of allocation of a scarce resource, protection of the environment, and easier commercial transfers. In resolving the issue, states, local governments, and courts have asked whether cities should have higher priorities than the countryside, how federal and state authority applies in water disputes, whether government can intervene for protection of water quality, whether water can be moved to address shortages and allocation proposals and who will do the moving, and what the legal status of water rights should be. For example, in *Long v. Great Spring Waters of America, Inc.*, 2002 WL 31813096 (Cal. App.), the California court dealt with a commerce issue and water use. Since at least 1930, Great Spring extracted water from federal forestlands to bottle and sell for profit. Great Spring had laid pipes, dug trenches, and developed wells with dimensions substantially exceeding those contained in the special use permit. One of Great Spring's bottled-water competitors brought suit on a number of grounds, including the failure of the California regulators to properly control water use. The court held that no permit was required for extraction of water from federal land, and since Great Spring has appropriated the water before anyone else, state law required recognition of its rights. Because of the source of the water, Great Spring also did not violate any of the state laws on extraction or dimensions of its facilities.

ETHICAL ISSUES

Evaluate Great Spring's approach to its water supplier. The court determined that it had not broken any law. Apply principles of ethics to determine the effects of its business model.

Perhaps at the heart of evolving changes in water rights is the classic economic issue of supply and demand. Water shortages were not a uniform issue at the time the traditional water rights were developed. Intervention may be necessary, and the law is adjusting to permit intervention with private property rights.

Protection of Property Rights

Trespass

Trespass is defined as the intentional interference with landowners' reasonable use and enjoyment of their property. General examples of trespass include parties' walking across another property owner's land or placing objects on another's land, although trespass can also arise from indirect objects intentionally set in motion by the trespasser. For example, if one landowner were to dam water so that it flooded an adjoining landowner's property, there has been a trespass. Even the simple act of opening shutters so that they extend across a boundary line to an adjoining property owner's land is an act of trespass. Bullets fired across the land of another also constitute trespass. In one unique trespass case, a child hurled a brick at a neighbor. When the neighbor reached across the boundary line and grabbed the child, he committed not only the torts of assault and battery but also that of trespass. A property owner who hires contractors to work on his or her land but does not verify boundaries is responsible if those contractors cross onto neighboring properties and cause harm, such as the destruction of trees.

Practical Tip

Landowners faced with periodic trespassers should take precautions in protecting themselves from liability. Signs and barriers should be erected so that trespassers do not gradually become classified as guests because of the owners' implied acquiescence through inaction. Furthermore, if physical action does not stop the trespass, a court injunction or damages may be appropriate so that the landowners have judicial records of their positions on and relationships to trespassers.

CONSIDER 3.5

Holmes and Doris Stockly have owned approximately 20 acres of undeveloped, forested land in Falmouth, Maine. Doil owns property adjacent to and with forestation similar to that of the Stockly Property. The Stocklys considered the trees on their property to be of tremendous personal value. Since 1966, they maintained, cultivated, and used the Stockly Property as a passive recreational area for activities such as hiking, walking, and cross-country skiing. They never harvested the trees or managed the property for any commercial value, and removed only fallen trees and cut brush as necessary to maintain trails. The Stocklys' sole goal in owning and maintaining the property was to maximize its beauty, aesthetic value, environmental benefits, and non-motorized recreational use for themselves and their family.

Sometime before April 2001, Doil contacted Mathew McCourt to discuss the selective cutting of trees on Doil's Property. On April 26, 2001, Doil signed a Timber Sales Agreement on a form provided by McCourt. One of its terms required McCourt to indemnify Doil in the event that his harvesting operation resulted in a trespass of abutting land. This provision was important to Doil because she was concerned about the possibility that trees might be removed from property she did not own. She did not authorize or direct McCourt to cut any timber on the Stockly Property.

Although there are stone walls located along the western and southern boundaries of the Stockly Property and along the eastern edge of the Doil Property, there are no monuments or other indicators of the common boundary between them. The Stocklys had also surveyed and flagged the northern, eastern and southern edges of their land.

Prior to the cutting, Doil never had her property or the common boundary line surveyed or marked in any way, and at the time the timber harvesting occurred that boundary was not flagged. Other than a tax map, Doil did not give McCourt a description of her property or the common property line; or any information on the dimensions of her lot; or a metes and bounds description of her property; or a copy of her deed. Doil did not ask or require McCourt to identify or locate the boundaries of her property.

CONSIDER 3.5

(continued)

Although Doil never walked her property with McCourt prior to the cutting, she understood that he had walked it and had identified some old stone walls on at least one of her boundaries. She also understood that McCourt had whatever information he needed to be able to locate the boundaries of her property, and she never asked whether he needed any additional information.

Sometime during the spring and summer of 2001, McCourt cut down and removed trees from approximately 30 acres of the Doil Property. He also cut down or destroyed over 725 trees on approximately 20 acres of the Stockly Property. The majority of those trees were larger, older hardwoods and softwoods. The Stocklys did not authorize the harvesting on their property and did not know about it until all of the cutting was done.

Although the Stocklys claim to have suffered emotional distress as a result of the trespass, neither of them sought or received any treatment, evaluation, or medication for emotional distress. While Mr. Stockly lost some sleep and felt like he had been "hit in the stomach" after learning of the cutting, Mrs. Stockly had no physical reaction to the loss of the trees.

The stumpage value of the trees on the Stockly Property that were cut down or destroyed by McCourt is $14,127.30. The forfeiture value of those trees is $59,525.00.49 [*sic*] ($59,525,49). The cost to restore the Stockly Property, as near as practicable, to its pre-casualty condition is approximately $370,000, comprised of (a) $35,750 to clean up the debris and slash left behind from the timber harvesting, (b) $330,000 to replant six hundred 2–2.5-inch diameter trees in a mix of species similar to those cut and destroyed, and (c) $4,000 to water and maintain the replanted trees.

Has there been a trespass? Who is liable to the Stocklys? For how much? *Stockly v. Doil*, 2004 WL 1433694 (Me.Super)

Nuisance

"Use your own property in such a manner as not to injure that of another *[Sic vere tuo et alienum non laedas]*." **Nuisance** is the unreasonable interference with others' use and enjoyment of their property. Nuisances are generally thought of as bad odors and excessive noise. Pollutants from a factory causing property damage and medical problems can constitute a nuisance. "A nuisance may be merely a right thing in the wrong place, like a pig in the parlor instead of the barnyard."[16]

Practical Tip

Verify property boundaries prior to sale, lease, purchase, listing, construction, landscaping, or excavation of that property.

Nuisances can be classified as private, public, or frequently a cross between the two. A nuisance affecting one property owner or a small group of property owners is a private nuisance. For example, a restaurant's storage of garbage bins behind a store is a private nuisance affecting the immediate neighbors.

However, the burning of used car materials to salvage metal can create smoke and smells affecting an entire community and would thus be labeled a public nuisance.

The remedies for nuisance usually fall into one of two categories: monetary or equitable relief. **Monetary relief** is compensation for illness and medical expenses or compensation for the reduction in property values because of the nuisance. For example, destruction of plants or paint caused by pollutants would be compensable. **Equitable relief** is injunctive relief where a court orders the nuisance-creating party to cease the nuisance activity. This injunctive relief is used sparingly, since in some circumstances the result will be the closing of a business. In determining whether

16. *Village of Euclid, Ohio v. Amber Realty Co.*, 272 U.S. 365 (1926).

injunctive relief will be afforded, courts balance the extent of the property owner's harm against the beneficial aspects of the wrongdoer's conduct. The following case deals with a nuisance issue, particularly in balancing landowners' interests against the economic interests of others as well as the interests of the public in a suit where the landowners have requested injunctive relief.

Spur Industries, Inc. v. Del E. Webb Development Co.

494 P.2d 700 (Az. 1972)

FACTS

Spur Industries operated a cattle feedlot near Youngtown and Sun City, Arizona (communities 14 to 15 miles west of Phoenix). Spur had been operating the feedlot since 1956, and the area had been agricultural since 1911.

In 1959 Del E. Webb began development of the Sun City area, a retirement community. Webb purchased the 20,000 acres of land for about $750 per acre.

In 1960 Spur began an expansion program in which its operating area grew from 5 acres to 115 acres.

At the time of the suit, Spur was feeding between 20,000 and 30,000 head of cattle, which produced 35 to 40 pounds of wet manure per head per day, or over one million pounds per day. And despite the admittedly good feedlot management and good housekeeping practices by Spur, the resulting odor and flies produced an annoying if not unhealthy situation as far as the senior citizens of southern Sun City were concerned. There is no doubt that some of the citizens of Sun City were unable to enjoy the outdoor living which Del Webb had advertised. Del Webb was faced with sales resistance from prospective purchasers as well as strong and persistent complaints from the people who had purchased homes in that area. Nearly 1,300 lots could not be sold. Webb then filed suit alleging Spur's operation was a nuisance because of flies and odors constantly drifting over Sun City. The trial court enjoined Spur's operations and Spur appealed.

JUDICIAL OPINION

Cameron, Vice Chief Justice. The difference between a private nuisance and a public nuisance is generally one of degree. A private nuisance is one affecting a single individual or a definite small number of persons in the enjoyment of private rights not common to the public, while a public nuisance is one affecting the rights enjoyed by citizens as a part of the public. To constitute a public nuisance, the nuisance must affect a considerable number of people or an entire community or neighborhood.

Where the injury is slight, the remedy for minor inconveniences lies in an action for damages rather than in one for an injunction. Moreover, some courts have held, in the "balancing of conveniences" cases, that damages may be the sole remedy.

Thus, it would appear from the admittedly incomplete record as developed in the trial court, that, at most, residents of Youngtown would be entitled to damages rather than injunctive relief.

We have no difficulty, however, in agreeing with the conclusion of the trial court that Spur's operation was an enjoinable public nuisance as far as the people in the southern portion of Del Webb's Sun City were concerned.

It is clear that as to the citizens of Sun City, the operation of Spur's feedlot was both a public and a private nuisance. They could have successfully maintained an action to abate the nuisance. Del Webb, having shown a special injury in the loss of sales, had a standing to bring suit to enjoin the nuisance. The judgment of the trial court permanently enjoining the operation of the feedlot is affirmed.

A suit to enjoin a nuisance sounds in equity and the courts have long recognized a special responsibility to the public when acting as a court of equity.

In addition to protecting the public interest, however, courts of equity are concerned with protecting the operator of a lawfully, albeit noxious, business from the result of a knowing and willful encroachment by others near his business.

In the so-called "coming to the nuisance" cases, the courts have held that the residential landowner may not have relief if he knowingly came into a neighborhood reserved for industrial or agricultural endeavors and has been damaged thereby:

Plaintiffs chose to live in an area uncontrolled by zoning laws or restrictive covenants and remote from urban development. In such an area plaintiffs cannot complain that legitimate agricultural pursuits are being carried on in the vicinity, nor can plaintiffs, having chosen to build in an agricultural area, complain that the agricultural pursuits carried on in the area depreciate the value of their homes. The area being primarily agricultural, and opinion reflecting the value of such property must take this factor into account. The standards affecting the value of residence property in an urban setting, subject to zoning controls and controlled planning techniques, cannot be the standards by which agricultural properties are judged.

"People employed in a city who build their homes in suburban areas of the county beyond the limits of a city and zoning regulations do so for a reason. Some do so to avoid the high taxation rate imposed by cities, or to avoid special assessments for street, sewer and water projects. They usually build on improved or hard surface highways, which have been built either at state or county expense and thereby avoid special assessments for these improvements. It may be that they desire to get away from the congestion of traffic, smoke, noise, foul air and the many other annoyances of city life. But with all these advantages in going beyond the area which is zoned and restricted to protect them in their homes, they must be prepared to take the disadvantages." And:

** * * a party cannot justly call upon the law to make that place suitable for his residence which was not so when he selected it. * * *.*

Were Webb the only party injured, we would feel justified in holding that the doctrine of "coming to the nuisance" would have been a bar to the relief asked by Webb, and, on the other hand, had Spur located the feedlot near the outskirts of a city and had the city grown toward the feedlot, Spur would have to suffer the cost of abating the nuisance as to those people locating within the growth pattern of the expanding city:

*The case affords, perhaps, an example where a business established at a place remote from population is gradually surrounded and becomes part of a populous center, so that a business which formerly was not an interference with the rights of others has become so by the encroachment of the population * * *.*

We agree, however, with the Massachusetts court that:

*The law of nuisance affords no rigid rule to be applied in all instances. It is elastic. It undertakes to require only that which is fair and reasonable under all the circumstances. In a commonwealth like this, which depends for its material prosperity so largely on the continued growth and enlargement of manufacturing of diverse varieties, "extreme rights" cannot be enforced. * * *.*

There was no indication in the instant case at the time Spur and its predecessors located in western Maricopa County that a new city would spring up, full-blown, alongside the feeding operation and that the developer of that city would ask the court to order Spur to move because of the new city. Spur is required to move not because of any wrongdoing on the part of Spur, but because of a proper and legitimate regard of the courts for the rights and interests of the public.

Del Webb, on the other hand, is entitled to the relief prayed for (a permanent injunction), not because Webb is blameless, but because of the damage to the people who have been encouraged to purchase homes in Sun City. It does not equitably or legally follow, however, that Webb, being entitled to the injunction, is then free of any liability to Spur if Webb has in fact been the cause of the damage Spur has sustained. It does not seem harsh to require a developer, who has taken advantage of the lesser land values in a rural area as well as the availability of large tracts of land on which to build and develop a new town or city in the area, to indemnify those who are forced to leave as a result.

Having brought people to the nuisance to the foreseeable detriment of Spur, Webb must indemnify Spur for a reasonable amount of the cost of moving or shutting down. It should be noted that this relief to Spur is limited to a case wherein a developer has, with foreseeability, brought into a previously agricultural or industrial area the population which makes necessary the granting of an injunction against a lawful business and for which the business has no adequate relief.

It is therefore the decision of this court that the matter be remanded to the trial court for a hearing upon the damages sustained by the defendant Spur as a reasonable and direct result of the granting of the permanent injunction. Since the result of the appeal may appear novel and both sides have obtained a measure of relief, it is ordered that each side will bear its own costs.

Affirmed in part, reversed in part, and remanded for further proceedings consistent with this opinion.

CASE QUESTIONS

1. Did Spur create a nuisance?

2. Should it make any difference that Spur was there first?

3. How does the court balance retirement communities and beef production, which are two of Arizona's biggest industries?

CONSIDER 3.6

In each of the following circumstances, determine whether a nuisance is involved, whether it is public or private, and what remedy would be appropriate. Determine any additional facts that would aid in the decision.

a. Damage and annoyance caused by blasting in a nearby quarry (the town developed because of the quarry)
b. Operation of a dog kennel
c. Construction of a proposed nuclear power plant
d. A neighbor with 55 cats residing in her three-bedroom/1200-square-feet home

Duties of Landowners

In addition to avoiding the problems of trespass and nuisance, landowners owe certain responsibilities to those entering their property. Those who enter property are classified into one of three categories: trespassers, licensees, and invitees. Traditionally, each category has a different status when on another's property, and landowners owe different degrees of responsibility to those in each category. While these differing categories and duties are discussed here, states are blending together the responsibilities and degree of care more and more so that the standard becomes one of reasonable care to all those who enter your property, regardless of their classification.

Trespassers

Trespassers are persons on the property of another without permission. Landowners may take the appropriate actions to have trespassers removed, but while trespassers are on their property, landowners have only the responsibility of not intentionally injuring them—that is, landowners may not intentionally injure trespassers or erect mantraps to injure or kill trespassers.

Licensees

Licensees are persons on the property of another who have some form of permission to be there. For example, in most states, fire protectors, police officers, and medical personnel would be classified as licensees. These groups have an implied invitation to a landowner's property so that their services are available to the landowner when needed. It is possible that meter readers would be classified as licensees because the implied invitation arises from the use of the utility or service. In some states, social guests are classified as licensees because although there may not be an express invitation to all social guests, an implied invitation arises from friendship.

To the licensees, landowners owe a greater duty of care. In addition to the duty not to injure intentionally is the responsibility of warning licensees of any defects of which landowners have knowledge. Thus, landowners must warn of broken steps, cracked concrete, or dangerous animals.

Invitees

Invitees are persons on the property of another by express invitation. Every public place offers an express invitation to all members of the public. Customers are always invitees in places of business. A repair person on the premises to fix a washer or refrigerator is there at the landowner's express request. Invitees are afforded the greatest degree of protection by landowners. Landowners must exercise reasonable care to protect invitees from injury. They owe a duty not only to warn invitees of any defects of which they have knowledge but also to inspect their property for defects and take reasonable steps to correct them. For example, a leaf of lettuce on the floor in the produce section of a grocery store is a hazard for invitees. Grocery store owners are required to periodically check and sweep aisle areas to protect invitees. Figure 3.4 provides a summary view of landowner liability and duty.

Practical Tip

Many malls and shopping centers are providing additional security guards. Grocery stores often mandate that customers be accompanied by an employee when they return to their cars in the parking lot. The issue of potential liability to their invitees has taken new prominence in security procedures for commercial areas.

Figure 3.4 Landowner Duties and Liabilities

Type of Person Entering Property	Landowner Duty	Liability*
Trespasser	Not to intentionally injure	Liable for intentional injury, mantraps, automatic traps, etc.
Licensee	Not to intentionally injure	Correct defects aware of; Liability for intentional injury; Injury caused by known defects
Invitee	Not to intentionally injure; Correct defects aware of or should be aware exist	Above, plus liability for should-have-known-defects

*There are several variations from state-to-state. For example, some states classify social guests as licensees whereas, others classify them as invitees, hence changing the duties and liability of the landowners.

CONSIDER 3.7

Classify each of the following parties in terms of landowner's responsibilities. Describe the landowner's duty to each.

a. Paramedic
b. Customer in a department store
c. Marketing researcher doing a door-to-door survey
d. Burglar

Breach of Duty

A landowner's breach of any of these stated responsibilities can result in the imposition of tremendous liability, especially if the trespasser, licensee, or invitee is seriously injured. Landowners must be cautious in exercising their responsibilities and can be further protected through maintenance of adequate insurance.

The following case deals with an evolving and important area of the liability of landowners. The case involves an issue of the landowner's liability to invitees when the invitee is injured by the criminal activity of a third party.

Paragon Family Restaurant v. Bartolini

799 N.E.2d 1048 (Ind.2003).

FACTS

Mario Bartolini had been a customer of Paragon Family Restaurant, d/b/a Round The Corner Pub ("the Pub"), on the Friday night of the incident, arriving about 11:00 p.m. Approximately 1:00 a.m., Jeffrey Todd and John Mattull arrived at the Pub. Mattull was 21 but Todd was under 21 years of age, and the Pub did not check for identification. The Pub served beer to both Todd and Mattull. Todd had frequented the Pub on 10 or 15 prior occasions and his identification had never been checked. While in the Pub, Todd and Mattull appeared loud and obnoxious to at least one other patron, yelling several times. Todd testified that he and Bartolini "had words" in the Pub, and there may have been "high anxiety" between them. At closing time, about 3:30 a.m., Bartolini left the bar with his female friend, and was walking her to her car in the Pub's parking lot. As Todd and Mattull left the Pub, one of them punched and knocked over a stop sign that was mounted in a tire or bucket of cement, and then Todd threw a bottle in the air which burst on the concrete. When Todd and Mattull got to the parking lot, they began taunting Bartolini. A waitress told the Pub's bartender and night manager of the disturbance in the parking lot. The ensuing verbal altercation between Todd and Bartolini became physical. Employees of the Pub, including the bouncer, stood by for five or six minutes without doing anything as the argument escalated in the parking lot. The bantering included Todd's threat to Bartolini, "Look, buddy, we're going to get you. We're going to kill you, and if it ain't tonight or tomorrow, but we're going to kill you." Eventually, Mattull lunged at Bartolini who fell to the ground, striking his head, and Todd and Mattull then both continued to viciously attack Bartolini. The bouncer eventually was able to pull Mattull away from Bartolini, but Todd continued kicking and hitting him. Bartolini suffered serious injuries.

The Pub appeals from a $280,000 jury verdict and judgment for Bartolini. The Court of Appeals affirmed in part, reversed in part, and remanded for a new trial. The parties appealed.

JUDICIAL OPINION

Dickson, Justice. Landowners have a duty to take reasonable precautions to protect their invitees from foreseeable criminal attacks. ***Delta Tau Delta v. Johnson*, 712 N.E.2d 968, 973 (Ind.1999).** In addition, we have observed that the duty of a business to exercise reasonable care extends to keeping its parking lot safe and providing a safe and suitable means of ingress and egress. We have further recognized that an individualized judicial determination of whether a duty exists in a particular case is not necessary where such a duty is well-settled. Thus, there is usually no need to redetermine what duty a business owner owes to its invitees because the law clearly recognizes that "[p]roprietors owe a duty to their business invitees to use reasonable care to protect them from injury caused by other patrons and guests on their premises, including providing adequate staff to police and control disorderly conduct." This duty only extends to harm from the conduct of third persons that, under the facts of a particular case, is reasonably foreseeable to the proprietor.

In three cases handed down together four years ago, this Court held that the determination of whether a landowner owed an invitee a duty to take reasonable care to protect the invitee against a third party criminal attack requires consideration of the totality of the circumstances to determine whether the criminal act was reasonably foreseeable. This analysis includes looking to "all of the circumstances surrounding an event, including the nature, condition, and location of the land, as well as prior similar incidents." While the number, nature, and location of prior similar incidents are substantial factors, "the lack of prior similar incidents will not preclude a claim where the landowner knew or should have known that the criminal act was foreseeable." We emphasized that "when the landowner is in a position to take reasonable precautions to protect his guest from a foreseeable criminal act, courts should not hesitate to hold that a duty exists."

There is no doubt, however, that reasonable foreseeability is an element of a landowner or business proprietor's duty of reasonable care. The issue is merely at what point and in what manner to evaluate the evidence regarding foreseeability. Where, as in this case, the alleged duty is well-established, there is no need for a new judicial redetermination of duty. The court's function was merely to adequately inform the jury of the applicable duty, and the jury was then to determine whether the Pub breached this duty of reasonable care to protect its invitees from foreseeable criminal attacks. In the present case, the well-settled duty was sufficiently established merely by evidence that Bartolini, a customer of the Pub, was beaten in the Pub parking lot as he was leaving. Upon receiving instructions as to the general nature of the Pub's duty, the jury was then able to evaluate whether Bartolini's injuries resulted from a criminal attack that was reasonably foreseeable to the Pub and for which it failed to exercise reasonable care.

Urging that there is sufficient evidence to support the trial court's determination of duty, Bartolini points to evidence that Todd and Matull were rowdy in the bar, that the Pub admitted and served underage drinkers, that Todd and Matull had exhibited violence at the stop sign as they left the bar in the presence of the bouncer, and that the bar manager and bouncer stood around for five or six minutes while the assailants engaged in an escalating argument with Bartolini. The Pub disputes each of these evidentiary claims, primarily emphasizing that Bartolini should not be able to use facts that arose long after the time when the Pub permitted his underage assailants to enter the bar. The Pub argues that the violence toward the stop sign does not suggest that the assailants would savagely beat a human being, and that its bouncer did not idly stand by but actively restrained one of the assailants and did everything possible to prevent the beating. These items of disputed evidence were matters for the jury to evaluate in determining whether the Pub breached its duty to exercise reasonable care to protect Bartolini from reasonably foreseeable intentional acts of other persons on its premises. We therefore decline to find error in the denial of the Pub's motion for judgment on the evidence with respect to the issue of duty.

The Pub also argues that the trial court should have granted its motion for judgment on the evidence because Bartolini's evidence failed to establish the element of proximate cause. In particular, the Pub argues that at the time of the Pub's negligence in permitting Todd to enter, it was not reasonably foreseeable that Todd would commit criminal battery on Bartolini, and that the criminal attack on Bartolini was an intervening superceding cause of his injuries.

Bartolini responds that the evidence indicated that the Pub was known as a place that underage drinkers could enter and be served; that the owner and manager knew that younger drinkers were more inclined to be rowdy and out of control; that if the Pub had turned Todd away, he and Matull would have left the Pub and gone elsewhere; that Todd had been loud and obnoxious in the bar that evening; that upon leaving the Pub he violently punched a stop sign, smashed a bottle, and then made threats against Bartolini in the parking lot; and that the Pub's night manager and bouncer stood by for several minutes as the verbal altercation escalated into the violent beating of Bartolini.

We conclude that there exists probative evidence or reasonable inferences to establish that Bartolini's injuries were reasonably foreseeable as the natural and probable consequence of the Pub's admitting and serving Todd, who was underage, and of its failing to act to prevent or interrupt the aggressive conduct of Todd and Mattull and their eventual attack upon Bartolini in the Pub's parking lot.

The Pub also asserts that it is entitled to a new trial because "the jury's allocation of fault is against the weight of the evidence." It argues that the verdict finding the Pub to be 80% at fault and Bartolini's attackers, Todd and Mattull, to each be 10% at fault "shocks the conscience and cannot stand," and that it has "no possible justification."

We acknowledge that the jury and the trial court in this case may have chosen to allocate a greater proportion of fault to the Pub than to the assailants because the opportunity for the beating would not even have existed had the Pub not failed to restrict Todd from entering its bar or had it taken appropriate action to prevent or stop the attack on its parking lot. In other words, the weight given to the causative role of the Pub may have exceeded that given the relative degree of intentionality of the perpetrators. We therefore decline to find an abuse of discretion by the trial court in refusing to order a new trial on the allocation of damages.

The Pub's final argument in favor of a new trial is that Bartolini's closing argument was improper. In particular, the Pub challenges the following portion of Bartolini's closing:

But your verdict can also do something else. It can send a message out, loud and clear, to every drinking establishment in our community by implicitly telling them it's their legal, it's their moral, it's their social responsibility to check I.D.'s at the door. Now, it won't always stop an intentional criminal act by an unruly patron. Some kids will slip through the cracks anyway. They've got pretty authentic looking I.D.'s. But it will go a long way towards stopping it, and it is beyond all doubt that it would have stopped it in this case. And so, at this moment, you are the conscience of our community. You can send this message to the restaurants and taverns. It isn't as though we're numbers or robots. We are people. We matter. And you could tell them, "You're not going to get away with this."

Noting that the Pub had not presented an objection to this argument during trial, the trial court denied the motion to correct error without considering this claim. Having failed to object at trial, the Pub may not present this issue on appeal.

The judgment of the trial court is affirmed.

CASE QUESTIONS

1. Describe what happened at the bar and the involvement of Pub employees.

2. Does the Pub have a duty to its patrons? Does that duty extend to protection from third-party harm? Was its duty breached?

3. What was the issue about allocation of fault?

4. What was the issue with the closing argument statement?

CONSIDER 3.8

Jane Doe, a 16-year-old runaway, using a pass obtained by another person, entered the Brainerd International Raceway (BIR) to watch the Quaker State Northstar National race. Doe indulged in alcohol and drugs, which were supplied to her by other patrons at the race.

An annual tradition at the race was a wet T-shirt contest. Flyers had been printed advertising the contest, and they were posted at the raceway at the time of the race. Doe participated in the contest, which began with sopping of the contestants' clothes and ended with Doe completely naked and subjected to crowd (consisting of 2,000 to 3,000 men) fondling for 45 minutes, all of which was captured on a videotape by one of the spectators.

Doe filed suit contending that BIR had breached its duty to her as an invitee in its failure to warn her about the contest and by not providing adequate security at the event. BIR maintains that Doe was a trespasser who did not have a valid pass for the event, which required that pass holders be age 18 or above.

Doe has requested damages for BIR's breach of duty as the property owner. Was Doe a trespasser or an invitee? Should BIR be held liable? *Doe v. Brainerd International Raceway*, 514 N.W.2d 811 (Ct. App. Minn. 1994)

Cautions and Conclusions

To avoid problems in this area of the extent of land ownership, parties should take precautions to establish their rights, the scope of those rights, and their liability for injuries that occur on their property. All parties in a sales transaction (seller, buyer, agents, and financiers) should analyze the sale with the following questions:

1. What water is available? Are the water rights protected?
2. Are mineral rights being transferred? What minerals are included? If minerals are not being transferred, who owns them and what do they own? What land-use rights do they have? What are the royalties or payments and who is entitled to receive them?
3. Is light available to the buildings, landscaping, and solar panels? If not, is an easement possible? Will future structures block the light?
4. Are the column and air lots included or have they been transferred? Who owns them?
5. Is air traffic unusually burdensome, close, or noisy?
6. Do any nuisances such as pollution, smell, or insects exist? Can they be remedied?
7. Are there any persons using the property? Do they hold any rights or are they trespassers?

This checklist helps buyers understand what they are getting and helps sellers be certain that they are disclosing relevant information about the extent of ownership and transfer.

When a property owner conveys mineral rights, the transaction may be clarified by answering the following questions:

1. What interest is being conveyed? What minerals? Subsurface only? Fee simple interest? Lease? Right of removal?
2. What rights are given on surface use? Will the lessee pay for restoration?
3. How much is the royalty? Are there any other fees to be paid? If no minerals are drawn, is there any payment?
4. Can the land be sold to someone else? Who gets the royalties?
5. Can the mineral rights be transferred to someone else? Will the same restrictions apply?

Property owners are responsible for the way they use their property and may want to answer these questions to limit or eliminate potential liability:

1. Are there significant noises, smells, or other emissions from the property? Do they interfere with others' use and enjoyment of their own property?
2. Are there individuals using the property in an unauthorized manner? Are there trespassers? Are there any mantraps to injure them? Have steps been taken to prevent trespass?
3. Do licensees enter the property? Are there appropriate signs and methods of warning them of dangers?

4. Do invitees enter the property? Are there any dangerous conditions? Have they been remedied? Are periodic inspections done to find and eliminate dangerous conditions?

5. Are nuisances from others affecting the property? Can action be taken to stop the conduct or recover damages?

Key Terms

air lot, 42
air rights, 39
centerline rule, 53
column lot, 42
Doctrine of Ancient Lights, 44
Doctrine of Correlative Rights, 51
equitable relief, 59
fee interest, 51
geothermal energy, 53
invitees, 62
licensees, 62
mineral interest, 52
mineral rights, 50
mineral servitude, 52
monetary relief, 59
nonownership states, 50
nuisance, 59
oil and gas lease, 52
ownership states, 50
Prior Appropriation Doctrine, 53
profit a prendre, 51
prorationing rules, 51
Riparian Doctrine, 53
royalty interest, 52
Rule of Capture, 50
solar easement laws, 43
Statute of Frauds, 52
trespass, 58
trespassers, 62
water rights, 53

Chapter Problems

1. In 1962, Rudolph and Bonnie Sher entered into a long-term lease agreement with Stanford University. The lot they leased was in a residential subdivision on the campus known as Pine Hill 2. Design approval by Stanford was required prior to construction of any homes on the lots. Herbert and Gloria Leiderman leased their lot located next to the Shers shortly after the Shers had signed their lease agreement.

The Shers' home was designed and built to take advantage of the winter sun for heat and light. Their home was placed on the lot so that its length faced the south. The windows on the south of their home are larger than the other windows in the house. The south side of the house is serrated to expose the maximum area to the sun. Roof overhangs were designed and constructed to block sun in the summer and permit winter sunlight to enter the home. Deciduous trees and shrubs on the south side of the house aid in shading and cooling in the summer, yet allow winter sunlight to reach the house. The Sher home is known as a "passive" solar home because it does not make use of any active solar collectors or panels.

The Leidermans undertook a landscaping scheme designed to attract birds and other small creatures and provide shade and privacy. By 1972, the Leiderman trees were casting shadows on the Sher house in the winter. The offending trees were removed at the Shers' expense. By 1979, the Shers had spent $4,000 on tree maintenance and removal in the Leidermans' yard. In 1979, the Leidermans refused to allow any further trimming at anyone's expense.

As a result of the ever-expanding trees, the Shers' house was cast in shadow between 10:00 a.m. and 2:00 p.m. A skylight was added in the kitchen but had little impact. Heat loss from the shadows amounted to 60 therms of natural gas. The Shers brought suit on the grounds of private nuisance, violation of the California Solar Shade Control Act, and negligent infliction of emotional distress. Is the Leidermans' landscaping a nuisance? Does it violate the Shade Control Act? Is it significant that the case involves passive solar devices and not solar panel access? *Sher v. Leiderman*, 226 Cal. Rptr. 698 (Cal. App. 1986)

2. Barclay and Marjorie Sloan own property directly north of and higher than the property of Robert, Joe, and Myrtle Wallbaum. Water drained from the Sloans' property through the Wallbaums' property through a grassy drainage ditch. In 1985, the Sloans tiled their land and had the ditch sloped and somewhat straightened. The result was erosion on the Wallbaums' property. The Wallbaums then blocked the ditch with a piece of tin and later fill dirt. The result was that the Sloans' property became flooded. The Sloans filed suit for an injunction ordering the removal of the blockage the Wallbaums had installed. Are the Sloans entitled to the injunction? Discuss the water rights issues. *Sloan v. Wallbaum*, 447 N.W.2d 148 (Iowa 1989)

3. Glen Prah constructed a residence during 1978 and 1979. He installed solar collectors on the roof for purposes of supplying energy for heat and hot water. Richard Maretti purchased the lot adjacent to Prah's and submitted proposed home plans that would result in a substantial obstruction of Prah's solar collectors and a corresponding reduction in the system's output and efficiency. Prah brought suit claiming that the construction of the home would be a private nuisance. If Maretti simply repositioned the layout of his home, the impact on Prah's system would be reduced, but Maretti has refused because his plans are in compliance with all zoning ordinances and other regulations. What factors should the court examine in balancing the parties' interests? *Prah v. Maretti*, 321 N.W.2d 182 (Wis. 1982)

4. Bruce Rankin occupies real estate in rural Platt County, Illinois, that is zoned for agricultural use. He has lived there since 1959 and, along with a partner, operates a business from his house known as Williams Trigger Specialties. In this business, Rankin, a federally registered gunsmith, works on firearm firing mechanisms.

Also located on the property, which has also been there since 1959, is a firing range. Rankin allows his friends to use the firing range in addition to using it himself. He does not permit strangers to use it. In the last several years, he has also permitted various law-enforcement agencies to use the range for training, practice, and qualification, including the Champaign Police Department, the Urbana Police Department, and the Ludlow Police Department. The Champaign Police Department Strategic Weapons and Tactics (SWAT) team, consisting of 12 people, has used the range 10 to 15 times in the last year.

Rankin has never charged a fee for use of the range. He has, however, considered putting his range to commercial use at some time in the future. Rankin is almost always present when the range is used by private individuals other than law-enforcement agencies. There has never been an injury or near injury or complaint to Rankin about the range or its use.

Charles Kolstad owns the property immediately west of Rankin's parcel. Mary Heath Hays and Mary Lucille Hays reside on another parcel of land to the west of Rankin's parcel. Kolstad and Mary Lucille Hays have children who play together.

The Kolstads and Hayses lived with the noise from the gunshots, but on October 4, 1988, they became alarmed when the new noise of rapid short bursts of gunfire sounded. Kolstad recognized the noise as the firing of automatic weapons. Both neighbors became concerned about their safety and filed suit for an injunction to halt the use of the property as a firing range. Should the court issue an injunction? Should it be an absolute prohibition on operation of the range or something less? *Kolstad v. Rankin*, 534 N.E.2d 1373 (Ill. 1989)

5. The Great Cove Boat Club had a wharf on the Piscataqua River in Maine. The Bureau of Public Lands, in its work for the preservation of public waterways, entered into lease agreements with private parties so that they could create and operate wharfs, floats, and moorings for public enjoyment. One such 30-year lease resulted in construction of public access wharfs that flooded the area of the Great Cove's wharf, cutting off access by the owners. Great Cove claimed, as a riparian, that its rights had been violated through the use of the water in such a fashion that its water access rights were destroyed. The Bureau of Public Lands claims that it has the right, as a state agency, to regulate land use and that leasing to parties is part of that regulation that Great Cove is subject to. Is the Bureau correct or have Great Cove's riparian rights been violated? *Great Cove Boat Club v. Bureau of Public Lands*, 672 A.2d 91 (Me. 1996)

6. Consider whether the following types of conduct would constitute a nuisance, and discuss the type of remedy available. Be sure to use the doctrine of balancing interests.

a. The operation of a dump causing smoke, odors, flies, rodents, and wild dogs to enter neighboring properties.
b. Stadium lights on at night that disturb a neighbor's sleep.
c. The operation of a 24-hour car wash next to a home when the car wash employees play loud music, curse, sell illegal drugs, urinate in plain view, and throw trash onto the grass surrounding the home. Would it matter if the customers were responsible for these activities? *Packett v. Herbert*, 377 S.E.2d 438 (Va. 1989)

7. The City of Spokane (City) has owned and operated Indian Canyon Golf Course, including its driving range, since the 1930s. The Episcopal Diocese of Spokane donated the driving range land to the City. In 1996, the Diocese sold developer Ronald C. McCloskey land at the end of the driving range. At that time it had never been enclosed or improved. Some portion of the property was the driving range rough.

In the 1960s, the City would retrieve hundreds of golf balls per month from the property. The number increased to approximately hundreds per week until 2000. The City did not seek permission from the Diocese to retrieve the balls. Exact boundaries between the properties were unknown. Initially, machetes were used to clear the underbrush. By the 1970s, City maintenance crews began clearing brush on the subject property two or three times a year with motorized equipment. From around 1985 to 1987, a City employee placed 8 to 10 "No Trespassing" signs on the subject property to keep people from stealing balls.

Mr. McCloskey divided the property into five lots (lots A–E), planning to build duplexes. Lot A was closest to the tee; lot E the furthest; lots A and B were most heavily hit by the golf balls. Mr. McCloskey conveyed the property to Canyon Greens, LLC, which in turn sold lot C to Ray and Kathryn Ayers, and lot D to Robert and Sue McVicars.

When Mr. McCloskey spoke with the City's golf pro about the situation, the pro was surprised the property did not belong to the City. Mr. McCloskey believed the golf course location would aid in development. Anticipating problems, the City offered to buy the property and discussed screening costs, but the parties could not agree on a price. When the City said it had adversely acquired an easement over the property, Mr. McCloskey ceased marketing lots A, B, and E.

Both the Ayers and McVicars built duplexes. During and after construction, the McVicars and the Ayers found golf balls on their lots. Windows were damaged in one of the duplexes. Despite the window damage, the falling golf balls did not interfere with the Ayers' ability to rent the duplexes. In 1998, the City filed a "Complaint for Declaratory and Injunctive Relief, and to Quiet Title" against Canyon Greens, McCloskey, the Ayers, and the McVicars (collectively Developers). The City filed an action for injunctive relief and quiet title, alleging a prescriptive easement right to hit golf balls onto the developers' property and retrieve them. The Developers' counterclaim sought trespass, nuisance, and inverse condemnation damages. Analyze the rights of the parties in the case. *City of Spokane v. Canyon Greens*, LLC, 107 Wash. App. 1005, Not Reported in P.3d, 2001 WL 772498 Wash. App. Div. 3,2001.

8. Neighbor A has installed a satellite dish on his roof and Neighbor B complains that the dish is unsightly and interferes with the pristine view Neighbor B had enjoyed previously. Neighbor B says the dish interferes with his "line of sight." Neighbor B has petitioned to have the receiving dish removed on the grounds that it is not protected by any solar energy statutes. Neighbor A indicates that there are no prohibitions on the installation of the receivers and no visual impairment statutes that protect Neighbor B. Neighbor A also argues that prohibiting the installation of such receiving dishes impairs technology. Discuss the issues and decide what a court or agency hearing the case should do. *In the Matter of Preemption of Local Zoning or Other Regulation of Receive-Only Satellite Earth Stations*, 59 Rad. Reg. 2d (P & F) 1073, 1986 WL 292763 (F.C.C. 1986)

9. Jane Doe was confronted by Billy Jo Hampton on February 23, 1994, as she was preparing to leave the Beckley Crossings Shopping Center in Raleigh County, West Virginia. She had been shopping at the Center's Wal-Mart store (defendants), which was managed by Belcher. The actual property itself was owned by B. C. Associates Ltd. Hampton placed a knife in her side, forced her into her car, drove the car out of the parking lot to a remote area, sexually assaulted her and then abandoned her and the car. Mr. Hampton was apprehended several days later in Greensboro, North Carolina, where he had abducted another woman. He was charged with attempted murder of Ms. Doe.

Ms. Doe filed suit against Wal-Mart and the limited partnership that owned and operated Beckley Crossings, alleging that they had failed to take reasonable precautions to prevent this kind of injury to customers invited to the shopping center. Is either Wal-Mart or the limited partnership liable? *Doe v. Wal-Mart Stores, Inc.*, 479 S.E.2d 610 (W.Va. 1996)

10. A private foundation has proposed the construction of a 72-bed facility for the mentally disabled persons in a residential neighborhood. Two neighbors have filed suit to halt construction as a nuisance on the basis of evidence that residents of existing facilities tend to roam the neighborhoods going through trash cans and approaching neighbors for money and food. Will the facility be enjoined? *Miniat v. McGinnis*, 762 S.W.2d 390 (Ark. 1988)

For research activities related to this chapter, go to our text companion website at www.thomsonedu.com/westbuslaw/jennings.

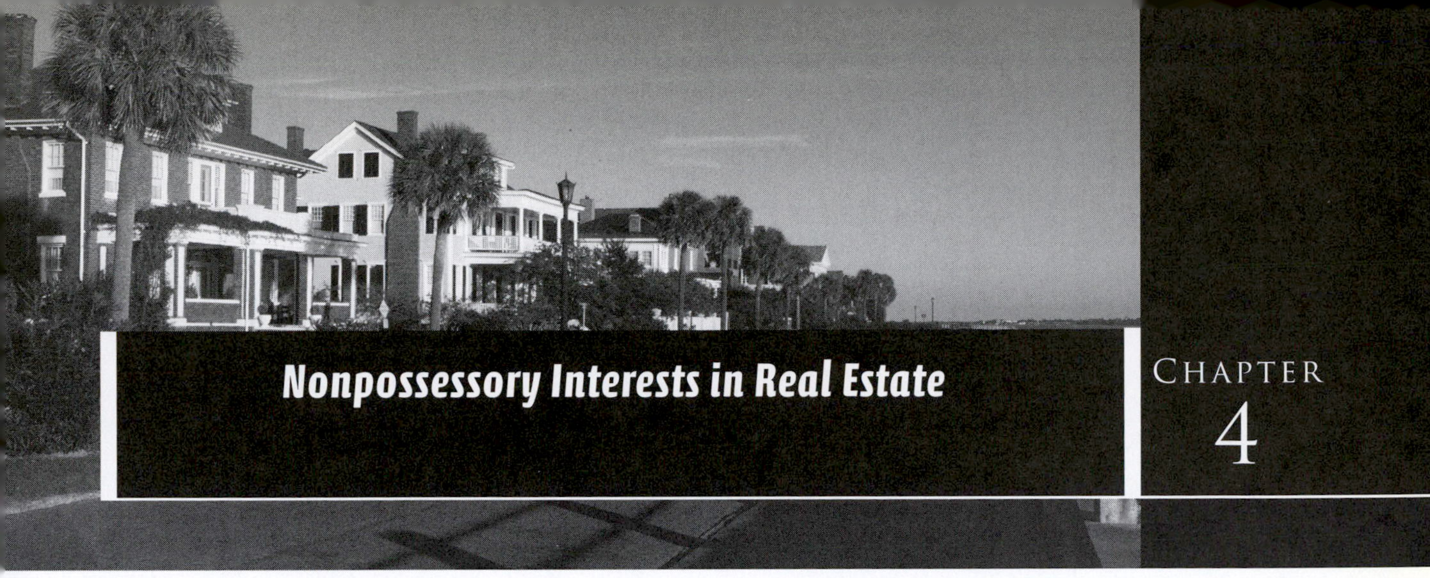

Good fences make good neighbors.

Robert Frost

Nonpossessory land interests are those that give rights that always fall short of possession of the land. These nonpossessory interests might be labeled privileges, liberties, or advantages. Nonpossessory interests give their holders some right of entry or use of the land of another. This chapter explains the creation and extent of these nonpossessory interests.

Easements

An **easement** is a liberty, privilege, or advantage in another's property. It is nonpossessory but can run on in perpetuity. There are many different types of easements and methods for their creation.

Types of Easements: Appurtenant v. Easements in Gross

An **easement appurtenant** is one that attaches to or benefits a particular tract of land. The purpose of an easement appurtenant is to provide benefit to a landowner.

For example, refer to Figure 4.1 and suppose both landowners C and A need access to the street that runs parallel to B's property. The dark strip represents the appurtenant easements held by C and A in B's land and C in A's land that give them access so that they can use and possess their land.

In contrast, an **easement in gross** is not created to benefit any landowner with respect to a particular tract of land; rather, it belongs to the holders regardless of whether they own any adjacent property. Generally, public utilities hold easements in gross through residential property (in the back six or eight feet of the lots, for example) so that cable, electrical, and water lines can be connected to all parcels of

Figure 4.1 Easement Appurtenant

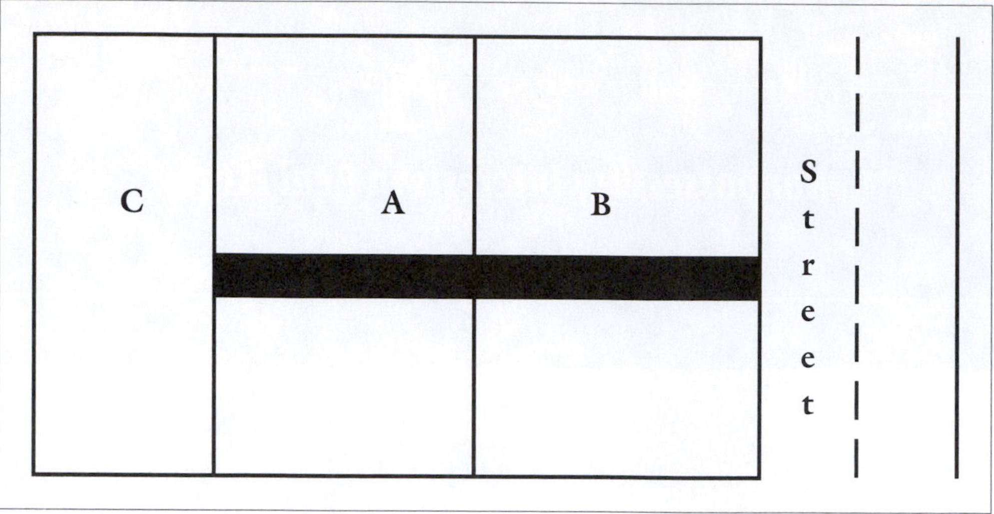

the property. At common law, easements in gross were not transferable, but in most states they are now transferable if they are commercial in nature.

Types of Easements: Affirmative v. Negative Easements

The situation diagrammed in Figure 4.1 is an example of an **affirmative easement**, which means that the owner of the easement right can use another's land (the land subject to the easement). In Figure 4.1, A and C have an affirmative easement in B's property. Likewise, C has an affirmative easement in A's property.

A **negative easement** is one in which the holders of the easements prevent other property owners from using their property in a particular way or prevent particular acts by other landowners; for example, an easement restricting the heights of buildings on adjoining property. These negative easements, often called *scenic easements*, can have a possible twofold tax advantage. First, the taxpayer/landowner can perhaps take a charitable contribution deduction. For example, a business might grant a neighboring church a negative easement that prevents the blockage of sunlight from the church's stained glass windows. The business can take the value reduction this easement causes in its property as a charitable contribution deduction. Second, the taxpayer/landowner's property taxes can be reduced by the decrease in value brought about by the easement restrictions. An easement that prevents the shading of solar panels (as discussed in Chapter 3) is an example of a negative easement.

Another type of negative easement that has been used extensively over the past few years is the **conservation easement**. A conservation easement is one granted by a landowner who owns property with historical, cultural, or architectural significance. These landowners grant negative easements that will prevent them from tearing down buildings on the property so that their historical significance is preserved. In many cases, again, these easements can be treated as charitable donations. These forms of easements are being used more and more as governments lack funds to buy or condemn the property. Private landowners accomplish the goal of conservation without the costs being borne by governments and taxpayers.

Recently, conservation easements have been used to preserve farmlands in those areas where development would otherwise force farmers, due to increased property taxes, to abandon their land to further development.[1] The farmers grant to their communities negative conservation easements, often referred to as *purchase and development rights (PDR) contracts,* in which they agree to limit their land uses. In exchange, the communities give the farmers reduced taxes for the promise to preserve their land as natural farmland. The result is a solution to encroaching development as well as to the high taxes faced in agricultural production.

The Parties: Dominant v. Servient Estates

In an easement relationship, the property owned by the easement holder is called the **dominant tenement** or **dominant estate,** and the property through which the easement runs is called the **servient tenement** or **servient estate**. In Figure 4.1, B holds the servient estate for dominant tenants A and C. Since C also has an easement through A's property, A is also a servient estate to C's dominant estate.

Creation of Easements

Easements by Express Grant or Express Reservation

An **easement by express grant** or **express reservation** is one in which the parties actually draw up papers as if transferring an interest in land. Since an easement is a land interest, creation of express easements must comply with all requirements in the state for the conveyance of land interests. Most states' Statutes of Frauds require the conveyance of a land interest to be in writing or evidenced by a record.

Whether an easement is created by express grant or express reservation depends on the physical layout of the land transferred: The two contrasting physical setups for easements are illustrated in Figure 4.2. In both situations, A was the original owner of the full parcel that contained an access route to the street that runs parallel to the tract. In the express grant situation, A retains that portion of the parcel with the access route and must therefore convey to B an easement by express grant. In the express reservation situation, A conveys that portion of the parcel with the access route and must therefore grant himself an easement by express reservation.

The same easement is involved in both circumstances, but the method of acquisition is different. In the deed transferring title to the property conveyed, A would either grant or convey the portion of the parcel B has purchased and would also include a grant to B of the easement for ingress or egress or, in the second circumstances, A would reserve that ingress and egress for himself when B is granted title to the land with that access.

An express easement is not limited to creation in situations of land partition. An express easement may be granted as a separate transaction. For example, a solar easement may be drafted and executed between two neighbors who already own their adjoining parcels of land. They might, for example, create a negative solar easement. The following case involves an issue of whether an express easement was created.

1. Some states use negative easements as a means of preserving historic farmlands. *U.S. v. Blackman,* 613 S.E.2d 442 (Va. 2005).

Figure 4.2 Express Grant and Express Reservation Easement

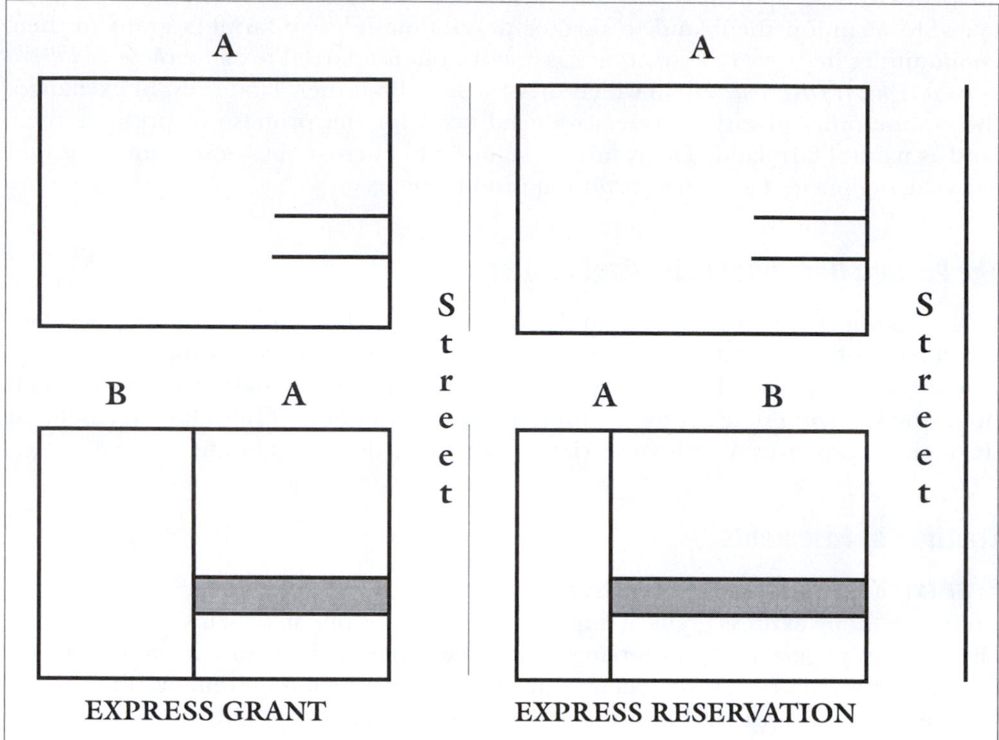

FRIERSON V. WATSON

636 S.E.2d 872 (S.C. App. 2006)

FACTS

The Friersons have a two-story building at the corner of East Main Street and Pendleton Street in Easley, South Carolina. The building shares a common wall with an adjacent two-story building owned by Watson and his wife. An outdoor stairway located on Watson's property provides access to the second floor of both buildings.

The Friersons' predecessors-in-interest, E.C., E.O., and D.M. Frierson, purchased the building in 1929 from the "Estate of R.F. Smith, Inc." The 1929 deed, dated January 14 and recorded on January 23, expressly conveyed "an easement in a certain four foot stairway in the back of the building, with right of ingress and egress on said stairway to the second story of said building."

On January 21, 1929, two days before the deed was recorded, the parties to the sale executed a "Memorandum of Agreement" concerning an easement for the use of the hallway. Although the agreement was signed, it was never recorded. The agreement stated in relevant part:

> *[T]he party of the first part [Estate of R.F. Smith, Inc.] has sold to the parties of the second part [E.C., E.O. and D.M. Frierson], a certain brick building at the corner of Main and Pendleton Streets, the second story of which is not partitioned, but one-half belongs to each of the parties hereto. There are offices constructed over the building of the parties of the second part covering practically the width of their building. As a part of the consideration of the sale of this property, the party of the first part grants to the parties of the second part, the right to use the hall-way on the second floor as long as the said room remains unpartioned [sic] by brick and continuous through to the roof.*

The Friersons currently use the first floor of their building to operate a drug store. Over the years, the family used the second floor for a variety of purposes. At one point, it was a Masonic lodge. Later, the family rented the second story to doctors, dentists, and others as office space and visitors used the hallway to access those offices. The second floor eventually became unusable and the family used it for storage and for private office space. The Frierson building passed through the estate of E.O. Frierson, one of the original parties named in the deed, to Virginia Frierson's husband, E.C. Frierson, III, and then through the husband's estate to Virginia.

In 2002, Watson and his wife purchased the two-story building adjacent to the Friersons' building from Goodwill Industries of Upper South Carolina, Inc. The deed, recorded June 6, 2002, noted an easement as follows: "This conveyance is made subject to an easement granted E.C. Frierson, et al. to use the stairway along this common line as ingress and egress to the second story of the Frierson building (See Deed Book 3-V at Page 229)." The 2002 deed also referenced "a plat prepared by J.C. Smith & Associates, Surveyors, for Goodwill Industries of Upper South Carolina, Inc. dated April 23, 2002..." The plat showed access to the second floor via an external door, a 28-foot stairway, and a 40-foot portion of an upstairs hallway.

Watson's closing attorney wrote a title opinion on June 3, 2002, prior to the closing, noting Goodwill was the owner of the property subject to easements for use of the exterior door, stairway, and hallway:

Goodwill Industries of Upper South Carolina, Inc. is the fee simple owner of said property subject, however, to the following exceptions... Easement as to Tract No. 2., granted to E.C. Frierson, E.O. Frierson and D.M. Frierson, their heirs and assigns... and such easements or rights-of-way to the exterior door, stairwell and hallway as [shown] on a plat dated April 23, 2002, by Smith Surveyors, Inc. for Goodwill Industries of Upper South Carolina, Inc.

The Friersons brought suit to establish an easement to the hallway. They also sought an injunction to stop Watson's construction and additionally asserted claims for trespass and breach of contract. The Friersons claimed Watson's construction violated their easement by eliminating the hallway, which denied them access to the second floor of their building. Watson maintains there is no easement for the hallway, and that the Friersons would not be denied access to the upper floor of their building because there is a stairway inside the Friersons' building.

The Friersons moved for summary judgment. The circuit court determined the Friersons had established an easement for use of the hallway by grant and by prescription and granted the Friersons' motion. Watson appealed.

JUDICIAL OPINION

Goolsby, Judge. During his deposition for discovery, Watson testified that he saw the survey containing the hallway easement either at closing or up to one week prior to closing, but he did not realize until after closing that the survey was actually part of the deed. Watson further testified that he received (1) either a copy of the 1929 deed or a document including the same language as the deed that granted an easement for the stairway and (2) a copy of the subsequent Memorandum of Agreement from 1929 that granted an easement for the hallway. Also prior to the closing, Watson and a previous owner of the building had a conversation about an ongoing dispute with the Friersons about the hallway; during this conversation the previous owner informed Watson that the Friersons were claiming a right to use the hallway.

An easement is a right which one person has to use the land of another for a specific purpose." This right of way over land may arise in three ways: (1) from necessity, (2) by grant, and (3) by prescription.

"A reservation of an easement in a deed by which lands are conveyed is equivalent, for the purpose of the creation of the easement, to an express grant of the easement by the grantee of the lands."

" 'A grant of an easement is to be construed in accordance with the rules applied to deeds and other written instruments.' " Both deeds and easements are valid to subsequent purchasers without notice when they are recorded. The purpose of the recording statute is to protect a subsequent buyer *without* notice. Additionally, one who already has notice of the existence of any instrument will be bound by such notice whether the instrument is recorded or not.

Notice of a deed is notice of its entire contents and whatever matters one would have learned upon the inquiry that the instrument made it one's duty to pursue. Further, "where a deed describes land as is shown as a certain plat, such becomes a part of the deed." The law imputes to a purchaser of real property notice of the recitals contained in the written instruments forming the purchaser's chain of title and charges him with the duty of making such reasonable inquiry and investigation as is suggested by the recitals and references therein contained.

An easement by grant is not required to be recorded to be valid. Although notice is assumed when a document conveying an interest in real property is recorded, recording is not necessary if the buyer has actual notice. In this case, Watson testified regarding the numerous ways in which he knew about the hallway easement-his deed contained a survey noting the hallway easement and the previous owner had informed him of an ongoing dispute over the hallway. Further, Watson testified that he received a document that granted the easement to the stairway and that he knew an easement only to the stairway itself provided the Friersons with no way of accessing their second story from the stairway. Additionally, Watson's attorney prepared a title opinion which included the hallway easement and, most importantly, Watson actually received a copy of the unrecorded document granting the hallway easement. Watson, moreover, testified at his deposition that he has been involved in purchasing and developing real estate for at least ten years. As the circuit court noted in its order, "Watson is a sophisticated businessman experienced in real estate." The unrecorded document clearly granted an easement to the hallway and Watson had the document prior to closing. We therefore hold the circuit court properly granted summary judgment to the Friersons on the basis they had established an easement by grant. Accordingly, the order of the circuit court is **Affirmed.**

CASE QUESTIONS

1. Trace the history of the properties to their present owners.
2. Is it significant that the easement was not recorded?
3. What type of easement existed?

Easements by Implication

An **easement by implication** arises when there is a necessity. Suppose, for example, that in the express grant of Figure 4.2, B's property is landlocked and that crossing A's parcel is B's only method of ingress and egress. Suppose further that the conveyance from A to B makes no provision or express grant in the deed to provide B with an easement. To prevent B from having to hold title to a worthless piece of inaccessible property, the courts developed the doctrine of easement by implication to remedy B's landlocked predicament.

An easement by implication exists if several factors are present. First, there must have been unity of ownership between the two tracts prior to the partition and sale. In this case there was unity of ownership, since A owned the entire parcel prior to the division. Second, there must have been a ***quasi* easement** at the time of the sole ownership of the parcel. A *quasi* easement is an access route used by the landowner when the land was not yet divided. Figure 4.2 indicates that A used the road as a means of access, and so a *quasi* easement existed. The term *quasi* is used because landowners cannot hold an easement in their own property. Third, the prior *quasi* easement must have been apparent and used continuously. This requirement is easily satisfied in Figure 4.2 and in most access cases because the road or path is visible. However, visibility is not required to meet the apparent standard in most jurisdictions. For example, sewer-line accesses, although not visible, are apparent because while we may not see sewer lines, we know that folks cannot live on property without their presence. Although not shown in the figure, continuous use can probably be assumed in most access cases where, as here, the roadway is the only means of access. Continuous use is normal use and does not require use every day.

The final requirement for an easement by implication is to establish that requiring the dominant estate to obtain access any other way would require unreasonable expense. In Figure 4.2, B's landlocked circumstances indicate that the access through just one parcel is the least expensive and least troublesome method of obtaining access.

There are both easements implied by grant and easements implied by reservation.

The following case deals with a question of whether an easement by implication exists.

THOMAS V. MADSEN

132 P.3d 392 (Idaho 2007)

FACTS

On May 5, 1970, Dale J. Thomas (Thomas/defendant) and his wife purchased a 50-acre parcel of property from Dale's father. The property had been in his family since 1878. The tract conveyed is almost square in shape and is bounded on its southern side by a public highway. There is also a canal that runs diagonally across the property from the southwest to the northeast.

A red brick house was placed onto the property in 1900, near the center of the southern boundary, not far off the highway. A dirt driveway provided access from the highway to the west side of the brick house and then turned northwestwardly to access the farm property, including a cattle-feeding operation located on it. Thomas moved into the brick house when he was six years old. His parents lived there until his father died in 1977 and his mother moved out in 1980.

On August 5, 1996, Thomas and his wife gifted a 1/2-acre parcel of the property to their son Dale L. "Dale Roy" Thomas (Dale Roy) and his second wife. That parcel is located just to the west of the red brick house, but is closer to the highway. It is bounded by the highway on its southern boundary, and it included the southern portion of the driveway used to access the brick house and the farmland. Prior to gifting the parcel to Dale Roy, Thomas and his wife had also gifted to their daughter a 1/2-acre parcel located east of the brick house.

Dale Roy and his second wife lived in the red brick house from about 1994 until 1996, when they put a manufactured home on the 1/2-acre parcel and moved into it. Some time later, a lending institution acquired title to the property through foreclosure proceedings, and on June 18, 2002, it sold the parcel to Daniel R. Madsen (Madsen).

In 2003, Madsen erected a fence along the boundary of his property, enclosing the southern portion of the dirt road inside the fence. He also installed a locked gate where the driveway connects to the public highway. Thomas had been regularly using the driveway to access his farming and cattle-feeding operations. He used it twice a day. When confronted with the locked gate and Madsen's refusal to unlock it, Thomas cut the chain so that he could have hay delivered to his cattle.

Thomas filed suit seeking a determination that he has an easement across Madsen's property, either by prescription or by implication. The lower court found that Thomas had an easement by prescription and an implied easement from prior use. Madsen appealed.

JUDICIAL OPINION

Eismann, Justice. In order to establish an implied easement by prior use, the party asserting the easement must prove three elements: (1) unity of title or ownership and a subsequent separation by grant of the dominant estate; (2) apparent continuous use long enough before separation of the dominant estate to show that the use was intended to be permanent; and (3) the easement must be reasonably necessary to the proper enjoyment of the dominant estate. There is no dispute regarding the first two elements. The dispute centers solely upon the district judge's finding that the easement across Madsen's property was reasonably necessary to the proper enjoyment of Thomas's property.

Strict necessity is not required for the creation of an implied easement by prior use. All that is required is reasonable necessity. Because the implied easement from prior use is created at the time of severance, the issue of reasonable necessity is based upon the circumstances that existed at that time. A later change in circumstances is not relevant to the creation of the easement.

The parcel now owned by Madsen was severed from Thomas's property by a gift deed dated August 5, 1996. The dirt driveway had been used continuously for almost 100 years. Thomas testified that the driveway has been in existence since 1898 and that it had been used to access the red brick house since 1900 when the house was moved onto the property. The driveway adjoined a parking area on the west side of the red brick house, where the house's main entrance was. The driveway was also the sole access to the feedlot, to various outbuildings, and to the adjoining farmland. It was used as needed, including for driving farm equipment to and from the field; for trucks hauling hay, corn, and silage; and for delivering fuel to the red brick house. At the time of severance, Thomas was using the road at least twice a day to access his feedlot, and the red brick house was occupied by Dale Roy and his wife.

Thomas's use of the dirt driveway was apparent. As the district judge found, "It is obvious to anyone going on the property of Madsen that the driveway provides access to the red brick house and Thomas' feed yard, stack yard, outbuildings and field."

It is obvious from the facts of this case that Thomas intended the driveway to be permanent. He testified that the driveway had been maintained as long as he could remember (he was age 74 at the time of trial), and since 1953 he had been maintaining it by spreading loads of gravel on it. When the parcel now owned by Madsen was severed in 1996, Thomas did not alter his use of the driveway, nor did he cease maintaining it.

Madsen argues that part of Thomas's property borders the public highway and therefore it was not landlocked. He could have simply built another access road. Because an implied easement from prior use requires only reasonable necessity, not great present necessity, there is no requirement that the dominant estate be landlocked. Thomas testified that because of the wet conditions in his adjoining field much of the year, he would have to build quite a foundation for a new road. The district judge found "that constructing a road of the same quality would require considerable expense and time." The district judge viewed the premises and therefore had the advantage of correlating the evidence to the actual situation on the ground. It was for him to balance the respective convenience, inconvenience, costs, and other pertinent facts. The district judge's finding that Thomas's claimed easement was reasonably necessary to the proper enjoyment of his property is supported by substantial and competent evidence. We therefore affirm the finding that Thomas has an implied easement by prior use.

The district judge also found that Thomas had an easement by prescription. The primary issue was whether Thomas's use of the driveway across the property of his son was adverse. Madsen argued that the family relationship between Thomas and his son should create a presumption that Thomas's use of the driveway was not adverse. Because we have upheld the implied easement by prior use, we need not address whether the facts also supported the district judge's finding that Thomas had obtained an easement by prescription.

Affirmed.

CASE QUESTIONS

1. Describe how the property was originally owned and transferred.

2. What are the requirements for an easement by implication and are they met in this case?

3. Why does the court not deal with the issue of prescription?

CONSIDER 4.1

For each of the following, determine what type of easement (affirmative, negative, appurtenant, gross) is being created and who will hold the dominant and servient estates:

a. Angela holds an easement that prevents Bill from planting willow trees. (Angela and Bill are adjoining landowners, and Angela obtained the easement because she felt the roots of willow trees would harm her in-ground swimming pool.)
b. Community Cable has just placed television wires along the back wall lines of several neighbors' lots in a new subdivision. The landowners object—they allege a trespass has occurred.
c. Oscar owns a passive solar home (dependent upon window sunlight for heat), and Oscar's neighbor has agreed not to plant trees or shrubs or construct walls on the boundary he shares with Oscar to prevent obstruction.
d. Nordstrom, the retail store, has its name placed on the top of the public parking garage (owned by the city of Scottsdale, AZ) located next to its store.

CONSIDER 4.2

Mary Eilen Thompson as Trustee of the Mary Eilen Trust, Lanny G. Brantner, Jerry O. Brantner, and Jon Airhart are the owners of Fanny Horner's Eating Establishment in Mitchell, South Dakota. Their restaurant is adjacent to the Palace Mall parking lot owned by E.I.G. Palace Mall, LLC. Western Sierra Contractors, Inc., is the construction contractor named to build the C.S.K. Auto Parts store. Thompson and the others maintain that they have easement rights in this area that would halt the intended development of the mall parking lot. The mall owner intended to sell this portion of the land to C.S.K. in order for it to build an auto parts store on the property.

At one time, Paul Bjornsen owned both the restaurant and mall properties. While Bjornsen owned the restaurant, the mall parking lot was used by restaurant patrons and delivery trucks. He deeded the restaurant property to the present owners on November 14, 1974. Because customer and delivery truck use of the mall parking has continued

CONSIDER 4.2

(continued)

since they purchased the restaurant, the restaurant owners claim that they have occupied the mall parking lot property for more than 20 years and have established open and notorious use and possession for purposes of customer parking, as well as for ingress and egress. The mall owner contends that the use of the mall's parking lot by the general public, including the restaurant customers, was permitted because it was not adverse to the mall's interests. Is there an easement? If an easement exists, how did it arise? Is it important to know whether it is possible to access restaurant parking in another way? *Thompson v. E.I.G. Palace Mall*, LLC, 657 N.W.2d 300 (S.D. 2003)

Easements by Necessity

An **easement by necessity** is one that can arise solely on the basis of necessity, and the requirements of prior use need not be established. However, this type of easement lasts only so long as the necessity continues, whereas an easement by implication may go on in perpetuity. In some states, condemnation procedures are available to assist landowners who need to obtain access to their property. In other states, an easement is automatically given when landlocked property is transferred.[2]

In Figure 4.1, B's circumstances could be changed to require an easement by necessity if the properties were surrounded by water. Then A's only method of access to the street would be through B's land, unless and until a bridge or causeway to B's land was constructed.

Some states have begun to follow doctrines on easements by implication and necessity that are less complex. For example, in *Carter v. County of Hanover*, 496 S.E.2d 42 (Va. 1998), the court found that without any deed restrictions, the "grantor of property conveys everything that is necessary for the beneficial use and enjoyment of the property."

Easements by Prescription

Obtaining an easement by **prescription** is somewhat similar to obtaining title to property through *adverse possession*. However, the term "adverse possession" (discussed in Chapter 13) is inappropriate for easements because easements are nonpossessory land interests. An easement by prescription requires the presence of the following:

1. *The easement must be used for the appropriate prescriptive period.* The prescriptive period will vary from state to state but generally corresponds to the state's adverse possession period, which ranges from 5 to 20 years throughout the United States.
2. *The use of the easement must be adverse (not permissive).* If the landowner has given the prescriptive taker an oral license, such use is permissive and does not qualify for prescription. The permissive use must be mutually agreed upon—a landowner's posting of a permission sign will not prevent prescriptive rights.
3. *The use of the easement must be open and notorious.* In most states, this requirement means that the prescriptive taker must use the property in such a way that a landowner would, under ordinary circumstances, be aware of the use. Because actual knowledge of use is not required, landowners who do not periodically inspect their property run the risk of having a prescriptive use accumulate.
4. *The use of the easement must be continuous and exclusive.* This requirement forces the prescriptive user to confine use to a particular area. The user is required to use

2. Fla. Stat. §704.01; see also *Restatement of Property* §476 and Colo. Const. Art. II §14. Other states may not have a statute or condemnation procedures but follow strong public policy in favor of an easement. *Big Sky Hidden Village Owners Ass'n v. Hidden Village, Inc.*, 915 P.2d 845 (Mont. 1996).

the same strip of land or access route consistently.[3] And parties acting together cannot create a prescriptive easement by ganging up on the property owner to obtain regular use. The prescriptiver user must be the exclusive user. One exception is the rule of tacking, which permits those in privity of contract (buyers and sellers) and those who inherit title to land to add their use to that of the seller or deceased in making up the prescriptive period. For example, a father using an easement for five years and then passing his property to his son by will also passes his five years of prescriptive use of the easement.

To stop a prescriptive taking, a landowner may take several prevention steps, most of which are recognized by the majority of states. Written protest is one method of interrupting the prescriptive period, as is physical interruption (for example, the use of a gate). Perhaps court-obtained injunctive relief is the best alternative, because such action provides the landowners with full records for establishing a cutoff of the prescriptive period. The following case deals with multiple issues in a claim of an easement by prescription.

Carnahan v. Moriah Property Owners Association, Inc.

716 N.E.2d 437 (Ind. 1999)

FACTS

Prior to 1972, Charles and Julia Drewry owned a 22-acre lake and the surrounding property. In November, 1972, Donald and Joyce Carnahan purchased a one-acre lot from the Drewrys and the purchase included a portion of the lake bed. The Carnahans used the lake for recreational activity including ice skating, fishing, swimming, and using various watercraft on the lake. In the spring of 1973, the Carnahans placed a houseboat on the lake and lived on it intermittently until 1976 when they finished building their lakeside home on their lot. They used a ski boat on the lake until 1986 and wave runners and jet skis through the summer of 1993.

In 1984, the Carnahans purchased an adjacent one-acre plot, one-fifth of which was bed in the lake. Subsequent to this purchase, the lake and adjoining lands were surveyed and platted into lots for subdivision additions to Lake County. In 1987, the Carnahans acquired another adjacent lot of 1.2 acres, one-eighth of which was lake bed. With their original purchase and the two subsequent ones, the Carnahans owned over half an acre or 2.5 percent of the 22-acre lake bed.

In 1991, the Moriah Property Owner's Association (Moriah) obtained the property rights to the majority of the lake bed including nearly all the water suitable for use by watercraft. Moriah then prepared restrictive covenants that were rules for use of the lake. One rule was "No motors are allowed on the lake except electric trolling motors powered by no more than two 12-volt batteries."

When the Carnahans received a copy of the new restrictions, they filed suit to establish their prescriptive easement in the lake. They also alleged interference with their real property, easement, and riparian rights. Moriah counterclaimed that the Carnahans' use of the lake was a threat to adults and children who swam there.

The trial court ruled that the Carnahans had a prescriptive easement but found that the restrictive covenants were valid. The court of appeals agreed that there was a prescriptive easement but reversed on the restrictive covenant validity. Moriah appealed.

JUDICIAL OPINION

Sullivan, Justice. Prescriptive easements are not favored in the law, and in Indiana, the party claiming one must meet "stringent requirements."...

3. *The Restatement (Third) of Property* (Servitudes) has four theories listed for granting prescriptive easements: (1) sufficiently long use can lead to entitlement; (2) use to perfect a flawed title meets the requirements; (3) long-term use is evidence of a right lost that must be restored; and (4) prescriptive claims arise and can exist but must be advanced within a limited time frame.

Adverse use has been defined as a "use of the property as the owner himself would exercise, disregarding the claims of others entirely, asking permission from no one, and using the property under a claim of right." The concept of adversity was developed in the context of establishing use rights over static paths or roads that crossed the property of adjoining landowners. The Court of Appeals affirmed the trial court's conclusion as to adversity by citing a prototypical path or road case for the proposition that "an unexplained use for 20 years is presumed to be adverse and sufficient to establish title by prescriptive easement."

We agree that "an unexplained use for 20 years" of an obvious path or road for ingress and egress over the lands of another creates a rebuttable presumption that a use was adverse. However, we are unwilling to recognize such a presumption in favor of a party trying to establish a prescriptive easement for the recreational use of a body of water. This is because recreational use (especially of a body of water) is of a very different character from use of a path or road or ingress and egress over land. Recreational use (especially of water which leaves no telltale path or road) seems to us likely to be permissive in accordance with the widely held view in Indiana that if the owner of one land "sees his neighbor also making use of it, under circumstances that in no way injures the land or interferes with the landowner's own use of it, it does not justify the inference that he is yielding to his neighbor's claim of right or that his neighbor is asserting any right; it signifies only that he is permitting his neighbor to use the land."

We thus conclude that claimants seeking to establish an easement based on the "recreational" use of another's property must make a special showing that those activities were in fact adverse; they will not be indulged a presumption to that effect.

Because the facts involve a conveyance of the servient estate during and near the end of the 20-year prescriptive period, we focus on the relationship between the Carnahans and the Drewrys, which comprised over 18 years of the relevant period.

The trial court's findings do not address whether the Carnahans' recreational use of the lake was adverse to the Drewrys. They only track the Carnahans' periodic change in the use of recreational equipment over the years. Therefore, the findings of fact do not support the court's conclusion that the Carnahans' recreational activities constituted the "adverse seasonal use of Lake Julia."

On the other hand, the record does contain ample evidence supporting the inference that the Carnahans' use of the lake was both non-confrontational and permissive in recognition of the Drewry's authority as title holders to a majority of the lake bed. For example, Mr. Carnahan testified that Mr. Drewry "would wave" to them as they anchored their houseboat in "plain sight of his house," but that they kept the houseboat "in the middle" as opposed to the "south side of the lake" so as not "to bother anybody." When asked why they retired their ski boat in 1986, Mr. Carnahan responded that they "didn't want to tick off the neighbors." There are other examples of the Carnahans' non-adversarial use of the Lake, such as Mr. Carnahan's statement that it had "been under his driving force that if people were on the lake fishing, the Carnahans stayed off," and Mrs. Carnahan's statement that "if there are children in the lake, we are either not out there or we are at the opposite end."

We find the evidence establishes that the Carnahans' use of Lake Julia was not adverse and was insufficient to overcome the special showing required with respect to establishing a recreational easement. The Carnahans were engaged in a nonconsumptive, leisurely use of Lake Julia which neither diminished nor adversely altered the quantity or quality of the water. We recognized that the law did not require an affirmative act of hostility of *[sic]* the part of the Carnahans; nevertheless, we conclude that their occasional, recreational use was not inconsistent with the Drewry's title as majority owners of the property underlying Lake Julia. Accordingly, as a matter of law the trial court's judgment was not sustained in its findings nor on the record on the basis that the Carnahans established a prescriptive easement.

We reverse the trial court's finding that the Carnahans had established a prescriptive easement.

CASE QUESTIONS

1. What did the Carnahans own and when did they own it?
2. How did the Carnahans use the lake and how much did they use?
3. Was there adverse use by the Carnahans?
4. Does the court find there is an easement by prescription?

CONSIDER 4.3

In the 1960s, the Pothiers sold to the Rickers Tax Lots 7353 and 7354, property near skiing resorts on Bald Mountain. The Rickers gave their neighbors permission to use an upper path which crossed their property to access Bald Mountain, but were unaware of a lower path (the Path). In 1975, the Rickers sold both lots to Dick Matthews. Sometime during 1975, others in the neighborhood began using the Path, but there was no

CONSIDER 4.3
(continued)

evidence as to whether Matthews gave permission to use the Path. Matthews sold the property to Fisher in 1978. Fisher lived on the property from 1978 to 1992, during which time he and his family used the Path to access Bald Mountain. Apparently, Fisher gave permission to use the Path to anyone who asked and was friendly to other users. When Fisher moved off the property in 1992, he instructed his tenants, who also used the Path, to allow the neighbors and the public to use it. In 2000, Fisher proposed to develop the portion of his property over which the Path crossed. Hughes, opposed to the development which would have blocked their use of the Path, filed suit to establish a prescriptive right to use the Path. Does he have such a right? *Hughes v. Fisher*, 129 P.3d 1223 (Idaho 2006)

Scope and Extent of Easements

The extent of permissive use of an easement is determined according to the type of easement. If an express easement has been created, determining the extent of the easement is simply a task of interpretation of the deed or contract granting the easement. A court must undertake this task of interpretation and will employ the **rule of reason** in executing its task. The rule of reason prohibits a court from imposing unreasonable burdens when the parties have expressed their desires and intentions in general terms. Under the rule of reason, a court cannot impose a strained construction of the language the parties chose.

For example, if the parties expressly provide for an easement across servient land in a definite location, then the court may not impose a different route for the easement. On the other hand, an express easement for a pipeline that does not specify depth can be interpreted to permit the dominant estate holder to move the pipe to a greater depth because of technological changes and necessities. Likewise, the grant of an easement to use a beach "for the purpose of boating, bathing, fishing, or other recreation" does not include the right to use the beach for the purpose of commercial boat rental. An easement for "foot passage" will not be expanded to permit vehicles, but an easement for "the right to pass" may be properly interpreted to permit vehicular traffic.

The extent, location, and use of a prescriptive easement is determined according to the type of use made during the prescriptive period. For example, a prescriptive right acquired through foot use does not include the right of vehicular use, and a vehicular private prescriptive use does not include an expansion to commercial use.

The task of determining the extent, use, and location of easements is perhaps most difficult in easements by implication. With this type of easement, courts assume that the parties would recognize the normal development of the dominant estate. Normal development is defined according to the initial use of the property. For example, if the dominant estate is used for residential purposes, normal development includes subdivision for numerous residences. However, it is not within normal development for the property to be used as a commercial rock bed with the accompanying use of large trucks. Also, the use of an easement by implication cannot be expanded to benefit properties other than the dominant estate.

However, all types of easements may be enlarged in their scope through prescription. For example, an easement "for the purpose of transporting milk to a factory" may be used for all purposes for a prescriptive period and expand into a general easement once the prescriptive elements are met. The following case deals with the interpretation of an easement granted to a condominium owner.

GARFINK V. CLOISTERS AT CHARLES, INC.

392 Md. 374 (Md. 2006)

FACTS

Danetta Garfink (Petitioner) owns a condominium unit at The Cloisters at Charles Condominiums(Respondent). Garfink purchased her unit (one of the model units) in 1991 during the development and construction phase of the project. The original construction included installed household appliances in each unit, a clothes dryer among them. As originally installed, the clothes dryer was connected and vented into the furnace room, rather than to the outside of the building, contrary to the terms of the construction contract, and in violation of prevailing building codes and regulations. The venting system ran from the clothes dryer through the kitchen floor and into the basement furnace room. During the normal operation of the clothes dryer, the vent system would carry and discharge the dryer's exhaust, heat, lint, and moisture into the furnace room. The furnace room contained two furnaces and a hot water heater, each of which were fired by gas burners. This potentially hazardous mixture of elements was extant for approximately nine years.

In 2000, the clothes dryer malfunctioned and Garfink purchased a replacement from Sears, Roebuck & Co. After viewing the existing vent system, however, Sears refused to install the replacement because a "fire hazzard *[sic]* was identified."

Garfink took it upon herself to have the venting system re-routed. The new system was routed from the dryer through the wall of the laundry room into the adjoining garage, then through the garage and through the exterior wall. A standard vent appliance, which discharged the dryer exhaust and lint to the outside, was installed into the exterior of the garage wall. Garfink neither sought nor obtained permission of The Cloisters to install the exterior vent.

Garfink's immediate neighbor, Dr. Oscar Kantt, found that the new vent was within 17 feet of the front door of his residence, and Dr. Kantt complained about the discharge. Litigation began when the parties could not reach an agreement.

The Circuit Court found in favor of The Cloisters and issued an injunction compelling petitioner to remove the exhaust vent. The Court of Special Appeals affirmed the judgment of the Circuit Court. Garfink appealed.

JUDICIAL OPINION

Cathel, Judge. The Condominium's Declaration states in Article 15.2:

In addition to any easement established by law, each unit shall have, appurtenant thereto, an easement in the common elements for the purposes of providing maintenance, support, repair or service for such unit to and for the ducts, pipes, conduits, vents, plumbing, wiring and other utility services to the unit.

The Court of Special Appeals' reasoning in regards to the treatment of the easement is flawed. The traditional law of easements applies to condominiums. Furthermore, the Condominium's Declaration specifically provides in Article 6.1 that "[e]ach unit in the Condominium has *all* the incidents of real property and the owner of a unit shall have such estate therein as may be acquired in real property..."

The generally accepted rule for an express easement is 'that [because] an easement is a restriction upon the rights of the servient property owner, no alteration can be made by the owner of the dominant estate which would increase such restriction except by mutual consent of both parties.' There are, however, in contrast to the Court of Special Appeals' opinion, instances in which a dominant and servient estate may *both* benefit and shoulder the burden of a particular covenant or easement. This can occur in the situation of an implied negative reciprocal easement.

In the case *sub judice* the language in Article 15.2 of the Condominium's Declaration creates an express easement. An easement is granted to the dominant estate, appurtenant to the individual condominium units (in this case petitioner's unit), "in the common elements," i.e., the exterior of the unit, by the servient estate, the Condominium... This easement was properly established when the Declaration was filed along with the Bylaws and Condominium plat, establishing the Condominium.

The Court of Special Appeals contends that there is an inherent conflict created by such a grant of an easement in the context of a condominium. The court argues that because the individual condominium unit owner is also a member of the Condominium unit owners as a whole, she has an interest in "both the servient *and* dominant estate[s]." In other words, petitioner is granted an easement over or through the common elements as the dominant estate represented by her condominium unit, but as a member of the Condominium she also has an interest in the servient estate by virtue of her interest in the common elements. The Court of Special Appeals finds this scenario to be distinguishable from the "traditional concept of easement, whereby one party obtains an easement for his or her benefit and another party must shoulder the obligations associated with that benefit." We find no conflict in this situation.

While petitioner "can be said to have a tenancy in common in the general common elements with all of the other Condominium unit owners," petitioner owns her individual condominium unit in fee simple. These are two wholly different types of estates. There is no conflict extant between the two types of ownership in regards to the existence of the express easement.

As such, we reiterate that traditional easement law applies to easements granted in condominium documents, in particular, to the easement granted by the Condominium Declaration in the case *sub judice*.

Our job now is to interpret what exactly the easement provides for. In doing this we look to standard constructs of contract interpretation. The establishment of an easement in a condominium declaration is analogous to the establishment of an easement by deed.

The pertinent language of the easement granted by Article 15.2 of the Condominium's Declaration is, as stated *supra:* "...each unit shall have, appurtenant thereto, *an easement in the common elements for the purposes of providing maintenance, support, repair or service for such unit to and for the ducts, pipes, conduits, vents, plumbing, wiring and other utility services to the unit.*" [Emphasis added.] From this language it is evident that condominium unit owners were to be provided with the ability to perform maintenance, support, repair or service on those items (ducts, pipes, conduits, vents, plumbing, wiring and other utility services) which pierced the "shell" of the unit, passing through the exterior walls or common element spaces. This type of easement is a logical extension of certain rights of individual unit owners. Otherwise, anytime something untoward occurred to one of the above-listed items the unit owner would be required to receive permission from respondent in order to remedy the situation.

The problem that arises in the case of petitioner's exercise of this easement, is that her particular exterior dryer installation was defective because the exhaust had not been properly vented at the time the unit was constructed and at the time of purchase in 1991, nor in fact did it exist when the Declaration establishing the easement was filed. Had a vent existed at the time the Declaration was filed, petitioner would clearly have an easement to pierce the common element in order to perform maintenance, support, repair or service on a pre-existing vent. In fact, every other condominium unit in the Condominium has such an exterior dryer exhaust vent and each unit's respective owner has an easement to service those vents as provided by Article 15.2 of the Declaration without the necessity of seeking the permission of the Board. The intent of the easement provision of the Declaration was to provide all unit owners with the ability to maintain the essential ducts and vents which run through, or were intended to run through, the common elements that surround their condominium units. It can be assumed that when the Declaration was drafted and the grant of easement made, the drafters believed that the condominium units would be, or had been, built to code and that all ducts, pipes, conduits, vents, plumbing, wiring and other utility services would be, or had been, properly constructed. There appears to be no dispute that a vent was contemplated for the respective unit, but failed to be installed during the construction phase—otherwise building codes and probably fire codes would have been violated. The fact that petitioner's unit was improperly constructed by the developer of The Cloisters does not negate this aspect of the easement.

It was reasonable for petitioner to remedy the hazard created by the improper original construction of the dryer exhaust system. In order to reasonably enjoy the grant of the easement, petitioner was entitled to install an exterior dryer exhaust vent.

"What is necessary for such reasonable and proper enjoyment of the way granted, and the limitations thereby imposed on the use of the land by the proprietor, depends upon the terms of the grant, *the purposes for which it was made, the nature and situation of the property subject to the easement,* and the manner in which it has been used and occupied."

We look to the intentions of the parties. It was the intention of the parties that existed at the time the Condominium was constructed and the Declaration placed on record that the condominium units be built to fire and building code specifications and therefore, a proper dryer exhaust system was required for the unit at inception—at which point no permission would have been necessary nor would there have been any respondent in existence. The installation of an exterior dryer exhaust vent is reasonable and necessary, and was fully contemplated, for the proper, and more importantly, safe, operation of the dryer and its presence and maintenance was fully contemplated by Article 15.2 of the Declaration.

Respondent concedes that the easement grants unit owners control over certain systems which run through the common elements of the Condominium, but asserts that the easement does not "serve to grant a unit owner the unfettered right to install a completely new system in an area in which it has previously not been installed." In support of this, respondent contends that such a holding would open and let loose a virtual Pandora's box of monstrosities on the Condominium, stating:

"then any unit owner could install a new gas heating system to replace the old electric heating system and run his new gas lines for same, in, through and around the exterior facade of the unit without seeking the approval of the Respondent. Moreover, any of the forty-seven (47) unit owners could punch holes in the exterior of their condominium unit whenever,

wherever, and however they pleased; replace a window with an exhaust fan; install a new heat pump on her parking pad; attach solar panels to the garage door; or attach a satellite dish to her front steps, all without any prior consent of the Respondent."

Respondent's concerns are not valid in this case. The installation of the exterior dryer exhaust vent by petitioner is not something that is new or in addition to the original construction of the other forty-seven condominium units. Every other condominium unit in The Cloisters already has such an exterior dryer exhaust vent system and the owners are able to maintain those systems without the approval of the Board because of the easement granted by Article 15.2 of the Declaration. That venting system is equally essential in order for petitioner's condominium unit to comply with Baltimore County Building Code and is, thus, reasonable and necessary. Our holding does not allow unit owners the unfettered ability to make changes to the exterior of their condominium unit without prior approval by respondent. Rather, it reasonably allows **only** the petitioner, where an obvious construction defect exists relating to safety, to install the exterior vent in reliance on the rights granted by the express easement (and for that matter in exercise of the rights inherent in an exception contained in the Bylaws).

Our holding is limited to instances where the inherent problem results from an initial construction defect and where the Condominium Declaration contains an express easement *and* there is a Bylaw exception permitting the repair without prior approval. Furthermore, as our decision relates only to the issue of whether prior approval of the Board was necessary, it does not affect other individual unit owners' rights of recourse if their individual rights are adversely affected. But, the Condominium's Bylaws under the particular facts and circumstances of this case did not require petitioner to obtain prior approval for the installation from the respondent because of the easement granted by the Condominium's Declaration, as well as the Bylaws exception.

The Circuit Court and the Court of Special Appeals, along with respondent, state that there were several alternate locations that the exterior vent could have been placed in order that it not interfere with Dr. Kantt's enjoyment of his property. The record, however, does not reflect this. Respondent identifies four alternate locations. The first alternative is running a new dryer exhaust system up though the main furnace duct, which would vent out through a chimney in the roof of the house. This proposal is unacceptable, as it would violate section 504.4 of the International Mechanical Code, 2000, which states that the "[c]lothes dryer exhaust ducts shall not be connected to a vent connector, vent or chimney." The second and third alternatives involved moving the exterior vent from its installed position either "a couple of inches or a couple of feet" or "twelve to sixteen inches." Neither of which is substantially different from where it was originally installed and would not serve to provide a remedy for Dr. Kantt's complaint. The final alternative was given when respondent's counsel questioned petitioner's expert witness at trial,

[Witness:] *Yeah. I believe my testimony was that we could move it six to twelve inches. And you asked me, if I heard you right, two things: Number 1, you said I said something out in the hallway that you didn't relate to and then you turn around and said to me that could it be moved and I said if you want to spend a lot of money. It is simple, we tear all the dry wall out of the garage, we tear out and drop the ceiling down and we can move the dryer to the second floor and shorten it up. We can move the dryer anyplace around that there is, move the garage out. If you want to spend the money, pal, give it to me.*

It is not a viable alternative to, effectively, completely remodel petitioner's condominium unit by tearing down walls and dropping ceilings in order to be able to provide exterior ventilation for the clothes dryer in a different location. Petitioner had the vent installed in the most logical place, as evidenced by the Court of Special Appeals' recitation of the facts of the case: Thus, we find the location of petitioner's original installation of the exterior dryer exhaust vent to be the most reasonable option under the facts presented in the case *sub judice.*

Reversed.

CASE QUESTIONS

1. Discuss the significance of the location of the original dryer vent.
2. Why is the fact that the other units had exterior vents important?
3. Which law has greater effect, the law on easements or condominium bylaws?

CONSIDER 4.4

John Wescoat owned property adjacent to a 176-acre parcel owned by Shooting Point, L.L.C. Wescoat's property was subject to a recorded easement that was 15 feet wide and 0.3 miles long and provided the only ingress and egress from Route 622 to Shooting Point's parcel.[4] When the easement was granted, both parcels were used for agricultural purposes and the easement was so bucolic and buried among the flora and fauna that it was barely visible to the eye and could not be seen from Route 622.

The parties, as dominant and servient tenements, enjoyed a peaceful coexistence from 1974 until 1999. In 1999, Shooting Point proposed the development of its parcel into 18 lots of approximately 5 acres each, which would surround a serene 50-acre "open-space" preservation. Shooting Point did inform purchasers that the easement for its parcel was limited to the 15-foot width and the plat plan incorporated that limitation.

When Mr. Wescoat learned of the proposed development, he filed suit alleging that such an expanded use of the parcel was "an additional and unreasonable burden" on the easement. From that point forward, the parties' relationship deteriorated as they argued over the true location of the easement and each side placed conflicting markers as to where they felt the easement was located.[5] Mr. Wescoat's son placed his wooden post markers in such as way that there were several very sharp 90-degree turns on the easement. The Shooting Point Property Owners Association then brought suit for fewer 90-degree turns.

The trial produced evidence that the presence of the new lot owners would result in 180 trips daily over the easement. In addition, the Wescoats introduced evidence that as more trips occurred on the road, there were more mudholes. The tendency of the lot owners was to drive around those mudholes and the result was that the easement was becoming increasingly wider at many points along the route to Route 622. Can the easement be expanded to accommodate the new land use and its development or is the expansion unjustified under the original terms of its grant? *Shooting Point, L.L.C. v. Wescoat*, 576 S.E. 2d 497 (Va. 2003)

Rights and Obligations of Estate Holders in an Easement

Each of the parties in an easement relationship has certain legal responsibilities and rights. The easement owner (dominant estate) must keep the easement on the servient estate in repair. This responsibility of repair exists even if the servient estate owner is responsible for damages or the state of disrepair in the easement. The easement owner has the right to enter the servient land for purposes of repair. Furthermore, the easement owner may improve the easement with pavement or gravel when the easement is a right of passage.

4. The easement is recorded as a metes and bounds description as follows: "[S]aid right-of-way easement to follow the present road leading from Virginia State Highway Route 622 to lands... known as Shooting Point Farm, said present road running generally in a northerly direction from a point in a turn of said Virginia State Highway Route 622 to a point at or near a corner of a certain woods, thence turning in a generally easterly direction and running along the northern edge of said woods to a point at or near the edge of said woods, thence turning in a generally northerly direction and following along the edge of said woods to a point at or near a corner of said woods, thence turning in a generally easterly direction and running along the edge of said woods until the boundary line separating Shooting Point Farm from the [Wescoat parcel] is reached, at which boundary line the said right-of-way easement terminates." 576 S.E. 2d at 498–499.
5. The overgrown nature of the easement and the metes and bounds description left plenty of room, as it were, for interpretation of the location.

The owners of servient estates have the right to use their property in any way that does not interfere with the dominant holder's use of the easement. For example, the servient owner may grant more than one easement to more than one party.

Servient estate owners may also construct fences along the easement and install gates so long as there is no interference with the easement owner's use of the easement.

The dominant estate has the right to transfer an easement. An easement is transferred along with the dominant estate even though it is not specifically mentioned in the deed. An "all other appurtenances" clause serves to transfer an easement. Likewise, a servient estate is sold subject to any prior-acquired easements.

Termination of Easements

The termination or extinguishment of an easement occurs in several different ways depending on the type of easement involved. All easements are terminated when there is one owner for both the dominant and servient estates or when the nonpossessory and possessory interests become united in one owner.

As discussed earlier, an easement by necessity is terminated when the necessity terminates.

All easements can be terminated through abandonment. Abandonment occurs through prescriptive nonuse. Two elements establish abandonment: (1) the easement owner must possess the intent to abandon; and (2) the intent to abandon must be accompanied by conduct indicating the intent to terminate. For example, the owner of a railroad easement who removes the tracks and destroys the shipping factory using the railway has manifested the intent to abandon through conduct. Permitting an easement to fall into a state of disrepair may constitute sufficient conduct manifesting an intent to abandon. For example, allowing an irrigation ditch to become inoperable is an example of disrepair indicating intent to abandon.

Practical Tip

When dealing with easements, follow this checklist for acquiring, maintaining, and protecting an easement:

1. *Be clear in establishing the scope of the easement*
2. *Specify use limitations in the easement granting language*
3. *If the dominant tenement is not using the easement, document that the nonuse is not to be taken as abandonment*
4. *Object to gates, locks, etc. erected by the servient tenement*
5. *Maintain the easement so as to establish ongoing intent*
6. *Keep the width and location of the easement clear*

CONSIDER 4.5

The Noyeses owned a tract of land that was subject to an easement for "road and utility" purposes for property owners Kaibel, Creech, and Scheffing. The easement, a gravel road, ran from County Road 631, through the Noyes property, across Bob's Creek. Bob's Creek became the crux of the parties' easement dispute because it overflowed in nearly all rainstorms, thereby washing away the dirt and gravel from the ends of the bridge, making the bridge impassable.

During the 1980s, the Kaibels acquired another tract of land and built an access road across that tract of land. The Creeches and Scheffings began using that road with the permission of the Kaibels. The Kaibels, Creeches, and Scheffings then complained to Noyes that the Bob's Creek passageway was impassable and Mr. Kaibel said that he was tired of "messing" with the creek. Noyes asked them to contribute to the cost of installing a culvert pipe, but the parties all declined.

In 1997, thinking that the parties were sufficiently irritated with Bob's Creek that they were no longer interested in passing through, Noyes built a locked gate across the easement. In 1998, Mr. Creech tried to "brushhog" the property, but Noyes appeared and ordered Creech off her property. Creech *et al.* then brought suit seeking an injunction against Noyes to keep her from blocking to the roadway. Had the easement been abandoned? *Creech v. Noyes*, 87 S.W.2d 3d 880 (Mo. App. 2002)

All easements may be terminated if the servient owner successfully prevents the dominant holder's use of the easement for the required prescriptive period. An easement may be created or terminated through prescription.

Some easements are created for a specific time or purpose and are terminated when the time period expires or the purpose is eliminated. For example, a right-of-way given so long as the dominant land is used for a stable would terminate if the land is used for other purposes.

An easement may be terminated through *estoppel*. Estoppel occurs when the servient owner, believing there has been abandonment, constructs improvements over the easement in reliance upon the abandonment. The idea supporting this theory of termination is that the easement owner should notify the servient landowner that such improvements interfere with the easement. If the easement owner were not required to object, then the servient landowner would make costly changes only to have them eliminated after completion. Estoppel requires prompt action to minimize expense.

CONSIDER 4.6

Would putting up a gate and posting a "No Trespassers" sign for two years be enough to stop an easement by prescription? *Kessinger v. Matulevich*, 925 P.2d 864 (Mont. 1996)

Profits

A **profit** (or ***profit a prendre***) is an easement plus the right of removal. A profit gives the holder the right not only of access to another's land, but also to remove oil, minerals, water, or some other part of the real property (see Chapter 3 for more discussion of oil and gas rights). A profit is not the same as the ownership of subsurface rights because such ownership is exclusive and unlimited. More than one party can hold a profit in a piece of property, and a profit can be limited by the types of minerals that may be taken, or the time allowed for taking.

A profit is not the sale of personal property, because the landowner does not sever the mineral or soil—the profit owner does. For example, the right to remove coal is a profit, whereas the right to buy coal after removal is the sale of personal property.

A profit can be appurtenant, as in the right to remove water for use on an adjoining tract; or it can be in gross, as when an oil company that owns no property in the area is given the right to remove oil from a particular parcel.

Apart from these definitional differences, the creation, rights, and obligations of the parties in a *profit a prendre* relationship are governed by the same principles of law discussed in the easement portion of this chapter.

One of the most frequently used profits is one for timber. Timber is considered a part of the real estate but can be severed through the award of a profit in the timber. Under the **Uniform Commercial Code (UCC)** (as adopted in most states), a contract for the sale of timber to be removed by the buyer is considered a contract for the sale of goods, but title to the timber does not pass to the buyer unless and until it is identified or removed from the land.

Licenses

A **license** is a right to use land in the possession of another, but it passes no land interest and does not alter or transfer property. A license only makes certain conduct on another's land lawful, such as hunting, fishing, or simply being on the property.

A licensee holds a privilege, and that privilege may be revoked at any time by the landowner. A license may be created by an oral agreement, since it is not an interest in land. If the parties attempt to create an easement by oral agreement, they instead create only a license.

CONSIDER 4.7

On April 4, 1955, Clarence McKinley received a patent granting him title to 480 acres of land in Carbon County, Wyoming. McKinley also owned an additional piece of land in section 22 that is now held by Seven Lakes. McKinley intended to subdivide the land in sections 22 and 27 and form a small community he called "Woodedge." He created 24 ten-acre plots that were to be sold with the intent that the buyers would erect cabins thereon. McKinley intended to build certain improvements on the land he retained, including a road, a toboggan run, and a lodge; however, such improvements were never completed. Two of the parcels that McKinley conveyed in this manner are now owned by the Maxsons. The deeds from McKinley to the Maxsons' predecessors contained language indicating that the original grantees were also granted a "privilege" to hunt and fish on the lands owned by McKinley. A large portion of the land in the Woodedge area that was subject to the "privilege" is now owned, through various conveyances, by others. Seven Lakes owns the land at issue in section 22 and David Kuhn owns the land in section 27.

The Maxsons own one of the McKinley properties and filed suit to have their "privileges" to hunt and fish declared a covenant that must be honored. Seven Lakes and Kuhn maintain that the Maxsons held only a profit. Help the court with its analysis of what was granted by McKinley. *Seven Lakes Development Co., L.L.C. v. Maxson,* 144 P.3d 1239 (WY 2006)

CONSIDER 4.8

In 1974, Beaufort County (the County) leased property located at the Hilton Head Airport to Hilton Head Air Service (Air Service). Air Service has operated an aviation business on the leased premises, providing services to the flying public such as maintenance and repair of aircraft. Air Service has also allowed rental car companies to operate on its leased premises.

In May 1979, the County and Air Service entered into a 25-year lease agreement. The lease agreement provided that the county would develop the airport according to a Master Plan Study accepted by the Federal Aviation Administration (FAA). A dispute arose regarding the presence of the rental car companies, which were not specifically or generally authorized by the plan. Air Service claims it can have the rental car companies removed at any time because there are no leases, many of their agreements are oral, and they hold only a license. Is Air Service correct in its characterization of the agreements with the car rental companies? *Hilton Head Air Service v. Beaufort County*, 418 S.E.2d 849 (S.C. 1992)

Covenants

A **covenant** is a restriction placed in a deed that is, in effect, a nonpossessory interest in land. Covenants restrict or control some aspect of the use of the land. The common law rule on covenants is that they are enforceable against the grantor and grantee but not against any subsequent transferees. For example, a covenant in a grant of land for a railway requiring the construction of a depot and station would be enforceable against the grantee but not against subsequent transferees. For this reason, covenants are not effective in enforcing residential use restrictions. However, **equitable servitudes** may provide a solution. Equitable servitudes are restrictions on the use of land that are enforceable against subsequent transferees in the restricted areas. Sometimes equitable servitudes are called "covenants that run with the land" because they carry through transfers of title to the property.

Equitable servitudes or covenants that run with the land provide residential home buyers with assurance that their neighborhoods will retain their residential character at a certain quality and level. Zoning laws are also helpful in restricting land use and are discussed at length in Chapter 18. The details on covenants and equitable servitudes can be found in Chapter 22.

Cautions and Conclusions

In applying the tools and risks described in this chapter, think through the following questions:

1. Is the property accessible or is it landlocked?
2. If the property is accessible, where is the access and who owns it?
3. If the property is landlocked, how can access be obtained?
4. Where is the access route (or where should it be) located?
5. How large an access route is necessary?
6. What types of uses can be made of the access route?
7. Is the access route recorded in any of the land records?
8. Will the deed in the transaction provide for an easement?
9. What parties are using the property, why, when, and for how long?
10. Who will be responsible for maintenance?

If buyers, sellers, agents, brokers, and financiers would take the time to check land records and physically inspect the property involved, many of the expensive easement litigations noted in this chapter could be avoided. The cases used in this chapter demonstrate the types of strong feelings and reactions that can result from misunderstandings on property use. This expensive hostility might be avoided by thinking through these 10 questions.

Key Terms

affirmative easement, 72
conservation easement, 72
covenant, 89
dominant tenement (estate), 73
easement, 71
easement appurtenant, 71
easement by express grant, 73
easement by express reservation, 73
easement by implication, 76
easement by necessity, 79
easement in gross, 71
equitable servitudes, 90
license, 88
negative easement, 72
prescription, 79
profit, 88
profit a prendre, 88
quasi easement, 76
rule of reason, 82
servient tenement (estate), 73
Uniform Commercial Code (UCC), 88

Chapter Problems

1. Charlotte Minogue and John Monette are sister and brother. Each inherited a home from their father through his last will and testament. Charlotte inherited her father's actual residence at 90 Hawthorne Avenue in Albany, New York. John inherited the contiguous parcel located at 88 Hawthorne Avenue.

A blacktop driveway, approximately 10-feet wide, runs between the two houses. A survey in 1988 showed the driveway to be located on John's property. A concrete cinder-block garage is located at the rear of Charlotte's two-family home. The driveway had provided access for her father to the garage and to Charlotte and her tenants until John blocked such use in 1988.

Charlotte filed suit seeking a declaration of easement for ingress and egress over the driveway. Is she entitled to one? What theory could she use? What type of easement might she have? *Minogue v. Monette,* 551 N.Y.S.2d 427 (1990)

2. Granite Properties Limited Partnership owned all of the parcels shown in the diagram below. Between 1963 and 1982, Granite conveyed certain of the parcels, and, in 1982, parcel B was conveyed to Larry Manns and others (defendants). The present status of the parcels is as follows:

- Parcel A contains a shopping center (built in 1967 and currently owned by Granite). To the north of the shopping center is an asphalt parking lot with 191 feet of frontage on Bethalto Drive.
- Parcel B is undeveloped and is owned by the defendants.

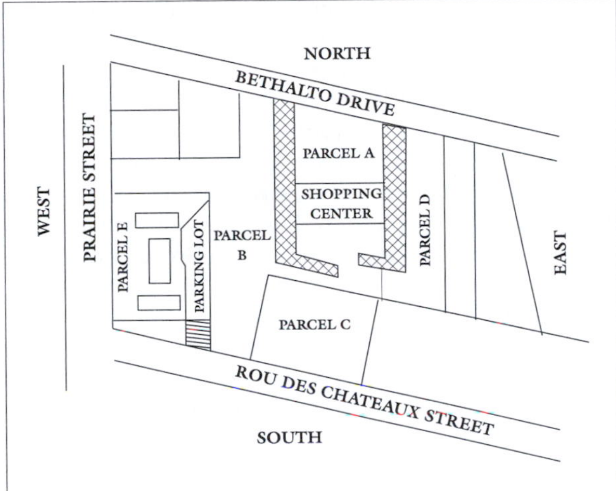

- Parcel C contains five four-family apartment buildings (owned by a third party).
- Parcel D contains a health club (owned by a third party).
- Parcel E contains the Chateau des Fleurs Apartments (owned by Granite).

The rear of the shopping center is used for deliveries, trash storage and removal, and utilities repair. To gain access to the rear of the shopping center for these purposes, trucks use a gravel driveway that runs along the lot line between parcel A and parcel B. A second driveway (noted in diagram), located to the east of the shopping center on parcel D, enables the trucks to circle the shopping center and deliver to the stores, including Save-a-Lot Grocery, without having to turn around in the limited space behind the stores. The trucks can thus make a convenient entrance, delivery stop, and exit.

The two pictured driveways existed before Manns purchased the property, and he saw them during an inspection of the land prior to his purchase. There are no references to the driveways in any of the deeds relating to the parcels.

Robert Mehann, owner of the Save-a-Lot grocery store located in the shopping center, testified that groceries, which are delivered to the rear of the store, are loaded by forklift on a concrete pad poured for that purpose. Mehann indicated that there are large, double-steel doors in the back of the store to accommodate items that will not fit through the front door. Mehann testified that semitrailer trucks make deliveries to the rear of the grocery store four days a week, with as many as two or three such trucks arriving daily. An average of 10 to 12 trucks a day, including semitrailer trucks, make deliveries to the grocery store. Mehann further explained that because the area behind the Save-a-Lot building extends only 50 feet to the rear property line, it would be difficult, if not impossible, for a semitrailer truck to turn around in the back and exit the same way it came in. In response to a question as to whether it would be feasible to have trucks make front-door deliveries, Mehann suggested that such deliveries would be very disruptive; pallets that would not fit through the front door would have to be broken down into parts, requiring extra work, and there would not be adequate space in the front of the store to do such work during business hours. Mehann admitted that he had not investigated the cost of installing a front door that would be big enough for pallets of groceries to be brought in by forklift. There would not be enough space to manipulate the forklift around the front of the store, although it could be run between the shelves of food to the back of the store.

Darrell Layman, a partner for Granite, testified that, although it was very difficult, he had seen semitrailer trucks exit the same way they came in. Layman also acknowledged that he had not investigated the cost of expanding the size of the front doors of the building. He also claimed it "would seem impossible" for him to put in any kind of a hallway or passageway that would allow equipment to bring supplies into the store from the front. Layman explained that the delivery trucks follow no set schedule and, therefore, their presence may overlap at times. He stated that he had seen as many as four or five delivery trucks backed up. Layman opined that there was "no way" the trucks could back up and turn around when there were multiple trucks present.

Granite claimed an easement by implication for the shopping center and the parcel E apartment complex. Is there an easement? Is Granite correct that it is an easement by implication? *Granite Properties Limited Partnership v. Manns*, 512 N.E.2d 1230 (Ill. 1987)

3. Christine and Steve Mallock buried their son in a burial plot purchased at Southern Memorial Park, Inc. Each year the Mallocks conducted a memorial service for their son at his burial plot. On the seventh anniversary of their son's death, the Mallocks went to their son's grave at 11:00 a.m. for the annual service, which generally took 30 minutes. When they arrived they discovered that a tent and chairs set up for funeral services on the plot next to their son's grave were actually resting on his gravesite. The Mallocks asked Southern's management if the tent and chairs could be moved until they could conduct their service. The managers refused, and the Mallocks went ahead with their ceremony, cutting it to five minutes, after they moved the chairs and tents by themselves.

Southern's managers called the police and had the Mallocks evicted. Southern claims the Mallocks had no rights on the property except for the grave. Their deed for the plot does not award an easement for access. Do the Mallocks have the right to access to the gravesite? *Mallock v. Southern Memorial Park, Inc.*, 561 So.2d 330 (Fla. Ct. App. 1990)

4. American University acquired a parcel of land (Lot 806) from Aetna Life Insurance Company. The university was given a Declaration of Easement and Agreement that provided that the grantor:

conveys to the owners from time to time of [Lot 806 and their] tenants, occupants, guests and business invites, a nonexclusive easement for vehicular parking of not less than 236 automobiles on the parking areas located from time to time upon [Lot 807].

New owners of Lot 807 decided to regulate parking and limit the number of spaces available to American University. Can a private agreement like this or regulations change the terms and scope of an easement? *Burka v. Aetna Life. Ins. Co.*, 945 F.Supp. 313 (D.D.C. 1996)

5. In 1962, Temco sold property located at 900 South Wakefield Street to Harvey and Rosabelle Wynn. The purchase contract contains the following provision: "use of apartment swimming pool to be available to purchaser and his family." The Wynns were told that subsequent purchasers of their property would also have use of the swimming pool, which is located in an apartment complex next to the Wynns' home. No reference to use of the swimming pool was made in the Wynns' deed.

In 1969, the Bunns purchased the Wynns' home. The Bunns were told of their right to use the pool but upon moving in were denied access. The Bunns insisted on access but were still denied. They filed suit against the owner of Temco, Offutt, seeking a declaration of the easement rights. Do the Bunns have easement rights? *Bunn v. Offutt*, 222 S.E.2d 522 (Va. 1976)

6. Sylvia Tenn owns a six-story building that has air conditioners in the windows. 889 Associates, Ltd., is planning to construct a 12-story building next to Tenn's building. The result will be that Tenn's window air conditioners will no longer be effective. Tenn claims that she has had the air conditioners for more than 20 years and that she has acquired a prescriptive easement for the air conditioners. Is she correct? *Tenn v. 889 Associates, Ltd.*, 500 A.2d 366 (N.H. 1985)

7. Pacific Theatres and Supply Company, Limited, acquired title to a lot in Waikiki near Seaside and Kalakaua Avenue. The lot deed also provided:

TOGETHER with the perpetual right of ingress and egress over the 10-foot strip of land on the Western side of Lot 2-B.

Consolidated Amusement bought Pacific's lot and has operated a movie theater there since 1936. Waikiki Business Plaza acquired title to an adjacent lot and planned to construct the Plaza Building and set up vendors' booths in the area. Before the vendors began business and during building construction, Consolidated and the Plaza agreed to allow a "pedestrian passageway" for Plaza activities when the Plaza commenced commercial business with the various booths. Consolidated maintains the booths interfere with its easement for theater patrons. Plaza claims that a small passageway is sufficient. Who is correct? Can the easement be reduced by agreement? *Waikiki Business Consolidated Amusement v. Plaza*, 719 P.2d 1119 (Haw. 1986)

8. Asa E. Phillips owned property in Seal Harbor, Maine. His deed included a 20-foot right-of-way over property owned by Kate Gregg and W. Layton Stewart. The right-of-way had long been reduced to a five-foot-wide footpath and was largely overgrown with trees. Gregg and Stewart had placed gates and warning signs along the path to discourage Phillips's use. Phillips brought suit for an injunction to prevent Gregg and Stewart from interfering with his use of his right-of-way. Gregg and Stewart claimed he had abandoned his easement through nonuse. Who is correct? How should the court determine abandonment? *Phillips v. Gregg*, 628 A.2d 151 (Me. 1993)

9. Paul Atkinson purchased land from Donald Mentzel that included an easement across Mentzel's land so that Atkinson could have access to his garage. Atkinson wished to install telephone cable along the easement so that he could more fully use his garage. At the time of the conveyance the Atkinson property did not have utility service. The easement was described as a right-of-way and including the following:

The purpose of this easement is to provide access from Lake Shore Drive to the following described real estate and shall allow access for all uses of said property other than retail sales.

Should Atkinson be permitted to install the telephone cable along the easement? *Atkinson v. Mentzel*, 566 N.W.2d 158 (Wis. App. 1997)

10. The Freeds and Margaret Sterner are owners of adjacent lots. Mrs. Sterner has used a driveway across the Freedses' land for access to her garage. The driveway has been there since 1957, when the Freedses' and Mrs. Sterner's lots were owned by a Mr. William Weaver as one parcel. In 1988, the Freeds erected a barrier and Mrs. Sterner could no longer use the driveway. Does Mrs. Sterner have any rights? Does she have an easement? If so, what type? *Sterner v. Freed*, 570 A.2d 1079 (Pa. 1990)

For research activities related to this chapter, go to our text companion website at www.thomsonedu.com/westbuslaw/jennings.

Fixtures

CHAPTER 5

Is the refrigerator included with the house?

The American Home Buyer

Every lawyer knows that cases can be found in this field that will support any proposition.

Powell, *Real Property*

A **fixture** is real property that was once personal property. It becomes attached to the real property, and when it does, it becomes a part of it. This chapter answers the following questions: What is a fixture and when does personal property become a fixture? How is the title to a fixture transferred? What rights do creditors have in fixtures?

Definition of a Fixture

Whether a particular item of personal property will become real property depends on several factors discussed in the following sections. No single factor controls; rather, the different factors must be considered together in their entirety in order to determine whether an item is real or personal property. The distinction between real and personal property is critical in two primary areas: First, a fixture passes with title to real property whereas personal property may be removed prior to the transfer of title to real property. Second, fixtures are subject to the interests of real property creditors, that is, how much the mortgage holder is entitled to on the property and how much belongs to the personal property creditor.

Degree of Annexation Test

The degree of annexation test is the first factor to be considered in determining the status of an item of property, and its purpose is to examine the fixture's degree of attachment. Under the English rule for fixtures, annexation was the controlling factor, and anything attached by mortar, nail, screw, or bolt was classified as a fixture.

Currently, annexation is defined as attachment to the realty with a use or purpose related to the realty. A furnace in a home is an example that meets the degree of annexation necessary for a fixture because the home cannot function without the presence of the furnace (which was once personal property). On the other hand, a ship or boat does not become part of the real property of a dock simply because an anchor is dropped, because its attachment to the realty is unrelated. A painting on a wall can be hung on any wall, but the sculptures within building columns are a part of the building and hence meet this annexation test.

The degree of annexation test applies to personal property attached to realty but not to accessions. Accessions are those items of personal property that are used in the construction of a building and become so integrated into the building that their identity is lost. Examples of accessions are lumber, bricks, and beams.

Nature and Use of the Property

The unique nature of the property attached and its necessity in relation to the effective functioning of the building are also factors in determining whether something is a fixture. For example, storm windows are especially built and installed for a particular home and work to help control heat in the home. Likewise, a pipe organ in a church with the pipes serving as decoration for the building has an intricate relation to the building. In a garage, an air compressor that is used to hoist cars for repair is central and necessary to the function of that building.

Relationship Between Annexor and Premises

Another factor to be examined is what type of land interest the party attaching the personal property (the annexor) owns. In brief, the higher the degree of interest in the land, the more likely it is that the item or property will be treated as a fixture. For example, a small cottage or bungalow placed on cement blocks on the land by a fee simple owner is a fixture. That same bungalow placed on leased land by a tenant will probably retain its characteristics of personal property.

A tenant does not hold as great an interest in the land as a life estate holder or a fee simple holder. Therefore, annexations by tenants are less likely to be treated as fixtures. There are two additional questions to examine in analyzing this factor: (1) Did the tenant intend the item to be a gift to the landlord (that is, did the tenant intend to leave the property at the termination of the lease?); and (2) will removal of the property cause substantial damage? For example, a floor replaced with a new covering by a tenant will be substantially damaged if the covering is removed upon termination of the tenancy. On the other hand, removal of temporary wall bookshelves may not cause irreparable damage and would be classified as a tenant's personal property.

Practical Tip

When in doubt, ask! Brokers should verify what is included in a property sale to avoid such items becoming an issue of negotiation and/or contention. Sellers should make their intentions clear and possibly remove any items that could confuse buyers. Buyers should list, count, and verify to be sure they know what they're getting.

Intent

The intent of the parties can be the controlling factor in cases where the issue of fixture versus personal property is a close decision, as well as in cases where the parties have reached an agreement (or have placed a provision in their contract or lease) covering the issue of whether an item will be real or personal property. For example, the refrigerators may be included in the sale of residences or apartments, and according to the parties involved may be considered a fixture. Likewise, washers and dryers may be part of the real estate according to the terms of the parties' agreement.

Trade Fixtures

The term **trade fixture** is a misnomer. This term covers a special rule for machines and equipment that treats items used in a trade or business as personal property, even though their degree of annexation may result in some damage upon removal. In the absence of an agreement between the parties, title to the equipment or machinery does not pass with the sale of the factory or business. For example, a large printing press bolted to the floor is a trade fixture and thus personal property. Likewise, display counters in stores are attached but are classified as trade fixtures.

CONSIDER 5.1

The Shapleigh, Maine, waste transfer station consists of a permanent, large garage-type structure with two levels that are both accessible by automobile. The upper level handles household trash, and the lower level handles recyclable and demolition materials. There are also trash bins outside of the lower level of the building that are used for larger items of trash. These bins are freestanding, have wheels, and are located in a parking lot.

An independent company, Pine Tree Waste, operates the upper level of the facility. An attendant employed by the Town supervises the lower level and the freestanding trash bins.

On August 3, 2002, Daniel Sanford went to the waste facility to dispose of some trash. First, he went to the upper level and disposed of household trash. He then drove to the lower level where an attendant directed him to one of the freestanding bins outside of the building. The door to the bin was closed. Sanford loaded some small, light pieces of scrap wood into the bin and then leaned a heavy piece of plywood against the bin. The attendant told Sanford to place the plywood inside the bin. As he lifted the plywood, Sanford felt a ripping sensation in his left bicep. Sanford testified that several days after the incident, the attendant's supervisor called Sanford and stated that the attendant should have helped him, the bin should have been open, and remedial actions would be taken.

Sanford filed a complaint against the Town alleging negligence in the design, operation, construction, maintenance, and supervision of the transfer station and seeking compensatory damages, punitive damages, and attorney fees. The Town raised the affirmative defense of immunity under a Maine statute, which provides that "all governmental entities shall be immune from suit on any and all tort claims seeking recovery of damages." The Act creates an exception to immunity when a governmental entity is negligent in "the construction, operation or maintenance of any public building or the appurtenances to any public building." Sanford argued that the trash bin was a fixture and the Town was not immune. Help in the analysis—is the bin a fixture? *Sanford v. Town of Shapleigh*, 850 A.2d 325 (Me 2004)

Who Wants to Know?

Although the treatises on real property do not list this factor as one to be used in the determination of real versus personal property, the question of "who wants to know" has affected judicial decisions in this area. Application of this factor produces differing results depending on what party seeks to determine the classification for an item of property.

For example, in litigation between a buyer and seller, the buyer is favored because the seller usually presents the form contract and has failed to make all intentions clear in that contract. In an eminent domain valuation procedure, the landowner is favored with a liberal finding of fixtures because just and fair compensation is the court's concern in these circumstances. If a question arises on the application of real property insurance for certain items, the insured will be favored with liberal fixture treatment because of the insurer's failure to clarify coverage provisions. In taxation valuations, fixtures are more liberally found because of the increased value of the property when the fixtures are included in the valuation determination.

The following cases are examples of courts applying the various factors used in the determination of whether an item is real or personal property. Note that the courts deal with fixture tests in different ways for different purposes.

KOHN V. DARLINGTON COMMUNITY SCHOOL DISTRICT

686 N.W.2d 455 (2004)

FACTS

On September 29, 2000, Elaine Kohn and her then four-year-old daughter, Lori Kohn, attended the homecoming football game at Darlington High School. At about 2:30 p.m. on a glorious Wisconsin Saturday afternoon, young Lori fell through the space at the foot of her seat in the home bleachers to the ground 15 feet below, sustaining injuries. The Kohns brought suit in 2001.

The home team bleachers at Darlington High School were manufactured by Standard Steel Industries, Inc. (Standard was later purchased by Illinois Tool Works (ITW)) and purchased by the school for $16,167 in 1969.

Initially, the Kohns filed suit against Darlington and its insurer for breach of their duty of care to the invitees in the bleachers. Later, however, the Kohns amended their complaint to include ITW as a defendant, alleging that Standard left the bleachers in a defective condition that was unreasonably dangerous and resulted in the accident involving their daughter. Still, the Kohns' suit was dismissed initially because Wisconsin has passed a statute of repose. Under Wis. §893.89(2), there is a 10-year statute of limitations on recovery for injuries caused by improvements to real property.

Following the dismissal of the Kohns' suit, the Wisconsin Court of Appeals reversed the lower court's dismissal. The court of appeals concluded that the bleachers were not an improvement to real property because there was no evidence that the bleachers were anchored to the ground. The court of appeals held that the Kohns' claims were governed by the three-year statute of limitation on personal injury and product liability actions (within which their 2001 filing date found them), rather than being dismissed under the 10-year period of repose. The Wisconsin Supreme Court then stepped, carefully, as it were, into the fray.

JUDICIAL OPINION

Wilcox, Justice. First, do the bleachers in question constitute an "improvement to real property" for purposes of §893.89 (the statute of repose)? Whether an item is an "improvement to real property" under §893.89 is a question of law that we review de novo. *Kallas Millwork Corp. v. Square D Co.*, 66 Wis.2d 382, 386, 225 N.W.2d 454 (1975) [hereinafter "*Kallas*"].

No one disputes that the installation of the bleachers at Darlington High School was substantially completed in 1969. The question is whether the bleachers constitute an "improvement to real property" under the statute. If they do, then the "exposure period" ended in 1979, and the Kohns' claims against ITW failed to accrue.

The parties dispute whether the bleachers are permanently anchored to the ground and whether this makes a difference in the analysis. The Kohns contend that the bleachers are not an improvement to real property because they are not anchored in the ground and are portable. The Kohns, like the court of appeals, rely on the "degree of physical annexation" of the bleachers to support their argument. The Kohns further contend that very little effort or expenditure was required to place the bleachers on the ground. They argue that the bleachers are simply "personal property resting upon the real estate" and are not "integral" to the usefulness of the property. Finally, the Kohns assert that the bleachers are not an improvement to real property because they were not specifically designed or manufactured for use at Darlington High School.

ITW argues that the bleachers are permanent as their permanency is a function of their purpose. ITW emphasizes that in the 30 years since they were erected, the bleachers have not been moved, and there is no evidence that they were ever intended to be moved. ITW also focuses on the size of the bleachers and the fact that they enhance the value and usefulness of the property. ITW states that it is significant that the bleachers are specifically adapted to the purpose for which the property is devoted. ITW also argues that the fact that the bleachers theoretically could be disassembled and moved is not dispositive, as most improvements to real estate, including the Eiffel Tower, can be disassembled and moved. Finally, ITW argues that the court of appeals inappropriately relied on *Massie v. City of Duluth,* 425 N.W.2d 858 (Minn.Ct.App.1988), to conclude that the bleachers here were not an improvement to property.

The appropriate question is whether the bleachers satisfy the test set forth in *Kallas.* The test first requires a "permanent addition to or betterment of real property." The parties disagree as to whether the word "permanent" modifies both "addition to" and "betterment of" such that a non-permanent betterment qualifies under the first part of the definition. However, we need not decide whether a non-permanent betterment satisfies the first part of the test for an improvement to real property because we conclude that the bleachers here are permanent.

The Kohns contend that the bleachers are not permanent because they are not anchored into the ground. While there may be a disputed issue of fact as to whether the bleachers are anchored into the ground, we conclude that this fact is not material to the question of whether the bleachers are "permanent" in this case. That is, we conclude that the bleachers here qualify as "permanent" regardless of whether they are anchored into the ground.

We disagree with the Kohns that "the degree of physical annexation" of the alleged improvement is dispositive. While the law of fixtures may focus on the degree of annexation of a chattel to land, courts, applying a commonsense definition to the term "improvement to real property," have "viewed the term 'improvement' as having broader significance than 'fixture' and ha[ve] indicated that the term comprehends all additions and betterments to the freehold, including everything that permanently enhances the value of the premises." Therefore, a given item need not be actually physically annexed to the land in order to constitute a permanent addition to or betterment of property.

We conclude that the bleachers at Darlington High School constitute a "permanent addition to" the Darlington High School stadium and track. First, examining the nature of the bleachers, we note that the home bleachers are a huge structure. They are 15 rows tall, over 100 feet long, and contain a 50-inch-wide walkway elevated 30 inches above the ground. They can seat nearly 1500 individuals. They adjoin a rather large press box and incorporate a wheelchair access ramp. While it is unclear whether they are anchored to the ground, they clearly are not readily moveable.

The Kohns focus on the fact that the bleachers can be disassembled and would not require any excavation to be removed. However, while the bleachers could theoretically be disassembled, that is true of almost any addition to property. Almost any structure that is assembled and installed can be dissembled and removed, even, as ITW artfully notes, a structure as large as the Eiffel Tower.

While the Kohns rely on the Minnesota Court of Appeals' decision in *Massie,* that decision is entirely distinguishable and actually beneficial to ITW in light of the distinctions drawn in that opinion. Massie involved a 30-foot tall water slide installed in a shallow lake that was bolted to concrete pads. "The slide was installed at the facility in 1974 and was used during the summers of 1975–83. At the end of each summer, the city would unbolt the slide from its base and apparently store it until the next season." The court concluded that the slide was not an improvement to real property, reasoning:

The water slide was not a permanent addition to the property. While it was bolted to concrete pads at the bottom of the pond, it was designed to be and was removed every winter for storage.... The slide was a removable piece of playground equi pment.... The slide was only used at the Twin Ponds area for three months out of the year and was permanently removed from the area after the 1983 season. There has been no decrease in the capital value of the Twin Ponds facility due to its removal.

Here, in contrast, the bleachers have never been taken apart or moved, much less permanently removed for an entire season. They are certainly not the equivalent of "a removable piece of playground equipment."

Further, it is quite apparent that the bleachers, unlike the slide in *Massie,* were never intended to be moved or taken apart. As evidence of this, we again note the length of time they have remained at Darlington High School—over 30 years. The fact that Darlington has constructed a large press box adjoining the bleachers is further evidence of the intent that the bleachers be permanent. Moreover, we note that Darlington has made significant improvements to the bleachers themselves, in the form of a wheelchair accessible ramp, new railings, and new footboards. Further evidence of the intended permanency of the bleachers is the fact that the utility of the stadium and track would be seriously diminished were the bleachers removed. In light of the above analysis, we do not find it significant that the bid contract Standard submitted to Darlington labeled the product as "portable bleachers." As such, we are satisfied that the bleachers constitute "a permanent addition to" the property.

The second and third prongs of the test for an improvement to real property under *Kallas* is that the permanent addition to the property must "'enhance[ ] its capital value and... involve[ ] the expenditure of labor or money and [be] designed to make the property more useful or valuable as distinguished from ordinary repairs.'" As these two prongs are interrelated, we shall consider them together.

Darlington contracted with Standard to provide the materials for the bleachers and supervise their installation at a cost of $16,167. Thus, the installation of the bleachers clearly involved the expenditure of labor and a significant amount of money. Further, we conclude that the bleachers increase the capital value of the track and football stadium at Darlington High School and make the property more useful or valuable. It seems patently obvious that a football stadium and track with a set of bleachers is more useful and valuable than an empty field and track. Clearly, the school would not be able to attract as many spectators and charge the same admission fee to see a game or meet if there were no bleachers in the stadium, as far less people would be able to have a clear line of vision to the field. Finally, it cannot seriously be argued that the installation of the bleachers constituted "ordinary repairs." Therefore, we conclude that the bleachers in this case meet all of the requirements of the test for an improvement to real property set forth in *Kallas.*

[W]e hold that the bleachers at Darlington High School constitute an "improvement to real property" for purposes of §893.89. The bleachers qualify as an "improvement to real property" because they are a permanent addition to Darlington's real property that enhance its capital value, involved the expenditure of labor and money, and were which it is used.

The decision of the court of appeals is reversed.

CASE QUESTIONS

1. Describe the structure, cost, and installation of the bleachers.
2. What are the differences between the bleachers and the water pipe slides that were part of another case?
3. Why is it important to the Kohns that the bleachers not constitute an improvement to real property?
4. What is the significance of the fact that the contracts for the bleachers described them as "portable"?
5. What is the purpose of statutes of repose?

CONSIDER 5.2

Is the test for improvements to real property different from or the same as the test for whether something is a fixture? Also, using the court's standards for what constitutes an improvement to real property, determine which of the following are improvements to real property:

1. Large steel tubes in a factory used to roll sheet metal
2. Cement block wall
3. Panic doors
4. Storm sewer systems
5. Hardwired smoke detector systems
6. Unfinished stairwell
7. Permanently installed electrical cables
8. Escalators

CUSTER V. BEDFORD COUNTY BD. OF ASSESSMENT AND REVISION OF TAXES

910 A.2d 113 (Pa. 2006)

FACTS

Robert S. Custer owns approximately 97 acres in Cumberland Valley Township, Bedford County, where he operates a nursery business. In March 2001, Custer purchased a used greenhouse for $1,500, disassembled it, transported it by flatbed pickup truck to his property, where he stored it until May 2004, and then reassembled it. The greenhouse is an arch-shaped structure that is 30 feet by 96 feet in size, and is approximately 12 feet high at its highest point. The greenhouse is constructed by 24 vertical pipes on each side. These vertical pipes are inserted two feet into the ground and are connected at the top to arch-shaped pipes. Plastic covering is attached to the arching pipes and serves as a covering for the structure.

Because of the addition of the greenhouse to the property, the Board increased the assessed value of the buildings on Custer's property for the 2004 tax year from $11,124 to $19,978, an increase of $8,854. Custer appealed to the Board contending that the greenhouse should not be assessed because it was not real estate. After the Board denied his appeal, he appealed to the trial court. The trial court affirmed the board's finding and Custer appealed.

JUDICIAL OPINION

Pelligrini, Justice. At the hearing before the trial court, Custer testified that to disassemble the greenhouse and move it to his property, the plastic was removed and then the pieces that held it together were unbolted. After transporting it to his property, he reassembled it without heavy equipment, using only clam shell diggers, shovels and wrenches. He testified that each of the posts/poles was placed two feet into the ground just past the frost line. Custer opined that it was never his intention for the greenhouse to be permanent, but only to serve as a "starter" greenhouse to be replaced in the future by a "better" greenhouse. He stated that if he were to move off the property or quit the nursery business, he would either sell the greenhouse or take it with him. Custer admitted, though, that he had no present intention of moving his business or relocating. As to the greenhouse's purpose, he testified that it assisted him by creating the necessary environment for raising plants going through a "transformation" from seed to plant to shrubbery to make them sellable.

Dawn Marie Custer, Custer's wife, gave similar testimony regarding the construction of the greenhouse and also stated that if they decided to move, they would take it with them.

Jacob Guyer, another Bedford County nursery owner, testified that he owned six similar greenhouses that were transported from his previous place of business in Princeton, New Jersey, to his current residence in Bedford County where he had them reassembled.

In deciding whether the greenhouse is subject to real property taxes, we take guidance from *In re Appeal of Sheetz, Inc.*, 657 A.2d 1011 (Pa.Cmwlth.), *petition for allowance of appeal denied,* 542 Pa. 653, 666 A.2d 1060 (1995), where we had to determine whether a gasoline pump canopy was a fixture, and, therefore, taxable as realty, or was personalty, and not subject to realty tax.

Chattels used in connection with real estate are of three classes: First, those which are manifestly furniture, as distinguished from improvements and not peculiarly fitted to the property with which they are used; these always remain personalty...Second, those which are so annexed to the property that they cannot be removed without material injury to the real estate or to themselves; these are realty, even in the face of an expressed intention that they should be considered personalty...Third, those which, although physically connected with the real estate, are so affixed as to be removable without destroying or materially injuring the chattels themselves, or the property to which they are annexed; these become part of the realty or remain personalty, depending upon the intention of the parties at the time of the annexation; in this class fall such chattels as boilers and machinery affixed for the use of an owner or tenant but readily removable.

Regarding the first classification, Custer asserts that the greenhouse is more furniture than an improvement because its purpose was not to enhance the value, beauty or utility of Custer's property or to adapt the property for a new or further purpose. Rather, he argues that the greenhouse was equipment that was necessary, useful and desirable for the purpose of raising plants for his nursery business. "Improvement" has been defined as a "permanent addition to or betterment of real property that enhances its capital value and that involves the expenditure of labor or money and is designed to make the property more useful or valuable as distinguished from ordinary repairs." While the greenhouse may not have been valuable from a monetary perspective ($1,500) or enhanced the beauty of the property from an aesthetic perspective, the greenhouse enhanced the utility of Custer's property by allowing Custer to grow more plants for his nursery business, making it an improvement, not furniture.

Regarding the third classification, Custer contends that because the greenhouse can be removed without harm to it or the property on which it was located, and it was his intention that the greenhouse was to be removed once a new greenhouse was bought or the nursery business failed, it cannot be considered real property. The test to determine whether a chattel becomes part of the realty follows:

A fixture is an article in the nature of personal property which has been so annexed to the realty that it is regarded as part and parcel of the land. BLACK'S LAW DICTIONARY 575 (5th ed.1979). The considerations to be made in determining whether or not a chattel becomes a fixture include (1) the manner in which it is physically attached or installed, (2) the extent to which it is essential to the permanent use of the building or other improvement, and (3) the intention of the parties who attached or installed it.

Applying this test to the greenhouse, beginning with the first consideration, the manner of attachment, Custer asserts that because the greenhouse can be removed without any damage to it or the property, it must be personalty. However, in categorizing the canopy as realty rather than personalty, we observed that the degree of attachment necessary to evidence permanence is not high. Further, we stated that:

The permanence required is not equated with perpetuity. Just because they have been and can be moved does not mean the intention was not to make them permanent. It is sufficient if the item is intended to remain where affixed until worn out, until the purpose to which the realty is devoted is accomplished or until the item is superseded by another item more suitable for the purpose.

We went on to observe that "[m]odern construction methods and types of structures allow material that stays for years on a piece of property to be moved with little damage to the property. Acoustic ceiling panels 'affixed' by gravity and removable with no damage to the property are nonetheless taxable as real estate as are door handles and kitchen faucets when attached to a structure." In the case of the greenhouse, each of the posts/poles are placed two feet into the ground, which possesses the requisite degree of "attachment."

As with the canopies in *Sheetz,* there is nothing in the record in the present case suggesting that the greenhouse is an item that was intended to be removed as long as the property was being used as a nursery to grow and cultivate plants. The greenhouse creates the necessary environment for raising plants and will be affixed to the property until it is worn out, the nursery business fails or Custer and his wife no longer occupy the property. Under the *Sheetz* test then, the greenhouse is realty and taxable as real estate.

Accordingly, because the greenhouse is "real estate" the trial court's order is affirmed.

DISSENTING OPINION

Kelley, Senior Judge. I respectfully dissent.

In determining whether the greenhouse became so affixed to the land that it became part of the real estate and was, therefore, subject to the realty tax under Section 201 of the Fourth to Eighth Class County Assessment Law (Law), this Court has outlined the relevant considerations, in pertinent part, as follows:

(1) the manner in which it is physically attached or installed (2) the extent to which it is essential to the permanent use of the building or other improvement, and (3) the intention of the parties who attached or installed it.

With respect to the third of these considerations, the Majority states the following, in pertinent part:

The greenhouse creates the necessary environment for raising plants and will be affixed to the property until it is worn out, the nursery business fails or Custer and his wife no longer own the property. Under the Sheetz *test then, the greenhouse is realty and taxable as real estate.*

To the contrary, Mr. Custer testified that the instant greenhouse was for temporary use in the nursery business until he and his wife could construct a more permanent structure, and that he would take the greenhouse if he should move the business like any other piece of equipment. Mr. Custer's testimony in this regard is supported by the testimony of his wife.

Specifically, Mr. Custer testified, in pertinent part, as follows:

Q. Okay. How long have you lived on the property, sir?

A. Three years since, in July it will be three years.

Q. Okay. If you were to move off the property would you take it with you?

A. Most definitely.

Q. Okay. Did you intend for the greenhouse to be permanent?

A. No. We kind of looked at this greenhouse as a starter greenhouse. And, you know, something that we could start to grow. It takes a long time to get any stock in this type of business when you're growing it yourself. And we always thought eventually we would have, you know, something, something different. But it's a-at the time it was the cheapest route for us to go. And that's why it was used and we went this way.

THE COURT: Mr.,—I want to ask you, Mr. Custer, you indicated initially that if you moved you'd take the greenhouse with you.

THE WITNESS: Yes.

THE COURT: And you indicated you would sell it; do you—

THE WITNESS: If I moved, I imagine that I would start, um, doing the same nursery business somewhere else.

THE COURT: Okay.

THE WITNESS: And I would take that as-well, as well as my other, you know, equipment that I need to do.

Specifically, Mrs. Custer testified, in pertinent part, as follows:

Q. Okay. Is there a possibility you could move off the property?
A. It is possible.
Q. Okay. And if you did would you create another nursery business?
A. Probably.
Q. Okay.
A. We would probably do that, yes.
Q. Okay. If you'd remain on the property do you intend for the greenhouse to be there as long as you are there?
A. Not that particular greenhouse-
Q. Okay.
A. —but the nursery business, yes.

There is simply no objective evidence in the record suggesting that the greenhouse was intended to be permanently affixed to the property so as to become part of the realty. Thus, even if it is assumed that the greenhouse in this case was sufficiently physically attached to the land, requiring an examination of the Custers' intent with respect to the greenhouse, the evidence in this case does not support the determination that the greenhouse was permanently affixed to the realty.

Accordingly, unlike the Majority, I would reverse the trial court's order in this case.

CASE QUESTIONS

1. What effect do you think the "who wants to know" question had on this case?
2. What does the dissenting judge say should be determinative in the case?
3. How does the degree of attachment test apply in this situation?
4. Discuss whether you agree with the majority decision or the dissent, and why.

CONSIDER 5.3

Applying the degree of annexation test, and other fixture tests, to each of the following, determine the likelihood of having the item treated as a fixture.

a. Roger W. Marsh, d/b/a (doing business as) Bestmade Wood Products, constructs wooden cabinets on special order and installs them in homes (usually new homes under construction). He installs the cabinets by placing them in the house and nailing them to the walls and floors. The Department of Revenue wished to collect sales tax from Marsh on the grounds that the cabinets were the sale of personal property. Marsh maintains the property is real estate once installed, he does not receive payment until after installation, and thus is not liable for sales tax for the sale of personal property. Who is correct? *Marsh v. Spradling*, 537 S.W.2d 402 (Mo. 1976)

b. J.K.S.P. Restaurant, Inc., purchased a prefabricated dining car from Pullman in 1965. The diner was transported in three sections from New Jersey to New York, where it was unloaded, assembled, and installed on a foundation that had been built in the ground. The three sections of the diner were bolted in place. J.K.S.P.'s president stated that the purpose of designing diners in this way was to retain their character and personality and allow for easy removal and movement. Nassau County has included the value of the diner in its assessment of J.K.S.P.'s real property value. Is this correct? *J.K.S.P. Restaurant, Inc. v. Nassau County*, 513 N.Y.S.2d 716 (1987)

c. As a result of an accident in the intersection near its place of business, one of A and A Market's gas pumps was struck and damaged by one of the errant vehicles. A and A is a convenience store/gas station. The total damages to the pump were $17,946.82, and A and A filed a claim with its insurer for the cost of repair. The insurance company has denied the claim because the policy covers personal property for A and A and the pumps are fixtures. Is the insurance company correct? *A and A Market v. Perkin Insurance Company*, 713 N.E.2d 1199 (Ill. App. 1999)

CONSIDER 5.4

Applying the factors for determining what constitutes a fixture and the preceding cases, determine the status of each of the following:

a. Floor-to-ceiling bookcases installed in an apartment by a tenant
b. Automatic garage door opener control
c. Landscaping
d. Electric ceiling fans
e. Stove and refrigerator purchased by the debtor for her mortgaged home (*In re Rolle*, 218 B.R. 636 [*Bkrptcy. v. S. D. Fla* 1998])
f. Modular commercial building attached to concrete pad by tenant (*Hot Shots Burgers and Fries, Inc. v. FAS FAX Corp.*, 169 B.R. 920 [E. D. Ark. 1994])
g. Partitions nailed to the floor in an office building
h. Paneled refrigerator (paneled to match kitchen cabinets)
i. Bank vault door
j. Murphy bed (bed that folds into wall)
k. Seats and screens in a theater
l. Ski lifts at a ski resort
m. Storage bins on a farm
n. Display cases in a department store
o. Bus passenger shelter on a sidewalk (*Ali v. City of Detroit*, 554 N.W.2d 384 [Mich. App. 1996])

A Word on Precautions

Once again, the cases in this chapter have demonstrated that emotions and litigation can arise very easily over what appear to be insignificant items. Also, most of the confusion, emotion, and litigation again could be avoided if parties would clearly determine their positions at the outset through written agreements. Figure 5.1 summarizes the questions that should be addressed in various types of land transactions to cover the issue of fixtures.

Attachments

Apart from fixtures, there are many other attachments to land. For example, most property contains trees, bushes, and grasses, which are referred to as ***fructus naturales*** and are considered part of the real property. When land is sold or mortgaged, these naturally growing elements are simultaneously sold or mortgaged.

CONSIDER 5.5

Phyllis and James Rose were married, but experienced the type of discordancy that necessitated their divorce. Phyllis received a judgment of $128,957 from the court in settlement of her marital property rights, a settlement that James neglected to pay. Phyllis reduced the judgment to a lien on their farm that they had jointly owned and operated when marital bliss was greater. After the lien was recorded, but before Phyllis executed on the lien, James planted crops on the property. Just as harvest time approached, the judicial sale of the farm, to satisfy the lien, took place. James demanded that he receive the value of the crops from the sale of the land. Phyllis maintains the crops were part of the real property and could be sold as part of the land. Who is correct and why? *Rose v. Rose*, 2004 WL 830957 (Ohio App. 3 Dist)

Figure 5.1 Fixture Analysis

Parties	Questions to be Answered
Landlord/Tenant	1. Does the lease contain a provision on what types of attachments the tenant may make and remove?
	2. Does the lease contain a provision on payment for damages for removal?
	3. Does the lease require prior notification before a tenant attaches property?
Buyer/Seller	1. What items are included with the real property?
	2. Are any items specifically excluded?
	3. Does the contract list questionable items, such as drapes?
	4. Does the contract prevent substitution or removal of fixtures before closing?
	5. Is a bill of sale drawn up for questionable items such as washers, dryers, and refrigerators?
Creditor/Attacher	1. Who owns the land where the property is being attached?
	2. How permanent will the attachment be?
	3. Can removal occur without damage to the property?
	4. Are there other creditors with protected interests in the real property?

Some property contains growing crops or ***fructus industriales*** (or **emblements**). These crops are not treated as part of real property; they are classified as personal property. If a tenant grows crops on leased property, the crops belong to the tenant even though they may not be ready for harvest at the time the tenant's lease terminates. This right of removal of crops planted by a tenant is called the **Doctrine of Emblements.**

Transfer of Title to Fixtures and Personal Property

If property is classified as a fixture and part of the real property, title to it will pass with the deed transferring title to the property. However, for items not classified as fixtures, some method of transferring title is necessary. Whenever a question exists as to whether an item is real or personal property, a bill of sale should be used to assure complete transfer of title.

Creditors' Rights in Fixtures

Creditors' rights in fixtures carry some unique complexities. Each state has provisions to protect creditors' interests in personal property that becomes attached to real estate and is then classified as a fixture.

This protection is afforded under **Article 9** of the **Uniform Commercial Code (UCC).** The UCC is a set of laws drafted by a group of scholars, attorneys, and businesspeople with the idea of having state-to-state uniformity in commercial transactions.

Article 9 covers creditors' rights and responsibilities in collateral pledged by debtors for loans. All of the states have adopted some version of Article 9. However, there have been revisions and technical amendments to Article 9 over the years that have been adopted in some states. In 2001, the majority of the states adopted Revised Article 9. These changes are covered in the following sections, and the courts are still struggling with interpretation.[1]

Scope of Article 9

Article 9 of the UCC governs the use of personal property or the use of fixtures as collateral. This book focuses on fixtures because of their relationship to real estate law.

Article 9 permits the creditor to obtain a **security interest** in the collateral, which provides the creditor with certain rights, opportunities, and priorities.

Creation (Attachment) of Security Interest (9-203)

There are three requirements for creating a valid security interest: a security agreement, a debtor with rights in collateral, and value given by the creditor.

Security Agreement (9-105)

A security interest begins with the execution of a **security agreement** by the creditor and debtor (9-203). A security agreement has several requirements: (1) it must be evidenced by a record; (2) it must be signed by the debtor (under Revised Article 9, the agreement must be "authenticated," which allows for signing via electronic record); (3) it must contain language indicating that a security interest is being created; and (4) it must contain a description of the collateral that reasonably identifies it. Since fixtures will be attached to real property, a description of the real property involved is helpful in clarifying the identity and location of the property. Form security agreements, available in each state, generally meet all of the requirements for a valid security agreement.

Debtor's Rights in Collateral (9-202)

In some cases, the debtor may already own the collateral and is simply pledging such property as security for a debt. In most fixture cases, however, the creditor is selling goods to the buyer, and the buyer is pledging the purchased goods as collateral. In these cases, the debtor has rights in the collateral at the time of delivery so that the pledge can be properly made. For example, a seller of air conditioners who has the buyer execute a security agreement will have a valid security interest when the buyer takes possession of the air conditioner. The security agreement can be executed in advance and become effective upon the buyer's possession.

Value Given by Creditor (9-203)

The creditor gives value through the binding commitment to extend credit. A creditor may give value in any way that would constitute consideration in a simple contract. In the case of fixtures, the promise to extend credit is most frequently given as value by the creditor.

Once all three requirements are met (authenticated security agreement, collateral interest, and value), the security interest attaches. Just having a security interest gives the creditor certain rights to a superior position over that of other creditors. A secured creditor is always given priority over unsecured creditors. Also, the creation

1. The section numbers used are those for Revised Article 9.

of a security interest entitles the creditor to repossession of the secured property in the event the debtor defaults on payments for the collateral. However, to enjoy the most complete protection available under Article 9, creditors should seek **perfection,** a process of creating notice of a security agreement's existence.

Purchase Money Security Interest in Fixtures (9-103)

Creditors with a **purchase money security interest (PMSI)** obtain more complete protection. A PMSI is given to secure all or part of the purchase price of the item purchased. For example, when a homeowner or business purchases an air conditioner on credit from a seller or manufacturer of such units and the seller or manufacturer takes a security interest, a PMSI exists. The distinction between a PMSI and a security interest is important because the PMSI creditor is entitled to certain priorities in the event the debtor (buyer) defaults on payments for the future.

Perfection of Security Interest (9-301)

Filing a financing statement (9-502) gives the creditor perfection (when fixtures are involved; for other items of personal property, there are other means of perfection). A **financing statement** is a record that will vary from state to state but must include the following items:

1. Names of the debtors and the secured party
2. Signature (authorization under Revised Article 9) of the debtor
3. Address of the secured party from which information can be obtained
4. Mailing address of the debtor
5. A statement describing the items of collateral

Fixture financing statements must be filed in the real estate records. Most of the information required on the financing statement is self-explanatory, but the description item is critical, including a property description for fixtures. While there have been substantial Article 9 changes on perfection, the fixture perfection has remained the same because of the need for filing with real property records.

Filing the Financing Statement

A valid or authenticated financing statement must be filed for fixtures locally, generally at the county level, where land records are kept. Under Revised Article 9, fixture filing remains local, or in property records.[2] For a fixture filing, the legal description of the property is a necessary part of the financing statement because otherwise there is insufficient notice about which property is affected.[3] Security interests for other types of personal property are filed centrally with the idea of creating a national electronic database, similar to the existing Canadian model, in which all types of perfected security interests around the country can be examined.

Upon filing of the financing statement in the proper office, the creditor's interest is perfected. This perfection entitles creditors to priority over subsequent creditors and even priority over some existing creditors. These priorities are discussed in the next section.

2. Section 9-502 covers "real-property–related financing statements," and requires that goods that are (or are to become) fixtures must be perfected by filing a financing statement in the real property records, which must include a description of the real property.
3. In *Webb v. Interstate Land Corp.*, 920 P.2d 1187 (Utah 1996), the court held that a fixture financing statement filed without a description of the land on which the sign is located was "totally ineffective to protect its interest in the sign against anyone except a buyer of the sign who saw it affixed."

Length of Perfection (9-515)

A filing under the UCC is good in most states for a period of five years. However, if the debt is paid prior to that time, the financing statement and security interest can be terminated. If necessary, the creditor may renew the financing statement any time during the final six months of the five-year term and will then receive the protection of perfection for another five years.

General Rules of Priority Among Secured Creditors (9-317)

To determine priorities among creditors in the event of the debtor's default, certain rules and exceptions apply. These general rules are the starting point for determining the priorities in payment rights when a debtor is in default on loans secured by mortgages and security interests in fixtures:

1. A secured creditor has priority over an unsecured creditor.
2. A perfected secured creditor has priority over an unperfected secured creditor.
3. A perfected secured creditor has priority over subsequent real estate interests. (For example, a filing on January 3 gives the secured party priority over filings occurring later in that month or simply later in time.)
4. A prior real estate interest (mortgage, deed of trust, lien, or judgment) has priority over a subsequently filed security interest.
5. Between perfected secured creditors the date of filing is controlling, with the first creditor to file having priority.

Exceptions to General Rules

PMSI Exception (9-324)/(9-334)

A PMSI creditor may take priority over prior real estate encumbrances if the financing statement is filed before the goods become fixtures or within 20 days after they become fixtures. This priority applies even though language in the mortgage provides that all after-attached property and fixtures are subject to the mortgage. To illustrate, suppose that a homeowner has a mortgage on his property, which was filed in August 2004. The homeowner wants to install a solar water-heating system. The homeowner purchases a system from Solar Systems Company on credit, and Solar Systems executes a security agreement and files a financing statement on June 3, 2007. Then Solar Systems installs the water-heating system. Solar Systems (as a PMSI) has priority over the 2004 mortgage holder.

The reason for the PMSI exception is that without some form of special priority for the secured party, creditors would be hesitant to finance improvements and fixtures to existing structures that are still subject to a mortgage. Improvements enhance or maintain property value and thereby protect the mortgagee's collateral.

Construction Mortgage Exception

A construction mortgage is a mortgage used to secure funds in advance for real property improvements. A construction mortgage has priority over fixture security interests for those fixtures that are installed during construction.

Readily Movable Exception

Secured creditors with perfected interests in readily removable office or factory machines or in replaced consumer goods and appliances have priority over conflicting real estate interests. Readily removable office equipment includes items such as fax machines, photocopy machines, and computers. These personal property interests are not real estate and are not subject to a mortgage (a real property interest).

Tenant Exception

Creditors of tenants who have attached fixtures to leased property have priority over other prior and subsequent real estate encumbrances so long as the tenant has the right to remove such items when the lease ends. For example, a secured creditor of a tenant who attaches the financed, movable air conditioner to the landlord's property has priority over a mortgage on the property executed by the landlord.

Good-Faith Purchaser Exception

Good-faith purchasers (9-320) who purchase real property or fixtures in the ordinary course of business will have priority over secured parties so long as they purchase for value. Purchasers of real estate with fixtures covered by security interests are protected regardless of whether the creditor or secured party files the required financing statement.

Figure 5.2 summarizes the priorities and exceptions of Article 9.

Figure 5.2 Priorities in Fixtures Under Article 9 (9-313)

Type of Party	Priority Over	Exceptions to General Priority Rules
Secured party	Unsecured party, secured party whose interest attached after	Good-faith purchasers
Perfected secured party	Secured party, unsecured party, subsequently filed real estate encumbrances (mortgages, deeds of trust, liens, judgments, security interests)	Good-faith purchasers
PMSI perfected secured party	Secured party, unsecured party, subsequently filed real estate encumbrances	Construction mortgages with advancements yet to be made; Good-faith purchasers
	Prior perfected security interests and real estate encumbrances if financing statement filed before annexation of the fixture or within 20 days of annexation	
Construction mortgage	All subsequent encumbrances and security interests	
Secured party for: readily removable office or factory machines	No fixture filing required; perfection required	Construction
Secured party for a tenant	Priority over all real estate encumbrances (prior and subsequent)	
	Priority over all real estate encumbrances regardless of perfection so long as tenant holds the right to remove property	
Good faith purchaser	Prior security interests if purchase is made in the ordinary course of business. For real estate, filing on fixtures gives creditor priority	

Default by Debtor and Rights of Secured Party (9-604)

Revised Article 9 includes a specific section for default procedures with regard to security interests in fixtures. The drafters have taken the time to clarify many issues that debtors with fixture collateral raised. First, the secured party can use either the real property remedies (i.e., foreclosure) or the Article 9 remedies (non-judicial but commercially reasonable sale). Second, the secured party can remove the fixture and, while liable for any damage caused by the removal, is not responsible for any diminution in value. Third, the secured party has a choice as to proceeding against the real property itself or the fixture. However, the effect of this new section on fixtures is to overrule all those previous cases which held that the only remedy a secured party with fixture collateral had was the removal of the fixtures.[4] Neither the debtor nor the secured party is responsible for paying any decrease in value caused by the removal of the fixture. For example, if mirrors are removed from a wall, the cost of repair may be $30 for restoring the wall surface. However, the $1,000 decrease in value of the property need not be paid.

CONSIDER 5.6

Edward and Terre Capers bought their home with a purchase money mortgage from Maplewood Bank and Trust. The mortgage was entered into on September 20, 1988, and recorded on October 5, 1988. The original amount of the mortgage was $121,000.

On May 31, 1989, Sears, Roebuck, and Company (Sears) filed a financing statement covering a completely new kitchen for the Caperses consisting of "new countertops, cabinets, sinks, disposal unit, dishwasher, oven, cooktop and hood" installed. Sears filed a financing statement on the Caperses' property after the Caperses gave Sears a security interest in their home as security for the remodeling of their kitchen on credit.

On August 18, 1989, the Caperses executed a second mortgage on their home to Savings Bank for the sum of $34,000. That mortgage was recorded on August 23, 1989.

When the Caperses defaulted in their payments to Maplewood and Sears, Maplewood declared the entire balance of its loan due. Maplewood filed for foreclosure of its mortgage on November 5, 1989. Sears filed an answer and counterclaim for the amount of its security interest in the kitchen remodeling.

Sears' claim was dismissed because the judge held Sears' only remedy was removal of the kitchen fixtures and work. Maplewood was allowed to foreclose. Sears appealed the dismissal of its claim. *Maplewood Bank and Trust v. Sears, Roebuck and Co.*, 625 A.2d 537 (N.J. Super. A.D. 1993). How and why would the parties rights be affected under Revised Article 9?

ETHICAL ISSUE

In the *Maplewood* case (Consider 5.6), re-examine the time between when the Caperses entered into the three credit contracts and their default. Were the Caperses overextended? Is it the creditors' responsibility to decline credit in these circumstances? Why don't laws place limitations on the amount of credit individuals can obtain? Is there an ethical component to the use and extension of credit? What responsibilities should both sides to a credit arrangement have beyond what the law requires?

4. For example, the case from the seventh edition *Maplewood Bank and Trust v. Sears, Roebuck and Co.*, 625 A.2d 557 (N.J. Super. A.D. 1993) has been overruled by the new provisions of Revised Article 9.

Cautions and Conclusions

Article 9 affords creditors tremendous protection in collateral rights and priorities. However, creditors need to be certain of their positions; the following questions should help ensure them the best position and best available protection for their secured debt:

1. Is there a written security agreement with all of the necessary information?
2. Has value been given?
3. Has the security interest attached?
4. To whose property is the item being attached?
5. What other creditors have interests in that property? Is there a construction mortgage? Have the land records been checked?
6. Is the financing statement complete? Is the legal description included and accurate? Is the collateral sufficiently identified?
7. Has the financing statement been filed and in the correct place?
8. Has the financing statement been filed within the appropriate time limits (20 days on a PMSI)?
9. Is renewal necessary? When?
10. Can removal damage be minimized?

By answering these questions and following through on tasks at the outset, creditors can avoid the problems of forgotten filings, incomplete documents, and the resulting lack of protection.

Before buying real property, check for Article 9 interests. An Article 9 interest that is undisclosed or overlooked opens the door for litigation and liability. The following checklist provides suggestions for buyers, sellers, brokers, agents, and others involved in real estate transactions:

1. Have the records been checked to determine if a perfected security interest exists?
2. If a perfected interest does exist, who is the creditor? What property is covered? How much is owed? What payments are made? Is all of the paperwork proper? Does this creditor have priority?
3. Does an unperfected security interest exist on any items on the property? Who is the creditor? How much is owed? What payments are made? Is all of the paperwork proper?
4. Who will pay the balance due? Will it be paid from sale proceeds? Is the buyer to assume responsibility for payments?
5. Is there a provision in the contract for the disposition of debts and collateral pledges?

Key Terms

Article 9, 104
Doctrine of Emblements, 103
emblements, 103
financing statement, 105
fixture, 93
fructus industriales, 103
fructus naturales, 102
perfection, 105
purchase money security interest (PMSI), 105
security agreement, 104
security interest, 104
trade fixture, 95
Uniform Commercial Code (UCC), 103

Chapter Problems

1. Determine whether each of the following would constitute a fixture. Discuss any further information that would be helpful in making the determination.

a. A marble monument with a cement foundation in a cemetery
b. Bookshelves in a library
c. Wall mirrors installed by a tenant
d. A furnace that is bolted to the floor in a factory
e. A hog house (with a cement foundation) on a farm
f. Ceiling fans in a home
g. A printing machine in a college copy center

(*Reynolds v. State Bd. Community Colleges,* 937 P.2d 774 [Colo. App. 1996])

2. Bill leased an apartment from Windmere Apartments, Inc. Under the lease agreement, Bill is permitted to remove all fixtures installed on the property. Bill arranged to have custom bookshelves placed along one wall (the shelves are attached to the wall). Bill financed the shelves with Carl's Cabinetry, and Carl's filed a valid financing statement for the fixtures on December 1, 2006. Windmere has had a mortgage on the property since 1992.

a. If Bill defaults, may Carl's remove the shelves?
b. What obligations does Carl's have?
c. If Windmere defaults, does its mortgagee get the shelves?
d. What is the position of Carl's if no filing is made?

3. William and Virginia Britton own a one-acre parcel of land near Detroit's Metropolitan Wayne County Airport. They operate several small industrial businesses in the industrial building located on their land. In 1992, Wayne County began acquiring a total of 550 acres around the airport for expansion purposes. Wayne County offered the Brittons $188,580 for their property. The Brittons disputed the amount for not including the value of their trade fixtures. Listed as trade fixtures were the following: tanks, air compressors, forklifts, scales, storage racks, hose-braiding machines, pipe-threading machinery, hydraulic pumps, grinding machinery, and work tables. It also included such miscellaneous items as a coat tree, an electric clock, a first-aid kit, file cabinets, a refrigerator, a metal folding chair, a flatbed truck, trash drums, and lawn mowers. Should the county be required to compensate the Brittons for these items in a taking of real property? *Wayne County v. Britton,* 563 N.W.2d 674 (Mich. 1997)

4. The Michigan Tax Tribunal held that Michigan National Bank's night depository equipment, drive-up window equipment, vault doors, and remote transactions units, which were physically integrated with the bank's land and buildings, were fixtures and subject to taxation as realty by the city of Lansing. Is the Tax Tribunal correct? Should the drive-up facilities be classified as fixtures or personal property? *Michigan National Bank, Lansing v. City of Lansing,* 293 N.W.2d 626 (Mich. App. 1980); aff'd 322 N.W.2d 173 (Mich. 1982)

5. Harry owns Harry's Discount Clothiers, Inc. Harry has a five-year lease on the building in which his store is located. The building had concrete flooring, which was not appropriate for a clothing store, so Harry had parquet flooring installed. The flooring was installed in the same fashion as tile flooring. Determine whether the flooring will be treated as a fixture, trade fixture, or personal property in the following situations:

a. When the lease terminates, Harry wants to take the flooring with him. What is the result?
b. Harry purchases the building and then sells it to Bob, who claims that the flooring goes with the building. What is the result?
c. Harry's fire insurance policy covers personal property but no real property. What is the result?
d. The county tax assessor wishes to increase the value of the property on the basis of the value added by the floor. What is the result?

6. On January 20, Tom purchased a new hot-water tank for his home from Tanks, Inc. Tanks agreed to carry Tom on part of the price of the tank and took a security interest in the tank. The tank was then installed. On February 1, Tom borrowed money from First Federal, and First Federal took a second mortgage on the house. On March 1, Fiesta Funtime Pools obtained a judgment against Tom and his house for the unpaid balance due on Tom's pool.

a. Who has priority?
b. What would be the result if Tanks had filed a financing statement on January 31?
c. What relation would a first mortgage have in the situation?
d. If Tom defaults to Tanks, what can be done under Article 9?

7. In 1990, the Hogers purchased a furnace and air conditioner from the Kansas Power and Light Company (KPL) to be installed in the Hogers' home. On March 2, 1990, the Hogers and KPL entered into an installment contract and the Hogers executed a promissory note to finance the purchase of the furnace and air conditioner. The furnace and air conditioner were installed on March 20. KPL filed financing statements covering the furnace and air conditioner in Johnson County on March 23, 1990. Capitol Federal, the Hogers' mortgage company, did not receive notice of either the purchase or the installation of the furnace and air conditioner and did not consent to the security agreement. The Hogers defaulted on both the Capitol Federal and the Western Resources loans. Capitol Federal filed a mortgage foreclosure action on December 28, 1992, and named both the Hogers and Western Resources as defendants. A second mortgage holder, Associates Financial Services Company of Kansas, Inc., was also named as a defendant. Western Resources (the successor to KPL) claimed for the $2,887.50 amount the Hogers still owed on their installment contract, claiming a first and prior right to the real estate mortgage foreclosure sale proceeds. How would the foreclosure proceeds be distributed? *Capitol Federal Sav. and Loan Ass'n v. Hoger,* 880 P.2d 281 (Kan. App. 1994)

8. Preston and Beverly Mulford purchased a parcel of land in Centreville, Fairfax County, in 1972, which is situated adjacent to and east of Old Centreville Road. As part of their purchase, the Mulfords were granted an easement situated on property owned now by Fairfax Center LLC (Fairfax Center/defendant), which connected Old Centreville Road westward to Route 28. The Mulfords turned the easement into an asphalt roadway and erected a sign, facing Route 28, to mark the location of the Mulford School and Camp, an operation the Mulfords began in 1972. The sign served as the primary source of advertising for the Mulford School and Camp.

In 1987 the Virginia Department of Transportation (VDOT) purchased from the Mulfords the portion of the easement which served as the access point to Route 28. In August 2002, Fairfax Center began construction on its property over which the grant of easement had existed. As a result of its construction work Fairfax Center destroyed the asphalt driveway as well as the Mulford School sign. In addition, Fairfax Center piled several feet of dirt and rock on the driveway, making what remained of the easement unusable to the Mulfords.

The Mulfords filed suit alleging that Fairfax Center, through its construction efforts, (1) interfered with the Mulfords' use of the easement and destroyed their easement and sign; and (2) effectively took the Mulfords' property—without the Mulfords' permission and without compensating the Mulfords—for its sole use and control. The Mulfords sought both compensatory and punitive damages.

Is a landowner liable for the destruction of improvements and/or personal property located on an extinguished easement? *Mulford v. Fairfax Center LLC 2003,* WL 1563430 (Va. Cir. Ct. 2003)

9. During construction of the Grand Beach Inn, heating and air-conditioning units were installed in the rooms and are part of the walls for each room. The Grand Beach Inn was to be a hotel with individual guest rooms with individually controlled heat and air-conditioning. In a foreclosure on the never-opened inn, the issue of whether the units are included in the real property has arisen. Are the heating and air-conditioning units personal property or fixtures? *Lewiston Bottled Gas Co. v. Key Bank of Maine,* 601 A.2d 91 (Maine 1992)

10. Cliff Ridge Skiing Corporation is in bankruptcy, and a priority dispute has arisen among creditors because of a question as to whether Cliff Ridge's chairlifts are fixtures. The chairlifts were attached to the real property Cliff Ridge had mortgaged to First National Bank. There were concrete pads poured into the realty, towers were bolted to the concrete pads, cables were strung between the towers, and about 100 chairs were attached to the cables. However, one creditor maintains that the chairlifts can be easily removed from the land and sold as a package to another ski resort. Another creditor maintains that the pads, towers, and cables are specifically designed to fit the topography of a particular ski resort and cannot be easily modified for another resort. Who is correct? *In re Cliff's Ridge Skiing Corp.,* 123 B.R. 753, 13 UCC Rep.2d 1309 (Mich. 1991)

For research activities related to this chapter, go to our text companion website at www.thomsonedu.com/westbuslaw/jennings.

Liens

CHAPTER 6

One thing Charles Keating, former CEO of a defunct California savings and loan, left behind is mechanic's liens. Nonpayment of subcontractors on his Phoenician Resort has created a ripple effect in terms of economic impact. The resort was a project of American Continental Corporation, the owner of the savings and loan. Court records list 61 subcontractors as being owed money, including $120,000 for metal work, $303,000 for glass and windows, $2,400,000 for electrical work, $31,000 for painting, and $18.5 million to the general contractor.

Mechanic's Liens—The Big Squeeze

A **lien** is a special encumbrance that makes real property the security for the payment of a debt or obligation. In some cases, property owners place liens on their property voluntarily as security for a loan. In other cases, creditors have the right to create liens on property because of contracts or work they have performed. This chapter focuses on the second type of lien—the liens of third parties attached for nonpayment.

This chapter answers several questions about liens. What types of liens exist? How are liens created and enforced? How can liens on real property be satisfied and removed from the property? By the end of the chapter, you will understand the significance of the facts in the epigraph.

Types of Liens

Statutory Liens

A **statutory lien** is a lien that exists because of an enabling statute. For example, a mechanic's lien is a statutory lien. **Mechanic's liens**, sometimes called materials and labor liens or construction liens, are created by statutes and allow those furnishing labor and materials for construction and improvement of real property to file a lien against that property for debt or payment security. Mechanic's lien statutes have existed since colonial times and exist now in all states, plus Puerto Rico and the District of Columbia. Some states, like California, afford these liens constitutional protection.[1] There are also state statutes that permit the attachment of a lien on real property when taxes are not paid.

Equitable Liens

An **equitable lien** is created through a mortgage. Sometimes referred to as a **contractual lien**, or voluntary lien, this lien is created to secure repayment of money borrowed to purchase the property or borrowed against the property.

Voluntary vs. Involuntary Liens

A **voluntary lien** is one created by both parties; a mortgage is an example. Both parties agree to place a lien on the property as security for the advance of money to purchase the property or simply as security for a loan (see Chapter 15).

An **involuntary lien** is attached to the property but is not done under a contractual arrangement. Involuntary liens are placed on property for satisfaction of property, state, or federal taxes (see Chapter 22).

Judicial Liens

A **judicial lien** arises from some action taken by a court. For example, plaintiffs must collect the judgments they are awarded. To collect the judgment, the plaintiff must attach the defendant's property. Plaintiffs can attach wages, bank accounts, equipment, inventory, and, more relevantly here, real property. A judicial or judgment lien allows the sale of defendant's property to satisfy the plaintiff's judgment.

Once a judgment is recorded against real property, it becomes a creditor's lien. If the property is sold, then the plaintiff with the judgment has the priority of a secured creditor in the proceeds from the sale. The priority of the judgment or judicial lien is determined on the basis of "first in time is first in right." If the property is already subject to a mortgage, then the judgment plaintiff is a secured creditor with priority after the mortgagee. In some cases, the judgment plaintiff can initiate sale action by foreclosing on the judicial lien. Even without foreclosure, the judgment lien is recorded against the property, and the title cannot be transfered or insured until the judgment has been paid or otherwise resolved between the parties.

Most states permit either the judgment that awards damages or an abstract of the judgment to be recorded in the land records, so that the lien is effective against any property owned by the judgment debtor.

Mechanic's and Materials Liens

Mechanic's and **materials liens** arise because companies or individuals have supplied labor, material, or both for the construction, improvement, alteration, or repair of real property or real property structures. This type of lien is the focus of the remainder of this chapter.

The laws on mechanic's liens vary significantly among the states. At one point in the late 1920s, a Uniform Mechanic's Lien Act was proposed. By 1943, the Commissioners on Uniform State Laws withdrew the proposal because "varied conditions made

1. Cal. Const. Art. XIV, §3 (1992) provides "Mechanics, persons furnishing materials, artisans, and laborers of every class, shall have a lien upon the property upon which they have bestowed labor or furnished material for the value of such labor done and material furnished."

uniformity impossible." However, the purposes of the laws are clear—to prevent unjust enrichment of property owners who do not pay for improvements.

In 1987, the National Conference of Commissioners on Uniform State Laws adopted its Uniform Construction Lien Act. The Act answers three basic questions: Who is entitled to a lien? Who has priority among lien holders? and What are the landowner's rights with respect to payment and liens? The Act has not yet been adopted by any state but its framework is an excellent one for discussing liens.

Creation of Mechanic's Liens

Who is Subject to Lien?

Any property owner who contracts expressly or by implication with another for the improvement of land or furnishing materials is subject to the provisions of state mechanic's lien provisions. However, the key phrase here is "property owner." Only the property owner or someone acting as an agent or representative of the owner has the authority to contract for improvements that can be the basis for a mechanic's lien. For example, a lessee who has improvements made on leased premises does not have the authority to bind the landlord/property owner for purposes of a lien unless the landlord consents or the lessee is acting as an agent for the landlord. The following case deals with the very common issue of liability among landlord, tenant, and lienor.

R.T.B.H., Inc. v. Simon Property Group

849 N.E.2d 764 (Ind. App. 2006)

FACTS

On February 20, 2003, Dick's Sporting Goods, Inc. ("Dick's"), entered into a lease with Simon Property Group for property Simon owned at the Greenwood Park Mall. The lease was for the express purpose of Dick's demolishing an MCL Cafeteria and Service Merchandise store that were on the property and for constructing a new Dick's store. The lease was for an initial term of 20 years, with options to extend it for a total of 50 years. In order to secure the consent of Simon's mortgage lender for the lease, Simon agreed to complete construction of the new building if Dick's did not do so.

The lease required Simon to pay Dick's a part of the costs associated with demolishing the MCL Cafeteria and constructing a courtyard. Otherwise, Dick's bore the cost of the construction. Simon reviewed and approved the plans for the Dick's store prior to entering into the lease but indicated on the plans, "Landlord's review of contract documents is for design intent and criteria compliance only." The building was to be surrendered to Simon when the lease ended.

Dick's retained S.C. Nestel, Inc., as general contractor for the construction project. Nestel, in turn, subcontracted window and glass work to McAndrews. McAndrews' representative interacted with representatives from Nestel and Dick's during construction of the store. There is no evidence that representatives from Simon ever interacted with any representative of McAndrews during the construction.

The new Dick's store was completed without Simon's intervention. However, Nestel refused to pay McAndrews for its work on the store. Nestel, in fact, filed a complaint for damages against McAndrews. McAndrews, in turn, filed a counterclaim against Nestel and against Simon, alleging that there was a valid mechanic's lien on the property and that it should be foreclosed. Simon moved for partial summary judgment, alleging that there was no valid mechanic's lien on its fee interest in the property. The trial court entered partial summary judgment in favor of Simon, concluding that there was no valid mechanic's lien as to Simon, and directed the entry of final judgment in favor of Simon. McAndrews appealed.

JUDICIAL OPINION

Barnes, Judge. In order for a mechanic's lien to attach to real estate, it is imperative that improvements to the property be made under the authority and direction of the landowner and something more than inactive or passive consent is required. A lien claimant's burden to prove active consent to improvements is especially important when they are requested by someone other than the landowner. Without the landowner's active consent, a lien claimant can only maintain a lien to the extent of his customer's interest in the land. A person about to improve real estate must take notice of the extent of his customer's rights in the land and of the rights of those in possession.

We find this case to be practically indistinguishable from *Stern & Son,* which our supreme court cited with approval in *Gill. Gill,* 810 N.E.2d at 1059. There, Gary Joint Venture ("GJV"), a mall owner, leased property to a group of individuals. The express purpose of the lease was to turn the property into a pizza restaurant. A corporation formed by some of the tenants undertook to build the restaurant, and it contracted with Stern & Son for that purpose. GJV approved the construction plans, provided Stern & Son with a set of rules for contractors performing construction work in the mall, and representatives of GJV regularly visited the work site to ensure that the mall's standards were adhered to. The restaurant eventually was completed, but Stern & Son was not paid for its work. It sought to enforce a mechanic's lien against the property. The trial court granted GJV's motion for summary judgment, concluding that no mechanic's lien existed as to GJV's interest in the property.

We first cited the existence of longstanding case law holding that "a lease calling for improvements, even very detailed improvements, will not prove the sort of active consent needed to maintain a mechanic's lien." Next, we noted that GJV's approval of the plans was perfunctory and technical, as was the onsite construction supervision. We stated, "while these facts certainly establish that GJV was aware of the construction, this awareness also does not establish the sort of active consent needed to maintain a mechanic's lien."

We also made the following observation:

"The exact nature and content of the owner's active consent in this context will vary from case to case; however, case law makes clear that the focus is not only on the degree of the owner's active participation in the decisions and the actual construction. Instead, the focus is also on how closely the improvements in question resemble a directly bargained-for benefit. In the present case, GJV did not receive a direct benefit from the improvements Stern constructed. The benefits GJV received were indirect in that they enabled the Tenants to produce income with which they could make lease payments."

Here, the fact that the lease between Simon and Dick's called for the construction of a new building does not mean that Simon actively consented to improvements provided by McAndrews. The only designated evidence in the record is that Simon had no interaction with McAndrews during the course of construction, nor for that matter is there any evidence that Simon had any significant interaction with the general contractor, Nestel. It also appears from the record that Simon's approval of the design plan for the Dick's store was largely technical and perfunctory, as evidenced by the stamp placed on the design by Simon, "Landlord's review of contract documents is for design intent and criteria compliance only." Additionally, evidence that Simon was aware of the construction of the Dick's store, and even McAndrews' involvement in it, is not enough to establish "the sort of active consent needed to maintain a mechanic's lien."

Simon did not receive a direct benefit from the construction of the Dick's store. The benefits it received from the construction of the store were indirect, including some assurance that Dick's would be able to pay the rent required by the lease by its construction and operation of the store, and whatever tangential value the new store would have to Greenwood Park Mall as a whole. The fact that the building would revert to Simon at the conclusion of the lease, which means anywhere from twenty to fifty years in the future, cannot be fairly construed as a primary bargained-for purpose of the lease or a direct benefit to Simon. In any event, it is difficult to conceive that Dick's would physically move the 75,000-square foot store or intentionally destroy it before the conclusion of the lease; it is natural to expect that Simon would take possession of the structure at that time.

Simon entered into an agreement with its mortgage lender to complete construction of the store if Dick's did not do so. We agree with Simon that this contingency agreement, which contingency never came to pass, is irrelevant to the question of whether Simon actively consented to the improvements provided by McAndrews. The actual facts of this case are that Simon did not participate actively in the construction of the Dick's store and made no payments for any construction to either Nestel or McAndrews.

McAndrews contends that this case is controlled by our opinion in *American Islam Society v. Bob Ulrich Decorating,* 126 Ind.App. 266, 132 N.E.2d 620 (1956). In that case, the American Islam Society ("the Society") owned a hotel and leased it to two individuals. The lease was expressly conditioned upon the lessees making repairs and improvements that were explicitly set forth in the lease. The lessees hired several contractors to perform the required improvements but failed to pay them for their work. Shortly after the work was completed, the lessees defaulted on the lease and possession of the hotel reverted to the Society. The trial court found that a mechanic's lien existed against the property and ordered its foreclosure to pay the amounts owed to the contractors.

We affirmed, concluding there was sufficient evidence the Society had actively consented to the improvements.

Although there are some superficial similarities between *American Islam Society* and the one before us now, there is a key difference that we noted in the following paragraph:

It seems to us on the record herein that the appellant leased its building to tenants of doubtful financial responsibility and that the lease required them to make improvements amounting to several thousand dollars. The lease was surrendered shortly thereafter and the appellants have obtained the benefit of the improvements. The facts illustrate the justice of the rule applied herein. To hold otherwise would permit appellant to unjustly enrich itself at the expense of appellees.

There is no indication here that the entity to whom Simon leased the property, Dick's, is of "doubtful financial responsibility." The lease is still in effect and it is Dick's, not Simon, who currently is enjoying the direct benefit of the construction performed by McAndrews. Simon has not "unjustly enriched" itself at McAndrews' expense. We conclude that the present case is distinguishable from *American Islam Society*. The trial court correctly concluded that, as a matter of law, McAndrews failed to establish the existence of a mechanic's lien against Simon's ownership interest in the property.

Affirmed.

CASE QUESTIONS

1. Describe the relationships of the parties.
2. What factors point to consent to the lien?
3. What factors indicate that there was no consent?
4. How would you describe the standard for consent now?

CONSIDER 6.1

Suppose that a property owner who originally contracted with a builder sold his property and the new owner signed nothing but allowed the builder to continue construction. Is the new owner subject to a lien? *Thomas Hake Enterprises, Inc. v. Betke*, 703 N.E.2d 114 (Ill. App. 1998)

Practical Tip

Some commercial landlords require contractors to register with them. Upon registration, the contractors are given a statement that limits the landlord's liability and explains that their contracts are with the tenant and not the landlord.

Any person who can contract and who has authority can subject property to a lien (the party subject to the lien is called the **lienee**). Corporations' properties are subject to mechanic's liens when others provide improvements for those properties. In the absence of a specific statutory provision, no one can impose a lien against the U.S. government or any of the state governments. This governmental exemption prevents the taking of state land for the satisfaction of a mechanic's lien. Construction of schools and public buildings such as courthouses and office complexes is exempt from attachment of mechanic's liens. For quasi-public entities, such as utilities, some states recognize an exemption, while others do not.

Most state lien statutes require that the **lienor** have an underlying contractual arrangement to enforce a lien. However, the degree and type of contractual arrangement varies significantly from state to state: Some states require only an express or implied agreement before a lien may be attached (**consent statutes**). Others require the owner of the property to sign a contract for the work or materials (**contract statutes**). The difference between these contract and consent statutes is that under the contract statutes, the lienor must establish that a contract exists in order to attach a lien. Under the consent statutes, the lienor need only establish that the owner consented through circumstances such as the owner allowing work to continue after seeing that work has begun.

The contract formalities required vary significantly across the states, but the following items are the basic ones that should be included:

1. Amount due under the contract (for labor, materials, and so on)
2. Amount of time within which work is to be completed

3. Amount of time permitted for payments and any schedule of payments
4. Description of the real property involved
5. Description of the work to be completed
6. Signature of the parties. (If the property is community property or held in tenancy by the entirety, then both spouses' signatures are required.)
7. If the property being repaired or improved is consumer property, Regulation Z (12 C.F.R. §226) requires the following disclosure to be made:

   The buyer may cancel this transaction at any time prior to midnight of the third business day after the date of this transaction.

   Under Regulation Z, the contract must also include cancellation information such as how and to whom cancellation notice must be given.
8. Provisions for breach of the agreement (i.e., nonpayment or nonperformance), such as withholding payment or obtaining another contractor.

It is possible, particularly in construction contracts, to have an open-end agreement so that supplies are purchased as necessary. It is also possible for a contract executed by an agent of the owner to be valid against the owner, so long as the agent held proper authority to enter into the contract. Unincorporated associations, such as churches and foundations, present special problems for lienors. The person who signs the agreement for the nonprofit organization should have some form of authority for the transaction, such as the resolution of the board or officer verification. Without proper authority for the improvements contract, the property of the church or foundation is not subject to a lien. Some states also have special laws that govern contracts with unincorporated associations, typically the structure for nonprofit organizations such as trusts and foundations. Trustees and executors of estates may also have authority to make improvements on real property that is part of the trust or estate, but their authority should be documented by court orders or appointments.

The description of the liened property is critical because the lien is recorded in the real property records. Only an accurate description of the property ensures that buyers, creditors, and others will be put on notice as to what interest is held by whom and in what property.

Who Is Entitled to a Lien?

Who is entitled to place liens on real property varies from state to state but is detailed in the state mechanic's lien statutes. Ordinarily, lien rights exist in mechanics and laborers, but state statutes extend lien rights to others. Some states grant lien rights to contractors, subcontractors, those furnishing materials, those acting in a supervisory capacity, and in some cases, to architects. For each of these categories, lien coverage may be limited or it may require special notice provisions for the landowner or at least that the landowner was aware of the work. In some states, only those who are properly licensed (if licensing is required) are entitled to liens on property. The following case deals with an issue about the types of lienors because environmental statutes and their requirements added new types of lien issues and lienors that were not anticipated when mechanic's lien statutes were drafted.

> **Practical Tip**
>
> *Verify who is working for whom. Verify title holders if you are a contractor, subcontractor, or supplier. Verify the subcontractors and suppliers if you are the property owner. Be certain you know the role of all potential parties.*

Haz-Mat Response, Inc. v. Certified Waste Services Limited

910 P.2d 839 (Kan. 1996)

FACTS

Coastal Refining and Marketing contracted with Certified Supply Corporation and Chief Supply Corporation to dispose of up to 500,000 pounds of Coastal's hazardous waste located on Coastal's property in four containers: two above-ground emulsion breaking tanks, one API separator, and one in-ground tank. Certified and Chief subcontracted with Haz-Mat Response, Inc. (plaintiff), to perform the work.

Problems arose during performance of the contract, and although Haz-Mat removed the waste from the storage tanks, it was not disposed of as required by contract. Coastal hired other contractors to complete the work. Coastal refused to pay Certified and Chief, who in turn refused to pay Haz-Mat. Haz-Mat filed a mechanic's lien and thereafter filed suit against Certified, Chief, Coastal, and CIC Industries, the owner of the real property on which Coastal conducted business. Haz-Mat asked for foreclosure of the mechanic's lien it had filed against the property.

Coastal filed a motion for summary judgment claiming that hazardous waste removal would not support a mechanic's lien because such removal is not improvement of the real property. Coastal also claimed that a subcontractor may not recover against a property owner on the basis of unjust enrichment in the absence of privity of contract. The trial court granted summary judgment for Coastal on both issues, and the court of appeals affirmed the decision on the mechanic's lien but reversed on the issue of unjust enrichment. Haz-Mat appealed.

JUDICIAL OPINION

Davis, Justice. We agree with the Court of Appeals' conclusion that the removal of hazardous waste in the circumstances of this case was not lienable.

Our mechanic's lien law is remedial in nature, enacted for the purpose of providing effective security to any persons furnishing labor, equipment, material, or supplies used or consumed for the improvement of real property under a contract with the owner. The theory underlying the granting of a lien against the property is that the property improved by the labor, equipment, material, or supplies should be charged with the payment of the labor, equipment, material, or supplies.

At the same time, a mechanic's lien is purely a creation of statute, and those claiming a mechanic's lien must bring themselves clearly within the provisions of the authorizing statute.

There is no dispute that Haz-Mat complied with all the statutory requisites in filing its mechanic's lien, that it provided labor and materials used in the removal of hazardous waste on the owner's real property, and that it has not been paid under its subcontract. The question before the trial court and on appeal is whether Haz-Mat's waste-removal activities constituted an *improvement of real property*.

The phrase "improvement of real property" is not defined in the Kansas mechanic's lien statute. The only reported Kansas case interpreting the term "improvement" as used in our mechanic's lien statute is *Mark Twain Kansas City Bank v. Kroh Bros. Dev. Co.*, 798 P.2d 511 (Kan. App. 1990). The question presented in *Mark Twain* was whether the architectural and engineering services provided by subcontractors constituted lienable labor resulting in an improvement to real property when construction was never commenced and there appeared no visible or physical manifestation of the subcontractors *[sic]* work on the property. *Mark Twain* held that the professional services provided were never used or consumed in any improvement of the real property within the meaning of the [statute].

Mark Twain concluded that there is a requirement of "[s]ome visible improvement" or some "visible effect on the real estate" in order to put those who seek to acquire an interest in the land on notice that building has commenced on the property.

Black's Law Dictionary's definition most closely reflects what is meant by use of the phrase "improvement of real property": "A valuable addition made to real property (usually real estate) or an amelioration in its condition, amounting to more than mere repairs or replacement, costing labor or capital, and intended to enhance its value, beauty or utility to adapt it for new or further purposes."

Applying the above definition, we find no evidence that the removal of the hazardous waste was part of an overall plan to improve the property or that removal would necessarily enhance the value of the real property. We agree with the Court of Appeals that the removal was not lienable because it was part of a maintenance program that was necessary in the normal course of Coastal's business.

The sole basis for the trial court's decision that a claim for unjust enrichment would not lie was the lack of privity between the owner, Coastal, and the subcontractor. Our past cases establish that recovery under quasi-contract or unjust enrichment is not prohibited simply because the subcontractor and the owner of the property are not in privity of contract.

Although Haz-Mat has submitted an affidavit stating that its president "believed" Coastal was responsible for the bill along with the prime contractor, Haz-Mat did not present any evidence nor did it claim that this supposed belief was based on any statement or promise by Coastal.

Moreover, the undisputed facts fail to establish that Coastal misled Haz-Mat to its detriment, that Coastal in some way induced a change of position in Haz-Mat to its detriment, or that any fraud existed. We conclude that the undisputed facts require affirmance of the trial court's decision that the theory of unjust enrichment was not available to Haz-Mat.

Affirmed in part and reversed in part.

CASE QUESTIONS

1. List the parties involved in the case and their relationships.
2. What is the key definitional issue for purposes of determining whether Haz-Mat has a lien?
3. Is the removal of hazardous waste an improvement? Doesn't such removal increase the value of the property?
4. Why is claim for unjust enrichment not allowed?

CONSIDER 6.2

Anderson Petroleum, Inc., a contractor, hired TPST Soil Recyclers to remove and dispose of contaminated soil found on the site of John and Mary Nobles' gas station. TPST removed the soil and recorded a mechanic's lien against the Nobles' real property for the outstanding invoice balance. The trial court granted summary judgment dismissing the lien and TPST appeals. Is the trial court correct? Does such work qualify TPST for a lien on the property? *TPST Soil Recyclers of Washington, Inc. v. W.F. Anderson Const., Inc.,* 957 P.2d 265 (Wash. App. Div. 2, 1998)

CONSIDER 6.3

GRW Engineers, Inc., entered into a contract to furnish architectural and engineering services to Chateau Royale, Inc. Chateau Royale was turning a historic building into a restaurant and hired GRW to prepare plans and specifications for the renovation and conversion. GRW worked on the plan and specs over a period of months. Bills were submitted to Chateau, but not paid. Chateau's attorney finally contacted GRW and said its bills were "out of reason." The attorney then offered GRW $25,000 to settle the account. The original contract amount was $340,000–$365,000 (depending on some contingencies in the work). GRW refused and filed a lien. Chateau claims GRW did not have the right to lien its property for services. Is Chateau correct? *GRW Engineers, Inc. v. Elam,* 504 So.2d 117 (La. 1987)

One additional issue is critical in determining who is entitled to a lien. The answer to the "Who?" question is in large part controlled by whether the state is a contract state or a consent state, or whether specific provisions have been made for those other than lienors in direct contract with the landowner. For example, if a property owner actually hires and has a direct contractual relationship with the contractor—there is privity of contract between them. On the other hand, the owner does not have a direct contractual relationship or privity with others involved in the construction project such as subcontractors, suppliers, and laborers. In the absence of some specific provisions in the applicable state statutes, the ability to lien stops at the direct contractual relationship.

Figure 6.1 Amounts of Lien Claims by State

Recovery Only to Extent of Amount Unpaid to General		Direct Lien for Full Amount	
Alabama	Massachusetts	Alaska	New Hampshire
Arkansas	Michigan	Arizona	New Jersey
Connecticut	Minnesota	California	New Mexico
Delaware	Mississippi	Colorado	North Dakota
District of Columbia	Nebraska	Hawaii	Oregon
Florida	New York	Idaho	Pennsylvania
Georgia	North Carolina	Indiana	Rhode Island
Illinois	Tennessee	Kansas*	South Dakota
Iowa*	Utah	Louisiana	Texas*
Kentucky	Virginia	Maryland	Vermont
Maine	West Virginia	Missouri	Washington
		Montana	Wisconsin
		Nevada	Wyoming

* Indicates some variation or limitation

To provide payment assurances for subcontractors, suppliers, and laborers not in privity with the landowner, state statutes usually permit them to place a lien on property provided they meet some notice and other preliminary requirements prior to the time the lien is filed. Basically, the statutes permit them to lien if the property owner is aware of their work.

In some states, it is possible that if all claims (of subcontractors, suppliers, and so on) are pursued and made into liens, the landowner could have liens in excess of the contract price. Other states follow the New York rule and limit the amount of the liens to the contract price less any amounts paid to the general contractor. Figure 6.1 is a summary of state laws on this issue.

Some states provide an exemption for residential property; that is, the owners of residential property cannot have liens in excess of the contract price with the general contractor. However, courts are also concerned when the homeowners have not paid the full amount to the contractor, and subcontractors have also not been paid. Many subcontractors bring suit on the basis of unjust enrichment in order to recover for the materials and work they have furnished. Courts work to balance the interests of the subcontractors with those of the homeowners. In the following case, the court deals with the application of the residential exemption to a lien by a supplier when the homeowner has made payments to a bankrupt general contractor but did not pay the full amount to that contractor.

Ontiveros v. Sanchez

3 P.3d 695 (N.M.C.A. 2000)

FACTS

Ricardo and Geraldine Sanchez and Nancy Bustamante (Homeowners) each contracted with William C. Parker, the general contractor, for the construction of their respective homes. The original contracts specified that the Sanchezes would pay $63,000 and Bustamante would pay $73,000 for the completed homes.

Parker purchased building materials, which included doors and windows, from Rawson and hired Ontiveros to install insulation and a heating system (Subcontractors). The services and materials were provided for the homes as contracted for by Parker, and the parties agree that, as a result, value was added to the homes.

Unfortunately for all involved, Parker, the general contractor, declared bankruptcy prior to completing construction of the homes, but after Subcontractors had provided the labor and materials. At the time of bankruptcy, Parker had finished some portion of the work. Also, at this point in time, the Sanchezes had paid Parker $26,000, or approximately 41 percent of the original contract price, and Bustamante had paid him $45,000, or approximately 62 percent of her original contract price.

Upon Parker's default, the Homeowners completed their homes by other means. Completion of each home ultimately cost the Sanchezes $125,456 and Bustamante $120,851, including the cost of purchasing the land. The post-construction appraisal of the Sanchez and Bustamante homes ultimately exceeded the actual costs of construction by approximately $19,000 and $20,000, respectively. While the stipulated facts do not indicate the pre-construction appraised value of Bustamante's home, such that any comparison can be made, the post-construction appraised value of the Sanchezes' home was $14,000 greater than the pre-construction appraisal.

Both Subcontractors filed suit for unjust enrichment seeking payment for their supplies and services. The district court found the Homeowners liable to Ontiveros Insulation Co., Inc., and Rawson, Inc., Builders Supply (collectively, Subcontractors) for a sum of $13,321.61, plus costs and prejudgment interest.[2]

JUDICIAL OPINION

Armijo, Judge. We now turn to the question presented: Are Homeowners entitled to prevail on their claim that any enrichment was not "unjust?" Homeowners argue that where a subcontractor seeks relief directly from the property owner with whom it has had no contact, it is virtually impossible for any claimed enrichment to be found "unjust." Subcontractors acknowledge that there is a paucity of New Mexico case law factually supportive of their position in this case; nonetheless, they contend that as is always the focus in equity, the only facts that matter are those here presented.

New Mexico has long recognized actions for unjust enrichment, that is, in quantum meruit or assumpsit. To prevail on such a claim, one must show that: (1) another has been knowingly benefitted at one's expense (2) in a manner such that allowance of the other to retain the benefit would be unjust. The theory has evolved largely to provide relief where, in the absence of privity, a party cannot claim relief in contract and instead must seek refuge in equity.

Subcontractors' suits against property owners are generally not favored. Remedy is instead viewed as best sought from the underlying general contractor. This general disfavor, however, is not required by anything intrinsic to the subcontractor–property owner relationship, but rather is a reflection of the jurisprudence of equity. Simply, equity does not take the place of remedies at law, it augments them; in this regard, an action in contract would be preferred to one in quasi-contract.

We decline, however, to apply this traditional reticence regarding consideration of equitable relief in the present context. To do so would ignore the basic foundation of equity. As the Missouri Court of Appeals has framed the issue:

Equity is reluctant to permit a wrong to be suffered without remedy. It seeks to do justice and is not bound by strict common law rules or the absence of precedents. It looks to the substance rather than the form. It will not sanction an unconscionable result merely because it may have been brought about by means which simulate legality. And once rightfully possessed of a case it will not relinquish it short of doing complete justice. It weighs the equities between the parties and adopts various devices to protect against unjust enrichment. Merrick v. Stephens, *337 S.W.2d 713, 719 (Mo. Ct. App. 1960)*

Accordingly, rather than shying from application of equitable principles in the present case, we inquire more closely as to the particular equities of this specific matter.

The parties agree that the labor and materials added value to the properties. It is axiomatic, however, that courts provide remedy in quantum meruit to prevent unjust enrichment. To prove their claim, therefore, it would not be enough that Homeowners were merely enriched at Subcontractors' expense: That enrichment must also be unjust. The well-founded cautionary rules Homeowners invoke are specific iterations of this basic principle. As a general matter, the limitations are premised on the bedrock principle that it makes little sense to remedy one wrong by inflicting another. The question before us, therefore, is whether the district court abused its discretion in not determining that Subcontractors' action failed because of one of the limitations upon actions for unjust enrichment which Homeowners assert. Homeowners argue, first, that they have paid to the general contractor a substantial portion of the original contract price and that they should not, therefore, be required to pay any further amount. Second, they argue that they did not request or know of the furnished work or materials and should not, therefore, be held liable. We are not persuaded by either argument.

Where a property owner pays to the general contractor "a very substantial part" of the monies due and owing, the subcontractor does not generally have an

2. Sadly, both Homeowners have declared bankruptcy as well and these proceedings are conducted simply for the purpose of determining the subcontractors' rights and priorities for payment in the bankruptcy court.

equitable claim for relief against the property owner. Such payment makes reasonable the presumption that the property owner has already paid for the conferred benefit. It follows, then, that if a defendant has already paid for the benefit, there has been no enrichment, much less unjust enrichment. As such, this limitation upon the action is consistent with the basic rule.

However, we find no abuse of discretion in the district court's implied finding that 42% and 61% payments—or, to aggregate, payments totaling 52%—on the underlying contracts are not "very substantial." First, as the stipulated record does not indicate what portion of the work remained unfinished upon the general contractor's default, we cannot tell what relation an aggregate payment of 52% on the original contracts bears to what services and materials the general contractor and Subcontractors had provided. The stipulated record does indicate, however, that Subcontractors received no compensation for the approximately $14,000 in work and materials they provided—work which the parties agree—added value to the homes. Moreover, it is clear that, in the aggregate, Homeowners never paid $65,000 out of $136,000 agreed upon in the original contract, but that their homes are now appraised, again in the aggregate, at $40,000 more than they expended. Given the state of the stipulated record, we cannot conclude that it was contrary to logic and reason for the district court's refusal to conclude that Homeowners had already paid for the services and materials Subcontractors had provided.

That they hired others to finish the work begun and abandoned does not of itself suggest that Homeowners have already paid for Subcontractors' labor and materials. Upon the standard of review applicable, the district court did not abuse its discretion by concluding that Homeowners did not pay for the benefit conferred upon them.

As to their claimed lack of request or knowledge, Homeowners claim they had no specific knowledge of Parker's hiring of Subcontractors or of purchasing materials. However, this is of little concern. While Homeowners may not have known the specifics of Parker's arrangement with the subcontractors, it would make little sense—certainly not at the prices of the homes at issue—for Homeowners to have contracted for homes to be built without heating systems, insulation, doors, and windows. In this regard, we conclude that the district court did not abuse its discretion in determining on the stipulated facts that Homeowners should have known such services and materials would be provided.

Finally, we note that while the record discloses no reason why any party should bear the blame for Parker's bankruptcy, abandonment of the underlying construction contract, or failure to pay Subcontractors, the equities weigh heavily in Subcontractors' favor. Among these considerations, the Subcontractors pursued all possible remedies before turning to the present action. Indeed, but for Homeowners' mortgage defaults and the resulting foreclosure and redemption, Subcontractors could claim an adequate remedy at law without resort to equity. Conversely, by virtue of the foreclosure actions, Homeowners redeemed the properties free and clear of any liens and now live in homes appraised at $19,000 and $21,000 more than expended. As to the work and materials for which Subcontractors now seek compensation, this turn of events has inured directly to their disadvantage and Homeowners' advantage. In light of this record, the district court did not abuse its discretion in providing equitable relief to Subcontractors.

In so holding, we wish to emphasize that recovery on such an action may not be had in every instance where a subcontractor has furnished labor or materials which benefit a third person with whom there is no privity of contract. Our decision today is limited to affirming the propriety of quasi contract as a remedy in a particular factual situation. Each case must be decided according to the essential elements of quasi contract. The most significant requirement for a subcontractor's successful recovery is that the enrichment be unjust. In the present case, Subcontractors exhausted their remedies against the person with whom they contracted, namely, Parker. Despite those efforts, they did not receive any value for the labor and services rendered.

Affirmed.

CASE QUESTIONS

1. What happened with the general contractor?
2. What percentage of the contract price had been paid?
3. Where are the homeowners now and how much are their homes worth?
4. Why does the court make an exception and allow the subcontractors to recover?
5. What is quasi contract? quantum meruit? unjust enrichment?

ETHICAL ISSUE

Evaluate the ethics of the homeowners in this case. Should they have paid the subscontractors? What additional information would you like to have before discussing the issues of fairness and forthrightness in handling this problem?

CONSIDER 6.4

Jimmy Gibson purchased an apartment complex located in Odessa, Texas, from the Federal Home Loan Mortgage Corporation. The same day, he entered into a contract for deed to sell the complex to Jim and Mary Nell Brown and Gerald and Johnnie Jones. Mary Nell and Johnnie are Gibson's sisters.

In 1993, a hailstorm hit Odessa and the roof of the complex was damaged. Jim Brown (Brown) received an estimate for the repair from Eddie Conner, an estimator and salesman for Bostick. Brown presented himself to Conner as the owner and advised that insurance would cover the damage. Conner admittedly took no steps to verify that Brown was indeed the owner of the property, nor were such steps customary in his business. Conner never dealt with Gibson.

Conner first estimated the cost of replacing the roof at $6,450. Because Brown also wanted to have the roof on his own residence repaired, the price was negotiated down to $5,500 for each roof. The work on the apartment complex was completed near the end of July 1993. Bostick never received payment.

Bostick began sending invoices to Brown. These invoices were prepared by Bostick's president Andy Reed, who was responsible for the company's record keeping and billing. Reed testified that the invoices were prepared in the regular course of business and were sent on a regular basis. After retaining counsel, Reed realized that Brown was not the only party with an interest in the property. He soon learned that Gibson was the legal owner while the Browns and the Joneses were the equitable owners. Reed filed an affidavit for a mechanic's and materialman's lien on March 4, 1994. Gibson was notified of the lien by letter, but Reed couldn't recall whether Gibson was notified before the lien was filed. Reed never dealt with Gibson and admitted that he had no contract whereby Gibson.

Gibson, a resident of Dallas, didn't know about the hail storm or that the roof of the complex needed to be or was being replaced.

After receiving demand letters, Gibson contacted Brown to inquire about the work. Brown admitted that he had a new roof put on the apartment complex, that it was covered by insurance, and that he would take care of everything. Gibson never followed up with the insurance company or his sisters. The insurance checks that were issued to pay for the repairs were sent to the complex; Brown forged Gibson's name, and cashed the checks.

On August 23, 1994, the Joneses transferred their interest in the complex to the Browns. In December 1995, Gibson repossessed the property and the Browns signed a quitclaim deed transferring their interest. The deed was never recorded. Gibson ultimately sold the property to the Thompsons on a contract for deed. Bostick filed suit on January 17, 1995. Can Bostick recover from Gibson? *Gibson v. Bostick Roofing and Sheet Metal Co.,* 148 S.W.3d 482 (Tex. App. 2004)

NORTH BAY CONST., INC. V. CITY OF PETALUMA

143 Cal.App.4th 552, 49 Cal.Rptr.3d 455 (2006)

FACTS

North Bay Construction, Inc. (plaintiff/North Bay), alleges that the City of Petaluma (City) is the owner of real property commonly known as the Redwood Empire Sportsplex that was leased to a developer for the purpose of constructing a sports complex. The developer contracted with North Bay, a licensed paving contractor, to perform grading work at the property, which North Bay has completed but for which it has not been paid. North Bay recorded a mechanic's lien against the property and served a "Notice of Potential Claim" on the City advising it that, as the owner and lessor of the property, it may be responsible for the reasonable value of the material and labor provided by North Bay. North Bay brought a cause of action to foreclose on the mechanic's lien. The trial court dismissed North Bay's complaint on the grounds that a mechanic's lien cannot be enforced against property owned by a municipality, even if the work was not performed as part of a "public work" project, and that a contractor cannot recover in quantum meruit for improvements to a municipality's property performed under a contract with a third party. North Bay appealed.

JUDICIAL OPINION

Pollak, J. "A mechanic's lien is a procedural device for obtaining payment of a debt owed by a property owner for the performance of labor or the furnishing of materials used in construction."

Section 3109, added by the Legislature in 1969, expressly provides that the mechanics' lien law "does not apply to any public work." "Public work" is defined as "any work of improvement contracted for by a public entity." North Bay argues that since the City did not contract for the performance of any of the work on the sports complex, the project is not a "public work" and therefore has no application. Since the work in question was contracted for by the lessee/developer, the argument continues, the mechanic's lien statute applies and, the City as owner having failed to file a notice of nonresponsibility, a lien may be imposed on the property on which the improvements were performed.

While there is no dispute that the express exemption for public work provided by section 3109 does not apply, it does not necessarily follow that a mechanic's lien may be impressed on property owned by the City. In 1891, the California Supreme Court held that a mechanic's lien could not be enforced against a school house owned by a local school district. (*Mayrhofer v. Board of Education* [1891] 89 Cal. 110, 112, 26 P. 646 [*Mayrhofer*].) The court explained that because of principles of sovereign immunity, any right to impress a mechanic's lien on public property must be expressly, not implicitly, provided for by statute. The court rejected the argument that "public buildings are included both in the word 'property,' used in the constitution, and in the phrase 'any building,' used in the code, and therefore it must necessarily follow that mechanics and material-men are, by these provisions, given a right to a lien upon such buildings." Since *Mayrhofer,* the general rule has been broadly stated, often without reference to section 3109, that "liens for labor or supplies on public property are not permitted." While most of these cases did involve public work projects, the prohibition is frequently stated as applying to "public *property*," not simply to public work projects. This is consistent with the rule in many other jurisdictions.

The holding in *Mayrhofer* remains good law. There is no right to impose a lien on property owned by a public entity unless such a right has been expressly conferred by statute.

North Bay argues that a distinction must be drawn between property owned by a municipality that is used for governmental as opposed to proprietary purposes. It contends that property held in a proprietary capacity—as it asserts is the case here—is subject to a lien as is any other privately held property. Although there is no California authority directly on point, some other jurisdictions have agreed that the purpose for which governmentally-owned property is used determines whether the property is subject to a mechanic's lien.

Contrariwise, the City suggests that although the property was to be developed by a private entity, the sportsplex retained a general public purpose and bore "more similarity to a public park or playground than a professional sports arena..." In view of the decision we reach rejecting the significance of such a distinction, we need not determine the proper characterization of the proposed use of the property. However, the elusive, if not illusory, nature of such a distinction and the uncertainty and inevitable litigation that recognizing such a distinction would generate are additional factors weighing against the adoption of such a distinction.

More directly on point, the Legislature has also enacted a separate comprehensive scheme prescribing the manner in which a judgment against a local public entity may be satisfied, and it does not include execution on public property.

Accordingly, while execution of a judgment lien against private property is authorized by Code of Civil

Procedure sections 697.010 through 697.060, no such procedure is now authorized in the relevant sections of the Government Code. Rather, the Government Code provides that "[a] writ of mandate is an appropriate remedy to compel a local public entity to perform any act required by this article" (§970.2), and "imposes a duty upon local public entities to pay tort judgments in the manner provided in this article and gives the judgment creditor the right to obtain a writ of mandate to enforce this duty. Depending upon the financial condition of the public entity, it can comply with the duty to pay a tort judgment by: (1) paying the judgment in the fiscal year in which it becomes final; (2) paying the judgment in the next fiscal year; (3) paying the judgment in not more than 10 annual installments; or (4) paying the judgment with the proceeds of a bond issue as authorized by Article 2 (commencing with Section 975) of this chapter." The procedure recommended above for enforcing money judgments against public entities takes into account their special nature. Making clear that execution is not available to enforce a judgment against a public entity will protect against the possibility of seizure and sale of public property to satisfy a judgment. Litigation to determine the status of public property will be avoided."

The legislative elimination of the right to execute upon governmentally owned property under any circumstances reflects a long-perceived recognition of the illusive nature of the distinction between property held in a governmental as opposed to a proprietary capacity. "[t]he government was created and shaped by the constitution. It is not an end in itself, but a mere instrumentality for public service. Its powers and functions exist only for the people. One of its functions is to enact laws for the government of the inhabitants within its limits, thereby affording them protection and advancing their general welfare. The property it holds is simply to enable it to perform the service required of it. It is as much devoted to public use as are the streets and highways, though in a different way; and it is generally held by a different tenure."

Since no legislation expressly authorizes the imposition of a mechanic's lien on this or other publicly owned property, North Bay may not pursue its claim to compensation by proceeding under the mechanic's lien law.

North Bay was not without a means of protecting its right to compensation. To enforce payment, a party contracting with a private lessee to perform work of improvement on publicly owned property may utilize the bonded stop notice procedure under sections 3159 and 3162, as can its subcontractors. These provisions enable the contractor to require a construction lender to withhold funds from the construction loan account to pay for uncompensated work performed on the project. Similarly, the contractor may insist that a payment bond be secured for work performed under its contract. But the contractor may not impose a lien on the underlying public property.

North Bay's third cause of action seeks to recover the value of its services based on a theory of quantum meruit. It has long been true, however, that a quasi-contract theory cannot be asserted against a municipality in a public works context. North Bay argues that this rule is not applicable here because, once again, "[t]he protection of the public is not at issue in the context of this private project."

North Bay offers no explanation for its assertion that this public policy is not implicated in the present case. But if a contractor cannot recover in quantum meruit against a city that has contracted for the performance of work without complying with competitive bidding requirements, there is hardly a basis for recovery in quantum meruit for work performed under a contract to which the city was not even a party. Certainly the risk of fraud, corruption or waste endangering the public treasury is as great, if not significantly greater, in this situation than where the municipality has at least agreed to pay for the work in question.

As to the understandable concern to avoid undue hardship, we quote the advice of the Supreme Court. "Persons dealing with the public agency are presumed to know the law with respect to the requirement of competitive bidding and act at their peril." Likewise, North Bay must be presumed to have known the law. As indicated above, it could have protected itself from the contractor's default by confirming the existence and sufficiency of a construction loan and following the statutory stop notice procedures, or by obtaining a payment bond or other security to ensure payment. Having failed to do so, North Bay cannot shift the burden of its loss to the City in disregard of a well established public policy to the contrary.

The judgment is affirmed.

CASE QUESTIONS

1. Describe the relationships of the parties and nature of the work.

2. What distinction does North Bay wish to draw between general government immunity and its work?

3. Explain the law on governmental immunity on quasi-public projects.

What Property is Subject to a Lien?

Once a lien is obtained, it applies to the whole property and not simply the portion of the structure that was the subject of the lienor's work, labor, or materials. The lien attaches to both the building and the lot on which the building is located (subject to the exemptions-noted page). A lienor could lien individual lots in a subdivision for work performed on each of those lots.

There are some lien exemptions. For example, government property is often exempt from liens. The following case deals with an interesting and common issue on quasi-government properties and lien rights.

Figure 6.2 summarizes the generic basics of lien rights.

> ***Practical Tip***
>
> *Mechanic's liens and the sale of residential property are a risky combination. Suppliers and subcontractors should be aware of their lien limitations. Buyers should do background checks on builders and observe the property to be certain lien claims do not arise, even though they may ultimately be defeated. All parties should know their state statutory protections for lien holders and buyers alike.*

Figure 6.2 Basics of Mechanic's Lien Rights

What Property Is Subject to Liens?

- All real property
- Exemptions:
  - Public property
  - Railways
  - Property devoted to public use
  - Property of quasi-public corporations

Who Can Claim Liens?

- Original or principal contractors
- Subcontractors
- Persons supplying labor
- Persons supplying materials

Types of Claims

- Written contracts
- Implied contracts (some states)

Procedural Aspects of Obtaining a Lien

Because mechanic's liens are statutory, the procedural aspects for creating and enforcing a lien vary from state to state, but the fundamentals are the same. Since the lien is a land interest, it must be recorded in the appropriate governmental land-record office to be valid. In most states, liens are probably filed in the same office as financing statements for fixtures (see Chapter 5). See Web Exhibits 6.1 and 6.2 for sample lien forms. Note that place on the first page of the form (not shown) for a real property description.

The times for filing, perfection, and period of validity for liens also differ among the states. Other times that vary include the days allowed for filing a lien and the date that the allowed time period for a lien filing begins. Some statutes begin the 60- or 90-days' period for filing the lien on the date the work is completed or on the date the supplies are delivered. Even completion of work is defined differently from state to state: it may mean the end of work or the completion of the project with the issuance of an architect's certificate.

Many states follow a prenotification procedure, especially for those performing work who do not have a direct contractual relationship with the property owner. Those without a contract who want lien protection must file a preliminary notice within a certain period of time after their work has begun or their supplies have been delivered. This notice is served on the property owner, the contractor (who has a contractual agreement with the property owner), and the construction lender. This notice serves to alert all concerned to the possibility of a lien. Because this notice gives a right to an eventual lien, the party giving the notice must be able to prove that notice was sent, to whom it was sent, and when it was sent. In some states, the notice must be served personally or sent through certified mail. This notice is not a lien; it simply makes all three parties aware of those working on the project, what they are doing, and the supplies and costs involved. The preliminary notice gives only the right to execute a lien in the future. In those states requiring the preliminary notice, failure to give the notice may cost the lienor the right of the lien. There are professional services across the states that perform the preliminary notice function for contractors and suppliers.

> ***Practical Tip***
>
> *Establish a payment mechanism for the contractor, subcontractors, and suppliers that ensures payment gets to the proper parties. Draws by the general contractor very often do not end up in the hands of the subcontractors and suppliers. Maintain adequate controls over payments so that your funds do not end up in the internal business of the general contractor instead of being paid to the subs and suppliers whose completed work is the basis for the draw.*

The time period for which the lien, once filed, is effective also varies. In some states, the valid lien period is six months (measured from the date of filing). If the owner does not make the necessary payments during the time the lien is effective, then the lienor will bring suit (a form of foreclosure suit) to execute the lien to satisfy payment due. If the lienor does not bring suit within the statutory period of effectiveness, the lien is lost.

Priority of Lien Interests

Attachment of Lien

The times and dates of perfection are also important issues in determining priority of recorded liens. In the majority of states, a lien for the construction of a building ordinarily dates back to the commencement of construction. If construction begins on January 1, 2007, and is completed on June 1, 2007, and a lien is filed on July 1, 2007 (assuming a proper filing time), then the priority of the lien dates back to January 1, 2007, when construction began. If new financing (also called permanent financing) were obtained for the building in June, the new lender's mortgage would be second in priority to the contractor's lien, because the contractor's lien has a priority date of the start of construction, or January 1, 2007. This principle is critically important for construction lenders, who must be certain construction has not begun prior to the recording of their mortgage in order not to lose priority. For permanent lenders, this means that all construction costs and subcontractors must be paid and all liens must be satisfied before the lenders record their mortgage or lend the money (so that they are not last in priority behind all those who have worked on the project and who have not yet been paid).

In another group of states, the priority date for liens is the date the particular lienor began work, not the date overall construction began.

In the final group of states, the lien is effective from the date of filing. For example, if the lender records the mortgage before the liens are filed, the lender would have priority because the liens would not date back to the time the construction was begun.

Rights of Purchasers

Whether a good faith or bona fide purchaser of property will be subject to a preexisting lien depends on the state's rule on lien attachment. For states that have a rule on attachments dating back to the time construction was commenced, purchasers are subject to liens. In other states, a purchaser would be subject to liens only if the liens were filed and recorded prior to the time of the purchase and transfer of title by deed, along with its recording in the land records (see Chapter 16 for more information on closing and Chapter 9 for more information on deeds and recording). In some states, a residential property exemption does not permit liens on newly constructed residences when the home has been purchased in good faith from a contractor for use as a residence.[3] This exemption protects the buyers even if the priority of liens dates back to the start of the home's construction. The following case deals with an issue of homeowners and problems with payments of subcontractors.

DLF Trucking, Inc. v. Bach

707 N.W.2d 606 (Mich. App. 2005)

FACTS

In August 2001, Steven and Lisa Bach contracted with Lucas Development, LLC (Lucas), to build a home. The Bachs financed the construction through a loan provided by ABN AMRO and secured by a mortgage. DLF Trucking (plaintiff) was subcontracted by Lucas to install a septic field and to do other excavating work for the home, which it commenced on August 21, 2001. On November 2, 2001, Lucas paid DLF for its work performed to that date and, in connection with that payment, executed a waiver and release of its lien for that work. DLF completed the remainder of its work on February 18, 2002, and, because it was concerned that Lucas might not pay the outstanding balance for that work, recorded a claim of lien against the property on February 25, 2002. That same day, however, Lucas provided ABN AMRO with a waiver of lien indicating that DLF had in fact been paid in full for its work and had waived and released all lien rights against the Bachs' property. This waiver of lien was a forgery fabricated from the earlier waiver of lien executed by DLF on November 2, 2001. In reliance on the waiver, however, ABN AMRO disbursed its final draw to Lucas on behalf of the Bachs on February 27, 2002.

When DLF failed to receive payment from Lucas on the balance due, it filed suit against Lucas, the Bachs, and ABN AMRO. In response, the Bachs filed with the trial court an affidavit averring that they had paid Lucas in full. ABN AMRO, along with the Bachs, thereafter moved for summary disposition, alleging, among other things, that the Bachs' affidavit of full payment prevented DLF's lien from attaching to the property pursuant to the Construction Lien Act (CLA), MCL 570.1101 *et seq.*, Although it granted summary disposition in favor of the Bachs and ordered that DLF's claim of lien be "removed," the trial court denied summary disposition in favor of ABN AMRO on the grounds that its constructive knowledge of the recorded claim of lien rendered its mortgage interest inferior to plaintiff's lien. DLF and ABN AMRO appealed.

Per Curiam. ABN AMRO argues that, because the Bachs have met the requirements of §203(1) of the CLA, MCL 570.1203(1), the construction lien asserted by plaintiff under the act does not attach to the property at issue and, therefore, summary disposition of plaintiff's action to foreclose on that lien was proper with respect to itself as well as the Bachs. We agree.

Subsection 1 of 203 of the CLA provides:

A claim of construction lien shall not attach to a residential structure, *to the extent payments have been made*, if the owner or lessee files an affidavit with the court indicating that the owner or lessee has done all of the following:

a. Paid the contractor for the improvement to the residential structure and the amount of the payment.
b. Not colluded with any person to obtain a payment from the [homeowner construction lien recovery) fund.

3. Fla. Stat. Ann. §627. 7842(c)

c. Cooperated and will continue to cooperate with the [Department of Licensing and Regulation, now the Department of Labor and Economic Growth] the Department of Labor and Economic Growth] in the defense of the fund. [MCL 570.1203(1) (emphasis added).]

Relying on the emphasized language, plaintiff argues that because it filed its claim of lien against the property before the Bachs' final payment to Lucas, §203(1) permits attachment of its lien against the property in an amount equal to the Bachs' final payment to Lucas. More specifically, plaintiff argues that §203(1) prevents the attachment of a construction lien only "to the extent payments have been made" and that, therefore, its filing of a claim of lien before the final payment by the Bachs entitles it to a lien against the property in an amount up to that of the subsequent final payment. We disagree.

Our fundamental obligation when interpreting statutes is "to ascertain the legislative intent that may reasonably be inferred from the words expressed in the statute."

It is well settled that the CLA is remedial in nature, and "shall be liberally construed to secure the beneficial results, intents, and purposes of [the] act." MCL 570.1302(1). It is similarly well settled that the CLA was enacted for the dual purposes of (1) protecting the rights of lien claimants to payment for expenses and (2) protecting property owners from paying twice for these expenses. Consistently with these dual purposes, subsection 1 of §203 of the CLA prevents a construction lien from attaching to the property of an owner who has paid the contractor. However, although the protection afforded a property owner under subsection 1 of §203 is expressly qualified by the language at issue, i.e., "to the extent payments have been made," there is nothing in the language of that section from which it can be inferred that this qualification is itself subject to a "first in time" qualification with respect to such payment and the filing of a claim of lien. To the contrary, and consistently with the purpose of protecting property owners from twice paying for an improvement, subsection 1 plainly provides only that property owners will be protected up to the amount paid by them. Therefore, to permit plaintiff's lien to attach to the property at issue here—thereby requiring the Bachs to pay twice for the improvements or suffer a lien against their property—merely because plaintiff filed a claim of lien before the Bachs' final payment to Lucas would be inconsistent with the plain language of §203, as well as the intent and purpose of the CLA. Consequently, the trial court did not err in granting summary disposition in favor the Bachs. However, because §203 of the CLA prevents plaintiff's lien from attaching to the property at issue, it is irrelevant whether such a lien would generally have priority over the mortgage if it had properly attached, see MCL 570.1119, and the trial court therefore erred in failing to also grant summary disposition in favor of ABN AMRO.

Accordingly, we affirm the trial court's grant of summary disposition in favor of the Bachs, but reverse its decision to deny that same relief to ABN AMRO.

CASE QUESTIONS

1. Outline the relationships between and among the parties.
2. What does the statutory exemption provide?
3. How does the mortgage company escape liability?

CONSIDER 6.5

Marvin and Carole Atlas entered into a contract with R. J. Eden Construction Company on November 19, 1985, for the construction of a residence on real property owned by the Atlases. The original contract payment amount was $331,554.09. The contract required Eden to furnish labor, services, and materials for construction of the house.

On December 31, 1985, Eden, acting as general contractor, entered into a written contract with Sundance Mechanical & Utility Corporation for Sundance to perform subcontract work on the Atlas house. Between September 2, 1986, and October 13, 1986, Eden and Sundance performed work on the Atlas residence.

On October 13, 1986, before construction was completed, the Atlases terminated Eden's contract as general contractor and began personally supervising construction of the residence. Between September 19, 1986, and June 18, 1987, the Atlases paid various subcontractors and suppliers $43,412.20 for work and materials.

Sundance completed its work on October 30, 1986. At this time Eden owed Sundance $14,637.80 for the work performed. On October 31, 1986, Sundance filed a claim of lien

CONSIDER 6.5

(continued)

against the Atlases in the County Clerk's office in Bernalillo County. On February 17, 1987, the Atlases paid Sundance $3,000 to reduce the claim to $11,637.80.

On March 13, 1987, Sundance filed suit to foreclose on its lien. Sundance filed for a motion for summary judgment, which the trial court granted. The Atlases settled the payment with Sundance by paying $18,557.39, the amount awarded by the trial court. They then filed a motion to have the judgment set aside. The trial court then found that the Atlases had paid Eden in full at the time it was discharged and that they were entitled to the statutory protection of a residential homeowner and exemption from any subcontractors' liens. Sundance's lien was declared invalid and Sundance was ordered to refund the money that had been paid. Sundance appealed. Is the lien valid? Are the homeowners subject to the lien? *Sundance Mechanical & Utility Corporation v. Atlas*, 880 P.2d 861 (N.M. 1994)

Priority Among Mechanic's Liens

The statutes on the priority among mechanic's liens are widely varied but can be grouped as follows according to attachment times, as discussed earlier:

1. Statutes in which all liens are treated equally, as if all began work at the start of the project
2. Statutes in which liens are given priority according to the time the liens were perfected
3. Statutes in which liens are given priority according to the time individual work began
4. Statutes in which liens are given priority on the basis of the lienor's status

The common law rule, which more than half the states follow, is that all mechanics are on equal footing, as it were, and there is no priority among them. Under common law, all liens go back to the time when construction of the project first began. The reason for this rule under common law was to protect those furnishing labor and materials at the end of a project from always being left without payment or recourse. For example, if first workers or suppliers were given priority, the foundation workers would always be paid but the carpet layers would not.

This method of dating all liens back to the time construction was begun gives all lienors an equal opportunity for recovery. The criteria for determining when construction began varies from state to state, but at common law the construction began with "the first stroke of the ax or spade." Many construction lenders will have the property inspected before a mortgage is recorded, so that they can be assured that no work has begun and that they will have priority over all other lienors who have rights once construction begins.

If there are insufficient funds available to pay lienors on an equal footing, they are paid on a pro rata basis. Suppose that there is $15,000 left to be distributed, and the following amounts are due to lienors Akron, Barkley, and Clark:

Akron	=$15,000
Barkley	=$10,000
Clark	=$5,000
Total liens	=$30,000

Pro rata distribution is based on proportions. Since the total amount of liens is $30,000, the proportions for the parties are as follows:

Akron $= 15{,}000 \div 30{,}000$, or 1/2
Barkley $= 10{,}000 \div 30{,}000$, or 1/3
Clark $= 5{,}000 \div 30{,}000$, or 1/6

Therefore, the $15,000 would be distributed as follows:

Akron $= 1/2 \times 15{,}000 = \$7{,}500$
Barkley $= 1/3 \times 15{,}000 = \$5{,}000$
Clark $= 1/6 \times 15{,}000 = \$2{,}400$

In the second group of states, lienor priority is determined by the times each lienor's project or portion of the work began. Again, this gives lienors involved with the initial stages of construction a greater chance of payment.

In the remaining two groups of states, lienors are paid according to the time their liens are filed. Laborers may be given special priority over other lienors, or subcontractors may obtain relief after general contractors have been satisfied.

Mechanic's Liens and Fixture Filings

It is possible for an Article 9 UCC fixture filing to have priority over a mechanic's lien. When the security interest is a purchase money security interest (see Chapter 5) and the filing was completed before the item became a fixture or within 20 days after its annexation as a fixture, then the Article 9 interest takes priority, even over previously filed mortgages and (in this case) previously filed or attached mechanic's liens.

Mechanic's Liens and Homestead Exemption

Some states provide for property protection for residential dwellers, called a **homestead exemption**. This exemption provides protection from the attachment of mechanic's liens or at least from the forced sale of property for the satisfaction of a mechanic's lien. Likewise, in those states with dower protection, a mechanic's lien may not attach to a dower or curtesy interest (see Chapter 8), or cause the sale of that interest. The homestead exemption can also preclude foreclosure on a judicial lien.

Mechanic's Liens and Mortgages

As mentioned in the discussion of attachment, whether a mortgage (construction or permanent) will have priority over a mechanic's lien depends on the state's law on the time of attachment. If the priority of liens dates back to the time construction was commenced, then the mortgage must have been recorded prior to that time in order to enjoy priority. If the time of attachment is determined from the date of filing, then the mortgage must have been recorded prior to the time the lien was filed in order to enjoy priority. This priority also applies to mortgages in which the funds are to be advanced in a series of construction draws over a period of time.

Termination of Mechanic's Liens

Waiver or Release by Agreement

A mechanic's lien may be eliminated by agreement of the parties. The first type of agreement is called a **waiver agreement**, in which a party waives the right (either before, during, or after construction) to file a lien for work on materials furnished.

Web Exhibit 6.3 is a sample waiver agreement. Some states recognize waivers in original contracts, which makes the waiver automatic and enforceable, while other states require the execution of a separate waiver agreement. Waivers executed during and after construction are recognized as valid in all states.

Some states have certain statutory language required for lien waivers. For example, California requires the following language in bold type on the lien waiver:

Notice: This document waives rights unconditionally and states that you have been paid for giving up those rights. This document is enforceable against you if you sign it, even if you have not been paid. If you have not been paid, use a conditional release form. Cal. Civ. Code §3262 (3) and (4).

The purpose of this waiver language is to help subcontractors and contractors understand the distinction between a conditional or limited release and an unconditional release. An unconditional release means that once the signing party is issued a check, all liens are released. Under a conditional or limited release, only the materials and work furnished to the date of the lien are released. The signing party still has lien rights for future work and materials.

Another type of release is the subordination release, which entitles the signing party to a lien, but the lien is secondary to other interests in the property such as those of the construction lender and any other named secured parties.

Lien Alternatives

The complexity of liens and the problems that arise for property owners as well as the cost of enforcement have caused many states to try to resolve construction payment issues by using non-lien methods. A number of jurisdictions[4] now have some form of **stop notice statutes** or **trapping statutes**. These statutes were passed with the subcontractor and supplier interests in mind. Under these statutes, suppliers and subcontractors can give notice to those who are disbursing funds for the project to stop payment to the general contractor until their rights, interests, and payments have been reviewed.

These statutes create many additional issues. For example, what is the liability of the fund holder if payment is not stopped? Also, the result of a stop notice is often that no one is getting paid at all. These relatively new statutes have issues that require resolution through case law.

Constitutionality of Mechanic's Liens

Several state and federal courts have examined the constitutionality of mechanic's lien statutes. Most have found them to be constitutional so long as there is adequate notice to the landowner of the lien or potential lien. Recent challenges to lien statutes have been grounded in a due process theory that the landowner is being deprived of a land interest without the chance to be heard because there are automatic qualities to the attachment and enforcement of these liens. For example, a lien can attach without a court hearing; the landowner's property and its value are affected and no court will have heard the story from both sides. However, most courts faced with this due process issue have held that no significant property interest is

4. Alabama, Arizona, California, Colorado, District of Columbia, Florida, Indiana, Louisiana, Michigan, Mississippi, New Jersey, New Mexico, New York, North Carolina, Ohio, Oklahoma, Pennsylvania, Rhode Island, South Dakota, Texas, and Washington.

taken, because although the lien decreases the property value, there is a corresponding increase in value for the improvements made. The liens are also upheld because the owner is given a chance to be heard before the amount of the lien is paid or the property is subjected to foreclosure.

Figure 6.3 Issues in Mechanic's Lien Rights, Waivers, and Collections

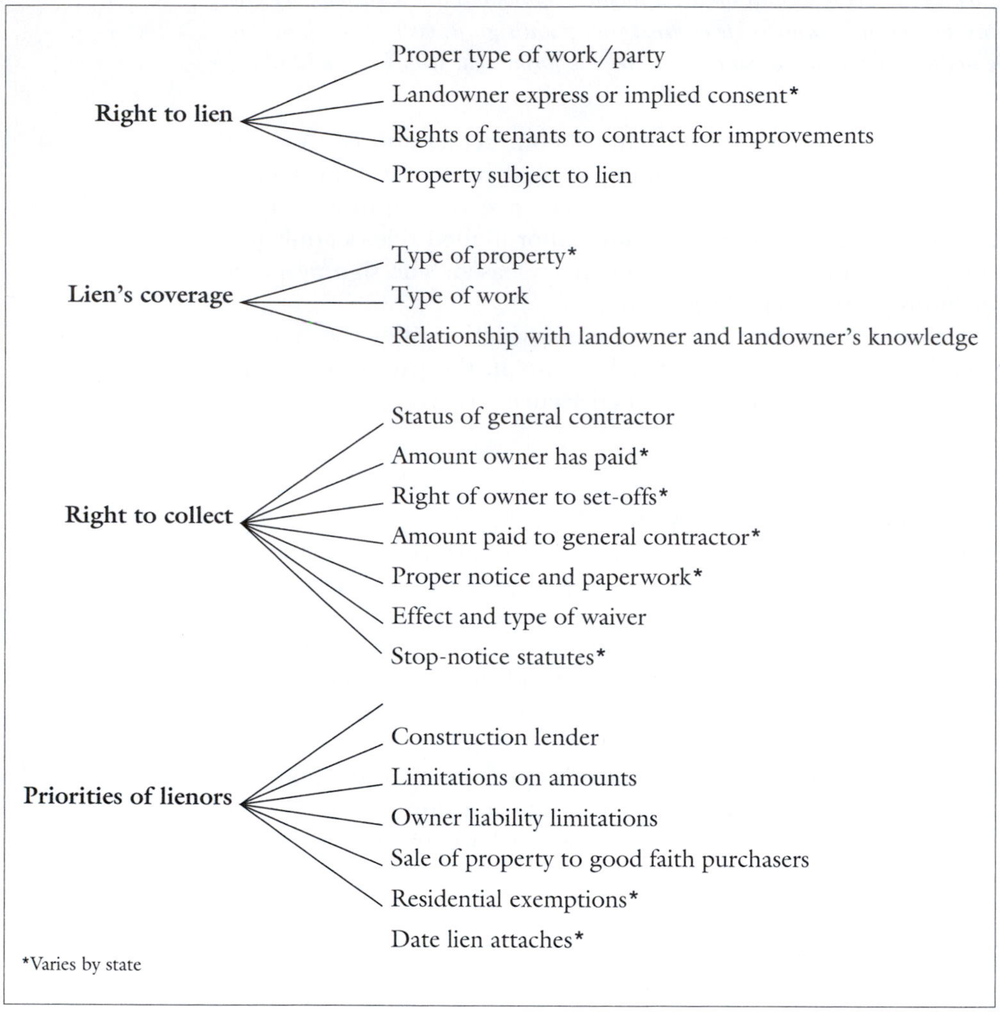

Right to lien
- Proper type of work/party
- Landowner express or implied consent*
- Rights of tenants to contract for improvements
- Property subject to lien

Lien's coverage
- Type of property*
- Type of work
- Relationship with landowner and landowner's knowledge

Right to collect
- Status of general contractor
- Amount owner has paid*
- Right of owner to set-offs*
- Amount paid to general contractor*
- Proper notice and paperwork*
- Effect and type of waiver
- Stop-notice statutes*

Priorities of lienors
- Construction lender
- Limitations on amounts
- Owner liability limitations
- Sale of property to good faith purchasers
- Residential exemptions*
- Date lien attaches*

*Varies by state

Cautions and Conclusions

The discussions in this chapter affect three parties: property owners, lienors, and lenders. Each group should take appropriate precautions to ensure that liens affect them in only a positive manner.

For property owners, the following questions should be answered:

1. Are licensed, reputable contractors being used?
2. If a general contractor is involved, what guarantees exist for payment of subcontractors and material suppliers? Is there adequate payment supervision?
3. Are there preliminary notice requirements for liens other than those by the general contractor?

For lienors, the following questions should be answered:

1. Who owns the property?
2. Is there a prior mortgage? A construction mortgage?
3. Is preliminary notice of a lien required? If so, how is it properly given?
4. Are there time limits for filing a lien?
5. How long is the lien effective?
6. How long may a lienor wait before foreclosing on a lien?
7. What priorities exist among lien holders?

For lenders, the following questions should be answered:

1. Who owns the property?
2. Is there a prior mortgage? Are there current liens?
3. Has construction or work already begun?
4. Are preliminary notices required?
5. Was the mortgage filed prior to the beginning of the work?
6. Who is the general contractor? What payment supervision is provided?

By assessing their positions and determining their rights and obligations at the outset, property owners, lienors, and lenders can often avoid the pitfalls of liens and enjoy the protections and benefits offered by them. Figure 6.3 provides a summary of the issues in mechanic's lien rights, waivers, and collections.

Key Terms

consent statutes, 117
contract statutes, 117
contractual lien, 114
equitable lien, 114
homestead exemption, 132
involuntary lien, 114
judicial lien, 114
lien, 113
lienee, 117
lienor, 117
materials liens, 114
mechanic's liens, 113
statutory lien, 113
stop notice statutes, 133
trapping statutes, 133
voluntary lien, 114
waiver agreement, 132

Chapter Problems

1. In 1977, Chagnon Lumber Company agreed to sell building materials on credit to Stone Mill Construction Corporation. Stone Mill had purchased land and intended to build houses on the property with Chagnon's and other suppliers' materials.

John and Ann Breiten purchased one of the Stone Mill homes. At closing of the sale, the Breitens were given an affidavit signed by an officer of Stone Mill that stated that the corporation had paid for all materials used in the house. The Breitens paid the purchase price and took title to the house.

Within 90 days after their last delivery of materials, but after the Breitens' closing, Chagnon filed in court for permission to attach a lien to the Breitens' property.

The Breitens objected to the lien on the grounds that they had no knowledge that any bills remained unpaid. Are the Breitens correct? Do they have any protection against the lien? *Chagnon Lumber Co., Inc. v. Stone Mill Construction Corp.*, 474 A.2d 588 (N.H. 1984)

2. In October 1981, Robert E. Hinkle leased to Raymond Arington the Dixie Plaza in Upshur County, West Virginia. The lease agreement contained the following clause:

Any improvements made to the leased premises shall, upon termination of this lease or the termination of any extension thereof, become the property of the lessor.

Arington hired Dunlap and others to do electrical and carpentry work to a building located on the premises. Arington went out of business shortly thereafter, owing Dunlap money for wages and materials.

On March 3, 1982, Dunlap filed a mechanic's lien against the property. That same day he filed a suit to enforce the lien against Arington and Hinkle. Can Arington and Hinkle be subject to a mechanic's lien and its foreclosure? *Dunlap v. Hinkle*, 317 S.E.2d 508 (W.Va. 1984)

3. Robert and Janet Barker had signed an installment contract to purchase a home from Roland and Gloria Barker and Eugene and Sandra Barker. Robert and Janet moved into the home in May 1975, and in December 1975, the home was partially destroyed by fire. Robert and Janet moved out of the home for five months so that repairs and restoration could be completed. Robert contracted with Tri-County Builders to repair the house. Robert paid $19,000 of the $20,000 contract price to Tri-County, but Tri-County did not complete the project and also failed to pay Brownsburg Lumber Company (the supplier of the lumber for the home repairs). Brownsburg filed a timely lien notice but notified only Robert and Janet of his supplier role. He did not notify the other Barkers who, under the terms of Robert and Janet's purchase contract, still held title to the house until the full purchase price was paid. Brownsburg filed suit to enforce its lien. Roland and Eugene claim that lien is invalid because they had no notice of Brownsburg's supplier role. Who is correct? Can Brownsburg collect on the lien? *Barker v. Brownsburg Lumber Co., Inc.*, 399 N.E.2d 426 (Ind. 1980) see also *Gravett v. Covenant Life Church*, 841 A.2d 342 (Md. App. 2004).

4. A is a carpenter and has completed the framing of eight homes for G, the general (prime) contractor. Prior to A's work, B had leveled and graded the property; C had put in the foundation; D had staked out the driveways and homes; and E had partially installed the plumbing fixtures. The tasks were completed on the following dates:

A, November 22, 2007
B, August 1, 2007
C, September 15, 2007
D, August 15, 2007
E, August 30, 2007

All parties properly served a preliminary notice. A construction mortgage was filed August 1, 2007. No one has been paid, and A, B, C, D, and E have all filed liens by December 1, 2007. Who has priority, the mortgage company or the lienors? What order of priority exists among the lienors? What happens if there is not enough money to pay the lienors?

5. Fifteen couples purchased homes in the Green Meadows subdivision, and they had all moved in by August 2007. Two days before Christmas, workmen's liens were filed against the homeowners' properties. Under state law, the filing of the liens dated back to the time construction began, May 2007. The homeowners wish to know their rights. What is the result? Would the result be different in your state?

6. Bank One filed a mortgage on May 31, 1989, on property owned by Sam and Grace Malz. The mortgage secured a $2,400,000 loan Bank One had made to the Malzes for purposes of constructing 10 six-unit buildings on the property. At the time the mortgage on the property was filed, Schalmo Builders, Inc., the contractor hired by the landowner to construct the buildings, had performed soil tests and staked out the locations for the buildings. The Malzes did not pay the builder and defaulted on the loan. The builder foreclosed on its lien and Bank One claimed priority. Who has first claim to the proceeds from the foreclosure sale of the property? *Schalmo Builders, Inc. v. Malz*, 629 N.W.2d 52 (Ohio App. 1993)

7. Allen Betke contracted with Thomas Hake Enterprises, Inc., to construct a home in Carpentersville, Illinois. As construction progressed, Betke was unable to pay, so he arranged for Charlotte Birck and her son, Jason Birck, to buy the house. Charlotte and Jason paid Betke $68,000, and Betke continued to supervise construction and hire subcontractors although Charlotte wrote checks for payment and channeled them through Betke for the contractors, subs, and suppliers.

The house was resold by Charlotte for $175,000 to the Coffmans. However, there were liens on the property from various parties not paid by Betke. The sale could not close until the lien issues were resolved. Charlotte claims she and Jason are not subject to the liens because they had no contracts with the lienors. Is she correct? *Thomas Hake Enterprises, Inc. v. Betke*, 703 N.E.2d 114 (Ill. App. 1998)

8. Morris was a general contractor that entered into a Master Work Agreement with Spire Communications to build the infrastructure for a fiber optic network around Atlanta, Georgia. Morris was responsible for directional boring, or digging trenches for the network to be placed underground. Spire eventually fell behind in payments and ultimately had many outstanding purchase orders unpaid. On November 27, 2001, Spire agreed to pay $2,167,366.05 to Morris as a "true-up" of all then-outstanding purchase orders. The settlement was evidenced by an e-mail from Mike Miller of Spire to D. L. Morris, Jr. ("Buddy Morris") of Morris Plumbing. In return, Morris agreed that it would continue to work on the network. However, the settlement payments were not made as quickly as Morris wanted and on December 11, 2001, Morris filed a mechanic's lien in the amount of $3.4 million in Fulton County, Georgia. The lien was filed in Fulton County, Georgia, but the work was done in several counties. The lien amount exceeded the amount the parties had agreed was owed. Morris did not file a commencement of work in relation to the lien. In your state, would Morris have a valid lien? *In re Spire Communications, Inc.* (Bank. Ct. D. Del, 2002) WL 1343463 (2002)

9. Edward and Elena Pucossi reside in Louisville, Kentucky, and purchased a lot on Nolin Lake in Edmonson County, Kentucky. They contracted with a builder to construct a lake house for them for a total contract price of $20,400. When the Pucossis had paid a total of $16,050 to the builder, the builder abandoned the project and could not be located. The lake house was never completed and was never occupied.

Bee Spring Lumber had furnished $8,292.68 in lumber and materials for the Pucossi project to the builder. Bee Spring Lumber had a lien against the property and brought suit to collect on that lien. The Pucossis claimed that they could not be held liable for more than the contract price because this was residential construction. The trial court held that the statutory exemption did not apply and held the Pucossis liable for the full amount ($8,292.68) owed Bee Spring Lumber. Is the trial court correct? *Bee Spring Lumber Co. v. Pucossi,* 943 S.W.2d 622 (Ky. 1997)

10. Are architects and engineers entitled to liens for the work they perform prior to construction? *Korsunsky Kank Erickson Architects, Inc. v. Walsh,* 370 N.W.2d 29 (Minn. 1985)

For research activities related to this chapter, go to our text companion website at www.thomsonedu.com/westbuslaw/jennings.

Describing Land Interests

CHAPTER 7

I hereby transfer 32 acres more or less in the southwest of lot no. 105 in the 13th District and 2nd section of my county.

Matthews v. Logan, 247 S.E.2d 865 (Ga. 1978)

[A deed must] comprehend the certainty of the land or tenements to be conveyed.

Sir Edward Coke

An error in a description of land can have multi-generational impact. And descriptions that do not meet legal requirements cannot pass valid title to property.

This chapter answers the following questions: What are the methods used to describe land? What precautions should be taken in drafting and checking land descriptions?

Methods of Describing Land Interests

Metes and Bounds

The metes and bounds method is a description technique that uses the boundary lines and marking points in a particular parcel as its basis for identification. **Metes** refers to distance, while **bounds** refers to the direction of the distance to be taken.

A **metes and bounds description** consists of a series of instructions that could be followed to walk out the boundary lines of the land parcel. A permanent beginning point can be natural (such as a stream or river) or artificial (such as a bridge). Monuments are frequently used as starting points for metes and bounds descriptions.

For example, a metes and bounds description of the shaded portion in Figure 7.1 would be as follows:

Figure 7.1 Sample Land Parcel for Metes and Bounds Description

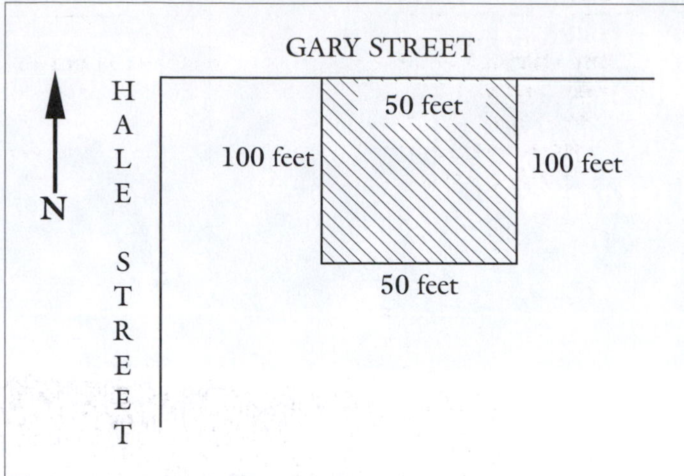

Beginning at a point on the south side of Gary Street, 200 feet east from the corner formed by the intersection of the south side of Gary Street and the east side of Hale Street, then proceeding south parallel to the east side of Hale Street 100 feet; then proceeding east parallel to the south side of Gary Street 50 feet; then proceeding north parallel to the east side of Hale Street 100 feet to the south side of Gary Street; and then proceeding west on the south side of Gary Street, 50 feet or to the beginning point.

Because of their dependency on starting points (which can be moved) and because of the potential for inaccurate measurement, metes and bounds descriptions can result in problems when land is transferred.

The following case deals with the adequacy of a metes and bounds description.

FOREMAN V. SHOLL

439 S.E.2d 169 (N.C. App. 1994), rehearing denied 456 S.E.2d 313 (N.C. 1995)

FACTS

Kenneth and Mary Foreman (Mr. and Mrs. Foreman, plaintiffs) spoke with Jeseppo Perrone in 1979 and indicated that they were interested in locating the heirs of "people who had bought property in Buncombe County, North Carolina, from the Mountain Retreat Association in 1907 or shortly afterwards" for the purpose of buying property from them.

In 1981, Mr. Perrone called Mr. Foreman and told him he had located the heirs and had a deed. Mr. Perrone offered to deed over, by quitclaim deed, title to the land. Mr. Perrone met Mr. Foreman on the sidewalk in front of the Radisson Hotel in Charlotte, North Carolina, on September 15, 1983. Mr. Foreman paid Mr. Perrone $2,400 and Mr. Perrone handed Mr. Foreman an envelope containing a quitclaim deed, which Mr. Foreman examined. The deed named "Kenneth J. Foreman, Jr., Trustee" and conveyed 59 tracts, 41 of which are described by reference to a 1906 drawing recorded in the Buncombe County Register of Deeds.

The drawing shows over 1,000 lots; distances are shown on some of the lots but there are no markers from which the distances can be measured. The bearings of the lines are not depicted. The radius or arc distance or chord length, chord bearing, and tangent distance of any arc are not shown. Nothing in the drawing refers to anything that can be located or identified with certainty.

In 1990, the Foremans, pursuant to a dispute with a number of landowners claiming title to the tracts (defendants), brought suit to quiet title to the land conveyed to them by Mr. Perrone. The trial court held that the description was insufficient and that the Foremans were not the title holders of the tracts. The Foremans appealed.

JUDICIAL OPINION

Greene, Judge. All conveyances purporting to be color of title, including deeds, must contain, as an essential element of the conveyance, "a description identifying the land." The description must be "either certain in itself or capable of being reduced to a certainty by a recurrence to something extrinsic to which the deed refers." It is the deed that must speak... [and] oral evidence must only interpret what has been said therein. In other words, a description, although indefinite, is sufficient if the court can, with the aid of extrinsic evidence which does not add to, enlarge, or in any way change the description, fit it to the property conveyed by the deed.

When it is apparent upon the face of the deed, itself, that there is uncertainty as to the land intended to be conveyed and the deed, itself, refers to nothing extrinsic by which such uncertainty can be resolved, the description is said to be patently ambiguous. A patent ambiguity is such an uncertainty appearing on the face of the instrument that the Court, reading the language in light of all the facts and circumstances *referred to in the instrument*, is unable to derive *therefrom* the intention of the parties as to what land was to be conveyed. Parol evidence may not be introduced to remove a patent ambiguity since to do so would not be a use of such evidence to fit the description to the land but a use of such evidence to create a description by adding to the words of the instrument.

Whether a description is patently ambiguous is a question of law. In this case, the deed upon which plaintiffs rely to establish color of title describes the property with reference to a drawing recorded in the Buncombe County Register of Deeds and known as the Drawing. Thus the Drawing becomes a part of the deed as if it were written therein. The question, therefore, is whether the Drawing provides a description having the same degree of certainty as [is] required of a description appearing only in the deed itself. The Drawing without question is not sufficient in itself to describe the land conveyed. The Drawing does not have any ascertainable monuments, does not indicate the size of the tracts of land shown, does not indicate any courses and very few distances, and has no ascertainable beginning points. The only issue is whether the description in the deed is capable of being reduced to certainty by use of something extrinsic to which the deed refers. We do not believe it is. The Drawing simply does not refer to anything extrinsic that would be of aid in identifying the property with certainty. The four surveyors, offered by plaintiffs, testified that they could, by reference solely to the Drawing, identify the property on the ground. This testimony, however, added to and enlarged the description given in the Drawing and was thus not competent.

Affirmed.

CASE QUESTIONS

1. What do you think about the circumstances surrounding the acquisition? List the circumstances in the parties' conduct and conveyance that seem different from the usual land transfers.
2. What were the problems with the Drawing?
3. Was the Drawing incorporated as part of the deed?
4. Was there a sufficient description? Do the Foremans hold title?
5. What was wrong with the testimony of the surveyors?

CONSIDER 7.1

A deed contains the following description:

> *Together with an easement for access purposes from State Highway 17 southerly over the existing driveway located on the back lot partitioned and conveyed to Marie Rotter and said easement to extend easterly over the N. 20 feet of the frontage lot partitioned and conveyed to Marie Rotter to the front lot above described of grantee.*

Is the description sufficient for legal purposes? *Kampinen v. Bierman*, 617 N.W.2d 908 (Wis. App. 2000)

Plat Map

The **plat map** is probably the most frequently used method for describing property in residential areas. This description method uses a map of a subdivision that is recorded at some state or local agency responsible for property records. Each plat map contains the size and

> ***Practical Tip***
>
> *Physical inspections help verify the accuracy or inaccuracy of descriptions. Compare physical boundaries with deed descriptions.*

shape of each lot, the numbers of blocks and lots, the names of all streets, indications of alleys and easements, and a list of covenants and restrictions. A sample plat description would be, "Lot 27 of Candlelight Estates IV, as per plat recorded in Book of Maps 30, page 80, in the Office of the County Recorder of Holim County, Utah."

The plat map itself must have certain minimal information to be valid. For example, county and town are critical information. If the deed description relies on an attached map, the map must be labeled with direction, street names, and lot numbers.

CONSIDER 7.2

A deed describes the property as "the property located at Municipal Address: ________, City Many, Parish Sabine, Louisiana, Legal description 4.87 acres on Hwy 6, see attached plat...." The plat map, which was attached, showed only the dimensions of the property and that it was located somewhere on Highway 6. The plat does not show landmarks or adjacent property owners. Is this description sufficient? *Wilson v. Head*, 707 So. 2d 127 (La. App. 1998)

ETHICAL ISSUE

Irene H. Jones owned 12.63 acres of land in the Seeley Swan valley. The land had various improvements, including a house constructed by Jones. Ownership of America approached Jones and requested that she convey two undeveloped acres from the 12-acre tract in exchange for Ownership's stock. There was no agreement specifying which two acres were to be conveyed.

A deed prepared by a friend, Vernon H. Peterson, on April 13, 1981, contained the following land description:

> *That portion of Lot numbered Seven (7) of Section Six (6) in Township Twenty (20) North of Range Sixteen (16) West of Montana Principal Meridian, Montana, lying West of Federal Aid Secondary 209 right-of-way and containing two acres more or less and further accurately described by plat on file with the party of the first part and the party of the second part. Party of the first part herein reserves all minerals under the above description.*

The deed did not specify which two undeveloped acres were to be conveyed, and no plat was ever filed with the Missoula County Clerk and Recorder. The Missoula County Clerk and Recorder erroneously treated the conveyance as a transfer of the full 12.63 acres. The Missoula County Treasurer changed the tax notice address and all notifications from that time were sent to Ownership.

In 1985, Missoula County transferred title to the property to Lee McDonald pursuant to a tax sale for Ownership's failure to pay property taxes. McDonald had notice of the two-acre limitation, but said nothing when the same deed description was used. Nonetheless, McDonald went to Ownership and asked for a quitclaim deed. Ownership did quitclaim any interest it had to McDonald in exchange for a $2,000 piece of property McDonald conveyed to Ownership.

Irene Jones, now married to Vernon Peterson, conveyed the remainder of the 12.63 acres to the Irene H. Peterson Limited Partnership.

The parties finally came face-to-face on the property, and McDonald filed suit to clear title. Who has title?

Did Irene Jones make a double gain here? Didn't she intend to convey the land and then just take it back? Are Ownership and McDonald owed anything? Does it make a difference that McDonald knew of the description problem and said nothing? *McDonald v. Jones*, 852 P.2d 588 (Mont. 1993)

Government Survey

History

Another method for describing a land interest is by the **United States government survey.** This survey was done in 1785 because there was such a vast section of land west of the original 13 colonies with so many conflicting claims of ownership. The purpose of the survey was to provide a uniform system for description based on dividing the vast lands into rectangular segments.

Principal Meridians and Baselines

The geographer for the United States who was assigned the survey task had to develop a system for the survey that would compensate for the Earth's curved surface.

The survey began with **prime** or **principal meridians** and **baselines.** These first guidelines serve as the solution for the curvature of the Earth's surface. The lines were positioned at uniform distances apart so that the curve would not affect the accuracy of the survey. There are 35 prime or principal meridian lines that run north to south, and 32 baselines that run east to west. The meridians are named according to their locations: Chickasaw, Michigan, San Bernardino, and Tallahassee are examples of principal meridians.

Guide Meridians and Parallels

Between each of the baselines and principal meridians, the surveyors placed correction lines to further compensate for the Earth's curved surface. **Guide meridians** were placed between principal meridians, and **parallels** were placed between baselines. These supplementary lines were placed every 24 miles. The result is that the surveyed land is divided into a **grid** of 24-mile squares.

Townships and Ranges

This grid of 24 miles is broken down even further with **township** lines placed every six miles between the parallels and **range** lines placed every six miles between the guide meridians.

Figure 7.2 (on next page) illustrates these divisions. In the figure, the six-mile squares (townships) are identified by their distances (in the number of squares) from the principal meridian. This distance is labeled as either east or west of the principal meridian. For example, in Figure 7.2 the upper right-hand square is one square west of the principal meridian, or R1W. However, because all squares adjacent to the meridian will have that same label, the townships are further identified according to their distance from the baseline. The upper right-hand square is the fourth square north of the baseline, or T4N.

Each six-mile square or township in Figure 7.2 is further broken down into 36 one-mile squares. Each one-mile square is called a **section.** Sections are numbered in a serpentine fashion starting at the upper right-hand corner and proceeding left (see Figure 7.3 on next page).

Each section is one-mile square or a total of 640 acres, and each section can be broken down into fractional portions to more precisely describe the land involved. These fractional portions are described according to directional locations. Figure 7.4 is an example of a section with fractional portions labeled. To start, each section can be divided into quarters. The upper right-hand corner is the northeast quarter, and the lower left-hand corner is the southwest quarter. In the same manner, each quarter can be broken into quarters and labeled.

Figure 7.2 Twenty-Four-Mile Grid of U.S. Government Survey

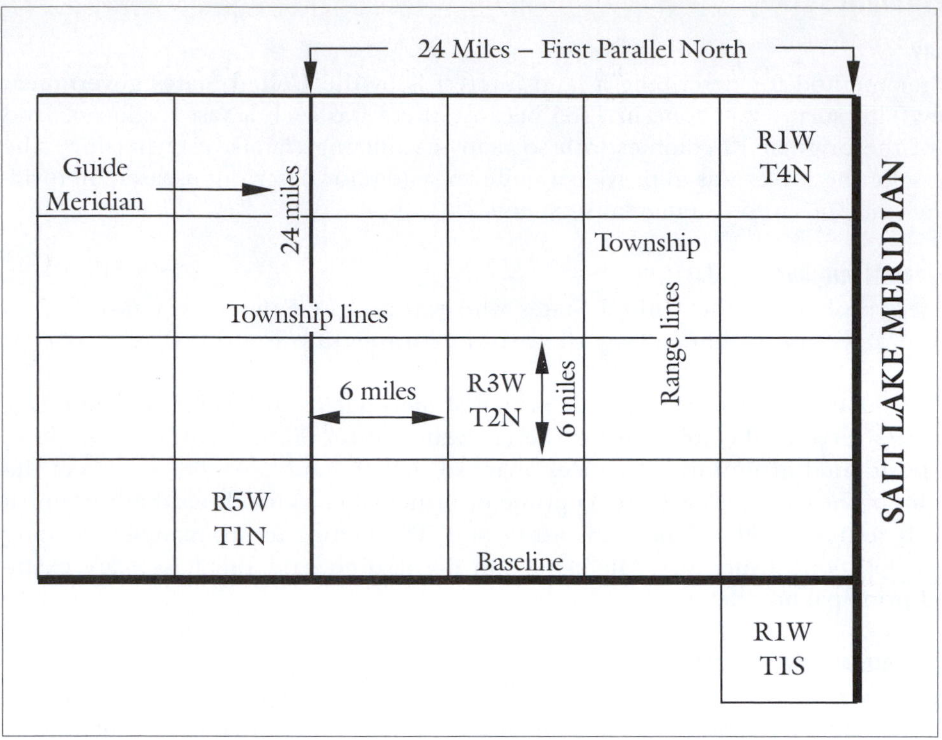

Figure 7.3 Sample Township

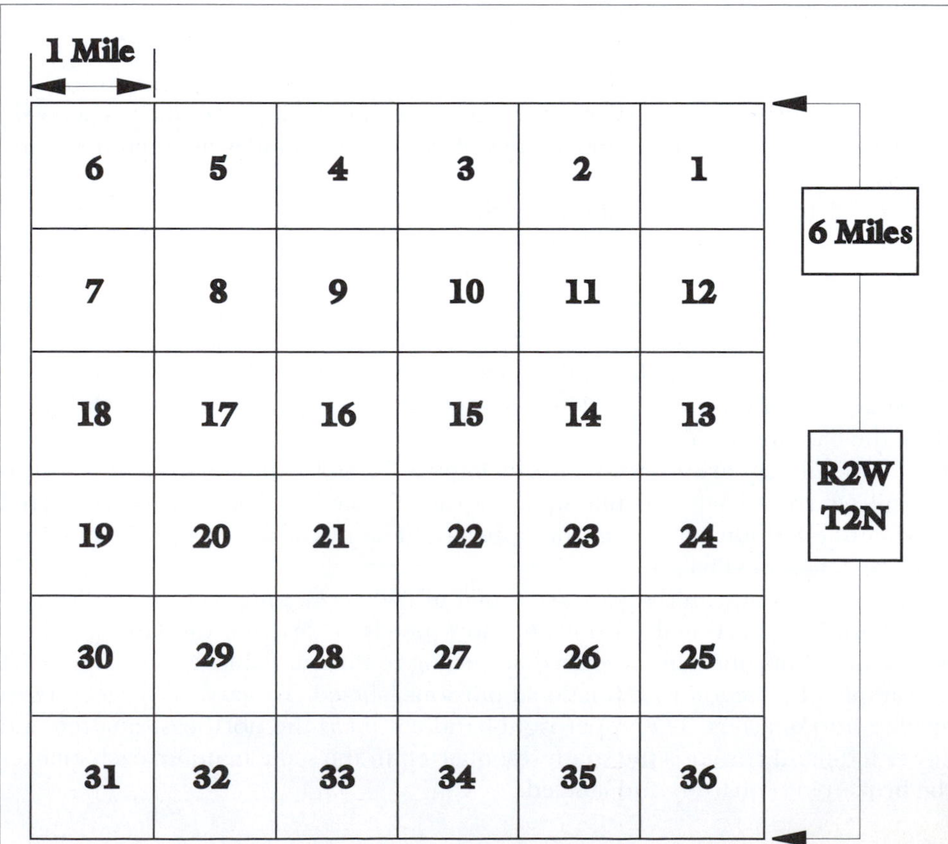

CONSIDER 7.3

Label each of the 21 blank squares in Figure 7.2 according to its location with respect to the Salt Lake Meridian and the baseline.

In Figure 7.4, finish filling in the descriptive names of the unmarked portions (A, B, C, D, and E) of each section.

Description and Size

Pulling together all divisions of the government survey, a sample land description would be "SE 1/4 of Section 12, Township 3 North, Range 2 East of the Salt Lake Meridian, Iron County, State of Utah." The addition of the county and state helps in determining which baseline is involved.

Because the government survey is uniform, it is possible to determine the size of a described parcel of land once the exact description is known. For example, if the land described is the NE 1/4 of a section, then the size of the parcel is 1/4 of 640 acres (the size of a section), or 160 acres. If the land described were the NE 1/4 of the NE 1/4, then the parcel would be 1/4 of 160, or 1/16 of 640, or 40 acres.

The following case deals with problems that result when the land is referenced to the government survey but still not adequately identified.

Figure 7.4 Sample Section

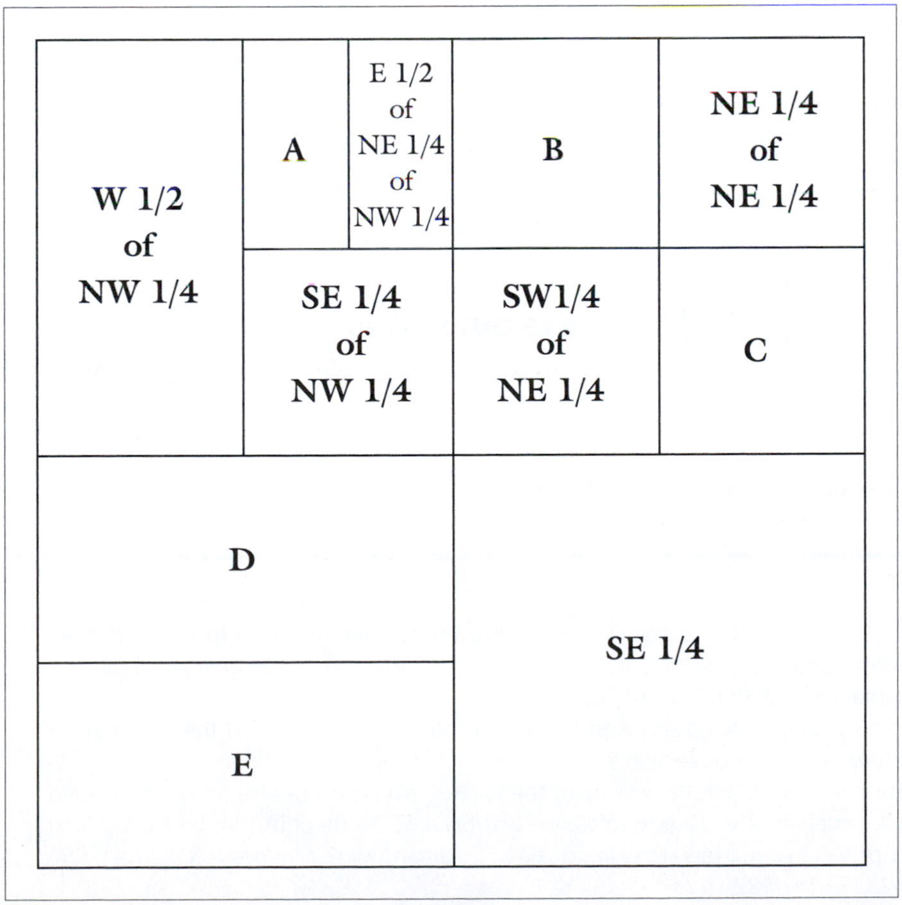

W 1/2 of NW 1/4
A
E 1/2 of NE 1/4 of NW 1/4
B
NE 1/4 of NE 1/4
SE 1/4 of NW 1/4
SW1/4 of NE 1/4
C
D
E
SE 1/4

TRIPLETT V. DAVID H. FULSTONE CO.

849 P.2d 334 (Nev. 1993)

FACTS

In 1907, 35 acres of land located in Lyon County and abutting the Walker River were owned by the Mason Townsite Company. In 1935, because of the failure of Mason Townsite to pay assessed taxes, the property was conveyed to Lyon County by tax deed. The property was described in the 1935 deed as follows:

Frac. W 1/2 of the SE 1/4; Frac. SW 1/4 of NE 1/4, Sec. 28, T. 13, N.R. 25 E., water only, for the total purchase price of $90.05.

In 1937, Lyon County conveyed title to Everett and Edna Triplett's predecessor in title. That deed contained the following description:

Fr. W 1/2; Fr. SE 1/4; Fr. SW 1/4; Fr. NE 1/4, Sec. 28, T. 13N., R. 25 E., M.D.B. & M., 60 acres, formerly assessed to Mason Townsite Company.

The word "of" was omitted twice in the first line of the 1937 deed and replaced with "Fr."

In 1939 and 1941, Lyon County, apparently not realizing it had conducted a tax sale of this land, held additional tax sales of the undisputed property. These deeds were to those who are the predecessors in title to the David H. Fulstone Company. The description in these deeds was almost identical to the 1935 deed conveyance to Lyon County. These deeds did not contain the omission of the words "of," as did the 1937 deed.

The Fulstones have paid taxes on the property and have used the property for pasturing, hunting, and woodcutting for 15 years. The Tripletts (plaintiffs/appellants) claimed title. The trial court held that the description in the deed for the Tripletts' predecessor in title was inadequate to transfer title to them and that the Fulstones had adversely possessed the property.

JUDICIAL OPINION

Per Curiam. The first issue presented is whether the 1937 tax deed to the Tripletts' predecessors in interest was a valid conveyance of the disputed property. This court has held that an inadequate legal description of the land in a deed may be remedied by extrinsic evidence.

The correct legal description of the 1937 deed can be easily ascertained by reference to the Lyon County assessment rolls. The 1937 tax deed specifically referenced land "formerly assessed to Mason Townsite Company," and because reference to the tax rolls establishes a description which encompasses the disputed property, we conclude that the holders of the first deed to the property have title to it. Because the deed to the Tripletts' predecessor in interest was validly conveyed and filed, it follows that this conveyance takes precedence over the subsequent conveyances to the Fulstones' predecessors in interest. Finally, although it appears that the 1937 deed should have provided sufficient warning for subsequent purchasers to be on notice of a previous conveyance, because this issue was not raised at the trial level or on appeal, we express no opinion with regard to this issue.

The Fulstones have occupied and claimed the property for at least 15 years. Because we believe the evidence adduced below affirmatively established adverse possession by clear and competent proof, we affirm the judgment of the district court.

Affirmed.

CASE QUESTIONS

1. Which of the descriptions was sufficient under the government survey method?
2. What was different about the 1937 deed from Lyon County?
3. Were the 1939 and 1941 deeds valid? Why?
4. Who ends up with title to the property and why?

CONSIDER 7.4

On December 13, 1945, Percy C. Harris conveyed by warranty deed to P. H. Coleman some land described as "twenty (20) acres out of the southwest quarter of Section 7 . . . containing one hundred sixty acres."

Harris actually owned the west half of the northeast quarter and the west half of the southeast quarter of Section 7.

Coleman claims that he now owns the full 160 acres because Harris was conveying the full parcel and the 20-acre reference was because he thought that he owned segments of various quarters. How much does Coleman own? *Mounce v. Coleman*, 650 P.2d 1233 (Ariz. 1982)

Adequacy of Descriptions

When properly followed, the three methods of description just discussed are legally sufficient descriptions. However, many other different methods of description are used, some of them legally sufficient and others only creating confusion and causing litigation. The most important criterion in evaluating the legal sufficiency of a description is whether the land is described in such a manner that only one possible tract can be identified from the description.

> ***Practical Tip***
>
> *The Triplett case shows how important it is for the description in a deed to be accurate, right down to the word "of." In this situation, 60 years of confusion resulted because of inadequate descriptions. Regardless of the means used for describing the property, make sure the description meets the legal tests for sufficiency under that method.*

Description by Popular Name

Often a popular name such as "my ranch, the Double T" is used as a description for conveying land. This type of description may or may not be sufficient, depending on whether the landowner holds one or several tracts of land.

In the following case, the issue of the legal sufficiency of a description by popular name is addressed.

WADSWORTH V. MOE

193 N.W.2d 645 (Wis. 1972)

FACTS

L. W. Anacker owned two parcels of land in the town of Stanton, Dunn County. One parcel consisted of a 130-acre farm with a dwelling and a number of other buildings. The other parcel was a one-acre piece of land with a remodeled schoolhouse in which Anacker lived. The schoolhouse was enclosed by a fence and was located 1/8 mile from the other buildings.

After his wife's death in 1962, Anacker became depressed and stopped farming. He lived in the schoolhouse near his daughter, Mabel Moe (appellant).

Anacker decided to sell the farm without the schoolhouse, and the farm was listed for $18,000. Wadsworth (respondent) learned of the listing, and he and Anacker went to a bank and had a real estate option document drawn up. (A standard legal form was used.)

In the blanks provided, the real estate was described as "The L. W. Anacker farm in the town of Stanton." Wadsworth paid Anacker $1,500 for the option and could buy the property by paying an additional $14,000 by January 4, 1968. The contract also provided:

Party of the second part may occupy the land and other buildings from this date forward. Party of the first part may occupy the dwelling and keep possession of the same up to November 1, 1968. Present insurance to be assigned to party of the second part free. The electric stove in the kitchen to remain for party of the second part.

On December 18, 1968, Wadsworth informed Anacker of his intention to exercise the option.

When Mabel Moe learned of the option she refused to let her father convey title, claiming that the legal description in the option was inadequate.

The trial court entered a judgment for Wadsworth and granted him specific performance. Mrs. Moe appealed.

JUDICIAL OPINION

Wilkie, Justice. An option to purchase real estate which does not conform to the statute of frauds is void and a nullity. To comply with the statute, the contract or memorandum must be reasonably definite as to the property conveyed. Here the trial court determined that the description of the real estate as "the L. W. Anacker farm in the town of Stanton" was not sufficiently definite but that the entire document, considered as a whole together with the stipulation of facts by the parties, did comply with the statute of frauds and was, therefore, valid.

The trial court was entirely correct in deciding that the bare description on the option did not comply with the statute of frauds. When an individual owns more than one parcel of land in the same general locality, the description in the document must be sufficiently definite so that a person might know to a reasonable certainty to which parcel or parcels the document relates.

The trial court did find, however, that although the option description was not sufficient, the whole option when taken together with information in the stipulation of facts was sufficient to meet the statute of frauds. All the terms of a contract may be considered when deciding whether the document conforms to the statute of frauds.

The land description in the option document was admittedly vague as to what constituted the "L. W. Anacker farm." The extent of the land is not shown. The other terms of the option contract do not clear up this ambiguity, neither does the stipulation. The extrinsic evidence shows either that both the farm and all of the schoolhouse land were conveyed; that only the schoolhouse land was conveyed; or that the farm, but not the schoolhouse was conveyed. In short, the contract, even when considered together with this extrinsic evidence, continues to be vague about the extent of the land sold.

In the end, the option contract here does not sufficiently show the extent of the land conveyed and for that reason must be held null and void.

Reversed and remanded for dismissal of the complaint.

CASE QUESTIONS

1. Describe the size, nature, amenities, and locations of Anacker's land.
2. Where did Anacker reside?
3. Did Anacker farm the land?
4. Who is Mabel Moe?
5. What type of agreement did Anacker and Wadsworth execute?
6. How was the land described?
7. Did Wadsworth exercise the option to purchase?
8. What were Mrs. Moe's objections to the agreement?
9. Who won at the trial court level?
10. Is the description legally sufficient?
11. Did the court examine extrinsic evidence?
12. What is the appellate court's decision?

Description by Street Number

Many times transfers of residential property have as a description just the street address of the property being conveyed. Although this type of description may be used as a supplement, and is sufficient for a contract, it should not be used in the deed or as the sole description. One reason is that street numbers and names may change. Also, the use of the street address alone does not describe the exact segment of land being transferred.

The following case deals with a description issue in which no real method of description was used and the issue of the deed's validity resulted.

REILAND V. PATRICK THOMAS PROPERTIES, INC.

213 S.W.3d 431 (Tex.App 2006)

FACTS

On February 18, 1977, Leonard Bythel Weis and Marjorie K. Weis granted to Beverly Faulkner a Right of First Refusal to acquire a 3.0152-acre tract of real property. The Right of First Refusal described the land as "3.0152 acres adjoining on the east side that certain 1.984 acre tract conveyed by Leonard Bythel Weis and wife, Marjorie K. Weis to Beverly Faulkner, Trustee on or about February 18, 1977," and it further identified the tract "as being 3.0152 acres in the William Walters Survey, Abstract 851, Harris County, Texas." The price is derived by the terms established in the Right of First Refusal:

Faulkner, Trustee, her successors or assigns shall have and does have the right of first refusal on the herein described real property on identical terms as those stated in an acceptable offer to Leonard Bythel Weis and wife, Marjorie K. Weis, but at ten cents (.10) per square foot less than such offer not to exceed a price of fifty cents (.50) per square foot.

The Right of First Refusal was declared valid for "so long as Leonard Bythel Weis, or wife, Marjorie K. Weis are alive plus twenty-one (21) years." Both Leonard and Marjorie Weis have died.

On November 15, 1999, Robert W. Mauk, Trustee of the Leonard B. Weis Trust, conveyed the tract to Reiland for $164,000. Five years later, Faulkner assigned the Right of First Refusal to PTP. Faulkner was unaware of the sale to Reiland and only became aware of the transaction when a real estate broker later informed her that Reiland was in the process of selling the property to someone else. Faulkner then informed PTP, and, upon further investigation, PTP discovered that the property was conveyed to Reiland in 1999. PTP sued Reiland and sought judgment to enforce its Right of First Refusal and claimed to be "ready, willing, and able to comply" with its terms to purchase the land, at the maximum price under the Right of First Refusal of $66,211.20. The market price of the property at the time of the suit was assessed at $203,229.18.

John Montgomery, PTP's director of operations, testified that PTP would have exercised its Right of First Refusal had it been notified of the earlier sale to Reiland, and it was "ready, willing and able to purchase the 3.0 Acre Tract pursuant to the terms stated in the Right of First Refusal." Montgomery had a document reflecting the survey of the property describing the metes and bounds. The survey was conducted in 1999, more than 22 years *after* the Right of First Refusal was created.

Reiland argued that the Right of First Refusal was void because the description is legally inadequate. In response, PTP submitted an affidavit from Greg Schmidt, a registered professional surveyor. In his affidavit, Schmidt testified that

I was able to locate the property, in part, because the Right of First Refusal refers to a deed which involved the same parties. I have reviewed the Harris County Real Property Records and there is only one other tract of real property which was owned by Leonard Bythel Weis and Marjorie K. Weis which was conveyed to Beverly Faulkner, Trustee. A copy of this deed is attached as Exhibit C. Therefore, the property which is described in the Right of First Refusal is adjacent to the property which was conveyed in the deed.

I have also reviewed another deed in which Robert W. Mauk, Trustee, conveyed the same property to Michael Reiland, Sr. A copy of this deed is attached as Exhibit D. This deed describes the real property by the use of a metes and bounds description. The real property which is described in the deed from Mauk to Reiland is the same property which is described in the Right of First Refusal which is attached as Exhibit B.

The trial court granted partial summary judgment in favor of PTP and denied Reiland's motion, holding that the legal description in the Right of First Refusal was adequate as a matter of law and therefore the Right of First Refusal was a valid and enforceable conveyance of real property. Reiland appealed.

JUDICIAL OPINION

Hanks, Jr., Justice. In point of error one, Reiland contends that the alleged Right of First Refusal from the Weises to Faulkner is void as a matter of law due to the fact that the legal description of the property conveyed in the document is legally inadequate.

On February 18, 1977, more than 20 years before Reiland's purchase, the Weises created a Right of First Refusal in which they granted to Beverly Faulkner, Trustee, her successors or assigns the right of first refusal to purchase the property identified as being 3.0152 acres adjoining on the east side that certain 1.984 acre tract conveyed by Leonard Bythel Weis and wife, Marjorie K. Weis to Beverly Faulkner, Trustee on or about February 18, 1977. The tract is further identified as being 3.0152 acres in the William Walters Survey, Abstract 851, Harris County, Texas.

There was no metes and bounds description of the 3.0152-acre tract attached to the Right of First Refusal.

In his motion for summary judgment, Reiland argued that the Right of First Refusal was deficient as a matter of law because "(1) there is nothing in the description that would allow an individual to identify the three-acre tract with reasonable certainty, and (2) the document wholly fails to define the size, shape or boundaries of the land to which it relates." We agree.

The well-settled rule to test the sufficiency of a description in a deed is that "the writing must furnish within itself or by reference to some other existing writing, the means or data by which the land to be conveyed may be identified with reasonable certainty." *Morrow v. Shotwell,* 477 S.W.2d 538, 539 (Tex.1972). In *Morrow,* the court examined a property description in a contract of sale. A description that identified property by tract, survey, and county was held to be an insufficient description because it did not refer to any other existing writing and because there were no means or data to tell a surveyor on what course and for what distances he will run.

The statute of conveyances and the statute of frauds require *[sic]* that conveyances and contracts of sale of real property be in writing and signed by the conveyor or party to be charged. In order for a conveyance or contract of sale to meet the requirements of the statute of frauds, the property description must furnish within itself or by reference to another *existing* writing the means or data to identify the particular land with reasonable certainty. The purpose of a description in a written conveyance is not to identify the land, but to afford a means of identification. The legal description in the conveyance must not only furnish enough information to locate the general area as in identifying it by tract survey and county, it also needs to contain information regarding the size, shape, and boundaries. If enough appears in the description so that a person familiar with the area can locate the premises with reasonable certainty, it is sufficient to satisfy the statute of frauds. Even when "the record leaves little doubt that the parties knew and understood what property was intended to be conveyed,... the knowledge and intent of the parties will not give validity to the contract and neither will a plat made from extrinsic evidence."

If a conveyance of an interest in real property does not sufficiently describe the land to be conveyed, it is void under the statute of frauds. Such a contract, deed, or conveyance will not support an action for specific performance or a suit for damages for a breach of contract.

Here, there is nothing "indicating the shape of the block or the courses and lengths of its border lines or those of the [3.0152] acres." To locate the 3.0152 acres with definiteness, it is necessary to first fix the location of the piece of land of which it is a part, and then locate the 3.0152 acres by boundaries, or metes and bounds of some character "adjoining on the east side that certain 1.984 tract." [w]e hold that, "under the established law of this state, the descriptive language used in this lease is vitally lacking in definiteness."

PTP attached a copy of the metes and bounds created when the property was surveyed in 1999. This evidence, however, is "inadmissible to aid the description in the written contract, because there is no reference to such [survey] in the contract which must be looked to in determining whether the statute of frauds is satisfied."

Further, in *Morrow,* after a search of the abstract records and on directions given by an attorney, a surveyor was able to locate the property on the ground and to make a plat showing its location and boundaries that was introduced into evidence. Similarly here, a surveyor did locate "the real property" by, "in part," reviewing the Harris County Real Property Records. The rule for the admissibility of extrinsic evidence to aid in descriptions for the conveyance of land, however, is that a "resort to extrinsic evidence... is not for the purpose of supplying the location or description of land, but only for the purpose of identifying it with reasonable certainty from the data *in the memorandum.*" There were no documents attached to or referenced by the Right of First Refusal that indicate the shape and boundaries of the 3.0152-acre tract.

We hold that the Right of First Refusal contains an inadequate land description and thus violates the statute of frauds. Accordingly, we sustain point of error one.

We reverse the trial court's judgment and render judgment in favor of Reiland quieting title and removing the cloud on Reiland's property.

Reversed.

CASE QUESTIONS

1. Describe what happened with the two conveyances.
2. What are the problems with the description?
3. If the description is not valid, what happens to the deed? Who has title to the property?

General Conveyances

Sometimes a legal description such as "all my real estate" is used. Such a description is inadequate because it does not provide the location, extent, and boundaries of the interest being conveyed.

Impermanent Descriptions

Often metes and bounds descriptions use a starting point that is impermanent in its character, such as "pile of rocks" or "fences." These types of descriptions create problems because there can be movement or even destruction of the beginning point, thus rendering the description invalid.

Interpretation of Descriptions

In determining the adequacy or meaning of a description, courts follow certain rules that are uniformly applied:

Rule 1 *The language of the description is construed against the grantor (seller) of the property and in favor of the grantee. This rule is based on the idea that the grantor drafted the deed and had the opportunity to check it for accuracy.*

Rule 2 *If there are two descriptions, one ambiguous and one nonambiguous, the nonambiguous description prevails so that a legally sufficient description is found.*

Rule 3 *Ambiguities may be clarified by reference to other portions of the document and to oral testimony. Outside evidence is permissible for clarification only if there is a latent as opposed to a patent ambiguity in the deed. A latent ambiguity is one that is not apparent to the parties when the deed is written. Examples of latent ambiguities are typing errors or the simple carryover of an erroneous legal description of which the parties are unaware. A patent ambiguity (as in the* Wadsworth *case) can be clarified only by reference to other parts of the deed or document and not by reference to extrinsic evidence.*

The following case brings together all of the problems that can arise with a description combining metes and bounds with plat map description, and ambiguities in both creating interpretation issues.

WITHINGTON V. DERRICK

572 A.2d 912 (Vt. 1990)

FACTS

James and Madeline Withington (plaintiffs) and Asa and Vivian Derrick (defendants) dispute the ownership of a piece of land located at the confluence of the parties' properties (as pictured on page 152). On October 10, 1959, in two separate transactions, two brothers, as common grantors, deeded the two pieces of property located in the Village of Wilder, Town of Hartford, Vermont, to the Withingtons and the Derricks. The Derricks' deed provides as follows:

Being Lot #36 as delineated on Hazen's Survey and Plan of Lots in the Village of Wilder, so-called, and which lot is bounded on the East by Lot #29, now owned by the grantees herein; on the north by Lot #35, now owned by the Benedicts; on the west by land now of Hoff; and on the south by the street known as Chandler Terrace.

The phrase in the Derricks' deed describing the western boundary of the property is incorrect: there was no adjacent landowner by the name of Hoff. At the time of the conveyance, people named Haff did own several lots about a block away. Even assuming that the drafter of the instrument was referring to Haff, the Haff property could not possibly have been the western boundary of lot 36. The Withingtons' deed includes the following description:

Also an irregular parcel of land described as follows: Beginning at a point marking the southeasterly corner of the Haff premises, and thence proceeding northerly along said Haff premises to the corner of Fern Street; thence easterly along Fern Street to the Benedict premises and St. John premises and the boundary of the right of way to said premises to Lot #36; thence southerly along the westerly boundary of Lot #36 to Chandler Terrace; thence westerly along the southerly boundary of the premises herein conveyed to the corner of Lot #44 which is the point of beginning.

This description has two problems. First, the Benedict and St. John deeds do not mention any right-of-way leading to or adjoining their land; however, it is uncontested that a narrow strip of land on the southerly end of the St. John premises separately existed as a right-of-way. Second, the last part of the description does not close the deeded property. Further, Fern Street and Union Street were never accepted as municipal roadways.

The trial court held that the grantors had intended to deed to the defendants the portion of the never-accepted Union Street directly west of lot 36 but that the drawer of defendants' deed has mistaken lot 44 for lot 37 and accordingly named the Hoff (meant to be Haff) property as the western boundary of lot 36. The trial court awarded title to the piece of property at issue to the Derricks, and the Withingtons appealed.

JUDICIAL OPINION

Gibson, Justice. Essentially, only two facts vaguely support the trial court's theory. First, since Union Street was not really a street at the time of the deed, one might infer that the grantors intended lot #36 to include the parcel of land adjoining lot #36 inaccurately marked as a street. Nonetheless, in addition to the fact that this is purely conjecture, we note that the same grantors had granted land in prior deeds (the Benedict and St. John properties) which adjoined, but did not include, Union Street. Thus, there is no reason to assume that Union Street would normally be considered part of one of its adjoining lots simply because it had never been accepted as a street.

Second, the trial court's theory, though attenuated, does provide an explanation of why the description in plaintiffs' deed does not close their property. Nevertheless, since the boundary of the "closing" segment of plaintiffs' land is not in dispute, the fact that plaintiffs' deed description does not close is of little consequence. Where there are several manifest errors and the proffered interpretation hinges on nothing more than speculation, that interpretation cannot prevail without first applying the established rules of construction to determine the intent of the parties.

"In construing a deed, we initially look at the instrument itself, which is deemed to declare the understanding and intent of the parties." Thus, it is the intention expressed by the words of the deed, not the unexpressed intention that the parties may have had, which prevails. Generally, a particular description will govern over a general description, but less significant aspects of a description will "[become] the controlling influence in determining the identity of premises where other parts of [the] description are not sufficiently certain," or are

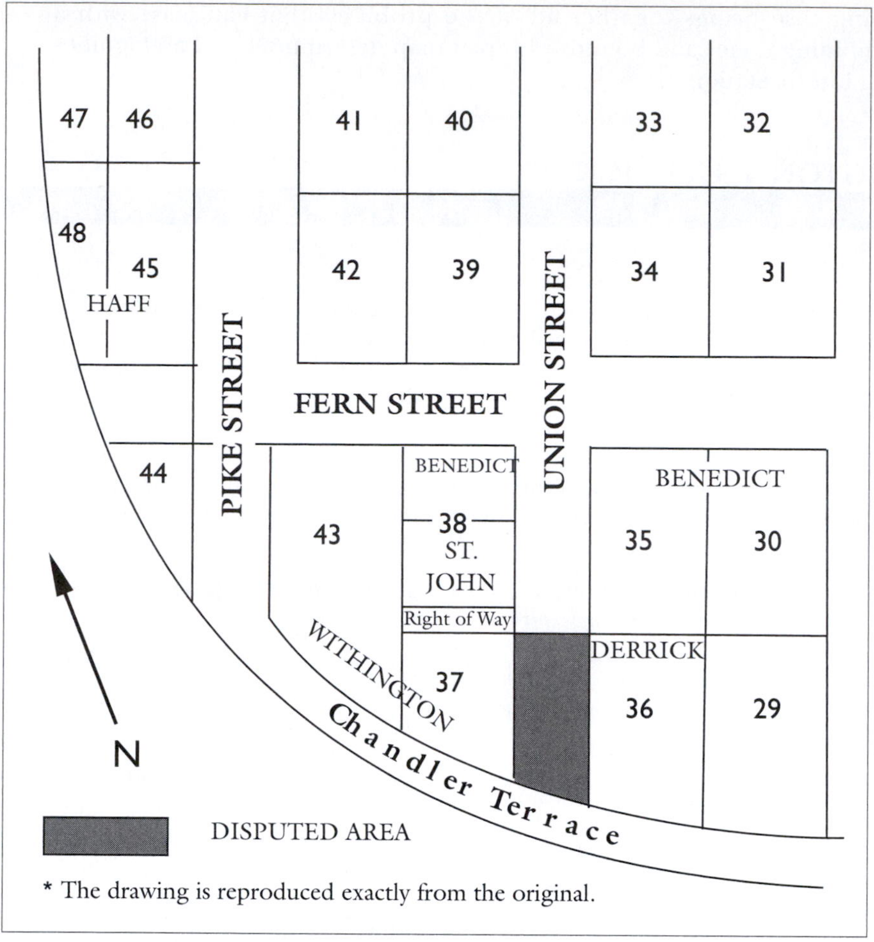

* The drawing is reproduced exactly from the original.

nonexistent. For instance, in *Spiller v. Scribner* 36 Vt. 365 (1863), where the deed described land as "being lots No. 22 and 23" and as "our home farm," this Court held that the disputed land, which was inside the home farm but outside lots No. 22 and 23, was not part of the deeded land because "land conveyed... by clear and well defined metes and bounds... shall prevail... over any general words of description that may have been used in the deed." The Court pointed out that an additional, more particular description could have overridden the reference to specific lot numbers, but that *the description of a lot by reference to its [number] is a description in its legal effect according to the lines of such lot as surveyed and established in the original division of town, and is just as definite, although not so particular, as it would be if the lines were given, and should receive the same construction and have the same legal effect, in one case as the other, and such description in this case must be the controlling description, and determine the extent of the land conveyed.*

In the instant case, the descriptions referring to the land of adjoining property owners are particular descriptions. Further, "[w]here an ambiguity or error exists with regard to the description in a deed, an attached map or survey relating to the ambiguity or error will control."

When there is a conflict between a specific description by metes and bounds and a lot as shown upon a map by which a tract of land is conveyed, the latter provision will control. When a deed the lot intended to be conveyed is properly designated by its number on a recorded plot, but the deed, in attempting to give a more particular description, incorrectly or inaccurately sets forth the dimensions of the same, such designation by lot number will prevail over such other description in the deed.

In the instant case, defendants' deed unambiguously describes their property as "[b]eing Lot 36 as delineated on Hazen's survey and Plan of Lots in the Village of Wilder," and plaintiffs' deed unambiguously describes the disputed property line as continuing "southerly along the westerly boundary of Lot #36." In contrast, the more detailed description of the disputed boundary line in defendants' deed is incorrect and ambiguous. Consequently, the unambiguous description by lot number should prevail over the erroneous reference to an adjoining property owner. The trial court's theory, created in an attempt to reconcile the ambiguities and inaccuracies in the deeds' description, is not supported by any evidence in the record and cannot supplant the plain meaning of the lot descriptions in the deeds.

Reversed and remanded.

CASE QUESTIONS

1. What deed language created the confusion about ownership?
2. To whom does the trial court award title and why? What does the appellate court do?
3. In reviewing the deeds and the ambiguities, what rules does the appellate court follow?
4. What is the significance of the map?
5. What is the significance of "Haff" vs. "Hoff"?

Cautions and Conclusions

In preparing or proofreading a land description, too much caution is never an issue. A sale of land may have been negotiated to the final detail, but if the deed description is inaccurate, litigation, liability, and other difficulties will result. The following questions should help avoid the difficulties of mistakes, inadequacies, or inaccuracies:

1. Is a legal description used? Is there more than a street address or common description?
2. If a metes and bounds description is used, is a better description available? If not, are permanent beginning points used?
3. If a government survey description is used, are all portions present? Is the prime meridian included?
4. If a plat map is used, is the location of the plat map in the land records accurately identified?
5. If two or more parcels are being conveyed, are they described separately? Are the descriptions distinct and run together?
6. Have two or more persons proofread the description?

The boxed excerpt from an article by Lewis Kanner lists the important factors to examine when a survey of property is done.

What You Should Know About Surveys

A private survey is more than a sketch of the boundaries of a parcel. A survey is apt to contain, in addition to the legal description of a parcel, information on the status of title to the parcel not disclosed by the usual title examination or title commitment and information on the ability to develop the property. A survey may disclose any of the following:

- Acreage content. The acreage content is important not only for purposes of determining the price of the property but is also important regarding information that must be furnished to many governmental agencies in any permitting process.
- Encroachments on the property. An examination may reveal that encroachments have ripened into established claims to a portion of the property or may indicate potential litigation that may delay development.
- Encroachments on adjoining property. An investigation may indicate that these encroachments may be a cause for potential litigation with the adjoining property owner.
- Public and private easements not of record. These easements may represent potential matters for litigation or may interfere with the plan of development.
- Undedicated roads. A claim of access across the client's property may be evidenced by an undedicated road. This claim may represent potential litigation or interference in the plan of development.
- Legal access. The survey may indicate that the property in question does not have legal access. If the survey does not reflect a dedicated road adjoining the property, an examination may determine that the property does not have legal access. Your client may therefore have to sue to obtain legal access.
- Gaps between parcels believed to be contiguous. The gaps may prevent your client from developing the parcels as a single parcel.
- The location of utility easements. These easements may interfere with the plan of development and may require relocation to proceed with development.
- The high water line of any water boundary. The high water line may indicate limits of ownership regardless of the legal description.
- Variations in the legal description of the property. Variations must be reconciled with previously utilized descriptions and may represent potential litigation.
- Fences upon the property. Fences may be evidence of adverse claims or boundary lines by agreement or acquiescence contrary to the title information.
- Agricultural use which may be evidence of possession inconsistent with record ownership.

- Historical or archeological sites which, in some areas, may not be disturbed and therefore will interfere with any plan of development.
- Existence of wetlands that may indicate the property cannot be developed.
- Existence of filled lands which may not physically be able to support the planned improvements. Further, an investigation may indicate that the requisite governmental permits to fill the property were not obtained, representing a potential matter for litigation.

Key Terms

baselines, 143
bounds, 139
grid, 143
guide meridians, 143
metes, 139
metes and bounds description, 139
parallels, 143
plat map, 141
prime meridians, 143
principal meridians, 143
range, 143
section, 143
township, 143
United States government survey, 143

Chapter Problems

1. Diagram each level of the following descriptions:
   a. SW 1/4 of the SW 1/4 of Section 27, T2N, R3E of the Gila Salt River Meridian.
   b. N 1/2 of the E 1/2 of the E 1/2 of the SW 1/4 of Section 12. How many acres of land does this describe?
   c. NE 1/4 of the NW 1/4 of Section 14, T3N, R4W, Gila Salt River Meridian.

2. Using metes and bounds, describe the property at the junction of Ash and Elm Streets as shown below. What happens if a metes and bounds description is not closed? *Undernehr v. Sandlin*, 827 S.W.2d 164 (Ark. App. 1992)

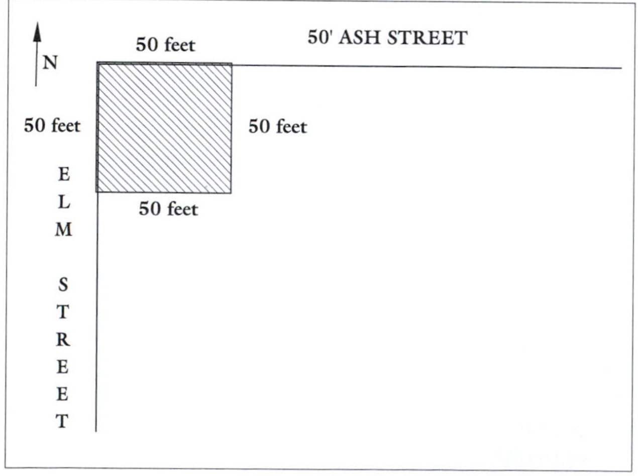

3. Corner Cupboard Craft Shop acquired title to real property from James and Shirley Smith. The legal description in the deed contains a metes and bounds description that contains several distance calls followed by the phrase "more or less" and general directions such as "northwesterly." A plat map is attached to the deed with the metes and bounds description. Is the legal description sufficient to pass title? *Lawyers Title Insurance Corp. v. Nash*, 396 S.E.2d 284 (Ga. 1990)

4. Determine and discuss the legal sufficiency of each of the following descriptions. In the applicable instances, determine if there is a patent or a latent ambiguity.
   a. "The real estate owned by the sellers and located in the town of Oak Grove, now known as the 'Dobie Inn,' and used in the business of sellers."
   b. "My house at Little Chicago."
   c. A metes and bounds description beginning with, "to an iron pipe and a line sighted with a gate marker."
   d. "All my property in Monroe County, Indiana." See *Partnership Props. Co. v. Sun Oil Co.*, 552 So.2d 246 (Fla. App. 1989).
   e. "All my real estate wherever situated."
   f. "My farm, Willamena Estates."

g. "Two acres in SE corner of SE 1/4 of SW 1/4 of Section 12."

5. The San Antonio Independent School District entered into a lease agreement with South Texas Sports, Inc., for the lease of Alamo Stadium and other tracts of land nearby. The validity of the lease was challenged by several homeowners associations, including River Road. The homeowners were challenging the lease on administrative grounds, potential nuisance effect, and the insufficiency of the lease agreement itself. The description in the lease was as follows:

that certain tract of land located in Bexar County, Texas, together with all improvements located thereon, such land and improvements being more particularly described and shown on the plot plan attached hereto as Exhibit 'A'.

Exhibit A is a map on which eight tracts of land are marked. Alamo Stadium is not shown as one of the tracts being leased. Is the description along with Exhibit A sufficient for a valid lease? *River Road Association v. South Texas Sports*, 720 S.W.2d 551 (Tex. 1986)

6. Joe Tanner, Commissioner of the Department of Natural Resources, brought suit against employees of the Department of Natural Resources (DNR), who were responsible for the management of Sapelo Island. Tanner brought suit because the employees prevented Tanner and others from landing their planes on two lots on Sapelo Island. The DNR employees claimed the state owned the lots (lot 7 and lot 4) and Tanner's claim to any interest or title in the lots was void. DNR claimed that the description in the deed to Tanner was insufficient to pass title. The legal description of lot 4 in the plaintiffs' deed is as follows:

All of that certain lot, tract or parcel of land situate, lying and being in the 1312 District, G.M., McIntosh County, Georgia, at Raccoon Bluff on Sapelo Island, containing Twenty-One (21) Acres, more or less and being Lot (4) Four of the Raccoon Bluff Subdivision of William Hillary. Said property being bounded Northerly by Lot 3, Easterly by Blackbeard Island River; Southerly by Lot 5; and Westerly by the out line [sic] of Raccoon Bluff Tract. This being that same property conveyed to Ben Brown by deed and plat from William Hillary dated July, 1882 and recorded in Deed Book 'U' at Page 298 and 299, to which said deed and plat reference is hereby made for all intents and purposes.

What type of description is this? Do you think it is sufficient to pass title to the property? *Brasher v. Tanner*, 353 S.E.2d 478 (Ga. 1987)

7. Diagram the following: Commencing at a point on the south side of Hale Street, 200 feet from the intersection of the south side of Hale Street and the east side of Gary Street; from thence south 10 feet parallel to the easterly side of Gary Street; from thence east 5 feet parallel to the southerly side of Hale Street; from thence north 10 feet parallel to the easterly side of Gary Street; from thence 5 feet west on the southerly side of Hale Street to the beginning point.

8. The following description appears in a deed: "Fairbrother farm recorded at West Fairlee Land Records Book 16, page 107." Is the description sufficient?

9. Since 1958, Ray and Barbara Mensen have leased on a month-to-month basis a house owned by Helen and Clarence Haines. (Clarence died in 1984.) In 1963, discussions began between the two couples about the possibility of a purchase of the home. The Haineses had hoped the Mensens would look after them in their old age, since the Haineses had no known relatives.

Several drafts of the deed were produced, along with discussions that the property was being deeded to the Mensens in exchange for care and assistance for the Haineses. The deed giving the Mensens "the farm" was transferred to them sometime in December 1980 or January 1981 and recorded on January 13, 1981. The deed also included the following language:

Part of the Northeast Quarter of the Northeast Quarter of Section 9 Township 16 North Range 13 East all in Douglas County Nebraska as recorded in the Douglas County Register of Deeds office.

The Mensens did not deliver the promised care, and Helen Haines brought suit to have the deed declared void for failure of consideration and inadequacy of the description. Is the description adequate? *Haines v. Mensen*, 446 N.W.2d 716 (Neb. 1989)

10. The Twain Harte Homeowners Association brought suit to quiet title in a recreational easement they alleged they held in the land of Earl Patterson. The easement provides for "recreational use and enjoyment for the benefit of the Twain Harte Tract." Patterson says the description of the dominant estate is inadequate because he remains uncertain as to who actually holds the easement. He maintains the grant of the easement is void because of an invalid description. The Association maintains that the description is sufficient to indicate they as homeowners are the owners and beneficiaries. Who is correct? *Twain Harte Homeowners Association v. Patterson*, 239 Cal. Rptr. 316 (1987)

For research activities related to this chapter, go to our text companion website at www.thomsonedu.com/westbuslaw/jennings.

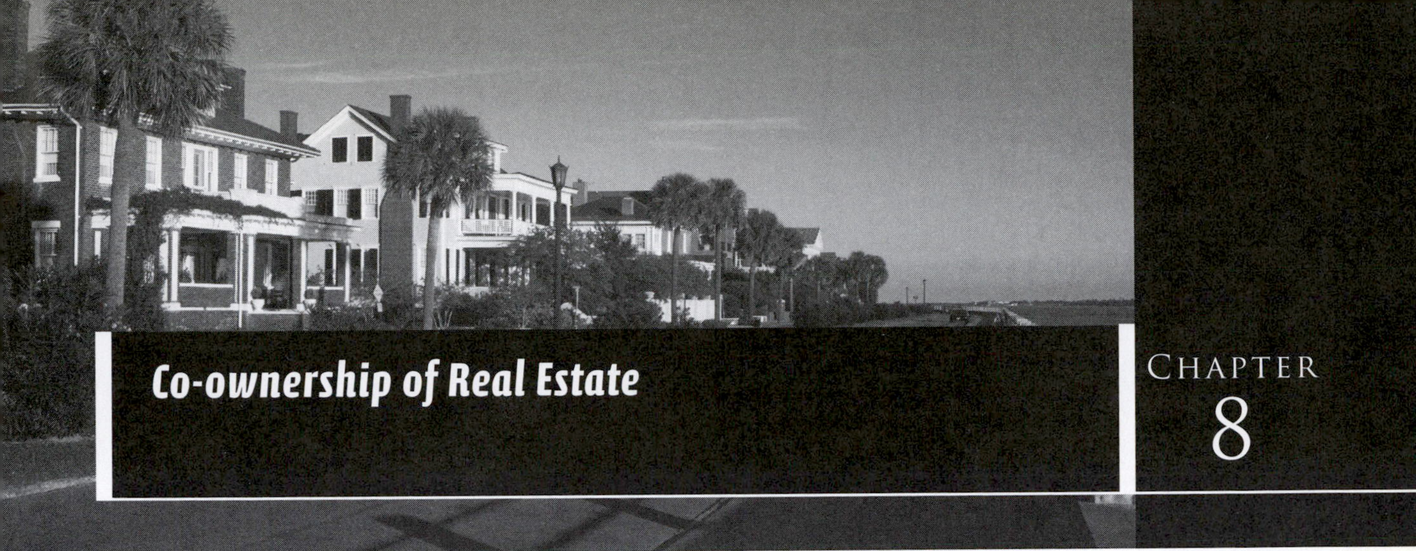

Co-ownership of Real Estate

CHAPTER 8

Prenup No-no's

- *Springing a prenup upon your intended*
- *Presenting the idea of a prenup as a fait accompli*
- *Suggesting a prenup at the last moment*
- *Being overbearing or heavy handed*

From "Broaching the 'P' Word," a chapter from *Prenups for Lovers* by Arlene G. Dubin (Villard Books, a division of Random House, Inc., 2001).

Often, title to real property is held by two or more people. Married couples hold title together to their homes. Children inherit a parcel of land from a parent as equal co-owners. Unmarried cohabitants have issues of property ownership and child support and those about to get married would like to avoid those issues in the event the marriage fails. **Co-ownership** of real estate is common and the issues complex, especially without an understanding of the basic rules and rights of such dual and multiple forms of ownership.

This chapter answers the following questions: How can title be held among several owners? What are the rights of each of the owners? What are the responsibilities of each of the owners? What action or actions may be taken in the event difficulties arise between or among the parties?

Methods of Co-ownership

There are four methods of co-ownership: tenancies in common, joint tenancies, tenancies by the entirety, and tenancies in partnership. These forms of co-ownership are often intermingled with statutory protections afforded by marital property protections.

Tenancies in Common

When parties hold title to property as tenants in common, they hold separate interests in a single piece of property. The tenants in common may hold equal or unequal shares in the land. For example, two tenants may hold a one-half interest in a tract of land or they may hold a one-third/two-thirds portion of the property. Tenants in common may acquire their interests at different times and may convey their interests to others. The conveyances can be made *inter vivos* (while the tenant in common is alive) or by will. For example, if X and Y hold title to a piece of property and X passes away, leaving, by will, his property to sons W and Z, then Y, W, and Z are all tenants in common.

Under a **tenancy in common**, each tenant is entitled to equal possession of the property. To the extent one cotenant has exclusive possession, the other cotenants are entitled to payment for their loss of use. For example, if cotenant A leased the property she owns with B and C to an architectural firm and kept the rent, B and C would be entitled to recover their share of the rental proceeds from A.

In the majority of states, the language necessary to create a tenancy in common is simply "To A and B." When this language is used, A and B will each have a 50 percent interest in the property. To create unequal interests, the amount of ownership must be specified. For example, "One-third of the above described property to my son B and two-thirds of the same to my daughter C" would be the language needed to create a tenancy in common with different shares or interests in the property. (For a discussion of the co-ownership of subsurface rights, see Chapter 3.)

Joint Tenancies

A **joint tenancy** is a form of co-ownership in which the parties hold equal shares and possess unique rights of ownership through survivorship. That is, when one joint tenant dies, title to the property remains with the surviving joint tenants. A joint tenancy interest cannot be given away by will because at the moment of death, title vests in the remaining joint tenants. If A, B, and C are joint tenants and C dies, A and B remain joint tenants and hold title to the property. C's heirs have no rights or interest in the property. If B then dies, A will hold full title to the property and B's heirs have no rights or interest in the property.

An interesting issue that arises in joint tenancy title is whether a joint tenant can make a valid *inter vivos* conveyance of his or her interest. Suppose, for example, that in the A, B, C joint tenancy, C conveys her interest to D. The result is that the unity of title is broken and the joint tenancy is partially severed. The result will be that D becomes a tenant in common with a one-third interest and A and B remain joint tenants for the remaining two-thirds of the property. Figure 8.1 illustrates the impact of joint tenancy transfers.

Practical Tip

The way title is carried has significant implications for the listing, sale, and purchase of property. Title insurers will not issue policies for property transfers attempted without the consent of all joint tenants. The rights and identity of all co-owners should be determined prior to marketing, buying, or selling property. When a joint tenant passes away, recording the death certificate is necessary in order for title to pass to the surviving joint tenant(s).

The Language of a Joint Tenancy

There are several requirements for the creation of a valid joint tenancy interest. The first requirement is the use of clear language to create a joint tenancy. Some states require the use of the phrase "as joint tenants with right of survivorship." Other states may simply require the use of the term "joint tenants."

Figure 8.1 The Severance of a Joint Tenancy

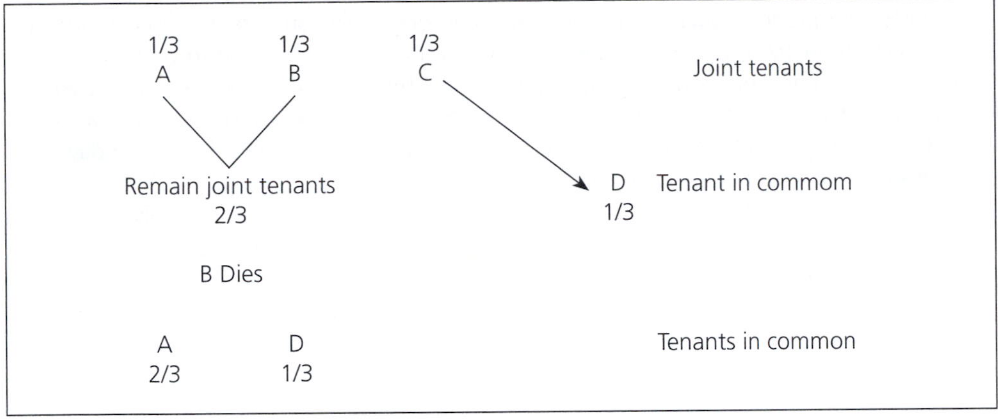

Other Requirements for Joint Tenancy Creation: The Unities

There are four other requirements for valid formation. They are referred to as the **unities** of a joint tenancy and they are time, title, interest, and possession.

Unity of Time Joint tenants must take their title to the property at the same time. For example, if O conveyed Blackacre to A and B on December 30, 2007, then A and B meet the unity of time requirement because they acquired their interest at the same time. However, if O conveyed half of Blackacre to A on December 30, 2007, and then conveyed the other half to B on June 30, 2008, then A and B cannot be joint tenants because they acquired their interests at different times. They are tenants in common.

In some states, this unity of time requirement presents problems when one party owns property prior to marriage and then after marriage seeks to hold the property with a spouse as joint tenants. For example, suppose Jane owns a home prior to marriage and upon marrying Bob seeks to transfer the property so that she and Bob will hold the property as joint tenants. If Jane transfers the property, the unity of time is not satisfied because Jane would have acquired her interest previously. This unity problem can be overcome by setting up what is called a **strawman transaction**. In this transaction, Jane transfers the property to a third party (the strawman), who then transfers the property back to Jane and Bob. Jane and Bob have thus satisfied the requirement of unity of time for joint tenancy. Although this transaction is simply procedural, it is necessary if this unity is to be satisfied. Some states have eliminated the requirement of unity of time in circumstances like Jane and Bob's and have passed statutes indicating the strawman transaction need not be conducted for the joint tenancy to be valid.[1]

CONSIDER 8.1

Terrell Taylor (Taylor) was the owner in fee simple of a 666-acre ranch in Fremont County, Colorado. On March 4, 1991, Taylor executed a warranty deed that conveyed that property from Taylor as sole owner to Taylor and Lucy I. Canterbury (Canterbury) as joint tenants. The validity of that deed is not in dispute.

1. For an example of a statute that eliminates the strawman requirement, see Mass. Gen. Laws Ann. Ch. 184, §8 (West 2003).

CONSIDER 8.1
(continued)

In 1997, Taylor executed a second deed: this time a quitclaim deed purporting to transfer the property back to himself and Canterbury as tenants in common. Taylor's intent to sever the joint tenancy between himself and Canterbury, and to create a tenancy in common, could not have been clearer. The second deed stated, "It is my intention by this deed to sever the joint tenancy created by [the 1991 deed], and to create a tenancy in common." The deed was duly recorded on June 16, 1997—the same day it was executed. Taylor died on August 20, 1999.

Canterbury filed an action to quiet title to the property to herself as surviving joint tenant. In that complaint, she also asked the trial court to set aside the 1997 conveyance and award her damages arising out of Taylor's attempted conveyance. What happens? Who owns the property and how much is owned? *Taylor v. Canterbury*, 92 P.3d 961 (Colo. 2004)

Unity of Title Parties are not joint tenants unless they derive their title from the same source or grantor. For example, if O conveys Blackacre to A and B, A and B can be joint tenants. However, if B then conveys his interest to C, A and C cannot be joint tenants since A derived her title from O and C derived his title from B. A and C are tenants in common.

Unity of Interest This unity requires that joint tenants have equal interests in the property. For example, A and B each holding a one-half interest qualify for joint tenancy. However, if A holds a one-third interest and B holds a two-thirds interest, then A and B can be only tenants in common.

Unity of Possession This requirement holds true for a valid tenancy in common as well. Under unity of possession, the parties must have equal rights to possess the property, and one party cannot dispossess the others of the land. If the land is divided either geographically or by time (into present and future interests; see Chapter 2), then the parties are no longer co-owners, and unity of possession is lost. For example, if O conveys Blackacre to A for life and then to B and C, B and C may be any type of tenants in the future, but they are not joint tenants with A because their interest in the property is divided.

The following case deals with the creation of a joint tenancy and whether it was severed through a partial transfer.

In re Estate of Quick

905 A.2d 471 (Pa. 2006)

FACTS

In July, 1957, A. Frank Jones and Grace A. Jones, by general warranty deed, conveyed fee simple title to 23 acres of land to Kenneth Quick, Robert Quick, and Robert Bean as joint tenants with right of survivorship (JTWROS). On December 26, 1957, the three joint tenants and their wives executed an oil and gas lease for the property subsurface rights to William and Marcus Seanor. Kenneth Quick died April 27, 1972, and title to the property vested in Robert Quick and Robert Bean as the surviving JTWROS.

On June 14, 1979, Bean executed an oil and gas lease on the property to Paul H. Gerrie & Associates, Inc. On September 15, 1979, Quick gave a similar oil and gas lease to Gerrie. Both leases were recorded September 20, 1979, assigned by Gerrie to Largent Investments May 15, 1980, and further assigned to Loyalhanna Drilling Program February 3, 1981.

The leases Bean and Quick executed are identical, except the Bean lease contains a typewritten addition that states, "Should any question of property ownership or royalty dispursements [*sic*] arise, the Lessor has agreed to accept full responsibility." The Quick lease does not contain this clause.

After drilling commenced, all royalties were paid to Bean and Quick with each receiving one-half of one-eighth (one-sixteenth) of the royalties from the drilling. These payments continued until Quick died September 25, 1981; after that date, the royalties were paid in the same amount, one-sixteenth each to Bean and the Estate of Quick. In 1992, Bean, through his attorney, Marilyn Bean Jeffers (appellee), transferred the property to Jeffers. Since 1992, one-sixteenth of the royalties have been paid to Jeffers, and one-sixteenth of the royalties have been held in escrow pending resolution of ownership interests.

Jeffers says title to the property vested in Bean upon Quick's death. She requested in her suit to quiet title that the court require Quick's estate to account for funds received as royalties under the lease. Robert H. Quick, II, as executor of the Estate of Quick, as well as Robert H. Quick, II, and Richard M. Quick individually, Robert Quick's sons and heirs (appellants), alleged that the JTWROS between Bean and Quick was severed by Bean's June 14, 1979, oil and gas lease to Gerrie, and therefore title to the property did not vest in Bean upon the death of Quick, since Bean and Quick held the property as tenants in common.

The trial court determined the 1979 leases did not sever the JTWROS, and thus, by operation of law, Bean became the sole owner of the property upon Quick's death. The appellate court affirmed the trial court's decision and the Quicks appealed.

JUDICIAL OPINION

Eakin, Justice. When two or more persons hold property as JTWROS, title to that property vests equally in those persons during their lifetimes, with sole ownership passing to the survivor at the death of the other joint tenant. In contrast, a tenancy in common is an estate in which there is unity of possession but separate and distinct titles. The essence of a JTWROS is the four unities: interest, title, time, and possession. A JTWROS must be created by express words or by necessary implication, but there are no particular words which must be used in its creation. In fact, courts have found the intent to create a JTWROS trumps the use of imprecise or improper language in creating it. While JTWROS has been said to be disfavored in Pennsylvania, it is a legitimate and permissible means by which individuals hold title.

Clearly and without dispute, the parties here intended to hold title as JTWROS. Appellants argue that following the execution of Bean's 1979 oil and gas lease, the JTWROS between Bean and Quick was severed, resulting in a tenancy in common. Appellants would have us adopt a rule that a lease executed by fewer than all of the joint tenants, in all instances severs a JTWROS. This we refuse to do. The intentions of the parties executing the leases cannot be ignored, lest we cause unwary title-holders to inadvertently undo that unity of title which they must purposefully create.

Intent is equally as significant when addressing the severance of a JTWROS as it is when considering whether a JTWROS was created. "[I]t is well settled in this state that a joint tenancy with right of survivorship is severable by the action, voluntary or involuntary, of either of the parties."

Therefore, to determine whether the 1979 oil and gas leases severed the JTWROS, we must consider the parties' intentions in executing them. As the trial court observed, the record is devoid of any action by either Bean or Quick which would signify the intent to destroy the joint tenancy. The separate dates on which the leases were signed is not determinative, for the parties may very well have intended to execute the leases contemporaneously. The same corporation was seeking the gas and oil rights, and obviously knew the permission of both tenants was needed before drilling could begin. Both leases were executed in favor of the same party, and neither was recorded until the other was signed—both were recorded on the same day. Both were simultaneously assigned to the same third party. The difference of execution dates of the oil and gas leases by the geographically distant owners does not evince an intent to sever the JTWROS. This is not a situation where each tenant changed the use of the property without the other's agreement. The difference in dates of the leases is simply not the definitive factor it might be in other scenarios.

The leases indicate Bean lived in Kissimmee, Florida, and Quick lived on Long Island, New York. Fax machines had not attained ubiquity in 1979, and overnight mail delivery was not then a routine means of sending business documents. Teleconferencing and the like, a staple today, was not the norm 27 years ago. Simultaneous signings by parties 1500 miles apart could not be expected, and more importantly, it was not legally significant, as nothing happened until both leases were executed. Taken in the context of technology and business practices in 1979, the time separating the execution of the leases is not indicative of differing visions of the owners, much less a desire to fundamentally alter the way the two held title.

The two leases themselves were virtually identical by their terms. The only difference in the two leases—an additional single type-written clause in the Bean lease—is hardly determinative of an intention to sever the JTWROS. The extra clause is so vague and ambiguous as to be meaningless, and is no basis for finding the leases are really different at all; these leases are essentially two copies of the same lease.

Moreover, drilling on the property did not commence until after both leases were executed and recorded.

Although the leases were executed at different times, in a business context, they were treated functionally as the attainment of but one lease.

There is no evidence the parties here intended the 1979 oil and gas leases to sever their JTWROS; their JTWROS remained intact and, by operation of law, Bean became the sole owner of the property upon Quick's death. Accordingly, we affirm the decision of the Superior Court.

DISSENTING OPINION

Justice NEWMAN, dissenting. A joint tenancy is severed whenever one or more of the four unities are destroyed. This may be achieved "by the action, voluntary or involuntary, of either of the parties [resulting in] the parties [becoming] tenants in common."

Prior to the matter *sub judice*, this Court had not addressed whether the execution of a lease by fewer than all of the joint tenants is sufficient to terminate the joint tenancy and to convert the interest into a tenancy in common. Pursuant to the old rule followed in England, when one of the joint tenants with a right of survivorship leased his interest to a stranger, the tenancy was severed. The courts in this country, however, have reached divergent opinions on this issue. The two leading authorities emerged from Maryland and California.

The Maryland courts have followed the traditional English rule. The state of California, however, reaches a different result. [w]hen a joint tenant leases his interest to a third person for a term of years, and dies during that term, the lease does not sever the joint tenancy, but expires upon the death of the lessor.

In finding the lease identical, the Majority was constrained to overlook, or rationalize away, the reality that **the leases are not the same**. The Majority acknowledges that unlike the document executed by Robert Quick, the agreement signed by Robert Bean contained a typewritten addition encumbering him with full liability for any dispute relating to property ownership or royalty payments. Further, the leases were not signed on the same day; instead, they were signed **three months apart**. This leads me to conclude that the leases were separate from each other and, as a result, failed to meet the essence of a JTWROS, which is four unities: interest, title, time, and possession.

I can not reconcile the fact that the leases were signed **three months apart** with the Majority's view that the separate signings were "not legally significant." Again, the Majority seeks to minimize this difference by surveying the changes in technology that have occurred since 1979, when fax machines, overnight mail delivery, and teleconferencing were not used as they are today. While I recognize that it may have been more difficult to effectuate simultaneous signings by parties in the 1970s, it was not impossible. The fact is that the leases were signed on different dates, violating the unity in time requirement for a JTWROS.

In the case before us, I see no difference between an "oil and gas" lease and a "run-of-the-mill" leasehold. In both instances, the lessee obtains the right to present enjoyment and utilization of the property for a predetermined period of time. Ultimately, applying the rule I propose today to the facts of this case, I find that by executing a lease in favor of Gerrie, Robert Bean irrevocably altered the nature of his interest in the land, changing from a present interest to a reversionary interest, thus destroying the unities of interest and possession and terminating the joint tenancy. The unity of time was destroyed by the three-month gap between the parties' signing of the leases. Thus, after Robert Bean leased his interest to Gerrie, both Robert Bean and Robert Quick owned undivided one-half interests in the property as tenants in common. Following his death in 1981, the interest of Robert Quick did not revert to Robert Bean, but remained an asset in his estate.

CASE QUESTIONS

1. Give a description of the history of the property ownership and transfers.
2. Why does the majority of the court find that the joint tenancy was not severed?
3. What point does the dissent make about joint tenancies in its disagreement with the majority's conclusion?

CONSIDER 8.2

Clayton and Margie Gulledge owned a house at 532 Somerset Place (the Somerset property). They had three children: Bernis Gulledge, Johnsie Walker, and Marion Watkins. After Margie Gulledge died in 1970, Clayton remarried, but the second marriage was not successful.

While the divorce proceedings were pending, and because of his fear of losing the house, Clayton borrowed money from his son, Bernis, in order to pay off the financial demands of the second Mrs. Gulledge. In exchange, Clayton created a joint tenancy of the Somerset property, naming himself and Bernis as joint tenants. Bernis expected, as a

CONSIDER 8.2

(continued)

joint tenant with right of survivorship, that he would, upon his father's death, take full title to the Somerset property and that his loan to his father would be satisfied.

In 1988, Clayton conveyed his interest in the Somerset property to his daughter, Marion Watkins, "in fee simple tenants in common."

In 1991, Clayton died, survived by his three children. However, Bernis died in 1993 and Johnsie died in 1994. The three estates were consolidated and there ensued quite a battle at the probate court level over the Somerset property. Bernis' personal representative, Deborah Walker, argued that Bernis was the sole owner of the Somerset property at Clayton's death. Marion Watkins argued that Clayton's conveyance to her severed the joint tenancy and she and Bernis were tenants in common at the time of Clayton's death and that she, therefore, owned one-half of the Somerset property. The trial court agreed with Ms. Watkins and Ms. Walker appealed. Who owns what, how much, and why? *Estate of Gulledge*, 673 A.2d 1278 (D.C. 1996)

Tenancies by Entirety and Other Survival Marital Property Interests

A **tenancy by entirety** requires the presence of the same four unities as for a joint tenancy plus one additional unity: unity of person. Unity of person requires that the tenants be married.

Tenancy by entirety also carries with it the right of survivorship; spouses are not permitted to dispose of the property by will. Severance of this tenancy requires the signature of the nonsevering spouse, and the property itself may be subject to dower and curtesy rights (discussed later in the chapter). Divorce (or dissolution of the marriage) severs the tenancy by entirety. In some states, divorce or dissolution converts the title to joint tenancy; in others, to tenancy in common.

Community property states (see page 169) follow a set of laws on marital property rights that give spouses a right of survivorship by statute in all assets determined to be marital assets. The spouses have all the survivorship rights of community property but also get the benefits of joint tenancy's ease of transfer upon death of one of the spouses.[2] The use of joint tenancy with right of survivorship in community property estates often caused questions about the underlying character of the property—is it separate or marital property? A newer form of title, **community property with right of survivorship**, allows married couples to hold title unequivocally: the asset is a marital asset and they have rights of survivorship in that asset.

The tax basis for property held as community property with right of survivorship can be stepped up to fair market value at the time one spouse dies and such a step-up can help minimize estate taxes (see Chapter 17).

Tenancy in Partnership

A **tenancy in partnership** exists either when partners have contributed property to the partnership or when the partnership has purchased property with partnership funds. The partners hold title to such property as co-owners or as tenants in partnership. A tenancy in partnership has the characteristics of a joint tenancy. Upon the death of one of the partners, the remaining partners are entitled to the deceased partner's share. Heirs and devisees of the partner have no rights to the partnership property itself, but they may be entitled to payment for the value of the deceased partner's share or interest in the partnership.

2. See, e.g., A.R.S. §33–341.

Although laws vary from state to state, a tenancy in partnership has characteristics common to all of the tenancies. Each partner has the right to possession and use of the property for partnership purposes, and one partner cannot dispossess the other partners or the partnership of the property. In many states, transfer of partnership property requires the signature of all partners. Parties who engage in a land transaction with a partner should verify how title is held and whether the partner has authority to transfer the property. (More information on partnerships and limited partnerships can be found in Chapter 21.)

CONSIDER 8.3

A, B, and C were partners in the operation of a grocery store. The partnership's major assets were the store and the land on which it was located. C has passed away, and the executor of C's estate now wants to sell the estate's one-third interest in the store and the land. A and B claim they now own the land. What is the result?

Creditors' Rights and Co-ownership

Because there is more than one method of co-ownership, creditors' rights in property vary. The extent of the creditor's rights in terms of repossession and sale is limited according to the rights of the cotenant. In a tenancy in common, tenants may mortgage, lien, or pledge their share of the property; and in the event of one tenant's default on the underlying debt, the creditor could become a tenant in common or could sell the tenant's portion of the property to satisfy the debt. Tenants may pledge only that portion of the property that they own and a creditor cannot foreclose on the entire property when one of the tenants defaults.

Creditors who accept pledges of property from joint tenants must realize the limitation of their interests. Because the estate is subject to survivorship, it is possible that their security will be lost if their debtors predecease other joint tenants. If a joint tenant defaults on an underlying debt secured by joint tenancy property, the creditor takes possession and title by foreclosure (or other method) and thus becomes a tenant in common.

In a tenancy by the entirety, creditors have no rights in the property unless the underlying debt is a joint debt of the husband and wife. A creditor cannot validly enforce a pledge of the property made unilaterally by one of the spouses.

A creditor taking only a partial property pledge from a co-owner should be aware of problems in priority that may arise if later all tenants pledge their interests to another creditor. In those circumstances, it is possible that the first partial creditor will be second in priority to a later full-pledge creditor.

The following case deals with a creditor's rights on co-owned property.

GAYTON V. KOVANDA

857 N.E.2d 929 (Ill. App. 2006)

FACTS

Monica and Joseph Gayton, husband and wife, held title to the property at 3524 Riverside Drive, Wilmette, Illinois, as joint tenants with rights of survivorship. On February 2, 2001, Joseph transferred his interest in the property via a quitclaim deed to his wife Monica.

Louis Kovanda was a creditor of Joseph Gayton and had a judgment of $414,000, plus court costs, entered in his favor against Joseph Gayton on November 20, 2003. Joseph Gayton died on November 26, 2003. Kovanda recorded the notice of judgment against the Wilmette property on December 3, 2003.

On March 15, 2004, Monica Gayton filed suit against Kovanda to quiet title to the property. Monica alleged that Kovanda had created a cloud on title by wrongfully recording the judgment as a lien against the property because she was the sole owner of the property and the judgment was against Joseph, who no longer had an interest in the property.

Kovanda filed a counterclaim alleging that Joseph's transfer of his interest in the property to Monica violated the Illinois Uniform Fraudulent Transfer Act.

Monica filed a motion for summary judgment on Kovanda's counterclaim, which the trial court granted. Kovanda appealed.

JUDICIAL OPINION

Karnezis, Justice. In her motion for summary judgment, Gayton argued that even if Joseph's transfer of his interest in the property was fraudulent, Kovanda still had no rights in the property because he did not perfect his judgment against the property prior to Joseph's death.

Assuming that Joseph's transfer of his interest in the property was fraudulent, we must address Kovanda's claim that when a joint tenant fraudulently conveys his or her interest in a property, the conveyance must be avoided and the property restored to a tenancy in common. Kovanda argues Joseph Gayton's voluntary transfer of his interest in the property amounted to an immediate severance of the unities required to maintain a joint tenancy, thereby extinguishing any rights of survivorship. Therefore, any title that would vest in Joseph Gayton, for purposes of his creditors, would vest in Joseph as a tenant in common and after his death, that interest would be owned by his estate.

A joint tenancy is an estate that two or more individuals hold jointly with equal rights. With joint tenancy comes the right of survivorship, which entitles the last surviving joint tenant to take the entire estate. A joint tenancy can be severed when one tenant voluntarily or involuntarily destroys one of the four unities (interest, time, title, and possession) that are crucial to the creation and continuance of a joint tenancy.

[a]ssuming that Joseph's conveyance of his interest in the property to Monica was fraudulent, the court should treat the property as if the fraudulent transfer had not been made. Therefore, subsequent to Joseph's transfer of his interest to Monica and prior to Joseph's death, Joseph and Monica owned the property in joint tenancy. When Joseph died, the property passed to Monica as a joint tenant through rights of survivorship. It is of no consequence that Kovanda obtained the judgment prior to Joseph's death because a judgment only becomes a lien on the real estate of the person against whom it is entered from the time the judgment is filed with the recorder of deeds in the county in which the property is located. Kovanda did not file the judgment until December 3, 2003, after Joseph ceased to have any interest in the property due to his death. Accordingly, based on the foregoing, we find that the trial court did not err in granting summary judgment for Monica.

The judgment of the trial court is affirmed.

Affirmed.

CASE QUESTIONS

1. Give a list of the transactions, issues, and timeline for the case.
2. Did Joseph sever the joint tenancy when he transferred his interest via quitclaim deed to Monica?
3. What is the effect of the fraud in the transfer?
4. Who owns the property and is it subject to the creditor's lien?

ETHICAL ISSUES

In looking back at the *Gayton v. Kovanda* case, does it seem as if Joseph got away with something? By pure luck? By interpretation of the law? Was his conduct legal? Was it ethical? Should Monica pay the debt?

Figure 8.2 compares the various kinds of tenancies—their creation, transfer, and creditor relations.

Rights and Responsibilities of Cotenants

Rents

In all tenancies, each tenant has the equal right of possession, and nonpossessing tenants are not permitted to collect rent from the tenant who is in possession of the property. However, the possessing tenant does not have the right to exclude the other

Figure 8.2 Comparison of Methods of Co-ownership

Characteristics	Methods of Co-Ownership			
Unities	Tenancy in Common	Joint Tenancy with Right of Survivorship	Tenancy by the Entireties	Tenancy in Partnership
		1. Time	1. Time	
		2. Title	2. Title	
		3. Interest	3. Interest	3. Interest
	4. Possession	4. Possession	4. Possession	4. Possession
			5. Person (marriage)	5. Person (partners)
Transferability	*Inter vivos* Testamentary transfer	*Inter vivos* (severs tenancy) No testamentary transfer	One spouse cannot sell Surviving spouse	One partner could sell Title goes to surviving partner
Creditors' Rights	Rights survive debtor Creditor can become tenant in common	Limited to rights of survivorship Creditor can become tenant in common	Must be debt of husband and wife	Only partnership debts

tenants from the property (see discussion on partition and ouster). If the tenant in possession is collecting rents and profits from third parties who are using the property, such receipts should be shared with the other tenants. The general rule is that the nonpossessing tenant is entitled to his or her share of the fair market rental value but must also honor the terms of the lease by the tenant in possession.

Expenditures

When cotenants do not pay equal amounts for the purchase of property, most courts have ruled that the shares in the property are not equal and have apportioned title according to the portion of the purchase price contributed.

Some payments are necessary to keep the land or its title clear; for example, taxes and mortgage payments. Cotenants are required to share in these expenses according to their proportionate share of title in the property. The proportion of these payments may be offset, in some states, if one of the cotenants has been in exclusive possession.

Expenditures for improvements are made solely at the discretion of the improving cotenant; there is neither a right to require contribution from the other tenants nor a right to offset costs by reducing the portion of mortgages and taxes paid by the improving cotenant. Expenditures for repairs are treated in the same way.

CONSIDER 8.4

X and Y own equal shares of a one-acre parcel of land in the White Mountains of Arizona. Y has built a cabin on it at a cost of $162,000. Y has also managed to rent the cabin for 50 of the 52 weeks in 2007 at $1000 per week. Mortgage payments on the cabin are $1,120 per month. Utilities vary from summer to winter but average about $190 per month. Taxes on the property are $180 per month with the cabin, but were $140 without it. Insurance is $970 per year. X has demanded an equal share of the profits. Y refuses but says X is responsible for half of the mortgage, utilities, taxes, and insurance. What is the result? Would the result be different depending upon what type of tenancy exists?

Partition and Ouster

Partition is the physical division of co-owned property with the result being that co-owners become adjoining landowners or neighbors. Severance, on the other hand, merely changes the form of co-ownership (as discussed earlier when a joint tenancy is severed).

A partition can be made voluntarily when co-owners agree to a geographical division of the property or it can be made by a court when circumstances require. The following circumstances require the partition of co-owned property: (1) when one tenant has dispossessed the other tenant or tenants and refuses to allow access (ouster), (2) when a tenant refuses to contribute for necessary expenditures, (3) when a tenant refuses to distribute rents and profits earned from exclusive possession (at common law), or (4) when other circumstances arise where the court deems a partition appropriate (such as feuding relatives).

If it is impossible or illogical to physically divide the property, a court may order the property sold and the proceeds divided among the cotenants according to their proportionate interests. For example, if a piece of property has water on only one portion, a division would be unfair but a sale would allow the parties to realize the value of their interests.

CONSIDER 8.5

In 1993, Nabil Asterbadi and Mrs. Asterbadi, then as now married to each other, acquired fee simple title to property located at Stone Harbor, Cape May County, New Jersey. The Asterbadis acquired title from the Sheriff of Cape May County, incident to a foreclosure sale, for $208,000, through a deed issued by the Sheriff to "Nabil J. Asterbadi and Maureen Bell Asterbadi." The deed identified the grantees as "Nabil J. Asterbadi and Maureen Bell Asterbadi, his wife."

The property is a single-family home located in a very desirable area near the Atlantic Ocean. The Asterbadis use the property during summer vacation for their family, and it currently has a value of several million dollars. In addition, the property could be rented and would have a significant income value, possibly $50,000 annually.

On October 4, 1993, a creditor obtained a judgment against Dr. Asterbadi (not Mrs. Asterbadi) in the amount of $2,286,009.97. On August 19, 2003, the judgment was docketed in New Jersey and on May 18, 2005, the Sheriff of Cape May County held a Sheriff's sale of Asterbadi's interest in the property, at which sale Capital Finance purchased Dr. Asterbadi's interest for $551,100. The Asterbadis have the following questions: Must Mrs. Asterbadi allow Capital to use the property? (Capital would like to lease the property as a time-sharing vacation spot.) What interest does Mrs. Asterbadi have in the property? What happens if Mrs. Asterbadi refuses to allow Capital to lease the property? Will a partition work? *Capital Finance Co. of Delaware Valley, Inc. v. Asterbadi*, 912 A.2d 191 (N.J. 2006)

Marital Property Rights—Co-ownership By Marriage

In every state, there are provisions to protect married persons holding title to property with their spouses. Tenancy by the entirety is one example, and other provisions and protections include dower and curtesy rights in some states and community property rights in other states.

The Common Law—Dower Rights

Under common law, **dower rights** existed for the protection of a widow. The common law rule was that a widow is entitled to a one-third interest for her life in any and all real property her husband owned at any time during their marriage.

Because of probable confusion and complications associated with dower rights, many states have changed dower rights to simply protect a surviving spouse by requiring that one-third to one-half of the deceased spouse's property of any character (real or personal) be given to the surviving spouse. Such statutes help prevent the problem of disinheritance by giving some property to the surviving spouse, but outright instead of in the form of a life estate interest. Some states have homestead exemptions that provide the surviving spouse with a minimum amount of property such as a residence, some personal property, a living allowance, and vehicles. This minimum amount is given to the surviving spouse before any distributions of property and before any creditors' obligations are satisfied.

Regardless of the form dower takes, it is a well-protected interest of a spouse. In the following case, the complexities of dower create a cloud on the title of another "wife."

FUNCHES V. FUNCHES

413 S.E.2d 44 (Va. 1992)

FACTS

Gisele Funches was married to Robert Funches until his death in March 1990. However, following Robert's death, Gisele discovered that Robert had married, at least by ceremony, Pranee Funches. Gisele and Robert had never been divorced.

Gisele (plaintiff/appellant) learned that during the course of his bigamous marriage to Pranee (defendant/appellee), Robert and Pranee had purchased real property near Alexandria, Virginia, and took title as "tenants by the entirety with right of survivorship." Upon Robert's death, Pranee claimed she had full title to the land. Gisele claimed that because they could not be legally married, Pranee and Robert could not hold title as tenants by the entirety. According to Gisele's suit, Pranee and Robert were thus tenants in common and Gisele, as Robert's heir, was entitled to one-half of the property.

The trial court held that Robert and Pranee did not have a tenancy by the entirety because they were not married but rather held title to the land as joint tenants with right of survivorship and that Gisele had no dower interest in the land. Gisele appealed.

JUDICIAL OPINION

Compton, Justice. The decision in this case is controlled by the principles which we recently enunciated in *Gant v. Gant*, 237 Va. 588, 379 S.E.2d 331 (1989). Indeed, the first sentence of the *Gant* opinion states the crucial issue in the present case: "In this appeal, we consider the effect of a deed purporting to convey an estate by the entirety, with words of survivorship, to parties who are not married."

In *Gant*, after a married couple divorced, they acquired a house and lot by a deed which purported to convey the property to the unmarried couple "to be held and owned by them...as tenants by the entireties with the right of survivorship as at common law. ..." Later, the man married another woman. Upon his death, his widow and their daughter filed a partition suit naming the ex-wife, among others, as a party defendant. We affirmed the trial court's ruling that, upon the decedent's death, the property had passed to the ex-wife by survivorship and that the widow and her daughter had no interest in the property.

In *Gant*, we stated: "Tenancies by the entirety are based upon five unities: those of title, estate, time, possession, and persons. The unity of persons relates to marriage and embodies the common law fiction that husband and wife are one. A tenancy which lacks the fifth unity but is based upon the other four is a joint tenancy, for which the first four unities are also prerequisite." We held that parties who are not married to each other, even though "they lack one of the essential unities prerequisite to the creation of a tenancy by the entirety,... may become joint tenants, and if the instrument creating the estate manifests the requisite intention, the joint tenancy will be clothed with the common law right of survivorship."

Only slight elaboration beyond the analysis of *Gant* is necessary to demonstrate that *Gant*'s principles govern the result in this case. Obviously, the deed which purports to establish a tenancy by the entirety between these persons who are not married to each other creates a joint tenancy. Clearly, the words of survivorship expressly manifest the requisite intent that the joint tenancy is clothed with the common law right of survivorship. And, this express manifestation of survivorship necessarily excludes plaintiff's dower interest.

Furthermore, the interest of the defendant, the surviving joint tenant, is superior to the dower interest of the plaintiff, the wife of the other joint tenant. "One joint tenant's right in the joint estate is superior to the contingent or inchoate dower of the wife of the other joint tenant. Joint tenants are seized *per mi et per tout*,—that is, each of them has the entire possession of his part as well as of the whole. One of them has not a seizen of one-half and the other the remaining half. Neither can one be exclusively seized of one acre and the other of another acre. Each has an undivided moiety of the whole, not the whole of an undivided moiety. The possession and seizen of one joint tenant is the possession and seizen of the other."

Finally, the plaintiff contends that the trial court erred when it did not recognize her dower interest and failed to modify the deed to reflect a tenancy in common "when the deed arose out of a criminal and illegal incident of bigamy." The complete answer to this contention, assuming as we must on demurrer that the decedent committed bigamy by marrying the defendant, is that the "marriage" did not confer the ownership or survivorship interests in the property. Instead, the deed created the right of survivorship in the defendant.

Here, survivorship was expressly created by the parties in the deed; no property rights were acquired by any wrongful acts. Thus, the fact of a void marriage affects neither defendant's ownership of the property nor her right of survivorship.

Affirmed.

CASE QUESTIONS

1. What is the relationship between and among Robert, Gisele, and Pranee?
2. What type of interest did Robert and Pranee create with their deed language?
3. What type of interest does Gisele say they had? Why?
4. What unity was lacking on the tenancy by the entirety? What is the effect of this missing unity?
5. How does the court deal with the issue of the underlying bigamous marriage?

The Common Law–Curtesy Rights

Curtesy is a surviving husband's protection that, at common law, gave the husband a life estate in all real property owned by his wife during their marriage. However, the **curtesy rights** existed only if there were issue born of the marriage. This right has been modified by the states today, and the above-discussed statutory protections now eliminate common law provisions on dower and curtesy but still protect surviving spouses.

Statutory Marital Law–Community Property

Community property is a system of ownership by spouses that has Spanish origins and exists, in some form, in 11 states, with many others adopting its 50–50 ownership principles. In states where community property is the basis for marital property rights, unless the parties agree and specify otherwise, property is held as community property.

The basic principle governing this system of co-ownership is that both partners in the marriage work for the benefit of the community and do so on an equal basis and therefore own half of all property acquired during the course of the marriage. This half-ownership principle is true regardless of whether the spouses were employed or unemployed during the course of the marriage.

If community property law is applicable to a marriage relationship, then all property acquired during the course of the marriage is classified as community property and is half owned by each spouse. However, the spouses may still have some separate property to which they hold complete title. For example, any property owned prior to marriage that is brought into the marriage is separate property. Also, gifts and inheritances received by individual spouses during the marriage are separate property. If, for example, a wife receives an inheritance from her father, the money would be her separate property and would not belong to the community.

Debts are also considered community obligations, and each spouse is responsible for 50 percent of the debts entered into for the benefit of the community.

Those dealing in real estate in community property states need the signature of both spouses for the listing, mortgaging, improvement, or sale of real property. Real estate partnerships operating in these states must obtain a waiver from the spouses of all partners, so that the property can be transferred without the risk of a spouse's interest being exercised at a later time. In noncommunity property states, the same process should be followed for dower and curtesy rights.

One of the benefits of the community property system is that both spouses acquire some property rights during the course of the marriage. In noncommunity property states, marriage for a lifetime does not guarantee a 50 percent share of the property acquired during the marriage. To equalize the states' laws on marital property, the **Uniform Marital Property Act** was drafted but has been adopted only in Wisconsin.[3] The purpose of the act is to bring community property principles to noncommunity property states.

The following case deals with an issue of a separate property contract entered into by a husband and wife after they are married.

Diosdado v. Diosdado

118 Cal. Rptr. 2d 494, 97 Cal. App. 4th 470 (2002)

FACTS

Donna and Manuel Diosdado were married in November 1988. In 1993, Manuel had an affair with another woman. When Donna learned of this, she and Manuel separated but did not divorce. Instead, they entered into a written "Marital Settlement Agreement" intended to "preserve, protect and assure the longevity and integrity of an amicable and beneficial marital relationship between them."

Section 1 of the agreement provides that if either party expresses concern that the goals of the marriage are not being met, they agree to seek counseling and make a good faith effort to resolve their problems to preserve the relationship.

Section 2 is labeled "Obligation of Fidelity," and provides as follows:

It is further acknowledged that the parties' marriage is intended to be an exclusive relationship between Husband and Wife that is premised upon the values of emotional and sexual fidelity, and mutual trust. The parties hereto are subject to a legal obligation of emotional and sexual fidelity to the other. It shall be considered a breach of such obligation of fidelity to volitionally engage in any act of kissing on the mouth or touching in any sexual manner of any person outside of said marital relationship, as determined by a trier of fact. The parties acknowledge their mutual understanding that any such breach of fidelity by one party hereto may cause serious emotional, physical and financial injury to the other.

Section 3 is labeled "Liquidated Damages." It provides as follows:

In the event it is shown by a preponderance of the evidence in a court of competent jurisdiction that either party has engaged in any breach of the obligation of sexual fidelity as defined hereinabove... and, additionally, that election is made by one or both parties to commence an action to terminate the marriage by divorce because of said breach, the following terms and conditions shall become effective:

a. *The party shown to have committed the breach shall vacate the family residence immediately upon the completion of a showing of breach as defined above;*
b. *The party shown to have committed the breach will be solely responsible for all attorney fees and court costs incurred as a result of or in connection with the litigation of any issue surrounding or relating to said breach;*

3. W.S.A. §§766.001 to 766.97.

c. *The party shown to have committed the breach will pay the other party (hereinafter, the 'recipient') liquidated damages for said breach in the sum of $50,000, said sum to be paid over and above, and irrespective of, any property settlement and/or support obligation imposed by law as a result of said divorce proceeding. Said damages shall be due and payable on a date that is no later than six (6) months following entry of judgment of dissolution of marriage by a court of competent jurisdiction. Said damages shall become the sole and separate property of the recipient, except that, should said recipient remarry at any time following such payment, said damages shall be fully and completely refunded to the party shown to have committed the breach. Said refund shall be due and payable on a date no later than six (6) months following the date of the recipient's remarriage.*

d. *Both parties shall cooperate in the negotiation and execution of a reasonable property settlement and support agreement for the resolution of said divorce proceeding so as to minimize the emotional and financial expense of said litigation.*

The agreement was drafted by Manuel's attorney, and both Donna and Manuel signed it voluntarily in December 1993. They resumed living together.

In 1998, Manuel again had an affair with another woman. When Donna learned of it, she confronted Manuel, who denied it. Donna obtained independent verification from a witness who saw Manuel kissing this other woman. The parties separated in August 1998, and thereafter divorced.

Donna then brought this action for breach of contract in February 2000, seeking to enforce the liquidated damages clause of the agreement. On the first day of trial, the trial court, on its own motion, granted a judgment on the pleadings in favor of Manuel. Donna appealed.

JUDICIAL OPINION

Epstein, Acting Presiding Judge. The only question before this court is whether the agreement is enforceable. The trial court found that it was not [enforceable] because it was contrary to the public policy underlying California's no- fault divorce laws. That reasoning is sound.

In 1969, California enacted Civil Code section 4506 (now Fam.Code, §2310), providing for dissolution of marriage based on irreconcilable differences which have caused the irremediable breakdown of the marriage. This change was explained in *In re Marriage of Walton* (1972) 28 Cal.App.3d 108, 119, 104 Cal.Rptr. 472: "After thorough study, the Legislature, for reasons of social policy deemed compelling, has seen fit to change the grounds for termination of marriage from a fault basis to a marriage breakdown basis."

With certain exceptions (such as child custody matters or restraining orders), "evidence of specific acts of misconduct is improper and inadmissible" in a pleading or proceeding for dissolution of marriage. Fault is simply not a relevant consideration in the legal process by which a marriage is dissolved. Recovery in no-fault dissolution proceedings "is basically limited to half the community property and appropriate support and attorney fee orders—no hefty premiums for emotional angst."

Contrary to the public policy underlying California's no-fault divorce laws, the agreement between Donna and Manuel attempts to impose just such a premium for the "emotional angst" caused by Manuel's breach of his promise of sexual fidelity. The agreement expressly states the parties' "mutual understanding that any such breach of fidelity by one party hereto may cause serious emotional, physical and financial injury to the other."

The family law court may not look to fault in dissolving the marriage, dividing property, or ordering support. Yet this agreement attempts to penalize the party who is at fault for having breached the obligation of sexual fidelity, and whose breach provided the basis for terminating the marriage. This penalty is in direct contravention of the public policy underlying no-fault divorce.

To be enforceable, a contract must have a "lawful object." (Civ.Code, §1550, subd. 3.) A contract is unlawful if it is contrary to an express provision of law, contrary to the policy of express law, or otherwise contrary to good morals. Here, where the agreement attempts to impose a penalty on one of the parties as a result of that party's "fault" during the marriage, it is contrary to the public policy underlying the no-fault provisions for dissolution of marriage. For that reason, the agreement is unenforceable.

Donna claims a different result is required, based on two Supreme Court cases. We find these cases inapplicable. In the first, *In re Marriage of Bonds* (2000) 24 Cal.4th 1, 99 Cal.Rptr.2d 252, 5 P.3d 815, the court addressed the enforceability of a premarital agreement. Its concern was that one party was not represented by independent counsel at the time the agreement was executed. The court held that circumstance is only one of several factors to be considered in determining whether a premarital agreement had been entered into voluntarily, and hence is enforceable pursuant to Family Code section 1615. There is no issue in our case concerning voluntariness.

What is informative in *Bonds* is the distinction the court drew between the freedom of contract found in ordinary commercial contracts and the existence of limitations in marital agreements. The court recognized that "marriage itself is a highly regulated institution of undisputed social value, and there are many limitations on the ability of persons to contract with respect to it, or to vary its statutory terms, that have nothing to do with maximizing the satisfaction of the parties or carrying out their intent.... These limitations demonstrate further that freedom of contract with respect to marital arrangements is tempered with statutory requirements and case law expressing social policy with respect to marriage."

Donna finds no greater support in the second case, *In re Marriage of Pendleton and Fireman* (2000) 24 Cal.4th 39, 99 Cal.Rptr.2d 278, 5 P.3d 839. In *Pendleton*, the Supreme Court held that a premarital agreement waiving spousal support does not violate public policy, and is not per se unenforceable. That decision provides no authority for enforceability of an agreement between spouses to pay damages in the event one party engages in sexual infidelity.

Affirmed.

CASE QUESTIONS

1. When was the agreement entered into?
2. What property rights are affected?
3. What public policy issue concerns the court?
4. Is the agreement enforceable? Why or why not?[4]

CONSIDER 8.6

Christopher Dargan (husband) had suffered an off-and-on addiction to cocaine for many years. He had several unsuccessful attempts to free himself from his addiction and after several years of marriage, Monica Mehren (his wife) separated after another episode resulting from Christopher's cocaine use. Months later, the parties agreed that husband would return to the family home. Mr. Dargan signed a postmarital agreement promising to grant to Monica Mehren (wife) all of his interest in certain of the their community property should he use illicit drugs. Subsequently, the parties entered into an "Agreement re Transfer of Property." The agreement recited that Monica "consented to the resumption of marital relations on the condition that [husband] abstain from the deliberate, intentional use or ingestion of any mind altering chemical or substance excluding such use that may be prescribed or approved by a medical doctor. In the event of such deliberate, intentional use or ingestion of mind altering chemicals or substances by [husband], [husband] agrees that he will forfeit all of his right, title and interest in [described property]." They signed the document before a notary public.

Unfortunately, Mr. Dargan did not keep his promise. Thereafter, Ms. Mehren filed for divorce, asking that the property described in the agreement be confirmed to her as her separate property. Mr. Dargan challenged the postmarital agreement as against public policy and void. Should the court enforce the agreement? Is this case different from the *Diosdado* case or should the decision be the same? *In re Marriage of Mehren & Dargan*, 118 Cal.App.4th 1167, 13 Cal.Rptr.3d 522 (2004)

CONSIDER 8.7

The very public divorce of Lorna Wendt, the wife of a GE executive, presented a test of property rights in Connecticut. Mrs. Wendt was awarded $20 million of the $100 million her husband had accumulated as a GE officer. Mrs. Wendt claimed she gave up her career as a music teacher in order to serve as a corporate wife. She had requested half of the $100 million. What is the nature of a marital partnership? What public policy issues are at stake in marital property divisions? Mrs. Wendt worked as a music teacher to allow her husband to obtain his MBA. Does she have any rights with respect to that investment?

4. There are some states that recognize so-called "covenant marriages." If the parties elect to have a covenant marriage, the statutes creating such marriages "bar divorce except under extreme circumstances like adultery, abandonment or, for 'cruel and barbarous treatment.'" Covenant marriage laws also require couples to participate in premarital and pre-divorce counseling, and "for cases that would correspond to current no-fault divorces, they extend the waiting time to up to two and a half years." Covenant Marriage Act of 2001, §4 (2001 Ark. Acts at 1486).

Extension of Property Rights to Relationships Beyond Marriage

In some states, the basic principles of community property rights have been applied in cases where the parties were not married but lived as husband and wife. The doctrine of common law marriage has traditionally been applied in those relationships that are long term and that carry the trappings of marriage, such as joint residence, children, and the sharing of property rights. However, common law marriages have imposed a higher standard of proof in terms of obtaining property rights, and perceived injustices can occur prior to the long-term establishment of a common law marriage. As a result, courts in community and noncommunity property states have allowed unmarried cohabitants rights in their partner's property acquired during the course of cohabitation. The basis for allowing these property recoveries has been a contract, express or implied, or a quasi-contract found to exist between the unmarried partners. The so-called palimony suits remain an active area of litigation, cases in which those who have lived together want compensation for the time spent in the relationship.[5] However, the courts do not allow palimony or support payments in those cases in which there is a valid marriage between one of the cohabitants and a third party.[6]

Courts are now dealing with domestic partnership dissolutions and unregistered domestic partnerships and property distributions when the couples have not taken off the state's imprimatur of reocgnition. Some states have recognized that both gay and straight couples are eligible for property rights under the doctrine of meritricious relationships whereas other states have held that such doctrines are limited to relationships that appear to be marriages (in those states that do not recognize same-gender marraiges) *Velez v. Smith*, 142 Cal.App.4th 1154, 48 Cal.Rptr.3d 642 (2006). The best protection for property rights is for couples to register under the state's domestic partnership or civil union laws. Those laws afford property rights and protections for domestic partners just as dower and curtesy provided marital property rights automatically at common law.[7]

> ***Practical Tip***
>
> *Marital and quasi-marital property rights are complex and carry significant impact in terms of real property interests and titles. The status of couples should be verified for both buyers and sellers prior to listing, selling, or buying property. Individuals should have their rights, obligations, and nuptial agreements reviewed by an attorney. The validity of such agreements should be verified according to individual state law.*

The following case deals with the difficulties of property rights when the parties are not married.

Champion v. Frazier

977 S.W.2d 61 (Mo. App. 1998)

FACTS

Leroy Frazier (defendant) and Helen Champion (plaintiff) began to see each other during the late 1970s. During the entire time of their relationship, they were married to other people. Prior to 1989, they maintained separate apartments, but in 1989, they moved into a house together on Lalite Street in St. Louis (Lalite property). Only Leroy's name was on the title and bank loan for the Lalite property.

5. *In re Estate of Sasson*, 904 A.2d 769 (N.J. 2006).
6. *Combs v. Tibbitts*, 148 P.3d 430 (Colo.App. 2006).
7. Hawaii adopted a "reciprocal beneficiary" law, which permits gay couples to register and thereby obtain some rights. Vermont's "civil union" law permits gay couples to register and obtain almost all of the private rights married couples have. California now permits a gay couple to file a "declaration of domestic partnership," but its effects are minimal. In Washington, heterosexual cohabitants can be treated as having a "meretricious" relationship (with shared property rights). J. Thomas Oldham, "Lessons from Jerry Hall v. Mick Jagger Regarding U.S. Regulation of Heterosexual Cohabitants or, Can't Get No Satisfaction," 76 *Notre Dame L. Rev.* 1409 (2003).

In May 1994, Leroy moved out of the Lalite property and Helen continued to live there with her two adult children and two grandchildren.

In June 1994, Helen brought suit against Leroy for, among other things, breach of contract with regard to Helen's rights in the Lalite property. Helen said that Leroy promised that she would own half of the property. The trial court found that there was a contract and awarded Helen half of the value of the Lalite property or $20,000 of the $40,000 appraised value. Leroy appealed.

JUDICIAL OPINION

Hoff, Judge. Plaintiff alleges Defendant breached a contract to share equally in all benefits obtained through ownership of the Lalite property. Plaintiff testified Defendant made two statements to indicate her ownership interest in the Lalite property.

Plaintiff testified Defendant took her to see the house and told her if she liked it "he would get it" for her. She understood this to mean that they would live together there and save money by not paying for two of everything. Plaintiff also testified that Defendant asked her to sign a "bank statement" for the loan to pay for the house. When she asked why she should sign it because he had not taken her to get the deed, she testified Defendant said, "Don't worry about that. Before I get the title I'll make sure your name is on it." Defendant denied making any of these statements. Defendant testified the only document Plaintiff ever signed from the bank was to put her name on his checking account. There were no other witnesses to corroborate the statements on which Plaintiff relied. Furthermore, Plaintiff concedes she is not obligated to pay the outstanding mortgage on the Lalite property.

An oral contract for specific performance to convey real estate cannot be based on conversations too loose or casual. The alleged statements that Plaintiff relied on are too loose and casual to indicate Defendant's intention to convey an interest in the Lalite property to Plaintiff. Defendant's alleged statements do not constitute an explicit promise to share equally in all benefits obtained through ownership of the Lalite property. We agree there was no express contract between the parties.

However, the trial court did find an implied-in-fact contract between the parties. Our research indicates the only Missouri case finding an implied-in-fact contract between unmarried cohabitants is *Hudson*. It explains courts should look to the conduct of the parties to determine whether there exists an implied contract between them. In *Hudson*, the court found an implied-in-fact contract based on the nature of the relationship between the parties. Marshall F. Hudson and Brigitte DeLonjay were unmarried cohabitants. They purchased a residence together, with both names on the title, and each financially contributed to the purchase. They owned a number of joint bank accounts to which each contributed. They paid most of their household expenses from the joint funds.

Additionally, the parties in *Hudson* created a business corporation, Affiliated, financed by both their joint checking account and a loan on which both parties were jointly obligated. Each party personally guaranteed the loan and their residence was pledged as security. Both parties worked at the business and each owned stock in the corporation. Various financial statements showed the parties owned all of their assets jointly. They also formed another business, Dollco, from jointly held capital.

The trial court in *Hudson* entered judgment in favor of DeLonjay based on an implied-in-fact contract, breach of a confidential relationship, constructive fraud, and constructive trust. This court affirmed the trial court's judgment.

A review of the conduct between Plaintiff and Defendant here indicates the evidence is insufficient to support a finding of an implied-in-fact contract to share equally in the Lalite property. The following facts are undisputed. In 1995, Plaintiff declared bankruptcy under Chapter 7. She did not indicate any interest in the Lalite property in the bankruptcy filing. A proposal for a new roof for the Lalite property was made out in the name of both Plaintiff and Defendant; and both Plaintiff and Defendant signed a remodeling contract for the property.

Defendant added Plaintiff's name to his checking account sometime between June 1989 and August 1990. Plaintiff wrote out all the checks for the bills. Defendant worked as a Deputy Sheriff for the City of St. Louis at a salary of $24,000. His paycheck was deposited in the joint account. Defendant also received income from rental properties. Plaintiff received $207 per month as child support from the state for her two children. That money was also deposited in the joint account. Plaintiff did not file any income tax returns until 1995. Plaintiff received food stamps which were used by Defendant to purchase groceries for the household.

The record also reveals the following. Defendant discovered he had glaucoma in 1984 and by 1991 he was no longer able to drive. Plaintiff testified she drove Defendant around for his job after he could no longer drive and without her help Defendant would not have been able to keep his job. However, Defendant testified ninety percent of the time he drove with Willie Smith. Willie Smith testified he and Defendant worked together most of the time and Willie drove during this time.

Although it is apparent Plaintiff contributed to the household, the conduct between Plaintiff and Defendant does not support a finding of an implied-in-fact contract to share equally in the Lalite property. Plaintiff did not substantially contribute to the purchase of the Lalite property nor is her name on the title or bank loan. The facts in this case are distinguishable from the facts in *Hudson.* Here, there is no "voluminous documentary evidence" of jointly held assets nor is there "extensive testimony" concerning the assets held by the parties to indicate an implied-in-fact contract between them. Moreover, Plaintiff and her family have continued to live in the Lalite property without paying rent since Defendant moved out in May 1994.

Here, Plaintiff and Defendant had a family relationship. Plaintiff did not introduce any evidence that she expected to be paid for the services she rendered. In addition, both parties benefited from Plaintiff's services. For instance, Plaintiff helped Defendant keep his job which was at a much higher salary than Plaintiff was able to obtain. As a result, Defendant could pay the mortgage and insurance on the Lalite property. Under the circumstances, Plaintiff's rendition of services alone does not justify a monetary award because there was no express contract or actual understanding between the parties that she would be paid for such services.

Upon review of the record, there is no substantial evidence to support the trial court's finding of an implied-in-fact contract. In addition, there is no substantial evidence to support the existence of an express contract.

We reverse and remand for the trial court to enter judgment in favor of Defendant on the breach of contract claim.

Reversed and remanded.

CASE QUESTIONS

1. What was the nature of the relationship between Helen and Leroy?
2. What was their understanding on the Lalite property?
3. What evidence does Helen point to in order to establish her rights?
4. Do you think the fact that Helen and Leroy were married to other people at the time influenced the appellate court's decision? Why or why not?

CONSIDER 8.8

Mick Jagger and Jerry Hall lived together for nearly two decades. They had four children together. At the time the couple decided to no longer reside together, Ms. Hall filed for divorce in Britain, citing their wedding ceremony in Bali as proof of their marriage. However, the court found that there was no marriage license and no compliance with Bali law for recognition of marriage there. Does Ms. Hall have any property rights?

CONSIDER 8.9

In 1981, William Hurt and Sandra Jennings began living together in New York City. Mr. Hurt was a movie actor, and Ms. Jennings was an accomplished member of a ballet company. In 1982, Ms. Jennings accompanied Mr. Hurt to South Carolina, where he was filming a movie. They lived together as husband and wife during the filming of the movie. Mr. Hurt was still married to another woman at that time, with the divorce becoming final in December 1982.

The relationship was volatile, but Mr. Hurt stated that "as far as he was concerned, we were married in the eyes of God" and "more married than married people." Ms. Jennings gave birth to a child later verified to be Mr. Hurt's. She then filed suit in 1988 seeking to establish her rights in Mr. Hurt's property and earnings. She claimed that Mr. Hurt had promised to support her if she would have his child and give up her career.

Should the court support an award of property and support for Ms. Jennings? *Jennings v. Hurt*, 554 N.Y.S.2d 220 (1990)

Premarital or Antenuptial Agreements

In recent years, and particularly with second marriages, many couples have entered into agreements minimizing or waiving their marital property rights. These agreements, called **premarital, prenuptial**, or **antenuptial agreements**, are subject to strict review by courts to determine if they are fair and were entered into voluntarily. Presently, 26 states have adopted the **Uniform Premarital Agreement Act**, or the UPAA, which was passed by the National Conference of Commissioners on Uniform State Laws (NCCUSL) in 1983. The UPAA recognizes these types of marital agreements, and most states that have not adopted the UPAA have passed some form of legislation that recognizes them.[8]

Ten Steps to an Airtight Prenup

1. Make sure there's no hint of coercion. To nail this down, make sure your spouse-to-be has his own lawyer. The American Academy of Matrimonial Lawyers will gladly supply a list of its members.
2. A lawyer for Donald Trump, Stanford Lotwin, says you can limit disclosure by stating merely that you have certain assets exceeding a certain value. Make sure you don't lie. If your spouse can prove you were hiding assets, you could be in big trouble.
3. Be prepared for a few surprises. Some are pleasant, some not.
4. Avoid any appearance of forcing a deal at the last minute. Sign at least a month before the wedding. Later than that an aggrieved spouse could claim he was made to sign under pressure.
5. Don't give the prospective spouse the idea that you regard your assets as more precious than her. "The more stringent and self-protective, the more likely the marriage is going to blow up in their faces," warns Beverly Hills lawyer Alexandra Leichtner.
6. Don't throw in anything mean: like the provision Stan Lotwin recently saw imposing a $1,000 penalty for every pound a wife gained. No court would enforce that kind of provision, and it could spur the judge to toss the whole thing out.
7. Consider increasing your spouse's cut over time to make the agreement more equitable. New York divorce litigator Carl Tunick recalls a phone call from a woman eager to divorce her husband immediately. Tunick pointed out that she was entitled to an extra $1 million for every year she stuck it out. "Can't you wait until Jan. 1?" asked Tunick. She did, and they're still married.
8. See that your spouse stands to inherit something if you die first. Without such a provision, taxes could soak up everything—including your 401(k).
9. Don't count on escaping alimony payment. In New York and a few other states, a spouse can waive the right to alimony. If the judge thinks it's unfair, he can order you to pay anyway, no matter what the agreement might say.
10. Be very careful about mixing premarital and post-marital assets. Because if you cannot absolutely prove what was yours before the marriage, you could stand to lose it.

DISCUSSION QUESTIONS

1. List three things you *should not* do in negotiating, drafting, or signing a prenuptial agreement.
2. What public policy issues do you see in honoring prenuptial agreements?

The area of prenuptial or antenuptial agreements has been clarified by courts and legislation over the past decade. The above excerpt from *Forbes* provides a good summary of the areas of concern in these agreements. See also Web Exhibit 8.1 for a sample prenuptial agreement.

The following case involving a well-known sports figure discusses the validity of an antenuptial agreement.

8. The adopting states are Arizona, Arkansas, California, Colorado, Connecticut, Delaware, District of Columbia, Hawaii, Idaho, Illinois, Indiana, Iowa, Kansas, Maine, Minnesota, Montana, Nebraska, Nevada, New Jersey, New Mexico, North Carolina, Oregon, Rhode Island, South Dakota, Texas, Utah, and Virginia.

IN RE MARRIAGE OF BONDS

5 P.3d 815 (Cal. 2000)

FACTS

Susann (known as Sun) Margreth Bonds (appellant) (referred to as respondent in lower court opinion) and Barry Lamar Bonds (respondent) met in Montreal in the summer of 1987 and maintained a relationship during ensuing months through telephone contacts. In October 1987, at Barry's invitation, Sun visited him for 10 days at his home in Phoenix, Arizona. In November 1987, Sun moved to Phoenix to take up residence with Barry and, one week later, the two became engaged to be married. In January 1988, they decided to marry before the commencement of professional baseball's spring training. On February 5, 1988, in Phoenix, the parties entered into a written premarital agreement in which each party waived any interest in the earnings and acquisitions of the other party during marriage. That same day, they flew to Las Vegas, and were married the following day.

Primarily at issue is paragraph 10 of the agreement, which provided, in pertinent part, as follows:

CONTROL AND EARNINGS OF BOTH HUSBAND AND WIFE DURING MARRIAGE. We agree that all the earnings and accumulations resulting from the other's personal services, skill, efforts and work, together with all property acquired with funds and income derived therefrom, shall be the separate property of that spouse.

The earnings from husband and wife during marriage shall be: separate property of that spouse.

The agreement also contained provisions concerning support obligations and the disposition of property upon dissolution of the marriage, including a proviso that

Each of us shall receive free and clear of all claim of the other spouse that property which was the separate property of each spouse prior to marriage... and as may be later acquired as separate property.

Sun and Barry were then 23 years of age. Barry, who had attended college for three years and who had begun his career in professional baseball in 1985, had a contract to play for the Pittsburgh Pirates. His annual salary at the time of the marriage ceremony was approximately $106,000. Sun had emigrated to Canada from Sweden in 1985, had worked as a waitress and bartender, and had undertaken some training as a cosmetologist, having expressed an interest in embarking upon a career as a makeup artist for celebrity clients. Although her native language was Swedish, she had used both French and English in her employment, education, and personal relationships when she lived in Canada. She was unemployed at the time she entered into the premarital agreement.

Barry petitioned for legal separation on May 27, 1994, and Sun requested custody of the couple's two children, then three and four years of age. In addition, she sought child and spousal support, attorney fees, and a determination of property rights. Child support was awarded in the amount of $10,000 per month per child. Spousal support was awarded in the amount of $10,000 per month, to terminate December 30, 1998.

The property disposition is disputed because Sun questions the validity of the prenuptial agreement. Barry testified that he was aware of teammates and other persons who had undergone bitter marital dissolution proceedings involving the division of property, and recalled that from the beginning of his relationship with Sun he told her that he believed his earnings and acquisitions during marriage should be his own. He informed her he would not marry without a premarital agreement, and she had no objection. He also recalled that from the beginning of the relationship, Sun agreed that their earnings and acquisitions should be separate, saying "what's mine is mine, what's yours is yours." Indeed, she informed him that this was the practice with respect to marital property in Sweden. She stated that she planned to pursue a career and wished to be financially independent.

Sun testified that her English language skills in 1987 and 1988 were limited. Out of pride, she did not disclose to Barry that she often did not understand him. She testified that she and Barry never discussed money or property during the relationship that preceded their marriage. She agreed that she had expressed interest in a career as a cosmetologist and had said she wished to be financially independent. She had very few assets when she took up residence with Barry, and he paid for all their needs. Their wedding arrangements were very informal, with no written invitations or caterer, and only Barry's parents and a couple of friends, including Barry's godfather Willie Mays, were invited to attend. No marriage license or venue had been arranged in advance of their arrival in Las Vegas.

Sun testified that on the evening before the premarital agreement was signed, Barry first informed her that they needed to go the following day to the offices of his lawyers, Leonard Brown and his associate Sabinus Megwa. She testified that only at the parking lot of the law office where the agreement was to be entered into did she learn, from Barry's financial adviser, Mel Wilcox, that Barry would not marry her unless she signed a premarital agreement.

Sun did not ask questions during the meeting in Barry's lawyers' offices, nor were any changes made to the agreement. She did not ask for more time, because she did not want to miss her flight and she was focussed on the forthcoming marriage ceremony. She did not believe that Barry understood the agreement either. She did not inform anyone at the meeting that she was concerned about the agreement; the meeting and discussion were not cut short, and no one forced her to sign the agreement.

Margarita Forsberg, a 51-year-old friend of Sun's, was present at the meeting and understood that Brown and Megwa were Barry's attorneys, not Sun's. She testified that when the attorneys explained the agreement, she did not recall any discussion of Sun's community property rights.

All three lawyers present for Bond recalled that Sun stated she did not want her own counsel, and Megwa recalled explaining that he and Brown did not represent her. Additionally, all three recalled that the attorneys read the agreement to her paragraph by paragraph and explained it as they went through it, also informing her of a spouse's basic community property rights in earnings and acquisitions and that Sun would be waiving these rights. Megwa recalled it was clearly explained that Barry's income and acquisitions during the marriage would remain Barry's separate property, and he recalled that Sun stated that such arrangements were the practice in Sweden. Furthermore, Barry and the two attorneys each confirmed that Sun and Forsberg asked questions during the meeting and were left alone on several occasions to discuss its terms, that Sun did not exhibit any confusion, and that Sun indicated she understood the agreement. They also testified that changes were made to the agreement at Sun's behest. Brown and Megwa experienced no difficulty in communicating with Sun, found her confident and happy, and had no indication that she was nervous or confused, intimidated, or pressured. No threat was uttered that unless she signed the agreement, the wedding would be cancelled, nor did they hear her express any reservations about signing the agreement. Additionally, legal secretary Illa Washington recalled that Wilcox waited in another room while the agreement was discussed, that Sun asked questions and that changes were made to the agreement at her behest, that Sun was informed she could secure independent counsel, that Sun said she understood the contract and did not want to consult another attorney, and that she appeared to understand the discussions and to feel comfortable and confident.

The trial court found for Barry Bonds and Sun appealed. The court of appeals reversed for a trial on voluntariness of the agreement. Bonds appealed.

JUDICIAL OPINION

George, Chief Justice. The trial court observed that the case turned upon the credibility of the witnesses. In support of its determination that Sun entered into the agreement voluntarily, "free from the taint of fraud, coercion and undue influence...with full knowledge of the property involved and her rights therein," the trial court made the following findings of fact:

> Respondent [Sun] knew Petitioner [Barry] wished to protect his present property and future earnings. Respondent knew...that the Agreement provided that...Petitioner's present and future earnings would remain his separate property....
>
> Respondent is an intelligent woman and though English is not her native language, she was capable of understanding the discussion by Attorney Brown and Attorney Megwa regarding the terms of the agreement and the effect of the Agreement on each [party's] rights. Respondent was not forced to execute the document, nor did anyone threaten Respondent in any way. Respondent never questioned signing the Agreement or requested that she not sign the Agreement. Respondent's refusal to sign the Agreement would have caused little embarrassment to her. The wedding was a small impromptu affair that could have been easily postponed....Respondent had sufficient awareness and understanding of her right to, and need for, independent counsel. Respondent also had an adequate and reasonable opportunity to obtain independent counsel prior to execution of the Agreement. Respondent was advised at a meeting with Attorney Brown at least one week prior to execution of the Agreement that she had the right to have an attorney represent her and that Attorneys Brown and Megwa represented Petitioner, not Respondent. On at least two occasions during the February 5, 1988, meeting, Respondent was told that she could have separate counsel if she chose. Respondent declined.

The Court of Appeal in a split decision reversed the judgment rendered by the trial court and directed a retrial on the issue of voluntariness. The majority opinion stressed that Sun lacked independent counsel, determined that she had not waived counsel effectively, and concluded that under such circumstances the evidence must be subjected to strict judicial scrutiny to determine whether the agreement was voluntary. The majority opinion asserted that Attorneys Brown and Megwa failed to explain that Sun's interests conflicted with Barry's, failed to urge her to retain separate counsel, and may have led Sun to believe they actually represented her interests as they explained the agreement paragraph by paragraph. The majority opinion concluded that the trial court erred in failing to give proper weight to the circumstance that Sun was not represented by independent counsel.

In California, a premarital agreement generally has been considered to be enforceable as a contract, although when there is proof of fraud, constructive fraud, duress, or undue influence, the contract is not enforceable.

Although the proposed Uniform Act initially contained a proviso stating that premarital agreements were presumptively valid unless the party against whom enforcement was sought was not represented by independent legal counsel or there was not full disclosure, the commissioners eventually removed any reference to independent counsel. [N]o state has made the presence of independent counsel a prerequisite to enforceability.

Finally, and perhaps most significantly, the rule created by the Court of Appeal would have the effect of shifting the burden of proof on the question of voluntariness to the party seeking enforcement of the premarital agreement, even though the statute expressly places the burden upon the party challenging the voluntariness of the agreement.

We conclude that although the ability of the party challenging the agreement to obtain independent counsel is an important factor in determining whether that party entered into the agreement voluntarily, the Court of Appeal majority erred in directing trial courts to subject premarital agreements to strict scrutiny where the less sophisticated party does not have independent counsel and has not waived counsel according to exacting waiver requirements.

We do not believe that the case before us presents an appropriate occasion to delineate the duties that must guide an attorney in drafting a premarital agreement. The issue before us is the enforceability of a premarital agreement, not the extent, if any, of counsel's duty to an unrepresented party to the agreement, or the imposition of discipline upon an attorney who does not comply with that duty. We do observe, however, that it is consistent with an attorney's duty to further the interest of his or her client for the attorney to take steps to ensure that the premarital agreement will be enforceable.

Finally, we observe that the evidence supports the inference that Sun was intrepid rather than a person whose will is easily overborne. She emigrated from her homeland at a young age, found employment and friends in a new country using two languages other than her native tongue, and in two years moved to yet another country, expressing the desire to take up a career and declaring to Barry that she "didn't want his money." These circumstances support the inference that any inequality in bargaining power—arising primarily from the absence of independent counsel who could have advised Sun not to sign the agreement or urged Barry to abandon the idea of keeping his earnings separate—was not coercive.

With respect to full disclosure of the property involved, the trial court found that Sun was aware of what separate property was held by Barry prior to the marriage, and as the Court of Appeal noted, she failed to identify any property of which she later became aware that was not on the list of property referred to by the parties when they executed the contract. The trial court also determined that Sun was aware of what was at stake—of what normally would be community property, namely the earnings and acquisitions of the parties during marriage. Substantial evidence supports this conclusion....

With respect to the question of knowledge, as already explained it is evident that the trial court was impressed with the extent of Sun's awareness.

Reversed.

CASE QUESTIONS

1. Describe the meeting at which the prenuptial agreement was signed.
2. Is the lack of independent legal counsel the sole factor that determines whether a prenuptial agreement is valid?
3. What persuaded the trial court and California Supreme Court that Sun's agreement was voluntary?

CONSIDER 8.10

Patricia met Joel F. Tamraz in December 1987, both having been previously married with children. At that time, Joel was in the process of purchasing a condominium in Malibu, California, for $220,000. Although Joel initially took title to the property in his name only, before escrow closed he signed a quitclaim deed in which he granted one-third of his separate property interest in the Malibu condominium to Patricia, as her separate property, with title to be held as tenants in common.

Patricia and Joel became engaged in February 1988 and the following month Patricia moved into the condominium. The parties lived together until September 1996. Thereafter, Patricia lived in Northern California, where she worked for The Gap, Inc., coordinating purchases and deliveries. Joel continued to live in the condominium and to maintain his law practice in Los Angeles.

CONSIDER 8.10

(continued)

Ten years after they met, on February 9, 1998, Joel made reservations for the parties to be married on February 14, 1998, in Las Vegas. Eight to ten people were invited to the wedding and Joel paid the airfare for many of the guests.

On the day before the wedding, Joel faxed an "Antenuptial Agreement," which he had drafted, from his office in Los Angeles to Patricia's place of employment in San Francisco. She was not aware the facsimile was coming and did not find it in her "in box" until after 4:00 p.m. She contacted Joel and told him that pages appeared to be missing, that she could not put the document together consecutively, and that she did not understand the terminology. Joel then faxed more pages, including duplicates, that did not appear to be a complete set.

The agreement, which was dated February 13, 1998, provided that if a petition for dissolution or nullity of the marriage was filed, Patricia would receive $20,000 as her full and complete share of the condominium and that she would be required to deed her one-third interest to Joel. The agreement was 10 pages in length and contained spaces at the bottom of each page for the parties' initials. Joel initialed each page, signed the agreement, and also signed the "Attorney's Certification for Prospective Husband," indicating that he was representing himself. Patricia did not see the version of the agreement signed by Joel until after their marriage. The copy of the agreement initialed and signed by Patricia, and faxed back to Joel, is missing the second page of the agreement, which contained, among other provisions, an express waiver by the parties of the right to any disclosure of the other's property and financial obligations. One page of the agreement signed by Patricia appears to have been cut off by the fax machine and another page is almost completely blank. Patricia herself signed the "Attorney's Certification for Prospective Wife," adding the handwritten notation, "I understand this agreement."

Prior to receiving the agreement, Patricia had at most two conversations about a premarital agreement. Joel told Patricia that the purpose of the agreement was to protect his interest in his law practice and in the condominium in the event that she initiated a divorce and to prevent her from being held liable for his debts. Patricia testified that she relied on Joel's representations as to the legal effect of the agreement. She did not read or understand most of the agreement and signed it because she "really loved" Joel and "believed in him" and "believed everything he said." Joel never advised Patricia to seek her own legal advice in regard to the agreement, and she did not do so.

Patricia felt a certain amount of pressure to sign the agreement because she was not convinced that Joel would marry her without the agreement and because everyone at her work knew that she was getting married. She was in "a terrible hurry" when she received the agreement because she had to leave work "within minutes" in order to pick up her luggage in Sausalito and then catch a flight to Las Vegas so that she and Joel could marry the next day. Once in Las Vegas, Joel did not mention the agreement.

Joel, who has practiced law in the state of California since 1967, had drafted at least five other prenuptial agreements for clients and had been engaged in litigation regarding such agreements. He had also previously successfully represented Patricia in helping her to obtain a larger award in her prior divorce.

Following the parties' marriage on February 14, 1998, Patricia continued to reside in Northern California until she moved back in with Joel in June 2000. Joel filed a petition for dissolution of marriage and sought to have marital and other property distributed according to the terms of the prenuptial agreement. Is the agreement valid? What makes this case the same as the *Bonds* case? What makes it different? *In re Marriage of Tamraz*, Not Reported in Cal.Rptr.3d, 2005 WL 1524199 (Cal.App. 2 Dist.) Not Officially Published.

ETHICAL ISSUE

Discuss the public policy and ethical issues in prenuptial agreements and in courts upholding their validity. One lawyer has commented, "I've never seen a marriage with a prenuptial agreement last." Why this observation?

Figure 8.3 provides a summary of famous prenuptial agreements and their eventual validity and fallout.

Figure 8.3 Prenuptial Agreements of the Rich and Famous

Name	Terms	Results
Donald Trump and Marla Maples	No alimony if adultery; child support; limited dollar amount	Prenup honored in divorce; Maples awarded limited amount.
Barry Bonds (San Francisco Giants) and Susann Branco	Agreement (14 pages) signed on the way to the wedding	Appellate court upheld the agreement (see case in chapter) and Mrs. Bonds was limited to $10,000 per month/per child support and no share of the earnings and property Barry Bonds acquired during their marriage.
Steven Spielberg and Amy Irving	Scrap of paper prenup, but Irving had no lawyer. Gave Irving no interest in Spielberg rights, royalties, revenues, and properties.	Judge set agreement aside for Irving's lack of representation. Spielberg settled for $100 million (4-year marriage).
Melinda and Bill Gates	Unknown	Still married
Jack and Jane Welch	Jane Welch had no interest in Jack Welch's stock, salary, options, and property during the first 10 years of their marriage. After 10 years, they shared in the assets.	Mrs. Welch filed for divorce after 13 years. Public filings in the divorce case caused General Electric shareholders to protest the expenditures and compensation of Welch, GE's retired CEO.

Cautions and Conclusions

Whether a party is a seller, buyer, or creditor, the status of property co-owners must be determined. The following are questions to be answered before entering into an obligation regarding the co-owned property:

1. Who are the co-owners?
2. What type of co-ownership exists?
3. Is one co-owner authorized to transfer title or to give a lien?
4. How much of an interest does the co-owner have?
5. Are additional signatures (spouses') required?

Key Terms

antenuptial agreements, 175
community property, 169
community property with right of survivorship, 163
co-ownership, 157
curtesy rights, 169
dower rights, 168
joint tenancy, 158
premarital agreements, 175
prenuptial agreements, 175
strawman transaction, 159
tenancy by entirety, 163
tenancy in common, 158
tenancy in partnership, 163
Uniform Marital Property Act, 170
Uniform Premarital Agreement Act, 176
unities, 159

Chapter Problems

1. On a deed dated November 1, 1928, an acre of land located on Gap Road near Peak Mountain in Rockingham County, Virginia, was conveyed to Add Shoemaker and his wife Bessie Shoemaker with the following provision:

It is hereby mutually understood and agreed, that the grantees herein named are to have and to hold the said land and tenements as joint tenants, and not as tenants in common.

Add Shoemaker died intestate (without a will) in 1951 and was survived by Bessie and several children. Bessie, at some point after Add's death, conveyed to Wilmer A. Shoemaker (one of her sons) a 0.542-acre portion of the land she and Add had acquired in the 1928 deed. Bessie died in 1984.

Wilmer died testate (with a will) sometime before 1988 and by his will devised the 0.542-acre tract of land to Shelby Jean Moubray. Moubray conveyed the tract to David Martin Smith and Vivian Secrist Smith on January 28, 1988.

On February 19, 1992, Susan Shoemaker Hoover, Catherine G. Shoemaker Smith, Sarah P. Shoemaker Pennington, and Margie C. Shoemaker Hoover (collectively, the Hoovers), the children of Add and Bessie, filed suit against Alvin Shoemaker, Nellie Craun, and Charles Shoemaker, also children of Add and Bessie (collectively, the Smiths). The suit alleged that by the language of the 1928 deed, Bessie and Add were tenants in common only and that upon Add's death his interest in the tract of land should have passed by intestate succession to his children. The children also asked that the land be sold and its proceeds distributed because it was not convenient to partition the land. Are the children right? *Hoover v. Smith*, 444 S.E.2d 546 (Va. 1994)

2. Althea Lynley and Agnes Peach hold title to a 640-acre section in Montana as joint tenants with right of survivorship. The two acquired the property in their younger days with the idea that they would always be there for each other, and that the survivor would carry on with the property's development as a ranch.

Within five years of their acquisition, Althea married and moved to San Diego, and Agnes was left in Montana, where she married and developed the property with her husband. The title to the property remained the same as it was when the deed was originally recorded. Agnes died in June 1994. Her husband and children assumed they would inherit the land because Agnes's will left everything she owned to them. However, Althea, who returned for Agnes's funeral, claims the land belongs to her. Who is correct?

3. George Herring and his wife had property conveyed to them as "Mr. and Mrs. Herring" with the following language:

TO HAVE AND TO HOLD unto said parties of the second part, and the Survivor of them, his heirs and assigns forever. It is the intention of this conveyance that said parties of the second part are to be vested with title as joint tenants, with the incident of survivorship, and not as tenants in common; so that upon the death of either said parties of the second part, the entire fee simple absolute title in and to said property shall ipso facto become vested in the Survivor of said parties of the second part.

Mrs. Herring conveyed her interest in the property to her son from a previous marriage, Clarence Carroll. Mr. Herring brought suit to have the conveyance set aside. During the judicial proceedings, Mr. Herring died and his children, Marshall Herring and Beatrice Midkiff, as Mr. Herring's sole heirs, continued the case, claiming they were entitled to receive title to the property. Mr. Carroll claims the conveyance by Mrs. Herring to him was valid and made him a tenant in common with Marshall and Beatrice. Who is correct? *Herring v. Carroll*, 300 S.E.2d 629 (Ct. App. W. Va. 1983)

4. Barbara Laudig and Robert Laudig were married in 1972. In 1987, Mr. Laudig discovered that Mrs. Laudig was involved in an extramarital relationship. Mr. Laudig left their home, but returned later that year and agreed to stay if Mrs. Laudig would sign a postnuptial agreement. The agreement provided that Mrs. Laudig, in exchange for $10,000, would waive all rights to marital property if she had an extramarital affair anytime during the next 15 years. The agreement was signed by both parties in August 1987.

In December 1988, Mrs. Laudig renewed her relationship with her former paramour, and Mr. Laudig filed for divorce in May 1989. Mr. Laudig sought to enforce the postnuptial agreement and be awarded all the marital property. Mrs. Laudig objected on the grounds that their postnuptial agreement was against public policy. Who is correct? *Laudig v. Laudig*, 624 A.2d 651 (Pa. 1993)

5. In February 1952, James and Syvilla Ballantyne acquired title, as joint tenants, to a lot in the city of Minot. They lived there in a house located on the lot. On April 10, 1959, James Ballantyne died, leaving a will that purported to devise the lot to his wife, Syvilla, for life, with the remainder to his eight children by a previous marriage. James and Syvilla had no children of their marriage, and the probate court awarded Syvilla a life estate and a remainder to the eight children as part of the final distribution of James's estate.

Syvilla occupied the home and paid the taxes on it until her death on May 11, 1973. She did not remarry and left a will that did not mention the lot but left the residue of her estate to her sisters and her brother. After Syvilla's death, James's eight children took possession of the property and attempted to sell it. At that time, the discovery of the joint tenancy was made, and Syvilla's sisters brought suit. What interest was created and who owns what and how following Syvilla's death? *Cranston v. Winters*, 238 N.W.2d 647 (N.D. 1976)

6. John Z. DeLorean and Cristina DeLorean entered into an antenuptial agreement on May 8, 1973 (only a few hours before they were married), that provided the following:

[A]ny and all property, income and earnings acquired by each before and after the marriage shall be the separate property of the person acquiring the same, without any rights, title or control vesting in the other person.

The marital assets (such as future earnings) could have exceeded $20 million, and practically all of them were in the name John. Without this agreement and considering that the marriage lasted 13 years and resulted in two minor children, Cristina would ordinarily be entitled to 50 percent of the marital assets at the time of divorce.

On DeLorean's petition for divorce, Cristina alleged that the agreement was invalid because she was not given full information about the extent of her husband's financial affairs before she signed and that her husband exercised undue influence on her in getting the agreement signed. The trial court upheld the validity of the agreement, and Mrs. DeLorean appealed. Is the agreement valid? *Delorean v. Delorean*, 511 A.2d 1257 (N.J. 1986)

(Note: Mr. DeLorean died at age 80 in 2005. He was acquitted in two criminal trials, one involving charges of conspiring to sell cocaine, and the other for financial fraud. His assets were depleted with a final sale to Donald Trump of his Bedminster estate, a property that is now a golf course.)

7. Robert and Bernice Fick lived together beginning in 1981. In 1984, they were married. Shortly before their wedding, they both signed a prenuptial agreement that had been drafted by Robert. Among other things, the agreement waived both parties' rights to alimony upon divorce. The agreement incorporated by attachment both Bernice's and Robert's financial statements of property ownership and debts. However, Robert's statement was not attached at the time the agreement was signed and was not produced for Bernice until a year after their wedding. In 1989, Bernice filed for divorce and asked that the prenuptial agreement be set aside. Robert maintained that the agreement was valid because Bernice signed voluntarily and was represented by counsel. Bernice says she was misled because Robert did not attach his financials and she signed without complete information. Should the court set aside the prenuptial agreement and award Bernice the alimony and property she is requesting? *Fick v. Fick*, 851 P.2d 445 (Nev. 1993)

8. Carolyn Cummings had been awarded a medical retirement and disability benefits from the state of Alaska during the 1970s. She then met and married Gary Cummings and continued to receive her benefits from Alaska because of her disability. She used the funds to purchase various items for their household as well as a camp trailer. During an action for divorce, Carolyn claimed the furnishings and the trailer were her separate property. Gary claimed the commingling of the funds made those items community property. Who is correct? *Cummings v. Cummings*, 765 P.2d 697 (Idaho 1988)

9. Otto and Oscar Olson built a footbridge on their property across the Smith River in 1949. A document called "Footbridge Access" was signed "Olson Brothers by Otto Olson" and gave E. G. Dunn the right to use the footbridge. A dispute later arose between the parties regarding the right to use the bridge. Oscar says Otto could not convey the access without his signature. Is he correct? *Smo v. Black*, 761 P.2d 1339 (Or. 1988)

10. William Pajak married his third wife, Audrey, one day after they entered into a prenuptial agreement by which Audrey waived any and all interests in William's estate. William had four children from his two previous marriages and wished for his property to go to them. Audrey was a secretary at Carolina Furniture Company, William's business. She had a tenth-grade education and did not read the agreement before signing it. The agreement was drafted by William's lawyer, and the lawyer was present while Audrey signed the agreement. Audrey also indicated she knew William owned the furniture store, but she knew of no other holdings. In fact, William's property and estate were quite extensive. Shortly after their marriage, William passed away. Audrey claimed an interest in the estate because the prenuptial agreement was invalid. The children claim Audrey understood the agreement and chose not to seek advice. Should Audrey be entitled to a spouse's share of the estate? *Pajak v. Pajak*, 385 S.E.2d 384 (W.Va. 1989)

For research activities related to this chapter, go to our text companion website at www.thomsonedu.com/westbuslaw/jennings.

The Landlord–Tenant Relationship

CHAPTER 9

Tenant's responsibilities/Landlord's rights:

- *Pay the rent on time.*
- *Keep the apartment and the surrounding area clean and in good condition.*
- *Keep noise to a level that will not disturb your neighbors.*
- *When moving out, give landlord proper advance notice.*
- *Notify the landlord immediately if the apartment needs repair through no fault of the tenant.*

Landlord's responsibilities/Tenant's rights:

- *A clean apartment when the tenant moves in;*
- *Clean common areas (hallways, stairs, yards, entryways);*
- *Well-lit hallways and entryways; and,*
- *Properly working plumbing and heating (both hot and cold running water).*

Adapted from the State of Connecticut, Judicial Branch, Landlord/Tenant Law, Frequently Asked Questions, http://www.jud.ct.gov/faq/landlord.html.

A lease may seem like a simple transaction—the tenant pays the rent and the landlord provides the premises. But, both sides have rights and responsibilities such as those listed in the chapter opening. This chapter answers the following questions: What types of lease agreements exist? What terms should be included in the lease agreement? What rights and responsibilities do each of the parties have? There are several sources of laws and principles for the landlord–tenant relationship, including common law, state statutory provisions, and the **Uniform Residential Landlord Tenant Act (URLTA)**, which has been adopted formally in about one-third of the states and is also followed in principle in most of the states. This chapter concentrates on residential leases, and Chapter 10 deals with commercial leases.

Types of Tenancies

The four types of tenancies that existed at common law are *tenancy for years, periodic tenancy, tenancy at will, and tenancy at sufferance.* These tenancies will apply to both commercial and residential leases except when there are specific statutory changes. A lease agreement can provide for its own type of lease and terms, but there are categories that common law still recognizes.

Tenancy for Years

A **tenancy for years** is created by a lease that will run for a specific period of time. Language used to create a tenancy for years includes "estate for years," "tenancy for a term," or "tenancy for a period." Every tenancy for years has a fixed beginning and ending date and is created by language such as "To A for 7 years" or "To A from 31 March 2007 until 30 June 2009." The lease terminates automatically when we reach the specified ending date.

In a tenancy for years, the parties involved have a continuing relationship and should have a written agreement that includes all their rights and obligations. A tenancy for years that runs for a period longer than one year must be in writing under most states' statutes of fraud. (Details on content of written leases are discussed later in this chapter.)

Periodic Tenancy

A **periodic tenancy** has no definite ending date: It continues until one of the parties takes proper legal steps to terminate the interest. A periodic tenancy can be expressly created, and an example of language used to create such an interest is, "To A on a month-to-month basis beginning 30 June 2007."

The periodic tenancy or estate from period to period need not be created expressly; it can be created through the conduct of the parties. For example, suppose that Ruth moves into one of Meryl's Maine beach houses on an oral lease agreement that is to run for 24 months. In Maine, leases that run for longer than one year must be in writing to be enforceable. Because of the writing requirement in the law, the parties do not have an enforceable lease agreement, but once Meryl accepts Ruth's rent, they have created a periodic tenancy by their conduct. Their lease can now be terminated only by meeting the requirements for ending a periodic tenancy.

Termination requirements for periodic tenancies are specified by statute in each state, but the key to termination in all states is notice. The type or length of notice will vary, but the requirement of notice is universal. The typical period, both at common law and by state statute on a month-to-month tenancy, is a full period's notice, or one month.

Tenancy at Will

A **tenancy at will** can be created expressly when the parties agree to a lease of property but provide no time period for the lease. Sample language to create a tenancy at will is, "To A at O's discretion or will."

In a tenancy at will, both parties have the right to terminate the tenancy at any time and are not required to provide advance notice. In some states, statutory provisions have changed this freedom and require some form of notice to terminate. In these states, the tenancy at will has been modified to a periodic tenancy by statute.

Tenancies at will can arise in situations with a financed property, where there is a default by the party possessing the property. For example, suppose Corey leases the land on which her mobile home is located, and her mobile home is financed through a bank. Corey leaves and the mobile home remains on the leased land. If Corey defaults on her payment and the bank is forced to repossess the mobile home, then the bank, as a creditor in possession, becomes a tenant at will on the land.

Tenancy at Sufferance

This final nonfreehold interest, **tenancy at sufferance**, arises when a tenant from another form of tenancy stays put, or, as the law refers to it, "holds over" on the landlord's property after the original tenancy ends. For example, suppose a landlord leased a bungalow in the Hollywood Hills to Amos Jacobs for two years with a lease termination date of March 31, 2007. Jacobs should vacate the premises by the termination date, but if he remains, he remains there as a trespasser. The landlord may have Jacobs, a holdover tenant, evicted. However, if Jacobs remains on the property without objection from his landlord, and if that landlord accepts rent after March 31, 2007, then Jacobs' lease went from a tenancy for years to a tenancy at sufferance and finally to a periodic tenancy once the rent is paid and accepted.

Terms of Lease Agreement

Need for Lease Agreement

As noted earlier, under the Statute of Frauds, a lease that is to run for a period longer than a year must usually be reduced to some form of writing or record. Under E-Sign and relevant state laws, records are defined to include faxes as well as electronically authorized contracts. In some states, the writing or record requirement may be imposed at six months. Residential and commercial leases are subject to the same Statute of Frauds requirements.

To satisfy the Statute of Frauds, the writing may be informal—in the form of a letter, memorandum, or series of documents. The basics needed are the parties, the signatures of the parties, a description of the leased premises, the term of the lease, and the amount of the rent. While some real estate transactions (deeds, for example) will still require formal written documents, leases enjoy the new freedom of flexibility in documenting lease agreements that fall under the Statute of Frauds. See Web Exhibits 9.1 and 9.2 for samples.

CONSIDER 9.1

Edson found, through Perry Development, an apartment in New York City. Edson told the leasing agent at Perry that he wanted a three-year lease. Perry's business manager wrote a letter to Edson confirming the location of the apartment, the dates of the lease term, the rent, and to whom the rent would be paid. After Edson had occupied the apartment for three months, he received a notice from Perry that the lease would terminate at the end of the fourth month. Edson objected, but Perry maintained that a lease for longer than a year must be in writing, and without anything in writing, Edson was a month-to-month tenant only. Edson wishes to know his rights.

In addition to the minimum requirements for a written lease already mentioned, there are many issues and details in leases that should be covered in the parties' lease agreement and are discussed in the following sections. If the parties do not deal specifically with these issues in a written lease agreement, statutory or common law provisions will apply, and the parties may not have the protection or obtain the results they expect.

Habitability

At common law, when tenants leased property, the doctrine of caveat tenant applied: Tenants leased the premises at their own risk and there were no warranties, covenants, promises, or guarantees that the premises were habitable. The common law did not impose an obligation on the landlord to deliver habitable premises. Without statutory protection, many tenants entered into leases for uninhabitable properties. They were obligated under the lease but faced the difficult task of obtaining repairs and services from the landlord.

To prevent the negative health and safety consequences of this doctrine, particularly in areas where there were housing shortages, most states (with cities imposing additional obligations) enacted laws that require landlords to deliver premises to tenants in habitable condition. The following statutory language is an example of a warranty of habitability requirement.

No persons shall rent or offer to rent any habitation, or the furnishings thereof, unless such a habitation and its furnishings are in a clean, safe, and sanitary condition; in repair; and free from rodents or vermin.

The effect of a breach of the warranty of habitability is to make the lease for the uninhabitable premises void. The effect of a void lease is that the tenant need not pay rent. Indeed, a breach of the warranty of habitability is a defense if a landlord brings action for eviction for nonpayment of rent.

Even in jurisdictions without a statute that applies specifically to leases, some tenants have been excused from performing lease agreements on other grounds. Leases of premises found to have building or fire code violations have been held void, and courts have excused tenants from performing on the grounds of illegality. The key to the cases is that the tenant must have given the landlord notice of the problems and also enough time to bring the premises into a habitable condition.[1] The following case deals with an issue of codes, statutes, and the implied warranty of habitability.

CHIODINI V. FOX

207 S.W.3d 174 (MO. App. 2006)

FACTS

Andrew Chiodini owns a house in Wildwood, Missouri, with a partially finished basement. The unfinished portion of the basement contains a room that Chiodini was in the process of turning into a billiard room, but, as of May 2003, the construction was not completed.

Chiodini wished to lease the house so he listed it with a rental agency called Apartment Search. Through that service Genia Fox and James Winkler (collectively Fox–Winkler) located the listing and Fox viewed the house on April 26, 2003. Winkler was unable to view the house at that time because he was out of state. Nevertheless, Fox–Winkler signed a one-year lease on May 3, 2003, and Chiodini signed it on May 8, 2003. Winkler viewed the house during the second week in May and learned that there was exposed wiring in the unfinished billiard room. At some point thereafter Winkler allegedly informed Chiodini that they would not be taking possession of the house on June 1, 2003,

1. If the tenant who withholds rent based on allegations of uninhabitable conditions fails to follow procedures under statute governing summary process actions, including notifying the landlord of the conditions prior to withholding rent, her refusal to pay some or all of the rent due will subject her to eviction proceedings to which she will have no defense; she cannot use the landlord's alleged breach of the habitability warranty as a defense to a notice to quit for nonpayment of rent unless there is compliance with legal requirements. *Jablonski v. Casey,* 835 N.E.2d 615 (Mass. App. 2005).

the date of the commencement of the lease. In addition, Fox–Winkler's attorney sent Apartment Search a letter on May 21, 2003, noting Fox–Winkler's intention to not take occupancy of the residence.

In an attempt to assuage Fox–Winkler's concerns, Chiodini executed an addendum to the lease ensuring the completion of the billiard room and a compensation scale for certain construction items if they were not completed as promised. The record reflects that neither of the parties signed the addendum.

In an attempt by Fox–Winkler to obtain the proper building permits and inspections, a Metro West Fire Protection District fire inspector inspected the billiard room on May 29, 2003, and found a violation with the fire-blocking. The same day, a county inspector inspected the building's electrical system, revealing the violation with the exposed wires. Fox–Winkler spoke with the fire marshal on May 30, 2003, and learned that the violations in the house could not be remedied by June 1. Fox–Winkler did not take possession of the house.

Chiodini repaired the fire-blocking system and on July 17, 2003, the fire inspector approved the premises. Chiodini repaired the electrical wiring and on June 25, 2003, the electrical system was approved. New tenants took possession of the house on August 20, 2003. Chiodini obtained a Certificate of Occupancy on October 23, 2003.

On December 5, 2003, Chiodini filed against Fox–Winkler for breach of lease. On January 21, 2004, Fox–Winkler filed an answer to Chiodini's petition, alleging as a defense that the premises were uninhabitable. On September 30, 2004 Fox–Winkler filed a counterclaim for the return of their security deposit. The trial court entered judgment for Fox–Winkler, finding that Chiodini breached the implied warranty of habitability by not possessing the appropriate permits and inspectionls. The court awarded Fox–Winkler the return of their security deposit as damages. Chiodini appealed.

JUDICIAL OPINION

Gaertner, SR., Judge. In his first point on appeal, Chiodini argues that the trial court erred in finding that he breached the implied warranty of habitability because any code violations were *de minimis.* It is well-settled in Missouri "that a landlord impliedly warrants the habitability of leased residential property." Habitability is measured by community standards, generally reflected in local housing and property maintenance codes. In order to state a cause of action for breach of an implied warranty of habitability, the tenant must prove four elements:

(1) entry into a lease for residential property; (2) the subsequent development of dangerous or unsanitary conditions on the premises materially affecting the life, health and safety of the tenant; (3) reasonable notice of the defects to the landlord; and (4) subsequent failure to restore the premises to habitability.

But minor housing code violations not affecting the habitability of the property are not considered breaches.

First, Fox–Winkler must prove entry into a residential lease. This element is undisputed.

Second, there must be dangerous or unsanitary conditions materially affecting the life, health, or safety of Fox–Winkler. The exposed electrical wires clearly posed a risk to Fox–Winkler and their children. Additionally, the fire-blocking issue posed a risk, inasmuch as the billiard room did not have the required protection if a fire were to start. Thus, the exposed electrical wires and fire-blocking issue constituted dangerous conditions materially affecting the safety of Fox–Winkler. Accordingly, these code violations were not merely *de minimis* as Chiodini contends.

The third element, notice, is also undisputed as Chiodini was aware of both defects due to notice of the violations from the inspectors.

And finally, Chiodini must have failed to repair the defects. Although Chiodini successfully repaired the electrical and fire-blocking defects by the end of June 2003, he failed to obtain an occupancy permit until October 23, 2003. Without an occupancy permit, Fox–Winkler could not have legally occupied the premises.

Therefore, the trial court did not err in finding that Chiodini breached the implied warranty of habitability. Point denied.

Chiodini contends that the trial court erred in finding that he breached the implied warranty of habitability because Fox–Winkler did not provide him with reasonable time to remedy the defects.

A tenant must give a landlord notice of the defects if the landlord is unaware of them, as well as reasonable time to alleviate the defects.

Chiodini argues that he was willing to put plates over the exposed electrical wires, as stated in the lease addendum, but he does not address the fire-blocking issue, save from arguing that it was merely a *de minimis* violation. Despite the temporary remedy proposed by Chiodini for the electrical wires, he did not and could not have obtained an occupancy permit by June 1, 2003, ensuring Fox–Winkler's legal occupancy of the house. In fact, it should be noted that Chiodini did not obtain an occupancy permit for the residence until October 23, 2003. We find that that is not a reasonable amount of time to remedy the defects.

Chiodini contends that the trial court erred in its calculation of damages. Chiodini argues that the lease addendum provided a compensation scale if certain construction items were not completed by the dates provided. It stated that Fox–Winkler could deduct $60 from their rent for each item not completed on time. Under this argument, Chiodini believes that $160 should be deducted from Fox–Winkler's damage deposit because nearly everything on the list was completed as scheduled.

But this argument is not supported by any authority, and furthermore, the record reflects that neither of the parties signed the addendum to the lease.

Based upon the foregoing, we affirm the judgment of the trial court.

Affirmed.

CASE QUESTIONS

1. What habitability issues existed on the property?
2. What is the significance of the term *de minimis*?
3. What is the effect of the absence of a signature on the addendum?
4. What does the court add as a remedy for tenants faced with breaches of the warranty of habitability on their leased premises?

There is yet another theory for requiring landlords to deliver habitable premises: some states, through statute or judicial decision, create an **implied warranty of habitability** in all lease agreements. The URLTA includes an implied warranty of habitability. For cases on the implied warranty of habitability, refer to Chapter 1.

Tenants should be sure to put in a habitability clause, which may be simple, as the following language indicates: "Owner (landlord) agrees to deliver premises to tenant in a fit and habitable condition."

If the tenant has the opportunity to inspect the premises prior to entering into the lease agreement, a clause may be added to the lease that requires the landlord to make certain repairs and adjustments. The addendum in the *Chiodini v. Fox* case would have worked if the parties had signed the addendum. The following language would require the landlord to make repairs before the tenant has an obligation to take possession and begin the lease: "Owner (landlord) agrees to repair the following or make the following changes prior to the date of the tenant's possession: ..." The *Schuman v. Kobets* case presents an interesting habitability issue as well as a damages question.

SCHUMAN V. KOBETS

760 N.E.2d 682 (Ind. App. 2002)

FACTS

Linda Schuman had an oral month-to-month tenancy with Ernest and Susan Kobets, d/b/a Lynnleigh Apartments, and had reported to them that pigeons had begun nesting in the broken window casing of her dining room window and in the wall next to the bathroom window. She asked in June 1990 that the holes in the walls be repaired, but the Kobetses were not forthcoming with the repairs.

By July of 1990, Ms. Schuman was experiencing fevers, swollen lymph nodes, and "other maladies." When she was diagnosed with histoplasmosis, she presented her doctor bills to the Kobetses for reimbursement. She did not press for payment and her illness passed by the fall of 1990. Histoplasmosis is "a fungus, which is spread by spores that are typically carried in bird excrement, particularly pigeon droppings."

In 1995, the disease appeared again, and Ms. Schuman had to be hospitalized and nearly died. She was taken home to Indiana to be cared for by her mother and forced to postpone her nursing career for one year. She had medical bills of $138,000. Histoplasmosis can reemerge at any time. Ms. Schuman's physicians warned her about the possibility of a lifetime of medical care and treatment for the disease.

Ms. Schuman filed suit against the Kobetses, seeking recovery for all of her medical and related damages. The trial court dismissed all of her claims and the court of appeals affirmed. The supreme court affirmed the dismissal except with regard to her claims for breach of the implied warranty of habitability. The trial court granted summary judgment on all claims except the warranty of habitability and the Kobetses appealed.

JUDICIAL OPINION

Friedlander, Judge. Following the trend of several other states, Indiana has reexamined the rights and duties governing the landlord–tenant relationship. Specifically, Indiana courts have progressively replaced the common-law doctrine of caveat lessee. This movement away from caveat emptor reflects the recognition that the modern tenant lacks the skill and "know-how" to inspect and repair housing to determine if it is fit for its particular purpose. Given the changing circumstances, imposing the doctrine of caveat lessee on residential leases would in effect shield landlords from liability and place tenants in an inferior bargaining position in comparison to that of the landlord. Thus, Indiana courts have consistently acknowledged the landlord's duty to render the premises habitable even in the absence of an express covenant.

Although Indiana clearly recognizes the implied warranty of habitability in the context of landlord–tenant disputes, it is less obvious whether the implied warranty provides the basis for relief on claims of personal injury. Upon review, Schuman requests that we extend the remedies available under contract law to include the expenses she has incurred as a result of the personal injuries sustained from the Kobetses' breach of implied warranty of habitability.

Schuman argues that consequential damages, including personal injury damages, are recoverable in Indiana under a claim for either breach of an implied warranty of quiet use and enjoyment or breach of an implied warranty of habitability. She maintains that when the consequential damages, including those for personal injury, are foreseeable, a tenant is entitled to recovery under a claim for breach of implied warranty of habitability.

"… Where the warranty is implied-in-fact, however, consequential damages may not be awarded because personal injury is outside the parties' contemplation." This language indicates that the supreme court intended, as a matter of law, to preclude the recovery of personal injury and property damages in a breach of implied warranty of habitability claim. Thus, we reject Schuman's claim that her personal injuries were within the contemplation of the parties at the inception of the lease.

The fact that the Kobetses carried $4,000,000 in liability coverage to pay for personal injury damages is insufficient to support the conclusion that Schuman's personal injuries were within the contemplation of the parties at the inception of the lease. Similarly, while violations of city ordinances or housing codes may serve as proof of breach of a warranty, they do not establish the fact that personal injuries were within the parties' contemplation at the inception of the lease. Although we acknowledge that consequential damages are available under certain circumstances, e.g., where there is an express warranty, we hold that personal injury damages are, as a matter of law, not recoverable under the theory of implied warranty of habitability.

Of course, Schuman's recovery on her contract claim will be defined by the law of contract. Her damages thus might be measured by the difference between the contract price and the market price of the apartment as delivered, for example, or by the difference between the value of the premises without promised repairs and with them.

Following the trend of other states in regards[*sic*] to landlord–tenant disputes, we hold that the warranty of habitability implied in a lease of a dwelling does not give rise to a cause of action for personal injuries as a matter of law. Accordingly, we affirm.

Judgment affirmed.

CASE QUESTIONS

1. What was the breach of the warranty of habitability?
2. Was the warranty express or implied?
3. Why is the answer to question number 2 significant for the court?
4. Will Schuman recover her medical damages? How much will she recover?

CONSIDER 9.2

Francine M. Fletcher and Michael G. Vazquez were tenants in the house in Scituate, Massachusetts, owned by Stephen F. Littleton. Their children, Paul and Stephen Fletcher, Maria and Dominique Vazquez, and Kristin Lynch, lived in the house with them. On April 4, 1995, while Francine and Michael were out to dinner and the children were at home with a babysitter, a fire broke out inside the living room wall. Maria, Paul, and Stephen were killed in the fire, and Dominique and Kristin were injured. The babysitter was not in any way responsible for the deaths or injuries.

The house, which was built prior to the 1930s, was purchased by Littleton's grandparents in the 1950s, and was later owned by Littleton's parents. They used the house as a summer vacation home until 1977, when they converted it to year-round use. Littleton inherited the house from his parents after their deaths in 1987 and 1988.

When Littleton's parents winterized the house in 1977, they had the walls filled with spray-in insulation but did not change the original wiring. That wiring was of the knob-and-tube variety, commonly used at the time the house was constructed and still

CONSIDER 9.2

(continued)

frequently in use, but no longer allowed to be used in repairs or new installations. Knob-and-tube wiring creates considerable heat and the presence of spray-in insulation can prevent the ventilation of that heat and increase the risk of fire. Littleton was not aware of the type of wiring in use in the house, of the presence of the spray-in insulation, or of the potential risk posed by the combination of the wiring and the insulation.

Fletcher and others brought suit against Littleton for wrongful death damages for Littleton's breach of the implied warranty of habitability. Fletcher argued that there was a code violation as well as a failure of Littleton to keep the property in a safe and sanitary condition and that both were grounds for breach of the implied warranty of merchantability. Littleton defended on the grounds that he was not aware of the wiring and insulation problem. Who is correct? How should the court decide the case and why? *Fletcher v. Littleton*, 859 N.E.2d 882 (Mass. App. 2007)

Some states have specific statutory requirements on certain conditions in rental property. For example, the presence of lead-based paint in residential property is now highly regulated. In some states, the landlord is required to remove the lead paint and repaint the apartment. In addition to the breach of the warranty of habitability, tenants may have statutory remedies when the habitability issue is one caused by the presence of this type of paint.

Under the Residential Lead-Based Paint Hazard Reduction Act of 1992, 42 U.S.C. §§4851–4856, both the Environmental Protection Agency (EPA) and the Department of Housing and Urban Development (HUD) were charged with disclosure standards for lead paints on their properties. Under the HUD/EPA rules, landlords must disclose the presence of lead paint on their property and provide a pamphlet explaining the hazards of lead-based paint (40 C.F.R. §745.100 *et seq.* and 24 CFR §35.80 *et seq.*). The effect of the rule has been that landlords are eliminating the lead paint because the disclosure makes properties difficult to rent.

The presence of mold in residential properties has resulted in a new wave of landlord forms and disclosure requirements across the states. For example, in Washington, landlords are required to notify tenants about the health risks of mold and provide information on how to spot mold issues and what to do in the event of any discovery of growing molds. Other states with similar requirements include California, Minnesota, Texas, and Wisconsin. Presently, there are no federal standards on the issue of mold and leases. If tenants are alert, molds formed because of humidity, condensation, or leaks can be cleaned up easily with just bleach and water. If, however, the molds grow, the spores infiltrate the property and require expertise and decontamination for removal. Regardless of statutory requirements, many landlords are obtaining inspections by certified mold inspectors prior to the start of leases because of the high health hazard and resulting liability exposure should molds be present.

Practical Tip

To deal with the mold issue, regardless of statutory requirements, landlords should

- *Have the property inspected by a certified mold inspector.*
- *Inform tenants of the risks of mold exposure.*
- *Provide tenants with information on how to spot and clean molds; some landlords provide tenants with mold test kits.*
- *Give tenants information on whom to contact in the event they see signs of growing molds.*
- *Have tenants sign off on special forms available from insurers that indicate they were furnished with the mold disclosure and information.*
- *Check insurance to be sure there is not a mold exclusion clause that eliminates mold cases as a recoverable issue; landlords can obtain a rider for coverage when mold is excluded but because of litigation (about 10,000 cases per year), the premium can double insurance costs on property.*

ETHICAL ISSUE

In some cases landlords are resistant to making repairs to properties that do not meet the standards for habitability. Many courts have undertaken creative remedies to this problem of resistance. For example, in Phoenix, Arizona, Sherwin Seyrafi, called a "slumlord" by various news organizations, was charged with misdemeanor violations for the conditions of his various properties and then ordered by a judge, as part of his sentence, to live in one of his properties for 30 days. What is the ethical standard the sentencing judge is applying to the landlord's conduct? Do you agree or disagree with the sentence?

CONSIDER 9.3

A 60-unit cooperative apartment building on West 142nd Street in Manhattan was severely damaged by fire on February 7, 1994, and rendered uninhabitable by the Department of Buildings. No action was taken to demolish or renovate the building, and in November 1994, the owners brought suit seeking a court order requiring the Owners Corporation and its managing agent to restore the premises to a safe and habitable condition. However, the property had not been adequately insured, and the Owners Corporation declared bankruptcy on November 23, 1994.

The Owners Corporation defended its inaction on the grounds that the cost of restoration would exceed the market value of the property. The owners maintain there is a statutory requirement for a landlord to keep his property in a safe and habitable condition. Could the warranty of habitability be used to mandate the reconstruction of a building? Should it be so used? *Bernard v. Scharf*, 656 N.Y.S.2d 583 (Sup. Ct. 1997)

Deposits

Most tenants are required to make some type of deposit when they enter into a lease agreement. The types of deposits include security deposit, cleaning deposit, and prepaid rent.

Security Deposit

The deposit most frequently required is the **security deposit**. Its purpose is to protect the landlord in the event of property damage or to cover lost rent if the tenant leaves before the lease ending date. The money held on deposit as security may be used to cover expenses or damages and may even be specified as liquidated damages in the event of an early termination by the tenant.

In some states, security deposits are regulated to a great extent; in other states, the landlord and tenant can agree on the purpose and effect of the security deposit. For example, under the URLTA, the amount of a security deposit is limited. Section 2.101(a) provides, "A landlord may not demand or receive security, however denominated, in an amount or value in excess of (one) month['s] period."

Once landlords have the tenant's security deposit, they retain it until termination of the lease. There are considerable differences among the states on how landlords may use security deposits received from tenants. The common law rule is that the landlord is a debtor to the tenant for the security deposit and is free to use the funds as if they were the landlord's own. However, some states require landlords to pay tenants a minimum amount of interest (such as 5 percent) for the time the deposit is held. Some states also require landlords to keep the security deposits in special trust accounts and maintain and submit periodic records of their balances and deposits received from tenants.

States also differ in their definitions of what constitutes a security deposit. For example, in some states prepaid rent is considered part of the security deposit, and in other states the landlord is not required to follow security deposit procedures on funds labeled prepaid rent.

The security deposit can also double as a liquidated damages provision. A liquidated damage clause is an advance agreement between the landlord and tenant as to how a breach will be determined and what the breach damages will be. The lease may provide that the liquidated damages for breach will be the security deposit. For example, if a tenant leases an apartment for $1000 per month for a six-month period and abandons the premises at four months, the landlord is entitled, with a proper liquidated damage provision in the lease, to keep the security deposit as damages for early termination by the tenant. When the tenant ends the apartment lease early, the landlord could re-rent the apartment the next day or the apartment could sit vacant for the remaining two months of the original lease. Because we cannot know in advance how, if, or to what degree the landlord will be harmed by an early termination, an agreement to allow the landlord to keep the security deposit as damages is a valid liquidated damage provision.

In some states and under the URLTA, if the landlord chooses the remedy of keeping the security deposit, then the amount of the security deposit is the total for the landlord's damages. A landlord cannot collect actual damages and keep the security deposit because the result would be an assessment of a penalty for breach against the tenant. Such penalties for breach of residential lease agreements are void. A landlord is not entitled to both liquidated and actual damages. Also under the URLTA, retention of the security deposit requires the landlord to account to the tenant for how much was kept and why.

The following language is an example of the type of clause necessary when the tenant is paying funds taken by the landlord as a security deposit:

SECURITY: In order to guarantee Resident's faithful performance of the terms and conditions contained herein, Resident hereby deposits with owner the sum of $____ as a security deposit to be applied to the payment of accrued but unpaid rent and any other damages suffered by reason of Resident's noncompliance or breach of any terms and conditions of the Rental Agreement.

If there are no statutory provisions governing security deposits in the state, the parties should specify in the lease agreement their rights to the security deposit, including procedures and time limitations for its use and return and its effect as a provision for liquidated damages.

Another issue that has arisen with leases is whether the landlord has a duty to mitigate damages by leasing the premises to another tenant. In the absence of an agreement, courts are reluctant to impose such a duty because of the resulting questions that arise, such as whether the landlord was diligent in finding a new tenant, whether the new lease was fair, and whether the costs the landlord incurred in mitigation are recoverable.

CONSIDER 9.4

Barbara Kent and her roommate, Sheila Barnes, have signed a nine-month lease on an apartment. The rent is $1,050 per month, and the roommates were required to make a $1,050 security deposit. At the end of four months, they decide to move to a house closer to their places of employment. The apartment owner is unable to lease the apartment for three months, and the apartment is vacant for that time. Discuss the use of the security deposit to cover damages according to the laws of your state.

Suppose the tenants abandon the leased apartment after performance of three months on a six-month, $1,050-per-month lease, and the landlord is able to rent the apartment for one of the three remaining months, what are the landlord's damages?

Cleaning Deposit

In addition to security deposits, which are intended to secure rental payments, landlords may require tenants to make other deposits. A **cleaning deposit** is a typical lease requirement and may take the form of a nonrefundable fee that all tenants are required to pay. Under the URLTA, a nonrefundable cleaning deposit must be disclosed and provided for in the lease agreement. The following is a sample clause from a lease: "Additionally, Resident hereby pays the sum of $____, which is a NONREFUNDABLE redecorating fee." The fees paid may be called cleaning, refurbishing, redecorating, or restoration fees, but they all require advance disclosure of retention under the URLTA.

Some cleaning fees are taken with the idea that they will be used, if necessary, at the time the tenant vacates the premises. The theory behind this type of deposit is that tenants will have greater incentive to keep the premises clean and well maintained and not destroy items of property. For example, some leases contain addenda that specify cleaning costs to be assessed if, at the end of the lease and upon the landlord's inspection, particular cleaning tasks are necessary. Specific items such as drapery cleaning or wall repainting may be represented as a dollar amount, so that tenants will know the potential assessments in advance.

Prepaid Rent

Many landlords require tenants to pay the first and last months' rent prior to taking possession of the property. Such a provision is for the protection of the landlord in the event the tenant vacates the premises without paying rent. However, the URLTA and many other states' provisions limit the amount of prepaid rent or total deposits that may be required of the tenant initially, and the limit may be as small as 1½ times the monthly rent. The lease agreement or an addendum to it should specify exactly what amounts are being received from the tenant and the purpose and application of those amounts. These limitations are not applicable in commercial leases.

Amount of Rent

In addition to specifying the amounts of deposits, the lease agreement should specify the monthly rental fee. The amount of rent becomes more of an issue in commercial leases where landlords are entitled to portions of profits (see Chapter 10). Residential lease agreements should specify how much rent is to be paid, the date the rent is due, to whom the rent is to be paid, and if there are any fees associated with late rental payments. The following is a sample rental fee clause:

RENTAL: The rental shall be $____ per month, plus sales tax thereon at the rate in effect from time to time, payable in advance on the FIRST day of each month at the on-site manager's office. An equitable proration of the first month's rent shall be made if the term of this Rental Agreement commences other than on the first day of the calendar month. A late charge of $10.00 per day shall be added as additional rent to any rent payment not paid in full on or before the due date. A $25.00 fee will be charged for all checks returned from the bank unpaid. Management reserves the right to demand that all sums due under the lease be paid in cash and to return any check previously accepted by Management and demand cash.

Rent Control

New York City and San Francisco are examples of cities with **rent controls** that limit the amount of rent landlords can charge to tenants. Nearly two-thirds of the rental market in both cities is rent regulated. Under rent regulation, a housing authority sets rates and determines any exceptions. A lease in violation of such rent control or rent stabilization statutes is void. A tenant cannot be evicted for refusal to pay more than the maximum rent permitted by the housing authority.

In areas where there is a rent stabilization regime, some landlords have converted their properties to "hotels" and charge higher rates to their occupants. However, rent control provisions also define what constitutes a "housing accommodation," and factors such as length of time of occupation, whether a key is retained on a regular basis by the occupant, what types of belongings the occupant has on the property, and whether the occupant does have a residence other than the occupied property are critical in defining housing. Even though the property owner may call the living area a "hotel," and collect rent on a weekly basis, it may still be subject to rent controls given the factors listed above (*Benroal Realty Associates, L.P. v. Lowe,* 9 Misc.3d 4, 801 N.Y.S.2d 114 (N.Y. Ct. App. 2005).

Other landlords have tried putting waivers of rent stabilizations in their lease agreements with tenants. These types of waivers are void because they contravene the purpose of rent stabilization, which is providing affordable housing for city dwellers (*Thornton v. Baron,* 4 A.D.3d 258, 772 N.Y.S.2d 326 (2004)).

Still others have tried to circumvent rent controls by arguing that there is a housing shortage. However, courts have not intervened in these debates and deferred to rent control statutes (*Santa Monica Beach, Ltd. v. Superior Court,* 968 P.2d 993 [Cal. 1999]). Some have also argued that such controls on use of property and rent constitute a taking in violation of the due process clause of the U.S. Constitution (see Chapter 19 and *San Remo Hotel L.P. v. City and County of San Francisco,* 41 P.3d 87 (Cal. 2002)).

The following case provides the U.S. Supreme Court's view on rent controls.

Fisher v. City of Berkeley California

475 U.S. 260 (1986)

FACTS

In June 1980, the city of Berkeley passed an initiative entitled Ordinance 5261-NS, Rent Stabilization and Eviction for Good Cause Ordinance (hereinafter Ordinance). The stated purposes of the ordinance were:

to regulate residential rent increases in the City of Berkeley and to protect tenants from unwarranted rent increases and arbitrary, discriminatory, or retaliatory evictions in order to help maintain the diversity of the Berkeley community and to ensure compliance with legal obligations relating to the rental of housing. This legislation is designed to address the City of Berkeley's housing crisis, preserve the public peace, health and safety, and advance the housing policies of the City with regard to low and fixed income persons, minorities, students, handicapped and the aged.

To accomplish the goals, the ordinance enacted strict rent controls. All rental properties (23,000) in Berkeley were given a base rate as of the May 1980 rental rate, and increases were permitted only pursuant to an annual general adjustment of rent ceilings by the Rent Stabilization Board or pursuant to a special petition approved by the same board. Failure to comply with the rent ceilings could result in suits by the tenants, the withholding of collected rents from the landlord, criminal penalties, or a combination.

Shortly after the ordinance was passed, a group of landlords (appellants) brought suit in California Superior Court challenging the ordinance as unconstitutional because it preempted federal antitrust laws. The Superior Court upheld the ordinance, and the Court of Appeals reversed. The California Supreme Court held that there was no conflict between the Ordinance and the Sherman Act. The landlords appealed.

JUDICIAL OPINION

Marshall, Justice. Recognizing that the function of government may often be to tamper with free markets, correcting their failures and aiding their victims, this Court noted that a state statute is not pre-empted by the federal antitrust laws simply because the state scheme may have an anticompetitive effect. We have therefore held that a state statute should be struck down on pre-emption grounds only if it mandates or authorizes conduct that necessarily constitutes a violation of the antitrust laws in all cases, or if it places irresistible pressure on a private party to violate the antitrust laws in order to comply with the statute.

Appellants argue that Berkeley's Rent Stabilization Ordinance is pre-empted because it imposes rent ceilings across the entire rental market for residential units. Such a regime, they contend, clearly falls within the per se rule against price fixing, a rule that has been one of the settled points of antitrust enforcement since the earliest days of the Sherman Act. That the prices set here are ceilings rather than floors and that the public interest has been invoked to justify this stabilization should not, appellants argue, save Berkeley's regulatory scheme from condemnation under the per se rule.

Certainly there is this much truth to appellants' argument: Had the owners of residential rental property in Berkeley voluntarily banded together to stabilize rents in the city, their activities would not be saved from antitrust attack by claims that they had set reasonable prices out of solicitude for the welfare of their tenants. Moreover, it cannot be denied that Berkeley's Ordinance will affect the residential housing rental market in much the same way as would the philanthropic activities of this hypothetical trade association. What distinguishes the operation of Berkeley's Ordinance from the activities of a benevolent landlords' cartel is not that the Ordinance will necessarily have a different economic effect, but that the rent ceilings imposed by the Ordinance and maintained by the Stabilization Board have been unilaterally imposed by government upon landlords to the exclusion of private control.

The distinction between unilateral and concerted action is critical here. Adhering to the language of §1, this Court has always limited the reach of that provision to unreasonable restraints of trade effected by a "contract, combination . . . or conspiracy" between separate entities. The ordinary relationship between the government and those who must obey its regulatory commands whether they wish to or not is not enough to establish a conspiracy. Similarly, the mere fact that all competing property owners must comply with the same provisions of the Ordinance is not enough to establish a conspiracy among landlords.

There may be cases in which what appears to be a state- or municipality-administered price stabilization scheme is really a private price-fixing conspiracy, concealed under a "gauzy cloak of state involvement." This might occur even where prices are ostensibly under the absolute control of government officials. However, we have been given no indication that such corruption has tainted the rent controls imposed by Berkeley's Ordinance. Adopted by popular initiative, the Ordinance can hardly be viewed as a cloak for any conspiracy among landlords or between the landlords and the municipality. Berkeley's landlords have simply been deprived of the power freely to raise their rents. That is why they are here. And that is why their role in the stabilization program does not alter the restraint's unilateral nature.

Because under settled principles of antitrust law, the rent controls established by Berkeley's Ordinance lack the element of concerted action needed before they can be characterized as a per se violation of §1 of the Sherman Act, we cannot say that the Ordinance is facially inconsistent with the federal antitrust laws. We therefore need not address whether, even if the controls were to mandate §1 violations, they would be exempt under the state-action doctrine from antitrust scrutiny.

Affirmed.

CASE QUESTIONS

1. Is there preemption of the Berkeley ordinance by the federal antitrust laws?
2. What arguments do the landlords make on their behalf?
3. Who is setting rent prices?
4. Do the landlords have any control?
5. Is the ordinance constitutional?

Note: Several other U.S. Supreme Court decisions indicate this type of activity is subject to scrutiny because property rights are affected.

CONSIDER 9.5

In San Francisco and New York, the following discoveries have been made:

a. Two-thirds of residential rental property are under rent controls and the average rent is $650.
b. The rent for the remaining one-third of properties is $1,500–$2,000, the apartments are small, in poor condition, and have a waiting list.

CONSIDER 9.5 (continued)

c. Landlords under rent control are converting their properties to commercial facilities or condominiums.
d. There is little tenant turnover in rent-controlled property, with relatives taking leases upon tenants' deaths.

What explains the price differences and problems? Give the economic analysis.

Lease Term

The portion of the lease agreement that specifies the term may simply state the beginning and ending dates of the lease. However, additional language may be necessary if the tenant wants an option to renew. The option to renew should specify when the option must be exercised, how it is to be exercised, how the rental amount for the option period is to be computed, and the maximum length of the option period.

Attorneys' Fees

In spite of careful drafting and execution of lease agreements, litigation does happen. All leases should include provisions for the payment of costs and attorneys' fees in the event the parties have a dispute that goes to arbitration or is litigated. The following clause is an example of an attorneys' fee provision:

In the event legal action is necessary for the enforcement of rights and obligations granted under this agreement, the prevailing party shall be entitled to an award including attorneys' fees and all attendant court costs regardless of the stage to which the legal action proceeds.

In states where attorneys' fees cannot be collected in contract actions, these clauses are unenforceable.

Rules and Regulations

Particularly in apartment complexes, rules of conduct and for use of the property are necessary for smooth functioning of joint facilities and for each tenant's peaceful enjoyment of the property. Under the URLTA and most state statutes, landlords can promulgate such rules. Section 3.102 of the URLTA permits rules and regulations that promote the convenience, safety, or welfare of the tenants; prevent abusive use of the landlord's property; or provide for a fair distribution of services and facilities held out for the tenants generally. To be valid, these rules of conduct and operation must apply to all tenants, be disclosed to all tenants, and not be applied unfairly. Rules and regulations cannot excuse the landlord from responsibilities or eliminate tenants' rights. Rules and regulations may be incorporated into the lease agreement in two ways:

1. They may actually be written into the section of the lease agreement on the applicability of rules and regulations.
2. They may be incorporated as an addendum or a schedule to the lease agreement or referenced in the lease. If they are referenced, the tenant is entitled to a copy.

The types of rules and regulations that are typical and meet the standards of the URLTA are hours of pool use, use of laundry facilities, parking regulations, and noise and pet restrictions. (A notice of change in the rules should be sent directly to each tenant.)

The following case deals with the reasonableness of a landlord's rule.

BERLINGER V. SUBURBAN APARTMENT MANAGEMENT

454 N.E.2d 1367 (Oh. 1982)

FACTS

Gary R. Berlinger (plaintiff/appellant) was a tenant in an apartment managed by Suburban Apartment Management (SAM/landlord/appellee). His security deposit was $420, and his monthly rent was $210.

In his lease agreement was the following paragraph:

No animals, birds, pets, motorcycles, waterbeds, trucks, jeeps, or vans shall be kept on the premises at any time.

The rule provided for a $50 fine for each violation. Berlinger had a motorcycle on his patio on October 10, 13, and 24, and November 7, 1979.

SAM notified Berlinger of the violation and the $200 fine. Berlinger did not pay the fine and moved out. SAM kept Berlinger's security deposit for a $200 fine, $210 in rent, and $10.50 in interest. Berlinger objected on the grounds that the fine was excessive and the rule was arbitrary. Berlinger sued to have his security deposit returned. The trial court awarded him $20 based on the following:

Security deposit	$420.00
Plus interest	+$10.50
Subtotal	$430.50
Less rent (for unpaid last month)	$210.00
Less 4×$50 (four days of motorcycle)	$200.00
Total	$20.50[2]

Berlinger appealed.

JUDICIAL OPINION

Jackson, Judge. It does not appear that the $50 per diem charge for the presence of a motorcycle was in the nature of a fee for parking or storage. The lease was not modified to permit possession of a motorcycle on the premises. Instead, the charge is in the nature of liquidated damages. It is a matter of common knowledge that motorcycles, if operated loudly, can be objects of great annoyance. This effect is magnified in densely populated places such as apartment complexes. Thus, it is not unconscionable for a landlord to prohibit the bringing of motorcycles on the premises.

A different issue is presented, however, by the liquidated damages clause. To be valid, a provision for liquidated damages must meet three criteria, expressed in the following excerpt from *American Financial Leasing v. Miller* (1974) 41 Ohio App.2d 69, 73, 322 N.E.2d 149 [70 O.O.2d 64] (quoting from 16 Ohio Jurisprudence 2d 155):

[I]t must, according to most cases, appear that the sum stipulated bears a reasonable proportion to the loss actually sustained; that the actual damages occasioned by the breach are uncertain or difficult to ascertain; and most important of all, that a construction of the contract as a whole evinces a conscious intention of the parties deliberately to consider and adjust the damages that might flow from the breach.

Actual damages occasioned by a breach of the "no motorcycle" provision of the lease are difficult to ascertain. However, the sum of $50 per day (which in a thirty-day month would amount to $1,500) does not bear a reasonable relationship to any loss which might foreseeably be sustained. A court could take judicial notice that the operation of a motorcycle might cause great damage to a landlord, because tenants who object to loud noise might move out. However, no evidence was introduced tending to show the amount of damages which might foreseeably result from the mere presence of a motorcycle.

The liquidated damages clause contained in the Disposition Advice is therefore invalid under the common law and under R.C. 5321.14, and is hereby ordered stricken from the lease.

In the absence of a valid provision for liquidated damages, the appellee was entitled to recover only the monetary equivalent of the actual damages caused by the appellant's breach. Again, however, the appellee failed to adduce any evidence tending to show that it sustained actual damages as a result of the presence of the motorcycle on the property, even if the motorcycle was there for one month, as claimed by appellee. In the absence of any evidence on this subject, compensatory damages may not be awarded.

The appellee did prove beyond any doubt that the appellant breached his promise not to bring a motorcycle on the property. The appellee is therefore entitled to judgment on its claim for breach of contract, and an award of nominal damages in the sum of one dollar.

The appellant proved that he was entitled to the return of his security deposit ($420) plus interest ($10.50) less one month's rent ($210), for a total of $220.50.

Reversed.

CASE QUESTIONS

1. What rule was at issue?
2. Was the fine excessive?

2. The trial court actually miscalculated and hence made the award at $20.00 as opposed to $20.50.

CONSIDER 9.6

In January 2002, Mary Jane Nealy entered into a one-year written lease agreement with Southlawn Palms Apartments (SPA). The lease provided that the term would run from January 22, 2002, to January 21, 2003, and would automatically renew on a month-to-month basis at the expiration of its initial term. The lease also provided that SPA could terminate the tenancy for (1) a serious or repeated violation of the terms and conditions of the lease; (2) a violation of federal, state, or local law; (3) criminal activity; or (4) other good cause. SPA had an addendum that listed the rules of conduct for the apartment complex. On April 28, 2004, SPA sent Nealy a "30 Day Notice to Vacate" the premises and listed two reasons for the notice to vacate: (1) "Owner desires possession" and (2) "Undesirable tenant behavior." SPA later filed a forcible detainer action against Nealy, citing "undesirable tenant behavior" as the sole ground for eviction. SPA indicated that "Ms. Nealy breached her lease by violating the rules of Southland Palms Apts. and by violated [*sic*] the Blue Star Addendum. Nealy rode a four-wheeler in the pedestrian areas of the apartment, and there were two reports that Nealy mooned other tenants or maintenance workers." Ms. Nealy points out that mooning and the four-wheeler issues were not covered in the addendum rules and that she was not warned about her conduct or given the opportunity to respond to the allegations by the other tenants. Can SPA evict Ms. Nealy? Why or why not?

Nealy v. Southlawn Palms Apartments, 196 S.W.3d 386 (Tex. App. 2006)

Practical Tip

A violation of the rules and regulations imposed by the landlord is also grounds for eviction. Most landlords provide tenants with notice of a violation before proceeding to an eviction.

Landlord's Right of Access

Although landlords own the property, tenants have the exclusive rights of possession even as against the landlords so long as a valid lease agreement exists. This principle of exclusive possession was applied at common law and has been codified in many states to protect tenants from landlords' unauthorized entry onto leased premises. Under Section 3.103 of the URLTA, a landlord can enter a tenant's dwelling if:

a. The tenant consents and the purpose is repair or services; and
b. In case of emergency (even without the tenant's consent). Except in emergencies the landlord must give the tenant at least (2) days' notice and must come at reasonable times.

In the lease agreement, the parties are free to agree to other terms of entry and arrangements for entry, and in most states these terms will be enforceable so long as the tenant has not been required to give up any statutory rights. With consent required, the tenant must act reasonably.

Assignments and Subleases

Assignments and **subleases** are similar in that they both bring third parties into the landlord–tenant relationship. However, there is a distinction between the two processes: In an assignment, tenants actually transfer their leasehold interests to third parties who will take over all obligations and assume all benefits associated with the original lease. In a subleasing arrangement, the tenants give up only a portion of their leasehold estate. For example, consider a tenant with a three-year lease of a New York City apartment. If while the tenant is studying in Europe for one year—year two of the lease—he has leased the apartment to someone, then he has sublet the apartment. But if the tenant decides to remain in Europe and the third party takes over years two and three completely, then there is an assignment of the lease.

At common law, a lease was freely transferable; both subleases and assignments were permitted and honored. However, landlords and tenants may agree to restrict transfers in their agreements. For example, some leases make any transfer void, although the enforceability of such a provision is questionable. Another type of transfer restriction is a provision that has tenants forfeit their leasehold interests if they attempt to transfer those interests to others. Under this type of provision, the assignment or sublease is not void, but the landlord has terminated both the original party's interest and the subtenant's or assignee's interest. Finally, the lease agreement may simply contain a provision that the tenant promises not to sublet or assign. If the tenant violates the provision and the landlord has resulting damages, the breaching tenant is liable to the landlord for those damages. In some leases, the sublease or assignment is not prohibited, but the tenant is required to obtain the landlord's approval for the transaction. If the landlord does not approve, one of the other types of provisions just mentioned would take effect. The following clause is an example in which prior consent is required: "Resident may not assign this Rental Agreement or sublet the premises, in whole or in part, without the prior written consent of management."

This consent to assignment was established as an ongoing right by the 1603 **Rule in Dumpor's Case**, which provided that if the landlord consented to one assignment, all other assignments were also deemed valid. In other words, at common law, once the landlord waived rights to prohibit an assignment, the right to prohibit was lost. Most states have abolished the effect of this rule.

Rights and Responsibilities of Parties to a Lease Assignment

Although an assignment is a complete relinquishment of the tenant's leasehold interest, the tenant's obligations do not end with an assignment. The tenant remains obligated to the landlord; if the assignee does not perform according to the terms of the lease agreement, the original tenant is liable for damages.

The assignee is not responsible for the obligations of the original tenant unless the assignee assumes these obligations. The assumption of responsibilities is not generally a problem since the assignee will be the recipient of the benefits—the right to the leasehold interest. The assignee does have the right to require the landlord to perform according to the terms of the lease agreement, as well as the right to sue in the event of nonperformance.

If an assignee does not perform under the lease or breaches the lease agreement, the landlord can pursue remedies from either the original tenant or the assignee. Although the landlord does not have privity of contract with the assignee, the landlord is still obligated to perform obligations as established by law or by the original parties' lease agreement.

Rights and Responsibilities of Parties to a Sublease

In a sublease, the subtenant becomes a tenant of the original lessee and not a tenant of the landlord. There is no legal relationship between landlord and subtenant and no rights of enforcement by one party against another. Any rights the parties have must be exercised indirectly through the tenant with whom they have a contractual relationship. For example, if a landlord who is required to maintain insurance on the leased premises fails to do so and a subtenant loses property because of it, the subtenant could proceed against the tenant. Although the tenant could then proceed against the landlord for recovery, the subtenant would have no direct cause of action against the landlord because the landlord's obligation to insure is to the tenant and not to the subtenant.

Unconscionability

As with most consumer contracts, leases are subject to judicial standards of fairness in language and bargaining power. Under the URLTA, a rental agreement is unconscionable if the tenant is required to waive any of the rights, remedies, or protections under the act.

Other areas in lease agreements that courts have found to be unconscionable include excessive cleaning deposits, excessive assessment of cleaning fees, excessive security deposit requirements, prohibitions on the right to organize, and waivers of judicial process. The basic standard in all cases is one that looks at the bargaining power of the parties and fairness.

Rights and Responsibilities of Parties to Lease Agreement

Both landlords and tenants have required responsibilities of performance as well as mandated rights. The following sections cover those rights and responsibilities.

Responsibilities of Landlords and Rights of Tenants

Maintenance of the Premises

At common law, a lease was a transfer of a land interest with no obligation of maintenance and repair for the landlord once the tenant began the lease period. Just as the doctrine of habitable premises has changed considerably, so has the doctrine governing the landlord's duty of repair. Several theories have now been used by courts or codified by states that require the landlord to keep the leased premises in repair. The theories are (1) constructive eviction, (2) self-help, (3) tort liability, and (4) lease termination.

1. *Constructive Eviction* One theory used to require repairs and thereby ensure the tenant of continued habitability is the doctrine of **constructive eviction**. For this doctrine to apply, the tenant must be able to establish that the landlord had an obligation to repair either through a covenant in the lease agreement or through some statutory or judicially imposed duty. Under URLTA Section 2.104, landlords are required to comply with building codes, make the repairs necessary to keep the leased premises habitable, keep the common areas clean and safe, keep all services and facilities in working order, arrange for trash collection and removal, and supply running water (hot and cold) and heat in winter and according to outside temperatures.

Once the tenant has established that the landlord was responsible for maintenance of the premises, the tenant must also prove that the landlord has failed to perform according to the statute or agreement. Furthermore, whatever the landlord's failure, it must be one that has made it difficult or impossible for the tenant to continue living on the premises. Under the doctrine of constructive eviction, the tenant in these circumstances has no choice but to leave and this profound act of leaving his or her home excuses the tenant from the lease obligations. The heart of the doctrine is also the greatest problem with the doctrine in a practical sense: the tenant must move out for the doctrine to apply. In areas where housing shortages exist, particularly for low-cost units, this requirement means going from substandard housing to no housing. In some states, the courts have permitted tenants who can establish all of the elements of constructive

> **Practical Tip**
>
> *When a landlord undertakes the responsibility of providing facilities, he or she must be certain those facilities remain in good repair and that no additional risks are created by the presence of the facilities.*

eviction to fix the problem areas and remain in the leased premises, deducting the cost of the repairs from their rent.

The following case presents an example of constructive eviction and illustrates one state's statutory remedies for the problem.

MINJAK CO. V. RANDOLPH

528 N.Y.S.2d 554 (1988)

FACTS

Diane Randolph and her roommates (respondents) leased a loft space from Minjak Company (petitioner) in 1976. Although the building was primarily used for residential purposes, Minjak had Randolph and the others sign a commercial lease. Their loft consisted of 1,700 square feet. Two-thirds of the square footage was used for Mr. Kikuchi's music studio, where he composes, rehearses, and stores his very expensive electronic equipment and musical instruments.

Late in 1977, the fifth-floor tenant began to operate a health spa equipment business that included the display of fully working Jacuzzis, bathtubs, and saunas. All the equipment was filled to capacity with water for display purposes. From November 1977 through February 1982, Randolph experienced at least 40 separate water leaks from the fifth floor. At times, water literally poured into their bedrooms and closets. Water leaked into the kitchen and onto Mr. Kikuchi's grand piano and other musical instruments. Randolph's complaints went unheeded by Minjak.

Sandblasting done by the fifth-floor tenant in 1978 caused dust to fall into the loft, their food, their eyes, and their beds. Construction on the stairs and elevators produced so much dust that the tenants were wearing masks, and Mr. Kikuchi ceased using the loft for his music studio in 1981. Randolph, Kikuchi, and the others ceased rent payment in 1981. In 1983 Minjak filed suit for nonpayment of rent. The tenants responded that they were unable to use two-thirds of the loft space, that there was a breach of the warranty of habitability, and that the landlord had failed to provide essential services.

Rent totals were $12,787.00, including $200 for October 1981, $450 for each month from November 1981 through December 1982, and $567 per month since January 1983. The jury awarded the tenants a rent abatement of 80 percent for part of the period, 40 percent for another part, and 10 percent for breach of the implied warranty of habitability. The jury also awarded $20,000 punitive damages and $5,000 in attorneys' fees. The appellate court reversed, holding that constructive eviction was not a defense to nonpayment of rent. The parties appealed.

JUDICIAL OPINION

Memorandum Decision. We reverse and hold that the tenants were entitled to avail themselves of the doctrine of constructive eviction based on their abandonment of a portion of the premises and that the award for punitive damages was permissible and warranted by these facts.

We agree with the holding and reasoning of *East Haven Associates v. Gurian*, 64 Misc. 2d 276, 313 N.Y.S.2d 276, that a tenant may assert as a defense to the nonpayment of rent the doctrine of constructive eviction, even if he or she has abandoned only a portion of the demised premises due to the landlord's acts in making that portion of the premises unusable by the tenant. The rule of *Edgerton v. Page*, 20 N.Y. 281, the first decision to establish the requirement of abandonment of premises as a condition to asserting the defense of constructive eviction, is not undermined by our acknowledgement of a defense for partial constructive eviction. *Edgerton v. Page, supra*, emphasized that the tenant's obligation to pay rent continues as long as the tenant remains in possession of the entire premises demised. ... It is not contrary to this rule nor against any established precedent to hold that when the tenant is constructively evicted from a portion of the premises by the landlord's actions, he should not be obligated to pay the full amount of the rent. Indeed, compelling considerations of social policy and fairness dictate such a result. None of the cases cited by the landlord reaches or warrants a contrary conclusion.

As for petitioner's argument on appeal that the tenants never abandoned any portion of the premises and, in fact, continued to use the entire loft even up until the day of trial, we note that this assertion is unaccompanied by any citation to the record. This was no mere inadvertent error, for there is absolutely nothing in the record to support such a claim. The evidence at trial fully supported a finding that respondents were compelled to abandon the music studio portion of the loft due to the landlord's wrongful acts [which] substantially and materially deprive[d] the tenant[s] of the beneficial use and enjoyment of the loft.

The award for punitive damages, as reduced by the Civil Court to $5,000, should be reinstated as well. Although no exception to the court's charge permitting the jury to award punitive damages was made, we discuss the issue of the propriety of submitting this issue to the jury in light of petitioner's argument that the award subjects it to a liability for which there is no support in the law and in light of Appellate Term's inconclusive comment on whether or not punitive damages could, as a matter of law, be awarded in habitability cases.

Although generally in breach of contract claims the damages to be awarded are compensatory, in certain instances punitive damages may be awarded when to do so would deter morally culpable conduct.

The determining factor is "not the form of the action... but the moral culpability of the defendant, and whether the conduct implies a criminal indifference to civil obligations."

With respect to this State's strict housing code standards and statutes, made enforceable through civil and criminal sanctions and other statutory remedies, it is within the public interest to deter conduct which undermines those standards when that conduct rises to the level of high moral culpability or indifference to a landlord's civil obligations. Therefore, it has been recognized that punitive damages may be awarded in breach of warranty of habitability cases where the landlord's actions or inactions were intentional and malicious.

Accordingly, the issue of punitive damages was properly submitted to the jury, and we are satisfied that this record supports the jury's finding of morally culpable conduct in light of the dangerous and offensive manner in which the landlord permitted the construction work to be performed, the landlord's indifference to the health and safety of others, and its disregard for the rights of others, so as to imply even a criminal indifference to civil obligations.

One particularly egregious example of the landlord's wanton disregard for the safety of others was the way in which the stair demolition was performed: steps were removed and no warning sign even posted. The landlord's indifference and lack of response to the tenants' repeated complaints of dust, sand and water leak problems demonstrated a complete indifference to their health and safety and a lack of concern for the damage these conditions could cause to the tenants' valuable personal property. Such indifference must be viewed as rising to the level of high moral culpability. Accordingly, the award of punitive damages is sustained.

We likewise reject petitioner's argument that respondents cannot rely on their lease in order to recover attorney's fees pursuant to the provisions of Real Property Law Sec. 234. This statute has the effect, *inter alia*, of implying into a lease for residential property which contains a provision permitting the landlord to recover attorney's fees in a summary proceeding brought pursuant to the lease a similarly binding covenant by the landlord to pay the tenant's reasonable attorney's fees incurred in the successful defense of a summary proceeding commenced by the landlord arising out of the lease.

The Civil Court judgment should be reinstated.[3]

CASE QUESTIONS

1. What type of property was leased?
2. How was the property used?
3. Describe the problems with the fifth-floor tenant.
4. Was the landlord aware of the problems with habitability?
5. Is constructive eviction a defense to nonpayment of rent?
6. Does the fact that the tenants did not move out affect their case?
7. Why were punitive damages awarded?

2. *Self-help* Common law did not permit the **repair and deduct** self-help method of remedying leased premises in disrepair. However, under the URLTA, this remedy of **self-help** has been adopted by an increasing number of states. Under Section 4.103 of the URLTA, the tenant can make repairs (up to $100) if the landlord does not respond within 14 days of a written demand for repair. The tenant can then send the landlord an itemized statement on the repair costs and deduct that amount from his rent. Tenants may not make repairs at the landlord's expense if the tenant or family member caused the condition.

Under this section of the URLTA, the tenant is given the statutory right to repair and deduct the cost of property problems that are not self-induced. Before repairing and deducting, the tenant should give notice to the landlord.

3. A contra result, requiring the party to move out in order to have constructive eviction apply, can be found at *Kenyon v. Regan*, 826 P.2d 140 (Ut. App. 1992).

3. *Tort Liability* In the absence of the statutorily or judicially imposed self-help right, tenants have another theory to recover from the landlord for correcting problems. In some decisions, the tenant has not been permitted to repair and deduct but has been permitted to repair and recover in tort for the damages caused or alleviated through the tenant's corrective actions. The difficulty with this remedy is that the tenant must take legal action to recover. This remedy provides the tenant with an opportunity for damages and remedies beyond just nonpayment of rent or a reduction in rent.

4. *Lease Termination* A final option available to a tenant faced with a lease of uninhabitable premises is to treat the state of disrepair as constructive eviction, vacate the premises, and regard the lease and the obligation to pay rents as terminated. This right of termination through constructive eviction was a common-law right that exists in all states in common law or statutory form. In the event a statute regulates constructive eviction, the tenant must comply with all procedural requirements before vacating the premises.

Retaliatory Action by Landlords

If a tenant exercises any of the rights and remedies afforded by self-help statutes, implied covenants, or tort liability, it is possible that the landlord may, in response to the tenant's action, retaliate with eviction. Because the purposes of these theories would be defeated if landlords used retaliatory eviction, the URLTA and many state statutes provide that landlords may not engage in retaliatory eviction against tenants who choose to exercise their self-help rights. For example, Section 5.101 of the URLTA provides that a tenant cannot be evicted and that a tenant's rental fee cannot be raised or his or her services decreased as a result of any of the following: (1) filing a complaint with housing authorities, (2) organizing or joining a tenant's union, or (3) using self-help procedures and remedies. If a tenant has engaged in these activities, there is usually a period during which the landlord's eviction would be presumptively retaliatory. For example, the URLTA presumptive retaliatory period is one year after the tenant has engaged in any of the protected activities. The effect is that it becomes the landlord's burden to establish that the tenant was evicted for reasons other than the exercise of statutorily protected rights. Naturally, the presumption can be overcome when the tenant has not paid rent or has in some way breached the lease agreement.

The following case deals with an issue of retaliatory conduct by a landlord.

Jablonski v. Clemons

803 N.E.2d 730 (Mass. App. 2004)

FACTS

In 1991, Thomas and Theresa Clemons (tenants) moved into unit 7K in the Eisenhower 7 building of the Presidential Acres, a large apartment complex in Randolph, Massachusetts, owned by H. Frank Jablonski (landlord). The tenants' unit was on the third floor. Immediately upon taking occupancy, the tenants discovered a ventilation problem in their unit. Apparently, dryers from other units were venting through their bathroom, causing both moisture and foul odor problems. The landlord knew about the ventilation problem from the inception of the tenancy.

The tenants reported the ventilation problem to the on-site property manager. While a solution to the problem was sought, the tenants kept the ceiling fan running in the bathroom 24 hours per day, seven days per week. They also kept the door to the bathroom closed. Despite several good faith attempts to correct it, the ventilation problem persisted up through the time of trial nine years later.

On the night of November 22, 2000, while the tenants were inside the apartment, a fire broke out in the bathroom, causing significant damage to the unit. The fire was caused by the overheated fan.

On November 25, 2000, the local board of health (board), which had been called in by the tenants, inspected the premises and cited the owners for several code violations, including the improper ventilation and an ant infestation that had been ongoing for "well over a year."

The landlord brought suit for eviction and nonpayment of rent. The trial court found in favor of the tenants on their counterclaim for breach of the implied warranty of habitability, and awarded the tenants the difference between the value of the premises as warranted and the value of the premises in defective condition. However, the trial court ruled in favor of the landlord on the tenants' counterclaims for breach of quiet enjoyment, and retaliatory eviction. This appeal followed.

JUDICIAL OPINION

Brown, J. Implied in every residential lease is a warranty that the leased premises are fit for human occupation and will remain so for the duration of the tenancy (i.e., there are no latent or patent defects in the facilities vital to the use of the premises). A violation of the code may (or may not) support a claim of breach of the implied warranty of habitability. The judge has wide discretion in determining whether the conditions in any given rental unit amount to a material breach of the implied warranty of habitability.

Presented with evidence of several substandard conditions and code violations here, the judge found two material breaches of warranty arising from the longstanding ant infestation and the ventilation problem. Indeed, by law, insect infestation and ventilation problems are considered serious code violations and are always deemed "conditions which may endanger or impair the health, or safety and well-being" of the occupants. The landlord did not appeal from these adverse findings.

The implied covenant of quiet enjoyment guarantees tenants the right to be free from "serious" interferences with their tenancies. A landlord violates, when its "acts or omissions impair the value of the leased premises."

Here, the judge found that the landlord knowingly rented the premises in a defective condition and failed to correct the ventilation problem – a serious code violation – for over nine years. Because of the defective ventilation, the tenants were forced to keep the bathroom door shut and to run the fan continuously, a dangerous situation which led to a fire in the apartment. The moisture and foul odor problems originating in other units, the judge found, were never eliminated and persisted to the time of trial. On these facts found by the judge, we think that the judge was required to find a serious interference with the tenancy and substantial impairment of the character and value of the leased premises. While it is true that the property manager made several attempts, albeit ineffectual, to correct the problem, there is no good faith defense to a counterclaim for breach of the covenant of quiet enjoyment.

We also conclude on review of the evidence that the tenants were entitled, as matter of law, to prevail on their counterclaim for retaliatory eviction. At trial, the tenants presented evidence that they had engaged in several protected activities in November, 2000 (organizing a tenants' petition for submission to the landlord and to the board, filing a complaint regarding code violations with the board, and withholding rent under G.L. c. 239, §8A). Proof that the landlord terminated their tenancy only a few months later in February, 2001, raised a rebuttable presumption of reprisal. Once the statutory presumption attached, it could be rebutted only by clear and convincing evidence that the landlord had "sufficient independent justification for taking such action, and would have in fact taken such action, in the same manner and at the same time the action was taken, regardless of tenants engaging in ... [protected] activities."

Here, the trial judge ruled, without any explanation, that the landlord had "rebutted any claim of a retaliatory eviction." Having reviewed the entire trial transcript and all the exhibits, we discern no clear and convincing evidence that would support this conclusion. According to the Appellate Division, the landlord testified that vacancy was necessary in order to fix the ventilation problem in the tenants' unit. This testimony may well have been sufficient to rebut the presumption. The problem is that there was no such testimony in the record presented for review. Nor was any inference warranted, contrary to the Appellate Division's conclusion, that there was "serious doubt as to the structural integrity of the building which could be remedied only if the tenants vacated the unit." In fact, as far as we can determine, the landlord failed to introduce any evidence on the issue of its motive for initiating the eviction action so quickly after the tenants engaged in their protected activity. It was not up to the tenants to introduce such evidence, as the landlord intimates in its brief. Because the landlord failed to meet its heavy evidentiary burden of rebutting the statutory presumption, the tenants should have prevailed on this claim.

Reversed. The trial judge erred in denying certain of the tenants' requests for rulings of law. Judgment shall enter for the tenants on their counterclaims of breach of the implied covenant of quiet enjoyment, and retaliatory eviction.

CASE QUESTIONS

1. What were the habitability issues? Was there constructive eviction?
2. What had the tenants done to try and remedy the problem?
3. How did the landlord respond?
4. Are the tenants evicted?

CONSIDER 9.7

Barbara Hill was a resident of Casa Blanca Mobile Home Park. Shannon Kearns was a resident of an apartment owned by Fair Plaza Associates. Both Hill and Kearns had month-to-month rental agreements with the property owners.

Hill began complaining in May 1996 about the level of noise from her neighbor's television. The manager of the mobile home park where she lived testified that he was awakened on 15 occasions between the hours of 12:30 and 1:00 A.M. to investigate the TV disturbances. Hill also complained during the day in July about the television set. At that point the manager served Hill with a 30-day notice of termination on her lease.

Kearns had sent two letters of complaint to the manager of her apartment complex about the noisy neighbors above her. Her manager also sent her a 30-day notice of termination.

Hill and Kearns filed suit alleging that the actions by their landlords were retaliatory and a violation of Uniform Owner–Resident Relations Act (UORRA). Both property owners won at trial with the court concluding they had the right to terminate the leases of Hill and Kearns for their complaints about noise. Hill and Kearns appealed. Should Hill and Kearns win? Why or why not? *Casa Blanca Mobile Home Park v. Hill*, 963 P.2d 542 (N.M. App. 1998)

Maintenance of the Common Areas

Regardless of any state's position on the landlord's responsibility to maintain individual dwelling units, all states require landlords to maintain the common areas of their leased properties. Common areas are those used by all tenants, such as staircases, halls, and laundry facilities. Although tenants may not be entitled to terminate their leases for disrepair of these areas, the landlord will be held liable for injuries resulting from the disrepair.

CONSIDER 9.8

Diane LaBorde moved into St. James Place Apartments with her two minor children in 1996. The apartment complex consisted of multiple apartment buildings with a common area between the buildings which was grassy and wooded. According to Mark Cardella, who performed lawn maintenance at the apartment complex from 1992 until March 1999, the common area contained tree roots and "quite a few" sawed-off tree stumps which protruded a few inches from holes in the ground. The same year they moved in, LaBorde's daughter told her that she had tripped and fallen in the common area due to a stump sticking out of a hole in the ground. LaBorde complained about the stump to the apartment complex's on-site manager, Margaret Kern, and assumed that it would be taken care of.

On May 27, 1999, LaBorde discovered a cat tearing into garbage bags on her porch. She had had problems with cats getting into her garbage in the past and became angry. She began chasing the cat through the common area in the hopes that it would leave her garbage alone in the future. While running after the cat, LaBorde's foot hit a

CONSIDER 9.8

(continued)

stump protruding from a hole in the ground and she fell, injuring her left ankle. LaBorde crawled back to her apartment and called Kern, who took her to the hospital. X-rays were performed, and LaBorde was diagnosed with a sprained ankle. She was put into a soft cast and instructed to follow-up with an orthopedic specialist.

LaBorde began treatment with Dr. Mark Hontas, an orthopedist, in June 1999. She was put into a walking cast and given physical therapy. An MRI revealed a bone fragment in her foot, for which surgery was performed in December 2000. She was briefly confined to a wheelchair after the surgery, then placed in a cast, and eventually underwent eight more weeks of physical therapy. Dr. Hontas discharged LaBorde in July 2001 and diagnosed her with a five percent total post-surgery disability. He also indicated that she would likely develop some degree of post-traumatic degenerative arthritis of the ankle. At the time of trial, LaBorde claimed to still suffer from ankle problems, and she wears orthopedic shoes and an ankle sleeve for this reason.

LaBorde filed suit against St. James Place Apartments, its owner, Money Hill Plantation, and their insurer, United National Group Insurance Company. The parties stipulated to LaBorde $50,000 as her damages, but they disagreed on liability. Are any of these parties liable for LaBorde's injury and damages? *Laborde v. St. James Place Apartments*, 928 So.2d 643 (La.App. 2006)

Duty to Maintain Premises to Prevent Injuries

The landlord has responsibility and liability for conditions on the leased premises. In many situations, the landlord has dangerous items and structures on the property that can cause injury to tenants even though those structures are not the leased premises and not technically part of the common areas of a building. Perhaps the greatest amount of landlord–tenant litigation in terms of premises liability is related to liability for the acts of third parties that injure tenants. The following is a case that established that the issue of landlord liability for criminal acts of third parties is a question of fact that requires proof of an underlying breach of duty.

Ambriz v. Kelegian

53 Cal.Rptr.3d, 700 (Ca. App.2007)

FACTS

On January 26, 2002, Celia Ambriz (plaintiff) was assaulted and raped by an intruder at Casa Escondida, the apartment complex in Escondido, California where she lived.

Casa Escondida has 330 rental units, a density that required a variance from the City of Escondido. As a condition of being granted the variance, Casa Escondida is required to rent to senior citizens or disabled individuals. Casa Escondida's tenant population consists of lower-income, elderly individuals, many of whom are female.

Ambriz had been told that Casa Escondida was a "secured community," and she had seen it marketed as a "controlled access" community, in that the complex claimed that it maintained a locked entry gate and that the doors to the buildings were secured. However, the entry gate was often chained open. An on-site security guard had reported to Casa Escondida management that male intruders were gaining access to the building interiors. At the time of Ambriz's rape, three of the four entrances to Ambriz's building did not close and lock properly because the mechanisms on the entrance doors were broken. Residents had complained, but the doors were not repaired.

The rapist was a transient who had been seen around the complex on a number of occasions over a period of more than eight months prior to the rape. He was often found sleeping on benches within the Casa Escondida complex. The transient regularly asked the residents, including Ambriz, for money. In December 2001, he became more aggressive and began to frighten Ambriz and other tenants. That month, Ambriz complained to the management that the doors to the buildings would not lock and that this transient was scaring her. Ambriz was told that management would "take care of it."

A police detective who investigated Ambriz's rape testified that the lack of evidence of a forced entry indicated that it was more likely than not that the rapist had entered the building through an open door.

Ambriz filed suit against the apartment owners and managers (respondents). The trial court granted the respondents' motion for summary judgment because the court determined that Ambriz could not, as a matter of law, establish causation in the premises liability case. Ambriz appealed.

JUDICIAL OPINION

Aaron, Judge. An action in negligence requires a showing that the defendant owed the plaintiff a legal duty, that the defendant breached that duty, and that the breach was a proximate or legal cause of injuries suffered by the plaintiff. In this case, the respondents assert that Ambriz could not have established in the premises liability action that the management of Casa Escondida owed her a duty to take additional security measures, or that any breach of a presumed duty was the proximate cause of her injuries.

Respondents contend that Ambriz could not have established that Casa Escondida owed her a duty to better secure the property from intruders, and thus, that she would have lost on summary judgment for this reason. We disagree.

The question whether a duty exists is to be resolved by the court, not a jury. Courts have determined that an actor has no legal duty to avoid harm that is not foreseeable. "The duty of a proprietor of a business establishment to business invitees generally includes a 'duty to take affirmative action to control the wrongful acts of third persons [that] threaten invitees where the occupant has reasonable cause to anticipate such acts and the probability of injury resulting therefrom."

"Out of the generic obligations owed by landowners to maintain property in a reasonably safe condition, the law of negligence in the landlord–tenant context has evolved to impose a duty of reasonable care on the owner of an apartment building to protect its tenants from foreseeable third party criminal assaults." With respect to a landowner's duty to provide invitees with protection from third party crime, "the scope of the duty is determined in part by balancing the foreseeability of the harm against the burden of the duty to be imposed. Duty in such circumstances is determined by a balancing of 'foreseeability' of the criminal acts against the 'burdensomeness, vagueness, and efficacy' of the proposed security measures." *Sharon P. v. Arman, Ltd.* (1999) 21 Cal.4th 1181, 1190, 91 Cal.Rptr.2d 35, 989 P.2d 121 (*Sharon P.*), disapproved of by *Aguilar v. Atlantic Richfield Co.* (2001) 25 Cal.4th 826, 107 Cal.Rptr.2d 841, 24 P.3d 493 [applying balancing test to assertion that security guards should have been provided].)

"In circumstances in which the burden of preventing future harm caused by third party criminal conduct is great or onerous, heightened foreseeability—shown by prior similar criminal incidents or other indications of a reasonably foreseeable risk of violent criminal assaults in that location—will be required. By contrast, in cases in which harm can be prevented by simple means or by imposing merely minimal burdens, only 'regular' reasonable foreseeability as opposed to heightened foreseeability is required.")

Ambriz asserted that Casa Escondida management should have taken a number of measures that could have prevented the harm she suffered as a result of third party criminal conduct. Among the various measures Ambriz raised was a duty to properly maintain the locks on the doors and gates intended to limit access to the Casa Escondida buildings. In the trial court, Ambriz presented evidence that a number of access points were either purposefully left open, allowing the general public unfettered access to Casa Escondida grounds, or that they did not function properly, such that the doors to the buildings failed to close completely and/or lock after use.

Because requiring a landlord to use, maintain and/or repair already existing doors and locks imposes only a minimal burden on the landlord, the degree of foreseeability required in this case need not be as great as that required in *Sharon P.* We conclude that Ambriz needed to show only "'regular' reasonable foreseeability" to establish the existence of such minimal duties. The record establishes that Ambriz could easily have met this burden.

There was evidence that a number of vagrants had been congregating just outside the Casa Escondida complex and that they were making their way in onto the complex grounds on a regular basis. Some were seen showering in the poolside showers. Ambriz saw them sleeping on benches at various locations on the property.

There was also evidence that male intruders had gained unauthorized access into the Casa Escondida buildings. The transient who attacked Ambriz had been seen inside her building on more than 19 occasions prior to the rape. He had become more aggressive in his panhandling of the residents at Casa Escondida in the weeks leading up to the attack. Ambriz and a couple of her neighbors had complained to the management that this transient "scared" them, and that the doors were not locking. The residents asked whether something could be done "about the doors and the man" and were assured by Casa Escondida management that they would "take care of it."

Under these circumstances, the management of Casa Escondida could foresee that a resident in Casa Escondida's vulnerable population might fall victim to an assault by an unauthorized intruder. Casa Escondida had previously installed locks in order to maintain the complex as a "controlled access" residential facility, evidencing a concern on the part of Casa Escondida management regarding the residents' safety, and they were on notice that their security had been repeatedly breached. In view of the repeated security breaches and the known presence of unauthorized male intruders, a violent attack by an intruder was sufficiently foreseeable that Casa Escondida management had a minimal duty to properly maintain the locks on the doors and gates to the complex and its buildings.

Further, as noted above, Casa Escondida was granted a density variance on the condition that the complex be maintained as a low-to-moderate income senior housing project. As part of its agreement to rent primarily to poor, elderly and/or disabled tenants, Casa Escondida was required to meet certain safety standards set forth by the Escondido City Council, which included that "[i]nternal and/or perimeter security measures... be provided as necessary to meet the special needs of senior residents." Casa Escondida thus knew that it was required to take certain security measures to protect its residents, and that its residents were in need of special protection. The recognition by Escondido City Council that senior citizens are a particularly vulnerable group and Casa Escondida's implicit acknowledgement of this, constitutes additional evidence that the harm Ambriz suffered was reasonably foreseeable.

The inferences from the circumstantial evidence in this case that are favorable to Ambriz are more reasonable than those against her. There was evidence that a number of entry doors to the buildings were not closing properly and were not locking. A security guard at the complex testified that during the time he worked at Casa Escondida, three of the four building entrances would not close and lock in the manner they were supposed to. Tenants had complained to the security guard that the doors would not close and lock behind them. The security guard was concerned about the fact that the entry doors were not in working order, believing that created an unsafe condition. He complained about the malfunctioning doors to management. Despite all of these complaints, the doors were not repaired prior to Ambriz's rape.

There was also evidence of numerous instances in which the rapist and other male "intruders" gained access to the inside of Ambriz's building prior to the rape. In addition, a police detective testified that there was no evidence of forced entry into the building at the time of the rape. A reasonable inference from this evidence is that it was more likely than not that the rapist gained entry through a door that failed to properly shut and/or lock.

The respondents suggest that the assailant might have entered Ambriz's building in any number of ways, including by being offered entry to the complex by a tenant, entering through a door that had been propped open by another resident, entering through a ground floor patio sliding glass door or unlocked window, or entering through a second floor balcony door or window. However, considering the lack of evidence supporting any of these other methods of entry, it is more likely that the assailant entered through a door that failed to lock than by any of these alternative methods.... here there is evidence, not merely speculation, that it was more probable than not that the rapist gained entry through an improperly maintained door rather than by any of the alternative methods respondents suggest.

In this case, Ambriz and Casa Escondida management *did* know the identity of Ambriz's attacker, and Ambriz had seen this same individual inside her building at Casa Escondida on more than 10 occasions prior to the attack. The assailant was a transient who did not live at Casa Escondida. We can infer that his entry was thus unauthorized. Based on the evidence Ambriz offered, we can also infer that the malfunctioning doors had allowed a number of people to gain unauthorized entry into the complex.

Ambriz has raised a triable issue of fact as to whether Casa Escondida's failure to properly maintain its doors and locks was a substantial factor in causing her injury. The trial court thus erred in determining as a matter of law that Ambriz would not have been able to establish the element of causation in the underlying premises liability action and in granting summary judgment in favor of respondents in the legal malpractice action on that basis.

Reversed.

CASE QUESTIONS

1. Describe how and why this case is different from other cases in which a third party causes harm to a tenant.

2. What factors point to the landlord's liability here?

3. What precautions should landlords be taking based on this decision?

CONSIDER 9.9

On June 21, 1997, Julio Ramos was helping his cousin move out of a second-floor apartment. He positioned himself on the outer side of the second-floor balcony railing, his feet between its spindles, in order to pass furniture to a friend on the ground below. While perched in this precarious position, Ramos held onto the railing with one hand, and used his other hand to move the furniture. The reason for this method of removing the furniture was that many pieces were too large to be taken down the stairs. After approximately an hour of moving furniture in this manner, Ramos heard some cracking and felt the railing giving way. He released the furniture and attempted to grab onto the railing with both hands, but the spindles broke, and Ramos fell to the ground.

Ramos brought suit against the landlord to recover for his injuries. Should the landlord be held liable? *Ramos v. Granajo*, 822 A.2d 936 (R.I. 2003)

Duty to Comply with Statutes and Regulations: The Americans with Disability Act

In addition to compliance with state and federal statutes already discussed, landlords must also be in compliance with the Americans with Disabilities Act (ADA) (42 U.S.C. §§12181–12189). The ADA requires the removal of "architectural barriers in places of public accommodation when those barriers are readily removable." While landlords must comply with ADA, the act does permit the landlord and tenant to allocate the compliance responsibility under the terms of their lease. In residential leases, the landlord makes the accommodations in the common areas and the tenant makes his accommodations in his individual dwelling. (See Chapter 10 for more details on commercial properties and the ADA.)

Duty to Comply with Statutes and Regulations: Convicts, Registrants, and Leasing

One of the developing areas of case law in the landlord–tenant relationship is that of a landlord's rights with regard to leasing to convicts and those who are registered as sex offenders. About 600,000 inmates are released from prisons each year and their housing choices generally involve leasing.[4] The federal government has addressed the issue with its public housing guidelines. The Department of Housing and Urban Development follows a policy called "One Strike and You're Out Screening and Eviction Guidelines for Public Housing Authorities," under which public housing authorities must screen and evict tenants for drug related or "safety threatening" behavior. Public housing authorities that receive federal funds must include a lease clause that requires automatic lease termination for any drug or violent criminal activity, even if the activity does not occur on the landlord's property. The following case is a landmark one that deals with such regulations

Department of Housing and Urban Development v. Rucker

535 U.S. 125 (2002)

FACTS

Several young men who are grandsons of William Lee and Barbara Hill (respondents), both of whom were residents on the leases of Oakland Housing Authority (OHA), were caught in the apartment complex parking lot smoking marijuana. The daughter of Pearlie Rucker, who resides with her and is listed on the OHA lease as a resident, was found with cocaine and a crack cocaine pipe three blocks from Rucker's apartment. On three instances within a two-month period, Herman Walker's caregiver and two others were found with cocaine in

4. Heidi Lee Cain, "Housing Our Criminals: Finding Housing for the Ex-Offender in the Twenty-First Century," 33 *Golden Gate U. L. Rev.* 131 (2003).

Walker's apartment. OHA had issued Walker notices of a lease violation on the first two occasions, before initiating the eviction action after the third violation.

After OHA initiated the eviction proceedings in state court against the Hills, Rucker, and Walker, they commenced actions against HUD, OHA, and OHA's director in U.S. District Court, challenging HUD's interpretation of the statute and arguing that the federal statute and HUD regulations do not require lease terms authorizing the eviction of so-called innocent tenants, and, in the alternative, that if it does, then the statute is unconstitutional.

The District Court issued a preliminary injunction, enjoining OHA from terminating the leases of tenants. A panel of the Court of Appeals reversed, holding that HUD regulations and the statutory authority under 42 U.S.C. §1437d(l)(6) unambiguously permits the eviction of tenants who violate the lease provision, regardless of whether the tenant was personally aware of the drug activity, and that the statute is constitutional. An en banc panel of the Court of Appeals reversed and affirmed the District Court's grant of the preliminary injunction. The U.S. Supreme Court granted *certiorari*.

JUDICIAL OPINION

Rehnquist, Chief Justice.... [4]2 U.S.C. §1437d(l)(6) unambiguously requires lease terms that vest local public housing authorities with the discretion to evict tenants for the drug-related activity of household members and guests whether or not the tenant knew, or should have known, about the activity.

That this is so seems evident from the plain language of the statute. It provides that "[e]ach public housing agency shall utilize leases which ... provide that ... any drug-related criminal activity on or off such premises, engaged in by a public housing tenant, any member of the tenant's household, or any guest or other person under the tenant's control, shall be cause for termination of tenancy."

Regardless of knowledge, a tenant who "cannot control drug crime, or other criminal activities by a household member which threaten health or safety of other residents, is a threat to other residents and the project." 56 Fed. Reg., at 51567. With drugs leading to "murders, muggings, and other forms of violence against tenants," and to the "deterioration of the physical environment that requires substantial government expenditures," 42 U.S.C. §11901(4) (1994 ed., Supp. V), it was reasonable for Congress to permit no-fault evictions in order to "provide public and other federally assisted low-income housing that is decent, safe, and free from illegal drugs," ...

There are, moreover, no "serious constitutional doubts" about Congress' affording local public housing authorities the discretion to conduct no-fault evictions for drug-related crime. The Court of Appeals sought to bolster its discussion of constitutional doubt by pointing to the fact that respondents have a property interest in their leasehold interest, citing *Greene v. Lindsey*, 456 U.S. 444, 102 S.Ct. 1874, 72 L.Ed.2d 249 (1982). This is undoubtedly true, and *Greene* held that an effort to deprive a tenant of such a right without proper notice violated the Due Process Clause of the Fourteenth Amendment. But, in the present cases, such deprivation will occur in the state court where OHA brought the unlawful detainer action against respondents. There is no indication that notice has not been given by OHA in the past, or that it will not be given in the future. Any individual factual disputes about whether the lease provision was actually violated can, of course, be resolved in these proceedings.

CASE QUESTIONS

1. Who was evicted and why?
2. Name the two bases for the challenges to the eviction.
3. What did the Supreme Court decide and why?

CONSIDER 9.10

Lakiasha Harris leased a Section 8 subsidized housing unit in an apartment complex in Cleveland, Ohio. Harris's lease requires Harris to "insure [*sic*] that Resident, household members, family members, guests or other persons, under the residents [*sic*] control, shall not engage in any drug related criminal activity ON or OFF C.M.H.A. premises."

On June 16, 2006, Cuyahoga Metropolitan Housing Authority police came to Harris's apartment to arrest a guest of Harris, Kevin Daniels, on a federal warrant. CMHA police searched Daniels and found a rock of crack cocaine in his pocket. CMHA conducted an inspection of Harris's apartment and found no drugs or drug paraphernalia. Harris testified that she was unaware that Daniels had the cocaine in his possession and Harris did not interfere with Daniels's arrest.

CMHA began eviction proceedings against Harris based upon violation of her lease; that Harris failed to ensure that her guest did not engage in drug-related criminal activity. Can Harris be evicted? *Cuyahoga Metro. Housing Auth. v. Harris,* 2006 WL 3859205 (Oh Mun Ct 2006)

Liability to Third Parties

In addition to the tenants, other party may enter the common areas of leased property or the dwelling units of tenants. For injuries occurring to third parties in the common areas, the landlord is liable in the same way as with tenants—that is, landlords are expected to exercise reasonable care in the maintenance of common areas.

The landlord's liability for injury to third parties while the third parties are actually in a dwelling unit varies according to the terms of the lease agreement. If the landlord has accepted the burden of repair and upkeep but fails to meet that burden, then resulting injuries to third parties are the responsibility of the landlord. On the other hand, if the tenant has undertaken the responsibility of repair and upkeep, then such injuries to third parties are the responsibility of the tenant.

Sometimes both the landlord and the tenant are liable. For example, in a case where the landlord is responsible for maintenance and a nonremedied problem exists (such as a loose step), the tenant must warn third parties of the problem until the landlord has the chance to repair. If the tenant fails to warn visitors of the problem during the interim, both landlord and tenant could be held liable.

If the leased premises have code violations, the landlord is responsible for injuries to third parties resulting from such violations. Furthermore, even if the landlord has no statutory or contractual duty to repair, it is his or her responsibility to warn the tenant of any hidden defects and to post notices for third parties who might enter the property.

Today, as noted earlier, landlords may have liability for the failure to provide adequate security or to screen those entering their property.

Use of Exculpatory Clauses

To attempt to avoid liability to both tenants and third parties, landlords frequently include exculpatory or hold-harmless clauses in leases. These clauses provide that the landlord will not be liable for any injuries or damages occurring on the premises because of the landlord's negligence or the negligence of any other parties. Although these clauses can be found in many lease agreements, their legal effect is minimal. In other words, landlords cannot by provisions in agreements hold themselves harmless for injuries caused by their failure to maintain the premises or to comply with building and safety codes. The courts have interpreted such clauses, at least in residential leases, to be unconscionable and unenforceable, or in some decisions, void. Some states have enacted specific statutes that prohibit exculpatory clauses; and in states that have adopted the URLTA, the section on unconscionability has been used to invalidate exculpatory clauses. The following is an example of an exculpatory clause in a residential lease:

Lessor and his Agent shall not be liable for any damage or inconvenience to either person or property, that may be sustained by Lessee, his family, invitees, licensees, or guests on or about the premises herein leased, including damage or inconvenience resulting from breakdown or delays.

Landlords may take two precautions to help reduce their potential liability for injuries caused to tenants and to visiting third parties. The first precaution is for landlords to obtain adequate insurance. The second is to use leases that specify who is responsible for repair and maintenance. A repair and maintenance clause may alleviate the effect of repair and deduct actions by tenants and may also serve to determine who is liable in the event disrepair causes an injury to a third party.

Rights of Landlords and Responsibilities of Tenants

Landlords have several basic rights under the lease agreement that, in turn, constitute the tenants' responsibilities under the agreement. The purpose of leasing property is to have the property produce income; the right of landlords to receive timely rental payments pursuant to the terms of the lease agreement is fundamental.

Tenants have an obligation to make timely rental payments according to the method and place of payment specified by the landlord. If a tenant does not make timely payment, there has been a breach of the lease agreement, and the landlord is permitted to take steps to minimize damages. Under URLTA Section 4.201, the landlord must give the tenant a written notice of nonpayment that states that the lease terminates within a specified period after receipt of the notice if rent is not paid. Although some states have changed the time constraints, the URLTA specifies that if rent is not received within 14 days from the time the tenant receives the notice of nonpayment, the lease will terminate within 30 days from receipt of the notice.

Most states provide specific procedures for having nonpaying tenants evicted from leased premises. Two names for this procedure are **forcible detainer** and **action for dispossession**. A distinct feature of these specialized procedures is that the defenses a tenant may assert are limited, so that the landlord is not kept in litigation for long periods while the tenant remains in possession of the property. For example, tenants may assert reasons for nonpayment that are justified under their states' landlord–tenant acts. Under the URLTA, defenses to nonpayment of rent are the landlord's failure to supply heat or water or the tenant's exercise of the right to repair and deduct for maintaining habitability of the premises. However, the right of asserting these defenses for nonpayment is limited to states that have recognized the right of habitability as being interrelated with the payment of rent and the existence of a valid lease agreement. In states not recognizing the doctrine of habitability, uninhabitability is not a defense to a landlord's action for possession.

In seeking to evict a tenant for nonpayment of rent, landlords must be able to establish that they have not waived their rights to timely payment. That is, if they have waited until the eighth day of the month for rent due on the first and have accepted the late payment, they will be bound by the delay period in the future unless they serve tenants with formal notice of the intent to exercise the right to timely payment.

In some states, landlords are afforded other remedies for nonpayment of rent. For example, suppose a tenant abandons the premises and leaves personal property. Some states give the landlord a lien, an interest, or a right to possession of that personal property. Although some landlords attempt the private remedy of changing locks for a truly short dispossession action, the courts have invalidated such conduct on the grounds that the tenant has been denied due process.

In some cases, a tenant stops paying rent upon vacating the premises prior to the expiration of the lease term. The landlord has possession of the premises but no tenant to produce rental income. In these circumstances, the landlord has a right of action for breach of contract against the tenant to collect the lost rents and associated expenses of the property sitting vacant. However, most states do require the landlord to mitigate damages, which means that if it is possible, the landlord must rent the premises and recover from the tenant only for the period during which the apartment was vacant.

Nonpayment of rent is the typical reason for a landlord's action for dispossession, but any breach of the rental agreement by the tenant may result in a termination notice and dispossession action by the landlord. Examples of other breaches include breaking the rules and regulations, failing to maintain the premises according to the lease agreement, and performing illegal activities on the premises.

Tenants are also under obligation to use the landlord's property in such a way that is not destructive of its future value. In the absence of express agreement or permission, tenants cannot destroy vegetation, reconstruct buildings, or destroy existing structures. A tenant's their basic right is use without change or destruction. The parties to the lease should agree in advance on the addition of fixtures and what will happen to the fixtures at the end of the lease term, so that their placement or removal is not interpreted to be a waste of the landlord's property.

CONSIDER 9.11

Richard Taylor was a resident of a Kenai low-income housing project owned by Gill Street Investments known as the Gill Street Apartments. Taylor's apartment badly needed cleaning and exuded a bad odor about which the neighbors complained. Taylor admitted that he left his drapes open and walked around his apartment nude, and his apartment was located near the children's play area in the complex. Taylor was known to sit in his car for extended periods of time and honk his car horn if someone had parked in his parking space, and would continue honking until the car in his place was moved. Taylor was frequently drunk and frightened children when he was intoxicated. Taylor was current in his rent, but Gill Street Investments served him with an eviction notice. Could Taylor be evicted? *Taylor v. Gill Street Investments*, 743 P.2d 345 (Alaska 1987)

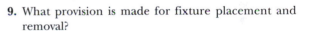

Cautions and Conclusions

In negotiating a lease, the following factors should be provided for, or at least considered:

1. What is the lease term? Must the lease be in writing? (Usually, leases for longer than one year must be in writing.)
2. When the lease expires, is there an option to renew? Can a month-to-month tenancy then exist?
3. How much notice, if any, is required for termination by both the landlord and the tenant?
4. Are there provisions for attorneys' fees? Does the tenant waive any legal rights?
5. Are pets and children permitted?
6. Are there rules and regulations on noise, pool use, and so on?
7. Is there an exculpatory clause? If so, what is its effect?
8. Who is responsible for maintenance in the dwelling unit and in the common areas?
9. What provision is made for fixture placement and removal?
10. Are assignments and subleases permitted?
11. When may the landlord enter the tenant's dwelling unit without permission?
12. How much is required in deposits? What is the purpose of each deposit? Are deposits refundable?
13. How are utilities paid?
14. Is there a warranty of habitability? Do any items need repair or replacement prior to the beginning of the lease term?
15. Are there late penalties for rental payments?

Although this list does not include all areas that should be covered in the lease, it serves as a checklist for the areas causing both landlords and tenants the most problems and the most litigation.

Key Terms

action for dispossession, 214
assignments, 200
cleaning deposit, 195
constructive eviction, 202
forcible detainer, 214
implied warranty of habitability, 190
periodic tenancy, 186
rent controls, 195
repair and deduct, 204
Rule in Dumpor's Case, 201
security deposit, 193
self-help, 204
subleases, 200
tenancy at sufferance, 187
tenancy at will, 186
tenancy for years, 186
Uniform Residential Landlord Tenant Act (URLTA), 185

Chapter Problems

1. Louis Varnado, a four-year-old child, sustained serious bodily burns from boiling water being carried in a pot by his grandmother from the kitchen to the bathtub of their apartment. The hot water in the apartment complex did not function and the landlord had not repaired the defective water heater despite complaints from the tenants. As a result, the tenants boiled water in their kitchens and carried it to their bathrooms in order to enjoy warm baths and basin water. Andrea Varnado brought suit against the landlord for her son's injuries that she says were caused by his failure to repair the water heater. Do you agree? Would you hold the landlord liable? *Bennett M. Lifter, Inc. v. Varnado*, 480 So.2d 1336 (Fla. 1985)

2. Garcia lived in a tenement house in the East Harlem section of Manhattan with his two young children. The paint in one of the rooms and in the bathroom was flaking off the walls, and Garcia's children were eating the paint and the flakes. In spite of Garcia's several complaints, the landlord did not remedy the problem. Garcia then expended $29.53 for materials and $70 for labor to replaster and repaint the walls in the rooms. He brought suit for the recovery of these amounts from his landlord. Could he recover these amounts from his landlord? *Garcia v. Freeland Realty, Inc.*, 314 N.Y.S.2d 215 (1972)

3. Thomas Campbell and Bonnie Glenn owned the apartment building located at 102–104 Bellevue Street, in the Dorchester section of Boston. Campbell was the day-to-day manager, supervising any renovations and collecting the rents.

On April 2, 1987, a Boston police officer, after observing heavy foot traffic in the building, made a drug-related raid and arrest in the building.

Break-ins were common at apartment no. 104-3. Following one of the break-ins, a different door was installed to apartment no. 104-3. The door had a hollow "peephole" below the traditional peephole and two "two by fours" were used to bar the inside of the door. After the new door was installed, transactions could occur by having the buyer put money through the lower peephole in the door. Drugs were pushed out the same hole to the buyer.

Campbell collected rents in the building. When he collected from apartment no. 104-3, he would be met by different individuals who claimed to be the occupant's cousin or brother. Campbell was never able to see inside apartment no. 104-3.

Three weeks after the new door was installed, Detective Sherman Griffiths of the Boston Police Department was shot and killed during the course of a raid on apartment no. 104-3. His widow (plaintiff) brought suit against Campbell and Glenn for their negligence in the operation and maintenance of their building. Are they liable? *Griffiths v. Campbell*, 679 N.E.2d 536 (Mass. 1997)

4. Mary Weatherall was a tenant in the Yorktown Townhome complex. She fell on the ice and snow accumulated outside her leased apartment and fractured her ankle. Can she recover from the landlord for her injury and the landlord's failure to maintain the premises? *Weatherall v. Yorktown Homeowner's Assn.*, 852 P.2d 815 (Okl. 1991)

5. Ricky Pierce owns a house located at 107 Beech Street, Roanoke Rapids, North Carolina. On April 5, 1999, Tammy Reichard signed a lease in which she agreed to rent the house from Pierce for $300 per month, plus a $300 security deposit. Approximately two weeks after Ms. Reichard moved into the house, the roof over the living room began to leak after a heavy rainfall. Ms. Reichard first complained about the leaks in August or September of 2000, and Pierce hired a repair person at that time to apply a coat of "Koolseal" to the roof. Ms. Reichard did not notice any difference in the leakage and complained about the leaks and water damage each time she paid her rent. In August 2001, Pierce had the old roof removed and new shingles installed, but did not repair any of the water damage inside the house. The living room continued to leak and Ms. Reichard moved out her furniture and used the room to "store junk."

During the roof repairs, Pierce's dump truck was parked in front of the house to contain roof debris. Ms. Reichard admitted that her four-year-old son may have sprayed water into the truck's open gas tank. Ms. Reichard and her husband agreed to siphon all of the gas out of the tank, and put in enough gas to get the truck to a gas station. They also agreed to reimburse Pierce for the cost of refilling the tank, but Pierce claimed that the truck broke down within a few yards of leaving the house and that the repairs cost him over $300. Pierce demanded that Ms. Reichard pay the repair bill, and she refused.

Ms. Reichard also complained to Pierce about a rotten tree on the property that she thought endangered her and her family. After Pierce failed to address this issue, a limb broke off the tree during a storm and damaged Ms. Reichard's car. The leaky roof continued through 2001 when Ms. Reichard left the property. She filed suit seeking damages for her property (living room furniture), a refund of rent, late fees, and other damages. Mr. Pierce counterclaimed for the damage to his truck. An expert testified that with the living room unusable, the property had a rental value of $150 per month. North Carolina allows for treble damages recovery for landlord breaches of warranty of habitability.

After a bench trial, the court awarded Ms. Reichard treble damages of $14,950, property damages of $200 for a broken windshield, a $200 refund of excessive late fees, the return of her $300 security deposit and attorney's fees of $4,085. The trial court awarded Pierce $318.07 for damage to his truck. Evaluate the court's award of damages. Was the warranty of habitability breached? What lessons in human nature do you learn from this two-year lease? *Pierce v. Reichard*, 593 S.E.2d 787 (N.C. App. 2007).

6. Mr. and Mrs. John Julian, Sr., rented a home from Mr. and Mrs. Donald Linden for $150 per month in Silverhill, Alabama. In March, when it came time to mow the grass around the home, Mrs. Julian inquired of the Lindens about the yard and was told to assume responsibility for mowing "from the bushes to the highway, to the dirt road, from the highway back to the pecan trees." Within this area was a thicket, dense with undergrowth and small trees, that concealed an old shed.

In September 1985, Johnny Julian, the Julians' ten-year-old son, chased his puppy into the thicket and encountered the shed, rotting and dilapidated, for the first time. When his puppy ran into the shed, Johnny pulled himself up on an outside wall to try to see inside; some bricks over the opening where he had placed his hands to lift himself dislodged as the shed collapsed, and three of his fingers were severed.

The Julians filed suit against the Lindens on the theory that they had negligently failed to warn of a known hidden danger. Should the Julians win? *Julian v. Linden*, 545 So.2d 23 (Ala. 1989)

7. Ella terminated her six-month lease agreement at the end of three months by abandoning her apartment. Her monthly rent was $800. Although the landlord had several opportunities to rent the apartment, he refused, stating, "Why hassle with another tenant when I can sue and collect the $2,400 from Ella?" Is the landlord correct in his assumption?

8. Paul Salmonte leased Richard and Mildred Eilertsons' Florida home in 1985. The Eilertsons lived in Houston, Texas, but sometimes returned to inspect the house. The Eilertsons also had an exterminator go to the home on a monthly basis. By May 1986, Salmonte decided that the inspections and extermination were occurring too often and began refusing regular access. The Eilertsons discovered that Salmonte had breached the terms of the lease agreement that prohibited changes in carpeting, wallpaper, and locks and then went to inspect the home and pets. The Eilertsons noticed that one of their rugs had been moved to the garage and had a car parked on it. They then filed a complaint for eviction for breach of the lease agreement. Could the Eilertsons have Salmonte evicted for violations of the rules? *Salmonte v. Eilertson*, 526 So.2d 179 (Ct. App. Fla. 1988)

9. Adam Armstrong rented Apartment 103-A located at 441 Kanekapolei Street in Honolulu from Jack Cione. The apartment was originally part of a two-bedroom unit within a cooperative building called the Waikiki Regent, which was constructed in 1959 and contained nine identical units.

On April 12, 1982, Armstrong's right hand and wrist were injured when a glass panel in the apartment's shower door shattered as he attempted to close it. The shower door was installed when the apartment was originally built and was constructed of three glass panels with hinged aluminum frames on an aluminum track. Safety glass was not used.

Cione says he was unaware of a crack in the door and Armstrong knew the door was difficult to close but never complained to Cione about the problem. Is this a breach of the warranty of habitability? *Armstrong v. Cione*, 736 P.2d 440 (Haw. 1987)

10. Margaret Skinner owned two adjacent parcels of land. She lived on one and leased the other to Bud Wellington on a month-to-month basis. The Bradys lived on the other side of Wellington. Skinner gave Wellington permission to keep two mules on the property. One was named Martin Luther and the other was named King. King acted like a typical, ornery mule. Basically he did not like anyone and would put his ears back and shy away when anyone got close to him. On the other hand, Martin Luther acted more like a horse than a mule. He was playful and friendly. The mules were docile and neither had ever kicked, bitten, or tried to injure anyone.

They were no more dangerous than any other mules, but like other mules, they were unpredictable.

One day Arthur Brady, Jr., who was four years old at the time, was kicked by one of the mules. No one seems to know which mule kicked him. The Bradys filed suit. Is Skinner liable? *Brady v. Skinner,* 646 P.2d 310 (Az. 1982)

For research activities related to this chapter, go to our text companion website at www.thomsonedu.com/westbuslaw/jennings.

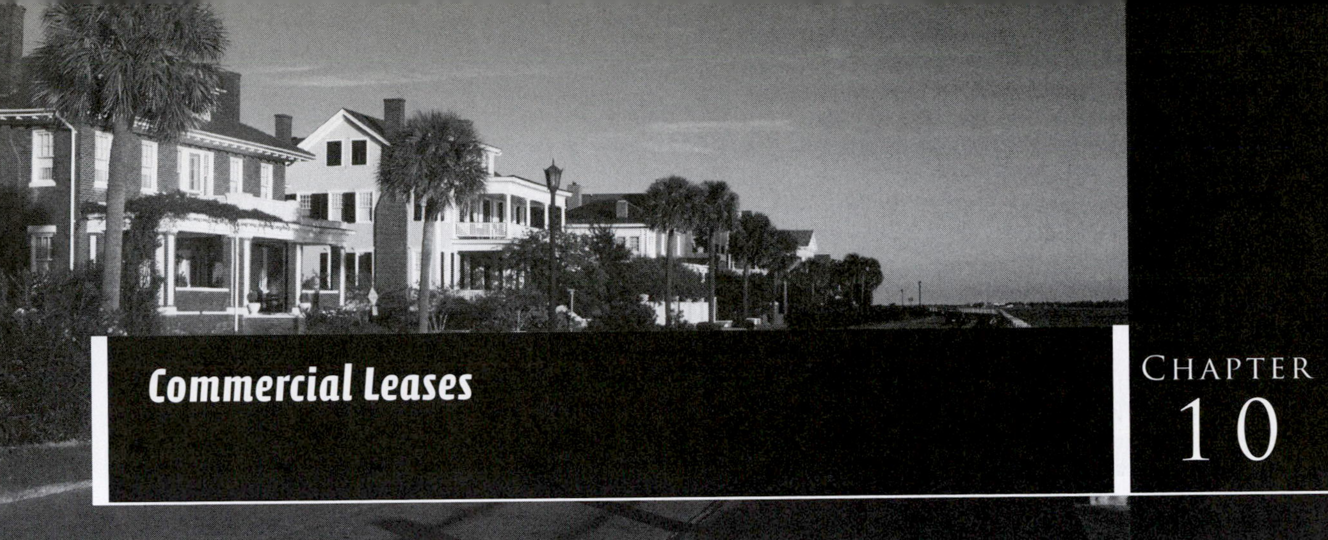

Chapter 10
Commercial Leases

"Real estate often represents a firm's largest single financial commitment and its largest annual expense other than payroll. A firm's facilities can have a major impact on earnings for many years from both the standpoint of direct cost and employee productivity."[1]

Beware the clause and its effect.

Phillip M. Perry, Attorney[2]

Commercial leases are complex beasts. From office space in the Sears Tower to the neighborhood shopping center, commercial leases are also different from the residential lease. The statutory provisions and protections discussed in Chapter 9 for residential leases do not exist in commercial transactions. Many states continue to rely primarily on case law for their commercial lease law, interpretation, and protections. While there is a Uniform Commercial Landlord and Tenant Act (UCLTA), it has not been adopted in toto by any states.[3] This chapter addresses the following questions: What are the requirements for the formation of a commercial lease? What topics and issues should a commercial lease address? What facts and information should be studied before entering into a commercial lease?

Formation of the Commercial Lease

Negotiations

Commercial leases have additional issues that are often contingent upon business conditions, timely completion of construction, and terms in agreements with other tenants. Potential commercial tenants need complete and accurate information

1. Gary Oldman, "Uniform Commercial Landlord and Tenant Act—A Proposal to Reform 'Law out of Context,'" 2002 *Trinity Law Review* 175 (2002).
2. "Clause and Effect," *Country Sampler and Country Business*, June 2000, p. 44.
3. Uniform Residential Landlord & Tenant Act, 7B U.L.A. 527 (2000).

because good neighbors are perhaps more important in commercial than residential leases. Who are the other tenants? What is the rental amount? How are the other tenants doing in their businesses? In the negotiation stage, the rules for contract formation on misrepresentation and fraud apply. However, relying on leasing agents and landlords for information is risky. In commercial lease negotiations, lessees need independent verification of information, as the following case illustrates.

Herring-Marathon Master Partnership B v. Boardwalk Fries, Inc.

979 F.2d 1326 (8th Cir. 1992)

FACTS

Marathon owns and operates the Park Plaza Mall in Little Rock, Arkansas. The mall opened in July 1988, and on March 21, 1989, Boardwalk entered into a ten-year lease agreement with Marathon to operate a Boardwalk Fries restaurant in the mall's food court.

Boardwalk, with Marathon's approval, sublet the Park Plaza Mall space to Ken Rittmueller and James Tandy as franchisees. Rittmueller and Tandy opened their mall restaurant on May 21, 1989.

In March 1990, Rittmueller and Tandy closed the mall restaurant and abandoned the premises due to poor sales. Marathon filed suit against Boardwalk for unpaid rents, and Boardwalk filed a third-party claim against Rittmueller and Tandy for the rent.

Boardwalk claimed that Marathon had misrepresented the sales of other tenants during the lease negotiations. When the annual rent was revealed to be $40,000 for the restaurant space, William Morris, Marathon's leasing agent explained, "Look, this mall is opening gangbusters.... We've got a couple of players in this food court that are going to do more than a million bucks." Jack Csicsek, Boardwalk's vice president for franchising and leasing, Rittmueller, and Tandy all described sales as the "only deciding factor" in their decision to lease in Park Plaza.

The trial court entered judgment for Marathon, and Boardwalk appealed.

JUDICIAL OPINION

Loken, Circuit Judge. Boardwalk based its fraud defense primarily upon the trial testimony of Rittmueller and Tandy. Rittmueller testified that he had more than a dozen conversations with Morris between October 1988 and the signing of the lease in March 1989. During four or five of those conversations, Morris orally provided sales figures for other tenants of the newly opened food court. According to Rittmueller, Morris sent him a typewritten sheet listing four months' sales for four or five of the food court tenants—a document Rittmueller subsequently lost—but never showed him a Cumulative Monthly Sales Report. If Rittmueller's testimony is believed, the sales figures that Morris provided were substantially inflated. Tandy's trial testimony supported Rittmueller. However, Rick Smith, manager of the franchise restaurant, testified that he, Tandy, and Rittmueller were given a Cumulative Monthly Sales Report.

Morris testified that he discussed the sales volumes of other food court tenants with Rittmueller and Tandy before the lease was signed and that he responded truthfully to Rittmueller's and Tandy's inquiries about sales figures. Specifically, he told Rittmueller that Chick-Fil-A reported $130,000 in sales in August 1988, and that Sbarro's pizza restaurant reported sales of $77,000 to $80,000 for part of November and December 1988—figures that are consistent with the Cumulative Monthly Sales Reports for that period.

On appeal, Boardwalk contends that the district court erred in finding that Marathon's agent, William Morris, committed no misrepresentation. The monthly sales of other food court tenants declined significantly between the Park Plaza Mall's opening in July 1988 and the signing of Boardwalk's lease in March 1989. Boardwalk argues that Morris had a continuing affirmative duty to disclose that fact. In addition, Boardwalk claims that Morris at least had an obligation to disclose those declining sales in response to repeated requests for sales figures by Rittmueller and Tandy over the course of the lease negotiations.

We reject Boardwalk's contention that, under Arkansas law, Marathon had an affirmative duty to disclose the declining sales experienced by other food court vendors. "As a general rule there is no duty between vendor and purchaser to disclose any information affecting the value of property in an arm's length transaction." There was no special relationship between these parties giving rise to such a duty. As the district court found, Boardwalk is an experienced and knowledgeable restaurant franchising company that can be expected to know what information it needs to obtain in negotiating leases of this type. In these circumstances, Arkansas law imposes no affirmative duty to disclose other tenants' declining sales figures over the course of the lease negotiations.

Arkansas law does impose a duty on parties negotiating a real estate transaction to respond truthfully to material inquiries:

[W]hen parties... deal at "arm's length" and in no confidential relationship, the prospective purchaser is under no obligation to volunteer information to the vendor; but if in such a situation, the vendor makes inquiry of material matters and the purchaser undertakes to make answers, then such answers must be truthful, unequivocal and non-evasive.

Relying on the testimony of Rittmueller and Tandy, testimony the district court expressly rejected, Boardwalk asserts that, in response to repeated inquiries, Morris provided Rittmueller and Tandy with a list of inflated sales figures. However, they claimed to have lost that list and, as the district court observed, "their explanation for the loss of this very important document is unconvincing and unsatisfactory."

Rittmueller and Tandy also testified that they never saw a computerized Cumulative Monthly Sales Report until after the lease was signed.

Morris testified that he responded truthfully to all inquiries about other food court vendors' sales, and the district court credited that testimony. The sales figures that Morris testified he provided orally to Tandy and Rittmueller were consistent with the Cumulative Monthly Sales Reports. On this record, we cannot conclude that the district court's finding that credited Morris's recollection of these conversations, rather than Rittmueller's and Tandy's, is clearly erroneous.

Finally, we note that the testimony of Boardwalk's vice president, Csicsek, provides independent support for the district court's decision. Csicsek testified that he, not the prospective franchisees, Rittmueller and Tandy, was solely responsible for negotiating the lease's economic terms. Csicsek testified that he made the decision to enter into the lease based upon one phone call to Morris. Csicsek admitted that he never saw a computer generated printout of other tenants' sales volumes, nor the document Rittmueller claimed to have received from Morris listing the sales figures for various tenants. In these circumstances, we agree with the district court that Boardwalk made an inadequate inquiry before signing the lease. If Boardwalk considered the prior sales of other tenants in the newly opened food court material, it should have unambiguously requested that Marathon provide the required information. Thus, Boardwalk's defense of fraud in the inducement is without merit.

Affirmed.

CASE QUESTIONS

1. Who entered into the lease agreement?
2. Why was there a sublease and to whom?
3. What misrepresentation is alleged to have occurred?
4. What information should the lessees have examined before entering into the lease?
5. Does a leasing agent owe any duty to a prospective tenant in terms of disclosure?

Ethical Issue

While the court in the *Boardwalk Fries* case did not find misrepresentation, do you think there was adequate disclosure of information about the mall's sales performance? Does the statement about the mall opening "gangbusters" accurately reflect its performance? Was it unfair to only answer specific questions? Is affirmative disclosure necessary?

CONSIDER 10.1

Barry Hinesley worked with Oakshade Town Center's agent and representative, Paul Petrovich, on leasing a suite for operating his business. Hinesley maintains that Petrovich told him that the regional restaurant chain Dos Coyotes, the international coffee shop chain Starbucks, and the international ice cream and yogurt vendor chain Baskin-Robbins would be leasing and occupying suites near the suite Hinesley was to lease. Hinesley said that Petrovich told him that all three chains would commence operations by the end of 1998. Hinesley and Oakshade later executed a lease, dated July 6, 1998, for a 1,200 square foot space at the Oakshade Town Center Shopping Center for a term of five years.

CONSIDER 10.1

(continued)

Starbucks and Baskin-Robbins never leased space from Oakshade. However, Marble Slab Creamery (an ice cream store) and Common Grounds (a coffee house) did become tenants. Dos Coyotes did become a tenant of Oakshade, but its lease did not commence until December 2000.

Paragraph 25.33 of the lease Hinesley signed provides: "Lessor reserves the right to effect such other tenancies in the Shopping Center as Lessor in the exercise of its judgment shall determine to bet [*sic*] promote the interest of the Shopping Center. *Lessee does not rely on the fact nor does Lessor represent that any specific Lessee of* [*sic*] *type or number of Lessees shall during the term of this Lease occupy any space in the Shopping Center.*"

Hinesley brought suit to rescind the lease on the basis of the misrepresentations by the landlord's agent on the development of the center and the promised tenants. Does Hinesley have any basis in law for allowing his rescission? Describe the pros and cons of his argument on misrepresentation. *Hinesley v. Oakshade Town Center*, 37 Cal.Rptr.3d 364 (2006)

The Lease Agreement

As odd as it may seem, many commercial tenants are operating under oral lease agreements. Generally, the statute of frauds requirement for commercial leases takes effect when leases run for more than six months (in some states) and one year (in most states). However, a month-to-month commercial lease would not be covered by the statute even though the lease may run on for years. Regardless of statute of frauds provisions, all commercial tenants should have their lease agreements in writing. Reliance on oral representations and understandings can be risky because recollections and understandings of oral promises can be fuzzy. See Web Exhibit 10.1 for a sample commercial lease.

> ***Practical Tip***
>
> *Due diligence, or the examination of all aspects of a transaction, is as necessary in commercial leasing as it is in sales of land. Lessees should verify the accuracy of square footage, sales, and income claims. They should look into demographics and planned changes in the area that might affect the sales base. Reliance on rental agents' and landlords' information is misplaced.*

Topics in the Commercial Lease

A successful commercial landlord–tenant relationship requires careful attention to details in the lease negotiations and in the lease itself. This section covers the typical provisions in a commercial lease.

The Lease Term

Commercial leases carry peculiarities in terms of start or beginning dates that residential leases will not have. For example, many commercial properties already have tenants with lease agreements before the property is constructed. In the Phoenix area, a developer who had taken on the responsibility of revitalizing the downtown area had commitments from businesses to be tenants in buildings that were to be constructed based on those commitments. The lease agreements existed before the buildings existed. Such arrangements are also typical with shopping centers and malls. The developer obtains commitments from large or anchor tenants prior to construction of the center or the mall, and the remaining tenants sign on for the yet-to-be-constructed stores on the basis of the anchor tenant's commitment.

In these types of leases, the start date of the leases is tied to completion of construction. However, completion of construction can change as the project progresses. Tenants should have protections for these fluctuations because of problems with planning and inventory holdings that will result. Tenants in malls and shopping centers will want start dates around seasonal swings to avoid opening a business or moving a business to a new location during a slow period in the sales year. For example, retail outlets have highest sales from October through January, so that commencing a lease in October would be a profit maximizer. On the other hand, commencing a lease in February begins an obligation during a slow period, with a long wait for increased sales. Likewise, moving a business during peak sales periods can hurt the business.

Another beginning-date issue is whether the tenant is allowed to move in before actual completion of the unit or the common areas and, if so, when rent will become due. Because of the uncertainty involved, it is probably best for the parties to put an outside date in the contract; that is, a date by which there must be occupancy or the lease is terminated. With an outside date, the lease provides for contingencies such as noncompletion, bankruptcy, and delays. The developer is not tied to a specific date of completion but has a range, and the tenant has a latest possible occupancy date for planning purposes. The lease may even provide an option for the tenant to extend the outside date if the date passes and the tenant still desires to continue with the lease.

Premises Condition

The implied warranty of habitability or usability generally does not exist in commercial leases. If a tenant wants a guarantee that the leased premises will be delivered with certain repairs, conditions, or improvements, a warranty for these items must be in the lease agreement. Problems such as faulty heating or air-conditioning, leaking roofs, and broken windows should be described in the lease as repairs that are conditions precedent to the tenant's performance under the terms of the lease.

In recent years, the courts have become more helpful to commercial tenants, finding in some instances that the condition of the premises is sufficiently bad to constitute constructive eviction of a commercial tenant.

In addition to the initial condition of the premises, the parties should agree on which party will be responsible for maintenance. The landlord may want to specify that the obligation to repair does not arise until the tenant brings the condition of disrepair to the landlord's attention through a written notice. Some obligations of repair may be imposed upon the tenant, such as keeping trade fixtures in good working condition. For example, many tenants have an electronic sign outside their business; the obligation of repair and upkeep of that sign belongs with the tenant.

The parties may also wish to make a provision for emergency repairs—an authorization for immediate work in circumstances where the parties are unable to contact each other and the repair is absolutely necessary. Water leaks are an example wherein immediate action may save later costs and damage, and an emergency repair by either party without the other's approval can save money for both. The following case is one of a growing number of decisions affording commercial tenants rights on repairs and habitability.[4]

4. For a case that held there was no right to reduce rent, see *Matte v. Shippee Auto, Inc.*, 876 A.2d 167 (N.H. 2005), in which the court held that because the statute did not allow for rent deductions in commercial leases, it could not allow the tenant damages for the failure to fix a leaky roof.

Richard Barton Enterprises, Inc. v. Tsern

928 P.2d 368 (Utah 1996)

FACTS

On November 21, 1991, Barton and Tsern entered into an agreement titled "Earnest Money Receipt and Offer to Lease," and on November 27, 1991, the parties executed a lease pursuant thereto for the first and second floors of a commercial building in downtown Salt Lake City. Barton agreed to pay rent at the rate of $3,000 per month for the one-year lease. The lease required Tsern to deliver possession of the premises to Barton on December 1, 1991. On November 27, Barton paid Tsern $9,000, covering the first and last months' rent and a $3,000 security deposit. Barton also paid an additional $3,000 as earnest money for an option to purchase the entire building.

Added to the terms of the printed earnest money form were the typed words, "Other than stated in lines 32 and 33, Tenant shall accept the building in 'As Is' condition." The language on lines 32 and 33 required Tsern to repair the building's leaky roof and the freight elevator to "good working order."

Barton's purpose in leasing the building was to establish an antiques dealership. The business inventory included large architectural pieces that, because of the dropped ceiling of the main floor and other limitations, had to be stored on the second floor. For that reason Barton required a freight elevator to transport the large, heavy pieces to the second floor. Barton's need for the elevator was communicated to Tsern repeatedly, both prior to signing the earnest money agreement, when Barton became aware that the elevator was inoperable, and after the lease was executed and Barton took occupancy of the leased premises.

Barton took possession of the ground floor on December 1, 1991, but could not obtain possession of the second floor until December 20, when a holdover tenant finally vacated the floor. The elevator was wholly inoperable, and Tsern had neither repaired the elevator nor entered into a contract to have it repaired. Moreover, the roof had not been repaired. The elevator remained inoperable until January 9, 1992, when Kimball Elevator Co., pursuant to a time and materials contract with Tsern, made certain repairs to the elevator. On Tsern's instructions, however, Kimball made only those repairs necessary to make the elevator operational in the sense that it would "go up and down." Tsern strictly limited the amount of money he would pay Kimball for repairs to $5,000 and expressly refused to authorize a number of repairs that Kimball stated were necessary to make the elevator operate reliably and safely. The strict limitations placed on Kimball's repairs and the failure to authorize additional needed repairs were not communicated to Barton. In fact, Tsern instructed Kimball not to mention those limitations to Barton.

The elevator operated from January 9, 1992, until January 24, 1992, when a city inspector ordered it shut down. After Kimball made an additional repair required by the city inspector on February 13, the elevator again operated until March 14. On April 10, a state elevator inspector found that the elevator was not in compliance with state law, directed Tsern to correct nine violations, and ordered the elevator shut down until it could pass a state safety inspection. Apparently believing that Barton intended to exercise its option to purchase the building, Tsern refused to spend the $5,552 to make those repairs. During the term of the lease, Barton continually demanded that the elevator be properly repaired. It never was and did not operate at all after March 14, 1992.

On December 10, 1991, Barton and Tsern each sent the other a communication concerning the possibility of a rent abatement. At that point Barton had not yet obtained occupancy of the second floor because of a holdover tenant, the leaky roof still had not been repaired, and the inoperable elevator. Barton suggested a rent abatement because of the difficulties. Independent of that request, Tsern on his own suggested a 50 percent rent abatement, but Barton never accepted his proposal.

Barton tendered less than the full rent for the months of January and February, and Tsern cashed the checks but maintained that he was entitled to the full rent of $3,000 for each month. Because the elevator operated during the latter part of January and the early part of February, Barton tendered full rent for February on February 1, minus a minor offset for something unrelated to the elevator. On April 15, 1992, Barton filed a complaint for a declaratory judgment to establish Tsern's legal duty to repair the elevator. Tsern counterclaimed with a three-day notice to pay the rent in full or quit the premises.

The counterclaim was dismissed and Barton later gave notice that he was exercising his option to purchase, and to cure any possible rental defaults, he deposited $19,000 with the court on October 29, 1992. On November 30, 1992, the court ruled that Barton could exercise the option to purchase prior to the conclusion of the bench trial on his declaratory judgment claim.

In its final judgment, the trial court found that the elevator had not been repaired to "good working order" as required by the lease, and entered judgment against Tsern for the cost of repairing the elevator to that standard. The court also ruled that although Barton and Tsern had never agreed on the amount of a rent abatement, Barton was entitled to have the rent abated to $2,000 a month and, in addition, that Barton's damages plus accrued interest should be deducted from the purchase price of the building. Finally, the court entered judgment against Tsern for attorney fees in the amount of $100,000. Tsern appealed.

JUDICIAL OPINION

Stewart, Associate Chief Justice. In *Union City Union Suit Co. v. Miller*, 162 A.D.2d 101, 556 N.Y.S.2d 864 (1990), a case remarkably similar to the instant case, a commercial lessor failed to repair, and eventually removed, a freight elevator from a leased building in violation of the lease. The court held that the lessor had constructively evicted the lessee from one floor of the building and that the lessee had no obligation to pay rent for the second floor.

In other cases, however, the doctrine of constructive eviction was inadequate to achieve a fair result. For example, if a lessor breached a covenant to repair and the lessee made the necessary repairs, the lessee could not offset the cost of those repairs against the rent owed. Even if the cost of repairs exceeded the rent, the lessee was subject to eviction for failure to pay rent.

Although the fiction of constructive eviction served the useful purpose of ameliorating the harshness of the rule of independent covenants while continuing to use recognized common law vocabulary and concepts, even the doctrine of constructive eviction had limited capacity to achieve fairness. With the evolution from an agrarian to an urbanized, industrialized society, improvements on the land became relatively more important. Improvements such as houses, apartments, office and commercial buildings, and plants and factories came to have greater value to the lessee than did the land itself. These developments have required courts to reassess the doctrines that underlie and define the legal rights and liabilities of parties to a lease.

In 1985, this Court recognized that certain property law rules that historically governed the leasing of land had become obsolete.

...[t]he reality of modern residential leases is that lessees bargain for the use of the structures, facilities, and services attached to the land rather than the land itself, so that the appurtenances to the land are the more important feature of the lease. We held that a contract concept of implied warranty should be extended to residential leases in the form of an implied warranty of habitability and that the covenant to pay rent was dependent on the lessor's compliance with the implied warranty of habitability.

We find that the principles...in the context of residential leases are equally applicable to the commercial context. In addition, several other states have held that under certain circumstances, commercial lessees may withhold rent. One group of states, which includes Texas and New Jersey, holds that covenants in commercial leases are mutually dependent. Texas offers the most expansive protection for commercial leases; it extends to commercial lessees all protections available to residential lessees, including an implied warranty of suitability that the leased premises are suitable "for their intended commercial purpose." *Davidow v. Inwood North Professional Group—Phase I*, 747 S.W.2d 373, 377 (Tex. 1988). The court in *Davidow* reasoned that a commercial lessee should have the same protections as those accorded a residential lessee and that contract principles rather than medieval property principles should apply. Although it stopped short of providing the same broad protections as Texas, the New Jersey Supreme Court held that "fair treatment for tenants with respect to latent defects remediable by the landlord...require[s] imposition on [the landlord] of an implied warranty against such defects." *Reste Realty Corp. v. Cooper*, 53 N.J. 444, 251 A.2d 268, 273 (1969). A New Jersey appellate court thereafter noted that the state supreme court's decision heralded "the demise of the doctrine of independent covenants." *Ringwood Assocs. v. Jack's of Route 23, Inc.*, 166 N.J.Super. 36, 398 A.2d 1315, 1319 (App. Div.1979)

A second group of states does not recognize implied warranties in commercial leases but nevertheless holds that covenants in commercial leases may be mutually dependent. Massachusetts and Indiana hold that the covenant to pay rent and the covenant to repair may be mutually dependent. *Erhard v. F.W. Woolworth Co.*, 374 Mass. 352, 372 N.E.2d 1277 (1978). [FN3] See *Welborn v. Society for Propagation of Faith*, 411 N.E.2d 1267, 1269 n. 4 (Ind. Ct. App. 1980)

Both groups of cases recognize that the covenant to pay rent under a commercial lease is dependent on the lessor's compliance with those covenants necessary to provide the lessee with the benefits that were the essence of the bargain as reflected in the lease. This approach relieves a lessee of the obligation to abandon the premises, as is necessary under the fiction of a constructive eviction. By making the lessee's covenant to pay rent dependent on the lessor's performance of essential covenants, the legal analysis can focus, as it should, on the essential elements and purposes of the bargain between the lessor and the lessee. By employing contract principles, a court's analysis of a dispute between a lessor and a lessee should provide a more fair, realistic, and forthright analysis of whether a lessee may abate rent. The result reached on such an analysis should better comport with modern leasing practices and expectations than the result under an analysis based on the principle of independent covenants as modified by the doctrine of constructive eviction.

Not all breaches of covenants by a lessor, however, justify a lessee in withholding rent. Only a significant breach of a covenant material to the purpose for which the lease was consummated justifies a lessee in abating rent. Temporary or minor breaches of routine covenants by a lessor do not. Thus, in assessing whether a lessor's breach is sufficient to justify the withholding of rent, a lessee first and a court later, if necessary, must gauge the materiality of the breach in light of the lessee's purpose in leasing the premises. Relevant to that determination may be whether the breach has a significant effect on the rental value of the premises.

In sum, we hold that the lessee's covenant to pay rent is dependent on the lessor's performance of covenants that were a significant inducement to the consummation of the lease or to the purpose for which the lessee entered into the lease.

Holding Barton liable for the full amount of rent when a significant part of the leased premises was practicably unusable for the purpose for which the premises were leased would be tantamount to requiring that Barton pay for something he could not use in the manner intended when the lease was executed, given the nature of his business and the nature of the building. Tsern knew that an operable elevator was essential to Barton's use of the second floor and that the lack of an operable elevator was not simply a matter of inconvenience. Tsern's promise to repair the elevator was a significant inducement to Barton to enter into the lease. Indeed, on several occasions before the lease was signed, Barton explicitly told Tsern that the business required an operable elevator. The absence of an operable and safe elevator had more than a peripheral effect on Barton's use of the premises; it impaired Barton's ability to conduct its business on the premises. It follows that Tsern was entitled to receive rent equal to the value of the premises without an operable freight elevator.

Affirmed.

Zimmerman, Chief Justice, concurring and dissenting. I join Justice Howe in concurring and dissenting as to part IV of the lead opinion. I find the logic of the lead opinion reasonable as to a basis for finding that Kimball's obligations under the modified contract were considerably less than Tsern's obligations to repair the elevator pursuant to its contract with Barton. However, I agree with Justice Howe that for such a rationale to provide a basis for affirmance, certain findings needed to be made by the trial court which were not made and upon which the evidence before us is conflicting.

Specifically, as Justice Howe separately notes, the record is devoid of the factual finding that Kimball and Tsern modified their elevator repair contract. The lead opinion ignores this allocation of responsibility between trial and appellate courts by supplying its own factual finding that a contract modification occurred. Even if we were to view the issue of whether a contract was modified as a question of law, we would assign the responsibility for initially making that highly fact-dependent determination to the trial court and give it a great deal of discretion in doing so. In short, appellate courts should not usurp the freedom given to trial judges "to make decisions which appellate judges might not make themselves ab initio but will not reverse." I understand that this case has dragged on and that the record is voluminous, as Justice Stewart notes, but none of that justifies our usurping the trial court's legitimate role in an effort to produce, today, the result we think appropriate, even if we think the trial court might reach the same result after remand.

For the foregoing reasons, I join Justice Howe in voting for a remand of this case to permit the trial court to make new findings regarding the parties' intent as to the meaning of the words "good working order."

Howe, Justice, concurring and dissenting. I dissent as to part IV, REPAIR OF THE ELEVATOR. The trial court held that Kimball fulfilled its contract to repair the elevator to a "safe operating condition" but that Tsern did not meet his lease requirement that he repair the elevator to "good working order." I cannot agree with the explanation offered by the trial court or with the lead opinion of this court as to why these holdings are not inconsistent.

The parties admit that the phrases "safe operating condition" and "good working order" are not recognized terms of art; they have no readily understood meaning outside of the contracts in which the parties inserted them. Because the meaning of these terms is uncertain, the trial court properly considered extrinsic evidence to determine what the parties intended them to mean. I would remand for a retrial on this issue.

CASE QUESTIONS

1. Describe the factual situation that led to the landlord–tenant dispute.

2. What is the significance of mutually dependent covenants in a lease?

3. Is the decision of this court in this case a majority or minority view in the United States with regard to commercial leases?

4. What do you conclude commercial tenants have the right to do in Utah when there are problems with their leased premises?

CONSIDER 10.2

Dr. Joseph Davidow entered into a five-year lease agreement with Inwood for medical office space. The lease required Dr. Davidow to pay Inwood $793.26 per month as rent. The lease also required Inwood to provide air-conditioning, electricity, hot water, janitor and maintenance services, light fixtures, and security services. Shortly after moving into the office space, Dr. Davidow began experiencing problems with the building. The air-conditioning did not work properly, often causing temperatures inside the office to rise above 85 degrees. The roof leaked whenever it rained, resulting in stained tiles and rotting, mildewed carpet. Patients were directed away from certain areas during rain so that they would not be dripped upon in the waiting room. Pests and rodents often infested the office. The hallways remained dark because hallway lights were unreplaced for months. Cleaning and maintenance were not provided. The parking lot was constantly filled with trash. Hot water was not provided, and on one occasion Dr. Davidow went without electricity for several days because Inwood failed to pay the electric bill. Several burglaries and various acts of vandalism occurred. Dr. Davidow finally moved out of the premises and discontinued rent payments approximately 14 months before the lease expired. Inwood sued Dr. Davidow for breach of contract. Could Inwood recover? Does Davidow have any defenses? *Davidow v. Inwood North Professional Group—Phase I*, 747 S.W.2d 373 (Tex. 1988)

One additional complication arises when there are repairs to commercial property: business interruption. During renovation, the tenant may experience an interruption of customer traffic or may lose ease of accessibility because of construction blockage or hazards. The following case deals with this issue of a tenant frustrated by construction interruption of business and the limited common law protection available to these commercial tenants.

BIJAN DESIGNER FOR MEN, INC. V. ST. REGIS SHERATON CORPORATION

536 N.Y.S.2d 951 (1989) aff'd, 543 N.Y.S.2d 296 (1989)

FACTS

The St. Regis Hotel (defendant), located at Fifth Avenue and 55th Street in Manhattan, was originally built in 1904. In November 1988, the hotel was designated by the Landmarks Preservation Committee as an official New York City landmark. The committee required that the hotel's heating, ventilating, air-conditioning, electrical, plumbing, and fire safety systems be installed or replaced.

Bijan Designer for Men (plaintiff) leases a two-story retail space situated in the St. Regis. Bijan has its own entrance from Fifth Avenue as well as entrances directly from the hotel's lobby and mezzanine. Bijan sells luxury-quality men's apparel and accessories, by appointment only, to a group it describes as "a distinguished and select domestic and international clientele of extremely well-to-do and renowned patrons." Bijan's lease commenced in 1981 for a period of 16 years. Bijan selected the site in the St. Regis because of the hotel's reputation, clientele, layout, security, and ambiance. Both parties expected Bijan to draw clientele from among the hotel's guests.

On June 30, 1988, the St. Regis was temporarily closed to commence the necessary reconstruction and renovation. The work was planned to take 14 to 18 months. The main doors to the hotel lobby were boarded up and access to the hotel lobby involved entering through a defunct restaurant and being cleared by a security guard.

Upon notification of the closure, Bijan informed the St. Regis that its rent would be paid into an escrow account. The St. Regis demanded payment, and Bijan filed suit to prevent the acceleration of rent.

JUDICIAL OPINION

Saxe, Justice. It is the plaintiff's position that by closing the St. Regis, the landlord rendered useless Bijan's contractually provided-for access to the hotel, resulting in an actual partial eviction of Bijan. An actual eviction, whether partial or complete, suspends in its entirety the tenant's obligation to pay rent.

The Defendant relies on paragraph 14.A of the lease, which permits the lessor to, *inter alia*, "make such decorations, repairs, alterations, improvements or additions as lessor may deem necessary or desirable either to the Hotel or the demised premises" and further on provides that "the rent shall in no way abate while the decorations, repairs, alterations, improvements or additions are being made and Lessor shall not be liable to Lessee by reason of loss or interruption of the business of Lessee because of the prosecution of any such work or otherwise."

For its part, Bijan points out that the very first paragraph of the lease promises the tenant that "[t]he first floor of the premises shall have access to the Hotel's main lobby" and also that "[t]he second floor of the premises shall have access to the Hotel's mezzanine." Its position is that this right of access may not be abrogated by the landlord's right to repair. In addition, the tenant contends that the implied covenant of good faith and fair dealing prohibits the actions taken by the landlord.

These motions confront the court with competing policies. Restoration and renovation of an old landmark building should be welcomed and encouraged, and in fact, here, the landlord attempted to contractually provide for that right. On the other hand, the rights accorded a tenant, such as the negotiated-for right of direct access to the hotel lobby, must be carefully protected from undue interference, particularly where, as here, that right provides a substantial economic benefit to the tenant.

Here, the tenant certainly consented to renovations; it is less clear, however, whether that consent was so broad as to permit its right of access to be subsumed or negated by those alterations or improvements.

More recently, in *Broadway Copy Service, Inc. v. Broad-Wall Co.*, 77 A.D.2d 827, 431 N.Y.S.2d 13, where a landlord painted over the clear glass doors leading from the rear of a tenant's store to the building's lobby, it was held as a matter of law that this act did not constitute an actual partial eviction which would excuse the tenant from paying rent. Noting, however, that painting over the glass door prevented prospective customers from knowing the nature of the tenant's business and potentially deprived the tenant of possible sales, the court indicated that the tenant might have a cause of action for compensatory damages.

It is apparent that a landlord's breach of an express or implied lease term does not necessarily result in an actual eviction, but merely gives rise to a cause of action for damages.

The tenant points to several cases in which a landlord's acts constituted an actual partial eviction. For instance, where a landlord sealed and blocked off a freight elevator which opened directly into tenant's store, it was found that this action constituted an actual partial eviction.

When the facts alleged by the plaintiff are viewed in light of the foregoing cases, it is apparent that the plaintiff's theory of actual eviction cannot be supported. The plaintiff agreed to repairs, alterations or improvements either in the store or in the hotel, and that the landlord would not be liable for loss or interruption of Bijan's business due to such work. If extensive alterations made upon consent *within* the leased premises cannot amount to an eviction, I fail to see how extensive renovations made upon consent *outside* the leased premises can be said to constitute an eviction. Moreover, where the exculpatory clause is so broad, for the court to construe the clause to permit extensive work except where the hotel must be closed to customers would constitute a re-writing of the contract by the court. Furthermore, although sealing off contracted-for access has been held to constitute actual eviction, whereas the defendants point out the plaintiff continues to have access to the lobby and mezzanine, albeit a lobby and mezzanine which are part of a hotel undergoing renovations.

It is apparent that the parties, particularly the tenant, did not contemplate that any building renovation might necessitate a lengthy closing of the hotel. I therefore take the opportunity to note that especially where—as here—the value of the leasehold takes into account the presence of the landlord's clientele, tenants are well advised to provide for the eventuality of temporary closing for renovation, or at least to specify some limits to the exculpatory clause concerning repairs.

In the absence of such a provision, Bijan is left with a situation which may clearly have a negative impact on the value of the leased premises, but which just as clearly does not constitute an actual partial eviction. This is not to say that a tenant in the plaintiff's position is necessarily without recourse. Notwithstanding the exculpatory clause permitting renovations, a right to compensatory damages may exist if the landlord exceeded the rights granted by the lease, and if its actions constitute a breach of another term of the lease, such as a right of access or an implied covenant of good faith or quiet enjoyment.

There was no partial eviction.

CASE QUESTIONS

1. Describe the layout of Bijan's leased premises.

2. Why was the hotel closed?

3. How long was the closure expected to last?

4. What arguments does Bijan make to justify its nonpayment of rent to St. Regis?

5. Will Bijan be given any relief?

6. What protections should have been drafted into the lease?

Condition of the Premises–The Sick Building Syndrome

When Benjamin Franklin was asked to testify about new legal requirements for building ventilation in the 1700s, he offered the following expertise: "I considered [fresh air] an enemy, and closed with extreme care every crevice in the rooms I inhabited. Experience has convinced me of my error. I now look upon fresh air as a friend: I even sleep with an open window. I am persuaded that no common air from without is so unwholesome as the air within a close[d] room that has been often breathed and not changed."[5] Since that statement, we have evolved from a fear that ventilation in buildings brings in disease to one that perhaps the lack of ventilation creates health problems. To combat the **sick building syndrome** (**SBS**), there are increasing health and safety regulations focusing on air in buildings as well as a rising trend in litigation related to health hazards being tied to building conditions.

The World Health Organization lists the following as eight common symptoms of SBS: (1) irritation of the eyes, nose, and throat, (2) dry mucous membranes and skin, (3) erythema (dermatitis erythematosa, redness of the skin, inflammation), (4) mental fatigue and headache, (5) respiratory infections and cough, (6) hoarseness of voice and wheezing, (7) hypersensitivity reactions, and (8) nausea and dizziness.

One possible cause of the change in interior conditions has been the decades-long drive to keep energy costs down, which results in the "sealing" of windows and doors to keep cold air out in the winter and hot air out in the summer. There are some dramatic examples of health impacts on employees. For example, Florida's $37 million Polk County Courthouse, a public building constructed in 1987, was evacuated in July 1992 after more than 460 of its 580 employees developed illnesses ranging from coughs to irreversible lung disease that were linked to the building itself. Renovations required to eliminate this telling example of SBS involved gutting the building and replacing air-handling units and vinyl wallpaper.[6]

The EPA and OSHA are working with professional associations to develop construction guidelines and suggestions for existing building modifications in order to minimize the health hazards that seem to occur in these highly contained commercial building settings. Tenants and landlords should provide clauses in their leases that address SBS issues, repairs, costs, and evacuation.

Rent and Rent Terminology

One unique aspect of the commercial lease is its terminology. Rental payments' terms and fees are very different from the flat monthly rates of residential leases. Although some older commercial leases do have flat per-month rates, called **gross rent**, this type of arrangement has been phased out over the past 30 years. Even if it is a part of the lease rent, the tenant will have some form of **escalation clause** that is a formula for extra rent beyond the base rent.

The most common form of commercial lease that has replaced the gross rent lease is the **triple net** or **net-net-net**. Under this arrangement, the tenant pays directly or reimburses the landlord for taxes, insurance, and maintenance expenses for the property and then pays the landlord a flat rate or **fixed rent** above and beyond the "net" amount paid for taxes, insurance, and maintenance.

5. Lewis W. Leeds, *Lectures on Ventilation at Franklin Institute, 1866–67 8* (New York: John Wiley and Sons, 1868) (quoting a letter by Benjamin Franklin to Dr. Ingenhaus, Physician to the Emperor at Vienna).
6. For full details and discussion on SBS, see Gene J. Heady, "Stuck Inside These Four Walls: Recognition of Sick Building Syndrome Has Laid the Foundation to Raise Toxic Tort Litigation to New Heights," 26 *Tex. Tech L. Rev.* 1041 (1995).

For purposes of the triple net lease, *taxes* includes real property taxes and assessments including those on fixtures regardless of whether the landlord or tenant owns them. *Insurance* includes fire, casualty, and liability insurance to cover the tenant's operations. *Maintenance* includes not only maintenance and repair but also operational expenses such as utilities and other services.

Even the fixed rent lease may be subject to adjustment. Many retail centers carry a **Consumer Price Index (CPI) adjustment clause**. This clause ties the flat rate to the CPI and allows the landlord to increase the fixed rent by the amount of increase in the CPI for the year. The lease may provide for a cap or a maximum increase that stipulates the rent will increase by the CPI increase or a maximum of 6 percent.

Some leases contain **specific happenings increase provisions**. For example, a lease may contain a provision that allows a rent increase in the event the developer or landlord is required to pay increased taxes.

As the popularity and hence size of shopping centers have grown, new rent payment ideas have been created to cover the costs of maintaining these large centers. For example, many tenants are responsible for their prorated share of **common area maintenance (CAM)** (sometimes called **operating expenses**).

Operating expenses can be a tricky part of lease negotiations for a tenant. Landlords have included everything from marketing expenses to elevator repairs in the operating expenses for their facilities. Some tenants negotiate out of their CAMs operating expenses the landlord's costs incurred because of the risk of operating a commercial facility. Such expenses would include the marketing expenses, because they increase when consumer spending is down. Other tenants rely on the landlord for promotion of a center or mall that they could not provide for themselves to generate business. Some expenses, such as those related to the elevators, may be capital improvements and should be amortized, as opposed to expensed all at once.

At a minimum, tenants should negotiate full access to the landlord's operating expense records so that they can see what is being included. These expenses can increase the rent substantially. For example, it would not be unusual for a base rent in a commercial building to be $32 per square foot; with expenses, the payment increases to $46 per square foot. Some leases place caps on expenses, with base year restrictions on expenses being no greater than 5 percent above those of comparable properties.

Once the operating expenses are clearly defined, the tenant should negotiate carefully for the percentage of operating expenses he or she will pay. The allocation of operating expenses, or CAM, can be complex, with the following representing one formula:

$$\frac{\text{Rental area of the tenant's premises}}{\text{Total of all rentable areas on the property (gross leasable area)}} \times \text{Total common area maintenance costs or CAM} = \text{Tenant's monthly fees}$$

The language used in the formula is critical. If, for example, the formula used "rented areas" as opposed to "rentable areas," then the effect would be to transfer to the occupying tenants the costs of CAM instead of having the landlord carry those costs until the premises are leased. The definition of even "rentable areas" may need clarification: whether mezzanines, basements, and other areas are included and the effect of having movable (cart) tenants selling smaller items in a mall.

Shopping center and mall leases usually carry a **percentage rent** that entitles the landlord to a given percentage of the tenant's gross receipts. When drafting a gross-percentage provision, the parties should remember the following details to facilitate collection of the intended fees:

1. A definition of gross sales, including what is and is not included in the computation of gross sales.
2. Record-keeping obligations of the tenant, along with the landlord's right of examination and right to an independent audit of the records.
3. Details of how often the percentage is to be paid, when it is to be paid, and whether the tenant is required to submit periodic reports.
4. A covenant of secrecy for the right of access. The landlord should be subject to suit and damages if information from the sales records is disclosed.

The following case illustrates one issue in these leases: the complexity of determining what constitutes "gross sales."

CIRCLE K CORPORATION V. COLLINS

98 F.3d 484 (9th Cir. 1996); aff'd 127 F.3d 904, cert. den. 522 U.S. 1148 (1998)

FACTS

Circle K Corporation leased property from landowner Frank Collins and agreed to pay rent calculated at 2 percent of "gross sales" on the premises, with some exceptions specified. The lease was a 20-year lease and also provided for a minimum base rent. The lease went into effect in 1975. The lease clause on rent provided as follows:

Lessee shall pay annually as hereinafter provided as additional rent, the amount, if any, by which two percent (2%) of Lessee's "gross sales" (as hereinafter defined) exceeds the guaranteed minimal annual rent plus the sum of the real estate taxes and insurance premiums on the leased premises for such year. Said additional rent is hereinafter referred to as "percentage rent."

The lease defined "gross sales" as follows:

Gross receipts of every kind and nature originating from sales and services on the demised premises, whether on credit or for cash, in every department operating on the leased premises, whether operated by Lessee, or by a Sublessee, or concessionaire excepting therefrom any rebates and/or refunds to customers, refundable deposits on beverage bottles, telephone tolls, gasoline sales, money order transactions, the transfer or exchange of merchandise between the stores of Lessee if any, . . . and the amount of any sales, privilege license, excise or other taxes on transactions collected and/or paid either directly or indirectly by Lessee to any government or governmental agency.

In July 1981, Arizona instituted a state lottery. In August 1981, Circle K sent a letter to Collins, advising him that Circle K wished to sell lottery tickets at the store located on Collins's property. At the bottom of the letter was the following statement and a place for Collins to sign:

I,____, the Lessor (or agent for same) do hereby accept and agree to allow participation in the Arizona Lottery by the Circle K Corporation upon and from the property/ies leased from me. I further agree to exempt and exclude any commissions and computation of sales of Arizona Lottery tickets from the calculation of any percentage rentals.

Collins did not sign the letter or return it to Circle K. Circle K began selling lottery tickets and did not pay Collins a percentage rate based on lottery ticket sales. Circle K filed for Chapter 11 bankruptcy in 1990. The bankruptcy court originally held that lottery proceeds were property of the state and should not be included in gross sales, but did include Circle K's commissions from the state for being a lottery agent. The Bankruptcy Appellate panel reversed and included gross sales revenue, and Circle K appealed.

JUDICIAL OPINION

Canby, Circuit Judge. This case requires us to interpret a contract. Although contract interpretation involves mixed questions of law and fact, the application of contractual principles is a matter of law.

It is a close question whether the Collins lease provides for percentage rent of two percent of Circle K's commissions from lottery sales, or two percent of total ticket sales price. We conclude, however, that the bankruptcy court's view is the correct one: percentage rent should be calculated only on the commissions. The parties have made comparisons to other types of receipts covered or not covered by the terms of the lease, but in our view state-sponsored lottery ticket sales fall into a class by themselves. They are quite unlike the general run of commercial operations mentioned in the lease. The State of Arizona has made Circle K one of its sales agents. State regulations require Circle K to pay over to the state its total proceeds from sales, less commissions and prizes awarded. The commission rate was originally five percent of ticket sales, and is now six percent.

In the hands of the State, lottery proceeds are used for various public purposes in the manner of tax revenues. In its ticket sales, Circle K acts more nearly as a tax collector for the State than as a retailer. It sells chances and takes custody of receipts, in which it has no interest beyond its commission, and remits them to the State. It is paid for its services by commission, and that commission is properly considered a "gross receipt" from "services" performed on the premises. We do not, however, interpret the lease as reaching the total funds received for the State in its calculation of percentage rent.

The only two cases squarely in point agree with this interpretation of similar leases. In *Cloverland Farms Dairy, Inc. v. Fry*, 587 A.2d 527 (1991), the Maryland Court of Appeals dealt with a lease, entered before Maryland authorized its lottery, that contained a clause as broad as the one before us. The lease provided for a percentage rent on "gross sales made in the store." It also provided that in computing "gross sales," the lessee was to take the total amount of sales of every kind made in the store and deduct therefrom the following, to the extent that same are included in such total amount: (1) refunds made to customers, (2) sales, excise and gross receipts taxes, and (3) proceeds from sale of money orders (fee received for issuance of money orders shall not be deducted).

Despite this broad language, the Court held that gross lottery sales did not fall within the percentage rent clause. The Court recognized that reasonable persons "would have thought that the additional rental percentage clause encompassed the sale of any and all items, not expressly excluded, which *Cloverland* would sell in its store in the course of its business activities." Lottery sales did not fall in that category.

The Maryland Court in *Cloverland* relied in part on the only other case cited to us that dealt with the same issue, *Anest v. Bellino*, 151 Ill. App.3d 818, 104 Ill. Dec. 861, 503 N.E.2d 576 (1987). *Anest* held that gross lottery sales did not fall within a percentage rental clause applying to "all gross sales." The Court stated:

Although the restaurant actually handled the money, that portion of the money belonging to the lottery system was not intended by the parties to be included in gross sales. Only the commissions and bonuses belong to the restaurant, and only those amounts increase the restaurant's sales.

Arizona has no decisions in point, but we have no reason to believe that its courts would diverge from these two decisions that are the only ones to have dealt with the lottery issue in connection with percentage rent clauses. The same factors that led Maryland's and Illinois' courts to exclude total lottery sales exist in this case. The money collected by Circle K, except for commissions, belongs to the State. Lottery sales were not part of the Circle K's regular business in the reasonable contemplation of the parties at the time the lease was entered into; they are in a class by themselves. If the parties had foreseen the future legalization of lottery sales, and had addressed the question specifically in the lease, the nature of other exceptions suggests that total proceeds other than commissions would have been excluded from "gross sales." The arguable-comparable activity of money order transactions was so excluded, as were receipts from refundable deposits on beverage bottles, and sales taxes that Circle K collected but transferred to the State. Thus the same kinds of considerations that led to the decisions in *Cloverland* and *Anest* are present here.

We conclude that the term "gross sales" in the percentage rent term of the lease agreement did not include the total sales price of state lottery tickets. "Gross sales" included only the commissions that Circle K received in exchange for its services in selling the tickets. The decision is therefore reversed.

Reversed.

CASE QUESTIONS

1. When was the lease negotiated? How were "gross sales" defined?

2. What have other states done with the issue of lottery sales with respect to rental percentage clauses?

3. Why is the issue of the sale of money orders similar?

4. Is it significant that Collins did not sign the letter on the lottery sales?

CONSIDER 10.3

On June 7, 1968, Sears entered into a "Shopping Center Lease" (lease) with Honey Creek Square, Inc. (Honey Creek), to lease space in its mall, Honey Creek Square Shopping Center. The lease became effective on November 1 of that year for a term of 30 years plus four 5-year options.

The lease is a standard Sears form that was modified pursuant to negotiations between Honey Creek and Sears. Rent due from Sears under the lease is based solely on a percentage basis of Sears' net sales made on the Honey Creek Store, with no guaranteed minimum. The monthly amount is calculated according to paragraph 8 of the lease, which reads in pertinent part:

a. Tenant, in consideration of said demise, does covenant and agree with Landlord to pay as rental for all of said demised premises (including the above mentioned retail store and attached Tire Service Station) a sum equal to three per cent (3%) of so much of "Net Sales" (as herein defined), made by Tenant upon the demised premises during any Lease Year (as herein defined) during the first three (3) years of the term hereinabove provided, as are not in excess of Eight Million Dollars ($8,000,000), and a sum equal to two and one-half per cent (21/2%) of so much of such Net Sales made by Tenant upon the demised premises during any Lease Year commencing with the fourth year of said term and continuing thereafter to the end of said term, as are not in excess of Eight Million Dollars ($8,000,000), and a further sum, applicable during the entire lease term, equal to one and one-half per cent (11/2%) of such Net Sales as are in excess of Eight Million Dollars ($8,000,000), said rentals to be paid in monthly installments within fifteen (15) days after the end of each calendar month during the term hereof.

b. The words "Net Sales" as used herein mean gross sales made upon the demised premises by Tenant and its departmental subleases, concessionaires and licensees occupying space upon said demised premises, but deducting or excluding, as the case may be, the following: (i) Sales of departments or divisions not located upon said demised premises; (ii) The amount of all sales, use, excise retailers' occupation or other similar taxes imposed in a specific amount, or percentage upon, or determined by, the amount of retail sales made upon said demised premises; (iii) Returns and allowances, as such terms are known and used by Tenant in the preparation of Tenant's profit and loss statements; (iv) Delivery, rental, installation and service charges; (v) Amounts in excess of Tenant's (or of its sublessees', concessionaires' and licensees'), cash sales price charged on sales made on credit or under a time payment plan; (vi) Sales of merchandise ordered through the use of Tenant's catalog order channels, regardless of the place of order, payment, or delivery; (vii) Policies of insurance sold on said demised premises and the premiums collected on policies of insurance; (viii) Sales made through the Commercial and Industrial Sales Department of Tenant.

Sears paid rent to Honey Creek Square, Inc., without incident until December 1981, when Honey Creek requested and carried out an audit in accordance with the terms of the lease. The auditor's report stated that in December 1981, Sears did not include in net sales the following:

Alteration sales	$____
Gift-wrapping sales	$1,262
Bike set-up sales	$112
Auto labor sales	$16,269
Service contract (maintenance agreement) sales	$53,513
Service center sales	$13,217

CONSIDER 10.3
(continued)

Sears admits that these amounts were not included in its report of net sales for December 1981. Sears stated that it had never included income from these categories in its net sales figure, except auto labor, which had been included from November 1977 through September 1981, because of a misunderstanding on the part of its in-store controller. Can Honey Creek recover rent based on the above exclusions from net sales? *Washington National Corporation v. Sears, Roebuck & Co.*, 474 N.E.2d 116 (Ind. 1985)

CONSIDER 10.4

On January 17, 1975, A & P entered into a 20-year commercial lease with Jerome Schostak, d/b/a Midland Venture, for property A & P intended to use for operation of a grocery store. The lease provided for a fixed rent of $8,630 per month plus an additional 1 percent of all sales in excess of $10,356,000.00. A & P did not have sufficient sales to owe the 1 percent until 1979. In July 1990, A & P ceased its operations on the property but continued to pay its fixed rent. In November 1990, A & P subleased the store to Dunham's Athleisure Corporation. Dunham's lease provided that it would pay 2 percent of its gross sales in excess of $3,000,000. Dunham also has never had sales sufficient to kick in the percentage portion of rent.

A & P has simply continued to pay the fixed monthly rent. Midland maintains that A & P owes more because the contract was negotiated with the underlying assumption that A & P would stay in business. Should A & P be required to pay more rent? *Plaza Forty-Eight, Inc. v. Great Atlantic & Pacific Tea Company, Inc.*, 817 F.Supp. 774 (E.D. Wis. 1993)

Security deposits are typical in commercial leases and can be substantial, so that the landlord is assured of payment. Because there is no uniform act on commercial leases, the parties should specify the purpose of the security deposit, whether it will be returned, on what grounds it can be retained, and whether there will be any time limits for returning the deposit upon termination of the lease.

Fixtures and Alterations

In most cases, commercial premises consist of walls, a roof, and a door. Generally, very little has been done to improve, finish, or decorate the interior of each retail space. There are substantial cost issues for necessary improvements, alterations, and construction to render the premises usable for a retail operation. Generally, the tenant is responsible for the costs of making the interior ready for operation because the landlord does not know the needs of the tenant's business or the tenant's business operations. This requirement of completion, plus any restrictions the tenant may have in altering the premises (because of building codes or the landlord's hesitancy or preference), should be covered in the lease. If the landlord wants restrictions on improvements, those limits should be specified.

What happens to all the improvements the tenant has made once the lease is terminated? In other words, are the improvements treated as trade fixtures or do they become permanent fixtures and property of the landlord? Although legal guidelines determine what a trade fixture is and what remains as the landlord's property (see Chapter 5), intent controls and the parties should address the issue of fixtures.

One common method for addressing tenant alterations in leases is to include a provision in the lease that requires the tenant to obtain prior written approval of the landlord. Under this arrangement, the tenant supplies the landlord with a written proposal that includes specifications for what constitutes a fixture in the proposed alteration and what will remain the property of the tenant as a trade fixture.

Operations

Commercial leases should cover hours of allowable operation as well as the days of closure. For example, many office buildings will be open for operation from 6:00 A.M. until 9:00 P.M. on weekdays, with limited access on Saturdays and Sundays. Many leases list specific holidays in which there will be no access or available amenities. In Arizona, critical portions of office building leases include those days during which the air-conditioning for the facility will not be running. In the summer months, the buildings would not be usable on those days.

Shopping center leases contain additional provisions, such as mandatory hours of operation. It does small tenants little good to be open for business if the large tenants in the center have different hours of operation and are not open to attract the foot traffic.

Common Areas

Managing Access

Commercial leases should contain specific provisions on the responsibilities and liabilities for maintenance and safety of the common areas. Businesses and offices will have operational difficulties themselves if the common areas are unsafe, unclean, or simply inaccessible. The landlord should assume responsibility for maintenance and security of these areas. Further, the lease should provide for tenant rights in the event the landlord fails with respect to this responsibility. A critical area in shopping center leases is the availability of parking for those using the tenants' offices and businesses. When there is shared parking among commercial tenants, lease provisions should address overflow issues and accommodations. For example, some tenants have specifically designated spaces in the center parking lot so that customers can gain access.

Managing Free Speech

One of the interesting aspects of shopping center operation is the presence of demonstrators for political causes. Their presence provides an interesting interaction between their First Amendment rights and the rights of the shopping center owners. Currently there is much litigation and debate over this issue, but the U.S. Supreme Court gave demonstrators certain rights in *Pruneyard Shopping Center v. Robins*, 474 U.S. 74 (1980), and various state and local regulation of such demonstrators' rights remains a topic of constitutional litigation. In the U.S. Supreme Court decision in *Hurley v. Irish-American Gay Group of Boston*, 515 U.S. 557 (1995), the Court held that interference with private speech rights by requiring public accommodation of all views presents First Amendment violations. States must be cautious in mandating speech rights of certain groups on commercial properties.

Twelve of the 17 states that have reviewed the issue of demonstrators' access to shopping centers have permitted the shopping center owners to restrict that access. California, Colorado, New Jersey, Massachusetts—the Massachusetts law was reviewed in the *Hurley* case—and Washington permit free speech on commercial properties but do vary in the type of speech allowed. For example, some states permit only the solicitation of signatures for ballot propositions and candidates under the theory that the modern commercial center is the equivalent of the town square where free speech was practiced and protected.[7]

7. For a look at some of the shopping center and free speech cases, see *New Jersey Coalition v. J.M.B. Realty Corp.*, 650 A.2d 757 (N.J. 1994); *Bock v. Westminster Mall Co.*, 819 P.2d 55 (Colo. 1991); *Betchelder v. Allied Stores Int'l, Inc.*, 445 N.E.2d 590 (Mass. 1983) and *Alderwood Associates v. Washington Environmental Council*, 635 P.2d 108 (Wash. 1981). Washington has a later limiting case: *Southcenter Joint Venture v. National Democratic Party Committee*, 780 P.2d 1282 (Wash. 1989).

Managing Safety

The liability of commercial landlords and property owners for injuries to tenants and tenants' employees by third parties who enter the leased property is an area of increasing litigation. The standard, as the following case illustrates, is similar to the residential landlord standard of foreseeability of the conduct of third parties.

Pichardo v. Big Diamond, Inc.

215 S.W.3d 479 (Tex. App. 2007)

FACTS

On the afternoon of November 23, 2002, James C. Luedtke, Jr., and his girlfriend, Heather Roberts, drove into the Diamond Shamrock gas station on White Settlement Road. The attendant activated the pump, and Roberts pumped gas into the vehicle. Roberts hopped in the vehicle, and Luedtke drove away without paying for the gas. As Luedtke drove off, an employee of the gas station ran outside and attempted to get the license plate number of the vehicle.

In an effort to escape, Luedtke accelerated the vehicle, ran a red light, and collided with a vehicle driven by Alexis Pichardo, Sr., who had his son Andrew Warren Pichardo with him. Peggy Pichardo, Alexis Pichardo, Jr., and Richard Anderson were following Alexis Pichardo, Sr., in a separate vehicle and witnessed the collision. Alexis Pichardo, Sr., and Andrew were injured in the collision.

On November 19, 2004, the Pichardos sued Luedtke; Selma Ann Roberts, the owner of the car Luedtke had been driving; and Big Diamond, the believed operator of the gas station. The Pichardos later added Diamond Shamrock, the correct operator of the gas station, as a defendant.

Big Diamond and Diamond Shamrock (Appellees) then filed a joint motion for summary judgment because neither breached a legal duty owed to the Pichardos, that Luedtke's actions were not foreseeable, and that any acts or omissions they committed were not a proximate cause of the Pichardos' injuries. The trial court granted the motion for summary judgment. The Pichardos appealed.

JUDICIAL OPINION

Walker, Justice. The common law doctrine of negligence consists of three elements: (1) a legal duty owed by one person to another; (2) a breach of that duty; and (3) damages proximately resulting from the breach. The threshold inquiry in a negligence case is duty. The plaintiff must establish both the existence and violation of a duty owed to the plaintiff by the defendant to establish liability in tort. Whether a duty exists is a question of law for the court to decide from the facts surrounding the occurrence in question.

As a general rule, "a person has no legal duty to protect another from the criminal acts of a third person." An exception is that "[o]ne who controls...premises does have a duty to use ordinary care to protect invitees from criminal acts of third parties if he knows or has reason to know of an unreasonable and foreseeable risk of harm to the invitee." The exception applies, of course, to a landlord who "retains control over the security and safety of the premises."

Likewise, third-party criminal conduct is a superseding cause of damages arising from a defendant's negligence unless the criminal conduct is a foreseeable result of the defendant's negligence. A defendant who seeks a summary judgment on the ground that the defendant has negated foreseeability as an element of proximate cause must prove, however, more than simply that the intervening third-party criminal conduct occurred. The defendant must show the third-party criminal conduct rises to the level of a superseding cause.

If the defendant does this, it has negated the ordinary foreseeability element of proximate cause, and the burden shifts to the plaintiff to raise a genuine issue of fact on foreseeability by presenting controverting evidence that, despite the extraordinary and abnormal nature of the intervening force, there was some indication at the time that such a crime would be committed.

We first evaluate Big Diamond's claim that it is not liable in any capacity because the summary judgment evidence clearly shows that it did not own the store property and did not operate or control the store property. The summary judgment evidence includes the oral deposition of Doug Miller, who is an officer of Big Diamond and vice president of Diamond Shamrock. During Miller's deposition, he stated that Big Diamond does not operate store # 723; instead, it is the holder of the alcohol licenses for that facility. Miller said that Diamond Shamrock owns the land, built the building, and operates store # 723. Based on this unrefuted testimony, it is clear that Big Diamond was not the owner of the property where the gas and dash occurred and therefore could not have owed the Pichardos a duty. Therefore, the trial court properly granted Big Diamond's motion for summary judgment.

The Pichardos argue that Diamond Shamrock knew that it was foreseeable that [not requiring] prepayment for gasoline purchases would in all likelihood result in foreseeable criminal activity such as theft of gasoline, and an attempt by the criminal to run away after the commission of the crime, and the possible injury of third persons such as [the Pichardos].

Here, the accident that injured the Pichardos occurred because Luedtke ran a red light after leaving the Diamond Shamrock gas station. The Pichardos were not invitees at the Diamond Shamrock gas station and the accident did not occur on the gas station premises. Consequently, we hold that the factors utilized to determine the scope of the duty owed by "[o]ne who controls… premises" to "protect *invitees* from criminal acts of third parties" is not applicable here.

[t]he "harm"—Alexis Sr.'s and Andrew's injuries—is a harm different in kind from that which would otherwise have resulted from the alleged negligence of not requiring prepayment for gasoline. Luedtke's actions in running a red light and striking the Pichardos' vehicle appear to be extraordinary rather than normal and appear to be independent of any negligence by Diamond Shamrock in not requiring prepayment for gasoline. Luedtke's action in running the red light is clearly due to his own decision to run the red light, and Luedtke is subject to liability to the Pichardos for his action in running the red light. Finally, we cannot see how Diamond Shamrock possesses more than possibly a minute degree of culpability for setting Luedtke's running of the red light in motion; the escape of any criminal following unauthorized criminal conduct could involve the running of a red light. Thus, we hold that Diamond Shamrock negated the foreseeability element of proximate cause by conclusively establishing that Luedtke's act of running the red light was a superseding cause of Alexis, Sr.'s and Andrew's injuries. The burden then shifted to the Pichardos to raise a genuine issue of fact on foreseeability by presenting controverting evidence that, despite the extraordinary and abnormal nature of the intervening force, there was some indication at the time that this crime—the running of the red light—would be committed.

The Pichardos presented no such controverting evidence. The record is devoid of any evidence showing that similar accidents had occurred, that the Diamond Shamrock gas station was a frequent victim of gas and dashes, or that the area was crime laden. The record contains no evidence that other crimes or gas and dashes had occurred on the property or in its immediate vicinity, or even that individuals committing a gas and dash frequently run red lights or drive recklessly. Because Diamond Shamrock conclusively negated the foreseeability element of the Pichardos' negligence claim, the trial court properly granted summary judgment in favor of Diamond Shamrock.

We affirm the trial court's take-nothing summary judgment rendered in favor of Big Diamond and Diamond Shamrock.

CASE QUESTIONS

1. What is the connection between Diamond Shamrock and the injuries the Pichardos experienced?
2. What evidence was missing from the Pichardos' case that was necessary?
3. What does the court say about extraordinary vs. normal acitivity?

CONSIDER 10.5

Sharon P. was an employee at a business located in the Coast Savings building located at 1180 South Beverly Drive, Los Angeles. On Thursday, April 8, 1993, Sharon P. entered the underground parking garage of the building at 11:00 A.M. and parked in her assigned space. While she was leaning back into her car to remove some items from her back seat, a man with a gun who was wearing a ski mask approached her. She was forced back into her car and sexually assaulted.

In the months preceding her attack, the condition of the parking garage had deteriorated. Lights were out (the lights were out in the immediate area of her attack that day), areas of the garage smelled of urine, and security cameras in the garage had not worked for months. In some places there were cots set up where apparently the homeless had moved into the garage.

CONSIDER 10.5

(continued)

Sharon P. brought suit against Arman, Ltd., the owner of the building and garage, and APCOA, the manager of the parking garage. APCOA's responsibilities were collection of revenues from those using the garage. The trial court entered summary judgment for Arman and APCOA. Sharon P. appealed. Should she recover? From whom? Discuss the standards for liability of commercial property owners and tenants for injury to those using the property. *Sharon P. v. Arman*, Ltd. 65 Cal. Rptr. 643 (Cal. App. 1997)

CONSIDER 10.6

One of the difficult issues many shopping center malls face is the presence and access of teenagers to the mall. Referred to as "mall rats," these teenagers often become aggressive and harass tenants and customers alike. They "travel" in groups in the malls and often congregate in intimidating large groups. Their activities can stretch through an entire day. What actions could a landlord take with regard to mall rats? Should a landlord take any action? Do tenants need protection against their presence? Do the mall rats present any security risks?

Americans with Disabilities Act

The Basics of the Law

The **Americans with Disabilities Act (ADA)** (42 U.S.C. §12007 [1990]) was passed "to provide a clear and comprehensive national mandate for the elimination of discrimination against individuals with disabilities," and to establish "clear, strong, consistent enforceable standards" for "scrutinizing such discrimination."

Section 302 of the ADA provides that "no individual shall be discriminated against on the basis of disability in the full and equal enjoyment of the goods, services, facilities, privileges, advantages, or accommodation by any person who owns, leases (or leases to), or operates a place of public accommodation."[8]

Those who fit the categories of owner, operator, lessee, and lessor must make "reasonable modifications" in "policies, practices, or procedures" that are necessary to allow individuals with disabilities access to their goods, services, or facilities.

The following case deals with an unusual ADA disability issue.

Staron v. McDonald's Corporation

51 F.3d 353 (2d Cir. 1995)

FACTS

Matthew Staron and others who joined him in this suit (plaintiffs) went to both a McDonald's and Burger King restaurant (defendants) in Connecticut. They found the air in both to be full of tobacco smoke. Because of their various physical conditions, including asthma, they were unable to enter these places without encountering breathing difficulties.

They registered complaints with the State of Connecticut Human Rights Commission and received no results to their satisfaction. They filed suit seeking

8. Examples of the traditional form of real property accommodations under ADA include sufficient width in aisles and restrooms for wheelchairs (*Pinnock v. International House of Pancakes,* 844 F. Supp. 574 [S.D. Cal. 1993]); permitting guide dogs for the visually impaired (*Crowder v. Kitagawa,* 842 F. Supp. 1257 [D. Haw. 1994]), installation of elevators (*Tyler v. City of Manhattan,* 849 F. Supp. 1429 [D. Kan. 1994]); resurfacing of streets and sidewalks to remove potholes and ensure smooth surfaces for wheelchairs (*Kinney v. Yerusalim,* 9 F.3d 1067 [C.A. 3 1993]); and reversal of policy prohibiting wheelchairs on the Little League field (*Anderson v. Little League Baseball, Inc.,* 794 F. Supp. 342 [D. Ariz. 1992]).

a judicial declaration that the smoke-filled restaurants were violations of the ADA and that the restaurants were required to adopt "No Smoking" policies in order to comply with the law.

The District Court dismissed the suit and the plaintiffs appealed.

JUDICIAL OPINION

Walker, Circuit Judge. The ADA was promulgated "to provide a clear and comprehensive national mandate for the elimination of discrimination against individuals with disabilities," as well as to establish "clear, strong, consistent, enforceable standards" for scrutinizing such discrimination... [d]efendants do not dispute that the section applies to them as owners and operators of public accommodations. They also concede at this point that plaintiffs qualify as "individuals with disabilities" under the ADA. The basis of the magistrate judge's Recommended Ruling, and the principal contention of McDonald's and Burger King on appeal, is that a total ban on smoking does not constitute a "reasonable modification" under the ADA.

The ADA and cases interpreting it do not articulate a precise test for determining whether a particular modification is "reasonable." However, because the Rehabilitation Act, which applies to recipients of federal funding, uses the same "reasonableness" analysis, cases interpreting that act provide some guidance.

The Supreme Court, addressing the issue of the reasonableness of accommodations under the Rehabilitation Act in the employment context, stated that "accommodation is not reasonable if it either imposes 'undue financial and administrative burdens'... or requires 'a fundamental alteration in the nature of [the] program.'" [O]ther courts have articulated factors that they consider relevant to the determination, including the nature and extent of plaintiff's disability.

Although neither the ADA nor the courts have defined the precise contours of the test for reasonableness, it is clear that the determination of whether a particular modification is "reasonable" involves a fact-specific, case-by-case inquiry that considers, among other factors, the effectiveness of the modification in light of the nature of the disability in question and the cost to the organization that would implement it.

While there may be claims requesting modification under the ADA that warrant dismissal as unreasonable as a matter of law, in the cases before us a fact-specific inquiry was required. None has occurred at this early stage of the suits. The magistrate judge instead concluded—and the district court agreed—that plaintiffs' request for a ban on smoking in all of defendants' restaurants was unreasonable as a matter of law. The magistrate judge offered two grounds for this conclusion: first, that "the ADA, by itself, does not mandate a 'blanket ban' on smoke in 'fast food' restaurants," and second, that "it is not reasonable, under the ADA, to impose a blanket ban on every McDonald's [and Burger King] restaurant where there are certain restaurants which reasonably can accommodate a 'no-smoking' area." We believe that neither ground justifies dismissal of the complaints.

The magistrate judge correctly noted that the ADA on its face does not ban smoking in all public accommodations or all fast-food restaurants. Defendants carry this point a significant step further, however, and argue that the ADA precludes a total smoking ban as a reasonable modification. They assert that Congress did not intend to restrict the range of legislative policy options open to state and local governments to deal with the issue of smoking. Their argument rests on §501(b) of the ADA:

Nothing in this chapter shall be construed to invalidate or limit the remedies, rights, and procedures of any Federal law or law of any State or political subdivision... that provides greater or equal protection for the rights of individuals with disabilities than are afforded by this chapter. Nothing in this chapter shall be construed to preclude the prohibition of, or the imposition of restrictions on, smoking... in places of public accommodation covered by subchapter III of this chapter.

42 U.S.C. §12201(b). The magistrate judge echoed a sentiment similar to defendants', stating that "the significant public policy issues regarding smoking in 'fast food' restaurants are better addressed by Congress or by the Connecticut General Assembly.... "

It is plain to us that Congress did not intend to isolate the effects of smoking from the protections of the ADA. The first sentence of §501(b) simply indicates that Congress, states, and municipalities remain free to offer greater protection for disabled individuals than the ADA provides. The passage does not state, and it does not follow, that violations of the ADA should go unredressed merely because a state has chosen to provide some degree of protection to those with disabilities.

Cases in which individuals claim under the ADA that allergies to smoke constitute a disability and require smoking restrictions are simply subject to the same general reasonableness analysis as are other cases under the Act.

The magistrate judge's principal objection to plaintiffs' proposed modification was that plaintiffs were seeking a total ban on smoking in all of defendants' restaurants even though "there are certain restaurants which reasonably can accommodate a 'no-smoking' area." We do not think that it is possible to conclude on the pleadings that plaintiffs' suggested modification in this case is necessarily unreasonable.

To be sure, the few courts that have addressed the question of reasonable modification for a smoke-sensitive disability have found a total ban unnecessary. Yet these courts only reached this conclusion after making a factual determination that existing accommodations were sufficient.

Plaintiffs in this case are entitled to prove that a ban on smoking is a reasonable modification to permit them access to defendants' restaurants. Given that McDonald's has voluntarily banned smoking in all corporate-owned restaurants, the factfinder may conclude that such a ban would fully accommodate plaintiffs' disabilities but impose little or no cost on the defendants. The magistrate judge's unsupported assumption that certain restaurants "reasonably can accommodate a 'no-smoking' area" does not obviate the need for a factual inquiry. Plaintiffs have alleged that, regardless of the different structural arrangements in various restaurants, the environment in each establishment visited by the plaintiffs contained too much smoke to allow them use of the facilities on an equal basis as other non-disabled patrons. These allegations belie the magistrate judge's assumption that no-smoking areas offer a sufficient accommodation to plaintiffs.

In addition, we note that plaintiffs do not solely request a ban on smoking. Their complaints ask that defendants be enjoined "from continuing or maintaining any policy" that denies plaintiffs access to their restaurants, as well as "such other and further relief as it may deem just and proper." While plaintiffs bear the eventual burden of showing that particular modifications are reasonable, we do not think that it is necessary at this point in the lawsuit to bind plaintiffs to the one specific modification they prefer. If plaintiffs should fail in their quest for an outright ban on smoking, they may still be able to demonstrate after discovery that modifications short of an outright ban, such as partitions or ventilation systems, are both "reasonable" and "necessary," *42 U.S.C. §12182(b)(2)(A)(ii)*, and plaintiffs should be allowed the opportunity to do so.

Reversed and remanded.

CASE QUESTIONS

1. What disability do the plaintiffs allege?
2. Does the court find that the ADA applies in these circumstances?
3. What must the plaintiffs establish when the case is remanded for trial?
4. Does the ADA address the issue of smoking?

ADA Lease Provisions

Without specific provisions on the ADA, legal requirements for access and alterations will be allocated under other lease terms such as those on alterations or repair. The ADA does apply to commercial facilities, referred to as "places of public accommodation" (PPA). Included in the PPA under the ADA would be shopping centers, medical offices, banks, and other professional service office buildings such as those for accountants, lawyers, and architects. The types of requirements for PPAs would include the removal of barriers and the presence of paths of entry for those with disabilities. Many of these requirements are met by modifications to property such as automatic doors and ramps.

> **Practical Tip**
>
> *In conducting a review of potential leased premises, the tenant should check for access routes, appropriate restroom facilities, automatic doors, drinking fountain heights, and elevators, and should evaluate the costs of compliance.*

Tenants should conduct a form of due diligence review of the property to determine ADA compliance. If modifications are required, the tenant should negotiate their addition and cost allocation. The lease agreement should allocate the costs of future compliance with the ADA and other laws as well as the cost of upkeep.

CONSIDER 10.7

Margo Neff is disabled and requires a wheelchair to gain mobility. Neff filed suit under section 308 of the ADA, 42 U.S.C. §12188(a) (1988), alleging that Dairy Queen (ADQ) had violated section 302 of the ADA, 42 U.S.C. §12182, by failing to make the San Antonio Dairy Queen stores accessible to her. In her complaint, Neff pointed to numerous barriers that she alleged made the San Antonio stores inaccessible to the disabled. Neff sought an injunction requiring ADQ to modify "its" San Antonio stores to eliminate

CONSIDER 10.7

(continued)

the alleged barriers, a declaratory judgment concerning ADQ's violation of the ADA, and attorneys' fees. The San Antonio stores indicate that they are simply leasing facilities from ADQ and are not responsible for ensuring that handicap-use modifications be made. Who is correct? Must the changes be made? Who is responsible for the changes? *Neff v. American Dairy Queen Corp.*, 58 F.3d 1063 (C.A. 5, 1995)

Landlord's Right of Entry

As in residential leases, tenants have the right to exclusive use of the leased property, but, on occasion, the landlord will need access. The lease should specify the hows and whens of the landlord's access, including when the landlord may enter the tenant's premises and for what purpose; how much notice is required before the landlord may enter, what form that notice must take, and how it is to be delivered; and whether notice provisions may be waived during emergency situations.

Destruction and Damage to Premises

The parties need to make provisions for what would happen to their relationship in the event that an accident or catastrophe destroys the shopping center property. For example, the 2001 destruction of the World Trade Center in New York City left many tenants without office facilities for substantial periods of time. Many tenants had contingency plans for operations. Other tenants have filed suit against various government agencies for the interruption of their leases and businesses.

The lease should cover several issues: If the premises are damaged or destroyed to the point of being unusable by the tenant, does the responsibility of rent abate? (During the time of nonuse, provision should be made for the tenant to stop paying rent.) May the tenant cancel the lease? At what point are the premises completely destroyed? Allowing the common law to cover these issues is inviting the ambiguity of the doctrine of impossibility and does not provide the parties with sufficient guidelines for their conduct.

In some cases, the parties incorporate into the lease an obligation of the landlord to rebuild the premises. Because of the unique nature of the shopping center, in which prime location can be the key to a successful business, this obligation to rebuild can be extremely important to the tenant. The tenant may not want to terminate the lease but may want to be back in business as soon as possible and can provide for time limitations on rebuilding. If there is a construction clause in the lease, there should also be a provision to require the landlord to carry appropriate insurance to cover reconstruction costs.

Breach

The last topic of concern to both parties in the commercial lease is what constitutes a breach and what the damages are in the event of a breach. For the landlord, nonpayment of rent is the major problem because businesses do face fiscal crises. If remedies for nonpayment of rent are not specified, the law affords the same protections in commercial leases as in residential leases. If rental payments are not made in a timely manner, the landlord may bring an action to dispossess the tenant. If the tenant breaches the lease agreement by terminating business prior to the lease expiration date, the landlord may have the responsibility to mitigate the situation by trying to find another tenant, but the parties could specify otherwise and could provide for a liquidated damage figure. In cases of breaches in other areas (such as failure to maintain or failure to grant access), the parties may agree to submit matters to arbitration prior to suit.

Landlord's Responsibility for Tenant's Conduct

A recent development in commercial leases is one of holding landlords responsible when their tenants are engaged in trademark infringement. For example, many landlords lease properties to stores that sell knock-off goods or goods that the stores are not licensed to sell. Such tenants are often found in outlet malls. To protect their trademarks, some manufacturers have joined together to bring suits against landlords so that landlords are more cautious about their tenants and the tenants' activities. For example, in *Polo Ralph Lauren Corp. v. Chinatown Gift Shop*, 855 F. Supp. 648 (S.D. N.Y. 1994), Polo Ralph Lauren, Rolex Watch USA, and Louis Vuitton brought suit against a landlord who was leasing property to three retailers who were selling goods that infringed on their trademarks for their clothing, watches, and leather goods, respectively. The court held that there was a cause of action against the landlord for its vicarious liability under federal law for facilitating the infringement by the tenants.

> ***Practical Tip***
>
> *Because of potential liability for infringement by the unauthorized sale of trademarked goods or the sale of knock-off goods, landlords will need to put a clause in the lease prohibiting such sales and also take precautions in screening tenants and knowing what activities are going on in the leased premises.*

Assignment of Leases

Most states readily permit the assignment of leases by tenants. But in nearly all commercial leases that have been drafted by the developer, assignments are prohibited without approval from the developer. Even if a lease does not contain an assignment prohibition, the type of assignment may be severely limited by the use restrictions clause. Since the tenant remains liable on the lease, the tenant would be responsible for a breach if an assignment were made to a retailer who sold goods that were unauthorized by the use provision.

Commercial leases involve complexities in assignments and subleases because of tenant mix. Many commercial leases have restrictions on assignments or require landlord approval because the landlord would breach his non-compete clauses with other tenants if, for example, an assignment meant there were two drugstores in one shopping center.

Shopping Center Leases—Specific Provisions

A successful shopping center is the result of a careful mix of tenants. To maximize the return on not just the owner's investment but also the profits earned by the individual tenants, the tenants need to complement rather than compete with one another. This section offers background on obtaining that mix.

The Anchor Tenant

Long before a center opens its doors and, in some cases, long before construction of the center begins, the developer or owner negotiates with an **anchor tenant** to begin creating the mix of tenants. The anchor tenant is generally the grocery store in a freestanding center or a major department store for a mall. In the case of a shopping mall, there may be two to five anchor tenants. The anchor tenants are responsible for drawing the majority of the customers to the center or mall and will do a significant amount of advertising that also brings in customers. The terms under which these anchor tenants will come to the center are critical because other tenants and lease terms will be controlled by the demands of the anchor tenant. For example, if a chain drugstore is to be the anchor tenant in a freestanding shopping center, the developer will not be able to lease to a small and locally owned drugstore a smaller space in the center. Likewise, if a discount clothing store is the anchor tenant, it would be difficult to lease the smaller spaces to retail clothing stores.

Commercial leases tend to be significantly longer than residential leases largely because of the degree of investment made by the developer and the time required for recoupment of the investment in the property. Periods of 15 to 20 years for the initial term of the lease are not unusual and are generally accompanied by four to five 5-year renewal options.

A portion of every commercial lease will cover restrictions on the developer's other tenants and future leases. For example, if a center will have a bakery, the bakery tenant will want a clause in the lease that prohibits both the landlord from leasing to another bakery and other tenants from assigning their leases to other bakeries.

One of the difficulties that can arise for a shopping center developer or owner occurs when an anchor tenant is signed and then fails to open for business. Because the developer is dependent upon the mix of tenants, and the tenants and their customer traffic are drawn by the anchor tenant, the failure of an anchor tenant to commence operations, even when rent is paid, can be devastating for the center. The following case deals with the issue of an anchor tenant's failure to open for business.

SLATER V. PEARLE VISION CENTER, INC.

546 A.2d 676 (Pa. 1988)

FACTS

Maurice Slater and Peter Kanton are the owners and developers of Bloomsburg Shopping Center (the shopping center/appellant/lessor). Pearle Vision Center (Pearle/lessee/appellee) is a tenant in this strip-type shopping center and has paid rent for its facilities but has never opened for business. Slater and Kanton, concerned about having such a large vacancy in their center, brought suit seeking an injunction requiring Pearle to occupy its premises and open for business.

Pearle filed a motion for summary judgment maintaining there was no breach of the lease agreement because there was no express provision in the lease agreement that required Pearle to occupy and use the premises. The trial court granted Pearle's motion, and Slater and Kanton appealed.

JUDICIAL OPINION

Beck, Judge. Shopping Center argues that the lease contains both an express and an implied requirement that Pearle occupy the premises. The express requirement is alleged to be found in Section 10 of the lease, which states:

A. Tenant covenants and agrees that it shall use the Premises solely as a "Pearle Vision Center" or such other name as is used by the other Tenant's businesses within the State of Pennsylvania for the retail sale and repair of eyeglasses, lenses and other optical merchandise and optical services, and eye examination and lens grinding and preparation and for no other purpose. . . .

The quoted language on its face would appear to impose an obligation on Pearle to occupy the premises and to use it as a vision center. However, Pennsylvania case law requires us to interpret such language in commercial leases to mean only that no use other than the use specified in the lease is permitted. The language does not address the question of the lessee's duty to occupy the premises.

In the seminal case of *Dickey v. Philadelphia Minit-Man Corp.*, 377 Pa. 549, 105 A.2d 580 (1954), the lease provided that the leased premises were to be occupied by the lessee in the business of washing and cleaning automobiles and for no other purpose. The lease also provided for rent based on a percentage of gross sales, with a fixed minimum annual rental. The defendant tenant occupied and used the premises for a number of years in accordance with the lease, but then limited its business to waxing cars and largely eliminated the car washing aspect of its business.

The lessor argued that in a lease where the rental is based upon gross sales, there is an implied obligation of the tenant to continue the business on the premises to the fullest extent possible. The Court rejected this argument, finding that the tenant's decision to change its business was made in good faith and in the exercise of legitimate business judgment and was not forbidden by an implied term of the lease. Interestingly, in so holding, the Court specifically distinguished a Louisiana case where a tenant had completely vacated the leased premises and conducted its business elsewhere.

Thus, the holding of *Dickey* would appear to be that a use covenant like that presented here cannot be read as an express requirement that the tenant use the premises for the precise permitted business purpose. Moreover, *Dickey* holds that there is no implied obligation that the tenant under a percentage lease refrain from conducting its business in good faith and in accordance with sound business judgment simply because doing so may decrease the rent payable.

More pertinent to the instant case is the fact that *Dickey* specifically does not address a situation where the tenant conducts no business on the leased premises. It also does not address a lease for premises which are part of a strip of stores where the economic health of each store may be dependent on the others.

Since there is no other directly controlling Pennsylvania precedent, we must necessarily rely on more general principles of lease construction.

Thus, where it is clear that an obligation is within the contemplation of the parties at the time of contracting or is necessary to carry out their intentions, the court will imply it.

[W]e find ample evidence in this lease that these parties may well have contemplated and intended that Pearle was obligated to occupy and use the premises. For example, sub-paragraph 9(E) of the lease provides that the tenant agrees to "open the Premises for business to the public not later than ninety (90) days after Landlord's approval of tenant's plans and specifications." Although we recognize that Shopping Center's complaint does not specifically allege when or if it ever approved Pearle's "plans and specification," thus triggering this provision, the complaint does allege that Pearle "failed to open the premises and utilize it in accordance with" this provision.

Moreover, we find that there are other provisions in the lease that suggest that actual occupancy and use of the premises by Pearle was in the contemplation of the parties when they executed the lease. Section 10(B) states that the tenant agrees "that it will conduct its business in the entire Premises." Section 30 includes "abandonment" as an Event of Default and contains the following noteworthy exception:

Notwithstanding anything to the contrary herein, Tenant may allow the demised premises to be vacant for a period not exceeding sixty (60) days, provided Landlord is given not less than ninety (90) days written notice that such vacancy will occur: said vacancy being necessary due to repairs or remodeling of the demised premises or transfer of possession to a franchisee or assignee pursuant to the terms of this lease.

This exception appears in type that differs from the body of the lease, which otherwise appears to be largely based on a standard form thus creating at least the suggestion that this provision was a separately negotiated term. The necessary implication of this provision, which severely circumscribes Pearle's ability to leave the premises vacant, is that except under the circumstances specifically outlined, Pearle cannot allow the premises to be vacant.

Finally, the lease contains references to the obligations of Pearle vis-a-vis the viability of the shopping mall as a whole. The "affirmative obligations" of Pearle set forth in Section 20(A) refer to Pearle's obligation to keep the premises in a manner consistent with the general character of the shopping mall and to refrain from any action or practice that "may damage, mar or deface the Premises or any other part of the Shopping Center."

In the face of such provisions, we cannot agree with the trial court's conclusion.

Reversed.

CASE QUESTIONS

1. Describe the landlord and tenant.
2. Did the tenant ever open for business?
3. Does the lease expressly require the tenant to open for business?
4. Does the lease imply that the tenant will open for business?
5. Does Pennsylvania have an exact case on point?
6. Is the intention of the parties important?
7. How does the court determine intention?

In many cases, anchor tenants pay a minimal or at least lower amount of rent than the other tenants. If the large spaces in the center go unoccupied, then all of the remaining tenants suffer. Tenants who occupy smaller units in the center do so with the idea that their services and goods will be unique to that center and that the landlord will not reduce their business by leasing to a competing venture in the same center. These ideas of traffic from anchor tenants and noncompetition are marketing tools that must be guaranteed by lease terms.[9]

Business Restrictions

The lessees in the shopping center may want to control the makeup of the center or even the types of merchandise sold by each retailer. Indeed, in some instances, the anchor tenant stipulates that it must review and approve all potential lessees for a center. For example, in some leases, anchor tenants have clauses that disallow the leasing of space to discount merchants. This is to prevent the anchor tenant from being undersold on certain items because a store in the same center has been leased to a discount merchant of those items.

The issue that arises from these clauses that limit the types of business operations is whether the clauses violate federal or state antitrust laws. Many such clauses have been challenged by the Federal Trade Commission and the Justice Department in an effort to eliminate them.

At this point, it is difficult to determine what clauses do or do not violate antitrust laws. Because the issues of the type of market, location, and competition vary from city to city, the validity of these clauses also varies. But for the most part, if the clauses are reasonably necessary for shopping center survival, they should be insisted upon by tenants. In the following case, the issue of use restriction is critical.

Child World, Inc. v. South Towne Centre, Ltd.

634 F. Supp. 1121 (S.D. Oh. 1986)

FACTS

Child World, Inc. (plaintiff), operates large retail toy stores throughout Ohio and other states called "Children's Palace." South Towne Centre, Ltd. (defendant), is a limited partnership in the state of Ohio and leases space in its South Towne shopping center complex to a Children's Palace store. Section 43(A) of the lease, executed in February 1976, provided as follows:

Except insofar as the following shall be unlawful, the parties mutually agree as follows:

A. Landlord shall not use or permit or suffer any other person, firm, corporation or other entity to use any portion of the Shopping Center or any other property located within six (6) miles from the Shopping Center and owned, leased or otherwise controlled by the landlord (meaning thereby the real property or parties in interest and not a "straw" person or entity) or any person or entity having a substantial identity of interest, for the operation of a toys and games store principally for the sale at retail of toys and games, juvenile furniture and sporting goods such as is exemplified by the Child World and Children's Palace stores operated by Tenant's parent company, Child World, Inc. at the demised premises and elsewhere.

The lease was a 20-year lease and was signed by Barbara Beerman Weprin, the sole general partner of South Towne. Mad River Ltd. is another limited partnership in which Weprin is the sole general partner. Mad River owns another parcel of land approximately one-half mile from the South Towne Center. On December 24, 1985, Mad River entered into an agreement to sell the parcel of land to Toys "R" Us, Inc. Toys "R" Us intends to construct a retail facility similar to the description in the just-noted lease clause. When Children's Palace was informed of the sale, they brought suit seeking to enforce the covenant not to lease or sell to a competitor of Children's Palace.

9. Recent decisions have some courts implying a covenant of continuing operations, particularly for anchor tenants. When a significant portion of the rent is tied to revenues, courts have held that the tenant must continue operations (*East Broadway Corp. v. Taco Bell Corp.*, 542 N.W.2d [Iowa 1996]).

JUDICIAL OPINION

Rice, Circuit Judge. The consensus of the federal courts which have considered covenants in shopping center leases is one with which this Court can agree; namely, that the varying terms, conditions, and economic justifications for such restrictions render them inappropriate subjects for application of the per se rule. Defendants have not alleged nor proven anything about Section 43(A) of the lease which would indicate that it has only anticompetitive consequences. Indeed, in Finding of Fact #9, Defendants agree that Section 43(A) was negotiated as an inducement for Plaintiff to erect a Children's Palace store on Defendants' premises and to enter into a twenty-year lease. This economic justification for exclusivity clauses such as Section 43(A) have [*sic*] not been found to be per se illegal, but rather have [*sic*] been found consistent with the public interest in economic development. Such laws can induce tenants to establish stores and to enter into a particular marketplace, often then encouraging the entry of other, often smaller, merchants.

A number of factors have been considered by the courts which have excluded restrictive covenants in shopping center leases: (1) the relevant product and geographic markets, together with the showing of unreasonable impact upon competition in these markets, due to the restrictive covenant; (2) the availability of alternate sites for the entity excluded by the operation of such a covenant; (3) the significance of the competition eliminated by the exclusivity clause, and whether present or future competitors were the parties excluded; (4) the scope of the restrictive covenant and whether it varied depending on particular circumstances; and (5) the economic justifications for the inclusion of the restrictive covenant in the lease.

Defendants have made no attempt to address the majority of these factors and to introduce evidence as to the markets affected by Section 43(A), the nature of the competition in these markets, and the like. Rather, Defendants focus exclusively upon the breadth of Section 43(A) and its prohibition of sale or lease by Defendants to competition of Plaintiff within a six-mile radius of the South Towne Centre shopping center. Defendants remind the Court that in none of the cases cited by Plaintiff was a restrictive covenant with a six-mile radius upheld under the rule of reason.

Due to the particular facts of this case, however, the Court needs not, and specifically does not, reach the validity of the six-mile limitation contained in Section 43(A). Regardless of possible overbreadth, a restrictive covenant challenged as unreasonable under Section 1 of the Sherman Act will be upheld to the extent that a breach of the covenant has occurred or is threatened to occur within a reasonable geographic area and time period. The parties have agreed, in Finding of Fact #12, that the parcel which Defendants seek to convey to Toys "R" Us is approximately one-half mile from the Children's Palace store covered by the Lease. The Court finds that Section 43(A) is lawful and enforceable to the extent of one-half mile, as required by the facts of this case.

Defendants have the burden of establishing that Section 43(A), enforced to the extent of one-half mile, would constitute an unreasonable restraint of trade. Defendants have not, however, presented any evidence to discharge their burden of demonstrating unreasonableness. Furthermore, the facts in this case, both those proven by the parties and those of which the Court takes judicial notice, tend to underscore the reasonableness of Section 43(A) as applied. Considering the latter set of facts first, this Court is quite familiar with the area of Miami Township within which the South Towne Centre is located. The Court takes judicial notice of the manner in which the real property in the Centre's vicinity has been developed, the rate at which economic development has proceeded, and the physical relationship of shopping centers, one to another, in this area. These current economic and geographic characteristics, of which judicial notice is taken, are among the factors which tend, even apart from Defendants' failure to meet their burden of showing unreasonableness, to support the enforceability of Section 43(A) to the extent of one-half mile.

Turning to the impact which enforcement of Section 43(A), as applied in this case, would have upon the Defendants, the burdens of enforcement are not unduly great. As noted *supra*, Section 43(A) does not appear to preclude rental or sale, even within a one-half mile radius, to any number of stores which can compete with a Children's Palace toy and game store but which are not "copycat" stores. On the financial level, there is testimony from a representative of Defendants in the record to the effect that the value of the parcel in question increases almost daily. Moreover, Defendants believe that they will have no difficulty in finding another purchaser, should Section 43(A) preclude their sale of the parcel to Toys "R" Us.

Enforcement of Section 43(A) to the extent of one-half mile would also not appear to foreclose the entry of Toys "R" Us into competition with Plaintiff's store in the environs of the South Towne Centre shopping center. In his deposition, J. Tim Logan indicated that, even were Section 43(A) upheld, presumably in its entirety, Toys "R" Us would still establish a store in the vicinity of Plaintiff's store.

Other courts have believed that restrictive covenants of a scope of one-half mile or more, albeit less than six miles, are legitimate lures by landlords in order for shopping center tenants to enter particular marketplaces and to thereby enhance the economic development of the community. The public has surely benefited from the development of South Towne Centre. As a restriction of six miles appeared reasonable to Defendants' predecessors at the time of bargaining, enforcement of Section 43(A) of the Lease to the extent of one-half mile is consistent with that original calculation of value, and certainly reasonable.

Judgment for plaintiff.

CASE QUESTIONS

1. Who leased what from whom?
2. What restrictions were there in the lease agreement?
3. How did Toys "R" Us become involved?
4. Is the sale a violation of the anticompetition clause?
5. Is the same shopping center involved?

CONSIDER 10.8

Walgreen operated a pharmacy in the Southgate Mall in Milwaukee since its opening in 1951. The current lease, signed in 1971 and carrying a 30-year, six-month term, contains, as had the only previous lease, a clause in which the landlord, Sara Creek, promises not to lease space in the mall to anyone else who wants to operate a pharmacy or a store containing a pharmacy. However, Sara Creek has lost its anchor tenant in the shopping center and has signed a lease agreement with Phar-Mor, a "deep discount" chain, rather than, like Walgreen, just a "discount" chain. Phar-Mor's store would occupy 100,000 square feet, of which 12,000 would be occupied by a pharmacy the same size as Walgreen's. The entrances to the two stores would be within a couple of hundred feet of each other.

Walgreen filed suit for an injunction halting the opening of the Phar-Mor. Sara Creek indicates that without another tenant in the space, Walgreen's sales will decline dramatically. Sara Creek argues that without the Phar-Mor, Walgreen's sales will drop $2,000,000 and that with the Phar-Mor, Walgreen will lose only $1,000,000 in sales. What do you think of Sara Creek's economic argument? Should those economic issues have a place in deciding whether to enforce restrictive covenants? Should Walgreen be permitted to terminate the lease if no injunction is granted? *Walgreen Co. v. Sara Creek Property Co.*, B.V. 966 F.2d 273 (C.A. 7. 1992)

Cautions and Conclusions

The commercial lease carries a unique set of legal problems from antitrust to liquidated damages to store hours. A checklist for commercial lease negotiations is a necessity, and the headings in this chapter can be used as a guideline in making sure all possible legal issues are covered. As is true with other areas of real estate, an investigation can never be too complete.

The following is a checklist for commercial leases.

1. Amount of rent. If there is a profit-sharing arrangement, specify exact terms. Is it gross or net profit? What percentage? Where is it paid?
2. In the case of a shopping center lease, what competition will be permitted?
3. Who is responsible for maintaining the common areas? Who will carry liability insurance for the common areas?
4. Can the lease be assigned? Is approval for assignment required?
5. Who will make repairs? Who pays?
6. Who will make improvements?
7. Are there mandatory hours of operation?
8. Is there an understanding on fixtures? Who keeps them?
9. What deposits are required? Are they refundable?
10. Is there compliance with all applicable laws, including ADA?

Key Terms

Americans with Disabilities Act (ADA), 238
anchor tenant, 242
common area maintenance (CAM), 230
Consumer Price Index (CPI) adjustment clause, 230
escalation clause, 229
fixed rent, 229
gross rent, 229
operating expenses, 230
percentage rent, 230
sick building syndrome, 229
specific happenings increase provisions, 230
triple net, net-net-net, 229

Chapter Problems

1. In April 1965, Berkeley Heights Shopping Center leased 11,514 square feet of space to A & P Supermarkets. Under the terms of the lease, Berkeley agreed not to lease any other shopping-center space to another grocery store. On April 16, 1977, A & P informed Berkeley that it was ceasing operations and subleasing the premises to Drug Fair, a modern chain drug store that also sells foodstuffs. In 1985, Berkeley sought to lease other space in the center to another grocery store, and Drug Fair objected on the grounds of the covenant not to compete. Berkeley maintains the covenant only applies when the premises Drug Fair occupies are used as a grocery store operation. Who is correct? *Berkeley Development Co. v. Great Atlantic & Pacific Tea Co.*, 518 A.2d 790 (N.J. 1986)

2. Douglas Theater Corporation (Douglas) operates the Ivanhoe Theater in Chicago. Gold Standard Enterprises, Inc. operates a liquor store. Both were tenants of a common landlord and shared a parking lot. Gold Standard's lease was dated May 22, 1978, and ran to September 30, 2003. The Douglas lease was dated March 15, 1982, and ran to June 30, 1987.

In 1982, Gold Standard purchased its underlying property as well as the common parking lot, subject to all tenants' rights under their leases. In 1987, Douglas exercised an option to purchase its underlying theater property. On June 30, 1987, Douglas entered into a parking lot lease with Gold Standard to run until September 30, 2003. The lease gave responsibility for maintenance and operation to Gold Standard. The use of the parking lot was granted in common on a first-come-first-serve basis.

Gold Standard was open for business from 10:00 A.M. to 10:00 P.M. weekdays and Saturdays and on Sundays from noon to 6:00 P.M. The theater was open 40 weeks per year, with shows running from 8:00 to 10:00 P.M. Tuesday through Saturday with 2:00 P.M. matinees on Saturday and Sunday. The theater was doing well, with the result that exits and access to Gold Standard were blocked. Both parties began having cars towed, and eventually the parties went to court over the issue. What should the court do? Has the landlord failed in his responsibilities? *Douglas Theater v. Gold Standard Enterprises, Inc.*, 544 N.E.2d 1053 (Ill. 1989)

3. Brophy College was a devisee in the will of Anastasia Nealon and received title to two parcels of real property through the probate of her will: lots 2337 and 2339 located on East McDowell Road in Phoenix. The Tovars claimed the right to occupy these lots under a purported lease agreement they had with Nick Mercer (purported to be the husband of Anastasia). The Tovars operated an adult bookstore and theater on the premises.

In 1977, most of the property on lots 2337 and 2339 was destroyed by fire, and Brophy College gave the Tovars notice of the right of termination on lot 2337 and notice of termination of a periodic tenancy on lot 2339. The notice on 2337 was pursuant to a lease agreement that permitted the tenant to terminate if there was a fire; and the notice for lot 2339 was a period's notice to terminate the periodic tenancy on that lot.

The Tovars claimed there was a lease for lot 2339 included in the lease for lot 2337, since there was a longhand addition to the lease that stated, "These premises primarily for expansion of Empress Theater 2339 E. McDowell." During their occupancy, the Tovars had spent $1,500 making improvements on lot 2339, including a stage, dressing room, sign, and carpeting. They did not use lot 2339 for six to eight months prior to the fire because of poor business but did pay rent for its use. Tovar testified that he and Mercer had orally agreed that the lease on lot 2337 applied to lot 2339.

The Tovars failed to vacate the premises, and Brophy College brought action in forcible detainer to require the Tovars to leave. The trial court found for the Tovars. Is the decision correct? *William Henry Brophy College v. Tovar*, 619 P.2d 19 (Ariz. 1980)

4. E. H. Webb and Ann Thomas Webb own a shopping center in Davidson County, Tennessee, and leased one of its spaces to Scooter Stores, Incorporated, in 1971. In 1975, Scooter assigned the lease to Borchert Enterprises. The Webbs approved the assignment, but various controversies arose between the parties, and Borchert filed suit.

The Webbs counterclaimed for rent due under a clause in the lease, which required a payment of 2 percent of gross sales as additional rent. The clause provided as follows:

Lessee, in addition, agrees to pay to Lessor as additional rental a sum equal to two (2%) percent of the gross sales in excess of Two Hundred Thousand ($200,000) Dollars per annum, excluding sales tax and money order sales, said payments to be made annually, within forty-five (45) days from each annual anniversary of this Lease. Lessee agrees to provide to Lessor annually a Certified Public Accountant's report of sales to substantiate the payments made hereunder.

Borchert was engaged in the operation of a convenience market and installed several pinball machines. The Webbs contended that Borchert had failed to pay the 2 percent due on the pinball revenues, and Borchert contended that revenue from the pinball machines was not included in the term *gross sales.* The trial court held that the pinball income was part of gross sales, and Borchert appealed. How should the case be decided? *Borchert Enterprises, Inc. v. Webb*, 584 S.W.2d 208 (Tenn. 1979)

5. Thom Rock Realty Company developed an interior design showroom center. The center, created by I. M. Pei & Partners was to total almost one million square feet and be devoted exclusively to showroom tenants. Herman Miller, Inc., a designer and manufacturer of high-end office furniture, leased space in the showroom facility. The 10-year lease was signed in 1986 and contained a clause that the facilities would "be used for showrooms and other related uses."

There was a downturn in the economy in the late 1980s, and the demand for contract furniture and showrooms declined. Thom Rock lost many tenants and began leasing the space in its showroom facility to video production firms and other types of companies. Herman Miller sued Thom Rock for breach of its rental agreement on the grounds that the lease contained a restrictive use clause. Can such a clause be enforced? How does the goal of the design center compare with the mix of a shopping center? *Herman Miller Inc. v. Thom Rock Realty Co.*, 46 F.3d 183 (2nd Cir. 1995)

6. Marc Fiedler is a quadriplegic moviegoer in Washington, D.C., who uses a wheelchair. American Multi-Cinema, Inc. ("AMC"), is a nationwide operator of movie theaters, one of which is the Avenue Grand, located on the basement concourse of Union Station, the principal passenger railway terminal in Washington, D.C. The only wheelchair seating available to Mr. Fiedler when he attends the Avenue Grand Theater is one of two wheelchair sites situated at the very back of the theater, in the last row of conventional seats farthest from the screen. Fiedler says that by relegating him to inferior seating in the back of the theater when he goes to see a movie at the Avenue Grand, AMC deprives him of full and equal enjoyment of the facilities to which he, as a disabled person, is entitled under the ADA. Fiedler has filed suit against AMC, the company that leases the facilities from the federal government (the owner of Union Station), which is managed by the Department of Transportation, also named as a defendant. AMC argues that the presence of a wheelchair and its occupant in the midst of able-bodied patrons in fear for their own safety could impede a mass exodus of the theater in the case of an emergency. Such seating would constitute a "direct threat to the health or safety of others," something that excuses ADA compliance. The federal government filed briefs in favor of Fiedler's position. Discuss the ADA issue, AMC's responsibility, and the actions of the federal government in support of a party including it as a defendant in his suit. What is the federal government's exposure in the case? *Fiedler v. American Multi-Cinema, Inc.*, 871 F.Supp. 35 (D.D.C. 1994)

7. David Gotlieb and Taco Bell Corporation entered into a 20-year lease on August 15, 1991 for the purpose of building a Taco Bell restaurant in Brooklyn, New York. There was a due diligence provision in the lease, and Taco Bell was permitted to cancel the lease if it could not obtain the necessary permits for the construction of the fast-food facility. Shortly after the lease was signed, community and religious groups began an organized effort to oppose the construction of the Taco Bell and any other fast-food franchises in the area. Taco Bell worked with community leaders for six months but was unable to make any progress. Taco Bell never applied for the permits but did cancel the lease. Gotlieb objected and sued Taco Bell for lost rents. What are Gotlieb's responsibilities upon Taco Bell's repudiation of the lease? What are Taco Bell's responsibilities? *Gotlieb v. Taco Bell Corporation*, 871 F.Supp. 147 (E.D.N.Y. 1994)

8. Elaine Barton entered into a five-year lease with the Mitchell Company for retail store premises for the purpose of operating her patio furniture store. The lease began November 1, 1985. In October 1984, the Mitchell Company leased the space adjoining Ms. Barton's store to Body Electric. Body Electric operated an exercise studio. Loud music, screams, shouts, and yells accompanied the operation of Body Electric during business hours. The intensity and volume of such caused the walls of Ms. Barton's space to vibrate. Paintings fell off the walls. Ms. Barton lost customers and salespeople because of the noise.

Ms. Barton complained of the noise, and Mitchell promised to add insulation to the walls. Nothing was done and the noise levels made it impossible for Ms. Barton to continue her operation. She vacated the premises on August 3, 1985. Mitchell then brought suit against Barton for rent due on the unexpired portion of the lease. Can Mitchell recover the rent? *Barton v. Mitchell Company*, 507 So.2d 148 (Fla. 1987)

9. Could a tenant who has agreed to a rental fee based on total number of square feet utilized withhold from his usual amount of rent when he discovers that the landlord has misrepresented the total amount of square feet? Or is it the tenant's responsibility to verify square footage? *MTS, Inc. v. 200 East 87th Street Associates*, 899 F. Supp. 1180 (S.D.N.Y. 1995)

10. On August 8, 1994, First Hawaiian Bank notified Colony Surf Development that its consent for any leases of mortgaged property was required under various mortgage agreements between the Bank and Colony Surf Development. On November 15, 1994, the Bank and Colony Surf Development entered into a Restructuring Agreement, which consolidated and restructured Colony Surf Development's debt. Colony Surf began negotiations for JCI to lease the Commercial Space. Colony Surf Development was represented by its agent, Radomile, in those negotiations.

Eventually, on April 27, 1995, Colony Surf Development and JCI entered into a 10-year lease. Radomile executed the lease on behalf of Colony Surf Development. Under the terms of the lease imposed by the Bank, JCI was required to construct, at its sole cost and expense, all interior improvements to the Commercial Space, the hard costs for which was not to be less than $500,000.00. The requirement was not disclosed to JCI, and the restructuring agreement with the Bank's requirements had not been recorded in the land records. JCI did put in $163,509.20 in improvements, but the Bank required more and claimed JCI was in breach. JCI filed suit for misrepresentation and asked that the lease be set aside. Colony Surf maintains that JCI was not entitled to rely on Radomile. What should the court decide? Is there a misrepresentation that allows the court to set aside the lease? Does it make any difference that the requirement on the expenditures was not public record? *First Hawaiian Bank v. Radomile*, 120 P.3d 1127 (Haw. 2005)

For research activities related to this chapter, go to our text companion website at www.thomsonedu.com/westbuslaw/jennings.

Real Estate Communities: Multiunit Interests and Owners' Associations

CHAPTER 11

Section 12.9. Window Coverings. The largest living room window of each Unit shall have a window covering, the back side of which (i.e., the side of the window covering facing the window pane and visible from the outside of the Building) will be of a color similar to Benjamin Moore #1065.

A sample rule from the CCRs of a condominium association

Since the time of Rome, Napoleon, and the Middle Ages, residential housing in limited space has been a struggle. A limited supply of land in those eras generated ownership of floors and "the subdivision of vertical space."[1] France first created multiunit housing and laws in the 1930s. When the supply of surface properties is limited, as discussed in Chapter 3, we turn to the air rights as a way of maximizing property use. Acquiring air rights has resulted in several types of home ownership in a group setting. The condominium, townhouse, cooperative, time-sharing, and recreational lease forms of housing are all answers to the home or second-home ownership dream when land is limited.

Whenever there are property owners in close proximity, as they are in multiunit housing, they need special rules for the use of their property, as well as rules that provide for rights and responsibilities. These special forms of housing create their own communities, with certain statutory controls and a complete set of private laws that govern the community and owner interaction. There is an increasing need for understanding how these private governance mechanisms work in housing ownership of all types. Planned single-family developments are often now required to have **owners' associations** in order to get municipal approval of the subdivision. These owners' or community associations are now the norm. In 1960, there were an estimated 500 owners' associations in the United States. By 1970, there were 10,000 associations, growing to 36,000 by 1980, 130,000 by 1990, 222,500 by 2000, and by 2006, the estimate

1. Warren Freedman and Jonathan B. Alter, *The Law of Condominia and Property Owners' Associations* 109–24 (1992).

was at 286,000 owners' associations, meaning that 57 million people, or roughly one in five Americans, were living under the governance of homeowners' associations.[2] In the largest metropolitan areas, more than half of new home sales are connected to an owners' association. With the rise of the gated community and planned housing developments, the regulatory framework for multiunit housing has been adopted and adapted to apply to owners and their housing, in whatever form.

This chapter first examines the forms of multiunit real estate interests and answers the following questions: What are the definitions of and distinctions among condominium, townhouse, cooperative, and time-sharing properties? How is each of the multiunit housing arrangements created? The second part of the chapter examines the governance issues in organized communities, such as in multiunit housing, in single-family housing subdivisions with owners' associations, and in private, gated communities, by looking at the following questions: What laws cover owners' associations? Who is responsible for the common areas? What can owners' associations require and control? What are the rights and responsibilities of associations and owners?

Multiunit Housing

The Applicable Laws

Each state has its own statutes to govern each of the types of multiunit real property ownership, and the statutes vary significantly from state to state. This concept of individual ownership of parts of buildings did not exist in the United States until the 1950s because of the relative ease with which a single-family dwelling could be built or purchased. Puerto Rico passed the first applicable laws in 1958 with the adoption of its Horizontal Property Act.

In 1961, Congress authorized the Federal Housing Administration (FHA) to insure mortgages on condominium units; subsequently, the attractiveness of condominiums was substantially enhanced, and state laws were passed. At the end of 1963, 39 states had some form of legislation; by 1969, all states had adopted some form of regulation on condominium and townhouse developments.

The tremendous growth in these multiunit forms of real estate ownership has resulted in some scrambling on the parts of legislatures and uniform law conferences to establish laws on these unique forms of real estate holdings. The oldest uniform law is the **Uniform Condominium Act**, which has been adopted in 10 states. States without the Uniform Condominium Act may still have legislation on ownership, but it may be referred to as **horizontal property regimes**. In some states, the laws are referred to as **horizontal property acts**.

Laws continue to evolve to address the complex issues that result from these creative forms of ownership. There is a **Model Real Estate Cooperative Act** and a **Model Real Estate Time-Share Act**. The relatively new **Uniform Common Interest Ownership Act** has been adopted in a handful of states. Its goal is to create one type of common ownership by defining a common interest in real property as one in which the owners of individual units also have an interest and/or obligation to pay for maintenance of other land areas, but it has met with resistance and concerns about ambiguity and

2. Community Associations Institute, www.caionline.org. See also, Steven Siegel, "The Public Role In Establishing Private Residential Communities: Towards A New Formulation Of Local Government Land Use Policies That Eliminates The Legal Requirements To Privatize New Communities In The United States," 38 *Urban Lawyer* 859 (2006).

overlapping statutes. All model acts that cover issues in multiunit land interests have seen only limited adoptions by the states.

The following sections cover the creation of the traditional forms of multiunit housing and generally applicable principles of law.

Condominiums

Definition and Characteristics

A **condominium** can take many physical forms: It can be a townhouse, an apartment, or part of a freestanding duplex house. Most states now allow the commercial condominium, with businesses able to enjoy horizontal property ownership in high-rise buildings. Ownership of a portion of a multi-story building allows a business to own real estate and avoid the variability and indefiniteness of lease agreements.

The physical form that the condominium takes, whether patio home or apartment-like unit, has no effect on the owner's legal status or rights. The owner owns a fee simple interest in the actual dwelling unit and is entitled to all the rights of a fee simple holder: The condominium may be sold, leased, or mortgaged and is subject to foreclosure, power of sale, and homestead rights. The owner is also given an undivided joint interest in all the common areas of the building. The owner of a condominium unit in the form of an apartment in a multistory building would have an undivided interest in areas such as the halls, stairs, lobby, and any recreational facilities.

Although the condominium unit owner has an interest in the common areas, only the actual dwelling unit may be mortgaged or pledged, and creditors of the unit owner may foreclose only on a per-unit basis, not on the entire unit. The use and decoration of the unit is controlled by bylaws, CC&Rs, and owners' associations (see later in the chapter for more discussion).

Creation of Condominium

A condominium development must be created according to statutory processes. If condominium developers do not follow the statutory requirements, they have not created the proper land interests for the owners.

Conversion Restrictions

Because of the large number of conversions of apartments to condominiums, most states have regulations requiring minimum notice periods before conversions can take place. The purpose of **conversion restrictions** is to give tenants the opportunity to decide whether to purchase the condominium unit in which they live or to move. The typical notice requirement under conversion statutes is 120 days. Also, most statutes provide that tenants who decline the opportunity to purchase the condominium unit must be given additional time to find other housing before they are required to end their tenancy. Many conversion statutes require that landlords honor the remainder of the tenants' leases.

Declaration of Condominium or Master Deed

The prerequisite for the creation of a condominium development is the fee simple ownership of a lot or lots of an existing building or buildings. The fee simple ownership may be held by an individual, several individuals, or a corporation. The owner (or owners) begins the condominium development by drafting and recording a master deed or a **declaration of condominium** (called a **declaration of horizontal**

property regime and covenants in some states). The **master deed** is, in effect, a description of the subdivision of the building. Every deed to every condominium unit owner will then refer to this master deed for a legal description of the unit. In addition to accomplishing the subdivision of the building, the declaration also covers the following:

1. Legal description of the property.
2. Detailed description of the building or buildings making up the complex, and the number of stories, basements, and units.
3. Mailing address of each unit and a physical description including the number of rooms, method of access, and other identifiable characteristics.
4. Detailed description of the common areas.
5. Limitations on the use of common areas.
6. Monetary value of the building and each unit.
7. How votes are to be assigned—per unit basis or per value basis.
8. Restrictions on land use; for example, all-adult restrictions.
9. Name and address of legal representative for the development.
10. Voting procedures.
11. Methods for amending the declaration of condominium.

In many states, the declaration or master deed for a condominium project may be called a **declaration of covenants, conditions, and restrictions (CC&Rs** or **CCRs)**.

Regardless of the name, the document that is filed has a certain permanence to it. Only by following amendment procedures can there be variations and changes from the original declaration.

Incorporation

Generally, most condominium projects are incorporated for a number of reasons, including the convenience of having the common areas owned by one entity instead of carrying title in the names of all unit owners, as well as the protection against personal liability of the unit owners for injuries in the common areas (discussed later in this chapter). But corporate ownership also creates a method of governance through shareholder voting (also covered later in the chapter under owners' associations). When disputes arise, there are far more legal precedents in corporate law than there are rights and procedures afforded under a declaration of condominium.

Deeds

Once the master deed is recorded, each unit owner is granted his or her interest through an individual deed. Condominium deeds must meet all requirements of property deeds (see Chapter 12) and should include the following specifics:

1. Legal description (includes a reference to the declaration of condominium and where it is recorded)
2. Mailing address
3. Use restrictions (may be a reference to another document)
4. Title warranties

Cooperatives

Nature of Cooperatives

Ownership of a cooperative is different from a fee simple ownership of real estate. A **cooperative** ownership is an undivided joint interest in the land and buildings that make up the cooperative. Ownership is most likely held by the cooperative as a non-profit organization, with each cooperative unit assigned a certain number of shares in the corporation. A cooperative unit dweller does not own a real estate interest but rather a share or shares in a corporation that owns the entire complex. In essence, the corporation of which the owner is a shareholder is the landlord for all units in the cooperative.

Another distinction between cooperative ownership and traditional fee simple ownership is the possibility that the cooperative shareholder may be restricted in the transfer of shares. Although cooperative unit owners may be free to sell their leasehold interests or shares, they may be required to obtain cooperative board approval or even offer their interests first to the corporation. They may also be restricted in how the property can be disposed of upon their death. New York City is filled with urban legends about co-op board denials to potential buyers. Co-op boards have the right to turn down any buyer, so long as the board does not discriminate on the basis of race or religion.

ETHICAL ISSUE

Co-op board denials have included one handed to former president Richard Nixon, after he resigned in disgrace following the Watergate political scandal. Other celebrities that have been denied by co-op boards include Madonna, Gloria Vanderbilt, Carly Simon, Mariah Carey, and Calvin Klein. The Dakota building, the location of John and Yoko Lennon's home and where Lennon was shot and killed, has other famous occupants (Lauren Bacall, Leonard Bernstein, Rudolph Nureyev, and Mia Farrow). But it is also famous for its public battle with actors Antonio Banderas and Melanie Griffith, who were turned down by the board when they tried to buy a unit. Banderas and Griffith called the decision "arbitrary" and "arrogant" and accused the board of "narrowness of vision." While the actions of the co-op boards in their denials are legal, are they ethical? What reasons could boards give for not wanting actors as residents?

"New York Apartment Buyers Face Powerful Co-Op Boards," *The Epoch Times*, January 27–February 2, 2005, p. 13.

In the following case, the court deals with the issue of the nature of ownership in a cooperative.

KADERA V. SUPERIOR COURT AND CONSOLIDATED COOPERATIVE OF SCOTTSDALE EAST, INC.

931 P.2d 1067 (Az. App. 1996)

FACTS

On January 22, 1993, Krag and Erin Kadera (petitioners) purchased one share of stock in Consolidated Cooperative of Scottsdale East, Inc. (respondent), from a former shareholder, paying $21,000 for their share. The Kaderas were required to sign a form designating how they were taking title to their interest, which they did in joint tenancy with right of survivorship.

When the Kaderas took possession of the unit, they were required to pay a $200.00 per month "carrying charge." This figure represented a proportionate one-twelfth of the cooperative's annual expenses.

After the Kaderas moved into their unit, they were served with a Notice of Default, Intention to Terminate Agreement, and Demand for Possession of the Premises. The cooperative, through its manager, alleged that the Kaderas had violated the nonfinancial terms of their occupancy agreement because they had a nonrelative living in their unit and were operating a babysitting service from it.

On August 16, 1995, the cooperative filed a forcible entry and detainer action seeking to have the Kaderas evicted from their unit. The Kaderas claimed they were not tenants but owners, and could not be evicted under landlord/tenant law. The trial court denied the Kaderas' motion to dismiss and they appealed.

JUDICIAL OPINION

Grant, Judge. The legislative purpose behind the Arizona Residential Landlord and Tenant Act ("ARLTA") is expressed in section 33–1302: ARLTA was passed both to "simplify, clarify, modernize and revise the law governing the rental of dwelling units and the rights and obligations of landlord and tenant," and to "encourage landlord and tenant to maintain and improve the quality of housing."

ARLTA undisputedly is inapplicable to the facts of this case. The legislature unequivocally excluded from the reach of ARLTA a residential occupant who is also an "owner of a proprietary lease in a cooperative."

Respondent Corporation does not argue it is entitled to exercise the ARLTA provisions; rather, it argues it is entitled to bring an action for forcible entry and detainer against Petitioners under A.R.S. section 12–1171 *et seq.* The forcible entry and detainer proceeding contained in this statute applies to a "holdover by a person to whom lands, tenements, or real property were let." Section 12–1171 *et seq.* applies only to landlord-tenant relationships.

While the legislature authorized the use of summary proceedings in the residential landlord-tenant context, it excluded a holder of a proprietary lease in a cooperative from the reach of these proceedings.

The legislature recognized that although the cooperative is a hybrid property arrangement wherein the line between ownership and leasehold blurs, the cooperator has a real property ownership interest. The term "proprietary lease," used frequently to identify the relationship between the cooperator and cooperative corporation, is oxymoronic. The cooperative corporation may indeed hold title to the real property, nevertheless, the cooperator also owns a real property interest. Precisely because the legislature recognized that hybrid property arrangements carry with them ownership interests, section 33–1308(6) of ARLTA excludes from its reach not only cooperatives, but also condominiums.

Petitioners argue since ARLTA's special detainer action, which incorporates section 12–1177, excludes cooperatives neither proceeding is appropriate. We agree. To hold otherwise would give cooperators far fewer protections than tenants are guaranteed under ARLTA. Surely the legislature did not intend this result. While an ordinary tenant may forfeit a deposit upon breach, the cooperator has considerably more at stake because the total investment is so much greater. Thus, we find ARLTA and summary proceedings inappropriate in the context of residential cooperative housing.

Respondent Corporation argues that since it has title to the real property, Petitioners cannot own a real property interest. We disagree. Respondent Corporation was established for the sole purpose of selling real property interests on a non-profit basis in the cooperative housing complex it owns, and Petitioners purchased such an interest. It was not necessary that title pass in order for Petitioners to have a real property interest. Moreover, the fact that this interest in land was not conveyed by a real estate sales contract is not fatal to the sale.

This court has clearly stated that with respect to real estate sales, we will not exalt form over substance.

With the exception of a title transfer, there are all of the indications of a residential real estate transaction here. Petitioners chose the location and neighborhood in which they wanted to live. No doubt their decision was partially based on Respondent Corporation's description of the benefits of cooperative ownership over renting in its "Introduction to Living at Consolidated Cooperative of Scottsdale East, Inc.":

Membership in Consolidated Co-Ops provides the member with many advantages of home ownership but without the mortgage liability and accompanying responsibilities. The most often cited advantage of Co-op living is economic. Co-ops are founded on the premise that cooperation leads to better services at lower cost and Co-op charges are usually lower than those for similar rental units. Cooperators pay actual housing costs, not a landlord's profit. Pride of ownership and sense of community also contribute to reduced housing costs.

Co-Op [sic] *housing offers its members the opportunity to help determine the kind of community they will live in, the quality of services it will provide and the way it will develop. Many members see this degree of control over their housing circumstances as an even greater advantage* than the continuing financial bargain in housing that Co-ops offer. [Emphasis added.]

Respondent argues that because Petitioners are its shareholders, they have no right, title, or interest in corporate property, and therefore they may not interfere with Respondent.

Given that Petitioners paid a large initial down payment and entered into a contract which requires that they pay on a monthly basis the principal and interest on the mortgage, as well as other operating costs, their real property interest is clearly in the nature of an ownership or fee interest.

When the legislature held that cooperatives are to be excluded from ARLTA, it excluded cooperatives from all summary proceedings, including those brought for forcible entry and detainer under A.R.S. section 12–1177 *et seq.*

Thus, we hold that a cooperative corporation's remedy for breach by a cooperator/shareholder lies in Arizona's real estate law.[3]

Reversed and Remanded.

CASE QUESTIONS

1. What interest did the Kaderas acquire?
2. Why did the cooperative want them out?
3. Can the cooperative use landlord–tenant law on the eviction of tenants?
4. Will the Kaderas be able to stay?
5. Who pays for the costs of this litigation?

Creation of a Cooperative

The following sections explain the basic documents needed for the creation of a cooperative.

Articles of Incorporation and Evidence of Incorporation

Since ownership of a cooperative is really ownership of an interest in a corporation, the first documents needed are the incorporation papers. Most states do require the filing of articles of incorporation before a certificate of incorporation or corporate charter is issued. The following information is generally required for incorporation:

1. Corporate name
2. Purpose of the corporation (cooperative)
3. Share structure, including voting rights and transferability
4. Name of legal agent or representative
5. Structure of the board of directors and makeup on initial board
6. Provisions for amendment to the articles

Bylaws

The **bylaws** for a cooperative are similar to those for both corporations and condominiums: Their purpose is to specify operating procedures. The bylaws provide the details for meetings, including place, time, notice, quorums, and voting requirements. Finally, the bylaws contain the procedures for transferring ownership rights to cooperative members and usually provide instructions for the proprietary lease.

Proprietary Lease

A **proprietary lease** is very similar to an ordinary lease, covering many of the topics and issues that arise in the landlord–tenant relationship. However, the following factors distinguish the two:

1. Length: If the proprietary lease provides for a termination date at all, the date will be well into the future. Otherwise, the termination of the lease is tied to the transfer of the tenant's interest in the cooperative corporation.
2. Rent: A proprietary lease has no provision for rent; instead, the tenant pays a maintenance fee. These maintenance fees can be increased and the lease may even provide for percentage increases according to a cost-of-living scale.

The proprietary lease also covers contingencies, such as the owner's option to sell if maintenance fees increase substantially and the owner's rights if the cooperative unit is uninhabitable for a period of time.

3. The decision was cited as valid Arizona law in *United Effort Plan Trust v. Holm,* 101 P.3d 641 (Az. App. 2004). For decisions contra, see *Quality Management Services, Inc. v. Banker,* 685 N.E.2d 367 (Ill. App. 1997) and *Gvozdanovic v. Woodford Corp.,* 742 N.E.2d 1145 (Ohio App. 2000).

Townhouses

Nature of Townhouses

The owner of a **townhouse** owns the land on which the townhouse is located, the actual dwelling unit, and an undivided joint interest in the common elements of the development such as a swimming pool or clubhouse. Actual land ownership distinguishes this form of multiunit housing from the others, where there is simply ownership of space.

Creation of Townhouses

As with the other forms of multiunit housing, there are specific requirements for creating townhouse ownership.

Declaration of Covenants, Conditions, and Restrictions

Similar to a master deed or declaration of condominium, the declaration of covenants, conditions, and restrictions (CC&Rs or CCRs) is the first step in creating a townhouse development. The CCRs contain all of the rights and responsibilities of the individual owners. Since the CCRs are recorded, everyone is presumed to know their content. Most states now have a requirement that buyers sign off on receipt of a copy of the CCRs. Once recorded, the CCRs serve as constructive notice of the regulations of and restrictions in the development. All-adult restrictions are often part of the CCRs. In the event of a conflict, the CCRs are the final authority for correcting ambiguities or clarifying legal rights.

Articles of Incorporation

The decision to incorporate is discretionary in some states as a more convenient way of holding title. Other states require that a corporation must be formed to hold title to common areas, and each owner is given a certain percentage share of the corporation.

Bylaws

The bylaws deal with the operation of the townhouse development, covering issues such as repairs and maintenance and compliance with all the CCR provisions. Although the bylaws set up voting procedures, such procedures must be consistent with the articles of incorporation to be valid. The bylaws may also establish various committees to aid in the enforcement of restrictions—an architectural control committee, for example. More details on bylaws appear later in the chapter in the discussion of owners' associations.

Regulations

The purpose of the regulations in a townhouse development is the same as the purpose of those in a condominium development: to keep common facilities in repair and reasonably available to residents in the development.

Time-Sharing Interests

Nature of Time-Sharing Ownership

In resort areas, the concept of **time-sharing** ownership or recreational ownership has become popular. The owner of a time-share owns a fee simple interest but can exercise the right of possession only for a limited time each year and during the same period of time each year. For example, a time-share may be the right to the use of a two-bedroom apartment in San Diego from June 1 to June 8 every year in perpetuity. This right of use may be transferred *inter vivos* or by will or intestate succession. The limitation on the property is the time of use. In addition to the right to use the dwelling unit, the owner is also given the right to use all common areas, including any recreational facilities such as pools, game rooms, and saunas.

Time-sharing units require clarification of whether a unit owner will always have a particular unit at a given time or whether a unit will simply be available for the buyer's use at the time purchased. The time-share regimen should specify how the time units are divided, the length of each owner's time unit, and whether a specific unit was assigned. A sample length-of-use clause appears below to illustrate the complexity of this task:

Week No. 1 is the seven consecutive days commencing at noon on the first Saturday of each year and continues till noon on the following Saturday. Week No. 2 is the seven consecutive days next succeeding Week No. 1. Successive weeks up to and including Week No. 51 are computed in a like manner. Week No. 52 contains the seven consecutive days next succeeding Week 51 together with any additional days not otherwise assigned continuing until the commencement of Week No. 1 of the following year. From Martin, "Timesharing in Colorado," 11 *The Colorado Lawyer* 2804 (1982)

Creation of Time-Sharing Interests

A time-sharing interest may take the form of a recreational lease, a proprietary lease, or a limited fee simple interest. A **recreational lease** is a financing device that allows the lessee to spread out over time the payment for use of another's recreational property. Generally, these recreational leases have rent-escalation clauses that increase the rent according to some scale over the perpetual period of the lease. The lease may be a true lease with a landlord–tenant relationship between the parties, or its character may depend more strictly on the terms of the agreement. Ninety-nine-year leases or those without a specific termination date are more likely to be proprietary leases for a cooperative form of ownership. Leases where the rental payment is determined according to a formula that is based on expenses of operation are also more likely to be proprietary leases for a cooperative form of ownership.

Time-sharing interests may also be interests in perpetuity but limited in use to a specified period during each year. It is possible for a time-sharing interest to be a fee simple interest with limited use rights.

The **vacation license** is an arrangement in which the developer retains a fee simple interest in the property and grants licenses for use for certain periods during the year. This type of arrangement is considered the sale of securities by the Securities and Exchange Commission (SEC) and is subject to securities registration requirements.

In some areas, time-sharing owners have developed time-sharing networks in which the owners trade off interests in one location for interests in another. In any of the arrangements, the documents should specify responsibilities and the liabilities for the cost of maintaining the premises.

> ***Practical Tip***
>
> *Townhouses and condominium and cooperative buildings may look very much the same. Sellers, buyers, lenders, and brokers should verify through the legal documents associated with a multiunit interest what type of ownership rights exist. Appearances are not controlling in terms of the rights afforded. For example, in* Orchard Glen East v. Bd. of Sup'rs, *492 S.E.2d 150 (Va. 1997), what looked like an apartment complex was really a condominium and its owner would pay real property taxes.*

Many states simply regulate their time-sharing properties through their condominium laws (California, Colorado, Maine, New Hampshire, New Mexico, Pennsylvania, Rhode Island, Utah, and West Virginia). Other states have enacted separate statutes to govern time-sharing projects (Arizona, Connecticut, Florida, Hawaii, Louisiana, Nebraska, New Mexico, South Carolina, Tennessee, and Virginia).

Hybrids

In some states, hybrid forms of ownership can be found under various labels such as **patio homes, garden homes**, and **attached homes**. In these hybrid forms, the owners may own the land and the entire dwelling but will have a party wall agreement for the joint wall between properties. The laws governing these hybrids vary from state to state. In some states, joint wall properties are treated as townhouses, while in others they are labeled condominiums.

Managing Close Quarters: The Issues of Owners' Associations

Onwers' associations are necessities in condominiums, co-ops, and townhomes, and their creation runs parallel with the conversion or creation of the multiunit interest. However, with the increases in planned communities and gated communities, the creation of an owners' association has also run parallel to a builder obtaining approval for the creation of a single-family home community and the fee simple ownership buyers will hold. In fact, owners' associations are often called a substitute for zoning in that they regulate the appearance of and types of structures in their communities.

The law on owners' associations is still developing and varies significantly from state to state. However, there are some developing uniform laws, at least portions of which can be found in state statutes. In addition to the provisions in the Uniform Condominium Act and the Model Real Estate Cooperative Act, mentioned earlier, there is also the Uniform Planned Community Act (UPCA) that addresses many of the issues of owners' associations that are common to multiunit owners' associations. There are three basic issues in all owners' associations: the structure for operating the association or the governance and authority issues, the interpretation and application of rules in the exercise of authority of owners' associations, and, finally, the liability of the association to owners and third parties.

GOVERNANCE: Running Communities Smoothly and Consistently

How do You Get an Owners' Association?

An owners' association is created simultaneously with the community.[4] The documents that are part of the creation of a community include the declaration of the land interest (as with the condominium declaration); the plat maps and deeds (including the CCRs); and then a series of documents that serve to create the owners' association as a corportation, including the articles of incorporation and the bylaws. These nonprofit corporation associations have three common characteristics: every property owner (regardless of the type of ownership) is automatically a member of the association; the individual unit or lot owners hold equal title to the common areas; and all of the individual owners are required to pay annual and/or monthly fees to their associations.

4. For ease of reference, the term "community" as used here includes condos, co-ops, townhomes, and gated and planned neighborhoods.

In the initial sale of the units in the communities, the developer/builder holds majority control of the corporation and, as a result, the owners' association. That control is then turned over to owners as the percentage of property owners exceeds the percentage of units or lots owned by the developer/builder. The presence of the corporate structure not only allows that transfer; it provides a means for the association to be run fairly and to take steps that ensure the quality of the community. One writer has described the role of owner's associations as follows: "(1) it maintains common areas; (2) it arranges for delivery of services; (3) it taxes members through regular and special assessments to pay for amenities and services; and (4) it protects neighborhood aesthetics and real estate values by enforcing the declaration."[5] Areas of contention and litigation include determining how much authority the association has and whether the association is acting properly in its contracting and enforcement.

Who is in Charge? The Association Board

The heart of association governance, as with all corporations, can be found in the articles of incorporation. The articles provide for the election of a board of directors, as elected representatives of the owners charged with the governance of the association and the community. The board will consist of owners in the community. In carrying out its responsibilities, the association board will take care of the four areas of association purposes noted earlier, responsibilities that can include everything from maintenance of common areas to policies on gate access to landscaping decisions.

The association board authority is limited by the powers granted in the declaration. The declaration includes the rights and restrictions that apply to all who purchase units or land in the community, and because the declaration is recorded, those rights and responsibilities run with the land. Under planned community laws now in effect in many states, there are mandatory rights and obligations for all planned communities and they are incorporated by statute.

The declaration can cover everything from the type of roof to the amount of time owners have to get landscaping. For example, they have 90 days from closing to install landscaping and 60 days from closing to have permanent window coverings such as curtains, blinds, or shutters. Many of the powers necessary for operating an association, including the right of assessment, cannot be put in place by the board after-the-fact because buyers purchased their interest in reliance on reasonable interpretation of the declaration. Under the association reform statutes being adopted by many states, bylaws and board resolutions creating new rights and obligations that were not in the declaration are subject to a judicial review for reasonableness. The following case deals with the issue of an unclear declaration and attempts by a board to remedy the lack of authority.

Armstrong v. Ledges Homeowners Association

633 S.E.2d 78 (N.C. 2006)

FACTS

Robert and Vivian Armstrong and others (Petitioners) own lots in The Ledges of Hidden Hills subdivision (Respondents). The Ledges was developed in 1988 by Vogel Development Corporation. Forty-nine lots are set out along two main roads that form a Y shape. There are four *cul de sacs.* The plat designates the roads as "public roads," which are maintained by the State. There are no common areas or amenities in The Ledges.

5. Brian Jason Fleming, "Regulation of Political Signs in Private Homeowner Associations: A New approach," 59 *Vanderbilt Law Review* 571, at 581 (2006).

The Declaration filed by Vogel did not contain any authorization for assessments. However, Vogel later decided to construct a lighted sign on private property in the Sunlight Ridge Drive right-of-way. Sunlight Ridge Drive is the entry road to the Ledges. Because lighting the sign required ongoing payment of a utility bill, Vogel included the following additional language in subsequent conveyances to the buyers in The Ledges:

The grantor herein contemplates the establishment of a non-profit corporation to be known as The Ledges of Hidden Hills Homeowners Association, and by acceptance of this deed the grantees agree to become and shall automatically so become members of said Homeowners Association when so formed by said grantor; and said grantees agree to abide by the corporate charter, bylaws, and rules and regulations of said Homeowners Association and agree to pay prorata [sic] charges and assessments which may be levied by said Homeowners Association when so formed. *Until the above contemplated Homeowners Association is formed or in the event the same is not formed, the grantor reserves the right to assess the above-described lot and the owners thereof an equal pro-rata* [sic] *share of the common expense* for electrical street lights and electrical subdivision entrance sign lights *and any other common utility expense for various lots within the Subdivision.*

This language appears in Armstrong's and the other owners' deeds, along with a reference to the Declaration.

Articles of Incorporation for the Ledges Homeowners' Association (Association) were not filed with the Secretary of State until 20 September 1994. The Articles provide that the Association is incorporated for the purposes of "upkeep, maintenance and beautification of the common amenities of [the Ledges]," "enforcement of the restrictive covenants of [the Ledges]," and "engag[ing] in any other lawful activities allowed for non-profit corporations under the laws of the State of North Carolina."

Sometime before the Association's first annual meeting in 1995, the Association's three-member Board of Directors adopted bylaws. These bylaws set forth the Association's powers and duties, which included the operation, improvement, and maintenance of common areas; determination of funds needed for operation, administration, maintenance, and management of the Ledges; collection of assessments and common expenses; and employment and dismissal of personnel.

At the first annual meeting, the bylaws were amended to provide that the Association would have a lien on the lot of any owner who failed to pay an assessment. Thereafter, the Association began assessing lot owners for the bills incurred for lighting the Ledges entrance sign. Additionally, the Association assessed owners for mowing the roadside on individual private lots along Sunlight Ridge Drive, for snow removal from subdivision roads, and for operating and legal expenses. The annual electrical bill for the sign is less than 60 cents per lot per month or approximately seven dollars and 20 cents per year; however, the Association has billed lot owners total assessments of approximately eighty to one hundred dollars per year.

On 18 June 2003, Armstrong sent an e-mail to the President of the Association, Marvin Katz, challenging the validity of these assessments and asking for a refund of $160.

At a meeting held on 16 July 2003, the board amended the Association bylaws again, greatly expanding the entity's enumerated powers and duties. The amended bylaws provided that the Association shall have the power to "[i]mpose charges for late payment of assessments and, after notice and an opportunity to be heard, levy reasonable fines not to exceed One Hundred Fifty Dollars ($150.00) per violation (on a daily basis for continuing violations) of the Restrictive Covenants, Bylaws, and Rules and Regulations of the Association pursuant to Section 47F-3–107.1 of the North Carolina Planned Community Act."

On 1 August 2003, the Armstrongs sent a letter to the Association requesting termination of their membership. On 8 August 2003, petitioners L.A. and E. Ann Moore requested termination of their Association membership as well. In their letter, the Moores stated:

We chose this particular property last year for several reasons. After a thorough search of Western North Carolina and the Hendersonville/Brevard area, in particular, we decided expressly against living in a gated community with "all the amenities." Golf courses, swimming pools and clubhouses are not our choice for daily living. Walking trails, while enjoyable and convenient, are but another source of assessment we don't need.

The Ledges appeared to be the answer to our desires, and until recent events we've been sure of it. The current Covenants are more restrictive than any other area in which we've resided, but not unreasonably so. While receptive to OPEN discussion of a small change or two, we are adamant in our opposition to the expressed plan of The Board to turn us into a Planned Community.[Emphasis added.]

The Armstrongs filed suit to have the assessments declared invalid. Both sides moved for summary judgment. The court granted the Ledges' motion for summary judgment and dismissed the Armstrongs' complaint. The court of appeals affirmed and the Armstrongs appealed.

JUDICIAL OPINION

Wainwright, Justice. We hold that amendments to a declaration of restrictive covenants must be reasonable. Reasonableness may be ascertained from the language of the declaration, deeds, and plats, together with other objective circumstances surrounding the parties' bargain, including the nature and character of the community.

Although petitioners' deeds contain an additional covenant requiring lot owners to pay a pro rata share of the utility bills incurred from lighting the entrance sign, it is clear from the language of this provision, together with the Declaration, the plat, and the circumstances surrounding installation of the sign, that the parties did not intend this provision to confer *unlimited* powers of assessment on the Association. The sole purpose of this additional deed covenant was to ensure that the developer did not remain responsible for lighting the entrance sign after the lots were conveyed. Payment of the utility bill is the single shared obligation contained in petitioners' deeds, and each lot owner's pro rata share of this expense totals approximately seven dollars and twenty cents per year.

In a community that is not subject to the North Carolina Planned Community Act, the powers of a homeowners' association are contractual and are limited to those powers granted to it by the declaration. [The North Carolina Planned Community Act was not in effect at the time of the Ledges creation and is, therefore, inapplicable.]

In the same way that the powers of a homeowners' association are limited to those powers granted to it by the original declaration, an amendment should not exceed the purpose of the original declaration.

In the case *sub judice*, petitioners argue that the affirmative covenants contained in their deeds authorize only nominal assessments for the maintenance of a lighted sign at the subdivision entrance; thus, the Association's subsequent amendment of the Declaration to authorize broad general assessments to "promot[e] the safety, welfare, recreation, health, common benefit, and enjoyment of the residents of Lots in The Ledges as may be more specifically authorized from time to time by the Board" is invalid and unenforceable. Respondents contend that the Declaration of Restrictive Covenants expressly permits the homeowners' association to amend the covenants; thus, *any* amendment that is adopted in accordance with association by-laws and is neither illegal nor against public policy is valid and enforceable, regardless of its breadth or subject matter. We hold that a provision authorizing a homeowners' association to amend a declaration of covenants does not permit amendments of unlimited scope; rather, every amendment must be *reasonable* in light of the contracting parties' original intent.

A number of other states considering amendments to the founding documents of common interest communities have also applied a reasonableness standard.

Here, petitioners purchased lots in a small residential neighborhood with public roads, no common areas, and no amenities. The neighborhood consists simply of forty-nine private lots set out along two main roads and four *cul de sacs*. Given the nature of this community, it makes sense that the Declaration itself did not contain any affirmative covenants authorizing assessments. Neither the Declaration nor the plat shows any source of common expense.

Although petitioners' deeds contain an additional covenant requiring lot owners to pay a pro rata share of the utility bills incurred from lighting the entrance sign, it is clear from the language of this provision, together with the Declaration, the plat, and the circumstances surrounding installation of the sign, that the parties did not intend this provision to confer *unlimited* powers of assessment on the Association. The sole purpose of this additional deed covenant was to ensure that the developer did not remain responsible for lighting the entrance sign after the lots were conveyed. Payment of the utility bill is the single shared obligation contained in petitioners' deeds, and each lot owner's pro rata share of this expense totals approximately seven dollars and twenty cents per year.

For these reasons, we determine that the Association's amendment to the Declaration which authorizes broad assessments "for the general purposes of promoting the safety, welfare, recreation, health, common benefit, and enjoyment of the residents of Lots in The Ledges as may be more specifically authorized from time to time by the Board" is unreasonable. The amendment grants the Association practically unlimited power to assess lot owners and is contrary to the original intent of the contracting parties.

Reversed.

CASE QUESTIONS

1. Was there a right of assessment in the declaration?
2. What factors does the court point to that indicate the right of assessment was not contemplated in the creation of this community?
3. What is the standard for allowing boards to change the powers given in the declaration?

CONSIDER 11.1

Puamana was established in 1968 as a Hawaii non-profit corporation. Several owners constructed "pop outs" that encroached onto the common areas owned by Puamana. The term "pop out" refers to an expansion of the dwelling by which the exterior walls are pushed out toward the area beneath the eaves of the building structure. The Board of Directors of Puamana initially assumed that the "pop outs" remained within the boundaries of the respective units because they did not protrude beyond the drip lines of the eaves. However, the Board subsequently discovered that the unit boundaries coincided with the original position of the exterior walls of the dwellings and that the "pop outs" encroached onto the common areas even though they remained under the eaves.

Dale W. Hillman was one of the unit owners desiring to construct a "pop out," and he proposed to extend nearly all of his 66-foot exterior wall two and one-half feet outward toward the eaves, creating an additional 165 square feet of floor space. The Board rejected Hillman's proposal unless and until the CC&Rs could be amended to expressly permit encroachments onto the common areas. On October 19, 1999, the Board recorded a document entitled "Amendment of Puamana Declaration, Covenants, Conditions and Restrictions." The amended CC&Rs authorized the Board to approve "minor encroachments" of up to 200 square feet per unit. Allan and Barbara Lee and other owners brought suit challenging the authority of the board to amend the CC&Rs to allow the "pop outs." The Lees also claimed that they enjoyed a scenic view of Kaho'olawe from their third-floor loft, which was blocked when their neighbor, Mark Ciaburri, impermissibly constructed his own third-floor loft. Did the board have the authority to allow the "pop out" through the amendment? In thinking about your answer, apply the tests of intent and the standards for change from the *Armstrong* case. *Lee v. Puamana Community Association*, 128 P.3d 874 (Hawaii 2006).

Board Operations: What can the Board Do and How Much Authority Does it Have?

As noted in the *Armstrong* case, the board and association can adopt bylaws, or the rules and procedures for running the association/corporation, subject to the powers granted and intent of the association and community formation documents.

The bylaws are generally drafted by the developer but may be adopted by the unit owners once the developer has sold all the units, lots, or houses. The bylaws should contain rules for the following areas:

1. Composition of a governing board or committee for the association and the methods and requirements for election of its members.
2. Details for meetings, such as place, time, notice, quorum, requirements, and voting processes.
3. Procedures for day-to-day maintenance authorization, equipment replacements, and routine repairs.
4. Amount of any association fees to be collected from unit owners for maintenance of common areas, and so on; the methods for collecting such fees; and the penalties for late payment or nonpayment. (See the discussion on enforcement for authority of associations for collection.)
5. Procedures for amending the bylaws.
6. Use restrictions, such as adult-only restrictions and limitations on transfer and rental.

CONSIDER 11.2

Louis Croce purchased 49 units in the Glenwood Park condominiums at a foreclosure sale in the mid-1970s. Through subsequent acquisitions, he was able to purchase more of the units and now owns 58 of the 60 units in the complex. Mr. Croce sent out a notice to all owners and lessees that he was raising the association fees from $30 to $160 per month. Josephine Artesani, one of the owners, says that she knew of no association meeting in which the increase was discussed. Can Mr. Croce raise the fees in this manner? *Artesani v. Glenwood Park Condominium*, 750 A.2d 961 (R.I. 2000)

Regulations

Regulations designed to ensure the smooth functioning of the community are valid. Regulations can cover items such as pets and the use of the pool, laundry room, and other recreational rooms and equipment. The bylaws should contain provisions for the development of and amendment to the regulations.

Enforcement

While boards have the authority to propose changes in the bylaws and regulations, they must still follow board processes and procedures and they cannot exceed unreasonably the authority given in the declaration. There are several other areas of considerable contention and litigation in owners' associations, and the following section on enforcement deals with those issues.

Enforcement tools are limited by both the legal documents of the community as well as, in most states, by statute. If those tools are not established as part of the bylaws, the association cannot use them. An effective homeowners' association is responsible for dealing with issues of noise, property use, property upkeep, and maintenance of the common areas. However, condominium homeowners' associations frequently end up in litigation because of the need for balance in managing common living conditions and individual property ownership. The amount of litigation related to homeowners' associations, particularly in condominium developments, has skyrocketed since 1990. Many states have passed Planned Community Acts (PCA) that establish the authority and rights of owners and boards. Listing the rights, responsibilities, and limits of associations and owners in these statutes has served as a way to decrease the contentious litigation surrounding associations as they provide the courts with definitive statutory guidance.

Standards for Association Enforcement

The courts use the following steps to determine whether they will uphold association actions.

Practical Tip

For avoiding litigation on condominium rules, the following tips are important:

1. *Enforce all the rules quickly and uniformly. Singling out owners for enforcement will give courts a reason for setting aside the rule and the enforcement.*
2. *Try other avenues for enforcement such as loss of voting privileges, ongoing but minimal fines, and loss of privileges on a temporary basis.*
3. *Be certain the rules are formally adopted and properly recorded as necessary.*
4. *Maintain minutes and records of meetings when rules are adopted so that a court could examine the intent of the owners and their governing body in adopting the rules.*
5. *Include a cost/benefit analysis of the rule in the adoption process.*
6. *Provide somewhere in the rules that attorneys' fees are recoverable when there is litigation.*

1. Whatever is being enforced must be grounded in law or the association's documents of creation or operation, either at the inception of the association or by vote of the owners, according to proper processes.
2. There must be enforcement authority given in the declaration, the CC&Rs, or by statute. A homeowners' association cannot take away rights given in the CCRs. Those CCRs are actually property rights and cannot simply be voted away at a board meeting for the association. For example, in *Woodside Village Condominium v. Jahren*, 754 So.2d 831 (Fla. App. 2000), the court declared an amendment to the CCRs of a condominium project void. The amendment would have prohibited owners of the units from leasing their units for more than nine months in any 12-month period. Originally, the CCRs provided that the unit owners could not lease or rent without prior approval for one year or less. While the court noted that the goal of the homeowners' association was a noble one of keeping the value of their properties from deteriorating due to too many tenants, the association simply could not change a property right those owners had through the CCRs when they purchased their units. They had a right to lease their real property interest and that interest was being partially taken away without the process required for taking a real property interest. *Shorewood West Condominium Ass'n v. Sadri*, 992 P.2d 1008 (Wash. 2000).
3. The substance of the rule or policy that the association wants to enforce must be valid. In determining validity, the courts use one of the three following tests.
   a. The reasonableness test, which examines both the rule or policy that is to be enforced and how it is to be enforced. The types of rules include everything from restricting hours for common area use to restrictions on pets.
   b. The business judgment rule test, which allows courts to follow corporation law and rely on the governing body of an association to make appropriate choices so long as those choices and decisions are made according to a valid process and in good faith.
   c. The contract law test, in which the courts treat the owners and the governing body as parties to a contract and, absent the usual contract defenses, they are free to contract. Under this test courts do not intervene in association governance.

Associations generally face three types of litigation: rules enforcement, appearance/modification issues, and use issues that carry constitutional questions.

Enforcement of Association Rules

Rules must have a purpose tied to benefiting the community; they must be reasonable, and they must be applied in egalitarian fashion. The following case is one example of a court facing a rules issue with the governing body of a condominium association and an owner who finds the rule oppressive. The case is widely cited, but there are similar cases that have reached the opposite decision because of the varying application of the tests discussed above.

NAHRSTEDT V. LAKESIDE VILLAGE CONDOMINIUM ASSOCIATION, INC.

878 P.2d 1275 (Cal. 1994)

FACTS

Natore Nahrstedt owned a condominium in a 530-unit complex called Lakeside Village in Culver City, California. The 530 units are spread throughout 12 separate three-story buildings. The residents share common lobbies and hallways in addition to laundry and trash facilities.

The Lakeside Village has CC&Rs that were included in the developer's declaration recorded with the Los Angeles County Recorder on April 17, 1978, at the inception of the development project. The CC&Rs include a pet restriction as follows:

No animals (which shall mean dogs and cats), livestock, reptiles or poultry shall be kept in any unit. [Domestic fish and birds are excluded.]

In January 1988, Nahrstedt (plaintiff) moved into her Lakeside Village condominium with her three cats. When the Association learned of the cats' presence, it demanded their removal and assessed fines against Nahrstedt for each month that she remained in violation of the pet restriction.

Nahrstedt then brought suit against the Association, its officers, and two of its employees asking the trial court to invalidate the assessments, to enjoin future assessments, to award damages for violation of her privacy when the Association "peered" into her condominium unit, to award damages for infliction of emotional distress, and to declare the pet restriction "unreasonable" as applied to indoor cats (such as hers) that are not allowed free run of the project's common areas. Nahrstedt said she did not know of the restriction when she purchased her unit.

The trial court dismissed Nahrstedt's complaint and she appealed. The court of appeal reversed the dismissal, and the Association appealed.

JUDICIAL OPINION

Kennard, Justice. Because a stable and predictable living environment is crucial to the success of condominiums and other common interest residential developments, and because recorded use restrictions are a primary means of ensuring this stability and predictability, the Legislature in section 1354 has afforded such restrictions a presumption of validity and has required of challengers that they demonstrate the restriction's "unreasonableness" by the deferential standard applicable to equitable servitudes. Under this standard established by the Legislature, enforcement of a restriction does not depend upon the conduct of a particular condominium owner. Rather, the restriction must be uniformly enforced in the condominium development to which it was intended to apply unless the plaintiff owner can show that the burdens it imposes on affected properties so substantially outweigh the benefits of the restriction that it should not be enforced against any owner.

Use restrictions are an inherent part of any common interest development and are crucial to the stable, planned environment of any shared ownership arrangement. The viability of shared ownership of improved real property rests on the existence of extensive reciprocal servitudes, together with the ability of each co-owner to prevent the property's partition.

Restrictions on property use are not the only characteristic of common interest ownership. Ordinarily, such ownership also entails mandatory membership in an owners association, which, through an elected board of directors, is empowered to enforce any use restrictions contained in the project's declaration or master deed and to enact new rules governing the use and occupancy of property within the project. As Professor Natelson observes, owners associations "can be a powerful force for good or for ill" in their members' lives. Therefore, anyone who buys a unit in a common interest development with knowledge of its owners association's discretionary power accepts "the risk that the power may be used in a way that benefits the commonality but harms the individual." Generally, courts will uphold decisions made by the governing board of an owners association so long as they represent good faith efforts to further the purposes of the common interest development, are consistent with the development's governing documents, and comply with public policy.

Thus, subordination of individual property rights to the collective judgment of the owners association together with restrictions on the use of real property comprise the chief attributes of owning property in a common interest development.

One significant factor in the continued popularity of the common interest form of property ownership is the ability of homeowners to enforce restrictive CC&R's against other owners (including future purchasers) of project units.

Restrictive covenants will run with the land, and thus bind successive owners, if the deed or other instrument containing the restrictive covenant particularly describes the lands to be benefited and burdened by the restriction and expressly provides that successors in interest of the covenantor's land will be bound for the benefit of the covenantee's land. Moreover, restrictions must relate to use, repair, maintenance, or improvement of the property, or to payment of taxes or assessments, and the instrument containing the restrictions must be recorded.

In California our Legislature has made common interest development use restrictions contained in a project's recorded declaration "enforceable... unless unreasonable."

Although no one definition of the term "reasonable" has gained universal acceptance, most courts have applied what one commentator calls "equitable reasonableness," upholding only those restrictions that provide a reasonable means to further the collective "health, happiness and enjoyment of life" of owners of a common interest development. Others would limit the "reasonableness" standard only to those restrictions adopted by majority vote of the homeowners or enacted under the rulemaking power of an association's governing board, and would not apply this test to restrictions included in a planned development project's recorded declaration or master deed. Because such restrictions are presumptively valid, these authorities would enforce them regardless of reasonableness.

An equitable servitude will be enforced unless it violates public policy; it bears no rational relationship to the protection, preservation, operation or purpose of the affected land; or it otherwise imposes burdens on the affected land that are so disproportionate to the restriction's beneficial effects that the restriction should not be enforced.

To allow one person to escape obligations under a written instrument upsets the expectations of all the other parties governed by that instrument (here, the owners of the other 529 units) that the instrument will be uniformly and predictably enforced.

Refusing to enforce the CC&R's contained in a recorded declaration, or enforcing them only after protracted litigation that would require justification of their application on a case-by-case basis, would impose great strain on the social fabric of the common interest development. It would frustrate owners who had purchased their units in reliance on the CC&R's. It would put the owners and the homeowners association in the difficult and divisive position of deciding whether particular CC&R's should be applied to a particular owner. Here, for example, deciding whether a particular animal is "confined to an owner's unit and create[s] no noise, odor, or nuisance" is a fact-intensive determination that can only be made by examining in detail the behavior of the particular animal and the behavior of the particular owner. Homeowners associations are ill-equipped to make such investigations, and any decision they might make in a particular case could be divisive or subject to claims of partiality.

Enforcing the CC&R's contained in a recorded declaration only after protracted case-by-case litigation would impose substantial litigation costs on the owners through their homeowners association, which would have to defend not only against owners contesting the application of the CC&R's to them, but also against owners contesting any case-by-case exceptions the homeowners association might make. In short, it is difficult to imagine what could more disrupt the harmony of a common interest development than the course proposed by the dissent.

Under the holding we adopt today, the reasonableness or unreasonableness of a condominium use restriction that the Legislature has made subject to section 1354 is to be determined not by reference to facts that are specific to the objecting homeowner, but by reference to the common interest development as a whole.

Accordingly, here Nahrstedt could prevent enforcement of the Lakeside Village pet restriction by proving that the restriction is arbitrary, that it is substantially more burdensome than beneficial to the affected properties, or that it violates a fundamental public policy.

We conclude, as a matter of law, that the recorded pet restriction of the Lakeside Village condominium development prohibiting cats or dogs but allowing some other pets is not arbitrary, but is rationally related to health, sanitation and noise concerns legitimately held by residents of a high-density condominium project such as Lakeside Village, which includes 530 units in 12 separate 3-story buildings.

Our conclusion that Nahrstedt's complaint states no claim entitling her to declaratory relief disposes of her primary cause of action challenging enforcement of the Lakeside Village condominium project's pet restriction, but does not address other causes of action (for invasion of privacy, invalidation of assessments, injunctive relief, and seeking damages for emotional distress) revived by the Court of Appeal. Because the Court of Appeal's decision regarding those other causes of action may have been influenced by its conclusion that Nehrstedt had stated a claim for declaratory relief, we remand this case to the Court of Appeal so it can reconsider whether Nahrstedt's complaint is sufficient to state those other causes of action.

Reversed.

CASE QUESTIONS

1. What did the pet restriction provide?
2. Why does Nahrstedt believe her pets should be exempt?
3. Of what importance is the fact that Nahrstedt said she did not have direct knowledge of the restriction at the time she purchased her unit?
4. What does the supreme court conclude about the cats and the restriction on pets?

ETHICAL ISSUE

Was it fair for Nahrstedt to continue to keep her pets while the Association assessed fines? What interests are being balanced with the rule? Would it be acceptable just to keep pets in secret?

CONSIDER 11.3

The Villa De Las Palmas project was formed in 1962 when the existing apartment units were conveyed to the original grantees by recorded grant deeds that contained various CCRs. The original grant deeds required the grantees to execute a management agreement and "covenant and agree to observe, perform and abide by any and all lawful [bylaws], rules, regulations and conditions with respect to the use and occupancy of said premises which may from time to time be adopted or prescribed by the Board of Governors constituted in said Management Agreement."

The grant deeds further provided that any violation would result in the forfeiture of the property, and permit other unit owners to sue for injunctive relief or damages. Lastly, the grant deeds specified that "[t]he benefits and obligations of this deed shall inure to and be binding upon the heirs, executors, administrators, successors and assigns of the respective parties hereto." The association subsequently adopted rules and regulations that provided in part that "[p]ets of any kind are forbidden to be kept in the apartment building or on the grounds at any time." These rules were never recorded.

In 1995, Paula Terifaj purchased a unit in the project. Although Terifaj had actual knowledge of the no-pets rule prior to purchasing her unit, she insisted on bringing her dog to the property. At the association meeting in 1996, Terifaj attempted to persuade the members to repeal the no-pets rule, but her proposal was rejected. The association repeatedly fined Terifaj for violating the no-pets rule, but she simply paid the fines and continued to bring her dog. Terifaj also had a guest who stayed at the property with his two dogs.

The association eventually filed suit, alleging causes of action for injunctive relief, declaratory relief, and nuisance, and requesting attorney fees and costs. The association subsequently adopted and recorded an amended declaration of CCRs. The amended declaration provided in pertinent part that "[n]o pets or animals of any kind, including without limitation, dogs, cats, birds, livestock, reptiles or poultry, may be kept or permitted in any Apartment or anywhere on the Property." It also provided that violations could be enjoined and declared them to be nuisances.

The association filed an amended complaint based on the provisions of the amended declaration, alleging the same three causes of action and requesting the same relief. Can the association obtain an injunction to stop Terifaj from bringing her dog to the property? Can it collect its fines? Attorneys' fees for bringing the suit? Which test should be applied to decide on the enforcement of the rule and the fines? *Villa De Las Palmas Homeowners Association v. Terifaj*, 99 Cal. App. 4th 1202 (Cal. App. 2002)

ENFORCEMENT FOR APPEARANCE AND MODIFICATION

Another issue of contention in associations is that of changing the appearance or structure of individual units. Many bylaws provide for the creation and operation of an architectural control committee (ACC). The goal of the ACC is to maintain uniformity in the appearance of condominium units. Particularly with regard to freestanding units, similar appearance preserves the value and continuity of the community, and individual owners' changes in colors, structure, or appearance can detract from the overall appearance of the development. The ACC reviews proposed construction changes and then either approves or disapproves them. The ACC can also check the neighborhood to ensure that there are no unauthorized changes or any failures to comply with CC&R requirements, such as maintainence and landscaping requirements.

In the following case, there is tense interaction among a condominium owner and her construction project, the association board, and city government.

LaSalle National Trust, N.A. (Carma McClure) v. Board of Directors of the 1100 Lake Shore Drive Condominium

677 N.E.2d 1378 (Ill. 1997), appeal denied, 686 N.E.2d 1163 (1998)

FACTS

Carma McClure, as the beneficiary of a trust, was the owner of a penthouse condominium in the Lake Shore Drive Condominiums located at 1100 North Lake Shore Drive. Her condominium consists of units 39A, 39B, and 40B, which have always been sold as one unit. An earlier owner added a roof house on the 41st floor that became part of McClure's penthouse. McClure had purchased the penthouse on March 20, 1991, for $1.4 million knowing that it was not in good condition. McClure and her husband, James Martin, decided to completely renovate the penthouse. They began in 1991 by demolishing its interior. McClure began this work without first notifying the Board of Directors of the Lake Shore Condominium (Board) (defendant). She also did not obtain the necessary city permits for the demolition.

The demolition resulted in the Board being cited by the city of Chicago for failure to obtain a permit. Also, an elevator cab was damaged, the alarm system in the building was cut off for a day, yard boxes and dumpsters were placed and removed illegally, and two other units in the building were damaged as a result.

McClure paid for the damage to the elevator cab. She also paid $16,552 to Elizabeth Rann, the owner of one of the damaged units as well as the president of the Lake Shore Condominium Association (association). McClure maintained Rann inflated her damages because of financial difficulty but that she paid them in order to get construction moving on her penthouse.

Demolition was complete in July 1991. McClure provided the Board and the city with a complete set of plans for the renovation in October 1991. Had the Board approved the plans, the work could have started and been completed in 26 weeks, or in May 1992.

On September 24, 1991, the Board passed a resolution that provided "[a]ll expenses incurred by the Board in connection with the modification by a unit owner to his unit or adjacent living [*sic*] comment [*sic*] elements shall be assessed to the unit owner. Expenses which will be assessed include, but are not limited to engineering, architectural and attorney fees and the cost of documents, plans and specifications."

The Board refused to approve McClure's plans unless and until she agreed to assume responsibility for the roof. McClure offered to pay one-third of the cost of replacing the main and machine room roofs if the Board would approve her plans.

Having still not approved the plans in March 1992, the Board proposed to McClure that she pay the Board expenses in reviewing the plans ($10,969); place money in escrow for covering any damages during renovation; repair, replace, and maintain the roof; and have a full-time on-site representative at the penthouse during construction.

Another unit was under renovation at the same time, and its owners were required to sign a similar agreement but were not assessed expenses of review nor required to assume the costs of repairing common elements.

McClure disagreed with many of the proposals but signed an agreement in May 1992 so that she could get her renovation started.

Once renovation began, the building began having infiltration problems. The Board maintained McClure had caused the problems with her construction. McClure said the infiltration was caused by cracks in the side of the building. Because of the infiltration problem, McClure could not finish her renovation in 1992, 1993, or 1994.

The parties were at a standstill until August 1994 when the Board and McClure entered into an agreement whereby she would pay for one half the cost of installing a new roof. The new roof was installed, but the water infiltration continued. A contractor indicated the infiltration would not stop until the Board caulked the walls of the building.

McClure then filed suit against the Board on several grounds including breach of fiduciary duty by the Board in withholding its approval, which amounted to constructive fraud. The trial court found for McClure and awarded her $896,609.52. The Board appealed.

JUDICIAL OPINION

Wolfson, Presiding Judge. The Condominium Declaration provides the Board can be liable to a unit owner only for "any acts or omissions found by a court to constitute gross negligence or fraud." Since there was no claim of gross negligence, and since there were no allegations or evidence of actual fraud, says the Board, there can be no liability. . . .

Condominium boards and board members owe a special duty to apartment owners. The Condominium Property Act provides:

*In the performance of their duties, the officers and members of the board *** shall exercise the care required of a fiduciary of the unit owners.*

This fiduciary duty is owed by boards as well as their individual members. The decisions make no distinction between a board and its members when describing fiduciary duty.

The failure of condominium board members to act in a manner reasonably related to their fiduciary duty results in "liability for the Board and its individual members."

The scope of that fiduciary duty can be limited by the declaration. In this case, the relevant part of the Declaration of Condominium is:

"Neither the directors, Board, officers of the Association, Trustee, nor Developer shall be personally liable to the Unit Owners for any mistake of judgment or for any other acts or omissions of any nature whatsoever as such directors, Board, officers, Trustee or Developer, except for any acts or omissions found by a court to constitute gross negligence or fraud." *[Emphasis added.]*

The first issue we must decide is whether the limitation of liability to acts or omissions that "constitute gross negligence or fraud" applies to McClure's count II. Gross negligence is not an issue in this case, but the Board contends the word "fraud" in the exclusion applies to actual fraud, not to the constructive fraud found by the trial court.

This case concerns a Declaration clause that seeks to exculpate the Board and its members and officers from personal liability except in narrow circumstances. Generally, exculpatory clauses "are not favored and are strictly construed and must have clear, explicit and unequivocal language showing that it was the intent of the parties."

If the Board wanted to limit its liability to actual fraud, it should have said so. Constructive fraud is a well-established doctrine in this State.

Constructive fraud does not require actual dishonesty or intent to deceive. "In a fiduciary relationship, where there is a breach of a legal or equitable duty, a presumption of fraud arises."

We find that the word "fraud" in the exculpatory clause includes both actual and constructive fraud. A holding to the contrary would virtually wipe out the Condominium Property Act's creation of a fiduciary duty between the Board and unit owners. If the Board were able to limit itself to actual fraud, there would be no liability for violation of its fiduciary duty. That is so because constructive fraud springs from the breach of a fiduciary duty.

Count II does not use the words "constructive fraud." Instead, it set out various ways the Board knowingly and willfully breached its fiduciary duty to Mrs. McClure. The allegations were fact-specific and, if believed, established a picture of delay, lack of cooperation, and obstruction.

To state a cause of action based on constructive fraud, "the facts constituting the alleged fraud must be set forth in the complaint."

Clearly, count II alleges that the Board breached its fiduciary duty to McClure. Where there is a breach of a legal or equitable duty arising out of a fiduciary relationship, a presumption of constructive fraud arises.

We find that the plaintiff adequately pled a constructive fraud.

McClure placed her confidence in the Board, which, by statute, owed her a fiduciary duty. In return, according to the trial court's findings, the Board virtually held her penthouse for ransom. This Board did not "act in good faith with due regard to the interests of the other."

We conclude the record supports the trial court's findings that: the Board's obstructive acts and lack of cooperation contributed to substantial delays in construction; damages for loss of use of the penthouse apartment, in the form of fair rental value, were recoverable and were properly proved.

Affirmed.

CASE QUESTIONS

1. Prepare an outline of the events in the penthouse renovation project.
2. What did the Board do wrong according to the court?
3. What does the court mean when it states that the Board held McClure's penthouse for ransom?
4. What is constructive fraud?
5. Who is liable to McClure?

CONSIDER 11.4

The Villas by the Sea condominiums are two-story condos located near a bay. Some of the condos have a third floor to them, known as lofts. The lofts are directly above the first two floors of the condo units. One of the owners of a condo with a loft, Michael Garrity, put in a pull-down staircase and finished the loft with some sheetrock and used it as an extra sleeping area. The association objected to the use of the loft as a taking of a common area. Two of the units had finished lofts completed by the developer and were sold that way to the original owners. Who owns the loft areas in the units? *Villas by the Sea Owners Ass'n v. Garrity*, 748 A.2d 457 (Me. 2000)

Tools for Enforcement

In associations, all owners are responsible for the costs of the association, which includes everything from administrative costs to management fees to the maintainence costs for common areas. Owners usually pay monthly fees and perhaps periodic capital assessment payments for special projects such as lighting installation or roof replacement on common area buildings. The amount of these fees may be specified in the declaration or bylaws and may be subject to change upon a vote or according to a formula included in the declaration or bylaws.

Every unit owner is required to pay these fees. In many cases, the fees are paid to the mortgagee, who in turn pays the association (since the mortgagee has an interest in keeping the property, which is held as security, well maintained).

Collection of these fees, without the help of a mortgage company, can be difficult. There are three tools of enforcement for associations: fines, liens, and, eventually, foreclosure. None of these tools can be used without authorization and their use is restricted by state laws. The following situation was so sympathetic and extreme that it resulted in reforms around the United States, reforms that restricted greatly what associations can do in terms of fines, liens, and foreclosure.

One dollar and fifty cents was all that stood between homeownership and homelessness for Anita and Thomas Radcliff. In early 2003 the couple moved into a home their sons built for them, located in Copperopolis, California. The home was part of a common interest development (CID), a type of housing development governed by a homeowners association and restricted by various covenants and conditions. After the Radcliffs failed to pay an annual association fee of $120, their CID initiated collection proceedings for the delinquent assessment. Anita Radcliff quickly hand-delivered a check for the annual fee, plus collection costs, but the check was $1.50 less than the total charges the CID sought and the collection agency the association hired returned the Radcliffs' check.

Less than a year after moving into their new home, the Radcliffs were confronted with what has been called the "extreme hammer of nonjudicial fore-closure." Within months, the addition of collection charges and attorneys' fees increased the Radcliffs' debt to nearly $2,000. When they failed to pay in time, their $285,000 home was sold at auction for a high bid of just $70,000.[6]

In California, where the Radcliffs lost their home, the legislature passed laws that give protection to property owners where the fines and resulting delinquent assessments from associations are less than $1,800. For amounts less than $1,800, the association may file a civil action in Small Claims Court. However, the association cannot foreclose on the homeowners' property for unpaid assessments until they exceed $1,800 or the assessments are more than 12 months delinquent.[7] Many states

6. Jim Wasserman, "For Want of $120, House Was Lost: More **Homeowners Associations** Using **Foreclosure** as Tool to Collect Dues," *Milwaukee J. Sentinel*, Feb. 22, 2004, at F1.
7. Code of Civil Procedure §§1367.4.

require some form of alternative dispute resolution before an association can file suit or impose a lien on owners' property. Some states, such as Arizona, have restricted the right of associations to place liens on property, requiring that there first be a judicial hearing before the lien for association fines, assessments, or penalties can be placed on the owner's property. Still other states have imposed mandatory steps and processes for both liens and foreclosures, requiring notification of owners as the association takes steps to try and collect the amounts due. Those steps also carry time requirements that allow the owners a guaranteed period of time within which they can respond and prevent further action by paying what is due. Some states prohibit foreclosure for association assessments altogether, leaving the association with the power to lien, something that can be collected only out of the proceeds of a sale if the property is ever transferred. However, under the Bankruptcy Abuse Prevention and Consumer Protection Act of 2005, pre-bankruptcy owners' association fees and fines are nondischargeable debts in bankruptcy.

Constitutional Issues in Enforcement

There are two frequent constitutional issues that involve owners' associations. The first type of case involves owners who post signs and other materials on their property that are a form of expression. These cases involve issues such as an owner flying a large U.S. flag from his property or the use of a community room for purposes of holding a political rally or for posting political materials on candidates and ballot issues. For the most part, the courts have held that associations are private entities and can impose aesthetic and other restrictions on these forms of speech that would otherwise be protected. However, there is an evolving line of cases that concludes that the private community is now a substitute for the public community and, as such, should be subject to constitutional limitations on the regulation of speech.[8]

The second type of case involves rules passed by owners' associations that prohibit owners from using their properties for certain purposes or impose restrictions on transfer of their properties to certain groups or individuals. In these situations, the homeowners' association, the bylaws, and CCRs often collide with public policy or even antidiscrimination laws. For example, in *Quinones v. Bd. of Managers of Regalwalk*, 673 N.Y.S.2d 450 (N.Y. A.D. 1998), the court held that a board did not have the authority to prohibit the operation of a day care center for adults in one of the condominium units because of the state's interest in promoting such homes and that such an interpretation of the CCRs was too restrictive. CCRs and their enforcement cannot deprive condominium owners of statutory protections or prohibit their exercise of rights. For example, prohibiting the installation of solar panels in a state that provides tax credits for such alternative energy use would be a violation of public policy and such CCRs or board policies would be unenforceable. See *Garden Lakes Community Ass'n, Inc. v. Madigan*, 62 P.3d 983 (Ariz. App. 2003).

Another use issue involves adult-only covenants in the CCRs. The age restrictions vary and generally limit occupation of units to those above a certain age, with 12, 18, and even 60 being typical ages for such restrictions. These restrictions have been declared constitutionally valid and are covered in Chapter 19.

A final and evolving area in owners' association powers relates to the transfer of property by owners, particularly, restritions on the sale of property to convicted sex offenders. The following case is one of the few appellate cases that addresses this issue and the power of owners' associations.

8. For a discussion of the private vs. public regulation, see *Committee for a Better Twin Rivers, v. Twin Rivers Homeowners' Association*, 890 A.2d 947 (N.J. App. 2006).

Mulligan v. Panther Valley Prop. Owners Ass'n

766 A.2d 1186 (N.J. App. 2001)

FACTS

Elinor Mulligan (Plaintiff) owns a home in Panther Valley, a private common-interest residential community. Panther Valley Property Owners Association (Defendant/Association) is a non-profit corporation that was organized in 1968 for the purpose of governing the community. The Association acts through an elected Board of Trustees.

In October 1998, the Association, through a vote of its membership, adopted six amendments to the community's Declaration of Covenants and Restrictions (Declarations) and the Association's bylaws. The amendment relevant here was the first of these amendments which required that no individual registered as a Tier 3 offender under N.J.S.A. 2C:7–8(c)(3) ("Megan's Law") could reside in Panther Valley. Tier 3 is the highest classification within Megan's Law. In order for an individual to be classified as a Tier 3 registrant, that individual must be a sex-offender who has been deemed to pose a high risk of re-offending. Factors that inform the decision whether an individual poses a high risk of re-offending include whether the conduct involved repetitive and compulsive behavior, N.J.S.A. 2C:7–8b(3)(a); whether the individual served the maximum term of confinement, N.J.S.A. 2C:7–8b(3)(b); and whether the sexual offense was committed against a child, N.J.S.A. 2C:7–8b(3)(c). Because such an individual poses a substantial risk to the community, the statute directs that notification of the presence of a Tier 3 offender within the community be more widespread than that provided in the instance of a Tier 1 or Tier 2 offender, who have been deemed to pose low and moderate risks of re-offending. Mulligan filed suit challenging the amendment and the trial court upheld the amendment precluding such Tier 3 registrants from residing within Panther Valley.

JUDICIAL OPINION

WEFING, Judge. The refusal to enforce arbitrary and capricious rules promulgated by governing boards of condominiums is simply an application of the "business judgment" rule. This rule requires the presence of fraud or lack of good faith in the conduct of a corporation's internal affairs before the decisions of a board of directors can be questioned. If the corporate directors' conduct is authorized, a showing must be made of fraud, self-dealing or unconscionable conduct to justify judicial review.... Although directors of a corporation have a fiduciary relationship to the shareholders, they are not expected to be incapable of error. All that is required is that persons in such positions act reasonably and in good faith in carrying out their duties. Courts will not second-guess the actions of directors unless it appears that they are the result of fraud, dishonesty or incompetence.

Plaintiff asserts three reasons why this amendment is invalid. She contends that it is an unlawful infringement on her right to alienate her property, that it compels her to violate the law by obligating her to seek out and identify such Tier 3 registrants and that it is contrary to public policy. The first two are wholly insubstantial in our view and if plaintiff's argument were confined to them, we would reject her position out of hand.

Defendants have supplied as part of the record in this case statistics that were compiled by the Office of the Attorney General in connection with its overall responsibility for monitoring Megan's Law matters. According to those figures, there were, as of July 30, 1999, only 80 Tier 3 registrants within the entire State of New Jersey. New Jersey has, as of the 2000 census, a population in excess of 8,400,000; that there may be 80 individuals out of a total of 8.4 million to whom plaintiff may not sell her home cannot, in our judgment, seriously be considered an unlawful restriction upon her right to sell or lease her home.

In addition, the restriction, if indeed it can be considered one, does not fall unfairly upon plaintiff; it affects all members of the Association equally. Thus, plaintiff, if she sought to sell or lease her home, would not be relegated to a smaller potential market than another Panther Valley resident. And it cannot escape remarking that the record is entirely barren of any indication that plaintiff has any present plans to sell or lease her home to anyone. To the extent plaintiff is seeking to vindicate the rights of a Tier 3 registrant to reside in Panther Valley, she is not the proper party.

Although not contained within the record before us, we are aware that other similar common interest communities within the State have passed similar restrictions upon residency by Tier 3 registrants. We do not know from the record how many common interest communities exist within the State and we do not know from the record how many of those communities have seen fit to adopt comparable restrictions and whether they have determined to include a broader group than Tier 3 registrants. We are thus unable to determine whether the result of such provisions is to make a large segment of the housing market unavailable to one category of individual and indeed perhaps to approach "the ogre of vigilantism and 1193 harassment," the potential dangers of which the Supreme Court recognized even while upholding the constitutionality of Megan's Law.

The record is deficient in another regard as well for it is entirely unclear if the Association performs quasi-municipal functions, such that its actions perhaps should be viewed as analogous to governmental actions in some regards. We do know, from *State v. Panther Valley, supra*, that the Association has turned over to the township the responsibility for traffic enforcement, for instance, and is precluded from acting independently in that sphere. The record does not disclose whether certain services are provided by the township and others by the Association. It may be somewhat instructive in this regard that we have concluded in another matter involving Panther Valley that the Association's newsletter, "The Panther," could not be compelled to publish an ad submitted by the plaintiff that was apparently critical of the local first-aid squad. *William G. Mulligan Found. for the Control of First Aid Squadders & Roving Paramedics v. Brooks*, 312 N.J.Super. 353, 711 A.2d 961 (App.Div.1998).

We recognize, of course, that Tier 3 registrants (and indeed convicted criminals) are not a protected group within the terms of New Jersey's Law Against Discrimination. N.J.S.A. 10:5–3. Nor have we been pointed to any authority deeming them handicapped. In this regard, however see *Arnold Murray Constr., L.L.C. v. Hicks*, 621 N.W.2d 171 (S.D.2001), in which the court upheld the eviction of a handicapped tenant who posed a direct threat to the health and safety of other tenants without the necessity of attempting to provide reasonable accommodations under the federal Fair Housing Act. It does not necessarily follow, however, that large segments of the State could entirely close their doors to such individuals, confining them to a narrow corridor and thus perhaps exposing those within that remaining corridor to a greater risk of harm than they might otherwise have had to confront.

Common interest communities fill a particular need in the housing market but they also pose unique problems for those who remain outside their gates, whether voluntarily or by economic necessity. The understandable desire of individuals to protect themselves and their families from some of the ravages of modern society and thus reside within such communities should not become a vehicle to ensure that those problems remain the burden of those least able to afford a viable solution.

We hasten to add that we recognize that not all gated communities are refuges for the wealthy. They are a spreading phenomenon that can be found among all economic strata. Their growth has been fueled by the public's fear of crime and need for safety.

The Supreme Court has long cautioned against the dangers inherent in courts, presented with a meager record, ruling upon questions having a broad social and legal impact. We decline to write a solution for a problem that has not been fully stated.

Because we have concluded, for the reasons we have set forth, that the record was insufficient to permit determination of the issue, we reverse that portion of the trial court's judgment upholding the validity of the amendment to the Association's Declaration.

CASE QUESTIONS

1. How was the restriction on transfer created?
2. What does the court say is the standard for reviewing the rules passed by owners' associations?
3. What are the court's concerns about the association rule and why does it decline to reach a decision?

Liability Issues in Associations

Owners' Association Liabilities: Management

Because the governing boards of owners' associations often make decisions on contentious issues, impose increases in association fees, and halt construction by individual unit owners for noncompliance with CCRs, they are often defendants in lawsuits brought by unit owners. Courts have had to determine association liabilities, defenses, and immunities. They have borrowed the standards of liability for governing boards from general corporation law.

The boards of owners' associations are protected by what is known in corporate law as the **business judgment rule** (see earlier discussion on conflicts for its use in determining the reasonableness of board action taken). So long as boards act in good faith and for articulated purposes related to the well-being of the property and unit owners, courts will not substitute their judgment for that of the board. Figure 11.1 is a checklist for owners and boards that both should follow in performing their various roles.

The following case deals with an issue of management and oversight by the condominium association.

Figure 11.1 Rules of Thumb for Owners, Owners' Associations, and Boards

1. The CCRs represent property rights and cannot be taken away or changed except in the same fashion that covenants on land parcels are changed or according to procedures outlined in the CCRs themselves.
2. Homeowners' associations and boards govern subject to the CCRs; they do not override the CCRs.
3. Bylaws cannot override CCRs; homeowners' association boards cannot override bylaws or CCRs except by proper process and procedure not in violation of unit owners' property rights.
4. All changes by homeowners' association boards require notice to unit owners and proper vote including raising association fees.
5. CCRs, bylaws, and homeowners' associations cannot pass or enforce rules and restrictions in violation of antidiscrimination laws or public policy.
6. Boards must be consistent in their enforcement of CCRs and bylaws; selective enforcement can be the basis of discriminatory conduct or the loss of protections under the CCRs for lax enforcement.

RANDOL V. ATKINSON

965 S.W.2d 338 (Mo. App. 1998)

FACTS

The Woodmoor Condominiums were created in 1990 and are managed by the Woodmoor Condominium Association (association). Woodmoor consists of 10 units with wooden decks.

On April 3, 1993, Susan Jochens (now Atkinson), who owned a condominium in Woodmoor, used her barbecue to make dinner for herself and her boyfriend. After finishing with the grill, neither Jochens nor her boyfriend went back onto the deck.

At approximately 2:00 A.M., fire swept through the condominium project and all 10 units were destroyed. The source of the fire was the grill on Jochens' deck.

Mr. and Mrs. Randol and others (appellants) filed suit against Jochens, the association, and the original development corporation, Wind River. They submitted an affidavit from a former fire marshal of Kansas City, Missouri, that indicated the use of charcoal grills on wooden decks was dangerous and a known fire hazard. The Randols and others who lost their units in the fire contend that the association should have adopted bylaws or rules prohibiting such use. The lower court dismissed the case, finding that there was no duty on the part of the association. The Randols and other owners appealed.

JUDICIAL OPINION

Howard, Judge. Appellants allege five theories for their argument that the Association and Wind River owed a duty of care to the condominium owners. Appellants first contend that the Association and Wind River owed a duty of care to the condominium owners under the Declaration of Condominium and bylaws for the Woodmoor Condominiums, as well as under Missouri statutory law.

We first address whether the bylaws or the Declaration created a duty on the part of the Association and Wind River to ban the use of charcoal grills by the unit owners. Condominium bylaws constitute the rules and regulations that govern the internal administration of the condominium complex. *Wescott v. Burtonwood Manor Condominium Ass'n Bd. of Managers*, 743 S.W.2d 555, 558 (Mo. App. E.D. 1987). The bylaws must be strictly construed. To support their argument, Appellants rely on a provision in the bylaws granting the Association and Wind River the power "to adopt, repeal or amend Rules and Regulations for the Woodmoor Condominiums." Appellants also rely on the section in the Declaration that regulates the use of limited common elements. We find nothing in the bylaws or the Declaration that, by itself, imposed a duty on the Association and Wind River to ban the use of charcoal grills.

We next address whether the Association and Wind River had a statutory duty to ban charcoal grills. Because the Woodmoor Condominiums were created after September 28, 1983, the Uniform Condominium Act, §§448.005 to 448.210 RSMo 1994, applies. Appellants argue that §448.3–103.1 of the Uniform Condominium Act imposed a duty on the Association and Wind River to prohibit charcoal grills. Section 448.3–103.1 provides, in pertinent part, that "[i]n the performance of their duties, the officers and members of the executive board are required to exercise (1) if appointed by the declarant, the care required of fiduciaries of the unit owners, and (2) if elected by the unit owners, ordinary and reasonable care." Although the facts are unclear, we will assume for the purpose of analysis that both Wind River and the Association were in control of the Woodmoor Condominiums at the time of the fire. That being the case, this section clearly imposes a fiduciary duty on Wind River and a duty of ordinary and reasonable care on the Association. However, we find that the Respondents' duties did not require them to ban the use of charcoal grills. Appellants presented no convincing evidence that the use of charcoal grills was such a dangerous practice that the failure of Respondents to ban the grills amounted to negligence.

Next Appellants contend that the Association and Wind River owed a duty of care to the owners of the Woodmoor Condominiums under a common law analysis of duty based on foreseeability, fairness, and public policy. However, the duties owed by the Association and Wind River to the unit owners are limited to those duties included in the bylaws and the provisions of Chapter 448 RSMo. Therefore, an analysis of common law duty is not appropriate in this case.

Third, Appellants contend that the Association and Wind River owed a duty of ordinary care to the owners of the Woodmoor Condominiums because condominium associations are analogous to landlords, who have a duty of ordinary care to their tenants. No Missouri court has found that condominium associations are analogous to landlords for the purpose of determining whether a duty is owed. We decline to make that analogy in this case.

Fourth, Appellants contend that the Association and Wind River owed a duty of care to the owners of the Woodmoor Condominiums because the Association and Wind River undertook the management of the Woodmoor Condominiums for the benefit of the condominium owners. However, where the existence of a duty is established, it is not one to protect against every possible injury which might occur. *Hoover's Dairy. Inc. v. Mid-America Dairymen, Inc./Special Products, Inc.*, 700 S.W.2d 426, 431 (Mo. 1985). Rather, it is generally measured by whether or not a reasonably prudent person would have anticipated the danger and provided against it. In this case, it was not the duty of the Association or Wind River to protect the owners from all potential sources of harm, particularly those caused by the negligence of third parties.

It is not negligence to fail to anticipate that another will be negligent, because one is entitled to assume and act upon the assumption that others will exercise due care for their own safety, in the absence of notice to the contrary. *Buck v. Union Elec. Co.*, 887 S.W.2d 430, 434–35 (Mo. App. E.D. 1994). The Appellants have not alleged that either the Association or Wind River had notice that any of the unit owners were being negligent in the use of their grills. Therefore, Respondents cannot be found negligent in their failure to anticipate Susan Jochens' negligence.

Fifth, Appellants contend that the Association and Wind River owed a duty of care to the owners of the Woodmoor Condominiums because the Association and Wind River had a special relationship with the condominium owners, who relied on the Association and Wind River to provide a place of safety. However, the condominium association-unit owner relationship is not recognized in Missouri as a special relationship which, by itself, gives rise to a duty. The judgment of the trial court is affirmed.

Affirmed.

CASE QUESTIONS

1. Who was responsible for the fire and how did the fire occur?
2. What theories do the owners of the units destroyed in the fire say apply in the case?
3. How does the court handle the theories?
4. Give a summary of the law on associations' responsibilities given the decision in this case.

CONSIDER 11.5

A building in a condominium development suffered from termite infestation. The board of directors of the development's community association decided to treat the infestation locally ("spot-treat"), rather than fumigate. Alleging the board's decision diminished the value of her unit, the owner of a condominium in the development sued the community association. In adjudicating her claims, under what standard should a court evaluate the board's decision? *Lamden v. La Jolla Shores Clubdominium Homeowners Assn.*, 980 P.2d 940 (Cal. 2002)

Owners' Association Liabilities: Maintenances

A major issue in associations is the liability for injuries occurring in common areas. If the association is a corporation, such as a nonprofit owners' association, then that corporation should carry insurance for liability in the common areas. Regardless of incorporation, the owners are liable together and individually (jointly and severally) for torts in common areas. The corporate organization with insurance simply makes the liability easier to bear, and the premium costs can be part of the assessment to each unit owner.

The liability for injuries occurring in common areas extends to visitors, repairpeople, governmental personnel (such as fire and medical personnel), and any others authorized to be on the premises, including unit owners. The responsibility of maintaining common areas extends to the responsibility for injuries resulting from faulty repair or lack of maintenance.

The following case deals with an issue of condominium associations' liability for harm to third parties in their common areas.

MARTINEZ V. WOODMAR IV CONDOMINIUMS

941 P.2d 218 (Ariz. 1997)

FACTS

Carlos Martinez (plaintiff) was attending a graduation party at the Woodmar IV 152-unit condominium project (defendant) as a guest of one of the unit owners. After 15 minutes of being at the party in the unit, Martinez and two fellow party-goers left to go to the complex's parking lot to check on their cars. They found a group of local ruffians sitting on the car of one of Martinez's friends. A "discussion ensued."

At some point, Martinez ran from the "discussion," and was shot in the back as he ran. The group scattered and no one has been charged with the Martinez shooting.

From descriptions given to the live-in security officer for the complex, the security officer concluded that the group was a gang of young people from a neighboring complex. This group would often gather in the Woodmar parking lot to sell drugs and "participate in other unsavory activities." The security guard would disperse the group when he saw them. However, because of budget constraints he was the only security guard and patrolled between the hours of 8 and 9 P.M. until 5 or 6 A.M. The shooting in the parking lot occurred one hour before the guard began his duties.

Martinez filed suit against the homeowners' association of Woodmar for its negligence in failing to provide adequate security. The trial court granted a motion for summary judgment, the court of appeals affirmed, and Martinez appealed.

JUDICIAL DECISION

Feldman, Justice. We focus on Defendant's status with relation to the land rather than the presence or absence of a special relationship between it and the tortfeasor or Plaintiff. We are concerned only with the question of whether Defendant, occupying a status similar to that of a landlord, had a duty of reasonable care to maintain the safety of its common areas because it had control over the land.

We believe this distinction is contrary to existing law when, as in this case, the danger causing the injury is located on property in the exclusive control of the landlord or condominium association. In Arizona, if there is no statute or case law on a particular subject, we have traditionally followed the Restatement of Laws. RESTATEMENT §360 states:

A possessor of land who leases a part thereof and retains in his own control any other part which the lessee is entitled to use as appurtenant to the part leased to him, is subject to liability to his lessee and others lawfully upon the land with the consent of the lessee or a sublessee for physical harm caused by a dangerous condition upon that part of the land retained in the lessor's control, if the lessor by the exercise of reasonable care could have discovered the condition and the unreasonable risk involved therein and could have made the condition safe.

We note Defendant in this case is not a lessor but a new type of possessor—a condominium association that has retained in its control common areas, such as the parking lot, that unit owners are entitled to use as appurtenant to their unit.

The element of control, we believe, is essential to a finding of duty for the condominium association. Like a landlord who maintains control and liability for conditions in common areas, the condominium association controls all aspects of maintenance and security for the common areas and, most likely, forbids individual unit owners from taking on these chores. Thus, if the association owes no duty of care over the common areas of the property, no one does because no one else possesses the ability to cure defects in the common area. We do not believe the law recognizes such a lack of responsibility for safety. We therefore hold that with respect to common areas under its exclusive control, a condominium association has the same duties as a landlord.

Thus, if we apply the rules of RESTATEMENT §360 and RESTATEMENT (SECOND) OF PROPERTY §17.3, a condominium association has a duty not only to the unit owners and their tenants but also to those who are on the land with their consent and who will inevitably be expected to use common areas such as the parking lot. This element of control creates an "affirmative obligation to exercise reasonable care to inspect and repair such parts of the premises for the protection of the lessee; and the duty extends also to members of the tenant's family, his employees, his invitees, his guests, and others on the land in the right of the tenant."

The duty to maintain the safety of common areas applies not only to physical conditions on the land but, we believe, also to dangerous activities on the land.

The court of appeals noted the Restatement rule but stated that "given plaintiff's legal status [as a licensee], Woodmar only owed a duty to 'refrain from knowingly letting him run upon a hidden peril or wantonly or willfully causing him harm.'" The court found the gang hanging out in the parking lot was not a hidden danger, stating the "transient harm created by third persons who commit crimes" is distinguishable from a dangerous physical condition that a landowner must make safe. The duty to those using the common areas with consent of the association, its unit owners, and their tenants, includes the use of reasonable care to prevent harm from criminal intrusion.

For the purpose of this section, the unreasonable risk of harm from criminal intrusion constitutes a dangerous condition, so that where the landlord could by the exercise of reasonable care have discovered the unreasonable risk of criminal intrusion and could have made the condition safe from such unreasonable risk of criminal intrusion, he is subject to liability for physical harm caused by criminal intrusion if he had not taken the necessary precautions. As regards parts of the property retained [under] *[sic]* the landlord's control, common entranceways, fire escapes, halls and other approaches to the leased property are included.

It is well recognized at present that failure to provide adequate lighting, door locks, or other security measures may subject certain landowners to liability for harm caused by a criminal attack on persons to whom the owner owes a duty of care.

Logically, it cannot be otherwise. If one owes a duty of reasonable care to those on one's land with permission, then the circumstances will dictate what is reasonable to protect others from foreseeable and preventable danger. The category of danger neither creates nor eradicates duty; it only indicates what conduct may be reasonable to fulfill the duty.

Our case is the type in which courts are tempted to blur the concepts of duty and negligence. As we have previously indicated, we disapprove of attempts to equate the concepts of duty with specific details of conduct. Duty is an issue "of the relation between individuals which imposes upon one a legal obligation for the benefit of the other. . . ." As the possessor of the common areas, Defendant has a relationship, similar to that of a landlord, with unit owners, their tenants, and persons on the land with consent and permission to use the common areas. That relationship required Defendant to use reasonable care to avoid causing the injury to those it permitted to use the property under its control. The relationship between Defendant, its unit owners, and persons given permission to enter the common areas thus imposed an obligation on Defendant to take reasonable precautions for the latter's safety. The type of foreseeable danger did not dictate the existence of duty but only the nature and extent of the conduct necessary to fulfill the duty. The true issue on summary judgment in this case, therefore, was not the question of duty but rather the question of negligence. We turn, then, to the specific facts to determine whether the trial judge correctly granted summary judgment.

In the response to the motion for summary judgment, there is evidence presented that Defendant knew of the incursion by gangs in the parking lot and other common areas of its property, knew the gangs engaged in drug dealing and other criminal activity, was warned by its own security guard of the need for 24-hour patrols, had hired a second guard for a short period but terminated him because of expense considerations, and knew a neighboring condominium complex had hired off-duty Phoenix police officers to patrol. We therefore hold there is sufficient evidence from which a jury could find the danger foreseeable and Defendant negligent.

On this record, also, we cannot say as a matter of law Defendant could not have taken reasonable measures that probably would have prevented the attack. It may be that increased security patrols, better fencing, calls for police control, or other measures might have prevented injury. This question of causation in fact is, of course, one especially for the jury.

Although Defendant did not owe Plaintiff a duty of care based on Defendant's special relationship to control the attacker in this case, with respect to the common areas under its control it had a duty like that of a landlord to maintain its property in a reasonably safe condition. This included the duty to take reasonable measures to protect against foreseeable activities creating danger, including criminal attacks, on the land it controlled.

Accordingly, summary judgment was improper. Therefore, we vacate the court of appeals' opinion, reverse the trial court's grant of summary judgment, and remand to the trial court for proceedings consistent with this opinion.

Reversed and Remanded.

CASE QUESTIONS

1. What happened and when?
2. What kind of security did Woodmar have available?
3. Did the homeowners' association have any duty to Martinez?
4. Does the court discuss any other duties the association may have?
5. What is the duty of condominium associations with regard to criminal activity on their premises?

Compare and contrast the finding in the following additional case on liability of condominium associations for criminal activity.

MEDCALF V. WASHINGTON CONDOMINIUM ASS'N

747 A.2d 532 (Conn. App. 2000)

FACTS

Mechelle Medcalf (plaintiff) and a friend, Deborah Michelson, arrived at 1633 Washington Boulevard in Stamford, Connecticut, to visit their friend, Tracy Skiades, who resides at the Washington Heights Condominiums.

Ms. Medcalf parked her car in the street level parking lot and walked to the lobby doors. The lighting in the parking lot was dim. She picked up the intercom and called Ms. Skiades. Ms. Skiades' brother-in-law answered and tried to let Ms. Metcalf in using the electronic buzzer system. The system did not work, so Ms. Skiades indicated she would come down and open the door. As she traveled down to the lobby, Ms. Medcalf was attacked and injured by Kenneth Strickler.

Ms. Medcalf filed suit against Washington Heights Condominium Association and Professional Property Management Company, Inc., its managing agent (defendants). Ms. Medcalf alleged that their failure to maintain the buzzer system was the cause of her assault and injuries. The jury found for Ms. Medcalf and the association and managing agent appealed.

JUDICIAL DECISION

Mihalakos, Judge. The dispositive issue in this appeal is whether there is a causal connection between the assault and the failure of the security system. We conclude that the jury could not reasonably have found that the failure to maintain the intercom security system was the proximate cause of the assault.

The elements in a negligence cause of action are duty, breach of that duty, causation and damages. "The first component of legal cause is causation in fact. Causation in fact is the purest legal application of... legal cause. The test for cause in fact is, simply, would the injury have occurred were it not for the actor's conduct."

The second component is proximate cause. "Proximate cause establishes a reasonable connection between an act or omission of a defendant and the harm suffered by a plaintiff." "The Connecticut Supreme Court has defined proximate cause as [a]n actual cause that is a substantial factor in the resulting harm.... The substantial factor test reflects the inquiry fundamental to all proximate cause questions, that is, whether the harm which occurred was of the same general nature as the foreseeable risk created by the defendant's negligence." Proximate cause is a question of fact to be decided by the trier of fact, but it becomes a question of law when the mind of a fair and reasonable person could reach only one conclusion. "Lines must be drawn determining how far down the causal continuum individuals will be held liable for the consequences of their actions.... This line is labeled proximate cause." In issues involving proximate cause analysis, this court has held that "an intervening intentional or criminal act relieves a negligent defendant of liability, except where the harm caused by the intervening act is within the scope of risk created by the defendant's conduct or where the intervening act is reasonably foreseeable.... As a general rule, the act of a third person in committing an intentional act or crime is a superseding cause of harm to another resulting therefrom.... In such a case, the third person has deliberately assumed control of the situation, and all responsibility for the consequences of his act is shifted to him." Recovery is barred in a negligence action where there is a lack of causal connection between the defendant's wrongful conduct and a plaintiff's injury.

In *Doe v. Manheimer*, 563 A.2d 699, our Supreme Court was not persuaded that the owner of a property should reasonably foresee that an overgrowth of vegetation would provide an inducement for the commission of a violent crime by a stranger. The court held that the overgrown vegetation was an incidental factor and not a substantial factor that would establish proximate cause.

In the present case, the plaintiff offered no evidence that the malfunctioning intercom system was designed to provide security to a person outside the building. The defendants' failure to maintain the intercom system was inconsequential and was not the proximate cause of the assault. The injury may likely have occurred without any negligence with respect to the intercom system.

The defendants could not have reasonably foreseen that a malfunctioning intercom system might provide a substantial incentive or inducement for the commission of a violent criminal assault on their property by one stranger upon another.

We rule that, as a matter of law, the jury could not reasonably have found that the assault on the plaintiff and the resultant injury were within the foreseeable scope of risk created by the defendants' failure to maintain the intercom system. Therefore, the plaintiff failed to establish the necessary causal relationship.

The judgment is reversed.

CASE QUESTIONS

1. What happened and when?
2. What does Ms. Medcalf allege is the cause of her injuries?
3. What is the difference between causation and proximate cause?
4. Is this case different from the *Woodmar* case? Do the two states' laws differ on injuries to visitors from third parties?

CONSIDER 11.6

Rose Stanley, who lives in a condominium project, was attacked by Elizabeth Rivera in the common hallway of the complex and pushed into her apartment, where she was stabbed several times and severely injured. Elizabeth Rivera was living in the complex because she was staying with another owner, without required authorization. Stanley filed suit against the condominium board for its failure to provide adequate security. The board defended on the grounds that there had been no other criminal activity on the premises and that Riviera's drug use made her incapable of proper judgment and also introduced a criminal element not affecting other members of the condominium community. Who is correct? What standard should the court apply in evaluating the actions of the condominium board? *Stanley v. Meriden Housing Authority,* 2002 WL 31172927 (Conn. Super. 2002)

Owners' Liability Issues in Associations

Owners of single-family dwellings buy insurance to cover liabilities they may have for injuries occurring on their premises. With single-family dwellings, it is clear that there is liability in ownership and that the liability rests with the homeowner. It is the owner's responsibility to maintain and repair the premises. However, in multiunit housing with common areas, the nature of multiple ownership makes the issues of liability and responsibility less clear.

Contractual Liability of Unit Owners

Three issues of contractual liability for owners are their liability for (1) unpaid bills of the developer, (2) assessment and maintenance fees, and (3) improvement and repair costs of common elements and individual units.

Liability for Unpaid Bills of Developers

A critical point in liability issues arises when control of the development is turned over to the association for operation. This juncture varies—some articles of incorporation or bylaws provide for a number turnover point (e.g., when three-fourths of all units have been sold), while others provide for an absolute point (when all units have been sold). When control is turned over to the development residents, the developer not only is no longer in control but also is no longer responsible for maintenance and repair costs.

One possible problem with turnover is when all construction elements of the development are not owned free and clear (when there are outstanding debts). In most cases, the developer would be responsible for payment of such obligations, since the homeowners' association probably would not have existed at the time of the debt contract. However, there are potential problems in spite of the developer's liability. First, the developer may not be able to pay, and fixtures may be repossessed from the development or liens may result. Second, even if the developer can pay, establishing the developer's liability may take litigation.

Additionally, owners may experience problems with the developer's delivery of promised services and quality of construction, particularly in the common areas. Owners have their various warranties for protection (see Chapter 14), but the association will need to have property inspections of common areas before it takes control so that it can recover from the developer for faulty construction and failed maintenance up to the time the developer turns over control to the association. For example, in gated communities, associations often have the developer make repairs to the private streets before the turnover because of the damage constuction vehicles do to the streets. Those costly repairs save the owners the cost of repaving streets.

Tort Liability of Unit Owners

Each owner is responsible for the maintenance and safety of his or her property and liable for any injuries that result from negligence. Owners have insurance on their property to cover such liability.

Cautions and Conclusions

Like other real estate purchases, multiunit housing and planned community ownership can be good investments, but, study before buying. Consider the following questions that relate to both nultiunit housing and owners' associaions before investing:

1. What is the structure of the community/building?
2. What is the condition of the property? What repairs are necessary? Who will make the repairs? Who will pay for the repairs?
3. When will the developer turn over control of the building operation? Who or what organization will control the building operation at that point? What system of government, maintenance, and repair has been set up?
4. Is there a provision to opt out (back out) if the units or homes do not sell?
5. Will the developer finish repairs? Are there any outstanding liens?
6. Is there an association? If so, how does it work and is it effective?
7. Are there assessments? If so, how much are they, and do the unit owners pay them?
8. What provisions for operations and restrictions are made in the declaration, charters, bylaws, and regulations?
9. Are the common areas well maintained?
10. What elements are included in the common areas, and what elements are the responsibility of individual unit owners?
11. How do other unit owners feel about the assessments and how the development is functioning?
12. Are there any pending lawsuits?
13. Is there adequate insurance coverage for the common areas?
14. Are the units rented or owner-occupied?
15. What type of ownership interest is being obtained?
16. Are there restrictions on transferability?
17. Are there use and age restrictions?
18. Are the units subject to architectural control?

The investigation can never be too thorough.

Key Terms

attached homes, 260
business judgment rule, 275
bylaws, 257
condominium, 253
conversion restrictions, 253
owners' associations, 251
cooperative, 254
declaration of condominium, 253
declaration of covenants, conditions, and restrictions (CC&Rs or CCRs), 254
declaration of horizontal property regime and covenants, 253
garden homes, 260
horizontal property acts, 252
horizontal property regimes, 252
master deed, 254
Model Real Estate Cooperative Act ,252
Model Real Estate Time-Share Act, 252
patio homes, 260
proprietary lease, 257
recreational lease, 259
time-sharing, 258
townhouse, 258
Uniform Common Interest Ownership Act, 252
Uniform Condominium Act, 252
vacation license, 259

Chapter Problems

1. Betty Grey and other condominium unit owners in Hawkins Landing brought suit against Coastal States Holding Company and others who also owned units in the Hawkins Landing condominium project for their expansion of their units by the construction of a second story onto each of their units. Grey and the others maintained that the defendants had thereby appropriated the airspace above their units, a common element belonging to the Hawkins Landing Association, Inc. Is Grey correct? *Grey v. Coastal States Holding Company*, 578 A.2d 1080 (Conn. 1980)

2. Roundtree Villas Association, Inc., is a nonprofit corporation whose primary function is to own and administer the common elements of the condominium project called "Roundtree Villas." Roundtree Corporation, Inc., was the original owner of a parcel of real estate that filed a deed under the Horizontal Property Act. Republic Mortgage Investment Services, Inc., was the financier of the project. Mortgage Investment Services, Inc., was an advisory service employed by Republic Mortgage, the lender.

The condominium project was constructed by Miles and Teal Builders at a time when money was short and sales were slow. Miles and Teal sold what they could and then 4701 Kings Corporation, a company created by Republic Mortgage to accept title to Roundtree Villas in lieu of Republic's foreclosure, took over the property. Shortly after the acquisition, the owners of the units began to complain about problems with the units' roofs and balconies. The lender attempted to remedy the problems, but only with stopgap measures. The problems continued.

The homeowners' association for Roundtree filed suit against Republic, the lender, and 4701 Kings Corporation for breach of the implied warranty of habitability and sought damages for the repair of the roofs and balconies. The jury entered a verdict against the lender and the lender appealed. Should the lender be held liable? *Roundtree Villas Association, Inc. v. 4701 Kings Corporation*, 321 S.E.2d 46 (S.C. 1984)

3. Melvin R. Luster and Harold E. Friedman formed a partnership to convert the 20 East Cedar property from rental property to condominium units. Deeds to each unit provided purchasers with title for the designated unit plus an undivided percentage of the "common elements." In each sales agreement, the partnership agreed to complete certain repair and rehabilitation work in the building.

In 1970 (during the conversion process), Luster and Friedman leased a canopy from White Way Electric Sign and Maintenance Company with a down payment of $6,128 and 60 monthly payments of $261.76 each. The canopy was ornamental and was installed at the front entrance of the 20 East Cedar building.

In 1973, the unit owners formed their own association, and Luster and Friedman were relieved of their responsibilities. After the release, the unit owners discovered the liability remaining on the canopy lease as well as several other unpaid expenses incurred by Luster and Friedman in the rehabilitation of the building.

The association brought suit, seeking a complete accounting and monetary relief from Luster and Friedman. The trial court ordered Luster and Friedman to pay for the canopy, and Luster and Friedman appealed. Who is liable? *20 East Cedar Condominium Association v. Luster* et al., 349 N.E.2d 586 (Ill. 1976)

4. Jay Johnson purchased a condominium in November 1978 but failed to pay the monthly maintenance fee after August 1979. The Condominium Declaration for his condominium apartments provided that the homeowner's council (First Southern) has a lien on each apartment for any unpaid assessments and authorized the council to enforce the lien through "non-judicial foreclosure through a power of sale."

Using the authority in the declaration of condominium, First Southern foreclosed on Johnson's unit. Johnson claimed he enjoyed a homestead exemption protection and that the council could not foreclose. Can the council foreclose? *Johnson v. First Southern Properties, Inc.*, 687 S.W.2d 399 (Tex. 1985)

5. William B. Miller, an owner of a condominium in San Antonio's Villa Del Sol, has failed to pay his share of common element assessments and owes $3,604.51 in back assessments. The bylaws authorize the directors to enforce the assessments by whatever means necessary. The directors shut off Mr. Miller's electricity. Is this proper under their bylaws? *San Antonio Villa Del Sol Homeowners Association v. Miller*, 761 S.W.2d 460 (Tx. 1988)

6. The Island House Association, Incorporated, a homeowners' association formed for the operation of the Island House condominiums and villas, assessed each unit for maintenance fees. The association required condominium owners to pay more for maintenance than villa owners because the condominium building was larger, had more units, and required more frequent repairs. The provision for fees was in the bylaws and had been voted on by the owners and approved by a majority. Thiess, a condominium owner, refused to pay his fees and claimed the assessment was inequitable and unfair. What was the result?

7. George E. Western is the owner of a condominium unit in Chardonnay Village. Chardonnay Village Condominium Association, Inc., is the association of condominium unit owners that governs and manages the condominium project. Under the Louisiana Condominium Act, associations are empowered to collect expenses of administration, maintenance, repair, and replacement of the common elements. The condominium declaration of Chardonnay Village authorizes the association to collect the costs of utilities for each unit as well as for the common areas.

Western has failed to pay the assessments for the common areas for approximately three years for a total of $4,962.08, which included late fees of $25.00 per month.

On October 1, 1986, the association turned off Western's water supply for failure to pay the assessment. Western filed for a temporary restraining order to prevent the water turnoff and was awarded such by the trial court. What should be the result? *Western v. Chardonnay Village Condominium Association, Inc.*, 519 So.2d 243 (La. 1988)

8. Donna Marie Morgan lived in the condominium building owned by 253 East Delaware Condominium Association (Delaware) and managed by Joseph Moss Realty (Moss). On September 18, 1986, at about 8:30 P.M., Morgan walked from her class at Loyola University's downtown campus to the building where she entered the lobby. She observed a man talking with the doorman when she first entered the building and was checking her mail. The man followed her onto the elevator.

When the elevator arrived at the tenth floor, the man poked a gun in her back and forced her off the elevator and into the stairwell. He pushed Morgan down to the ninth floor, robbed and beat her with the gun, and caused severe injuries.

Morgan filed suit alleging that Delaware and Moss were negligent for their failure to protect her from criminal acts of unknown parties. Should Delaware and Moss be held liable? *Morgan v. 253 East Delaware Condominium Association*, 595 N.E.2d 36 (Ill. 1992)

9. Ronald and Roseanne Ebner are shareholders and tenants under a proprietary lease of an apartment in a Manhattan multiple dwelling owned by 91st Street Tenants Corporation. The Ebners sought to assign their shares and their lease to Janusz Gorzynski. They made application to the corporation's board of directors, but the consent to transfer was denied on the grounds that Gorzynski is a psychiatrist who intends to use the apartment primarily for treating patients and only secondarily as a residence. The board also pointed out that Gorzynski would allow other physicians to use his residence when he is out of the city.

The Ebners then used Article II, Section 6, of the proprietary lease, which permits a tenant to make an assignment without the consent of the board so long as there is written consent from a majority of lessees owning capital stock. The Ebners believe they have obtained such consent, but they have obtained only one signature in many cases when the shares are jointly owned. Describe the types of interests involved in this situation and advise the parties on their rights. *Ebner v. 91st Street Tenants Corp.*, 481 N.Y.S.2d 198 (1984)

10. William and Joan Madigan and Henry and LaVonne Speak owned homes in the Garden Lakes subdivision. The Association recorded a Declaration of Covenants, Conditions, Restrictions and Easements for Garden Lakes ("Declaration"). The Declaration applies to all owners of property within Garden Lakes who purchased a lot after the Declaration was recorded on January 28, 1986. The Madigans and the Speaks purchased their lots after the Declaration and accepted their deeds subject to the following provision in the Declaration:

No improvements, alterations... or other work which in any way alters the exterior appearance of any property or improvements thereon... shall be made or done... unless and until the Architectural Review Committee has, in each such case, reviewed and approved the nature of the proposed work, alteration, structure or grading and the plans and specifications therefor.

The Association established an architectural review committee ("ARC") and architectural review guidelines ("guidelines") that included the following.

1. All solar energy devices Visible from Neighboring Property or public view must be approved by the Architectural Review Committee prior to installation.
2. Panels must be an integrated part of the roof design and mounted directly to the roof plane. Solar units must not break the roof ridge line, must not be visible from public view and must be screened from neighboring property in a manner approved by the Board of Directors or its designee(s). Roof mounted hot water storage systems must not be Visible from Neighboring Property. Tracker-type systems will be allowed only when not Visible from Neighboring Property.
3. The criteria for screening set forth in Section III(M) "Machinery and Equipment", shall apply to solar panels and equipment.

Under the "Machinery and Equipment" section, the guidelines provided:

[S]creening or concealment shall be solid and integrated architecturally with the design of the building or structure, shall not have the appearance of a separate piece or pieces of machinery, fixtures or equipment, and shall be constructed and positioned in such a manner so it is level and plumb with vertical building components and shall be structurally stable in accordance with sound engineering principles.

The Madigans and the Speaks installed solar energy devices ("SEDs") on the roofs of their respective homes without ARC or Association approval. These SEDs included solar panels to collect and transfer heat to their swimming pools. The Association sued the Madigans and the Speaks in separate actions, alleging failure to comply with the guidelines and breach of the Declaration. The Association sought permanent injunctions compelling the removal of the SEDs, monetary penalties, and attorneys' fees and costs. The Madigans and Speaks say that the state gives tax credits for these solar panels and that the Association's rules runs contrary to public policy designed to encourage solar energy use. What are the rights of the owners? The Association? The state? *Garden Lakes Community Ass'n, Inc. v. Madigan*, 62 P.3d 983 (Ariz. 2003)

For research activities related to this chapter, go to our text companion website at www.thomsonedu.com/westbuslaw/jennings.

The Broker's Role in the Transfer of Real Estate

CHAPTER 12

Robert Schwalb and Suzanne Schwalb were thinking of buying a farm owned by Ruth McCormack. The Schwalbs were shown the farm by William V. Kulaski III, a broker and agent with Kulaski Realty. Mr. Kulaski said to the Schwalbs, "You gotta see this room," referring to a room located in the second story of the farm's barn, a barn that was built in 1910. Mr. Schwalb broke his leg when he fell through the second-story floorboards of the room above the barn. Needless to say, the Schwalbs did not buy the farm, but they did file suit against Kulaski and his real estate firm for their negligence in failing to disclose and discover the dangerous condition in the barn. Can the Schwalbs recover?[1]

The opening scenario shows the liability issues that brokers and agents face. This business of selling property for others has prickly legal issues at every step, as it were. There are ever-evolving dilemmas and questions surrounding the conduct and role of brokers. This chapter answers the following questions: Does the broker represent the seller or the buyer in the transaction? Is the broker responsible for defects the seller fails to disclose? Is the broker entitled to be paid when a sale falls through? What happens if a potential buyer falls through, literally and figuratively? What is the agency relationship of the broker? What responsibilities and liabilities does the broker have as an agent? What ethical constraints should a broker follow? What areas should a broker focus on when listing and selling a property?

Nature of Broker's/Agent's Role

Definition

A **broker** is an agent[2] hired either by the owner of a property to aid in its sale or by a potential owner (buyer) to find property suitable for specified needs. A broker is the

1. *Schwalb v. Kulaski,* 814 N.Y.S.2d 696 (2006).
2. Note: The term *broker* is used here in a generic sense to reflect that person hired to represent either the seller or buyer in a real estate transaction. *Broker* and *agent* have distinct meanings in the real estate industry, with differing

middle person acting to bring buyer and seller together. Generally, a broker works on a commission basis rather than on salary. That commission is usually specified as some percentage of the sales price and will probably not be paid until the actual sales transaction is complete (see the consideration discussion in this chapter).

Traditional Principal/Agent Concepts vs. Principal/Broker Roles

Under the traditional principal/agent relationship, the **agent** works on behalf of the principal, owes a duty of loyalty to the principal, would not breach confidences of the principal, and would not profit at the principal's expense. The principal and the agent are a team, working together with a common interest. However, the nature of property transactions creates flowing, instead of rigid, relationships for the real estate broker. Interactions and methods of conducting business blur the traditional lines and rules of agency. While the industry is still evolving with respect to the role of brokers, there are certain types of broker relationships that are common in the industry. Those types of relationships are found in the following section.

The Types of Real Estate Broker Relationships

The Listing Agent

The listing agent works directly with the seller to list the property, advertise it, and contribute other marketing services. However, even the listing agent will be involved in showing property to buyers and hence has contact with both the buyer and seller. A Federal Trade Commission survey found that even though the listing agent is the only one involved in a sales transaction, 72 percent of purchasers of real estate still believed that the listing agent represented them and not the seller.

The Dual Agency

Given the confusion of buyers with respect to the role of brokers, many states allow **dual agency** relationships. A dual agency permits an agent to represent both sides in a transaction so long as the parties are aware of the dual representation.

All states have some form of mandatory disclosure requirements by agents, regardless of the type of agency relationship that the parties have agreed to have. Before buyers or sellers sign with a broker for representation, there must be full disclosure about the broker's role and responsibilities. In addition, the **National Association of Realtors** (**NAR**), the professional association for brokers and agents, requires under its code of ethics that NAR members make specific disclosures to all parties.[3]

If these disclosures are not made, the real estate broker will lose the commission or be required to pay back the commission. Web Exhibits 12.1 and 12.2 are sample disclosure forms for Massachusetts and Florida.

In the case of dual representation, the disclosure form, known as a "Consent to Act," must be signed by the parties hiring the broker. Web Exhibit 12.3 is a sample dual representation consent form.

training and education requirements. A real estate agent must work for a broker but can serve as an agent in the legal sense for seller or buyer. That real estate agent's broker is also a legal agent for the listing seller or the represented buyer. The terms *broker* and *agent* are used interchangeably throughout the chapter.

3. Standard of practice 1–6 of the Code of Ethics and Standards of Practice for the National Association of Realtors (effective January 1, 2007) provides that a Realtor may not represent the landlord and tenant or the buyer and seller until there has been full disclosure to and informed consent by both parties.

ETHICAL ISSUE

Is it possible for a dual agent to be loyal to both parties? Does one side suffer in a dual agency relationship? Is the dual agent simply protecting information the buyer would never gain access to if there were separate agents?

The Buyer Broker

It is also possible to have an agency relationship in which the buyer is represented by a broker.[4] The buyer broker may require a nonrefundable up-front fee but is generally paid the bulk of his or her fee as percentage commission from the eventual property sale. Fees are usually in the range of 2–3%. The question of conflict arises with this commission arrangement because the buyer broker's compensation is tied to the purchase price: Will the buyer broker negotiate the lowest possible price when compensation increases as the price increases? The key to managing this conflict under codes of ethics in the broker profession is dislosure of all terms and all relationships or potential relationships.[5]

The Open Listing Agency

An **open listing** agreement is used when an owner lists the property to be sold with more than one broker. Under this form of listing, not common in residential transactions, the seller owes only one commission to the broker who actually sells the property. Furthermore, the seller retains the right to sell the property personally; and if the seller does produce the buyer, no commission is owed to any broker.

Other brokers are free to solicit listings from sellers who have open listing arrangements with other brokers, and the only commission paid will be the one to the broker who actually produced the buyer.

The Exclusive Agency

An **exclusive agency listing** arrangement is one in which the seller is required to pay a commission to the listing broker if that broker sells the property. However, the seller still retains the right to sell the property independently; and if the seller does sell the listed property, the listing broker earns no commission. If the seller hires another broker, the original broker retains the right to commission and the seller will be obligated for two commissions.

The major distinction between the open listing agreement and the exclusive agency listing agreement is that the open listing permits the seller to list the property with other brokers. Under the exclusive agency listing, sellers should not list with other brokers, because they will still be responsible to the exclusive broker for the commission and may end up paying more than one commission. In both types of listings, the seller may still sell the property independently without being required to pay the commission. See Web Exhibit 12.4 for sample open and exclusive listings.

The Exclusive Right-to-Sell or Exclusive Listing-to-Sell Agency

Under the **exclusive right-to-sell** or **exclusive listing-to-sell** arrangement, the seller agrees to pay a commission to the broker regardless of who produces a buyer. The broker

4. There is the National Association of Exclusive Buyer Agents (NAEBA), founded in 1995, that is comprised of agents who represent only buyers in real estate transactions. These agents also have their own code of ethics.
5. Standard Practice 1–13 of the NAR's code requires the Realtor to disclose the compensation and whether there are any arrangements between the buyer-broker and other brokers.

earns the commission even if the seller produces a buyer independently of the broker. This type of listing agreement, which is beneficial to the broker, is the one used most frequently in the real estate industry.

Multiple Listing Agency

The **multiple listing** agreement is not really a form of agency between seller and broker, but rather a service available to brokers who are members of a multiple listing service. An example of a **multiple listing service** is the **MLS**, a network of exclusive right-to-sell listings that affords brokers and sellers a larger market for their properties. Through MLS, broker members are able to show the listed properties of other brokers. The listing broker then shares in the commission if a another broker obtains a buyer for the broker's listed property. The split commission is prenegotiated and determined by the MLS members. Since there is still only one listing agreement, the seller is liable for only one commission. The MLS is a marketing tool that allows brokers to assist each other in finding buyers and gives sellers greater exposure for their properties.

The Subagency

The subagency relationship is a product of MLS arrangements. Under an MLS listing, there is the listing broker (who represents the seller) and then, quite often, the selling broker (who brings the buyers who eventually buy the property). In a subagency, the selling broker is a subagent of the seller because the selling broker derives his/her authority from the listing broker. However, there remains a problem with buyers' perceptions in this type of arrangement—the buyers still feel both brokers work for them. Further, many sellers believe the selling broker works for the buyer rather than for them.[6] In 1993, NAR changed its position that subagents were mandatory agents of the seller, and the result has been a shift to more buyers' agents participating in sales of MLS-listed properties. A new term, "the cooperating broker," has emerged. A cooperating broker is one who is working as a subagent of the listing broker and has agreed to a commission arrangement in the event the cooperating broker finds a buyer for the property. All subagents must disclose their relationship and compensation to the seller's agent when they have contact with the property and again if there is an offer or contract on the property. Subagents who are agents of the seller must disclose that information to any prospective buyers. Listing brokers also have obligations to disclose their commission arrangements to cooperating and potentially cooperating brokers.

Net Listing Agency

In the **net listing** agreement, the seller and broker may have any of the previous types of listing arrangements for determining who is entitled to the commission. This arrangement, illegal in residential listing in some states, merely provides a different method for determining the amount of commission the broker is entitled to receive. Generally, the commission is some percentage of the selling price. However, in net listings, the sellers establish a predetermined amount that they must receive from the sale of the property after expenses, insurance, and so on. The broker's commission is anything received above that predetermined amount. For example, if the seller

6. Ann Moales Olazábal, "Redefining Realtor Relationships and Responsibilities: The Failure of State Regulatory Responses," 40 *Harvard J. of Legislation* 65 (2003).

sets the net figure at $40,000 and $41,500 remains after expenses, etc., the broker receives a $1,500 commission. Again, this form of commission determination may be coupled with an open listing, exclusive agency listing, or exclusive right-to-sell format.

The Designated Agency

A **designated agency** relationship arises when one firm represents both the buyer and seller in a transaction. The broker for the firm designates one salesperson to represent the seller and another salesperson to represent the buyer. The designated agency differs from the dual agency in that two different agents are representing the parties, with the theory being that the representation is more objective. Most states also have disclosure requirements for designated agency arrangements so that sellers and buyers are aware that their agents work for the same broker or agency.

The Nonagent Broker

A **nonagent broker** may be known as a **transaction broker, intermediary, limited agent**, or **statutory broker**. At least 18 states recognize this relationship in which brokers represent both buyer and seller in closing a transaction.[7] They are simply facilitators for closing. States vary on their requirements for creating a nonagency relationship.

ETHICAL ISSUE

Tom Caines is acting as an agent for Luci and Neil Dayton, a couple looking to purchase a home. Tom has located a home in Ventura Canyon that nearly perfectly suits the needs Luci and Neil have described to him. Tom approaches the owner, Mel Cusack, and explains that he is representing Luci and Neil Dayton as buyers. Tom then adds, "Look, you have what they want. You can pretty much get your asking price. It helps me because I am on commission in addition to the fee they paid up front." Has Tom acted ethically? What conflict does Tom have in acting as a buyer broker and earning a commission?

The Internet as an Agent

Stocks, bonds, antiques, and anything e-Bay sellers can think of have sold well over the Internet. The free market exchange of information and quick transactions have produced selling booms in everything from books to toys. The idea of matching buyers and sellers of real estate with an Internet database seemed to be a possibility that would eliminate the need for any type of agent or broker. However, those responsible for Microsoft's Internet site for home buyers, http://www.HomeAdvisor.com, have conceded that agents play a critical role in the buying and selling of real estate, particularly when it comes to homes. The most successful Internet real estate sites are those that partner with agents. Not all real estate buyers are ready to negotiate the purchase of a home without a physical view and are not prepared enough to handle the contracting and negotiations by themselves.

Internet listing services are not so different from other types of listings or even the MLS. The seller lists property with the Internet service, which plays the role of the listing broker. Buyers may come to the site with their own agent or broker, or they may use an agent or broker offered by the site. That broker or agent then is entitled to split the commission with the Internet listing service. The laws and codes of ethics

7. Ann Moales Olazábal, "Redefining Realtor Relationships and Responsibilities: The Failure of State Regulatory Responses," 40 *Harvard J. of Legislation* 65 (2003).

provisions on disclosures still aply to brokers acting for sellers and buyers over the many Internet sites for sales of homes.

Listing Agreements for Hiring Brokers/Agents

The agency arrangement between broker and seller is called a **listing agreement**. State requirements for valid listing agreements vary, but the parties should be cautious about including provisions that specify their rights, duties, and responsibilities. The goal is to cover all fundamentals so that their intentions are made absolutely clear.

Agreements in Writing

Under most state laws and the code of ethics for Realtors, the agency agreement must be in writing. In most states where a written listing agreement is required, the failure to execute a written agreement will cost the broker or salesperson the commission. States now allow faxed agreements as well as electronic communications applications that have been part of the reforms since the federal E-Sign provisions that require parity for electronic forms of communication with paper documents. However, oral agreements for real estate agency contracts remain unenforceable in most states. Even if a broker sells the property pursuant to an oral agreement, the seller need not pay the commission. Exceptions to the writing requirement are rare.

Ethical Issue

Jeffrey Sisson owned a sports bar and restaurant in Charles City. In early 1999, he contacted Larry Stewart about selling the restaurant. Stewart is a licensed real estate broker in Charles City. Sisson told Stewart he wanted a sales price of around $615,000, and he would pay him 10 percent of the sales price if he found a buyer. However, Sisson did not want Stewart to list the property because he thought he would lose sales and value from the business if the public was aware it was for sale. Stewart agreed to find a buyer, but the parties never reduced the agreement to writing.

Stewart began looking for a buyer for the property. One person he contacted was Michael Walter, who Stewart thought would be interested in the business. Stewart obtained financial information about the business from Sisson and told Sisson he intended to disclose it to Walter. Stewart required Walter to sign an agreement to keep the information confidential and to prevent him from negotiating directly with Sisson.

On November 13, 2001, Sisson sold the business to Walter without notifying or involving Stewart. Stewart subsequently learned about the sale and wrote Sisson to inquire about his commission. Sisson replied and asked Stewart for written documentation to verify the agreement. Stewart could not provide a writing.

After trying and failing to resolve the dispute, Stewart filed an action against Sisson for breach of contract in March 2002. Sisson responded by filing a motion to dismiss. He claimed Iowa Administrative Code rule 193E-1.23 [now rule 193E-11.1] barred Stewart's claim. ("All listing agreements shall be in writing, properly identifying the property and containing all of the terms and conditions under which the property is to be sold, including the price, the commission to be paid, the signatures of all parties concerned and a definite expiration date.") The district court dismissed the breach-of-contract claim. Was the result fair? Think of an argument you could make to have the agreement for the 10 percent commission be enforceable. Was Sisson's conduct ethical? *Stewart v. Sisson*, 711 N.W.2d 713 (Iowa 2006)

Signature by Owner

The listing agreement must be signed (according to the state law provisions on electronic communication and statutes on authentication) by the owner of the property. The true or record owner must sign the agreement and if there is more than one owner, all owners must sign. In the case of land owned by a corporation or partnership, the officer, director, or partner signing the listing agreement must have the authority to do so, such as a resolution by the board for a corporate officer's authority. The authority of a trustee, executor, administrator, or personal representative can be found in a court order or the letters of administration, along with any restrictions on the authority to transfer title to the property. For example, some executors of estates may have authority to list the property but not to sell it without prior court approval.

Importance of Careful Drafting and Completion of Standard Form Agreements

Both brokers and sellers should be cautious in drafting the listing agreement, even if drafting consists only of completing forms, so that the type of listing is clear and the commission issue is not clouded with ambiguities. Generally, with higher prices in real estate now prevalent, brokers stand to receive substantial commissions. With so much money involved, it is only natural that many legal battles have been fought and are pending in the courts over the issue of who is entitled to receive a commission. The best way to avoid litigation is to make sure the listing agreement is drafted carefully and unambiguously.

Expiration Date

Most states have some type of law or regulation requiring a definite expiration date for a listing agreement to be valid. When an expiration date is required and there is none in the agreement, the listing is an unenforceable contract and can cost the broker the commission in spite of a sale. Some states impose maximum time limits for listing agreements, with 90 days being a typical maximum length.

Brokers may put a clause in the listing agreement that entitles them to a commission for a certain period of time after the expiration of the listing agreement if there is a post-expiration sale to prospective buyers originally introduced to the property by the broker during the listing period.

A sample clause follows:

If within ninety (90) days after the expiration of this listing agreement, a sale is made directly by the broker to any person to whom this property has been shown by you or the broker or an agent of the broker, the same fee shall prevail, unless this listing is renewed or the property is relisted on the same basis with another broker, and in that case, this stipulation shall be void.

In some states there are statutory requirements for the right to earn a commission on a listing agreement that has expired if a sale is made to a prospect the broker brought to the seller. Requirements often include the broker providing a seller with a list of "protected persons," or those persons to whom the property has been shown, so that the seller is aware of the broker's claim for a commission should a sale to any of them occur. In many states, statutes or regulations require that this list be a formal document that must be delivered in a relatively short time limit, such as within 72 hours after the listing agreement ends.

One additional danger in having a listing agreement without an expiration date and extension clause, even in those states recognizing the validity of open-end listings, is that the seller may cancel the agreement at any time. Such a right of cancellation is often used to avoid paying a commission. The courts have implied a duty of good faith on the part of the parties to an indefinite-duration listing agreement to preclude commission avoidance.

The rights of termination under the listing agreements are also an important timing issue. Issues that should be addressed in the listing agreement include whether the listing may be terminated, how termination occurs, what type of notice of termination is required, and what damages will be due and owing, if any.

The following case deals with a termination and commission issue on a residential listing agreement.

Island Realty v. Bibbo

748 A.2d 620 (N.J. App. 2000)

FACTS

Island Realty (plaintiff/appellant) listed Susan Bibbo's (defendant) property in Loveladies, New Jersey. The listing agreement was an MLS exclusive right to sell effective from May 13, 1998, until November 13, 1998. The listing price was $359,000 and the commission for Island was 6 percent.

On July 23, 1998, Ms. Bibbo notified Island that she wanted to remove her house from the market. She confirmed that decision the next day with a letter to the Island offices.

On July 27, 1998, Island faxed to Bibbo an unsigned, illegible agreement for sale for the listing price from a buyer produced by another realtor. A legible version was faxed the next day, but the actual agreement was not signed by the buyer until July 29, 1998. Bibbo never received a signed copy of the purchase agreement and she did not sign either document that she received. In short, Bibbo refused to sell the property. She also refused demands by Island for its commission.

Island filed suit for its full commission of $21,540. The lower court granted Bibbo's motion for summary judgment and Island Realty appealed.

JUDICIAL OPINION

Kestin, Judge. In a written statement attached to the dismissal order, Judge Ford expressed her reasons for granting defendant's motion for summary judgment and dismissing the complaint.

The statement recited in part: Mrs. Bibbo did not sign the agreement, since she felt she had removed the house from the market, and further, since she found the terms to be unacceptable; although the offer was for full price, the initial deposit of $1,000 and the additional deposit of $35,900 were not paid, and the offer had not been signed by the prospective purchaser. . . .

The listing agreement does not address the issue of termination in the event that the seller, as is purported occurred here, has a change of heart. For purposes of this motion, however, I am assuming that the listing agreement was in effect and the question is whether or not the right to a commission, setting aside the enforceability of the agreement, ever occurred. It appears that it was within the prerogative of the seller to reject even a full price offer based upon unacceptable terms, in this case, the deficiency of the down payment, and the failure of the purchaser to follow through with the offer.

Therefore, there was not a ready, willing and able buyer making a bona fide offer, and thus the right to receive the commission never accrued. Since there is no factual dispute to be resolved, summary judgment is appropriate.

In denying plaintiff's motion for reconsideration, Judge Ford expressed her reasons in an oral opinion:

I agree that somebody could make a full price offer knowing that someone is not going to accept it for whatever reason, and under this theory they could always guarantee themselves a source of income because to say that just as long as somebody offers the full price, then that triggers the commission. I don't think. . . I agree.

What this is governed by is what was the agreement between the parties. And the agreement was that Island Realty would market the property for sale. I think that the ultimate decision about whether or not to accept a contract always resided with the seller of the property and no matter what the circumstances were, the decision about whether or not to sell the property was always reposed with the seller.

I don't think that by entering in a listing agreement that the seller intends to surrender that aspect of the ownership of the property because otherwise they would be, in effect, surrendering all of the decision making for the sale of the property. And I think that's something that goes with the incident of ownership of property that resides with the seller. What they are giving up is the right to *market the property. And when there is a meeting of the minds in terms of a transaction and even if that transaction doesn't consummate in an actual sale, if there's a meeting of the minds and if the seller backed out of that, then there would be a right to some type of real estate commission. And I agree that Island Realty would then be entitled to the commission it would have realized on the transaction which in this case would have been approximately $10,000, not the full commission but the commission that they would have realized because they would have split it with the other—they're the listing broker and there was a broker here that actually produced this potential customer. But for whatever reason, there was no meeting of the minds in terms of the terms and conditions of this contract. And there may be some question as to whether or not this particular [purchaser] rose to the level of being a ready, willing, and able [purchaser] and whether or not the terms were acceptable to the [seller].*

But in any event, because of the seller's personal circumstances she decided to take this property off the market. And so long as she did not go to another agency and market it, if she was taking it off the market at that point in time, then I think that it is implicit within her agency agreement that she have the right to do that. This again doesn't do violence to the right of Island Realty to get a commission on a sale or where they produce a ready, willing, and able buyer. But here because there just wasn't a meeting of the minds and because a reasonable seller cold [could] disagree with certain terms and conditions of this contract, then I think that my initial decision was accurate and that the application for a commission is denied. . . ."

In general, the seller is liable for the commission where, during the listing term the realtor was the "efficient producing cause" of an actual sale.

Where the property has been withdrawn from the market before the broker's efforts have produced a buyer who stands ready to consummate the transaction, the owner is responsible to the broker only for such damages as may be established for breach of contract or on a quantum meruit basis for special services rendered in connection with reasonable efforts to sell the property, undertaken before it was withdrawn from the market.

Instead of seeking the full sales commission where no sale had occurred, plaintiff could have sought damages based on breach of contract or on quantum meruit. Even though one cannot prevail on both a contract claim and a quantum meruit (implied contract) claim covering the same services, our liberal approaches to pleading practice permit a party to seek relief on alternative grounds. However, when questioned at oral argument before us on the subjects of quantum meruit and breach of contract damages, plaintiff expressly disavowed any interest in pursuing a claim other than for its full commission, notwithstanding that count four of the complaint, viewed with the customary liberality employed in construing the scope of pleadings. We note, as well, that during the pendency of this matter plaintiff never asserted that it had incurred damages from defendant's alleged breach of contract apart from its loss of the full sales commission.

Affirmed.

CASE QUESTIONS

1. When was the listing agreement signed? When was it terminated?
2. When was the offer faxed? When was it signed?
3. Does a seller have the right to refuse an offer for the full listing price?
4. Is the broker entitled to the commission in this case? Is the broker entitled to damages in this case?

CONSIDER 12.1

Palmer and Elva Loyning entered into a real estate listing agreement with Property Brokers, Inc., to sell their ranch near Roberts, Montana. The agreement employed Property Brokers "to sell or exchange" the property, and would give them an 8 percent commission under the following circumstances:

In the event that you or any other brokers cooperating with you, shall find a buyer ready and willing to enter into a deal for said price and terms, or such other terms and price as I may accept, or that during your employment you supply me with a name of or place me in contact with a buyer to or through whom at any time within 180 days after the termination of said employment I may sell or convey said property, I hereby agree to pay you in cash for your services a commission equal in amount to 8 percent of the above-stated selling price.

CONSIDER 12.1
(continued)

The agreement was entered into on June 25, 1979, and was to expire June 25, 1980.

Vern Schoulte and a broker cooperating with Property Brokers showed the Loyning ranch to John and Anyce Gerhardt. The Gerhardts and Loynings entered into a buy–sell agreement on October 23, 1979. An earnest money deposit of $1,000 was given to Schoulte to hold until closing.

The buy–sell agreement was made entirely contingent upon the sale of the Gerhardts' property near Sidney, Montana. Meanwhile, the Gerhardts would take possession of the Loyning ranch as tenants. The buy–sell agreement, including the tenancy provision, was to expire March 31, 1980. If another buyer was found prior to March 31, 1980, the Gerhardts would have 72 hours to finalize their agreement.

The Gerhardts were not able to sell their property near Sidney before March 31, 1980, and no other buyer was found. The Loynings allowed the Gerhardts to stay at their ranch as tenants beyond the March 31 deadline. On August 6, 1980, however, the $1,000 earnest money deposit was forfeited.

On December 31, 1980, the Gerhardts eventually sold their property near Sidney, and were then able to buy the Loyning ranch. On January 29, 1981, the Gerhardts finalized the purchase of the Loyning ranch.

Property Brokers and Schoulte brought suit for their commission. Are they entitled to their commission? *Property Brokers, Inc. v. Loyning*, 654 P.2d 521 (Mont. 1982)

Amount of the Commission

Particularly in multiple listing arrangements, there has been a uniformity in commission rates that has caused the Justice Department to bring suit alleging a conspiracy among real estate brokers to fix prices. Most listing agreements include language similar to the following to attempt to countermand the allegations of price fixing: "*The commissions payable for the sale, lease, or management of property are not set by any board of Realtors, multiple listing service, or in any manner other than between the broker and the client.*"

While there has not been a judicial decision directly addressing real estate commissions and their antitrust implications, the United States Supreme Court has ruled in *McClain et al. v. Real Estate Board of New Orleans, Inc. et al.*, 441 U.S. 942 (1980) that real estate brokerage has a sufficient impact on interstate commerce for it to be subject to federal antitrust laws such as the Sherman Act and its prohibition on price fixing. Some states now require that brokers' disclosure forms include language informing consumers that the commission rate is negotiable.

Because the MLS listing enables brokers to tap into an entire community's market, its accessibility is often critical for success in the business. Sales statistics indicate that 80 percent of all residential purchases involve a multiple listing service broker. However, in recent years these organizations have, like other trade and professional associations, faced review of their anticompetitive effects. Membership restrictions for such boards are particularly suspect when the result is that those denied memberships, on the basis of unjustified criteria, are effectively precluded from the business benefits and activities afforded members.

CONSIDER 12.2

The newly elected president of a professional organization of real estate agents held a dinner at an exclusive country club. He invited his colleagues who would help him manage the organization during his tenure of office. Their discussion at dinner centered around a new membership drive and the organization of committees. The new president then stood at the meeting and said the following:

CONSIDER 12.2
(continued)

My business is dying fast. I have already borrowed $75,000 to keep afloat. If I am going bankrupt at 6 percent, I might as well go bankrupt at 7 percent. I don't care what the rest of you do, that is what I am going to do.

Has there been an antitrust violation? *U.S. v. Foley*, 598 F.2d 1323 (C.A. Md. 1979).

Because of the Internet, buyers have ease of access to information outside an MLS, and a means for easier and less expensive access to property information. Despite this plethora of information, however, there is still great market power through the MLS, along with relationship issues regarding the use of MLS and the fees associated with it. The following significant case explores the interrelationships of various MLS services and their antitrust implications.

FREEMAN V. SAN DIEGO ASS'N OF REALTORS

322 F.3d 1133 (9th Cir. 2003), *cert. denied* 540 U.S. 940 (2003)

FACTS

At one time, there were 11 regional associations of real estate agents in San Diego County. These 11 associations operated three separate MLS's (defendants), each of which provided a partial and fragmented listing of the real estate for sale in San Diego County.

The separate 11 MLS services in one county proved chaotic, and in December 1991, the 11 local associations combined their separate MLS's and created a new MLS listing of all properties for sale throughout San Diego County. To create this new product, the local associations formed Sandicor, a corporate entity in which they were shareholders. Sandicor owns and operates a county-wide MLS. Sandicor's MLS is an essential tool for real estate agents, and nearly all real estate agents actively engaged in buying or selling real estate in San Diego County use Sandicor's MLS.

Despite the unified front and consolidation, the Realtors felt that the maintenance of the listing information was best handled by the 11 individual MLS associations. However, the new consortium discovered that the fees among the associations varied significantly, with some charging as little as $10 per subscriber per month for maintenance and others charging as much as $50. The San Diego Association of Realtors (SDAR), the largest of the associations, charged only $10 per month, and Sandicor officials worried that if they allowed the fees to be charged by individual associations that SDAR would simply withdraw and undercut the efficacy of the consolidation.

As a result, Sandicor agreed to a universal maintenance fee of $25 per month per subscriber. Every member of every association would now pay a uniform fee of $25 per month for the Sandicor MLS subscription. Those who had paid $10 now paid $25 and those who paid $50 formerly now had their fees cut in half. Sandicor kept only a portion of that $25 fee but returned the bulk of it to the association for maintenance completion, something they had already decided was best done by the individual associations. Those kept funds became the crux of the antitrust litigation.

Arleen Freeman, a Realtor, along with other Realtors (plaintiffs/petitioners) and subscribers to Sandicor, brought suit alleging that the retention of a portion of the fees paid by Sandicor constituted monopolization under the Sherman Act. The lower court granted summary judgment to Sandicor and Freeman appealed.

JUDICIAL OPINION

Kozinski, Circuit Judge. Competition is the mainspring of a capitalist economy. Sometimes, however, cooperation can make markets more efficient; setting industry standards and pooling market data are two examples of arrangements that often benefit consumers. Antitrust laws acknowledge these benefits, but still treat the arrangements with skepticism, for seemingly benign agreements may conceal highly anticompetitive schemes. We apply these principles to a case involving a real estate Multiple Listing Service.

Real estate agents make a living matching buyers and sellers. Up-to-date information about properties on the market is a must. Long gone are the days when agents trawled the neighborhood on horseback in search of telltale "For Sale" signs. We're now in the era of the Multiple Listing Service, or "MLS," which lets agents share information about properties on the market with the help of a computerized database. Agents who subscribe to the MLS can peruse the listings of other subscribers and post their own.

Care and feeding of an MLS involves more than just maintaining a database. Someone must enroll new MLS subscribers, bill and collect payments, ensure that postings comply with guidelines and provide support staff to answer subscribers' questions. These "support services" are part of the necessary overhead of delivering an MLS.

The Sherman Act applies to restraints of trade or commerce "among the several States." 15 U.S.C. §§1–2. Monopolizing the local lemonade stand doesn't get you into federal court. To make a federal case, a plaintiff must show that the activities in question, although conducted within a state, have a "substantial effect on interstate commerce." *McLain v. Real Estate Bd. of New Orleans, Inc.*, 444 U.S. 232, 242, 100 S.Ct. 502, 62 L.Ed.2d 441 (1980). Uncontradicted evidence shows that Sandicor's MLS mediated more than $23 billion of home sales over a four-year period, affecting approximately $10 billion in interstate home-mortgage financing. The effects of home sales on the interstate mortgage market are a sufficient connection with interstate commerce, and $10 billion is "substantial" by any standard.

Defendants urge that we consider only the interstate effects caused by the illegal conduct itself. According to their economics expert, the cost of an MLS subscription is trivial compared to the typical real estate sales commission. Thus, even if the cost of the MLS was inflated, it would have only a de minimis effect on the commissions real estate agents charge, and thus no effect on the number of houses sold. Defendants misunderstand the legal standard. The Supreme Court has explained:

To establish the jurisdictional element of a Sherman Act violation it would be sufficient for petitioners to demonstrate a substantial effect on interstate commerce generated by respondents' ["infected"] activity. Petitioners need not make the more particularized showing of an effect on interstate commerce caused by the alleged conspiracy to fix [prices], or by those other aspects of respondents' activity that are alleged to be unlawful.

Thus, we examine the MLS, not the alleged price fixing. Even if the price of the MLS has no substantial effect on interstate commerce, the MLS itself does. Defendants' economist may be right, but he answered the wrong question.

PRICE FIXING

The dispositive question generally is not whether any price fixing was justified, but simply whether it occurred.

They [the associations] admit that they fixed the fee in order to ensure that financially weaker associations would make more money than under a competitive regime, and thus concede by implication that they intentionally fixed the fee at a supracompetitive level.

Sandicor is paying for something. What it's buying is the contractual right to have the associations provide support services to its MLS subscribers. That the subscribers receive the support services as third-party beneficiaries doesn't change the fact that Sandicor is the buyer and the associations are the sellers. If Elle Woods pays someone to walk her dog, she's the buyer and the dog-walker is the seller, even though Bruiser gets the exercise. And if the Cambridge dog-walking cartel starts fixing prices, it's hardly a defense for them to say "We just walk dogs!"

Sandicor charges subscribers for their use of the MLS; its MLS fee includes the support services provided by the associations. The support fee Sandicor in turn pays the associations for support services was fixed at a level more than twice what it cost the most efficient association to provide them. These inflated support fees harm subscribers if Sandicor passes them on in the form of higher MLS fees.

There is unmistakable evidence that Sandicor not only considered its costs in setting MLS fees but, in fact, priced near cost and thus may have passed on the inflated support fees almost dollar for dollar. For example, an April 1997 association bulletin explains that "[Sandicor's] pricing takes the total amount required to run Sandicor and divides by the total number of agents on the system. The amount to run Sandicor includes ... the amount Sandicor sends back to each Association, by contractual arrangement, to provide you with local service." This evidence is sufficient to show that Sandicor's prices reflected its costs to some extent and thus that an inflated support fee injured plaintiffs. In contrast, the record does not support the counterintuitive claim that Sandicor is some sort of accounting pyrrhonist that sets its prices in utter disregard of its costs of doing business.

Were we to grant immunity from section 1 merely because defendants nominally sell services through another entity rather than to consumers directly, we would risk opening a major loophole for resale price maintenance and retailer collusion. Consider the following: Ford can't sell cars to its dealers wholesale for $20,000 and require them to mark up the price exactly $4,000 before reselling them to the public—that would be resale price maintenance, a per se violation of section 1. Nor can the dealers collude among themselves to peg the retail markup at $4,000. Can Ford and its dealers circumvent these prohibitions by agreeing that the dealers, while continuing to bear the same economic risks, will nominally sell the cars on Ford's behalf for $24,000 and receive a $4,000 "reimbursement" from Ford for each car sold? We think not. Yet this is in material respects analogous to what Sandicor and the associations did here. Sandicor charges MLS subscribers $44 per month; an association collects this fee from each subscriber and hands it over to Sandicor, which then returns $22.50 to the association as the support fee. But the association might as well simply collect $44, send $21.50 to Sandicor and keep the other $22.50 for itself; defendants' counsel forthrightly conceded that "economically, it could be described either way." For that matter, the associations could purchase MLS database access from Sandicor for $21.50 on an as-needed basis and then agree among themselves to resell it with support services for exactly $22.50 more—again, there's no practical economic difference. Defendants can't turn a horizontal agreement to fix prices into something innocuous just by changing the way they keep their books.

No one doubts that Sandicor and the associations may set policies necessary to maintain the MLS database. See *United States v. Realty Multi-List, Inc.*, 629 F.2d 1351, 1368 (5th Cir. 1980) (allowing an MLS operator to enforce "reasonably ancillary restraints"). Obviously, for example, they can dictate standards for data entry. Sandicor also retains considerable freedom to specify services that the associations must provide. But this flexibility does not extend to what the associations did here.

The associations engaged in price fixing, and plaintiffs have standing to sue them. The associations purposely fixed the support fee they charged Sandicor at a supracompetitive level. Sandicor passed on some portion of that inflated support fee to agents, who paid higher prices for the MLS as a result. This is precisely the type of injury the antitrust laws are designed to prevent.

We find all the asserted defenses legally deficient or factually unsupported. The record compels the conclusion that defendants violated section 1 of the Sherman Act by fixing support fees. The district court should have denied summary judgment to defendants and granted it to plaintiffs instead.

Reversed.

CASE QUESTIONS

1. Describe what the multilist groups on the San Diego area had agreed to do and why. What does the court say is the effect of the agreement?
2. Is the agreement a violation of the Sherman Act?
3. Why does the court use an example from *Legally Blonde*? What point does it illustrate?

When Commission is Due and Owing

Most form listing agreements provide, and the majority of courts hold (in the absence of an agreement to the contrary), that the broker is entitled to the commission when a purchaser who is ready, willing, and able to meet the terms of the listing agreement has been brought to the seller. Actual closing of the deal is not necessary for the broker to collect the commission.[8] However, the listing agreement should spell out this right to a commission, regardless of closing.

Also, the listing agreement must contain all the material terms and conditions for sale of the property, since the broker's entitlement to commission is tied to those terms.

Producing a buyer who is ready and willing simply means that a buyer is ready to purchase according to the seller's listing terms and has made necessary deposits on the property. The *able* portion of the test for earning a commission requires the broker to establish that the buyer had the financial ability, credit, or resources necessary to go through with the transaction.

If the seller contacts the buyer directly and gets the buyer to cancel, this attempt to thwart the transaction still results in the broker earning the commission.

In some states, courts have eliminated the ready, willing, and able standards and now require that the deal actually close before the broker is entitled to a commission.[8] These states are limited, and even in these states the parties must specify a **no deal, no commission clause** in their listing agreement.

Description of Property and Sale Terms

Because the listing agreement will be the basis for advertising the property and a representation of its quality, size, location, and character, brokers must collect and disclose accurate information about the property.

8 Some that follow a "no deal, no commission" rule are Oregon, Idaho, Kansas, Massachusetts, and Nebraska. Louisiana remains unclear on its standard, while Vermont and Alaska point to the virtues of "no deal, no commission" while adhering to the "ready, willing, and able" standard.

The listing agreement should cover price, method of financing, date property may be transferred, fixtures included and not included, any conditions for rental or occupancy of the property, any easements or other use restrictions, and any restrictions such as a requirement of court approval. Another important issue for a listing agreement is spelling out what happens to the earnest money if the buyer defaults. The more detail in the listing, the less confusion there will be when an offer comes in and during the process of completing the sale.

Conditions Precedent

A **condition precedent** is a requirement or event placed in a contract that must be fulfiled or should occur before the parties are required to perform their obligations under that contract. Conditions precedent in the listing agreement include court approval for sale of the property or the buyer being able to qualify for financing. With these uncertain future events in the listing agreement, the parties know the contract performance issues before offer and acceptance on the sale of the property.

Liability Limitations

Many brokers insert clauses in their listing agreement limiting their liability to the seller to the amount of commissions they are to be paid under the listing agreement. In some cases, such limitations are effective, but when the seller experiences damages because of the broker's negligence, such clauses may be set aside. (Brokers' duty of care is discussed later in this chapter.) Furthermore, with third parties now able to recover damages directly from brokers, these liability limitations are limited to contract parties, if they are honored at all (third-party liability is discussed later in the chapter).

Other Details

The listing agreement should also contain permission clauses that allow the broker to advertise, place signs on the property, bring prospective buyers to the property, and use a multiple listing service to market the property.

Figure 12.1 is a checklist for preparing an effective listing agreement.

Responsibilities of Brokers/Agents

Authority

The listing agreement gives the broker the authority to market the listed property and bring prospective buyers to the seller. Any restrictions and limitations on that authority should be part of the listing agreement. Brokers who engage in conduct beyond the scope of their authority are liable for any damages or obligations that result. For example, a broker who reduces the listing price without the seller's consent would be liable for the price difference. A broker who accepts an offer for a seller without authority to do so would be liable to the buyer and seller for damages caused by the unauthorized agreement.

Antisolicitation Statutes

Some states have enacted antisolicitation statutes that prohibit brokers and agents from soliciting property owners to list their properties for sale. In many cases, these

*Figure 12.1 Checklist for an Effective Listing Agreement**

1. Name of owner
   a. Are they authorized?
   b. Who holds title?
   c. Is there more than one owner?
   d. Signatures
2. Type of listing agreement
   a. Open
   b. Agency
   c. Exclusive right to sell
   d. Net
   e. Multiple listing
3. Duration of the listing
   a. Length
   b. Extension clause for buyers introduced to the property by the broker
   c. Termination: reasons, methods, notice, damages
4. Entitlement to commission
   a. Ready, willing, and able
   b. No sale, no commission
   c. Fraud or bad faith by the seller
5. Description of the property
   a. Accurate legal description
   b. Correct parcels
6. Selling Terms
   a. Price
   b. Financing
   c. Date of transfer
   d. Good title
   e. Rental or occupancy
   f. Easements
7. Condition precedent
   a. Court approval
   b. Buyer financing
   c. Sale or other property
8. Marketing rights
   a. Advertise
   b. Place sign on property
   c. Showings
   d. Multiple listing
9. Rights upon buyer's default
   a. Earnest money
   b. Effect on listing
10. Liability limitations

*Should be written

antisolicitation statutes are enacted to prevent "blockbusting," which is the practice of controlling the racial composition of neighborhoods by soliciting listings and sales through use of fear in depicting the neighborhood's racial composition as one that is changing (see Chapter 19 for a more complete discussion). The relevant portion of Illinois' antisolicitation statute provides as follows:

It shall be unlawful for any person or corporation knowingly:
d) to solicit any owner of residential property to sell or list such residential property at any time after such person or corporation has notice that such owner does not desire to sell such residential property.

Antiblockbusting statutes that attempt to restrict access of real estate agents to certain areas for purposes of obtaining listings have not survived constitutional challenges (*New York State Association of Realtors, Inc. v. Shaffer*, 27 F.3d 834 [2nd Cir. 1994]). A restriction such as that in Illinois that permits the property owner to prevent *future* contacts by agents would survive constitutional challenges. However, prohibiting solicitations in certain areas without justification could be challenged as a violation of commercial speech rights.

Duty of Care

A broker is required to exercise care in listing the seller's property, presenting offers, and handling the details of closing.

This duty of care requires the broker to list the property at a reasonable market value figure. Because of commission pay structures, underappraising properties and listing them accordingly can result in rapid, easy sales, complete with the broker's percentage earnings. The listing price should be set according to market comparables with the overarching goal of assisting the seller with the sale of the property that brings a fair return. Brokers should exercise caution in making overzealous statements about sales potential of the property and their abilities because inflated expectations of the seller can cause problems for the broker later.

If the seller needs to net a certain minimum from the transaction, the broker's computation of the sales price is even more critical. The broker should take into account all fees and contingencies and understand every cost associated with the sale, from transfer fees to title insurance, to commissions.

The broker's duty of care continues throughout the period of the relationship. Brokers must present all offers to their sellers and provide their expertise in helping sellers evaluate the soundness of those offers, including the hazards or pitfalls, such as the advantages or disadvantages of financing alternatives as well as the risks of contingencies, involved in each offer. Brokers do not advise which offer a seller should take, but they can explain offers' weaknesses and strengths.

In explaining offers, however, brokers should not cross over the fine line between exercising care and practicing law. A broker may explain to a seller the customs and practices of the real estate industry but not the law. Brokers should refer clients who have questions about legal details or issues to their attorneys.

Brokers should also proofread documents such as the listing agreement, the offer, the contract for the property, and closing documents by checking for errors in figures, descriptions, and dates. In some states brokers may fill out contracts, but they are under a high duty of care to be sure all terms are present, carefully drafted, and accurately stated. When brokers use form contracts, offers, and agreements, they should be cautious and be sure that the form language reflects the parties' intentions.

Brokers who prequalify prospective buyers can match properties and sellers with buyers more easily and avoid the problems that arise when a contract falls through because the buyers cannot obtain financing. Also, a broker who knowingly presents an offer from an unqualified buyer exposes himself to liability.

Clauses in listing agreements that try to exculpate brokers for breach of their duty of care are invalid, as they are for accountants, lawyers, engineers, and other professionals. No professional may be held harmless by a clause when they have failed to exercise the standards of care for their profession.

Fiduciary Duty

Once a broker is employed by a principal, that broker is expected to act only in the best interests of the principal, regardless of the negative effects and consequences that may result for the broker. However, the nature and extent of the fiduciary duty is controlled by the nature of the agency relationship, covered in the beginning of the chapter under the types of listings. This section discusses the duty from a seller's perspective. However, depending upon the state, these duties could be imposed on the buyer's broker as well.

CONSIDER 12.3

Joseph and Jacqueline Lombardo were behind in their mortgage payments on their Fountain Hills, Arizona, home. One of their lenders had extended the payment period for the Lombardos in order to give them a chance to sell the home.

In February 1994, the Lombardos listed their home with MCO Realty, Inc., with Doris Elco as the listing agent. Shortly thereafter, Elaine Albu of Century 21 Realty presented the Lombardos with an offer to purchase by Roberta Codney. The parties met minds and agreed to a June 30, 1994, closing date.

In April 1994, Mrs. Codney explained to Mrs. Albu that she was buying the property in her name only because her husband had filed for bankruptcy and was subject to IRS liens. Mrs. Albu kept this secret between herself and Mrs. Codney even as the Lombardos waited around for a closing that was postponed and never happened, even as they kept their house off the market assuming that Mrs. Codney was an "able" buyer. As a result, the Lombardos' home was sold at a trustee's sale when their ever-patient lenders concluded that they had had quite enough of the extensions.

The Lombardos filed suit against the Codneys, their listing agent, and Mrs. Albu for their negligent misrepresentation. Their complaint noted that the real estate agents knew of the precarious financial position of the buyer, did not disclose such and, indeed, persuaded the Lombardos to postpone the closing several times before dreams turned to dust and the Codney purchase fell through.

The trial court granted summary judgment against the Lombardos, holding that, as a matter of law, a buyer's agent owes the seller no legal duty. The Lombardos appealed and the court of appeals agreed with the trial court. The Supreme Court granted review. What should the Supreme Court do and why? *Lombardo v. Albu*, 14 P.3d 288 (Ariz. 2000)

Brokers must not lead their sellers into unsound transactions for the sake of a commission and should inform their sellers when problems arise in the negotiation or closing of a transaction. All aspects of the transaction should be represented accurately and disclosed in a timely manner. Any changes affecting the principal's rights or interests must be revealed immediately.

Most states impose a separate fiduciary duty upon brokers with respect to earnest money deposits. Money that belongs to the seller should not be commingled with the broker's own funds. Most states require that deposits be placed in trust accounts or escrow accounts, or else require the establishment of escrow funds within a short time after receipt. Brokers in these states who retain deposits for unreasonable lengths of time may be held liable for this loss and may face license revocation or suspension.

Duty of Loyalty

A broker may not work both ends of the transaction by representing both parties unless there has been full disclosure and both parties consent to such dual representation. (See earlier clarifications on state variations on duties and types of agencies.)

A broker may not profit secretly from a transaction involving the principal. Brokers must disclose to their clients all they know about all parties involved in the transaction. If a broker chooses to deal in listed property, he or she must make a full and complete disclosure of the interests to the client. A broker who is a partner, shareholder, or relative of a party to the transaction must disclose those ties as well. If a broker does not make the appropriate disclosure and realizes a secret profit, that profit belongs to the principal.

Under dual agency relationships, the duty of loyalty becomes complicated. For example, suppose that a broker representing both buyer and seller knows that the buyer is a credit risk? Does the duty of loyalty require the broker to disclose that to the seller? Does such a disclosure breach the duty of loyalty to the buyer? Most states that permit dual agency also list categories of information the dual agent must keep confidential, such as (1) the seller being willing to take less than the asking price; (2) the buyer's willingness to pay more than the asking price; (3) the motivation of the parties in buying and selling; and (4) the willingness of either party to accept less favorable financing terms. The following case deals with the issues of broker duty and disclosure.

WARREN V. MERRILL

49 Cal.Rptr.3d 122 (Cal. App. 2006)

FACTS

John Warren (plaintiff and respondent) suffered from Tourette's syndrome and other related neurological disorders affecting his short-term memory and cognitive abilities. His movie set rental business was having financial difficulties and he was also in the process of getting divorced. He met Hildegard Merrill (defendant and appellant) at an open house for a condominium. Merrill, doing business as Calabasas Realty, was the agent for the seller of the condominium. Merrill had acquired her real estate license in 1967 and had been a licensed real estate broker since 1981. She sometimes referred to herself by her professional nickname of the "condo queen." Merrill also held a mortgage broker's license.

Merrill told Warren the condominium was a good investment and that the seller was motivated to sell. Warren was interested, but he had sustained a $1 million judgment for nonpayment of rent when one of his business ventures collapsed. As a result, Warren's credit rating was poor. Merrill told Warren he needed a co-borrower with a good credit rating in order to secure a mortgage at a reasonable rate. Merrill suggested her own daughter, Charmaine Merrill, would be the co-owner and co-borrower on the loan. Once the loan/credit hurdle was overcome and escrow closed, Charmaine would execute a quit claim deed to him to remove her name from title in exchange for the $10,000.

As the loan broker Merrill knew it was important to make a 20 percent down payment in order to secure a reasonable interest rate. Because Warren did not have the money Merrill offered to defer her commissions of $27,000 and to loan this amount to Warren in order to attain a 20 percent down payment of $77,000. Their entire arrangement was never put into written form.

Merrill wrote up a purchase offer for the condominium with Charmaine and Warren as co-purchasers. Merrill never had Warren fill out a loan application form and Merrill never attempted to secure a loan with Warren as a co-borrower with her daughter Charmaine. Instead Merrill applied for and secured a loan in Charmaine's name alone.

Merrill misrepresented the facts when she filled out Charmaine's loan application. For example, Merrill stated the source of the proposed $77,000 down payment was a combination of savings and gifts. The application stated Charmaine then resided in a condominium at 5800 Kanan Road in Agoura Hills, conducted catering and shuttle businesses out of the residence on Kanan Road, and had been doing so since 2001, earning a monthly income of $7,500 from those businesses. In reality, Charmaine had resided for years in Aspen, Colorado, and had never lived at or conducted a business out of the 5800 Kanan Road residence. Also, the businesses Charmaine conducted had shut down sometime in 1990. Charmaine was instead employed as a waitress in Aspen, Colorado, and periodically conducted her shuttle business there. She otherwise relied on her mother for support. Merrill indicated on the loan application that Charmaine intended the condominium to be her primary residence. Merrill later conceded that she would never have gotten the loan had she been truthful in the loan application. The trial court was so alarmed by Merrill's testimony and her apparent lack of concern about admitting she had committed a form of fraud on the lender that the court recessed the proceedings to permit Merrill to consult with counsel regarding her Fifth Amendment right not to incriminate herself.

How the $77,000 down payment was cobbled together remained a mystery. According to Warren, he paid the entire $77,000 down payment: $50,000 into escrow by writing checks to different persons and entities as directed by Merrill and by repaying the $27,000 Merrill loaned him toward the down payment. Warren testified he and Charmaine each deposited a check for $10,000 into escrow. Then at Merrill's direction, he repaid Charmaine this $10,000 by writing two checks of approximately $5,000 each: one to pay toward Charmaine's

Chase Platinum credit card balance and the other to pay toward Charmaine's MBNA credit card balance.

Warren wrote a check for $30,000 to Merrill's boyfriend, again at Merrill's direction. Merrill then deposited into escrow a check for $30,000 written on her and her boyfriend Paine Webber's investment account. In exchange for her boyfriend's services, Merrill had Warren write her boyfriend another check for $2,000.

Merrill deferred her combined sales commission and loan broker commission of $27,000 to complete the $77,000 down payment. Warren wrote Merrill a check for $27,000, which Merrill held uncashed until Warren repaid her this amount. He accomplished repayment of the $27,000 by writing Merrill checks of between $3,000 and $4,000 over the course of about six months. Unbeknownst to Warren, the seller had agreed to credit $6,000 in escrow to defray closing costs, which should have reduced the amount Warren repaid Merrill.

Merrill knew the lender would not fund the loan request with different people proposed to hold legal title than had applied for the loan. Merrill had Warren sign an amendment in escrow to remove his name from title, explaining the document was just a formality required to secure the loan and to close escrow. The amendment stated title would vest solely in Charmaine Merrill. The amendment further stated, "John Warren is no longer a party to this escrow. All monies currently on deposit to this date shall accrue to Charmaine Merrill. ..."

Escrow closed in October 2001 and Warren moved into the condominium. Merrill did not have Charmaine execute a quit claim deed to transfer title to Warren after escrow closed.

Warren and/or his attorney made the mortgage payments directly to the lender for several months. However, Warren developed substance abuse problems. He checked into the Betty Ford Center for treatment. He had not made arrangements for someone to handle his personal and financial affairs in his absence. Merrill learned the homeowners' association was about to foreclose on Warren's unit. A few days before the scheduled foreclosure date, Merrill paid the association the approximately $5,000 then claimed as arrearages to prevent the foreclosure.

Merrill filed an unlawful detainer action to have him removed from the unit. While Warren was still in the Betty Ford Center receiving treatment, Merrill secured a judgment against Warren, got a writ of possession and evicted him from the premises. She removed all his belongings and placed them either in a storage facility or in the garage of her home in Woodland Hills. Warren's belongings included original artwork, sports memorabilia, the personal papers of his grandfather, the former California Governor and Chief Justice of the United States, Earl Warren, antique furniture, jewelry, medals, and several filing cabinets containing all his business records. Merrill held a lien sale of Warren's personal property and was herself the successful bidder at the sale.

When he left the Betty Ford Center in September 2002 Warren talked to Merrill many times but she would not permit him to return to the residence. In his last conversation with Merrill, Warren explained he was desperate and homeless. Over a four-month period, he had stayed with various friends or slept in his car, but was then sleeping in the park and using public facilities to attend to his personal hygiene. Merrill told Warren he just "didn't get it." Merrill informed Warren he did not owe her any money and directed Warren not to call her any more. After evicting Warren, Merrill rented the condominium to a series of renters.

Warren filed suit against Merrill, Charmaine and others. The trial court found that Merrill had acted outrageously and with reckless disregard in perpetrating the fraud on Warren and made an award of punitive damages of $50,000. The court also entered judgment quieting title in favor of Warren. The court also awarded Warren noneconomic damages in the amount of $15,000 on his causes of action for fraud, breach of fiduciary duty and ejectment. Merrill agreed to return all of Warren's personal property and in exchange Warren agreed to pay the storage fees. The court also awarded Warren costs and attorney's fees.

Merrill appealed.

JUDICIAL OPINION

Johnson, Judge. There should be no dispute Merrill owed a fiduciary duty to Warren once she undertook to represent him in the real estate transaction. Merrill herself acknowledged at trial she held a fiduciary position of trust toward Warren. Because she owed Warren a fiduciary duty Merrill further acknowledged she was required to place his interests above her own in the real estate transaction. Nevertheless, she claims there was no evidence of misrepresentation, no evidence of fraud and no evidence of a breach of her fiduciary duties to sustain the court's judgment. She claims this is true because whatever fiduciary duties she owed Warren terminated when he "withdrew" from the escrow.

The record in the present case contains substantial evidence satisfying each of the elements of both constructive and actual fraud. The evidence showed Merrill breached her fiduciary duties toward Warren and committed fraud by deliberately and falsely promising him she would place his name on title to the condominium if he went along with her plan on how to structure the transaction. From the beginning of the transaction she did not intend to perform her promise of placing his name on title. Merrill instead intended to procure the condominium for herself but did not disclose her role as a principal in the transaction. Merrill in fact kept the condominium.

If this was a legitimate transaction, writing checks to third parties would have been wholly unnecessary. However for Merrill's purposes it made it appear, at least superficially, she, and not Warren, had contributed the $30,000 check into escrow, Charmaine had contributed $10,000 into escrow and Merrill had deferred her earned commissions of $27,000 as a credit into escrow (while holding Warren responsible for repayment).

Merrill led Warren to believe he had to sign the amendment in escrow removing his name from the title and gifting his contributions to Charmaine in order to secure financing. Warren obviously trusted Merrill's representation because he signed the amendment. Through these deceptive maneuvers Merrill secured for herself an investment property in her daughter's name by lying to her principal and misappropriating his funds.

In these circumstances it seems preposterous to argue, as does Merrill, Warren "withdrew" from escrow and for this reason she owed him no fiduciary duty and thus could not be guilty of fraud. Instead, it may be more accurate to say Warren was "coerced" into signing the amendment and into "withdrawing" from escrow based on Merrill's representations the loan would not fund and the whole deal would fall apart unless he signed the amendment taking his name off title. If Warren truly "withdrew" from the escrow then all of the money he had contributed to the down payment should have been returned. It was not.

In sum, we agree with the trial court the evidence in this case was more than sufficient to show an egregious violation of the duties of loyalty and undivided interest by a fiduciary toward her principal, as well as a deliberate plan to defraud him out of his down payment and the property.

Merrill argues Warren was not entitled to equitable relief of any sort because he was guilty of unclean hands. She asserts his entire claim for relief was premised on an illegal scheme to conspire to defraud the lender by having Charmaine secure the loan in her name and then fraudulently concealing from the lender Warren's ownership interest in the property. In addition, Merrill points out because of Warren's personal and substance abuse problems he would have lost the property altogether but for her efforts stopping the foreclosure and paying the arrearages.

Although Warren's behavior was far from exemplary, we do not believe under the circumstances he and Merrill were equally at fault. True, Warren agreed to, and acquiesced in, what would have been an improper, if not impossible, plan to use Charmaine as a front in order for him to secure the loan. We note it was Merrill, not Warren, who proposed the "illegal plan." We also note the "illegal plan" never happened and thus Warren never participated in any "illegal scheme." Of course, the "illegal scheme" was not carried out because the fiduciary's own undisclosed plan was to instead take the property for her personal benefit. In the process of carrying out her plan Merrill defrauded her client out of the property and his $77,000 down payment. And she did this to the very person to whom she owed fiduciary duties of loyalty, trust and full disclosure.

In these circumstances the trial court properly weighed the equities and found the doctrine of unclean hands did not automatically bar Warren from receiving relief in this case.

The judgment is affirmed.

CASE QUESTIONS

1. List all of the actions by Merrill that were a breach of her duty of loyalty, the law, or her ethics as a real estate agent.

2. How does the court respond to Merrill's argument that Warren had joined in on the plan to dupe the lender?

3. If Warren did indeed remove himself from the escrow, what should Merrill have done?

Legal Duties and Responsibilities to Third Parties

The broker who lists the property and the buyer of the listed property do not have a direct contractual relationship. However, in some states, the broker may still have liability to the buyer for misrepresentations as to the condition of and defects in the property. This liability is based on the common law tort of misrepresentation, liability that has been expanded dramatically.

Misrepresentation

Misrepresentations about property generally fall into two categories: (1) those made intentionally and (2) those made negligently. Intentional misrepresentation occurs when the broker knows of a fact and then either misstates it to the buyer or simply fails to disclose it. Negligent misrepresentation occurs when (1) the broker failed to make a reasonable effort to determine whether the fact represented was true or false and (2) the buyer justifiably relied on that misrepresentation in purchasing the property.

Under negligent misrepresentation, a broker who makes statements about the property without a sufficient knowledge base may be liable to the buyer. An example of negligent misrepresentation occurs when the broker makes statements about the cost of heating, air-conditioning, or electricity and does so without a statement of cost from the seller or without an actual investigation or verification of the cost.

With negligent misrepresentation, ignorance as to whether a statement is true or false does not allow the broker to avoid liability; it is the broker's responsibility to determine whether information is true or false. When the prospective buyer asks if city sewer, water, and gas are available for the property, the appropriate response for a broker who is uncertain is, "I don't know, but I can check." Brokers are liable for misrepresentations that they make to the buyer orally, for descriptions of the property, for the content in fliers and ads about the property, and for information and photos posted on websites about the property. In short, all the marketing materials count for purposes of misrepresentation.

Nondisclosure

Misrepresentation occurs when the broker is aware of the problems or defects in property but fails to disclose that material information to prospective buyers. Cosmetically covered wall cracks and foundation cracks should be disclosed. The traditional water-in-the-basement problem should also be disclosed. The fact that an existing property use violates the city code is another example of a required disclosure.

CONSIDER 12.4

Suppose a broker misrepresented the length of time that a piece of property had been listed. Would such a misrepresentation be a basis for liability? Does the broker harm a seller by such a disclosure? *Beard v. Gress*, 413 N.E.2d 488 (Ill. 1980)

Sales Puffing

Misrepresentation can result from the sales-puffing techniques of brokers. The classic line given to induce buyers is, "if you are going to do anything, you had better do it quickly because I have another buyer on the line for this property." The statement is innocent enough so long as there is, in fact, another buyer. If no other buyer exists, such statements inflate the value and desirability of the property and constitute misrepresentation to the buyer who was led to believe the property was in demand. The following case deals with an issue of misrepresentation and whether the broker's language was a basis for a claim by a buyer or was simply puffing.

Capiccioni v. Brennan Naperville, Inc.

791 N.E.2d 553 (Ill. App. 2003)

FACTS

In 1998, Dean and Majel Capiccioni (Plaintiffs-Appellants) moved from Ohio to Illinois and purchased a home in Bolingbrook. Brennan Naperville, a residential real estate brokerage company, and Sharon Clermont, a licensed real estate broker and one of Brennan's agents (defendants), represented the Bolingbrook property's sellers. The sales brochure for the Bolingbrook property listed as one of the home's features "Acclaimed [school] District 204."

The Capiccionis moved into the home, and their three children attended school in District 204 for three years. However, the children were unable to attend District 204 classes during the 2001–2002 academic year after the Capiccionis discovered that their property was actually located in District 365-U. The Capiccionis subsequently sold the property and purchased another home. Their new home was located in District 204.

In June 2001, the Capiccionis filed suit against Clermont and Brennan for giving them false, untruthful, and misleading information. They maintained that they would not have purchased the home if they had known of the true district alignment, that they paid more for the home because of the school district's reputation, and that they had incurred the cost of selling the house and moving in order to be located within the school district boundaries.

The trial court dismissed the Capiccionis' complaint and they appealed.

JUDICIAL OPINION

Callum, Justice. We conclude that plaintiffs set forth sufficient facts to show that defendants intended that plaintiffs rely upon their representations. Plaintiffs alleged that the "Acclaimed District 204" statement was included in a sales brochure for the Bolingbrook property. Given the nature of this communication, plaintiffs adequately pleaded this element.

Plaintiffs properly pleaded that the misrepresentation occurred in the course of conduct involving trade and commerce. They alleged that defendants represented the Bolingbrook property's sellers and that they made their representations in the course of selling the property.

We conclude that plaintiffs adequately pleaded that they suffered damages, in that they alleged that they purchased a home that they would not have otherwise purchased; they paid more for the property than it was worth; the property did not appreciate as much as one in District 204; and they paid moving-related expenses associated with the purchase.

Defendants contend that plaintiffs did not adequately plead proximate cause. They argue that plaintiffs' admission that District 204 employees confirmed that the Bolingbrook property was within its boundaries makes plaintiffs unable to plead that the single reference to District 204 in their sales brochure proximately caused plaintiffs' damages. We disagree.

Proximate cause means any cause which, in natural or probable sequence, produced the injury complained of. It need not be the sole cause or the last or nearest cause. The requirement of an allegation of proximate cause in a pleading has been termed "minimal" because the determination is best left to the trier of fact. Here, plaintiffs alleged in all of their counts that they purchased the home based on defendants' misrepresentations regarding the home's location in District 204; that they paid more for the home than it was worth; and that they would not have purchased it if they had known otherwise. We are not convinced by defendants' assertion that plaintiffs' admission that they spoke with District 204 employees prior to their purchase somehow breaks the causal chain. We note that there can be more than one proximate cause contributing to any one injury. We cannot conclude that plaintiffs have not adequately pleaded proximate causation.

Negligent misrepresentation consists of: (1) a false statement of a material fact; (2) carelessness or negligence in ascertaining the truth of the statement by the party making it; (3) an intention to induce the other party to act; (4) action by the other party in reliance on the truth of the statement; and (5) damage to the other party resulting from such reliance when the party making the statement is under a duty to communicate accurate information.

This court has indicated that negligent misrepresentations of material fact made by a realtor "could well be the basis" for a negligent misrepresentation claim.

In *Richmond v. Blair*, 142 Ill.App.3d 251, 256, 94 Ill.Dec. 564, 488 N.E.2d 563 (1985), the Appellate Court, First District, decided that such an action can be brought against a realtor. In *Richmond*, the plaintiff toured a home with the sellers' real estate broker. The broker informed the plaintiff that the house had experienced water leakage in the basement. When the plaintiff requested assurance that the problem had been fixed, the broker assured her that the home was completely free of water leaks or seepage. The plaintiff purchased the home, and it subsequently flooded. She sued the broker and her employer alleging, *inter alia*, negligent misrepresentation. The trial court granted the defendants' motion to dismiss, and the appellate court reversed and remanded the cause, finding that the plaintiff adequately pleaded the required elements of negligent misrepresentation. The plaintiff alleged that the broker owed to her a duty to be knowledgeable and accurate in her representations about the property; that the broker breached her duty by negligently making statements about the basement without actual knowledge about their truth or falsity; and that the broker's breach proximately caused the plaintiff's injuries.

[R]ealtors occupy a position of trust with respect to prospective buyers and...they owe to them a duty to exercise good faith in their dealings with them, even absent an agency relationship between the parties.

With respect to the second element, plaintiffs alleged in their negligent misrepresentation count that defendants owed to them a duty to use due care in obtaining and communicating information that they knew plaintiffs would rely upon in deciding to purchase the Bolingbrook property; that defendants breached this duty and were negligent in marketing the property as being located in District 204 when it was widely known in the real estate industry that misinformation exists about Bolingbrook school district boundaries; and that Clermont took no action to determine the property's school district. We conclude that plaintiffs properly pleaded negligence.

With respect to the third element—intent—we conclude, as we discussed above, that plaintiffs adequately pleaded this element. They alleged that defendants made the representations in an advertising brochure in the course of selling the Bolingbrook property.

We next address the reliance elements. Plaintiffs contend that they adequately pleaded reliance, where they alleged that they relied on Clermont's false representations and took reasonable steps to confirm the information by contacting District 204 employees.

In the common-law fraud context, the plaintiff's reliance must be justified, i.e., the plaintiff must have had a right to rely. The same requirement applies for a negligent misrepresentation claim. A party is not justified in relying on representations when he or she had ample opportunity to ascertain the truth of the representations before acting.

Here, we conclude that the facts in plaintiffs' amended complaint indicate that plaintiffs would have been entitled to rely on defendants' alleged misrepresentations. Plaintiffs alleged that District 204 employees confirmed that their property was located in the district, and plaintiffs' children were permitted to enroll in District 204 schools for several years. Based on these allegations, we cannot conclude that plaintiffs could not prove a set of facts to establish reasonable reliance. Although plaintiffs' allegations regarding their discussions with school district employees might establish that they did not exclusively rely upon defendants' representations, we cannot conclude, based on the pleadings, that the discussions completely undermine their reliance argument.

Finally, we conclude that plaintiffs properly pleaded damages. They alleged that they were damaged as a direct result of defendants' negligence, in that they purchased a home they would not have otherwise purchased; they paid more for the property than it was worth; the property did not appreciate as much as if it were within the boundaries of District 204; and they paid moving-related expenses associated with the purchase.

For these reasons, we conclude that the trial court erred in granting defendants' motion to dismiss on plaintiffs negligent misrepresentation count.

Reversed.

CASE QUESTIONS

1. Where did the representation on the schools appear?
2. What is the significance of proximate cause in this case?
3. How does the court handle the issue that the buyers could have checked on the school district themselves?

Safety Standards

A broker may be held liable for conditions on a property that violate codes or are unsafe if the conditions were not disclosed to prospective buyers or remedied prior to the closing of a deal. Brokers should check for hazards while showing the property so that they can note new developments or hazards.

Broker liability for concealment or the failure to disclose material information to potential buyers varies from state to state. In Alaska, the District of Columbia, Illinois, Minnesota, South Carolina, Texas, Utah, and Wisconsin, brokers are even held liable for innocent misrepresentation. Some states impose liability for only intentional or negligent misrepresentation. For example, Washington does not hold brokers liable for innocent misrepresentation because the effect of imposing such liability would be that of a "strict liability" standard for brokers.

"As Is" Clauses

Often property will be sold with a provision in the contract that says it is sold **as is**, meaning that the buyer is taking the property as it stands with all existing defects and no promises of repair. Such a clause would appear to relieve the broker of liability for latent defects and the failure to disclose material information. However, the courts have held that the use of the "as is" clause is not a blanket of immunity for the broker from allegations of fraud. If a broker actively misrepresents the condition of the property or fails to disclose true facts, the "as is" clause will have no effect, and the broker will still be held liable for the silent or affirmative misrepresentation. A dilapidated building sold "as is" will not provide immunity from liability for the broker who failed to disclose that the building had been condemned.

Statutory Duties of Disclosure

About one-half of the states have some form of mandatory disclosure statutes that require the seller to disclose varying types of information about the property as part of the listing process. In many states, these disclosure statutes were passed as a result of lobbying efforts by brokers who desired some protection from the increasing liability from the lack of clarity on disclosure responsibilities and resulting liabilities.

Generally called "Residential Property Disclosure Acts," the acts are indeed limited to the sales of residential property and may not apply when residential property is being sold by an owner without the use of a broker. Remedies for the failure to make required disclosures include the right to rescind the purchase contract as well as the usual damage remedies available for misrepresentation or fraud.

Some disclosure statutes are specific, with itemized topics related to structure, plumbing, environmental conditions, foundation issues, and other material types of issues in property transactions. However, other state disclosure statutes are more general, requiring purchasers to disclose whatever information would influence the decision to purchase the property or the price that the buyer would pay. Still another type of state statute simply requires a sworn statement from the seller that the buyer has had all material information disclosed to him or her by the seller.

Both sides enjoy protection under the disclosure statutes. That is, the seller is protected from liability for misrepresentation or fraud when there is compliance with the disclosure statutes, and the buyer enjoys more complete information going into the transaction. In addition, brokers in many states enjoy limited liability when they have complied with the disclosure statutes and required their seller-clients to do the same.

The following case deals with the issues of misrepresentation and its relationship to statutory disclosure requirements.

FULLER V. CROSTON

725 N.W.2d 600 (SD 2006)

FACTS

In the fall of 2002, Ivan R. Fuller was interested in purchasing a Sioux Falls home owned by James and Patricia Croston, the sole owners of the house since its construction. Fuller received a signed and completed seller's property disclosure statement, as required by SDCL 43-4-38, from the Crostons.

The disclosure statement indicated that the home had not experienced any water penetration problems. However, when the Crostons signed the disclosure statement in November 2002 they were aware of two to three occasions between 1969 and 1977 when water had seeped into the basement. They maintain that they did not include this information in the disclosure statement on the recommendation of their real estate agent, Janey Johnson (a licensed real estate agent), who allegedly advised the Crostons that if they believed the problem was fixed they did not have to disclose it. She denies these allegations. The Crostons, believing that the water problems had been resolved, did not disclose the prior seepage on the disclosure statement. Their disclosure statement also indicated there were no cracks in the interior walls of the house. However, the Crostons were aware of some cracks in the walls in the basement behind the washer and dryer. They puttied and painted over these cracks two to three years before selling the house to Fuller.

Before signing the purchase agreement, Fuller visited the home with the Crostons. He noticed some flaking on one of the basement walls. When he asked about this, Crostons informed Fuller of a "little bit of water there sometime back." They told him that they had experienced some water in the basement on two to three occasions between 1969 and 1977, but they had not experienced any additional water problems since adding a sunroom to the home in 1977. Fuller also noticed some "roughness of the paneling in the family room." The Crostons explained that when they added a sunroom and a garage, they had some water come into the basement. As a result, they did landscaping to seal off the water and also placed wood paneling over the drywall in the basement.

After the conversation with the Crostons about water in the basement, Fuller still offered to purchase the Crostons' home for $158,000. The Crostons accepted this offer and the purchase agreement provided that Fuller would have 10 days to complete a professional home inspection and notify the Crostons of any unacceptable conditions discovered.

Fuller hired David Kemper of Kemper Inspection Services to perform the inspection. The report noted a small horizontal crack and minor bowing at the north and south foundation walls. The report explained that the north wall had been patched and there was no new cracking. According to the inspection report, this was not unusual and was of no structural significance at the time. The inspection report further indicated some signs of past dampness in the basement which appeared to be old.

The cracking and dampness issues raised by the inspection report were not addressed by the addendum because Kemper felt these matters were not significant.

On January 17, 2003, the parties closed the sale on the home. By August 2003, Fuller completely moved into the home. On June 16, 2004, the total rainfall for Sioux Falls was approximately eight inches. According to a FEMA Report, Sioux Falls accumulated a total of 12.74 inches of rain from May 17 to June 16 of 2004, a record amount for a 31-day period. At some point during or immediately after this rainfall, Fuller noticed water entering his basement, but could not determine precisely where it was coming in. He stated that the water appeared to be "seeping in around the foundation and the walls." The water created "puddles here and there" until the carpet was largely saturated.

Fuller contacted Roy Johnson, a contractor, to evaluate and remedy the water problem. When Johnson removed some of the paneling in the basement, the "stuff behind the paneling crumbled" in his hands. Johnson advised Fuller that it appeared there had been previous water penetration in the home. He blamed the water infiltration on the existence of cracks in the home's foundation and bowing of the walls. He also told Fuller that there had been major water damage in the past and that frequent water problems would persist unless action was taken. Johnson then installed drain tile around the perimeter of the basement and a sump pump, and reinforced the foundation walls. Fuller also purchased and installed new padding and carpet for the basement.

At about the same time Fuller encountered the water issues, he noticed the garage roof was sagging once again. He contacted Duane Boice, an engineer, to evaluate the roof. Boice advised Fuller that installation of the support beam actually weakened the roof and made it worse. Boice explained that the roof would have to be fixed, or it would collapse. Fuller then hired Able Construction to repair the roof.

Fuller filed suit on the grounds that he was not made aware of the extent of the previous water damage or all of the cracks in the basement walls and that the Crostons were aware of damage behind the paneling.

The circuit court entered summary judgment in favor of the Crostons and the real estate agents (defendants) and Fuller appealed.

JUDICIAL OPINION

Miller, Justice. Crostons admit they had knowledge of previous water damage and a crack in the basement at the time they signed the disclosure statement, and that they did not reveal this knowledge on the disclosure statement. They contend that disclosure of these defects was not necessary. First, they claim their real estate agent (Janey Johnson) advised them not to disclose the prior water penetration because the problems occurred so long ago and were believed to have been fixed. However, the disclosure form mandated by statute simply asks, "have you experienced any water penetration problems in the walls, windows, doors, basement, or crawl space?" Crostons checked "no" to this question. By its plain terms, the question does not ask only for ongoing water penetration problems. Indeed, it is silent as to whether the problems have been fixed or persist. The disclosure statement simply asks if the sellers "experienced" water penetration problems. Crostons own admissions reveal they had.

Second, Crostons contend that disclosure of the crack was not necessary because it appeared insignificant to them. They also claim that their understanding of the question related only to cracks in the sidewalk and driveway. Again, the disclosure form provided in SDCL 44-3-44 asks, "are there any interior cracked walls or floors, or cracks or defects in exterior driveways, sidewalks, patios, or other hard surface areas." The disclosure question does not qualify the cracks in any manner, and it does not ask for significant cracks only. Rather, it asks for cracks in the walls and floors as well as those in the sidewalk and driveway. Based on these facts, viewed in a light most favorable to Fuller, it does not appear Crostons completed the disclosure statement truthfully, completely, and in good faith as required by South Dakota's disclosure laws. At the very least, there is a genuine issue of material fact whether they did so.

Despite the absence of completeness and candor in the disclosure statement, Crostons contend that they nevertheless fulfilled the disclosure requirements of SDCL chapter 43-4. They claim that their oral disclosures to Fuller of prior water penetration alleviated any earlier misrepresentation or omission in the disclosure statement. Whether an oral disclosure is sufficient to fulfill South Dakota's disclosure requirements is a matter of first impression.

Again, SDCL 43-4-44 provides a mandatory written form that "shall be used for the property condition disclosure statement." Also, SDCL 43-4-38 requires written amendments to the property condition disclosure statement. That statute provides in relevant part:

If after delivering the disclosure statement to the buyer or the buyer's agent and prior to the date of closing for the property or the date of possession of the property, whichever comes first, the seller becomes aware of any change of material fact which would affect the disclosure statement, the seller shall furnish a written amendment disclosing the change of material fact.

The statutes are otherwise silent as to the issue of oral or written disclosures. This Court has held that "[s]tatutory disclosure statements essentially create a contract between the parties to a land sale." Fuller argues that this contract must be in writing, and that any modifications to the written contract must also be in writing.

The allowance of oral disclosures would defeat the purpose and clear language of the statute requiring written amendments as well as the statute providing the mandatory form. Were we to conclude that oral disclosures were sufficient to satisfy the disclosure statutes, these statutes would effectively be rendered moot. We are not willing to do so. That is the prerogative of the Legislature.

Crostons contend Fuller's knowledge of previous water damage, cracking and roughness in the paneling, which was based on oral disclosures, inspections and observations, defeats their liability. They claim Fuller's knowledge of the defects demonstrates a lack of reliance on the incorrect disclosure statement, and without reliance, the violation of the disclosure statute was not the cause of Fuller's damages. Whether a lack of reliance on the disclosure statement can defeat a seller's liability is also a matter of first impression in South Dakota.

SDCL 43-4-42 provides in pertinent part, "a person who intentionally or who negligently violates §§43-4-37 to 43-4-44, inclusive, is liable to the buyer for the amount of the actual damages and repairs suffered by the buyer as a result of the violation or failure." This language seems to imply that reliance and causation are necessary elements for a cause of action based on a failure to comply with the disclosure statement requirements.

Several surrounding jurisdictions have discussed whether reliance on the property condition disclosure statement is necessary to create liability. For instance, an Illinois court held, "[a] seller who knowingly makes a false statement is subject to liability under the Act; no exception is made because of a buyer's knowledge of the defect." *Woods v. Pence,* 303 Ill.App.3d 573, 236 Ill.Dec. 977, 708 N.E.2d 563, 565 (1999) (citing 765 ILCS 77/25 (West 1996)). The *Woods* court did provide, however, that a buyer's knowledge was relevant to the amount of damages awarded because any defect of which the buyer was aware would be reflected in the purchase price of the house, thereby reducing those damages. Another Illinois court "reject[ed] defendant's inference that plaintiffs' actual notice of any alleged problems is a bar to their cause of action under the Disclosure Act."

Furthermore, a Nebraska court agreed with the *Woods* analysis and held "the buyer's knowledge of undisclosed damage in a cause of action for failure to provide a disclosure statement is relevant on the extent of damages, but does not provide a total defense." That court held this was "logical and consistent with the obvious purpose of [the] statute, which at its core is to get sellers to give buyers the written disclosure statement." Nebraska's disclosure statute allows for recovery of actual damages, which the buyer has sustained as a result of the violation of the statute.

Fuller is not appealing the summary judgment disposition of his fraud and fraudulent concealment claims. He is appealing the disposition of his claim under SDCL chapter 43-4. The claims have different elements.

In this case, Fuller's knowledge is based upon oral disclosures from Crostons and an inspection he hired conducted. By requiring reliance on the disclosure statement, this Court would allow sellers to misrepresent defects in the disclosure statement and cover themselves later by making oral disclosures. Also, this Court would effectively penalize the prudent buyer who conducts an independent inspection and investigation. Anything the buyer learned or was put on notice of would defeat a cause of action for a disclosure-statement violation by the seller. A seller could simply claim the buyer relied on the inspection and investigation instead of the disclosure statement. The legislative intent of protecting consumers would not be upheld if the statutes were construed in such a manner.

Therefore, this Court agrees that a buyer's knowledge of undisclosed damage in a cause of action for violation of the disclosure statutes does not provide a complete defense. However, the buyer's knowledge may be relevant to the amount of damages awarded because any defect of which the buyer was aware would be reflected in the purchase price of the house, thereby reducing damages. This raises a genuine issue of material fact concerning the extent of damages resulting from the violation of the disclosure statutes.

This conclusion, however, should not imply that strict liability results from a seller's nondisclosure under SDCL 43-4-38. Strict liability is not the requisite standard under South Dakota's disclosure statutes, because liability attaches only if the nondisclosure is negligent or intentional. Therefore, a mere nondisclosure without some form of culpability will not result in liability. We hold that a buyer's knowledge does not affect liability and is not a complete bar to the cause of action. However, according to SDCL 43-4-42, a buyer's knowledge is relevant to the extent of damages because recoverable damages are only those suffered "as a result of" the nondisclosure. Damages, therefore, may still be affected by the buyer's knowledge.

Fuller contends there are genuine issues of material fact concerning Johnson's and her employer's liability for misrepresentation and/or nondisclosure. SDCL chapter 36-21A provides rules and regulations for real estate licensing. A section of this chapter states in part, "no licensee is liable for a misrepresentation of the licensee's client arising out of the agency agreement unless the licensee knew of the misrepresentation." In this case, Johnson is a licensed real estate agent and admits to representing Crostons in the sale of their home.

Taking the evidence in the light most favorable to Fuller, Crostons assert Johnson told them not to disclose the prior water damage to the home on the disclosure statement. And, as stated earlier, Johnson denies that assertion. Crostons claim she advised them not to disclose because they told her the damage occurred many years ago and was fixed. Johnson, therefore, allegedly was aware of prior water penetration in the home. If that is true, she not only failed to prevent Crostons' nondisclosure, but actually encouraged it. This observation, however, does not end our inquiry. According to SDCL 36-21A-148, a licensee is liable for misrepresentations of the client if the licensee had knowledge of the misrepresentation. Therefore, before Johnson could be held liable, the Court must determine whether the nondisclosure of prior water damage was a misrepresentation by Crostons.

The crux of this issue is whether reliance is an element of misrepresentations as used in SDCL 36-21A-148. If so, Fuller's failure to rely on the misrepresentation of no prior water damage in the disclosure statement defeats his claim against Johnson. Johnson attempts to equate misrepresentation as used in SDCL 36-21A-148 with the elements for a cause of action for deceit or negligent or intentional misrepresentation. However, this is not how the term is used in the statute. This Court has determined that a misrepresentation is "essentially a false statement of material fact." The summary judgment in favor of Johnson must be reversed.

Affirmed in part, reversed in part, and remanded.

CASE QUESTIONS

1. What does the court establish as the law on the failure to disclose pre-existing but repaired defects in a home?
2. What does the court establish was the law on oral disclosures that supplements the disclosure requirements?
3. Is there potential liability for real estate brokers who do not advise their clients to make property disclosures?
NOTE: For differing results in cases similar to this in which knowledge did make a difference in the buyer's right to recover from the seller, see, for example, *Sherman v. Elkowitz*, 130 S.W.3d 316 (Tex. App. 2004) (full disclosure of cracks in driveway and presence of termites were sufficient for directed verdict for seller and broker when both were disclosed but buyer later brought suit out of frustration over repairs and costs); *Alires v. McGehee*, 85 P.3d 1191 (Kan. 2004) (no reasonable reliance on seller's statements about the water and the basement); *Funk v. Durant*, 799 N.E.2d 221(Oh. App. 2003) (buyers were aware of problems with basement prior to purchase); and *Alires v. McGehee*, 77 P.3d 1008 (Kan App. 2003) (leaking basement, but court held the buyers could not rely on statements as a basis for a claim).

CONSIDER 12.5

John Helm, an architect, designed and built a large home in 1989. Anne Marie Grossman was a co-owner of the home and property with Helm. Because the home was built on hilly terrain, Helm used a pier and grade beam foundation. Helm and Grossman moved into the home in 1990 and listed it for sale with California Prudential Realty with Marti Gellens-Stubbs as the listing agent.

On the real estate disclosure form, Helm and Grossman stated that they were unaware of any significant defects in the foundation, exterior walls, windows, ceilings or other parts of the home. When Ms. Gellens-Stubbs inspected the property, she noticed hairline stucco cracks, which Helm assured were only cosmetic. Ms. Gellens-Stubbs did not note the cracks on her portion of the disclosure statement but did write, "property appears to be in good condition...I see nothing to contradict what the seller has mentioned...." Later, Gellens-Stubbs noticed that the interior paint was peeling near a dining room window. Helm explained that the peeling had been caused by water infiltration during construction, but that the problem had been remedied. Gellens-Stubbs did not note this information either.

Mark and Susan Robinson looked at the home several times in 1991 and noticed the stucco cracks. When they discussed the cracks with their agent, Gracinda Maier, she recommended that they have the home professionally inspected. Helm told the Robinsons that the cracks "were caused by the finish of the house, which is called a Santa Barbara finish, and there was a product called elastomeric that...would alleviate the stucco cracks."

Helm and Grossman accepted an offer of $653,750 from the Robinsons. The purchase contract of May 22, 1991, required Helm and Grossman to furnish the Robinsons with a geological report by Ninyo & Moore. The contract permitted the Robinsons to cancel the agreement if any of the geological reports or testing commissioned by the Robinsons revealed problems they would be unwilling or unable to correct.

On May 24, 1991, Maier added the following to the disclosure statement:

My visual inspection found numerous cracks in the house. Buyer's agent recommends buyer to have property inspected by a professional home inspector and have the land checked by a geologist.

Gellens-Stubbs then added the following:

Stucco cracks on home are cosmetic in nature according to the seller because of finish and type of stucco.

The Robinsons hired Ameritec Home Inspection Service. Robert Brand, an employee, listed the "very old" water stain in the dining room and "normal settling cracking" of the stucco. Brand found no soils-related distress and the report concluded, "the house was very well built,...[and] was not going anyplace...."

During final inspection in July 1991, Mrs. Robinson noticed more water stains in the ceiling and wall of the entryway. There were patched stucco cracks and some water damage on the deck. Grossman assured that the cracks were cosmetic and the small hole in the deck had been repaired. The final inspection report included the phrase "per seller—stucco cracks are cosmetic." Gellens-Stubbs sent Mr. Robinson a letter stating, "The ceiling and wall in the downstairs sitting area will be repainted where the stains are and according to seller, the stucco cracks are cosmetic in nature and were patched with a stucco and glue mixture." Escrow closed.

A few weeks after moving into the home, as they were attempting to have a swimming pool installed, the entire excavation around the house collapsed. The Robinsons sued Helm, Grossman, Gellens-Stubbs, Prudential, and others for professional negligence, and negligent and intentional misrepresentation.

CONSIDER 12.5

(continued)

The trial court dismissed the fraud accusations against Prudential and Gellens-Stubbs. The jury found there had been negligent misrepresentation, professional negligence and awarded the Robinsons $16,827. They had asked for the value of the home or $719,130 (if it had been as represented plus the approximate cost of reconstruction). The jury found Grossman had no liability and awarded her attorney's fees of $10,980.13 from the Robinsons. The Robinsons appealed. Who should win? Be sure to discuss the law and cases you have studied and consider whether the broker and owner should be held liable. *Robinson v. Grossman* 67 Cal. Rptr.2d 380 (Cal. App. 1997)

Disclosure, Discrimination, and Silence

Brokers and agents have faced increasingly complex issues of disclosure with respect to properties they are listing or showing. Should the fact that a crime has been committed on the property be revealed? Should the fact that someone with HIV/AIDS owned the property previously be revealed? What if, as the quotes opening this chapter discuss, there is a registered sex offender living in the neighborhood where the property is located? In some of these disclosure situations, brokers and agents have statutory duties that prohibit them from affirmatively disclosing the information about the property. In other situations, an affirmative duty to disclose is imposed by statute. However, even in those situations in which the information is protected by statute and the broker is prohibited from affirmatively disclosing it, the broker or agent cannot lie in the event the buyer asks a question and the broker or agent has the information. In some states, these disclosure and nondisclosure rules include "shield statutes," which protect the broker from liability for maintaining the statutory silence about the covered subject areas.

The presence or absence of criminal activity on a property or the presence of a released sex offender near a particular property is deemed to be material information because it does affect the value of the property.

NAR has adopted a position on the issue of sex offender information that provides,

> *all public disclosures should emanate directly from the appropriate law enforcement agency, and no affirmative disclosure duty regarding the location of released sex offenders should be placed on real estate licensees as a result of state public notification programs.*

In NAR's position statement, information on sex offenders must come from the government records themselves and not from brokers or agents. Brokers and agents need only respond to questions from buyers by referring them to the public records.

Practical Tip

The following is a checklist for brokers undertaking a new listing and handling prospective buyers of that property:

- *Ask about the property repair record.*
- *Ask about the utilities.*
- *Ask about the condition of appliances, roof, walls, and basement.*
- *Include pertinent information about physical condition in the listing agreement.*
- *Make an independent investigation of the property, carefully looking for recent cover-ups, redecorating, and hidden defects.*
- *Consider a warranty policy for the home.*
- *Consider having a professional home inspection.*
- *Make no statement that is not based on your firsthand information or knowledge.*
- *Have available a list of addresses and phone numbers for municipal, state, and country offices, so that the prospective buyer may make independent checks on information.*
- *Do not fail to disclose pertinent information, and do not participate with the seller in a nondisclosure scheme.*
- *Take measurements to verify room sizes and square footage.*
- *Follow up on the buyer's questions for which you have no answer or knowledge.*

Practical Tip

Good or bad, the buyer should have full information about the property. The failure to disclose negative information only leads to litigation against the broker, the agent, and the agency. Negative information finds its way to the surface, as it were, and the resulting liability is significant.

All states currently have some form of statute on the responsibility for disclosure of sex offender information. Some states exempt real estate agents from disclosure, while others include required language in contracts referring buyers to appropriate agencies for information. Further discussion of these disclosure protections and mandates and the broker's responsibilities and liabilities are found in Chapter 13 as well as Chapter 19.

Insurance Protection

Suits against brokers for misrepresentation are a constant in the industry. Actual and punitive damages, for either intentional or negligent misrepresentation by brokers, have been quite large. As noted earlier, a broker may be held liable under a pretense of knowledge even when the broker has no actual knowledge. As a result of the amount of litigation and the size of verdicts and settlements, brokers purchase **errors and omissions insurance** coverage, which is a form of malpractice insurance for brokers, salespeople, and their companies, all of which can be held liable in these types of suits. The amount of coverage available usually begins at $100,000 with a deductible of $1,000 for small claims.

Self-Protection

Perhaps the best protection a broker may obtain against a suit for misrepresentation is preventive protection. Preventive protection includes understanding the property to be sold and all of its defects, restrictions, and limitations.

Web Exhibit 12.5 will link to a seller's disclosure form used by brokers and agents to try to be certain that they know all the material information they are expected to know about a property they have listed. "I didn't know" is no longer a defense for brokers and agents with regard to property conditions and issues affecting the value of the property. Brokers' and agents' liability is determined by whether they *should* have known, not whether they actually did know.

Licensing Requirements for Brokers/Agents

All states and the District of Columbia have licensing requirements for brokers and agents. Licensing affords protection to the public by requiring real estate practitioners to meet certain uniform standards of competency and practice. Second, licensing protects existing licensees from unscrupulous or illegal conduct by new entrants.

Every state has a statute that establishes licensing requirements for those seeking status as real estate practitioners. In each state statute, some type of administrative agency is created to be responsible for the issuing of licenses to real estate practitioners and will have a title such as the real estate board, board of real estate, real estate commission, or department of real estate. These administrative agencies are responsible for establishing licensing procedures and qualifications and for enforcing statutorily imposed licensing procedures and qualifications. Agencies also serve to clarify and interpret applicable legislative provisions. In addition, they are usually responsible for the supervision of licensees, investigations of alleged misconduct, and appropriate disciplinary measures such as license revocation or referrals for criminal prosecution.

Requirements for Obtaining Licenses

Two types of agents may work for the principal buyer or seller in the real estate transaction. Brokers are licensed to operate their own real estate brokerage businesses. A **salesperson** (sometimes called an **agent**) is licensed only to work for a broker, with the broker assuming responsibility for the salesperson's actions. Licensing requirements for brokers are more stringent than those for salespeople, and a salesperson's license is almost universally a prerequisite for a broker's license.

Most state license laws follow the model license law written by the National Association of Real Estate License Law Officials (NARELLO). Each state will have its own variations, but the following list of requirements is part of the NARELLO model.

a. *Educational requirements.* State educational prerequisites for licensing vary from none to an accredited college or university degree.
b. *Experience.* This requirement is limited to broker licenses. Most states require two years' experience as a salesperson or two years' experience in the real estate field as a prerequisite for licensing as a broker.
c. *Examination.* All states require both salespeople and brokers to pass examinations to obtain licensing.
d. *Sponsorship.* About half of the states require candidates for salespeople's licenses to be sponsored by a licensed broker who will be responsible for the salesperson when the license is awarded.
e. *Minimum age.* In most states, the minimum age for licensure is the age of majority in the state (about half of the states list 18 years of age).
f. *Citizenship.* Some states still require U.S. citizenship status as a prerequisite for licensing; however, this requirement with respect to other forms of licensing has been struck down on constitutional grounds.
g. *Residency.* Some states require that license applicants be residents of the state for 30 to 90 days before application may be made. Again, such requirements for other license cases have been subject to constitutional challenges.
h. *Criminal record.* Nearly all of the states have provisions prohibiting licensing if the applicant has been convicted of a felony. However, these states usually limit the length of time for this restriction.
i. *Application.* All states require potential licensees to submit a completed form provided and developed by the regulating agency. Commonly, the application will require the applicant to give character references from persons in the community or from persons already established in the real estate business.
j. *Payment of fees.* All states require the payment of a licensing fee upon original application. Furthermore, a renewal fee is required to be paid at intervals established by the states.

Issuance of Licenses

Once applicants have satisfied the requirements, their state license will be issued. In all states, all licenses must be displayed in the agent or broker's place of business. Some states also have a requirement whereby licensees must carry pocket cards indicating their licensed status.

Doing Business without Licenses

Attempting to act as a salesperson or broker without proper licensing is illegal. The licensing of brokers and salespeople is a regulatory scheme, and any contract for commission between an unlicensed salesperson or broker and a seller would also be void. Court enforcement of such a contract is not available. In addition, a fee paid to an unlicensed salesperson or broker may be recovered.

License renewals have become significant over the past few years, with many states requiring evidence of continuing education as well as the payment of license fees. Continuing education requirements may include college course credits as well as professional seminars. Some states require training in fair housing laws, for both initial licensing and renewals.

The following case deals with a commission issue when a broker's license expires.

Douglas v. Schuette

607 N.W. 2d 142 (Minn. App. 2000)

FACTS

Terry Lee Douglas (appellant) listed the property of Dennis and Lucille Schuette (respondents). The property consisted of 420 acres of land in Sherburne County. On April 29, 1990, Beverly A. Aubol signed a purchase agreement for the property with escrow to occur on or before September 15, 1990.

On June 30, 1990, Douglas's real estate license expired. On July 9, 1990, the listing agreement between Douglas and the Schuettes expired and was not renewed. Under Minnesota law, a broker or agent can provide the sellers with a list of "protected persons," or those persons to whom they have shown the property in order to protect the commission in the event the property is sold to one of those prospects. Douglas did not provide the Schuettes with such a list.

In late spring 1990, Aubol began to question Douglas's business practices. Because she had planned to purchase the property to develop it jointly with Douglas, she notified the Schuettes that she would no longer be willing to buy the land because of what she had discovered about Douglas.

The Schuettes then listed their property with another agent and Aubol notified them on November 11, 1990, that she was once again interested in the property. Aubol and the Schuettes signed a purchase contract for the property which closed on April 18, 1991.

On August 2, 1995, Douglas brought suit against the Schuettes demanding his commission on the property. The trial court granted summary judgment to the Schuettes and also awarded them sanctions against Douglas in the amount of $18,500. Douglas appealed.

JUDICIAL OPINION

Foley, Judge. The listing agreement provides that appellant is entitled to a commission

upon the happening of any of the following events: (1) the closing of the sale, (2) [seller's] refusal to close the sale, or (3) [seller's] refusal to sell at the price and terms required in this contract.

Under the listing agreement, appellant was entitled to a commission if a closing occurred. Appellant admitted, however, that there was never a closing under the first purchase agreement. Under the stipulated facts, the first purchase agreement was cancelled on October 30, 1990. While the property was eventually sold to the same buyer on April 18, 1991, (1) that sale was governed by a different purchase agreement, (2) it was arranged with another agent, (3) the listing agreement between the parties had already expired, and (4) appellant's real estate license was no longer in effect.

The listing agreement also provided that if the seller refused to close, appellant would be entitled to a commission. Respondents did not refuse to close. Aubol stated in her December 17, 1997, affidavit that "she was no longer willing to purchase the property because [she] was ending [her] association with [appellant]." After learning of Aubol's unwillingness to purchase the property, respondents agreed to cancel the purchase agreement. Because there is no evidence in the record of collusion between respondents and the buyer to cancel the purchase agreement in order to prevent appellant from earning his commission, the district court properly concluded that it was Aubol, not respondents, who refused to close.

Appellant could also have earned a commission if respondents had refused to sell the property at the price and terms required under the contract. However, in her affidavit Aubol states that she was not willing to buy the property. Because appellant failed to produce a buyer willing to purchase the property at the price and terms required in the listing contract, appellant cannot rely on this provision to retain a commission.

By complying with the override clause of the listing agreement, appellant could have recovered a commission. The override clause stated:

If within 180 days after the end of this contract [respondents] sell or agree to sell the property to anyone who:

(1) During this contract made inquiry of [respondents] about the property and [respondents] did not tell [appellant] about the inquiry; or

(2) During this contract made an alternative showing of interest in the property or was physically shown the property by [appellant] and whose name is on a written list [appellant gives respondents] within 72 hours after the end of this contract, then [respondents] will pay [appellant a] commission on the selling price, even if [respondents] sell the property without [appellant's] assistance.

The record shows that appellant failed to provide respondents with a list of protected persons. Under Minnesota law,

licensees shall not seek to enforce an override clause unless a protective list has been furnished to the seller within 72 hours after the expiration of the listing agreement. Minn.Stat. §82.195, subd. 4 (1998)

Because appellant failed to provide a protective list within the statutory period, appellant is precluded from recovering his commission under the override clause.

Appellant claims that the purchase agreement served as a substitute for the protective list. This court has explicitly held that a purchase agreement cannot substitute for a protective list.

The listing agreement stated:

I understand that I do not have to pay your commission if I sign another valid listing contract after the expiration of this contract, under which I am obligated to pay a commission to another licensed real estate broker.

The district court concluded that because respondents entered into a listing agreement with another licensed real estate agent after their listing agreement with appellant had expired, appellant is barred from seeking a commission under this provision. We agree.

Appellant claims that because he procured the buyer who eventually bought the property, he is entitled to a commission. However, this court has held that a real estate agent cannot recover a commission by relying on the procuring-cause doctrine. Here, the listing agreement included a provision that relieved respondents of any obligation to pay a commission to the appellant if, after the expiration of the listing agreement with appellant, respondents entered into another listing agreement with a different agent. The district court did not err in its determination that no commission was earned.

Appellant argues that the district court erred in concluding that he did not have standing to bring suit for his commission because he was not a licensed real estate agent when the sale between respondents and Aubol was consummated.

No person shall bring or maintain any action in the courts of this state for the collection of compensation for the performance of any of the acts for which a license is required under this chapter without alleging and proving that the person was a duly licensed real estate broker, salesperson, or closing agent at the time the alleged cause of action arose. Minn.Stat. §2.33, subd. 1 (1998)

"This section is penal in nature and will defeat a claim for commissions if a plaintiff fails to allege and prove that [he or she was] duly licensed."

On June 30, 1990, appellant's real estate agent license expired.

The record proves that respondents never (1) closed under the first purchase agreement, (2) refused to close, or (3) refused to sell the property at the price and terms required under the listing agreement. In addition, appellant failed to provide respondents with a list of protected persons within the statutory period and thus cannot recover under the override clause. Therefore, the only dates on which any cause of action of appellant could have arisen were December 13, 1990, when the second purchase agreement was signed, or April 18, 1991, when the property was eventually sold to Aubol. Because appellant was not a licensed real estate agent on either of these dates, he had no standing to raise a claim.

Appellant argues that so long as he was licensed when he began his services, he can recover a commission. Appellant cites no Minnesota law to support this proposition.

Appellant also argues that the statute does not preclude his claim because his partner was a licensed real estate agent. The evidence demonstrates that respondents dealt exclusively with appellant, who was not licensed at the time of the sale.

Affirmed.

CASE QUESTIONS

1. Give the sequence of events on the listing and sale of the property.

2. Why did Aubol not go forward with the original purchase of the property?

3. What did Douglas fail to do that might have entitled him to a commission?

4. What happens if a real estate agent is not licensed at the time of closing?

CONSIDER 12.6

Ceas Mortgage Company brought suit against Walnut Hills Associates, Ltd., for an unpaid commission. Ceas alleged that it was a real estate broker for the sale of property to Walnut Hills. Ceas Mortgage did not have a real estate broker's license, but an employee of Ceas who handled the transaction was a licensed broker. The transaction took place in Illinois where the following statute governs the payment of real estate commissions:

No action or suit shall be instituted, nor recovery therein be had, in any court of this State by any person, partnership, limited liability company, or corporation for compensation for any act done or service performed, the doing or performing of which is prohibited by this Act to other than licensed brokers or sales persons unless such person, partnership, limited liability company, or corporation was duly licensed hereunder as a broker or salesperson at the time that any such act was done or service performed which would give rise to a cause of action for compensation.

Should Ceas collect a commission? Is there a legal or ethical obligation to pay the commission? *Ceas Mortgage Co. v. Walnut Hills Associates, Ltd.*, 726 N.E.2d 695 (Ill. App. 2000)

Exemptions from Licensing

All states have some exemptions from the licensing requirement. For example, individuals selling real estate for themselves need not be licensed. In all states, attorneys acting for clients in real estate transactions are not required to be licensed as brokers. Those acting as personal representatives, executors, administrators, or trustees for estates need not be licensed to sell or offer to sell property of the estate. All states also have exemptions for public officials dealing with land and its purchase and sale as part of their official duties and responsibilities.

Professional Organizations

The largest professional association in the real estate industry is the National Association of Realtors (NAR). Only those who are members may use the designation **Realtor**, which is a registered trade name of the association. When used by real estate practitioners, this term indicates that they subscribe to the code of ethics of NAR. NAR also promotes and provides educational opportunities for Realtors, and local and state chapters often have publications mailed to members that provide updates and information on changes in the field of real estate.

There are also affiliates of NAR for specific real estate professions. The following list is not comprehensive but indicative of the various specialized affiliates of NAR:

1. American Institute of Real Estate Appraisers (AIREA)
2. Institute of Real Estate Management (IREM)
3. Realtors National Marketing Institute (RNMI)
4. Society of Industrial Realtors (SIR)
5. Women's Council of Realtors

Broker's/Agent's Legal Duties and Responsibilities to State

State

Because they are licensed by the state, brokers must also comply with state laws and regulations. Violations can result in penalties that include fines, penalties, and suspension or revocation of license.

Suspension or Revocation of Real Estate License

Each state has its own requirements and penalties for forms of illegal conduct, but certain types of conduct are universally prohibited by the states and usually result in suspension or revocation of license.

1. *Commingling of funds.* All states have some provision prohibiting brokers from commingling clients' funds with their own funds and require the maintenance of separate escrow or trust funds.
2. *Discriminating practices.* Refusing to show property on the basis of a prospect's race, color, sex, or national origin may bring about not only a loss of license, but also the imposition of federal penalties and other state penalties for violations of the fair housing laws. Discriminatory practices include *steering* (where brokers direct certain races to certain areas and away from other areas) and *redlining* (where sales or listings are agreed to on the basis of the neighborhood racial composition). (See Chapter 19 for a full discussion of these issues.)
3. *Conviction of a felony.* A felony conviction may preclude initial licensing and also result in the loss of license.
4. *Advertising.* Placing media advertising that contains misrepresentations results in disciplinary action in all states. Some states require the written consent of the owner for advertising.
5. *Splitting commissions with an unlicensed party.* Only licensed individuals may split commissions.
6. *Failure to deliver required documents.* Those who fail to deliver required copies of documents to clients, such as purchase contracts and listing agreements, are subject to suspension or revocation.
7. *Failure to submit all offers.* All offers received prior to written acceptance must be submitted to the seller.
8. *Breach of duties to seller and unethical conduct.*
9. *The unauthorized practice of law.* As noted earlier, some states permit brokers to fill in purchase contract forms and closing documents, while other states require attorneys. Brokers who exceed their authorized authority are subject to disciplinary action by both their licensing agency and the state bar.

Rights upon Suspension or Revocation

Constitutional standards of due process for license suspension or revocation are satisfied with administrative proceedings. That is, the licensing agency may conduct appropriate hearings and impose penalties even though such an agency is not a court.

The broker or agent charged with a violation has the right to be informed of the charges and to advance notice of the hearing so that he or she can appear and defend the charges and present evidence and witnesses. The state, through its agency, must give the broker or agent advance notice of those witnesses who will be called to testify in the hearing, so that the broker or agent can prepare a response or call rebuttal witnesses.

The following case involves a broker's suspension and the issues of fitness for continued licensing.

DEARBORN V. REAL ESTATE AGENCY

53 P.3d 436 (Or. 2002)

FACTS

On October 4, 1996, Harold Dearborn (petitioner), then a licensed real estate agent, broker, and designated broker, was arrested at his home. Police officers found small amounts of cocaine and methamphetamine in his home. Police officers were at his home pursuant to an investigation of Dearborn's sexual activities with transients in exchange for drugs. One of the transients with whom he had sexual relations was a 17-year-old. Dearborn was indicted for possession of controlled substances as well as prostitution, endangering the welfare of a minor, and furnishing obscene materials to a minor. Dearborn entered a guilty plea to two counts of possession of a controlled substance and the other counts were dismissed. He was placed on probation for 18 months, ordered to serve 10 days in jail, perform community services, and pay a $500 fine. He was also ordered to have no contact with juveniles without prior approval from his probation officer.

The Real Estate Commissioner began proceedings to have his broker's license suspended. At the time of the hearing, Dearborn had paid his fine, performed his community service, had his driver's license reinstated (which had been suspended upon the guilty plea), and had his probation changed to unsupervised probation. The Commissioner ordered that Dearborn's license be suspended pending successful completion of the terms of his probation. Upon successful completion of probation, his broker's license would be revoked and he would be issued a limited salesperson license for two years. Assuming no further difficulties, he could then have an unrestricted license. Dearborn appealed the agency's decision. The Court of Appeals reversed and the Commissioner appealed to the Oregon Supreme Court.

JUDICIAL OPINION

Gillette, Justice. We conclude that there must be a substantial relationship between the conduct at issue and a licensee's real estate activities. We next consider whether the conduct at issue in this case would support revocation of broker's license under one or both of those subsections. We begin with ORS 696.301(26) (1995), which authorizes disciplinary action when a broker is convicted of a crime that is "substantially related" to the broker's fitness to engage in real estate activity.

It is important, at this juncture, to identify which facts are relevant to our analysis. Although the Court of Appeals and the Commissioner appear to have treated all the conduct identified in the Commissioner's findings as relevant to subsection (26), it is clear to this court that only a relatively small subset of that conduct is germane. ORS 696.301(26) (1995) authorizes professional discipline against brokers who have been convicted of a felony or misdemeanor of a specified sort. Evidence pertaining to other, unrelated criminal charges that the court dismissed, or to acts that the authorities discovered in the course of the criminal investigation, do not support revocation or suspension of a license under that subsection.

The Agency suggests that subsection (26) is not so limited. It contends that the provision must be read in the context of ORS 670.280, which provides:

Except as provided in ORS 342.143 or 342.175, no licensing board shall deny, suspend or revoke an occupational or professional license or certification solely for the reason that the applicant or licensee has been convicted of a crime, but it may consider the relationship of the facts which support the conviction and all intervening circumstances to the specific occupational or professional standards in determining the fitness of the person to receive or hold such license or certificate.

The Agency argues that, although it is a more general statute, ORS 670.280 nonetheless modifies ORS 696.301(26) (1995), thereby extending the scope of the latter statute to include conduct and circumstances surrounding the crime and ultimate conviction. That category would include, in the Agency's view, any conduct mentioned in any of the voluminous law enforcement investigative reports that relate to broker's convictions, including discussions of broker's sexual behavior and his pattern of giving drugs to sex partners.

We disagree. Although ORS 670.280 explicitly confers some authority to look at the "facts which support the conviction" and "intervening facts" when applying ORS 696.301(26) (1995), that statute cannot reasonably be read as expanding the scope of subsection (26) to permit imposing a sanction under that subsection for acts extraneous to broker's actual convictions. What the Commissioner may consider ... are such facts as the broker's conviction of possession of cocaine and methamphetamine, that both substances are controlled substances, that small amounts of those substances were found in his home, and that he admitted to purchasing and using both substances on more than one occasion. If, in light of those facts, the Commissioner can conclude that broker's crimes were "substantially related" to his trustworthiness or competence to engage in professional real estate activity at the time that he committed them, then the Commissioner had authority to discipline him under section (26).

However, he cannot so conclude. The Commissioner's order on reconsideration fails to recognize that the reference in ORS 696.301 (1995) to acts that a licensee "has done" places a temporal element in the statutory inquiry: The acts that give rise to the Commissioner's authority must have occurred in the past and, at the time that they occurred, must have been substantially related to broker's real estate activities. As the Commissioner acknowledges in his order, however, there is "no evidence" that broker's criminal activities arose out of broker's "use of his position as a real estate licensee." It follows that the Commissioner had no authority to sanction broker under ORS 696.301(26) (1995).

We recognize that the Commissioner offers two justifications in the "Reasoning" section of his opinion that he believes to justify disciplining broker under ORS 696.301(26) (1995). They are: (1) the statement that, when a real estate licensee has used highly addictive drugs (as broker has), there is a risk that the licensee will use his or her access to people's homes to steal prescription drugs, cash, or valuables; and (2) the statement that there is an additional risk that the licensee will use funds held in trust for clients to support his or her drug habit. Those statements miss the mark, because they purport to justify the Commissioner's choice to sanction broker on the possibility that broker might do something in the future that would violate some subsection of ORS 696.301 (1995). As we have explained, however, the Commissioner's right to discipline must arise out of something that a licensee has done, not out of something that a licensee might do. So far as this record discloses, none of broker's criminal acts had anything to do with his real estate activities. None involved clients, real estate, or money entrusted to broker. Without such a nexus, the Commissioner could not permissibly conclude that broker had violated ORS 696.301(26) (1995). We hold, in short, that the Commissioner erred in concluding that broker's drug possession convictions were "substantially related" to broker's real estate activities.

We turn to the question whether the Commissioner properly could revoke broker's license for violating ORS 696.301(31) (1995). Subsection (31) is broader than subsection (26), inasmuch as it authorizes the Commissioner to revoke a broker's license for engaging in any conduct that "demonstrates" untrustworthiness, incompetence, or improper dealings. On some level, all the conduct described in the Commissioner's order may be said to fit into that category. However, as we have discussed, the range of acts to which subsection (31) applies is limited by the implicit requirement that the conduct in question relate substantially to the broker's fitness and ability to engage in real estate activity.

As noted, the Commissioner explained his decision to revoke broker's license in terms of certain perceived risks to broker's future real estate clients—that, e.g., broker might offer drugs in exchange for sex to a client's children or to other juveniles whom broker might meet through his real estate dealings, that broker might use his access to client's homes to steal prescription drugs, cash, or valuables, or that broker might convert money held in trust for clients to his own use to support his possible drug habit. In doing so, the Commissioner is positing a predictive relationship between broker's past conduct, which the Commissioner acknowledges did not involve real estate activities, and broker's future professional conduct, i.e., the Commissioner is asserting that broker's crimes, sexual behavior, and drug use create or increase the probability that broker will abuse his position as a real estate professional in one or more of the suggested ways.

That is not the question, however. Instead, the question is whether the acts that broker committed, at the time that he committed them, "demonstrated" untrustworthiness, incompetence, or improper dealings with respect to broker's real estate activities. As we have explained with respect to subsection (26), they did not: They did not involve real estate, clients, or funds of clients. They were private acts, separate from broker's professional life. And, because they were, the Commissioner had no authority under them to discipline broker under ORS 696.301(31) (1995).

The Court of Appeals reversed the Commissioner's order because it found "no factual support in the record to justify the concerns [that the Commissioner] identified" therein. As we have explained, we see the problem somewhat differently, but our analysis leads to the same conclusion: The Commissioner erred.

The order of the Real Estate Commissioner is reversed.

CASE QUESTIONS

1. Describe the nature of the real estate broker's criminal convictions.
2. Is a criminal conviction grounds for not issuing a license? When is a criminal conviction grounds for revocation or suspension of a license?
3. Will the suspension be upheld?
4. What mistake did the Commissioner make in issuing the suspension?

Relationships Among Brokers/Agents

In this final section the focus of discussion is on duties and responsibilities among the interrelationships of those acting within the industry.

Broker-Salesperson Relationship

A broker will probably have salespeople working in a common office and should establish the rights of all the agents who will be working together. The office broker should have a contract with each agent that spells out the details of their relationship, including the following:

- Broker will maintain a properly equipped office.
- Salesperson will maintain licensing status (including the payment of fees).
- Broker makes all listings available to agent (salesperson).
- Broker may not dictate which parties salesperson will solicit.
- Salesperson will work diligently for sales and listings.
- Salesperson and broker will abide by the Code of Ethics of the National Association of Realtors, as well as state, national, and local laws.
- Commission-splitting arrangements will be set and followed.
- Terms for ending relationship are set.
- Arbitration procedures are specified.

Salesperson-Salesperson Relationship

Because there is generally more than one salesperson per office, brokers have rules and regulations governing their interrelationships. For example, most offices have a policy on commission splits for those sales in which more than one agent is involved in getting the deal closed. Offices also have policies on handling walk-ins and the distribution of information about prospects to avoid misunderstandings, resentment, and undercutting.

Broker-Broker Relationship

Often in open listing agreements, the issue of who actually obtained a buyer for a sale—and, hence, who is entitled to a commission—becomes critical. The standard used for determining this is the **procuring cause of the sale standard**. To be entitled to a commission under this standard, the broker need not be the one to obtain the actual sale terms but must establish that he or she brought seller and buyer together.

Bringing seller and buyer together can result from direct contact or newspaper advertisement. If the broker finds and introduces to the principal a person who is ready, willing, and able to purchase or exchange the property according to the principal's terms, the commission is earned. It is immaterial if the final contract is made without the presence or knowledge of the procuring broker.

The following case deals with a dispute over commissions and the procuring cause of the sale.

Telluride Real Estate Company v. Penthouse Affiliates, LLC

996 P.2d 151 (Co. Ct. App. 1999); cert. denied

FACTS

Jeffrey Brooks and Prospect Real Estate listed the Revenue Penthouse (defendants) in Telluride, Colorado, on MLS. In September 1995, Steven Hilbert (plaintiff) was introduced to Richard Furlaud (defendant), a potential purchaser of the property. Hilbert showed Furlaud and his wife several properties in the Telluride area, including the Revenue Penthouse.

The Furlauds were interested in the Penthouse and made a follow-up appointment with Hilbert to see the property again. At that time they asked questions about taxes, homeowners' fees, and the amount of an offer.

The Furlauds returned to New York, and Hilbert gave them his cell phone and fax number because he would be on a trip for the next few days. He also gave the Furlauds the name of another agent in his office for them to reach for further questions if he could not be reached. Hilbert called Brooks that evening and told him he had a definite prospect for the Revenue Penthouse.

On the flight home, Furlaud had decided against the Penthouse, but called a friend who owned property in Telluride and expressed dissatisfaction with Hilbert. Furlaud's friend spoke with Brooks and asked Brooks to call Furlaud. Furlaud and Brooks then reached a "handshake deal" for Furlaud to purchase the Penthouse.

No one returned Hilbert's calls and Hilbert sent a letter confirming his right to a commission. Both Brooks and Furlaud responded that they were "dissatisfied" with Hilbert's services. The property closed and Hilbert and his firm brought suit for their commission. The trial court awarded them $70,000 and Brooks and Furlaud appealed.

JUDICIAL OPINION

Rothenberg, Judge. The doctrine of procuring cause has long been a part of the common law in Colorado. Under this doctrine, the determination whether a broker is the procuring cause rests on whether the broker set in motion a chain of events which, without break in continuity, resulted in a sale. When the buyer and seller involved in a real estate contract intentionally exclude a broker from negotiations, they are precluded as a matter of law from defending on the basis that the broker was not the procuring cause. *Winston Financial Group, Inc. v. Fults Management, Inc.*, 872 P.2d 1356 (Colo. App. 1994). Application of the procuring cause doctrine does not depend on the existence of a written agreement.

In 1993, the General Assembly enacted, effective January 1, 1994, "An Act Concerning Brokerage Relationships in Real Estate Transactions." Defendants assert that the 1994 Act was intended to supplant completely existing law pertaining to brokerage relationships. However, the trial court concluded that there was nothing in the statutory scheme addressing the issue of procuring cause and, therefore, that it was not an issue considered or addressed by the statutory amendments. We agree with the trial court that the plain language of the statutory scheme does not support defendants' assertion.

Statutes in derogation of the common law must be strictly construed. The legislative declaration contained in the 1994 Act states:

(1) The general assembly finds, determines, and declares that the public will best be served through a better understanding of the public's legal and working relationships with real estate brokers and by being able to engage any such real estate broker on terms and under conditions that the public and the real estate broker find acceptable. This includes engaging a broker as a single agent, subagent, dual agent, or transaction-broker. Further, the public should be advised by the general duties, obligations, and responsibilities of a real estate broker in any particular real estate transaction.

(2) This part 8 is enacted to govern the relationships between real estate brokers and sellers, landlords, buyers, and tenants in real estate transactions.

Thus, the expressed purpose of the legislation is to protect consumers in their interactions with real estate professionals. The 1994 Act does not address comprehensively the area of commissions and/or compensation earned by brokers. In addition, the parties have agreed that there was no mention of the procuring cause doctrine in the legislative history surrounding the 1994 Act. Accordingly, we conclude, as did the trial court, that the Act did not eradicate the common law concept of procuring cause.

Applying the principle of procuring cause to the facts here, the trial court found that:

Hilbert showed the unit, provided information, diligently attempted to provide assistance but was 'frozen out' by Defendants who all expected that this would save $70,000 to all concerned in the transaction ... 'But for' Hilbert's three showings (two of the Revenue unit) this transaction would not have occurred.

There is record support for the trial court's determination that Hilbert was the procuring cause of the transaction and defendants do not dispute that fact. Rather, their assertion, which we have rejected, is that the realty agents cannot prevail as a matter of law because the Act eradicated the common law concept of procuring cause.

In view of our conclusion that the procuring cause doctrine still permits recovery, we need not reach the separate issue whether under §12-61-803(2), C.R.S. 1998, Hilbert also was a "transaction-broker," given the undisputed fact that he failed to comply with §12-61-808(2)(a)(I) and §12-61-808(2)(d), C.R.S. 1998. See 12-61-802(6), C.R.S. 1998 (defining "transaction-broker" as: a broker who assists one or more parties throughout a contemplated real estate transaction with communication, interposition, advisement, negotiation, contract terms, and the closing of such real estate transaction without being an agent or advocate for the interests of any party to such transaction).

In summary, we uphold the trial court's determination that the realty agents were entitled to a commission as the procuring cause of the sale.

On cross-appeal, the realty agents contend the trial court erred in refusing to award them damages for tortious interference with contract and for civil conspiracy.

Tortious interference with a contract requires that: (1) the plaintiff have a contract with another party; (2) the defendant knew or should have known of such contract's existence; (3) the defendant intentionally induced the other party to the contract not to perform the contract with the plaintiff; and (4) the defendant's actions caused plaintiff to incur damages.

Here, the realty agents maintain that all of the required elements were met, and that the trial court misapplied the law to the facts. Specifically, they point to the trial court's finding that Furlaud had participated in "freezing out" Hilbert in order to save $70,000 in commissions. However, the court also found that Furlaud was dissatisfied with Hilbert, that a buyer is entitled to work with any real estate professional he or she chooses, and that the required element of intentional inducement had not been proven.

Affirmed.

CASE QUESTIONS

1. Who brought the Furlauds to the property? Who was the listing agent?
2. Who finished the deal with Furlaud?
3. Does the statute eliminate the doctrine of "procuring cause of the sale"?
4. Does Hilbert get his commission?

Cautions and Conclusions

The real estate broker plays an integral role in the transfer of real estate. The role is not only complex in terms of the knowledge requirements and duties of the broker and agent, it is also complex in its relationships with the many parties involved in real estate transactions. Because of these complexities, brokers and agents should be have clear and written agreements on these relationships that cover the following issues: whom the agent or broker represents, how long that relationship will last, how compensation is to be paid, and when that compensation is due. Even relationships between and among agents and brokers in their own firms require written agreements so that issues such as commission arrangements are clear.

All states have statutory requirements for agent and broker licensing and statutory requirements for disclosures to clients on representation. Brokers and agents should be very careful to comply with the requirements when there is a dual representation of both buyer and seller.

Brokers and agents should be cautious in their descriptions of and representations about the properties they show to potential buyers and the listings they take. Brokers need to verify statements and representations about the property through physical inspection. Full disclosure statutes now impose duties of disclosure on both sellers and their brokers.

Brokers and agents are licensed professionals subject to annual license renewal, as well as reviews of their conduct by agencies and professional groups. They cannot earn commissions without a valid license. That license can be suspended or revoked for misconduct, such as a violation of the law or taking clients' funds.

Key Terms

agent, 288
as is, 310
broker, 287
condition precedent, 300
designated agency, 291
dual agency, 288
errors and omissions insurance, 316
exclusive agency listing, 289
exclusive listing-to-sell, 289
exclusive right-to-sell, 289
intermediary, 291
limited agent, 291
listing agreement, 292
multiple listing, 290
multiple listing service (MLS), 290
National Association of Realtors (NAR), 288
net listing, 290
no deal, no commission clause, 299
nonagent broker, 291
open listing, 289
procuring cause of the sale standard, 324
Realtor, 320
salesperson, 317
statutory broker, 291
transaction broker, 291

Chapter Problems

1. Lucy Mae Jones entered into a contract to purchase a home listed by Century 21 Mary Carr & Associates Realty. The contract had a clause that required Jones to promptly apply for financing for the property. The loan was approved by Home South Mortgage Corporation on the condition that Jones pay off the balance due on a Visa account. Jones refused, although she had the funds available, because the account belonged to her boyfriend and he was unemployed and could not pay. The result was that the financing was not granted. The realty brought suit for its commission alleging bad faith on the part of Jones. Should the agency be able to collect its commission in this case? *Century 21 Mary Carr & Assoc. v. Jones*, 418 S.E.2d 435 (Ga. 1992)

2. Fines and Earnestine Hagans purchased a home through Woodruff & Associates Realty. After the Hagans moved into their home, they discovered there was a fault in their neighborhood. The subdivision streets had different levels, and they began to notice separations in their home, between the entry door, in the den, between the garage door, and in the air conditioning unit. The Hagans filed suit against Woodruff for their failure to disclose the presence of a fault line through the neighborhood. Woodruff did not know of the presence of the fault. The Hagans maintain it was Woodruff's responsibility to find these things out because buyers rely on real estate agents for information. Should Woodruff be held liable? *Hagans v. Woodruff*, 830 S.W.2d 732 (Tx. 1992)

3. Suzanne Young (seller) owned 50 acres of land near Bloomington that she wanted to sell. She contacted a real estate broker and offered him $75,000 as a commission if he found a buyer for the $2.8 million property. She then had occasion to speak to Mark Adams, a real estate broker whose license had expired, and he offered to take just a $50,000 commission if he found a buyer for the property. Ms. Young orally signed up for the discount, albeit unlicensed, broker. With all the clarity of an oral agreement for a $50,000 commission on a multimillion dollar piece of property, the parties proceeded to wreak havoc on the statute of frauds.

Young suggested to Adams that he might mention her interest in selling her property to the owner of the neighboring property, Kenneth Blackwell, and see if Blackwell was interested in purchasing the property. Blackwell had previously indicated he was interested in buying the Young property. Adams did indeed run into Blackwell at the gym where their sons played basketball together. Adams told Blackwell that Young wanted to sell the property and offered to show Blackwell the house located on the property. Blackwell was in fact interested, and Adams showed Blackwell around the house.

As a result of the fortuitous gym meeting, Blackwell and Young eventually entered into an agreement in which Blackwell would purchase the property for $2,800,000, contingent on the approval of a zoning change. The zoning change was not granted, and the contract expired. Blackwell then found additional investors and eventually purchased the property from Young for $2,600,000.

Adams then requested that Young pay him the $50,000 commission. Young refused, asserting, with all the force of a mere oral agreement, that they never agreed to such. Adams filed suit for breach of contract. Young defended against the claim on several grounds: (1) Adams was not entitled to the commission because the statute of frauds barred his claim; (2) Adams was acting as an unlicensed real estate broker; (3) no contract was formed; and (4) Adams did not "find" Blackwell. Using what you have learned in this chapter, address these four arguments. *Young v. Adams*, 830 N.E.2d 138 (Ind. Ct. App. 2005) (Problem factual statement is adapted from Marianne M. Jennings, Real Estate Commissions: Of Writings, Fraud, and the Continual Desire for Exceptions, 35 *Real Estate Law Journal* 145 (2006)).

4. Ballard signed an open listing agreement with Barrett for the sale of real property. Barrett ran an advertisement in the local newspaper. In response to the advertisement, Scilley visited the property and talked directly with Ballard. The two were able to reach an agreement. When Ballard refused to pay the commission, Barrett brought suit. Barrett maintains she was the procuring cause of the sale. What is the result?

5. In each of the following hypotheticals, discuss the brokers' duties and liabilities.

- A brokerage firm has a property management subsidiary and its leasing agents are approaching clients in their firms' management subsidiary properties to place them in other properties.
- A broker is a leasing agent for a major anchor tenant and has two listings that will work for the tenant, but only mentions one to the tenant because of his compensation arrangement with the owner of that property.
- A broker accepts a listing on a property located next to land he owns. A buyer approaches the broker about purchasing the broker's land and the broker does not disclose the offer to the listing client/owner of the adjoining land.
- A broker lists a property without results. He then decides to purchase the property. While escrow is pending, he receives an offer on the property for $23,000 more than he has paid. What should the broker do? *Letsos v. Century 21-New West Realty*, 675 N.E. 2d 217 (Ill. App. 1996); *Foley v. Mathias*, 233 N.W. 106 (Iowa 1930); *Reinhold v. Mallery*, 599 A.2d 126 (N.H. 1991); *Baskin v. Dam*, 239 A. 2d 549 (Conn. Cir. Ct. 1967)

6. J. Pagel Realty and Insurance Co. acted as real estate brokers for the sale of property owned by Clifton and Mary Morley. The brokers arranged for the sale of a home in Bisbee, Arizona, with the buyers paying for the home with a down payment and a $12,500 note to the Morleys. The phrase, "This note is secured by a mortgage on real property" was crossed off the note. The brokers, as permitted by Arizona law, completed all of the paperwork for the transaction but did not discuss the need for a mortgage to enforce the note. The buyers defaulted on the note and sold the house to another party. The Morleys sued Pagel for damages, claiming that they should have been told of the need for a mortgage. Pagel defended on the grounds that such advice would have been practicing law. Should the mortgage issue have been discussed? *Morley v. J. Pagel Realty & Insurance*, 550 P.2d 1104 (Ariz. 1976)

7. Lori Hanegan's broker's license was up for renewal in 1994. In Colorado, a broker applying for renewal is required to complete a minimum of "twenty-four hours of credit, of which shall be credits developed by the real estate commission." Ms. Hanegan completed 36 hours of continuing education but those hours did not include the mandatory eight hours developed by the real estate commission.

Hanegan's failure to take the mandated eight hours was discovered in an audit of licensee's continuing education units. Disciplinary proceedings were initiated and following a hearing, Hanegan was fined $50 and a public censure was recommended. Is the punishment appropriate? *Colorado State Real Estate Commission v. Hanegan*, 924 P.2d 1170 (Co. Ct. App. 1996)

8. Andrew Letsos listed his property for sale with Andrew Brusha, an agent with Century 21-New West Realty, on June 15, 1990. The property was listed at a price of $229,000, and Letsos agreed to pay a 6 percent commission. After eight consecutive listing renewals and no buyers, the property was listed again at a price of $129,000 on September 16, 1992. Following a listing period at the new price that ran one and one-half years with no success, Mr. Brusha contracted with Mr. Letsos to buy the property for $92,000 on March 9, 1993. Sometime later in March 1993, Mr. Brusha met Anthony Hernandez, another real estate broker. In May, Mr. Brusha and Mr. Hernandez contracted for the sale and purchase of the Letsos property for $115,000, with closing to take place on or before July 27, 1993.

Letsos and Brusha closed their deal on the property in July 1993. When Letsos's attorney called Brusha for a follow-up payment, Brusha asked for some time because he would have the money as soon as his sale of the property to Hernandez closed. Letsos's attorney then told Letsos about the Hernandez sale and Letsos filed suit against Brusha and Century 21 alleging breach of fiduciary duty by Brusha in his failure to disclose the sale to Hernandez. Should Letsos recover for breach of fiduciary duty? *Letsos v. Century 21-New West Realty*, 675 N.E.2d 217 (Ill. App. 1996)

9. Leticia Easton purchased a one-acre parcel of land in the city of Diablo, California, with a 3,000-square-foot home, swimming pool, and a large guest house for $170,000 in May 1976 from the Strassburgers through Valley Realty.

Shortly after Easton purchased the property, there was a massive earth movement and subsequent slides in 1977 and 1978 that destroyed a portion of the driveway. Experts testified that the slides occurred because a portion of the property was fill that had not been properly engineered and compacted. The slides caused the foundation of the house to settle, which in turn caused cracks in the walls and warped doorways. After the damage, the value of the property was set at $20,000. Cost estimates for repairs were $213,000.

Agents Simkin and Mourning represented Valley Realty and inspected the property several times prior to sale. "Red flags" indicated problems, but the agents did not have soil tests done and did not mention to Easton any potential soil problems.

Easton filed suit against the Strassburgers and Valley Realty. Is Valley Realty liable to Easton? Are the Strassburgers liable? *Easton v. Strassburger*, 199 Cal. Rptr. 383 (1984)

10. Kohn is a licensed real estate broker associated with his father's firm, Louis T. Kohn Realty. As managing agent for the Levee Building at the Laclede's Landing area of St. Louis, one of Kohn's responsibilities was to seek tenants for the building. One of the building owners suggested Kohn look into the possibility of Spaghetti Factory locating a restaurant in the building. The following sequence of events took place:

- *April 1975*: Kohn visited Denver's Spaghetti Factory and presented the idea to the executives.
- *May 1, 1975*: Kohn presented the idea to the Spaghetti Factory home office in Portland.
- *May 22, 1975*: Kohn met with three representatives of the Spaghetti Factory at the Levee Building. The Levee Building was determined to be unacceptable in size. Kohn took the three to Cohn's (defendant/appellee) office to examine his building. Spaghetti Factory executives asked for a floor plan. Kohn, in the presence of Cohn, said he would take care of the details.
- *June 26, 1975*: Kohn and Cohn met, and Kohn indicated he was seeking a tenant for Cohn's building. Cohn said he would go to Portland, but did not go.
- *October 1975*: Kohn and Spaghetti Factory executives met.
- *October 23, 1975*: Cohn and Spaghetti Factory executives met.
- *October 29, 1975*: Spaghetti Factory executives wrote Kohn and declined to lease the Cohn building.
- *September 16, 1976*: Cohn and Spaghetti Factory reached a five-year lease agreement.

Assuming there is no written agreement, could Kohn collect a commission in your state? *Kohn v. Cohn*, 567 S.W.2d 441 (Mo. 1978)

For research activities related to this chapter, go to our text companion website at www.thomsonedu.com/westbuslaw/jennings.

Methods of Transfer and Conveyance in Real Estate

CHAPTER 13

A New Orleans lawyer provided the FHA with an Abstract of Title for a client's loan. The abstract traced title back only to 1803 and the FHA demanded a search back to its origins. The lawyer responded:

Your letter regarding title in Case 189156 has been received. I note that you wish to have title extended further than the 194 years covered by the present application. I was unaware that any educated person in this country, particularly those working in the property area, would not know that Louisiana was purchased by the U.S. from France in 1803, the year of origin identified in our application. For the edification of uninformed FHA bureaucrats, the title to land prior to U.S. ownership was obtained from France, which had acquired it by Right of Conquest from Spain. The land came into possession of Spain by Right of Discovery made in the year 1492 by a sea captain named Christopher Columbus, who had been granted the privilege of seeking a new route to India by then reigning monarch, Isabella. The good queen, being a pious woman and careful about titles, almost as much as the FHA, took the precaution of securing the blessing of the Pope before she sold her jewels to fund Columbus' expedition. Now the Pope, as I'm sure you know, is the emissary of Jesus Christ, the Son of God. And God, it is commonly accepted, created this world. Therefore, I believe it is safe to presume that He also made that part of the world called Louisiana. He, therefore, would be the owner of origin. I hope to hell you find His original claim to be satisfactory. Now, may we have our damn loan?

According to Internet legend, the client got the title abstract approved and the loan.

When people think of the transfer of title to real property, they often think of it as a buyer and seller exchanging paperwork. However, title to property may be transferred in many different ways including transfer by adverse possession. Every property transfer must meet minimum legal requirements to be effective. And the parties should take precautions to make certain that the title obtained is what was intended and that it will remain protected. This chapter answers the following questions: What are the methods for transferring property? What rules and requirements apply to the methods of transfer? What protections are there for title transfer?

Transfer of Property by Deed

In England, the transfer of title was originally accomplished by a symbolic ceremony called the **livery of seisin**. In the ceremony, the grantor and grantee stood with witnesses on the property to be transferred, and the grantor gave the grantee some portion of the property such as a clump of dirt or a twig to symbolize the conveyance of the land. The grantor also spoke certain words at the time of this physical transfer to indicate what land and what type of interest (such as simple or fee tail (see Chapter 2)) was being conveyed. This oral ceremony for passing title to land made it difficult to establish who owned what parcels and where the boundaries were located (see discussion of adverse possession in this chapter).

With the Statute for the Prevention of Frauds and Perjuries, passed in 1677, England required a written instrument to validly convey title to property. This written conveyance became known as the **deed**. Today, each of the states here in the United States has its own Statute of Frauds and set of requirements for a valid deed.

Requirements for Valid Deed

The general requirements for a valid deed are the following: (1) grantor with legal capacity, (2) signature of the grantor, (3) grantee named with reasonable certainty, (4) recital of consideration, (5) words of conveyance (items 4 and 5 are referred to as the **premises**), (6) habendum or type of interest conveyed, (7) description of land conveyed, (8) acknowledgment, (9) delivery, and (10) acceptance.

Grantor with Legal Capacity: Age and Mental Capacity

States have varying rules for what constitutes mental capacity on the part of the grantor. For grantors who are natural persons, the requirements are a minimum age (the age of majority) and a sound mind. A sound mind, or legal capacity, does not preclude those who are old or eccentric from passing valid title to their property. In order to meet the capacity test, grantors must just understand three things: the legal significance of a deed (an understanding that they are transferring the title to their land), to whom they are conveying their property, and the nature and value of the property they are conveying.

Most grantor competency cases involve issues related to undue influence in a confidential relationship. A confidential relationship exists when one party places continuous trust in another party and relies on that party for almost everything from management of financial affairs to assistance with day-to-day activities. If mental weakness is accompanied by a factual situation in which the grantor has a confidential relationship with the grantee, most courts find a presumption of undue influence that requires any grantee who was part of that relationship to overcome the presumption.

Typically, a confidential relationship arises in the following circumstances: between parent and child when the parent is elderly; between one who is afflicted or weak (for example, between priest and parishioner); and between one who is younger and stronger and provides care, help, or assistance (for example, between client and attorney). When the stronger party uses the trust gained in the confidential relationships to obtain property or funds, the issue of undue influence arises. If there has been undue influence, the deed that has conveyed the title will be set aside. For more on what constitutes undue influence, see Chapter 16.

CONSIDER 13.1

Gladys Whatley was hospitalized for blindness, diabetes, and various problems with her hips. At the time of her admission, hospital personnel described her as "considerably impaired" mentally. She received various medications while in the hospital and the medical records refer to her as "ill" and "appearing very weak."

While she was in the hospital, her daughter Kay brought Gladys a new will in which some beach property owned by Gladys was conveyed to Kay and her husband. Kay had Gladys execute the new will. After Gladys was released from the hospital to Kay's care, Kay had a deed drawn up in which the beach property was conveyed to Kay and her husband outright. When the remaining children learned of the conveyance, they sought an easement so that they could use the beach on the property. When Kay refused, they sought to have the will and deed set aside for undue influence. Can they succeed? *Avery v. Whatley*, 670 A.2d 922 (Me. 1996)

Grantor with Legal Capacity: Identification of Grantor

Individual grantors should be identified clearly in the deed. Spelling of the grantors' names is important, and if the grantors have used other names or initials, a separate identity statement can clarify that the grantors with varying names are the same person. For example, "Marianne M. Jennings," "Marianne Jennings," and "Marianne Moody Jennings" are the same person, but the names vary. An identity sheet that the title company records verifies in the public records that the three names are names for the same person. The grantor's name should appear in the deed in the same way the grantor's name appeared as grantee in the instrument conveying title. The identity statement can clarify. For example, "John Edward Doe" is not the same as "J. E. Doe" and would require an additional verification through an identity sheet.

The deed should also give the status of the grantor, such as, "unmarried male" or "single female." On deeds in the eighteenth and nineteenth centuries, single women were referred to as "widow" or "spinster." The term "divorced and not remarried" is used today to clarify the presence or absence of marital rights. Status clauses are assurance that those who execute the deed have proper authority to do so independently. A grantor acting on another's behalf must provide that capacity on the deed. For example, an executor for an estate would have a status description clause: "Paul H. Ramsay as executor for the Last Will and Testament of Mary R. Ramsay, whose will was admitted on *date* in *court* in case *number*."

Grantors need not be individuals; they can also be business organizations, such as corporations. Corporations, partnerships, limited partnerships, LLCs and LLPs may all hold and convey title. Agents of the business organization will actually execute the deed. Most title companies require a board resolution or other form of agency authority when a business (in whatever form) is transferring property. Documented proof of such authority helps to keep the title chain clear. In the following case, the parties became terribly confused and cost themselves a great deal of time and money because their deeds were executed using the wrong grantor.

Michaelson v. Michaelson

939 P.2d 835 (Colo. 1997)

FACTS

Ervin and Ruth Michaelson were married in 1946. During their marriage they formed a Colorado corporation called Michaelson's Originals, Inc. They each owned 50 percent of the corporation with 2,500 shares of stock each.

The Michaelsons were divorced on November 10, 1965, but the permanent orders on the division of their marital property were not entered until 1989. The reason for the delay was a great deal of confusion over three parcels of land. Ruth Michaelson quitclaimed the three parcels to Ervin.

No stock in the corporation was exchanged.

In 1990, following Ervin's mismanagement of some assets of the corporation, Ruth filed suit against him for breach of fiduciary duty. Ervin claimed that Ruth was no longer a shareholder and could not bring suit. The trial court held that Ruth was a shareholder and could bring suit. The trial court further held that Ruth's quitclaim conveyed only her interest in the land and not in the corporation and that she was entitled to compensation for the value of the land quitclaimed. The Court of Appeals dismissed the case and Ruth appealed.

JUDICIAL OPINION

Hobbs, Justice. The [trial] court found that Ruth Michaelson's share of the post-1965 increased value of the corporate property was $277,093. The court ruled that Ruth Michaelson was also entitled to $78,665, which amount was one-half of new assets acquired by the corporation after 1965.

The court of appeals reasoned that Ruth Michaelson had already received a settlement for the properties for their increase in value from 1965 to 1989 and had conveyed, by the quitclaim deed, her equitable interest in the real property. We do not agree. To the contrary, the marital property award included a corporate property valuation only up to the date of the divorce, November 10, 1965, and did not include post-1965 appreciation on the corporate property, nor did the quitclaim deed operate to alter Ruth Michaelson's rights as a shareholder, including her *pro rata* share in all of the property and assets of the corporation upon dissolution, after creditors were satisfied. Accordingly, we reverse the judgment of the court of appeals.

The case before us deals primarily with the effect of Ruth Michaelson's quitclaim deed. The court of appeals determined that, upon dissolution of the corporation, equitable title to corporate property passes to all record shareholders. Therefore, the execution of the quitclaim deed by Ruth Michaelson operated to divest her of any claim she had to the corporate properties enumerated in the deed. We disagree. Under Colorado law, title to corporate property remains in the corporation upon dissolution. The quitclaim deed had no effect on Ruth Michaelson's status as a shareholder or the distribution of corporate property and assets to which she was entitled as a *pro rata* participant.

In construing any deed, our purpose is to give effect to the instrument. Unless ambiguity exists, "the intent should be determined from the four corners of the instrument." We must consider the deed in its entirety, harmonize all its provisions, and give force and effect to all of its language if possible. We must not ascertain intent from "portions presented in isolated sentences and clauses," but from the deed as a whole.

With these principles in mind, we examine the language of this quitclaim deed. The granting clause states:

WITNESSETH, That the grantor for and in consideration of the sum of other valuable consideration and Ten and no/100 DOLLARS the receipt and sufficiency of which is hereby acknowledged, has remised, released, sold, conveyed and QUIT CLAIMED, and by these presents does remise, release, sell, convey and QUIT CLAIM unto the grantee [Ervin Michaelson], his heirs, successors and assigns, forever, all the right, title, interest, claim and demand which the grantor has in and to the real property, *together with improvements, if any, situate, lying and being in the City and County of Denver and State of Colorado....*

[Emphasis added.] The property to be conveyed was described as follows:

Lots 1 through 13, Block 1, Norwood Addition;
Lots 9 through 15, Block 2, Norwood Addition; and
Lots 9 through 15, Block 6, Sumners Addition to Denver
also known by street and number as:
123–135 South Kalamath
164–176 South Kalamath
401–435 Santa Fe Drive
931–935 West 4th Avenue

Ervin Michaelson argues that the language of the deed indicates an intent on the part of Ruth Michaelson to convey not only her then present individual interest in the parcels of property, but also her "equitable title" in the properties as a shareholder upon dissolution of the corporation. We disagree. The grant constituted a clear and unambiguous conveyance of her individual ownership interest, if any, in the three enumerated parcels of land.

The language of the deed does not convey Ruth Michaelson's shares of the corporation or her right to receive a shareholder distribution upon dissolution. To determine what Ruth Michaelson conveyed, we must identify what interest she owned in the three parcels, if any, at the time of the conveyance. Two of the three properties listed on the quitclaim deed were owned by the corporation; the titles to Norwood, Block 1, and Sumners, Block 6, were in the name of Michaelson's Originals, Inc. Ruth Michaelson had no ownership interest in those two parcels and conveyed none by reason of the quitclaim deed. Rather, she was a shareholder of the corporation that owned those two parcels. However, Norwood, Block 2 was held by the Michaelsons individually as partners, not the corporation. When she executed the quitclaim deed, Ruth Michaelson conveyed her ownership interest in Norwood, Block 2, to Ervin Michaelson. The trial court correctly did not include this property in the damages for breach of fiduciary duty.

Although ownership of two of the properties remained in the corporation after dissolution, Ervin Michaelson nevertheless argues that Ruth Michaelson obtained an equitable title to the parcels and conveyed that interest to him.

In Colorado, "equitable title" to real property owned by a corporation does not pass to the shareholders upon dissolution of that corporation. Title remains in the corporation pending distribution to the shareholders of the remaining assets, in cash or in kind, after creditors of the corporation are satisfied.

Likewise, no merit exists in Ervin Michaelson's claim that the quitclaim deed on November 22, 1989, operated to waive Ruth Michaelson's claim for breach of fiduciary duty. The 1965 divorce action did not terminate the corporate existence. Ruth Michaelson did not transfer her shares of stock to Ervin Michaelson, and she continued to be a shareholder of record.

As an officer and director of Michaelson Originals, Inc., Ervin Michaelson had a fiduciary duty to act in good faith and in a manner he reasonably believed to be in the best interests of the corporation and all of its shareholders, in this case Ruth Michaelson. The record is replete with evidence of Ervin Michaelson's breach of fiduciary duty to Ruth Michaelson.

The court of appeals determined that Ruth Michaelson had already "been paid the value of her share of the real estate plus an appropriate amount for the increase of value of the real estate from 1965 to 1989," and so negated her award. However, the record does not support this determination.

Two relationships existed here. The first was the marital relationship which existed between 1946 and 1965. In this regard, the marital property division reflected: (1) the value of marital property up to the 1965 divorce date; and (2) the corporate property valued only from 1952 up to the 1965 divorce date. The second was the corporate relationship. The corporate property's *increase* in value from 1965 to 1989 was not included in the marital property division, nor were any properties acquired by the corporation after 1965.

Reversed.

CASE QUESTIONS

1. What did Ruth have the authority to convey?
2. Did Ruth give up title to the land?
3. Was Ruth entitled to compensation for giving up the title?
4. Does a deed convey title to the stock shares?
5. Do you think Ervin believed he owned the land and could manage it as he pleased? What deed would transfer to Ervin the property and the right of control? Who would be the grantor in such a deed?

An example of a grantor without legal capacity is a charitable organization that is an unincorporated association. In most states, associations such as these have no legal existence and hence may not hold or convey title to property. In these associations, title must be held and conveyed through the association officers or trustees, unless there is a specific state statute authorizing the holding of legal title by unincorporated associations (see footnote h, Figure 13.1, p.).

Governmental bodies have no inherent authority to convey title and must have statutory authorization to do so. Agencies must comply with all the guidelines and restrictions in their statutory authorizations.

Executors, guardians, trustees, and administrators have legal authority to convey title on behalf of their estates or protected persons but must do so according to the terms of the will, trust, or court orders and possibly only with court approval.

Grantor's Signature

A grantor with proper capacity must sign the deed, and if the grantor is not signing as an individual there must be an indication of any representative or agent capacity. If two persons hold title, both signatures are required. In most states the signatures of both spouses are required to convey title even in cases where only one holds such title. Those who sign for business organizations, estates, minors, and nonprofits should have some verification of authority.

Practical Tip

Nonprofit corporations have played an increasing role in property transfer. Under a HUD program, nonprofits could qualify for low-interest government loans if they had a proven track record of rehabilitation of housing. In areas such as Harlem, nonprofits could qualify for significant federal funds for the purchase, fix-up, and resale of properties there. However, many shell nonprofit corporations were formed for the purpose of obtaining the loan funds without any record or plans for rehabilitation.[1] Real estate speculation using government funds and then reselling quickly, or flipping, to inflate the price, has resulted in many buyers owning property that is now the subject of litigation and foreclosure by the federal government. Checking the records for the history of a nonprofit grantor is important to assure good title.

A party who signs on behalf of a grantor should have a power of attorney. In some states, that power of attorney must be recorded along with the actual deed. The power of attorney should be either a general one, that gives the signer the authority of a general agent, or one specifically authorizing the transfer of real estate or the transfer of the particular parcel.

Grantors who are incapable of signing may place an "X" along with a verification clause to indicate who placed the X. The name may be typed in for the grantor.

In the case of a corporate agent signing for a corporation, many states require that the corporate seal also be placed on the deed. The signature must indicate that the deed is being executed on behalf of the corporation.

Figure 13.1 summarizes the types of grantors and the identification and signatures necessary for meeting the requirements for a valid deed.

CONSIDER 13.2

The following language appears in a deed:

THIS DEED OF CONVEYANCE, made and entered into this 8th day of April, 1975, between LOGAN MIDDLETON, President of the V.T.C. Lines Incorporated, Harlan, Harlan County, Kentucky, party of the first part, and JOHN CHRISTIAN, Evarts, Harlan County, Kentucky, party of the second part.

The signatory portion of the document in its entirety appears thusly:

/s/ Logan Middleton
Logan Middleton, President
V.T.C. Lines, Incorporated

The only other reference to the corporate entity is contained in the attestation clause:

/Subscribed, sworn to, and acknowledged before me by Logan Middleton, President, V.T.C. Lines, Incorporated, to be his own free act and deed, and the act and deed of said corporation on this the 8th day of April 1975.
<u>/s/ Mary Alice Hutbank</u>
Notary Public
My Commission Expires: 2/27/79

Christian is now attempting to convey the property to Johnny Pace. The Johnsons have levied the property as creditors of V.T.C. Lines. Christian claims he is the property owner and that the levy is improper. Using Figure 13.1 and the chapter discussion, determine if title was conveyed to Christian. *Christian v. Johnson*, 556 S.W.2d 172 (Ky. 1977)

1. Terry Pristin, "Despite Inquiry into Fraud, Buyers Still Seek Harlem Homes," *New York Times*, Jan. 15, 2001, A16.

Figure 13.1 Grantor Capacity, Identification, and Signatures

Grantor	Sample Identification	Signature
Individual	"John Edward Doe, a single man" "John Edward Doe, and Mary Frances Doe, his wife." "Eileen Jones Doe, a widow"	"John Edward Doe" "John Edward Doe/Mary Frances Doe" "Eileen Jones Doe"
Incompetent	"John Edwards Doe, a conservator for the estate of Eileen Jones Doe, an adult protected person" (an incompetent)	"Eileen Jones Doe by John Edward Doe, conservator for the estate of Eileen Jones Doe"[a]
Partnership	"ABC Partnership, a partnership organized and authorized to do business under the laws of the state of Arizona."	"ABC Partnership by John Edward Doe, general partner"[b]
Corporation	"LMN Company, Inc.,[c] a corporation incorporated and authorized to do business under the laws of the State of Arizona with its principal place of business in Phoenix"	"LMN Company, Inc., by John Edward Doe, president[d] (corporate seal)"[e]
Executor	"John Edwards Doe, as executor of the last will and testament of Eileen Jones Doe, deceased at Mesa, County of Maricopa, State of Arizona"	"John Edwards Doe as executor of the last will and testament of Eileen Jones Doe"[a]
Minor	"John Edwards Doe, a minor under the age of 18 years"[f]	"John Edwards Doe by Willard Scott Doe, as legal guardian of John Edwards Doe, as minor"
Individual with power of attorney (attorney in fact)	"John Edwards Doe, a single man"	"John Edwards Doe by Willard Scott Doe, his attorney in fact"[g]
Illiterate	"John Edwards Doe, a single man"	"*X*," with verification clause to indicate who made the "*X*." Name of grantor should be typed below the "*X*."
Unincorporated Association[h]	Need individual(s) signatures	"John Doe"

a. Court approval may be required for transfer.
b. Authority of partner to convey as general partner should be confirmed.
c. Use name under which it was incorporated.
d. Authority to transfer should be verified; board resolution required; check to see if it is an extraordinary corporate transaction (additional approval required).
e. Should be attested to or verified by corporation's secretary.
f. Or whatever age of majority happens to be.
g. Power of attorney must authorize real property transfers.
h. Ten states have adopted the Uniform Unincorporated Nonprofit Association Act, an act that qualifies nonprofit associations as a legal entity (Alabama, Arkansas, Colorado, Delaware, Hawaii, Idaho, Texas, West Virginia, Wisconsin, and Wyoming) and the signature would be "Tri-City Arts League, by John Doe, President."

Grantee Named with Reasonable Certainty

Grantees must also be identified with reasonable certainty because the usefulness and validity of public land records on land transfers depend on the accuracy of the spelling and identity of grantors and grantees. Accurate spelling is the basis for an effective indexing system for land transactions. Aliases or AKAs (also known as) should be noted on the deed or on a separate, acknowledged form.

The status of the grantee should also be included in the deed. For example, just as with grantors, individuals should be identified as single or married, and corporations should be identified as to their location and place of incorporation. The following case deals with a fascinating issue on the legal capacity of the LLC grantee.

Allen v. Scott, Hewitt & Mize

186 S.W.3d 782 (Mo. App. 2006)

FACTS

David and Veronica Allen bought land in Independence, Missouri during 1994 for $22,000. In January 1998, they listed it for sale with a broker, Chuck Zuvers, asking $88,000. The property remained on the market until May 1999, when Thomas C. Scott contracted to buy it for $90,000. Scott signed the sales contract as "Thomas C. Scott, or assigns" because he was organizing Scott, Hewitt and Mize as a limited liability company and wanted the land deeded to the firm. Scott and his partners planned to list it for sale at a high price, knowing that the price might delay a sale for several years.

At closing, and following Scott's instruction, the Allens deeded the property to "Scott, Hewitt & Mize, LLC." Although Scott and his partners had filed articles of organization for Scott, Hewitt and Mize with the Secretary of State before closing, the Secretary of State rejected the articles because of errors contained in them. Scott corrected the errors, and the Secretary of State issued a certificate of organization to Scott, Hewitt and Mize nine days after closing. Scott, Hewitt and Mize immediately listed the property for sale for more than $1 million.

Approximately 20 days after closing, the Allens, seeing the Scott, Hewitt and Mize listing, tendered a $99,900 check to Scott and asked him to rescind the sale. Scott refused. The Allens sued to rescind the contract, their theory for rescinding the contract being mistake. The circuit court issued summary judgment for Scott, Hewitt and Mize.

JUDICIAL OPINION

Spinden, Presiding Judge. We consider first the Allens' argument on appeal that the sale and conveyance should be rescinded because Scott, Hewitt and Mize did not exist until nine days after closing. Even assuming all facts in favor of the Allens, it is wholly irrelevant that Scott, Hewitt and Mize was not organized at the time that the Allens contracted with Scott. The Allens contract was with Scott. It is of no consequence to the Allens that Scott assigned his interest to an entity that, because of a defect in its organizational paperwork, had not finished the organizational process. The formation issues of Scott, Hewitt and Mize are irrelevant to the Allens' contract with Scott.

Even if this were not the case, Scott, Hewitt and Mize was capable of receiving a valid conveyance despite its not having complete the organizational process. Generally, to be valid, a conveyance requires a grantee in *esse* capable of taking and holding title to property when the conveyance occurs. However, "equitable rights may result in favor of a subsequently formed corporation named as a grantee." The Allens cannot challenge the transfer on the basis that Scott, Hewitt and Mize was not yet a *de jure* entity.

The Allens' petition contended that they should be permitted to void the contract because of their mistake as to the property's value. Value is a matter of opinion—not fact—resting in conjecture. To be a basis for rescinding a contract, a mistake must "relate to the existence or non-existence of a fact, past or present, material to the contract, and not as to a future contingency. The mistake must be as to a matter of fact, not as to a matter resting in mere conjecture or belief."

Property values depend on multiple variables, and a property's value can increase or decrease following sale. The Allens and Scott, Hewitt and Mize agreed on a price that reflected the property's value at the time of contracting. Allowing the Allens to rescind creates a rule whereby sellers could argue mistake after deciding that he or she did not receive a fair deal.

The Allens were not unaware of a fact affecting value. They understood exactly what they were selling. They understood all of the pertinent details surrounding the sale. Their purported mistake was their opinion of what the land was worth. After Scott, Hewitt and Mize bought it from them and listed it for sale at more than $1 million, the Allens simply became dissatisfied with the bargained-for exchange, a risk inherent in any sale.

Affirmed.[2]

CASE QUESTIONS

1. Why was the LLC not formed at the time of the deed transfer?
2. What theory are the Allens using under deed requirements?
3. What does the court find on the Allens' argument on mistake?

2. For a case that reached the opposite result on an LLC not being able to take title if it is not yet formed, see *Sullivan v. Buckhorn Ranch Partnership*, 119 P.3d 192 (Ok. 2005).

The deed should also describe the interests and forms of ownership being conveyed to the grantees. For example, the proper language should be used if the grantees wish to be joint tenants (see Chapter 8). If the grantees are taking unequal shares, then the deed should include the fractional divisions, for example, "one-third to John Edward Doe, a single man, and two-thirds to Jane Elizabeth Doe, a single woman, as tenants in common."

There are statutory presumptions in some states as to how title is taken if the deed does not include a form of ownership for the grantees. For example, in many states, grantees who are married will take the property as tenants by the entireties unless the deed specifies otherwise.

Recital of Consideration

A recital of consideration does not require the parties to actually include the price paid for the land in the deed. In fact, deeds that convey title to real property as gifts generally have a simple recital of consideration, such as, "for the consideration of ten dollars, and other good and valuable consideration" (see Web Exhibit 13.1 for a sample warranty deed and the recital clause). The use of a nominal sum presents no problems for the deed's validity. So long as some consideration was actually paid, the deed's transfer of title may be enforced.

Words of Conveyance

The recital of consideration and words of conveyance portions of the deed are known as the premises of the deed. The words of conveyance reflect the grantor's true intent to transfer some title or interest in the property. The words of conveyance can place limits on the title to the property (see discussion of warranties later in this chapter). Standard form deeds use language such as "do hereby grant and convey," "do hereby grant," "do hereby convey and specially warrant," or "do hereby quitclaim." These words determine the warranties or promises made by the grantor to the grantee in the transfer of title.

Habendum: The Type of Interest Conveyed

"Habendum et tenendum" means "to have and to hold." The habendum clause in a deed declares what type of land interest, such as fee simple, fee tail, or fee simple defeasible, the grantor is conveying. The language used in the **habendum clause** of the deed is discussed in Chapter 2, similar to these limited examples:

- *Fee simple*: "To A," "To A and her heirs"
- *Fee simple determinable*: "To A so long as the premises are used for a school"

Any restrictions, such as easements or liens, must be included after the habendum clause. These restrictions generally begin "subject to"; for example, "the Carolina Power easement in the four feet along the ..."

Description of Land Conveyed

Chapter 7 covered the requirements for an adequate legal description to convey property. The grantee's protection of title is dependent upon this description and it is a key to effective title searches and protection.

Acknowledgment

The **acknowledgment clause** establishes that the act of conveying was indeed done by the grantor. In most states the deed need not be acknowledged to be valid between the parties to the deed, but acknowledgment is required before the deed can be recorded in the public land records.

Acknowledgment means that the parties have appeared before a notary (or otherwise authorized state official), signed their names, indicated through identification that they are the parties identified in the deed, and that they are executing the deed voluntarily.

The acknowledgment format varies from state to state, but generally includes the venue (the county and state), the date, the name of the notary or other official, and that the signature of the person on the deed was indeed the person who appeared before the notary. In most states, the notary must affix some form of seal or stamp.

Witnesses may or may not be required for an acknowledgment. In some states, witnesses can serve as a substitute for an acknowledgment.

Delivery

The transfer of title is not complete until the deed has been delivered to the grantee. In most transactions, this step is a simple one; the deed is given in exchange for a consideration. However, **delivery** can be actual or constructive. That is, delivery can occur when the grantor places the deed irrevocably in the hands of a third party or in a location that only the grantee has access to. When delivery is not a direct exchange between grantor and grantee, the intent of the grantor is critical. In delivery to a third party, the grantor must relinquish all control of the deed, otherwise the intent is not there, and delivery to the grantee has not yet been made. If the deed is placed in escrow with instructions to convey it to the grantee upon receipt of funds, there again is no delivery because a condition is attached. Once the funds are received, then the delivery can take place. Often grantors execute deeds to grantees and then place them in a safe-deposit box, with instructions to relatives for delivery after the grantor's death. Such a transfer is not delivery and, once death has occurred, title cannot pass without going through proper probate processes. The standards for delivery of deeds are the same as the standards for delivery of gifts (discussed later in the chapter).

CONSIDER 13.3

Holstein wanted his niece to have a parcel of land upon which she could build a home after her completion of law school. Holstein signed and executed a deed for a small parcel that he owned and turned it over to his attorney with instructions that the deed be recorded upon the niece's graduation. Holstein told his niece of the pending gift to inspire her in her last year of law school, but he died before the niece graduated. Both the niece and other heirs claim the parcel. Who wins?

In most states, a deed that has been executed, acknowledged, and recorded (discussed later in this chapter) carries a presumption of delivery.

Once delivery has occurred, the grantor's destruction of the deed, change of heart, or even a grant to another grantee do not change the fact that the title has passed.

Acceptance

Although the law does not foist land onto grantees, if the transfer of property is beneficial to the grantee, then acceptance is presumed. This presumption applies even when the grantee has no knowledge of the conveyance. Also, if the grantee has possession of the deed, acceptance is presumed.

Types of Deeds

The type of deed makes a difference in the grantor's promises about the title. The types of deeds are (1) quitclaim deed, (2) warranty deed, (3) special warranty deed, (4) deed of bargain and sale, and (5) judicial deed.

Quitclaim Deed

A **quitclaim deed** is a deed of no promises. A quitclaim deed makes no bones about it; it does not purport to transfer or convey title to property. A quitclaim deed conveys only any right, title, and interest the grantor may have in the property. But grantors on a quitclaim deed make no promise that they hold any such right, title, or interest in the property. A quitclaim deed is often used as a release for purposes of clearing a cloud on a title or correcting title defects. This form of deed is also used to convey lesser land interests such as life estates. The language of conveyance in a quitclaim is "I (grantor) hereby quitclaim to . . ." or "I (grantor) hereby remise, release, and quitclaim unto. . . ."

In the *Michaelson v. Michaelson* case (p. 334), a quitclaim deed was used, but with regard to several of the properties, the grantor did not have title.

Warranty Deed

Most land transactions require the grantor to transfer title by warranty deed. In most states, a **warranty deed** springs from the language used by the grantor in the words of conveyance, which usually includes "warrant" but by statute may instead include "grant" or "convey."

The warranty deed title describes its purpose. At common law, the grantor who uses a warranty deed gives six warranties: seisin, right to convey, freedom from encumbrances, covenant of warranty, quiet enjoyment, and further assurances. In most states, the warranty or covenant of seisin is a promise that the grantor has title to the property. In other states, the warranty of seisin means that the grantor is in possession of the property. Easements or other noted encumbrances such as liens are not a breach of this warranty.

The right to convey warranty promises that the grantor has the authority to pass title to the property. In states where seisin means only possession, this warranty guarantees the right to transfer more than just possession.

Freedom from encumbrances warrants that the title is free from defects. That is, the grantor warrants that the property is free from both title and physical encumbrances on the property. However, the deed may include a list of any encumbrances that the grantor is passing along, such as an outstanding mortgage or an easement. The types of title defects warranted against (unless specifically listed as excluded) are mortgages, unpaid taxes, assessments, leases, judgment liens, right of redemption, and dower rights. Physical defects warranted against (unless specifically mentioned) are building restrictions, encroachments, easements, profits, party wall agreements, fences, and mineral rights.

The covenant of warranty requires the grantor to compensate the grantee for any losses that result from the grantor's failure to convey title to the property. If a grantee loses title to the conveyed property or is required to pay an amount to retain title, the grantor agrees to identify the grantee for such loss, costs, and expenses. In the following case, the court deals with an issue of damages when a grantor who conveyed title by warranty deed conveyed a defective title.

SCHORSCH V. BLADER

563 N.W.2d 538 (Wis. App. 1997)

FACTS

On April 30, 1985, Anton F. Schorsch and his son purchased a schoolhouse and 1.8 acres of land from the Wautoma Area School District for $20,400. The District signed a warranty deed transferring property to the Schorsches.

In 1993, the Schorsches entered into an agreement to sell the property, but their purchasers refused to close when they discovered that James, Chester, and Louise Blader held title to 0.8 of an acre of the property. The

Blader portion of the land included the parcel's only access to State Highway 22. The Schorsches brought suit against the Bladers for adverse possession of the 0.8 acre and against the District for misrepresentation and breach of warranty. At trial, the Schorsches lost on the adverse possession claim but prevailed on the breach of warranty. After a separate trial on damages, the trial court awarded the Schorsches $13,600 in lost profits and $12,243 in attorney fees and litigation expenses. The District appealed, challenging the damage award.

JUDICIAL OPINION

Roggensack, Judge. The Schorsches maintain that the common law measure of damages for a breach of warranty of seisin is irrelevant, because it has been superseded by §706.10(5), STATS., which they assert requires the use of the common law of damages for breach of contract. No citation is offered for their assertion, and the District disputes that they are correct.

When we are asked to apply a statute whose meaning is in dispute, our efforts are directed at determining legislative intent. In attempting to determine the intent of the legislature, we begin with the plain meaning of the language used in the statute.

The Schorsches rely on the following words from §706.10(5), STATS., for their theory of damages: "A conveyance...shall be construed according to its terms, under rules of law for construction of contract." They argue that because §706.10(5) requires deeds to be construed as contracts, the common law of damages for breach of contract applies, not the common law of damages for breach of warranty of title. Their argument requires us to decide whether the phrase "construction of contracts" refers to the process of determining the meaning of words used in the deed or whether that phrase refers to the types of damages awardable for breach of specific covenants.

A deed must also be interpreted to determine its meaning. It may contain several types of promises or covenants, which are collateral to the conveyance of property. At common law, a deed was construed according to rules of construction for other written documents.

If a warranty deed is given without a stated exception, at common law, the grantor of a warranty deed, his heirs and personal representatives, covenanted with the grantee, his heirs and assigns, that: (1) the grantor is lawfully seized of the premises and has the right to convey the same; (2) the grantee shall have quiet enjoyment of the property; (3) the property is free from encumbrances; and (4) the grantor will defend the grantee's title and right of possession.

Section 706.10(5), STATS., codified certain common law covenants for the benefit of the grantee, which sometimes had been excepted from deeds, and established a rebuttable presumption that they were included, unless the terms of the deed provided to the contrary. It was upon these warranties that the Schorsches sued.

Section 706.10(5), STATS., did not change the rules which were used to interpret the meaning of deeds. Stated another way, §706.10(5) confirms that the rules of law for construction of contracts are to be used to determine the substance of the covenants from the grantor to the grantee of a deed. Nothing in the language of the statute implies any change whatsoever in the measure of damages for a breach of any covenant. Therefore, we conclude that the common law measure of damages for breach of warranty of title was not changed by §706.10(5).

We now examine the Schorsches claim, under the common law of damages for breach of warranty of title. They were entitled to recover the portion of the purchase price which they proved to be attributable to the .8 of an acre of land to which title failed, plus statutory interest on that amount from the date of purchase. This recovery includes the intrinsic value of the .8 of an acre, as well as any extrinsic value the trial court finds it provided to the parcel on which good title was conveyed, on the date of purchase.

The Schorsches paid $20,400 for the schoolhouse and 1.8 acres of land. Its then current tax assessment was $20,500, with $2,500 attributable to the land. There was testimony that the .8 of an acre, standing alone, was worth $5,000 on the date of trial. However, there was also testimony that the current market value of the parcel, as a whole, was $36,000 and the .8 of an acre represented 45 percent of that amount. There was no direct testimony about what part of the purchase price the .8 of an acre represented. We remand to the trial court to make that determination and thereafter to calculate interest on that amount at the statutory rate from the date of purchase. The amount so determined, together with the attorney fees and costs already awarded, are the Schorsches damages for breach of warranty of title of the .8 of an acre.

For the reasons set forth above, we set aside $19,203.50 of the $35,002.67 damage award, and remand for a determination of additional damages measured by that portion of the $20,400 purchase price, which is attributable to the .8 of an acre on which title failed, and interest thereon at the statutory rate, from the date of purchase.

Reversed and remanded.

CASE QUESTIONS

1. What warranty of title did the District breach?

2. What is the common law method for computation of damages?

3. What damages are the Schorsches awarded and why?

4. Can the Schorsches sell a portion of the property and warrant good title?

Under the warranty of quiet enjoyment, the grantor makes the same promise as under the covenant of warranty, which is that the grantor will reimburse the grantee for expenses and losses incurred if a problem with title arises.

The warranty of further assurances requires the grantor to execute documents or institute suits to protect any defects in title that might exist and which the grantee desires corrected.

In the majority of states, these six common law warranties have been combined into the following three basic warranties:

1. The grantor possesses an indefeasible fee simple estate, or the grantor has good title and the transfer is proper.
2. There are no encumbrances against the property except those specifically noted.
3. The grantee shall have quiet enjoyment of the property, and the grantor will warrant and defend title against all claims.

If there is an unbroken chain of warranty deeds conveying title to the property, each grantor is liable to all subsequent grantees on the warranties provided (see Web Exhibit 13.1 for a sample warranty deed).

Special Warranty Deed

A special warranty deed offers the same warranties as a warranty deed but limits the time of application. Under a special warranty deed, a grantor's warranties apply only for the period of that grantor's ownership. A grantor who owns property from June 1, 2004, to June 1, 2007, and conveys title with a special warranty deed would warrant only for that period of ownership and would provide no warranties for defects and encumbrances created or arising prior to or after that time period. In a special warranty deed, the covenants are not listed, and the language used is similar to the following: "Grantor hereby covenants that he has not done anything whereby the above described property has been encumbered in any way whatsoever." Some states allow shortened language in the granting clause, such as "do hereby specially warrant and convey."

Deed of Bargain and Sale

This form of deed is another name, in some states, for a special warranty deed. A **deed of bargain and sale** offers the limited warranty protection of the special warranty deed.

Judicial Deed

A **judicial deed** is a deed executed under court orders. Examples include the deeds of the following: executors and administrators of estates, conservators of estates, guardians of minors or incompetents, and sheriffs. **Sheriffs' deeds** are issued to parties who have purchased properties at foreclosure sales and are issued after the period of the debtor's right of redemption (see Chapter 15). Assuming that all legal procedures have been followed, these deeds serve to convey good title.

CONSIDER 13.4

A deed contained the language, "I, Jacob Smith, of Washington County, warrant and defend unto Christena Smith...the following real estate. ..." Although the deed included all the necessary requirements, the parties are now unclear as to the type of deed given and what warranties, if any, were given. Discuss. *Hummelman v. Mounts*, 87 Ind. 178 (1882)

Transfer of Property by Adverse Possession

Acquiring title to real property through **adverse possession** (often called **squatter's rights**) can be traced to the Middle Ages. Adverse possession rights arose during that time because there was no proper system for keeping records of land titles, and property owners inevitably lost the documents that established ownership rights. Adverse possession allows owners to prove title through possession for a certain period of time. Even when the American colonies were first settled, the use of adverse possession continued because recording systems were nonexistent or unsophisticated and important documents were still lost by landowners. Also, adverse possession rights were used by property owners to establish boundary lines on large tracts of land when they themselves were unsure of the exact boundaries of their properties. Boundary disputes were settled by proof of adverse possession. These uses and application of adverse possession continue today.

Obtaining title to property through adverse possession is similar to obtaining an easement by prescription (discussed in Chapter 4). There is no exchange of a document of title and no closing or deed conveyance under adverse possession. Instead, title is awarded because of certain types of actions related to land. Adverse possession is a statutory doctrine, and the requirements vary from state to state. However, if the statutory requirements are met, title passes as though there had been a conveyance through the traditional methods of deed transfers. The generic requirements for adverse possession are

- Actual and exclusive possession
- Open, visible, and notorious possession
- Continuous and peaceable possession
- Hostile and adverse possession
- Possession for the required statutory period

The adverse possessor has the burden of proving the coexistence of the requirements, discussed in the following sections.

Actual and Exclusive Possession

Actual and exclusive possession means that the adverse possessor (acquirer) must have sole physical occupancy of the property. The extent of physical occupancy required is determined by the nature of the land. The extent of physical occupancy must correspond with the customary and appropriate uses made on land of that nature and size. The issue of what constitutes possession is a question of fact for a jury, but several common factors help illustrate the standards for customary and appropriate uses.

For residential property, the adverse possessor is required to take up residence in the appropriate structure on the premises; for farmland, the adverse possessor is required to farm the acres sought to be acquired; and for ranch or grazing property, the adverse possessor is required to use the land for the grazing of livestock. In adverse possession of open acreage, such as farm or ranch land, the fencing in of the possessor's acreage is a commonly recognized method of establishing a customary and appropriate use of the property.

Open, Visible, and Notorious Possession

Under this requirement, the adverse possessor must use the property in a manner that is open to the public and sufficient to put those who see the property regularly on notice that there is occupation. This possession must not be secret or clandestine; it must be obvious. Open and visible possession is "calculated to apprise the world that the land is occupied and who the occupant is; and such an appropriation of the land by claimant as to apprise, or convey visible notice to the community or neighborhood in which it is situated that it is in his exclusive use" (*Marengo Cave Co. v. Ross*, 10 N.E.2d 917 [Ind. 1937]). Courts have labeled this element as one of the disseisor (adverse possessor) unfurling a flag over the land and keeping it flying so the owner can see the enemy and the planned conquest.

Continuous and Peaceable Possession

Continuous and peaceable possession requires that the adverse claimant be in possession of the property for the requisite statutory period without being evicted either physically or through court action. The requisite statutory period varies from state to state and is discussed on page 348. This continuity of possession may be established even if the property is used only for certain periods during the year, so long as those periods are consistent and regular.

The doctrine of tacking can be used to establish continuous possession. This doctrine allows a purchaser or someone inheriting a land interest to incorporate the adverse use of the predecessor into meeting the required statutory period. Tacking may be used between predecessor and adverse possessor where there is privity. Privity requires the parties to have a reasonable connection such as a contract, will transfer, or intestate distribution of the predecessor's interest. For example, if A is adversely possessing tract 1 and dies leaving all his property to B after having completed five years on tract 1, B could incorporate those five years in meeting the statutory period of continuous possession.

Hostile and Adverse Possession

This element of adverse possession requires that the adverse possessor establish that the property possession was against the rights of the property's true owner and such action is inconsistent with the title of the true owner. However, the adverse possessor (disseisor) need not establish ill will, bad feelings, or hatred toward the true owner.

The state of mind of the possessor is the issue in establishing this requirement. The appropriate state of mind may be drawn from the concept of either claim of right or color of title. Under claim of right, the possessor claims to be the owner of the property, whether or not such claim has any justification. Under color of title, the possessor has an instrument that is believed to convey title, when in reality such instrument is ineffective or inoperative. Unless specified differently by statute, the claimant may establish hostile and adverse possession under either one of these mental intents. In some states, adverse possession may be established regardless of the presence of either of these two mental states.

Often, factual circumstances arise in which an adverse claim is maintained because there has been a mistake in the placement of a boundary line, and the parties wish to base their claim on that mistaken boundary for the requisite statutory period. Most states find that a mistaken belief about a boundary line is enough to meet the intent requirements for adverse possession.

If a party is given permission by the true title holder to use the property, such permission prevents the user from asserting an adverse claim because permissive use is not hostile and adverse. When the true owner of the property grants a license or easement or gives permission for some other use of property, the user or possessor's use or possession cannot ripen into an adverse claim.

It is possible for co-owners of property to make adverse claims against one another. Thus a cotenant may oust others of their possession and gain title by possessing the entire interest for the requisite statutory period.

CONSIDER 13.5

The Kapinskis owned and occupied lot 18 from 1935 to 1950. In 1950, the lot was conveyed to the Wyroskis. The Laurins purchased lot 19 in 1954. The lots were the sites of summer homes. A row of lilac bushes marked the boundary between lots 18 and 19, and the Kapinskis and Wyroskis put in and maintained a lawn and flower bed that bordered the lilacs. A boathouse for lot 18 was also located next to the lilac bushes. Laurin claimed the boundary line was too far on his property and in 1960 brought an action to clear title. The Wyroskis claimed they had obtained title by adverse possession. What is the result? Is there sufficient actual possession? *Laurin v. Wyroski*, 121 N.W.2d 764 (Wis. 1963)

Possession for Required Statutory Period

The possession of the property with the requisite characteristics previously listed must occur for a certain statutory period of time. Although times vary from state to state, the typical adverse period is 20 years. In some states, such as Arizona, the period is as short as 10 years (see Figure 13.2). The adverse claimant must maintain possession continuously for the period of time specified by state statute.

The following case deals with several of the elements of adverse possession and the rights of the parties.

*Figure 13.2 Number of Years Required for Adverse Possession**

State	Years	State	Years	State	Years	State	Years
Alabama	20	Illinois	20	Montana	5	Rhode Island	10
Alaska	10	Indiana	10	Nebraska	10	South Carolina	10
Arizona	10	Iowa	10	Nevada	5	South Dakota	20
Arkansas	7	Kansas	15	New Hampshire	20	Tennessee	7
California	5	Kentucky	15	New Jersey	30	Texas	3
Colorado	18	Louisiana	30	New Mexico	10	Utah	7
Connecticut	15	Maine	20	New York	10	Vermont	15
Delaware	20	Maryland	20	North Carolina	20	Virginia	25
District of Columbia	15	Massachusetts	20	North Dakota	20	Washington	7
Florida	7	Michigan	15	Ohio	21	West Virginia	10
Georgia	20	Minnesota	15	Oklahoma	15	Wisconsin	20
Hawaii	20	Mississippi	10	Oregon	10	Wyoming	40
Idaho	5	Missouri	10	Pennsylvania	21		

* These figures represent the general time period. Many states have variations depending on issues such as payment of taxes, possession of deed, etc. For example, Texas periods run from 3 to 25 years.

Williams v. Estate of Williams

952 So.2d 950 (Miss.App.2006)

FACTS

In 1895, Travis and Florence Williams purchased a parcel of land in what is now known as Wiggins, Stone County, Mississippi. Travis died intestate in 1935, and Florence died intestate in 1960. The land, consisting of 51 acres, went to their nine children as tenants in common. These children were R.T. Williams, Petral Williams, Evert Williams Bullock, Flora Williams Johnson, John Horace "Preacher" Williams, Tommy Williams, Kizer Williams, Louis Charles Williams, and Rachel Williams Fairley. Robert Williams (plaintiff and appellant) is Kizer's son, and the estate's executrix Gloria Fairley is Rachel's daughter.

In 1966, John returned home from the military and moved onto the property. From that time on, he insisted that anyone, including his family, who wanted to visit or use the property get permission from him first. The prevailing belief in the community was that the property belonged to John. Although his sister Rachel and her children lived in the house with John, it was only through his permission. Gloria returned to the home in 1982 to take care of her sick, elderly mother and uncle. John's daughter Jenice Williams Clendening lived in the house as well. John was in charge of all maintenance and improvements to the land. Kizer and another brother helped around the property, such as repairing the roof. However, John always paid them for their work. John's brothers and sisters referred to the land as John's. On a few occasions, John asked his brothers to leave the property, and they did.

During 1994 through 1995, John obtained deeds from two of Flora's children and two of Rachel's children which purported to give him their interest in the land. The deeds stated, however, that they already recognized John as the sole, exclusive owner of the property. From 1997 to 1999, Robert obtained deeds from R.T., Petral, and all five of his own sisters which purported to give their interest in the property to him. On March 29, 2001, shortly before his death, John deeded 1/32 of his interest in the property to Gloria.

The only time that a family member's animals went on the land without John's permission was when Robert placed them there. However, he did not do this until 2001, when John became hospitalized and confined to a wheelchair. When John returned home and found out, he was so angered that he threatened to shoot the cows and Robert. Gloria's son, Derrick Fairley, hid John's guns to keep John from killing Robert and his animals.

John died later that year. The beneficiaries of his will include Jenice, Gloria, and Derrick. On November 8, 2002, John's estate filed suit against Robert and Travis's and Florence's estates to declare John's estate as the sole owner of the property. The Estate of John Horace Williams, represented by the executrix Gloria Fairley, filed suit against Robert H. Williams and the unknown heirs of Travis and Florence Williams to confirm title to the property. Robert filed a counterclaim to quiet and confirm an undivided interest in title in himself. The trial court ruled that John had adversely possessed the property since 1960 and confirmed title in John's estate. Robert appealed.

JUDICIAL OPINION

Griffis, Judge. John's estate had to prove that his possession or occupancy of the property was (1) under claim of ownership, (2) actual or hostile, (3) open, notorious, and visible, (4) continuous and uninterrupted for ten years, (5) exclusive, and (6) peaceful. There is an additional element in order to adversely possess the interests of co-tenants. His estate must also prove ouster. Ouster is unequivocal notice by one co-tenant that he intends to adversely possess the claims of his fellow co-tenants. Robert contends that John's estate failed on three elements: exclusivity, hostility, and ouster.

Exclusive use was expressly admitted. As for hostility, it means "an assertion of title superior to the potential competing claims of anyone else; it can be rebutted by showing that the actual record title owner gave permission to begin the possession." By virtue of the admissions, Robert conceded that John asserted that he had a superior title to the land than that of his co-tenants.

It was then Robert's burden to prove that John's possession began permissively, in order to rebut Robert's own admission that it was hostile.

There was testimony from Robert's sister, Elva Joyce Husband, that around 1965, Kizer objected to John being on the land. This, coupled with Gloria's testimony and Robert's admissions, indicated that the siblings, most notably Kizer, were fighting with John over the land before he came into possession of it. This was substantial credible evidence for the chancellor to conclude that Robert did not carry his burden of rebutting the prima facie case of hostility. If anything, he produced conflicting evidence as to whether John's use was permissive. This issue has no merit.

Next, we examine Robert's argument that there was no evidence of ouster. The chancellor found John ousted his siblings by unequivocal actual notice since

1960. "An ouster of a co-tenant not in possession must be unequivocal notice of some kind to the co-tenant not in possession that the one in possession intends to hold and claim ownership of the property to the exclusion of all others." It must be distinctly hostile to the rights of the others so that the intent to adversely possess is clear and unmistakable. The co-tenant alleging ouster has the burden to prove that the others were "unequivocally ousted by actual notice or conduct equivalent thereto."

Archie Batson testified that he was a long-time neighbor and family friend of the Williamses. He was familiar with the family and the land in question since the early 1950s. All of his life, Archie was under the impression it was John's property. He said the prevailing belief in the community was that the fifty-one acres belonged to only John. He testified that John was mean and even required his siblings to get his permission to go on or use the property. He testified that the siblings did not dare go on the property without getting John's permission. He said he never witnessed John physically evict his siblings from the land. Batson stated that from the 1950s until the present litigation, he never heard anyone in John's family claim an interest in the land. Batson testified that the Williams family, including R.T. and Kizer, referred to the land as "John's place."

Derrick said he had lived on the property with John since he was born. Derrick maintained that for the first twenty-nine years of his life, there was no other belief in the family but that the property was John's. At trial in 2004, Derrick was thirty-nine years old. Derrick additionally corroborated Batson's testimony that family members had to get John's permission to come onto the property. If the family did not ask permission first, they were asked to leave. When the family members were asked to leave, they did. Derrick testified that although he and Kizer made improvements to the land, they did so at John's request and were compensated by him. No other family member placed animals on the land with the exception of Robert. However, [o]nce John found out, he threatened to kill Robert and his animals.

Maurice Redeemer testified that he came into the family thirty years ago when he married Joanna Fairley Redeemer, one of Rachel's daughters. He lives down the road from the property in question and worked for John for the last twenty years of his life. He has lived in the community since 1964 and testified that the prevailing belief was that the property was John's. He never heard John's co-tenants, including Joanna, claim an interest. He testified that all John's co-tenants knew that John claimed the land for himself.

Voncile Martin testified that she has been a friend of the Williams family since 1956. John returned home from the service in the early 1960s. She testified that the community had always believed it was John's property. She verified that he was mean and would not let his co-tenants go on the property without his permission. She said the heirs refer to the farm as John's place.

Gloria asserted that John's siblings "knew they could not come there to do anything." She said he had no hesitancy in telling his siblings that he owned the property from the time the present house was built until his death in 2001. He told them and her repeatedly that he was the sole owner. Gloria said this occurred continuously, as long as she can remember. She said he did not allow any of his siblings "to build anything or tear down or remove anything on or from that property." She testified that the 1995 deeds from some of the heirs which purported to give their interest to John was done at an attorney's suggestion. She said those heirs were surprised, because they believed that John was already the sole owner of the property. Nevertheless they signed the deeds at his request with no compensation. The deeds recite that they recognize that John is the sole owner.

Lovelt…admitted that the property was referred to by the family as "John H. Williams' [s] estate."

On this record, we find that there is substantial credible evidence to support the chancellor's findings of ouster. Every one of John's co-tenants had actual, unequivocal notice that John was asserting exclusive title and he would not recognize their rights as co-tenants. There was evidence that this occurred as early as Florence's death in 1960 and as late as John's retirement in 1966. His exclusive possession continued uninterrupted until 2001. Accordingly, we affirm.

CASE QUESTIONS

1. Give the length of time John had possession and use of the property.

2. Was John's use exclusive? Why is this issue important in the case?

3. What are the facts that point to ouster and why is ouster important in this case?

Be sure to discuss the impact of the admissions in the case.

CONSIDER 13.6

On April 11, 1946, Lawrence and Pearl Pepka obtained a warranty deed for their residential property, which was Outlot 37 and a portion of Outlot 40 of Big Stone City. In 1991, the Pepkas conveyed their property to their children, holding back a life estate for themselves (see Chapter 2 for more information on life estates).

The Dews' chain of title is somewhat more complex but involves the remaining two-thirds of Outlot 40 and was eventually conveyed to Thomas C. Dew and Denise A. Dew as husband and wife (the Dews).

The Pepkas believed their driveway on Outlot 40 was on their property and they used it without the Dews' permission. However, as the Outlot existed at the time of the Pepkas' acquisition, their driveway was actually located well onto the Dews' property. Lawrence Pepka put gravel on the driveway and then later paved it with asphalt. He also mowed the lawn for six feet west of the driveway because he believed that to be the boundary point between his property and the Dews'. Sometime in the 1960s, Lawrence and his son Bernard planted seven evergreen trees along the driveway in the area now disputed. Bernard had received the trees as a gift from a local minister for serving as an altar boy.

The Pepkas did not put up a fence and the Dews and Pepkas had a good relationship. As the Pepkas aged, Tom Dew helped them maintain their property by mowing their lawn and shoveling their snow. Pearl took the Dews baked goods in exchange for the help. Tom even put up the snow fence for Pearl after Lawrence passed away and the snow fence was located along what she believed to be the boundary line for their properties.

In 1993, Pearl decided to sell the property. Because of a survey that revealed the true boundary line to be different from that used by the Pepkas, the Dews asserted ownership of the property through the Pepkas' driveway. Pearl attempted to settle the matter and even offered to purchase the disputed strip. When no agreement could be reached, Pearl filed suit to clear title to the strip by adverse possession. The trial court found no disputed facts and declared the Pepkas the owners of the property. Discuss what the court should decide and why. *Schultz v. Dew*, 564 N.W.2d 320 (S.D. 1997)

Observations about Adverse Possession

One question often brought out in adverse possession cases is, Who was paying the taxes during the alleged period of adverse possession? Unless a state's statute specifies, the adverse possessor is not required to pay taxes to be allowed to claim title. California's statute, for example, does require the payment of taxes for an adverse claim to be successful. In some states, the failure to pay taxes weakens but does not destroy a claim for adverse possession.

When a title holder is faced with an adverse claimant, the proper method for halting such a claim is to bring a legal action in trespass to have the claimant removed by court order or injunction. This removal serves to interrupt the claimant's continuous possession and ends the adverse period. Once suit is filed, the claimant's right to possession stops. The clock stops running on the adverse period. Such a proceeding may be brought by seeking an injunction or through a quiet title action in which the court will determine the parties' rights and interests in the property. A **quiet title action** requires that notice be given to all interested in the property in advance of a

Practical Tip

Even for those who are occupying land with permission, some form of written agreement about their presence can avoid complication and possibly adverse possession. The presence of possession by permissive use should be clarified, if not by agreement, at least by a letter memorializing the arrangement.

hearing on the property (as was done with all the heirs in the *Williams* case. Once title is quieted, any adverse claimant would have to begin anew to establish the requisite statutory period.

Transfer of Property by Gifts

Title to property may be transferred through an ***inter vivos*** **gift** from **donor** (grantor) to **donee** (grantee); that is, the gift is made while the donor is alive. A gift is defined as a voluntary transfer of property by donor to donee where there is no consideration or compensation for the transfer. There are three requirements for passing title by gift. There must be (1) donative intent by the donor or grantor, (2) delivery of the gift, and (3) acceptance by the donee or grantee.

Donative Intent

Donative intent requires proof that the donor intended to pass title absolutely and irrevocably and to relinquish all rights in the property. The best proof of donative intent is a party in possession of a written instrument conveying title.

Delivery

Delivery of a deed can be done through a physical act, or, as noted earlier on delivery of deeds, by proving that the donor intended to part with possession, control, and ownership. In most cases, delivery comes through the simple physical transfer of possession of the written instrument (the deed) from the donor to the donee. Actual delivery occurs when the donee is physically given the deed. **Constructive delivery**, as noted earlier, is tied to exclusive access. For example, if the donor locks the deed in a desk and gives the donee the only key, there has been constructive delivery. Again, a gift is complete if control is relinquished, and the gift fails if the donor maintains control. Joint ownership of a safe deposit box or delivery of a deed to a third person to hold are transfers of possession, but not a sufficient delivery for purposes of making a gift.

Acceptance

The final requirement for a valid gift is acceptance by the donee. As noted earlier, this element of a gift is presumed unless the donee makes a clear refusal, as by tearing up the deed or refusing to accept the appropriate paperwork.

Gifts may be set aside on some of the same grounds used to set aside apparently valid contracts. For example, a donor (grantor) who executed a deed under duress (force or threat of force or wrongful act) or undue influence may have the gift set aside. Or in the event of the donor's death, heirs or devisees may petition to have the gift deed set aside on these bases. **Undue influence** exists when a party in a confidential relationship is able to exert great influence over the donor for the party's own benefit.

CONSIDER 13.7

Mary Blettell was in poor health and went to live with her daughter, Darlene Snider. Herman, Mary's second husband and stepfather to Darlene, continued to live in a house owned by Mary. He was unable to care for Mary and Mary wanted him to live at the house she owned even though he was not on the title for the property.

CONSIDER 13.7

(continued)

Mary instructed Darlene to bring her all the deeds to her property. She signed over the deed to the home where Herman lived and told Darlene to record the deed after Mary died. Darlene then placed the deed in her own safe-deposit box and held onto it for two years until Mary died in 1989. The day after Mary died, Darlene recorded the deed. Herman was not aware of Mary's conveyance to him until after Mary died and Darlene had recorded the deed.

Mary's heirs filed suit, contending that there was not a valid transfer of the property to Herman and that they were entitled to the property as heirs to her estate. The lower court held there had been a valid transfer and the heirs appealed. Who has title to the property? Was there a valid conveyance? *Estate of Mary Blettell v. Snider*, 834 P.2d 505 (Or. App. 1992)

Transfer of Property by Will or Intestate Succession

Title to property may be transferred upon the death of the title holder by the title holder's will; or if no will was executed, it may be transferred pursuant to a state statutory scheme of distribution for those dying intestate. The passage of title by will and intestate succession are covered in detail in Chapter 17.

Transfer of Property by Eminent Domain

Eminent domain is the taking of private property by a governmental entity for use for the general public good. Such a taking is permissible and serves to transfer full and complete title to the state if the state provides the existing owners with appropriate compensation. Chapter 19 provides details on eminent domain.

Protection of Title

The discussions of deeds, adverse possession, and other methods of transfer of real estate demonstrate the confusion that can arise with regard to title to property. The deed and the possessory rights are between the parties. However, the issue of third parties and their rights in the land arises if conveyances between grantor and grantee are not documented in the public records. Recording and other forms of public registration are used to protect title and resolve title disputes.

Recording

The process of **recording** as a method of title protection has been practiced in the United States since the days of the colonies. Indeed, the Massachusetts Bay Act of 1634 required records of land transfer to be filed with the court so that an accurate record of land ownership could be maintained. These early acts required the extra work of copying every instrument of conveyance. Every state now has some form of recording act. Although the acts differ, the same topics are covered in each: (1) the documents required to be recorded, (2) the mechanics of recording, (3) a system for maintaining and organizing records, and (4) a method for determining priorities of interests.

Documents Required to be Recorded

All of the recording acts provide that instruments affecting title to land are to be recorded. These instruments include deeds, mortgages, liens, judgments, and, as discussed in Chapter 5, Article 9 financing statements.

The recording of a land-related document affords both protection and public notice. Not everyone could be expected to have actual knowledge or notice about every land transaction. Recording serves to give everyone the chance to verify transactions. Recording is constructive notice of the rights of the parties in the land.

Mechanics of Recording

Recording is accomplished at statutorily designated offices. Offices may be local, such as a county recorder office, or may be a state agency or a town clerk. As discussed in Chapters 3, 4, 5, and 6, other documents such as easements, liens, and fixture filings are recorded in the same place. In most states, recording is accomplished at a county office for the location of the property. Some states may have a separate land records office in counties where the population is large.

The difference between filing and recording is that in filing, the document is retained by the governmental agency. In recording, the document is copied and the copy is retained by the governmental agency in an appropriate organizational system (discussed later in this chapter).

Fees for recording, required in every state, are set according to the type of document and the number of pages in it.

When the fee is paid, the party recording the instrument is given a receipt with the date and time stamped on it. The document being recorded will also have a stamp of date and time. Since many documents are accepted at the same time, each document will also be numbered (the number is sometimes called a *fee number*) to indicate the exact order of filing. The receipts and time stamps are often critical in establishing title and lien rights in the property. Each document also indicates where in the agency's records it will be filed, such as "Book 425 of Deeds, p. 585" or "Docket 300 of Book of Maps, p. 700."

System for Maintaining and Organizing Records

Every state has some system for organizing land records so that information about title to a piece of property can be readily obtained. The purposes of such recording systems are to provide a method whereby the chain of title for a particular piece of property can be effectively traced and to provide title protection. Chain of title simply provides a history of how a piece of real estate has been transferred over the years between successive owners. To establish ownership of property today, the current owner must establish that the chain of title is unbroken; in other words, that title has been conveyed without any breaks through successive owners.

To be able to trace chains of title, the records must follow an index system. States have either a grantor/grantee system of indexing, a tract system, or both. Most states have a grantor/grantee system, which is easy to understand but more difficult to use when establishing the chain of title. In a **grantor/grantee index system**, the agency responsible for recording maintains a running index of transactions alphabetized by the grantor's and grantee's names.

Figures 13.3 and 13.4 are sample grantor and grantee index entries. Suppose the Joneses were purchasing lot 388 from the Jenningses. The Joneses could establish the chain of title by first looking for the Jenningses in the grantee index (Figure 13.4) and then verifying the transfer by looking at American Continental in the grantor index (Figure 13.3). To trace further back, they would check American Continental

Figure 13.3 Sample Grantor Index

Date of Recording	Grantor	Grantee	Type of Document	Brief Land Description	Docket or Volume	Page
4/9/90	American Continental Corporation	Terry H. and Marianne Moody Jennings	Joint Tenancy Deed	Lot 388 of Hohokam Village, Unit Two	14342	913

in the grantee index to find its grantor and so on. The docket or volume number and the page number in the index permit the tracing party to turn to the records and actually examine the joint tenancy deed of conveyance.

Although tracing the chain of title seems uncomplicated here, many titles require more thorough searches. Also, the grantor/grantee system of indexing has inherent problems: the use of different names, initials, or married names can cause confusion and an apparent break in the chain of title. (See earlier discussion of grantor and grantee.) Title obtained in other ways such as by will may not appear in the land records. Also, not all title defects such as judgments and tax liens will appear in the grantor/grantee index.

The second system of indexing, called the **tract index system** (also known as *block indexing* or *numerical indexing*), avoids some of the inherent problems of the grantor/grantee system. Many states have both systems, but title companies, which sell insurance for chains of title, use the tract index system to avoid the problems in the grantor/grantee system. Furthermore, tracing the chain of title under the tract index system is much faster than under the grantor/grantee system. Under the tract index system, the entire county is divided into tracts and the chain of title for each tract is traced back to the time when the land was given in a government grant. Each piece of land is then indexed to a tract, so that every piece of property can have its origins traced quickly to the origination of title.

Method for Determining Priorities of Interests

State recording acts provide a public record of land transfers and interests. Constructive notice serves as notice to the world. Once a document is recorded, everyone has notice of the recorded interest even without seeing a recorded document.

However, without immediate recording of transferred land interests, the door is open for fraudulent conveyances. Unscrupulous grantors have conveyed the same land interests to different parties. Who, then, is entitled to the property and who is left to collect damages from the fraudulent grantor on the basis of breach of

Figure 13.4 Sample Grantee Index

Date of Recording	Grantee	Grantor	Type of Document	Brief Land Description	Docket or Volume	Page
4/9/90	Terry H. and Marianne Moody Jennings	American Continental Corporation	Joint Tenancy Deed	Lot 388 of Hohokam Village, Unit Two	14342	913

warranty? Three types of state statutes are used for determining rights and priorities in the property: (1) pure race, (2) notice, and (3) race/notice.

1. *Pure Race* North Carolina's statute is a pure race statute and provides as follows:

§47–18. Conveyances, contracts to convey, options and leases of land.

Unless otherwise stated either on the recorded instrument or on a separate recorded instrument duly executed by the party whose priority interest is adversely affected, instruments registered in the public record shall be presumed to have priority based on the order of recordation as determined by the time of recordation. If instruments are recorded simultaneously, then the order of recordation shall be presumed as follows, in order of priority:

(1) The earliest document number set forth on the recorded instrument.

(2) The sequential book and page number set forth on the document if no document number is set forth on the recorded instrument.

A **pure race statute**[3] means first to record is first in right, or the first party to record the instrument in the proper place will hold title to the property. This rule applies even though deeds may have been executed to the parties prior to the time the recording party received the same interests. An example follows.

- *Day 1*: Grantor conveys Blackacre to A.
- *Day 2*: Grantor conveys Blackacre to B.
- *Day 3*: B records interest.
- *Day 4*: A records interest.

In a pure race jurisdiction, B takes title as the first to record even though the interest in Blackacre was conveyed first to A.

2. *Notice* Arizona's statute [ARS §33–412] is an example of a notice statute:

§33–412. Invalidity of unrecorded instruments as to bona fide purchaser or creditor

A. All bargains, sales and other conveyances whatever of lands, tenements and hereditaments, whether made for passing an estate of freehold or inheritance or an estate for a term of years, and deeds of settlement upon marriage, whether of land, money or other personal property, and deeds of trust and mortgages of whatever kind, shall be void as to creditors and subsequent purchasers for valuable consideration without notice, unless they are acknowledged and recorded in the office of the county recorder as required by law.

B. Unrecorded instruments . . . as to all subsequent purchasers with notice thereof, shall be valid and binding.[4]

The key to understanding the system of priorities in notice states[5] is the term **good-faith purchaser** or **bona fide purchaser (BFP)**. Under **notice statutes**, the last good faith purchaser keeps the land interest. However, if a deed is not recorded in a notice state, the purchaser may lose title to a subsequent bona fide purchaser. A **good faith** or **bona fide purchaser** is defined as one who has no knowledge of a prior conveyance either constructive (no prior recorded interest) or actual (no knowledge of a transfer or sale). A notice example follows.

- *Day 1*: Grantor conveys to A (a BFP).
- *Day 2*: Grantor conveys to B (a BFP).
- *Day 3*: Grantor conveys to C (a BFP).

3. Pure race states are Louisiana and North Carolina.
4. There are some authorities who believe that Arizona is a race/notice state by case interpretation of this statute.
5. Notice states are Alabama, Arizona, and Colorado (race/notice by judicial decisions), Arkansas (except mortgages), Connecticut, Delaware, Florida, Illinois, Kansas, Kentucky, Maine, Massachusetts, Missouri, New Hampshire, New Mexico, Ohio (except mortgages), Oklahoma, Rhode Island, South Carolina, Tennessee, Texas, Vermont, Virginia, and West Virginia.

In this case, since A and B did not record, C takes title. This would be true even if A and B recorded their interests on day 4 before C recorded on day 5. In a notice jurisdiction, the failure to record may cost the parties their interests.

3. *Race/Notice* New York is a jurisdiction following the **race/notice system** of priorities (Real Property §291):

A conveyance of real property, within the state, on being duly acknowledged by the person executing the same, . . . may be recorded in the office of the clerk of the county where such real property is situated, . . . Every such conveyance not so recorded is void as against any person who subsequently purchases or acquires by exchange or contracts to purchase or acquire by exchange, the same real property or any portion thereof, or acquires by assignment the rent to accrue, therefrom valuable consideration, from the same vendor or assignor, his distributees or devisees, and whose conveyance, contract or assignment is first duly recorded, and is void as against the lien upon the same real property or any portion thereof arising from payments made upon the execution of or pursuant to the terms of a contract with the same vendor, his distributees or devisees, if such contract is made in good faith and is first duly recorded.

Race/notice statutes entitle the property to go to a good faith purchaser, but it will go to the good faith purchaser who is the first to record. An example would be as follows.

- *Day 1*: Grantor conveys property to A (BFP).
- *Day 2*: Grantor conveys property to B (BFP).
- *Day 3*: Grantor conveys property to C (BFP).
- *Day 4*: B records.
- *Day 5*: A records.
- *Day 6*: C records.

In a race/notice jurisdiction,[6] B would take title to the property because B was the first BFP to record the interest; in a notice system, C would take title; and in a pure race system, B would take title. However, if B were not a BFP, in a race/notice jurisdiction A would take title; in a notice jurisdiction, B's status is irrelevant and C would still take title; and in a pure race jurisdiction, B would still take title.

The following case provides a discussion of priorities for title.

GENSHEIMER V. KNEISLEY

778 S.W.2d 138 (Tex. 1989)

FACTS

On May 15, 1985, Gilbert and Vivian Beall executed a general warranty deed to Mark Gensheimer. On September 9, 1985, Kevin Kneisley obtained a judgment against Gilbert Beall for $124,895.90. Kneisley recorded an abstract of the judgment on October 28, 1985. On October 29, 1985, Gensheimer's deed from the Bealls was recorded. Kneisley filed suit against Gensheimer, who had already been living in the property, claiming superior title. The court found for Kneisley and Gensheimer appealed.

JUDICIAL OPINION

Bleil, Justice. Gensheimer maintains that the trial court erred in granting Kneisley's summary judgment because the abstract of the judgment acquired by Kneisley against Gilbert Beall failed to include Vivian Beall's name. Since her name was not included on the judgment, Gensheimer argues, no lien exists on the property; alternatively, if a lien exists at all, it is only as to the community one-half interest of Gilbert Beall. Tex.Prop. Code Ann. §52.004(b)(2) (Vernon 1984) provides that an abstract of judgment must be recorded and indexed

6. Race/notice states are Alaska, California, Georgia, Hawaii, Idaho, Indiana, Maryland, Michigan, Minnesota, Mississippi, Montana, Nebraska, Nevada, New Jersey, New York, North Dakota, Oregon, Pennsylvania (except mortgages), South Carolina, South Dakota, Utah, Washington, Wisconsin, Wyoming, and the District of Columbia.

alphabetically showing the name of each defendant in the judgment. No requirement exists that an abstract show the names of the parties to the suit or the names of the defendants in the suit; the only requirement is that the defendants against whom a judgment was taken be listed. Although Vivian Beall was named as a party, the judgment was taken only against Gilbert Beall. The abstract of the judgment shows the name of the party against whom the judgment was taken—Gilbert Beall. Community property subject to a spouse's sole or joint management, control, and disposition is subject to the liabilities incurred before or during marriage. Therefore, the abstract of judgment against Gilbert Beall constituted a valid lien against the entirety of the property held in community by Gilbert and Vivian Beall.

Kneisley's judgment against Beall was on file when Gensheimer recorded his deed from Beall. Kneisley recorded first, on October 28, 1985; Gensheimer's deed from Beall, dated May 15, 1985, was not *recorded* until October 29, 1985. A lien of a judgment creditor who has fixed a lien upon real estate by abstracting a judgment takes precedence over a prior unrecorded deed executed by the judgment debtor, unless the creditor has notice of the unrecorded deed at or before the time the lien was fixed on the land. Kneisley stated by affidavit that he had no knowledge or notice of a deed dated May 15, 1985. Gensheimer did not controvert this fact. A valid lien against the property was established and foreclosed upon, and Kneisley's recorded judgment lien takes precedence over Gensheimer's prior unrecorded warranty deed, thus vesting superior title to the property in Kneisley.

Nevertheless, Gensheimer also complains that the trial court erred in granting judgment because a fact issue exists as to whether Kneisley had knowledge of the warranty deed dated May 15, 1985, from the Bealls to Gensheimer. When Kneisley abstracted his judgment on October 28, 1985, Gensheimer's warranty deed was not in his chain of title, since it was not recorded until the following day. An unrecorded deed does not give constructive notice. Kneisley's uncontroverted affidavit established that he had no actual knowledge or notice of the deed.

Affirmed.

CASE QUESTIONS

1. Write out a chronology of events with respect to the title and recording interests.
2. Was there actual notice of the Gensheimer deed?
3. Was there constructive notice of the Gensheimer deed?
4. Does the judgment take priority over a warranty deed?
5. Who has title to the property in this case?

CONSIDER 13.8

Day 1: O conveys to A (BFP).
Day 2: O conveys to B (BFP).
Day 3: A records.
Day 4: B records.
In the above example, who takes title under all three types of recording statutes?

Torrens System

Another method of title protection used instead of a recording system is the **Torrens system**—named after Sir Robert Torrens, who introduced it in Australia in 1858. The system is one of land title registration; that is, documents of transfer are not recorded, but title to land is registered once by making an entry reflecting the owner. That owner is then given an official certificate of title. If the owner wishes to transfer title to the land, the certificate and a deed are given to the purchaser. The purchaser then takes these documents to the land registration office where the old certificate is surrendered, a change of ownership is entered, and a new certificate is issued to the purchaser. This system eliminates the need for establishing the chain of title.

Initial registration under the Torrens system requires a form of quiet title action, so that all parties with interests or potential interests may be heard before title is registered.

Title Abstracts

In many states, parties transferring property interests will hire attorneys to trace the chain of title on a piece of property and then issue an opinion on that chain. That opinion, in written form, is called an **abstract of title** and is defined as a concise statement of the substance of documents or facts appearing on the public records that affect the title.

The abstract begins with the legal description of the property, often called a **caption** or **head**, and then proceeds with copies of all documents, in chronological order, affecting title. Acknowledgments and signatures are not included so long as the abstractor views them as being in order and proper.

Part of the abstract also includes the **abstractor's certificate**, which summarizes what the abstractor did not examine. For example, it would be very typical for the abstractor to state that zoning violations may affect the title's marketability but that information on such violations is not available from the recorder's records. The abstractor then directs the users to the appropriate agency for determining whether zoning violations exist.

The buyer's attorney then examines the abstract and issues an opinion that includes a description of the property and time covered by the abstract, who holds title to the property, what defects or imperfections exist, and any recommendations for clearing up these defects and imperfections. The abstract will include summaries of items such as deeds, mortgages, deeds of trusts, ***lis pendens*** (pending legal action on the property), sheriffs' sales certificates, liens, taxes, assessments, judgments, and bankruptcy petitions.

Title Insurance

Recording and title abstracts still do not provide protection if a title defect arises. Neither system of title protection offers a guarantee that no problems will arise. In most parts of the United States today, **title insurance** affords the property purchaser financial protection in the event certain types of defects arise in the property.

A title insurer may operate in one of two ways. First, it may hire an attorney to do an abstract and then issue insurance on the basis of that opinion. Second, the title insurer may be a complete operation by actually doing the search and abstract and then issuing insurance. Those insurers operating the second type of business maintain a title plant for conducting their operations. A title plant consists of copies of documents taken from the public records. Generally, title companies will organize their records pursuant to a tract index system.

Title insurers issue different policies according to the type of applicant for insurance and the use to be made of the property. For example, there are different policy forms for commercial and residential property. Also, different policies are issued for owners of property and for those who wish insurance as mortgage lenders. Neither policy is issued until the insurance company has had an opportunity to examine the records and establish the chain of title.

Process of Issuing a Policy

Most contracts for the purchase and sale of property have marketable title, often obtained through the purchase and issuance of a title insurance policy, as a prerequisite to closing the transaction. **Marketable title** is a title free of problems in the chain of title, the quality of title, and the seller's right to convey the property. Although the definition of marketable title may vary, adding a requirement that a title insurer issue a policy gives the buyer assurance and financial backing in the event of a problem.

A policy will not be issued unless the insurer is reasonably sure no loss will be incurred.

The seller applies for a policy with a title insurance company. The title company prepares an abstract, and any defects are considered by the title examiner, who decides whether the defects are a risk or whether the property is insurable. If there is a favorable decision, the title insurer issues a preliminary binder that is not a policy but a commitment to insure contingent upon the transaction's closing and the title's being delivered to the buyer.

If the company finds defects that make the property uninsurable, the seller may be given the opportunity to correct those defects to make the title insurable. For example, the title abstract will provide a list of all judgments against persons having the same name as the seller. The seller may by affidavit establish that he or she is not the same person as named in those judgments. Tax liens may be removed through payment. When the discovered problems are remedied, the insurer will then issue the preliminary binder.

The fees for preparation of the abstract and issuance of the policy vary. In many states, the fee charged will be based on an escalating scale set by a state regulatory body, which allows the fee charged to increase with the value of the property. The reason for the escalating scale is that a title problem on a more expensive piece of property will cost the insurer more in terms of correction or compensation. In some states the fees are set by a board composed of industry members and then approved by the state as adopted by the board. Such arrangements have been subject to antitrust scrutiny. In *F.T.C. v. Ticor Title Ins. Co.*, 504 U.S. 621 (1992), the U.S. Supreme Court held that these private board mechanisms for establishing title insurance fees must be subject to adequate state review in order to survive an antitrust charge of horizontal price fixing.

Many companies will physically inspect the property to be insured in order to determine any adverse possession or occupancy not reflected in the public records. Also, when insuring a construction lender, the title insurer must be certain that construction or work has not begun prior to the recordation of the mortgage. As noted in Chapter 6, any start of construction, from the presence of equipment to digging one shovelful of dirt, will place the mechanics in first priority if those acts are done prior to recording.

Coverage Afforded by the Title Policy

Title insurance differs significantly from ordinary fire or auto insurance in covering only defects in title in existence at the time of the transfer. Title insurance does not afford protection for new problems developing after the closing of the transaction and the transfer of title to the buyer.

The Title Policy

The American Land Title Association (ALTA) has developed the most widely used form policies and the ones used by major title insurers.

ALTA issues policy forms for lenders, owners, construction lenders, and leaseholds (for either tenants or landlords). The basic title policy, with the 2006 reforms, expanded greatly the coverage for owners and lenders, and includes the following sections:

1. Insuring clauses (outline the coverage), which cover
   a. failure of title to the property (covers forgery, fraud, unauthorized signatures, electronic recording failure and a host of other problems that arise in recording titles to property and executing deeds)

   b. defects in title such as liens[7]
   c. lack of right of access
   d. unmarketable title
   e. encroachments (new in 2006)
2. Exclusions (which outline those items not covered) (see the next section)
3. Schedules, generally A and B (which outline the added protections or endorsements purchased by the policy holder)
4. Conditions (requirements for the issuance of the policy, such as removal of liens)
5. Stipulations (certain statements of fact that the parties agree are part of their assumptions for the policy, such as the new definition of what constitutes a "public record")

The ALTA policies also include a unilateral arbitration clause when the amount involved exceeds $2 million. The insurance amount must cover the value of the land when a building is constructed, and not just insurance for the cost of the raw land. Title policy buyers must now purchase title insurance based on the proposed value of the land with completed construction.

The ATLA policy also requires that the title insurer undertake its obligation to defend a title "diligently." This change adds an element of good faith to the title insurer's role in defending claims against the insured property.

Exclusions in Title Insurance Coverage

Exclusions from coverage are listed in what is called schedule B of the policy. Title insurance does not provide protection for facts, rights, or claims that are not noted in the public records but are visible upon inspection. Zoning restrictions are not covered. Additional exclusions from coverage are

- Violations of environmental laws unless recorded in the public records (see Chapter 20 for a discussion of these environmental laws and see the *Stewart* case and note that the ATLA revisions have a new definition of "public records").
- Litigation defense costs for items excluded under schedule B exceptions.
- Purchasers who are not bona fide purchasers.
- Problems noted in public records other than those that are part of the property records designated by the state as the proper filing place for matters affecting property(see, again, *Stewart* case).
- "Unmarketability of title" items (see Chapter 14).
- Problems with title based on usury (see Chapter 15).
- Mechanic's liens (see Chapter 6) that arise from work contracted for and commenced after the date of the policy.
- Eminent domain rights (see Chapter 19) unless there is notice in the public records of eminent domain proceedings prior to the date of the policy.

The Enhanced Title Policy—Special Protection Through Endorsements

Title insurers do offer additional coverage of these and other exemptions for a fee. For example, mechanic's lien protections may be added to a policy.

Other types of endorsements include coverage for violation of protective covenants (see Chapter 21) and violation of zoning laws. The California Land Title Association policy, which is becoming more popular outside California, can include

7. A 2006 survey by the American Land Title Association found that 36% of residential titles had a defect in them, the most common pay-out was on liens not discovered in the course of issuing the title policy. The liens involved taxes, unpaid child or spousal support, and first- and second-mortgages.

hundreds of endorsements available to title policy purchasers. Sometimes referred to as "the California 100," these endorsements give purchasers a wide choice of options for protections. Some states, such as Texas, do not permit the use of these complex endorsement policies.

Another type of special endorsement would be a successorship and assignment endorsement that allows corporations to transfer the policy protection to subsidiaries or newly formed corporations that result from mergers and consolidations so that the policy rights are not lost to corporate reorganizations.

Who is Protected Under Title Policy?

The policy affords protection to the insured (or insureds) named in the policy (a mortgagee or buyer). If the mortgagee is protected and a property loss results from a title defect, the insurer will pay the balance due on the mortgage, thereby relieving the owner of liability for the mortgage. However, the owner will lose the property and any existing investment or equity. Title policies are not transferable, and the protection afforded a buyer in one transaction may not be passed along to the next buyer.

CONSIDER 13.9

The Gebhardts, husband and wife, owned a 31.7-acre parcel of property, upon which they held an owner's title insurance policy. In 1995, they discovered that another party was paying property taxes on 4.75 acres of the property. They submitted a claim to their title insurer, demanding that the insurer correct the situation by "negotiating a purchase from the alleged owner (who also has a cloud on title)...and obtaining a quitclaim in favor of [the Gebhardts]." In 1996, before the claim was resolved, the Gebhardts executed, for estate-planning purposes, a special warranty deed conveying all of the property to a Virginia L.L.C. of which they were the sole members. The deed recited a consideration of approximately $161,000.

In 1997, the Gebhardts sued the title insurer for breach of contract for failing to resolve the title dispute. The title insurer refused to pay because the Gebhardts were no longer the policy holders. Mr. Gebhardt said that no consideration changed hands (despite the deed recitation of consideration in the amount of $161,000), and that the only reason for the deed recitation was so that the State of Maryland could "assess the transfer taxes from the individual to the L.L.C."

The Gebhardts argued that they nonetheless remained insured parties under the title policy because the conveyance was, in effect, to themselves, and therefore they still retained an "interest" in the property. Are the Gebhardts correct? *Gebhardt Family Restaurant, L.L.C. v. Nation's Title Ins. Co. of New York*, 132 Md. App. 457, 752 A.2d 1222 (2000)

The seller is not protected by the purchaser's title insurance policy. The seller remains liable to the buyer for breach of any warranties if defects in title arise. In fact, it is not unusual for a title insurer to pay the buyer the loss resulting from the title defect and then through subrogation proceed against the seller for the seller's breach of warranty to the buyer.

Damages

All title policies have a section dealing with the determination and payment of losses. Under the standard policy, the loss is defined as the least of

1. The actual loss of the insured claimed; or
2. The amount of the insurance set forth in the policy; or
3. If the policy is for a mortgagee, the amount necessary to pay off the mortgage debt.

In addition to actual loss, the title insurer will pay the costs, attorneys' fees, and expenses imposed upon an insured in litigation carried out by the insurer for the insured. The following case deals with the complexities of title insurance and its coverage.

NEW ENGLAND FEDERAL CREDIT UNION V. STEWART TITLE GUAR. CO.

765 A.2d 450 (Vt. 2000)

FACTS

On July 14, 1976, Alfred and Dorothy Lafrance conveyed a parcel of land in Essex, together with a modular home and a mobile home, to Gordon Reinhart and retained a parcel of land about 10 acres in size in the area. Because the retained parcel was less than 10 acres, Alfred Lafrance was given a deferral of permit on the property from the Vermont Department of Environmental Conservation (DEC). The permit prohibited the "construction or erection of a structure or building that would require the installation of plumbing and sewage treatment facilities" without first complying with Vermont's subdivision regulations. The deferral of permit was not recorded in the Town of Essex land records.

In August 1986, the Lafrances conveyed their retained parcel of property to Eugenia Evans. In August 1988, Evans conveyed the property and premises to Edward Fleming. In 1989, Fleming obtained a building permit from the Town of Essex to replace a mobile home that was located on the lot with a two-story house. In July 1991, the New England Federal Credit Union (NEFCU) made a $67,000 loan to Fleming for a refinancing of the land and premises. Stewart Title issued a title insurance commitment to NEFCU to provide title insurance in the amount of the loan. Stewart Title's insurance contract to NEFCU provided as follows:

SUBJECT TO THE EXCLUSIONS FROM COVERAGE, THE EXCEPTIONS FROM COVERAGE CONTAINED IN SCHEDULE B AND THE CONDITIONS AND STIPULATIONS, STEWART TITLE GUARANTY COMPANY... insures, as of Date of Policy shown in Schedule A, against loss or damage, not exceeding the Amount of Insurance stated in Schedule A, sustained or incurred by the insured by reason of:...

(2) Any defect in or lien or encumbrance on the title...

The policy excluded loss, damage, costs, attorneys' fees or expenses which arise by reason of:

Any law, ordinance or governmental regulation (including by not limited to building and zoning laws, ordinances, or regulations) restricting, regulating, prohibiting or relating to (i) the occupancy, use, or enjoyment of the land... (iv) environmental protection, or the effect of any violation of these laws, ordinances or governmental regulations, except to the extent that a notice of the enforcement thereof or a notice of a defect, lien or encumbrance resulting from a violation or alleged violation affecting the land has been recorded in the public records at Date of Policy.

In 1992, Fleming died, and his estate contracted to sell the property for $94,000. The sale fell through, however, when the buyer discovered the violation of the deferral of permit resulting from the construction of a dwelling and wastewater system on the property without a subdivision permit. NEFCU foreclosed on the property and sold it for $10,734. NEFCU forwarded a notice of claim to Stewart Title. Stewart Title denied NEFCU's request for coverage and compensation under the policy.

NEFCU filed suit and for summary judgment. The trial court denied NEFCU's motion and instead granted Stewart Title's motion for summary judgment. NEFCU appealed.

JUDICIAL OPINION

Amestoy, Chief Justice. NEFCU first contends the trial court erred in ruling that the violation of Vermont's public health regulation requiring a subdivision permit was not an encumbrance on title covered under the policy. In so holding, the court noted that encumbrances generally fall into two categories—those that infringe on the title, and those that involve physical facts concerning the premises. It concluded that the subdivision permit restricted only the use of the land, and therefore was not an encumbrance on title under the policy.

[t]he policy excludes from coverage any law regulating the occupancy, use, enjoyment or environmental regulation of land, or the effect of any violation of these laws. An exception to the exclusion, however, provides that coverage will not be denied if "a notice of a defect, lien, or *encumbrance* resulting from a violation or alleged violation affecting the land has been recorded in the public records" at the date of the policy. Thus, read in its entirety, the policy language evinces a clear intent to include violations of land-use regulations within the meaning of "encumbrance," and within the scope of coverage, *to the extent that they had been recorded in the public records on the date of the policy.*

We are aware that decisions from other states have reached varying conclusions as to whether land use regulations that restrict the use, occupancy, or enjoyment of land may constitute an encumbrance on title. In *Bear Fritz Land Co. v. Kachemak Bay Title Agency, Inc.*, 920 P.2d 759, 761–62 (Alaska 1996), however, the court held that a federal wetlands permit containing restrictions was not an encumbrance on title under the title insurance policy, and therefore was outside the scope of coverage. There, however, the subject policy expressly excluded from the definition of public records "**any of the offices of federal, state or local environmental protection, zoning, building, health or public safety authorities**." Because policy language varies from case to case, these decisions are of limited value.

The question of coverage in this case thus pivots on whether notice of the violation was recorded in the "public records." Turning once again to the policy, we find that it defines "public records" as:

records established under state statutes at Date of Policy for the purpose of imparting constructive notice of matters relating to real property to purchaser for value and without knowledge.

Without explanation, the trial court construed this definition to include only matters of record in the "public *land* records." In both *Hunter Broadcasting*, 164 Vt. at 396–97, 670 A.2d at 840, and *Bianchi v. Lorenz*, 166 Vt. 555, 560–61, 701 A.2d 1037, 1040–41 (1997), however, we held that records imparting constructive notice of matters relating to real property are not confined under our statutory scheme solely to documents recorded in the municipal land records. Like the instant case, *Hunter Broadcasting* involved the failure to obtain a subdivision permit in violation of Vermont's public health regulations. At the time of the relevant events in *Hunter Broadcasting*, subdivision permits were not required by statute to be recorded in the land records. Nevertheless, we concluded that, because "Vermont's subdivision regulations are sufficiently precise that an ordinary person, using ordinary common sense, can understand and comply with them," the city's violation of the subdivision regulations when it conveyed the 9.7 acre parcel should have been obvious from the very nature of the transaction. Indeed, although the concurring opinion in *Bianchi* anticipated the difficulties of searching for encumbrances outside of the land records, that concern did not extend to the search necessary to determine whether a state subdivision permit had been obtained or violated. The concurrence distinguished its concern about searching municipal records from a search of a state agency's records when it explained:

In Hunter Broadcasting *the seller knew that a state subdivision permit had not been obtained when it conveyed the property. A subsequent seller could easily verify the existence or nonexistence of the state subdivision permit by contacting the issuing agency for permits required to be issued before September 1, 1994, or by searching the land records for permits issued after that date.*

Our construction of the policy in question here imposes no additional or unreasonable burdens upon title searchers beyond the normal scope of due diligence.

Stewart Title relies on 18 V.S.A. §1221b, which provides that notice of a subdivision permit violation must be "recorded on the land records of any municipality in which the land subdivision or development is located." While we agree that 18 V.S.A. §1221b provides a clear directive as to where, precisely, such permits or violations should be recorded, this statute was not in effect at the date of policy, and did not become so until September 1, 1994, approximately three years after Stewart Title issued the policy in question. Therefore, as in *Hunter Broadcasting*, where, at the time of the events in question, subdivision permits were not required by state statute to be recorded in the land records, the public-records exception at issue here plainly encompassed the records of the DEC—a public agency which, pursuant to state law, imparts constructive notice of matters relating to real estate and subdivision permits or violations arising prior to the enactment of §1221b.

Our conclusion finds support outside of Vermont in analogous cases addressing the meaning of public records in the title insurance context. For example, in *Hahn v. Alaska Title Guaranty Co.*, 557 P.2d 143, 145–47 (Alaska 1976), the court concluded that the plain language of the subject title insurance policy did not exclude from the definition of "public records" a public land order filed with the office of the Federal Registrar in Washington, D.C. And in *Radovanov v. Land Title Co. of America*, 189 Ill.App.3d 433, 136 Ill.Dec. 827, 545 N.E.2d 351, 355 (1989), the court held that a title insurance policy that defined "public records" as those records which by law imparted constructive notice of matters relating to subject land included the records of the circuit court of the county.

Finally, we note that Stewart Title could have readily achieved the more narrow definition of public records that it seeks here simply by excluding from the definition certain locations where public records containing information about matters relating to land are maintained. In *Somerset Savings Bank v. Chicago Title Insurance Co.*, 420 Mass. 422, 649 N.E.2d 1123, 1126 (1995), the title insurance policy, like the Stewart Title policy, excluded from coverage any encumbrance resulting from a violation of any law or governmental regulation restricting or regulating the use or enjoyment of land unless notice of the encumbrance was recorded "**in those records in which under state statutes, deeds, mortgages, *lis pendens*, liens or other title encumbrances must be recorded in order to impart constructive notice to purchasers of the land**..." Unlike the Stewart Title policy, however, the title insurer in ***Somerset*** added language explaining that, "***without limitation, such records shall not be construed to include records in any of the offices of federal, state or local environmental protection, zoning, building, health or public safety authorities.***" Absent any limiting language such as that in the ***Somerset*** insurance policy, and prior to the enactment of 18 V.S.A. §1221b, the policy language here, providing that "records established under state statutes . . . for the purpose of imparting constructive notice of matters relating to real property" plainly includes the deferral of permit at the DEC, a public agency which imparts constructive notice of matters relating to real estate.

A final issue concerns the type of notice contemplated by the policy. The trial court concluded in part that because no actual notice of violation or alleged violation was recorded, the exception to the exclusion did not apply. A search by Stewart Title of the DEC filings would have revealed the deferral of permit prohibiting the construction of a structure on the property that required plumbing and sewage treatment facilities. This notice was sufficient for purposes of the policy.

Reversed and remanded.

CASE QUESTIONS

1. What is the significance of the meaning of "public records"? What definition would Stewart Title like to have? Why is its definition different from that of NEFCU?
2. What changes would Stewart have had to make in its policy to be certain the DEC filings were not covered?
3. What additional duties does the decision impose on title companies?

ETHICAL ISSUE

The same property at issue in the *Stewart Title* case was at issue in *Estate of Fleming v. Nicholson*, 168 Vt. 495, 724 A.2d 1026 (1998). In conducting a title search for Fleming before he purchased the property, Fleming's attorney discovered the violation of the deferral of permit and lack of subdivision permit for the dwelling and wastewater system, but failed to inform Fleming. The Vermont Supreme Court affirmed the superior court's decision on Fleming's motion for summary judgment, finding the attorney and law firm's omission negligence as a matter of law. Did Fleming, his estate, or the lawyer have an ethical responsibility to let anyone know of the problem with the property? Notice that the case explains that the buyer discovered the problem with the permit, not that the problem was disclosed. Reconcile this withholding of information with the disclosure requirements discussed in Chapter 12 and the misrepresentation issues covered in Chapter 14.

Uniform Laws and Proposals

The complications of deeds, title, and recording have produced several uniform acts. Two of them, the Uniform Simplification of Land Transfers Act and the Uniform Marketable Title Act, both drafted for use in 1990, have not yet been adopted in any state. The Uniform Recognition of Acknowledgments Act, which applies to both deeds and wills, has been adopted in 16 states.

Cautions and Conclusions

Transferring title to property requires a great deal of detailed attention to the paperwork and the background of the property itself. Parties involved in a transfer of title by deed should check the following:

1. Does the grantor have the authority to transfer the title to the property?
2. Does the grantor have full and complete title to the property?
3. Is the description for the property accurate?
4. Are there any boundary issues that are evident from a physical inspection of the property?
5. Do the public records reveal any title issues such as judgments or liens?
6. Are there restrictions on the use of the land such as zoning or covenants?
7. Can I obtain title insurance for the property?

8. What will the title insurance cover?
9. How does recording work in my state and is my title protected if I am first to record my deed?
10. What type of title am I getting and do I get any warranties with my title?
11. Is there a good chain of title? Do I need a title abstract?
12. Have I checked the rights of those occupying the property and are there any possible claims for title by adverse possession?
13. Have I proofed the deed for correct spelling and adequate descriptions of the property?
14. Have I met the formal requirements for signature?

The devil is in deeds and these questions should help the parties walk through those potential pitfalls in transferring title.

Key Terms

abstract of title, 357
abstractor's certificate, 357
acknowledgment clause, 339
adverse possession, 344
bona fide purchaser (BFP), 354
caption (head), 357
constructive delivery, 350
deed, 332
deed of bargain and sale, 343
delivery, 340
donee, 350
donor, 350
good faith purchaser, 354
grantor/grantee index system, 352
habendum clause, 339
inter vivos gift, 350
judicial deed, 343
lis pendens, 357
livery of seisin, 332
marketable title, 357
notice statutes, 354
premises, 332
pure race statute, 354
quiet title action, 350
quitclaim deed, 341
race/notice system, 355
recording, 351
sheriffs' deeds, 343
special warranty deed, 343
squatter's rights, 344
title insurance, 357
Torrens system, 356
tract index system, 353
undue influence, 350
warranty deed, 341

Chapter Problems

1. In the late spring or summer of 1970, Dan Jutting's father planted grass on his lot, including a 10-foot strip bordering adjoining property belonging to Jack and Georgine Hendrix, and kept it watered as it grew. During that summer, he also planted two trees on the strip of property near the boundary. These trees are now fully grown. Jutting's father also constructed a clothesline on the property that ran from the west to the east. The west support for the clothesline was also located on the strip. Later, a swing was hung from that support and used by the Jutting children and grandchildren. Behind the west support, Jutting's father planted lilac bushes. From the summer of 1970 until 1998, the Jutting family has continuously watered and mowed the grass on the disputed strip and raked it when necessary.

Jutting's father died in the early 1990s and Jutting's mother remained in the home until 1997 when she sold it to Jutting. Before Jutting purchased the property, a surveyor was hired to do a location survey for the title insurance company. The survey showed that the west boundary of the property was where it was presumed to be, i.e., approximately 10 feet from the west side of the Jutting residence.

The Hendrix residence has had a number of different owners since its construction in the late 1960s. The Hendrixes purchased the property in late 1997. Through subsequent discussions with Jutting, Mr. Hendrix learned there was uncertainty over the exact location of the line between their two properties. In the summer of 1998, he hired a surveyor to do a complete survey to determine the boundaries. The surveyor discovered a 10-foot error in the original platting of the subdivision that "slid" the boundaries of the Hendrix and Jutting properties 10 feet to the east. This pushed the east line of the Hendrix property to within an inch of the west side of Jutting's residence.

Although Jutting was made aware of the true property line, he persisted in trying to maintain the disputed strip of property. Harsh words were eventually exchanged between Jutting and Mr. Hendrix, and Hendrix began to construct a split rail fence along the property line within an inch or so of Jutting's residence. Jutting sued the Hendrixes for an injunction to prevent construction of the fence and to quiet title to the disputed strip of property. Jutting also raised claims for trespass and property damage and claimed adverse possession of the disputed strip. Who owns the strip? *Jutting v. Hendrix*, 606 N.W.2d 140 (S.D. 2000)

2. The following is an actual deed recorded on page 215 of volume 40, Cass County, Illinois, deed records.

I, J. Henry Shaw, the grantor, herein
Who lives at Beardstown the county within,
For seven hundred dollars to me paid today
By Charles E. Wyman, do sell and convey
Lot two (2) in Block Forty (40), said county and town,
Where Illinois River flows placidly down,
And warrant the title forever and aye,
Waiving homestead and mansion to both a goodbye,
And pledging this deed is valid in law
I add here my signature, J. Henry Shaw
[Seal] Dated July 2, 1881

The acknowledgment on the deed is as follows:

I, Sylvester Emmons, who lives at Beardstown,
A Justice of Peace of fame and renown,
Of the county of Cass in Illinois state,
Do certify here that on the same date
One J. Henry Shaw to me did make known
That the deed above and name were his own,
And he stated he sealed and delivered the same
Voluntarily, freely, and never would claim
His homestead therein, but left all alone,
Turned his face to the street and his back to his home.
[Seal] S. Emmons J.P. Dated August 1, 1881

Is this a valid deed? What type of deed is it?

3. Under each of the three types of recording systems, who takes title?

- *Day 1*: O conveys to A (BFP).
- *Day 2*: A conveys to B (BFP). B records.
- *Day 3*: O conveys to C (BFP). C records.

4. Clarence and Lillian Ellison and Clifford and Mary Grace Bearden are adjoining landowners with a dispute regarding the location of the boundary line between their properties. A fence built by the Beardens has separated the two parcels of property for more than 40 years. The Ellisons have raised gardens, cut timber, grazed cattle, and otherwise used the property on their side of the fence for more than 38 years. An error in the location of the fence was discovered, but the Ellisons claimed title to the land up to the fence through adverse possession. The Beardens' son knocked down the southernmost portion of the fence, and the Ellisons filed suit. The trial court found the Ellisons held title to the disputed boundary property and ordered a survey to have the deed reformed. Is this a correct outcome? *Bearden v. Ellison*, 560 So.2d 1042 (Ala. 1990)

5. Prepare a deed on the basis of the following information. Be sure to attach to it any comments on missing information or information that is not necessary.

a. Land to be conveyed.
b. Grantors. Mr. and Mrs. Paul S. Smith living in a home on the pictured lot, 4141 Waverly Street, Phoenix, Arizona 85003. They own the property as joint tenants. Mrs. Smith's name is Helen.
c. Grantees. Mr. and Mrs. Samuel P. Polk, 3232 Holly Drive, Phoenix, Arizona 85204. They wish to own the property as joint tenants. Mrs. Polk's name is Janice.
d. Date of transaction. September 12, 2007.
e. Amount Polks will pay to Smiths. $252,500.00.
f. A neighbor of the Smiths, Thomas Jones, is a notary public who will furnish his services for free. His commission expires September 15, 2010.
g. The Smiths wish to warrant title only for the time they have held the property.
h. The Smiths have lined up their neighbors, Brad Georges and Bill Daves, to witness the transaction.
i. A school water pipeline runs through the back two feet of the property. There are no other easements, encumbrances, unpaid taxes, or liens on the property.
j. The Polks are paying cash.

6. Determine who gets title to the property under each of the three types of jurisdictions in the following circumstances.

Day 1: O conveys to A (BFP).
Day 2: O conveys to B (not BFP).
Day 3: O conveys to C (BFP).
Day 4: B records.
Day 5: A records.

7. Irene Franzen and Joseph and Shirley Cassarino are neighbors. As is often the case, the boundary line between their properties is described one way in their deeds but appears to be physically different. Indeed, part of the Cassarinos' garage is on Franzen's property, and the Cassarinos have used other parts of the area in dispute as a vegetable garden. They have also mowed the yard in the disputed area and planted trees and shrubs. They have so used the land since they moved into their home in 1964. Irene Franzen claims title to the strip of land through her deed. The Cassarinos counterclaim for the land on the grounds of adverse possession. Who holds title to the land strip? *Franzen v. Cassarino*, 552 N.Y.S.2d 789 (1990)

8. In 1968, Colonial Motel Properties, Inc., acquired title to a 7.746 acre tract of land next to land owned by Marathon Petroleum. Colonial decided to expand its motel business by appealing to trailer truck drivers. The southern portion of its acreage and .27 acres of Marathon's property were covered with dirt and gravel for use for parking by the drivers. Since 1970, trucks have parked on this lot. A sign that read as follows was posted: *Free Parking for Colonial Inn Motel Guests Only. All Others $20.00 per night. Violators impounded at owner's expense. All vehicles must register.*

The motel also employed a security guard for the lot to ensure that all vehicles were registered. The lot, the sign, and the security guard were all visible from Marathon's property.

In 1985, Marathon was approached by a buyer for its property and the .27 acre encroachment was discovered. Colonial claimed title through adverse possession. Is Colonial correct? *Marathon Petroleum Co. v. Colonial Motel Properties, Inc.*, 550 N.E.2d 778 (Ind. 1990)

9. William Bryant constructed an air strip on what he believed to be his property. He used the airstrip for landing his plane, but he also permitted other pilots in the area to land there. The airstrip was used for 40 years and was located on land that was primarily used for timber and mining. When Bryant brought suit against the coal mining company that owned the land seeking to establish title to the airstrip by adverse possession, the coal company defended itself by noting that Bryant's use was not exclusive and not sufficiently open and notorious to qualify for a taking by adverse possession. Does Bryant have title by adverse possession? *Bryant v. Palmer Coaking Coal Co.*, 936 P.2d 1163 (Wash. App. 1997)

10. Somerset Savings Bank agreed to finance a 72-unit condominium project and Chicago Title issued a policy for Somerset's $9.5 million mortgage. After the title policy was issued, the city of Revere, Massachusetts, refused to issue a permit for the project because of issues with existing zoning laws, including a railroad right-of-way through the property. Somerset was left with a $9.5 million mortgage on condominiums that would never be built. Somerset brought suit against Chicago Title for its failure to note the zoning issue. The trial court held that the zoning issue was not covered under the policy, the court of appeals reversed on one issue, and Somerset appealed. Who is correct? The title insurance company or Somerset, and why? *Somerset Savings Bank v. Chicago Title Insurance Company*, 649 N.E.2d 1123 (Mass. 1995)

For research activities related to this chapter, go to our text companion website at www.thomsonedu.com/westbuslaw/jennings.

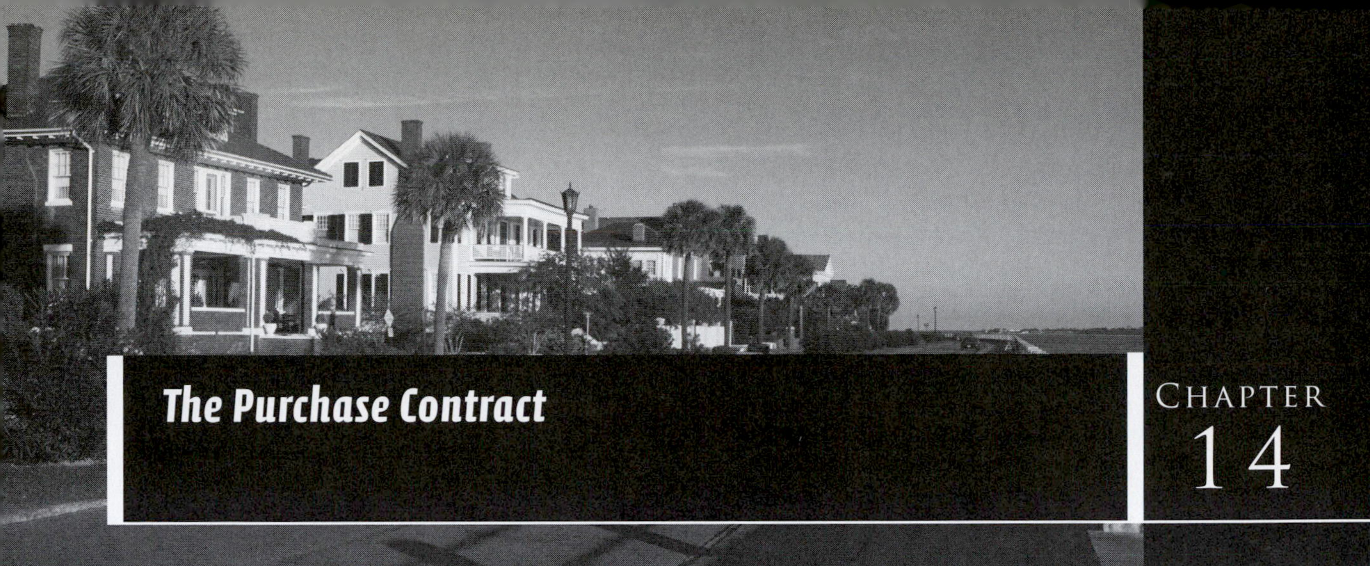

The Purchase Contract

CHAPTER 14

"People will go to great lengths to get out of a legally binding transaction."
-Larry Sorsby, CFO, Hovnanian Enterprises, Inc.[1]

We wonder when an enforceable contract for the purchase of real property is formed. We also wonder whether there are outs, breaches, and bases for cancellation. This chapter provides the insights and information you need on contracts for the sale of real estate: what is required for a valid contract; what it helps to include in a valid contract; and what remedies you have for nonperformance of a valid real estate contract.

Common Law Principles of Formation as Applied to Real Estate Contracts

Although contracts for the purchase and sale of real estate have certain specific requirements, they must still meet the general requirements that all contracts must have for formation. A contract does not exist until there has been an offer, acceptance, and consideration.

Offer

The **offer**, the first step in the real estate transaction, is generally made by the buyer. Listing agreements, advertisements, auction flyers, and notices of public sales are just invitations for offers. These marketing tools make buyers aware of the property and catch the buyer's attention, but they are not offers.

1. Michael Corkery and Ruth Simon, "As Market Cools, Home Buyers Seek a Way Out," *Wall Street Journal*, May 4, 2007, p. A1.

Elements

To be valid, an offer must show a present intent to contract, its terms must be certain and definite, and it must be communicated to the offeree. Most real estate purchase offers are made when the buyer actually fills out, signs, and presents to the seller a form or contract of purchase. The language in such forms has definite evidence of intent to contract: "________ as seller, agrees to sell to ________ as buyer, and buyer agrees to purchase from seller the following described property. . . ."

Often, contracts are negotiated not through the use of forms but through very informal procedures. For example, the buyer's offer may come in the form of a letter or memorandum, and we need to find language that shows present intent to contract. Language such as, "I'm considering buying," "Would you consider selling?" or "What would your asking price be?" is not indicative of present intent to contract. These are inquiries or invitations for offers.

Likewise, memoranda or correspondence from seller to buyer that includes language such as, "I might sell," "I'd consider selling," "I'm thinking of offering," or "In December, I'll offer" is too conditional and is not enough for an offer.

Not only must the offer show intent to contract, it must also contain sufficient information and details: the identity of the parties, the description of the property, the price, and the terms (to be discussed in detail). Form purchase contracts list all required information. If one of the basic requirements for formation is missing, then the offer is really just an invitation for an offer or simply a step in the negotiation process. A complete sales contract can be seen at the text website for this chapter.

The final requirement for a valid offer is communication to the offeree. In practice, communication to the offeree comes when the purchase contract form with the buyer's signature is given to the seller or the agent or broker of the seller.

CONSIDER 14.1

Determine if the following language from a letter by Thompson to Hale (the lot owner) meets the requirements for a valid offer:

I am very much interested in your lot, zoned C-2, which is located at the southeastern corner of Gilbert and Southern Roads. If the price is $475,000 or less, I can pay cash. I will need it for construction by 6/1/08.

/s/ Walter Thompson

Termination

An offer is not legally binding and may be revoked or withdrawn at any time prior to acceptance by the offeree (note, as discussed in the section following, an option is a different type of offer). When an offer is voluntarily withdrawn prior to acceptance, the offeror has not breached any contract because it was not yet formed and has no liability for any damages others may have incurred in relying on the offer.

An offer can be limited in time, with a specified ending date, but unless it is an option, it can still be revoked prior to that ending date. The offeror must let the offeree know of the revocation because the offeree still has the power of acceptance until he or she knows of the revocation. For example, a valid offer may include as one of its terms, "This offer good only until noon on April 5, 2008." This offer would automatically terminate at that time and date unless the offeree accepts prior to that time. Even offers without specific time limits terminate after a reasonable amount of time, although it is probably best for the offerors to withdraw or revoke any long-outstanding offers. What is a reasonable time varies according to the nature and location of the property and the terms of the offer.

The death of either an offeror or the offeree terminates the offer (with an exception noted in the next section "Options"). At the moment of death, the offer is automatically terminated or withdrawn.

Rejection of the offer by the offeree terminates the original offer. A rejection is a negative response, such as, "No, I'm not interested." But a rejection may be given indirectly. If an offeree makes the acceptance of an offer conditional on certain additional terms and requirements, the acceptance is both a rejection of the original offer and a **counteroffer**, placing the original offeree in an offeror position. The following sequence of excerpts from correspondence illustrates this point.

a. Offeror: "*I will buy Blackacre (legal description) from you for $300,000 cash, to close 6/1/08.*"
b. Offeree (counteroffer): "*I accept your offer, but must have cash in hand by 5/1/08.*"
c. Offeree (original offeror): "*That is agreeable.*"

When the offeree conditioned acceptance on a change in closing date (b), the acceptance was a counteroffer that the original offeror, now an offeree, was free to accept or reject. The contract was formed when the original offeror (now offeree) agreed to the change in terms.

In practice, when brokers and salespeople run between buyer and seller with changes in terms and addenda to the purchase contract, they are engaging in negotiation and the parties are constantly changing roles as offerors and offerees. The offeree must accept all of the offeror's terms without change or qualification for a contract to be formed. Any change, under the common law rules that apply to all real estate contracts, results in a rejection and a counteroffer.

Options

Requirements

Often a buyer is unsure about purchasing property and wants time to do research or just to make the decision. However, since an offer may be revoked by the offeror any time prior to acceptance, the opportunity to purchase may pass while the buyer researches and debates the purchase. The buyer would like some type of guarantee that the offer will remain open for a stated period of time. However, simply having the seller include a time provision in the offer ("This offer to remain open until June 15, 2008") is not foolproof, as noted earlier. The offeror can still revoke the offer any time prior to acceptance and with notice of that revocation.

However, if the buyer obtains an option from the seller, this problem is alleviated. An **option** is a contract for time whereby the seller agrees to hold an offer open for a specified period in exchange for consideration (payment). Either a buyer or seller can turn an offer into an option with proper consideration from the offeree.

An option is different from an ordinary offer because the offeree gives consideration to the offeror to keep the offer open. An option is, in effect, a contract for time that is paid for. If an offeror has been paid for an option on property and sells the property to another party, the offeror is in breach of contract and will be required to pay damages to the option holder. The amount of consideration is not important so long as it is actually paid. The following case deals with the issue of consideration in options.

Board of Control of Eastern Michigan University v. Burgess

206 N.W.2d 256 (Mich. 1973)

FACTS

On February 15, 1966, Burgess (defendant/appellant) signed a document that provided Eastern Michigan University (EMU/plaintiff/appellee) a 60-day option for the purchase of Burgess's home. The document, drafted by an agent of Burgess, indicated receipt of "one and no/100 Dollar ($1.00) and other valuable consideration." The dollar was never paid. On April 14, 1966, EMU notified Burgess of its acceptance, but Burgess refused to close and deliver title. EMU brought suit for delivery of the property or specific performance. The trial court found for EMU, and Burgess appealed.

JUDICIAL OPINION

Burns, Judge. Options for the purchase of land, if based on valid consideration, are contracts which may be specifically enforced. Conversely, that which purports to be an option, but which is not based on valid consideration, is not a contract and will not be enforced. In the instant case defendant received no consideration for the purported option of February 15, 1966.

A written acknowledgment of receipt of consideration merely creates a rebuttable presumption that consideration has, in fact, passed. Neither the parol evidence rule nor the doctrine of estoppel bars the presentation of evidence to contradict any such acknowledgment.

It is our opinion that the document signed by Burgess on February 15, 1966, is not an enforceable option, and that Burgess is not barred from so asserting. In the instant case Burgess claims that she never received any of the consideration promised here.

That which purports to be an option for the purchase of land, but which is not based on valid consideration, is a simple offer to sell the same land. An option is a contract collateral to an offer to sell whereby the offer is made irrevocable for a specified period. Ordinarily, an offer is revocable at the will of the offeror. Accordingly, a failure of consideration affects only the collateral contract to keep the offer open, not the underlying offer.

A simple offer may be revoked for any reason or for no reason by the offeror at any time prior to its acceptance by the offeree. Thus, the question in this case becomes, "Did defendant effectively revoke her offer to sell before plaintiff accepted that offer?"

Defendant testified that within hours of signing the purported option she telephoned plaintiff's agent and informed him that she would not abide by the option unless the purchase price was increased. Defendant also testified that when plaintiff's agent delivered to her on April 14, 1966, plaintiff's notice of its intention to exercise the purported option, she told him that "the option was off."

Plaintiff's agent testified that defendant did not communicate to him any dissatisfaction until sometime in July 1966.

If defendant is telling the truth, she effectively revoked her offer several weeks before plaintiff accepted that offer, and no contract of sale was created. If plaintiff's agent is telling the truth, defendant's offer was still open when plaintiff accepted that offer, and an enforceable contract was created. The trial judge thought it unnecessary to resolve this particular dispute. In light of our holding the dispute must be resolved.

An appellate court cannot assess the credibility of witnesses. We have neither seen nor heard them testify.

Accordingly, we remand this case to the trial court for additional findings of fact based on the record already before the court.

Reversed and remanded.

CASE QUESTIONS

1. How long was the option?
2. What property was involved?
3. How much was the consideration?
4. Was the consideration paid?
5. Was there a valid option?
6. What issue remains to be determined?

CONSIDER 14.2

On February 7, 2007, A entered into negotiations with B for the purchase of B's farm. After consulting with an attorney and having the property appraised, B agreed to sell for $750,000. A and B agreed in writing that in exchange for $1,000 then received from A, B would hold the offer open for nine months. After six months, A wrote B that he was no longer interested in buying the farm. Several days later, A received notice from B that he was negotiating with C to sell the farm for $950,000. A immediately called B, who

(continued)

suggested that if A would agree to pay $875,000 and conclude the deal within 10 days, then B would still be willing to sell to A. A protested that B was driving a hard bargain, but finally agreed by telegram that evening to buy the farm for $875,000 within 10 days. A purchased the farm as agreed and then sought to recover $125,000 from B or alternatively to rescind the purchase (in other words, get out of the contract). What result and why?

CONSIDER 14.3

A seller and buyer signed a memorandum entitled "*PROPOSED OPTION AGREEMENT COMPONENTS.*" The memorandum agreement states,

1. Grant of $500 for a six-week option to purchase property with amount paid credited against the purchase price in the event option is exercised; any amounts paid in option extension(s) will also be credited.

Is there an option? Is it enforceable? What advice could you give the parties on their memorandum? *Reardon v. Lautner*, 1997 WL 33343924 (Mich.App. unpublished opinion)

Termination

Another distinguishing feature about an option is that, unlike an ordinary offer, it does not terminate with the death of the offeror or the option holder. In other words, the estate of an option holder could elect to exercise the option for the estate. Likewise, the estate of the offeror is required to honor the option if the option holder decides to exercise the right after the death of the offeror.

Another issue in options is what happens when the option holder rejects the option prior to the given ending date. For example, A gives B an option on some property to run from February 1, 2007, to March 2, 2007, and B pays A $1,000 for the option. On February 16, 2007, B notifies A that he is rejecting the offer. The following questions arise: (1) Must A still hold the offer open until March 2, 2007? (2) Is B entitled to a refund of a portion of the option payment? (3) Must A refund a portion of the option payment in order to sell the property prior to March 2, 2007?

The jurisdictions are split on the answers to the questions raised by the option holder's rejection prior to the option's expiration date. One view is that rejection is rejection; that is, an option is an offer that terminates once rejected by the option holder (offeree). The majority view is that a rejection before the option term has no effect on the option; that is, that the option continues until the ending date unless the offeror has materially changed position. Under this view, if the parties agreed to a partial refund and signed a mutual release terminating the option, then the offeror would be free to sell the property to another. Under the first view, release and refund would not be required for the offeror to be free to transfer the property.

In light of the split among the courts on how options are to be handled in the event of rejection prior to their expiration, it is probably best for the parties to put a clause in their option agreement that deals with early rejection and the offeror's and option holder's rights.

The following list of topics is important when negotiating and drafting option agreements:

- Legal description of the property
- Proper names of the parties
- Signatures of the parties
- Length of the option

- Beginning and ending dates of the option period
- Amount of consideration to be paid
- Destiny of the consideration if
  a. the option is exercised: Can it be a down payment?
  b. the option expires without acceptance: Does the offeror retain the money?
  c. the option holder rejects prior to expiration: Will there be a prorated refund?
  d. the property is destroyed during the option period
  e. one of the parties dies
- Recording of the option in the public records and its removal if not exercised
- Procedures and notifications required for exercise of the option
- All terms or provisions of the sales contract:
  a. marketable title (type of deed, insurance, and so on)
  b. rights of lessees
  c. presence of mortgages and new liens during the option period
- Assignability of the option

Options are not earnest money deposits—the down payments by buyers that accompany offers for buying real property. Earnest money is appropriately named because it is customarily required to show the offeror's good faith and is actually part of the payment for the purchase price. Options generally come from sellers and are promises to hold offers open for periods of time. Payment for an option is not necessarily a payment of part of the purchase price. Furthermore, consideration is required for an option to be valid, whereas earnest money is not required for a valid contract to purchase (although it may be good business practice).

Acceptance

Acceptance is conduct by the offeree that indicates a willingness to take the terms of the offer. Acceptance is the second part of the so-called meeting-of-the-minds requirement for formation of a contract. Like the offer, acceptance has certain requirements: (1) it must be by the party with the power of acceptance; (2) it must be absolute, unequivocal, and unconditional; and (3) it must be communicated to the offeror.

Power of Acceptance

The only party with the power of acceptance is the party to whom the offer is made. Offers are not transferable. Options are an exception to this rule. Options, like all nonpersonal contracts, are transferable. An assignment of an option right gives the assignee the right to exercise the option.

Absolute, Unequivocal, and Unconditional Acceptance

This requirement for acceptance was briefly explained in the discussion of termination of offers. The offeree must accept the offer on its terms and must not change those or make acceptance conditional on new or different terms. If the offeree does make any changes in the terms, then there is no acceptance; rather, there is a counteroffer that the original offeror (now offeree) is free to accept or reject.

CONSIDER 14.4

Terry and Marianne Jennings listed their home for sale with Stapley Realty. When the listing agent, Brad Reed, came to the home, he asked if there was anything that was attached to the house that would not be sold with the house. Mr. Jennings pointed to an original Hunter ceiling fan and said it would not stay with the house since he had installed it himself. Reed told the Jennings that it would be best to remove the fan and

CONSIDER 14.4

(continued)

replace it with another lighting fixture or fan. They agreed and planned to do the replacement on Saturday. On Friday afternoon, the "For Sale" sign and the lock-box for real estate agent access went on their property. On Saturday morning another agent taking a couple to another home noticed the Jennings's house, which had not yet appeared in the multiple listing. He took the couple through it and that night they made an offer on it. The Jennings accepted all the terms because they had only 90 days to sell their home and move to another one. Mr. Jennings noted above his signature, "Ceiling fan in family room is not included." The buyers then refused to go through with the sale. The Jennings wish to know if they have any rights. Is there a contract?

Communication of Acceptance to Offeror

The signature on the purchase contract alone is insufficient acceptance: A copy of that agreement must be delivered to the offeror or the offeror's agent for a valid contract to exist. When there is electronic communication (see discussion under the writing requirement that follows), an electronic record is sent when it is properly directed to the system used by the receipient for electronic communication (e.g. john.smith@cpan.net), it is in a form that can be read by the recipient, and only the recipient can control access to the content of the record.

Many times, an offer will dictate the means of acceptance. It may require acceptance to be by mail or personal delivery, or to be given within a certain period of time. The offeree must comply with these requirements for the acceptance to be valid; otherwise, acceptance by some means other than what the offeree specified is a counteroffer.

The following case deals with several issues of offer and acceptance.

Norkunas v. Cochran

895 A.2d 1101 (Ca. App. Md. 2006)

FACTS

Eileen Norkunas (appellant) owns a residence at 835 McHenry Street, Baltimore City, Maryland. Robert and Hope Grove and Robert and Rebecca Cochran (appellees) approached Ms. Norkunas and expressed their interest in purchasing the property. Assisted by a real estate agent, the four hopeful buyers gave Ms. Norkunas a handwritten letter of intent together with a check for a $5,000 deposit. The text of the letter of intent is as follows:

3/7/04

LETTER OF INTENT

We, Rebecca Cochran, Robert Cochran, Hope Grove and Robert Grove, Buyers-offer to buy 835 McHenry Street, Baltimore, Md. 21230 for $162,000. Payment by $5,000 check, this date and $157,000 by certified or cashiers funds not later than April 17, 2004.

A standard form Maryland Realtors contract will be delivered to Seller within 48 hours. Seller to pay only 1/2 normal transfer taxes and a 3% commission to Long & Foster. All other costs of closing to be paid by buyers.

The contract will contain a financing requirement for buyers, but buyers will guarantee closing and not invoke the financing contingency.

We will delete the standard home inspection contingency. [written in margin:] Buyer to honor Seller's lease and offer tenants any renewal up to 12 months.

The letter of intent was signed by the Groves and the Cochrans under "Buyers," by Ms. Norkunas under "Seller," and by Brian Best under "Agent."

Within a day or so after signing the letter of intent, Ms. Norkunas received a package of documents from the buyers' agent with a cover letter that stated:

Dear Ms. Norkunas,

It was a pleasure meeting you yesterday. Enclosed with this folder are all the documents needed to complete the sale of your home. The basic Real Estate contract, along with a couple of documents I need you to fill out to ratify the contract. The first is a Disclosure/Disclaimer. You can either fill out the first 3 pages (the Disclosure) or you can just sign the last page (the Disclaimer). Also included is a property fact sheet. This is just basic information on the property that needs to accompany the

contract. The Groves and the Cochrans are so excited about your home. If you have ANY questions please feel free to call me or have someone near you look over the contract. Rest assure[d] that we want this to go as smooth as possible for you and both the Groves and Cochrans asked me to tell you if there is anything they can do please feel free to ask. I look forward to hearing from you.
You can either fax me the contract and disclaimer back or I[']ll include a Fed-X envelope for you to send back.
Thank you again[.]

The package of documents ("the buyers' offer") contained a number of pre-printed forms, including a form titled "Residential Contract of Sale," published by the Maryland Association of Realtors®, together with 10 or more form addenda. Many of the addenda appear to be forms. At least one of the addenda appears to be a form that the buyers' broker developed. Some of the documents had blanks filled in or altered by the buyers. The price and description of the property were the same as in the letter of intent. The form financing contingency had been filled in with details. A separate Property Inspections contingency addendum was included, but appears to have been struck through as promised in the letter of intent.

Ms. Norkunas never did return the documents to the buyers or their agent. Nor did she otherwise communicate to the buyers or their agent that their offer had been accepted. After a week or so had passed, the buyers were eventually told that Ms. Norkunas was "taking the property off the market."

The buyers filed suit seeking specific performance of the letter of intent. Ms. Norkunas had, in the privacy of her home, signed the documents, striking through two paragraphs relating to the financing contingency, and making some other marks on the documents. At her deposition, Ms. Norkunas explained:

I was probably going through it at the time and kind of getting overwhelmed the more I went through it and questioning parts and kind of scratching out some parts. This was what I thought was going to be my counteroffer. I signed what I thought was going to be a counteroffer, and then it just got so overwhelming, it was too much. It was just too much.

The Circuit Court for Baltimore City granted summary judgment for the buyers. Ms. Norkunas appealed.

JUDICIAL OPINION

Meredith, Judge. Letters of intent have led to much misunderstanding, litigation, and commercial chaos. Courts have expressed reservation concerning the binding nature of "letters of intent" because traditionally, the purpose and function of a preliminary letter of intent has been to merely provide the initial framework from which the parties might later negotiate a final binding agreement. Calling a document a "letter of intent" implies, *unless circumstances suggest otherwise*, that the parties intended it to be a nonbinding expression in contemplation of a future contract. As is commonly the case with contract disputes, prime significance attaches to the intentions of the parties and to their manifestations of intent. Labels such as "letter of intent" or "commitment letter" are not necessarily controlling, although they may be helpful indicators of the parties' intentions.

The buyers in this case contend that the letter of intent signed by Ms. Norkunas falls into that first category of enforceable agreement, and that it therefore required no further formalization. When we analyze the language of the letter of intent, however, we find that the parties merely agreed that the buyers would submit a more detailed formal offer.

The buyers argue that a reasonable person in the position of Ms. Norkunas should have known when she signed the letter of intent that she had already sold her home to these buyers, and that there would be no further negotiations and no opportunity for her to further consider whether she wanted to sell her property upon the terms set forth in the letter. The plain language of the letter, however, simply does not say that.

In the first paragraph, the letter of intent states that the buyers "offer to buy" the property, but there is no statement anywhere in the letter that could be construed as a statement that Ms. Norkunas agrees to accept the offer or agrees to sell the property upon the terms set forth. The letter states that a "standard form Maryland Realtors contract will be delivered to Seller." The letter further states that "[t]he contract will contain ..." certain language, and that other language "will" be deleted from the contract. In our view, a reasonable person in the position of a seller who was approached by buyers indicating they wanted to purchase her home would have understood the letter of intent to mean that a formal contract offer would soon follow. The reasonable person in Ms. Norkunas's position would have understood that these buyers wanted her to know the terms they were prepared to offer and that they were very seriously interested in purchasing the property. The terms of this letter would not communicate to such a seller, however, that if she signed this document she was irrevocably locked into a contract of sale.

The delivery of the referenced check for $5,000 does not elevate the letter beyond the status of an offer. It is customary for most real estate offers to be accompanied by a check tendered as a good faith deposit or "earnest money." Moreover, the buyers did not allege, either in their complaint or in the documents filed in connection with the cross motions for summary judgment, that Ms. Norkunas ever negotiated the $5,000 check that accompanied the letter of intent.

The letter of intent did not contain any commitment by Ms. Norkunas to sell her property to the buyers upon the terms they indicated they would include in a more formal offer to follow. Her signature did nothing more than acknowledge that she was aware of the letter of intent.

The buyers argue, in the alternative, that even if the letter of intent was not an enforceable contract, the buyers' formal offer as expressed in the subsequent package of documents became a binding enforceable contract when Ms. Norkunas placed her signature on the documents. We do not agree that there has been irrevocable acceptance when an offeree privately signs an offer but then decides not to communicate her acceptance to the offeror. It is apparent that Ms. Norkunas had second thoughts about the advisability of this transaction, and she never communicated to the buyers or their agent that she had signed the buyers' offer. We do not agree, however, that the buyers' offer was transformed into a contract the instant that the offeree privately signed the offer.

[T]he Court of Appeals noted that Maryland has long followed the rule known as the "postal acceptance rule" or "The Rule in *Adams v. Lindsell* [1, Barn. & Ald. 681, 106 Eng. Rep. 250 (1818, King's Bench)]" for determining when an offer received via mail has been accepted.

Professor Corbin, after reviewing the logical difficulties which the rule presents and the considerations of policy for and against the continuation of the rule, concludes that it is probably wiser to continue it. He aptly stated in 1 *Corbin*, §78, page 337:

One of the parties must carry the risk of loss and inconvenience. We need a definite and uniform rule as to this. We can choose either rule; but we must choose one. We can put the risk on either party; but we must not leave it in doubt. The party not carrying the risk can then act promptly and with confidence in reliance on the contract; the party carrying the risk can insure against it if he so desires. The business community could no doubt adjust itself to either rule; but the rule throwing the risk on the offeror has the merit of closing the deal more quickly and enabling performance more promptly. It must be remembered that in the vast majority of cases the acceptance is neither lost nor delayed; and promptness of action is of importance in all of them. Also it is the offeror who has invited the acceptance.

The analogous rule for when acceptance takes effect appears in the RESTATEMENT (SECOND) OF CONTRACTS (1981) in Section 63, which states:
Unless the offer provides otherwise,

(a) an acceptance made in a manner and by a medium invited by an offer is operative and completes the manifestation of mutual assent as soon as put out of the offeree's possession, without regard to whether it ever reaches the offeror; but

(b) an acceptance under an option contract is not operative until received by the offeror.

Applying these rules to the undisputed facts of this case, it is clear that, even if Ms. Norkunas's signature of the buyers' offer was intended to be an acceptance (as opposed to a counter-offer), acceptance would not have taken effect until the signed documents were either mailed by her, or until they were otherwise put out of her possession, for example by fax or transmittal to the buyers' agent. The evidence was undisputed that she did neither, but rather, retained possession of the documents until being forced by the rules of discovery to permit her opponents to inspect and copy the papers.

Here, the buyers urge us to adopt a rule that considers the offeree's acceptance binding and irrevocable as soon as the offeree affixes her signature to the offer. We observe that such a rule could create more controversies than it resolved.

Because the evidence was undisputed that Ms. Norkunas never transmitted to the buyers or their agent the documents she had marked up, we need not further analyze whether the changes made by her to the buyers' offer were of such significance to the transaction that her alleged acceptance was in fact a counter-offer. In this case, Ms. Norkunas communicated nothing to the buyers until she advised them that she was taking her property off the market. Consequently, we need not determine whether the changes made by her to the documents would have required further assent from the buyers to complete formation of the alleged contract.

It is not clear from the record what became of the buyers' check for earnest money. Nor is it clear whether there are any further issues to be resolved by the circuit court in light of our holding that there was no enforceable contract for the sale of 835 McHenry Street. The buyers did not allege in the complaint or in their cross motion for summary judgment that Ms. Norkunas negotiated the $5,000 check, but if the deposit check was negotiated, the position asserted by Ms. Norkunas in this case provides no basis for her to refuse to return any funds she received from the buyers.

Reversed.

CASE QUESTIONS

1. What is the law on letters of intent and contract formation?
2. Why is Ms. Norkunas's signature on the contract forms not formation of a contract?
3. What requirement for formation is missing and why does the court find this element to be required and controlling?

CONSIDER 14.5

Reed Gilmore filed an oil and gas application for Parcel NV-148 in June 1987 with the Bureau of Land Management (BLM). His application was selected in a computerized random drawing. BLM notified Gilmore by an August 26 letter sent certified mail that included the following language:

Enclosed is the original and two copies of Form No. 3100–11, "Offer to Lease and Lease for Oil and Gas" for your execution. The applicant (or the applicant's attorney-in-fact, as provided by 43 C.F.R. [§]3112.6–1(a) and (b) [(1986)]), must manually sign and date each copy on the reverse side of the form.

All copies of the lease form must be properly executed and filed in this office within thirty (30) days from your receipt of this decision, which constitutes a compliance period. Failure to do so will result in the rejection of your offer without further notice.

Gilmore received the letter on August 29, 1987. He signed the copies and sent them certified mail from his office in Kimball, Nebraska, on September 21, 1987, with a return receipt requested. On the morning of September 28, 1987, Gilmore's secretary, Debra Bohac, noticed that she had not yet received the return receipt card. September 28 was the 30-day deadline.

Bohac called the BLM and spoke with Joan Woodin to see if the forms had been received. While there was subsequent disagreement about the full content of the conversation, Woodin and Bohac agreed that Woodin told her the forms had not been received.

Bohac then tried to book a flight for Gilmore to Reno, but there were no flights available that would get Gilmore there before the BLM office closed. Bohac then called the BLM back and spoke with Bernita Dawson, a Land Law Examiner in the BLM. Bohac offered to telefax (fax) the lease forms and maintains Dawson agreed to take the faxes as acceptance. Dawson denies making such a statement.

Gilmore then sent a telecopy to Robert McCarthy, a Reno attorney, who delivered it to the BLM at 11:15 A.M. on September 28. The mailed originals were received in the BLM office the next day, September 29. BLM informed Gilmore on September 29 that his offer was rejected for failure to comply with the terms. The decision was affirmed by the overall agency and Gilmore filed suit in federal district court. The district court dismissed the case, and Gilmore appealed. *Gilmore v. Lujan*, 947 F.2d 1409 (9th Cir. 1991)

ETHICAL ISSUE

Andrew and Joyce Kay Pride moved to a farm and placed their house for sale with Priority One Realty. The house sat empty for some time; Mr. and Mrs. Pride then found a tenant to rent the house until such time as it sold. The tenant rented the house for $450 per month.

In April 2003 Larry Lewis made an offer to purchase the house for $55,000, with earnest money in the amount of $1,500. During this time, Mr. Lewis was married to Issoline Lewis. The first contract offered by Mr. Lewis required Mr. and Mrs. Pride to owner finance the transaction. This offer was rejected by Mr. and Mrs. Pride. Mr. Lewis then presented a second contract. Mr. and Mrs. Pride also presented a second contract, already signed by Mr. Lewis and his real estate agent. This contract specified conventional bank financing would be used. The contract stated that Mr. and Mrs. Pride were selling the house to Larry and Issoline Lewis. Mr. Lewis signed the contract on April 9, 2003. His agent also signed the contract, although the date is not indicated. Mrs. Lewis never signed the contract. Mr. and Mrs. Pride, as well as their agent, signed the real estate contract on April 11, 2003. Upon signing the contract, Mr. and Mrs. Pride informed their tenant that she would have to vacate the house by June 1, 2003. The contract provided by Mr. Lewis had a closing date of May 15, 2003. Mr. and Mrs. Pride changed this date, by hand, to June 1, 2003. This change was initialed by Mr. and Mrs. Pride, but not by Mr. Lewis or Mrs. Lewis.

ETHICAL ISSUE

(continued)

Mr. and Mrs. Pride were prepared to close on the property on June 1, 2004, but neither Mr. Lewis, Mrs. Lewis, nor their agent ever appeared. Mr. and Mrs. Pride's agent contacted Mr. Lewis's agent and was informed that Mr. Lewis had not responded to phone calls or otherwise communicated. Mr. Lewis testified that he thought "they were going to try to [close] early June, and that's the last I knew." When the closing with Mr. Lewis failed to occur, Mr. and Mrs. Pride sent him a letter notifying him of his default and their electing not to take the $1,500 earnest money as damages.

Mr. and Mrs. Pride sued Mr. Lewis for breach of contract. They sought damages for the difference between the $55,000 contract price with Mr. Lewis and the $40,000 for which the house actually sold, for the lost rent for a year, for which they were unable to find another tenant, and for attorney's fees, as provided in the contract. The trial court entered judgment in favor of Mr. and Mrs. Pride. Mr. Lewis appealed. Determine the parties' contractual rights. Then evaluate the ethics of their conduct with each other. *Pride v. Lewis*, 179 S.W.3d 375 (Mo. App. 2005)

PROBLEM OF MULTIPLE OFFERS

Because acceptance is effective upon communication to the offeror, an offeror who has made more than one offer may find two acceptances being communicated before one or both of the offers can be revoked. It is a major legal risk for an offeror to have more than one offer outstanding. Consider the following sequence of events as an example:

> ***Practical Tip***
>
> *Deal with one party at a time. Multiple offers create confusion and liability. Make sure there is only one outstanding valid offer at a time. Don't extend another offer until an outstanding offer is revoked.*

Day 1: Buyer A submits an offer to seller.
Day 2: Seller counteroffers to buyer A. Buyer B submits an offer to seller.
Day 3: Seller counteroffers to buyer B. Buyer A accepts. Before seller can revoke, buyer B accepts.

The seller in the example has formed two valid contracts and would have to convey the property to one buyer and pay damages for breach to the other buyer.

CONSIDER 14.6

Cynthia has listed her home with We Sell 'Em Realty, Incorporated. Buyer A conveys a written offer of $283,000 to Cynthia on March 1, 2008. Buyer B conveys an offer of $284,000 to Cynthia on March 2, 2008. On March 2, 2008, Cynthia issues counteroffers of $285,000 to both A and B. On the counteroffers, Cynthia adds the following: "This offer good until March 4, 2008, 6 P.M."

Suppose Buyer A accepts on March 3, 2008 (written forms signed), and communicates the acceptance to Cynthia at 7 P.M. that day. Cynthia then contacts Buyer B and says, "I revoke the counteroffer." What is the result?

a. Suppose that before Cynthia contacts B, B contacts Cynthia and accepts at 2:15 P.M. (written forms signed). What would be the result?
b. Suppose that B paid Cynthia $500 to hold the offer open until March 4, 2008, 6 P.M. What would be the result?
c. Suppose same facts as part b except that B calls Cynthia at 1 P.M., March 3, 2008, and states, "I reject," whereupon Cynthia receives A's acceptance. What would be the result?

Consideration

The third and final requirement for formation of a valid contract is consideration. **Consideration** is something of value given up by each party to the contract. In most cases involving a sale of real property, consideration is easily established: The seller gives up title to the property, and the buyer gives up money, assumes a mortgage, or both in order to pay for that property.

Consideration need not be money. As noted, the buyer's promise to take over a loan is sufficient consideration. The traditional earnest money deposit received from buyers in a real estate transaction is a form of consideration but is not required for the contract to be valid and binding. Both parties' promises to give something up in the transaction promises constitute sufficient consideration. However, earnest money does demonstrate sincerity and good faith on the part of the buyer and may be used as a source of funds for damages in the event of a problem.

The amount of consideration is not of legal concern to the courts, so long as there is consideration and it passes from one party to the other. A promise to pay $50,000 for property worth $200,000 is valid consideration provided that each party voluntarily agrees to the terms.

The following case deals with the sufficiency of consideration in a real estate purchase agreement.

Trengen v. Mongeon

206 N.W.2d 284 (N.D. 1973)

FACTS

On May 9, 1967, Louis and Margaret Mongeon executed a warranty deed conveying approximately 960 acres of land to their son Ernest and his wife, Pearl (defendant/appellee). The deed contained an acknowledgment of the receipt of $38,400 as consideration for the conveyance. At the same time, the parties entered into an agreement whereby Ernest and Pearl agreed to pay to Louis and Margaret the sum of $1,800 annually for as long as both or the survivor of them shall live. At the time of the agreement, Louis was 87 and Margaret was 83. Ernest's sister, Elaine Trengen (plaintiff/appellant, as guardian for her parents), brought suit seeking to set the deed aside on the grounds of lack of consideration. The trial court found for Ernest and Pearl, and Elaine appealed.

JUDICIAL OPINION

Teigen, Judge. In the present case the consideration is of an indeterminable value. Monetarily, payment of the sum of $1,800 was made in the fall of 1967, and that sum will continue to be payable on or before November 1 of every year for as long as both or the survivor of the plaintiffs shall live. Payments received by the plaintiffs to the present time total $10,800.

... Since adequacy of consideration is not necessary to sustain a deed, and any valuable consideration, however small, is sufficient, the consideration need not equal the value of the property conveyed, especially where no creditor's rights are affected. Indeed, the merely nominal consideration of one dollar, which is frequently recited in deeds, evidences a sufficient consideration. So, where, as compared with the actual value of the property or interest received, the consideration is adequate, the deed will stand, whether such consideration be merely a valuable one without any monetary payment or a valuable one coupled with pecuniary advances. Adequacy of monetary consideration is not an important element in a conveyance which has for its principal purpose the conferring of a gift or endowment rather than financial gain. The adequacy of consideration is not to be viewed with hindsight, but it should rather be considered from the viewpoint of the parties at the time the deed was executed. The ordinary standard for testing the adequacy of consideration to support a transfer of property is not applicable to a deed conveying realty on condition that the grantee care for the grantor during the remainder of the grantor's life because of the uncertainty of life involved in such agreements. In considering the adequacy of consideration of a promise to care for and support a grantor for the remainder of his life in exchange for a conveyance of land, conditions existing at the time the contract is made are controlling, and subsequent events, such as the early death of the person to be cared for cannot be used to determine the adequacy of the consideration.

The trial court also found that the plaintiff's love and affection for their son Ernest was both a motivating factor and part of the consideration for the transaction.

Natural love and affection has always been held to be sufficient consideration for a deed where the relationship of the parties is such as to justify the presumption that love and affection exists.

The love and affection the plaintiffs (parents) felt toward Ernest is evidenced by the fact that, as stated in the agreement, the land in question had been devised to Ernest by the wills of both Louis and Margaret, and nine days after the land was conveyed to Ernest and the defendant (Pearl), Louis and Margaret executed new wills, each of which contained this provision:

I have purposely omitted my son, Ernest Mongeon, as a devisee or legatee under this Will, for the reason that my [wife, Margaret Mongeon] [husband, Louis Mongeon] and I have made disposition of substantial farmlands to him during our lifetime for a fair consideration ... [emphasis added].

We conclude that, in the absence of a finding of fraud or undue influence, the evidence is sufficient to support a finding that there was adequate consideration to uphold the conveyance of the land from the plaintiffs to Ernest and the defendant.

Affirmed.

CASE QUESTIONS

1. What was the relationship between Louis and Margaret and Ernest and Pearl?
2. How much land was conveyed?
3. What was the total price?
4. How was the price to be paid?
5. How old were Louis and Margaret at the time of the conveyance?
6. Was there consideration?

Specific Requirements for Real Estate Contracts

In addition to meeting the common law requirements just discussed, a valid real estate purchase contract must also meet certain specific requirements that are peculiar to real estate transactions. The following are the requirements: (1) that the contract be in the form of a record, such as a written agreement, (2) that the parties sign or authenticate the contract, and (3) that the description of the property be adequate.

Writing or Record Requirements

As discussed in Chapter 13, the Statute of Frauds includes real estate contracts as the type of agreement that must be evidenced by a record. The nature of the requirements for the Statute of Frauds has changed with the use of electronic communication. The Electronic Signatures in Global and National Commerce Act (E-Sign), passed by the federal government, requires that electronically signed contracts be given equal legal effect with traditional paper contracts. Under E-Sign, the states can modify the effects of E-Sign if they enact the Uniform Electronic Transactions Act (UETA), which allows electronic signatures, even signatures of notaries for contract formation, in audits, and as evidence in court and other legal proceedings. Called the rule of parity, UETA provides that electronic and paper records and signatures are given the same legal effect, with some exceptions. Exceptions include wills and codicials (See Chapter 17), testamentary trusts, and commercial paper such as checks and letters of credit. When consumers are involved in the contracts, they must agree to communication and negotiation via electronic means before they can be bound by electronic records. Before electronic communication, the type of record had to be a written contract. Now with the impact of E-Sign, courts must recognize electronic forms of communication, such as faxes and electronic agreements. However, even with the recognition of electronic contracts, there is a form of a record of a transaction. Oral agreements for the transfer of property remain unenforceable. And, standard industry practice for the listing, sale, and purchase of real property is to have all documents and signatures reduced to paper form. While those in the real estate field rely on fax communications, they continue to finalize with paper agreements and signatures.

> **Practical Tip**
>
> *Always follow up on electronic communications, particularly acceptances, to be sure that the party received the communications and that whoever is accepting an offer truly is the same party who is sending the e-mail. Most lawyers always follow up electronic or fax communication with paper verification to close the loop on proof that the electronic communication was with the correct party and was indeed received.*

A contract and its terms may be pieced together from informal exchanges, whether on paper or electronically, as long as all the requirements for formation are met and the necessary elements are present.

One of the exceptions to the writing or record requirements for real estate contracts under the Statute of Frauds is the doctrine of part performance. Under this doctrine, a party may be entitled to enforce an oral agreement for the sale of property on the basis of conduct. Under Section 197 of the *Restatement of Contracts*, the party who wants to use the doctrine of part performance to enforce an oral agreement must establish one of the following:

1. That valuable improvements have been made to the property; or
2. That there has been full or partial payment of the purchase price and that the party who has paid money has possession of the property.

Establishing either of these circumstances provides some tangible physical evidence that the parties had an agreement. In other words, if a contract did not exist, why would the improvements have been made, or why was payment accepted but the paying party not permitted to possess the property? While some states do not recognize the doctrine of part performance at all, some states recognize variations. For example, some states require possession only, while other states require payment, or improvements, or both.

CONSIDER 14.7

Hancock Construction maintained that it had an oral agreement to purchase property from Kempton & Snedigar Dairy. On the basis of the oral contract, Hancock had engineering studies done on the property and arranged to obtain a loan for $292,830. Kempton & Snedigar refused to go through with the contract, alleging a defense of the Statute of Frauds. Hancock brought suit for specific performance relying on the doctrine of part performance. What is the result?

Signature of Parties

Authentication, through written signature or electronic verification, is required for real estate contracts. Again, each state is left to determine appropriate standards for electronic contracts and signatures and verification of their authenticity.

In addition to obtaining authentication, the parties should verify that the correct and necessary parties have authenticated. In the case of joint owners, both parties must authenticate. In many states both husband and wife must authenticate contracts for the transfer of their property held jointly.

In the case of business organizations such as partnerships and corporations, the authenticating parties must have the authority to transfer property and must indicate their capacity. For example, a corporate officer signing for the corporation should have the following signature line:

ABC Company, Inc.

by ______________________________

Steven Doe, President

Attest ______________________________

John Doe, Secretary

Adequate Description of Property

To satisfy the Statute of Frauds, the property to be conveyed must be adequately described. While the legal description is not required for the purchase contract, it is perhaps the best way to reasonably identify the property and avoid confusion. Without an adequate description, the agreement cannot be enforced. (Chapter 7 provides details on property identification.)

Terms of Purchase Contracts

Mere compliance with Statute of Frauds requirements may not give the parties enough detail for performance or reflect adequately their intentions.

A complete contract begins with a careful review and inspection of the property. Figure 14.1 is a checklist for buyers to complete before purchasing any property.

Figure 14.1 Checklist for Negotiation of Real Estate Contracts

1. Determine exact boundaries of buildings, driveways, and fences.
2. Determine easements and underground utilities.
3. Determine zoning laws and other governmental regulations applicable to property.
4. Determine future or present uses of surrounding property.
5. Determine quality of available utilities and fire protection.
6. Determine rights-of-way or easements if necessary for use of property.
7. Determine locations of schools, public transportation, churches, and shopping centers.
8. Determine physical condition of building: termites, plumbing, electric, and water in basement.
9. Determine traffic conditions on street and surrounding streets.
10. Determine possible changes in traffic and street structure (such as a proposed freeway).
11. Determine possible nuisances: factories, aircraft, playgrounds, smoke, fumes, and noise.
12. Determine title: judgments and assessments.
13. Determine status of inhabitants (if any).
14. Determine soil suitability if intention is to build.
15. Determine if seller is married or was previously married.
16. Determine utility costs.
17. Determine reputation of builder if new development, verify warranties, approval, conformity with Interstate Land Sales Full Disclosure Act (ILSFDA), bonding, and licensing of builder.
18. Determine if any warranty protection is available.
19. Determine whether any toxic wastes exist or have existed on the property and whether any environmental agencies have actions pending.
20. Determine whether the property is located in a natural hazard area: faults, floodplains, and/or shifting soil.

A binder or an intent to contract that is then followed by a formal purchase contract can, as noted in the *Norkunas v. Cochran* case, create a confusing situation. Such binders are hazardous for two reasons: On one hand, it may be so loosely drafted that the parties really have no protections and no locked-in price or terms. On the other hand, it may be drafted carefully enough to legally bind the parties without containing all the terms desired, and the parties may be bound by a general agreement that does not reflect their understanding.

The following sections cover specific issues that the parties' contract should address.

Property Identification

Most purchase contracts (other than those for acreage) give the street address, followed by a clause such as, "and more particularly described as" or "more fully described as" and then the legal description. In many cases, brokers or salespeople will take the description from the listing agreement; however, the best source for the description is the seller's deed.

Following the legal description, a general protection clause (found in many form contracts) should be inserted:

together with all the right, title, and interest of the seller in and to the land lying in the street in front of or adjoining the above described property, to the center lines thereof respectively.

If there is any personal property that will be conveyed with the title to the real property, that property should be listed in the contract. A clause reading, "together with the following personal property ..." may be inserted along with a list of the personal property. Because a deed transfers title to real property only, title to personal property should be handled through a bill of sale, which is in effect a deed for personal property.

The personal property clause is particularly important in the purchase of multiunit dwellings. Since the standards for what constitutes a fixture may vary, it is best to list the property included if there is any doubt. Buyers should verify that the seller actually owns the personal property and whether there are any Article 9 security interests in the property. (See Chapter 5 for a full discussion of security interests.) Identification of the property by serial number provides the buyer with protection against the seller swapping out personal property items prior to closing.

If there are any title limitations such as assessments, easements, or rights-of-way, they should be noted in the contract. A typical provision reads, "subject to rights, rights-of-way, easements, including those for public utilities, water companies, alleys, and streets; assessments and other encumbrances of record." If there are restrictive covenants on the property, they too should be noted. And if the seller needs to reserve or grant an easement, a clause covering and describing that easement issue should also follow the description.

Practical Tip

Be sure to carefully identify the parties to the contract. Below is a checklist.

1. *Name: full name, aliases, and AKAs (also known as). How does a seller's name appear on deed granting title?*
2. *Marital status.*
3. *If legal entity (corporation) is involved:*
   a. *Place incorporated and proper corporate name.*
   b. *Name of president.*
   c. *Name of secretary.*
   d. *Authority of individual signing.*
4. *If partnership is involved:*
   a. *Proper partnership name.*
   b. *Type of partnership (general or limited).*
   c. *Name of partner.*
   d. *Authority of partner.*
5. *If executor for estate is involved:*
   a. *Name of estate.*
   b. *Executor's name and aliases.*
   c. *Executor's appointment and authority.*
6. *If agent acting for another is involved:*
   a. *Name of agent and aliases.*
   b. *Authority of agent (power of attorney).*

Note: Numbers 3–5 are critical so that the correct name(s) are used in the transaction and deed.

Earnest Money

As discussed earlier, **earnest money** is not required for a valid purchase contract but it does demonstrate the buyer's good faith. The following phrases provide the necessary information for a security deposit:

1. $1,000.00 earnest deposit payable to Security Title.
2. $1,000.00 cash or check drawn to the order of ——— to be held in escrow by ———.

Financing

This element of the contract is critical. For example, suppose a buyer purchases a home for $310,000 and the earnest money is $1,000 with an additional payment of $49,000 at closing. The remaining amount to be paid is $260,000 and this $260,000 may be paid in a number of ways. The payment methods used most often are (1) assumption of an existing mortgage, (2) purchase money mortgage by the seller, (3) new financing, or (4) any combination of the first three.

Assumption of an Existing Mortgage

In order to pay the remaining $260,000 of the purchase price, the buyer could agree to assume responsibility for the $260,000 mortgage on the property, or take over the seller's payments on the property. (The problems and liabilities of assumption are discussed in Chapter 15.) A sample clause providing for an assumption is as follows:

As part of the total purchase price, the Buyer agrees to assume and pay the existing first mortgage on the property described above with (mortgagee) and having an approximate balance of ——— dollars ($ ———.00), with said balance to be established by Seller furnishing a mortgagee's statement with payments of principal, interest, taxes, and insurance of $ ———per month with an annual interest rate of———% and running until ———, 20 ———.

Some drafters prefer to list the exact balance at drafting and provide for an update at closing. The monthly payments, rate, and ending date of the loan must be accurate.

If approval by the mortgagee is required for an assumption, then a clause stating "subject to the mortgagee's approval" is needed. Furthermore, some states permit the mortgagee to increase the interest rate upon assumption, and the contract should disclose such an increase.

Purchase Money Mortgage by the Seller

In some land transfers, the seller will act as the lender either by retaining title until the money is paid or by taking a mortgage on the property. In the example, if there were no mortgage to be assumed and the $260,000 still remained to be paid, the seller could finance the buyer's purchase. The language used would be as follows:

As part of the total purchase price, Seller agrees to take a purchase money note secured by a mortgage covering the above described property in the amount of ——— dollars ($ ———.00), with the principal amount of the note being that sum and the rate of interest being ———% per annum, with both principal and interest payable in the amount of $ ——— on the ——— day of each month beginning on the ——— day of ———, 20 ———, and continuing until ———, 20 ———, when the balance shall be paid in full. It is further agreed that the Buyer will execute the necessary note and mortgage reflecting these terms at or before closing on the property.

The seller may ask the buyer to furnish a balance statement or credit report as a condition to the granting of the note and mortgage. If the seller provides financing on a residential transaction, the seller will need to comply with the federal **Truth-in-Lending Act** and make certain disclosures on financing cost (see Chapter 15).

New Financing

To complete payment of the purchase price, the buyer may agree to obtain new financing for the balance due ($260,000 in the example). At the time the parties agree to the terms of the sale, the buyer's ability to obtain financing may be unknown. This portion of the purchase contract must be phrased as a condition precedent to performance or contingency.

A condition or contingency, known as a condition precedent, is an event that must occur before the parties or one party is obligated to perform under the contract. If a condition precedent never occurs, then the parties are not obligated to perform but are released from their contractual obligations. Although the contract is binding and creates legal obligations, conditions or contingencies control whether those obligations must be performed.

At a minimum, such a conditional financing clause should contain the most important terms, such as the principal amount, interest rate, maturity date, amount and frequency of installments, number of points (lender's commitment fee), and source of the financing (bank, trust company, or other source). Also, the clause should place time limitations on the buyer: "The loan application must be made within 14 days of the agreement," plus a maximum time for qualification. The following is a typical conditional financing clause:

This agreement is subject to the Buyer's securing a new first mortgage loan on the property described in this agreement in an amount of not less than ——— dollars ($ ———.00) from (bank, savings and loan, Federal Housing Administration, or other source), principal and interest payable in equal monthly payments of not more than $ ——— at an interest rate of not more than ——— % per annum, said mortgage loan being all due and payable ——— years from date of consummating this agreement.

A conditional financing clause gives the buyer a specified period within which to obtain financing and then gives the seller the opportunity to find financing for the buyer. Carefully drafted time limits and notification requirements are important in condition clauses.

Combinations of Financing Methods

The buyer can pay the purchase price through a combination of the various methods of financing. In the same example of a buyer purchasing a home for $310,000, the financing might be arranged as follows: If the property was already mortgaged for $200,000, the buyer could pay $1,000 earnest money, put $49,000 down, and assume the $200,000 mortgage; and the seller could take a second mortgage and carry the remaining $60,000. The arrangements could be written in the contract as follows:

The purchase price of three hundred ten thousand dollars ($310,000) is to be paid as follows:

a. *$1,000.00 Earnest money to be deposited with ABC escrow in the form of cash or check.*
b. *$49,000.00 Additional down payment to be paid on or before the close of escrow.*
c. *$200,000.00 Approximate balance of first mortgage with California Pacific Mortgage to be assumed by the buyer with monthly payments of principal, interest, taxes, and insurance of ——— due and payable on the ——— day of each month and an annual rate of ———%, with final payment being made on ———, 20 ———.*
d. *$60,000.00 Buyer agrees to execute note and second mortgage to seller on the above described property in the amount of $60,000 at a rate of ——% per annum payable in monthly installments of ——— on the ——— day of each month beginning on the ——— day of ———, 20 ———.*

CONSIDER 14.8

Highlands Plaza, Incorporated, entered into an agreement to purchase property from Viking Investment Corporation. The purchase was conditioned upon Highlands obtaining a $725,000 mortgage on the property. Highlands was able to obtain the $725,000 only through a first and second mortgage with different institutions, but still sought to go through with the sale. Viking refused on the grounds that the financing condition was not met. Highlands has brought suit for specific performance. What is the result?

Property Reports

Often buyers contract to purchase property before actually knowing the condition (in detail) of the property. However, the contract may require, as conditions precedent to the buyer's performance, expert reports on the property.

Property Condition Reports

One such condition often inserted in the contract is a clean termite report. An example of a termite clause follows:

The Sellers shall, at their expense and prior to closing, furnish the Buyers with a certificate from a reputable exterminator (a) certifying that the building(s) are free and clear from infestation and any resulting damage caused by termites or other wood-boring insects, and (b) guaranteeing such status for a period of one year from the date of closing. If such infestation or damage is found, buyer shall have the option of terminating all rights and obligations under this contract or requiring the sellers to cure and/or repair any infestation or damage on the property caused by termites or other wood-boring insects.

Another type of report buyers may require is a soil report, particularly in circumstances where buyers are purchasing land for development and construction. The quality of the soil will control the feasibility of constructing homes or other buildings on the property.

In recent years, Phase I, II, and III investigations of environmental issues on properties have been a critical part of pre-closing activity. Buyers begin by checking federal records to determine whether the Environmental Protection Agency (see Chapter 20) has designated the site as a "Superfund" site, a land tract that needs environmental cleanup. Even without that designation, Phase II checks for soil may provide information about contamination that is not yet known to the EPA. Buying property with environmental issues subjects the buyer to liability for cleanup. (See Chapter 20 for discussion of asbestos, radon, and toxic waste.)

Geological reports can provide buyers with information about whether the property is a risk because of its location in a fault or floodplain.

Federal Disclosure Requirements

In the 1960s, because of an increase in available leisure time and disposable income, land for the construction of recreational, second, or vacation homes became an in-demand commodity. Unfortunately, mail-order lots were offered by less-than-reputable sellers who capitalized on the high demand. Buyers were left with land that was moon-surface quality despite brochures that featured green and lush property. The land they had purchased was raw and undeveloped, often lacking roads, utilities, and water.

Because of the fraud in raw-land sales, Congress passed the **Interstate Land Sales Full Disclosure Act (ILSFDA)** (15 U.S.C. §1701 *et seq.*)—see Appendix D—which regulates sellers of undeveloped properties. The basic purpose of the act is to provide full and accurate information so that buyers are in an equal bargaining position with sellers when making purchase decisions. The ILSFDA is administered by the Office of Interstate Land Sales Registration (OILSR), a division of the **Department of Housing and Urban Development (HUD)**.

Who is Covered Under the ILSFDA?

Since the ILSFDA is a federal enactment, it applies only to sales of land involving or affecting interstate commerce—generally, to the sale or lease of 50 or more unimproved lots in interstate commerce. The act defines what constitutes interstate commerce in a negative manner by excluding those sales it does not cover:

a. Sales or lease of real estate pursuant to court order
b. Sales of securities by real estate investment trusts
c. Sales or lease by governments or government agencies
d. Sales of cemetery lots
e. Sales or leases in subdivisions with fewer than 25 lots
f. Sales or lease of lots 20 acres or more in size
g. Sales of lots where there is a residential, commercial, or industrial building

The ILSFDA also provides an exemption for intrastate land developers if the developer complies with the following requirements:

a. Prospective buyers or spouses make on-site inspection of the lots before purchasing.
b. Sales contract (1) identifies who will be responsible for roads and utilities, (2) provides deeds free and clear of any blanket encumbrances, and (3) grants a rescission period of seven business days.
c. Developer provides good-faith estimates of cost of getting services such as electric, water, sewer, and gas and when they will be complete.

> ***Practical Tip***
>
> *Check state and federal regulations on land sales before developing promotional materials, listings, and contracts. Be certain you are in compliance with all filing and disclosure requirements. If you believe an exemption applies, be careful to analyze why you can claim an exemption.*

Content of Filing Reports for Nonexempt Developers

Developers who are nonexempt must file a **statement of record** with the following information:

a. Names and addresses of the developers and their interests in the property
b. Legal description of the topography, climate, nuisances, subdivision map, permits, and licenses
c. General terms and conditions of the lot offer, including selling price and buyer's right of revocation for 48 hours
d. Access to nearby communities and roads
e. Availability of utilities; and if the utilities are developer-controlled, estimates for completion
f. Copies of articles of incorporation, partnership, or other entity creation of the developers and the development

The statement of record is really a form of registration of the property sales that takes effect in 30 days unless HUD notifies the developer that the record is incomplete. HUD's notification stops the running of the 30 days and the developer must then comply with HUD's requests for more information.

In addition to filing a statement of record, the developer must file a copy of the **property report**. Every buyer who signs a contract for purchase of the property must also be given a copy of the property report. The report is set up in an easily understood question-and-answer format and includes the same basic information as the statement of record but in a more readable manner. The developer cannot give out property reports until the HUD has approved the statement of record.

Penalties for Violation of ILSFDA

Developers who fail to comply with ILSFDA disclosure requirements face both civil and criminal penalties. Buyers may recover from developers who have not complied with ILSFDA requirements. Buyers can recover damages or obtain specific performance or any other relief the court deems fair, just, and equitable. Purchasers may also recover interest, court costs, attorneys' fees, appraisal fees, and cost of travel to and from the lots. Buyers can recover for fraud or misrepresentation in the property report even without proving their actual reliance on the report. The criminal penalties for willful violations of the Act are $10,000, and/or imprisonment for five years. Civil penalties range from $1,000 to $1,000,000.

In addition to regulation by the ILSFDA, all developers (even those exempt under the federal act) may be required to comply with state land sales acts and disclosures.

CONSIDER 14.9

Would the ILSFDA apply to:

a. The sale of condominium units?
b. The sale of mobile home lots?
c. The sale of 200 40-acre parcels?
d. The sale of homes in a tract subdivision with 375 lots?
e. A developer who has filed with the state?

Condition of Premises

A contract clause on the property's condition requires the seller to deliver the property in the same condition it is in at the time of the contract. This requirement imposes a duty on the seller to maintain the property as the details of closing are worked out. In addition, any repairs the buyer wants should also be included as conditions of the buyer's performance. The following clause would be appropriate:

The Sellers agree to keep the property in the same condition as it exists as of the date of the contract. Sellers further agree to repair the following items: ________ ________ ________. If such repairs are not completed or if the condition of the property has deteriorated, the buyers shall have the option of terminating all rights and obligations under this contract, or having said repairs made, or having conditions corrected at the sellers' expense, or requiring sellers to make said repairs or remedies.

Implied Warranty of Habitability

Purchasers of new homes have **implied warranty of habitability** protection from builders and vendors. The cases on habitability have given us a body of law with the following warranty protections and standards:

1. It is possible for a new home to be in substantial compliance with building codes and still be uninhabitable.
2. The primary function of a new home is to shelter its inhabitants from the elements. If a new home does not keep out the elements because of a substantial defect of construction, such home is not habitable within the meaning of the implied warranty of habitability.

3. Another function of a new home is to provide its inhabitants with a reasonably safe place to live, without fear of injury to person, health, safety, or property. If a new home is not structurally sound because of a substantial defect of construction, such a home is not habitable within the meaning of the implied warranty of habitability.
4. If a new home is not aesthetically satisfying because of a defect of construction, such a defect does not make the home uninhabitable.

Many states have passed statutes that specifically dictate when warranties are made and also codify the judicially afforded protection of the implied warranties. One critical issue in warranty protection is whether the warranty of habitability extends to purchasers of homes beyond just the original purchaser from the builder. Some states limit the warranty protection to the original buyer. Some states have permitted the extension of the warranty and added a time restriction. That is, the warranty runs for an 8-year or 10-year period regardless of how many buyers have owned the home.

CONSIDER 14.10

In 1992 Mark Cummings entered into a contract with Asilomar, a licensed contractor, to construct a single family home. Asilomar substantially completed construction by June 2, 1992. Cummings then occupied the home until November 1998, when he sold the property to the Maycocks.

After moving into the home, the Maycocks experienced problems with the residence. They noticed movements in the slab and walls throughout the home, as well as buckling in walls and sagging and cracking of the garage floor. In September 2000, Tom Thomas, a civil engineer hired by the Maycocks to evaluate the property, concluded that the unusual movements in the structure indicated inadequate compaction of the backfill soils during construction.

The Maycocks filed suit against Asilomar in January 2001, alleging negligence and breach of express and implied warranties. Asilomar says that since it did not sell the home to the Maycocks it is not liable and that there has been too much time that has passed to allow the Maycocks to recover. What should the court do with the suit? *Maycock v. Asilomar Development, Inc.*, 88 P.3d 565 (Ariz.App. 2004).

Many sellers, in order to avoid litigation, are selling their homes "as is" (see Chapter 12); that is, they are disclosing that there may be defects but that they are not responsible for them and buyers have been given the opportunity to inspect the property for any problems. In addition, many buyers are purchasing a warranty policy for their homes so that should problems arise, they will have insurance protection for repairs and renovation. In the following case, one court, however, found that an "as is" clause does not relieve the seller of disclosure requirements, even in commercial transactions.

S Development Co. v. Pima Capital Management Co.

31 P.3d 123 (Az. App. 2002), review denied

FACTS

The S Development Company and Presidio North Limited Partnership (appellees/purchasers/buyers) entered into a contract to purchase two apartment buildings, Presidio North and Bell Tower, from Pima Capital Management Company and Lincoln Life & Casualty (appellants) in July 1993. Both purchase contracts contained substantially similar provisions, which stated:

Disclaimer of Warranties. Buyer acknowledges that except as expressly set forth in this Agreement, Seller makes and has made no representations or warranties of any kind whatsoever, including but not limited to warranties concerning the condition of title, physical condition, encroachments, access, zoning, value, future value, income potential, any survey, environmental report or other information prepared by third parties, loan assumability, or the presence on or absence from the Property of any hazardous materials or underground storage tanks. Buyer is purchasing the Property as a result of its own examination thereof in its "AS IS" condition, and upon the exercise of its own judgment and investigation.

Prior to the close of escrows, the purchasers retained two engineering firms to inspect each of the buildings to be purchased. The inspections did not reveal any substantial problems with the plumbing in the buildings. Approximately two years after closing, however, the purchasers appellees learned that polybutylene pipe (PB pipe) had been used in both Presidio North's and Bell Tower's plumbing. PB pipe is a defective type of flexible tubing that will fail and leak when it is used to transport warm water under normal water pressures. The sellers claim that they were not aware that PB pipe had been used in the buildings when they sold the buildings.

The purchasers claimed that had they known of the defective pipe, they would have paid $5–6 million less than the $15 million they had paid. The purchasers filed suit against the sellers for their failure to disclose the material information about the defective pipe. The sellers defended on the grounds that the contract contained an "AS IS" clause and that the purchasers were given the opportunity to inspect using experts. Following a trial, a jury awarded $3,690,000 in damages to the purchasers and the sellers appealed.

JUDICIAL OPINION

Garbarino, Presiding Judge. We are called upon to determine the effect, if any, that a disclaimer of warranties, or an "as is" provision, in a purchase contract for commercial property has on a vendor's duty to disclose defects in the physical condition of a property being sold. We hold that latent defects in a property sold "as is" that are known to the vendor must be disclosed to the purchaser. We also hold that a vendor may be held liable for negligent nondisclosure of facts basic to the transaction when the purchaser is precluded by the vendor from discovering those facts.

The appellants do not dispute that the appellees argued, and the jury was instructed, that the appellants' duty to disclose arose under §551(2)(e) of the Restatement (Second) of Torts, which provides as follows:

(2) One party to a business transaction is under a duty to exercise reasonable care to disclose to the other before the transaction is consummated,

. . .

(e) facts basic to the transaction, if he knows that the other is about to enter into it under a mistake as to them, and that the other, because of the relationship between them, the customs of the trade or other objective circumstances, would reasonably expect a disclosure of those facts. Restatement (Second) of Torts §551(2)(e).

Essentially, the appellants argue that they were under no duty to disclose the defective plumbing to the appellees by operation of the "as is" clauses; that the "as is" clauses effectively shifted the burden of discovering the defect to the appellees and, therefore, the appellants are not liable for the appellees' failure to discover the defect, and they should have been granted judgment as a matter of law.

First, we find merit in the appellees' argument that the existence of an "as is" provision in a purchase contract generally operates only as a waiver of breach of warranty claims, not tort claims.

[A]rizona law "implies a covenant of good faith and fair dealing in every contract" so that "neither party will act to impair the right of the other to receive the benefits which flow from their agreement or contractual relationship." In keeping with the covenant of good faith and fair dealing, we hold that a vendor must disclose latent defects in property that are known to the vendor, notwithstanding the existence of a burden-shifting "as is" clause or disclaimer of warranties.

A latent defect is defined as "[a] hidden or concealed defect. One which could not be discovered by reasonable and customary observation or inspection. ..." *Black's Law Dictionary 611* (Abridged 6th ed. 1991). Nondisclosure to the purchaser of latent defects known to the vendor "impair[s] the right of the [purchaser] to receive the benefits" of the contract. The very nature of a latent defect precludes the discovery of the defect upon a reasonable inspection. To hold otherwise would allow vendors to conceal latent problems with the property and "hide behind contract language purporting to shift the risk of nondisclosure to the purchaser."

Even if we assume that the plumbing defect in this case was a "patent defect," the jury was free to conclude that the "as is" clauses did not protect the appellants because the buyers were not given a chance to investigate. The *Restatement (Second) of Torts* further indicates that "when the plaintiff has equal opportunity for obtaining information that he may be expected to utilize if he cares to do so," then the defendant is not under a duty to disclose. The evidence developed at trial demonstrates that, even if the plumbing defects were patent defects, the appellees did not have an "equal opportunity" to discover the defects because (1) the defective pipe was buried six inches inside the walls; (2) the contracts precluded the appellees from damaging the property; (3) the appellants' property manager would not allow the appellees to inspect inside the walls of either building; and (4) all visible plumbing was copper piping. This is logical because, although a defect could be discovered upon inspection, preventing a party from conducting an inspection effectively turns what may be a patent defect into an undiscoverable-in-fact latent defect.

Simply stated, in the face of an "as is" sale, the rule of *caveat emptor* continues to apply and the vendor may be insulated from liability for nondisclosure of facts basic to the transaction if the facts at issue are patent, or if the purchaser has been given an appropriate opportunity to discover latent defects.

Affirmed.

DISSENTING OPINION

Ehrlich, Judge. Whether a buyer may reasonably expect disclosure of a basic fact depends on the contract—the relationship between the parties, the customs of the trade or other objective circumstances. Again according to comment j of Section 551, "if the parties expressly or impliedly place the risk as to the existence of a fact on one party ... the other party has no duty of disclosure."

By expressly providing that the property was being sold "as is," the purchase contracts between the appellants and the appellees placed the risk as to the existence of defects on the appellees.

CASE QUESTIONS

1. What was the defect in the property?
2. What is the effect of the "as is" clause?
3. What is the difference between a patent and a latent defect?
4. What point does the dissent make?

CONSIDER 14.11

On the basis of the four statements on the warranty of habitability (on pages 390–391), determine whether the following defects would be a breach of the warranty. (Assume all buyers purchased new homes.)

a. A septic tank that does not function properly
b. Water seepage into a home
c. A mudslide damaging a homeowner's patio area
d. A cracked foundation
e. Cracked basement walls
f. Mold in a house

CONSIDER 14.12

Would the failure to disclose a problem with errant golf balls landing on the roof of a house be misrepresentation? What if the house is located across the street from a golf course? *Murray v. Crank*, 945 S.W.2d 28 (Mo. Ct. App. 1997)

A final issue in home warranties is whether the implied warranty of habitability can be disclaimed. States that permit such disclaimers require that the buyers be aware of the limitation. That awareness can come from conspicuous language, actual signing of a disclaimer, or any other type of conduct that shows the buyers knew of the limitation before they purchased the home. Some states permit a disclaimer of the implied warranty only if some other type of warranty is given in exchange. An example of a disclaimer upheld in a New York case follows:

> ***Practical Tip***
>
> *Professor Thomas John Rhoads has offered the following advice to sellers and their agents in making their decision to disclose information: "Seek out all the information that you would want to have yourself and remember the simple rule, 'If you don't want to disclose, then you probably should.'"*[1]

It is further understood that THE SPONSOR MAKES NO HOUSING MERCHANT IMPLIED WARRANTY OR ANY OTHER WARRANTIES, EXPRESS OR IMPLIED, IN CONNECTION WITH

1. Thomas John Rhoads, "Caveat Venditor: Seller Disclosure in California Residential Real Estate Transactions," 2 *Journal of the Pacific Southwest Academy of Legal Studies in Business* 45 (1996).

THIS PURCHASE AGREEMENT OR THE UNIT, AND ALL SUCH WARRANTIES ARE EXCLUDED EXCEPT AS PROVIDED IN THE LIMITED WARRANTY ANNEXED TO THIS PURCHASE AGREEMENT. THE EXPRESS TERMS OF THE ANNEXED LIMITED WARRANTY ARE HEREBY INCORPORATED IN AND MADE A PART OF THIS PURCHASE AGREEMENT; THEY SHALL SURVIVE THE CLOSING OF TITLE; AND THERE ARE NO OTHER WARRANTIES WHICH EXTEND BEYOND THE FACE THEREOF.

New Damages and the Implied Warranty

Liability theory with respect to home buyers is evolving in California with the imposition of damages for emotional harm to buyers when their homes are defective. In *Salka v. Dean Homes of Beverly Hills, Inc.* (22 Cal. Rptr. 2d 902 (Ca. App. 1993); 877 P.2d 761 (Cal. 1994)), the owner of a home that became waterlogged because of a defective foundation recovered not only the economic damages, but also $50,000 for emotional harm. The appellate court in affirming the emotional harm award stated,

The purchase of a home isn't only the largest investment people make in their lifetime, it is also a highly personal choice concerning how and where one lives his or her life. Generally, no other material acquisition is of equivalent personal importance.

Home Warranty Policies

There are really two uses of the term *home warranty*. The first use is that covered by state statutes in which the builder is required, for specified times, to offer a warranty on construction of the house. The second use is that often seen on listing signs placed on property, such as "one-year warranty available." This protection is for the buyer and is a form of insurance that covers defects and problems on the home for one year from closing.

If a buyer is not in a position of being protected by either a statutory or implied warranty, the purchase contract may still be afford protection in the event defects arise. One way to obtain such protection is to require the seller to purchase one of the available home warranty protection plans. Most policies for used homes will run for a period of a year, but varying coverage exists. The buyer should specify in the contract what type of protection is sought. Another protection can be obtained by requiring the seller to personally warrant the property. A sample seller's warranty clause follows:

The Seller warrants that the plumbing, heating, air conditioning, and electrical systems in the buildings on the property are in good working order and condition, and will be in good working order and condition at the time of closing. In the event such items are not in working order at closing, the Seller agrees to deduct the cost of repair or replacement from the amount due from the buyer at settlement.

A warranty clause such as this may be coupled with a warranty policy.

Environmental Contingency Clause

Because of so many issues regarding environmental hazards (see Chapter 20), many contracts now have environmental inspections as conditions precedent to performance. These **environmental contingency clauses** require inspection of the property for problems relating to the presence of toxic waste, radon, asbestos, and other toxins. Some states have statutory disclosure requirements. For example, New York, Rhode Island, and Florida require radon-disclosure notices in residential sales contracts. In some contracts, the cost of reducing an elevated level of radon is charged against the seller at closing. Even developers have soil testing in their purchase contracts so that radon issues are addressed before they purchase undeveloped land.

Risk of Loss

In most jurisdictions, the risk of loss for property damage is with the buyer from the time the purchase contract is executed. Buyers have an insurable interest from the time the contract is executed, and may hold a valid policy on the property even though they do not have title or possession.

However, in most cases, the seller will maintain insurance on the property until closing. To avoid the duplication of insurance and costs, purchase contracts usually provide that the seller will maintain insurance on the property until closing. The buyers can be added to the existing policy along with a notation establishing their interest in the property.

Recording the Contract

The purchase contract need not be recorded to be effective between the parties. However, without recording, liens can attach and recorded interests would have priority over the buyer's interests. Nonetheless, recording a sales contract is uncommon. One reason for not recording is a very practical one: The contract has conditions and contingencies that might not be met; therefore, it is always subject to the buyer's default. If the recorded contract falls through, the seller is not free to sell to anyone else until a release is signed and the contract is stricken from the records. Without the defaulting purchaser's release, clearing the contract could be an expensive matter requiring a court hearing.

Closing Date and Escrow Instructions

Although the purchase contract establishes the terms of the sale, it does not contain all the details for the execution of documents, transfer of title, and payment of money. The purchase contract will provide an escrow date, such as in the following clause:

1. *Closing shall take place within ——— days of the date of this agreement.*
2. *Closing shall be on ———, 20 ———.*

In many states, the closing is handled by a third party (see Chapter 16), and a contract is required among the buyer, seller, and third party to properly complete the transaction. Standard forms provide for this type of escrow clause:

Buyer and Seller shall execute escrow instructions to fulfill the terms hereof and deliver the same to the escrow agent within 15 days of the date of execution of this agreement.

Also, if applicable, a simple clause such as "time is of the essence in the performance of this agreement" may be included to indicate the parties' intention that delays mean the contract will not go forward. This type of clause halts the often endless extensions either party could otherwise demand for his or her execution of the contract. Without an indication of the parties' intent on time being of the essence, the courts are likely to permit extensions that may exceed the parties' original intentions on time for performance.

Apportionments

Property is not always transferred at times when taxes, insurance, and rent are due. To be absolutely fair to the parties, amounts paid for six-month or year-long blocks, such as taxes and insurance premiums, must be apportioned between the buyer and seller as of the date of transfer of title. Specific clauses may be used for the apportionment of each type of fund or a general apportionment clause may be used. The following are examples of specific types of clauses:

1. *Proration of Rent* All rent on any and all portions of the property shall be prorated to the date of closing, with the seller receiving all rents due to the date of closing and the buyer receiving all rents due thereafter. All prepaid rents shall be prorated in the same manner.
2. *Taxes* All taxes due and owing on the property shall be prorated to the date of closing, with the seller paying all taxes due to the date of closing and the buyer paying all taxes due thereafter. Any prepaid taxes shall be prorated in the same manner.

Marketable Title

The clause on **marketable title** in the purchase contract is a condition precedent to the buyer's performance that requires the seller to deliver a certain quality of title. The clause may be very simple, requiring the seller to furnish a title insurance policy, or it may be demanding and restrictive, by requiring the seller to remove liens or obtain zoning changes. The following are examples of the title clauses:

1. *In the event title to said property herein described is found by a title insurance company to be unmarketable at the time of closing, the purchaser is excused from performance.*
2. *Title to the premises shall be good and marketable and free and clear of all liens, restrictions, easements, encumbrances, leases, tenancies, and other title objections, and shall be insurable as such at ordinary rates by any reputable title insurance company selected by the buyer.*

Marketable title is generally defined as one a prudent person would accept even with full knowledge of all facts about the property. Marketable title is a title that is free from reasonable doubt or controversy and which is not subject to any liens or encumbrances. Marketability is determined on a case-by-case basis. One general standard applied in reviewing the marketability of a title is, Would a prudent person accept this title in exchange for a fair purchase price?

In many purchase contracts, the seller is given time to cure defects in title discovered before closing. For example, if the preliminary title report shows a defect, the seller may be given an extension on closing of 30 or 60 days to cure the defect. Figure 14.2 provides a list of marketable title issues.

Many states have adopted the **Uniform Marketable Title Act**, which provides that a person who has unbroken record title for 50 years has marketable title. There are certain exceptions to the act, but it was designed to create a 50-year statute of limitations on various title claims and provide a mechanism whereby titles could be cleared of unrenewed and unenforced clouds.

CONSIDER 14.13

The following clause is a marketable title clause in a purchase contract.

Title is to be conveyed free from all encumbrances except: Any state of facts an accurate survey may show, provided same does not render title unmarketable.

A title search revealed that a telephone easement was recorded for the property, and that the height of the sidewalk on the property violated a city ordinance, although a waiver had been obtained for its construction. The title company offered to insure title except for the sidewalk waiver and the telephone easement. The buyers refuse to perform on the grounds of lack of marketable title. What is the result?

Figure 14.2 Marketable Title

Affects Marketable Title*	Does Not Affect Marketable Title
Unrecorded easements	Zoning
Easements (unless visible)	CC&Rs
Quiet title litigation pending	Visible easements
Liens	
Leases	
Encroachments	
Mortgages	
Tenancies	
Water rights	
Tax issues	
Disputes among heirs on property rights	
Land contracts	
Prescriptive and adverse possession rights	

* The buyer could agree to accept title subject to any of these and such willingness would be noted in the contract.

Remedies

Liquidated Damages

Many contracts provide that the earnest money or deposit will be used for damages in the event of a breach by one of the parties. That deposit should be large enough to cover damages. The following is an example of such a clause:

Should the undersigned Buyer fail to carry out this agreement, all money paid hereunder, including any additional earnest money, shall, at the option of the Seller, be forfeited as liquidated damages and shall be paid to or retained by the Seller, subject to deductions of broker's commission and disbursements, if any. In the event neither party has commenced a law suit within one (1) year after the closing date set forth herein, the broker is authorized to disburse the earnest money as liquidated damages, and if the Seller has not notified the Buyer of election to consider the earnest money as liquidated damages within six (6) months of said closing date, broker is authorized to refund all earnest money to the Buyer.

Should the Seller be unable to carry out this agreement by reason of a valid legal defect in title which the Buyer is unwilling to waive, all money paid hereunder shall be returned to the buyer forthwith, and this contract will be void.

In most cases, the courts will enforce the award of the earnest money as a valid **liquidated damages** clause; that is, a clause in which the parties agree on the amount of damages before any breach of contract occurs. However, the seller may not keep the earnest money deposit and collect actual damages in addition. Such double compensation is a penalty and void. Whatever the amount of liquidated damages the parties agree to, it must be reasonable. The courts uphold liquidated damage provisions that reflect the potential loss the seller could or does suffer because of the buyer's breach.

Because of so much litigation over liquidated damage clauses, some states have passed statutes requiring specific language to have an enforceable provision for liquidated damages. Many of these statutes also require that the parties sign or initial the clause in the contract so that a court can be certain the parties were aware of its existence. Still other states require a "second look" at liquidated damages clauses, or a review of reasonableness of the damages provided for in the contract after the breach of contract has occurred.

The following case deals with the issue of appropriate damages when there has been a breach.

PERRONCELLO V. DONAHUE

859 N.E.2d 827 (Mass. 2007)

FACTS

On April 3, 1998, Joseph F. Perroncello (buyer/plaintiff) and Paul J. Donahue, Sr. (as trustee) (seller/defendant), signed a purchase and sale contract for property at 198 Beacon Street in Boston for $2,250,000. The contract contained a clause that provided that "acceptance of deed by the BUYER, shall be deemed to be a full performance and discharge of every agreement and obligation herein contained or expressed." It also contained a liquidated damages clause providing that if "the BUYER shall fail to fulfill the BUYER's agreements herein, all deposits made hereunder by the BUYER shall be retained by the SELLER and this shall be SELLER's sole remedy at law or in equity." The buyer paid a deposit of $150,000. The sale was to close by May 6, 1998, but the agreement provided that the buyer could seek one 30-day extension (until June 5), which he did, during which time he would be obligated to pay the seller's carrying costs of up to $500 per day. Carrying costs included "seller's financing costs, taxes, insurance and the like."

The contract did not include a mortgage contingency clause, and recited that time was of the essence.

As of June 4, 1998, Perroncello had not finalized the mortgage financing he needed to purchase the property. His attorney sent a request to the Donahue's attorney seeking an extension of the closing to June 16. Donahue's attorney responded on June 5 with a letter stating that Donahue was ready to deliver the deed on June 5. Perroncello asserts that Donahue told him to continue working with his bank to secure the mortgage and that any correspondence sent by the attorney stating that June 5 was the deadline should be disregarded. On June 12, Donahue's attorney sent written notice to the Perroncello's attorney that, no closing having occurred, the contract was breached and the deposit forfeited. Perroncello and Donahue had further discussions and meetings about the real estate through the month of June. On June 23, 1998, the bank approved Perroncello's mortgage, and he notified Donahue. Thereafter, Donahue did not return Perroncello's telephone calls, and put a "For Sale" sign on the property.

On June 30, 1998, Perroncello filed a complaint in the Superior Court for breach of contract, specific performance, deceit, and conversion and also sought both a restraining order preventing the seller from marketing the property, his $150,000 deposit returned, and a *lis pendens*. Donahue counterclaimed for abuse of process, breach of contract, and unfair and deceptive trade practice.

A trial court granted summary judgment against the seller and the Appeals Court reversed. The buyer appealed.

JUDICIAL OPINION

Cordy, Justice. It is a settled principle that when the purchaser of real property breaches a contract for sale, the seller may retain the property and bring an action for damages or may request specific performance of the contract by offering to perform, and bringing an action for the purchase price. If the purchase and sale contract contains a provision awarding liquidated damages to the seller in the event of the purchaser's breach, that clause will be enforced so long as "at the time the agreement was made, potential damages were difficult to determine and the clause was a reasonable forecast of damages expected to occur in the event of a breach." ***Kelly v. Marx*, 428 Mass. 877, 878, 705 N.E.2d 1114 (1999)**. Liquidated damages clauses providing that a real estate seller may retain the buyer's deposit on breach are a common real estate practice recognized in Massachusetts.

When seeking specific performance of a contract, the seller offers to surrender title to the property and collect the purchase price. In bringing an action for damages on the breach of the contract, the seller proposes to retain the property and have his compensation in damages. While these remedies may not be inconsistent in the sense that they are both premised on the validity of the contract, ordinarily a seller is not entitled to seek both remedies; the retention of a deposit as liquidated damages is an alternative to specific performance, not an additional remedy.

The seller directs our attention to, and the Appeals Court largely relied on, our decision in ***Kelly v. Marx*,** ***supra***. Such reliance is unwarranted. The ***Kelly*** case is inapposite. There, the judge permitted the seller to keep the buyer's deposit as liquidated damages following the buyer's failure to tender payment for the real estate. Specific performance was sought by neither party. Rather, after the buyer's breach, the seller found another buyer who purchased the property for $5,000 more than the original contract price. The question presented was whether it was appropriate to enforce the liquidated damages clause of the contract, where the seller ultimately sold the property at a higher price to another party, thereby suffering no loss. We held that the liquidated damages clause was enforceable because potential damages were difficult to determine at the time of the contract formation, and the amount agreed to was a reasonable forecast of damages in the event of a future breach, at that time. In so holding, we rejected the "second look" approach to liquidated damages. We did not imply that liquidated damages could be obtained, in addition to specific performance from the buyer.

Here, the seller sought an order from the judge directing the buyer to purchase the property by September 15, 1998, at the agreed on purchase price, and the buyer complied. The only additional damages the seller was entitled to seek under the contract were for the carrying costs he incurred as a result of the delay between the expected date of performance and the time of actual conveyance. These carrying costs were separately provided for in the contract and ancillary to its performance. The obligation to pay the costs was triggered by the buyer's election to delay the closing for thirty days. This award is not inconsistent with specific performance. Restatement (Second) of Contracts, at §378 comment d ("A party who seeks specific performance or an injunction may ... be entitled to damages to compensate him for delay in performance").

The law of contracts is intended to give an injured party the benefit of the bargain, not the benefit of the bargain and a windfall. To award liquidated damages against the buyer for his failure to close and also specific performance to the seller requiring the buyer to acquire the property by a date certain at the contracted price, would violate the fundamental principles of contract law.

The order granting summary judgment to the buyer on the issue of liquidated damages is affirmed.

CASE QUESTIONS

1. List the mistakes the parties made in their purchase contract as well as in their conduct between the time of the contract and the litigation.

2. Does the court distinguish between and among actual damages, specific performance, and liquidated damages?

3. What is the rule on "second looks" on damage clauses in real estate purchase contracts in Massachusetts?

CONSIDER 14.14

On September 4, 1996, Gable Ridge and Barberry Homes entered into a purchase and sale agreement concerning the sale of 18 undeveloped house lots located in Westborough, Massachusetts. Under the agreement, Barberry Homes would purchase the lots from Gable Ridge in three phases, with closing dates on October 21, 1996; June 1, 1997; and October 15, 1997. Six lots were to change hands at the first closing, three at the second, and nine at the third. The total purchase price for the lots was $2,700,000, or $150,000 per lot.

The agreement provided for Gable Ridge's remedy if Barberry Homes breached the relevant portion, captioned BUYER'S DEFAULT: DAMAGES, which states: "If the BUYER shall fail to fulfill the BUYER's agreements herein, all deposits made hereunder by the BUYER shall be retained by the SELLER as liquidated damages and this shall be the SELLER'S sole remedy at law and equity."

Before the first closing date, the parties executed an amendment to the agreement. In the amendment, the parties agreed that Barberry Homes would pay $50,000 less than the previously agreed-to price for one of the six lots (Lot 16) set to change hands on the first closing date. The amendment, however, did not lower the total purchase price. Rather, the $50,000 was to be reallocated over the remaining 17 lots being sold, so that the individual lot price for the remaining lots would become $152,942, rather than $150,000. The amendment repeats the default provision.

On October 21, 1996, the parties closed on the first six lots. Barberry Homes paid $100,000 for one lot (Lot 16) and $152,941 for each of the five other lots, as provided

CONSIDER 14.14
(continued)

for in the amendment. The total paid was therefore $864,705. In February 1997, Peter Gallipeau, the president of Barberry Homes who signed the agreement and the amendment, resigned his position. In March 1997, David Carter (Carter) succeeded Gallipeau as president of Barberry Homes. On June 1, 1997, the second scheduled closing date under the agreement, Barberry Homes failed to close on the next set of lots. Carter decided not to close on the remaining lots because Gable Ridge would not change the sequences in which the remaining lots were to be purchased.

Gable Ridge took possession of Barberry Homes' $50,000 deposit. Barberry Homes disputes that retention as a penalty because Gable Ridge was able to sell the lots to others for more than the original agreed-upon contract price. Is Barberry Homes correct? *Carroll v. Barberry Homes, Inc.*, 10 Mass.L.Rptr. 668, 1999 WL 1204020 (Mass. Super. 1999)

Actual Damages

The decision to keep the earnest money as damages is often left to the discretion of the seller. The seller may elect to proceed and collect the actual damages sustained by the buyer's breach. Such damages could include all the monies expended by the seller in preparing for closing, such as the cost of reports. It could also include a commission to the broker or lost rental value if the property remains vacant or if a lease is terminated in anticipation of the buyer's takeover.

Likewise, the buyer may opt to collect actual damages for the seller's breach, which could include the costs of preparation for closing in the form of loan origination or commitment fees, appraisal fees, survey costs, and so on.

The party asking for actual damages has the burden of establishing the amount of the damages and that those damages were a result of the other party's breach.

The **Uniform Land Transactions Act (ULTA)**, drafted for passage by the states in 1975, has several formulas for determining actual damages in the event of a breach of a land sales contract. For example, a seller reselling at a lower price recovers from the breaching buyer the difference in price plus the incidental costs of resale.

Specific Performance

Specific performance is a remedy for buyers that requires the seller to go forward with the transaction according to the terms of the contract.

Generally, specific performance is not awarded to sellers who have breaching buyers; in such cases sellers are left to the remedies of actual damages or the collection of liquidated damages.

Rescission

Rescission entitles the parties to rescind their agreement and return to the positions they were in before they entered into the contract. The buyer is given back any compensation paid and the seller is no longer obligated to sell the land. Rescission is most commonly used in cases where the seller has misrepresented the property or its condition.

Misrepresentation

Misrepresentation is a defense to the formation of a contract. Misrepresentation occurs when the seller has misled the buyer about the nature or condition of the property. Misrepresentation can be innocent; that is, one party through misinformation or lack of knowledge provides the other party with inaccurate and misleading information. Misrepresentation can also be fraudulent, as when one party intentionally provides inaccurate information for purposes of inducing a sale. Finally, misrepresentation can occur because of a party's failure to disclose information that would have affected the purchasing decision. Misrepresentation allows the party affected to rescind the contract. However, all types of misrepresentation require proof of the following:

1. A statement of material fact has been made or omitted—the type of information involved would affect the buying decision.
2. There is reliance on the statement of fact—the buyer uses the fact in making the decision of whether to buy (see earlier discussion under "AS IS" clauses for disclosures about patent and latent defects).
3. There is detriment—the buyer suffers through loss of property value or cost of repair.

CONSIDER 14.15

Decide whether the following statements would or would not be a basis for misrepresentation in a real estate contract.

a. "The test/scores for this area's public schools are the highest in the state."
b. "This roof has a 30-year warranty."
c. "This well could never run dry."
d. "That easement is not recorded, but it's valid."
e. "This property was certified in 2006 as termite free."
f. "The crime rate is very low here."
g. "The city has no plans for a stadium next to this house."
h. "The value on this house just keeps going up."
i. "Basements in this area don't leak."

The next case illustrates the application of the three elements in a case in which the misrepresentation was a fraudulent one about a latent defect in the property.

Reed v. King

193 Cal. Rptr. 130 (1983)

FACTS

Dorris Joni Reed (plaintiff/appellant) purchased a house from Robert King through his real estate agents (defendants/respondents). No one informed Reed that a woman and her four children had been murdered in the house 10 years earlier. When Reed learned of the murders, she brought suit seeking rescission and damages. The trial court dismissed the suit and Reed appealed.

JUDICIAL OPINION

Blease, Associate Justice. In the sale of a house, must the seller disclose it was the site of a multiple murder? Neither King nor his agents told Reed that a woman and her four children were murdered there. However, it seems "truth will come to light; murder cannot be hid long." (Shakespeare, *Merchant of Venice,* Act II, Scene II.) Reed learned of the gruesome episode from a neighbor after the sale.

King and his real estate agent knew about the murders and knew the event materially affected the market value of the house when they listed it for sale. They represented to Reed the premises were in good condition and fit for an "elderly lady" living alone. They did not disclose the fact of the murders. At some point King asked a neighbor not to inform Reed of that event. Nonetheless, after Reed moved in neighbors informed her no one was interested in purchasing the house because of the stigma. Reed paid $75,000, but the house is only worth $65,000 because of its past.

Does Reed's pleading state a cause of action? Concealed within this question is the nettlesome problem of the duty of disclosure of blemishes on real property which are not physical defects or legal impairments to use.

Reed seeks to state a cause of action sounding in contract, i.e., rescission, or in tort, i.e., deceit. In either event her allegations must reveal a fraud. "The elements of actual fraud, whether as the basis of the remedy in contract or tort, may be stated as follows: There must be (1) *a false representation* or concealment of a material fact (or, in some cases, an opinion) susceptible of knowledge, (2) made with *knowledge* of its falsity or without sufficient knowledge on the subject to warrant a representation, (3) with the *intent* to induce the person to whom it is made to act upon it; and such person must (4) act in *reliance* upon the representation (5) to his damage."

The trial court perceived the defect in Reed's complaint to be a failure to allege concealment of a material fact. "Concealment" and "material" are legal conclusions concerning the effect of the issuable facts pled. As appears, the analytic pathways to these conclusions are intertwined.

Concealment is a term of art which includes mere non-disclosure when a party has a duty to disclose. Reed's complaint reveals only non-disclosure despite the allegation King asked a neighbor to hold his peace. There is no allegation the attempt at suppression was a cause in fact of Reed's ignorance. Accordingly, the critical question is: does the seller have a duty to disclose here? Resolution of this question depends on the materiality of the fact of the murders.

In general, a seller of real property has a duty to disclose: "where the seller knows of facts *materially* affecting the value or desirability of the property which are known or accessible only to him and also knows that such facts are not known to, or within the reach of the diligent attention and observation of the buyer, the seller is under a duty to disclose them to the buyer. This broad statement of duty has led one commentator to conclude: 'The ancient maxim *caveat emptor* ('let the buyer beware') has little or no application to California real estate transactions.'"

Whether information "is of sufficient materiality to affect the value or desirability of the property ... depends on the facts of the particular case." Materiality "is a question of law, and is part of the concept of right to rely or justifiable reliance." Accordingly the term is essentially a label affixed to a normative conclusion. Three considerations bear on this legal conclusion: the gravity of the harm inflicted by non-disclosure; the fairness of imposing a duty of discovery on the buyer as an alternative to compelling disclosure, and its impact on the stability of contracts if rescission is permitted.

Numerous cases have found non-disclosure of physical defects and legal impediments to use of real property are material. However, to our knowledge, no prior real estate sale case has faced an issue of non-disclosure of the kind presented here. Should this variety of ill-repute be required to be disclosed? Is this a circumstance where "non-disclosure of the fact amounts to a failure to act in good faith and in accordance with reasonable standards of fair dealing[?]"

The paramount argument against an affirmative conclusion is it permits the camel's nose of unrestrained irrationality admission to the tent. If such an "irrational" consideration is permitted as a basis of rescission the stability of all conveyances will be seriously undermined. Any fact that might disquiet the enjoyment of some segment of the buying public may be seized upon by a disgruntled purchaser to void a bargain. In our view, keeping this genie in the bottle is not as difficult a task as these arguments assume. We do not view a decision allowing Reed to survive a demurrer in these unusual circumstances as endorsing the materiality of facts predicating peripheral, insubstantial, or fancied harms.

The murder of innocents is highly unusual in its potential for so disturbing buyers they may be unable to reside in a home where it has occurred. This fact may foreseeably deprive a buyer of the intended use of the purchase. Murder is not such a common occurrence that buyers should be charged with anticipating and discovering this disquieting possibility. Accordingly, the fact is not one for which a duty of inquiry and discovery can sensibly be imposed upon the buyer.

Reed alleges the fact of the murders has a quantifiable effect on the market value of the premises. We cannot say this allegation is inherently wrong and, in the pleading posture of the case, we assume it to be true. If information known or accessible only to the seller has a significant and measurable effect on market value and, as is alleged here, the seller is aware of this effect, we see no principled basis for making the duty to disclose turn upon the character of the information. Physical usefulness is not and never has been the sole criterion of valuation. Stamp collections and gold speculation would be insane activities if utilitarian considerations were the sole measure of value.

Reputation and history can have a significant effect on the value of realty. "George Washington slept here" is worth something, however physically inconsequential that consideration may be. Ill-repute or "bad will" conversely may depress the value of property. Failure to disclose such a negative fact where it will have a foreseeably depressing effect on income expected to be generated by a business is tortious. Some cases have held that *unreasonable* fears of the potential buying public that a gas or oil pipeline may rupture may depress the market value of land and entitle the owner to incremental compensation in eminent domain.

Whether Reed will be able to prove her allegation the decade-old multiple murder has a significant effect on market value we cannot determine. If she is able to do so by competent evidence she is entitled to a favorable ruling on the issues of materiality and duty to disclose. Her demonstration of objective tangible harm would still the concern that permitting her to go forward will open the floodgates to rescission on subjective and idiosyncratic grounds.

A more troublesome question would arise if a buyer in similar circumstances were unable to plead or establish a significant and quantifiable effect on market value. However, this question is not presented in the posture of this case. Reed has not alleged the fact of the murders has rendered the premises useless to her as a residence. As currently pled, the gravamen of her case is pecuniary harm. We decline to speculate on the abstract alternative.

Reversed.

CASE QUESTIONS

1. What happened in the house?
2. How did Reed discover it?
3. What effect did it have on the value?
4. Is concealment fraud? When?
5. Can Reed proceed with her case?
6. Give examples of other types of disclosures that would be necessary.[2]

CONSIDER 14.16

In 1989, Jeffrey and Patrice Stambovsky bought an 18-room mansion in Nyack, New York, for $650,000. They talked with a local architect who said, "Oh, you're buying the haunted house." The Victorian house has had gifts left by ghosts and the Amazing Kreskin has sought to hold a seance there. The Stambovskys were not given this information before they signed the contract, and they now wish to have their earnest money returned ($32,500). In fact, the house had been written up in *Reader's Digest* in 1977; in the article the owner described a ghost who looked like Santa Claus. In a description in a house tour book, the house description read: "riverfront Victorian—with ghost." Mr. Stambovsky feels he and his wife are the victims of "ectoplasmic fraud." Is he correct? *Stambovsky v. Ackley*, 572 N.Y.S.2d 672 (1991)[3]

Remedies for misrepresentation include rescission, actual damages, and, if fraudulent, punitive damages. If a real estate agent or broker colludes with a party to defraud or misrepresent, the agent or broker faces license suspension or revocation.

Disclosure Statutes

Because of many problems with innocent and intentional misrepresentation in the sale of property, the National Association of Realtors and other groups worked together to have states adopt disclosure laws. In most states sellers are required to fill out questionnaires to disclose any known defects including problems with plumbing, the electrical system, walls, floors, insulation, and the home's foundation. Over half of the states recommend such disclosure. Known as **transfer disclosure statements**

2. Serial killer Jeffrey Dahmer's apartment building was so stigmatized that a community redevelopment group bought it, razed the building, and, to this day, the lot remains vacant. Likewise, John Wayne Gacy's home, a site of burial for his child victims, was razed.The Ramsey home in Boulder. Colorado, where Jon Benet Ramsey was killed sold for nearly $2 million less than its value. Likewise, Nicole Brown Simpson's condo sold for $200,000 less than its market value. The Rancho Santa Fe home where the Heaven's Gate cult committed mass suicide sold for less than half its value. Roman Polanski's home, where Charles Manson and his followers killed his actress wife, has never been on the market since the director fled the country following charges that Polanski committed statutory rape in the house. On the other hand, the Miami mansion of Gianni Versace (where he was shot and killed) brought the highest selling price ever in the area. Catherine Rempell, "For Sale: Scene of a Crime," *USA Today*, August 7, 2006. pp. 1A and 2A. "The Scandal Effect," *Wall Street Journal*, August 4, 2006, pp. W1, W6.
3. The Hudson Valley of New York is infamous for its tales of haunted houses, including the alleged home of Icahbod Crane, Washington Irving's legendary character. Kathryn Matthews, "This Old House Has Ghosts," *New York Times*, October 13, 2006, pp. D1, D4.

(TDS), these forms, in the states where they are required, must be presented to potential buyers *before* they enter into a purchase contract. The result of these mandatory disclosure forms has been growth of real estate inspection firms and the warranty industry that affords buyers protection for defects that arise despite all the caution in inspection and disclosure. In addition to finding defects, the inspections determine compliance with code, e.g., the presence of smoke alarms, carbon monoxide detectors, or pool fencing.

The duty of disclosure has also been recognized by many courts regardless of statutory obligations, and all relevant information that would affect a decision to purchase should be disclosed by the seller. An evolving area of disclosure debate is the disclosure required when the property being sold was used as a production facility for methamphetamine, or was a so-called "meth lab." Even in those states that protect sellers from failing to disclose criminal activity, the presence of "meth labs" on the property must be disclosed because of possible health risks.[4]

Practical Tip

Before buying property, talk to the neighbors. Find out about noises and check with others for the history of the property. Have experts check the physical condition of the property for everything from leaky roofs to malfunctioning air conditioners.

Ethical Issue

Roberts purchased a home through a realty. When she learned that one of the sellers had died of hepatitis and the other from pneumonia, she suspected that the sellers had AIDS and she brought suit against their estates and the realty for their failure to disclose this psychologically important information about the property. Should Roberts be permitted to rescind the contract? Do you think she has the right to that information about the sellers? If you were the real estate agent, would you feel an obligation to disclose such information? What response is appropriate in those states where the agent is prohibited from disclosing whether the seller had AIDS?

Psychological Disclosure Statutes

A new form of disclosure statute has resulted from cases such as *Reed* and because of additional issues that could have a psychological impact on the buyer and possible resulting reduction in value.[5] More appropriately named "nondisclosure statutes," these laws shield sellers and their agents from liability for the nondisclosure of murder, suicide, or other felonies committed on the property or that a resident or former resident suffers from AIDS (see Chapter 12 for more discussion of broker/agent responsibilities regarding these types of disclosures). Some states require disclosure for three years and then protect sellers and real estate agents against nondisclosure.

Currently, nearly all states have some form of statute on nondisclosure of information that could have a psychological impact and on liability shields. However, the statutes often leave open the question as to the seller's

Practical Tip

Issues of disclosure often conflict with sellers' and brokers' duties under the Fair Housing Act (see Chapter 19). In other words, answering a question may result in a pattern of not selling certain properties. Some real estate agents answer buyers' questions about stigmatized (psychologically impacted) property as follows: "It is the policy of our firm not to answer inquires of this nature one way or the other. In addition, any type of response to such inquiries by me or other agents may be a violation of federal fair housing laws. If you believe that this information is relevant to your decision to buy the property, you must pursue this investigation on your own."

4. A.R.S. §32-2156 exempts sellers from liability for failure to disclose criminal activity, but Arizona mandates disclosure if meth labs existed on the property. A.R.S. §32-101.
5. For example, Connecticut's statute provides (at Conn. Gen. Stat. 20-329cc) "'psychologically impacted' means. ... ., but is not limited to: (1) the fact that an occupant of real property is, or was at any time suspected to be, infected or has been infected with the human immunodeficiency syndrome, as defined in section 19a-581; or (2) the fact that the property was at any time suspected to have been the site of a homicide, other felony or suicide."

Practical Tip

Avoid misrepresentation issues:

1. *Don't state unverified information.*
2. *Don't predict the future for property conditions or equipment (e.g., "This air conditioner will last 10 years").*
3. *Get independent confirmation of material information.*
4. *Carefully and visually inspect the property.*
5. *Document what you say and the questions you answer.*
6. *Know the "red flags" of real property (see Chapters 12 and 19).*
7. *Disclose all material issues, defects, and conditions.*

or agent's response if the buyer specifically asks a question about such activity on the property. Most legal experts agree that if there is a specific question from a buyer, the seller or his agent cannot lie about the property and would be required to disclose such information.

CONSIDER 14.17

Must a seller disclose to a buyer that his neighbors are unusually noisy, that is, that their parties sometimes cause the seller's house to shake? *Shapiro v. Sutherland*, 76 Cal. Rptr. 2d 101 (1998)

Cautions and Conclusions

To be certain a real estate contract is complete and enforceable, the parties must not only follow the basic contract rules for formation, they must be certain they have covered all the contingencies and issues. This chapter has explained the most common pitfalls in real estate contracts, which include:

- The danger of multiple offers and having two parties accept.
- The need to have minds meet on all the terms, whether material or immaterial.
- Contingency clauses so that performance is not required until certain events occur, such as the buyer obtaining financing, the seller being able to deliver marketable title, or experts concluding the property is termite-free.
- The need for care in the folllowing:

a. Details of transfer, such as how the buyer will take title, how the rent and taxes will be apportioned, who will carry insurance until closing, and how the condition of the property will be preserved

b. Providing for damages through a liquidated damages clause so that the earnest money becomes the damages for breach.

c. Adequate disclosure about the property's nature and history that will include everything from soil conditions to whether there was a murder there.

d. Federal law compliance with the ILSDFA and the Truth-in-Lending laws.

A contract for the sale and purchase of real estate may seem like a simple exchange of title, but it is a complex transaction with many layers that requires careful negotiation and drafting.

Key Terms

acceptance, 372
consideration, 378
counteroffer, 369
Department of Housing and Urban Development (HUD), 386
earnest money, 383
environmental contingency clauses, 391
implied warranty of habitability, 387
Interstate Land Sales Full Disclosure Act (ILSFDA), 385
liquidated damages, 394
marketable title, 393
misrepresentation, 397
offer, 367
option, 369
property report, 386
rescission, 397
specific performance, 397
statement of record, 386
transfer disclosure statement (TDS), 400
Truth-in-Lending Act, 384
Uniform Land Transactions Act (ULTA), 397
Uniform Marketable Title Act, 393

Chapter Problems

1. The following excerpts from letter negotiations on land occurred between Magnus Matthews and Elaine Brown.

January 4, 2006
Dear Magnus,
I am interested in buying that lot you showed me last Saturday. You talked about $40,000 as a price. That sounds good to me. Let's meet Wednesday at Frisco Kid's to iron out details.
Elaine

January 4, 2006 (via fax)
Elaine,
$40,000 is the price. Cash only. I'll see you Wednesday at 5:30.
Magnus

On January 5, 2006, a developer came to Magnus with $40,000 cash and asked to buy the lot. Magnus signed a contract and accepted a $4,000 earnest money deposit. On January 6, 2006, Magnus met Elaine at Frisco Kid's and said when he first spotted her, "Sorry, kid. I sold the lot yesterday. Cash straight up. Let's talk about any of my other lots." Did Magnus and Elaine have a contract?

2. Reese Aherns signed a contract to purchase a mountain home from Mr. and Mrs. Jack Johnson. The contract included the following condition (handwritten in an addendum signed by both parties):

Closing is subject to buyer's inspection of property by him and his designated specialist and complete satisfaction of specialist with property condition.

Aherns's specialist inspected the property and said he thought the roof would need to be replaced in a few years. He also felt some wood near the front of the cabin should be replaced. Aherns demanded that the Johnsons fix these items or he would not close. The Johnsons maintain they did not agree to any repairs; the condition was for Aherns' protection so that he could opt out of the agreement. Aherns has threatened to sue for breach of contract. Who should win?

3. State which of the following defects would be covered under the implied warranty of habitability (assuming new-home purchasers):

a. Defective air-conditioning system
b. Use of ungalvanized nails in walls
c. Variations in the color of carpet (one color ordered)
d. Sagging roof
e. Lack of insulation

4. Tommy Smith negotiated the sale of what was called the "Smith Farm" to Alex Boone. Tommy negotiated separately with Boone and had agreed to deliver to Boone option contracts from all of his relatives who held an interest in the Smith Farm. Boone had agreed to pay Tommy for obtaining the agreements and signature of his relatives who all held an interest in the Smith Farm. Boone represented a kaolin company. Kaolin is a mineral that had been discovered in great quantities beneath the Smith Farm. The mineral rights for the Smith Farm had been leased for a number of years, but no company had ever done any significant amount of mining of that subsurface area.

After the relatives had signed all the agreements to sell and the transaction had closed, they were told of Boone's relationship with a kaolin company and his payments to Tommy in exchange for Tommy assuring the relatives that the $85,000 price obtained was the best that they could hope for. The relatives brought suit to have the transaction set aside because of misrepresentation by the buyer in the transaction. Is this possible? Can a buyer be guilty of misrepresentation? Do you think Tommy had any duty to disclose what he was doing to his relatives? Did Boone have any duty to disclose who he was representing? *O.L. McClendon v. Georgia Kaolin Co., Inc.*, 837 F. Supp. 1231 (M.D. Ga. 1993)

5. Theresa S. Polk owned 181 acres of land in Polk County and she listed the property for sale with a real estate agent at a sale price of $1,299,000. On January 24, 2005, Avon made an offer to buy the property. Polk rejected the offer by making counteroffers on February 2 and February 3, 2005. There were some differences between the two counteroffers. However, both counteroffers provided that Avon had until 5 P.M. on February 7, 2005, to accept or reject them: "Seller counters Buyer's offer (to accept the counter offer, Buyer must sign or initial the counter offered terms and deliver a copy of the acceptance to the Seller by 5:00 p.m. on 2/7/05)."

On February 4, 2005, Avon made another offer, which altered the material terms of the counteroffers. Polk did not respond to the February 4 offer, and Avon signed both of Polk's counteroffers and delivered them before the February 7 deadline. Avon also delivered a $25,000 deposit check to Polk's attorney, who accepted the check but eventually wrote "VOID" on it instead of cashing it.

When Polk refused to perform her duties under the signed counteroffers, Avon filed a suit seeking specific performance.

Was there a contract formed? In determining the answer, be sure to do a chronological listing of all the back-and-forth between Polk and Avon. ***Polk v. BHRGU Avon Properties, LLC***, 946 So.2d 1120 (Fla. App. 2006).

6. Otto and Frank Mattuschek owned a ranch in Montana consisting of 3,540 acres. Carnell, a real estate broker, discovered their interest in selling the ranch, and the following instrument was executed:

PLAINTIFF'S EXHIBIT "A"

APPOINTMENT OF AGENT

I hereby appoint E. F. Carnell of Lewistown, Montana, whose office is located in said City and State, my agent with the exclusive right to sell the following property:

Our Ranch property 3540 acres, T.23 & 22-R-19 & 20-Fergus County Mont.

For the Sum of $30,000.

Conditions and terms of the sale are as follows:

Cash to seller. Possession Dec. 1, 1953, seller retain 5% landowner Royalty. Seller pay 1953 taxes, seller transfers all lease land to buyer.

And I agree to furnish a title as outlined in the following paragraph:

A. An abstract of title showing a good merchantable title to said property together with a warranty deed properly executed.

Said sale may be made for a less amount if hereafter authorized by me; you are further authorized to receive a deposit on the sale price. I agree to pay a commission of $1,000—on the sale price and the commission shall be payable as soon as the sale is made and a down payment has been made, or sale price paid in full at the time of sale, and, or as soon as a binder fee has been collected on the sale, whichever be first.

This authorization is to remain in effect and full force for 30 days and thereafter until revoked by me in writing.

Dated at Lewistown, Montana this 14th day of May 1953—

x Otto Mattuschek

x Frank Mattuschek

Carnell then met Ward, a prospective buyer, and accepted from him a check for $2,500 as a binder. The check looked as follows:

PLAINTIFF'S EXHIBIT B

93-73/921

1st Bank Stock Corporation
First National Bank of Lewistown

Lewistown, Montana, May 20, 1953 No.

Pay To The Order of *Red Carnell* $2500xx
twenty five hundred and no/100 Dollars
s/s E. E. Ward
For down Payment on land
Mattuschek
(Endorsement E. F. Carnell)

At the same time Carnell had the following executed on his letterhead:

PLAINTIFF'S EXHIBIT "C"
(Defendant's Exhibit no. 1)

Real Estate	Fergus Realty City	Property
Insurance	213 Main St. Phone 598	Farms
Rentals	Lewistown, Montana	Ranches
May 20 – 1953		

I hereby agree to buy the Mattuschek place in accordance with the terms of the agreement between E. F. Carnell and the Mattuscheks.

Dated May 14, 1953.

/s/ E. E. Ward

To Buy or Sell—See "Red" Carnell

Carnell drove to the ranch and advised the Mattuschecks of the sale. They asked if Ward would be willing to lease back the property. When closing was attempted, the Mattuscheks refused to convey the property, and the Wards filed suit seeking specific performance and damages. Is there a contract? Are any damages or remedies appropriate? *Ward v. Mattuscheks*, 330 P.2d 971 (Mont. 1958)

7. Carl and Cleo Nordstrom entered into a contract to purchase 480 acres of farmland from John Lee and Marilee Miller. The purchase price was $480,000. The advertisements for the property described it as "irrigated cropland" and stated that the property had two wells. One advertisement read:

480 acres of Prime Developed irrigation land located northwest of Garden City in Finnery County, Kansas. Two irrigation wells and approximately 14,000 ft. of underground pipe. This land is flood-irrigated and all runs are one-half mile long. THIS IS ONE YOU HAVE TO SEE TO BELIEVE.

Robert Legere, a real estate broker, contacted the Nordstroms and showed them the property. Nordstrom inspected the land, the buildings, and the wells. The Nordstroms paid $15,000 down, sold their home and store in Colorado, and purchased the property and moved in on March 2, 1976.

During the summer of 1976, one of the irrigation wells went dry. On further investigation, Nordstrom discovered that insufficient water was available to supply either well and the farm could no longer be operated owing to its geological limitations.

Nordstrom confronted the defendants with the information, and the defendants offered to drill another well and change the contract payment terms. The Nordstroms refused and brought suit for fraud and misrepresentation seeking rescission of the agreement. Should they win? *Nordstrom v. Miller*, 605 P.2d 545 (Kans. 1980)

8. The Rosens contracted to purchase from the Luttingers some property in Stamford for $85,000 and paid an $8,500 deposit. The contract contained the following contingency:

subject to and conditional upon the buyers obtaining first mortgage financing on said premises from a bank or other lending institution in an amount of $45,000 for a term of not less than twenty (20) years and at an interest rate which does not exceed 81/2 percent per annum.

The Rosens agreed to use due diligence in attempting to obtain such financing. The parties further agreed that if the Rosens were unsuccessful in obtaining financing as provided in the contract, and notified the Luttingers within a specific time, all sums paid on the contract would be refunded and the contract would terminate without further obligation of either party.

In applying for a mortgage that would satisfy the contingency clause in the contract, the Rosens relied on their attorney, who applied at a New Haven lending institution for a $45,000 loan at 8¼% per annum interest over a period of 25 years. The Rosens' attorney knew that this lending institution was the only one that would at that time lend as much as $45,000 on a mortgage for a single-family dwelling. A mortgage commitment for $45,000 was obtained with "interest at the prevailing rate at the time of closing but not less than 8¾%." Since the commitment failed to meet the contract requirement, timely notice was given to the Luttingers, and demand was made for the return of the down payment. The Luttingers' counsel thereafter offered to make up the difference between the 8¾% interest rate offered by the bank and the 8½% rate provided in the contract for the entire 25 years by a funding arrangement, the exact terms of which were not defined. The Rosens did not accept this offer and, on the Luttingers' refusal to return the deposit, an action was brought. Who should win? *Luttinger v. Rosen*, 316 A.2d 757 (Conn. 1972)

9. Patrick and Laurie Doyle submitted a form real estate purchase contract to Tom Ortega to purchase his property for $28,000. Ortega countered for $30,000. The Doyles accepted his counteroffer but changed a checked box on who would pay escrow fees. Ortega then agreed to the revisions and sent back the form changing the escrow agent from Rock Springs National Bank to an Idaho Bank. Do the Doyles and Ortega have a contract? *Doyle v. Ortega*, 872 P.2d 721 (Idaho 1994)

10. Marriott Corporation entered into a real estate purchase contract with Creyts Complex, Inc., for the purchase of some land located in Oak Creek, Wisconsin. Marriott wished to construct a Courtyard Hotel on the site. Their agreement was contingent upon Creyts Complex being able to purchase a parcel contiguous to the land it owned, called the Moss-Glowacki parcel (named for its two owners). Marriott wanted the full parcel of both the Creyts Complex tract and that of Moss-Glowacki. The agreement provided that time was of the essence and closing was to occur within 60 days. Marriott extended the agreement twice. Problems in securing title to the Moss-Glowacki parcel arose when the city of Oak Creek stepped in and demanded certain accommodations in exchange for its approval of Marriott's proposed use. The efforts to buy the property continued along with negotiations with the city for a year after the expiration date of the contract. The last written agreement on the closing date for the sale put that date as October 3, 1988. In September 1989, Marriott refused to renegotiate its contract terms in order to permit the Moss-Glowacki acquisition as well as the city's approval. Creyts Complex alleges Marriott breached its contract. Marriott claims its contract expired on October 3, 1988, and that there was no writing indicating an extension of the agreement. Must an extension for a land sale contract be in writing? *Creyts Complex, Inc. v. Marriott Corporation*, 98 F.3d 321 (7th Cir. 1996)

Would an oral modification of a real estate contract be enforceable? *Bradshaw v. Ewing*, 376 S.E.2d 264 (S.C. 1984)

11. On March 18, 1994, John and Pamela Kelly signed an offer to purchase residential property from Steven and Merrill Marx (defendants) for $335,000. The Kellys gave $1,000 earnest money with the offer.

By early May, 1994, the Kellys and Marxes had signed a purchase and sale agreement and deposited another $16,750. Clause 18 of their agreement provided:

If the BUYER shall fail to fulfill the BUYER'S agreements herein, all deposits made hereunder by the BUYER shall be retained by the SELLER as liquidated damages.

The closing date was set as September 1, 1994, but the Kellys never purchased the property because they were unable to sell their house. The Kellys notified the Marxes on August 9, 1994, that they would not be closing on the transaction.

On August 24, 1994, the Marxes accepted another offer to purchase and eventually sold the property on September 20, 1994, to new buyers for a purchase price of $360,000. The Marxes kept the Kellys' total deposit of $17,750 and the Kellys brought suit to recover it. The trial court granted the Marxes' motion for summary judgment and the court of appeals reversed. The Marxes appealed. What decision should the appellate court make? Kelly v. Marx, 705 N.E.2d 1114 (Mass. 1999)

For research activities related to this chapter, go to our text companion website at www.thomsonedu.com/westbuslaw/jennings.

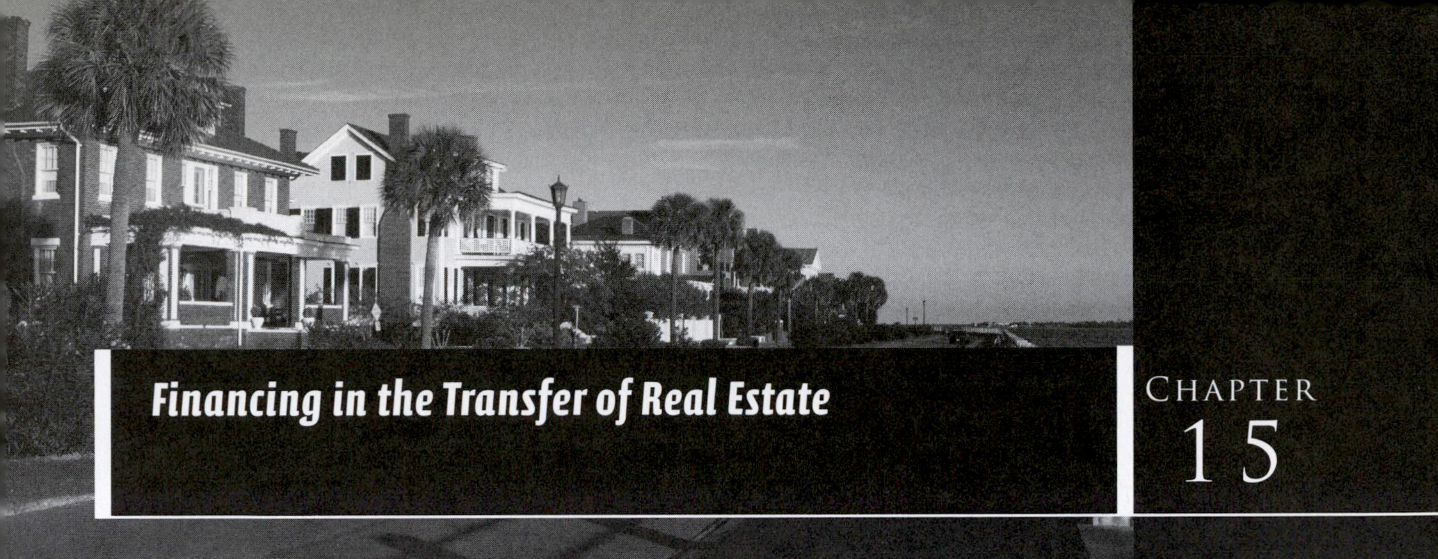

Financing in the Transfer of Real Estate

CHAPTER 15

Test Your Knowledge

Do you know the meanings of the most commonly used terms in buying a home? Check this list and then take the test at the end of the chapter (pages 458, 459).

point	*government loan*	*FHA*
deed of trust	*ARM*	*prepaids*
lock	*caveat emptor*	*conventional loan*
annual percentage rate	*loan-to-value ratio*	*balloon payment*
amortization	*creative financing*	*walk-through*
escrow	*earnest money*	*PITI*

As this partial list of terms shows, financing the purchase of real property is a complex critical element of our personal lives, but real estate finance is also a key part of any economy. This chapter discusses the processes, rights, remedies, and obligations in financing the purchase of land.

The Mortgage

Ancient civilizations, such as those in Egypt and Babylonia, pledged property to finance their purchase or to simply secure loans. Called *fiducia* in ancient Rome, obtaining security in real property required the borrower to transfer title to the lender, who retained title until the borrower had completely repaid the loan. Later, under the concept of *pignus*, the borrower retained title, but the lender was entitled to take possession at any time if the borrower defaulted.

Although the Roman concepts of *fiducia* and *pignus* were used later in Europe as methods for financing the purchase of real property, the term **mortgage** was not introduced into the English legal system until after the 1066 invasion of England by William I (William the Conqueror). Mortgage is derived from the French word *mort*, which means dead or frozen (to indicate that the borrower could not transfer the property freely), and *gage*, which means pledge.

Black's Law Dictionary defines a mortgage as

a pledge or security of a particular property for the payment of a debt or the performance of some other obligation, whatever form the transaction may take, but is not now regarded as a conveyance; a written instrument providing security for payment of a debt.

This basic definition applies to all forms of mortgages and mortgage theories. However, the details on the creation, enforcement, and rights of parties do vary among the states.

Parties to the Mortgage

A mortgage is a two-party relationship. The borrower who is buying or pledging property is referred to as the **mortgagor**. The mortgagor may be borrowing the funds to purchase the property being pledged, called a **purchase money mortgage**. Alternatively, the mortgagor may be pledging property already owned as security for a loan for other reasons.

The lender who advances the mortgagor the funds for the loan is referred to as the **mortgagee**. In a mortgage relationship, one of these two parties (mortgagor or mortgagee) will hold title to the property and the other will have an interest in the property.

Title Theory versus Lien Theory

Although all states permit the use of mortgages, how the security of a mortgage is accomplished varies. There are three theories of mortgage security: title theory, lien theory, and intermediate theory (a combination of the two).

Title theory states give the mortgagee some type of legal title to the property. This theory is the older of the two and is used primarily in the eastern states. Under title theory, the mortgagee has the right to possession and the right to collect rents on the property.

In **lien theory** states, the mortgagee has only a lien on the property and is entitled to possession and rents only upon foreclosure. Under this theory, the mortgagor actually holds title to the property. The lien theory is followed by the majority of states west of the Mississippi.

Some states follow an intermediate theory, which is a combination of the title and lien theories. In these states, the mortgagee is entitled to possession and rents upon the default of the mortgagor. However, unlike the lien theory, the mortgagee is not required to wait until after foreclosure; and unlike the title theory, the mortgagee does not hold title until after completion of proceedings mandated by statute but short of full foreclosure.

The following case illustrates the effect of a lien theory mortgage when a mortgagor is in default. The court clarifies the principle that title and all its rights remain with the mortgagor until court process reviews the default of the mortgagor.

Siffring Farms, Inc. v. Juranek

561 N.W.2d 203 (Neb. 1997)

FACTS

Donald Juranek was in default on the mortgage on his property held by Farm Credit Bank of Omaha, and a decree of foreclosure was signed on March 20, 1992. The mortgaged property was sold to Siffring Farms at a foreclosure sale held on September 3, 1993. The sale was confirmed on October 8, 1993, and a sheriff's deed to the Juranek property was delivered to Siffring on November 16, 1993.

In April 1993, Juranek and his son had entered into an agreement with J. C. Robinson Seed Company to grow seed corn. Juranek and his son grew the seed corn on the property that was subject to a mortgage. The seed contract was signed by both Juranek and his son, as well as by a representative of Robinson. While the contract provided that Robinson would supply the seed and would at all times remain owner of the crop unless Robinson chose to release it, the grower was required, among other things, to plant and fertilize according to Robinson's timing and specifications; to "rogue out" volunteer corn near the seed acreage; to protect the crop against insects, weeds, and other conditions that could damage it; and to destroy all male plants. Payment under the contract was based upon a formula and the work that had been required by Robinson. The contract further provided that the payment would be divided, with 20 percent going to Juranek's son as the grower and 80 percent to Juranek as the landlord. Under the formula for payment, the grower had the ability to establish a settlement price (or prices) per 5,000 bushels at any time (or times) between May 1, 1993, and April 21, 1994. Regardless of when the settlement price was determined; however, payments under the contract could not be made before December 16, 1993.

On November 10, 1993, Siffring filed suit against the Juraneks, Robinson, and Farm Credit for payment under the Robinson contract. Robinson deposited the money with the court and participated no further in the litigation. The lower court held that because the seed corn crop had been harvested prior to November 16, 1993, the date of the delivery of title to the property, the proceeds from the sale to Robinson had already become the personal property of Juranek and that the money from Robinson belonged to Juranek. Siffring appealed.

JUDICIAL OPINION

Flowers, District Judge. Siffring claims the district court erred in (1) finding that the payment due Juranek under the Robinson contract was personal property and not rent, (2) failing to find that the payment due Juranek was rent and that the right to it passed to Siffring with the delivery of the sheriff's deed, and (3) finding the lease to be a crop share arrangement.

The first question we must decide is whether the payment due Juranek under the Robinson contract is rent. Juranek and *amicus curiae*, Farm Credit Services of the Midlands, suggest that it is something different. The contracts identifies Juranek as the landlord and his son as the grower. The contract imposed no obligations upon Juranek. The payment due him was for the use of the land. While the testimony at trial shows that Juranek may not have been as passive as the Robinson contract contemplated, it does not necessitate a different conclusion. In this case, the payment due Juranek was for the use of his land, which, by definition, is rent.

The next question is whether the rent was unaccrued at the time the sheriff's deed was delivered to Siffring. At the time the sheriff's deed was delivered, Juranek and his son had done all that was required of them to receive payment. The seed corn had been grown, harvested, and delivered to Robinson. The right to receive payment was a fully vested and enforceable right, and Robinson was no longer using Juranek's land for any purpose under the contract. We find that under the circumstances the rent had accrued, even though the time for payment had not yet arrived. Siffring cites *Conservative Sav. & Loan Assn. v. Karp*, 218 Neb. 217, 352, N.W.2d 900 (1984), for the proposition that a purchaser at a judicial sale is entitled to all rents collected after the date the purchaser receives the sheriff's deed. What *Conservative Sav. & Loan Assn.* actually held was that the purchaser was entitled to all rents collected for the period after the date of the sheriff's deed. The case says nothing about the right to receive rents that had accrued for a prior period but had remained unpaid. In the instant case, the rent due Juranek was for the 1993 corn crop season. That season ended with the harvest of the seed corn, which was prior to the delivery of the sheriff's deed to Siffring. Robinson was no longer using Juranek's land when Siffring took title, and there was no rent due under the contract for the period that commenced on November 16, 1993.

Because the rent had accrued prior to the date Siffring took title and was for a period of time during which Juranek was the owner, we need not determine whether the rent was crop share or cash, or what difference, if any, that would make.

The payment due Juranek for the crop grown under the contract with Robinson covered a period of time prior to Siffring's ownership and had accrued prior to November 16, 1993. The payment did not pass to Siffring with the sheriff's deed.

Affirmed.

CASE QUESTIONS

1. Even though Juranek was in default during the period in which he contracted with Robinson, why does he get to keep the proceeds from the contract with Robinson?

2. What would have happened in the case if the foreclosure had occurred prior to the harvest of the seed corn?

3. What clauses could be put in a mortgage to allow the mortgagee to collect the benefits of any contract entered into during a time of default or foreclosure?

4. Who had title to the property between April 1993 and November 16, 1993? Why?

CONSIDER 15.1

Bishop Estate is the fee simple owner and was the lessor of two lots of commercial real property located in Kaka'ako, Hawai'i (the Kaka'ako Properties). Bishop Estate leased each lot for a 40-year term. Bishop Estate had pledged the lots in a mortgage to several different lenders and has defaulted on those loans. The lenders have stepped in and are collecting the rents from the two tenants. Bishop Estate objects because there has been no foreclosure. Can the lenders take the rents? Will the answer vary from state to state? *Hawaii Nat. Bank v. Cook*, 55 P.3d 827 (Haw. 2000)

Creation of Mortgage Relationship

Writing Requirement

As with all real estate transactions, the mortgage must have some form of writing or record. In addition to compliance with the Statute of Frauds, the rights of the mortgagee in the property are to a certain extent protected by public notification of the mortgagee's interest. Public notification comes through recording the mortgage with the appropriate government agency—the same agency where deeds (Chapter 13) and security interests (Chapters 5 and 6) are recorded. Mortgages are complex land interests and recorded documents control the parties' interests, rights, and remedies. As is the case with all other written requirements, the documents and signatures can now be electronic.

Underlying Debt Requirement

The Debt Instrument A mortgage is invalid unless there is some underlying debt. In other words, a mortgage cannot be enforced unless the mortgagor owes some debt to the mortgagee. Generally, and particularly in the sale and purchase of residential property, that underlying debt is evidenced by a **promissory note**. The promissory note is the actual contractual arrangement between the parties for the loan of funds. It is usually a very simple instrument specifying the principal amount, the rate of interest, and the payment terms. Also, the promissory note indicates that its payment is secured by a mortgage or deed of trust. Figure 15.1 is an example of a note secured by a mortgage.

The promissory note usually contains terms that make it negotiable—a quality that enables the lender to easily transfer and sell the note to third parties. Also, the note contains various clauses relating to acceleration, default, and attorneys' fees. These provisions are closely tied to the rights afforded mortgagees and are discussed later in this chapter in conjunction with mortgage terms. Without an underlying debt, there can be no mortgage and resulting security for a lender. The following case deals with an issue of whether a mortgage existed.

Figure 15.1 Promissory Note

$ ____________ City, State ____________ Date ____________, 2007

For value received ____________________ promises (s) to pay

to ____________________ or order, at ____________________

the sum of ____________________ DOLLARS ($ ____________).

Should default be made in the payment of any installment when due, then the whole sum of principal and interest shall become immediately due and payable at the option of the holder of this note, with interest from date of such default at the highest legal rate until paid on the entire unpaid principal and accrued interest.

Should any installment due hereunder not be paid as it matures, the amount of such installment which has matured shall, at the option of the holder of this note, bear interest at 10 percent per annum from its maturity date until paid.

Principal and interest payable in lawful money of the United States of America.

Should suit be brought to recover on this note ____________ promise(s) to pay as attorneys' fees a reasonable amount additional to the amount found hereunder.

The makers and indorsers hereof severally waive diligence, demand, presentment for payment and protest, and consent to the extension of time of payment of this note without notice.

This note is secured by a mortgage upon real property.

____________________ ____________________

____________________ ____________________

Moon v. Moon

776 N.Y.S.2d 324 (2004).

FACTS

Bonnie Sue Moon (Plaintiff) and Francis Moon (defendant) were married in 1974, separated in 2000, and divorced in 2001 after a trial. In 1995 they had purchased their marital residence from Bonnie Sue's mother, Frances Goehring (also a defendant), for $150,000, which the parties financed by a bank mortgage in the amount of $100,000. Bonnie and Francis do not dispute that they made an oral promise to pay the $50,000 balance to Goehring in installments over time. In fact, they made payments through May 2001.

After a trial, the lower court found that the terms of the oral loan agreement included 7 percent interest on the loan balance and that the loan was not subject to the Statute of Frauds and was enforceable. The court determined that the loan balance was marital debt, that Francis and Bonnie Sue are responsible for one-half of the remaining debt, and directed the balance to be paid in full upon sale of the marital residence. Goehring was permitted to intervene in the case.

JUDICIAL OPINION

Spain, Judge. Initially, we find no merit to defendant's contention that [the] Court erred in determining that the agreement at issue constituted an enforceable loan and not a mortgage, and that it was not barred by the statute of frauds. Although at trial both Goehring and plaintiff referred to this loan as a "mortgage" and the parties appear to have improperly reported the loan interest they paid to Goehring as "mortgage interest" on joint income tax returns, the record does not support a finding that the financial arrangement between the parties and Goehring was indeed a mortgage, either in law or in equity.

Specifically, "[a] mortgage is an interest in land created by a written instrument providing security for the performance of a duty or the payment of a debt." Further, "[a]n equitable mortgage has been defined as a transaction that has the intent but not the form of a mortgage and that a court will enforce in equity to the same extent as a mortgage." Here, no mortgage instrument or written agreement to make a mortgage exists, and no other evidence was presented that Goehring was to hold any interest in the real property as a security for the loan. Rather, the overwhelming evidence supports [the] Court's determination that this financial arrangement was an unsecured loan and that "there [was] no attempt to enforce or create a mortgage."

Further, [the] Court credited the testimony of plaintiff and Goehring that they all agreed that the loan payments would be $300 per month at 7% interest, with a balloon payment after 10 years. The court found defendant's testimony lacking in credibility - including his denial that the parties agreed to pay 7% interest - in light of his admission that their joint tax returns reflect a tax deduction for interest paid on the loan at that rate. The court's assessment of the credibility of the witnesses is entitled to great weight and its determination of the terms of the loan and its calculation of the balance owed as of May 15, 2001 will not be disturbed as they are amply supported by the record.

Next, [the] Court properly rejected defendant's assertion that the oral agreement was unenforceable under the statute of frauds. Of course, an agreement which cannot be performed within one year is void and therefore unenforceable, by its terms, under the statute of frauds unless it is in writing and subscribed by the party to be charged. However, if "there might be any possible means of performance within one year * * * the one-year provision" does not apply. Here, the oral agreement between the parties was devoid of any restriction against prepayment within one year and, as such, the possibility remained of complete performance within one year without breaching the agreement.

The judgment is affirmed.

CASE QUESTIONS

1. If there is not a mortgage, what was the parties' relationship?
2. How did the parties classify their relationship?
3. Why was their agreement enforceable despite the Statute of Frauds? Don't mortgages have to be in writing to be enforceable?

Federal Regulation of Mortgage Debt Instruments

Federal Disclosure Requirements in Mortgage Debt

Federal Disclosure Regulations The note underlying a mortgage must comply with all applicable federal regulations. The **Truth-in-Lending laws** are part of the **Federal Consumer Credit Protection Act**. The Federal Reserve Board promulgated the specifics on loan disclosures and forms, which are referred to as **Regulation Z** (12 C.F.R. §226 *et seq.*). Over the past few years, Regulation Z has undergone what has been called a simplification process. The goal of the rule changes was to provide as much limited and straightforward language in the disclosure requirements as possible. Regulation Z, which applies to consumer credit transactions, including mortgages, requires specific disclosures to the consumer borrowers. Electronic notification and signatures are now acceptable, with the following specific provisions on electronic disclosure:

- Federal agencies follow E-Sign Act (15 U.S.C. §7001 *et seq.*) and any electronic signature qualifies for regulation requirements for a signature or initials.
- A creditor may provide any Regulation Z disclosure requirement by electronic communication.
- A consumer's electronic consent qualifies as a signature.
- A creditor that uses electronic communication to provide disclosures must
  (1) Send the disclosure to the consumer's electronic address; or
  (2) Make the disclosure available at another location such as an Internet website; and
    (i) Alert the consumer of the disclosure's availability by sending a notice to the consumer's electronic address (or to a postal address, at the creditor's option).

(ii) Make the disclosure available for at least 90 days from the date the disclosure first becomes available or from the date of the notice to the consumer, whichever is later.[1]

Regulation Z applies to mortgage lenders who make consumer loans, but also applies to brokers and other private parties involved in installment sales and other creative financing methods (discussed later in this chapter). However, Regulation Z does not apply to the following:

1. Business transactions
2. Commercial transactions
3. Agricultural transactions
4. Organizational credit transactions

If Regulation Z does apply to a transaction, then the lender/creditor must furnish the following information to the borrower:

1. Identity of creditor
2. Cash price
3. Annual percentage rate (APR)
4. Finance charge including any prepaid finance charges
5. Amount financed and itemization
6. Total payment amount
7. Number of payments
8. Amount per payment
9. Due date for payments
10. Late payment charges

These disclosures are usually made on a statement separate from the promissory note and mortgage documents.

ETHICAL ISSUE

What are the ethics of disclosure when a real estate professional is dealing with an inexperienced borrower or buyer? Is it the job of the mortgage broker or real estate broker to inform the borrower/buyer of all his or her rights? What are the ethics of obtaining a higher interest rate from a borrower because of his or her inexperience?

Federal Debt Rescission Regulations Although Regulation Z provides for a three-day rescission period for security interests and second mortgages, this rescission period does not apply to **residential mortgage transactions** for first mortgages on property being purchased by a consumer for use as a residence. However, the consumer who executes a second note and mortgage on his residence does enjoy the protection of the three-day rescission period. In these types of secondary consumer financings, including home equity loans, the lender must disclose the right of rescission and also provide the consumer/borrower, in written form, the procedures for exercising their right of rescission. Figure 15.2 is a sample right-to-rescission form from the regulations with the new plain English requirements. If the lender makes an error in its required disclosures on APR and other terms of the loan, the consumer is given a three-year right of rescission. The *Carmichael* case is an important decision on what happens when credit disclosures are inaccurate.

1 Full details on electronic communication by lenders can be found at 12 C.F.R. §226.36.

Figure 15.2 Notice of Right to Cancel

G-8—Rescission Model Form (When Adding a Security Interest)

1. Your Right to Cancel.

You have agreed to give us a [mortgage/lien/security interest] [on/in] your home as security for your existing open-end credit account. You have a legal right under federal law to cancel the [mortgage/lien/security interest], without cost, within three business days after the latest of the following events:

(1) the date of the [mortgage/lien/security interest] which is ____________ ; or
(2) the date you received your Truth-in-Lending disclosures; or
(3) the date you received this notice of your right to cancel the [mortgage/lien/security interest].

If you cancel the [mortgage/lien/security interest], your cancellation will apply only to the [mortgage/lien/security interest]. It will not affect the amount you owe on your account. Within 20 calendar days after we receive your notice of cancellation, we must take the necessary steps to reflect that any [mortgage/lien/security interest] [on/in] your home has been cancelled. We must also return to you any money or property you have given to us or to anyone else in connection with this increase.

You may keep any money or property we have given you until we have done the things mentioned above, but you must then offer to return the money or property. If it is impractical or unfair for you to return the property, you must offer its reasonable value. You may make the offer at your home or at the location of the property. Money must be returned to the address shown below. If we do not take possession of the money or property within 20 calendar days of your offer, you may keep it without further obligation.

How to Cancel.

If you decide to cancel the [mortgage/lien/security interest], you may do so by notifying us, in writing, at

________________________.

(creditor's name and business address).

You may use any written statement that is signed and dated by you and states your intention to cancel, or you may use this notice by dating and signing below. Keep one copy of this notice no matter how you notify us because it contains important information about your rights.

If you cancel by mail or telegram, you must send the notice no later than midnight of (date) ____________ (or midnight of the third business day following the latest of the three events listed above). If you send or deliver your written notice to cancel some other way, it must be delivered to the above address no later than that time.

I WISH TO CANCEL.

______________________________ ______________

Consumer's Signature Date

CARMICHAEL V. THE PAYMENT CENTER, INC.

336 F.3d 636 (C.A.7 2003); cert. denied, 541 U.S. 987 (2004)

FACTS

In March 2001, The Payment Center, Inc. (PCI), lent Harry and Louise Carmichael $69,000 for home remodeling, which they secured through a mortgage on their house. The promissory note called for a series of 12 monthly payments of $709.74, followed by a final balloon payment of all remaining principal and interest in the 13th month, although the Carmichaels had the option of prepayment. In an effort to comply with the Act, PCI submitted a TILA statement to the Carmichaels. The statement was accurate except for two glaring errors: it greatly overstated the finance charge as $188,716.76, and it likewise overstated that the Carmichaels' total of payments would be $257,716.76. Both amounts due under the loan contract were only a fraction of the numbers listed. Despite the obvious mistakes in the TILA document, the Carmichaels made several of the $709.74 monthly payments to PCI. In October 2001, they then made several attempts to rescind the loan, each of which PCI rebuffed.

Harry and Louise Carmichael sued PCI alleging that PCI violated the Truth-in-Lending Act (TILA or the Act), 15 U.S.C. §1601, *et seq.*, by failing to make adequate disclosures regarding their loan, and by failing to allow them the extended rescission period of three years required when a creditor fails to make a material disclosure. The district court granted summary judgment, holding that PCI's disclosures were adequate under the Act and that the extended rescission period was therefore unavailable to the Carmichaels. The Carmichaels appealed.

JUDICIAL OPINION

Manion, Circuit Judge. The first issue on appeal is whether PCI adhered to §1638(a)(6)'s amount requirement regarding the 13th payment. It is undisputed that PCI's TILA document describes the 13th payment's amount as encompassing "the balance of unpaid principal and interest to be paid in full"; there is no dollar figure for the 13th payment. Therefore, we must first decide whether, as the Carmichaels maintain, only a dollar figure can satisfy §1638(a)(6)'s amount requirement. This is an issue of first impression in this jurisdiction and, as far as we can discern, a question that none of our sister circuits has answered.

The Act's definition section does not define the term "amount."

Regulation Z, however, shows that the broader concept of amount applies within the context of TILA. It provides that, "[i]n a transaction in which a series of payments varies because a finance charge is applied to the unpaid principal balance, the creditor *may* comply with this paragraph by disclosing... (i)[t]he *dollar amounts* of the largest and smallest payments in the series." This provision illustrates that "amount" does not necessarily equate to "dollar figure" within the scheme of TILA and its implementing regulations. First, the provision's use of the word "may" indicates that providing a dollar figure as to the largest and smallest payments is a permissive, instead of mandatory, means of satisfying §1638(a)(6)'s amount requirement, which leads unavoidably to the conclusion that there must be other ways to satisfy the requirement. The provision also implies the possibility that the dollar figures of the other payments in the series need not be given, which leads to the same conclusion.

Regulation Z makes clear that there are instances in which a creditor may satisfy the amount requirement without providing a dollar figure. In light of that consideration, it is safe to conclude that the word "amount" in §1638(a)(6) does not necessarily equate to "dollar figure."

Reading the Act and its implementing regulations as a whole, and in light of analogous precedent, we hold that providing a dollar figure is not the only means of adhering to §1638(a)(6)'s amount requirement. That leads us, then, to the more fundamental question of whether the disclosure that PCI made regarding the 13th payment, although not in the form of a dollar figure, satisfied §1638(a)(6).

A creditor's TILA disclosures must meet an objective standard, providing the relevant information in a form that a "reasonable person" would understand. Here, a reasonable person in the Carmichaels' position would have comprehended what "the balance of unpaid principal and interest to be paid in full" meant. The loan was for $69,000 at an APR of 12%. The loan called for 12 monthly payments of a minimum of $709.74 each, which adds to $8,516.88 over the course of a year. Thus, a reasonable consumer who paid the minimum payments for the first twelve months would have known that the first twelve payments would cover mostly interest, and that the 13th payment would be slightly less than the principal loan of $69,000, which is what one would expect to be the case for a construction loan with a balloon payment. *See generally* Marianne Moody Jennings, *Real Estate Law* 579 (5th ed.1999). Had he, or someone on his behalf, made the calculations, our reasonable consumer could have learned that the precise number was $68,727.37. In short, this case is an example of how the amount requirement can be satisfied by providing a method that would enable a reasonable consumer to calculate the dollar figure of a final payment where the dollar figure of that final payment depends on the actual payments the consumer had made beforehand.

The Carmichaels disagree, contending that because the reasonable consumer is "left to guess the amount of the 13th payment," he "could easily assume the 13th payment to be $249,199.88, *e.g.* -subtracting 12 monthly payments of $709.74 each ($8,516.88) from the total of payments of $257,716.76 ($257,716.76–$8516.88 = $ 49,199.88)." We do not subscribe to that point of view. Such an "easy" assumption would be ridiculous where, as here, the original loan was for $69,000.

Aside from that obvious defect, there is another fundamental flaw in the Carmichaels' position. The Carmichaels are essentially saying that PCI violated §1638(a)(6) because, by grossly overstating the total of payments, PCI insinuated that the 13th payment was far larger than actually was the case. PCI, relying upon 15 U.S.C. §1605(f)(1)(B), argues that TILA immunizes creditors from liability under the Act where, as here, they overstate a disclosure affected by a finance charge. Section 1605(f)(1)(B), through which Congress amended the Act in 1995, provides as follows:

In connection with credit transactions not under an open end credit plan that are secured by real property or a dwelling, the disclosure of the finance charge and other disclosures affected by any finance charge-

(1) shall be treated as being accurate for purposes of this subchapter if the amount disclosed as the finance charge...

(B) is greater than the amount required to be disclosed under this subchapter... 15 U.S.C. §1605(f)(1)(B) (emphasis added).

Theoretically, the $257,716.76 total-of-payments figure, although patently incorrect, was "affected by any finance charge," because it corresponds to the addition of the $69,000 principal to the inaccurately listed finance charge of $188,716.76. Therefore, the $249,199.88 amount of the 13th payment that, the Carmichaels argue, derives from the total-of-payments number was itself "affected by [the overstated] finance charge" and, pursuant to §1605(f)(1)(B), must be "treated as being accurate." Thus, even after drawing all factual inferences in the Carmichaels' favor, we hold that there is no genuine issue of fact as to the Carmichaels' claim under §1638(a)(6). The Act protects consumers only when the stated amount is *less* than the amount required to be disclosed.

We turn now to the Carmichaels' second claim: that PCI violated §1638(a)(4), which requires creditors accurately to disclose the contractual APR. To be accurate, such a disclosure must "reflect the terms of the legal obligation between the parties," which, of course, derive from the loan contract. Here, the loan contract was the parties' promissory note, which required the Carmichaels to pay an APR of 12%. It would therefore seem obvious that the 12% APR listed on the TILA document was accurate and that PCI is not liable under §1638(a)(4).

The Carmichaels' position, nonetheless, is that the APR should be calculated not from the loan contract, but should be "based on [PCI's] disclosed Finance Charge of $188,716.76, [the] Amount Financed of $69,000, 12 monthly payments of $709.74 each and a 13th installment of the remaining balance," which equates to an APR of "130.7721 percent." Because PCI did not list an APR of 130.7721% on the TILA document, so the argument goes, it violated §1638(a)(4). This contention is incorrect because it ignores the fundamental point that the terms of the contract dictate the TILA disclosure, not vice versa.

In their reply brief, the Carmichaels try a different approach, arguing for the first time that "the APR is impossible to calculate." Because they have waited until this juncture to contend that no calculation of the APR is possible, that argument is waived. Moreover, to the extent that the Carmichaels' argument might be construed to imply that the creditor overstated the APR, the Carmichaels still would lose. The APR is a disclosure affected by the finance charge. Therefore, where the APR is overstated, §1605(f)(1)(B) immunizes a creditor from liability for that technical inaccuracy. Even where the overstatement is so obviously an error (to everyone except the Carmichaels), they cannot prove that PCI violated §1638(a)(4).

The Carmichaels' final argument on appeal is that they were entitled to an extended period of recision [*sic*] under §1635(f). The Act provides that a consumer may rescind, *inter alia*, a consumer credit transaction in which the creditor retains a security interest on the consumer's home. In the typical case, this right extends until the third business day after the later of two dates: the date on which the parties consummate the transaction, or the date on which disclosure and recision [*sic*] forms are delivered to the consumer 15 U.S.C. §1635(a). If, however, the creditor fails to deliver the forms, or fails to provide the required information, the right to rescind extends for three years after the transaction's consummation.

The Carmichaels base their right to the three-year recision [*sic*] period on the contention that PCI failed to provide the information that §§1638(a)(4) and (a)(6) require. Because we have held as a matter of law that PCI did provide the requisite information, it follows that the Carmichaels were not entitled to the extended recision period of §1635(f).

We affirm summary judgment in favor of PCI.

CASE QUESTIONS

1. Describe the errors that the Carmichaels allege were made by their lender.
2. How does the court acknowledge the errors but find no violation of TILA? What do we learn is the purpose of the TILA?
3. Why are the Carmichaels not entitled to the three-year, as opposed to three-day, rescission period?
4. What authority did the court cite on real estate financing?

ETHICS ISSUE

Evaluate the ethics of the Carmichaels in their effort to be released from their debt obligation.

Federal Debt Credit Advertising Regulation Regulation Z also regulates the advertisement of the credit terms by lenders. Regulation Z defines an **advertisement** as "a commercial message in any media that promotes, directly or indirectly, a credit transaction." Regulation Z also covers electronic types of messages, and those messages must comply with hard-copy advertising disclosure requirements. Advertisements must be accurate, but are also subject to mandatory disclosure requirements. If a lender advertises finance charge rates, it must include an APR, an expression of the cost of credit according to its yearly rate. Regulation Z provides the formulas for computing APR. Finance charges are one example of **triggering language** in ads that is also regulated. Once triggering language appears in an ad, the lender must make additional disclosures. Other triggering language includes:

1. Amount or percentage of any down payment
2. Number of payments or period of repayment
3. Amount of any payment
4. Amount of any finance charge

The additional disclosures that must be made in advertisements using triggering terms are as follows:

1. Amount or percentage of down payment
2. Terms of repayment
3. Annual percentage rate
4. Disclosures of any increases in payments or rates that may occur

Two examples of down-payment triggering language are "total move-in costs of $1,000" or "as low as 10 percent down." The phrase "30-year loan" is an example of a triggering term because it indicates the repayment period. "Payable in monthly installments of $550" is triggering language related to the amount of the payments. Triggering language related to the finance charge includes "total cost of credit is..." and "$90,000 mortgage with two points." Use of any of these triggering phrases requires more disclosure. However, general language such as "no down payment," "years to repay," and "monthly installments to suit your budget" may be used without triggering additional disclosure requirements.

CONSIDER 15.2

Do the following advertisements contain any triggering language requiring further disclosure?

a. NEW LISTING—Exciting three-bedroom home. Excellent Northeast Mesa location. Pool and tennis court. Low rates and low down payment.
b. 5% DOWN, 121/2% INTEREST LOAN—Country style two-bedroom and guest house.

Federal Regulation of Home Equity Loans

Interest on home mortgages is deductible and lenders for home equity lines of credit have been aggressively marketing their services and urging consumers to convert their debt into a home equity loan. Regulation Z requires the following disclosures to consumers for these credit arrangements:

1. That the line of credit creates a security interest in their home and that they could lose their home if the obligation is not repaid.
2. That they need to consult a tax advisor regarding limitations on the deductibility of the interest.

3. What charges are incurred in obtaining the line of credit (such as application fees, points, and annual maintenance fees).
4. All the standard Regulation Z disclosures regarding rates, rate changes, minimum payments, APR, and the right of rescission (also three days for all lines of credit and loans that create a security interest in a debtor's home).

Model disclosure forms have been developed by the Federal Reserve Board for these types of credit arrangements as well. Web Exhibit 15.1 is a sample disclosure form for a home equity credit line.

Federal Regulation of the Decision to Extend Credit for Real Property Financing

The federal government also regulates lenders in their decisions to extend credit for the owner's purchase of real property.

Equal Credit Opportunity Act Mortgage lenders are also subject to the provisions of the **Equal Credit Opportunity Act (ECOA)** (15 U.S.C. §1691), which prohibits lenders from refusing loans or discriminating in lending on the basis of sex, marital status, race, religion, or national origin. Penalties for violations include private suits as well as fines. Under the ECOA, lenders must base their decisions on issues of creditworthiness that can be substantiated, and not on race, gender, religion, and other protected class grouping under the act.[2]

The application of the ECOA to real estate loans is slightly different from other credit arrangements because, as a practical matter, the real estate lender will generally need the signature of the spouse for the mortgage or deed of trust to ensure protection of its security in real property for the loan. A dower or marital property right can deprive a lender of one-half of the security in a piece of land when a spouse claims that marital interest. A creditor cannot enforce sale and foreclosure rights that run contra to state marital property protections. So, requiring a spouse's signature for a real estate loan is not necessarily a violation of the ECOA. (*Evans v. Centralfed Mortgage Co.*, 815 F.2d 348 [5th Cir. 1987] and *Rooms With a View, Inc. v. Private Nat. Mortg. Ass'n, Inc.*, 7 S.W.3d 840, 850 [Tex. App. 1999].

Figure 15.3 lists the Federal Trade Commission guidelines on the Equal Credit Opportunity Act.

Fair Housing Act and Community Reinvestment Act Under the **Home Mortgage Disclosure Act**, lenders are required to furnish to the federal government information about the nature of loan applicants and their approval rates for loans by race. The latest figures (2006 Federal Financial Institutions Examination Council) show the following rates for home mortgage purchase loan denials on conventional mortgage loans: Whites (22.4%); Asian Americans (17.3%); Blacks (33.1%); Native Americans (36.2%); and Hispanics (29.7%). The reporting requirements are seen as a means for determining violations of the Fair Housing Act as well as a way to curb "redlining," the red circling of certain areas on a map by lenders as a means of targeting high-risk areas and then using location of property in those areas as their lending criterion as opposed to individual qualifications (see Chapter 19 for more details on redlining).

2 The application of the ECOA has been extended in some jurisdictions from consumer transactions to commercial transactions. *Bagley v. Lumbermens Mut. Cas. Co.*, 100 F. Supp.2d 879 (N.D. Ill. 2002)

Figure 15.3 Federal Trade Commission Guidelines on ECOA

When You Apply For Credit, A Creditor May Not . . .

- Discourage you from applying because of your sex, marital status, age, race, national origin, or because you receive public assistance income.
- Ask you to reveal your sex, race, national origin, or religion. A creditor may ask you to voluntarily disclose this information (except for religion) if you're applying for a real estate loan. This information helps federal agencies enforce antidiscrimination laws. You may be asked about your residence or immigration status.
- Ask if you're widowed or divorced. When permitted to ask marital status, a creditor may only use the terms: married, unmarried, or separated.
- Ask about your marital status if you're applying for a separate, unsecured account. A creditor may ask you to provide this information if you live in "community property" states: Arizona, California, Idaho, Louisiana, Nevada, New Mexico, Texas, and Washington. A creditor in any state may ask for this information if you apply for a joint account or one secured by property.
- Request information about your spouse, except when your spouse is applying with you; your spouse will be allowed to use the account; you are relying on your spouse's income or on alimony or child support income from a former spouse; or if you reside in a community property state.
- Inquire about your plans for having or raising children.
- Ask if you receive alimony, child support, or separate maintenance payments, unless you're first told that you don't have to provide this information if you won't rely on these payments to get credit. A creditor may ask if you have to pay alimony, child support, or separate maintenance payments.

When Deciding To Give You Credit, A Creditor May Not . . .

- Consider your sex, marital status, race, national origin, or religion.
- Consider whether you have a telephone listing in your name. A creditor may consider whether you have a phone.
- Consider the race of people in the neighborhood where you want to buy, refinance, or improve a house with borrowed money.
- Consider your age, unless:
    - you're too young to sign contracts, generally younger than 18 years of age;
    - you're 62 or older, and the creditor will favor you because of your age;
    - it's used to determine the meaning of other factors important to creditworthiness. For example, a creditor could use your age to determine if your income might drop because you're about to retire;
    - it's used in a valid scoring system that favors applicants age 62 and older. A credit-scoring system assigns points to answers you provide to credit application questions. For example, your length of employment might be scored differently depending on your age.

When Evaluating Your Income, A Creditor May Not . . .

- Refuse to consider public assistance income the same way as other income.
- Discount income because of your sex or marital status. For example, a creditor cannot count a man's salary at 100 percent and a woman's at 75 percent. A creditor may not assume a woman of childbearing age will stop working to raise children.
- Discount or refuse to consider income because it comes from part-time employment or pension, annuity, or retirement benefits programs.
- Refuse to consider regular alimony, child support, or separate maintenance payments. A creditor may ask you to prove you have received this income consistently.

You Also Have The Right To . . .

- Have credit in your birth name (Mary Smith), your first and your spouse's last name (Mary Jones), or your first name and a combined last name (Mary Smith-Jones).
- Get credit without a cosigner, if you meet the creditor's standards.
- Have a cosigner other than your husband or wife, if one is necessary.
- Keep your own accounts after you change your name, marital status, reach a certain age, or retire, unless the creditor has evidence that you're not willing or able to pay.
- Know whether your application was accepted or rejected within 30 days of filing a complete application.
- Know why your application was rejected. The creditor must give you a notice that tells you either the specific reasons for your rejection or your right to learn the reasons if you ask within 60 days.
- Acceptable reasons include: "Your income was low," or "You haven't been employed long enough." Unacceptable reasons are: "You didn't meet our minimum standards," or "You didn't receive enough points on our credit-scoring system." Indefinite and vague reasons are illegal, so ask the creditor to be specific.
- Find out why you were offered less favorable terms than you applied for—unless you accept the terms. Ask for details. Examples of less favorable terms include higher finance charges or less money than you requested.
- Find out why your account was closed or why the terms of the account were made less favorable unless the account was inactive or delinquent.

A Special Note To Women

A good credit history—a record of how you paid past bills—often is necessary to get credit. Unfortunately, this hurts many married, separated, divorced, and widowed women. There are two common reasons women don't have credit histories in their own names: they lost their credit histories when they married and changed their names, or creditors reported accounts shared by married couples in the husband's name only.

If you're married, divorced, separated, or widowed, contact your local credit bureau(s) to make sure all relevant information is in a file under your own name.

The 1977 **Community Reinvestment Act (CRA)** requires banks to meet the lending needs of their community, including loans to both individuals and small businesses in low-income areas. The Federal Reserve Board, responsible for the enforcement of CRA, requires great detail in reports filed by lenders on their loan portfolios, including information on loans for multiunit housing, small businesses, and rehabilitation of neighborhoods.

Additionally, many institutional shareholders are asking for loan information from banks and requesting proxy proposals for disclosure to shareholders of bank compliance with the CRA.

Debtor's Rights in Mortgage Credit Transactions

Finding financing for a real property purchase is often difficult, involves complex paperwork, and too often requires meeting deadlines. Lenders who are not cautious in handling loan applications and decisions have been held liable to credit applicants for their bad faith. Lenders have an obligation of good faith and fair dealing and are liable to buyer/borrowers for negligence in responding to loan applications. Lenders are liable for the lack of timely approval or the withdrawal of an approval for financing already issued.

Debtor's Rights on Interest Rates: Usury

Most states have laws fixing the maximum interest rates that may be charged legally. If the lender charges a rate in excess of that statutory maximum, that is **usury**. The usury rate varies significantly from state to state and also according to changes in the economic climate and the type of credit transaction involved.

Although most lenders would never use an interest rate that exceeds the statutory maximum, they may step into usury accidentally with fees on top of the loan interest, such as financier's charges and points. However, some of these fees and charges may be made without making the loan usurious. The following list explains such charges:

a. *Charges for costs actually incurred.* Additional charges by a lender for necessary expenditures actually made in making the loan will not make the transaction usurious. Examples include appraisal fees, credit report fees, survey costs, title search and insurance costs, recording fees, and actual costs incurred in the preparation of loan documents.
b. *Charges for commissions by loan brokers.* Brokers, in negotiating a loan between parties, may charge commissions and such commissions will not make the loan usurious. However, such a commission charge must be paid to a third party and not the lender.
c. *Standby commitment charges.* Often builders have construction loans for a project but not permanent financing. Instead, the builder arranges for a standby commitment for permanent financing from a lender. Because the standby commitment requires the lender to produce the money upon the builder's demand, with no guarantee that the builder will make such a demand, the lender's funds are tied up for a period of time. The lender can charge a commitment fee in addition to the maximum legal interest rate for the loan because of the funds commitment.
d. *Late charges.* Late fees are not considered usurious because of the expense, time, and paperwork involved in collecting and posting late payments. Regulation Z does require disclosure of late fees up front. The following is the recommended Federal Reserve Board clause for late fees or penalties:

Late Charge: If a payment is late, you will be charged——% of the payment.

e. *Government loan charges.* When a borrower seeks a government insured loan (such as a Federal Housing Administration [FHA] loan), there is additional paperwork involved, and the lender is also required to pay a premium for government loan insurance. These expenses may be charged to the borrower without tipping the loan into usurious territory.
f. *Construction loan charges.* Construction lenders generally have more paperwork and tasks than consumer lenders. The principal amount of a construction loan is paid in installments as construction progresses, with the lender inspecting before releasing funds and doing the additional paperwork (including mechanic's liens as discussed in Chapter 6) for payment of subcontractors and suppliers. Fees for these services do not cause usury problems.
g. *Life insurance premiums.* Many lenders require the borrower to maintain life insurance, with the benefits to be used to retire the note debt. Life insurance premiums for such mandatory policies related to the borrower are not part of the loan's interest charges.
h. *Prepayment penalties.* Whether early loan repayment charges are included in the total interest charges varies from state to state. However, even in states where prepayment penalties are not included in the interest rate, the amount of the charges may be limited by state statutes.
i. *Brundage clauses.* A **Brundage clause** requires the borrower to pay any tax that may be imposed on the lender's mortgage. However, in some states the loan will be usurious if the tax plus the interest charged exceeds the statutory maximum.

Each state provides that certain types of lenders and transactions are exempt from the usury laws. For example, all states with usury laws have some type of exemption for business loans, and many states exempt FHA-insured loans from their usury statutes.

The penalties for charging a usurious rate vary from state to state. In some states, the lender forfeits all interest and recovers only the principal. In others, the lender forfeits only that amount of interest above the maximum. In yet other states, the entire contract is void, and the lender forfeits both interest and principal.

Debtor's Rights, Subprime Loans, and Predatory Lending

Troubled credit history is a problem for debtors when they want to buy a home. Nonetheless, when there is bad credit repentance and lender redemption, the latter can be profitable. Over the last decade there has been significant growth in the subprime mortgage market. The subprime mortgage market is defined to include those borrowers with a FICO (Fair Isaac Co.) score below 570. The median FICO score is 720, with a perfect score being 850. The subprime home mortgage market, from 1994 to 2004, grew from $35 billion to $401 billion. The foreclosure rates range from 20 to 50% on subprime loans, with the likelihood of default higher on many of the loans because of loan structure that includes high interest rates as well as balloon payments (see below for more discussion). The high default and foreclosure rates carried a secondary market impact at the beginning of 2007 as subprime lenders collapsed under the weight of their foreclosure portfolios in a soft real estate market.

ETHICS ISSUE

"We made so much money, you couldn't believe it. And you didn't have to do anything. You just had to show up,"[3] was the comment of Kal Elsayed, a former executive at New Century Financial, a mortgage brokerage firm based in Irvine, California. With his red Ferrari, Mr. Elsayed enjoyed the benefits of the growth in the subprime mortgage market. However, those risky debtors, whose credit histories spelled trouble, are now defaulting on their loans. Century Financial is under federal investigation for stock sales and accounting irregularities as it tries to deal with his portfolio of $39.4 billion in subprime loans. "Subprime mortgage lending is easy," is the comment of mortgage brokers and analysts, until the market changes. What are the ethical issues in subprime mortgage loans? Do the lenders fill a market niche? What could or should they have done differently? Why do you think so many of the subprime lenders experienced financial collapse in the 2006–2007 period?

The subprime market is fraught with complexities that the average consumer may not fully understand as he or she realizes the dream of home ownership or a means for paying off credit-card debt through a home equity loan. Some subprime borrowers are able to make payments initially because they have interest-only loans for a three- to five-year period. After that initial phase-in, their payments escalate to include principal, with the result being an inability to pay or keep current. In many subprime loans, the lender builds in very high costs for closing, appraisal, and other fees with a result known as "equity stripping." The loan amount is so high that the borrower owes more than 100 percent of the value of the home. The lenders often return to customers and use a practice known as "flipping." The borrowers refinance their homes on the promise of lower payments, a lower rate, or some benefit that may actually be real. However, the costs of refinancing, known as "packing" the loan, increase the lender's interest in the home. The lender's additional interest, coupled with an escalating interest rate produce higher and higher loan balances with longer payment periods and a greater likelihood of foreclosure.

These practices, coupled with marketing techniques of subprime lenders that target the poor and elderly, have resulted in significant state and local legislation designed to curb subprime lender activities. Known as "Homeowner Security Protection Acts" or "High Cost Home Loan Acts" or "Home Loan Protection Acts," these state laws take various approaches to protecting consumers from predatory lending practices.[4] Some states limit charges or interest rates. Other states limit foreclosures or refinancings within certain time frames. Some, such as Cleveland's ordinance, simply prohibit predatory practices, making such activity a criminal misdemeanor. Cleveland's ordinance was described by a court as follows:

"Predatory loan" in Cleveland is defined as any residential loan bearing interest at an annual rate that exceeds the yield on comparable Treasury securities by either four and one-half to eight percentage points for first mortgage loans or six and one-half to ten percentage points for junior mortgages. In addition, loans are considered predatory if they were made under circumstances involving the following practices or include the following terms: loan flipping, balloon payments, negative amortization, points and fees in excess of four percent of the loan amount or in excess of $800 on loans below $16,000, an increased interest rate on default, advance payments, mandatory arbitration, prepayment penalties, financing of credit insurance, lending without home counseling,

3 Julie Creswell and Vikas Bajas, "A Mortgage Crisis Begins to Spiral, and the Casualties Mount," *New York Times*, March 5, 2007, pp. C1, C4.

4 For a summary of the state legislation on predatory lending practices, see *Therese G. Franzén* and *Leslie M. Howell*, "Predatory Lending Legislation in 2004," 60 *Business Lawyer* 677 (2005).

lending without due regard to repayment, or certain payments to home-improvement contractors under certain circumstances.[5]

Cleveland's ordinance, like so many of the anti-predatory statutes, has been successfully, judicially challenged by lenders who have argued that the regulation of home loans is preempted by the extensive federal regulation of both home mortgages and consumer credit.[6] (See Chapter 19 for more discussion of the constitutional issue of preemption).

Debtor's Rights with Recording

A mortgage need not be recorded to be valid. However, an unrecorded mortgage gives rights only between the borrower (mortgagor) and the lender (mortgagee). In order to protect the mortgagee against others' rights or to give the mortgagee priority in relation to other creditors, the mortgage must be recorded in the appropriate government office. Recording the mortgage gives the lender priority over subsequently recorded and unrecorded land interests. (See discussion of priorities later in this chapter.)

Terms of the Mortgage

Additional terms in the mortgage agreement, beyond just the basic requirements, protect and define the rights of the parties. The same provisions can often be found in the underlying promissory note.

Acceleration Clause

An **acceleration clause** permits the mortgagee to accelerate the maturity date of the note if the mortgagor defaults. The second paragraph in Figure 15.1 is a typical example of an acceleration clause. Virtually all mortgage notes contain an acceleration clause because without them the mortgagee's only recourse for default would be a suit to collect the payments missed or a partial foreclosure for the amount of those missed payments. The mortgagee would be required to bring suit each time there was a default. Acceleration clauses are valid in all states and are also permitted in government-insured loans for real estate.

One of the common issues with acceleration clauses is whether the lender can accelerate the loan when the lender has a history of allowing late payments. Suppose, for example, that your mortgage payment was due on the first of each month. You have never paid before the 15th of the month and have occasionally paid a late penalty. Your mortgage company has always accepted your late payments. One month you pay on the 16th of the month, with the late fee, and the lender declares you in default and accelerates your loan. In some states, the lender could not take such action until it gave notice that timely payment was now reinstated as a requirement under the mortgage. States that follow this principle of reinstatement of timeliness do not allow lenders to accelerate and foreclose until the late payment *after* reinstatement of timely performance. Lenders eliminate the problems of late payments, timeliness in reinstatement, and acceleration by putting a clause such as this in their mortgages:

5 *Am. Financial Serv. Assn. v. Cleveland*, 824 N.E.2d 553 at 557 (Oh. App. 2004).

6 *Am. Fin. Servs. Ass'n v. City of Cleveland, No. 83676,* 2004 WL 2755808, (Ohio Ct. App. 2004); *City of Dayton v. State*, No. 02-CV-3441 (Ohio Ct. Common Pleas Aug. 26, 2003); 813 N.E.2d 707 (Ohio Ct. App. 2004) *Am. Fin. Servs. Ass'n v. City of Oakland, 23 Cal. Rptr. 3d 453, 461–62* (Cal. 2005); and *Mayor of New York v. Council of New York*, 780 N.Y.S.2d 266 (N.Y. Sup. Ct. 2004). Cleveland's ordinance was held to be preempted by Ohio's laws on predatory lending.

> ***Practical Tip***
>
> *A "prior forbearance" clause is one that allows the lender to accelerate a loan when payment is late even if late payments have been made in the past. Under a prior forbearance clause, the lender does not need to reinstate his or her right to prompt payment before declaring the loan in default and accelerating the loan for the full amount due.*

Holder may exercise this option [to accelerate] during any default by maker regardless of any prior forbearance.

Interest Acceleration Clause

This clause increases the interest rate to either the maximum amount permitted by law or some other amount when some event, such as a default, occurs. Many subprime loans have **interest acceleration clauses** such as the following:

Should default occur and acceleration of the full amount of the entire indebtedness is called for, interest on the entire amount of the indebtedness shall accrue thereafter at the maximum rate of interest then permitted under the laws of the state of ____________________ or continue at the rate provided herein, whichever of said rates is greater.

Balloon Payment Clause

Usually, a mortgage is amortized over a certain number of years so that the full amount of the mortgage loan and the interest are paid when the term of the mortgage has expired. For example, after 30 years of a typical residential 30-year mortgage, the mortgagor will have paid the full amount of the debt and interest due on the mortgage.

Under a mortgage with a balloon payment, the mortgagor is still required to make periodic installment payments, but those payments do not fully amortize the amount of the loan; hence, the mortgagor will be required to pay the balance of the amount due at the end of the mortgage term. The lump sum due at the end of the mortgage term is called a **balloon payment**.

Balloon payments are typical in commercial and subprime loans. Government-insured loans cannot include balloon payment provisions.

Prepayment Penalty Clauses

The mortgagee has the right to earn the interest on the money invested in the mortgage loan for the term of the loan. Unless the note or the mortgage specifically provides, the mortgagor has no right to prepay the loan before the end of the mortgage term.

Most mortgages require the mortgagor to pay a penalty in order to prepay the loan. The penalty is compensation for the lender for having to find a new investment outlet and incurring the expenses of finding and making that reinvestment. The penalty may apply only during the first 5 to 10 years of the mortgage or can run for the full mortgage term. The Federal Reserve Board has suggested the following disclosure in consumer mortgages:

Prepayment: If you pay off early, you
may will not have to pay a penalty
may will not be entitled to a refund of part of the finance charge.

All states allow prepayment penalties; however, certain types of government-insured loans prohibit them. Also, loans that are to be sold or transferred to certain government corporations (Freddie Mac or Fannie Mae) cannot include prepayment penalties.

Late Payment Clause

Late payment clauses are usually included in mortgage documents, promissory notes, or both. These clauses allow the mortgagee to charge a late fee for payments received a certain number of days after the due date. The fee covers the bookkeeping expenses of having to post late payments as well as the loss of use of funds. Late payment clauses are legal in all types of loans. As noted earlier, acceptance of a late payment may or may not waive the right to acceleration.

Due-on-Sale Clause

The **due-on-sale clause** is a provision in the mortgage agreement that is similar to the acceleration clause. The difference is that it takes effect upon the attempted sale of the property by the mortgagor to a buyer who will take over mortgage payments. The due-on-sale clause gives the mortgagee the right to call the entire balance of an indebtedness due and payable if the borrower sells the mortgaged property. The following is an example of a due-on-sale clause:

TRANSFER OF THE PROPERTY; ASSUMPTION. If all or any part of the property or an interest therein is sold or transferred by Borrower without Lender's prior consent, excluding (a) the creation of a lien or encumbrance subordinate to this deed of trust; (b) the creation of a purchase money security interest for household appliances; (c) transfer by devise, descent, or by operation of law upon the death of a joint tenant; or (d) the grant of any leasehold interest of three years or less not containing an option to purchase, LENDER MAY, AT LENDER'S OPTION, DECLARE ALL SUMS SECURED BY THIS DEED OF TRUST TO BE IMMEDIATELY DUE AND PAYABLE.

As interest rates increase, such a clause helps the mortgagee because mortgage notes at older, unprofitable rates can be eliminated with the funds reinvested at higher rates. However, the clauses do create problems for mortgagors trying to sell property when interest rates are high. If the buyer cannot take over an existing loan and the cost of borrowing is prohibitive, then the seller's pool of buyers is small.

Although there was much confusion and debate over the validity of due-on-sale clauses during the economic downturn of the early 1980s, the issue was settled when the U.S. Supreme Court held in *Fidelity Federal Savings and Loan v. de la Cuesta*, 458 U.S. 141 (1982), that the clauses were valid and could be enforced in federally related mortgage loans. State laws declaring the clauses invalid were preempted by the federal standards that permitted enforcement.

Following the Supreme Court's decision, Congress enacted the Garn–St. Germain Depository Institutions Act of 1982 (called the Garn Bill; 12 U.S.C. §226), which provides that states may not restrict the enforcement of due-on-sale clauses with respect to real property loans except to protect home buyers who relied on due-on-sale restrictions and reasonably believed they had assumable loans. The Garn Bill clarified the rights of both mortgagors and mortgagees when there is a due-on-sale clause in their agreement.

Types of Mortgages

Government-Insured Mortgages—FHA and VA Mortgages

The acronyms **FHA** and **VA** are used widely in advertisements, discussions, and news about the housing market. Both terms signify a government-backed loan, which means that if the borrower defaults on repayment of the loan, the lender can recover the loan amount from the federal agency insuring the loan. The Federal Housing Administration (FHA) and the Veterans Administration (VA), respectively, serve as the insuring agencies for these types of loans.

These loans have restrictions, most of which are imposed for the protection of the mortgagor. For example, the interest rate on such loans is set by the federal government, and the borrower must qualify for the loan through the government agency. Also, the terms of the mortgage and note are regulated by the federal government, and certain types of clauses just discussed are prohibited. For example, as noted earlier, the balloon payment provision is prohibited in FHA and VA loans. Both FHA and VA carry maximum loan amounts, so these loans are not available for higher-priced residences. Also, the borrower is required to pay the premium for the government insurance, which is a fixed percentage of the outstanding balance for the life of the loan. There may also be down-payment minimums required on government loans.

Many different types of FHA loans have been developed to enable buyers to qualify for and afford homes. For example, FHA introduced the graduated-payment mortgage (FHA 245), which provided for a lower beginning monthly payment that is gradually increased each year over the next five years until reaching a level payment in the sixth year of the loan. FHA also provided incentives for the development of low-income housing to help those in lower-income brackets purchase homes.

In addition to the government as an insurer, a mortgagee with a VA or FHA loan also has a secondary market for these mortgages through government-owned corporations. These government-owned corporations, such as the **Federal National Mortgage Association** (**FNMA** or **Fannie Mae**) and the **Government National Mortgage Association** (**GNMA** or **Ginnie Mae**), purchase blocks of government-insured mortgages and, in some cases, conventional mortgages. These secondary-market corporations were created to encourage primary lenders to participate in the home mortgage market.

Federal Regulatory Agencies for Mortgage Lending

In 1989, the **Financial Institutions Reform, Recovery and Enforcement Act of 1989** (**FIRREA**) was passed as part of a sweeping reform of the federal thrift industry. FIRREA created a new federal regulatory scheme for financial institutions primarily responsible for real estate loans. Both the **Federal Home Loan Bank Board** (**FHLBB**) and the **Federal Savings and Loan Insurance Corporation** (**FSLIC**), original regulators of federal savings and loans, were dissolved, with their responsibilities given to the **Office of Thrift Supervision** and the **Federal Deposit Insurance Corporation** (**FDIC**). The **Resolution Trust Corporation** (**RTC**) was created to temporarily manage thrift institutions placed in conservatorship or receivership. The RTC remained an active force in the real estate industry through 1996. All remaining RTC issues are handled by the FDIC.

FIRREA also established standards for real estate appraisals as well as internal controls for federal financial institutions on their appraisals and evaluations of the qualifications of their appraisers because of the role appraisers played in the over-valuation of so many properties that led to inflated savings and loans portfolios and, ultimately, their collapses. In addition, courts have imposed professional liability on appraisers, holding them liable to third parties who rely on their appraisals in the same manner that accountants are held liable to certain third parties for their financial opinions.[7]

Conventional Mortgages

The **conventional mortgage** is a mortgage made by a private lender that is not insured by a government agency and, therefore, not subject to the government restrictions on

7 *First State Savings Bank v. Albright Associates of Ocala, Inc.*, 561 So.2d 1326 (Fla. App. 1990), but see, for a differing view: *Garden v. Frier*, 602 So.2d 1273 (Fla. 1992); *Huntington Mortg. Co. v. Mortgage Power Financial Services, Inc.*, 90 F.Supp.2d 670 (D.Md. 2000); *Cooper v. Brakora & Associates, Inc.*, 838 So.2d 679 (Fla.App. 2003) *Gibb v. Citicorp Mortg., Inc.*, 518 N.W.2d 910 (Neb. 1994).

loan structure. Conventional mortgages are offered by the same institutions offering FHA and VA loans.

Conventional mortgage interest rates will probably be higher; the down payment will probably be greater; and the lender will be able to easily incorporate balloon payments, interest acceleration clauses, and other terms restricted or regulated in government loans.

Purchase Money Mortgage

The purchase money mortgage is one in which the mortgagor is using the borrowed funds to buy the property that will serve as the security for the loan. Most residential mortgages are purchase money mortgages. Pledging your home in order to borrow money for a college education is not a purchase money mortgage.

Master Mortgage

Mortgages, with all their clauses and enforcement issues, can be long and complex. Furthermore, a lender may be using the same mortgage forms for all borrowers, recording the same document each time, complete with another filing fee. To avoid this duplication, some states have **master mortgage** statutes that permit lenders to record one master mortgage and then record one piece of paper with the land description for each new mortgage that refers to the record location of the master mortgage so that the terms are still available for those who want the details.

Straight Term Mortgages or Interest-Only Mortgages

A **straight term mortgage**, now known in the decade from 1998 to 2008 as the "interest only mortgage," is a mortgage in which there is no amortization of principal over the loan period. The borrower makes only interest payments and then repays the unpaid principal along with any accrued interest at the end of the term (usually three to five years). For those of you reading closely, this is a form of a balloon payment. "Interest-only mortgages" allowed buyers who might not qualify to afford the high-priced homes of this era. By making only interest payments, their monthly housing costs were lower. In the subprime market, the interest-only loans were typical and the repossession/foreclosure rates high once the balloon payment came due. The **interest-only mortgage** is known as one of the creative financing techniques (see the discussion later in the chapter).

Subordinate or Wrap-Around Mortgages

A **subordinate mortgage** (or **wrap-around mortgage**) is one in which sellers act as lenders for their buyers who cannot afford a loan from a commercial lender because of high rates. This type of mortgage is discussed in the alternative financing section of this chapter.

Piggyback Mortgage

This type of mortgage is also part of the subprime market. A home buyer/borrower structures an 80 percent loan, one in which the borrower/home buyer puts down 20 percent and qualifies for a conventional or government mortgage at a lower rate and without the cost of mortgage insurance. However, straightaway, the buyer/borrower then puts a second mortgage on the property (usually at a much higher interest rate) to recoup the 20 percent down. The money from that loan is then used to purchase yet another property. The property is mortgaged to its full value without the first lender being aware of the **piggybacked mortgage**. And the buyer has now linked properties together, all with the hope of being able to "flip" or sell the property quickly and for a gain (if the market remains on an upswing).

Anaconda or Dragnet Mortgages

An **anaconda mortgage** or **dragnet mortgage** secures all items of indebtedness that the mortgagor may, at any time during the period of mortgage, owe to the mortgagee. Under a dragnet mortgage, a lender could acquire all the mortgagor's debts at a discount and then collect 100 percent through the mortgage transaction.

Adjustable Rate Mortgages

The **adjustable rate mortgage** (**ARM**) has a fluctuating interest rate throughout the life of the loan, the loan's rate being tied to some index such as the FHA rate, the treasury securities index, or treasury bill rates. The rates fluctuate according to the terms of the note or loan agreement, but the following should be part of the mortgage agreement:

1. What index will be used? Short-term indices (like treasury bills) tend to be more volatile. The only restrictions on use are that the index be public and not controllable by the lender.
2. What will be the margin? The margin is the difference between the index rate and the contract rate. In other words, the borrower's rate is the index plus the margin. The margin could be from 1 to 4 percent.
3. What adjustment period will be used? Will the ARM be adjusted every six months? Every year? Shorter periods are more beneficial for the lender.
4. Is there a rate cap? Is there a maximum interest rate for the loan?
5. If the loan is assumed, is the cap readjusted upon assumption?
6. Is the rate for loan qualifying different from the rate for the first year? If so, there may be negative amortization, which means the monthly payments are low the first year but the size of the mortgage increases during that time.

Regulation Z has mandatory disclosure forms for ARMs that have been greatly simplified. Figure 15.4 is the required form for disclosure of all ARM information.

Reverse Mortgages

With a retired population on the rise, and most with large amounts of equity in their homes, lenders have found profits high in the **reverse mortgage** business. Reverse mortgages allow retired homeowners to supplement their retirement income by borrowing on the equity in their homes. In a reverse mortgage, the mortgage company agrees to loan the homeowners a sum that will be distributed to them in monthly payments over a specified term, or until their death. The owners do not repay the loan; repayment comes when they die and the house is sold. The reverse mortgagee is repaid the principal amount of the loan plus interest from the proceeds from the sale of the house. Because of excessive fees and inadequate disclosure in reverse mortgages, HUD and the FDIC developed disclosure requirements for such mortgages. Mandatory disclosure forms require mortgagees to disclose the amount of the withdrawals, the total cost of the process, and the implications of the reverse mortgage with regard to market price.

Commercial Mortgages

The focus of this chapter has been primarily on residential mortgages, but commercial buildings are also financed through mortgages. However, commercial loans involve additional issues such as what happens to the lessees in the building and whether there will be assignment of rents presently or in the event of a default. Commercial lenders must also perform due diligence on prior and current uses of the property for purposes of environmental issues and liabilities.

Figure 15.4 Sample Variable Rate Mortgage Disclosure Form

H-14—VARIABLE-RATE MORTGAGE SAMPLE

This disclosure describes the features of the adjustable-rate mortgage (ARM) program you are considering. Information on other ARM programs is available upon request.

How Your Interest Rate and Payment Are Determined

- Your interest rate will be based on an index rate plus a margin.
- Your payment will be based on the interest rate, loan balance, and loan term.
  —The interest rate will be based on the weekly average yield on United States Treasury securities adjusted to a constant maturity of 1 year (your index), plus our margin. Ask us for our current interest rate and margin.
  —Information about the index rate is published weekly in the *Wall Street Journal.*
- Your interest rate will equal the index rate plus our margin unless your interest rate "caps" limit the amount of change in the interest rate.

How Your Interest Rate Can Change

- Your interest rate can change yearly.
- Your interest rate cannot increase or decrease more than 2 percentage points per year.
- Your interest rate cannot increase or decrease more than 5 percentage points over the term of the loan.

How Your Monthly Payment Can Change

- Your monthly payment can increase or decrease substantially based on annual changes in the interest rate. [For example, on a $10,000, 30-year loan with an initial interest rate of 12.41 percent in effect in July 1996, the maximum amount that the interest rate can rise under this program is 5 percentage points, to 17.41 percent, and the monthly payment can rise from a first-year payment of $106.03 to a maximum of $145.34 in the fourth year. To see what your payment is, divide your mortgage amount by $10,000; then multiply the monthly payment by that amount. (For example, the monthly payment for a mortgage amount of $60,000 would be: $60,000 / $10,000 = 6; 6 × $106.03 = $636.18 per month.)
- You will be notified in writing 25 days before the annual payment adjustment may be made. This notice will contain information about your interest rates, payment amount, and loan balance.

Example

The example below shows how your payments would have changed under this ARM program based on actual changes in the index from 1982 to 1996. This does not necessarily indicate how your index will change in the future. The example is based on the following assumptions:

Amount	**$10,000**
Term	30 years
Payment adjustment	1 year
Interest adjustment	1 year
Margin	3 percentage points

Caps ________ 2 percentage points annual interest rate ________ 5 percentage points lifetime interest rate

Index ________ Weekly average yield on U.S. Treasury securities adjusted to a constant maturity of one year.

{{12-31-97 p.6678.26}}

Year (as of 1st week ending in July)	Index (%)	Margin* (percentage points)	Interest Rate (%)	Monthly Payment ($)	Remaining Balance ($)
1982	14.41	3	17.41	145.90	9,989.37
1983	9.78	3	**15.41	129.81	9,969.66
1984	12.17	3	15.17	127.91	9,945.51
1985	7.66	3	**13.17	112.43	9,903.70
1986	6.36	3	***12.41	106.73	9,848.94
1987	6.71	3	***12.41	106.73	9,786.98
1988	7.52	3	***12.41	106.73	9,716.88
1989	7.97	3	***12.41	106.73	9,637.56
1990	8.06	3	***12.41	106.73	9,547.83
1991	6.40	3	***12.41	106.73	9,446.29
1992	3.96	3	***12.41	106.73	9,331.56
1993	3.42	3	***12.41	106.73	9,201.61
1994	5.47	3	***12.41	106.73	9,054.72
1995	5.53	3	***12.41	106.73	8,888.52
1996	5.82	3	***12.41	106.73	8,700.37

*This is a margin we have used recently; your margin may be different.
**This interest rate reflects a 2 percentage point annual interest rate cap.
***This interest rate reflects a 5 percentage point lifetime interest rate cap.
Note: To see what your payments would have been during that period, divide your mortgage amount by $10,000; then multiply the monthly payment by that amount. (For example, in 1996 the monthly payment for a mortgage amount of $60,000 taken out in 1982 would be: $60,000 ÷ $10,000 = 6; 6 × $106.73 = $640.38.)

- You will be notified in writing 25 days before the annual payment adjustment may be made. This notice will contain information about your interest rates, payment amount and loan balance.

Rights and Responsibilities of Mortgagor and Mortgagee

If the parties fail to specify all the necessary terms of their relationship, the law does step in to provide certain rules for governing the relationship.

Rents and Leases

The rights of the parties for rents from the property will vary (as discussed earlier) according to whether the property is located in a title or a lien theory state. In the title theory states, the mortgagee has the right to the rents upon execution of the mortgage. In the lien theory states, the mortgagee is not entitled to rents or possession until after default and foreclosure.

However, in some lien theory states, the parties are permitted to put a clause in their mortgage agreement that gives the mortgagee the right to possession and rents immediately upon default by the mortgagor. In other lien theory states, such a clause is void.

In any state where the mortgagee is properly in possession of the mortgaged property and collecting rents, the mortgagee must provide an accounting to the mortgagor for the rents received during the possession. In some lien theory states, the rents received while the mortgagee is in possession must be applied to the reduction of the mortgage debt.

One final issue in commercial properties is that of the tenant's rights. Tenants of mortgaged property have rights that vary according to when the lease was executed. For those leases that antedate the mortgage, the mortgagee is required to honor the tenant's rights, even when the mortgagee forecloses. In a postdated lease, the mortgagee is permitted to terminate the lease simply because of the mortgagor's default. Of course, the mortgagor and the mortgagee could have a clause in the lease that made tenants' rights subject to all mortgages.

Both tenants and mortgagees should scrutinize documents carefully. For example, a tenant who leases property after the mortgage exists should check the mortgage for termination and cancellation provisions. A mortgagee taking a mortgage on property subject to existing leases should review the leases prior to execution of the mortgage.

The following case illustrates the rights of mortgagor, mortgagee, and tenants upon default by the mortgagor. After reading the case, determine whether the result would be the same under the theory of mortgages followed by your state.

Comerica Bank–Illinois v. Harris Bank Hinsdale

673 N.E.2d 380 (Ill. App. Ct. 1996)

FACTS

Affiliated Bank/North Shore National issued a first mortgage on the Family Square Shopping Center in Hillside, Illinois (mortgagor). Comerica Bank–Illinois is the successor to Affiliated. Upon taking over the loan, Comerica recorded both a mortgage and an assignment of rents as security for the loan. The assignment provided that Comerica could collect rents from the property without taking possession of the property, and without exercising any of its other options under the property. Chicago Title and Trust held a second mortgage on the same property.

The mortgagor paid the first installment of real estate taxes on the property in 1990, but failed to make further payments. Comerica first learned of the tax delinquency in 1993 when a real estate buyer notified Comerica that it had purchased the property at a public sale. The tax obligation on the property exceeded $600,000. The mortgage agreement did require the mortgagor to make the tax payments to a Comerica escrow, but Comerica had waived the requirement.

Comerica was free to foreclose at that time, but, instead, in April 1994, Comerica notified the mortgagor that it was in default and that Comerica would exercise its legal remedies if the default was not cured. The mortgagor did not cure the default and Comerica chose to exercise its rights under the assignment of rents clause in the mortgage. Comerica began collecting rents from the tenants in the property without foreclosing on it. By collecting rents, Comerica was able to reduce the debt on the property without assuming responsibility for the large tax obligation.

On May 20, 1994, Comerica filed for an accounting and relief against the mortgagor and its guarantors. The mortgagor filed a counterclaim seeking the appointment of a receiver and mandating Comerica's maintenance and operation of the mortgaged property. The trial court dismissed the counterclaim. On August 5, 1994, Chicago Title filed an action for foreclosure on its second mortgage and appointment of a receiver for an accounting of the rents. The trial court found that the rents collected by Comerica belonged to the mortgagor. Comerica appealed.

JUDICIAL OPINION

Theis, Justice. The trial court awarded the rents to the mortgagor. On appeal, Comerica claims that the trial court erred in awarding the rents to the mortgagor as Comerica should have been allowed to exercise its right to collect rents under the assignment of rents.

The trustee first argues that Comerica's assignment of rents, which permits Comerica to collect the rents without any other action, cannot supersede the common law requirement of possession. In resolving this issue, we have relied on Illinois case law. However, we have also found relevant bankruptcy decisions and Federal case law to be thorough and persuasive. Because the Supreme Court has required bankruptcy courts to apply State law in determining mortgagee's entitlements to rents, we find bankruptcy decisions useful in resolving this issue.

Courts will not enforce private agreements that are contrary to public policy. At common law, it was strictly held that the mortgagee must take actual possession before he was entitled to rents. "[A] clause in a real estate mortgage pledging rents and profits creates an equitable lien upon such rents and profits of the land, which may be enforced by the mortgagee upon default by taking possession of the mortgaged property."

The possession requirement reflects the public policy in Illinois which seeks to prevent mortgagees from stripping the rents from the property and leaving the mortgagor and the tenants without resources for maintenance or repair. Applying Illinois law, the court in Monarch stated that:

To obtain the benefits of possession in the form of rents, the mortgagee must also accept the burdens associated with possession—the responsibilities and potential liability that follow whenever a mortgage goes into default. The mortgagee's right to rents, then, is not automatic but arises only when the mortgagee has affirmatively sought possession with its attendant benefits and burdens. In re J.D. Monarch Development Co., *153 B.R. 829, 833 (Bankr.S.D.Ill. 1993).*

We recognize that there is a modern trend in this area of the law which permits a mortgagee to collect rents once it has taken constructive, as opposed to actual, possession of the property. Courts have recently allowed mortgagees to collect rents after taking some affirmative action to gain possession of the property such as obtaining judicial intervention by way of injunctive relief. Similarly, courts have ruled that mortgagees may be entitled to rents once a receiver has been appointed.

While the trustee concedes that actual possession is not necessary to collect rents, it argues that Comerica failed to take the affirmative action which would constitute constructive possession of the property. In the absence of such action, Comerica's enforcement of the assignment of rents permits Comerica to strip the property of its value without accepting responsibility for its maintenance. The trustee claims that such conduct contravenes Illinois' public policy. We agree.

We find that even under the more progressive "affirmative action" cases, a mortgagee still needs to obtain a court's authorization before he may collect rents without taking possession. Such a requirement ensures that the [*sic*] all of the parties' interests will be before the court, and will not be subject to the unilateral acts of the mortgagee. We agree with the trustee's claim that actual or constructive possession of the property is required before a mortgagee may collect rents. Because Comerica's assignment of rents permitted Comerica to collect rents in contravention of Illinois public policy, we refuse to recognize that provision of the agreement.

This is not the end of our discussion, however, as the trustee argues that it took the necessary affirmative action and that it is therefore entitled to the rents. The trustee claims that filing a foreclosure action and seeking the appointment of a receiver constitute the necessary affirmative action which entitled it to the rents.

We find that the mere filing of the foreclosure action or request for a receiver is not sufficient to trigger the mortgagee's right to collect rents. First, in a foreclosure action, the mortgagee is not entitled to rents until judgment has actually been entered unless the mortgage agreement permits the mortgagee to obtain prejudgment possession. Similarly, the mere request for the appointment of a receiver is not sufficient. "[T]he mortgagee is not entitled to the rents until the mortgagee or a receiver appointed on the mortgagee's behalf has taken actual possession of the real estate after default."

Accordingly, we find that it is not the mere filing of certain pleadings, but rather the trial court's affirmative ruling on such filings which entitles the mortgagee to the rents.

It is undisputed that the trustee did not obtain prejudgment possession of the property. The rents in dispute were collected during the time that the mortgagor was in possession of the property but before the receiver was appointed. Therefore, we find that the trial court was correct in ruling that the rents collected properly belong to the mortgagor.

Affirmed.

CASE QUESTIONS

1. Outline the parties and their roles in the transaction.
2. Why did Comerica want to collect rents and not proceed with foreclosure?
3. What reasons are given for requiring possession before collection of rents is permitted?
4. What effect does this case have on assignment of rent clauses in mortgages?

Property Covered by the Mortgage

Unless otherwise specified, the mortgage covers all property (houses, buildings, fixtures, easements) on the land described in the mortgage. The mortgage covers all buildings, fixtures, easements, and any other items classified as real property. The mortgagee should specify any questionable items that might be construed as personal instead of real property. The following clause is an example of a thorough inclusion clause that would follow the legal description of the property in the mortgage agreement.

TOGETHER with all articles and fixtures used in occupying, operating, or renting the building on the premises, including but not limited to gas and electric fixtures, radiators, heaters, washers, driers, engines and machinery, boilers, ranges, elevators, escalators, incinerators, motors, bathtubs, sinks, pipes, faucets, and other heating and plumbing fixtures, air conditioning equipment, mirrors, cabinets, refrigerators, stoves, fire prevention and extinguishing devices, furniture, shades, blinds, curtains, draperies, drapery and curtain rods, rugs, carpets and all other floor coverings, lamps, wall hangings and pictures, and all replacements thereof and additions thereto from this point on and such additions and replacements shall be deemed to form a part of the realty and are thus covered by the lien of this mortgage.

This clause also includes an **after-acquired property clause**, a provision that serves to add to the mortgage coverage any buildings, fixtures, or other attachments that are made after the mortgage is attached.

Transfers and Assignments by Mortgagor

In many mortgage arrangements, the mortgagor will not remain in possession or use of the property for the entire term of the mortgage. In both residential and commercial transactions, the original mortgagor may need to sell or transfer the mortgaged property. The following sections cover the methods of transfer and the rights and duties of the parties.

The Assumption

In many cases, the original mortgagor's interest rate is lower than the rates available at the time the transfer of the property becomes necessary. If the buyer can purchase the property by agreeing to assume the responsibility for repayment of the original mortgage, the seller will have a much better chance of being able to sell the property at a good price.

The following factual example illustrates how this method of transferring the mortgage debt as part of the purchase price of the property works:

Hal Wood purchased a small home for $275,000 in 2004. In 2007, Hal had to sell the home. Hal had a mortgage balance of approximately $265,000 on the home, and he advertised to sell the home for $298,000. Bob Freeman has made an offer to purchase the home for $295,000, with Bob paying Hal $30,000 cash and agreeing to assume responsibility for repayment of the $265,000 mortgage.

The following diagram illustrates the transfer:

FIRST MORTGAGEE ⇆ *HAL WOOD, MORTGAGOR*
↓
BOB FREEMAN, BUYER

The transaction is a simple assignment of contract benefits and a delegation of contract duties. Bob will enjoy the benefits of residing in the property but will assume responsibility for the mortgage payments. The transaction is referred to as an **assumption**, or, frequently, as a **cash-to-mortgage sale**, since Bob is paying enough cash down to be able to assume the mortgage.

An assumption does not relieve the original mortgagor (Hal) of liability under the mortgage arrangement. The mortgagor remains liable for repayment of the debt and, if the buyer defaults, the mortgagor must still pay the mortgage debt. The mortgagee has the right to enforce repayment against either one of the parties and always retains the right of foreclosure in the event both parties default (discussed later).

The only way the mortgagor can be relieved of liability under the mortgage agreement is if the mortgagee consents to a release. Many mortgages require a release once the mortgagee has qualified or is satisfied with the purchaser and has consented in writing to the transfer and assumption.

Many mortgages are subject to a due-on-sale provision, which effectively prevents the mortgagor from transferring the rights available under the mortgage.

The Subject-to Sale

In a sale of property by a mortgagor to a buyer in which the buyer takes *subject to* the existing mortgage, the mortgagor remains personally liable on the mortgage; the buyer undertakes no personal responsibility for payment of the mortgage; and the property remains subject to the foreclosure. In a **subject-to sale**, the seller continues to be responsible for the payments on the mortgage. The mortgagee's rights are not affected by a transfer of property subject to its existing mortgage. The subject-to sale can be used very effectively in some of the alternative financing techniques discussed later in the chapter.

> **Practical Tip**
>
> *The assumption of a loan is often a more efficient way to transfer property. However, the creditworthiness of the transferee is a critical issue in such a transfer. Also, knowing the state's position on deficiency judgments in the event the transferee defaults is important information to have prior to sale. Absent statutory protection, if the transferee defaults, the transferor remains liable for the balance of the loan.*

Refinancing

In some property sales where the cash-to-mortgage balance is too high for the buyer, the buyer will need to finance the purchase of the property by borrowing the money under a new note secured by a new mortgage. This new mortgage is called **refinancing** the purchase of the property. The original mortgagee is paid the full amount due on the mortgage, the seller gets the cash difference between the sale price and the mortgage balance, and the new mortgagee puts a new mortgage on the property. The seller is no longer liable and the old, original mortgagee no longer has any rights in the property.

Transfers and Assignments of Mortgages by Mortgagees

Many property owners are confused when they receive notification that their mortgage has been sold. Some believe that their loan or credit rating will be affected by such a transfer. Actually, the assignment of a mortgage has been and remains motivated by a thriving secondary market for mortgages. A mortgage may be sold several times over the course of the loan period. Following the savings and loan crisis of the 1980s, many homeowners experienced seven to ten or more transfers of their mortgages over the terms of their loans as the industry consolidated.

Upon an assignment of a mortgage loan, the mortgagor's rights remain the same. The change in payment place occurs only after the new mortgagee notifies the mortgagor of the change for future payments. Such an assignment cannot affect the mortgage and the assignment has no effect on the mortgagor's credit rating.

Satisfaction of the Mortgage

As discussed earlier, a mortgage must be supported by some underlying debt to be valid. Once that debt is repaid, the mortgage ends through the execution and recording of an agreement called a **satisfaction of mortgage**.

The satisfaction of mortgage requires only an adequate description of the property and the signature of the mortgagee (usually notarized). Figure 15.5 is an example of the simple language that may be used to satisfy the requirements for clearing title to the property of the mortgage.

The satisfaction of the mortgage is recorded with all other land interests and, when recorded, clears the mortgage lien in lien states or vests title in the mortgagor in title states. All states have some type of statutory penalty for mortgagees who wrongfully refuse to execute a release or satisfaction of the mortgage. The penalty can be a one-time sum or a weekly fee that continues until the title is cleared by the mortgagee.

Foreclosure

Default of the Mortgagor

Foreclosure is a mortgagee's right when the mortgagor defaults. A **default** occurs when the mortgagor fails to comply with some provision of the mortgage. The most

Figure 15.5 Satisfaction of Mortgage

KNOW ALL MEN BY THESE PRESENTS: That the mortgage executed by ________________
to ________________ dated ________________ and recorded ________________ in Docket
________________ pages ________________ in the Office of the County Recorder of
________________ County, ________________ , together with the debt thereby secured, is
fully paid, satisfied, and discharged.

DATED THIS ________________ day of ________________ , 20 ________________

____

MORTGAGEE

common form of default occurs when the mortgagor fails to make timely payments. However, any breach of the mortgage or note or violation of any of the other provisions of either is a default. For example, most mortgagees require the mortgagor to maintain hazard insurance on the property and to make timely payments of taxes and assessments. Failure to comply with these provisions is a default.

If the mortgagor causes destruction, devaluation, or general decline of the property, known as *waste*, the mortgagee may declare a default.

The mortgage agreement should define default. In other words, the mortgage should include a list of the triggers for default. All states afford remedies for mortgagees upon the mortgagor's default, but very few state statutes specify what a default is. The mortgage acceleration clause will also be tied to violations of the mortgage terms and the resulting default. A typical trigger for a default and acceleration is a failure to maintain hazard insurance.

Processes of Foreclosure

When mortgages first existed in England, the mortgagor was required to make debt payments by a certain date. If a payment was not made, the mortgagor lost all right and interest in the property to the mortgagee. Today, upon the mortgagor's default, it is quite possible that the mortgagor will lose all interest in the property, but such a forfeiture requires substantial judicial procedures and notification plus a second chance or two for the mortgagor to regain the interest in the property.

Foreclosure follows state law and each state has different procedures for the mortgagee to follow in exercising foreclosure rights. There are two basic groups of foreclosure proceedings: judicial foreclosure and strict foreclosure.

Judicial Foreclosure

Under **judicial foreclosure**, required in about 40 percent of the states, the mortgagee is required to bring suit to have the rights of the parties established. The court then has the power, following its findings, to order the sale of the property to satisfy the debt due. In order to pass good title to the property, the judicial foreclosure sale must follow all procedural requirements. The failure to follow these steps (a critical part of the mortgagor's due process) means that the foreclosure may be set aside.

1. **Filing the Petition** for judicial foreclosure, usually in the state and county where the property is located. The petition must include the factual basis for the foreclosure action, including the dates and amounts of all defaults, the exact amount of principal due on the underlying debt, and the relief requested, such as a judicial sale.
2. **Notifying Required Parties** Once the petition is filed, it must be served on all parties who will be affected by the foreclosure. Other parties could include tenants, second or junior mortgagees, holders of mechanic's liens, UCC Article 9 secured creditors, any government agencies with tax claims, and any other lienors. A search of the land records will give the names of those who should have a notice of foreclosure.
3. **Filing a Notice of Action (*Lis Pendens*)** Court backlogs and statutory waiting periods mean that it may be some time before the foreclosure sale actually occurs. But public notification of the pending foreclosure prevents others from further burdening the property between the filing of the petition and the actual sale of the property. Also, the public notice gives lienors and potential lienors notice that any lien amount on the property in foreclosure is not likely to bring proceeds sufficient enough to help with their repayment. The notice that a mortgage foreclosure action has been filed is called a ***lis pendens***. The notice is filed under

all parties' names to ensure that others can pull up the information if they search the records.

4. **Foreclosure Trial or Hearing** The proof required at a foreclosure is that there has been a default and that the mortgage agreement authorizes judicial action and sale. Generally, the hearing is a formality, with the mortgagor rarely appearing to challenge the action.
5. **Order of Foreclosure**. Once the court finds that the foreclosure is appropriate, it orders foreclosure. In strict foreclosure states, the order has a definitive time for final sale, such as a three- or four-month period. If the mortgagor is not able to pay the amount due within that time, the order provides for a sale of the property. Once the sale has occurred, the mortgagor loses forever all interest in the property and the right to reacquire the property. In other states, the court orders a sale for as soon as possible, but the mortgagor is still given one last chance to redeem the property interest. For a statutory period ranging from six months to a year after the foreclosure sale, the mortgagor may pay the full amount due and regain title to the property (even if the property has in fact been sold). This right to pay the debt after the judicial sale is referred to as the **statutory right of redemption**. The effects of the statutory period are twofold: (1) the mortgagee is required to wait before closing the case file completely and (2) the purchaser of the property is required to wait before actually obtaining full and complete title.
6. **The Sale Logistics**. A foreclosure sale is held as a public sale or as a private sale for which there has been published notice. The sale is carried out by an officer of the judiciary, such as a sheriff, and is an auction, with the property being transferred to the highest bidder. In strict foreclosure states, the purchaser is given a **sheriff's deed**, which serves to convey title but does not include any warranties of title. The deed is only as good as the judicial procedures were proper. In statutory redemption states, the purchaser is given some type of document such as a certificate of sale, but the purchaser cannot be given title to the property until the statutory redemption period has passed. At the end of the statutory redemption period, the purchaser is also given a sheriff's deed (also called a **judicial deed**, see Chapter 9).

Most challenges to foreclosure proceedings focus on the way the sale was conducted. The sale must be advertised and the bidding must be conducted in a fair and proper manner. Mortgagors often feel that the sale price at the judicial sale was inadequate. The low-price complaint is seldom a basis for setting aside the sale. Successful challenges deal with failures to follow procedures.

The following case involves issues of the relationship between foreclosure and judgment on the underlying note.

First Union Nat. Bank v. Penn Salem Marina, Inc.

893 A.2d 1 (N.J. Super. 2006)

FACTS

On May 4, 2001, Marvin Hitchner, Jr. (Hitchner), and Penn Salem Marina (collectively, defendants) executed a promissory note to Interbay Funding for $750,000. The note was secured by a mortgage and guaranteed by Marvin Hitchner, III. The mortgage was a lien against Penn Salem's Marina in Pennsville. Interbay assigned the note and mortgage to First Union National Bank (plaintiff/bank).

The note called for defendants to pay interest at the rate of 13.5 percent per year, with monthly installments commencing July 1, 2001, and the entire principal and all accrued and unpaid interest payable on June 1, 2016.

Penn Salem defaulted in its monthly payments and on January 13, 2003, the bank filed a complaint in the Law Division seeking to collect the balance due on the note. Penn Salem failed to answer the complaint and on August 8, 2003, the court entered a final judgment by default for the bank for $845,779.72.

While this Law Division action was pending, on February 4, 2003, the bank commenced a foreclosure action. The court subsequently granted plaintiff's summary judgment motion on the foreclosure and remanded the complaint to the Foreclosure Unit.

In June 2004, the bank moved for entry of final judgment in the Foreclosure Unit. Accompanying the motion was a certification of amount due of $1,043,085.10. The primary difference between the amount of the judgment on the note ($845,779.72) entered in August 2003 and the amount requested in the 2004 foreclosure action represented additional accrued interest; advances made by the bank, which were authorized under the terms of the mortgage for real estate taxes, forced placement of insurance, and property preservation; and for prepayment penalties. The bank did not seek to recover those damages in the Law Division action.

In a letter to the Foreclosure Unit on November 1, 2004, Penn Salem claimed that because the Law Division judgment was based on the same underlying indebtedness as the foreclosure action—the May 4, 2001 promissory note—the foreclosure judgment should not exceed $845,779.72, the amount of the final judgment entered in the Law Division. The Foreclosure Unit granted the $1,043,085.10 foreclosure amount.

JUDICIAL OPINION

Winkelstein, Judge. A note, or bond, is a contract by the obligor to pay a debt. The mortgage, "which is a conveyance of an estate in the mortgaged premises," is security for the payment of the underlying debt. To enforce the terms of a note and a mortgage requires discrete actions. A suit on a note is *in personam*, that is, against an individual involving personal rights, while an action in foreclosure is *quasi in rem*, providing relief only against the property subject to the mortgage lien.

Though a judgment arising out of a suit on a note constitutes a lien against all of a defendant's real property, a mortgage foreclosure suit gives the creditor the right to collect the amount due only from the land subject to the mortgage lien. Nevertheless, the foreclosure suit does not preclude a creditor from seeking a deficiency against a debtor's assets other than that subject to the lien of the mortgage.

When a debt is secured for a business or commercial purpose, as here, it is not necessary that the mortgage be foreclosed before an action on the note is brought; the creditor may bring an action on the note alone.

A mortgage lien survives after a judgment is entered on the underlying note. Until the mortgage debt is actually satisfied, "the recovery of a judgment on the obligation secured by a mortgage, without the foreclosure of the mortgage, although merging the debt in the judgment, has no effect upon the mortgage or its lien, does not merge it, and does not preclude its foreclosure in a subsequent suit instituted for that purpose...." And, even while the underlying obligation may become unenforceable by reason of the expiration of the statute of limitations, or a bankruptcy by the maker of the obligation, a mortgagee may nevertheless enforce the mortgage through a foreclosure action.

Thus, it is clear that our jurisprudence has traditionally treated a lawsuit to enforce the terms of a note as distinct from a mortgage foreclosure action. While the lawsuits are connected in the sense that they arise from a default by the debtor on one or more terms of the note and/or mortgage, each action presents a creditor with different remedies, each independent of the other. In a Law Division action, the lender seeks a money judgment. In a foreclosure action, the lender seeks not only to fix the amount due on the note and mortgage, but possession of the mortgaged premises; that the debtors be foreclosed of all equity of redemption in the mortgaged property; and the property be sold to satisfy the debt.

As an additional indication of the difference between the two actions, it is notable that a suit on the underlying indebtedness is specifically precluded by court rule from being joined in a foreclosure action.

Facing a similar but not identical issue, a bankruptcy court in Maine found that because an action on a promissory note and a foreclosure action on a securing mortgage are distinct, *res judicata*, or claim preclusion, "will not bar recovery on a mortgage after judgment on the underlying debt." *Bache–Wiig v. Fournier*, 299 *B.R.* 245, 249 (Bankr.D.Me.2003). The court grounded its decision on the difference between the actions—that the lawsuit to enforce the note was *in personam*, while the mortgage foreclosure was *quasi in rem.*

Given the differences between actions to collect a debt under a note and to foreclose a mortgage, to limit the foreclosure judgment to the amount recovered in the Law Division action would not foster the principles of either *res judicata* or collateral estoppel—"to insulate courts from the relitigation of claims and issues, and to prevent harassment to parties." Simply put, the actions reflect different claims with different issues. Fairness to defendants does not require the process to end after the first lawsuit, which is a primary justification for the application of either *res judicata* or collateral estoppel.

Defendants also contend that because at the time plaintiff filed suit on the note it was in a position to seek, in that suit, reimbursement for advances made under the mortgage through that date, it waived the right to seek those advances in the subsequent foreclosure proceeding. We disagree. Paragraph four of the note recited that in the event defendants defaulted, "at the option of Lender...all other monies agreed or provided to be paid by [defendants] in this Note, [and] the [mortgage]...shall...become immediately due and payable." This language did not require the lender to seek those additional charges in a suit on the note, but simply gave the lender the option to do so. And too, the note provided that plaintiff could waive the note's provisions without affecting defendant's liability.

The mortgage instrument also afforded plaintiff the option of how and in what manner to collect the debt in the event defendants defaulted. It allowed plaintiff to

> *take action to recover the Debt, or any portion thereof, or to enforce any covenant hereof without prejudice to the right of [plaintiff] thereafter to foreclose this [mortgage]. The rights of [plaintiff] under this [mortgage] shall be separate, distinct and cumulative and none shall be given effect to the exclusion of the others.*

Plaintiff was permitted to seek judgment either under the note or mortgage, or both, and in no particular order. Hence, defendants' argument that plaintiff is collaterally estopped from collecting sums not demanded in its suit on the note is belied by defendants' specific agreement to the contrary in both the note and the mortgage.

As authority for their position, defendants rely upon *In re Mitchell,* 281 *B.R.* 90 (Bankr.S.D.Ala.2001). In *Mitchell,* the issue was whether the mortgage lien survived after the note was reduced to judgment, or if by electing to sue on the note, the lender gave up its security status and waived its rights under the mortgage. Defendants point to the language in *Mitchell* that states: "[a]s to all issues concerning the note, including the amount owed, the judgment is a final determination of those issues and *res judicata* applies. Although the judgment does not destroy the lien of the mortgage, it judicially determines the amount thereof."

For two reasons, we respectfully disagree with the court's conclusion that the judgment on the note judicially determines the amount of the mortgage. First, both by contract—the note and mortgage—and by established legal precedent, plaintiff had the option to seek redress either from the note or mortgage; and, seeking a judgment under one does not bar, or limit, a judgment under the other. Second, the *Mitchell* court relied on *In re Clark,* 738 *F.*2d 869 (7th Cir.1984), for its conclusion that the judgment arising out of the suit on the note determines the amount due under the mortgage. In *Clark,* however, the "judgment" that determined the amount of the mortgage was not a separate judgment on a note, but the foreclosure judgment itself. The *Mitchell* court's reliance on *Clark,* therefore, to conclude that the suit on the note judicially determined the amount of the mortgage, was, in our opinion, misplaced.

In sum, plaintiff's remedies under the mortgage remained, despite the previously obtained judgment on the note. Defendants' position would blur the lines between the two proceedings, and disturb over one hundred years of legal precedent. Actions to enforce a mortgage and its underlying promissory instruments are separate, and should be so treated.

We affirm the judgment of foreclosure.

CASE QUESTIONS

1. What was the difference in amount between the action on the note and the foreclosure and why?
2. What is the debtor's argument on the relationship between foreclosure and judgment on the underlying note?
3. Why does the court reject the debtor's interpretation of the law?

CONSIDER 15.3

Edward Knudsen owned a nine-acre ranch, adjacent to a country club, that was appraised at $900,000. Knudsens's monthly mortgage payments of $4,008 became too burdensome, and he defaulted. The mortgage company, after public notice, sold the ranch for $214,460—a mere $5.66 more than the mortgage on the property. Has the mortgage company acted properly?

7. **The Soldiers and Sailors Civil Relief Act (50 U.S.C. §501)** This federal act can have a substantial effect on mortgage foreclosure proceedings. The **Soldiers and Sailors Civil Relief Act (SSCRA)** was passed to protect those drafted into the military service from losing their homes while they were on active duty. The act also permits

the court to postpone foreclosure proceedings if the default of the mortgagor results from a pay reduction because of induction into the armed services.[8]

Among the many protections in the SSCRA, an interest rate can be no higher than 6 percent during the time of active service and for three months after that active service ends; computation of statutory redemption cannot include the mortgagor's active military service (i.e., the period does not begin until active service terminates); and any civil proceedings must be delayed so long as the mortgagor is on active duty. The wars in Afghanistan and Iraq in 2001 and 2003 resulted in amendments to this law to cover National Guard reservists who were called to active duty and experienced economic hardship.

Foreclosure by Power of Sale

Many states permit mortgagees to sell the property, upon the mortgagor's default without court proceedings. This **power of sale** is a characteristic of the deed of trust financing arrangement (discussed later).

Under this method of foreclosure, a rather quick and nonjudicial sale may be held. The following are the typical procedures the mortgagee must follow to execute a valid sale.

1. **Notice and Advertisement**. The mortgagee must furnish notice to all interested parties (the mortgagor, secondary or junior creditors, lienors, and so on) and also advertise or publish notice of the impending sale, including time and place of the sale. In some states, this notice is such a critical part of this process that this method of foreclosure is referred to as **foreclosure by advertisement**. Many states have time requirements on the notice such as the notice and advertisement be given 90 days prior to the date of sale.

   In many states, the ease of the power of sale is not without some cost to the mortgagee: the mortgagee loses the right to a deficiency action by exercising the power of sale. In other words, the mortgagee is entitled to a speedy foreclosure; but if the sale does not bring enough to satisfy the debt, the mortgagee cannot collect the deficiency. Challenges to these sales are successful when the mortgagee has not complied with the process requirements, including notice.
2. **Right of Redemption**. An additional distinction between the power of sale and foreclosure procedures is that under the power of sale, the debtor loses the statutory redemption period. The debtor has time only up until the sale to redeem the property. Once the property is sold, the buyer gets full title to the property, and the debtor does not have a redemption period (as under judicial foreclosures). The power of sale process is swift, clean, and permanent.
3. **The Soldiers and Sailors Civil Relief Act**. This act applies to the power of sale foreclosure as well. Procedures must simply be postponed for all those who qualify. The postponement runs for the period of active service.

Deed in Lieu of Foreclosure

Chances are that before foreclosure occurs there have been substantial efforts to work with the mortgagor to correct the default. On government-insured loans, the average duration of default before foreclosure is initiated is 6 months. If the mortgagor tries to correct the default—in most cases by making up back payments—the average default period before foreclosure is 10 months. The lender/mortgagee also works with the borrower before foreclosure. Lenders/mortgagees encourage mortgagors to try to sell the property in an effort to salvage any equity interest it may have in the property.

8 The act has been expanded to cover leases, including real property and auto leases.

After the default period efforts, from workouts to sales, have failed, the parties may still reach an agreement to avoid the costs and delays of foreclosure. The parties agree that the mortgagor will quitclaim the property to the mortgagee. This transaction is called a **deed in lieu of foreclosure**. When the deed is signed over by the mortgagor, the underlying debt is canceled. Perhaps one of the most famous deed-in-lieu-of transactions occurred in 1994 when Sears turned over the deed to the Chicago Sears Tower to a trust set up for the benefit of all the mortgage holders on the property. After facing mounting costs and years of declining real estate values, Sears walked away from the financings and cost involved.

Some states require the mortgagee to pay something to the mortgagor (in addition to canceling the debt) in order to be a bona fide and protected purchaser. Many mortgagors simply pay an additional $500 so that the mortgagee is a purchaser for value and entitled to full protection as a transferee. The transaction must also be free of coercion and the mortgagee must be able to prove that the mortgagor acted voluntarily. To avoid difficulties and questions about voluntariness, particularly if the mortgagor subsequently declares bankruptcy, the parties should sign an agreement explaining their transaction or at least have the mortgagor execute an affidavit explaining the reason for the transfer and the consideration being paid for it.

The following case provides some insight into the complexities of mortgages and the relationship between lenders and borrower as well as the effect of layered mortgages.

HULL V. NORTH ADAMS HOOSAC SAVINGS BANK

730 N.E.2d 910 (Mass. App. 2000)

FACTS

Before his marriage to Kathleen Hull, M. Harry Hull (Harry) had a variety of real estate investments, including one acquired in 1985 and located at East Quincy Street and another also acquired in 1985 at Millard Avenue. The Quincy Street property had a first mortgage to the sellers and the Millard Avenue property had a first mortgage to North Adams Bank.

Following his marriage to Kathleen, Harry conveyed the properties to himself and Kathleen as tenants by the entirety and subject to the mortgages. Immediately upon conveyance to them jointly, the two used the properties to obtain an additional property, located on Yale Street, subject to a mortgage. The Hulls lived in a rental unit in the Millard Avenue property. The following diagram illustrates the Hulls' complex mortgage relationships.

By 1988, and still more mortgages later, the marriage was over and Harry had all loans in default. The banks threatened foreclosure and Kathleen borrowed $15,000 from her parents to bring the payments on the properties current.

Harry filed for divorce in 1989 and conveyed his interests in the East Quincy and Yale properties to Kathleen, subject to the mortgages. Kathleen also agreed to assume the payments for these properties. The divorce court awarded her the Millard Avenue property.

Kathleen fell into arrears trying to make payments on all three properties and asked the bank to separate them out. The bank maintained the liens were indistinguishable and filed for foreclosure shortly after Kathleen filed suit to have her rights under the mortgages determined and for the bank's bad faith in its refusal to separate the loans and properties.

The jury at the trial court awarded Kathleen $300,000 and the trial court judge granted the bank's motion for judgment n.o.v. Kathleen appealed.

Millard Avenue		**East Quincy Street**	**Yale Street**
1985 loan (to Harry)	1st mortgage (from Harry)	1st mortgage (from Harry & Kathleen)	1st mortgage (from Harry)
1986 loan (to Harry & Kathleen)	2nd mortgage (from Harry & Kathleen)		
1988 loan (to Harry)	3rd mortgage (from Harry)		

JUDICIAL OPINION

Kass, Judge. We have laid out the facts in some detail and at some length to test the correctness of the grant of judgment n.o.v. Kathleen's primary contention is that the bank owed her a duty to explain that she was not liable on Yale Street. Failing to do so, she says, saddled her with operating and attempting to maintain mortgage service on all three properties, a burden that was her undoing. The jury found (by special verdict) that the bank's insistence on payment of mortgages on all three properties was a failure on the part of the bank to exercise good faith in the bank's dealings with Kathleen and that this inflicted $300,000 in damages on her.

The facts do not admit of the finding of failure by the bank to exercise good faith; the question of damages falls by the wayside with that conclusion. Although Kathleen was not on the Yale Street mortgage note in October, 1988, when the bank first asked her for payment on that property along with the other two loans, she had already acquired an undivided interest in the primary security for that note, i.e., the Yale Street property, by deed from Harry dated February 16, 1988. In addition, the Yale Street loan from the bank was cross-collateralized by a third mortgage loan on Millard Avenue. Consequently, a default on Yale Street triggered a default on Millard Avenue. In turn, a default on Millard Avenue caused a default on East Quincy Street because those two properties had been mortgaged to the bank together to secure the September 9, 1986, loan. On the basis of the loan documents between the bank and the Hulls, the bank was quite within its rights in asking that the loans involving all three properties be made current, on pain of foreclosure if they were not.

Had there been any doubt about Kathleen's interest in Yale Street, that was resolved by her accepting sole title to it on May 31, 1989, with a proviso in the deed that the grantee, by accepting the deed, assumed and agreed to pay the mortgage to the bank. She then became personally liable on the Yale Street debt. She also acquired the title to the Millard Avenue and East Quincy Street properties.

Between the time of Kathleen's acquisition of sole title to the three properties on May 31, 1989, more than five years went by before the bank foreclosed on the three loans in November, 1994. The forbearance of the bank did not work a waiver of its rights as a mortgagee under the loan documents nor was it inequitable for the bank to exercise its contractual rights under the governing documents.

If follows that the judge correctly allowed the motion for judgment n.o.v.

Affirmed.

CASE QUESTIONS

1. Why did the bank treat all the loans as one?
2. Did Kathleen agree to assume personal liability? Were all the properties subject to foreclosure?
3. Does it matter that Kathleen was not an original party to all the mortgages?
4. Does Kathleen still owe the money if she wants to keep the property?

Loan Workouts

A **workout** is a negotiated restructuring of a real estate loan between the borrower and lender that is used as an alternative to foreclosure, litigation, or bankruptcy. Typically, a workout results when there is reduced market or rental value to the mortgaged property. Often property values are depressed because a major local industry has closed or moved, there has been overbuilding, or an economic boom in a nearby area draws away growth.

A workout can involve an extension of the loan repayment and amortization period; a temporary suspension of loan payments; a reduction or elimination of accrued future loan interest; additional security; a reduction in the loan's principal; personal guarantees from officers or directors; or additional or new control on borrower operations, cash disbursements, or accounts receivables.

Many lenders use the workout period as a way to avoid **lender liability** suits that are usually brought as counterclaims by borrowers in foreclosure actions. These counterclaims often allege malice or bad faith on the part of the lender in dealing with an ailing borrower who can establish that recovery and repayment were possible. Many lenders have borrowers waive these liability claims as part of the workout conditions. The key for lenders in avoiding liability in a workout is avoiding coercion and misrepresentation. Having the mortgagor sign workout agreements that spell out all conditions, consequences, and costs helps avoid liability. In *State National Bank v. Farah Manufacturing Co.*, 678 S.W.2d 661 (Tex. 1984), the court imposed tort liability on a bank for its excesses in handling a troubled debtor.

Proceeds and Priorities upon Foreclosure

Very often when a mortgagor defaults, more than one creditor has an interest in the property. The priority of the parties will determine rights of foreclosure and will also determine who will be entitled to payment first upon sale of the mortgaged property at a foreclosure sale. The priority of the various creditors will determine the order of distribution of the proceeds from the sale of the property.

Recorded Interests

As mentioned earlier, a mortgage is valid even if not recorded, but only as between mortgagor and mortgagee. An unrecorded mortgage takes last position against any interests in the mortgaged property that are recorded either prior to the mortgage execution or subsequent to it.

If a mortgage is recorded, the general rule for priority of interests is "first in time is first in right." That is, the mortgage recorded first will enjoy priority over junior or second mortgages recorded later in time. Generally, the same rule applies for the priority of mortgage interests over other recorded land interests such as lien or security interests: If the mortgagee recorded the mortgage prior to the recording of these other interests, then the mortgagee will have priority. There are exceptions as discussed in Chapters 5 and 6. For example, purchase money security interests (PMSIs) in fixtures take priority over previously recorded mortgages if the PMSI is recorded before annexation of the fixture to the land or within 10 days after its annexation; and mechanics' liens take priority over previously recorded mortgages if work on the land began before the mortgage was recorded.

Applications of Proceeds from Foreclosure

The determination of priority among the various interest holders is the preliminary step in determining who will or will not be paid in the event foreclosure on the property becomes necessary. It is very likely that a foreclosure sale will bring only a minimal amount—perhaps simply the amount of the outstanding debt. However, the order of the distribution of funds is as follows:

1. Payment of the costs of sale: court costs, fees, notice and publication costs, and so on
2. Payment of the mortgage debt having first priority
3. Payment of any junior liens, claims, or mortgages in the order of their priority
4. If there is any surplus, it is distributed to the mortgagor

There are some exceptions to the general priority rule of first in time is first in right. One such exception is the priority of liens for federal and state taxes. Although a mortgage recorded prior to the filing of the tax lien will enjoy priority, the expenses associated with foreclosure may be subordinate to the tax lien.

The foreclosure sale extinguishes all mortgages and liens on the property regardless of whether the sale proceeds were sufficient to cover all of them.

CONSIDER 15.4

M gave a mortgage to C1, who recorded the mortgage that day (May 30, 2007) at 8 A.M. in the county recorder's office. M had previously given a mortgage to C on May 15, 2007, which C recorded at 11 A.M. on May 30, 2004. Who, between C and C1, has priority?

CONSIDER 15.5

A foreclosure sale on a parcel of property took place on September 11, 2007. The amount received from the sale is $175,000. The following list indicates the parties holding interests in the property sold. Distribute the funds according to the priority of the parties.

- First Federal: balance of $132,000 due on note secured by mortgage recorded January 21, 2000
- Great Western: balance of $8,000 due on note secured by mortgage recorded October 16, 2001
- Federal tax lien: balance of $22,000 due, with notice of lien recorded on January 5, 2001
- First Federal's costs and expenses of foreclosure: $5,000
- Judgment lien against the property owner for $10,000 recorded December 23, 1997
- American Finance: purchase money security interest in solar water heater, filed before attachment on December 1, 2001, in the amount of $3,000

Postforeclosure Remedies—The Deficiency Judgment

In many cases, the sale of the mortgaged property at a foreclosure sale does not bring enough to satisfy the mortgage debt and foreclosure expenses. Many states allow a **deficiency judgment**, or allow the mortgagee to seek a personal judgment against the mortgagor to collect what the foreclosure process did not bring.

In some states, courts grant a personal judgment against the mortgagor at the same time the decree of foreclosure is entered. In other states, an action for deficiency cannot be brought until the foreclosure sale is held and the exact amount of the deficiency is known. In yet other states, deficiency judgments are not permitted in certain types of mortgages, particularly in purchase money mortgages for residential property.

Statistics indicate that deficiency actions, particularly in the case of residential purchase money mortgages (even where permitted), are not frequently used because of the unseemliness of taking more from debtors who just lost their homes to foreclosure.

In some states, mortgagees must take certain steps before they are permitted to pursue a deficiency judgment. One common prerequisite is establishing that they have exhausted the foreclosure remedy. In some states, if the mortgagee pursues a personal judgment on the note against the mortgagor, that mortgagee loses the right of foreclosure. The following case deals with a deficiency judgment issue.

KAWAI AMERICA CORP. V. HILTON

613 N.Y.S.2d 989 (1994)

FACTS

On February 16, 1984, Kawai America Corp. (plaintiff) executed a one-year "musical instruments dealer agreement" with A. H. Music Corporation, doing business as Hilton Music Stores (defendant and hereinafter the corporation). R. Arthur Hilton (defendant and hereinafter Hilton), sole shareholder of the corporation, at the same time executed a personal guarantee to pay all debts incurred by the corporation "now and in the future." Similar one-year dealer contracts were signed each year, extending into 1990.

Kawai, seeking additional security in 1989, requested that Hilton and Harleen E. Hilton, his wife, sign a mortgage in the sum of $50,000 on certain real property they owned. This mortgage was executed by them on September 12, 1989. Kawai then shipped and billed over $50,000 worth of merchandise to the corporation.

Neither the corporation nor Hilton made payments, and Kawai declared the full amount of the mortgage due and payable in December 1990 and then commenced foreclosure in March 1991. Meanwhile, the corporation filed for bankruptcy in June 1991. The lower court found a lack of consideration and the absence of any obligation underlying the mortgage. The court stated that it could not "take the gigantic leap needed to find that the personal guarantee of defendant R. Arthur Hilton served as the underlying obligation of the parties," noting that if the parties so intended, they "had the opportunity to include such in the mortgage or the nonexistent Bond or Note." Kawai appealed.

DECISION

Mikoll, Presiding Justice. Plaintiff's contention that the mortgage was supported by valid consideration as it secured Hilton's future obligation to plaintiff is meritorious. Although there was no bond or note, their absence was not fatal since a bond or note is not the consideration for a mortgage, but rather merely evidence of the obligation. When an obligation secured by a mortgage exists aside from the note or bond, the mortgage is not invalidated by the invalidity of the note or bond manifesting the debt. Further, "a future debt or obligation, may be sufficient to support a mortgage." The instant mortgage provided that "[i]n addition to the above Debt the Bond or Note and this Mortgage is intended to secure any more debts now or in the future owed by the Mortgagor to the Mortgagee." Plaintiff sought the mortgage because it wanted added security for its account with the corporation. After the mortgage was executed, plaintiff shipped added goods and Hilton was personally obligated to pay plaintiff as guarantor of the corporation's debts to it. Thus, the mortgage was supported by sufficient consideration. Hilton's wife was not personally obligated to pay the corporation's debts by any personal guarantee, as was Hilton. However, her execution of the mortgage was a benefit to Hilton and therefore sufficient consideration to support her mortgaging of the property.

Plaintiff's contention that it is entitled to a deficiency judgment against both Hiltons, since as mortgagors they are personally liable for the debt under the provisions of the mortgage and the dealer agreement, is rejected. The statement in the mortgage that it is made to secure a debt of $50,000 is not a covenant to pay the indebtedness under Real Property Law §254(3). This language indicating that the property stands as security for a debt must be stated to make the instrument a mortgage. However, without express wording binding the mortgagor to pay the debt secured, a promise to do so "cannot be implied." Plaintiff's argument that the dealer agreement is the "other separate instrument" that contains the required covenant referred to in Real Property Law §249 is in error. The dealer agreement obligated only the corporation, not the mortgagors. However, as Hilton is obligated due to his personal guarantee, which serves as the underlying obligation for the mortgage, he may be found liable for any deficiency.

Reversed, on the law, with costs, and summary judgment awarded to plaintiff.

CASE QUESTIONS

1. What argument did the Hiltons make to try to maintain there was no mortgage?
2. Does the court agree with the Hiltons?
3. Will a deficiency judgment be allowed? Why or why not?

The Uniform Nonjudicial Foreclosure Act

In 2002, the Uniform Nonjudicial Foreclosure Act was promulgated by the National Conference of Commissioners on Uniform State Laws. Following four years of study and debate, the goal of the panel was to offer some uniformity on the foreclosure process across state lines because of the increasingly national real estate market with an underlying investment market. The goal of the act is to enhance negotiated foreclosures while providing prompt relief and protections, particularly for residential debtors. Perhaps its most attractive provision is that foreclosure sales would be handled not through the courts, but through the use of a real estate broker and a listing, just as with the sale of non-foreclosure properties. The act's elimination of the public auction, the typical type of sale in both judicial and non-judicial foreclosure, should increase the sale proceeds. One goal of the UNFA, a mutually beneficial one, is to preserve property value and bring as much in sales proceeds as possible.

The UNFA would also bring uniformity to redemption periods, a problem with a national investment market because it is unclear how long it will take, with properties in various states, before the purchaser at a foreclosure public sale has title to the property.

The UNFA has not been adopted by any states, but there is currently movement to have it adopted by Congress because of the substantial benefits to both Freddie Mac and Fannie Mae and their secondary national markets.

Deeds of Trust

The typical mortgage involves only two parties: the mortgagor and the mortgagee. The **deed of trust** (also known as the trust deed form of securing debts with real property) is a type of mortgage or security agreement that involves three parties. The property owner (buyer/trustor) conveys title to a third party (trustee) who then holds title for the benefit of the lender (beneficiary).

This three-party financing arrangement holds several advantages for the lender. First, the lender in most states has the right of foreclosure in the event of default without judicial process (called the **power of sale**). The power of sale requires only notice to the trustor and publication of the proposed sale date. Although there is a statutory minimum waiting period before the sale can take place, that waiting period is much shorter than that required for foreclosure. This simple notice and private sale is also much cheaper than judicial foreclosure.

A second advantage for the lender is that the lender's involvement can be kept secret, since only the trustee's name need appear in the records.

Another advantage is that the deed of trust facilitates the borrowing of large sums. Sales of bonds and other debentures by corporations to many parties can be secured by one deed of trust on corporate property, which will be held by a third party.

Relationship to Mortgages

Even though a deed of trust may be used instead of a mortgage to secure an underlying debt, the rights and relationships of the parties, with the exception of foreclosure, remain the same. That is, the trustor still has the obligations of timely payment, nonwaste, insurance, and so on. Furthermore, the deed of trust contains the same types of clauses and provisions as mortgages.

The lender must use the correct language to set up a deed of trust, or in many states, the arrangement will be treated as a mortgage. Perhaps the most important part of the deed of trust instrument is that the parties spell out the separation of title, with a named trustee.

The power of sale characteristic of the deed of trust eliminates or limits redemption rights of the trustor/borrower. Under the deed of trust, the borrower is usually given a right of reinstatement, which is the right to pay the amount due and owing the trustor at any time prior to the time of the sale (thereby redeeming the property). Reinstatement must take place prior to the sale. Under a deed of trust, once the sale takes place, all of the borrower's rights end. Under a mortgage, the period of redemption actually begins at the time of the sale and runs for six months to a year afterwards.

In some states, reinstatement requires the trustor to pay only the amount due in back payments plus costs and expenses. In other words, when the power of sale is exercised, the right of reinstatement may be exercised without the trustor paying the full, accelerated amount of the loan then due. This type of provision permits borrowers to reinstate more easily.

Duties and Responsibilities of the Trustee

The trustee in a deed of trust financing arrangement acts for the benefit of both parties. The trustee is the administrator responsible for carrying out the financing arrangement according to the terms set forth.

In many states, a statute specifies what parties are permitted to serve as trustees in a financing arrangement. In all states recognizing this form of financing, the trustee must be someone other than the lender. Typically, those authorized to serve as trustees are lawyers, brokers, title insurers, and escrow companies.

When conflicts arise between the parties or when a default has occurred, the trustee must adhere to the provisions of the trust agreement and conduct a sale pursuant to the terms of the agreement and any statutory procedures in the state where the property is located.

CONSIDER 15.6

Fill in the chart to indicate the distinctions between mortgages and deeds of trust. Be sure to list under the mortgage sections the provisions applicable in title theory and lien theory states.

	Number of Parties	Title	Remedies upon Default	Right of Redemption
Mortages				
Deeds of Trust				

Installment Land Contracts

The **installment land contract** is an alternative to a mortgage or a deed of trust as a method of financing the purchase of property. The installment contract is used frequently when the buyer is unable to obtain financing, when the buyer cannot come up with a large-enough down payment, or when interest rates are very high. Often called a **contract for deed** or a **long-term land contract**, the installment contract is also used to finance the purchase of property in areas where lenders have been reluctant to lend.

Each state has different statutes and regulations for land contracts, but all states follow a basic formula for this method of financing. The installment land contract is not a purchase contract with earnest money. Rather, the installment land contract is an agreement that covers the rights and responsibilities of the parties for the life of the debt, which is being carried by the seller and repaid by the buyer. The installment land contract, unlike the purchase contract, is not executed until closing.

The Forfeiture Aspect

One of the unique features of the installment land contract is that in some states the seller has a very strong remedy in the event of the buyer's default: **forfeiture**. In other words, some states provide that a buyer who defaults under an installment contract will forfeit all interest acquired in the property to the seller and the forfeiture occurs without judicial process according to time periods established by statute. All states require the seller to give some form of notice of default to the buyer/borrower that includes a statement of the intent to exercise forfeiture rights.

The amount of notice and grace period for installment contracts varies. For example, some states provide that if a defaulting buyer has paid less than 20 percent of the property's purchase price, then that buyer's interest is forfeited within 30 days after the notification of the default. The 30 days is a grace period that allows the buyer to redeem the property by paying what is then due and owing. The length of the grace period varies according to the amount the buyer has paid in to the seller; in some states it may last up to a year.

A seller who wants to keep forfeiture rights must be cautious in accepting late payments from the buyer. If the seller has been accepting late payments, the forfeiture provisions cannot be invoked unless the seller provides the buyer with notice of the reinstatement of timely payments. Some states still require a form of foreclosure proceedings for a forfeiture of an interest held under an installment contract. In these states, the courts require sellers to give buyers a chance for redemption rather than subject them to the time limits of strict forfeiture.

Title Problems

A clean title is the secret to the stability of the mortgagee's security. However, in an installment contract, no third party is involved in the financing. The parties have only to deal with each other, and there is a good chance that the title check will slip. Tax liens and other deficiencies lessen the value of the land for the buyer and the extent of security for the seller.

Furthermore, without the involvement of a third-party lender, many buyers neglect to record the installment contract and their rights are at risk for anything recorded after the fact. The time span of the contract is also a challenge in terms of preserving title.

For the seller of the property, recording the land contract can present problems if the buyer defaults and forfeits all interest in the property. The seller would have a recorded land contract as a defect on the title to the property, and a quiet title action would be required to remove the cloud of the forfeited contract from the records.

Tax Consequences

One of the benefits of using the installment contract is that the seller may defer recognition of gain made on the sale of the property to the buyer. By meeting certain Internal Revenue Service regulations, the seller avoids having to report an entire gain on the sale of property in one year. The specific tax benefits available in installment sales are discussed in Chapter 22.

Regulation Z Application

The seller in an installment contract must comply with certain disclosure requirements if Regulation Z (12 C.F.R. §226) is applicable to the property sale. Many lots for second or resort homes are purchased on an installment basis and Regulation Z applies (see Appendixes D and E).

Sellers subject to Regulation Z must comply with two major disclosure provisions. First, the buyer must be notified of the right of rescission. For example, in the purchase of nonprimary residential property, the buyer is entitled to the 72-hour rescission period and must be given a form to sign indicating that the right exists and how it can be exercised.

The seller must also disclose all minimum requirements for a closed-end transaction under Regulation Z. (Minimum disclosure requirements, discussed earlier, include such information as the amount of the payments, the number of payments, the annual percentage rate, and so on.)

Subdivision Trusts

The **subdivision trust** is available only in a limited number of states. This method of financing is a three-party arrangement that involves a trust relationship, but the parties have different roles from those in the deed of trust financing arrangement. Both the buyer and the seller are beneficiaries of a trust managed by a third-party trustee. The seller transfers title to the property to the trustee, and the buyer and seller execute a note or other contract that contains the payment terms governing the parties' relationship.

In addition, the parties will execute a trust agreement that assigns duties and responsibilities to a trustee, who will hold title to the property. The trust agreement determines when the trustee may take action and how payments are to be made. The diagram shows the subdivision trust relationship.

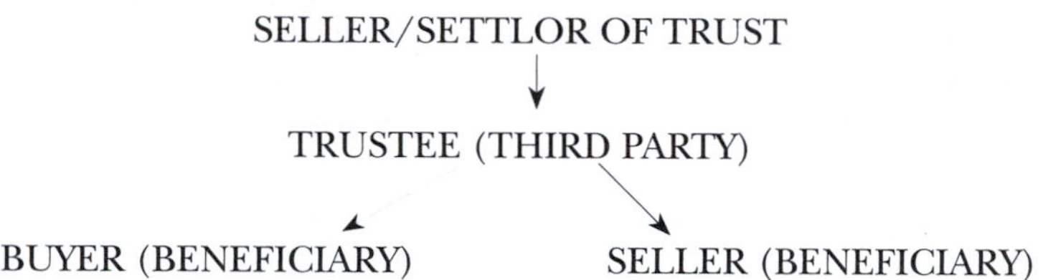

If the buyer defaults on the payments due, the trust agreement gives the trustee with the right of sale of the property, or perhaps a right of reconveyance of title to the seller with a forfeiture of the buyer's interest in the property. This method of financing permits the seller quick relief in the event of a buyer default.

Typically, the subdivision trust is used by developers (buyers) with great ideas but little cash for the development of land parcels. Under this arrangement, the buyer and seller have the protection of a third party holding title, and the benefit of having the trust continue once the developer is able to sell or lease the development. Both buyer and seller share in the profits obtained as the development is completed and sold. The seller not only is paid a certain amount for the property, but also collects a certain portion of the development profits after the buyer begins to earn on the investment.

An example of a subdivision trust arrangement is when a farmer sells a substantial portion of prime-location real estate to a shopping center developer. During the construction of the shopping center, the farmer would take minimal or no payments for the property. Upon completion of the shopping center, the leasing of the property, and the collection of rents and perhaps percentages of the sales of tenants, the farmer would collect the purchase price of the property, an additional share of the profits received for a certain period of time, or both. The relationship is shown in the diagram.

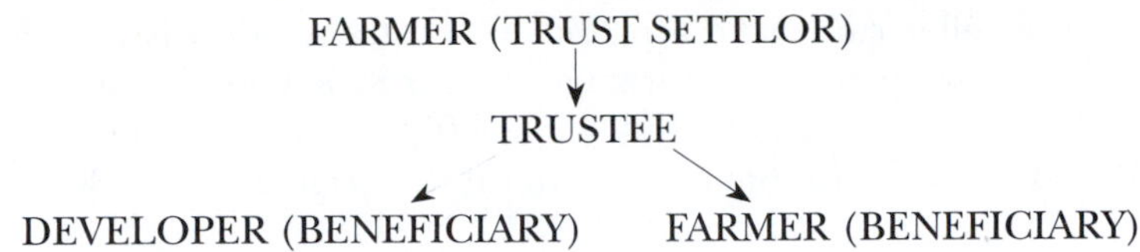

In states that recognize the subdivision trust method of financing, the rules on foreclosure, redemption, power of sale, and reinstatement rights are simply inapplicable. Rather, the parties are governed only by the law of trusts. In these states, the parties have provisions in their trust agreements for the trustee to follow in the event of nonpayment or any other form of default.

Alternative Financing Methods

During economic downturns, price increases and high interest rates create financial barriers to the purchase and ownership of real estate. Those barriers include large down payments and high monthly payments, which effectively shut out many willing buyers. To break down those barriers, many lenders, sellers, buyers, and brokers have developed financing methods that combine traditional methods, create new methods, and often combine these two. The following sections cover some of the new and combined financing methods.

Shared-Appreciation or Equity-Participation Financing Mortgages

The **shared-appreciation mortgage** or **equity-participation financing** is a creation of the commercial lender that involves a trade-off: The lender offers lower monthly interest rates in exchange for a share in the appreciation of the property, pledged as security. Under this approach, the lender will finance a loan at, say, 7 percent as opposed to 8 percent and, upon the borrower's sale of the property, will receive some percentage of the profit made—usually no more than 40 percent. The lender enjoys a gain on the transfer of the property, and the buyer enjoys the benefit of lower monthly payments by giving up a portion of the property appreciation.

Wrap-Around Mortgages

This type of financing arrangement is used in the purchase of property that already has financing not subject to a due-on-sale clause upon transfer. The wrap-around mortgage is similar to an assumption except that the seller is involved more and gets more security.

For example, suppose that a residence is being sold for $285,000, and there is an existing mortgage balance of $250,000 on the property. The buyer can afford to put $20,000 down. In an assumption, the buyer would then assume the $250,000 obligation, and the seller would take a second mortgage on the property to come up with the remaining $15,000 difference. Under a wrap-around arrangement, the buyer simply takes title to the property subject to the mortgage. The buyer is given a loan by the seller for $285,000, which is secured by an all-inclusive mortgage. The seller will continue to make the payments on the $250,000 loan, and the buyer will make payments to the seller on a full $285,000 at a lower-than-market rate. The seller keeps that portion of the buyer's monthly payment that is above the amount due on the $250,000 mortgage.

One way the seller can make a profit on the transaction is to charge a higher rate on the entire wrap-around mortgage. If the $250,000 original mortgage is at 7 percent, the seller could carry the full $285,000 at 8 percent and would make 8 percent on $35,000 and an additional 1 percent on the original $250,000 obligation.

Exchange or Trades

In a property exchange, the parties involved swap the equity in their properties as a means of purchasing each other's property. This type of financing is used more commonly in commercial transactions and when consumers have second homes that they use as investment properties (a 1031 exchange). When employees in the same firm are being transferred to each other's respective location, each needs a house in the other's location, and the equities are simply swapped as a means of purchase.

The primary concern of the parties using a property exchange is that the equities are even. If the equities in the exchanged properties are not even, one of the parties must pay the other the difference in cash. When an individual sells one second residence and buys another, the IRS has strict timing requirements as well as the requirement that the proceeds move from escrow to escrow, not through the owner's accounts.

Lease-Purchase Agreements

If it is difficult for the buyer to obtain financing, and if the seller does not want to carry the buyer's purchase, then the parties may enter into an agreement of sale along with a lease agreement. The purchase agreement will have a delayed closing date.

The parties will agree to the purchase price and to a future date for closing the sale when financing will be more reasonable. Usually, the buyer will make a deposit toward the down payment and will also make monthly rental payments to the seller. The amount of the monthly rental payments will cover at least the underlying mortgage debt, and it may exceed that amount as a benefit to the seller carrying the lease or as partial payment of the eventual down payment that will be required.

With the **lease-purchase mortgage**, the buyer has a definite purchase price locked in at the current market price as well as the opportunity to wait for better loan terms. The seller enjoys the tax benefits of leasing the property (discussed in Chapter 22) and has a sale guaranteed at some future date. The seller also has the generally afforded remedy of retaining the buyer's deposit in the event the sale falls through or the buyer terminates the lease.

A variation of this method of financing is the lease with an option to buy. Under this type of arrangement, the parties do not actually enter into a purchase contract, but the buyer is given the right to exercise an option to purchase at any time during the period of the lease. The parties' agreement may also provide that the rental payments may be used toward the down payment if the option to purchase is exercised.

The Broker, Regulation Z, and Alternative Financing

Alternative methods of financing carry with them complexities that require the assistance of brokers and lawyers. In addition, these methods of financing may carry hidden legal pitfalls for the broker assisting a seller or a buyer.

The broker who is regularly involved in the arrangement of credit must meet all of the Regulation Z disclosure requirements. "Regularly involved in credit arrangements" means that the broker has participated in the arrangement of credit for "more than 5-secured by a dwelling" financing arrangements, or for more than 25 transactions in which a dwelling was not used as credit. A financing arrangement is one that involves more than four installments.

Brokers should also consult with an attorney to determine whether the acts of individual salespeople in arranging credit transactions can be attributed to them as part of the "regularly involved in credit arrangements." A broker may also be required to make disclosures if the salespeople working in the same office have met the criteria for the firm as a whole.

Mortgage brokers also serve as a link between potential customers and lenders who will eventually underwrite the loan. These **mortgage brokers** are independent businesses that do not represent any particular company. Their job is to shop for the customer and find the best mortgage interest rate. As noted earlier, their involvement in the subprime market has brought some risk and is also a focus of ongoing legislative hearings and possible reforms, including additional licensing, educational requirements, and restrictions.

Cautions and Conclusions

The many complexities and loopholes of all the methods of financing discussed in this chapter are potentially costly to one or both of the parties to the transaction. It is important that all parties involved in the financing arrangement for the purchase of real property consider the following questions before entering into an agreement, so that problems and pitfalls can be avoided initially rather than encountered during the course of performance.

- Is there some form of security for loan repayment?
- What constitutes default under the agreement? Is it defined?
- Are late payments permitted? Can the acceptance of late payments cause rights to be waived?
- Is Regulation Z compliance required? Who must comply?
- Are there other secured interests in the property? Who has priority?
- May the security instrument be recorded for protection?
- If there is a default, will the debtor be given some type of grace period?
- What happens if the property is transferred?
- What tax benefits or implications exist?
- Does the written document (or documents) reflect all desires and intents?

Key Terms

acceleration clause, 423
adjustable rate mortgage (ARM), 428
advertisement, 417
after-acquired property clause, 432
anaconda mortgage or dragnet mortgage, 428
assumption, 433
balloon payment, 424
balloon payment clause, 424
Brundage clause, 421
cash-to-mortgage sale, 433
commercial mortgage, 428
Community Reinvestment Act (CRA), 420
contract for deed, 446
conventional mortgage, 426
deed in lieu of foreclosure, 440
deed of trust, 445
default, 434
deficiency judgment, 443
due-on-sale clause, 425
Equal Credit Opportunity Act (ECOA), 418
equity-participation financing, 449
Federal Consumer Credit Protection Act, 412
Federal Deposit Insurance Corporation (FDIC), 426
Federal Home Loan Bank Board (FHLBB), 426
Federal National Mortgage Association (FNMA) or Fannie Mae, 426
Federal Savings and Loan Insurance Corporation (FSLIC), 426
FHA, 425
Financial Institutions Reform, Recovery and Enforcement Act of 1989 (FIRREA), 426
foreclosure, 434
foreclosure by advertisement, 439
forfeiture, 446
Government National Mortgage Association (GNMA) or Ginnie Mae, 426

Home Mortgage Disclosure Act, 418
installment land contract, 446
interest acceleration clause, 424
judicial deed, 436
judicial foreclosure, 435
lease-purchase mortgage, 450
lender liability, 441
lien theory, 408
lis pendens, 435
long-term land contract, 446
master mortgage, 427
mortgage, 407
mortgage brokers, 451
mortgagee, 408
mortgagor, 408
Office of Thrift Supervision, 426
power of sale, 439
prepayment penalty clause, 424
promissory note, 410
purchase money mortgage, 408
refinancing, 433
Regulation Z, 412
residential mortgage transactions, 413
Resolution Trust Corporation (RTC), 426
reverse mortgage, 428
satisfaction of mortgage, 434
shared-appreciation mortgage, 449
sheriff's deed, 436
Soldiers and Sailors Civil Relief Act (SSCRA), 438
statutory right of redemption, 436
straight term mortgage, 427
subdivision trust, 448
subject-to sale, 433
triggering language, 417
Truth-in-Lending laws, 412
usury, 420
VA, 425
workout, 441

Chapter Problems

1. A purchased B's home through a cash-to-mortgage arrangement with A assuming B's $140,000 Federal Housing Administration (FHA) loan. Three months after the purchase, A has lost his job and is unable to meet the monthly payments. The mortgagee has turned to B for the payments, and B protests, claiming he is no longer liable on the underlying mortgage note. The mortgagee, complying with proper procedures, forecloses on the property and sells it for $125,000. The mortgagee is now interested in obtaining a deficiency judgment and has therefore sued both A and B. Has the mortgagee acted properly under the circumstances? Is B correct about his liability? Is a deficiency judgment possible under the circumstances? Would it make any difference if a deed of trust arrangement were involved?

2. The following summarizes the sequence of events involved on a parcel of property located in Nevada and owned by the Lundgrens:

- *November 30, 1970*: The Lundgrens executed a note in favor of Nevada Wholesale Lumber in the amount of $7,767.44, secured by a deed of trust, with Title Insurance and Trust Company as trustee.
- *May 8, 1972*: The Lundgrens, without notifying Nevada Wholesale, conveyed fee simple title to Rampart Corporation.
- *December 6, 1972*: The Lundgrens executed a second note to Nevada Wholesale for $12,126.99. The note was secured by a dragnet clause in the November 30, 1970, deed of trust.
- *January 16, 1973*: Rampart Corporation executed a note and deed of trust to Myers Realty.
- *February 7, 1973*: Nevada Wholesale recorded a notice of default and election to sell the property.
- *February 12, 1973*: Nevada Wholesale filed suit on the $12,126.99 note.
- *June 28, 1973*: Default judgment was awarded Nevada Wholesale on suit and the land was attached.
- *August 17, 1973*: Myers Realty filed notice of foreclosure on its deed of trust from Rampart Corporation.

Assuming the sale of the property does not bring enough to satisfy all parties in the transactions, who has priority?

3. W. J. Minderhout has entered into a lease agreement with Coast Bank under which Minderhout will lease an office building (worth $200,000) from Coast for rental payments of $25,000 per year. The agreement also provides that at the end of the 10-year lease period established in the agreement, Minderhout will have the option to purchase the building for $40,000. Minderhout wishes to know if the arrangement is a mortgage or a lease and what rights both he and Coast will have in the event he defaults on the lease payments. *Coast Bank v. Minderhout*, 392 P.2d 265 (Calif. 1964)

4. Seven Palms Motor Inn obtained financing from Commerce Mortgage Company for the purchase of a motel. Commerce secured the purchase through a duly recorded mortgage on the property, which contained an after-acquired property clause. Seven Palms then contracted, through a security agreement perfected by the filing of the financing statement, with Sears, Roebuck and Company for the purchase of drapery rods, drapes, and matching bedspreads for each of the rooms in the motel. Seven Palms defaulted and Commerce foreclosed. Sears claimed priority in the items it furnished, since the items were personal property. Commerce claimed the items were fixtures and were covered by the mortgage. What was the result? *Sears, Roebuck & Co. v. Seven Palms Motor Inn, Inc.*, 530 S.W.2d 695 (Mo. 1975)

5. Leon Zeibert had given his nephew, Alan Sloane, large amounts of cash over the years. Zeibert maintained that Sloane and his wife, Gloria, had signed a mortgage on their home as security for the loans. However, Zeibert did not have a copy of the note.

Zeibert claimed priority over other creditors of Sloane in a state receivership proceeding. First American Bank objected to Zeibert's claim of a mortgage. The lower court held that there was no mortgage because Zeibert's cash advances were gifts not intended to be secured by a mortgage. Zeibert appealed. What should the appellate court do and why? *First American Bank of New York v. Sloane*, 651 N.Y.S.2d 734 (Sup. Ct. App. 1997)

6. Lynley and Samuel Crabtree purchased their first home in 1996 for $195,000. Their purchase was financed by Western Mortgage and secured by a deed of trust. Two years later, the Crabtrees decided to put in a swimming pool. They were given a loan by Valley National Bank for pool construction. The loan was secured by a second deed of trust. In 2002, the Crabtrees sold their home to John and Julia Gardner. The Gardners assumed the Western Mortgage. The Crabtrees agreed to carry the Valley pool loan in the form of a wrap-around financing. Valley was not notified of the sale of the property.

Both of the Gardners were victims of layoffs in their companies, and they fell behind on all their payments. Western has begun foreclosure proceedings. The property is worth $214,000. The Gardners owe $7,000 in back payments. The mortgage amount due is $189,000. The pool loan balance is $10,000. The expenses of the sale are $7,000 (including a real estate agent's commission). The property is sold for $212,000. How will the amounts be distributed?

7. Stuckenberg, through a straw party, purchased a ranchette-style apartment building with five apartments under one roof. Stuckenberg purchased the property with funds from a note signed with First Federal, which was secured with a deed of trust on the property. Paragraph 7 of the deed of trust provided:

> *First Federal shall have power and authority to take possession of the said real estate and to manage, control, and lease the same and collect all rents, issues and profits therefrom for the purpose of paying the note secured by the deed of trust.*

The full amount of the loan was due in February 1969, and Stuckenberg defaulted on both the January and February 1969 payments. After the default, First Federal notified Stuckenberg's son of its intention to exercise its rights under paragraph 7 and requested information on the tenants, the rental amounts, and the rental due dates. First Federal then sent to Stuckenberg, his attorney, and all the tenants a notice of First Federal's rights under paragraph 7 and its intent to exercise those rights. A management corporation was hired by First Federal, and personal service of the letter was given to three of the five tenants in the building (the other tenants could not be reached). Can First Federal collect the rents and take over the property in this manner? *In re Stuckenberg*, 374 F.Supp. 15 (Mo. 1974)

8. Do any of the following statements contain triggering terms that require further disclosure under Regulation Z?

a. "$70,000 balance payable in 120 monthly installments"
b. "Total interest payments are $40,000 less"
c. "Fantastic assumption terms available"
d. "Assume low-interest FHA loan"

9. A construction lender had an obligation to loan $250,000 to a builder/mortgagor. The mortgage was recorded upon execution of the note. The funds were to be dispersed to the mortgagor as follows: 20 percent when the foundation was set, 20 percent when the building was roofed in, 20 percent when the interior plaster was set, 20 percent when the certificate of occupancy was issued, and 20 percent 30 days later. Will the lender have priority at the time of recording or at the time and amount of each advance? *Larson Cement Stone Co. v. Redlem Realty Co.*, 137 N.W.2d 241 (1965)

10. Dynamic Development Corporation (Dynamic) is a developer that builds and sells residential and commercial property. In May 1985, Mid Kansas Federal Savings and Loan Association of Wichita (Mid Kansas) loaned Dynamic $803,250 for the construction of 10 "spec" homes in a subdivision Dynamic owned in Prescott, Arizona. There were 10 separate loans made, with a note and deed of trust (see page 406) on each of the 10 lots.

By January 1986, Dynamic needed additional funds to complete the homes and Mid Kansas loaned another $150,000, which was secured by a second note and deed of trust on seven of the lots for the spec homes that had not been sold.

The first and second notes were both due in the summer of 1986. Two more lots were sold and released from the deeds of trust. In fall 1986, Mid Kansas notified Dynamic that the five remaining properties would be sold at a trustee's sale if the total debt owed was not paid. Dynamic could not pay the loan amount but did sell one additional lot and applied the proceeds to the loans.

Mid Kansas gave notice of a trustee's sale on the four remaining lots. At the time of the sale, Dynamic owed Mid Kansas $102,000 on the second note and $425,000 on the first note. Mid Kansas foreclosed on the second notes and bought the properties for a credit balance at the sale. Mid Kansas never foreclosed on the first notes, but brought suit, waiving the security, against Dynamic for the efficiency. Can the deficiency be collected? *Mid Kansas Federal Savings and Loan Association of Wichita v. Dynamic Development Corporation*, 804 P.2d 1310 (Ariz. 1991)

For research activities related to this chapter, go to our text companion website at www.thomsonedu.com/westbuslaw/jennings.

Test Your Knowledge of Home Buying Terms

Think you are ready to buy a home? There's more to it than looking through a myriad of floor plans and qualifying for a loan. This quiz will test your real estate savvy. There are 20 commonly used real estate terms: Pick the answer that most closely defines the boldfaced word or words.

1. POINT
(a) A fact or idea made by a loan officer.
(b) A charge that equals 1 percent of the loan amount.
(c) A discount offered on the loan.
(d) An upfront charge derived from the mortgage interest rate.

2. DEED OF TRUST
(a) Used instead of a mortgage in Arizona.
(b) A note signed by the borrower indicating intent to purchase.
(c) A note signed by the mortgage company indicating it believes the borrower will repay the loan.
(d) A deed entrusting the borrower to pay the closing costs.

3. LOCK
(a) An electronic security device that restricts access to a home until after closing.
(b) A period of time for which a certain interest rate is good.
(c) Securing a certain lot in a subdivision.
(d) A chamber of compressed air within a house.

4. ANNUAL PERCENTAGE RATE
(a) The percentage of the principal that is paid off yearly.
(b) The relationship between the principal to the interest paid annually.
(c) The percentage of the borrower's annual income needed for the mortgage payments.
(d) The effective rate of interest.

5. AMORTIZATION
(a) Repayment of a mortgage through payments made over a set period of time at regular intervals.
(b) Prepayment of a loan.
(c) A deed that lists principal and interest payments of a mortgage.
(d) A schedule listing how much interest is due.

6. ESCROW
(a) Fancy, scrolled molding.
(b) Property used as collateral.
(c) An agreement made between the buyer and the builder.
(d) Property, documents, and/or money held for safe-keeping until specified terms of a sales contract are completed.

7. GOVERNMENT LOAN
(a) A loan given to governmental agencies for construction of affordable homes.
(b) A loan awarded to the highest bidder for a foreclosed-upon home offered through the U.S. Department of Housing and Urban Development.
(c) A loan insured or guaranteed by a government housing agency, such as the Veterans Administration.
(d) A mortgage issued to government workers.

8. ARM STANDS FOR:
(a) Annualized-ratio mortgage.
(b) Annualized-rate mortgage.
(c) Adjustable-rate mortgage.
(d) Arbitrary-rate mortgage.

9. CAVEAT EMPTOR IS LATIN FOR:
(a) "Let the buyer beware."
(b) "Let the seller beware."
(c) "Home is where the heart is."
(d) "Let the emperor eat caviar."

10. LOAN-TO-VALUE RATIO
(a) The relationship between the mortgage amount and the amount of appreciation a home is expected to have.
(b) The mortgage amount compared with the value of other homes in a given neighborhood.
(c) A comparison of loan terms among various lenders.
(d) The amount borrowed compared with the appraised value or sales price of a home.

11. CREATIVE FINANCING
(a) New and innovative types of lending institutions.
(b) New and innovative types of loans.
(c) New and innovative ways that borrowers come up with down-payment money.
(d) A loan specifically geared for artists.

12. EARNEST MONEY
(a) Money given by a builder to a lending institution showing a buyer's intent to purchase a home.
(b) Money that is set aside by a builder in case a buyer defaults.
(c) Money given by a buyer to a seller or builder showing intent to buy the home.
(d) 20 percent of a purchase price of a home.

13. FHA STANDS FOR:
(a) Federal Housing Administration.
(b) Federal Home Association.
(c) Federal Home Administration.
(d) Federal Housing Association.

14. PREPAIDS
(a) A reserve of interest and tax payments set aside in an impound account.
(b) Prepayment of a mortgage.
(c) Earnest money applied to the down payment.
(d) Payments made before a home is built.

15. CONVENTIONAL LOAN
(a) A loan for a standard three- or four-bedroom, two-bathroom home.
(b) A loan not insured by the Veterans Administration or guaranteed by the FHA.
(c) A mortgage worded in easy-to-understand language.
(d) A loan for a conventional single-family home, not a town home or condo.

16. BALLOON PAYMENT
(a) Mortgage payments that rise gradually over the life of the loan.
(b) The final payment of a loan, celebrating the ending of the debt.
(c) The last payment of a mortgage, with the amount of that payment being much greater than that of the previous payments.
(d) A second mortgage that is paid in one lump-sum payment.

17. SETBACK
(a) An interruption in the loan process.
(b) The amount of money the borrower has to pay out for closing costs.
(c) The number of feet a patio extends into the back yard.
(d) The distance from a street that a house must be placed, as required by zoning laws.

18. HAZARD INSURANCE
(a) Insurance against theft.
(b) Insurance against physical damage due to fire, storms, and other hazards.
(c) Insurance given to lenders to protect against borrowers defaulting on their loans.
(d) Insurance given to builders to protect against natural disasters occurring while a home is under construction.

19. WALK-THROUGH
(a) The initial viewing of a floor plan by the prospective buyers.
(b) An inspection by a city building inspector of a home under construction.
(c) An inspection by the builder of a newly constructed home.
(d) An inspection of a new home by the buyers just before closing.

20. PITI STANDS FOR:
(a) Principal, interest, taxes, and insurance.
(b) Payments of interest, taxes, and insurance.
(c) Principal, interest, title, and investment.
(d) Property, investment, taxes, and insurance.

Score: 20 correct: You've mastered home buying. Pass Go and move into your new home. 17–19: You're ready to buy. 16 or below: Is someone else buying a home for you? Better do some home-buying research.

Source: © Arizona Republic. Susan Doerfler, "The Language of Real Estate Loans," Arizona Republic, October 1, 1994. AH1. Used with permission. Permission does not imply endorsement.

Answers

1-b, 2-a, 3-b, 4-d, 5-a, 6-d, 7-c, 8-c, 9-a, 10-d, 11-b, 12-c, 13-a, 14-a, 15-b, 16-c, 17-d, 18-b, 19-d, 20-a.

Closing the Deal

CHAPTER 16

It ain't over until it's over.

Attributed to Yogi Berra

"Close of escrow" shall mean the day documents are filed for record. The exterior landscaping to be the responsibility of the buyer herein. Buyer agrees to provide Seller with landscaping rendering within sixty (60) days, seller herein to approve of same. Buyer and Seller to walk though subject property on or before March 31, 2007, to review and approve finishing details. Buyers are aware flooring allowance is $50,000, any additional costs shall be buyers [sic] *expense. Seller herein agrees to provide buyer with a copy of the appraisal of Lot 60, completed by ________________________ MAI in the amount of $2,150,000. Buyer acknowledges that there is currently a construction loan in the amount of $1,300,000.00 on subject property.*

From sample escrow instructions

Close of escrow is not simple, and a contract for purchase of real property does mean the deal is done. Closing is a legal and logistical challenge. Buying property isn't the same as buying Raisinets at the grocery store. That transaction is simple, done face-to-face with title and payment passing at the same time. However, a piece of property is not as neat and compact as a box of candy. The issues of others' interest in the land, financing, and property inspections must all come together somewhere, sometime, and somehow—"It ain't over until the closing." This chapter covers all the issues related to closing a real estate transaction: How is a closing done? What documents are necessary for closing? What parties will be involved in closing? What are their responsibilities during the closing process?

The Nature of Closing

Where?

The nature of a closing varies from state to state, and even within states. In some states a closing is held at the government office responsible for recording land documents, such as county clerk, county recorder, or recorder of deeds. The closing may be held after the office closes (or the document recording for that day ends) so that the problems of title covered in Chapter 13 do not arise.

In other states, closing is held in title company offices, again usually at a time when the title search is complete up until the recording office is closed.

In many states, closing takes place at an attorney's office, with the attorney representing one of the parties. Again, the time will be controlled by closure on the title search.

In still other states, there are escrow companies established exclusively for the purpose of handling the documents, funds, and people necessary for the transaction to close.

What?

In some states, closing is a formal process in which the parties gather in a room for signing and exchanging documents. In other states, a designated party, such as an escrow agent or title company, gathers the necessary documents and signatures and sets a date for closing.

Regardless of the method or place, there is one consistent factor among all the states' methods of closing: getting all the conditions for closing met. Regardless of how, the closings all occur at the same time: when all parties have fulfilled their obligations under the contract and the closing agreement or escrow instructions.

Who?

The closing or **escrow** setup generally involves three or four parties. The buyer and seller who set up the escrow arrangement are the first two parties. If there is a lender involved in either the financing or assumption of financing of the property, the lender is also a party to the transaction. The final party is an independent party (as noted above) who handles the collection of necessary documents and the actual transfer of funds and title.

While the term *escrow* is used throughout the remainder of the chapter, it is used for convenience. Regardless of the method for closing, the parties must designate an agent to handle the preparation for the closing. The agent selected, regardless of name, has the same obligations as an escrow agent. Further, the parties must establish a contractual relationship with this third party no matter how the physical closing takes place.

State law dictates who the third party can be such as an escrow company, attorney, title company and, in some states, insurance companies and certified public accountants are permitted to handle closings.

An escrow agent should be carefully screened because the agent will handle title and funds. Background checks on the proposed agent have become quite common, complete with references and a history of the agent or company.

The Closing Setup

Requirements for Setting Up the Escrow or Closing

Valid and Enforceable Contract for Purchase and Sale of Real Estate

An escrow is not valid without an underlying contract between the parties. Without such a purchase contract, the escrow agent is carrying out an agency relationship that has no binding effect on either of the parties, since there is no direct contractual relationship between them. Many parties believe they can move more quickly by going directly to escrow instructions, but such a timesaving step can be costly in that there is no enforceable contract between buyer and seller—only an agency contract between the escrow agent and buyer and seller. The two can be combined, as when the parties sign a "Purchase Agreement and Escrow Instructions."

Deposit of Deed with an Agent

A valid escrow requires irrevocability, which means that the parties are not permitted to withdraw their funds and documents at will, but only if the provisions in their contract and escrow instructions are not met. If the seller is free to revoke the deed at any time or if the buyer is able to withdraw the funds at any time, the agent's responsibilities would be frustrated, liabilities complicated, and the deal never closed. The seller must deposit a validly executed deed with the escrow agent as the first step of irrevocability.

Valid Escrow Instructions

Even the irrevocable deposit of the deed with the third party will not create an escrow unless the agent and the parties execute a contract, called **escrow instructions**, which will direct the agent on the hows, whens, and whats of closing the property transaction. The escrow can do only what is prescribed in the escrow instructions; without instructions, the third party has no authority to consummate a sale.

Contents of Escrow or Closing Instructions

Mandatory Matters

Because the escrow involves the transfer of a land interest, the agent's authority must be documented by a record. In addition, escrow instructions should include these mandatory items:

1. Name of the agent, third party, or depository
2. Names of the buyer (buyers) and seller (sellers) and their proper designation (partnership, corporation, married couple, single person, and so on)
3. Legal description of the property to be transferred
4. Purchase price of the property
5. Conditions of transfer and payment
6. Allocation of expenses, costs, insurance, taxes, assessments, and so on
7. Signatures of the buyer and seller

Recommended Provisions

The minimum requirements do not always provide for the contingencies that arise in closing a property transaction. The parties are wise to include additional provisions. Although many states and regions have customs that might apply when the escrow instructions lack provisions, disputes over such customs can mean expensive and time-consuming litigation.

Allocating Costs The escrow instructions should specify who will pay which costs associated with closing the transaction. Again, there are many customs for such allocations, but it is easier and legally binding to list such cost breakdowns as part of the escrow instructions. The following list covers the typical costs of closing:

1. Escrow fee
2. Fees for title search, title abstract, title insurance, and attorneys' work associated with such
3. Recording fees for the deed, mortgage, deed of trust, and any other documents required
4. Mortgage transfer or release fees
5. Loan origination fees
6. Termite inspection report
7. Appraisal or survey fees
8. Credit report fees
9. Loan discount points
10. Other attorneys' fees such as for drafting documents

By agreeing on allocation of costs in advance, the parties avoid confusion and delay in closing. However, the parties should not violate any lender restrictions on closing costs. For example, with certain government-insured loans, federal regulations specify which party must pay which costs. With some government loans, the seller is required to pay the loan discount points.

> ***Practical Tip***
>
> *More and more closing agreements include mandatory arbitration clauses. These clauses are helpful in situations in which the parties disagree over compliance with the conditions and the escrow deposit sits in limbo. Arbitration is often faster than litigation.*

Closing fees are often a sticky point for the parties. Someone—an attorney, a title company, or an escrow firm—will collect a fee for closing the transaction. In the case of title companies used as escrow agents, there is a fee for both the closing and the title insurance policy. In many states, those fees are set by statute or regulation; that is, the title companies' fees are regulated. In some of those states the fees are established by a board composed of members of the title industry in that state. (See Chapter 13 for more details on this fee issue as it relates to title insurers.)

Prorating Prepaids As noted in Chapter 14, prorating insurance, property taxes, and other fees paid annually or semi-annually is part of the transfer process. Escrow instructions should spell out prorata formulas for allocation. The formulas follow one of two general theories. Theory 1 breaks the year into 360 days with 12 months of 30 days each. Theory 2 holds that the year consists of 365 days and prorates prepaids on a daily basis of 1/365th of the total annual cost. Suppose, for example, that the seller had paid a $360 insurance premium in January for a six-month period to run through the end of June. Assuming the closing took place on March 15, in the example above, under theory 1 the seller would receive a credit of $210 or 3 months at $60 plus a half-month at $30. Under theory 2, the seller would receive a credit of $1.97 per day ($720÷365). Taking the number of days from March 15 to June 30, the total credit would be $210.79 (107×$1.97).

CONSIDER 16.1

A seller has prepaid both taxes and insurance on the property about to be transferred. The taxes are $6000 per year, and the insurance premiums are $1200 per year. The seller prepaid both in January for the entire year through December 31. The closing on the property will take place on March 15, and the parties wish to know what formulas can be used to prorate these prepaids. Explain the results to them under both the 360-day year and the 365-day year formulas.

Sale of Personal Property The seller should furnish the escrow agent with a bill of sale if the transfer of personal property, such as washers, dryers, and refrigerators, is part of the transaction. The bill of sale should describe the property being transferred, including model number and serial number if available. If furniture is being transferred, as in the sale of an apartment complex, the description should be specific and include the size, color, and purpose of the furniture; for example, "one 96-inch green and yellow plaid living-room sofa." The bill of sale should also warrant that the seller has title to the property and is authorized to transfer title, and that there are no liens or encumbrances on the transferred property.

Documents to be Delivered by Each Party

There are other documents that both seller and buyer must deposit for the closing. The following list is not comprehensive but shows the layers of detail needed for a closing.

1. By the seller
   a. Title documents: abstract, opinion, and insurance
   b. Most recent tax bill
   c. Insurance policies
   d. Plans and specifications for original construction and modifications
   e. Warranties on any appliances, heating systems, and so on
   f. Uniform Commercial Code (UCC) bulk sale affidavit for business transfer (where applicable—Article 6 on Bulk Sales has been repealed in some states)
   g. Soil, termite, and other property condition reports, including reports from environmental agencies
   h. Keys
   i. Notes, mortgages, deeds of trust, UCC Article 9 security agreements and financing statements
   j. List of tenants and copies of leases
   k. Building code inspection and compliance
2. By the buyer
   a. Earnest money check
   b. Loan commitment
   c. List of defects to be remedied prior to closing
   d. Corporate authorization if corporate buyer is involved
3. By the lender
   a. Mortgage, deed of trust, and promissory note
   b. Truth-in-lending statement (see Chapter 15)
   c. Real Estate Settlement Procedures Act (RESPA) statement (see later for discussion)
   d. Required forms if Federal Housing Administration (FHA) or Veterans Administration (VA) loan is availed
   e. Required inspections if FHA or VA loan is involved

Cancellation of Escrow

The escrow agent can consummate the transaction only when conditions specified in the instructions are met. If those conditions are not met, the parties are excused from their performance under the contract and the escrow is canceled.

Many states have provisions for cancellation, but it is best for the escrow instructions to specify when and how cancellation occurs. The cancellation clause

Practical Tip

The escrow agent must follow the instructions as the parties drafted them. An escrow agent is not in a position to make a "close enough" decision. Either the documentation and requirements have been met or they have not. Any change in the conditions requires a modification of the instructions signed by both parties. The parties together must make a "close enough" decision. One party cannot talk an escrow agent into deviating from the instructions.

should cover three issues. First, the escrow instructions should include the grounds for cancellation. The grounds may be a simple statement such as "if either party fails to comply with the terms hereof," or some items may be spelled out, such as the failure of the seller to supply a clean soil report. Second, the instructions should make clear the procedures for cancellation. The cancellation notice requirements could include, for example, that the cancellation be in writing and how notice is communicated (personally, through the escrow agent, or by mail). Third, the cancellation clause should include time elements: when the cancellation takes effect and whether the other party will be allowed a time to comply with a missed requirement before the cancellation takes effect.

Cancellations, Contingencies, and Contract Performance

Complex issues on contract provisions and contingencies often create confusion in the closing process. The following sections highlight some key issues.

Relationship Between Purchase Contract and Escrow Instructions

In the majority of real estate transactions, the parties have used both form purchase contracts and escrow instructions. One difficulty with such form agreements is that they are not carefully cross-compared and may include contradictory terms. Often the contract may have a remedy or procedure different from that remedy provided in the escrow instructions. The question becomes, Which document is controlling? Some states hold that the escrow instructions control, since they were executed later in time and can be viewed as superseding the contract. Other states hold that the contract is better evidence of the parties' intent, since the escrow agreement is merely a set of instructions to a third party and not the parties' original agreement.

The following case is a landmark one that shows a majority view on the relationship between purchase contracts and escrow instructions.

Allan v. Martin

574 P.2d 457 (Ariz. 1978)

FACTS

Kirby and Felicienne Allan (defendants/appellants), both licensed real estate agents, approached George and Pamela Martin (plaintiffs/appellees) about purchasing the Martins' property, which was located in Mesa, Arizona. The Martins wished to sell the property to obtain funds to complete and move into a home they were building in the mountains. The parties entered into a purchase and sale contract, which provided that escrow would close on or before July 31, 1974. The Martins needed the funds by that date so that their mountain home could be completed and they could be in it before cold weather began. Escrow instructions were prepared by a title company and signed by both parties.

The closing did not take place on July 31, but the Martins agreed to a 15-day extension. The Martins checked with the title company on August 15, the last day of the extension, and discovered that the money necessary to purchase their property had not been deposited into escrow. The Martins sent a telegram to the Allans which read, "Due to delay in the sale to you of our home we will no longer sell as the contract expired 7-31-74." The Allans received the telegram on August 15.

The next day, the Martins signed a "thirteen day letter," which instructed the title company to cancel the escrow if the Allans did not comply with the escrow instructions within 13 days from the date of the letter. The 13-day provision for notice and compliance was part of the escrow instructions. The Martins indicated that they believed the 13-day notice was given only for the purpose of canceling the escrow. The Allans complied within the 13 days, but the Martins refused to sell. The Martins brought suit seeking cancellation of the contract. The trial court found for the Martins, rescinding the contract and awarding them $1,000 in damages. The Allans appealed.

JUDICIAL OPINION

Hays, Justice. A contract to sell real estate and an escrow arrangement are not the same thing. There must exist a binding contract to sell the real estate which is the subject of the escrow, or the escrow instructions are unenforceable. An escrow primarily is a conveyance device designed to carry out the terms of a binding contract of sale previously entered into by the parties. Therefore, the escrow instructions are not a part of the underlying real estate sales contract and the terms of the instructions cannot alter or modify the sales contract unless the parties specifically and clearly state such alteration or modification in writing with specific reference to the fact it changes the original contract.

The appellants (Allans) base their appeal almost entirely upon a fine print form provision in the escrow instructions:

Cancellation

16. If either party, who has duly performed hereunder, elects to cancel these instructions because of the failure of the other party to comply with any of the terms hereof within the time limits provided herein, said party so electing to cancel shall deliver to Escrow agent a written notice to the other party and Escrow agent demanding that said other party comply with the terms hereof within thirteen days from the receipt of said notice by Escrow agent or that these instructions shall thereupon become canceled.

This term clearly applies only to the procedure for canceling the escrow instructions; it has nothing to do with how and under what circumstances the real estate contract may be rescinded. The time for performance of the contract was the date designated in the contract for the close of escrow. The latest date agreed upon by the parties was August 15, 1974. The sales contract stated that time was of the essence, and appellees [Martins] informed appellants that the time for the closing of the transaction was very important to them. The latest date for closing was a bargained for term, clearly material in this case. The cancellation provision in the escrow instructions cannot be construed to permit the appellants to perform their contract obligation any later than August 15, 1974.

On August 15 the appellant still had not complied with the sales contract; the money to purchase the property had not been delivered to the escrow agent. When time for performance is material to a contract and one party fails to perform by the contract deadline date, the other party may treat the contract as ended. Thus, when the purchase price was not paid into escrow on the last day agreed upon for closing, the appellees had the legal right to refuse to convey their property and to cancel the contract. They notified appellants they were exercising this right by telegram on August 15.

When appellees exercised their right to treat the contract as ended, the escrow instructions became unenforceable because there was no longer a binding contract to sell the property which was the subject of escrow. The "thirteen day letter" canceling the escrow then became only a formality to prove that the escrow was now void. The fact that the quoted provision on cancellation of the escrow instructions gives a party thirteen days to comply with the terms of the escrow does not mean that one may belatedly comply with the breached sales contract when the nonbreaching party has given notice that he elects to treat the contract as ended. Nothing in the escrow instructions can revive an already dead underlying contract.

Appellants also urge that by signing the "thirteen day letter" appellees elected the escrow cancellation remedy and thus are bound to convey the property because appellants met their obligations under the escrow within thirteen days. As explained previously, this is incorrect because the escrow was already void at the time the letter was issued and also because the escrow cancellation procedure does not apply to a sales contract.

Affirmed.

CASE QUESTIONS

1. Who are the buyers in the transaction? Who are the sellers?
2. What was the original closing date as provided in the purchase contract?
3. Why was a timely closing important to the Martins?
4. What happened when closing did not occur on the original closing date?
5. What happened when closing did not occur on the second date?
6. What is the significance of the "13-day letter" in the escrow instructions?
7. Did the Allans comply with the 13-day provision?
8. Is the 13-day provision controlling?
9. Which document controls, the contract or the escrow instructions?

Mutual Cancellation Provisions

In addition to a unilateral cancellation clause, the parties may want a procedure for cancellation by mutual agreement. The escrow instructions should then cover the distribution of funds and costs in the event of cancellation. All the provisions should be consistent with the sales contract, but the escrow instructions can address their intent to have the escrow instructions control. For example, the following clause would give the escrow instructions control:

In the event of any conflict in the provisions of these escrow instructions and the underlying sales agreement, it is the intent and desire of the parties that the terms of these escrow instructions be controlling.

Contingencies for Closing

Contingencies vary significantly from transaction to transaction, but spelling out carefully all the contingencies is an important part of escrow instructions. There are several types of contingencies that show up in both residential and commercial transactions. For example, a requirement that the seller establish compliance with building codes and zoning restrictions may be a contingency. As discussed in Chapter 14, delivery of marketable title is yet another coningency to closing.

Other contingencies include the assignment of all lease and service contracts associated with the property, furnishing a favorable pest report, providing evidence of repair of items agreed to, furnishing of an architect's certificate of completion on a newly constructed building, providing a final property inspection, verifying boundaries with a survey, and, for business sales, furnishing audited financial statements. The number and types of contingencies are limitless, but in drafting the escrow instructions, the parties should think through their interests that require protection before money and title change hands.

Responsibilities of the Lender in Closing—The Real Estate Settlement Procedures Act

Lenders involved in property transfers must furnish the promissory note, the Truth-in-Lending disclosures statement, and also the mortgage or deed of trust to be recorded to protect the lender's interest. However, the **Real Estate Settlement Procedures Act** (**RESPA**) (12 U.S.C. §2601 *et seq.*), if it applies, imposes some additional disclosure requirements. RESPA and its regulations, promulgated by the **Department of Housing and Urban Development** (**HUD**), referred to collectively as Regulation X, place strict controls on the closing process.

Purpose of RESPA

The Real Estate Settlement Procedures Act was passed by Congress in 1974 in reaction to evidence that buyers of residential property were surprised at closings with additional fees and expenses that were not disclosed to them in advance. The result was that neither buyers nor sellers could meet these substantial additional costs, or if they could meet them, there was a loss on the expected return on the sale. The first section of RESPA provides the four purposes of the act:

1. To provide more effective advance disclosure to home buyers and home sellers of settlement costs.
2. To eliminate kickback or referral fees that tend to increase the costs of settlement services.

3. To reduce the amounts buyers are required to pay into escrow for taxes and insurance.
4. To reform local record keeping and land title information.

Application of RESPA

RESPA applies to "federally related mortgage loans," which includes first and second mortgages, refinancings, home equity loans, and lines of credit using a home as security for the loan. The required RESPA information (discussed later) must be furnished at the time the lender makes a commitment to offer any of these types of loans. RESPA does not apply to loans for commercial transactions.

Disclosures Under RESPA

Buyer's Information Handbook

When a RESPA lender receives a loan application, the lender must give the applicant a borrower's information handbook within three days. The handbook may be printed by the lender or purchased from HUD. Written by HUD, the handbook includes explanations of RESPA, the selection of an escrow agent, the role of the real estate broker, and the lender's responsibilities. It also contains sample disclosure forms and explanations for fees charged.

Good Faith Estimate of Settlement Costs (the GFE)

As originally passed, RESPA required lenders to make advance disclosures of closing costs to buyers. However, RESPA has evolved to require the lender to give a good faith estimate (known as a GFE) of the charges expected at closing. Figure 16.1 lists the requirements for the GFE.

RESPA requires the lender to estimate only those figures that the lender "anticipates the buyer will pay at settlement based upon the lender's general experience as to which party normally pays each charge in the locality." Although HUD offers no precise formula for determining what constitutes a GFE, there must be dollar amounts and the estimate must bear "a reasonable relationship to the charges the buyer is likely to experience at closing." For figures that may change substantially between application and closing (such as points), HUD suggests that the lender also include a disclosure on the possible fluctuation, perhaps in the form of a range.

The lender can use HUD's **Uniform Settlement Statement** (**USS**, discussed on page 471) or HUD's sample GFE form (see Web Exihibits). RESPA requires that the GFE meet the following four criteria:

1. The form must be clear and concise.
2. The form must include the lender's name.
3. The form must include the following statement or its equivalent in boldface type:

THIS FORM DOES NOT COVER ALL ITEMS YOU WILL BE REQUIRED TO PAY IN CASH AT SETTLEMENT, FOR EXAMPLE, DEPOSITS IN ESCROW FOR REAL ESTATE TAXES AND INSURANCE. YOU MAY WISH TO INQUIRE AS TO THE AMOUNTS OF OTHER SUCH ITEMS. YOU MAY BE REQUIRED TO PAY OTHER ADDITIONAL AMOUNTS AT SETTLEMENT.

4. The names of the charges in the estimate should be identical or as near as possible to the names used in the Uniform Settlement Statement.

Both the handbook and the good faith estimate must be delivered within three days of loan application regardless of whether the lender ultimately approves the loan of the applicant. The new content of the HUD-suggested GFE follows a plain-English format and allows the loan applicant to compare mortgage and settlement costs (see Web Exhibit 16.1).

Figure 16.1 Sample Good Faith Estimate Form from HUD

Loan origination fee	$XXXX
Loan discount fee	$XXXX
Appraisal fee	$XXXX
Credit report	$XXXX
Inspection fee	$XXXX
Mortgage broker fee	$XXXX
CLO access fee	$XXXX
Tax related service fee	$XXXX
Interest for [X] days at $XXXX per day	$XXXX
Mortgage insurance premium	$XXXX
Hazard insurance premiums	$XXXX
Reserves	$XXXX
Settlement fee	$XXXX
Abstract or title search	$XXXX
Title examination	$XXXX
Document preparation fee	$XXXX
Attorney's fee	$XXXX
Title insurance	$XXXX
Recording fees	$XXXX
City/County tax stamps	$XXXX
State tax	$XXXX
Survey	$XXXX
Pest inspection	$XXXX
[Other fees—list here]	$XXXX

Applicant Authorized Official

Date

These estimates are provided pursuant to the Real Estate Settlement Procedures Act of 1974, as amended (RESPA). Additional information can be found in the HUD Special Information Booklet, which is to be provided to you by your mortgage broker or lender, if your application is to purchase residential real property and the Lender will take a first lien on the property.

1. The name of the lender shall be placed at the top of the form. Additional information identifying the loan application and property may appear at the bottom of the form or on a separate page. Exception: If the disclosure is being made by a mortgage broker who is not an exclusive agent of the lender, the lender's name will not appear at the top of the form, but the following legend must appear:

This Good Faith Estimate is being provided by XXXXXXXX, a mortgage broker, and no lender has yet been obtained.

2. Items for which there is estimated to be no charge to the borrower are not required to be listed. Any additional items for which there is estimated to be a charge to the borrower shall be listed if required on the HUD—1.

While originally Congress provided buyers/borrowers with a private right of suit for falling short of GFE requirements, that provision was eliminated, and federal courts have held that there is no private cause of action for the violation of the RESPA's GFE. Rather, enforcement is handled by HUD (*Collins v. FMHA-USDA*, 105 F.3d 1366 [11th Cir. 1997] *cert. denied*, 521 U.S. 1127 [1998]; *Beard v. Worldwide Mortgage Corp.*, 354 F.Supp.2d 789 (W.D. Tenn. 2005)). However, other courts are still grappling with whether loan applicants could use state tort laws when lenders fall short on RESPA GFEs. One court has held that RESPA does not preempt such suits (*Washington Mutual Bank v. Superior Court*, 89 Cal. Rptr. 2d 560 [1999]), but courts have not yet addressed the substance of such an action and its foundation in tort law. *Ruiz v. Decision One Mortg. Co., LLC*, Not Reported in F.Supp.2d, 2006 WL 2067072 (N.D.Cal.) and *McKell v. Washington Mut., Inc.*, 49 Cal.Rptr.3d 227 (Cal. App. 2006).

Disclosures Relating to Assignments

RESPA has been expanded to require certain disclosures when there is an assignment, sale, or transfer of the loan or the servicing of a loan account. At the time of the loan application, the following information must be given to the potential borrower(s):

- Whether the loan may be assigned, sold, or transferred.
- For each of the most recent three calendar years completed, the percentage of loans made for which servicing has been assigned, sold, or transferred.
- If the person making the loan does not engage in the servicing of loans (as is the case with mortgage brokers), that there is a present intent to assign, sell, or transfer the loan.

The borrowers must sign the disclosures to verify that they have read and understood the disclosures. The RESPA amendments also provide procedures for notification of borrowers when there is a sale, transfer, or assignment. That notification must be made within 15 days after the effective date of the transfer. Borrowers have procedural rights and protections to object to any inaccuracies in figures and balances when there is a transfer. The disclosures relating to assignments can be seen in Web Exhibits 16.2 and 16.3.

Uniform Settlement Statement and Advance Disclosure

The RESPA Uniform Settlement Statement (USS) provides the buyer with a final summary and explanation of all costs paid at closing. Buyers are permitted to inspect the USS one day in advance of the settlement. Any buyer who does not request the USS in advance is entitled to receive a copy at the time of closing, or if the buyer is not present at closing, as soon as possible after closing.

The form used for the USS was developed by HUD, and a sample appears in Web Exhibit 16.4. All of the charges listed on the form must be disclosed. In some circumstances, the buyer will be required to pay a fee before closing, but such a fee is required by the lender, not by HUD. In cases of outside payment such as for pest inspection, the cost must still be noted on the USS but will be followed by the abbreviation **poc** (**paid outside closing**).

The USS is not required if the buyer is to pay one flat fee at closing, as long as the fixed fee is given to the buyer as a dollar amount at the time of the loan application. This exemption applies when the buyer is purchasing a new home from the developer, who is offering fixed closing costs as an incentive for purchase.

Penalties for Failure to Make Disclosures

RESPA does not provide any express penalties for failure to make the disclosures. HUD, charged with enforcement of RESPA, would have the usual remedies of complaint, injunction, and other forms of civil enforcement mechanisms to stop violations.

Relationship of State Laws

RESPA preempts only those state laws that are inconsistent. Lenders and escrow agents may be required to comply with even higher standards of disclosure and possible penalties if their states' laws have higher standards. Lenders must comply with both RESPA and state regulations and statutes. As noted earlier, some state tort remedies may be available for RESPA violations.

Prohibited Conduct Under RESPA

RESPA was also passed to eliminate the kickback and referral costs, which were increasing the cost of closing for buyers. The following sections cover the prohibited fees and relationships.

Kickbacks and Unearned Fees

Prior to the passage of RESPA, it was common practice for escrow agents to pay fees for business referred to them by lenders, brokers, and salespeople. Such fees were paid as percentage commissions. RESPA prohibits giving or accepting "any fee, kickback, or thing of value" for the referral of business. Cash payments, special discounts, stock, and special prices are all prohibited. One of the areas of intense class action litigation has focused on fees paid between mortgage brokers and mortgage companies that are part of the lending transaction. The following case explains one view on this fee, its payment, and whether there is a violation of RESPA.

Schuetz v. Banc One Mortg. Corp.

292 F.3d 1004 (C.A.9 Ariz.,2002).*cert. denied* 537 U.S. 1171 (2003).[1]

FACTS

Bettina J. Scheutz found a house that she wanted to buy in the Sun Lakes Country Club development in Sun Lakes, Arizona, and she hired Home Mortgage Financial Corporation, a mortgage broker, to arrange a loan. Mortgage brokers are intermediaries who bring borrower and lender together.

Home Mortgage obtained Schuetz a 30-year loan in the principal amount of $68,000 with a 7.5 percent interest rate from Banc One, which is a wholesale lender. This was above Banc One's par rate. "Par rate" refers to the rate at which the lender will fund 100 percent of a loan with no premiums or discounts to the broker. For each loan product, Banc One estimates the secondary market value of a model loan and derives a "par" price (taking into account its own costs and return requirements) that it uses in developing rate sheets for brokers. If the interest rate on a particular loan exceeds the rate assumed by Banc One's par price model, Banc One will pay the broker a "yield spread premium" equal to the value of the additional interest.

Schuetz paid her broker direct fees of $1,661.00, consisting of $688.00 for loan origination, $688.00 for loan discount, and $285.00 for processing. Banc One also paid Home Mortgage a yield spread premium (YSP) of $516.00. This payment was identified on Schuetz's HUD-1 Settlement Statement as "Mortgage Broker fee to Home Mortgage from BANC ONE."

1. For a contra view, see *Culpepper v. Inland Mortg. Corp*, 132 F.3d 692 (C.A. 11, 1998). However, the case here reflects a view of more of the federal circuits, although there are strong dissents in the cases. This issue may be resolved ultimately by the U.S. Supreme Court.

Scheutz sued Banc One on behalf of a class of borrowers whose loan settlements included a YSP, claiming that the YSP violates RESPA because it is a kickback for referral of a federally related mortgage loan. The district court denied class certification because this issue of YSP was too fact-intensive to be resolved on a class-wide basis.

The district then granted summary judgment in favor of Banc One. Scheutz appealed.

JUDICIAL OPINION

This appeal requires us to decide whether yield spread premiums, which are fees paid by mortgage lenders to mortgage brokers that are based on the difference between the interest rate at which the broker originates the loan and the par, or market rate offered by the lender, are lawful under the Real Estate Settlement Procedures Act (RESPA), 12 U.S.C. §2601 *et seq.* (West 2001). RESPA prohibits the giving or receiving of fees for referral as part of a real estate settlement service but permits fees that are paid for facilities actually furnished or services actually performed in the making of a loan.

Lender payments to mortgage brokers may reduce the up-front costs to consumers. This allows consumers to obtain loans without paying direct fees themselves. Where a broker is not compensated by the consumer through a direct fee, or is partially compensated through a direct fee, the interest rate of the loan is increased to compensate the broker or the fee is added to principal. In any of the compensation methods described, all costs are ultimately paid by the consumer, whether through direct fees or through the interest rate.

In a nutshell, Schuetz contends that the direct fees which she paid fully compensated Home Mortgage for the services it performed and that the yield spread premium paid by Banc One, which was not tied to-or in exchange for-any particular services, is necessarily a fee for referral. In her view, HUD and the district court got the liability test wrong, and the Eleventh Circuit got it right in *Culpepper v. Irwin Mortgage Corp.*, 253 F.3d 1324 (11th Cir.2001). Banc One counters that HUD's test is binding and that courts must defer to it.

HUD issued a Statement of Policy March 1, 1999 after consulting industry groups, federal agencies, consumer groups and other interested parties. 1999 Statement of Policy, 64 Fed.Reg. at 10084. The heart of HUD's position is that lender payments to mortgage brokers are not illegal per se; yield spread premium payments may be legal (or illegal) in individual cases or classes of transactions. Accordingly, the Policy Statement prescribes the following test:

In determining whether a payment from a lender to a mortgage broker is permissible under Section 8 of RESPA, the first question is whether goods or facilities were actually furnished or services were actually performed for the compensation paid. The fact that goods or facilities have been actually furnished or that services have been actually performed by the mortgage broker does not by itself make the payment legal. The second question is whether the payments are reasonably related to the value of the goods or facilities that were actually furnished or services that were actually performed.

In applying this test, HUD believes that total compensation should be scrutinized to assure that it is reasonably related to goods, facilities, or services furnished or performed to determine whether it is legal under RESPA. Total compensation to a broker includes direct origination and other fees paid by the borrower, indirect fees, including those that are derived from the interest rate paid by the borrower, or a combination of some or all. The Department considers that higher interest rates alone cannot justify higher total fees to mortgage brokers. All fees will be scrutinized as part of total compensation to determine that total compensation is reasonably related to the goods or facilities actually furnished or services actually performed. HUD believes that total compensation should be carefully considered in relation to price structures and practices in similar transactions and in similar markets.

The HUD test focuses on whether compensable services of the sort identified in the 1999 Statement are provided, and if they are, then on whether the total compensation (without regard to whether it comes from the borrower, the lender, or both) is reasonably related to the services provided. This is consistent with the general intent of Congress in enacting RESPA, which is to foster home ownership. By allowing lenders to pay mortgage brokers yield spread premiums, prospective homeowners with a dearth of cash at the time of settlement can front less money and pay for some of their mortgage broker's services over time. Nor is HUD's test inconsistent with the prohibition on fees for referral; §8 can reasonably be construed as only prohibiting payments that are for nothing else than the referral of business. HUD's test prevents this, too, for the first prong requires actual performance of compensable services. By the same token, the second prong requires that the total compensation, including the YSP if it is a component, be in the ball park. If it isn't, then regardless of whether there is a YSP or the YSP is high or low, an illegal referral may be inferred.

Neither is [HUD's] 2001 Statement inconsistent with HUD's prior communications. It carries forward the same principles articulated in the 1999 Statement, and we do not read the 2001 Statement as backing off the 1999 position that services must still actually have been performed for the compensation paid. Likewise, we do not see any conflict between the regulations and the Policy Statement.

For these reasons, we agree with the district court that deference is due the HUD policy statements.

Having resolved that the two-prong test contained in HUD's 2001 Statement of Policy provides the appropriate standard of liability for yield spread premiums under RESPA, we apply that test to Schuetz's case. With respect to the first prong, there is substantial evidence that Schuetz's mortgage broker provided her a host of compensable goods, facilities, and services. There is no evidence to the contrary. Under the second prong, the record demonstrates that Home Financial offered Schuetz the best interest rate it could based upon her situation, the rates available at the time, and its need to be compensated. It would not have originated her loan only for the direct fees that she personally paid up front. The evidence shows that the broker's total compensation, including direct as well as indirect fees, was consistent with local practice and reasonably related to the value that Home Financial contributed to Schuetz's transaction. Schuetz offered no evidence to the contrary, and none to show that her broker's services weren't worth what it was paid. In these circumstances, the district court correctly concluded that payment of the yield spread premium did not violate §8.

Affirmed.

CASE QUESTIONS

1. Explain why Schuetz maintains that there was a violation of RESPA in her closing fees.
2. What did HUD do in 1999 and 2001 to try to clarify the law?
3. What is the test for the validity of a YSP under RESPA?

In an effort to deal with the YSP issue, HUD has proposed the **Guaranteed Mortgage Package (GMP)** (see Web Exhibit 16.4) that would give a RESPA liability exemption to lenders who package all of the settlement services required by the lender and guarantee the cost as well as the interest rate up front to the borrower. The GMP would be disclosed using special HUD forms at the same time the GFE would be required. The GMP discloses and promises the following:

- A guaranteed price for the loan origination and virtually all other lender-required settlement services needed to close the mortgage (application, origination, underwriting, appraisal, pest inspection, flood and tax review, title services and insurance, and any other lender-required services, including mortgage insurance but not including items that fluctuate based on the borrower's choice, such as hazard insurance, per diem interest, and optional owner's title insurance
- A mortgage loan with an interest rate guarantee, subject to change (prior to borrower lock in) only from a change in observable and verifiable index or based on other appropriate data
- A GMP agreement that is binding through settlement

While some lenders currently offer a GMP, HUD has not promulgated its rules on GMPs and continues to face opposition from both the lending and real estate brokerage industries on the proposal.

Practical Tip

HUD referred to its GMP as the heart of its "Bill of Rights for Homebuyers." The following HUD goals, called "homebuyer bill of rights," are consumer-driven principles that should guide the settlement process. These principles mandate that home buyers have the right:

- *To receive settlement cost information early in the process, allowing them to shop for the mortgage product and settlement services that best meet their needs;*
- *To have the disclosed costs be as firm as possible, thereby avoiding surprises at settlement;*
- *To benefit from new products, competition, and technological innovations that could lower settlement costs;*
- *To have access to better borrower education and simplified disclosure; and,*
- *To know they are protected through vigorous RESPA enforcement and a level-playing field for all industry providers.*

REQUIRING THE USE OF A SPECIFIC TITLE COMPANY

RESPA also prohibits sellers from requiring "that title insurance be purchased by the buyer from any particular title company." This provision stopped the practice of developers receiving substantial discounts in their title policies in exchange for the promise to send all of their purchasers to the title insurer for their policies. Prohibitions on kickbacks also apply to referrals on refinancings, lines of credit, and home equity loans.

Controlling Business Arrangement and RESPA

One of the more intricate RESPA issues that Regulation X addresses is a referral by a real estate agent, lender, or attorney of a buyer/borrower to a mortgage company or title firm in which the real estate agent, attorney, or lender owns an interest. There is no kickback or referral fee for the business sent, but the agent, attorney, or lender does enjoy the benefit of higher earnings and perhaps dividends from the title company or mortgage firm. Under Regulation X, a referral by someone who owns a 1 percent or greater interest in the company receiving the referral must make a disclosure to the buyer/borrower. These referrals are not prohibited under RESPA, but the buyer must be furnished with the following information:

1. That the referring party owns a controlling interest in the provider;
2. An estimate of the charges the provider will make;
3. A statement that use of the provider is not mandatory.

A separate piece of paper must be used to make this disclosure and it must be provided no later than the time of the referral. Web Exhibit 16.5 is a sample Affiliated Business Arrangement Disclosure Statement form developed by HUD.

Those real estate firms that provide in-house computerized loan origination services must disclose not only their charges for such services, but also any interests they hold in the service or any mortgage firms included in the databases.

CONSIDER 16.2

Security Escrow kept $250,000 in an account with Southwestern Savings and Loan at no interest. Southwestern was a substantial residential mortgage lender in the area and had all of its borrowers use Security Escrow to close their residential purchases. Would this no-interest account present any problems under RESPA?

Ethical Issue

In 2003, HUD settled a civil complaint brought against 13 attorneys in New York for violating RESPA. HUD alleged the lawyers improperly referred their clients to title companies they formed, earning payments based solely on the volume of business referred.

As principal shareholders, the attorneys received referral fees from the title company that they established. As part of the agreement, the title company was required to file amended tax returns for the prior three years.

The attorneys had established Covenant Abstract Company, Inc., and two affiliated title companies—Citation Abstract Company and Titlewaves Abstract. The attorneys agreed to pay $200,000 for the settlement of the RESPA allegations and to divest themselves of any interest in a title company for three years.

How would the federal government know of the arrangement? How would it learn of the ownership? Aren't the lawyers in technical compliance with RESPA? Evaluate the lawyers' conduct from an ethical perspective.

RESPA Consumer Rights on Questions on Mortgage Accounts

Consumers' RESPA rights continue through to the servicing of their loans. If they make a written inquiry on their loan, the mortgage service provider must acknowledge the request within 20 days and take action on it within 60 days. The mortgage service provider must do an investigation that results either in a credit to the consumer's account for any errors or a full explanation that answers the consumer's question or dispute. Violations of these sections of RESPA carry civil class action remedies of up to $1,000 for each litigant, not to exceed $500,000 or 1 percent of the net worth of the loan service company, whichever is less.

CONSIDER 16.3

Jacqueline P. Walker and Kevin R. Franklyn took out a second mortgage on their 4,000-square foot home so that they could obtain the funds they needed to replace their carpeting. They signed the paperwork for the loans and the carpet was installed. Jacqueline Walker signed a certificate of completion on the carpet and the mortgage service company released the funds to the carpet company. Kevin Franklyn called to object to the release of the funds because Jacqueline had no ownership interest in the property and did not have the authority to sign. He demanded a return of the carpet funds to his escrow account there. The mortgage service company refused, and after six months, Franklyn filed suit under RESPA. Does RESPA apply? Did the mortgage service company violate Franklyn's rights?

RESPA Penalties

Unlike the disclosure sections of RESPA, the prohibition sections contain specific penalties for violation. The penalty for violating the kickback section is a fine of $10,000, one year of imprisonment, or both; plus liability to the harmed party in the amount of three times the kickback paid or received; plus court costs and attorneys' fees. The penalty for requiring the use of a particular title company is three times the amount charged for the title insurance (paid to the buyer), plus court costs and attorneys' fees. The treble recovery is permitted even if the charge for the policy was reasonable and conformed to charges acceptable within the area.

The following case deals with issues of whether RESPA violations took place.

Krzalic v. Republic Title Co.

314 F.3d 875 (7th Cir. 2002)

FACTS

Nedzad and Danijela Krzalic and other property purchasers (plaintiffs) brought a class action suit against Republic Title, the closing agent in their purchase of a home, for charging them $50 for recording their mortgage yet paying the county recorder only $36. The Krzalics claim that the $14 difference pocketed by the defendant represented the receipt of a portion of a charge other than for a service actually performed, and so violated Section 8(b) of the Real Estate Settlement Procedures Act.

The trial court dismissed the suit and the Krzalics and others appealed.

JUDICIAL OPINION

Posner, Circuit Judge. In *Echevarria v. Chicago Title & Trust Co.*, 256 F.3d 623, 626–28 (7th Cir.2001), we held, as have other courts, see *Boulware v. Crossland Mortgage Corp.*, 291 F.3d 261, 265–68 (4th Cir.2002); *Willis v. Quality Mortgage USA, Inc.*, 5 F.Supp.2d 1306, 1309 (M.D.Ala.1998), that section 8(b) is an anti-kickback provision. There was no kickback in that case, and there is none here. But in response to our decision, the Department of Housing and Urban Development issued a policy statement in which, clarifying its previous views on the subject, which had been ambiguous, it stated its disagreement with our decision and made clear its view that section 8(b) is not "limited to situations where at least two persons split or share an unearned fee." HUD, *Real Estate Settlement Procedures Act Statement of Policy 2001–1*, 66 Fed.Reg. 53052, 53057 (Oct. 18, 2001).

When a statute administered by a federal agency is unclear and the agency is authorized to interpret it, the agency's interpretation, unless unreasonable, may bind a reviewing court in accordance with *Chevron U.S.A. Inc. v. Natural Resources Defense Council, Inc.*, 467 U.S. 837, 842–44, 104 S.Ct. 2778, 81 L.Ed.2d 694 (1984).

Small-d democrats might question *Chevron*'s shift of legislative power to the bureaucracy. But realists, while acknowledging the point and also that it is a fiction to suppose *Chevron* itself an interpretation of the statutes to which it applies or that the exercise of power by appointed officials is democratic merely because it is authorized by elected officials, will applaud the Supreme Court's recognition that the interpretation of an ambiguous statute is an exercise in policy formulation rather than in reading.

We need not penetrate more deeply into this thicket; for even if HUD's interpretations of RESPA are entitled to *Chevron* deference, that deference is not total and as it happens section 8(b) of RESPA will not bear, as a matter of straightforward judicial interpretation (for if such interpretation dissipates any possible statutory ambiguity and fills any possible gap in the statute, *Chevron* deference is not owed), the meaning that HUD wants to give it. Republic Title did not "accept any portion, split, or percentage of any charge." No one agreed to divide a receipt with Republic. The statutory language describes a situation in which *A* charges *B* (the borrower) a fee of some sort collects it, and then either splits it with *C* or gives *C* a portion or percentage (other than 50 percent—the situation that the statutory term "split" most naturally describes) of it. *A* might be a lawyer, and *C* a closing agent like Republic Title, and *A* might charge a legal fee to *B* and kick back a share of it to *C* for recommending to the borrower that he use *A*' s services. That would be a form of commercial bribery and is the target of section 8(b). Republic, however, received no part of a fee charged by someone else. The plaintiffs' beef is that the county recorder did *not* charge $50 to record their mortgage; and so he could not have divided it with Republic. Recall, too, that the statute forbids the giving as well as the receiving of any portion, split, or percentage. On the plaintiffs' understanding, they themselves violated the statute because they gave Republic a portion of the fee charged by the county recorder!

In this case, however, context *reinforces* the implications of the statutory language. On the plaintiffs' and HUD's view, section 8(b) forbids a lender or closing agent to reprice any of the charges that it has incurred and is passing on to the borrower. This would make sense if RESPA were a public-utility or other rate-regulating statute, but it is not. The statute places no ceiling on the amount that a closing agent can charge for its services. At the closing on the Krzalics' real estate transaction, Republic charged them a closing fee of $315 plus various expenses that included the $50 recording fee. Had Republic charged the Krzalics only the actual recording fee of $36, it could have raised its closing fee to $329 and be in the identical economic position that it was in with the repricing of the fee. The plaintiffs and HUD argue that Republic would have been reluctant to do this because then the plaintiffs might have taken their business to a closing agent that charged a lower closing fee. But all that borrowers care about is the bottom line—which in this case was approximately $165,000—and that would not have been affected by which line contained the $14; the sum of $315 and $50 is identical to the sum of $329 and $36. If borrowers are as price conscious as the Krzalics claim to be (and more power to them), then their lawyers (for the Krzalics were represented by counsel at the closing), who know what the county recorder charges for routine services, will shop for closing agents who neither reprice such charges nor make compensating upward adjustments in their closing fees.

Nothing is more common than for professionals to reprice the incidental charges that they incur on behalf of their clients. Law firms, for example, typically reprice their copying expenses in their bills to their clients. The client is not hurt because he can easily find out what those expenses actually were, and so it is with the government's charges for routine services in connection with real estate transactions—the charges are not secret. If the real estate settlements industry is competitive, a member of the industry cannot increase the market price for its services by how it allocates its overhead among the different components of its invoices. What is more, if the effect of the plaintiffs' suit were to induce closing agents like Republic to defer levying the charge for recording until it did the recording and thus knew the exact fee, it would be more rather than less difficult for consumers to comparison shop among closing agents.

Maybe, though, there is some hanky-panky going on here that we are missing by assuming away costs of information. When asked at argument why his client reprices the recording fee, Republic's lawyer answered that the precise fee is not known until the documents are recorded, and that occurs after the closing. True, but it's easy enough to estimate within pennies. A visit to the Cook County recorder's website reveals that the fee for recording a mortgage is $23 for the first two pages and $2 for each additional page plus 50 cents for service by return mail; so for the eight-page mortgage involved here, the total fee could readily be estimated at $35.50, which is well short of the $50 that Republic charged. And anyway Republic does not refund any overcharge that emerges when the precise fee is learned. Still, to repeat an earlier point, we have difficulty seeing what difference it can make to the consumer where the $14 "overcharge" appears on the closing statement. And if there is a fraud here, there are plenty of legal remedies, though none so far as we know under RESPA.

But the most important point is that if the practice of repricing incidental charges is a fraud or market failure or abuse of some sort, still it is not a market failure that section 8(b) can reasonably be thought to address, and so a reading of the section that leaves the failure uncured is not a reading that creates a loophole. If RESPA were a price-control statute a loophole would be opened if the firms subject to the statute were allowed to mark up cost items in their bills to whatever height they wanted. It is not a price-control statute.

There is not enough play in the statutory joints to allow HUD to impose its own "interpretation" under the aegis of *Chevron.* And there is a further point. If an agency is to assume the judicial prerogative of statutory interpretation that *Chevron* bestowed upon it, it must use, not necessarily formal adjudicative procedures or its closest nonadjudicative counterpart, which is notice and comment rulemaking but, still, something more formal, more deliberative, than a simple announcement. A simple announcement is too far removed from the process by which courts interpret statutes to earn deference. A simple announcement is all we have here. One fine day the policy statement simply appeared in the Federal Register. No public process preceded it—or at least the part of it that concerns section 8(b), for the policy statement deals with other matters as well.

HUD's amicus brief alarmingly warns that repricing is "putting home ownership beyond the reach of many Americans," that "HUD is currently investigating over 100 complaints," and that if we don't adopt its interpretation we will be permitting "unscrupulous providers to inflate settlement charges without limit." None of this appears in the policy statement, perhaps because it is silly; a $14 overcharge (if that is how it should be viewed) in a $165,000 purchase is not going to make the difference between owning and renting.

Affirmed.

CASE QUESTIONS

1. What is the fee being challenged in the case and why?
2. What does the court say about HUD's authority on interpretation of RESPA?
3. Why does the court not find a violation of RESPA?

CONSIDER 16.4

Amy and Peter Haug obtained a mortgage loan and, under the terms of their GFE and USS paid $50.00 for a credit report, $300.00 for an appraisal, and $25.00 for document delivery services in connection with the loan. The Haugs discovered that their lender, Bank of America, obtained their credit report from a third party vendor for less than $15.00, and that the appraisal and document delivery services from a third party vendor cost significantly less than the amount they were charged. The Haugs brought suit alleging that the overcharges constituted a "split of fees" or "unearned fees" in violation of Section 8(b) of RESPA. Are they Haugs correct? *Haug v. Bank of America, N.A.* 317 F.3d 832 (C.A.3 2003)

CONSIDER 16.5

Hollis Grissom was president of State Savings and Loan of Clovis, New Mexico, in June 1983. He was asked by a principal of Eaton Investors, Thomas Hartley, if State Savings would finance construction of a medical building in Denver, Colorado. Grissom also owned 72 percent of the stock of State Savings. On July 5, 1983, Grissom wrote Hartley a six-month financing commitment for $450,000. The loan commitment provided for a 2 percent origination fee, half of which was payable upon Hartley's acceptance of the commitment.

Hartley sent an acceptance letter and a check for $4,500 (1 percent of the commitment). The check was made out to Grissom personally rather than to State Savings, apparently the result of a clerical error. Grissom applied the check to his personal use, allotting part of it to a personal loan and taking the remainder in cash.

In November 1983, the Federal Savings and Loan Insurance Corporation (FSLIC) placed State Savings into receivership. FSLIC refused to honor the loan commitment because there was no record that State Savings had ever received the 1 percent origination fee. Grissom refused to discuss the matter and was thereafter indicted for embezzlement and RESPA violations. He was convicted and appealed on the grounds that the $4,500 was earned as compensation for services he performed. Was Grissom guilty of a violation of RESPA? *U.S. v. Grissom*, 814 F.2d 577 (10th Cir. 1987)

Limitations on Escrow Deposits Under RESPA

RESPA also eliminates excessive prepaids and deposits that were once required of buyers before escrow could close. Lenders required the prepaids and deposits to be certain that the property was insured and that no tax liens arose quickly after closing. For the buyer, the prepaids were a form of forced savings, but they also created difficulties because coming up with the cash necessary for closing precluded too many from home ownership. RESPA limits the amount for deposits that the lender may require at escrow and also limits the amount that the lender require as monthly payments for taxes and insurance.

At escrow, the maximum payment is calculated as the amount that would normally have been paid into escrow from the date the charge would have been last paid until (but not including) the date of the first full mortgage payment, plus the equivalent of two-months' payment (actually, the wording of the statute is one-sixth of 12 months). For example, suppose annual taxes on the property are $1,200 (or $100 per month), due on April 30. Closing on the property will occur on July 15, and the first full mortgage payment will be made on September 1. Under RESPA, the maximum deposit would be $600, computed as follows: $100 would be paid on May 1, June 1, July 1, and August 1 before the first full mortgage payment is due, for a total of $400. The two-month cushion is $200, so the total is $600.

After settlement, RESPA prohibits the lender from requiring large monthly deposits for taxes and insurance. Monthly payments for taxes and insurance are limited to one-twelfth of the amount that will become due during the year on such charges. About one-third of the states have regulations that require lenders to pay borrowers the interest on their escrow accounts earned during the year.

There are no civil or criminal penalties in RESPA for violation of these deposit limitations, but there have been several suits by harmed buyers in which federal district courts have taken jurisdiction and have held that the buyers do have a civil remedy under the act for their actual damages.

CONSIDER 16.6

The Calhouns are purchasing property. The taxes on the property are $1,200 per year, and the insurance is $600 per year. Both taxes and insurance are due on June 30. Closing on the property will take place on September 15, with the Calhouns' first mortgage payment due on November 1. How much is the lender permitted to be paid at closing? How much may the lender require in monthly deposits?

Escrow Agent's Responsibilities

The difficulty with the role of the escrow agent is that the relationship is not a true agency, since both parties' interests are carried forth by a single agent. The unique position of the agent in closing is created and clarified in duties and responsibilities spelled out in the escrow instructions.

Escrow Agent's Duty to Follow Instructions

The escrow agent must follow the directions and limitations in the escrow instructions. The agent can do no more and no less than what is specified in that agreement because the escrow agent holds only the authority given in the escrow instructions. Escrow agents who exceed their authority are liable for any resulting harm. For example, if an agent is required to pay all tax liens on the property before turning funds over to the seller and fails to do so, the agent is liable to the buyer for the amount of the tax liens.

The escrow agent often faces the same difficulties the buyer and seller face, namely, which document controls the closing? In the absence of a speicifc provision, the agent must follow only the escrow instructions because that is the only agreement to which the escrow agent is a party. The following case illustrates this principle of limiting the duties of the agent to the escrow instructions.

First Montana Title Company of Billings v. North Point Square Association

782 P.2d 376 (Mont. 1989)

FACTS

Loyd Kimble was the owner of a parcel of land in Yellowstone County, Montana. He borrowed $3,000,000 from Commerce Mortgage Company for which he executed to Commerce a note and mortgage on the land parcel on May 12, 1980. The note and mortgage were assigned to American Guaranty Life Insurance Company, and the assignment was recorded on June 4, 1981. Loyd Kimble also borrowed an additional $150,000 using the same land parcel as security, and he executed a note and mortgage to Commerce Mortgage Company, which mortgage was recorded on July 1, 1981.

Loyd Kimble defaulted on his loan payments, and the mortgages went into default. American and Commerce obtained a judgment against Kimble on the mortgage loans on July 3, 1986. There was no sheriff's sale of the land.

On July 21, 1986, Kimble entered into an option agreement for the purchase of the land parcel by North Point Square and others (defendants/appellants). The option was exercisable on or before January 24, 1987. An abstract of the option was recorded on July 24, 1986.

The escrow agreement with First Montana Title Company provided that First Montana (plaintiff and respondent) would hold a partial release of *lis pendens* (See Chapter 15, a legal document recorded to indicate litigation pending on a parcel of land), a release of the judgment in the foreclosure, and a release of American Guaranty's and Commerce's mortgages to clear the title to parcel if the option was exercised. In exchange, American and Commerce would receive the sale proceeds from the exercise of the option.

On August 22, 1986, First Interstate Bank of Billings obtained a judgment lien on the parcel for $77,041.01, and First Interstate Bank of Missoula obtained a judgment lien on the parcel for $27,000 on September 30, 1986. Interstate Production Credit Association obtained yet another judgment on the same parcel.

On January 21, 1987, North Point Square exercised the option by timely delivery of $336,674.05 to First Montana Title Company. Paragraph 6 of the escrow agreement provided:

Escrow agent is hereby authorized to use said funds to clear title to the property and to then distribute the balance of the funds to the two underlying mortgagees as follows:

(a) To American Guaranty Life Insurance Company—97 percent
(b) Commerce Mortgage Company—3 percent

When the option agreement had been exercised and the money received, First Montana Title took the position that under paragraph 6 it must pay off the judgment liens before distributing the balance of the funds to American and Commerce. American and Commerce disagreed with this interpretation. First Montana then interpleaded (deposited) the funds with the district court for a determination of which parties were entitled to them. The trial court entered a judgment for the judgment lien holders and against the mortgagees, and the mortgagees appealed.

JUDICIAL OPINION

Sheehy, Justice. The position of American Guaranty Life Insurance Company and Commerce Mortgage Company is that an option which is recorded prior to the establishment of judgment liens on the same property gives the holder of the option a priority over such subsequent judgment liens. They contend that the escrow agreement had the effect of an assignment for consideration prior to the entry of the judgments and that therefore under the escrow agreement the funds should pass to American Guaranty and Commerce Mortgage Company free of said judgment liens.

The controlling issue in this case is the contractual effect of the language in the escrow agreement.

If the escrow holder was required to "clear title" before the mortgagees could receive the balance of the funds, the relative priorities between a recorded option and judgment liens become irrelevant. We hold it was the escrow holder's duty to clear title for the optionee under the escrow agreement.

It is clear to us that the decision in this case should turn on the language of the escrow agreement, as a matter of contract. Under paragraph 6 above quoted, the escrow agent was authorized by all of the parties to the agreement to "use said funds to clear title to the property," and then to distribute the proceeds to the mortgagees.

In *Ogg v. Herman, et al.* (1924), 71 Mont. 10, 15–16, 227 P. 476, 477, this Court said:

While provision is made that plaintiff shall furnish an abstract showing clear title, good title, and a marketable title, it is apparent that these terms were used interchangeably, and that they are in fact synonymous. A clear title means that the land is free from encumbrances. A good title is one free from litigation, palpable defects and grave doubts, comprising both legal and equitable titles, and fairly deducible of record. A clear title means a good title (citing authority) and a good title means a marketable or merchantable title. A contract to convey in fee simple, clear of all encumbrances, implies a marketable title (citing authority), and a marketable title is one of such character as assures to the purchaser the quiet and peaceable enjoyment of the property and one which is free from encumbrances.

This Court further noted in *Gantt v. Harper* (1928), 82 Mont. 393, 405, 267 P. 296, 298, the following:

Webster's *definition of the word "clear" as here employed is "free from encumbrance, obstruction, burden, limitation," etc., and the word "title," in the sense here used, "the union of all elements which constitutes ownership, at common law, divided into possession, right of possession, and right of property, the last two now, however, being considered essentially the same."*

In our opinion, the words, "clear title" as employed in the plaintiff's letter, denied admission in evidence, means title to the property free from any encumbrance, burden or litigation, uniting all the elements constituting ownership, including right of possession and right of property—i.e., fee-simple title. Such was in effect the contract upon which the defendant agreed to pay a brokerage commission on the sale of the property, and a tender of the performance was complete as in accordance with the defendant's terms.

The contractual duty of the escrow agent in this case, agreed to by all the parties, was that the escrow holder should distribute the funds so as to deliver clear title to the optionee upon the exercise of the option. The judgment liens were indeed clouds on the title, and clear title could not be delivered until those judgment liens were satisfied and removed.

Affirmed.

CASE QUESTIONS

1. Give a list and chronology of events regarding the parcel of land.
2. What did paragraph 6 require the escrow agent to do?
3. What was disputed about the escrow agent's obligation under paragraph 6?
4. What definition of clear title does the court use?
5. Who will get paid first? How much will be left over for American and Commerce?

Escrow Agent's Fiduciary Responsibilities

Along with the duty of following instructions, the escrow agent also has the responsibility to act only in the best interests of the parties to the transaction. The agent cannot jeopardize either party's rights by closing for the sake of earning the closing fee if the required terms and conditions of the instructions have not been met. If an escrow agent breaches this fiduciary responsibility, any party who experiences a loss as a result can recover that loss from the agent.

Embezzlement of deposited funds by the escrow agent is definitely a breach of fiduciary duty, but the problem is that usually the agent has disappeared or has squandered the funds. This lack of remedy leaves the parties to the underlying sales contract to determine who will absorb the loss of the embezzled funds. The risk of loss will be determined according to the degree of compliance with the contract contingencies. That is, if the buyer has complied with all contingencies and the money has been deposited with the agent, then title to the money technically belongs to the seller, who would absorb the loss. Likewise, if the money has been deposited but the contingencies necessary for transfer have not been completed (e.g., the buyer does not qualify), title to the funds (and hence the risk of loss) would remain with the seller. The following case deals with the issue of misconduct by an escrow agent.

Baker v. Stewart Title & Trust of Phoenix, Inc.

5 P.3d 249 (Ariz. App. 2000)

FACTS

Ben Friedman, an attorney, obtained investments from Baker and others (plaintiffs) for a number of limited partnerships he created. However, the limited partnerships were a scam for Friedman to reap secret profits.

Friedman would find a property, and, using a fictitious name, buy it through an escrow established at a title company. While the escrow for the property was open, he would create a limited partnership and solicit investors for the down payment. After the escrow closed, he would then sell the property to the partnership for a far greater price than the purchase price he had paid to the seller of the property. By using fictitious names and shell entities, he was able to conceal the fact that he was making substantial gains each time a partnership was created.

However, Friedman required assistance in making these transactions work. He had that help from Bonnie DeAngio, an employee of Stewart Title & Trust (defendant/appellee). Ms. DeAngio handled at least eight of the Friedman escrows and on at least one of the escrows she notarized the signature of a fictitious person on a deed of trust. On another escrow she helped Friedman impersonate a fictitious buyer in a face-to-face meeting with the seller. DeAngio also handled the transfer of the properties to the limited partnerships and the affidavits of value in these transfers showed the fictitious buyer, who DeAngio knew to be Friedman, was receiving the profits from the transfer. Following each closing and transfer, an associate of Friedman's, Tom Lynch, paid DeAngio several hundred dollars.

There is no evidence to indicate that Stewart Title knew of DeAngio's fraudulent actions. DeAngio did leave Stewart Title and went to work for Chicago Title where she continued her work for Friedman.

When the limited partnerships failed, all of the investors (plaintiffs/appellants) filed suit against Stewart Title alleging its liability for the fraud of its employee. The trial court granted Stewart Title summary judgment on this issue as well as their racketeering claim (alleged violation of federal RICO statutes). The investors appealed.

JUDICIAL OPINION

Berber, Judge. An employer is vicariously liable for the negligent or tortious acts of its employee acting within the scope and course of employment. Conduct falls within the scope if it is the kind the employee is employed to perform, it occurs within the authorized time and space limits, and furthers the employer's business even if the employer has expressly forbidden it.

Here, DeAngio's actions fell within the scope of her employment because she typically notarized documents and opened and closed escrows. Opening escrows using fictitious names by itself is legal; DeAngio's opening of these escrows was thus not wrongful unless she knew that Friedman was acting with intent to defraud.

DeAngio's more apparent wrongful actions involved notarizing documents for Friedman that she knew he had signed under fictitious names and then concealing his fraudulent signature. Tom Lynch gave her cash after these closings. When Friedman was asked in his deposition, "So basically, anything that you asked her to do with respect to the defrauding of the investors, she [DeAngio] did?" He answered "yes." He also described her as "a very important facilitator" in his schemes. Though Stewart Title argues that appellants cannot show that DeAngio knew of Friedman's actions, the parties' depositions suggest that she may well have knowingly engaged in misconduct while at Stewart Title by notarizing signatures she knew to be false.

Stewart Title further claims that it would have received escrow fees, collection account fees and title insurance fees even if DeAngio had acted legitimately and, further, that the increase in purchase prices of properties due to her malfeasance did not affect its fees. Nevertheless, DeAngio's activity benefitted and furthered the business of Stewart Title because of the repeat business that she generated with Friedman. In fact, DeAngio stated that Stewart Title encouraged its escrow officers to procure new clients and develop business with existing clients. These clients would usually follow the escrow officers when they changed employment. Generating such benefits may suffice for liability. Due to DeAngio's conduct furthering its business, Stewart Title may incur vicarious liability. Whether Stewart Title would have received the same fees if she had acted properly is irrelevant.

The appellants claim that DeAngio is liable for conspiracy to defraud and, therefore, Stewart Title incurs liability under respondeat superior for all fraud-based claims. We address Stewart Title's liability for conspiracy as it applies to each group of plaintiffs and to each summary judgment.

The preliminary issue is whether DeAngio herself is liable for conspiracy. "For a civil conspiracy to occur two or more people must agree to accomplish an unlawful purpose or to accomplish a lawful object by unlawful means, causing damages."

However, the central issue remains whether Stewart Title could be liable under *respondeat superior* for DeAngio's acts in furthering the Friedman conspiracy. We find no case that holds an employer liable for its employee's acts to perpetuate a conspiracy to defraud under *respondeat superior*. The absence of such case law may result from the term "conspiracy" generally indicating vicarious liability for concerted action. If Stewart Title is liable for conspiracy through respondeat superior, two layers or "double" vicarious liability would result: DeAngio would be liable for a concerted action she did not personally perform and Stewart Title would be further liable. The nexus between Stewart Title and all the appellants thereby becomes too remote.

Reversed and remanded.

CASE QUESTIONS

1. Explain what scheme to defraud existed and what the title company employee's role in it was.
2. What is respondeat superior and how does it apply in this case?
3. Will the title company be held liable for the problems with the investment?
4. Do you think DeAngio understood what she was doing?

Escrow Agent's Duty of Care

The escrow agent has a duty to exercise reasonable care and skill during the closing. An escrow agent is expected to understand and comply with title procedures and recording requirements. In other words, the agent is held to the professional standards of those who are involved in real estate transactions. The following case illustrates the difficulties an escrow agent can encounter as a result of an oversight.

BOATRIGHT V. TEXAS AMERICAN TITLE COMPANY

790 S.W.2d 722 (Tx. 1990)

FACTS

Philip and Linda Boatright negotiated for the purchase of 2.013 acres of land from Meadowbrook, Ltd. The Boatrights paid cash and executed a note payable to Meadowbrook for $63,200. A deed of trust secured the note, and Meadowbrook executed a general warranty deed to the Boatrights. Texas American Title acted as escrow agent for this transaction.

The Boatrights immediately entered into a "flip transaction," meaning that they found an immediate buyer for the property. Akro-Tex was the buyer, and Texas American was again designated as the escrow agent. Akro-Tex paid $33,000 cash and executed two promissory notes: (1) one for $63,200 and (2) one for $36,025. The escrow agreement provided that the notes would be secured by deeds of trust, and the Boatrights executed a general warranty deed. However, the warranty deed failed to mention the Akro-Tex lien. Only the deed of trust for the $63,200 note was recorded by Texas American. Unknown to the Boatrights, the $36,025 deed of trust was never recorded.

Akro-Tex made only three payments on the $36,025 note and defaulted. The Boatrights hired Harold F. Harris to pursue collection of the note. The lack of the deed of trust was then discovered, and the Boatrights had additional difficulties in their relationship with Meadowbrook as a result of the default and lack of deed of trust. The Boatrights sued Texas American for breach of fiduciary duty. The trial court granted a judgment notwithstanding the verdict for Texas American, and the Boatrights appealed.

JUDICIAL OPINION

Fuller, Justice. When an escrow agent undertakes to act in an escrow relationship with the parties by performing such actions as preparing the escrow papers, advising both parties and accepting and cashing checks, a fiduciary duty arises between the escrow agent and both parties.

Donald R. Conoway, senior vice president and general counsel for Southern, testified that title companies such as Texas American perform escrow functions in the ordinary course of their business and agreed that they hold critical real estate documents and money in escrow.

Dan Oliver, an attorney offered as an expert by the Boatrights, testified that title companies acting as escrow agents owe a fiduciary duty to both closing parties. He testified that he would not perform a closing without the deed of trust and that a breach of fiduciary duty occurred to the seller if the escrow agent in the title company failed to deliver one of the two deeds of trust. Texas American admitted that a deed of trust covering the $36,025.00 note was never recorded.

Patricia Sweisthal, an escrow officer with Texas American that handled the Boatright–Akro-Tex transaction agreed that it is part of the function of an escrow officer to match the real estate documents just to see that everything has been done. She could not swear there was ever a deed of trust for the $36,025.00 note. She was asked: "And part of your responsibility as an escrow officer is seeing that you have the proper deeds of trust securing the notes involved?" She agreed and was then asked: "That much was not done?" She answered: "Evidently not." There was sufficient evidence before the jury to find Texas American negligent. The elements needed to provide negligence, duty, breach and injury were presented.

Gerald Anthony Colbert, a real estate broker, testified that all of the papers, including the deeds of trust were present at the closing. Texas American was to forward the documents to Akro-Tex.

There was sufficient evidence for submission of the issues as to the negligence of Texas American for jury determination and sufficient evidence to justify the jury's findings as to Texas American's negligence and the actual damages suffered by the Boatrights. We also find there was evidence that supported the jury's finding that Texas American was grossly negligent in failing to see that all supporting documents were executed and properly recorded, thereby indicating a conscious indifference as to the Boatrights' welfare.

The trial court should have entered judgment for the Boatrights against Texas American.

Reversed.

CASE QUESTIONS

1. Describe the series of sales and deeds of trust.
2. What is a "flip transaction"?
3. What document was missing and in what transaction?
4. What was the effect of the missing document?
5. Is the escrow agent a fiduciary for both parties?
6. Was the escrow agent negligent here?

Escrow Agents and the USA Patriot Act

Any time large sums of money are part of transactions, there is the potential that those types of transactions could be used for money laundering. Until 2002, federal laws that were designed to curb money laundering were applicable to just financial institutions. With the passage of the USA Patriot Act following the September 11, 2001 terrorist attacks on buildings in the United States, Congress expanded the money laundering protections to escrow agents, title companies, and others involved in closing real estate transactions, the types of transactions in which large sums of money change hands.[2] Section 352 of the USA Patriot Act applies to anyone involved in real estate closings and requires them to do the following:

1. Develop policies and procedures for effective internal controls on the use and source of funds coming into the organization for real estate closings
2. Designate a compliance officer to oversee the organization's compliance with the Act
3. Develop training programs for employees on compliance and detection of money-laundering schemes
4. Create an independent audit function to sort through transactions to determine compliance

2. The real name of the act is "Strengthening America by Providing Appropriate Tools Required to Intercept and Obstruct Terrorism Act of 2001," and the specific provisions that apply to real estate transactions are known as the International Money Laundering and Anti-Terrorist Financing Act of 2001, amended the Bank Secrecy Act of 1970 ("BSA") and it can be found codified at 12 U.S.C. §§ 1829b, 1951–1959 and 31 U.S.C. §§ 5311–5322 (2001)).

The USA Patriot Act requires those who close real estate transactions to use due diligence in preventing their transactions from being used for money-laundering purposes. For example, one of the industry's best practices is to require that buyers provide copies of account statements that show the source of the funds they are using as either a deposit (if over $10,000) or down payment. For example, if a buyer were making a $120,000 down payment from his or her bank account, the closing agent would ask for a copy of the bank account statement as well as an affidavit from the account holder that explains the source of the $120,000 in the account, something that could verify the source as the sale of another piece of property, a distribution of a gift from an estate, or the payment of royalties or dividends. Due diligence requires the closing agent to show legitimate sources and uses of funds. Without this direct linkage with fund sources, closings have been used as a means for laundering money for terrorist organizations.

Cautions and Conclusions

The devil is once again in the details. Closing a property transaction is a matter of careful attention to the paperwork and timing. When preparing to close on a property:

1. Be sure you have all the necessary paperwork.
2. Make sure the paperwork is signed by someone with authority.
3. Make sure the paperwork is dated.
4. Make sure the paperwork has all the blanks completed.
5. Make sure that you have placed deadlines and timelines in your closing agreement.
6. Be sure to choose a reputable company and parties for handling the closing.
7. Be sure that you have complied with all the required paperwork for federal and state laws in the closing documents.
8. Make sure your escrow and closing instructions are detailed enough for the agent to handle all issues and handle them so that your risk is minimized.
9. Be sure you are clear on the relationship between your contract and the closing agreement or escrow instructions.
10. Keep copies of all closing documents.
11. Make sure you comply with RESPA and the USA Patriot Act.

Key Terms

Department of Housing and Urban Development (HUD), 464
escrow, 458
escrow instructions, 459
Guaranteed Mortgage package (GMP), 470
poc (paid outside closing), 467
Real Estate Settlement Procedures Act (RESPA). 464
Uniform Settlement Statement (USS), 465

Chapter Problems

1. Herbert Walsh is the owner of valuable commercial/industrial acreage located near a municipal airport. Sam Stanton is interested in purchasing the property and informs Walsh that he has deposited $25,000 with First American Escrow, along with signed escrow instructions to purchase the property for a total cash price of $750,000. If Walsh signs the escrow instructions, do the parties have an enforceable contract?

2. Kenneth Durr received a Uniform Settlement Statement (USS) that reflected charges in excess of actual costs of closing. Durr, along with other property purchasers, filed a class-action suit alleging violation of RESPA by Intercounty Title Company. Durr's alleged errors were that he was charged a $25 deed recording fee, when in fact the deed recording fee was $23, and that he was charged $37 for recording of his mortgage when in fact that recording fee was $31.50.

Durr alleged that the collection of such fees above actual charges incurred constituted a violation of RESPA in that Intercounty was thereby accepting a charge for services other than those actually rendered. Intercounty filed a motion to dismiss. What is the result? *Durr v. Intercounty Title Co. of Illinois* 826 F. Supp. 259 (N.D. Ill. 1993); *cert. den.*, 513 U.S. 811 (1994)

3. Dearborn paid United Financial Mortgage $100 rent for every closing that it conducted at United's office that involved United as a lender. Dearborn paid $300 rent for every closing that involved another lender. Is this a RESPA violation? *Lawyers Title Ins. Corp. v. Dearborn Title Corp.*, 118 F.3d 1157 (7th Cir. 1997); remanded at 22 F. Supp. 2d 820 (N.D. Ill. 1998)

4. First Trust was the escrow agent designated to handle a property closing for Reinhold as seller and Cazalet as buyer. Escrow instructions were executed and provided for payment to Reinhold in one lump sum upon the satisfaction of certain contingencies. Shortly after the instructions were executed, Cazalet wrote to First Trust and asked that payment be made in three installments rather than in a lump sum and that payment be delayed. First Trust complied with Cazalet's letter and Reinhold objected. What was the result?

5. Jeff and Kathy Briggs obtained a mortgage loan from Madison Equity Mortgage Company, Inc. Madison Equity lent the Briggses funds that they used to refinance their residence. Madison Equity is a mortgage broker, and once the loan had been made to the Briggses, Madison transferred the loan to Countrywide Funding Corporation in exchange for a $528.75 payment. Countrywide maintains that the payment is simply a yield spread premium all lenders pay to brokers and that the Alabama state legislature has authorized such payments from lenders to brokers. The Briggses maintain the fee is a kickback that violates RESPA. Who is correct? Do you think state law or federal law will govern the payment? *Briggs v. Countrywide Funding Corp.*, 931 F. Supp. 1545 (M.D. Ala. 1996)

6. Prepare a good faith estimate of closing costs and a settlement statement from the following information:

- *Sales price*: $70,000
- *Term of loan*: 30 years
- *Loan*: $63,000; 90 percent FHA loan; $450 origination fee; 2 percent discount
- *Principal and interest*: $652
- *FHA insurance*: 1 percent
- *Location of property*: 5730 E. Grand Ave., Mesa, AZ 85203, Maricopa County
- *Tax information*: $1,200 per year for city, county, and state taxes; taxes due July 1, 2008
- *Estimated settlement date*: June 15, 2008, with first payment on August 1, 2008

What additional information is needed to complete the good faith and settlement statement?

7. Which of the following loans and lenders would be subject to RESPA?

a. A loan for a single-family dwelling by First Federal Savings and Loan
b. A loan for the purchase of one condominium unit for use as a residence in a complex consisting of 450 such units
c. A loan for the purchase of a 20-unit apartment complex by a bank insured by the Federal Deposit Insurance Corporation (FDIC)
d. A loan secured by a second mortgage for the construction of a swimming pool in the backyard of a residence
e. A loan for the purchase of a cooperative that was formerly an apartment
f. Refinancing a home mortgage to take advantage of lower interest rates
g. Home equity line of credit with funds to be used for a child's college education costs
h. A loan for the purchase of a mobile home (*Campbell v. Machias Sav. Bank*, 865 F. Supp. 26 [D. Me. 1994])

8. Is an escrow company liable for embezzlement by an employee?

9. William R. Bliss agreed to sell George P. Salemo, Jr. (and later his nominee, Catherine Salemo, his wife), a piece of residential property in the Phoenix area for $795,000. U.S. Life Title Company of Arizona was employed as the escrow agent for the transaction. Written escrow instructions were executed and delivered to U.S. Life Title.

The buyer's agent gave a certified check for $114,023.80 to U.S. Life Title at the time of closing. The certification was forged, and Chase Manhattan Bank, on which the check was drawn, refused payment. Before the forgery was discovered, U.S. Life Title delivered the closing documents, including the deed, from Bliss to Salemo and disbursed $74,422.28 to Bliss. U.S. Life Title recorded a *lis pendens* and brought suit against Salemo for the amount of the forged check. The suit was later amended to include Bliss as an additional defendant on the grounds of an indemnity provision in the escrow instructions.

After the forgery was discovered on October 22, Bliss purchased a home from the Tillotsons and as part payment assigned the note he had received from Salemo. That note was secured by a deed of trust on the property. Tillotson foreclosed on the deed of trust and resold it to Bliss, who in turn sold it to another buyer for $755,000. Thus, Bliss received $49,745 from Salemo through escrow and $74,422.28 at closing and then recovered the property that he had sold. Bliss therefore received benefits of $310,000 to $375,000 from the various transactions. Who will bear liability for the forgery? *U.S. Life Title v. Bliss*, 722 P.2d 356 (Ariz. 1986)

10. From September 1975 through May 1979, Graham Mortgage Corporation provided Rose Hill Realty, Inc., with interim financing of Rose Hill's purchase, rehabilitation, and resale of Detroit-area residences. For each loan it received, Rose Hill agreed to refer to GMC two mortgage loan applicants from its brokerage business, in addition to referring the purchaser of the rehabilitated house. In turn, GMC, when making FHA or VA mortgage loans to purchasers of the rehabilitated residences sold by Rose Hill, charged Rose Hill fewer points than it charged other sellers. To recoup the income lost through the reduction in points charged to Rose Hill, GMC increased the points charged to buyers of residences referred to Rose Hill and financed by FHA or VA loans.

Richard E. Chapin, executive vice president and director of GMC; Thomas P. Heinz, a vice president and manager of GMC; and Manford Colbert, president of Rose Hill Realty, were charged along with GMC with violations of Section 8(a) of RESPA. (Kickbacks Section).

GMC moved at the trial court to have the indictment dismissed on the grounds that the making of a mortgage loan is not "a real estate settlement service." Is this correct? *U.S. v. Graham Mortgage Corp.*, 740 F.2d 414 (6th Cir. 1984)

For research activities related to this chapter, go to our text companion website at www.thomsonedu.com/westbuslaw/jennings.

Chapter 17

Transferring Real Estate after Death: Wills, Estates, and Probate

Let's talk of graves, of worms, and epitaphs;
Make dust our paper, and with rainy eyes
Write sorrow on the bosom of the earth.
Let's choose executors and talk of wills.

William Shakespeare, *King Richard II*, Act III, Scene 2

- *Malcolm Forbes left $1,000 each to owners of nine New York restaurants, including Lutece, the Four Seasons, and Mortimer's; and $1,000 each to 30 motorcycle clubs.*
- *Bob Fosse left $25,000 to be divided among 66 friends including Dustin Hoffman, Liza Minelli, and Neil Simon "to go out and have dinner on me."*
- *Cole Porter left his clothes to the Salvation Army.*
- *Lillian Hellman gave her Toulouse-Lautrec poster to Mike Nichols.*
- *Jim Morrison left everything to his wife, who died three years later, so Morrison's estate went to his father-in-law.*
- *Alan Jay Lerner, among other bequests in his will, left $1,000 to two friends: "The purpose of this modest remembrance is to defray the cost of one evening's merriment to be devoted to cheerful recollections of their departed friend."*
- *Philip, fifth Earl of Pembroke, used his will to get back at a friend: "I give to the Lieutenant-General Cromwell one of my words... which he must want, seeing that he hath never kept any of his own."*
- *John Lennon's will disinherited anyone who contested it.*
- *Judy Garland left $250,000 to each child to be paid twice at ages 25 and 35, but the probate located only $40,000 in assets and $1,000,000 in debts.*[1]

1. Sources: Stephen M. Silverman, *Where There's a Will* (HarperCollins 1991) and Jeff Stryker, "Poison-Pen Wills: They Couldn't Resist: Oh, One Last Thing," *The New York Times*, May 31, 2000, WK 7.

Death is inevitable, but what happens to your property can be dictated by you or by the law. The law of wills and estates determines who gets what when you die.

All of the previous information about odd wills and estates raises questions about your property and what happens to it when you die. Can a will direct any disposition of property? Can you disinherit a spouse, children, or other relatives? How are creditors paid? What if there are insufficient assets to pay the creditors? Will taxes be paid first? What if there is no will, what happens to your property? This chapter answers these questions and others about your property and its transfer and disposition upon death.

Law of Wills, Estates, and Probate

In all areas of real estate law, we have seen significant variations from state to state. This degree of variation is greatly exaggerated in the law of wills, estates, and probate—so much so that it would take an entire series of texts to fully explain it all. So, this chapter deals with the subject in general terms.

However, there is a uniform law in the area, called the **Uniform Probate Code (UPC),** which by 2004 had been adopted in some form by about one-third of the states.[2] Because of the likelihood of expanded adoption of the UPC and because of its simplicity, the provisions of this code are discussed throughout the chapter.

Intestate Estates

If a person dies without a valid will or fails to dispose of certain items of property in a will, the person is said to have died **intestate** or partially intestate. In the case of an intestate death, the property of the decedent is distributed according to the state's law on **intestate succession**. The method of distributing the intestate's property follows different formulas in different states, but in all states intestate distribution is tied to the decedent's familial situation at the time of death.

Intestacy with Surviving Spouse

Generally, each state statute begins by attempting to have the decedent's property go to the closest living relatives. All state intestacy statutes focus first on surviving spouses, leaving all or some portion of the property to the surviving spouse. In some states, the surviving spouse will share the amount of the estate with any surviving children. As early as 1670, England's statute of distribution gave one-third of the intestate's property to the surviving spouse and two-thirds to the surviving children.

Under the UPC (as modified in 1999), the surviving spouse of the intestate will inherit the entire estate if no parent survives the decedent and there are no surviving children or their descendants. However, if there are surviving children and they are all children of the surviving spouse and the surviving spouse has no other children, the surviving spouse will still receive the full estate. This last portion comes from the

2. Not all states have the same version of the UPC. The UPC has been adopted in Alaska, Arizona, Colorado, Florida, Hawaii, Idaho, Maine, Michigan, Minnesota, Montana, Nebraska, New Mexico, North Dakota, South Carolina, South Dakota, and Utah. Twenty other states have adopted portions of the UPC: Arkansas, California, Georgia, Illinois, Indiana, Kansas, Kentucky, Maryland, Missouri, New Jersey, Ohio, Oklahoma, Oregon, Pennsylvania, Texas, Virginia, Washington, West Virginia, Wisconsin, and Wyoming. The predominant form of the UPC continues to be the 1969 version, but the 1999 version is gaining in popularity, with some states adopting various sections from it and integrating it with the 1969 version.

"Cinderella" problem. The theory is that a surviving spouse left with children from two marriages might favor the children from a previous marriage and shortchange the decedent's children.

Certain marital property rights in some states may supersede intestate formulas for distribution. For example, in community property states (see Chapter 8), the surviving spouse would always be entitled to his or her one-half of all community assets. The more complex the family relationships, the greater the need for a will to clarify desires with respect to family members. Most states do not include domestic partners in their intestate distribution statutes.[3] Also, federal tax laws do not recognize domestic partners for purposes of the marital/life estate tax benefits (generation-skipping trusts).[4]

Intestacy with No Surviving Spouse but with Descendants

Under the UPC, if a decedent has no surviving spouse, the estate property will pass to his or her descendants. The UPC uses the term "descendants" to refer to children, grandchildren, and other direct lineal descendants of the intestate decedent. The UPC follows the policy that, where possible, property should pass to future generations and not back to older generations. The terms and amounts of distribution among the descendants are covered later in this chapter.

Intestacy with No Surviving Spouse and No Descendants

If the decedent has no surviving spouse or descendants, the estate property goes back to the decedent's parents in equal shares. If there is one parent, that parent will receive the full estate.

If the decedent has no surviving spouse, no descendants, and no parents, the property is then inherited by the descendants of the parents, or, in lay terms, the brothers and sisters of the decedent and their descendants (the decedent's nieces and nephews).

If there are no descendants of the parents, the grandparents of the decedent inherit the property, with one-half going to the maternal grandparents and one-half going to the paternal grandparents. Likewise, the descendant rules apply here so that if the grandparents are deceased, their descendants (or the aunts and uncles of the decedent) would inherit the property.

CONSIDER 17.1

Ralph married Cora in 1949. Ralph and Cora had two children, Steven and Alice. Cora died in 1959, and Ralph married Susan in 1963. Ralph and Susan had two children, Alan and Erica. Ralph has just died intestate and his estate is valued at $800,000. How would Ralph's property be distributed under the intestacy laws of your state? How would it be distributed under the UPC?

Ron, a single young man, has just passed away. Survivors include his parents, a brother, a sister, both sets of grandparents, and two uncles. How would Ron's property be distributed under the laws of intestacy of your state? How would it be distributed under the UPC?

3. Some courts have clarified state intestate succession laws by holding that their property rights are limited to spouses who are of the opposite sex, thereby concluding that intestate succession laws are not applicable to unmarried couples or domestic partnerships. *Storrs v. Holcomb*, 168 Misc. 2d 898, 645 N.Y.S.2d 286 (Sup. Ct. 1996). Changes in marital status laws will now affect interstate distributions in states that permit same-sex unions.

4. The Defense of Marriage Act, *1 U.S.C.A. §7*, provides that "[i]n determining the meaning of any Act of Congress…the word 'spouse' refers only to a person of the opposite sex who is a husband or a wife.",

Intestacy with No Surviving Relatives

All states have some provision for the destiny of the decedent's property when a decedent has no surviving relatives. At some point in all of the state statutes, the property will go to the state or some public fund, or will **escheat** to the state. The degree to which a state statute permits distant relatives to inherit varies. Under the UPC, the property will escheat if there are no lineal descendants of the maternal or paternal grandparents; the UPC does not permit second or collateral heirs to inherit.

The escheat provisions of state intestate statutes are often referred to as **laughing heir statutes** because an escheat occurs before distant heirs, who may not have known the decedent, inherit the decedent's property.

Intestacy Terminology and Special Provisions

The following sections cover the terms and special provisions that are used in intestacy statutes to determine how property is distributed.

Per Stirpes vs. Per Capita Distribution

The formulas for distribution of intestate property make it clear that there could be many relatives who would be heirs of an intestate decedent. A question that arises is who gets how much?

There are basically three theories for distribution of intestate property. Under a **per capita** theory, the parties take an equal share. Under a **per stirpes** theory, the parties take by degree of relationship. Under the UPC theory (for which there are pre- and post-1999 versions that result in different distributions even across UPC states, since not all states have adopted the 1999 modifications), the results for distribution are somewhat of a cross between per capita and per stirpes, often called a right of representation theory.

The best way to understand these theories of distribution is by an example, complete with variations. Suppose that G is the intestate grandfather (decedent) and he has three children: A, B, and C. C has two children, Y and Z. B has one child, X. A has no children. The family relationships are diagrammed as follows:

Suppose that all three children have survived G. In this case, all three systems reach the same solution: A, B, and C take one-third each.

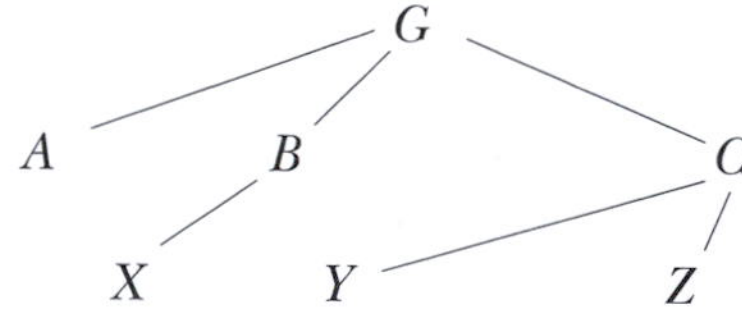

Suppose that one child, C, predeceases G. The other two children survive G. Under a straight per capita distribution, A, B, Y, and Z each take one-fourth of the estate. Under per stirpes and the UPC, A and B take one-third each and Y and Z have one-half of one-third, or one-sixth of the estate of G for each.

Suppose that all three children predecease G. Under the per capita and pre-1999 and post-1999 UPC, the result is the same: X, Y, and Z each take one-third of the estate. However, under the per stirpes method, X takes one-half, and Y and Z each take one-half of one-half, or one-quarter.

Suppose A and B predecease G, but C survives G. Under the old UPC, which is the same as per stirpes distribution, the result would be that C and X would each take one-half of G's estate. The result is the same under a per capita distribution because there are only two surviving heirs. Under the revised UPC (per capita at each generation), the solution is often debated. One view is that C would take one-half of the estate, with the remainder (one-half) combined into a single share and distributed equally among the surviving grandchildren of G (with the exception of C's children), so that X would get one-half of the estate. Another view is that after C's one-half interest, the remaining one-half is distributed equally among all the grandchildren so that X, Y, and Z would receive one-third of one-half of the estate or one-sixth of G's estate.

CONSIDER 17.2

H and W were married in 1949. They had four children, A, B, C, and D. H died in 2000 and left all of his property to W. W passed away two months ago, intestate. A died in 1999 but had three children, X, Y, and Z. B, C, and D are alive at the time of W's death. B has one child, R; and C has two children, T and S. How would the property of W be distributed in your state? How would the property be distributed by per stirpes distribution under the UPC?

Relatives by Marriage

In most states, relatives by marriage other than the surviving spouse are not entitled to receive property through intestate distribution. Stepchildren, nieces, nephews, and spouses of predeceased children are all part of this excluded group.

Half-Blood Relatives

No state has a provision that absolutely excludes half-blood relatives of the intestate from taking a share under the statutory scheme of distribution. Many states and the UPC treat a half-blood relative the same as a full-blood relative. Other states have provisions requiring half-blood relatives to take a lesser proportion of the estate than full-blood relatives.

Posthumous Heirs

At common law and under all state statutes and the UPC, children born after the intestate's death are still treated as heirs.

Some states stipulate that the **posthumous** or **afterborn heir** must be born within 10 months of the decedent's death in order to be treated as an heir. Because of scientific developments, there are now heirs being born years after the decedent has passed away. One writer has noted, "Modern reproductive technologies have enabled physicians and scientists to intervene in the procreative process in infinite ways. The ability to conceive a child after the death of one or both of the parents has become a reality."[5] Some states do not permit any such posthumous relatives to take property under intestate distribution; other states stipulate that these relatives must be at least in the embryonic stages of development at the time of the intestate's death to be eligible to take property. The Uniform Status of Children of Assisted Conception Act ("USCACA") is a relatively new uniform law that addresses the issues of science meeting probate law, but only three states have adopted it.[6] Courts have yet to sort out the rights of these very delayed posthumous children and the decisions vary among the states. The following case represents one state's view.

5. Michael K. Elliott, "TALES OF PARENTHOOD FROM THE CRYPT: THE PREDICAMENT OF THE POSTHUMOUSLY CONCEIVED CHILD," 39 Real Prop. Prob. & Tr. J. 47 (2004).
6. North Dakota, Florida, and West Virginia.

Gillett-Netting v. Barnhart

371 F.3d 593 (9th Cir. 2004)[7]

Some of the factual background was taken from the lower court decision at 231 F.Supp.2d 961 (D. Ariz. 2002)

FACTS

On March 13, 1993, Rhonda Gillett (plaintiff/appellant), 32, a student, and Robert Netting, 59, a professor of anthropology, were married. They lived in Tucson, Arizona, and they began trying to conceive a child. After Rhonda suffered two miscarriages, she was diagnosed with medical conditions which interfered with her ability to conceive a child and to carry the child to full term without medical intervention. Thereafter, she began fertility treatments.

In mid-December, 1994, Robert was diagnosed with multiple myeloma, a form of cancer. Rhonda and Robert jointly decided to continue with their efforts to have a child. On December 16, 1994, Robert was taken to the emergency room in severe pain. His treating physician recommended that he immediately undergo chemotherapy treatment for the cancer. Because the chemotherapy could have rendered him sterile, Robert delayed treatment so he could deposit and preserve his sperm for Rhonda's fertility treatments.

Throughout Robert's illness, Rhonda continued with her fertility treatments. Robert died on February 4, 1995.

After Robert's death, Rhonda's doctor performed an *in vitro* fertilization procedure on December 19, 1995. The embryo transfer occurred on December 21, 1995, and on August 6, 1996, Rhonda gave birth to twins, a female named Juliet and a male named Piers.

In March 1997, Robert's estate was distributed. Each of Robert's three children from his previous marriage received one-sixth of his retirement account. Rhonda received the rest of the account, her and Robert's house in Tucson, and the remainder of the estate. Rhonda also received proceeds as beneficiary from a life insurance policy which she used to provide for the twins.

Gillett-Netting filed a complaint in district court, alleging that the decision denying Juliet and Piers Social Security benefits was not supported by substantial evidence, was not in accordance with the law, and denied them equal protection of the laws. The district court granted summary judgment for the Commissioner of Social Security, holding that Juliet and Piers do not qualify for child's insurance benefits because they are not Netting's "children" under the Act and they were not dependent on Netting at the time of his death. Gillett-Netting appealed.

JUDICIAL OPINION

Fletcher, Circuit Judge. Developing reproductive technology has outpaced federal and state laws, which currently do not address directly the legal issues created by posthumous conception. Neither the Social Security Act nor the Arizona family law that is relevant to determining whether Juliet and Piers have a right to child's insurance benefits makes clear the rights of children conceived posthumously. Our task is to determine whether Juliet and Piers have a right to child's insurance benefits under the law as currently formulated.

Under the Act, every child is entitled to benefits if the claimant is the child, as defined in 42 U.S.C. §416(e), of an individual who dies fully or currently insured; the child or the child's representative files an application for benefits; the child is unmarried and a minor (or meets disability requirements) at the time of application; and the child was dependent on the insured wage earner at the time of his death. It is undisputed that Netting was fully insured under the Act when he died, that Juliet and Piers are his biological children and are unmarried minors, and that Gillett-Netting filed an application for child's insurance benefits on their behalf.

The Act defines "child" broadly to include any "child or legally adopted child of an individual," as well as a stepchild who was the insured person's stepchild for at least nine months before the insured person died, and a grandchild or stepgrandchild of the insured person under certain circumstances. Courts and the SSA have interpreted the word "child" used in the definition of "child" to mean the natural, or biological, child of the insured.

As the district court stated, "[b]ecause Juliet and Piers were not in existence at the time of Robert's death, they cannot demonstrate actual dependency" on him at the time of his death. The only remaining issue is whether Juliet and Piers, the undisputed biological children of a deceased, insured individual, are statutorily deemed dependent on Netting without proof of actual dependency.

In summary, through the Act's statutorily deemed dependency, any legitimate child, a child entitled under the intestacy laws of the insured parent's domicile to inherit personal property from the parent, a child whose illegitimacy results from a formal defect in the parents' purported marriage ceremony, and a child acknowledged in writing by the insured father as his son or daughter or judicially decreed (during the father's

7. For a contra view, see *Stephen v. Commissioner of Social Sec.*, 386 F.Supp.2d 1257 (M.D. Fla. 2005).

lifetime) to be such, are all deemed under the Act to be dependent upon the parent, unless the child has been adopted by some other individual, and thus are relieved of otherwise proving actual dependency.

Moreover, the Act is construed liberally to ensure that children are provided for financially after the death of a parent. Under Arizona law, Netting would be treated as the natural parent of Juliet and Piers and would have a legal obligation to support them if he were alive, although they were conceived using *in-vitro* fertilization, because he is their biological father and was married to the mother of the children. Although Arizona law does not deal specifically with posthumously-conceived children, *every* child in Arizona, which necessarily includes Juliet and Piers, is the legitimate child of her or his natural parents.

The Commissioner nevertheless argues that Juliet and Piers do not satisfy the "legitimate child" requirement, and therefore cannot be deemed dependent, unless they also are able to inherit from Netting under state intestacy laws. This is not the case. Legitimacy is determined in accordance with state law.

Because Juliet and Piers are Netting's legitimate children under Arizona law, they are deemed dependents [for purposes of Social Security benefits].

Accordingly, we REVERSE the decision of the district court and REMAND with instructions to further remand to the Commissioner of Social Security for an award of benefits.

Reversed and Remanded

CASE QUESTIONS

1. What law does the court use in making the Social Security–dependent determination?
2. What effect will this decision have on the rights of children under Arizona intestate laws?
3. What concerns would the Social Security administration have about the effects of the decision?

ETHICAL ISSUE

Could the decision allowing the recovery of Social Security benefits by a posthumous child create incentives for conception and birth for profit? What limits will the Social Security administration need to put in place to control the use of posthumous children for claims?

ILLEGITIMATE CHILDREN

Under the UPC and in all states, illegitimate children who have not been adopted by anyone are treated as natural children of their mothers and are entitled to inherit from their mothers and their mothers' relatives. Unless legitimized, these children are not treated as the natural children of their fathers. Paternity suits establish the right of the child to inherit once the determination of paternity is made judicially or the father acknowledges paternity.

ADOPTED CHILDREN

The legislative trend has been for adopted children to be treated as the natural children of the parents adopting them. The UPC also follows this doctrine for purposes of intestate distribution.

CONSIDER 17.3

When Hank Williams, Sr., the country western singer, died in 1953, he left a single living heir: his son, Williams, Jr. In the month before his death, however, Williams, Sr. entered into an agreement with Bobbie Jett regarding the care of a child that Jett was then carrying. Under the terms of the agreement, Jett surrendered all parental rights in the child and Williams, Sr., without specifically claiming the child as his own, undertook to raise and support it. This child was born five days after Williams, Sr.'s death. The child, now an adult, is Cathy Louise Deupree Adkinson. After her birth, pursuant to the agreement between Williams, Sr., Jett, and Adkinson's mother, Adkinson was adopted by Lillian Stone, the mother of Williams, Sr. At Mrs. Stone's death two years later, however, Adkinson was placed in foster care and eventually adopted out of the Williams family. Adkinson's adoptive parents did not tell Adkinson of her connection to Williams, Sr.

CONSIDER 17.3
(CONTINUED)

In 1967, the Williams family petitioned the Montgomery Circuit Court for final settlement of the estate of Williams, Sr. At this time, the trustees of the estate advised the court of Adkinson's potential claim on the estate, in light of the agreement between Williams, Sr. and Adkinson's mother. Because Adkinson's adoptive parents chose not to participate in the distribution, the court appointed a guardian to represent Adkinson's interests. As a result of proceedings held in 1967 and 1968, the court ruled that Williams, Jr. was the sole heir to the estate and that, according to state law, Adkinson, as an illegitimate child who had been twice adopted, was not entitled to inherit from Williams, Sr., even if she were found to be his natural child. The guardian *ad litem* appealed this ruling on behalf of Adkinson but the trial court denied permission to appeal. In 1975, the Williams estate was closed.

Sometime after 1974, when she reached the age of majority, Adkinson discovered her connection to the Williams family and the possibility that she might be the natural child of Williams, Sr. In 1985, Adkinson wrote Williams, Jr. demanding a share in the renewal copyrights of her father's songs. Anticipating litigation over the renewal copyrights, Williams, Jr. filed suit to re-establish his property rights through the estate. Who is the rightful heir? Are the songs included as his inheritance? Should the estate be reopened? *Stone v. Williams,* 766 F. Supp. 158 (S.D.N.Y. 1991); *Stone v. Gulf American Fire & Casualty Ins. Co.*, 554 So.2d 346 (Ala.1989); *Williams v. Adkinson,* 792 F. Supp. 755 (M.D. Ala., 1992), *cert. den*. 508 U.S. 906 (1993).

Aliens

Aliens are entitled to receive property through intestate distribution. Their citizenship is not an issue in their right to inherit.

Convicts

A convict is permitted to inherit property and have it distributed through intestate succession at the time of death. Convicts' property does not escheat to the state.

Murder

Under the UPC and in most states, an heir convicted of murdering (intentionally and feloniously) the intestate is not entitled to the intestate share of property that ordinarily would be awarded. State provisions vary as to the type of conviction required before the inheritance is lost. The following case deals with an issue of murder and inheritance.

In the Matter of the Estate of Morris P. Van Der Veen

935 P.2d 1042 (Kan. 1997)

FACTS

On or about April 30, 1993, Kent Van Der Veen murdered his parents, Morris and Deanne Van Der Veen. Kent was 19 years old at the time and had fathered a child two years earlier who had been legally adopted by persons not identified in the court proceedings. Morris and Deanne were not aware of the existence of Kent's child prior to their deaths.

The 1989 joint will of Morris and Deanne Van Der Veen provides for the following distribution of their estate after debts and obligations are paid:

Upon the death of the survivor of us, each of us hereby gives, devises, and bequeaths all of the rest, residue, and remainder of our property of every kind, character, and description, and wherever located, unto our children, Laura Ann Van Der Veen and Kent Phillip Van Der Veen, equally and per stirpes.

Kent Van Der Veen was disqualified from inheriting any portion of his parents' estate under Kansas's slayer statute. Kent's child, the biological grandchild of Morris and Deanne, petitioned to inherit one-half of her biological grandparents' estate. The grandchild is identified in the case only as D.B.B. The trial court denied the grandchild any interest in the estate, and the grandchild appealed.

JUDICIAL OPINION

Allegruccci, Justice. In their will, the Van Der Veens bequeathed one-half of their estate to each of their children, Laura and Kent. It is agreed that Kent is statutorily disqualified from inheriting property from his parents. At all pertinent times, it has been provided by statute:

No person convicted of feloniously killing, or procuring the killing of, another personal shall inherit or take by will[,] by intestate succession, as a surviving joint tenant, as a beneficiary under a trust or otherwise from such other person any portion of the estate or property in which the decedent had an interest. K.S.A. 1996 Supp. 59-513.

This appeal challenges the district court's determination that the statute prevails over the express terms of the Van Der Veens' will, resulting in D.B.B.'s being disinherited. The argument made on behalf of D.B.B. by her guardian *ad litem* is that the language of her grandparents' bequest to their children, "equally and per stirpes," must be construed to give what would have been Kent's share, if he had not been disqualified, to his heir, D.B.B. D.B.B.'s guardian *ad litem* further argues that D.B.B.'s adoptive status is irrelevant because K.S.A. 59-2118(b) provides that "[a]n adoption shall not terminate the right of the child to inherit... through the birth parent."

Appellee Laura Van Der Veen counters that the language of 59-2118(b), on which D.B.B. relies, was added in 1993 and became effective after the Van Der Veens' deaths. If the effective date of the amendment does not prevent it from applying in the present case, appellee further argues, the statute should be construed to restrict inheritance "through the birth parent" to instances where the birth parent has died. In other words, it should be interpreted so as to exclude inheritance through a birth parent who is alive but disqualified. In appellee's words, the statute should be interpreted so that the disqualified killer is treated as if he never existed rather than as if he had died.

We first address whether D.B.B.'s adoption affects her right to inherit from her biological grandparents. There is no doubt that the legislature intended that 59-2118(b), at all pertinent times, permitted an adoptee to inherit from and through his or her biological parents.

In that enactment, the sentence, "An adoption shall not terminate the right of the child to inherit from or through the birth parent," was added to 59-2118(b).

The Court of Appeals in [*In re Estate of Hirderliter*, 882. P.2d 1001 (Kan. 1994)] concluded that the 1993 amendment to 59-2118 merely codified existing law so that the rule should be given effect whether decedent died before or after the effective date of the statutory amendment, July 1, 1993.

We find the Court of Appeals' rationale persuasive and conclude that D.B.B.'s adoption would not bar her from inheriting from or through her biological parent.

We next consider whether Kent's being barred from inheriting from his parents prevents the inheritance from passing through him to his child. This was the basis for the trial court's decision and has not been decided by the appellate courts of this state. The question has arisen in other jurisdictions, however, and has been pondered by commentators, scholars, and the National Conference of Commissioners on Uniform State Laws.

With regard to the UPC, the Tennessee Court of Appeals, in *Carter v. Hutchison*, 707 S.W.2d 533, 537 n. 10 (Tenn. App. 1985), noted:

A vast majority of states enacting the forfeiture statutes have patterned them after the model statute proposed by Dean Wade in 1936, see J. Wade, [Acquisition of Property by Willfully Killing Another—A Statutory Solution, 49 Harv. L. Rev. 715, 753–55 (1936)], *or the Uniform Probate Code. Thus, in twenty-nine states there is a statutory presumption that the victim's property passes to his estate as if the slayer had predeceased the decedent. Four states provide for forfeiture but are silent as to distribution. Tennessee is among ten states that provide for forfeiture and for distribution to the decedent's heirs through the laws of intestate succession. The eight remaining states without statutes have forfeiture provisions by court decision.*

It appears that Kansas is one of the few states that does not expressly provide for distribution of the forfeited share.

Turning to the present case, it is clear that under either version of the UPC, appellee would take one-half of the estate of her parents. The other half would be taken by her disqualified brother's minor child.

The disposition of the slayer's share is one of four issues identified as unresolved by 59-513 and discussed in a 1984 law review article. Kuether, *Barring the Slayer's Bounty: An Analysis of Kansas' Troubled Experience,* 23 *Washburn L. J.*, 494, 495, 519–26 (1984).

Professor Kuether undertook to show why two possible objections to considering the slayer to have predeceased the victim were not significant. The first is that the slayer might act in order to benefit his heirs. He suggests that "[t]his will be rare since it is a very costly gift by the slayer." Furthermore, to bar all taking by representation and any antilapse with the exceptional slayer in mind would be unjust and typically contrary to the victim's intent. The second "is Kansas' traditional position that those who take by representation take subject to the equities against their ancestors." Kuether's analysis why this principle is not applicable in the case of a slayer/beneficiary is convincing. He states that the principle was developed in cases where an heir claims through a person who was indebted to the decedent. The shares of the other beneficiaries were reduced by the amount of the indebtedness. In contrast, the other beneficiaries' shares have not been reduced by the slayer's killing the decedent. In fact, their benefits have been accelerated. Thus, just treatment of the other beneficiaries does not demand that the slayer's heirs be disqualified or penalized. To illustrate this proposition in the circumstances of the present case, we need only look at appellee's situation. She would take one-half of her parents' estate if they had died from natural causes, and she would take the same if Kent is disqualified for killing their parents and his share passes as if he predeceased them. In contrast, if Kent's child were disqualified because Kent killed his parents, the innocent child would be penalized, and appellee would take twice what the testators intended and what she expected.

We conclude that the better rule where the slayer's heir or heirs are wholly innocent would be to dispose of the disqualified slayer's share as if the slayer predeceased the victim(s).

The Van Der Veens intended for their daughter to take one-half of their estate. Their knowledge of Kent's troubled nature is reflected in a provision of the Van Der Veens' will that nominates Laura to serve as Kent's guardian and conservator. Nonetheless, they bequeathed one-half of their estate to him. There is nothing in the instrument from which the court could conclude that the Van Der Veens intended for Laura to receive the entire estate in the event of Kent's incapacity or disqualification. By extension, it may reasonably be inferred that they would not have intended for Kent's innocent child to be disqualified in order for Laura to receive the entire estate.

Appellee invites the court to speculate that the Van Der Veens would not have intended for their unknown, illegitimate grandchild to share in their estate. We decline the invitation and note there is no factual support in the record for such a speculation.

The judgment of the district court is reversed.

CASE QUESTIONS

1. What is a "slayer statute"?
2. What does the court find about adopted children inheriting from their biological parents?
3. What does the court find about grandchildren of murderers inheriting the barred murderer's share of an estate?
4. Is Laura's position different from what it would have been if the inheritance by the grandchild were disallowed?
5. Why does the court discuss the concept of innocence?

ETHICAL ISSUE

What ethical and public policy issues exist in the dilemma of slayers, beneficiaries, and decedents? What concerns are courts and legislators trying to address with slayer statutes?

ADVANCEMENTS

At common law, the doctrine of **advancements** required that any gifts made by the intestate while alive to his or her heirs had to be subtracted from that heir's share of the intestate estate. For example, suppose three heirs were entitled to receive equal shares of a $90,000 estate. If one heir had received $10,000 as an *inter vivos* gift, that heir would get only $20,000 under the doctrine of advancements. The remaining two heirs split the extra $10,000. Some states still follow the doctrine, but it is recognized under the UPC only if the intestate indicated in writing that the gift was an advance.

Property Interests Not Passing by Intestate Succession

Some land interests do not transfer by intestate distribution because of their characteristics. These interests, which were discussed in Part I, are life estates, joint tenancies by the entireties, and rights under dower and curtesy (discussed in Chapter 8). These interests automatically pass title at the time of death and are not distributed under intestacy rules. Life insurance benefits also pass to beneficiaries named in the policy, not by the laws of intestacy.

Simultaneous Death

In cases of accidents and air disasters, husbands and wives, who would ordinarily receive each other's estates, perish together or will die under circumstances where it is impossible to tell who predeceased the other. Some states have survival period requirements before an heir may inherit through intestate distribution. Under the UPC, heirs must survive by 120 hours before they are permitted to inherit. Survival clauses make intestate distribution easier. For example, a husband might survive his wife in an auto crash by only a few hours or a day and then pass away. In the absence of a survival provision, the property of the wife would pass to her husband's estate, which would in turn pass according to the remaining rules of intestate succession. With a survival provision, the property of each would be directly distributed to those next in line.

Some states have passed a uniform law related to the UPC, the **Uniform Simultaneous Death Act (USDA),** which provides that if a married couple dies under circumstances where it is impossible to determine the order of their deaths, then property of each spouse is distributed as if the other spouse had predeceased them. The wife's property would be distributed as if she died without a surviving spouse and the husband's property would be distributed in the same manner. Perhaps the most famous application of this provision was in the case of the deaths of John Kennedy and Caroline Bessette-Kennedy in a plane crash. Their estates would have gone to each other, but because of their simultaneous deaths, and no children, his estate went to the children of his sister, Caroline Kennedy Schlossberg.

Wills

Purpose of a Will

A **will** is a series of written instructions that sets forth what is to be done with the decedent's property upon death. The will transfer takes place only after the death of the testator.

A will reflects the wishes of the decedent and can expedite the distribution of property. Under the UPC, probate procedures require a minimal number of court appearances and substantially reduce paperwork, court costs, and attorneys' fees.

A will can also name who will be responsible for handling and distributing the property, who should be appointed as guardian for minor children, who will make funeral arrangements, and the type of funeral arrangements.

Wills can also create trusts to protect the income of minor children and to minimize estate taxes.

> ***Practical Tip***
>
> *Everyone needs a will. It saves time and the assets of the estate. However, the number of Americans with a will is limited:*
>
> | *Age Group* | *Percent with a Will* |
> |---|---|
> | *35–44* | *41%* |
> | *45–54* | *63%* |
> | *55–64* | *62%* |
> | *65 and older* | *75%* |
>
> *On average, 55% of Americans do not have a will.*
>
> *Source: (www.findlaw.com 2005)*

Requirements for a Valid Will

The requirements for executing a valid will vary from state to state as significantly as intestate distribution rules. However, all of the states have provisions on these basic requirements: writing, testamentary capacity, signature, witnesses, and acknowledgment.

Writing

Like all other documents conveying interests in real property, a will is generally required to be in writing. The writing requirement is true for wills even if the testator is not disposing of any real property in the will. A few states do recognize oral or **nuncupative wills**, but often such wills are limited to the disposal of personal property and must be created under circumstances of near death. In many states, the nuncupative will requirements are similar to the gift in contemplation of death (gift *causa mortis*) requirements. Electronic forms of wills and faxes, the type of documentation now permitted in other areas, still will not serve as a writing because of the need for notaries and other attestations on wills. In fact, the most frequently litigated issue in estate distributions is whether the document submitted for probate actually constitutes a will. The following sections discuss the validity of such will substitutes.

Holographic Will Most wills are thought of as formally typed documents drafted by attorneys, backed by blue paper, and written in very formal language. However, other types of writings can qualify as wills that have none of those characteristics. Many states and the UPC recognize the holographic will as valid. The **holographic will** is a will that is written entirely in the handwriting of the testator and signed by the testator. Former Chief Justice Warren Berger had a 176-word holographic will in which he left his property to his children. Some states now permit holographic wills to be placed on a preprinted form.

Some states require that the holographic instrument be witnessed to be valid, while others recognize the will as valid so long as it is signed. One problem with the holographic will, particularly in states where the will need not be witnessed, is establishing the authenticity of the handwriting and the signature as that of the testator. The long-lasting probate battle over the will of billionaire Howard Hughes resulted because there were several purported holographic wills submitted to the court, all of which had different property distributions.

CONSIDER 17.4

The following language was found in a holographic will left in the residence of William P. Avery and Deborah Smalling who were unmarried but lived together in the house they had built with their earnings and savings:

I would like Deborah to have my home and property to maintain and keep with the hope that she may find the comfort and independence that has been denied me. She has been my love and faithful consort and has given me untold support and happiness. Words fail me. /s/William P. Avery

Does the will qualify as a holographic will? Does the language have any ambiguities? Would the will also pass to Deborah the 32 acres of land on which the house sat? *Smalling v. Terrell*, 943 S.W.2d 397 (Tenn. App. 1996)

Contracts to Make Wills and Joint or Mutual Wills Husbands and wives often enter into contracts to make joint or mutual wills that will serve to dispose of the property belonging to the two in a certain way. The idea behind the contract to make a will is to bind the spouse so that the agreed-upon distribution cannot be changed by the surviving spouse. The contract to make the wills is not a will. However, once the wills are executed, the terms of both the agreement and the wills can be enforced. To be enforceable, a contract to make a will must be supported by consideration. Husbands and wives offer consideration through their mutual relinquishment of the right to distribute their property according to their desires. Theoretically, each party is bound even after the death of one of the parties to the agreement. In practice, these contracts cause litigation.

A **joint will** is the same will executed by different parties as their own will. **Mutual wills** are the separate wills of parties that are reciprocal in their provisions and are probably based on a mutual agreement, understanding, or contract to make a will. States vary in their recognition of the validity of joint wills, but all states recognize mutual wills. Because of their nature, mutual wills are also often the subject of will contests. One of the issues often arising in the case of a mutual will is whether its provisions can be revoked. The provisions can be revoked with the mutual consent of the parties. Unilateral revocation usually brings litigation by the heirs or potential heirs.

Content of the Writing There are no requirements for specific provisions in a valid will (with the exception of execution requirements discussed later). However, all wills should clearly explain the testator's intentions and desires for the distribution of their property and the handling of their affairs upon death.

Generally, wills can be broken down into the following topics, although the topics and their content may vary from state to state and according to the needs of the testator's family.

1. *Declaration clause*: Declares the age, capacity, and residence of the testator and that the document is a will.
2. *Definition clause or clauses*: Lists wife, husband, children, and so on. Defines terms such as *children* and *issue*.
3. *Funeral and burial arrangements clause*: If desired, specifies funeral procedures.
4. *Debt clause*: Provides for payments of all debts, estate and inheritance taxes, and so on.
5. *Appointment clause or clauses*: Appoints the party responsible for the administration of the estate. May also specify the powers of the appointed person.
6. *Gift clause or clauses*: Disposes of the estate property, by either specific dispositions or a general disposition.
7. *Execution and signature clauses*: See the discussion later in this chapter.

Testamentary Capacity

There are two requirements for **testamentary capacity**: age capacity and mental capacity.

1. **Age Capacity** Every state has a statute that fixes the minimum age requirement for executing a valid will. In most states, the age of testamentary capacity is the age of majority, which in most states is 18. The age requirement must be met at the time the will is executed.

2. **Mental Capacity** Many wills begin their declaration clause with "I,—————, being of sound mind...." This clause establishes the mental capacity requirement for the execution of a valid will, which is that the testator must be of sound mind. Mental capacity is not synonymous with intelligence, logic, or distributing

property only to relatives. Rather, mental capacity requires proof that the testator understood the following at the time the will was executed:

1. The nature or extent of his or her property
2. What persons would be the natural recipients
3. What disposition is being made of the property
4. The relationship between items 1 to 3
5. How to form an orderly distribution of property

Eccentricity or old age alone do not establish a lack of testamentary capacity. Each case on testamentary capacity presents a different set of factual circumstances and requires the court to apply each of the five factors listed according to the familial situation of the individual testator. The following case illustrates how the determination of testamentary capacity is made.

BRACEWELL V. BRACEWELL

20 S.W.3d 14 (Tex. App. 2000)

FACTS

Irene Bracewell was married to W.T. Bracewell and they had two children: Bobbie, born in 1932, and Charles, born in 1936. In 1961, Irene executed a will that left all of her estate to Charles. During the 1960s, Irene left W.T., who had named a lake on their ranch, Lake Irene, and moved in with Charles at his home in Houston, Texas. Irene returned to W.T. in 1975 and executed another will that left everything to W.T. if she died first. W.T.'s will left everything to her if he died first.

During the 1970s, Irene suffered from nervousness, anxiety, hypertension, hypothyroidism, and degenerative joint disease. In 1984, Irene was hospitalized with Parkinson's disease. She added to her long list of medications, including tranquilizers, prescriptions for Parkinson's.

While Irene loved both W.T. and Charles, all agreed that W.T. and Charles did not get along. In 1989, W.T. executed another will that left all of his property to Bobbie. Irene, upon learning of this change, deeded property to Charles and executed a new will. Following the execution of the will, Irene's mental and physical health deteriorated and she died in 1995 following a year in a nursing home.

W.T. wanted the 1975 will probated and Charles petitioned to have the 1989 will recognized as valid. A jury agreed with W.T.'s position that Irene lacked competency to execute the 1989 will and the judge then admitted the 1975 will to probate. Charles appealed.

JUDICIAL OPINION

Wanda McKee Fowler, Justice. In the instant appeal, Charles complains that the evidence adduced at trial is legally and factually insufficient to support the jury's finding that Irene lacked testamentary capacity to execute a valid will on August 17, 1989.

In his brief, W.T. contends that the trial record shows that Irene lacked testamentary capacity on the day the 1989 will was executed. At trial, W.T. testified that Irene was hospitalized in 1984. According to W.T., Irene was "sick a lot" from that time on, and that she was a different woman. W.T. stated that, following her diagnosis with Parkinson's Disease, Irene quit driving a car, quit going to church, and "didn't want no company." W.T. concluded that, in 1989 "Irene was in pretty bad shape." In addition to his own testimony, W.T. offered the following witnesses in support of his contention that Irene was not legally competent to execute the 1989 will: (1) Bobbie Bracewell Rigby; (2) Linda Grisset; (3) Dr. Luke Scamardo; and (4) Dr. Gary Newsome. That testimony is summarized below.

W.T. and Irene's daughter, Bobbie Bracewell Rigby, testified on W.T.'s behalf. According to Bobbie, Irene's health "got bad in 1984." She added that, although Irene had been a devout woman previously, her mother quit going to church because of her condition. Bobbie stated further that, after 1984, Irene socialized with other people less frequently. Bobbie reported that, during 1987, and most of 1988, she visited Irene every day so that she could bathe her mother, brush her teeth, and fix her hair. Bobbie added that Irene "acted like a little child" while her daughter brushed her teeth for her. Bobbie testified that Charles sent a letter to "Dr. Jankovic" in Houston, Texas, in October of 1987, which recited Irene's medical history. In that letter, Charles reported that his mother had been taking "pain pills, tranquilizers, and sleeping pills" for thirty years or "maybe longer." Charles wrote further that Irene's Parkinson's Disease was "continu[ing] to get worse." During the summer of 1989, Bobbie and her husband traveled to Pennsylvania to pursue his work in the oil pipeline industry. Bobbie noted that she "didn't think" that Irene was "of sound mind" during the 1989 time period "because the way she was about church and everything."

Linda Grisset is Bobbie's youngest daughter and W.T.'s granddaughter. Linda described her relationship with her grandmother, Irene, as a "close" one. Linda testified that, from 1975 through 1979, Irene never missed a single Sunday church service, and that she went to the beauty parlor every Wednesday. In addition, Irene helped out at her church by cleaning, vacuuming, wiping song books, and doing "whatever needed to be done." During that time, Irene loved to read and would help Linda with her schoolwork. Linda, described Irene as a "nervous lady." Linda testified that, in 1984, after a stay in the Madison County Hospital, Irene stopped driving and quit going to church altogether. Linda was married on August 21, 1989. Linda testified that she visited Irene on the afternoon of Thursday, August 17, 1989, to tell her grandmother about her wedding plans. According to Linda, Irene would not "respond to anything" and "couldn't relate" to her granddaughter at all on that day. Linda testified further that Irene was "absolutely not" in a sound frame of mind on August 17, 1989, that she was in that same condition "[m]ost of the time, and had been for awhile."

Dr. Scamardo testified that he was informed by Charles, in 1987, that Irene was experiencing "periods of incoherence" at home. Dr. Scamardo added that Irene's family had to supply information for her when she came in for treatment because she was incoherent "ninety-nine percent" of the time.

Dr. Scamardo testified that, in his opinion, Irene would not have had testamentary capacity on the day she executed the 1989 will. Dr. Scamardo explained that he based this opinion on Irene's "anxiety course" during her entire treatment history. He elaborated further that, during the time he treated Irene, she had periods in which she would become "more anxious, [and] more incoherent." According to Dr. Scamardo, on August 17, 1989, Irene would have been unable to "keep up with all the complicated dealings of making out a will, [and] dealing with business dealings."

Dr. Newsome reviewed Irene's medical records dating from the 1970s, and he also reviewed records from the Clouser Pharmacy for the year 1989. Dr. Newsome observed that Irene was "taking some pretty heavy duty medication" during the time she signed the 1989 will. He noted further that "she was having evidence of confusion" as early as 1984. Dr. Newsome explained that people who are diagnosed with Parkinson's Disease later in life have a "much greater incidence of... having significant depression, dementia and even worse psychiatric symptoms of delusions and hallucinations and paranoia." Dr. Newsome added that Irene's condition may have been worsened by the fact that Irene misused her medication.

In Dr. Newsome's opinion, Irene's lack of competency wasn't even a "close" question. Dr. Newsome added that, given the medications described in the Clouser Pharmacy records, he was "not sure if [she] would know what planet [she] took these medicines [on]." Dr. Newsome commented further that Irene's decision to lock herself in the bathroom for the purpose of executing her will could be considered an indication of the level of her paranoia at the time. Dr. Newsome also noted that Irene's decision to leave the bulk of her estate to Charles showed that she was unaware of her "bounty" and unaware that she had any children "other than Charles Bracewell."

The overall evidence supports the doctors' testimony. Therefore, we hold that the verdict was supported by legally sufficient evidence and overrule the challenge by Charles on that issue.

After reviewing all of the evidence, we do not consider the jury's finding so contrary to the overwhelming weight of the evidence as to clearly wrong and unjust. Accordingly, we overrule Charles's factual sufficiency challenge.

Affirmed.

CASE QUESTIONS

1. Are health problems alone grounds for a finding of lack of mental capacity for executing a will?
2. Is age alone grounds for a finding of lack of mental capacity for executing a will?
3. Explain what testimony was the basis for a finding of a lack of mental capacity.
4. What lessons do you learn about multiple wills, health issues, and family relationships from this case?

CONSIDER 17.5

Burnell Young died on December 18, 1995, leaving a will that left all of his property to his daughter, Martha Young. Freeman Young, his son, challenged the validity of the will on the grounds that Burnell could not read. Should a will be set aside because the testator cannot read? *Succession of Young*, 692 So.2d 1149 (La. App. 1997)

CONSIDER 17.6

Dr. Albert Blakes had separated from his wife Alyce 12 years before his death. Despite the separation, Blakes continued to provide Alyce with financial support. Additionally, Blakes maintained his relationship with his stepson Richard and treated him as one of his children. Blakes was diagnosed with malignant melanoma about one year before his death. During that year, Blakes underwent various treatments for his cancer. By January or February of 1999, Blakes's condition was classified as stage four, indicating the cancer had spread within his body. His condition continued to deteriorate and on May 20, 1999, he was admitted to the hospital suffering from confusion and dehydration.

On May 25, 1999, William Podsednik, Blakes's friend, was informed by Reeta Parlin (a nurse from Blakes's medical practice with whom Blakes was romantically involved) that Blakes wanted to make a will. Podsednik testified he was generally aware of how Dr. Blakes wanted to dispose of his property from conversations during past years. Podsednik specifically asked Blakes what he wanted to do about Richard to which Blakes responded, "Nothing." Podsednik relayed what he believed to be Blakes's wishes to attorney Jack Garbo.

Based on information provided by Podsednik, Garbo prepared a will for Blakes. Podsednik then brought the will to the hospital on May 26, 1999, for Blakes's signature. Podsednik, two witnesses, and a notary were present when Blakes executed the will in the afternoon. During the will execution, Blakes got tired and asked to finish the next day. Parlin and Podsednik urged Blakes to continue and he completed the signing. Garbo never spoke directly to Blakes about the will he prepared and did not go to the hospital to supervise its execution. Blakes died at midnight on May 26, 1999. Among other things, the will purported to leave Blakes's interest in his medical practice to his partner Dr. Sharon Rae and the remainder of his estate to his three biological children. The will left nothing to his wife Alyce and stepson Richard Blakes. Is the will valid? *In re Estate of Blakes*, 104 S.W.3d 333 (Tex. App. 2003)

Signature

All states require, as part of the formal prerequisites for a valid will, that the will be signed by the testator. The signature requirement is straightforward when the testator is able to sign. However, there are circumstances when the testator, because of disease or hospital equipment, is unable to personally sign the will. In these circumstances and under the UPC, the testator may direct someone else to sign the will so long as the testator acknowledges the will and is present at the signing of it.

Those who are unable to write may still authenticate a will by placing an *X* on the signature portion of the will, witnessed by others as being placed by the testator.

The signature of the testator should appear at the end of the will to make clear what portions and provisions were intended to be included in the will. As a matter of practice or law, the testator should also initial each page of the will to prevent pages from being added or altered after the execution occurs.

Witnesses

The witness requirements for a valid will vary from state to state. The number of witnesses required for a valid will is either two or three; under the UPC, the requirement is two. In addition, some states require that the witnesses be disinterested parties; that is, the witnesses must not be beneficiaries under the will. The UPC does not impose this requirement of having disinterested witnesses.

Many states also specify the manner in which the witnesses witness the transaction. For example, some states require that all of the witnesses be present in the same room at the time the testator signs the will, and that the witnesses sign in the presence of the testator and in the presence of one another. Other states and the UPC do not require the witnesses to actually witness the signing by the testator so long as the testator indicates the signature is authentic before the witness signs.

CONSIDER 17.7

George Baxter Gordon executed a will that provided that the Church of Christ of New Boston, Texas, would receive a substantial amount of his property. The will was executed with two members of the church serving as witnesses for the will. Upon Gordon's death, several heirs contested the admission of the will to probate on the grounds that the witnesses were interested parties. What was the result? *In re Estate of Gordon*, 519 S.W.2d 902 (Tx. 1975)

ACKNOWLEDGMENTS

Many states and the UPC provide all testators with the opportunity to execute a **self-proving will**. In a self-proving will, the signatures of the testator and the witnesses are notarized following a clause that is a form of affidavit for the parties. If the proper acknowledgment procedures are followed, then the will enjoys a presumption that it was validly executed. Figure 17.1 is an example of an acknowledgment clause used in a UPC state. The clause follows after the testator and witness signatures.

Will Contests

The validity of a will may be challenged by anyone who might have an interest in the estate of the decedent—someone named in the will or an heir omitted from the will. Some of the grounds for such challenges include the testator's lack of testamentary capacity or the failure to meet the requirements for sigantures or witnesses.

One frequent reason wills are set aside is that thre has been **undue influence** in its execution. When undue influence is raised in a will contest, the party challenging the will does not dispute the valid execution of the will, but rather raises the defense that the will was not executed of the testator's own free will and choice—that someone else influenced the testator in an unfair manner to execute the will.

Undue influence is a difficult concept to define. There need not be force to establish undue influence, but there must be something more than advice, persuasion, and kindness. The following elements are required to be able to set aside a will on the grounds of undue influence:

1. The testator must be established as a person who could be subject to undue influence.
2. A party must be shown to have had the opportunity to exercise undue influence.
3. A party must have been disposed to exercise undue influence.
4. There must be a will that reflects the results of undue influence.

Undue influence, like testamentary capacity, is based on the factual circumstances. Classically, undue influence occurs when an elderly party becomes dependent on a friend or relative for assistance in day-to-day living, then executes a will leaving all or the majority of his or her estate to that person while other relatives are ignored in the testamentary disposition.

Relationships of dependency and trust are called *confidential* relationships. In many states, there is a presumption that undue influence was involved in the execution of a

Figure 17.1 Sample Will Acknowledgment

STATE OF ______________________________)

SS. ACKNOWLEDGMENT/AFFADAVIT)

County of ______________________________)

We, ____________________ , ____________________ , and ____________________ , the Testator and the witnesses, respectively, whose names are signed to the foregoing instrument, being first duly sworn, do hereby declare to the undersigned authority that the Testator signed and executed the instrument as his Last Will and Testament and that he signed willingly, and that he executed it as his free and voluntary act for the purposes therein expressed, and that each of the witnesses, in the presence of the Testator, signed the will as witness and that to the best of their knowledge the Testator was at that time eighteen or more years of age, of eighteen or more years of age, of sound mind, and under no constraint or undue influence.

Testator ______________________________

Witness ______________________________

Witness ______________________________

Subscribed and sworn to and acknowledged before me by ____________________, the ____________________, Testator, and subscribed and sworn to before me by ____________________, and ____________________, witnesses, this _____ day of ________________, 20 _____

Notary ______________________________

will if there is a confidential or fiduciary relationship between the testator and the party who is a major beneficiary and who also procured the execution of the will.

The following case deals with an issue of undue influence.

Slusarenko v. Slusarenko

147 P.3d 920 (Or. App. 2006)

FACTS

Jack Slusarenko's (the decedent) first wife, Juanita Slusarenko, died in 1986. Around early 1988, Jack met Wilma, a woman 26 years his junior. In April 1988, Jack wrote that he had been sad since Juanita's death, but that he had been spending time with Wilma and she took his mind off his pain. He added that his children "seem to resent me keeping company with her. But [I] think I have my life to live & I'm a lot happier now since I met her."

Jack and Wilma married in March 1990. Jack did not tell his children ahead of time, and tensions soon developed between Wilma and the children. According to Jack's friend Rosa Howton, Wilma did not encourage Jack to be with his family and "seemed to want to keep Jack in a box." Jack and Wilma also had a turbulent relationship. Jack complained to his children and his friends about Wilma's cooking, her failure to get a job or help with the farmwork, and her spending. After Jack and Wilma married, the house and yard were extremely dirty and ill-maintained. Jack and Wilma separated and reconciled in 1991, separated again in 1997, divorced in January 1998, and remarried in December 1998.

Between 1986 and 1998, Jack made five different written estate plans. In late 1998, Jack and Wilma began seeing attorney David Gallaher's office. Gallaher's 13 years of private practice included a good deal of estate planning and work on many mental commitment cases. When Gallaher realized that Jack wanted to talk about a will, he explained that he would be representing Jack and that he needed to speak with Jack alone. Gallaher met with Jack for a little over half an hour on the first visit and had five or six total meetings with him in November and December. Although Wilma came along to the meetings, Gallaher preferred to talk with Jack alone.

Jack told Gallaher that he loved and had no ill will toward his children but wanted to use his assets to ensure that he would be taken care of. Jack told Gallaher that his children were successful, implying, without expressly stating, that the children did not need an inheritance. Jack did not want to tell his children about the change in his estate plan until it was done.

Jack loved his children but had some disputes with them. Jack sometimes expressed frustration with his sons Ronald Slusarenko and David Slusarenko for not calling or visiting more often.

In the 1998 will, Jack left all of his property to Wilma or, if she predeceased him, to his church. Jack and Wilma did not obtain a marriage license until after all of the documents pertaining to the will were executed. Wilma testified that Jack was still in the hospital when the documents were signed but that they got married as soon after that as possible. On December 22, Jack and Wilma remarried.

At that same time, Jack signed a bargain-and-sale deed (the 1998 deed) transferring the farm from himself individually to himself and Wilma with a right of survivorship. Jack died in July 2000. Wilma sought to enforce the 1998 will and claimed to be the sole beneficiary of his estate and the sole owner of the farm, Ronald J. Slusarenko, Louise Hofer, Patricia D. Shaver, Donald L. Slusarenko, and Terri J. Eisele, and David Slusarenko (Plaintiffs), all but one of Jack's children from his first marriage, challenged Jack's will and deed to Wilma because of undue influence.

The trial court found that Jack had capacity and that there had been no undue influence. The children appealed.

JUDICIAL OPINION

Ortega, Judge. Plaintiffs first contend that Wilma exerted undue influence over Jack when he executed the 1998 will and deed. Undue influence "has been characterized as 'a species of fraud'" involving a beneficiary's reaping unfair advantage from wrongful conduct. "[e]very will is the product of some kind of influence. It is the task of the courts to determine whether the influence in the particular case is 'undue.'"

In such cases, the first question is whether there was a confidential relationship, in which the testator placed confidence in the beneficiary and the beneficiary exercised dominance over the testator. Plaintiffs contend that, given Wilma's role in administering Jack's medication and taking him to medical appointments, among other factors, there was a confidential relationship. Although Wilma emphasizes Gallaher's testimony that Jack appeared to be the dominant person in their relationship and Dr. Hoehn's testimony that he did not observe manipulative behavior around the time that the 1998 will and deed were executed, she does not seriously dispute that a confidential relationship existed. Because Jack was living with Wilma and relying on her to manage his medications and doctor's appointments, we conclude that theirs was a confidential relationship.

When a confidential relationship exists, we consider whether suspicious circumstances were present. If the will contestant presents slight evidence of suspicious circumstances, then a presumption of undue influence arises, and the beneficiary must come forward with evidence to rebut the presumption. The following factors may constitute suspicious circumstances: (1) the participation of the beneficiary in the preparation of the will; (2) a lack of independent and disinterested advice; (3) secrecy and haste in the preparation of the will; (4) an unexplained change in the testator's attitude toward others; (5) a change in the testator's estate plan; (6) an unnatural or unfair disposition of property; and (7) the testator's susceptibility to undue influence. We also examine "the consequences of upholding the influenced gift."

We conclude that some, but not all, of those circumstances were present. Wilma did participate in the making of the will and the deed, making specific demands in those regards. There also was some degree of secrecy: Jack instructed Gallaher not to tell Jack's children until his plans were complete. Jack deviated from his previous plans: the 1998 will marks the first time that Jack made no testamentary provision whatsoever for his children. Even if Jack had wished to treat Wilma as he did Juanita in his 1986 will, that earlier will made gifts to Jack's children if Juanita predeceased him; there was no such provision in the 1998 will. As to the deed, by putting the orchards and the home place up for sale before, Jack demonstrated that he did not necessarily intend to pass on the farm to his children; however, he previously had been unwilling to give Wilma an ownership interest. Finally, because of medical problems, Jack was susceptible to influence in November and December 1998. During that period, he suffered from serious illnesses and was very concerned about living alone.

The other factors, however, were not present. Jack received independent advice from Gallaher. Although Gallaher happened to have time to prepare the documents quickly, there was no pressure for haste. Jack's attitude toward his children did not change. Although Wilma sometimes discouraged visits or limited information from health care providers, Jack's family and friends continued to see him and sometimes saw him alone. In light of Jack and Wilma's relationship and discussion of remarriage, the will and deed are not an unnatural gift. Their relationship had improved, and Jack wished Wilma to care for him.

Because some suspicious circumstances were present, we examine whether sufficient evidence was present to overcome the inference of undue influence. Here, we conclude that there was, because the suspicious circumstances are accounted for by Jack's desire to have Wilma take care of him for the rest of his life.

Both Wilma's participation in the preparation of the will and deed and Jack's deviation from his earlier estate plans were the result of a bargaining process between Wilma and Jack. Dr. Hoehn observed Jack and Wilma bargaining about their respective needs and potential reconciliation during and after the dissolution of their first marriage, with Jack trying to get Wilma back and Wilma insisting that they first reach some financial understandings. That view of the bargaining between Jack and Wilma is borne out by the testimony of Gallaher, who thought that Jack was making a decision to trade his assets in exchange for Wilma's care and that Jack knew what he was doing. We further note that the effect of Wilma's participation in the preparation of the 1998 will and deed was lessened by Jack's obtaining independent advice from Gallaher.

Although there was some secrecy, Jack was not entirely secretive about his plans. Moreover, the initial secrecy was Jack's choice, a result of his understanding that his children would not approve of his reunion with Wilma. In any event, after Gallaher wrote to Patricia in late December 1998 about the revocation of the family trust, Patricia was aware that Jack's estate plans had likely changed.

Jack's susceptibility to influence is troubling. However, Jack began to pursue reconciliation with Wilma long before he was hospitalized in November and December 1998. Hoehn counseled them about their relationship and was aware that they were considering reconciling as early as July 1998. The initial appointment with Gallaher to discuss estate planning also was made before Jack's hospitalizations, and Gallaher, meeting with Jack alone, observed that Jack appeared to be in control of his situation.

By the time that Jack executed the 1998 will and deed, he had known Wilma about a decade. Their relationship had been stormy. However, after going through with the dissolution of his marriage to Wilma, Jack tried to reunite with her for months before he became ill and required hospitalization. Witnesses who saw them together after the dissolution believed that their relationship had improved. Jack knew Wilma well and chose to give her the financial promises that she had long desired in exchange for her returning to him and taking care of him. Despite conflicts between Wilma and Jack's children and Wilma's occasional interference with the children's access to Jack, he continued to see his children, as well as other family and friends, and was not isolated. He received independent legal advice regarding the deed and will, and his lawyer and doctor seem to agree that Jack sometimes manipulated Wilma. After he executed the will and deed, he lived with Wilma for one and one-half years and appeared to be fairly content; he did not try to rearrange his finances after executing the will. In short, Jack's disposition of his property was a result of his choices regarding the care that he wanted to receive at the end of his life, not wrongful conduct by Wilma. We accordingly affirm the trial court's rejection of plaintiff's undue influence claims.

CASE QUESTIONS

1. List the factors that point to undue influence along with the factors that mitigate that finding.
2. What do you learn from the case about the steps a testator should take when executing a will?
3. What influence does the disinheritance of the children have on the court's decision?

CONSIDER 17.8

Bill Cruxton died in November 1992. He was widowed, childless, and past 80. In his will he left $500,000, the bulk of his estate, to a 17-year-old waitress who had been kind to him as part of her job as a waitress at Dink's Restaurant in Chagrin Falls, Ohio. Cruxton had lunch and dinner there every day for 13 months preceding his death. He was very public about leaving the money to her because he knew that her father had died and that she wanted to attend college. Cora Bruck, Cruxton's 86-year-old sister, is challenging the will as Cruxton's only relative. Cruxton left her only sufficient funds to cover her funeral expenses. Mark Fishman, Bruck's attorney, has stated, "Mr. Cruxton's longtime friends all agree that this was not the same guy. The Bill Cruxton that they knew was a very conservative and down-to-earth guy. This is the last thing they would have expected from the true Bill Cruxton." Are there valid grounds for challenging the will?

Disinheritance and Limitations on Distribution

Most states have provisions that prevent **disinheritance** of certain family members. In fact, all states have some protections for the surviving spouse. Although a will may purport to disinherit a surviving spouse, the surviving spouse will be entitled to one or more of the following depending on the state's system of property allocation between husband and wife.

1. *Dower*: In some states, the wife is entitled to a certain portion of her husband's estate. If she is not provided for in the will, she will still receive her statutory dower percentage.
2. *Curtesy*: In some states, the husband is entitled to a portion of the wife's estate, and the result will be the same as in the dower situation above.
3. *Community property*: In community property states, the surviving spouse is entitled to half of the community property even if the testator spouse has attempted to disinherit by the terms of the will.
4. *Homesteads, exemptions, and family allowances*: Most states have some provision that requires that the home and often specific personal property (usually furnishings) pass to the family (spouse and children) of the decedent. These items are thus given to the family regardless of disinheritance provisions in the will. Also, many states provide for an allowance to be given to the spouse and children of the decedent for the purposes of support during the probate of the estate.

In some cases, the surviving spouse has been provided for in the will but would be entitled to receive more under the afforded statutory protections. Under these circumstances, many states permit the surviving spouse to elect whether to take what was provided under the will or to take the statutory share as provided by the applicable protections. The election must be formally filed as part of the probate proceedings, usually within a certain limited period.

Relatives other than the surviving spouse may be disinherited. Testators who disinherit relatives should make sure that all property is given to others, because if there is any unbequeathed property, it is still possible that the disinherited relative will inherit it under intestate succession. Some states require a clause in the will naming the disinherited relative and the testator's intent to disinherit that relative. Even when such a clause is not required, it may help to have it in the will to show the testator's intent and awareness.

CONSIDER 17.9

James G. Newkirk left his wife and daughter in 1951. Shortly thereafter, he met Pauline Knight and began living with her; they held themselves out as husband and wife in all places where they resided. In 1952, Newkirk executed a will that left all of his property to Pauline and made no provision for his wife or daughter except the following clause:

> *Third: I have a daughter, Joan Janick, who is married, and for whom I have heretofore provided, and I do not wish her to participate in my will.*

Newkirk died in 1964, and Pauline presented the will for probate. Newkirk's daughter challenged the will on the grounds of undue influence because the will had been made less than a year after Newkirk left and was made at a time when he was still married and had a child to provide for. What was the result? *In re Estate of Newkirk*, 456 P.2d 104 (Ok. 1969)

Tortious Interference with Expectation of Inheritance

A new theory for will contests has emerged. Many heirs who are left out or whose inheritances are challenged by other heirs are using **tortious interference with expectation of inheritance** as a basis for contesting a will. Perhaps the most famous case involving tortious interference with expectation of inheritance involved a former Playmate of the Year, the late Anna Nicole Smith (aka Vicki Lynn Marshall). Ms. Smith's husband, 90-year-old J. Howard Marshall II, a wealthy oil company owner, died leaving a $1.6 billion estate. Ms. Smith was given $90 million, not from Mr. Marshall's estate, but rather from Mr. Marshall's son for what Ms. Smith proved was his interference with the execution of a will by the late Mr. Marshall that would have allowed her to be an heir.[8] Ms. Smith did challenge her husband's trusts (there were seven) in Texas courts, but she was awarded nothing from them, per his expressed intention. A California bankruptcy court awarded her the damages from her husband's son.[9] The son appealed the jurisdictional issues, challenging the federal court's authority to grant the tortious interference claim when a Texas probate court had jurisdiction over the estate. The U.S. Supreme Court sided with Ms. Smith.

The U.S. Supreme Court's decision in the case confirms that this tort is an action outside of probate created to prevent fraud in the execution of wills; some state legislatures and more courts are developing statutes and precedent that provide a right to recover for such interference. About one-half of the states recognize the tort, while ten refuse to recognize it. The remaining states are unclear or have not yet addressed the issue.

Living Wills

The term **living will** has been a part of a national dialogue since 2004, when the country was gripped by the legal saga of Terri Schiavo, a woman in a persistent vegetative state whose husband had won the right to withhold food because of his belief that she would not want to live in such a condition.[10] A living will is a document that verifies the wishes of the testator to be taken off artificial life-support systems when there is no reasonable prospect of recovery. States that recognize living wills have statutory requirements for their validity. For example, disinterested witnesses and specific language are required in many states. Whatever requirements a state has must be followed if the living will is to be valid. Web Exhibit 17.1 is a sample living will form.

The **Uniform Rights of the Terminally Ill Act**, as approved by the Conference on Uniform Laws and endorsed by the American Bar Association, provides a comprehensive statement of law regarding the rights of the terminally ill. This act gives legal rules for living wills, authorization of appointment of an agent to make healthcare decisions, rules for determination of which family members may make decisions on healthcare for the incapacitated, and rules on immunities and liabilities of healthcare givers in cases covered under the act. Living wills under the act are labeled "Declaration Relating to the Use of Life-Sustaining Treatment."

In *Cruzan v. Director, Missouri Dept. of Health*, 497 U.S. 261 (1990), the Supreme Court required that the right to be removed from life support systems is valid if the individual evidenced a desire to exercise that right in advance of illness or

8. *In re Marshall*, 253 B.R. 550, 553 (Bankr. C.D. Cal. 2000). Ms. Smith's real name is Vickie Lynn Marshall. She was married to Mr. Marshall for 14 months before he passed.
9. *Marshall v. Marshall*, 547 U.S. 293 (2006). Sadly, Ms. Smith passed away from drug ingestion in February 2007. Ironically, there are now both will challenges pending on Ms. Smith's estate, which includes the $90 million from the Marshall tortious interference case.

disability. The court also ruled that the decision can be made by others for the individual, according to requirements and standards established by the states. Most states now have laws that establish the procedures for allowing others to make the decision for those who are in coma or, as in the Schiavo matter, in a persistent vegetative state. Known as "absence of advance directive statutes," these laws provide authority to spouses, parents, and children to petition a court for withdrawal of life support and life-sustaining systems if they can provide proof "supported by clear and convincing evidence that the decision would have been the one the patient would have chosen had the patient been competent or, if there is no indication of what the patient would have chosen, that the decision is in the patient's best interest."[11] The original *Schiavo* case on the Florida lack-of-advance-directive statute provides insight into how these statutes are applied.

In re Guardianship of Schiavo

851 So.2d 182 (Fla. App. 2003)

FACTS

Theresa Marie Schindler was born on December 3, 1963, and lived with or near her parents, Robert and Mary Schlindler, in Pennsylvania until she married Michael Schiavo on November 10, 1984. Michael and Theresa moved to Florida in 1986. They were happily married and both were employed. They had no children.

On February 25, 1990, Theresa, age 27, suffered a cardiac arrest as a result of a potassium imbalance. Michael called 911, and Theresa was rushed to the hospital. She never regained consciousness.

Since 1990, Theresa has lived in nursing homes with constant care. She is fed and hydrated by tubes. The staff changes her diapers regularly. She has had numerous health problems, but none have been life threatening.[12]

The Schindlers appeal the guardianship court's order denying their motion for relief from a judgment that ordered their daughter's guardian to withdraw life-prolonging procedures.

JUDICIAL OPINION

Altenbernd, Chief Judge. This is the fourth time that this court has reviewed an order from the guardianship court in this controversy. This case has a long and difficult history, which we will not detail in this opinion. As we explained in our last opinion, we affirmed the trial court's decision ordering Mrs. Schiavo's guardian to withdraw life-prolonging procedures. In so doing, we affirmed the trial court's rulings that (1) Mrs. Schiavo's medical condition was the type of end-stage condition that permits the withdrawal of life-prolonging procedures, (2) she did not have a reasonable medical probability of recovering capacity so that she could make her own decision to maintain or withdraw life-prolonging procedures, (3) the trial court had the authority to make such a decision when a conflict within the family prevented a qualified person from effectively exercising the responsibilities of a proxy, and (4) clear and convincing evidence at the time of trial supported a determination that Mrs. Schiavo would have chosen in February 2000 to withdraw the life-prolonging procedures.

In our last opinion we stated that the Schindlers had "presented no medical evidence suggesting that any new treatment could restore to Mrs. Schiavo a level of function within the cerebral cortex that would allow her to understand her perceptions of sight and sound or to communicate or respond cognitively to those perceptions." Although we have expressed some lay skepticism about the new affidavits, the Schindlers now have presented some evidence, in the form of the affidavit of Dr. [Fred] Webber, of such a potential new treatment.

On remand, we permitted the parents to present evidence to establish by a preponderance of the evidence that the judgment was no longer equitable.

10. *Bush v. Schiavo,* 885 So.2d 321 (Fla. 2004).
11. F. S. A. §765.401(2007).
12. Because there have been so many decisions in the Schiavo matter, this statement of facts was taken from *In re Guardianship of Schiavo,* 780 So.2d 176, 177 (Fla. 2d DCA 2001) *(Schiavo I)* to provide some background.

In order to minimize disputes between the parties, this court's last opinion also provided guidance to the guardianship court concerning the nature of the hearing to be held on remand. We required an additional set of medical examinations of Theresa Schiavo and the selection of no more than five physicians to provide expert testimony on the issue presented. We instructed that one of the five physicians must be a new, independent physician selected either by the agreement of the parties or, if they could not agree, by the appointment of the guardianship court. We indicated that this physician should be board certified in neurology or neurosurgery, with expertise if possible "in the treatment of brain damage and in the diagnosis and treatment of persistent vegetative state."

Instead, the parents provided testimony from Dr. William Maxfield, a board-certified physician in radiology and nuclear medicine, and Dr. William Hammesfahr, a board-certified neurologist. Michael Schiavo, Mrs. Schiavo's husband and guardian, selected Dr. Ronald Cranford and Dr. Melvin Greer, both board-certified neurologists, to testify. The fifth physician, selected by the guardianship court when the parties could not agree, was Dr. Peter Bambakidis, a board-certified neurologist practicing in the Department of Neurology at the Cleveland Clinic Foundation in Cleveland, Ohio. He is a clinical professor of neurology at Case Western Reserve University. His credentials fulfilled the requirements of our prior opinion.

Through the assistance of Mrs. Schiavo's treating physician, Dr. Victor Gambone, the physicians obtained current medical information about Theresa Schiavo including high-quality brain scans. Each physician reviewed her medical records and personally conducted a neurological examination of Mrs. Schiavo. Lengthy videotapes of some of the medical examinations were created and introduced into evidence. Thus, the quality of the evidence presented to the guardianship court was very high, and each side had ample opportunity to present detailed medical evidence, all of which was subjected to thorough cross-examination. It is likely that no guardianship court has ever received as much high-quality medical evidence in such a proceeding.

On the issue that caused this court to reverse in our last decision, whether new treatment exists which offers such promise of increased cognitive function in Mrs. Schiavo's cerebral cortex that she herself would elect to undergo this treatment and would reverse the prior decision to withdraw life-prolonging procedures, the parents presented little testimony. Dr. William Hammesfahr claimed that vasodilation therapy and hyberbaric therapy "could help her improve." These therapies cannot replace dead tissue. Although the physicians are not in complete agreement concerning the extent of Mrs. Schiavo's brain damage, they all agree that the brain scans show extensive permanent damage to her brain. The only debate between the doctors is whether she has a small amount of isolated living tissue in her cerebral cortex or whether she has no living tissue in her cerebral cortex.

The parents contended that Mrs. Schiavo was not in a persistent or permanent vegetative state. Both Dr. Maxfield and Dr. Hammesfahr opined that she was not in such a state. They based their opinions primarily upon their assessment of Mrs. Schiavo's actions or responses to a few brief stimuli, primarily involving physical and verbal contact with her mother. The three other physicians all testified that Mrs. Schiavo was in a permanent or persistent vegetative state.

The guardianship court concluded that there was no evidence of a treatment in existence that offered such promise of increased cognitive function in Mrs. Schiavo's cerebral cortex that she herself would elect to undergo it at this time.

In this case, the guardianship court followed the instructions in our last decision. It conducted a thorough hearing and prepared an extensive order. We cannot conclude that the guardianship court abused its discretion when it denied the motion.

The Schindlers have urged this court to conduct a *de novo* review of the evidence in this case, primarily because of the finality of this decision for their daughter. This court can review the evidence in the record with only its training in the law and its lay experience. It is simply not proper for this court to review such a fact-intensive determination using a de novo standard.

Despite our decision that the appropriate standard of review is abuse of discretion, this court has closely examined all of the evidence in this record. We have repeatedly examined the videotapes, not merely watching short segments but carefully observing the tapes in their entirety. We have examined the brain scans with the eyes of educated laypersons and considered the explanations provided by the doctors in the transcripts. We have concluded that, if we were called upon to review the guardianship court's decision *de novo*, we would still affirm it.

The judges on this panel are called upon to make a collective, objective decision concerning a question of law. Each of us, however, has our own family, our own loved ones, our own children. From our review of the videotapes of Mrs. Schiavo, despite the irrefutable evidence that her cerebral cortex has sustained the most severe of irreparable injuries, we understand why a parent who had raised and nurtured a child from conception would hold out hope that some level of cognitive function remained. If Mrs. Schiavo were our own daughter, we could not but hold to such a faith.

But in the end, this case is not about the aspirations that loving parents have for their children. It is about Theresa Schiavo's right to make her own decision, independent of her parents and independent of her husband. In circumstances such as these, when families cannot agree, the law has opened the doors of the circuit courts to permit trial judges to serve as surrogates or proxies to make decisions about life-prolonging procedures. It is the trial judge's duty not to make the decision that the judge would make for himself or herself or for a loved one. Instead, the trial judge must make a decision that the clear and convincing evidence shows the ward would have made for herself. It is a thankless task, and one to be undertaken with care, objectivity, and a cautious legal standard designed to promote the value of life. But it is also a necessary function if all people are to be entitled to a personalized decision about life-prolonging procedures independent of the subjective and conflicting assessments of their friends and relatives. It may be unfortunate that when families cannot agree, the best forum we can offer for this private, personal decision is a public courtroom and the best decision-maker we can provide is a judge with no prior knowledge of the ward, but the law currently provides no better solution that adequately protects the interests of promoting the value of life.

At the conclusion of our first opinion, we stated:

In the final analysis, the difficult question that faced the trial court was whether Theresa Marie Schindler Schiavo, not after a few weeks in a coma, but after ten years in a persistent vegetative state that has robbed her of most of her cerebrum and all but the most instinctive of neurological functions, with no hope of a medical cure but with sufficient money and strength of body to live indefinitely, would choose to continue the constant nursing care and the supporting tubes in hopes that a miracle would somehow recreate her missing brain tissue, or whether she would wish to permit a natural death process to take its course and for her family members and loved ones to be free to continue their lives. After due consideration, we conclude that the trial judge had clear and convincing evidence to answer this question as he did.

The guardianship court should schedule another hearing solely for the purpose of entering a new order scheduling the removal of the nutrition and hydration tube.

Affirmed.

CASE QUESTIONS

1. What is the standard in Florida for withdrawing life support or life-sustaining measures when there is no advance directive?
2. What is the standard of proof?
3. How does the court address the emotional issues surrounding the decision to withdraw life support or life-sustaining procedures?

Living Trusts

One of the more popular property transfer forms over the past five years is the **living trust**. The living trust is a revocable trust established during the testator's life. It can be revoked at any time and the testator still retains control of the trust assets. However, upon the testator's death, the trust property passes according to the provisions of the trust and probate is avoided.

> **Practical Tip**
>
> *The living will must be done cautiously, methodically, and with a full understanding of the laws that apply.*

These trusts must be executed formally and can involve large amounts of paperwork for compliance with the tax laws. While touted as a tax-avoidance device, there is nothing accomplished with a living trust that cannot be done through a will and the use of joint tenancy ownership (see Chapter 8).

Revocation of Wills

A will can be revoked in several different ways: (1) by physical destruction of the document, (2) by execution of a subsequent document, or (3) by operation of law.

Revocation by Physical Destruction

Revocation occurs when there is mutilation or destruction of the will by either the testator or by someone acting at the testator's request. In addition to the physical destruction of the document, the testator must have intent to destroy the will. The degree of destruction varies across states. For example, some states recognize crossing out portions of a will as a revocation of those portions of the will, whereas other states treat such an act as a destruction of the entire will.

The types of acts sufficient for physical destruction include cutting, tearing, burning, and writing *void* or *canceled* across the will. If there are copies of the will, some states provide that the destruction of one of the copies constitutes revocation of the will, while other states require the destruction of the original.

Revocation by Execution of a Subsequent Document

A will can be revoked by the subsequent execution of another instrument. A second will serves to revoke a prior will. An addition to a will (called a **codicil**), which may contain provisions inconsistent with the original will, also serves to revoke certain portions of the will. Revocation by a subsequent document is valid only if the subsequent document is executed with the same formalities required for the execution of the original will.

Generally, a subsequent will contains a clause that provides that the testator "hereby revokes any prior wills and codicils." However, such a clause is not required. The will that is latest in time of execution serves to revoke prior wills.

In jurisdictions that recognize holographic wills, a holographic will or codicil can serve to revoke a prior formally executed will so long as the holographic instrument complies with all validity requirements.

CONSIDER 17.10

Charles Uhl executed a will in 1946, found in his safe-deposit box after his death. The will contained several interlineations and markings made by Uhl in colored pencil, including a notation in the left-hand margin of the first page that stated, "Revise whole mess."

Uhl's sister visited him while he was alive and they found the will. His sister told him the will would not be valid and Uhl replied, "The will is still good and is good anywhere. Oh, nuts! I am going to make a new one. I will get it done. Don't worry about it."

When the will was offered for probate, the sister objected because her share was small and she contended the will had been revoked. What was the result? *In re Estate of Uhl,* 81 Cal. Rptr. 436 (1969)

Revocation by Operation of Law

Most states have provisions that require the revocation or partial revocation of a will when the testator's family circumstances change between the time of the will's execution and the testator's death. For example, many states provide that divorce automatically serves to revoke a will at least with regard to property left to the former spouse. In other states, marriage after the execution of the will entitles the new spouse to at least an intestate share of the property.

Perhaps one of the most common partial revocations of wills occurs when testators have children after execution of the will but before death. Children born or adopted after will execution are called **pretermitted** children. Many states provide that these children are entitled to receive the amount they would have received through intestate succession.

Probate

Purpose of Probate

Probate includes all legal proceedings required to accomplish the passing of title of the decedent's property to those for whom it was intended. Probate involves determination of the existence of a valid will and defenses to the will, the existence of heirs if no will exists, the proper construction of the will, the collection of the decedent's assets, the payment of debts, and the distribution of the estate. The procedures and terminology vary from state to state, but the following sections cover the basic processes.

Appointment of Party to Administer Probate

In every state, some party or parties is appointed to carry out the administrative details involved in probate. If the decedent died intestate, the party is often called an **administrator** or **administratix**. If the decedent died testate, the party is often called an **executor** or **executrix**. Under the UPC, the party is called a **personal representative** regardless of whether the decedent died testate or intestate.

No matter which name applies, the probate administrator is responsible for all transfers, payments, and distributions of the estate. In many cases, because of the substantial sums and valuable property in an estate, the administrators are required to post a bond for the duration of the probate. Under the UPC and in most states, the bond requirement can be waived in the testator's will or by statute, particularly in cases where the sole beneficiary will act as the personal representative. Waiving the bond can mean a substantial savings in the cost of administering the estate.

Who serves as the probate administrator (when not specified in the will) is provided for by state statute. If the party appointed in the will is unable to serve or if the decedent died intestate, the court follows the state statute that specifies who qualifies and in what order for serving as a probate administrator. In many states the surviving spouse has first priority for appointment.

Application for or Opening of Probate

Probate proceedings are opened when an application or petition is filed, generally with the probate division or probate court located in the area where the decedent lived. However, other courts may have jurisdiction. For example, if the decedent owned property in a second state, the probate court in that area would also have jurisdiction for probate. In the case of an estate located in multiple jurisdictions, one probate court will serve as the court for hearings, petitions, and so on, and the other courts will then recognize those proceedings for purposes of property distribution and carrying out that court's orders.

Parties who can petition for probate include heirs, devisees, persons entitled to appointment as personal representatives, and creditors. Basically, any party with an interest in the estate can open probate.

The application or petition will attach any (and all) wills if the decedent died testate. The petitioner must serve notice upon potential heirs and interested parties that application has been filed, and the notice includes a hearing date. Because the purpose of the hearing is to determine the validity of the will, anyone who wants to challenge the will must prepare to present evidence at the hearing on the will's admission to probate. Many of the cases in this chapter involved appeals from hearings where wills were challenged.

Collection of Assets

Once the will is admitted to probate or the finding of intestacy has been made, the administrator or personal representative must collect the estate's assets. Most states and the UPC require the personal representative to file an inventory with the court within a certain period after appointment. The inventory is sent to heirs and devisees. The administrator is fully accountable for all assets and also fully responsible for collecting any funds due to the estate and all property the decedent owned.

Determination and Payment of Debts

In addition to collecting and reporting assets, the personal representative must determine whether valid debts exist and if they should be paid. Most states require the publication of a notice of probate in a public newspaper to alert creditors to file a claim with the estate. For example, under the UPC, the personal representative is required to publish notice of the opening of probate once a week for three weeks in a newspaper of general circulation. Creditors then have four months from the time of first publication to file a claim with the estate or have their claim forever barred from collection.

Once the personal representative receives a creditor's claim, the personal representative reviews it and makes the decision to allow or disallow it. If a claim is disallowed, the creditor always has the opportunity to bring an action against the estate to have a judicial determination on the claim's validity.

Distribution of Estate

Whether the decedent died testate or intestate, probate determines who will be entitled to what portions of the estate after creditors' claims, taxes, and administrative expenses have been paid.

In the case of intestacy, the court will hold a hearing or trial for the adjudication of heirs. In the case of a testate estate, the court may still be required to construe the provisions of an ambiguous will. In interpreting a will, the court's primary rule is to follow the intent of the testator. If intent is not clear from the document itself, the court may use extrinsic evidence to clarify the intentions of the testator.

After the determination of heirs and the interpretation of the will, the property is distributed to the appropriate parties. Different terms describe the types of gifts given to heirs of the decedent. A gift of real property is called a **devise** and the recipient a **devisee**; a gift of money is called a **legacy** and the recipient a **legatee**; a gift of personal property is called a **bequest** (general term that includes legacies).

Occasionally, the distribution of gifts is impossible. For example, a testator may have left a specific item of property or a legacy to an heir who has predeceased the testator. In the absence of the testator's provision or a state statute that permits such a gift to go to the heirs of the predeceased recipient, the gift will **lapse**, become part of the residuary estate, and revert to those who are entitled to that portion of the estate. If there is no clause devising the residuary estate, the specific gift would be distributed according to the laws of intestacy.

Also, there are times when a testator has left a specific item of property to an heir; and although the heir is still in existence, the property is not. For example, a testator may have left a "1996 Honda Accord to my nephew Ralph." If the testator does not own the Honda Accord at death, the gift adeems or fails completely. This doctrine of **ademption** will apply regardless of the intention of the testator.

Closing of Probate

Once all of the preceding steps are complete, the personal representative can close the estate. Closing the estate may require a hearing or, as under the UPC, may be done through an informal filing of a closing inventory and accounting. Once the proper procedures are complete, the estate is closed and cannot be reopened to relitigate creditors' and heirs' claims. Closing an estate operates as an estoppel for future actions unless there has been fraud or misconduct in the administration of the estate or a failure to follow the statutory processes.

Practical Tip

Will contests, even among families with the best of feelings, are not uncommon. Clarity in language is critical. Careful drafting avoids confusion and will contests.

Estate Tax Implications

The transfer of property from the decedent to the heirs may involve tax issues on parts of the estate and the heirs. Several types of taxes may apply. First is the possible estate tax at both the federal and state levels. The amount of tax due on an estate subject to taxation is computed according to tables provided by the federal government, and certain deductions are allowed before the taxable value is actually determined. For example, at the federal level, a marital deduction is given for a probate transfer of property between spouses for the entire amount of the estate. Currently, the federal estate tax is on an annual increasing exclusion schedule.[13] Estates valued below the federal exclusion are not required to pay federal estate taxes.

In addition, there are larger exemptions for family-owned businesses when the death of one of the principals in that business occurs. The time limitation for filing a federal estate tax return is nine months, which can be extended upon an estimation of no tax or a payment of the amount estimated to be due.

There are also estate and inheritance taxes at the state level. In addition to a tax on the estate, an inheritance tax may apply to heirs. Inheritance tax is computed as a percentage of the amount received by the heir. The inheritance tax is an obligation of the heir, not the estate.

Cautions and Conclusions

There are two ways to die: intestate and testate. If you die intestate, there are laws in each state to provide for the distribution of your estate. Those laws can be complex and may not distribute your property according to your desires. The other way to die, testate, is preferred. The execution of a will not only assures that your property is distributed the way you would like to see it distributed, it can save time and money in the administration of your estate.

A will should be executed with witnesses and at a time when those witnesses can verify that the will is done voluntarily and with a clear-enough presence of mind to understand what property is being given away in the will and who the beneficiaries are.

When executing codicils or new wills, use great caution to be certain that the right will and your correct intentions are carried out by the valid document.

Living wills provide for withdrawal from life support or life-sustaining processes.

The probate process is a series of mandatory notices and hearings that ensure the correct and orderly distribution of the decedent's property.

13. The issue of estate tax has become a political one with a strong movement for elimination of the so-called "death tax." Currently, the phase is as follows: 2004–2005: $1,500,000; 2006–2008: $2,000,000; and 2009: $3,500,000. The unified credits move from $345,800 to $1,445,800.

Key Terms

ademption, 512
administrator, 511
administratrix, 511
advancements, 494
bequest, 512
codicil, 510
devise, 512
devisee, 512
disinheritance, 505
escheat, 488
executor, 511
executrix, 511
holographic will, 496
intestate, 486
intestate succession, 486
joint will, 497
lapse, 512
laughing heir statutes, 488
legacy, 512
legatee, 512
living trust, 509
living will, 506
mutual wills, 497
nuncupative wills, 496
per capita, 488
per stirpes, 488
personal representative, 511
posthumous or afterborn heir, 489
pretermitted, 510
probate, 510
self-proving will, 501
testamentary capacity, 497
tortious interference with expectation of inheritance, 506
undue influence, 501
Uniform Probate Code (UPC), 486
Uniform Rights of the Terminally Ill Act, 506
Uniform Simultaneous Death Act (USDA), 495
will, 495

Chapter Problems

1. On August 9, 1983, Mr. Emmett King was taken to the emergency room at Halifax Memorial Hospital with a leaking abdominal aneurysm. He was in extreme pain and suffering from shock from the loss of blood. He was given considerable pain medication including meperidine (Demerol), morphine, and diazepam (Valium). Meperidine and morphine both may decrease mental awareness.

He was placed on a respirator with an intratracheal tube and taken to intensive care. At about 1 P.M., Delores King, one of King's daughters, visited him with Jeff Crowder, King's grandson. Jeff went to the waiting area and asked Patsy West and Rhoda Joyner to come and witness a codicil that King was executing. When they arrived, Delores read the codicil to King and asked him if he understood that he was giving Jeff his business and the real property on which it was located. King nodded that he did. Delores helped guide King's hand across the document for a signature. Patsy and Rhoda signed as witnesses. The witnesses indicated Mr. King was aware of them and what was happening. The codicil was executed at 1 P.M., and King died at 2:15 P.M. Dr. Richard Frazier, King's doctor, said that King was in a semicoma during most of the morning and had been sedated. Dr. Frazier believed that King would have been incapable of knowingly executing the document.

Prior to the execution of the codicil, King's wife, children, and grandchildren received his estate. With the codicil, Jeff got most of it. The trial court found the will and codicil to be valid, and Thomas King, a son, appealed. Is the will/codicil valid? Discuss all issues. *In the Matter of the Will of Emmett J. King*, 342 S.E.2d 394 (N.C. 1986)

2. In 1984, Alexander Tolin executed a will under which the residue of his estate was to be devised to his friend Adair Creaig. The will was prepared by Steven Fine, Tolin's attorney, and executed in Fine's office. The original will was retained by Fine, and a blue-backed photocopy was given to Tolin. In 1989, Tolin executed a codicil to the will that changed the residuary beneficiary from Creaig to Broward Art Guild, Inc. The codicil was also prepared by Fine, who retained the original and gave Tolin a blue-backed photocopy of the original executed codicil. Tolin died in 1990. Six months before his death, he told his neighbor, Ed Weinstein, who was a retired attorney, that he made a mistake and wished to revoke the codicil and reinstate Creaig as the residuary beneficiary. Weinstein told Tolin he could do this by tearing up the original codicil. Tolin handed Weinstein a blue-backed document that Tolin said was the original codicil. Weinstein looked at the document—it appeared to him to be the original—and gave it back to Tolin. Tolin then tore up and destroyed the document with the intent and for the purpose of revocation. Some time after Tolin's death, Weinstein spoke with Fine and found out for the first time that the original will and codicil had been held by Fine. Tolin had torn up the blue-backed copy that had been given to Tolin at the time of execution. The document that Tolin tore up was an exact photocopy of the will. Tolin's personal representative petitioned the court to have the will and codicil admitted to probate. Creaig filed a petition to determine if there had been a revocation of the codicil. Had there been a revocation of the will? *In re Estate of Tolin*, 622 So. 2d 988 (Fla. Dist. Ct. App. 1993)

3. The heirs of Vern V. Walls filed a will contest alleging that the last will and testament of Vern V. Walls was the result of undue influence by Cyril DeClercq (brother of Kathryn Walls, Vern's predeceased wife) and Floyd DeClercq (nephew of Kathryn).

Vern V. Walls died on March 31, 1986, at the age of 79. Kathryn had died two months earlier after a long illness. Walls and Kathryn had one child who had predeceased them at age 14. Walls was survived by several brothers and sisters. Cyril is Kathryn's brother. Prior to Kathryn's death, Vern's and Kathryn's wills provided that on the death of the survivor, their estate would be divided equally between the Walls heirs and the DeClercq heirs. On March 15, 1986, Vern, then in the hospital for emphysema, executed a new will that directed the bulk of Vern's estate, valued at approximately $300,000, be given to the DeClercq heirs. Only $34,000 in cash bequests were given to the Walls heirs. Harold Tenney, the original lawyer for the 1985 wills, testified that he represented Vern on a roof problem subsequent to the will execution but that their relationship terminated over the roof problem. Donald G. Baird, Cyril's lawyer, drew up the new will as well as a power of attorney from Vern to Cyril. He was contacted by Cyril to handle these matters for Vern. Is there undue influence? *In the Matter of the Estate of Walls*, 561 N.E.2d 344 (Ill. 1990)

4. William and Margaret Pearl Phillips, husband and wife, executed a joint will for the disposition of their property. The will contained the following clause:

It is the intention of the testators that the surviving testator shall have the right by codicil to change the bequests of equal division referred to said testator's heirs, but may not change the bequests to the heirs of the first deceased testator.

William died first. Margaret drafted a codicil that changed the distribution of the property to William's heirs. Upon her death, William's heirs challenged the admission of the will to probate on the grounds that the codicil violated a joint contract to make a will. What is the result? *In re Estate of Philips*, 195 N.W.2d 486 (Wis. 1972)

5. D. W. Elmer died testate, and a provision in his will was as follows: "*THIRD: I make no provision for my brothers, Jake N. Elmer, Henry Elmer, nor for my sisters, Lena Elmer, Rachel Martell, and Marie Brown, all of whom are financially so fixed that they can well live without any benefits from my estate.*"

Unfortunately, D. W. did not dispose of all of his property under the provisions of the will. To whom will the property be given? *In re Estate of Elmer*, 210 N.W.2d 815 (N.D. 1973)

6. On February 13, 1956, Philip Bogner made his last will and testament. One portion of the will gave a one-half interest in some real and personal property to his daughter Helen Bogner Fallgren and her husband, Curtis Fallgren. At the time of the execution of the will, Helen and Curtis were married and had eight children. From 1946 to 1956, Curtis was employed by Philip and received a salary of $5,800 as well as a furnished home.

In 1956, the Fallgrens moved to Oregon to run a poultry ranch that had been purchased using a loan on an insurance policy Philip had purchased for Helen. Philip repaid that loan when it became evident the Fallgrens would not. Sometime thereafter, a physician and Helen told Philip that Curtis had been involved in depraved moral conduct including incestuous relationships with one of his daughters and that such activity had continued for a number of years.

Helen obtained a divorce from Curtis in 1965 on the grounds of infidelity and returned home to North Dakota with her children to live with her father. Bogner told several people including a family counselor, his sister, and one of his employees that he was going to disinherit his son-in-law. Bogner died on September 3, 1968, and portions of his will read as follows:

THIRD: To my daughter, Helen Bogner Falgren and her husband Curtis Falgren, or to the survivor of them...

SIXTH: I appoint my daughter, Helen Bogner Falgren, to be my Executrix under this Will, and if she fails or ceases to act, I appoint Curtis Falgren Sr., husband of my daughter, Helen Bogner Falgren, to be the Executor and successor Trustee of the trust hereinabove provided. If my daughter does not survive me, or dies before a grandchild of mine attains the age of 21 years, without having appointed a guardian of the persons and estates of my grandchildren, I appoint Curtis Falgren, Sr. to be guardian of the persons of such grandchildren and their estates.

Lines had been forcefully drawn through the references to Curtis. The obliterations did not exist at the time the will was originally executed. Has there been an effective revocation? *In re Estate of Bogner*, 184 N.W.2d 718 (N.D. 1971)

7. John C. Ramsey Sr. (Senior) executed a will in the last months of his life that left the bulk of his estate to Melody Taylor, his paramour. Senior's relationships with his son and grandsons were strained and his will included the following clause:

I have intentionally provided significant, yet smaller amounts for my son and grandsons because they have for several years alienated my affections by being irresponsible, contentious, and constantly seeking financial support from me rather than providing for themselves.

I have made provisions for MELODY J. TAYLOR because MELODY J. TAYLOR provides me care and support.

Senior was suffering from cancer and renal failure and his pain was extraordinary. His doctors prescribed high doses of morphine which Melody administered. Senior died from an overdose of morphine.

John Ramsey Jr. (John II), Senior's son, challenged the validity of the will on the grounds of undue influence as well as felonious killing of a testator by a beneficiary. The trial court found there was undue influence and refused to admit the will to probate. Melody appealed. *Ramsey v. Taylor*, 999 P.2d 1178 (Or. App. 2000)

8. Tom is in the hospital and is dying, having suffered a stroke that has left him partially paralyzed. Tom's will has been prepared for him (he is of sound mind), but Tom cannot control the movement of his hand to sign or make a mark on the will. Tom's wife guides his hand over the paper, making an *X*. Is the will valid?

9. Wilma has passed away intestate and is survived by the following relatives: her mother, Catherine; her sister, Chris; her granddaughter, Elizabeth (daughter of Wilma's deceased daughter Jill); a grandson, Joe (son of Wilma's living daughter Buddy); daughter Buddy; and a single daughter, Diane. Who is entitled to Wilma's estate?

10. Egon Engers II murdered his mother, Dorothy Engers. Dorothy died testate and her Last Will and Testament left specified personal property to her two children, Egon and a daughter, Laura Jo Jones (formerly Engers), and the estate residue to a testamentary trust. In that Egon murdered his mother he is disqualified from taking any interest in her estate by Oklahoma's slayer statute, 84 O.S.Supp.1994, §231. However, unbeknownst to Dorothy and Laura, Egon had an illegitimate son, Jason Kyle Hulett, a minor, who now wishes to inherit what his father would have inherited from his mother were he not barred by the statute that precludes a murderer from inheriting from his victim. Laura objects because her mother's will did not acknowledge the existence of such a child and because it would be against public policy to allow the relatives of murderers to inherit. Who is correct? Does Jason have an interest in his grandmother's estate? *Hulett v. First Nat. Bank and Trust Co. in Clinton*, 956 P.2d 879 (Ok. 1998)

For research activities related to this chapter, go to our text companion website at www.thomsonedu.com/westbuslaw/jennings.

Zoning

CHAPTER 18

> *Property is in its nature timid and seeks protection, and nothing is more gratifying to government than becoming a protector.*
>
> John C. Calhoun, March 21, 1834

Local laws that control land use are grouped into one term that describes their effect: **zoning**. The zoning on a piece of property can affect its value, price, and marketability. This chapter answers the following questions: What is zoning? What types of zoning exist? What terms are used in zoning and zoning procedures? Are all forms of zoning constitutional? Is it possible to change or make exceptions?

Purposes

Each community is divided into areas, districts, or zones in which certain activities are permitted and others prohibited. Zoning laws classify property areas and permissible activities. Zoning controls building heights and whether apartments or single-family dwellings may be constructed in any area. Zoning sometimes prohibits construction altogether, such as when homes on a mountain side are prohibited. Zoning is a method of controlling community development. Zoning follows and enforces a **general** or **master plan** for the community so that the community develops in an orderly fashion. Zoning and a master plan prevent the problems and nuisances that result when residential areas are next to factories.

Zoning laws are, for the most part, local governmental ordinances. Cities and towns act under an enabling statute. In most cases, the enabling statute is based on the **Standard State Zoning Enabling Act**, which was drafted by the United States Department of Commerce in the 1920s. This act authorizes the local governmental entities to pass zoning laws that "lessen congestion . . . promote safety . . . prevent overcrowding . . . avoid undue concentration of population . . . and promote health and general welfare."

Authority

"Promot[ing] health and general welfare" is a broad grant of authority to local government that is grounded, as it were, in the police power clause of the United States Constitution (Section 8, cl. 1), which provides that governments exist for the promotion of the health, safety, morals, and general welfare of people. Zoning laws passed for the general welfare purpose fit within this constitutional framework.

To meet the constitutional standard of police power, zoning laws passed must serve some public health, safety, or morals interest. In addition, zoning laws cannot be arbitrary or discriminatory. (These issues are discussed later in the "Methods" section.) Another constitutional issue that arises is whether zoning use restrictions constitute a taking without due process of law as required under the Fourteenth Amendment, an issue covered in see Chapter 19.

In the *Village of Euclid, Ohio v. Ambler Realty Co.*, 272 U.S. 365 (1926), the United States Supreme Court recognized zoning as constitutional in general, a permissible exercise of police power. Any decreases in land values that result from zoning are not takings that require compensation (see p 537).

Methods

Generally, zoning begins with a master plan that divides the geographical area (county, city, or town) into districts with varying shapes that will supervise safety, traffic flow, and so on. Once these districts are created, the government entity then passes ordinances for each district. While the zoning standards can vary from district to district, all districts have the same procedural rules and regulations for exemptions and variances. The following sections address the types of rules and regulations in a zoning structure.

Use Restrictions

Use restrictions can be classified into four general categories: residential, commercial or business, industrial, and agricultural. These categories can have subcategories, as when residential is divided into R-1 for single-family dwellings, R-2 for duplex houses, and R-3 for apartments or mobile homes. Industrial districts may be classified according to the nature of the noise, waste, activity, danger, odor, and so on. When subcategories are created, the number 1 is usually associated with the most restrictive land use as in the example of R-1, which includes generally only single-family dwellings.

Zoning classifications may be cumulative or noncumulative. In a **cumulative classification**, the lesser restricted areas allow all of the activities permitted in more restrictive areas. If cumulative zoning existed in the R-1 example above, then R-2 districts would allow single-family dwellings to be included along with R-2 duplex houses, and R-3 districts would allow single-family dwellings and duplex houses, along with R-3 apartments and mobile homes. Classifications are ranked as follows:

1. Residential, single family
2. Residential, multiple family
3. Residential, apartment
4. Commercial, office
5. Commercial, business
6. Industrial

For example, an area zoned commercial could have residential uses within it under cumulative zoning. However, the reverse does not apply, and no industrial or commercial activity would be permitted in residential areas.

In a **noncumulative classification**, only the activities specified by the applicable zone are permitted. For example, in R-2 areas, there would be no single-family dwellings. An area zoned industrial or commercial in a noncumulative system cannot have residences. Noncumulative zoning prevents nuisance actions by prohibiting homes and apartments in industrial areas.

In developing their zoning systems, local governments are restricted only by constitutional restraint. One of the issues raised repeatedly in challenging zoning ordinances is single-family dwelling limitations, particularly in areas where housing costs are high and, with zoning, less costly forms of housing are not available for a significant portion of the population. In the following case, a court was faced with determining the validity of a zoning law that strictly controlled the use of manufactured homes.

Mississippi Manufactured Housing Ass'n v. Board of Sup'rs of Tate County

878 So.2d 180 (Miss.App., 2004); *cert. denied*, Assoc. v. Bd. of Super., 878 So.2d 67 (Miss. 2004)

FACTS

In September of 2000, Tate County began preparing to revise its county comprehensive zoning plan that had been adopted in 1972. The Allen and Hoshall firm assisted the county in the revision of the comprehensive zoning plan. Charlie Goforth, a representative of Allen and Hoshall, discussed at a public hearing the increased growth in the western and northern areas of the county and presented an amended comprehensive zoning plan to accommodate this growth, a plan that the board of supervisors adopted.

The 1972 ordinance established three residential districts: R-1 (single family), R-2 (single family), and R-3 (multi-family). Manufactured homes were prohibited in R-1 and R-2, but allowed in R-3 "[u]pon written approval of the Planning Commission." The 1972 ordinance also allowed manufactured housing in A-1 (agricultural) districts as "single family residences including mobile homes." The amended ordinance had five, rather than the previous three, residential districts: R-R (single family rural population density), R-1 (single family low population density), R-2 (single family medium population density), R-3 (multiple family medium population density), and R-M (low population density manufactured and modular homes, including single family). The amended ordinance included an AG district (agricultural) on which manufactured housing was permitted in very low population density areas. The amended ordinance also "grandfathered in" non-conforming uses, whereby if a property owner had a manufactured housing unit on his property, and the unit was destroyed, he could replace the unit with one of equal or greater value, so long as it met federal construction regulations.

Mississippi Manufactured Housing Association (MMHA) (plaintiffs) brought suit challenging the comprehensive zoning plan as an illegal restriction on manufactured housing. MMHA also challenged the plan as arbitrary and capricious and a violation of its rights to due process secured under the Fourteenth Amendment to the United States Constitution.

The trial court found that the comprehensive zoning plan was adopted in accordance with Mississippi statutes, which were enacted pursuant to "a valid reason for local governing authorities to regulate and zone areas for the use of manufactured movable homes," and that Tate County's revision of it's comprehensive zoning plan allowed manufactured housing to be placed in 86.4% of the land located within the county.

MMHA appealed.

JUDICIAL DECISION

Chandler, Judge. It is inevitable that the antiquated, traditional and affluent residential areas and estates of the past must give way to modern, progressive, gadget-equipped buildings of the future. The quiet life of yesterday is being swept aside and swamped by a tide of phenomenal, sudden growth. Where yesterday a fisherman pulled his little boat out on a sandy beach, today 16,000 boxes of bananas are being unloaded each hour from ocean-going ships. The quiet life of yesterday is shattered by the blating and groaning traffic piercing the veil of peaceful tranquility. There is no turning back, and those who would be in quiet serenity will eventually retreat from the battle and fatigue of modern progress. Change is inevitable. Those who guide the destiny of urban development must meet the challenge of a new era. They must stay abreast of modern times, and the hustle and bustle of this modern age. It is not only legally permissible for the municipal authorities to reexamine the zoning ordinances of their city as to necessary changes and new classifications essential to the welfare of the city, but it is their duty to do so where there is substantial evidence shown before the municipal authorities on which to base their determination. The court will not substitute its judgment for that of the municipal authorities.

The supreme court addressed the express issue of due process in the operation of zoning ordinances affecting manufactured housing in ***Carpenter v. City of Petal*, 699 So.2d 928** (**Miss**.1997).

In ***Carpenter***, the supreme court struck down a zoning ordinance which restricted manufactured housing except in designated mobile home parks, while at the same time allowing such uses as commercial stables and kennels, poultry, livestock and small animal raising in RF (rural fringe) districts where manufactured housing was prohibited.

In this case, the zoning ordinance is of the type that the ***Carpenter*** court found would be "fairly debatable," and therefore constitutionally permissible. Therefore, the zoning ordinance in question in this case is not precluded by ***Carpenter***. Nevertheless, MMHA raises specific assertions of substantial due process deprivations.

The contract between Tate County and Allen and Hoshall expressly stated the purpose was to "establish long range goals for the county. These goals shall include: residential, commercial and industrial development, parks, open space and recreation, street or road improvement; and public schools and other community facilities." There is no judicial finding that the "express purpose" was to prevent the proliferation of manufactured housing. However, in the public hearing the board residents expressed concern that the proposed comprehensive plan and maps would allow for the proliferation of manufactured housing. One exchange concerning a map showing existing mobile or manufactured housing units within the county provided:

Mr. Smith: You still hadn't answered my question, sir. Are they [manufactured housing]—are they concentrated, meaning there's just 100 of them there? Are there just three there or—because I don't understand why you've chosen arbitrarily to put trailer homes in certain areas and not in others.

Mr. Goforth: Well, I mean, right here there's probably twenty in that one little area right there. There are hundreds in this area.

Mr. Smith: Well if you zone it that way there will be millions of them there.

Mr. Goforth: There will be more; yes sir.

Therefore, nothing in the record indicates that the zoning ordinance amendment was solely to prevent the proliferation of manufactured housing. This issue is without merit.

Courts throughout the nation continue to hold that local zoning laws may regulate the location of manufactured housing by excluding manufactured housing from some residential classifications on the basis of their differences in construction from other types of housing. There is no merit to this assignment of error.

MMHA argues that Mississippi's adoption of the uniform standards code for factory manufactured moveable homes, precludes zoning requirements from considering safety as an issue. Nothing in the record shows the board considered manufactured housing to be unsafe, or that safety was a consideration in amending the zoning ordinance. To the extent that this is asserted as an issue, it is without merit.

In this state, the supreme court found it was "fairly debatable" whether manufactured housing could be excluded from other single residential housing construction to further the legitimate government purpose of "preserving surrounding residential property values." An ordinance that is found "fairly debatable" in furthering a legitimate governmental purpose, such as protecting property values, passes due process muster. Therefore, this issue is without merit.

Nevertheless, the evidence in the record does tend to show that Tate County's amended zoning ordinance requires manufactured housing to be placed on larger residential lots than other forms of construction, such as site built. Manufactured housing on "residential" lots was required to have a lot of one acre, while residential lots for site built housing were set at 15,000 and 12,000 square feet.

In this case, MMHA presented no testimony in the public hearings as to why or how the differences in density requirements precluded citizens being able to purchase manufactured housing. Moreover, Goforth also stated that other adjacent counties, which were fueling Tate County's population growth, had even stricter restrictions on manufactured housing by requiring even greater acreage for manufactured housing, and MMHA conceded in its briefs that the amended zoning ordinance at issue in this case actually *reduced* the acreage requirements that the zoning ordinance required prior to its amendment. However, the most dispositive fact in the record is that MMHA admitted a manufactured home will cost less per square foot than a site built home. It is reasonable that the board wanted to protect the values of site built homes by requiring manufactured homes to be placed a reasonable distance from the site built homes. Therefore, we find that the record does not present facts to overcome the presumption of validity and to show that the board acted arbitrarily or capriciously in adopting density and lot size requirements in the amended zoning ordinance. There is no merit to this assignment of error.

The arguments of Plaintiffs that there is nothing inherently different about manufactured housing which justifies such different treatment, and that manufactured housing is not necessarily incompatible with site-built housing, preservation of the tax base or preservation of market values of site-built homes, are arguments to be addressed to each legislative body concerned and to the citizens of these communities, rather than to the courts. Whether Plaintiffs' arguments concerning these issues are better reasoned than public perception does not trump the democratic process; the remedy is public debate and persuasion and not judicial fiat or ukase. In the absence of invidious discrimination based upon such illicit factors as race, religion or national origin, a majoritarian preference or persuasion, however "accurate," is a legitimate basis for local legislation.

If the municipal council deemed any of the reasons which have been suggested, or any other substantial reason, a sufficient reason for adopting the ordinance in question, it is not the province of the courts to take issue with the council. We have nothing to do with the question of the wisdom or good policy of municipal ordinances. If they are not satisfying to a majority of the citizens, their recourse is to the ballot—not the courts. *Village of Euclid*, 272 U.S. at 393.

The record shows that the board adopted the amendment in reasonable response to the needs of the citizens of Tate County, with input from those citizens and any interested party. Judicial review will not overturn such a decision, as it properly belongs to the elected officials of Tate County.

Affirmed.

CASE QUESTIONS

1. What was the process for Tate County's change in its zoning plan?
2. What grounds does the MMHA raise for challenging the new zoning plan?
3. What does the court say is its role with regard to county and state bodies on zoning issues?

CONSIDER 18.1

The town of Chester, New Hampshire, has a zoning ordinance, in effect since 1985, that provides for a single-family home on a two-acre lot, a duplex on a three-acre lot, and excludes multifamily housing from all five zoning districts. Planned residential developments (PRD) would be permitted to have multifamily structures.

Chester consists principally of single-family homes with the majority of its residents commuting to work in Manchester. A bedroom community, Chester, at the time of the case, was projected to have one of the highest growth rates in New Hampshire.

Raymond Remillard, a resident of Chester who owns 23 acres, tried for 11 years to obtain a permit to construct a multiunit housing complex primarily for low- to moderate-income families. He was unsuccessful until he brought suit challenging the validity of Chester's zoning ordinances. Can he challenge the zoning plan successfully? *Britton v. Town of Chester*, 595 A.2d 492 (N.H. 1991)

Intensity Zoning

Intensity zoning regulates location and size of structures on land. Intensity regulations generally take the following forms:

1. Building-height limitations
2. Setbacks for buildings (minimum distance between the street or sidewalk and the structure)
3. Minimum lot sizes (may be total square feet or minimum length and width)

4. Maximum structures per area (often called *density*—specifies, for example, the number of houses that may be built in an R-1 tract)
5. Floor area ratios (sets a maximum amount of floor area per lot; for example, a 10-to-1 ratio would permit a 10-story building to occupy an entire lot or a 20-story building to occupy half the lot).

Aesthetic Zoning

The purpose of **aesthetic zoning** is to control or improve the beauty of an area. Zoning that is purely aesthetic is not valid in a majority of the states. However, if aesthetic controls can be tied to or coupled with a health or welfare purpose, then they are valid. Courts recognize the public interest in aesthetic controls and uphold such zoning. For example, an aesthetic zoning ordinance that prohibits construction of homes on the side of a mountain to preserve the beauty of the mountain is not a stand-alone reason for upholding the ordinance. However, the city or county could show that there is great risk in constructing homes on the mountainside because of possible slides, destruction of the homes, injury to others, and the need for city safety and rescue equipment. With this explanation, the ordinance becomes a valid exercise of police power for safety reasons, not just aesthetic ones.

Aesthetic zoning has been used to preserve historical towns and portions of cities by controlling the type of architecture, its repair, and alteration.[1] These types of zoning ordinances are valid because they preserve historical areas as well as the resulting tourist business.

The following case deals with an issue of zoning aesthetics.

SALIB V. CITY OF MESA

133 P.3d 756 (Ariz. App. 2006)

FACTS

Edward Salib ("Salib") owns a Winchell's Donut House franchise within a designated redevelopment area of Mesa. To attract customers, Salib displays signs affixed to his store windows that advertise his products. On August 5, 2002, after giving Salib several warnings, a Mesa code enforcement officer ordered Salib to remove his window signs because their display violated Mesa's Sign Code (the "Sign Code"), which Mesa had enacted the prior November. Salib's display violated Sign Code 11-19-6, which prohibited businesses from covering more than 30 percent of their windows with signs.

In March, 2003, the Sign Code was amended to define "window" to include a series of neighboring windows not separated by more than six inches. The effect of the amendment was to allow larger signs because the 30 percent would be measured against a larger area.

On January 8, 2003, Salib filed suit against Mesa alleging the Sign Code violates his free speech rights under the Arizona and United States Constitutions. He asked the court to declare the Sign Code unconstitutional and enjoin Mesa from enforcing it. The trial court granted summary judgment in favor of Mesa.

JUDICIAL OPINION

Irvine, Judge. With regard to government regulations of signs, the Supreme Court has explained:

While signs are a form of expression protected by the Free Speech Clause, they pose distinctive problems that are subject to municipalities' police powers. Unlike oral speech, signs take up space and may obstruct views, distract motorists, displace alternative uses for land, and pose other problems that legitimately call for regulation. It is common ground that governments may regulate the physical characteristics of signs—just as they can, within reasonable bounds and absent censorial purpose, regulate audible expression in its capacity as noise. City of Ladue v. Gilleo, *512 U.S. 43, 48, 114 S.Ct. 2038, 129 L.Ed.2d 36 (1994)*

1. *Brick Haus, Inc. v. Board of Adjustment*, 2006 WL 2266299 (Ia. App).

Commercial speech that concerns unlawful activity or is misleading is not protected by the First Amendment. Commercial speech that falls into neither of these categories may be regulated if the government satisfies a three-prong test. First, the government must assert a substantial interest in support of the regulation. Second, the government must demonstrate that the restriction on commercial speech directly and materially advances that regulation. Third, the regulation must be narrowly drawn. Mesa does not argue that Salib's signs are misleading or concern unlawful activity, so the Sign Code must meet the three-part test. Mesa argues, and Salib concedes, that the governmental regulation of aesthetics constitutes a substantial interest.

Mesa also asserts safety as a goal, stating that it will be easier for police to see through windows that are not totally blocked. Salib responds that seeing through windows is not a valid concern because businesses are not required to have any windows and are free to cover windows entirely with blinds or shades. Because Mesa's interest in aesthetics is sufficient to support the Sign Code, we do not address safety as an independent justification.

[The] government "must demonstrate that the challenged regulation advances [its] interest in a direct and material way." This burden is "not satisfied by mere speculation or conjecture; rather, [the government] ... must demonstrate that the harms it recites are real and that its restriction will in fact alleviate them to a material degree." Nevertheless, the Supreme Court does not "require that empirical data come to [the courts] accompanied by a surfeit of background information" and has "permitted litigants to justify speech restrictions by reference to studies and anecdotes pertaining to different locales altogether, or even ... based solely on history, consensus, and 'simple common sense.'"

Salib argues that this prong has not been met because the Code "is arbitrary and incapable of actually furthering a significant governmental purpose." Salib asserts that no studies were conducted to determine what aesthetic or safety problems existed and how the Sign Code could solve such problems, so the Sign Code has not been proven to advance governmental interests.

Mesa responds that the Sign Code was enacted because of legitimate concerns among business owners that many businesses in the area had 100% coverage of their storefront windows and that this total coverage was unattractive and detracted from the aesthetics of the city. Mesa further argues that because the Sign Code clearly listed statements of purpose and intent, the Sign Code directly advances substantial governmental interests. It also argues that the city council researched the effects of the Sign Code on aesthetics, although copies of the research were not kept. The record does contain a 1999 Council Report from the City Manager to the City Council listing aesthetics as a reason for the limit on window coverage to 30%. The same report noted the "primary task of [amending the Sign Code] is to provide an encouraging environment for investment in the redevelopment area."

To update the Sign Ordinance Mesa created a Project Team, which included business owners and City staff. After receiving recommendations from the Project Team, city staff held public meetings seeking input regarding the suggested changes, including the suggestion to limit window coverage to 30%. The proposed amendments were then reviewed and approved by the Downtown Development Committee and approved by the city council.

Here, the Sign Code is accompanied by clear statements of purpose and intent that address aesthetic concerns. The Sign Code states, in part:

(A) The purpose of this Sign Ordinance regulating signs of all types is to:

1. Preserve and protect the public health, safety and welfare within the City of Mesa.

....

(B) The intent of the application of this Ordinance is to:

....

3. Provide an improved visual environment for the citizens of and visitors to the City of Mesa, Arizona.

Mesa's city council plainly concluded that regulating signs directly furthered its interest in promoting aesthetics. This determination is entitled to reasonable deference.

As for proof, the First Amendment does not require a formal study before a regulation may be enacted. The record shows that the city council received considerable input on the subject of window coverage and aesthetics before enacting the Sign Code. Although its final adoption of the Sign Code may have rested on anecdote, history, consensus or simple common sense, rather than a formal study or survey addressed specifically to the window coverage provision, the constitution requires no greater proof. Therefore, Mesa has shown that the Sign Code was enacted to, and does in fact, directly advance the substantial government interests of aesthetics.

Next, Salib argues the restriction is not narrow enough. It is clear from the First Amendment cases that narrowly tailored or narrowly drawn does not mean that the least restrictive means must be used. Rather, a "reasonable fit" between the intent and purpose of the regulation and the means chosen to accomplish those goals is required. The regulation does not have to be perfect, but its scope must be in proportion to the interest served.

Salib argues that the regulation is not a reasonable fit to the desired goals of improved aesthetics because Mesa never explained how the 30% blockage figure was reached or why the regulation was drafted to only affect signs within the window sill and not outside the sill area. He also argues that Mesa's Senior Redevelopment Specialist, Patrick Murphy, admitted during a deposition that a less restrictive Sign Code would have been equally effective.

We read Mr. Murphy's testimony differently. While Mr. Murphy did state that any reduction from allowing 100% window coverage would be an improvement over no restriction at all, he did not state that all reductions would have an equal effect on aesthetics. In fact, he stated in his deposition that a reduction to 45% would be less aesthetically effective than a reduction to 30%.

As noted above, there were concerns among business owners that many businesses in the area had 100% coverage. The Sign Code was adopted to address this problem, and Mesa argues that 30% is a reasonable compromise between 100% coverage and a total ban of signage. Further, Mesa argues, the Sign Code is narrow because it only addresses signs that are inside the pane, and the Code allows alternative methods of communication, including signs hanging outside of the window sill area. Additionally, Mesa conducted comparisons with other communities and found that the 30% restriction on window coverage was comparable to other cities' restrictions.

To ask the City to justify a size restriction of 120 square feet over, say 200 square feet or 300 square feet would impose great costs on local governments and at any rate would do little to improve our ability to review the law—because any further explanation assuredly would contain the kind of aesthetic and subjective judgment that judges are not well-equipped to second guess.

For similar reasons, we are not in a position to determine what percentage of window coverage is optimal. Rather, we only decide if the 30% figure that was adopted by the Sign Code is a reasonable fit to further the goal of improving aesthetics. We conclude that it is. Signs are not completely banned, but the windows will largely remain uncovered. Reasonable minds can differ as to whether Mesa's interest would best be served by a 15%, 25%, 30% or 40% limitation on window coverage, but under the facts of this case we cannot conclude that these differences of degree are of a constitutional dimension. The exact balance between the size of the signs and the aesthetic benefits attained is ultimately a subjective decision best left to the city council to determine through its decision-making processes.

We also disagree with Salib's argument that because Mesa never justified why the Sign Code does not address signs outside the window area, the Sign Code is not a reasonable fit to the goal of aesthetics. The First Amendment does not "impose upon [regulators] the burden of demonstrating that…the manner of restriction is absolutely the least severe that will achieve the desired end" but simply a reasonable fit.

We conclude the Sign Code directly advances a substantial governmental interest and is narrowly tailored to directly advance the goal of improved aesthetics. Therefore, it meets the test for regulation of commercial speech and is constitutional under the First Amendment.

We therefore affirm the trial court's granting of Mesa's Motion for Summary Judgment.

CASE QUESTIONS

1. When was the ordinance on signs adopted and why?

2. What First Amendment standards must the sign code meet?

3. Why does Mr. Salib raise the question of no regulation of outdoor signs?

CONSIDER 18.2

Nestled in the Mount Washington Valley, the town of Conway, New Hampshire, historically has been a tourist destination for activities in the White Mountain National Forest. Route 16 links the villages of Conway and North Conway and offers striking views of the mountains and ledges to the west. Substantial commercial development, primarily along this highway, has rendered part of the town a shoppers' Mecca. Hundreds of signs draw tourists in the day and evening hours to the shopping centers, lodging facilities, and restaurants clustered in the villages of Conway and North Conway.

In 1982, the town of Conway passed a zoning ordinance requiring all property owners to obtain a permit from the town zoning officer before erecting a sign. The same zoning ordinance prohibited signs "illuminated from within," but allows signs illuminated by external lights.

Michael Asselin, the owner of Mario's, a restaurant on Route 16, purchased a sign that was illuminated from within and erected it on his property. The town notified

CONSIDER 18.2

(continued)

Asselin that the sign was in violation of the ordinance. Asselin challenged the authority of Conway to regulate commercial speech (his sign) solely for the purpose of "preserving scenic vistas" and "retaining the character of a country community." Is Conway's restriction of the types of signs for its businesses covered as permissible zoning? *Asselin v. Town of Conway*, 628 A.2d 247 (N.H. 1993)

Telecommunications, Aesthetic Zoning, and NIMBYs

Cellular phone service is now the preferred method of communication. Many individuals opt not to have landlines and the result is an increasing number of wireless tower sites needed to accommodate this new form of telecommunications. However, the sites for those towers continue to be problematic for local zoning boards. The so-called NIMBYs, an acronym for "not in my back yard," along with the BANANAs (build absolutely nothing anywhere near anything), and the NoWIMPs (not with my property) were vocal presences at local zoning hearings when telecommunications companies applied for approval for locating cellular phone towers. Responding to active and vocal constituencies, local authorities created blocks for cellular telecommunications companies and their towers.

Congress intervened with Section 332(c) of the Telecommunications Act of 1996, which covers "Mobile Services."[2] The federal law does not preempt local zoning authority over tower locations, but it does place some limitations on that local government over siting in discreet ways. For example, state and local governments cannot engage in unreasonable discrimination among "providers of functionally equivalent services." If they allow telephone wires and cables, then they must allow towers. The Act also prevents state and local governments from prohibiting "the provision of personal wireless services."

To prevent stalling, the Act requires state and local governments to respond within a reasonable time to tower-siting requests. Denials require written reports that include "substantial evidence" supporting that denial. If the denial is based on health claims, the state and local authority must provide something more than community hysteria in its report. There must be scientific and medical evidence to support a denial based upon health claims. For example, a denial on the basis of aesthetics violates the standards of the Act. Telecommunications companies are entitled to expedited judicial review of the denial. The following case deals with the limitations on local zoning authorities when there is an issue of telecommunications structures.

CROWN COMMUNICATION OF NEW YORK V. DEPARTMENT OF TRANSPORTATION

824 N.E.2d 934 (A. N.Y. 2005)

FACTS

In 1997, the New York State Police and the Department of Transportation (DOT or collectively the State) entered into an agreement with Crown Communication to construct and operate telecommunications towers on state-owned lands and rights-of-way. Under the agreement, Crown could license space on the towers to localities and commercial wireless providers, and the State could co-locate its own communications equipment on the towers.

2 47 U.S.C.A. §332(c).

After Crown identified two potential locations for towers on state-owned property within the City of New Rochelle (the City), the State approved construction of both towers.

In June 2000, Crown and the State gave a public presentation to the Mayor and City Council regarding the purpose and intended use of the two proposed towers. At this meeting, the City voiced no objection to the siting or construction of the towers, and Crown offered space on the facilities to the municipality for use by its public safety agencies. DOT performed an environmental review of both sites. DOT's study found that neither the replacement tower nor the maintenance yard tower would result in any significant adverse environmental or aesthetic impact.

Crown proceeded with the construction of the towers and entered into license agreements with a number of commercial wireless telecommunications providers to lease space on the towers for their equipment. During construction, the City issued a stop work order, contending that the towers were subject to the City's zoning laws and that Crown must apply for a special permit from the City's Planning Board.

The Supreme Court determined that Crown need not comply with local zoning requirements. The Appellate Division also determined that the wireless telecommunications providers are not subject to local zoning regulation and affirmed. The parties appealed.

JUDICIAL OPINION

Graffeo, Justice. In this case we are asked whether the installation of private antennae on two state-owned telecommunications towers is exempt from local zoning regulation. Under the particular facts and circumstances of this case, we conclude that the commercial telecommunications providers involved in this state project are not required to make applications for special permits.

The City argues that, although the towers themselves are exempt from regulation, no justification exists to extend such immunity to the installation of commercial equipment on the towers. Specifically, the City asserts that it has the right pursuant to its zoning authority to evaluate whether private antennae are necessary to close cellular telecommunications coverage gaps or should be placed elsewhere, and to require some form of aesthetic camouflaging of equipment. In response, Crown and the State contend that the private carriers are entitled to share in the immunity already enjoyed by the state-owned towers. They claim that the State's plan envisions a public-private partnership and that the joint use of its towers facilitates the State's public safety and environmental goals.

[t]he State submitted evidence of numerous benefits the government's use of the towers would afford the public, which Supreme Court took into account in finding the towers immune from local regulation under the balancing test. For example, the State is currently in the process of developing its telecommunications infrastructure in anticipation of establishing a Statewide Wireless Network (SWN), which will replace outdated systems with a state-of-the-art digital land mobile radio network designed to permit interagency and intergovernmental communications across the state in emergency situations. Consultants retained by the State Police have indicated that in order to operate in the higher frequency range, it will be necessary to construct three to four times the approximately 150 existing state-maintained radio sites. The State has therefore reserved space on the replacement and maintenance yard towers for anticipated SWN use when the network becomes operational.

Additionally, DOT has developed an Intelligent Transportation System (ITS), which monitors traffic flow, weather and road conditions. DOT's Director of Traffic Engineering and Safety stated that the collection of such data aids DOT and public safety entities in being able to "respond to emergency situations, manage and divert traffic, and provide real-time traffic information to motorists," thereby improving the safety of the traveling public and reducing travel times.

Finally, the State has followed a policy of offering space on its towers to local public safety authorities and offered such space on the two towers to the City in this case. Currently, Westchester County has placed antennae on the replacement tower for use by its Department of Public Safety.

[we] agree with the Appellate Division that the installation of licensed commercial antennae on the towers should also be accorded immunity because co-location serves a number of significant public interests that are advanced by the State's overall telecommunications plan. At this time, there are apparently more private than public antennae on the towers, but the presence of commercial equipment does not exclusively serve private interests. The private antennae will improve the availability of 911 emergency cellular calls made by the public, thereby promoting the public safety interest central to construction of the State's towers. Significantly, the co-location of public and private equipment also eliminates the need for the proliferation of telecommunications towers, an important environmental and aesthetic public concern. Furthermore, profits derived from licensing space to wireless providers will ultimately aid in financing the construction of the State's telecommunications infrastructure plan.

The fact that the wireless providers will also realize profit from their services does not undermine the public interests served by co-location. In sum, the public and private uses of the towers are sufficiently intertwined to justify exemption of the wireless providers from local zoning regulations.

Accordingly, the order of the Appellate Division should be affirmed, with costs.

CIPARICK, J. (dissenting). Because I do not believe the exemption from local zoning regulation accorded to the state-owned telecommunications towers should be applied to the private telecommunications providers here, I respectfully dissent.

Placement of private wireless service facilities is ordinarily subject to local zoning requirements. This case differs from the typical scenario because the private providers locate their antennae on a state tower that is immune from local regulation. The issue before this Court is whether that immunity should be extended to benefit the private providers—allowing them immunity from local zoning simply because they opt to co-locate on a state, rather than a private, tower.

The State's immunity from local zoning requirements should not be extended to the private providers. The State has not preempted this area and there is no indication that the local zoning regulations would conflict with the State's purposes. Thus, I would reverse the order of the Appellate Division and reinstate the order of Supreme Court.

CASE QUESTIONS

1. Why is the presence of private users an issue in the case?
2. What test does the court apply in determining whether the towers are exempt from local ordinances?
3. What is the focus of the dissenting justice's opinion?

ETHICAL ISSUE

What interests are the zoning boards balancing as they make the decision to site a telecommunications tower? What economic issues are at stake? One city council member said that not allowing the towers would sentence his city to being a second-class citizen in the business world. What does he mean by that? Who is affected by the tower sitings? What arguments can be made in their favor? What arguments against?

Exclusionary Zoning

Exclusionary zoning controls who comes into the community and in what numbers. Antigrowth ordinances are invalid if they are a permanent block to any use of the land. Restrictions on the rate of development so that services and governmental organization can grow to meet needs serve a legitimate public interest and are permissible forms of regulation.

An area of zoning contention has been that of the exclusion of religious structures and church buildings and developments. In 2000, Congress passed the Religious Land Use and Institutionalized Persons Act (RLUIPA). RLUIPA requires that local government land use regulation on religious organizations must meet a standard of strict judicial scrutiny.[3] The federal protections have engendered emotional battles over local zoning and federal control. Cases under the law include church expansions, the creation of church educational facilities, and church use and alteration of storefront properties.

Exclusionary zoning laws used to eliminate all but single-family dwellings are subject to strict judicial scrutiny.

Interim Zoning

It may take a city or town some time to make a study and develop a master plan. In the time it takes for such study and planning, developers may develop segments to

3. 42 U.S.C. §2000cc(a)(1) (2000).

Practical Tip

NIMBYs protest about other issues such as the location of waste and nuclear depositories, utility plants, and even Wal-Marts. Before applying for zoning approval, applicants should be aware of the psychological impact and likely outcry from the type of facility they propose. Working with the NIMBYs before application for zoning approval may be the key to obtaining approval. For example, some telecommunications companies have turned their cellular towers into works of art that rally the NIMBYs and the community to their side.

frustrate the plan and enjoy the protections of nonconforming use. To alleviate this problem, cities and towns may adopt **interim** or **hold zoning** to prevent uncontrolled development before a comprehensive plan and ordinances are adopted. The interim zoning may be as simple as a requirement of approval before construction or development begins. This prior approval gives the city or town government control before permanent zoning takes effect.

Social Issue Zoning

Social issue zoning battles social issues through land use controls. For example, zoning ordinances have been used to disperse adult theaters and bookstores. In *Young v. American Mini Theaters*, 427 U.S. 50 (1976), the United States Supreme Court held that zoning ordinances may classify these types of businesses differently from other movie houses and bookstores for safety purposes, thus upholding the disbursement treatment required by the ordinances. In *City of Renton v. Playtime Theaters, Inc.*, 475 U.S. 41 (1986), the United States Supreme Court held that zoning restrictions on adult bookstores are valid under the First Amendment so long as nothing prevents such businesses from locating in other areas of the city. In the following case, a federal appellate court faces the issue of alternative availability.

Lim v. City of Long Beach

217 F.3d 1050 (9th Cir. 2000)

FACTS

In 1995, the city of Long Beach passed an ordinance that amended its existing adult entertainment zoning ordinance by prohibiting adult entertainment businesses within 300 feet of a residential zoning district, 1,000 feet of any public or private school, 600 feet of any city park, 500 feet of a church, and 1,000 feet of another adult entertainment business.

Seung Chung Lim and his corporation, Fluffy, Inc., challenged the constitutionality of the newly amended ordinance. He and Fluffy, Inc., own and operate two adult entertainment businesses located within 300 feet of residential districts. The district court found the ordinance to be valid and Mr. Lim appealed.

JUDICIAL OPINION

Michael Daly Hawkins, Circuit Judge. As a threshold matter, we note that it is clear that the burden of proving alternative avenues of communication rests on Long Beach.

The issue before this court—one that is decidedly less clear—is the level of specificity about each particular site Long Beach is required to provide to sustain its burden.

A city allows for alternative avenues of communication if it offers adult businesses a "reasonable opportunity to open and operate...within the city...," *Renton*, 475 U.S. at 54, 106 S.Ct. 925. We have applied a two-step approach to determining whether this condition is satisfied: (1) relocation sites provided to adult businesses must be considered part of an actual business real estate market for commercial enterprises generally; and (2) after excluding those sites that may not properly be considered part of the relevant real estate market, there are an adequate number of relocation sites. See *Topanga Press v. City of Los Angeles*, 989 F.2d, 1524, 1529 (9th Cir. 1993).

In *Topanga Press*, we noted that "[w]e are left to the simple, yet slippery, test of reasonableness when attempting to discern whether land is or is not part of a market in which any business may compete." We then listed five considerations in making the reasonableness determination: (1) a relocation site is not part of the market if it is "unreasonable to believe that it would ever become available to any commercial enterprise," (2) a relocation site in a manufacturing or industrial zone that is "reasonably accessible to the general public" may also be part of the market; (3) a site in a manufacturing zone that has proper infrastructure may be included in the market; (4) a site must be reasonable for some generic commercial enterprise, although not every particular enterprise, before it can be considered part of the market; and (5) a site that is commercially zoned is part of the relevant market. In addition, a site must obviously satisfy the conditions of the zoning ordinance in question.

Plaintiffs argue that the district court erred in considering sites with restrictive leases banning adult entertainment establishments. Under *Topanga Press*, however, sites must only reasonably become available to some generic commercial enterprise, not specifically to adult businesses. Plaintiffs also argue that the district court improperly considered certain currently occupied property as part of the actual business real estate market. *Topanga Press* stated that the requirement that property potentially become available (the first factor, above) "connotes genuine possibility." Thus, for example, property subject to a long-term lease might not meet the *Topanga Press* test. Plaintiffs contend that under *Topanga Press*, Long Beach should have been required to prove that the currently occupied property would reasonably become available to any commercial enterprise. Long Beach came forward with a list of 115 sites it contended were potentially available. According to the district court opinion, Long Beach provided pertinent, specific, and detailed information about each site. Based on this information, the district court found that Long Beach made a good faith and reasonable attempt to prove that it was providing the Plaintiffs with a reasonable opportunity to open and operate.

A city cannot merely point to a random assortment of properties and simply assert that they are reasonably available to adult businesses. The city's duty to demonstrate the availability of properties is defined, at a bare minimum, by reasonableness and good faith. If a plaintiff can show that a city's attempt is not in fact in good faith or reasonable, by, for example, showing that a representative sample of properties are on their face unavailable, then the city will be required to put forth more detailed evidence. But where a city has provided a good faith and reasonable list of potentially available properties, it is for the Plaintiffs to show that, in fact, certain sites would not reasonably become available. There is no reason to conclude that Long Beach acted in bad faith or unreasonably in identifying potentially available properties. The burden of showing that particular sites would not reasonably become available therefore rests with the Plaintiffs.

Once the relevant market has been properly defined in light of any additional evidence presented by Plaintiffs on remand, the district court will have to reexamine whether the market contains a sufficient number of potential relocation sites for Plaintiffs' adult businesses. Because it is unclear how many sites will be part of the relevant market, we cannot determine whether the district court correctly concluded that a sufficient number of sites exist to allow Plaintiffs a reasonable opportunity to open and operate.

Here, there is evidence that Long Beach had a rational reason for enforcing the adult business ordinance and not enforcing other zoning ordinances. Long Beach enforces its adult business ordinance become of its interest in curbing the secondary effects of adult businesses. Long Beach does not have a similar interest in enforcing its other ordinances. As such, the district court did not err in denying Plaintiffs' equal protection claim.

Remanded for further trial on the sufficiency of locations.

CASE QUESTIONS

1. What does the ordinance restrict?
2. Are there other sites available for adult businesses?
3. Are these sites offered by the city sufficient?
4. What does the appellate court rule must be done?

CONSIDER 18.3

The city of Tampa passed a zoning ordinance that prohibits the location of an adult business within 500 feet of a residential or office district. The ordinance was passed to revitalize inner-city neighborhoods and was not based on studies of the effects of these businesses on residential neighborhoods. Specialty Malls was denied a permit to operate an exotic dance club in an office district and then filed suit alleging that the ordinance serves no substantial governmental interest. The aldermen of the city maintain that these adult businesses attract transients and were not conducive to a "stable, growing, vibrant neighborhood." Is the zoning ordinance constitutional? *Specialty Malls of Tampa v. City of Tampa*, 916 F. Supp.1222 (M.D. Fla. 1996)

ETHICAL ISSUE

The city of Southborough, Massachusetts, passed a zoning ordinance that prohibited the operation of abortion clinics within the town. Framingham Clinic attempted to establish a clinic that would perform first-trimester abortions and challenged the ordinance. Is the regulation permissible? *Framingham Clinic, Inc. v. Board of Selectmen*, 367 N.E.2d 606 (Mass. 1977)

Would it be constitutional for a city to restrict protestors outside abortion clinics? What if the city could establish that the protests caused congestion and noise? *Madsen v. Women's Health Center, Inc.*, 512 U.S. 753 (1994)

One social zoning issue that has emerged over the past few years is the concept of group homes for those with terminal illness or mental or physical disabilities. The following case reflects the U.S. Supreme Court position on how requests for such group homes in residential areas should be resolved.

CITY OF EDMONDS V. OXFORD HOUSE, INC.

514 U.S. 725 (1995)

FACTS

In the summer of 1990, respondent Oxford House opened a group home in the city of Edmonds, Washington (City), for 10 to 12 adults recovering from alcoholism and drug addiction. The group home, called Oxford House–Edmonds, is located in a neighborhood zoned for single-family residences. Upon learning that Oxford House had leased and was operating a home in Edmonds, the City issued criminal citations to the owner and a resident of the house. The citations charged violation of the zoning code rule that defines who may live in single-family dwelling units. The occupants of such units must compose a "family," and family, under the City's defining rule, "means an individual or two or more persons related by genetics, adoption, or marriage, or a group of five or fewer persons who are not related by genetics, adoption, or marriage." ECDC §21.30.010. Oxford House–Edmonds houses more than five unrelated persons, and therefore does not conform to the code.

Oxford House relied on the Fair Housing Act, 102 Stat. 1619, 42 U.S.C. §3601 *et seq.*, which declares it unlawful "[t]o discriminate in the sale or rental, or to otherwise make unavailable or deny, a dwelling to any buyer or renter because of a handicap of...that buyer or renter." §3604(f)(1)(A). The parties have stipulated, for purposes of this litigation, that the residents of Oxford House–Edmonds "are recovering alcoholics and drug addicts and are handicapped persons within the meaning" of the Act.

The District Court granted summary judgment to the City. The Court of Appeals reversed and remanded, and the City and the group home appealed.

JUDICIAL OPINION

Ginsburg, Justice. Discrimination covered by the FHA includes "a refusal to make reasonable accommodations in rules, policies, practices, or services, when such accommodations may be necessary to afford [handicapped] person[s] equal opportunity to use and enjoy a dwelling." §3604(f)(3)(B). Oxford House asked Edmonds to make a "reasonable accommodation" by allowing it to remain in the single-family dwelling it had leased. Group homes for recovering substance abusers, Oxford urged, need 8 to 12 residents to be financially and therapeutically viable. Edmonds declined to permit Oxford House to stay in a single-family residential zone, but passed an ordinance listing group homes as permitted uses in multifamily and general commercial zones.

On May 17, 1993, the State of Washington enacted a law providing

No city may enact or maintain an ordinance, development regulation, zoning regulation or official control, policy, or administrative practice which treats a residential structure occupied by persons with handicaps differently than a similar residential structure occupied by a family or other unrelated individuals. As used in this section, "handicaps" are as defined in the federal fair housing amendments act of 1988 (42 U.S.C. Sec. 3602).

Wash. Rev. Code §35.63.220 (1994).

The United States asserts that Washington's new law invalidates ECDC §21.30.010, Edmonds' family composition rule, as applied to Oxford House–Edmonds. Edmonds responds that the effect of the new law is "far from clear."

The sole question before the Court is whether Edmonds' family composition rule qualifies as a "restrictio[n] regarding the maximum number of occupants permitted to occupy a dwelling" within the meaning of the FHA's absolute exemption. In answering this question, we are mindful of the Act's stated policy "to provide, within constitutional limitations, for fair housing throughout the United States." We also note precedent recognizing the FHA's "broad and inclusive" compass, and therefore according a "generous construction" to the Act's complaint-filing provision. Accordingly, we regard this case as an instance in which an exception to "a general statement of policy" is sensibly read "narrowly in order to preserve the primary operation of the [policy]."

Congress enacted §3607(b)(1) against the backdrop of an evident distinction between municipal land-use restrictions and maximum occupancy restrictions.

Land-use restrictions designate "districts in which only compatible uses are allowed and incompatible uses are excluded. These restrictions typically categorize uses as single-family residential, multiple-family residential, commercial, or industrial. In particular, reserving land for single-family residences preserves the character of neighborhoods, securing "zones where family values, youth values, and the blessings of quiet seclusion and clean air make the area a sanctuary for people." *Village of Belle Terre v. Boraas*, 416 U.S. 1 (1974). To limit land use to single-family residences, a municipality must define the term "family"; thus family composition rules are an essential component of single-family residential use restrictions.

Maximum occupancy restrictions, in contradistinction, cap the number of occupants per dwelling, typically in relation to available floor space or the number and type of rooms.

Turning specifically to the City's Community Development Code, we note that the provisions Edmonds invoked against Oxford House, ECDC §§16.20.010 and 21.30.010, are classic examples of a use restriction and complementing family composition rule. These provisions do not cap the number of people who may live in a dwelling. In plain terms, they direct that dwellings be used only to house families. Captioned "USES," ECDC §16.20.010 provides that the sole "Permitted Primary Us[e]" in a single-family residential zone is "[s]ingle-family dwelling units." Edmonds itself recognizes that this provision simply "defines those uses permitted in a single family residential zone."

A separate provision caps the number of occupants a dwelling may house, based on floor area:

Floor Area. Every dwelling unit shall have at least one room which shall have not less than 120 square feet of floor area. Other habitable rooms, except kitchens, shall have an area of not less than 70 square feet. Where more than two persons occupy a room used for sleeping purposes, the required floor area shall be increased at the rate of 50 square feet for each occupant in excess of two.

ECDC §19.10.000.

This space and occupancy standard is a prototypical maximum occupancy restriction.

Edmonds nevertheless argues that its family composition rule, ECDC §21.30.010, falls within §3607(b)(1), the FHA exemption for maximum occupancy restrictions, because the rule caps at five the number of unrelated persons allowed to occupy a single-family dwelling. But Edmonds' family composition rule surely does not answer the question: "What is the maximum number of occupants permitted to occupy a house?" So long as they are related "by genetics, adoption, or marriage," any number of people can live in a house. Ten siblings, their parents and grandparents, for example, could dwell in a house in Edmonds' single-family residential zone without offending Edmonds' family composition rule. Family living, not living space per occupant, is what ECDC §21.30.010 describes. Defining family primarily by biological and legal relationships, the provision also accommodates another group association: Five or fewer unrelated people are allowed to live together as though they were family. This accommodation is the peg on which Edmonds rests its plea for §3607(b)(1) exemption. Had the City defined a family solely by biological and legal links, §3607(b)(1) would not have been the ground on which Edmonds staked its case. It is curious reasoning indeed that converts a family values preserver into a maximum occupancy restriction once a town adds to a related persons prescription "and also two unrelated persons."

This curious reasoning drives the dissent. If Edmonds allowed only related persons (whatever their number) to dwell in a house in a single-family zone, then the dissent, it appears, would agree that the §3607(b)(1) exemption is unavailable. But so long as the City introduces a specific number—any number (two will do)—the City can insulate its single-family zone entirely from FHA coverage. The exception-takes-the-rule reading the dissent advances is hardly the "generous construction" warranted for antidiscrimination prescriptions.

Edmonds additionally contends that subjecting single-family zoning to FHA scrutiny will "overturn Euclidian zoning" and "destroy the effectiveness and purpose of single-family zoning." This contention both ignores the limited scope of the issue before us and exaggerates the force of the FHA's antidiscrimination provisions. We address only whether Edmonds' family composition rule qualifies for §3607(b)(1) exemption. Moreover, the FHA antidiscrimination provisions, when applicable, require only "reasonable" accommodations to afford persons with handicaps "equal opportunity to use and enjoy" housing.

The parties have presented, and we have decided, only a threshold question: Edmonds' zoning code provision describing who may compose a "family" is not a maximum occupancy restriction exempt from the FHA under §3607(b)(1). It remains for the lower courts to decide whether Edmonds' actions against Oxford House violate the FHA's prohibitions against discrimination set out in §§3604(f)(1)(A) and (f)(3)(B).

For the reasons stated, the judgment is affirmed.

DISSENTING OPINION

Scalia, Thomas, and Kennedy, Justices. Consider a real estate agent who is assigned responsibility for the city of Edmonds. Desiring to learn all he can about his new territory, the agent inquires: "Does the city have any restrictions regarding the maximum number of occupants permitted to occupy a dwelling?" The accurate answer must surely be in the affirmative—yes, the maximum number of unrelated persons permitted to occupy a dwelling in a single-family neighborhood is five. Or consider a different example. Assume that the Federal Republic of Germany imposes no restrictions on the speed of "cars" that drive on the Autobahn but does cap the speed of "trucks" (which are defined as all other vehicles). If a conscientious visitor to Germany asks whether there are "any restrictions regarding the maximum speed of motor vehicles permitted to drive on the Autobahn," the accurate answer again is surely the affirmative one—yes, there is a restriction regarding the maximum speed of trucks on the Autobahn.

The majority does not ask whether petitioner's zoning code imposes any restrictions regarding the maximum number of occupants permitted to occupy a dwelling. Instead, observing that pursuant to ECDC §21.30.010, "any number of people can live in a house," so long as they are "related 'by genetics, adoption, or marriage,'" the majority concludes that §21.30.010 does not qualify for §3607(b)(1)'s exemption because it "surely does not answer the question: 'What is the maximum number of occupants permitted to occupy a house?'..."The majority's question, however, does not accord with the text of the statute. To take advantage of the exemption, a local, state, or federal law need not impose a restriction establishing an absolute maximum number of occupants; under §3607(b)(1), it is necessary only that such law impose a restriction "regarding" the maximum number of occupants. Surely, a restriction can "regar[d]"—or "concern," "relate to," or "bear on"—the maximum number of occupants without establishing an absolute maximum number in all cases.

CASE QUESTIONS

1. What is the nature of the group home in this case?
2. What federal and local laws are in conflict?
3. What must the local law do to avoid conflict with the federal law?
4. What is the dissent's point?
5. What would you say is the rule for group homes and zoning?

CONSIDER 18.4

Harry Eichlin appealed the decision of a New Hope Borough Zoning and Hearing Board decision to grant a zoning permit to Buck Villa, Inc. (BVI), for use of a single-family dwelling as a group home for eight unrelated HIV-infected persons. Section 218(3) of the Ordinance defines the term "family" to include:

A home for no more than eight unrelated persons which is sponsored and operated by a non-profit group, organization, or corporation for a group of persons to live together in a single communal living arrangement where the residents permanently live together as the functional equivalent of a traditional family in a non-profit dwelling unit maintaining a non-transient common household with single cooking and dining facilities and sharing a permanent unity of social life. This shall be referred to as a "family group home". Groups contemplated by this use include, but are not limited to, the handicapped, the elderly, and the disabled, but excludes halfway houses for ex-convicts and for drug or alcohol rehabilitation, or for licensed personal care homes or any other use specifically provided for in this Ordinance. A family group home may have no more than two residential managers living at the home in addition to the residents. Residential managers are agents or employees of the agency or organization sponsoring and operating the group home.

CONSIDER 18.4

(continued)

New Hope Borough Zoning Ordinance No. 1933-2, art. 1 §1(3)

Applying the *Edmonds* case, determine whether the ordinance is valid and whether the group home can remain. *Eichlin v. Zoning Hearing Board of New Hope Borough*, 671 A.2d 1173 (Comm. Ct. Pa. 1996)

Zoning as a Taking

Many who have had their permissible land uses restricted by zoning have raised the issue of whether such regulation constitutes a "taking" under the United States Constitution's Fifth Amendment, which would require that they be compensated for the loss in value of their land. (See Chapter 19 for additional details on eminent domain and just compensation.) One **takings issue** that has been the focus of litigation relates to restrictions on beachfront and **wetlands** development. In the following landmark case, the United States Supreme Court faced the issue of a "taking" because of development restrictions on wetlands.

LUCAS V. SOUTH CAROLINA COASTAL COUNCIL

505 U.S. 1003 (1992)

FACTS

In 1986, David H. Lucas (petitioner) paid $975,000 for two residential lots on the Isle of Palms in Charleston County, South Carolina. Lucas intended to build single-family homes on the lots. In 1988, South Carolina's legislature enacted the Beachfront Management Act. The effect of the act was to prohibit Lucas from erecting any permanent habitable structures on his two lots. Lucas filed suit challenging the legislation as a taking under the Fifth and Fourteenth Amendment, which requires that he be compensated. The trial court found that the law rendered Lucas' land valueless. The South Carolina Supreme Court reversed, and Lucas appealed.

JUDICIAL OPINION

Scalia, Justice. Prior to Justice Holmes' exposition in *Pennsylvania Coal Co. v. Mahon*, 260 U.S. 393, 43 S.Ct. 158, 67 L.Ed. 322 (1922), it was generally thought that the Takings Clause reached only a "direct appropriation" of property.

Justice Holmes recognized in *Mahon*, however, that if the protection against physical appropriations of private property was to be meaningfully enforced, the government's power to redefine the range of interests included in the ownership of property was necessarily constrained by constitutional limits. If, instead, the uses of private property were subject to unbridled, uncompensated qualification under the police power, "the natural tendency of human nature [would be] to extend the qualification more and more until at last private property disappear[ed]." These considerations gave birth in that case to the oft-cited maxim that, "while property may be regulated to a certain extent, if regulation goes too far it will be recognized as a taking."

We have, however, described at least two discrete categories of regulatory action as compensable without case-specific inquiry into the public interest advanced in support of the restraint. The first encompasses regulations that compel the property owner to suffer a physical "invasion" of his property. In general (at least with regard to permanent invasions), no matter how minute the intrusion, and no matter how weighty the public purpose behind it, we have required compensation. For example, in *Loretto v. Teleprompter Manhattan CATV Corp.*, 458 U.S. 419, 102 S.Ct. 3164, 73 L.Ed.2d 868 (1982), we determined that New York's law requiring landlords to allow television cable companies to emplace cable facilities in their apartment buildings constituted a taking, even though the facilities occupied at most only 1½ cubic feet of the landlords' property.

The second situation in which we have found categorical treatment appropriate is where regulation denies all economically beneficial or productive use of land.

As we have said on numerous occasions, the Fifth Amendment is violated when land-use regulation "does not substantially advance legitimate state interests *or denies an owner economically viable use of his land.*"

On the other side of the balance, affirmatively supporting a compensation requirement, is the fact that regulations that leave the owner of land without economically beneficial or productive options for its use—typically, as here, by requiring land to be left substantially in its natural state—carry with them a heightened risk that private property is being pressed into some form of public service under the guise of mitigating serious public harm.

We think, in short, that there are good reasons for our frequently expressed belief that when the owner of real property has been called upon to sacrifice *all* economically beneficial uses in the name of the common good, that is, to leave his property economically idle, he has suffered a taking.

Under Lucas's theory of the case, which rested upon our "no economically viable use" statements, that finding entitled him to compensation. Lucas believed it unnecessary to take issue with either the purposes behind the *Beachfront Management Act*, or the means chosen by the South Carolina Legislature to effectuate those purposes. The South Carolina Supreme Court, however, thought otherwise. In its view, the *Beachfront Management Act* was no ordinary enactment, but involved an exercise of South Carolina's "police powers" to mitigate the harm to the public interest that petitioner's use of his land might occasion. By neglecting to dispute the findings enumerated in the Act or otherwise to challenge the legislature's purposes, petitioner "concede[d] that the beach/dune area of South Carolina's shores is an extremely valuable public resource; that the erection of new construction, *inter alia*, contributes to the erosion and destruction of this public resource; and that discouraging new construction in close proximity to the beach/dune area is necessary to prevent a great public harm."

It is correct that many of our prior opinions have suggested that "harmful or noxious uses" of property may be proscribed by government regulation without the requirement of compensation. For a number of reasons, however, we think the South Carolina Supreme Court was too quick to conclude that that principle decides the present case.

("[T]he problem [in this area] is not one of noxiousness or harm-creating activity at all; rather it is a problem of inconsistency between perfectly innocent and independently desirable uses"). Whether Lucas's construction of single-family residences on his parcels should be described as bringing "harm" to South Carolina's adjacent ecological resources thus depends principally upon whether the describer believes that the State's use interest in nurturing those resources is so important that *any* competing adjacent use must yield.

When it is understood that "prevention of harmful use" was merely our early formulation of the police power justification necessary to sustain (without compensation) *any* regulatory diminution in value; and that the distinction between regulation that "prevents harmful use" and that which "confers benefits" is difficult, if not impossible, to discern on an objective, value-free basis; it becomes self-evident that noxious-use logic cannot serve as a touchstone to distinguish regulatory "takings"—which require compensation—from regulatory deprivations that do not require compensation. *A fortiori* the legislature's recitation of a noxious-use justification cannot be the basis for departing from our categorical rule that total regulatory takings must be compensated. If it were, departure would virtually always be allowed.

Where the State seeks to sustain regulation that deprives land of all economically beneficial use, we think it may resist compensation only if the logically antecedent inquiry into the nature of the owner's estate shows that the proscribed use interests were not part of his title to begin with. This accords, we think, with our "takings" jurisprudence, which has traditionally been guided by the understandings of our citizens regarding the content of, and the State's power over, the "bundle of rights" that they acquire when they obtain title to property. It seems to us that the property owner necessarily expects the uses of his property to be restricted, from time to time, by various measures newly enacted by the State in legitimate exercise of its police powers; "[a]s long recognized, some values are enjoyed under an implied limitation and must yield to the police power."

In the case of land, however, we think the notion pressed by the Council that title is somehow held subject to the "implied limitation" that the State may subsequently eliminate all economically valuable use is inconsistent with the historical compact recorded in the Takings Clause that has become part of our constitutional culture.

On this analysis, the owner of a lake bed, for example, would not be entitled to compensation when he is denied the requisite permit to engage in a landfilling operation that would have the effect of flooding others' land. Nor the corporate owner of a nuclear generating plant, when it is directed to remove all improvements from its land upon discovery that the plant sits astride an earthquake fault. Such regulatory action may well have the effect of eliminating the land's only economically productive use, but it does not proscribe a productive use that was previously permissible under relevant property and nuisance principles.

As we have said, a "State, by *ipse dixit*, may not transform private property into public property without compensation. . . ." *Webb's Fabulous Pharmacies, Inc. v. Beckwith*, 449 U.S. 155, 164, 101 S.Ct. 446, 452, 66 L.Ed.2d 358 (1980). Instead, as it would be required to do if it sought to restrain Lucas in a common law action for public nuisance, South Carolina must identify background principles of nuisance and property law that prohibit the uses he now intends in the circumstances in which the property is presently found. Only on this showing can the State fairly claim that, in proscribing all such beneficial uses, the *Beachfront Management Act* is taking nothing.

The judgment is reversed.

CASE QUESTIONS

1. What did Lucas purchase and for how much? When?
2. When was the law on beachfront construction passed?
3. Does South Carolina allege an important public purpose?
4. What is the distinction between this case and one in which a landowner is required to remove a business because it is a nuisance?
5. Will Lucas be able to build on his lots?
6. What implications does this case have for future wetlands development?
7. What implications does this case have for government preservation of wetlands properties?

Procedural Aspects

Adoption of Zoning Regulations

As already stated, local governments obtain their authority for zoning from an enabling act, and most states have adopted some form of the Standard State Zoning Enabling Act. This act consists of nine basic sections summarized as follows.

- *Section 1—Grant of Power*: In this section, the governmental unit is given the authority to zone on the basis of a need to preserve health, safety, morals, and the general welfare of the community.
- *Section 2—Districts*: In this section, the governmental unit is given the authority to divide its area of jurisdiction into any size, shape, and number of districts for purposes of regulating activities or structures in those districts.
- *Section 3—Purposes in View*: This section requires the governmental unit to exercise its power under Section 2 pursuant to a master plan designed to provide all areas with adequate safety protection, schools, water, sewage, parks, and all other amenities.
- *Section 4—Method of Procedures*: In this section, the governmental unit is authorized to establish procedures for adopting and amending zoning regulations.
- *Section 5—Changes*: This section specifies that changes in zoning may be made but can be stopped if 20 percent or more of the owners of lots in the area in question oppose the change. The 20 percent may also include those who own lots within a certain distance of the area subject to the change. The distance (in feet) is left blank, to be determined by the adopting governmental unit.
- *Section 6—Zoning Commission*: This section establishes the right of the governmental unit to appoint a **zoning commission** to set up the original zoning plan on the basis of studies of the area.
- *Section 7—Board of Adjustment*: The purpose of this section is to allow the local governments to set up a **board of adjustment** that can, in cases and circumstances they deem appropriate, make exceptions to the zoning regulations in particular areas, so long as the exceptions are in keeping with the idea of the master plan and basic district division. These exceptions are called **variances** under the act.

Practical Tip

Over the past few years, many wetlands cases have been brought challenging developmental restrictions. Property purchasers considering coastal property should check not only local zoning, but state and federal restrictions as well prior to purchasing.

- *Section 8—Enforcement*: In this section, the local governmental body is authorized to call zoning violations misdemeanors and to provide for penalties of either fines or imprisonment. Also, the local governmental body is authorized to bring suit to stop construction or use of property that is in violation of the zoning regulations; in other words, to seek an injunction for violative activity.
- *Section 9—Conflicts*: This section serves to clarify which set of laws will govern in the event two governmental units have established zoning for the same area; for example, if a county has adopted zoning for the county, but the cities within the county have adopted their own zoning ordinances. This section provides that city ordinances will be controlling to the extent they are more strict than the county ordinances.

Today, although the Standard State Zoning Enabling Act is still the law in the majority of states, it provokes some dissatisfaction. The American Law Institute has drafted a Model Land Development Code that some states have adopted as a supplement. Although there may be slight variations, zoning control must meet the basic requirements and follow basic procedures to guarantee due process.

Exceptions from Zoning Regulations

Section 7 of the Standard State Zoning Enabling Act provides for a board of adjustment that can grant exceptions or variances for uses that differ from assigned zoning. An application for a variance must show two things:

1. That an undue hardship results if the ordinance is enforced
2. That the granting of the variance will not be excessively disruptive of the surrounding land or the master plan

Factors considered by boards in granting variances include the effect of the use on surrounding land, the benefit to the public of the varied use, whether the property is different in its surface character from other property in the district, whether loss results without the variance, and whether the master plan's purposes would be defeated through the grant of the variance.

One of the most frequently approved variances involves an exception to building-height restrictions. It may be economically beneficial to the community and not a burden on surrounding property to permit a large business to build a multistory building in a single-story zoned district.

Another exception to a zoned use is **special permit**. A special permit allows an exception for the construction of a church or school in a residential area provided certain restrictions or conditions are met. A variance or special permit is, more or less, a matter of opinion.

If a variance or special permit is denied, there is a right of judicial review on the grounds of abuse of discretion, constitutionality, or arbitrariness. Figure 18.1 (on page 541) summarizes the procedural aspects of zoning.

Nonconforming Uses

A **nonconforming use** is a grandfather clause protection in zoning. A zoning ordinance now prohibits a use that already existed. An example would be a store or business operating in an area that has just been zoned residential. Because of *ex post facto* issues, these grandfathered uses remain (although see Chapter 19 for more discussion of economic development and takings issues).

Figure 18.1 Zoning Process

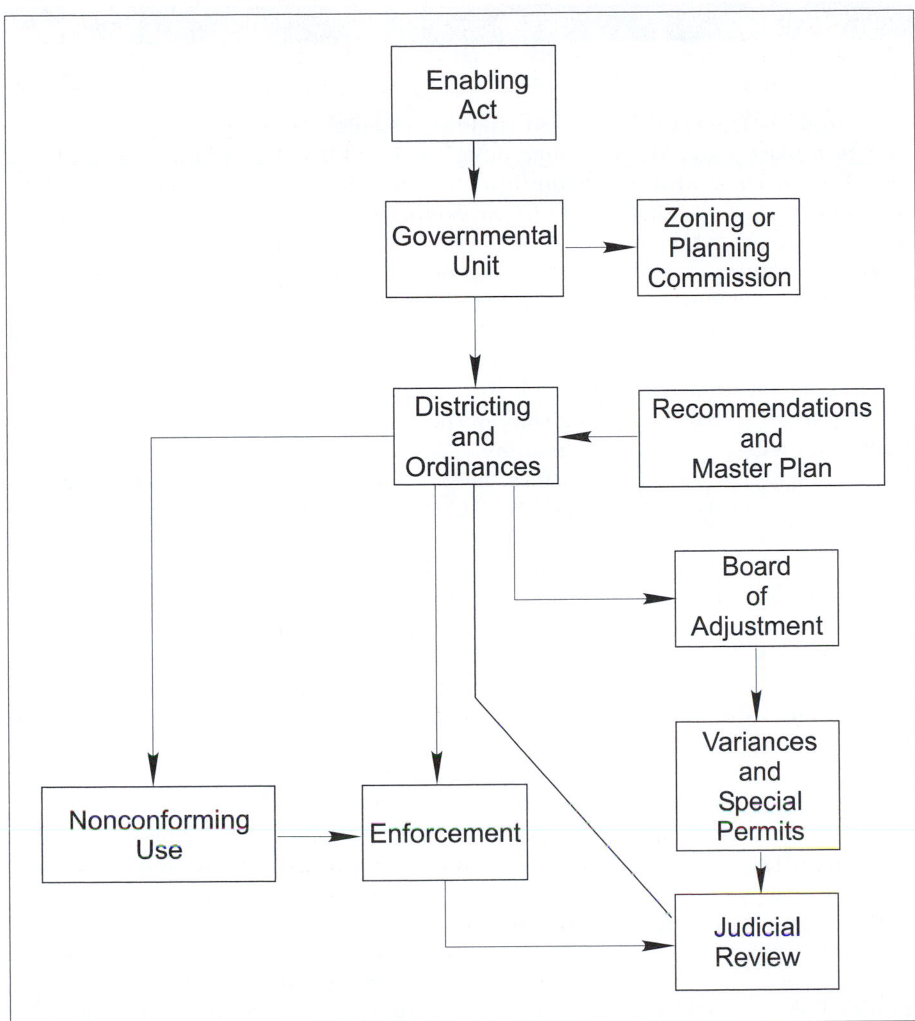

For a nonconforming use to be immune from zoning, it must be in existence at the time the zoning is passed. Furthermore, the nonconforming use cannot be expanded beyond the use at the time the zoning was passed.

A right to nonconforming use can be lost if the nonconforming activity is abandoned or if the nonconforming building is destroyed by fire or natural events. The zoning ordinances specify a time period for abandonment as well as what constitutes destruction for purposes of ending a nonconforming use.

Recently, many local governments, in an effort to carry out their community planning objectives, have sought to eliminate nonconforming uses over time and have passed ordinances that require amortization of nonconforming uses. These amortization sections require nonconforming uses to be eliminated over a specified period—usually five years. Amortization periods allow landowners some time to convert their property to appropriately zoned activities or buildings. The following case deals with an issue of a continuing nonconforming use.

MONEY V. ZONING HEARING BOARD OF HAVERFORD TOWNSHIP

755 A.2d 732 (Pa. 2000)

FACTS

David Money (landowner) applied to Haverford Township for a building permit to replace a deteriorated, nonconforming garage/chicken coop with a nonconforming garage that took up less space but that was a larger garage than the current size limits for his property's zoning. Mr. Money petitioned to be allowed to build the garage larger than existing maximums as the replacement of an existing nonconforming use with another nonconforming use.

The Township denied his application and Mr. Money appealed to the Zoning and Hearing Board (ZHB). The ZHB denied his appeal. Mr. Money appealed.

JUDICIAL OPINION

Friedman, Judge. In his appeal to this court, Landowner contends that the ZHB committed an abuse of discretion and an error of law when it denied Landowner a building permit because the area of Landowner's proposed garage exceeds the maximum permitted by section 182-7111. B(2) of the Zoning Ordinance. Specifically, Landowner claims that the ZHB erred in rejecting Landowner's argument that he is entitled to erect the proposed garage as a continuation of a nonconforming use—i.e., the replacement of a lawful nonconforming structure. Landowner also asserts that the trial court erred in relying upon the proposition that the replacement of "one nonconforming structure with another nonconforming structure" is prohibited.

We agree.

Here, the sole issue is whether Landowner abandoned the nonconforming use. The Township contends that Landowner abandoned the nonconforming use by allowing the old garage/chicken coop to fall into a state of disrepair. The Township argues that the dilapidated condition of the garage/chicken coop prevented the structure from being used as a garage for a substantial period of time and supports the conclusion that the use was abandoned.

As the party claiming the abandonment, the Township bears the burden of proving that Landowner abandoned the nonconforming use. To sustain its burden of proof, the Township must show that (1) Landowner intended to abandon the nonconforming use and (2) Landowner actually abandoned the use consonant with his intention. Here, the Township has failed to meet its burden of proving either Landowner's intent to abandon or actual abandonment.

[A] landowner's failure to use property for a period of time designated by a zoning ordinance is evidence of the intention to abandon. Here, section 182-802. C(1) of the Zoning Ordinance provides, "If a nonconforming use of land or building ceases operations for a continuous period of more than six (6) months, then this shall be deemed to be an intent to abandon such use, and any subsequent use of land shall conform to the regulations of this chapter." The effect of this ordinance is to create a presumption in favor of an intent to abandon where a use is discontinued for more than six months.

Here, however, the Township did not prove that Landowner had failed to use the old garage/chicken coop for more than six months before he applied for the building permit. Indeed, the evidence is to the contrary. At the hearing, Landowner testified that he used the dilapidated garage/chicken coop to store a car, "some wood and...couple of cases of...coffee mugs." The ZHB did not reject or discredit that testimony; nor did any evidence contradict Landowner's testimony in that regard.

However, we acknowledge that, even where a landowner has used the building within the prior designated time period, structural alterations to a building that are inconsistent with continuance of the nonconforming use may establish both intent to abandon and actual abandonment.

Here, Landowner proposes to replace the old garage/chicken coop with a similar structure—a garage. Because both structures are nonconforming as to area, it cannot be said that Landowner is abandoning the nonconforming use by building the new garage. Landowner's proposed replacement garage is a continuation, not an abandonment, of a nonconforming use.

Courts have permitted landowners to demolish nonconforming structures and replace them with new nonconforming structures.

Reversed.

CASE QUESTIONS

1. What was the extent of Mr. Money's use of his existing garage/chicken coop?

2. Had Mr. Money abandoned the use of the garage/chicken coop?

3. Is the new garage a change or a continuation?

Some courts have even declared certain nonconforming uses to be nuisances and have had them eliminated by legal action for nuisance. Through the litigation by surrounding landowners, nonconforming use can be eliminated by court injunction. For example, a smelting plant in a residential area could easily be enjoined as a nuisance and the problem of nonconforming use eliminated.

ETHICAL ISSUE

Ralph Horowitz owned land in the Los Angeles area that had been zoned for manufacturing and warehousing. When he acquired the land, it had not been used for those purposes since 1992, when about 350 local residents had begun a communal garden there. The garden, complete with fruit-bearing trees, had been praised by the Los Angeles mayor as a wonderful community touch among the industrial plants and warehouses. Among the gardeners and their supporters were Danny Glover, Laura Dern, Joan Baez, and Daryl Hannah. Mr. Horowitz had to seek judicial help to get the gardeners removed from his property. He even had the sheriff postpone their removal until they could harvest their seasonal gardens. Ms. Hannah sat in one of the garden trees for days to resist the execution of the court order for removal. Ms. Hannah was removed from a tree by police, who had to employ the help of a fire truck ladder from one of the nearby stations. Ms. Hannah, upon her removal, made the following statement to the media, "I'm very confident this is the morally right thing to do, to take a principled stand in solidarity with the farmers." Some violence broke out as police removed other protestors who had chained themselves to a walnut tree in the garden. The gardeners said they wanted Mr. Horowitz to commit the land to an urban garden.

What are their rights? What are Mr. Horowitz's rights? Evaluate the ethics on both sides of the use of the land.

Cautions and Conclusions

From the information and cases in this chapter, it is not difficult to see that the issue of zoning can be controlling in the value of property and is certainly controlling in the use to be made of property. Before purchasing land or beginning construction, make a zoning check. In addition, check surrounding tracts and plats to see the effects of growth and expansion and also the resulting effect on property values. Finally, evaluate the master plan to determine any future problems and possible changes or variances that might affect the land's value. When it comes to the issue of zoning, there can never be enough research.

Key Terms

aesthetic zoning, 522
board of adjustment, 535
cumulative classification, 518
exclusionary zoning, 527
general plan, 517
hold zoning, 528
intensity zoning, 521
interim zoning, 528
master plan, 517
nonconforming use, 536
noncumulative classification, 519
social issue zoning, 528
special permit, 536
Standard State Zoning Enabling Act, 517
takings issues, 533
variances, 535
wetlands, 533
zoning, 517
zoning commission, 535

Chapter Problems

1. The city of Philadelphia's Department of Licensing and Inspections denied Midnight Sessions, Ltd., a permit for the operation of an exotic dance club because of a history of disturbances and crime when such dance clubs operated. The city, through police department records, was able to establish that there was an increase in noise, trash, drug activity, loitering, and public urination in every area where an exotic dance club was given a permit for operation. In addition, the clubs attracted between 3,000 and 5,000 patrons on weekend event nights, and after the show many of those patrons roamed the surrounding neighborhoods in a state of drunkenness. Could the city prohibit the clubs altogether? *Midnight Sessions, Ltd. v. City of Philadelphia*, 945 F.2d 667 (3rd Cir. 1991)

2. New Orleans passed an ordinance governing its historic Vieux Carré section that detailed the types of structures and permissible repairs, maintenance, and alterations in the area. The ordinance has been challenged on the grounds that it exceeds the police power. What is the result?

3. Marina Limited Partners applied for a zoning variance to relocate part of their 700-slip marina to a new marina to be constructed at another location on the Geist Reservoir in Hamilton County, Indiana. Marina would move 300 of its slips to the new marina. The construction of the new marina required approval of a variance by the Board of Zoning Appeals for the city of Noblesville. At the hearing, John Allen and others who owned property in the area appeared and objected to the marina's construction. They presented evidence that construction of the marina would lower their property values. There was additional evidence regarding noise, traffic, smoke, fumes, and odors. The board's staff recommended approval, but the board denied the variance. Marina Partners filed suit alleging the finding was arbitrary. Are they correct? *Allen v. Board of Zoning Appeals for the City of Noblesville*, 594 N.E.2d 480 (Ind. 1992)

4. The Township of Brady has zoning restrictions on the number of animals that can be kept on properties in certain areas. More pigs are permitted per acre than cows. A farmer has brought suit alleging that the zoning restriction is arbitrary and not based on a public welfare basis. Township officials say that pig waste does not smell as much as cow waste and hence they permit more pigs than cows. Is the zoning restriction valid? *Richardson v. Township of Brady*, 218 F.3d 508 (6th Cir. 2000)

5. The Madison County Livestock and Fair Association owns a tract of land that has been used as the location for county fairs. The tract is now located in an area in which zoning changes prohibited such uses. The use of the tract as a fairgrounds has been a nonconforming use. The Association filed for a permit to build a race track on the tract. Neighbors objected because they said that such a proposed use could not be grandfathered in under the nonconforming use. Are they correct? *Perkins v. Madison County Livestock & Fair, Ass'n.*, 613 N.W.2d 264 (Iowa 2000)

6. The city of St. Louis passed an ordinance that required all for-sale signs posted on properties within the city to include an indication of the zoning for the property. Green failed to place the zoning on the sign for one of his listed properties and was convicted of a misdemeanor. Green appealed the conviction on the grounds that the ordinance was an excessive exercise of power by the city. What was the result?

7. Stanley Carpenter owns a 92-acre parcel of land in a rural area of Petal, Mississippi. Mr. Carpenter wanted to put a mobile home on a small area of the property located near the road and protected from view by mature trees. Mr. Carpenter would then have his son living there.

Mr. Carpenter's property is located in an RF District, a zoning classification that permits agriculture, farming, forestry, livestock production, nurseries, truck gardens, public or commercial stables and kennels, poultry, livestock and small animal raising; single-family dwellings, two-family dwellings, and accessory uses including home occupations and signs.

Ordinance 1979 (42-A-70) prohibited placement of mobile home units outside of approved mobile home parks:

The purpose of this Section is for the establishment of areas within Petal, Mississippi, for the development and expansion of mobile home parks. These mobile home parks shall be developed and located so as to provide safe and sanitary living conditions for the occupants and to be convenient to employment, shopping centers, schools and other community facilities, and to prohibit Single Mobile Home Units from being used and utilized within the City Limits unless placement is in an approved Mobile Home Park, as described in this ordinance.

The Board of Aldermen unanimously denied Mr. Carpenter's position. Mr. Carpenter appealed and the circuit court affirmed the Aldermen's decision. Mr. Carpenter appealed. How should the court decide the case? *Petition of Carpenter*, 699 So.2d 928 (Miss. 1997)

8. The Stoyanoffs sought to build a home of an ultramodern design in Ladue, Missouri. The home was to be built in a neighborhood in which all of the homes were of two-story conventional architectural design such as Colonial, French, or English.

The city of Ladue has a zoning ordinance that requires that a proposed structure conform to certain minimum architectural standards of appearance and conformity with surrounding structures, and that unsightly, grotesque, and unsuitable structures, detrimental to the stability of value and the welfare of surrounding property, structures, and residents, and to the general welfare and happiness of the community, be avoided, and that appropriate standards of beauty and conformity be fostered and encouraged.

Can the city stop construction of the Stoyanoff home? *State of Missouri Ex Rel. Stoyanoff v. Ladue*, 458 S.W.2d 305 (Mo. 1970)

9. Bernard Smookler and his wife purchased a 123-acre tract of land at the intersection of Jolly and Meridian Roads in Wheatfield Township in 1968. Ninety acres were used for agriculture, and 1.5 acres were rented to a tenant for residential use. Two years later, they requested a zoning change from rural agricultural to mobile home park with a 300-foot strip for commercial zoning. The planned mobile home park would be called Wheatfield Acres Mobile Home Park, would include five units per acre, and would have 535 total units.

The 1970 census put the population of Wheatfield Township at 1,117 with 325 housing units. There is no master plan for the township, which is 36 square miles with 18,297 acres and only about 5 percent developed. Three residential areas are in the township, with most of them located in the northern part. The proposed park would be in the northwest section. At the time of the application, Wheatfield had one commercial development: a gas station along Interstate 96. The township had no police or fire department and relied on the adjoining cities, counties, and the state for such services. There are no mobile home parks in the township and nothing that could be characterized as low-cost housing, but there has been some discussion of creating mobile home parks.

The Zoning and Planning Commission denied the Smooklers' application, stating that the area would be better for residential use, there would be an added burden to police and fire services, and to the schools, and no benefit to the surrounding community.

The Smooklers appealed the commission's decision to the trial court. There the Smooklers and the commission stipulated that there would be no traffic problem nor any problems with the sanitary or sewage systems. The Smooklers alleged at the trial court that the decision of the commission was evidence of a preconceived scheme to eliminate or prohibit mobile home parks. Can zoning be used in this way to control population growth? *Smookler v. Township of Wheatfield*, 232 N.W.2d 616 (Mich. 1975)

10. The Houghtalings are the owners of a travel business known as "Pleasure Cruises." Pleasure Cruises is operated out of the Houghtalings' home on East Liberty Street in Medina, Ohio. Mr. Houghtaling had installed a metal replica of an anchor on the lawn of their home in 1997. The anchor is seven and one-half feet in height and the crossbar is six feet long. Two lights were added to the ends of the crossbar a few months later.

In May 1997, the Medina City Planning Director, Richard Grice, sent a letter asking the Houghtalings to remove the anchor. The letter stated that the anchor violated City Zoning Code 1113.07.

The Houghtalings appealed Grice's decision to the board. The board ordered the sign removed. Lower courts found for the Houghtalings and the board appealed. How should the court decide the case? *Houghtaling v. City of Medina Board of Zoning Appeals*, 731 N.E.2d 733 (Ohio App. 1999)

For research activities related to this chapter, go to our text companion website at www.thomsonedu.com/westbuslaw/jennings.

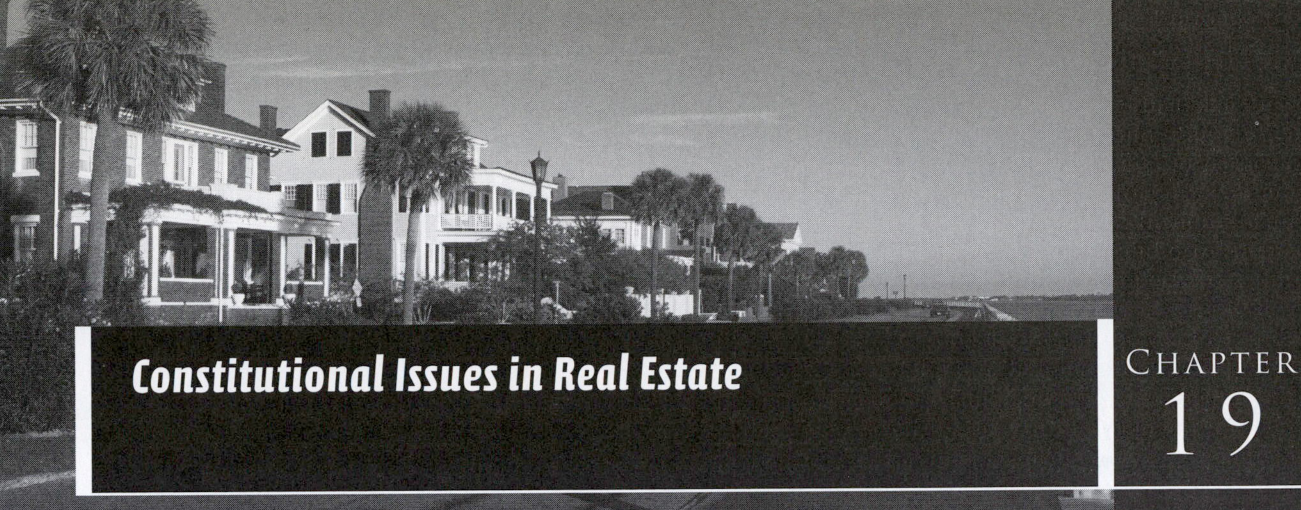

Constitutional Issues in Real Estate

CHAPTER 19

Supreme Court Justice Sandra O'Connor is stepping down. She didn't want to resign—she just wants to make sure she's home so nobody can seize her house.[1]

Jay Leno's comment in his monologue after the U.S. Supreme Court issued its eminent domain decision in *Kelo v. City of New London*

Owning and transferring title to real property also includes certain constitutional rights that entitle property owners to certain guarantees with regard to their property ownership. This chapter discusses the constitutional protections for real property owners and purchasers.

Land Title and Constitutional Issues–Eminent Domain

The right of a governmental body to take title to property for a public use is called **eminent domain**. This right is found in the Fifth Amendment to the Constitution as well as in certain state constitutions. Private individuals cannot require property owners to sell their property, but governmental entities can require them to transfer title for public projects for the public good. The Fifth Amendment provides that "property shall not be taken for a public use without just compensation." A governmental entity can exercise eminent domain only when three standards come together: the taking is for a public purpose, there is a taking (as opposed to use regulation), and the owner is given just compensation.

Public Purpose

Eminent domain requires proof of a government purpose. "Public purpose" brings to mind taking land for highways and schools. However, government purposes for

1. "Notable and Quotable," *Time*, July 18, 2005, p. 21.

eminent domain extend much further. The following uses are considered public purposes: the condemnation of slum housing (for purposes of improving city areas), the limitation of mining and excavation within city limits, the declaration of property as a historic landmark, and economic development. That last purpose has created a firestorm of judicial, legislative, and public controversy over the last few years. The following case was the U.S. Supreme Court decision that changed the eminent domain landscape, as it were.

Kelo v. City of New London

545 U.S. 469 (2005)

FACTS

In 1978, the city of New London, Connecticut, undertook a redevelopment plan for purposes of creating a redeveloped area in and around the existing park at Fort Trumball. The plan had the goals of achieving all the related ambience a state park should have, including the absence of pink cottages and other architecturally eclectic homes. Part of the redevelopment plan was the city's deal with Pfizer Corporation for the location of its research facility in the area. The preface to the city's development plan included the following statement of goals and purpose:

to create a development that would complement the facility that Pfizer was planning to build, create jobs, increase tax and other revenues, encourage public access to and use of the city's waterfront, and eventually "build momentum" for the revitalization of the rest of the city, including its downtown area.

The redevelopment plan included detailed and extensive documentation on its socioeconomic impact. The affected property owners, including Susette Kelo, live in homes and cottages (15 total) located in and around other existing structures that will be permitted to stay in the area for the proposed new structures that will consist of primarily private land developers and corporations. In fact, the city was assisted by a private, nonprofit corporation, the New London Development Corporation (NLDC), in the development of the economic plan and the ferrying of it through the various governmental processes, including that of city council approval. The city council created the NLDC. The central focus of the plan was attracting Pfizer to the Fort Trumbull area (where the homeowners and their properties were located) with the hope of the economic boost and benefits a major corporate employer can bring to an area.

Kelo and the other landowners whose homes would be razed to make room for Pfizer and the accompanying and resulting economic development plan filed suit challenging New London's legal authority to take their homes. The trial court issued an injunction preventing New London from taking certain of the properties but allowing others to be taken. Following an injunction, the property owners who were denied relief appealed and the city cross-appealed. On appeal, the landowners were held subject to eminent domains.

The appellate court found for New London on all the claims, and the landowners (petitioners) appealed.

JUDICIAL OPINION

Stevens, Justice. Two polar propositions are perfectly clear. On the one hand, it has long been accepted that the sovereign may not take the property of A for the sole purpose of transferring it to another private party B, even though A is paid just compensation. On the other hand, it is equally clear that a State may transfer property from one private party to another if future "use by the public" is the purpose of the taking; the condemnation of land for a railroad with common-carrier duties is a familiar example. Neither of these propositions, however, determines the disposition of this case.

As for the first proposition, the City would no doubt be forbidden from taking petitioners' land for the purpose of conferring a private benefit on a particular private party. Nor would the City be allowed to take property under the mere pretext of a public purpose, when its actual purpose was to bestow a private benefit. The takings before us, however, would be executed pursuant to a "carefully considered" development plan.

The disposition of this case therefore turns on the question whether the City's development plan serves a "public purpose." Without exception, our cases have defined that concept broadly, reflecting our longstanding policy of deference to legislative judgments in this field.

In *Berman v. Parker*, 348 U.S. 26, 75 S.Ct. 98, 99 L.Ed. 27 (1954), this Court upheld a redevelopment plan targeting a blighted area of Washington, D.C., in which most of the housing for the area's 5,000 inhabitants was beyond repair. Under the plan, the area would be condemned and part of it utilized for the construction of streets, schools, and other public facilities. The remainder of the land would be leased or sold to private parties for the purpose of redevelopment, including the construction of low-cost housing.

The owner of a department store located in the area challenged the condemnation, pointing out that his store was not itself blighted and arguing that the creation of a "better balanced, more attractive community" was not a valid public use. Writing for a unanimous Court, Justice Douglas refused to evaluate this claim in isolation, deferring instead to the legislative and agency judgment that the area "must be planned as a whole" for the plan to be successful. The Court explained that "community redevelopment programs need not, by force of the Constitution, be on a piecemeal basis—lot by lot, building by building."

"We do not sit to determine whether a particular housing project is or is not desirable. The concept of the public welfare is broad and inclusive.... The values it represents are spiritual as well as physical, aesthetic as well as monetary. It is within the power of the legislature to determine that the community should be beautiful as well as healthy, spacious as well as clean, well-balanced as well as carefully patrolled. If those who govern the District of Columbia decide that the Nation's Capital should be beautiful as well as sanitary, there is nothing in the Fifth Amendment that stands in the way."

Those who govern the City were not confronted with the need to remove blight in the Fort Trumbull area, but their determination that the area was sufficiently distressed to justify a program of economic rejuvenation is entitled to our deference. The City has carefully formulated an economic development plan that it believes will provide appreciable benefits to the community, including—but by no means limited to—new jobs and increased tax revenue. As with other exercises in urban planning and development, the City is endeavoring to coordinate a variety of commercial, residential, and recreational uses of land, with the hope that they will form a whole greater than the sum of its parts. To effectuate this plan, the City has invoked a state statute that specifically authorizes the use of eminent domain to promote economic development. Given the comprehensive character of the plan, the thorough deliberation that preceded its adoption, and the limited scope of our review, it is appropriate for us to resolve the challenges of the individual owners, not on a piecemeal basis, but rather in light of the entire plan. Because that plan unquestionably serves a public purpose, the takings challenged here satisfy the public use requirement of the Fifth Amendment.

[P]etitioners urge us to adopt a new bright-line rule that economic development does not qualify as a public use. Putting aside the unpersuasive suggestion that the City's plan will provide only purely economic benefits, neither precedent nor logic supports petitioners' proposal. Promoting economic development is a traditional and long accepted function of government. There is, moreover, no principled way of distinguishing economic development from the other public purposes that we have recognized. In our cases upholding takings that facilitated agriculture and mining, for example, we emphasized the importance of those industries to the welfare of the States in question. It would be incongruous to hold that the City's interest in the economic benefits to be derived from the development of the Fort Trumbull area has less of a public character than any of those other interests. Clearly, there is no basis for exempting economic development from our traditionally broad understanding of public purpose.

Petitioners contend that using eminent domain for economic development impermissibly blurs the boundary between public and private takings. Again, our cases foreclose this objection. "The public end may be as well or better served through an agency of private enterprise than through a department of government—or so the Congress might conclude. We cannot say that public ownership is the sole method of promoting the public purposes of community redevelopment projects." It is further argued that without a bright-line rule nothing would stop a city from transferring citizen A's property to citizen B for the sole reason that citizen B will put the property to a more productive use and thus pay more taxes. Such a one-to-one transfer of property, executed outside the confines of an integrated development plan, is not presented in this case. While such an unusual exercise of government power would certainly raise a suspicion that a private purpose was afoot, the hypothetical cases posited by petitioners can be confronted if and when they arise. They do not warrant the crafting of an artificial restriction on the concept of public use.

Just as we decline to second-guess the City's considered judgments about the efficacy of its development plan, we also decline to second-guess the City's determinations as to what lands it needs to acquire in order to effectuate the project. "It is not for the courts to oversee the choice of the boundary line nor to sit in review on the size of a particular project area. Once the question of the public purpose has been decided, the amount and character of land to be taken for the project and the need for a particular tract to complete the integrated plan rests in the discretion of the legislative branch."

The judgment of the Supreme Court of Connecticut is affirmed.

It is so ordered.

DISSENTING OPINION

O'Connor, Justice, joined by Justices Scalia, Thomas and Rehnquist. Under the banner of economic development, all private property is now vulnerable to being taken and transferred to another private owner, so long as it might be upgraded—i.e., given to an owner who will use it in a way that the legislature deems more beneficial to the public—in the process. To reason, as the Court does, that the incidental public benefits resulting from the subsequent ordinary use of private property render economic development takings "for public use" is to wash out any distinction between private and public use of property—and thereby effectively to delete the words "for public use" from the Takings Clause of the Fifth Amendment. Accordingly I respectfully dissent.

Where is the line between "public" and "private" property use? We give considerable deference to legislatures' determinations about what governmental activities will advantage the public. But were the political branches the sole arbiters of the public-private distinction, the Public Use Clause would amount to little more than hortatory fluff. An external, judicial check on how the public use requirement is interpreted, however limited, is necessary if this constraint on government power is to retain any meaning.

Even if there were a practical way to isolate the motives behind a given taking, the gesture toward a purpose test is theoretically flawed. If it is true that incidental public benefits from new private use are enough to ensure the "public purpose" in a taking, why should it matter, as far as the Fifth Amendment is concerned, what inspired the taking in the first place? How much the government does or does not desire to benefit a favored private party has no bearing on whether an economic development taking will or will not generate secondary benefit for the public. And whatever the reason for a given condemnation, the effect is the same from the constitutional perspective—private property is forcibly relinquished to new private ownership.

CASE QUESTIONS

1. What is different from this case and a case in which property is taken for a freeway?
2. What is the concern of the dissent about the decision?
3. Why does the majority state that the courts should be reluctant to get involved in local government eminent domain activities?

The impact of the *Kelo* case has been substantial. The decision unleashed new uncertainty in the minds of landowners and paved the way for legislative reforms that curb eminent domain powers at the state and local levels. Following the November 2006 general elections, nearly one-half of the states had passed ballot propositions limiting the exercise of eminent domain, adopted constitutional amendments restricting economic development eminent domain, or passed legislation with similar limitations.[2]

Taking or Regulating

A governmental entity is required to pay a landowner compensation when there has been a **taking** of the property. A taking occurs when landowner is deprived of any use of the property. In the landmark case of *Pennsylvania Coal v. Mahon*, 260 U.S. 393 (1922), the U.S. Supreme Court established standards for what constitutes a taking. A Pennsylvania statute prohibited the mining of coal under any land surface

2. Florida, Georgia, Louisiana, Michigan, New Hampshire, North Dakota, and South Carolina passed constitutional amendments. Florida, Georgia, Michigan, and New Hampshire, along with Alabama, Alaska, Colorado, Illinois, Kansas, Maine, Minnesota, Missouri, Nevada, Pennsylvania, South Dakota, Utah (had reform prior to *Kelo*), Vermont, West Virginia, Wisconsin, and Texas, passed legislation limiting eminent domain reforms. The ballot states are Oregon, California, Idaho, Washington, Montana, and Arizona. Oregon has already codified its ballot proposition. In November 2005, the U.S. House of Representatives passed "The Private Property Rights Protection Act of 2005" (also known as House Resolution 4128) by a vote of 376 to 38. The bill died in the Senate.

where the result would be the subsidence of any structure used for human habitation. The subsurface owners, the coal companies, brought suit challenging the statute as a taking without compensation. The court held that the statute was more than regulation and, in fact, was an actual taking of the subsurface property rights.

Technology has brought many new and subtly different issues in takings. In the following case, the Supreme Court dealt with technology, minimal land use, and the takings issue.

LORETTO V. TELEPROMPTER MANHATTAN CATV CORP. ET AL.

458 U.S. 419 (1982)

FACTS

A New York statute required landlords to permit cable television companies to install cable facilities on landlords' property so that tenants could subscribe to cable television services. Teleprompter Manhattan CATV (defendant/appellant) installed its equipment on the roof and side of Loretto's (plaintiff/appellant) building. The equipment was to permanently occupy Loretto's property, and Loretto was paid the usual $1 fee to which a landlord is entitled upon installation of such equipment. Loretto filed suit alleging that this minor but permanent physical occupation of her property constituted a taking under the Fifth Amendment without just compensation. The New York Court of Appeals ruled the installation did not constitute a taking, and Loretto appealed.

JUDICIAL OPINION

Marshall, Justice. The Court of Appeals ruled that the law serves a legitimate police power purpose—eliminating landlord fees and conditions that inhibit the development of CATV, which has important educational and community benefits. Rejecting the argument that a physical occupation authorized by government is necessarily a taking, the court stated that the regulation does not have an excessive economic impact upon appellant when measured against her aggregate property rights, and that it does not interfere with any reasonable investment-backed expectations. In a concurring opinion by Judge Gabrielli, it was stated that the law works a taking but concluded that the $1.00 presumptive award, together with procedures permitting a landlord to demonstrate a greater entitlement, afford just compensation.

We conclude that a permanent physical occupation authorized by government is a taking without regard to the public interests that it may serve. Our constitutional history confirms the rule, recent cases do not question it, and the purposes of the Takings Clause compel its retention.

In *United States v. Pewee Coal Co.*, 341 U.S. 114 (1951), the Court unanimously held that the Government's seizure and direction of operation of a coal mine to prevent a national strike of coal miners constituted a taking, though members of the Court differed over which losses suffered during the period of Government control were compensable. The plurality had little difficulty concluding that because there had been an "actual taking of possession and control," the taking was as clear as if the Government held full title and ownership.... In *United States v. Central Eureka Mining Co.*, 357 U.S. 155 (1958), by contrast, the Court found no taking where the Government had issued a war-time order requiring nonessential gold mines to cease operations for the purpose of conserving equipment and manpower for use in mines more essential to the war effort.... The Court reasoned that "the Government did not occupy, use, or in any manner take physical possession of the gold mines or the equipment connected with them." The Court concluded that the temporary though severe restriction on use was justified by the exigency of war.

The historical rule that a permanent physical occupation of another's property is a taking has more than tradition to commend it. Such an appropriation is perhaps the most serious form of invasion of an owner's property interests.

Constitutional protections for rights of private property cannot be made to depend on the size of the area permanently occupied.

This Court has consistently affirmed that States have broad power to regulate housing conditions in general and the landlord-tenant relationship in particular without paying just compensation for all economic injuries that such regulation entails. In none of the cases, however, did the government authorize permanent occupation of the landlord's property by a third party. Consequently, our holding today in no way alters the analysis governing the State's power to require landlords to comply with building codes and provide utility connections, mailboxes, smoke detectors, fire extinguishers, and the like in the common area of a building. So long as these regulations do not require the landlord to suffer the physical occupation of a portion of his building by a third party, they will be analyzed under the multi-factor inquiry generally applicable to nonpossessory governmental activity.

Our holding today is very narrow. We affirm the traditional rule that a permanent physical occupation of property is a taking. In such a case, the property owner entertains a historically rooted expectation of compensation, and the character of invasion is qualitatively more intrusive than perhaps any other category of property regulation.

The issue of the amount of compensation that is due... is a matter for the state courts.

Reversed.

CASE QUESTIONS

1. What regulation is at issue?
2. What form of physical occupation of property is alleged?
3. Was Loretto paid for the occupation?
4. What public purpose did the New York Court of Appeals find existed?
5. The Supreme Court cites two cases in reaching its decision—what are they? their facts? the decisions?
6. In determining whether a taking has occurred, what is the significance of physical occupation?
7. What distinction is offered between television equipment and items such as smoke alarms and fire extinguishers?
8. How much compensation will Loretto be paid?

NOLLAN V. CALIFORNIA COASTAL COMMISSION

483 U.S. 825 (1987)

FACTS

James and Marilyn Nollan own a beachfront lot in Ventura County, California. A quarter-mile north of their property is Faria Park, an oceanside public park with a public beach and recreation area. Another public beach, known as "the Cove," lies 1,800 feet south of their lot. A concrete seawall approximately eight feet high separates the beach portion of the Nollan's property from the rest of the lot.

The Nollans originally leased their property with an option to buy and had only a small bungalow (504 square feet) located on the lot. The Nollans' option to purchase was conditioned on their promise to demolish the bungalow and replace it. To do that, the Nollans had to apply for a coastal development permit from the California Coastal Commission. They filed for such a permit and proposed construction of a three-bedroom home similar to other residences in the area.

The Nollans were informed that their application was on the calendar and the staff had recommended approval provided that the Nollans allow a public easement to make it easier for the public to get to the Cove and Faria County Park.

The Nollans filed suit the Ventura County Superior Court asking them to invalidate the easement condition. The court agreed and remanded the matter to the commission for a full hearing. The commission found the new house would block the view of the beach and also inhibit the public psychologically from using the beach.

The Nollans filed another suit and said the condition constituted a taking of their property. The trial court agreed and remanded to the commission. The commission appealed, and the appellate court reversed. The Nollans appealed to the United States Supreme Court.

JUDICIAL OPINION

Scalia, Justice. Had California simply required the Nollans to make an easement across their beachfront available to the public on a permanent basis in order to increase public access to the beach, rather than conditioning their permit to rebuild their house on their agreeing to do so, we have no doubt there would have been a taking. To say that the appropriation of a public easement across a landowner's premises does not constitute the taking of a property interest but rather, "a mere restriction on its use," is to use words in a manner that deprives them of all their ordinary meaning. Indeed, one of the principal uses of the eminent domain power is to assure that the government be able to require conveyance of just such interests, so long as it pays for them. Perhaps because the point is so obvious, we have never been confronted with a controversy that required us to rule upon it, but our cases' analysis of the effect of other governmental action leads to the same conclusion. We have repeatedly held that, as to property reserved by its owner for private use, "the right to exclude [others is] one of the most essential sticks in the bundle of rights that are commonly characterized as property."

Given, then, that requiring uncompensated conveyance of the easement outright would violate the Fourteenth Amendment, the question becomes whether requiring it to be conveyed as a condition for issuing a land use permit alters the outcome. We have long recognized that land use regulation does not effect a taking if it "substantially advance[s] legitimate state interests" and does not "den[y] an owner economically viable use of his land." The parties have not elaborated on the standards for determining what constitutes a "legitimate state interest" or what type of connection between the regulation and the state interest satisfies the requirement that the former "substantially advance" the latter. They have made clear, however, that a broad range of governmental purposes and regulations satisfies these requirements.

The Commission argues that among these permissible purposes are protecting the public's ability to see the beach, assisting the public in overcoming the "psychological barrier" to using the beach created by a developed shorefront, and preventing congestion on the public beaches. We assume, without deciding, that this is so—in which case the Commission unquestionably would be able to deny the Nollans their permit outright if their new house (alone or by reason of the cumulative impact produced in conjunction with other construction) would substantially impede these purposes, unless the denial would interfere so drastically with the Nollans' use of their property as to constitute a taking.

The Commission argues that a permit condition that serves the same legitimate police-power purpose as a refusal to issue the permit should not be found to be a taking if the refusal to issue the permit would not constitute a taking. We agree. Thus, if the Commission attached to the permit some condition that would have protected the public's ability to see the beach notwithstanding construction of the new house—for example, a height limitation, a width restriction, or a ban on fences—so long as the Commission could have exercised its police power (as we have assumed it could) to forbid construction of the house altogether, imposition of the condition would also be constitutional. Moreover (and here we come closer to the facts of the present case), the condition would be constitutional even if it consisted of the requirement that the Nollans provide a viewing spot on their property for passersby with whose sighting of the ocean their new house would interfere. Although such a requirement, constituting a permanent grant of continuous access to the property, would have to be considered a taking if it were not attached to a development permit, the Commission's assumed power to forbid construction of the house in order to protect the public's view of the beach must surely include the power to condition construction upon some concession by the owner, even a concession of property rights, that serves the same end. If a prohibition designed to accomplish that purpose would be a legitimate exercise of the police power rather than a taking, it would be strange to conclude that providing the owner an alternative to that prohibition which accomplishes the same purpose is not.

The evident constitutional propriety disappears, however, if the condition substituted for the prohibition utterly fails to further the end advanced as the justification for the prohibition. When that essential nexus is eliminated, the situation becomes the same as if California law forbade shouting fire in a crowded theater, but granted dispensations to those willing to contribute $100 to the state treasury. While a ban on shouting fire can be a core exercise of the State's police power to protect the public safety, and can thus meet even our stringent standards for regulation of speech, adding the unrelated condition alters the purpose to one, which, while it may be legitimate, is inadequate to sustain the ban. Therefore, even though, in a sense, requiring a $100 tax contribution in order to shout fire is a lesser restriction on speech than an outright ban, it would not pass constitutional muster. Similarly here, the lack of nexus between the condition and the original purpose of the building restriction converts that purpose to something other than what it was. The purpose then becomes, quite simply, the obtaining of an easement to serve some valid governmental purpose, but without payment of compensation. Whatever may be the outer limits of "legitimate state interests" in the takings and land use context, this is not one of them. In short, unless the permit condition serves the same governmental purpose as the development ban, the building restriction is not a valid regulation of land use but "an out-and-out plan of extortion."

We view the Fifth Amendment's property clause to be more than a pleading requirement, and compliance with it to be more than an exercise in cleverness and imagination. As indicated earlier, our cases describe the condition for abridgement of property rights through the police power as a "substantial advanc[ing]" of a legitimate State interest. We are inclined to be particularly careful about the adjective where the actual conveyance of property is made a condition to the lifting of a land use restriction, since in that context there is heightened risk that the purpose is avoidance of the compensation requirement, rather than the stated police power objective.

We are left, then, with the Commission's justification for the access requirement unrelated to land use regulation:

Finally, the Commission notes that there are several existing provisions of pass and repass lateral access benefits already given by past Faria Beach Tract applicants as a result of prior coastal permit decisions. The access required as a condition of this permit is part of a comprehensive program to provide continuous public access along Faria Beach as the lots undergo development or redevelopment.

The Commission [believes] that the public interest will be served by a continuous strip of publicly accessible beach along the coast.

The Commission may well be right that it is a good idea, but that does not establish that the Nollans (and other coastal residents) alone can be compelled to contribute to its realization. Rather, California is free to advance its "comprehensive program," if it wishes, by using its power of eminent domain for the "public purpose," but if it wants an easement across the Nollans' property, it must pay for it.

Rewriting the argument to eliminate the play on words makes clear that there is nothing to it. It is quite impossible to understand how a requirement that people already on the public beaches be able to walk across the Nollans' property reduces any obstacles to viewing the beach created by the new house. It is also impossible to understand how it lowers any "psychological barrier" to using the public beaches, or how it helps to remedy any additional congestion on them caused by construction of the Nollans' new house. We therefore find that the Commission's imposition of the permit condition cannot be treated as an exercise of its land use power for any of these purposes.

Reversed.

CASE QUESTIONS

1. What was the proposed use of the Nollans' land?
2. What condition did the Commission wish to impose?
3. If the Commission could not have the condition, were they willing to grant the permit?
4. Is the condition a taking of the Nollans' property?
5. What arguments did the Commission make?

For additional cases and information on "takings," please refer to pages 537 in Chapter 18.

Just Compensation

The final requirement for the proper exercise of eminent domain is **just compensation**. The issue of just compensation is a difficult question of fact. The compensation for the owner is not measured by the governmental entity's gain. In *United States v. Miller*, 317 U.S. 369 (1943), the Supreme Court held that, in cases where it can be determined, fair market value is the measure of compensation. And in *United States ex rel. T.V.A. v. Powelson*, 319 U.S. 266 (1943), the Supreme Court defined fair market value to be "what a willing buyer would pay in cash to a willing seller."

Problems in applying these relatively simple standards include peculiar value to the owner, consequential damages, and greater value of the land because of the proposed governmental project. Basically, the issue of just compensation becomes an issue of appraisal, which is affected by all the various factors involved.

CONSIDER 19.1

The U.S. Energy Department located its now-failed supercollider project in Ellis County, Texas. Generally, land prices in the area had been $500 to $800 an acre. However, during the two years preceding the announcement of the now-defunct project, as anticipation about the area getting the supercollider project grew, land began selling for as high as $7,000 an acre. The U.S. government's policy is to pay "fair market value" for the land that it needs. How was the fair market value for the nearly 7,000 acres taken by eminent domain for the project determined?

As noted with the *Lucas* case in Chapter 18, there are times when regulation can constitute a taking. The following is a landmark case in the constitutionality of use regulations.

Constitutional Issues in Land-Use Restrictions

The use of land is restricted through zoning requirements (Chapter 18), future interests (Chapter 2), and covenants or restrictions in deeds that control the use of the property being transferred (Chapter 21). Restrictions on land use are subject to judicial scrutiny. All three forms of restrictions have met with constitutional challenges, discussed in the following sections.

Zoning

Constitutional challenges to zoning have already been discussed in the *Nollan* case and in Chapter 18, including the discussion on group homes.

Annexation

The decision to annex property to a city is a difficult one that is marked by strong emotions on both sides of the issue. The United States Supreme Court has dealt with the issue of whether a city's annexation process violated federal Voting Rights Act. In *City of Pleasant Grove v. United States*, 479 U.S. 462 (1987), the court held that the decision on annexation cannot be based on race.

Future Interests

Although fee simples determinable and fee simples subject to conditions subsequent do restrict the use and transferability of property, the courts have not intervened in these land interests unless the restrictions have violated any constitutional rights. Racial restrictions violate constitutional rights. In *Capitol Federal Savings and Loan Association v. Smith*, 316 P.2d 252 (Colo. 1957), the Colorado Supreme Court, in a decision followed by other courts, held that racially based fee simples determinable are unconstitutional.

Ethical Issue

Consider the following excerpts from insurance memos during the 1950s and 1960s, prior to civil rights laws in the United States.

Non-whites present special insurance problems traceable to their generally less favorable living conditions and greater instability of the family among them.

From a Met Life internal memo on insurance underwriting in 1964

I am concerned about the likelihood that if we continue to write business extensively in certain portions of cities, such as Washington, Baltimore, Detroit, Chicago and New York, where the proportion of the total population that is colored is increasing, we may, say in ten years, wind up with a serious handicap. . . .[3]

Edward A. Lew, Internal memo Actuary and statistician, MetLife, 1959

Both documents emerged in a racial discrimination suit filed in 2001 in a federal district court in New York City. Were the actions of the companies legal? Were they ethical?

All-Adult Covenants

In many areas, particularly in retirement communities, owners impose a restrictive covenant that allows only persons above the age of 18 or 21 to reside in a particular area: an **all-adult covenant**. The validity of these all-adult covenants and communities has been an issue before the courts, and the following case is one of those judicial reviews.

Practical Tip

Many racially restrictive covenants can still be found in the chain of title for property. Although they are often used for sensational effect, as when the title to Chief Justice William Rehnquist's Arizona land was revealed in the newspaper, when his Senate confirmation was pending, as having a racial restriction, they are simply invalid and unenforceable. No one can control the language in deeds used prior to the time of their ownership.

3. Scott Paltrow, "Old Memos Lay Bare MetLife's Use of Race to Screen Customers," *Wall Street Journal*, July 21, 2001, A1, A10.

Schmidt v. Superior Court

769 P.2d 932 (Calif. 1989)

FACTS

Teri Lynn Schmidt and her sister and daughter (plaintiffs) wanted to purchase a mobile home in a mobile home park managed by Valley Mobile Park Investments (defendants). The purchase was conditioned on Valley's acceptance of the Schmidts' application for space. Valley rejected the application, citing a rule that permitted only persons age 25 or older to live in the park. Schmidt then brought suit alleging that her constitutional rights as well as the Unruh Civil Rights Act had been violated. The trial court dismissed the case. The Court of Appeals ruled that the mobile home park was not specifically designated for senior citizens and reversed. Valley appealed.

JUDICIAL OPINION

Arguelles, Justice. In this case we must determine the validity, under California law, of a private mobilehome park rule limiting residence in the park to persons 25 years or older. The trial court found the rule valid, but the Court of Appeal disagreed, concluding that Civil Code section 798.76 barred a private mobilehome park owner from adopting or enforcing such a rule.

In September 1988, while this matter was pending before us, Congress enacted new legislation (Pub. L. No. 100–430 (Sept. 13, 1988) 102 Stat. 1619, 1988 U.S. Code Cong. & Admin. News, No. 8), effective March 1989, which defendant mobilehome park owners acknowledge will render their 25-year or older policy invalid in the future, at least as applied to families with minor children. Contrary to plaintiffs' suggestion, however, the new federal legislation does not render this proceeding inconsequential or moot, because plaintiffs seek damages for the mobilehome park owners' enforcement of the 25-years-or-older rule prior to the effective date of the new federal legislation and the validity of the park owners' conduct at that time necessarily turns on the proper interpretation of California law. Furthermore, the interpretation of the applicable California statutes will continue to affect the nature of the residence policies which private mobilehome parks in California may establish in the future in light of the new federal legislation. Thus, the state law issue posed by this case continues to have general significance.

In September 1988, Congress enacted the Fair Housing Amendments Act of 1988 (Pub. L. No. 100–430 (Sept. 13, 1988) 102 Stat. 1619, 1988 U.S. Code Cong. & Admin. News, No. 8), an act which makes substantial changes in the preexisting federal fair housing law. Among other significant changes, the act makes it unlawful for a business which engages in residential real estate related transactions to discriminate on the basis of "familial status," as well as on the previously forbidden grounds of race, color, religion, sex or national origin. (42 U.S.C. §3605.) "Familial status" is defined to mean families which include children under the age of 18. (42 U.S.C. §3602(k).)

While the new act generally bars discrimination in housing against families with children under 18, it also creates an exception for "housing for older persons" in which discrimination on the basis of familial status is not prohibited. (42 U.S.C. §3607(b)(1).) "Housing for older persons," in turn, is defined to include, *inter alia*, housing which is (1) "intended for, and solely occupied by, persons 62 years of age or older," or (2) "intended and operated for occupancy by at least one person 55 years of age or older per unit" provided that such housing is specifically designed to meet the physical or social needs of older persons and meets other specified criteria. (42 U.S.C. §3607(b)(2)(B) and (b)(2)(C).)

Plaintiffs contend that because, under traditional supremacy principles, the new federal legislation takes precedence over conflicting state law, and because, under the new legislation, defendants' 25-years-or-older rule may not be validly applied to exclude families with children under the age of 18, the issue of state law presented by this case has been rendered insignificant. For several reasons, we cannot agree.

First, and most obviously, the new federal act clearly does not control plaintiffs' damage claim in this case. By its terms, the federal act does not take effect until 180 days after its enactment and nothing in the act purports to govern conduct—such as the actions of the mobilehome park owners at issue here—which occurred prior to the effective date of the statute.

Second, even with respect to the future, the new federal act does not totally eclipse the question of state law presented here. As we shall see, one of the points at issue in this case is whether the relevant California provisions prohibit a mobilehome park owner from adopting any age-based policy other than an 18-years-or-older rule. If state law does limit a mobilehome park owner's discretion in this fashion, then in the future mobilehome parks in California might well be prohibited from adopting the type of more narrowly defined age-based policies—i.e., a 62-years-or-older rule or a properly limited 55-years-or-older rule—which would qualify for the "housing for older persons" exemption under federal law. (See 42 U.S.C. §3607(b)(2)(B) and (b)(2)(C).) Accordingly, the question of statutory interpretation before us is by no means eliminated by the recent federal enactment.

Section 798.76 provides in full: "The management [of a mobilehome park] may require that a purchaser of a mobilehome which will remain in the park, comply with any rule or regulation limiting residence to *adults only*."

In asserting that defendants' 25-years-or-older rule is invalid under section 798.76, plaintiffs advance two distinct, and somewhat inconsistent, arguments. First, plaintiffs maintain that the statutory language permitting a park owner to require compliance with "any rule or regulation limiting residence to adults only" [emphasis added] should properly be construed to authorize only a rule or regulation limiting residence to "senior citizens," and that the 25-year-or-older rule is invalid because it does not limit residence to senior citizens. Second, plaintiffs alternatively contend that if "adults only" is not interpreted to mean "senior citizens only," then the statute must necessarily be read to permit a mobilehome park owner only to adopt a rule limiting residence in the park to persons 18 years or older—i.e., the park owner must permit the residence of all "adults"—and that the statute may not be construed to permit a park owner to adopt any rule which limits residence to a subcategory of adults—e.g., a rule limiting residents to those 25 years or older, or 45 years or older or 62 years or older. We conclude that neither of plaintiffs' arguments can be sustained.

With respect to the initial contention, we think it is clear that the plain language of the statute will not bear the meaning plaintiffs propose. "Adult" is, of course, plainly not the equivalent of "senior citizen," and other statutory provisions concerning senior citizens and mobilehomes—enacted contemporaneously with section 798.76—demonstrate that the Legislature has used quite clear and specific language when it has intended to refer to senior or elderly citizens.

Furthermore, there is absolutely no indication in the background or legislative history of section 798.76 to suggest that the Legislature, in adopting this provision, intended to use the term "adults only" in such an unconventional manner. As we have seen, when this statutory language was first adopted in 1975, no case had either held or intimated that age-based housing policies were valid only within the senior citizen context. In this setting, there simply is no realistic basis for reading the "adults only" language of section 798.76 as bearing such an unnatural meaning. Insofar as the meaning of section 798.76 itself is concerned, we find no legitimate ground for interpreting the section to permit only "senior citizens only" rules.

With respect to plaintiffs' alternative contention—that section 798.76 should be read to permit mobilehome parks to enforce only a rule limiting residence to those 18 years or older, and to preclude the enforcement of any other rule limiting residence, for example, to those 25 years or older, or 45 years or older, or 62 years or older—we again conclude that the claim is untenable in light of both the language and legislative history of the section.

Finally, viewing the matter in very practical terms, we cannot reasonably conclude that the Legislature, in adopting section 798.76, intended to prohibit mobilehome park owners from adopting any age-based rule other than an 18-years-or-older rule. A recent survey of mobilehome parks in California indicates that mobilehome parks throughout the state have adopted a great variety of age-based rules or regulations, with minimum age limits ranging from 18 years of age, to 25 years, 45 years, 50 years, and 60 years. (See *Cal. Dept. of Housing & Community Development, Mobilehome Parks in California: A Survey of Mobilehome Park Owners Pursuant to S.B. 1835* (Feb. 1986) pp. 31, 33.) Although the survey did not seek to determine how long such policies have been in effect, there is nothing to suggest that this variation is only of recent vintage. To read section 798.76 as plaintiffs propose, we would have to conclude that the Legislature, in enacting the predecessor to section 798.76 in 1975, intended to invalidate all age-based rules in mobilehome parks other than 18-years-and-older rules, thus prohibiting a mobilehome park owner from establishing a park reserved, for example, for persons 55 years or over. In light of the language and legislative history of the provision reviewed above, we cannot reasonably ascribe any such intention to the Legislature.

Finally, plaintiffs claim that if section 798.76 permits a mobilehome park owner to enforce a rule excluding persons under 25 from a mobilehome park, as we have held, the statute is unconstitutional, violating their rights of familial privacy and equal protection. In support of their constitutional claims, plaintiffs rely, *inter alia*, on *Moore v. City of East Cleveland* (1977) 431 U.S. 494, 97 S.Ct. 1932, 52 L.Ed.2d 531 and *City of Santa Barbara v. Adamson* (1980) 27 Cal.3d 123, 164 Cal.Rptr. 539, 610 P.2d 436, decisions in which the United States Supreme Court and this court invalidated local zoning ordinances which impinged on an individual's right to live with members of an extended family (*Moore*) or with unrelated persons (*Adamson*). For a number of reasons, plaintiffs' constitutional challenge lacks merit.

First, both the *Moore, supra*, 431 U.S. 494, 97 S.Ct. 1932, 52 L.Ed.2d 531 and *Adamson, supra*, 27 Cal.3d 123, 164 (Cal.Rptr. 539, 610 P.2d 436), decisions are clearly distinguishable from the present case in a crucial respect. The restriction at issue in each of those cases was a state-imposed rule directly limiting an individual's right to live with whom he or she wanted; in each case, a governmental body had made the substantive decision to limit individual living arrangements within a community. In this case, by contrast, the state, in adopting section 798.76, has not itself established a rule limiting living arrangements or restricting housing to particular age groups, but has simply left that decision—in the private mobilehome park context—to the owner of the mobilehome park. Contrary to plaintiffs' contention, it is not true that, absent section 798.76, a private mobilehome park owner would not have the authority to adopt an age-based housing policy for its park; a park owner's authority to adopt such a rule arises from its general common law property rights in the mobilehome park, rights which clearly preexisted the enactment of section 798.76. Nothing in *Adamson* or *Moore* suggests that constitutional guarantees are violated by the enactment of a statute which simply recognizes the continuing existence of a private property owner's authority in this respect.

Second, even if plaintiffs were able to successfully surmount the "state action" hurdle in this case, their constitutional challenge to defendants' age-based housing policy would still lack merit. To begin with, although plaintiffs contend that all classifications on the basis of age should be viewed as constitutionally "suspect" and should be subjected to "strict scrutiny" under the equal protection clause, past decisions—both in this state and in other jurisdictions—have declined to consider age classifications on a constitutional par with classifications which treat persons differently because of their race or ethnic origin.

For the reasons discussed above, we conclude that the private mobilehome park rule at issue here—limiting residence to persons 25 years or older—is not invalid under current California law. Although recent federal legislation will in the future apparently affect the validity of such a rule as applied to families with minor children, defendants did not violate plaintiffs' statutory or constitutional rights in applying the rule during the time period at issue in this case.

Reversed.[4]

CASE QUESTIONS

1. What restriction was placed on residence in the mobile home park?
2. How does the restriction differ from other restrictions?
3. How does the court deal with the issue of providing housing for families?
4. Is the mobilehome park restriction unconstitutional?
5. Do results on these restrictions differ in retirement states?

CONSIDER 19.2

In August of 1976, Morgan Gayvert, age 29, purchased a mobile home in the Colony Cove Mobile Home Park Community in Carson. Thereafter, Morgan Gayvert married, and his wife, Susan, moved into the park in May of 1984. In November of 1984, David Brown, age 23, and his wife, Laurie, also purchased a mobile home in the same community. The Gayverts and the Browns leased spaces for their mobile homes on month-to-month tenancies from the Colony Cove Associates, which rented a total of 429 spaces in the community. The terms of the rental agreements included acknowledgment of and agreement to abide by the mobile home park's present and future rules and regulations. One of the rules and regulations in effect at the time when both the Browns and Gayverts rented spaces in the park specified that "Colony Cove is an adult Park. Persons under 21 years of age will not be accepted as Residents of the Park.... If a family is expected, it will be necessary for the Resident to vacate."

On March 20, 1985, and April 25, 1985, tenants in the Colony Cove Mobile Home Park were advised by the management of a rule change effective October 15, 1985, whereby the park was to be "limited to senior adults only," meaning adults "55 years of age or older." By the terms of the new rule, "only those persons who meet the requirements of the seniors-only rule shall be admitted as tenants of the Park" in the future. However, the rule also provided that "No person who was a tenant of the Park on March 20, 1985, when notice of this rule change was first given, shall be deemed in violation of the seniors-only rule, regardless of whether or not such person is a senior adult on or before this amendment becomes effective."

In September of 1985, the Browns' child was born. In December of 1987, the Gayverts' child was born. The Browns and Gayverts were given notices of their failure to comply with park rules.

The Browns and Gayverts filed suit challenging the constitutionality of the mobile home park rules. Will they prevail? *Colony Cove Associates v. Brown*, 220 Cal.App.3d 195 (Cal. App. 1990)

4. The federal circuits are in agreement with this California decision that all-adult covenants are constitutional. See *Taylor v. Rancho Santa Barbara*, 206 F.3d 932 (9th Cir. 2000).

Constitutional Issues in Transfer of Property

One of the major issues in the transfer of property is discrimination against certain buyers. The Fair Housing Act, passed in 1968 (42 U.S.C. §3601 *et seq.*), provides that it is

unlawful to refuse to sell or rent after the making of a bona fide offer, or to refuse to negotiate for the sale or rental of, or otherwise make unavailable or deny, a dwelling to any person because of race, color, religion, sex, familial status, or national origin.

The basis for this statutory regulation is the Equal Protection Clause of the Fourteenth Amendment. As discussed in Chapter 1, the Fourteenth Amendment ensures that all citizens are treated equally under state laws. The Fourteenth Amendment is the basis for many of the racial, religious, and national origin discrimination cases.

The Fair Housing Act applies not only to sellers of properties, but also to real estate brokers and salespeople, mortgage lenders, property insurers, and property appraisers. The following sections cover application of the Fair Housing Act.

Application of the Fair Housing Act

The Fair Housing Act applies to residential housing and prohibits discrimination in selling, renting, lending, or insuring residential property on the basis of race, color, religion, sex, handicap, family status, or national origin. Some states may have additional classes protected under state law.

A handicap is defined as it is under the Americans with Disabilities Act (see Chapters 10 and 11 on leases). A *handicap* is a mental or physical impairment that limits one or more major life activities. Examples of impairment protected under the Fair Housing Act include impairments in sight, mobility, and hearing. Mental illness, heart disease, cancer, cerebral palsy, multiple sclerosis, diabetes, AIDS, HIV, and treatment for substance abuse are also protected. Smokers and current drug users are not protected.

There are some Fair Housing Act exemptions. The owner exemption applies when an owner is selling his or her own home, does not use a real estate agent or broker, does not own more than three single-family homes, and does not use any form of discriminatory advertising. Another owner exemption applies to the owner of a residential dwelling in which he or she also resides and that has four or fewer units that are leased to others. There is also a religious exemption for religious organizations. These organizations can discriminate on the basis of religion in selling and leasing residential properties. Another exemption covered earlier in the chapter is for senior housing, or housing for senior citizens exclusively. There are a substantial number of requirements for senior housing, such as having 80 percent or more of the units occupied by at least one resident who is age 55 or above.

Types of Discriminatory Conduct Under the Fair Housing Act

Advertising

Brokers, agents, and even newspapers that run residential property ads must use caution in their descriptive terms so that the ads do not suggest limitations on availability of the property to certain protected classes. For example, language that suggests the property is "great for a mature person" would be discriminatory. To comply, brokers and agents should try to describe the property, not potential buyers or lessees or the seller or the neighbors. The following is an excerpt from a HUD memo offering guidelines for advertising real property.

1. Race, color, national origin. *Real estate advertisements should state no discriminatory preference or limitation on account of race, color, or national origin. Use of words describing the housing, the current or potential residents, or the neighbors or neighborhood in racial or ethnic terms (e.g., white family home, no Irish) will create liability under this section.*

   However, advertisements which are facially neutral will not create liability. Thus, complaints over the use of phrases such as master bedroom, rare find, and desirable neighborhood should not be filed.
2. Religion. *Advertisements should not contain an explicit preference, limitation, or discrimination on account of religion (e.g., no Jews, Christian home). Advertisements which use the legal name of an entity which contains a religious reference (for example, Roselawn Catholic Home), or those which contain a religious symbol (such as a cross), standing alone, may indicate a religious preference. However, if such an advertisement includes a disclaimer (such as the statement, "This Home does not discriminate on the basis of race, color, religion, national origin, sex, handicap, or familial status"), it will not violate the Act. Advertisements containing descriptions of properties (apartment complex with chapel), or services (kosher meals available) do not on their face state a preference for persons likely to make use of those facilities, and are not violations of the Act.*

   The use of secularized terms or symbols relating to religious holidays such as Santa Claus, Easter Bunny, or St. Valentine's Day images, or phrases such as "Merry Christmas" or "Happy Easter," or the like does not constitute a violation of the Act.
3. Sex. *Advertisements for single-family dwellings or separate units in a multi-family dwelling should contain no explicit preference, limitation, or discrimination based on sex. Use of the term master bedroom does not constitute a violation of either the sex discrimination provisions or the race discrimination provisions. Terms such as "mother-in-law suite" and "bachelor apartment" are commonly used as physical descriptions of housing units and do not violate the Act.*
4. Handicap. *Real estate advertisements should not contain explicit exclusions, limitations, or other indications of discrimination based on handicap (e.g., no wheelchairs). Advertisements containing descriptions of properties (great view, fourth floor walk-up, walk-in closet), services or facilities (jogging trails), or neighborhoods (walk to bus stops) do not violate the Act. Advertisements describing the conduct required of residents ("non-smoking," "sober") do not violate the Act. Advertisements containing descriptions of accessibility features are lawful (wheelchair ramp).*
5. Familial status. *Advertisements may not state an explicit preference, limitation, or discrimination based on familial status. Advertisements may not contain limitations on the number or ages of children, or state a preference for adults, couples, or singles. Advertisements describing the properties (two bedroom, cozy, family room), services and facilities (no bicycle allowed), or neighborhoods (quiet streets) are not facially discriminatory and do not violate the Act.*

For additional guidance on advertising, see the HUD Advertising Guide reproduced in the Fair Housing Handbook.

CONSIDER 19.3

Evaluate the following language and determine whether there is a violation of the Fair Housing Act in running an ad with these terms.

a. "Spacious 1- & 2-bedroom apartments in quiet mature complex. No pets, please."
b. "2-person limit."
c. "Adults pref."
d. "No children."

CONSIDER 19.3

(continued)

e. "Mature Christian handyman wanted to share house."
f. "Ideal for professionals."
g. "Mature setting."
h. "For one person."
i. "Within walking distance."
j. "Handyman's dream."
k. "No alcoholics."
l. "Female tenant wanted."
m. "Near church."
n. "Desirable neighborhood."
o. "Call Betsy."
p. "No pets."

Blockbusting

Blockbusting, a violation of the Fair Housing Act, is a method of controlling the racial composition of neighborhoods and is usually attributed to the actions of real estate brokers or salespeople. For example, in *United States v. Mitchell*, 327 F.Supp. 476 (N.D. Ga. 1971), a real estate agent went from house to house in a neighborhood informing the residents that "negroes were coming into the neighborhood" and that houses should be sold as quickly as possible. All of the white residents in the neighborhood sold their homes, and the neighborhood became all black. Mitchell was convicted of violating the Fair Housing Act.

Steering

Steering is another violation of the FHA that is generally attributed to real estate brokers and salespeople. It is an attempt to direct buyers to specific sections of town that are labeled as either white or black areas. In *Zuch v. Hussey*, 394 F. Supp. 1028 (E.D. Mich. 1975), salespeople found to have violated the act made statements such as, "Do you read the newspapers? Even the police are afraid to live in the area and they are supposed to protect the rest of us" and "You wouldn't want that home, the coloreds have moved in pretty good there." In the same case, salespeople discouraged black buyers from buying in white areas by temporarily taking homes off the market. Through these tactics (which were declared illegal), several real estate firms were able to maintain racially segregated neighborhoods in the Detroit area for a time. The following case deals with the extent of liability for FHA violations by brokers and agents.

Meyer v. Holley

537 U.S. 280 (2003)

FACTS[5]

Emma Mary Ellen Holley is African American, her husband, David Holley, is Caucasian, and their son, Michael Holley, is African American. The Holleys (Respondents) visited Triad Realty's office during October 1996 in Twenty-Nine Palms, California, where they met with Triad agent Grove Crank and inquired about listings for new houses in the range of $100,000 to $150,000. Crank showed them four houses in the area, all above $150,000. In mid-November 1996, the Holleys located a home on their own that happened to be listed by Triad. In response to the Holleys' inquiry about the home, Triad agent Terry Stump informed them that the asking price for the house was $145,000. The Holleys expressed interest in purchasing the home and offered to pay the

5. Some of the facts were added from the lower court opinions in the series of cases surrounding this final decision, such as *Holley v. Crank*, 258 F.3d 1127 (9th Cir. 2001).

asking price and to put $5,000 in escrow for the builder to hold the house until April or May 1997 when they closed escrow on their existing home.

Stump told the Holleys that their offer seemed fair, as did the builder, Brooks Bauer, when Mrs. Holley called him with the same offer. Bauer did express, however, that the offer would have to go through Triad. Later, Stump called Mrs. Holley to tell her that more experienced agents in the office, one of whom was later identified as Grove Crank, felt that $5,000 was insufficient to get the builder to hold the house for six months. The Holleys decided not to raise their offer and Triad never presented the original offer to Bauer. One week later, Bauer inquired at Triad about the status of the Holleys' offer. Crank then allegedly used racial invectives in referring to the Holleys, telling Bauer that he did not want to deal with those "n" and called them a "salt and pepper team." The Holleys eventually hired a builder to construct a house for them and Bauer later sold his house for approximately $20,000 less than the Holleys had offered.

Bauer and the Holleys filed a complaint on November 14, 1997, alleging that Crank and Triad violated federal and state fair housing laws. They later filed a separate action against David Meyer as officer/broker, president, and owner of Triad, covering the same allegations and adding several new claims. They claimed that Meyer was vicariously liable in one or more of these capacities for Crank's unlawful actions.

The District Court consolidated the two lawsuits. It dismissed all claims other than the Fair Housing Act claim. It dismissed the claims against Meyer in his capacity as officer of Triad because (1) it considered those claims as assertions of vicarious liability, and (2) it believed that the Fair Housing Act did not impose personal vicarious liability upon a corporate officer.

The Ninth Circuit reversed those determination. Meyer sought certiorari and the U.S. Supreme Court granted his petition.

JUDICIAL OPINION

Breyer, Justice. The Fair Housing Act forbids racial discrimination in respect to the sale or rental of a dwelling. 42 U.S.C. §§3604(b), 3605(a). The question before us is whether the Act imposes personal liability without fault upon an officer or owner of a residential real estate corporation for the unlawful activity of the corporation's employee or agent. We conclude that the Act imposes liability without fault upon the employer in accordance with traditional agency principles, i.e., it normally imposes vicarious liability upon the corporation but not upon its officers or owners.

The Fair Housing Act itself focuses on prohibited acts. In relevant part the Act forbids "any person or other entity whose business includes engaging in residential real estate-related transactions to discriminate," for example, because of "race." 42 U.S.C. §3605(a). It adds that "[p]erson" includes, for example, individuals, corporations, partnerships, associations, labor unions, and other organizations. It says nothing about vicarious liability.

Nonetheless, it is well established that the Act provides for vicarious liability. This Court has noted that an action brought for compensation by a victim of housing discrimination is, in effect, a tort action. And the Court has assumed that, when Congress creates a tort action, it legislates against a legal background of ordinary tort-related vicarious liability rules and consequently intends its legislation to incorporate those rules.

The Ninth Circuit held that the Fair Housing Act imposed more extensive vicarious liability—that the Act went well beyond traditional principles. The Court of Appeals held that the Act made corporate owners and officers liable for the unlawful acts of a corporate employee simply on the basis that the owner or officer controlled (or had the right to control) the actions of that employee. We do not agree with the Ninth Circuit that the Act extended traditional vicarious liability rules in this way.

For one thing, Congress said nothing in the statute or in the legislative history about extending vicarious liability in this manner. And Congress' silence, while permitting an inference that Congress intended to apply ordinary background tort principles, cannot show that it intended to apply an unusual modification of those rules.

For another thing, the Department of Housing and Urban Development (HUD), the federal agency primarily charged with the implementation and administration of the statute, 42 U.S.C. §3608, has specified that ordinary vicarious liability rules apply in this area. And we ordinarily defer to an administering agency's reasonable interpretation of a statute.

Neither does it help to characterize the statute's objective as an "overriding societal priority." We agree with the characterization. But we do not agree that the characterization carries with it a legal rule that would hold every corporate supervisor personally liable without fault for the unlawful act of every corporate employee whom he or she has the right to supervise. Rather, which "of two innocent people must suffer," and just when, is a complex matter. We believe that courts ordinarily should determine that matter in accordance with traditional principles of vicarious liability—unless, of course, Congress, better able than courts to weigh the relevant policy considerations, has instructed the courts differently.

The Ninth Circuit did not decide whether other aspects of the California broker relationship, when added to the "right to control," would, under traditional legal principles and consistent with "the general common law of agency," establish the necessary relationship. But in the absence of consideration of that matter by the Court of Appeals, we shall not consider it.

Respondents also point out that, when traditional vicarious liability principles impose liability upon a corporation, the corporation's liability may be imputed to the corporation's owner in an appropriate case through a "'piercing of the corporate veil.'" *United States v. Bestfoods,* 524 U.S. 51. The Court of Appeals, however, did not decide the application of "veil piercing" in this matter either. It falls outside the scope of the question presented on certiorari. And we shall not here consider it.

The Ninth Circuit nonetheless remains free on remand to determine whether these questions were properly raised and, if so, to consider them.

The judgment of the Court of Appeals is vacated, and the case is remanded for further proceedings consistent with this opinion.

CASE QUESTIONS

1. Describe the scenario that led to the Holleys' suit against the agent, broker, and realty company.
2. When is vicarious liability for violation of the FHA imposed?
3. What does the Court do with the issue of piercing the corporate veil?
4. What conclusions can you draw about broker liability under FHA for the acts of his or her agents?

REDLINING

Redlining, yet another FHA violation, is the refusal by a lender to lend or an insurer to insure on property because of its location within a predetermined geographic area. The name for this practice arose because lenders and insurers were literally drawing red lines on maps around areas in which property loans and insurance should not be made or should be made on less than favorable terms. The Fair Housing Act and many state statutes prohibit redlining; in many cases, they require lending institutions to submit loan figures so that an agency can verify the institutions' lending records. For example, federal institutions are required to submit loan figures under the Home Mortgage Disclosure Act (12 U.S.C. §§2801 *et seq.*). Also, the Community Reinvestment Act of 1977 (12 U.S.C. §§2901 *et seq.*) imposes an affirmative obligation on federal financial institutions to meet the community's loan needs regardless of property location or area condition.

> ***Practical Tip***
>
> *With this new standard on vicarious liability under the FHA, brokers and their companies should take steps to prevent liability. First, the office should have clear policies on discrimination and provide training on the FHA. Second, the broker may have to perform occasional checks or audits on offers and how they are processed. Finally, agents should be reminded of their obligation to present all offers from buyers to sellers.*[6]

Redlining can occur in a number of different ways. The most obvious is when lenders openly refuse to make loans in particular areas. Other, more subtle processes still classified as redlining include the arbitrary variation of loan application processes and loan terms. For example, redlining can consist of requiring a higher down payment, higher closing costs, minimum loan amounts, lowered percentage of loan amount to appraised value, or underappraisal of property. Whether a lender has made a predetermined lending decision on the basis of property location is a question of fact.

CONSIDER 19.4

Great Eastern Bank has been sued by several members of the Navajo Tribe for redlining on home loans located on the reservation. Great Eastern has supplied statistics indicating that over 75 percent of all home mortgage loans on reservation property end in default and foreclosure. Is Great Eastern's statistic a valid basis for denying future reservation loans?

6. There are cases pending regarding the landlord's vicarious liability for the acts of his agents in leasing properties; see, e.g., *Alexander v. Rigas,* 208 F.3d 419 (3rd Cir. 2000)

A new lending practice, known as "customized" home mortgage loans, has created yet another redlining issue. The terms of a customized mortgage are dictated by market specifics. For example, lenders have determined that Cincinnati home buyers keep their homes for longer periods than most home buyers, thereby generating more profits on the loans. So, lenders reduce interest rates for Cincinnati home mortgage debtors. The federal regulators are concerned about these geographic breakdowns and differences as a form of redlining, particularly when racial composition varies.

Redlining is also an issue in setting appraisal values. In the following case, the appraisal standards of the American Institute of Real Estate Appraisers were challenged as violative of the Fair Housing Act. The case extends FHA liability to yet another aspect of the process of buying and selling property.

UNITED STATES V. AMERICAN INSTITUTE OF REAL ESTATE APPRAISERS

442 F. Supp. 1072 (Ill. 1977) affirmed 590 F.2d 242 (8th Cir. 1978)

FACTS

The United States filed suit against two organizations, the American Institute of Real Estate Appraisers (AIREA) and the Society of Real Estate Appraisers (defendants), for violation of the Fair Housing Act. The suit alleged that since the effective date of the Fair Housing Act, these two organizations had engaged in unlawful discriminatory practices by promulgating standards that have caused appraisers and lenders to treat race and national origin as negative factors in determining the value of dwellings and in evaluating the soundness of home loans. The suit further alleged that the organizations failed to take adequate steps to correct the continuing effects of past discrimination and ensure nondiscrimination by appraisers and lenders, whose practices are subject to the influence of the organizations.

The United States sought injunctive relief, and after extensive negotiations the United States and the AIREA agreed not to litigate the matter; instead, they asked for the approval of a settlement order, which would include the adoption of the following statements as policies of the AIREA:

1. It is improper to base a conclusion or opinion of value upon the premise that the racial, ethnic or religious homogeneity of the inhabitants of an area is necessary for maximum value.
2. Racial, religious or ethnic factors are deemed unreliable predictors of value trends or price variance.
3. It is improper to base a conclusion or opinion of value, or a conclusion with respect to neighborhood trends, upon stereotyped or biased presumptions relating to race, color, religion, sex or national origin or upon unsupported presumptions relating to the effective age or remaining life of the property being appraised or the life expectancy of the neighborhood in which it is located.

Opelka and others, as members of the AIREA, brought suit challenging the settlement order on grounds that appraisal was not within the coverage of the Fair Housing Act and that the AIREA has no authority to enter into such a settlement.

JUDICIAL OPINION

Leighton, District Judge. The first and fundamental objection is that the court lacks jurisdiction (to approve the settlement) because the Fair Housing Act does not apply to appraisers.... [T]he court takes this opportunity to hold that the Fair Housing Act does apply to appraisers of real estate.... The principal argument advanced is that the sections of the Fair Housing Act do not mention appraisers. Section 3604 provides in pertinent part:

It shall be unlawful—

(a) To refuse to sell or rent after the making of a bona fide offer, or to refuse to negotiate for the sale or rental of, or otherwise make unavailable or deny, a dwelling to any person because of race, color, religion, sex or national origin.

It shall be unlawful to coerce, intimidate, threaten, or interfere with any person in the exercise or enjoyment of, or on account of his having exercised or enjoyed, or on account of his having aided or encouraged any other person in the exercise or enjoyment of, any right [granted under this Act].

It is clear from the plain language of the provisions that appraisers are not exempted from their coverage; both sections are unrestricted with respect to the class of persons subject to their prohibition. The "otherwise make unavailable or deny" language has been applied to a variety of conduct to prohibit all practices which have the effect of denying dwellings on prohibited grounds. For example, the Act applies to racially exclusionary land use practices by a municipality. It applies to "redlining" by financial institutions. It applies to delaying tactics and discouragement of rental applications used by resident managers and rental agents, and top management and owners who fail to set objective and reviewable procedures for rental applications.

The "or interfere with" language has been similarly broadly applied to reach all practices which have the effect of interfering with the exercise of rights under the Act. The Act requires a liberal construction if the statute is to prohibit effectively "all forms of discrimination, sophisticated, as well as simple-minded." Given a broad interpretation of these provisions, it becomes clear that the United States has stated a claim for relief under their terms. The promulgation of standards which cause appraisers and lenders to treat race and national origin as a negative factor in determining the value of dwellings and in evaluating the soundness of home loans may effectively "make unavailable or deny" a "dwelling" and may interfere with persons in the exercise and enjoyment of rights guaranteed by the Act.

The settlement order is approved.

CASE QUESTIONS

1. Who are the defendants in the case?
2. What does the settlement order provide?
3. Who is challenging the settlement?
4. What is the basis of the challenge?
5. Does the Fair Housing Act apply to appraisers?

Section 8 Housing and the Fair Housing Act

One of the complex issues in the area of fair housing arises when there is an intersection of several federal statutes that provide housing rights. For example, the so-called Section 8 housing program now places low-income families in mainstream housing and does so through rent vouchers. Landlords who participate in the program were once required by HUD regulation and federal statute to take all the Section 8 tenants sent their way, with the only limitation being HUD's restrictions on the number of Section 8 tenants within a particular apartment complex or area. Known as the "take one, take all" provisions, the impact on landlords and properties was substantial and the requirement was repealed by Congress. A landlord need not take all Section 8 tenants, but the decision not to rent must be based on something other than receipt of public assistance.[7]

The Americans with Disabilities Act and Fair Housing

Both the Fair Housing Act and the laws and regulations on Section 8 housing prohibit discrimination on the basis of disability. One form of discrimination is the refusal of a landlord to make reasonable accommodations for tenants with disabilities. For example, a landlord must provide a tenant with multiple sclerosis an assigned parking space rather than the usual "first-come, first-serve" policy because of the tenant's difficulty with walking, her incontinence, and the space she needed for negotiating getting in and out of her car. Courts are often was faced with yet another wrinkle as ADA intersects with FHA as it intersects with Section 8 housing recipients. For example, in *Salute v. Stratford Greens Apartments*, 136 F.3d 293 (2nd Cir. 1998) Richard Salute and Marie Kravette both had disabilities but were also qualified to receive Section 8 housing assistance. They were denied an apartment at the Stratford Greens Garden Apartments because the owner refused to take

7. *Becker v. Our Lady of Angels Apartments, Inc.*, 192 F.3d 601 (6th Cir. 1999).

Section 8 tenants. Salute and Kravette filed suit alleging that they were refused an apartment because of their disabilities. The court found for the landlord, holding that because "the Section 8 program is voluntary and nonparticipating owners routinely reject Section 8 tenants, the owners' 'non-participation constitutes a legitimate reason for their refusal to accept Section 8 tenants and... we therefore cannot hold them liable for... discrimination under the disparate impact theory.'" Not all courts have followed this line of reasoning in such cases. Resolving the conflicting rights of landlords to refuse to rent to Section 8 tenants along with the protections of FHA and ADA has resulted in differing views among the federal courts. The perfect storm of federal laws and rights will require U.S. Supreme Court resolution.

CONSIDER 19.5

John Giebeler had worked as a psychiatric technician for approximately five years before becoming disabled by AIDS. At the time Giebeler had to leave work because of his disability, he was earning approximately $36,000 per year. Since 1996, Giebeler has supported himself through monthly disability benefits under the Social Security Disability Insurance (SSDI) program and housing assistance from the Housing Opportunities for People with AIDS program (HOPWA).

In May 1997, Giebeler sought to move from his two-bedroom apartment at the Elan at River Oaks complex (Elan) to an available one-bedroom unit at the Park Branham Apartments (Branham), a rental property owned by M & B. Giebeler wanted to move to the Branham unit because the rent, $875 per month, was less expensive than the $1,545 per month rent at Elan, and the Branham unit was closer to his mother's home. At the time Giebeler inquired about the Branham unit, he was receiving $837 from SSDI per month, $300 to $400 per month in a HOPWA subsidy, and varied amounts of financial support from his mother. He had a record of consistent and prompt payment of rent during his six years of residency at Elan, and his credit record contained no negative notations.

Branham resident manager Jan Duffus informed Giebeler that he did not qualify for tenancy at Branham because he did not meet the minimum income requirements. Duffus stated that Branham required prospective tenants to have a minimum gross monthly income equaling three times the monthly rent. For the apartment Giebeler wished to rent, the minimum required income was $2,625 per month, an amount less than Giebeler had earned before he became ill.

After he was informed of his ineligibility, Giebeler asked his mother, Anne Giebeler, to assist him in renting the apartment. Anne Giebeler went to the Branham office the next day for the purpose of renting an apartment that would be occupied by her son.

Like her son, Anne Giebeler had a credit record with no negative entries. Anne Giebeler had owned the same home for 27 years and had completely paid off her mortgage. The home was located less than a mile from Branham. Anne Giebeler's income was $3,770.26 per month.

Both John Giebeler and Anne Giebeler filled out application forms for the one-bedroom Branham apartment, indicating that John Giebeler would be the only resident. On his rental application, Giebeler listed his current gross income as $837 and his present occupation as "disabled." The Branham property manager rejected the applications on the basis that M & B considered Anne Giebeler a cosigner and has a policy against allowing cosigners on lease agreements.

Following the denial of his rental application, Giebeler contacted AIDS Legal Services for assistance. Attorney John Doherty wrote a letter to the Branham property manager on Giebeler's behalf, stating that Giebeler was disabled and that, under 42 U.S.C. §3604(f)(3)(B) of the FHAA, unlawful discrimination against disabled persons in housing

CONSIDER 19.5

(continued)

includes "a refusal to make *reasonable accommodations* in rules, policies, practices, or services, when such accommodations may be necessary to afford such person *equal opportunity to use and enjoy a dwelling.*" Is the landlord in violation of FHAA by the refusal to rent? *Giebeler v. M & B Associates*, 343 F.3d 1143 (9th Cir. 2003)

Penalties Under the Fair Housing Act

The Fair Housing Act is enforced through civil suits by individuals and through complaints filed by state agencies, HUD, or special interest groups on behalf of protected classes. Even testers, or individuals sent out to pose as potential buyers or renters, can bring actions for violations. Administrative law judges assigned to hear complaints brought by HUD have the authority to issue injunctions to halt an activity. They also have the authority to assess fines and penalties which range from $10,000 to $50,000, depending upon the nature of the violation and the violator's past history of violations. Individuals can recover damages for emotional distress, mental anguish, and any other damages resulting from the discrimination.

Many cases brought by HUD are settled through a consent decree that requires a remedy for the disparity in housing opportunities. Compliance with the consent decree terms is critical because the courts have upheld fines against officers and government officials when they fail to comply with the requirements of the decree. In *Spallone v. United States*, 493 U.S. 265 (1990), the city of Yonkers, New York, was charged with engaging in a pattern and practice of housing discrimination. The charges were brought in 1980, and a consent decree was entered into. By 1988, however, the requirements of the decree to remedy past housing discrimination had not been met, and a federal district court held city council members in contempt and imposed a daily fine. The U.S. Supreme Court eventually reversed the contempt holding and the fines against the individuals as a violation of some portions of the First Amendment but did uphold sanctions against the city for failure to comply. The case made clear the authority of the federal government to collect fines from municipalities.

Due Process and Real Property

Throughout the preceding chapters, the concept of due process has crept into the discussion. For example, mortgage foreclosures are a huge group of due process rights. With respect to real property taxes, landowners must be given opportunities to be heard on the valuations of their properties. Tax sales require advance notice to the property owner and an opportunity for redemption. All of these protections are afforded through the Fifth and Fourteenth Amendments' due process clauses of the Constitution. Due process protections may be satisfied through judicial or administrative proceedings, as long as there is the opportunity to be heard.

Cautions and Conclusions

This chapter discussed only a few issues of constitutional law affecting real property rights. The opportunities for constitutional challenges to real property rights and procedures are as limitless as the field of constitutional law. Basically, the areas of constitutional law affecting real property are concerned with fairness, the deprivation of rights in existing property, or the right to own property. Constitutional protections offer security for property owners holding title and provide potential property owners the opportunity to purchase.

Key Terms

all-adult covenant, 551
blockbusting, 557
eminent domain, 543
just compensation, 550
redlining, 559
steering, 557
taking, 546

Chapter Problems

1. The Laufmans attempted to purchase property in an area of Cincinnati that was changing in racial composition from white to black. Oakley Building and Loan denied the Laufmans' loan application on grounds that the neighborhood was declining and they would not have sufficient security by taking a mortgage on the property located there. The Laufmans filed suit alleging that Oakley Building and Loan had violated the Fair Housing Act. Is there a violation? *Laufman v. Oakley Building & Loan Co.*, 408 F. Supp. 489 (Ohio 1976)

2. Florence Dolan owns a plumbing and supply store located on Main Street in the central business district of Tigard, Oregon. The store covers approximately 9,700 square feet on the eastern side of a 1.67-acre parcel that includes a gravel parking lot. Fanno Creek flows through the southwestern corner of the lot and along its western boundary. The year-round flow of the creek renders the area within the creek's 100-year floodplain virtually unusable for commercial development. The city's comprehensive plan includes the Fanno Creek floodplain as part of the city's greenway system.

Dolan applied to the city for a permit to redevelop the site. Her proposed plans called for nearly doubling the size of the store to 17,600 square feet, and paving a 39-space parking lot. The existing store, located on the opposite side of the parcel, would be razed in sections as construction progressed on the new building. In the second phase of the project, Dolan proposed to build an additional structure on the northeast side of the site for complementary businesses and to provide more parking. The proposal by Dolan is consistent with the city's zoning scheme in the central business district.

The City Planning Commission granted Dolan's permit application subject to conditions imposed by the city's Community Development Code (CDC). The commission required, as a condition to approval of the permit application, that Dolan dedicate the portion of her property lying within the 100-year floodplain for improvement of a storm drainage system along Fanno Creek and that she dedicate an additional 15-foot strip of land adjacent to the flood plain as a pedestrian/bicycle pathway. The dedication required Dolan to give up approximately 7,000 square feet, or roughly 10 percent of the property. In accordance with city practice, Dolan could rely on the dedicated property to meet the 15 percent open space and landscaping requirement mandated by the city's zoning scheme. The city would bear the cost of maintaining a landscaped buffer between the dedicated area and the new store. Can the city require Dolan to do this? *Dolan v. City of Tigard*, 512 U.S. 374 (1994)

3. William G. Haas & Company purchased land and procured a site permit from the city of San Francisco for the construction of a high-rise project. The site permit was later invalidated because of violations of the Environmental Quality Act and later because of the rezoning of the property, which prohibited high-rise projects in the area. Haas brought suit claiming the rezoning and the imposition of other land-use restrictions diminished the value of his property to such an extent that the regulations constituted a taking. What was the result?

4. Midwestern Indemnity refused to write insurance policies for homes located in neighborhoods that were predominantly black. Midwestern's reasons were high theft, vandalism, and arson rates in the areas, and company officials had the areas marked on maps in their offices. Several black home owners brought suit, alleging the insurer was redlining. Midwestern maintains insurers are not subject to the Fair Housing Act. What is the result?

5. Brigid Healy has resided in Apt. 3B at 30 Eastchester Road, New Rochelle, New York, since December 1, 1996. An initial written lease was entered into between the parties on November 1, 1996, to commence December 1, 1996, and end one year later. In connection with such initial lease, Healy entered into a Housing Assistance Payment Contract (the "HAP Contract") with the City of New Rochelle as the Section 8 Administrator. HAP was to pay the Landlord pursuant to the Section 8 program a subsidy of $607.00 per month; Healy had the responsibility to pay the balance of the rent.

The lease was renewed for additional periods, and the proportion of the rent paid through the Section 8 program subsidy was periodically adjusted so that as of November 1, 2001, of a total contract rent of $986.00, tenant was to pay $7.00 and the Administrator was to pay $979.00 to the Landlord. The lease as renewed was to end by its terms on November 30, 2001.

Several months prior to the November 30 termination date, by letter dated August 13, 2001, the Landlord notified the Administrator's Section 8 office that the Landlord "no longer wish[ed] to accept the Section 8 Program" and that the Landlord "will be terminating the tenant's lease when it expires (11-30-01)." However HAP continued to pay the rent and December 2001 and January 2002 had been paid, but Healy did not pay her portion of the rent for those months. Now the landlord wishes to evict for nonpayment of rent. Can Healy be evicted for nonpayment of rent or does Section 8 Housing protection apply? Can the landlord simply decide not to rent to Section 8 tenants? *30 Eastchester LLC v. Healy*, 2002 WL 553709 (N.Y. City Ct. 2002); see also *Rosario v. Diagonal Realty LLC*, 803 N.Y. S.2d 343 (N.Y. 2005)

6. The city of Phoenix announced the taking of 60 homes located near the airport for the purpose of expanding the airport runways to support increased air traffic. The home owners claim that the appraisals should reflect the commercial value of their property because of the closer proximity to the airstrips. The city of Phoenix maintains that value is determined before the change. What is the result?

7. In 1927, W. T. Shore and T. C. Wilson gave property to the city of Charlotte "so long as the property was used for municipal parks, golf courses, or playgrounds for whites only." Several black citizens have brought suit, alleging the restriction is unconstitutional. What type of interest was created, and what is the result?

8. Bradley Winker owned a duplex dwelling unit in Brookings, South Dakota. The duplex was located in an "R-2" residential zoning area that permits two-family dwellings but limits the number of unrelated adults who may constitute a "family." An inspection of one unit in the duplex on November 8, 1994, revealed the presence of at least four unrelated adult college students residing in one unit of the duplex. Brookings filed a complaint against Winker, charging him with a violation of the Brookings ordinance that restricts the number of unrelated adults per unit. Winker sued, challenging the Brookings ordinance as a violation of the due process and equal protection clauses with its restrictive definition of family. Is the zoning restriction valid or unconstitutional? Be sure to refer to cases in this chapter and Chapter 18 to help you analyze the question. *City of Brookings v. Winker*, 554 N.W.2d 827 (S.D. 1996)

9. The Montgomery Newspapers, Inc., ran ads for rental properties in their six newspapers with the following language:

a. "mature person"
b. "ideal for quiet and reserved single and/or couple"
c. "professional male . . . only"
d. "quiet mature setting"

Do any of these phrases violate the Fair Housing Act?

Fair Housing Council of Suburban Philadelphia v. Montgomery Newspapers, 141 F.3d 71 (3rd Cir. 1998)

10. Bert and Cleone Reece own an apartment building near Logan Field in Billings, Montana. Their policy was to refuse to rent any of their apartments to single women who did not have cars. Further, they did not consider alimony or child support in determining whether a woman could meet monthly rental payments. Do their policies create any constitutional problems? *United States v. Reece*, 457 F. Supp. 43 (Utah 1978)

For research activities related to this chapter, go to our text companion website at www.thomsonedu.com/westbuslaw/jennings.

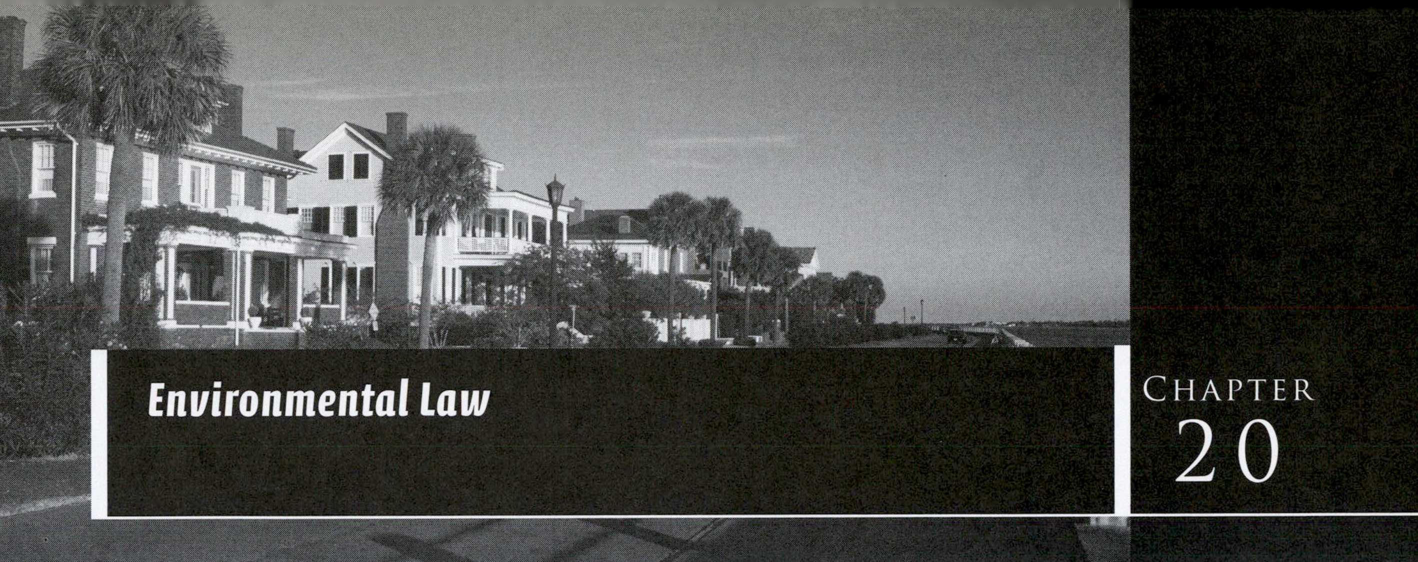

Environmental Law

CHAPTER 20

The landscape and the language are the same
For we ourselves are landscape and land.

Conrad Aiken, *A Letter from Li Po and Other Poems* (1955)

This chapter discusses land use and answers the following questions: What types of governmental regulations affect property use and ownership rights? Who is responsible for enforcing governmental regulations? What are the penalties for violation of the regulations? In the event of conflicts between common law rights and governmental regulations, which group of laws will control?

Statutory Environmental Laws

At the federal level, most environmental laws fall into one of three categories: those regulating air pollution, those regulating water pollution, and those regulating land pollution.

Air Pollution Regulation

Early Legislation

The first legislation dealing with the problem of air pollution, the **Air Pollution Control Act**, was passed in 1955, but it lacked enforcement teeth. Federal regulation in this area continued to be ineffective in the 1960s. However, under the **Air Quality Act** of 1967, the then–Department of Health, Education, and Welfare was authorized to oversee the states' adoption of air quality standards and the implementation of those plans. Still, by 1970 no state had adopted a comprehensive plan.

1970 Amendments to Clean Air Act—New Standards

Because the states did not take action, Congress passed the 1970 Clean Air Act (42 U.S.C. §7401)—the first federal legislation with any real authority for enforcement. Under the act, the **Environmental Protection Agency (EPA)** was authorized to establish air quality standards. The EPA air quality standards specify how much of a particular air substance is permissible. Once those standards were developed, states were required to adopt implementation plans to achieve those standards. These **state implementation plans (SIPs)** had to be approved by the EPA, and adoption and enforcement of the plans were no longer discretionary but mandatory. To obtain EPA approval, the implementation plans had to meet deadlines for compliance with the standards.

The states then had to measure the presence of substances such as sulfur dioxide, carbon monoxide, and hydrocarbons. Based on the results, the states then took appropriate steps to reduce those substances that exceeded federal standards.

In industrialized states, nearly all manufacturers were required to install pollution control equipment. Many companies filed suits challenging the state and EPA requirements because the equipment was expensive and often technologically infeasible. Courts concluded that the **Clean Air Act** was and is intended to be technology forcing, a principle that the Clean Air Act Amendments in 1977 and 1990 codified.

1977 Amendments

The 1977 amendments also gave the EPA authority to regulate business growth to achieve air quality standards. The EPA then developed two areas for measuring air standards for purposes of controlling growth of industry and the resulting pollution. **Nonattainment areas** included those areas with existing, significant air quality problems, the so-called dirty areas. **Prevention of significant deterioration (PSD) areas** were clean areas that the EPA protected.

EPA Economic Controls for Nonattainment Areas

For nonattainment areas, the EPA developed its **Emissions Offset Policy**, which requires new facilities to meet three requirements before they can operate in nonattainment areas:

1. The new plant must have the greatest possible emissions controls. In some cases, this means the plant will be required to meet standards higher than existing standards.
2. The proposed plant must have all other operations in compliance with standards.
3. The new plant's emissions must be offset by reductions from other facilities in the area. These offsets have to be greater than the new emissions.

The EPA follows the **bubble concept**, which treats all air pollutants in the area as if they came from a single source. If a new plant will have no net effect on the air quality in the area (after offsets from other plants), then the EPA allows the new facility.

Although the EPA did not initially regulate the construction of plants in areas already meeting air quality standards, environmentalists' protests and suits brought about the application of EPA regulations to PSD areas. PSD regulations give the EPA the right to review proposed plants prior to construction. Proposed plants must establish through their applications to the EPA that their operations will have no significant effect on air quality and that they will control emissions with appropriate devices.

Latest Controls—Clean Air Act Amendments of 1990

The **Clean Air Act Amendments of 1990** focus on issues such as **acid rain**, urban smog, airborne toxins, ozone-depleting chemicals, and regional economic concerns, as well as resulting political issues.

At the time of the passage of the 1990 amendments, 96 cities had not yet reached their attainment levels under their SIPs (required to be reached under the 1977 amendments by 1987), and 41 cities had carbon monoxide levels exceeding the goals in their SIPs. Under the 1990 amendments, the EPA must establish a **federal implementation plan (FIP)** within two years of a state's failure to submit an adequate SIP to the EPA. The 1990 Act established compliance deadlines and annual pollution-reduction goals for cities at a rate of 3 to 4 percent per year.

The amendments had a substantial impact on smaller businesses such as dry cleaners, paint shops, and bakeries because the definition of a major source of pollution was changed from those businesses emitting 100 tons or more per year to those emitting 50 tons or more per year.

Motor vehicle manufacturers experienced substantial impact under the 1990 amendments. The nine worst nonattainment areas are required to use reformulated gasolines that have reduced emissions by 25 percent. Tighter tailpipe standards were phased in to require emission reductions in various pollutants ranging from 30 to 60 percent.

Plants that are major sources of toxic emissions are now required to use **maximum achievable control technology (MACT)**.

Utilities now have a cap on sulfur dioxide emissions. Putting in scrubbers for meeting the maximum sulfur dioxide emissions became mandatory unless new technology achieved the same result.

The penalties under the act were increased to allow field citations and civil penalties of up to $25,000 per day in general fines and criminal penalties increased, from 1 to 15 years' imprisonment, depending on the nature of the violation and past violations. The EPA was given the authority to pay $10,000 rewards to people who provide information leading to criminal convictions or civil penalties.

New Development in Air Quality: The Kyoto Protocol At the Kyoto meeting of the United Nations Framework Convention for Climate Change (UNFCCC), the delegates adopted the *Kyoto Protocol*, a plan for reducing six greenhouse gases, primarily in the United States and other industrial nations. Under the Protocol, signatory countries will reduce their carbon dioxide levels to less than their 1990 levels, a reduction that will require transfer of industries to other countries. The Protocol took effect in 2005 and as of July 2006, had 164 signatory countries. The United States has not adopted the Kyoto Protocol. There is strong opposition to it from businesses that believe the goal is the transfer of wealth from developed nations to undeveloped nations. The treaty enjoys strong support from environmental groups. In 2006, intense focus on air pollution continued with debate over global warming and the need to reduce carbon emissions. In *Environmental Defense v.Duke Energy*, 127 S. Ct. 1423 (2007), the U.S. Supreme Court heard a case in which EPA had brought suit against Duke Energy for modifications of its coal-fired electricity plants without prior filing and approval from the agency. Duke maintained that only major modifications to power plants required EPA approval under the Clean Air Act. However, the EPA based its expanded authority for action on even minor modification under the PSD regulations. That is, the prevention of carbon emissions and the problems with global warming required more intense and detailed intervention by the agency to carry out its PSD mandate. The utilities challenged the agency's authority to act on greenhouse gases and global warming issues because there was no statutory provision that covered such an expansion. Environmental groups also intervened in the suit. In the *Duke* case as well as in *Massachusetts v. EPA*, 127 S.Ct. 1438 (2007), the court held that the Clean Air Act mandated EPA action on greenhouse gases and global warming, "Under the clear terms of the Clean Air Act, EPA can avoid taking further action only if it determines that greenhouse gases do not contribute to climate change or if it provides some reasonable explanation." In a dissent written by Chief Justice Roberts, three justice maintained that redress of the EPA inaction on global warming is with Congress and the president, not the federal courts. The justices added that their position was one of jurisdiction and authority and "involves no judgment on whether global warming exists, what causes it, or the extent of the problem." Given the decision, there will be additional enforcement actions as well as new regulations under the Clean Air Act.

Practical Tip

One of the results of the 1990 amendments to the Clean Air Act and subsequent regulatory actions and developments has been the development of a market for sulfur dioxide emissions permits. If, for example, one company has an EPA permit to discharge one ton of sulfur dioxide per year, but its equipment allows it to run much cleaner, the company can sell its permit to another utility. The purchase of a particular tract of land may be tied to the buyer being able to obtain the necessary emissions permits. The Chicago Board of Trade deals with emissions permits in much the same way it sells other commodities. The first trading in these emissions permits occurred on March 30, 1993, with a permit for emission of one ton of sulfur dioxide selling for between $122 and $450. Environmental groups currently own about 10 percent of all emissions permits. In 2006, the carbon credits market also emerged. Companies and individuals can purchase, from companies that specialize in renewable energy sources, credits for their own carbon emissions as a means of offsetting their contributions to global warming.

CONSIDER 20.1

Do you think the emissions permits are real or personal property? What issues do you see arising if the permits are classified as real property? What concerns arise if the permits are classified as personal property? What issues do you see with the sale of carbon credits?

CONSIDER 20.2

Union Electric Company is an electric utility company servicing St. Louis and large portions of Illinois and Iowa. It operates three coal-fired generating plants in metropolitan St. Louis that are subject to sulfur dioxide restrictions under the state of Missouri's implementation plan. Union Electric did not seek review of the implementation plan but applied for and obtained variances from the emissions limitations. When an extension for the variances was denied, Union Electric challenged the implementation plan on the grounds that it was technologically and economically infeasible and should therefore be amended. Will Union Electric succeed in having the plan amended? What in the Clean Air Act provides the response to Union? *Union Electric Co. v. EPA*, 427 U.S. 246 (1976)

Water Pollution Regulation

In 1965, the **Water Quality Act**, the first federal legislation on water quality standards was passed. The act established a separate enforcement agency—the **Federal Water Pollution Control Administration (FWPCA)**—and, like the pattern for air pollution legislation, required states to establish quality levels for the water. The act had few enforcement procedures, so only about half of the states had developed their zones and standards by 1970, and none were engaging in active enforcement.

Because of the states' lack of involvement and the ineffectiveness of the 1965 act, the rediscovery of an old act, the **Rivers and Harbors Act of 1899**, became the heart of water pollution control. The act prohibited the discharge of refuse into navigable rivers and harbors, which caused interference with navigation. Release of "any refuse matter of any kind or description" into navigable waters in the United States required a permit from the Army Corps of Engineers. For a time, the act controlled the issuance of permits and was the basis for prosecuting industrial polluters who were discharging without permit. The act was self-limiting because it did not prohibit what was released or the amount of releases, so long as a permit was obtained.

Present Legislation

In 1972 the first meaningful and enforceable federal legislation came with the passage of the **Federal Water Pollution Control Act of 1972** (33 U.S.C. §1401). This act had two goals: (1) swimmable and fishable waters by 1983 and (2) zero discharge of pollutants by 1985. The 1977 amendments allowed extensions and flexibility in meeting the goals and renamed the central statute for water pollution control the **Clean Water Act**. The act moved water pollution from local to federal controls. Federal standards for water discharges were established on an industry basis and all industries across states must meet the standards.

Under the act, all direct industrial dischargers are placed into 27 groups, and the EPA (now responsible for water pollution control since the FWPCA was merged with it) establishes ranges of discharge for each industrial group. The ranges for pulp mills will differ from those for textile manufacturers, but all plants in the same industry must operate within the same ranges.

The ranges of discharges in each industrial group are referred to as **effluent guidelines**. The EPA has also established a specific permissible amount of discharge for each plant within an industrial group, which is the effluent limitation. Finally, for a plant to be able to discharge wastes into waterways, it must obtain a **National Pollution Discharge Elimination System (NPDES)** permit from the EPA. This type of permit is required only for direct dischargers, or **point sources**, and is not required of plants that discharge into sewer systems (although these secondary dischargers may still be required to pretreat their discharges).

In issuing permits, the EPA prescribes standards for release. Generally, the standards that are set depend upon the type of discharge. For setting standards, the EPA has developed three categories of pollutants: **conventional, nonconventional**, and **toxic**. For **conventional pollutants**, the EPA can require pretreat with the **best conventional treatment (BCT)**. If the discharge is either toxic or nonconventional, the EPA can require the **best available treatment (BAT)**, which is the highest standard imposed. In imposing the requirements for permits, the EPA need only consider environmental effects and not the economic effects on the applicant discharger.

CONSIDER 20.3

Inland Steel Company applied for a permit from the EPA under the Federal Water Pollution Control Act of 1972. Although Inland was granted the permit, the EPA made the permit modifiable as new standards for toxic releases and treatment were developed. Inland claimed the modification restriction on the permit was invalid because the EPA did not have such authority and also because Inland would be subject to every technological change or discovery made during the course of the permit. Inland filed suit. Was the restriction invalid? *Inland Steel Company v. Environmental Protection Agency*, 574 F.2d 367 (7th Cir. 1978)

In 1986, Congress passed the **Safe Drinking Water Act**, which requires the EPA to establish national standards for contaminant levels in drinking water. The states are primarily responsible for enforcement and can have higher standards than the federal standards, but must at least enforce the federal minimums for drinking-water systems.

Large oil tanker spills, such as the one that resulted from the grounding of the *Exxon Valdez* in Prince William Sound, Alaska, and dumped 11 million gallons of crude oil that coated 1,000 miles of the Alaskan coastline, brought public outcry for additional federal regulation for pollution of waterways. In 1990, Congress enacted the **Oil Pollution Act (OPA)** of 1990. The OPA applies to all navigable waters up to 200 miles offshore and confers the power for cleanups on the EPA. The EPA may clean up the spill itself and seek compensation from the party responsible, or it may require the party to do the cleanup.

The OPA also established the Oil Spill Liability Trust Fund, which is funded by a five-cent-per-barrel tax that is used to cover the costs of cleanup in those cases where the party responsible does not have the resources to pay for the cleanup.

Penalties under the OPA range from $25,000 per day civil penalties and up to $3,000 per barrel if the spill is willful or negligent. The failure to report an oil spill carries a penalty of $250,000 and/or five years imprisonment for individuals, and $1,000,000 for corporations. Civil penalties run higher and include the full cost of cleanup (up to $50,000,000) should those responsible not clean up the oil spill.

Solid-Waste Disposal Regulation

Early Regulation

The disposal of solid waste (garbage) has been a significant problem in the United States because of the long history and popularity of the open-dumping method of disposal. As with other pollution issues, the disposal of solid wastes was assigned to state and local governments, with few changes resulting. In 1965, Congress passed the **Solid Waste Disposal Act**, which provided money to state and local governments for research in solid-waste disposal. In 1970, this 1965 act was amended with the passage of the **Resource Recovery Act**. It was this act that encouraged the recycling process by offering aid to local governments with recycling projects. The act had guidelines for solid-waste disposal, but no real enforcement provisions.

Later Responses—Toxic Substance Control

After several major open-dumping problems, such as the Love Canal chemical dumping near Buffalo, New York, two federal acts granted some enforcement power to the federal government. The **Toxic Substances Control Act (TOSCA)** (15 U.S.C. §2601) was passed in 1976 and authorized the EPA to control the manufacture, use, and disposal of toxic substances. Under the act, the EPA is authorized to prevent future, and stop ongoing, manufacture of dangerous substances.

Also passed by Congress in 1976 was the **Resource Conservation and Recovery Act of 1976 (RCRA)** (42 U.S.C. §6901). The two goals of the act are to control the disposal of potentially harmful substances and to encourage resource conservation and recovery. A critical part of the act's control is a manifest or permit system that requires manufacturers to obtain a permit for the storage or transfer of hazardous wastes so that the location of wastes can be traced through permits issued.

Superfund

In 1980, Congress passed the **Comprehensive Environmental Response, Compensation, and Liability Act (CERCLA)** (42 U.S.C. §9601), which authorized the president to issue funds for the cleanup of areas that were once disposal sites for hazardous wastes. The act established a **Hazardous Substance Response Trust Fund** to provide funding for cleanup. If funds are expended in such a cleanup, then the company responsible for the disposal of the hazardous wastes can be required to repay the amounts expended from the trust fund. Often called the **Superfund**, the funds are available for governmental use but cannot be obtained through suit by private citizens affected by the hazardous disposals. (See below for a full discussion of clean-up liability.)

In 1986, CERCLA was amended by the **Superfund Amendment and Reauthorization Act**. Under the amendments in that act, the EPA can recover cleanup funds from those responsible for the release of hazardous substances. Approximately 700 hazardous substances are now covered (they are listed at 40 C.F.R. §302). Since the passage of the 1986 amendments, the courts have expanded greatly "responsibility" to include those who purchased the property without performing adequate checks on its history.

CERCLA Lender Liability

One of the more intriguing issues that resulted from CERCLA liability was whether a lender has the responsibility of cleanup because it held property due to a foreclosure sale or a deed in lieu of foreclosure. In *United States v. Fleet Factors Corp.*, 901 F.2d 1550 (11th Cir. 1990), the court held that a lender could be held responsible for the cleanup of real property held due to a loan default. The decision created significant exposure for lenders when they did not have control over the conduct of the mortgagor prior to their repossession or foreclosure. The EPA promulgated rules on lender liability in 1992 but the rules did not provide lenders with guidelines for managing property obtained through default or foreclosure. To clarify, Congress passed the **Asset Conservation, Lender Liability, and Deposit Insurance Protection Act of 1996**. This statute provides a specific exclusion for lenders in that the definition of "owner/operator" (see below) does not include someone who "holds indicia of ownership primarily to protect his security interest." This provision has been labeled the "secured lender exemption" from CERCLA liability. However, a lender can lose its exempt status if it "actually participate[s] in the management or operational affairs of a vessel or facility." But, the "capacity" to assert control does not result in lender liability. A lender can do the following and still not be exposed to CERCLA liability:

- Monitor or enforce terms of the security agreement
- Monitor or inspect the premises or facility
- Mandate that the debtor take action on hazardous materials
- Provide financial advice or counseling
- Restructure or renegotiate the loan terms
- Exercise any remedies available at law
- Foreclose on the property
- Sell the property
- Lease the property

CERCLA—Four Classes of Liability Rules

There are four classes of parties liable under CERCLA. "Owners and operators" are the first group. While "owner" is self-explanatory, "operator" includes those who lease property and then contaminate it, such as those who lease factories, operate storage facilities, and so forth. A second group would be owners and operators at the time the property was contaminated. This group brings those who were responsible for the property contamination, as opposed to present owners who had the problem deeded to them, under CERCLA. For example, many gas stations have been converted to other businesses. Suppose that one of the underground gas tanks once used by the gas station has been leaking hazardous materials into the surrounding soil. Not only would the present owners be liable, but also all those who owned the gasoline station previously. The final two groups consist of those who transport hazardous materials and those who arrange for the transportation of hazardous materials. There are virtually no liability exemptions for those who fit into these four groups. Further, CERCLA liability includes both corporations and corporate officers. For example, the EPA has successfully prosecuted officers of corporations who have been ordered to conduct a cleanup but who failed to do so. The following case deals with a CERCLA liability issue.

Acushnet Company v. Mohasco

191 F.3d 69 (1st Cir. 1999)

FACTS

Sullivan's Ledge, once a popular swimming, hiking, and impromptu gathering area located near New Bedford, Massachusetts, has become little more than an industrial dumping ground for scrap rubber, waste oils, gas, combustion ash, and old telephone poles. The sludge became so toxic, the refuse so thick, and the stench so overwhelming, that the city closed down the area in the 1970s.

The EPA eventually identified a number of business entities and their successors in interest as responsible for the cleanup of the area. Following lengthy negotiations, those businesses entered into a consent decree in 1992 that required them to implement a remediation plan and shoulder the costs of that plan for returning Sullivan's Ledge to a nonhazardous site.

Following the agreement, Acushnet Company and others in the consent decree group (plaintiffs) filed suit seeking financial contribution from Mohasco Corporation and others including American Flexible Conduit (AFC), New England Telephone & Telegraph Company (NETT), and Ottaway Newspapers, Inc. (defendants/appellees).

The trial court found that there was insufficient evidence to find these companies liable under CERCLA and granted them summary judgment. The plaintiffs appealed.

JUDICIAL OPINION

Bownes, Senior Circuit Judge. CERCLA, as we have said on other occasions, sketches the contours of a strict liability regime. Broad categories of persons are swept within its ambit, including the current owner and operator of a vessel or facility; the owner or operator of a facility at the time hazardous waste was disposed of; any person who arranged for the transportation of hazardous substances for disposal or treatment; and anyone who accepted hazardous waste for transportation. *See* 42 U.S.C. §9607(a)(1)–(4). There are a few affirmative defenses available, but they are generally difficult to satisfy (they include showing that the release or threat of release was caused solely by an act of God or an act of war). By and large, a person who falls within one of the four categories defined in §9607(a) is exposed to CERCLA liability.

While CERCLA casts the widest possible net over responsible parties, there are some limits to its reach. The courts of appeals have generally recognized that "although joint and several liability is commonly imposed in CERCLA cases, it is not mandatory in all such cases."

The Sullivan's Ledge Group mounts a three-fold attack on the district court's reasoning in resolving the respective motions. Its arguments on appeal are broad-brushed in nature, focusing almost entirely on the legal meaning of "causation" and CERCLA's underlying policy goals. First, plaintiffs insist that reading any causal element into CERCLA is inconsistent with the principle of strict liability. Second, they contend that doing so would run counter to the remedial purpose of CERCLA because, among other things, it will let smaller polluters off the hook and discourage responsible parties from entering into consent agreements with the government. Third, to the extent the district court may have considered equitable factors in ruling in favor of Mohasco, Ottaway, and AFC, plaintiffs claim that the court did so without providing a "full and fair allocation trial" within the meaning of section 9613(f).

Defendants-appellees, for their part, contend that it makes sense to say that a *de minimis* polluter has not caused a responsible party to incur clean up costs; and that, in all events, plaintiffs' contribution claims against them founder for a more fundamental reason: the record did not permit a finding that each should bear a meaningful share of the costs associated with restoring Sullivan's Ledge. In their view, these fatal weaknesses in the plaintiffs' case justified judgment as a matter of law in their favor.

We have strong reservations about interpreting the statute's causation element to require that a defendant be responsible for a minimum quantity of hazardous waste before liability may be imposed. The text of the statute does not support such a construction—CERCLA itself does not expressly distinguish between releases (or threats of releases) by the quantity of hazardous waste attributable to a particular party. At least on its face; any reasonable danger of release, however insignificant, would seem to give rise to liability. On this point the courts of appeals are in unison.

To read a quantitative threshold into the language "causes the incurrence of response costs" would cast the plaintiff in the impossible role of tracing chemical waste to particular sources in particular amounts, a task that is often technologically infeasible due to the fluctuating quantity and varied nature of the pollution at a site over the course of many years.

Moreover, it would be extremely difficult, if not impossible, to articulate a workable numerical threshold in defining causation. How low would a polluter's contribution to the mix have to be before a judge could find, with equanimity, that the polluter was not a but-for "cause" of the clean up efforts? Less than 0.5 percent or 1 percent? We do not see how much a line, based on the quantity or concentration of the hazardous substance at issue, can be drawn on a principled basis in defining causation. To even begin down that path, we feel, is to invite endless confusion.

This does not mean, however, that the *de minimis* polluter must necessarily be held liable for all response costs. The approach taken by the Second Circuit is instructive. The Second Circuit reaffirmed the Restatement (Second) of Torts approach to fleshing out the scope of CERCLA liability, holding that where environmental harms are divisible, a defendant may be held responsible only for his proportional share of the response costs. In extending the principle a half-step, the Second Circuit went on to say that:

> *[A defendant] may escape any liability for response costs if it either succeeds in proving that its [waste], when mixed with other hazardous wastes, did not contribute to the release and cleanup that followed, or contributed at most to only a divisible portion of the harm.*

We therefore hold that a defendant may avoid joint and several liability for response costs in a contribution action under §9613(f) if it demonstrates that its share of hazardous waste deposited at the site constitutes no more than background amounts of such substances in the environment and cannot concentrate with other wastes to produce higher amounts. This rule is not based on CERCLA's causation requirement, but is logically derived from §9613(f)'s express authorization that a court take equity into account when fixing each defendant's fair share of response casts. We caution, however, that not every *de minimis* polluter will elude liability in this way. As always, an equitable determination must be justified by the record.

There is nothing to suggest that Congress intended to impose far-reaching liability on every party who is responsible for only trace levels of waste. Several courts, albeit taking different paths to a similar result, have rejected the notion that CERCLA liability "attaches upon release of any quantity of a hazardous substance."

Allowing a CERCLA defendant to prevail on issues of fair apportionment even at the summary judgment stage, is consistent with Congress's intent that joint and several liability not be imposed mechanically in all cases. Permitting a result that is tantamount to a no-liability finding, is in keeping with the legislative goal that clean up efforts begin in a speedy fashion and that litigation over the details of actual responsibility follow. In fact, to require an inconsequential polluter to litigate until the bitter end, we believe, would run counter to Congress's mandate that CERCLA actions be resolved as fairly and efficiently as possible. On the whole, the costs and inherent unfairness in saddling a party who has contributed only trace amounts of hazardous waste with joint and several liability for all costs incurred outweigh the public interest in requiring full contribution from *de minimis* polluters.

Plaintiffs complain that any consideration of causation is at odds with CERCLA's objectives and would discourage responsible parties from entering into consent decrees. Because we ground the quantum inquiry solidly in §9613(f), we are satisfied their prophesy will not come to pass. The ultimate failure of a contribution claim because someone did only a negligible amount of harm does not impede enforcement by the EPA or frustrate any of CERCLA's objectives.

Affirmed.

CASE QUESTIONS

1. Explain why companies are litigating against each other under CERCLA.
2. What is a *de minimis* violation of CERCLA?
3. Does the court require that the standard for liability be based on an amount or number?
4. Will the decision excusing companies from cleanup costs defeat the purposes of CERCLA?

CONSIDER 20.4

Grand Auto Parts Stores receives used automotive batteries from customers as trade-ins. Grand Auto drives a screwdriver through spent batteries and then sells them to Morris Kirk & Sons, a battery-cracking plant that extracts and smelts leads. Tons of crushed battery casings were found on Kirk's land. The EPA sought to hold Grand Auto liable for cleanup. Can Grand Auto be held liable? *Catellus Dev. Corp. v. United States*, 34 F.3d 748 (9th Cir. 1994)

CERCLA and Corporate Liability

CERCLA liability has also extended to corporate board members and corporate successors and officers in cases where a company is purchased by another firm. Those who merge or buy corporations also buy into CERCLA liability—liability under CERCLA continues after a transfer of ownership. The U.S. Supreme Court has ruled in *United States v. Bestfoods*, 528 U.S. 810 (1999), that a parent corporation is not automatically liable under CERCLA for a subsidiary corporation's conduct, but may be responsible if the subsidiary is simply a shell. In other words, CERCLA liability of parent corporations for the actions of their subsidiaries is governed by corporate law on piercing the corporate veil. Under the *Bestfoods* case, liability of the parent corporation for actions of a subsidiary results if:

a. the parent corporation operates the facility, is a joint venturer in the operation of the facility, or works side-by-side with the subsidiary in operations;
b. the parent and subsidiary corporations share officers and directors such that it becomes impossible to separate out the decision-making processes; or
c. an officer of the parent corporation (or other designated or authorized employee) operates the facility of the subsidiary.[1]

CERCLA and Buying Property

Before buying property, a buyer should use *due diligence*, which is an investigation into the current and past uses of the land to determine possible CERCLA liability. There are three phases in a due diligence review. Phase 1 consists of a search to determine whether there is evidence of past or current environmental problems on the property. A Phase 1 search involves looking at private and public records, aerial photographs, and a site inspection. If Phase 1 reveals some concerns, then the parties proceed to Phase 2, which consists of chemical analysis of soil, structures, and water from the property. If Phase 2 finds contaminants, the report for Phase 2 will estimate the cost of cleanup. Phase 3 is the actual cleanup plan.

CERCLA and Brownfields

CERCLA has perhaps been a too-effective environmental law. Because of the liability exposure on sites that were designated as Superfund sites, there were, as of 2002, over 450,000 sites around the country that were undeveloped and untouchable because of contamination. Called "**brownfields,**" these sites are defined by the EPA as "real property, the expansion, redevelopment, or reuse of which may be complicated by the presence or potential presence of a hazardous substance, pollutant, or contaminant." Brownfields often contribute to urban blight and present a barrier to economic

1. The work of Professors Cindy A. Schipani and Lynda J. Oswald is an excellent resource for discussions on parent liability for CERCLA violations, as well as a history of the development and scope of CERCLA. See, e.g., Lynda J. Oswald and Cinday A. Schipani, "CERCLA and the 'Erosion' of Traditional Corporate Law Doctrine," 86 *Northwestern Law Review* 259 (1990). Their work was referred to in the *Bestfoods* case.

development and revitalization.[2] As a result, the Small Business Liability Relief and Brownfields Revitalization Act was passed to allow 75 federal agencies to work together, called the *Federal Partnership Action Agenda,* to provide funding for proposals to clean up and use these brownfields.[3] EPA rules on the act now provide a process for application to become an "innocent landowner," or someone who seeks to develop the brownfield but wants an exemption from CERCLA exposure. That designation then allows the applicant to obtain federal funding for purposes of cleaning up and developing the brownfield.

> **Practical Tip**
>
> *Due diligence is necessary not only when buying property but also when buying companies with land holdings. Liability under CERCLA transfers via land ownership or corporate ownership.*

Insurers and CERCLA

An issue that continues to evolve is whether property insurance can be used to cover CERCLA liability. Environmental exposure is a risk that contractors and owners try to manage, but most insurers now include an exclusion policy on CERCLA exposure. Courts are left with interpretation issues on these policies, and on what is excluded as CERCLA liability and what is a hazard or risk on the property. For example, in *Gainsco Ins. Co. v. Amoco Production Co.*, 53 P.3d 1051 (Wyo. 2002), the court held that a pollution exclusion clause did not apply in a situation in which workers were exposed to poisonous gas. However, the courts are willing to enforce clearly written exclusion clauses (i.e., unambiguous) when there are issues with standard environmental contaminants. For example, in *Bituminous Cas. Corp. v. Cowen Const., Inc.*, 55 P.3d 1030 (Okl. 2002), the court held that an insurer need not cover the contractor's exposure when lead crept into the water supply of a kidney dialysis center because lead exposure was a typical type of environmental hazard that would be intended by an environmental exclusion. Contractors and owners can obtain pollution coverage, but it is a policy rider and requires additional premiums.

The Self-Audit

Companies have responded to CERCLA liability with voluntary disclosures through the EPA's self-audit procedures. The EPA has established a program called **Incentives for Self-Policing, Disclosure, Correction, and Prevention of Violations.**[4] Under the program, those companies that come forward voluntarily, having met certain conditions, will have their penalties reduced for any violations uncovered. The following are the conditions for reduced penalties:

> **Practical Tip**
>
> *When negotiating for environmental hazard insurance, be sure to cover both known and unknown hazards. Be sure to cover on-site and off-site hazards so that the issue of, for example, lead creeping into the water supply from adjoining land is covered for the contractor who builds on clean land.*

1. The violations were uncovered as part of a self-audit or due diligence done on property.
2. The violations were uncovered voluntarily.
3. The violations were reported to the EPA within 10 days.
4. The violations were discovered independently and disclosed independently, not because someone else was reporting or threatening to report.
5. There is correction of the violation within 60 days.
6. There is a written agreement that the conduct will not recur.
7. There can be no repeat violations or patterns of violations.
8. There is no serious harm to anyone as a result of the violation.
9. The company cooperates completely with the EPA.

2. For more information about brownfields, go to http://www.epa.gov/brownfields/about.htm.
3. *42 U.S.C.A. §9601.*
4. For more information, see http://www.epa.gov.

> ***Practical Tip***
>
> *Companies have hired executive-level managers such as vice presidents for environment or vice presidents for health, safety, and environment to manage a staff of in-house professionals who do everything from supervising a company's current activities to investigating past activities to determine environmental problems. These problems are then reported to the EPA and the company and agency work together to solve the problem and ascertain that cleanup is done where warranted. These self-audits and disclosures also help the companies be more accurate in their disclosures in materials for shareholders and analysts.*

The EPA will reduce fines and penalties by 75 percent if substantially all these conditions are met. If a company falls into the 75 percent mitigation category, the EPA will not recommend criminal prosecution to the Department of Justice. The documents related to the audit can be protected by the attorney/client privilege, including even those that are disclosed to the EPA. The clarification of the privilege has resulted in most companies taking advantage of the EPA's self-reporting protections.

> **ETHICAL ISSUE**
>
> The Superfund has been used quite frequently since its inception. The result is that more funding is needed to keep it going. Congress has proposed expanding the tax used for funding to include all manufacturers. When expansion of the funding sources for the Superfund has been proposed in Congress, the businesses not currently subject to the Superfund tax have opposed additional impositions on them. Do these firms have an obligation to assist in the cleanup? Can some firms claim that they do not affect the environment? Is the cleanup a general business obligation?

STATE REGULATION OF HAZARDOUS WASTE

Many states have their own regulatory schemes to provide mechanisms and funding for cleanup, and penalties for failure to follow their requirements. All 50 states have some form of hazardous waste regulation, and the definitions of hazardous wastes as well as the penalties vary. Arizona includes garbage in its definition, and Oregon establishes fines on the basis of a fee per animal destroyed as a result of the waste. The death of one mountain goat due to hazardous waste will cost the violator $3,500 in Oregon.

Four states (California, Connecticut, Illinois, and Indiana) now impose mandatory disclosure requirements in certain real estate transactions. New Jersey has similar regulations that cover other types of transfers such as stock sales that might result in the indirect transfer of property. The purpose of these disclosure statutes is to have the seller reveal the types of activities that have occurred on the premises. The goal is to either have the parties then agree to have cleanup done prior to closing, or force the selling party into a cleanup because the disclosure of environmental hazards can permit a rescission of the sales agreement.

Environmental Quality Regulation

Environmental controls of air, water, and waste are directed at private parties in the use of their land. However, as part of the environmental control scheme, Congress also passed an act that regulates what governmental entities can do in the use of their properties. The **National Environmental Policy Act (NEPA) of 1969** (42 U.S. §4321) was passed to require federal agencies to take into account the environmental impact of their proposed actions and to prepare an **environmental impact statement (EIS)** prior to taking any proposed action.

An EIS must be prepared and filed with the EPA whenever an agency sends a proposed law to Congress and whenever an agency will take major federal action significantly affecting the quality of the environment. The information required in an EIS is as follows:

1. The proposed action's environmental impact
2. Adverse environmental effects (if any)
3. Alternative methods for accomplishing the task
4. Short-term effects versus long-term maintenance, enhancement, and productivity
5. Irreversible and irretrievable resource uses

Examples of federal agency actions that have required the preparation of EISs include the Alaska oil pipeline, the extermination of wild horses on federal lands, the construction of government buildings such as post offices, and any highway construction built with federal funds. Even the North American Free Trade Agreement (NAFTA) was challenged on the basis that an EIS was required.

The following case involves an issue of whether an EIS was required.

SIERRA CLUB V. UNITED STATES DEPARTMENT OF TRANSPORTATION

753 F.2d 120 (D.C. 1985)

FACTS

In 1983, the Federal Aviation Administration (FAA) issued two orders amending the operations specifications for Frontier Airlines, Inc., and Western Airlines, Inc. These amendments gave the airlines permanent authorizations to operate Boeing 737 jet airplanes (B-737s) out of Jackson Hole Airport, which is located within the Grand Teton National Park in Wyoming. These two airlines are the only major commercial carriers that schedule flights to and from Jackson Hole.

Private jets have flown into the airport since 1960. Western Airlines has been flying into Jackson Hole since 1941. The airport is the only one in the country located in a national park, and Congress has continually funded expansions and improvements of the once single dirt-runway airport.

In 1978, Frontier applied for permission to fly B-737s into the Jackson Hole Airport. The FAA released its EIS on the application in 1980. The EIS found that B-737s were comparable with C-580 propeller aircraft (the type then being used by Western and Frontier) for noise intrusion, but were substantially quieter than the private jets using the airport. The study also showed that fewer flights would be necessary since the B-737 could carry more passengers and that different flight paths could reduce noise. Based on this EIS, Frontier was given the right to use B-737s for two years. When Frontier applied for permanent approval, the FAA used the 1980 EIS statement and found that with flight time restrictions, the impact would not harm the environment.

The Sierra Club, a national conservation organization, brought suit for the failure to file an EIS for the 1983 amendments and for the use of national park facilities for commercial air traffic without considering alternatives.

JUDICIAL OPINION

Bork, Circuit Judge. We do not think the FAA violated NEPA by failing to prepare an additional EIS. Under NEPA, an EIS must be prepared before approval of any major federal action that will "significantly affect the quality of the human environment." The purpose of the Act is to require agencies to consider environmental issues before taking any major action. Under the statute, agencies have the initial and primary responsibility to determine the extent of the impact and whether it is significant enough to warrant preparation of an EIS. This is accomplished by preparing an Environmental Assessment (EA). An EA allows the agency to consider environmental concerns, while reserving agency resources to prepare full EIS's for appropriate cases. If a finding of no significant impact is made after analyzing the EA, then preparation of an EIS is unnecessary. An agency has broad discretion in making this determination, and the decision is reviewable only if it was arbitrary, capricious or an abuse of discretion.

This court has established four criteria for reviewing an agency's decision to forego preparation of an EIS. First, the agency must have accurately identified the relevant environmental concern. Second, once the agency has identified the problem, it must take a "hard look" at the problem in preparing the EA. Third, if a finding of no significant impact is made, the agency must be able to make a convincing case for its finding. Last, if the agency does find an impact of true significance, preparation of an EIS can be avoided only if the agency finds that changes or safeguards in the project sufficiently reduce the impact to a minimum.

The first test is not at issue here. Both the FAA and Sierra Club have identified the relevant environmental concern as noise by jet aircraft within Grand Teton National Park. The real issues raised by Sierra Club are whether the FAA took a "hard look" at the problem, and whether the methodology used by the agency in its alleged hard look was proper.

We find that the FAA did take a hard look at the problem. The FAA properly prepared an EA to examine the additional impact on the environment of the plan. The EA went forward from the 1980 EIS. The 1980 EIS, which was based on extensive research by Dr. Hakes of the University of Wyoming, noise testing by the FAA, and data derived from manufacturer information, showed that noise intrusions of B-737 jets over the level caused by C-580 propeller aircraft amounted to only 1 dbl near the Airport and decreased in proportion to the distance from the Airport. The agency, exercising its expertise, has found that an increase this minute is not significant for any environment. In addition, the EIS and Hakes studies were based on a worst case scenario, and it was determined that if certain precautions were taken the actual noise levels could be diminished greatly.

Petitioner (Sierra Club) argues that because Jackson Hole Airport is located within national parkland a different standard—i.e., individual event noise level analysis—is mandated. Both individual event and cumulative data were amassed in preparing the 1980 EIS on which the EAs were based. The fact that the agency in exercising its expertise relied on the cumulative impact levels as being more indicative of the actual environmental disturbance is well within the area of discretion given to the agency. We agree with petitioner that although noise is a problem in any setting, "airplane noise is a problem fundamentally inconsistent with the type of recreational experience Park visitors are seeking" and should be minimized. Here the FAA found that a cumulative noise increase of 1 dbl or less is not significant—even for the pristine environment in which Jackson Hole Airport is located.

Given all of these facts, we think the FAA was not required to prepare yet another EIS before granting permanent authorizations for the use of B-737s.

The orders of the FAA are hereby affirmed.

CASE QUESTIONS

1. What airport noise is at issue?
2. Who is involved in the case?
3. Was an EIS prepared?
4. What is the basis for the appeal?
5. What has the FAA allowed? Will the authorizations stand?

Other Federal Environmental Regulations

In addition to the major environmental laws, there are specific environmental federal statutes.

Surface Mining

The **Surface Mining and Reclamation Act of 1977** (42 U.S.C. §6907) requires those who mine coal to obtain a permit and to restore land surfaces to their original condition.

Noise Control

Under the **Noise Control Act of 1972** (42 U.S.C. §4901), the EPA, along with the Federal Aviation Administration (FAA), can control the amount of noise emissions from low-flying aircraft for the protection of landowners in flight paths.

Pesticide Control

The **Federal Environmental Pesticide Control Act** controls the use of pesticides through registration with the EPA. Registration is required for the sale, shipment, distribution, or receipt of pesticides. The EPA also classifies pesticides according to their effects and dangers.

OSHA

The **Occupational Safety and Health Administration (OSHA)** is responsible for the works environment. OSHA controls the levels of exposure to toxic substances and requires safety precautions for exposure to such dangerous substances as asbestos, benzene, and chloride.

> ***Practical Tip***
>
> *When considering a purchase of real property, look into the following issues: Are there asbestos-containing materials and/or asbestos itself on the property? Look in walls, ceiling, and pipes. Is there any lead-based paint on the property? Check for decaying, flaking, and peeling paint as signs of possible lead-paint problems. Lead paint is outlawed now, but many older properties may still have it. Is there a radon problem on the property? The only way to determine whether a property has radon is to have testing done. Radon often enters through foundations or cracks in basement floors. Only experts can detect its presence.*
>
> *Checking for these environmental hazards prior to purchase is important for safety, for the decision to buy, and for setting the right price for a property that may need some cleaning up.*

Asbestos

Buildings that contain asbestos materials remain a problem for buyers, sellers, and occupants. The **Asbestos Hazard Emergency Response Act (AHERA)**, passed in 1986, required all public and private schools to arrange for the inspection of their facilities to determine whether their buildings had asbestos-containing materials (ACMs). The Clean Air Act defines airborne asbestos as a **toxic pollutant.** An amendment to the Superfund Act classifies asbestos as a **Community-Right-to-Know substance**, which means that there is a duty to disclose the presence of asbestos to buyers, tenants, and employees. The issues of the degree of harm and the cost of replacement continue to be debated among property owners and is also a subject of much of the asbestos-related litigation.

Endangered Species

In 1973, Congress passed the **Endangered Species Act**, a law that has been a powerful tool for environmentalists in protecting certain species when commercial use and development threaten the habitats of protected animals under the act.

The secretary of the interior is responsible for identifying endangered terrestrial species, and the secretary of commerce identifies endangered marine species. In addition, these cabinet members designate protected habitats considered crucial for these species. Once a species is on the list, its critical habitat cannot be disturbed by development, noise, or destruction. The following case is one that gave federal agencies broad authority in protecting endangered species.

Babbitt v. Sweet Home Chapter of Communities for a Great Oregon

515 U.S. 687 (1995)

FACTS

Two U.S. agencies halted logging in the Pacific Northwest because it endangered the habitat of the northern spotted owl and the red-cockaded woodpecker, both endangered species. Sweet Home Chapter (respondents) is a group of landowners, logging companies, and families dependent on the forest products industries in the Pacific Northwest. They brought suit seeking clarification of the authority of the secretary of the interior and the director of the Fish and Wildlife Service (petitioners) to include habitation modification as a harm covered by the Endangered Species Act (ESA).

The federal district court found for the secretary and director and held that they had the authority to protect the northern spotted owl through a halt to logging. The court of appeals reversed. Babbitt, the secretary of the interior, appealed.

JUDICIAL OPINION

Stevens, Justice. Section 9(a)(1) of the Endangered Species Act provides the following protection for endangered species:

Except as provided in sections 1535(g)(2) and 1539 of this title, with respect to any endangered species of fish or wildlife listed pursuant to section 1533 of this title it is unlawful for any person subject to the jurisdiction of the United States to—(B) take any such species within the United States or the territorial sea of the United States[.] 16 U.S.C. §1538(a)(1).

Section 3(19) of the Act defines the statutory term "take":

The term 'take' means to harass, harm, pursue, hunt, shoot, wound, kill, trap, capture, or collect, or to attempt to engage in any such conduct. 16 U.S.C. §1532(19).

The Act does not further define the terms it uses to define "take." The Interior Department regulations that implement the statute, however, define the statutory term "harm":

Harm in the definition of 'take' in the Act means an act which actually kills or injures wildlife. Such act may include significant habitat modification or degradation where it actually kills or injures wildlife by significantly impairing essential behavioral patterns, including breeding, feeding, or sheltering. 50 C.F.R. §17.3 (1994).

We assume respondents have no desire to harm either the red-cockaded woodpecker or the spotted owl; they merely wish to continue logging activities that would be entirely proper if not prohibited by the ESA. On the other hand, we must assume *arguendo* that those activities will have the effect, even though unintended, of detrimentally changing the natural habitat of both listed species and that, as a consequence, members of those species will be killed or injured. Under respondents' view of the law, the Secretary's only means of forestalling that grave result—even when the actor knows it is certain to occur—is to use his §5 authority to purchase the lands on which the survival of the species depends. The Secretary, on the other hand, submits that the §9 prohibition on takings, which Congress defined to include "harm," places on respondents a duty to avoid harm that habitat alteration will cause the birds unless respondents first obtain a permit pursuant to §10.

The text of the Act provides three reasons for concluding that the Secretary's interpretation is reasonable. First, an ordinary understanding of the word "harm" supports it. The dictionary definition of the verb form of "harm" is "to cause hurt or damage to: injure." *Webster's Third New International Dictionary* 1034 (1966). In the context of the ESA, that definition naturally encompasses habitat modification that results in actual injury or death to members of an endangered or threatened species.

Respondents argue that the Secretary should have limited the purview of "harm" to direct applications of force against protected species, but the dictionary definition does not include the word "directly" or suggest in any way that only direct or willful action that leads to injury constitutes "harm." Moreover, unless the statutory term "harm" encompasses indirect as well as direct injuries, the word has no meaning that does not duplicate the meaning of other words that §3 uses to define "take." A reluctance to treat statutory terms as surplusage supports the reasonableness of the Secretary's interpretation.

Second, the broad purpose of the ESA supports the Secretary's decision to extend protection against activities that cause the precise harms Congress enacted the statute to avoid. As stated in §2 of the Act, among its central purposes is "to provide a means whereby the ecosystems upon which endangered species and threatened species depend may be conserved."

Third, the fact that Congress in 1982 authorized the Secretary to issue permits for takings that §9(a)(1)(B) would otherwise prohibit, "if such taking is incidental to, and not the purpose of, the carrying out of an otherwise lawful activity," 16 U.S.C. §1539(a)(1)(B), strongly suggests that Congress understood §9(a)(1)(B) to prohibit indirect as well as deliberate takings. The permit process requires the applicant to prepare a "conservation plan" that specifies how he intends to "minimize and mitigate" the "impact" of his activity on endangered and threatened species, 16 U.S.C. §1539(a)(2)(A), making clear that Congress had in mind foreseeable rather than merely accidental effects on listed species.

The Court of Appeals made three errors in asserting that "harm" must refer to a direct application of force because the words around it do. First, the court's premise was flawed. Several of the words that accompany "harm" in the §3 definition of "take," especially "harass," "pursue," "wound," and "kill," refer to actions or effects that do not require direct applications of force. Second, to the extent the court read a requirement of intent or purpose into the words used to define "take," it ignored §9's express provision that a "knowing" action is enough to violate the Act. Third, the court employed *noscitur a sociis* to give "harm" essentially the same function as other words in the definition, thereby denying it independent meaning. The canon, to the contrary, counsels that a word "gathers meaning from the words around it." The statutory context of "harm" suggests that Congress meant that term to serve a particular function in the ESA, consistent with but distinct from the functions of the other verbs used to define "take." The Secretary's interpretation of "harm" to include indirectly injuring endangered animals through habitat modification permissibly interprets "harm" to have "a character of its own not to be submerged by its association."

When it enacted the ESA, Congress delegated broad administrative and interpretive power to the Secretary. The task of defining and listing endangered and threatened species requires an expertise and attention to detail that exceeds the normal province of Congress. The proper interpretation of a term such as "harm" involves a complex policy choice. When Congress has entrusted the Secretary with broad discretion, we are especially reluctant to substitute our views of wise policy for his. In this case, that reluctance accords with our conclusion, based on the text, structure, and legislative history of the ESA, that the Secretary reasonably construed the intent of Congress when he defined "harm" to include "significant habitat modification or degradation that actually kills or injures wildlife."

In the elaboration and enforcement of the ESA, the Secretary and all persons who must comply with the law will confront difficult questions of proximity and degree; for, as all recognize, the act encompasses a vast range of economic and social enterprises and endeavors. These questions must be addressed in the usual course of the law, through case-by-case resolution and adjudication.

Reversed.

CASE QUESTIONS

1. Is habitat modification harming endangered species?
2. Does the Court's interpretation mean no intent is required to violate ESA?
3. Did Congress intend to give the secretary authority to shut down an industry?
4. Is logging prevented now?
5. What ethical issues arise from this case?

Since the time of these head-on confrontations, the logging and paper industries have adopted a "Sustainable Forestry Initiative." The Initiative, adopted by 200 members of the American Forest and Paper Association, supports eco-friendly logging. The Nature Conservancy supports the Initiative, which has had the effect of negotiated solutions to the issue of logging versus environmental protection. No further legislation has been needed at the federal level because of the cooperation between and among these groups.

ETHICAL ISSUE

Asia Pacific Resources International Holdings, Ltd. (called April), is about to sign a landmark agreement with the World Wildlife Fund, an environmental activist group. April has agreed to curb timber-cutting areas in Sumatra, Indonesia, to preserve a natural rainforest with great biodiversity. Over the past 20 years, more than half of the forest has been cut down for lumber.

April's customers, such as Procter & Gamble (makers of Charmin and Bounty paper towels), were shunning April as a supplier because of its damage in Indonesia. While April complied with Indonesian law (leaving 20 percent of the forest untouched), it left long ribbon strips that could not support the local wildlife.

Terms of the deal include the following:

- April will not allow other loggers to use its transportation system (barges and roads).
- April will verify the source of all logs it purchases.
- April will cultivate tree plantations and expects to be able to sell only plantation-grown wood by 2009.

Local residents resent these agreements with environmental groups because their livelihoods have been blocked as April closes its road and prohibits use by illegal loggers.

What advantages do you see in these private contract promises on environmental policy? What disadvantages do you see? What ethical issues exist for April?

Source: Steve Stecklow, "Environmentalists, Loggers Near Deal on Asian Rainforest," *Wall Street Journal*, February 23, 2006, pp. A1, A14.

In the following case, the U.S. Supreme Court interpreted the Endangered Species Act as also permitting lawsuits by landowners who are affected by the statute's application.

BENNETT V. SPEAR

520 U.S. 154 (1997)

FACTS

The Fish and Wildlife Service issued an opinion on the operation of the Klamath Irrigation Project and the project's impact on two varieties of endangered fish. The Klamath Project is one of the oldest of the federal reclamation projects and is a series of lakes, rivers, dams, and irrigation canals in northern California and southern Oregon. The opinion concluded that the operation of the project might impact on the Lost River Sucker (*Deltistes luxatus*) and Shortnose Sucker (*Chasmistes brevirostris*) species of fish that were listed as endangered in 1988. The opinion further provided for alternative means of operation for the project that included the maintenance of minimum water levels in certain portions of the project.

Brad Bennett and other ranchers (petitioners) operate their ranches within the areas designated to receive less water pursuant to the biological opinion issued. Bennett filed suit alleging that the opinion was incorrect in its conclusions on the impact of the project on the two species of fish and that the opinion failed to take into account the resulting economic impact of lessening the water levels. Bennett's complaint alleged that the Endangered Species Act (ESA) and the Administrative Procedure Act (APA) required the federal government to take his interests into account in making the determination as to what to do about the project. The federal district court dismissed the complaint and the court of appeals affirmed the dismissal. Mr. Bennett appealed.

JUDICIAL OPINION

Scalia, Justice. We first turn to the question the Court of Appeals found dispositive: whether petitioners lack standing by virtue of the zone-of-interests test. Although petitioners contend that their claims lie both under the ESA and the APA, we look first at the ESA because it may permit petitioners to recover their litigation costs, and because the APA by its terms independently authorizes review only when "there is no other adequate remedy in a court."

The question of standing "involves both constitutional limitations on federal-court jurisdiction and prudential limitations on its exercise."

Numbered among these prudential requirements is the doctrine of particular concern in this case: that a plaintiff's grievance must arguably fall within the zone of interests protected or regulated by the statutory provision or constitutional guarantee invoked in the suit.

We have made clear, however, that the breadth of the zone of interests varies according to the provisions of law at issue, so that what comes within the zone of interests of a statute for purposes of obtaining judicial review of administrative action under the "generous review provisions" of the APA may not do so for other purposes.

The first question in the present case is whether the ESA's citizen-suit provision, set forth in pertinent part in the margin, negates the zone-of-interests test (or, perhaps more accurately, expands the zone of interests). We think it does. The first operative portion of the provision says that "any person may commence a civil suit"—an authorization of remarkable breadth when compared with the language Congress ordinarily uses. Even in some other environmental statutes, Congress has used more restrictive formulations, such as "[any person] having an interest which is or may be adversely affected," or "any person having a valid legal interest which is or may be adversely affected...whenever such action constitutes a case or controversy." And in contexts other than the environment, Congress has often been even more restrictive. In statutes concerning unfair trade practices and other commercial matters, for example, it has authorized suit only by "[a]ny person injured in his business or property."

Our readiness to take the term "any person" at face value is greatly augmented by two interrelated considerations: that the overall subject matter of this legislation is the environment (a matter in which it is common to think all persons have an interest) and that the obvious purpose of the particular provision in question is to encourage enforcement by so-called "private attorneys general"—evidenced by its elimination of the usual amount-in-controversy and diversity-of-citizenship requirements, its provision for recovery of the costs of litigation (including even expert witness fees), and its reservation to the Government of a right of first refusal to pursue the action initially and a right to intervene later. Given these factors, we think the conclusion of expanded standing follows.

It is true that the plaintiffs here are seeking to prevent application of environmental restrictions rather than to implement them. But the "any person" formulation applies to all the causes of action authorized by §1540(g)—not only to actions against private violators of environmental restrictions, and not only to actions against the Secretary asserting underenforcement under §1533, but also to actions against the Secretary asserting overenforcement under §1533. As we shall discuss below, the citizen-suit provision does favor environmentalists in that it covers all private violations of the Act but not all failures of the Secretary to meet his administrative responsibilities; but there is no textual basis for saying that its expansion of standing requirements applies to environmentalists alone. The Court of Appeals therefore erred in concluding that petitioners lacked standing under the zone-of-interests test to bring their claims under the ESA's citizen-suit provision.

By the Government's own account, while the Service's Biological Opinion theoretically serves an "advisory function," 51 Fed. Reg. 19928 (1986), in reality it has a powerful coercive effect on the action agency:

The statutory scheme...presupposes that the biological opinion will play a central role in the action agency's decision-making process, and that it will typically be based on an administrative record that is fully adequate for the action agency's decision insofar as ESA issues are concerned.... [A] federal agency that chooses to deviate from the recommendations contained in a biological opinion bears the burden of 'articulat[ing] in its administrative record its reasons for disagreeing with the conclusions of a biological opinion,' 51 Fed.Reg. 19, 956 (1986).

What this concession omits to say, moreover, is that the action agency must not only articulate its reasons for disagreement (which ordinarily requires species and habitat investigations that are not within the action agency's expertise), but that it runs a substantial risk if its (inexpert) reasons turn out to be wrong. A Biological Opinion of the sort rendered here alters the legal regime to which the action agency is subject. When it "offers reasonable and prudent alternatives" to the proposed action, a Biological Opinion must include a so-called "Incidental Take Statement"—a written statement specifying, among other things, those "measures that the [Service] considers necessary or appropriate to minimize [the action's impact on the affected species]" and the "terms and conditions...that must be complied with by the Federal agency...to implement [such] measures."

The Service itself is, to put it mildly, keenly aware of the virtually determinative effect of its biological opinions. The Incidental Take Statement at issue in the present case begins by instructing the reader that any taking of a listed species is prohibited unless "such taking is in compliance with this incidental take statement," and warning that "[t]he measures described below are nondiscretionary, and must be taken by [the Bureau]." Given all of this, and given petitioners' allegations that the Bureau had, until issuance of the Biological Opinion, operated the Klamath Project in the same manner throughout the twentieth century, it is not difficult to conclude that petitioners have met their burden—which is relatively modest at this state of the litigation—of alleging that their injury is "fairly traceable" to the Service's Biological Opinion and that it will "likely" be redressed—i.e., the Bureau will not impose such water level restrictions—if the Biological Opinion is set aside.

Whether a plaintiff's interest is "arguably...protected...by the statute" within the meaning of the zone-of-interests test is to be determined not by reference to the overall purpose of the Act in question (here, species preservation), but by reference to the particular provision of law upon which the plaintiff relies. It is difficult to understand how the Ninth Circuit could have failed to see this from our cases. As we said with the utmost clarity in National Wildlife Federal, "the plaintiff must establish that the injury he complains of...falls within the 'zone of interests' sought to be protected by the statutory provision whose violation forms the legal basis for his complaint."

The Court of Appeals erred in affirming the District Court's dismissal of petitioners' claims for lack of jurisdiction. Petitioners' complaint alleges facts sufficient to meet the requirements of Article III standing, and none of their ESA claims is precluded by the zone-of-interests test. Petitioners' §1533 claim is reviewable under the ESA's citizen-suit provision, and petitioners' remaining claims are reviewable under the APA.

Reversed.

CASE QUESTIONS

1. Who has brought the suit and why?
2. Can those affected by the protection of an endangered species bring suit under the ESA?
3. How does the Court deal with the issue raised by the government that the opinion is only an opinion and not government action?
4. Do the ranchers have standing to challenge the endangered species protection under the ESA?
5. The Court's opinion was unanimous. Do you agree that both sides in an environmental case, those representing the interests of the species and those representing economic interests, should have the right to challenge a finding by the federal government?

EMINENT DOMAIN ESA

A new issue that arose under ESA is whether restrictions on land use that are imposed pursuant to the ESA constitute a taking for purposes of eminent domain. Several cases have now held that ESA restrictions are neither takings nor compensable claims. *Seiber v. U.S.*, 364 F.3d 1356 (4th Circ. 2004)

State Environmental Laws

In addition to the federal enactments, 30 states have enacted some form of environmental laws and have established their own environmental policies and agencies. Some states may require new industrial businesses to obtain a state permit along with the required federal permits for the operation of their plants. As noted earlier, all 50 states have some form of hazardous waste regulation.

Enforcement of Environmental Laws

Federal environmental law can be enforced through criminal sanctions, penalties, injunctions, and suits by private citizens. In addition to the federal enforcement rights, there are common law remedies such as nuisance or trespass that can be used to protect property and property rights.

Parties Responsible for Enforcement

The EPA is responsible for enforcement of the major environmental laws on air and water pollution, solid-waste disposal, toxic substance management, and noise pollution. The EPA promulgates specific standards and seeks remedies and sanctions for violations. The EPA works with state EPAs on enforcement issues.

The **Council on Environmental Quality (CEQ)** was established in 1966 under the National Environment Protection Act and is part of the executive branch. Its role is that of policy maker. The CEQ formulates national policies on the quality of the environment and makes recommendations to lawmakers regarding its policy statements.

In addition to these agencies, other federal agencies such as the Atomic Energy Commission, the Federal Power Commission, the Department of Housing and Urban Development, the Department of the Interior, the Forest Service, the Bureau of Land Management, and the Department of Commerce have specific areas for which they have enforcement authority. All federal agencies that deal with the use of lands, water, and air are involved in compliance with and enforcement of the environmental laws.

Criminal Sanctions for Violations

Most of the federal statutes discussed above carry criminal sanctions for violations. See Figure 20.1 for penalties. The following case deals with criminal sanctions for environment violations.

UNITED STATES V. JOHNSON & TOWERS, INC.

741 F.2d 662 (3d Cir. 1984)

FACTS

Johnson & Towers repairs and overhauls large motor vehicles. In its operations, Johnson uses degreasers and other industrial chemicals that contain methylene chloride and trichlorethylene, which are classified as "hazardous wastes" under the Resource Conservation and Recovery Act (RCRA) and pollutants under the Clean Water Act.

The waste chemicals from Johnson & Towers' cleaning operations were drained into a holding tank, and when the tank was full, pumped into a trench. The trench flowed from the plant property into Parker's Creek, a tributary of the Delaware River. Under RCRA, generators of such wastes must obtain a permit from the EPA. Johnson & Towers had not received or even applied for such a permit.

Jack Hopkins, a foreman, and Peter Angel, the service manager for Johnson, were charged with criminal violations of the RCRA and the Clean Water Act. Johnson & Towers was also charged and pled guilty. Hopkins and Angel pled not guilty on the grounds that they were not "owners" or "operators" as required for RCRA violations. The trial court agreed and dismissed all charges against Hopkins and Angel except the criminal conspiracy charges.

The government appealed the dismissal.

JUDICIAL OPINION

Sloviter, Circuit Judge. The single issue in this appeal is whether the individual defendants are subject to prosecution under RCRA's criminal provision, which applies to:

any person who—(2) knowingly treats, stores, or disposes of any hazardous waste identified or listed under this subchapter either—

(A) without having obtained a permit under Section 6925 of this title... or
(B) in knowing violation of any material condition or requirement of such permit.

If we view the statutory language in its totality, the congressional plan becomes...apparent. First, "person" is defined in the statute as "an individual, trust, firm, joint stock company, corporation (including a government corporation), partnership, association, State, municipality, commission, political subdivision of a State, or any interstate body." Had Congress meant to take aim more narrowly, it could have used more narrow language.

Second, under the plain language of the statute, the only explicit basis for exoneration is the existence of a permit covering the action. Nothing in the language of the statute suggests that we should infer another provision exonerating persons who knowingly treat, store or dispose of hazardous waste but are not owners or operators.

Finally, though the result may appear harsh, it is well established that criminal penalties attached to regulatory statutes intended to protect public health, in contrast to statutes based on common law crimes, are to be construed to effectuate the regulatory purpose.

In summary, we conclude that the individual defendants are "persons" within the RCRA, that all elements of that offense must be shown to have been knowing, but that such knowledge, including that of the permit requirement, may be inferred by the jury as to those individuals who hold the requisite responsible positions with the corporate defendant.

Reversed and remanded.

CASE QUESTIONS

1. Who is charged with criminal violations?
2. What violations are charged?
3. What violations did the lower court dismiss?
4. Did Congress intend to prosecute corporate employees?
5. Does the appellate court reinstate the charges?
6. What proof is required to show violations by the "persons" involved?

Figure 20.1 Penalties for Violation of Federal Environmental Laws

Act	Penalties	Private Suit
Clean Air Act	$25,000 per day, up to 1 year imprisonment; 15 years for willful or repeat violations $10,000 rewards	Citizen suits; authorized EPA suit for injunctive relief
Clean Water Act	$25,000 per day, up to 1 year $50,000 and/or 3 years for violations with knowledge; $100,000 and/or 6 years for subsequent violations	Citizen suits; authorized EPA suit for injunctive relief
Resource Conservation and Recovery Act (Solid Waste Disposal Act)	$250,000 and/or 15 years imprisonment for intentional violation; $1,000,000 for corporations $50,000 and/or 5 years for others	Citizen and negligence suits after EPA refuses to handle
Hazardous Substance/ Response Trust	Fund for cleanup	EPA suit for injunctive relief and reimbursement of trust funds
Oil Pollution Act	$25,000 per day, or $1,000 per barrel $3,000 per barrel if willful or negligent $250,000 and/or 5 years for failure to report	Private actions in negligence

Civil Liability for Violations

Injunctive Relief

Although the criminal sanctions imposed on violators may be costly, adjoining landowners may just want to stop the polluting activity. As indicated in Figure 20.1, under each federal statute, the EPA has the authority to bring suit for injunctive relief. In seeking injunctive relief, the EPA asks the court to order a business to stop an activity or other violation of one of the acts. In addition to the EPA's power to seek injunctive relief, each federal act (except NCRA) allows private citizens to bring suit for damages for violations and also for obtaining injunctive relief.

Common Law Relief

In spite of the complex federal regulatory scheme, the elimination of pollution has frequently come through private suits based on the common law doctrine of nuisance. Nuisance was covered in Chapter 3. However, **nuisance** is applied by courts to allow landowners living near contaminated sites to recover for damages to their property as a result of the contamination. Other theories that can be used to challenge uses of land include negligence and trespass. (See Chapter 3 for more details).

In the following landmark case, the New Jersey Supreme Court deals with the issue of whether a purchaser can recover from a seller for the sale of contaminated property.[5]

T&E Industries, Inc. v. Safety Light Corp.

587 A.2d 1249 (N.J. 1991)

FACTS

United States Radium Corporation (USRC) owned an industrial site on Alden Street in Orange, New Jersey, where it processed radium from 1917 until 1926. USRC sold the radium for medical purposes and also used it to manufacture luminous paint for instrument dials, watches, and other products. Radium processing permitted recovery of only 80 percent of the radium from the carnotite ore, transported to the plant from Colorado and Utah. The unextracted radium was contained in "tailings" that USRC discarded into unimproved portions of the Alden Street site.

Through a complex series of chemical processes, the discarded radium emits radon, which can cause lung cancer when inhaled. Epidemiological studies had not been done at the time the tailings were discarded, and the federal government did not regulate the disposal of the tailings until 1978. However, many people had suspicions about handling radium and, as early as 1917, USRC employees measured the radioactivity of radium. One story told of how Dr. Van Sochocky, the president of USRC, "hacked" off his fingertip when radium lodged beneath his fingernail because he feared the effects of radium.

Radium processing ceased at the Alden site in 1926, and the site was leased to various commercial tenants until it was sold in 1943 to Arpin, a plastics manufacturer. The tailings were not removed from the site in spite of continually developing evidence about the danger. In fact, Arpin constructed a new portion of plant that rested on the discarded tailings. The property changed hands several times. T&E (plaintiff), a manufacturer of electronic components, leased the premises in 1969 and purchased it in 1974.

The Uranium Mill Tailings Radiation Control Act (1978) calls for the evaluation of inactive mill-tailing sites. New Jersey's Department of Environmental Protection (DEP) inspected the plaintiff's site and found radon levels exceeding state and federal standards. In spite of soil removal and other actions, the site could not be brought into compliance; T&E was forced to move its operations. The site could not be sold until cleanup of the tailings was complete.

In 1981 T&E sued Safety Light Corporation (a successor corporation to USRC) (defendant) and others (all corporations that bought from USRC or its transferees) based on nuisance, negligence, misrepresentation,

5. For a contra view by a court that did not allow nuisance recovery, see *Rosenblatt v. Exxon Co., U.S.A.*, 642 A.2d 180 (Md. 1994).

fraud, and strict liability of abnormally dangerous activity. The trial court dismissed the strict liability claim and found that USRC had no knowledge of the dangers when the tailings were disposed. The jury found for T&E, but the trial court entered a judgment N.O.V. for Safety Light. T&E appealed. The appellate court reversed the trial court's decision. Safety Light appealed.

JUDICIAL OPINION

Clifford, Justice. At the outset we must determine whether a property owner can assert against a predecessor in title a cause of action sounding in strict liability for abnormally dangerous activities. Defendant suggests that only neighboring property owners, not successors in title, can maintain such a suit, and that successors in the title must rely on contract law to recover from a prior owner. According to defendant, a wealth of case law, including the Third Circuit decision in *Philadelphia Electric Co. v. Hercules, Inc.*, 762 F.2d 303 (1985), and the historical development of the abnormally dangerous-activity doctrine support that distinction.

In *Philadelphia Electric Co.* the court considered whether a property owner could recover damages for toxic-waste contamination from its predecessor in title. Relying on the doctrine of *caveat emptor* and the historical role of private nuisance law, the court concluded that the property owner could not bring a private-nuisance claim against its former owner and could not recover damages.

In reaching that conclusion, the court explained the traditional view of a seller's liability:

Under the ancient doctrine of caveat emptor, the original rule was that, in the absence of express agreement, the vendor of land was not liable to his vendee, or a fortiori to any other person, for the condition of the land existing at the time of transfer. As to sales of land this rule has retained much of its original force, and the implied warrantees which have grown up around the sale of chattels never have developed. This is perhaps because great importance always has been attached to the deed of conveyance, which is taken to represent the full agreement of the parties, and to exclude all other terms and liabilities. The vendee is required to make his own inspection of the premises, and the vendor is not responsible to him for their defective condition, existing at the time of transfer.

Drawing from the rationale of the *Philadelphia Electric Co.* opinion, defendant argues that we should adopt a similar analysis. Defendant stresses that a successor in title, unlike an innocent neighbor, could have inspected the property or demanded a warranty deed. We are not persuaded, however, that a landowner who engages in abnormally dangerous activities should be liable only to neighboring property owners.

The abnormally dangerous-activity doctrine emphasizes the dangerousness and inappropriateness of the activity. Despite the social utility of the activity, that doctrine imposes liability on those who, for their own benefit, introduce an extraordinary risk of harm into the community.

Because some conditions and activities can be so hazardous and of "such relative infrequent occurrence," the risk of loss is justifiably allocated as a cost of business to the enterpriser who engages in such conduct. Although the law will tolerate the hazardous activity, the enterpriser must pay its way.

Because the former owner of the property whose activities caused the hazard might have been in the best position to bear or spread the loss, liability for the harm caused by abnormally dangerous activities does not necessarily cease with the transfer of property.

Nor are we satisfied that the doctrine of *caveat emptor* as developed in New Jersey should bar plaintiff's cause of action. Although the principle of *caveat emptor* dictates that in the absence of express agreement, a seller is not liable to the buyer or others for the condition of the land existing at the time of transfer.

A real-estate contract that does not disclose the abnormally dangerous condition or activity does not shield from liability the seller who created that condition or engaged in that activity.

We focus now on the elements of the abnormally dangerous-activity doctrine. That doctrine is premised on the principles that "one who carries on an abnormally dangerous activity is subject to liability for harm to the person, land or chattels of another resulting from the activity, although he has exercised the utmost care to prevent the harm." The *Restatement* sets forth six factors that a court should consider in determining whether an activity is "abnormally dangerous." They are:

(a) existence of a high degree of risk of some harm to the person, land or chattels of others;
(b) likelihood that the harm that results from it will be great;
(c) inability to eliminate the risk by the exercise of reasonable care;
(d) extent to which the activity is not a matter of common usage;
(e) inappropriateness of the activity to the place where it is carried on; and
(f) extent to which its value to the community is outweighed by its dangerous attributes.

Defendant does not dispute that liability can be imposed on enterprisers who engage in abnormally dangerous activities that harm others; but it contends that such liability is contingent on proof that the enterpriser knew or should have known of the "abnormally dangerous character of the activity."

Defendant adds that knowledge, or the ability to acquire such knowledge, must be assessed as of the time the enterpriser engaged in the activity, not at a later time—that is, if the risk of harm from the activity was scientifically unknowable at that time, an enterpriser should not be liable.

We need not, however, determine whether knowledge is a requirement in the context of a strict-liability claim predicated on an abnormally dangerous activity. Even if the law imposes such a requirement, we are convinced, for the reasons set forth more fully below, that defendant should have known about the risks of its activity, and that its constructive knowledge would fully satisfy any such requirement.

That brings us to the question of whether defendant's activity was such as to fall within the meaning of "abnormally dangerous-activity."

Radium has always been and continues to be an extraordinarily dangerous substance. Although radium processing has never been a common activity, the injudicious handling, processing, and disposal of radium has for decades caused concern; it has long been suspected of posing a serious threat to the health of those who are exposed to it.

Furthermore, although the risks involved in the processing and disposal of radium might be curtailed, one cannot safely dispose of radium by dumping it onto the vacant portions of an urban lot. Because of the extraordinarily hazardous nature of radium, the processing and disposal of that substance is particularly inappropriate in an urban setting. We conclude that despite the usefulness of radium, defendant's processing, handling, and disposal of that substance under the facts of this case constituted an abnormally dangerous activity. Plaintiff's property is befouled with radium because of defendant's abnormally dangerous activity. Radiation levels at the site exceed those permitted under governmental health regulations. Moreover, the property has been earmarked as a Superfund site. Because plaintiff vacated the premises in response to the health concern posed by the radium-contaminated site and because the danger to health is "the kind of harm, the possibility of which [made defendant's] activity abnormally dangerous," defendant is strictly liable for the resulting harm.

Despite that wealth of knowledge concerning the harmful effects of radium exposure, defendant contends that it could not have known that disposal of the radium-saturated by-products behind the plant would produce a hazard. That contention appears to rest on the idea that somehow the radium's potential for harm miraculously disappeared once the material had been deposited in a vacant corner of an urban lot, or at the least that one might reasonably reach that conclusion—a proposition that we do not accept.

Surely someone engaged in a business as riddled with hazards as defendant's demonstrably was should realize the potential for harm in every aspect of that dangerous business. If knowledge be a requirement, defendant knew enough about the abnormally dangerous character of radium processing to be charged with knowledge of the dangers of disposal.

Finally, we reflect on the "parade of horribles" argument, namely, that our decision will create such uncertainty as to render it impossible for today's business community to regulate its affairs effectively. We have already noted the limited scope of our holding in that it extends only to that rare form of conduct that meets the criteria of an abnormally dangerous activity. Second, we note that almost without exception any conveyance of industrial property today would be made not in vacuum but in full appreciation of regulatory requirements that would surely embrace a condition such as the one on the Alden Street property. Parties to such transactions will be able to accommodate themselves to the necessities of the situation. A seller of land dealing in an abnormally dangerous activity such as the processing of radium can arrange to have the cost of cure shifted to a purchaser and obtain indemnification from such purchaser against any downstream claims. Although the recording of such an agreement might not create a bar to third-party claims, it will surely alter the equities in respect of any claim of benefit-of-the-bargain damages by a successor in the chain.

Affirmed.

CASE QUESTIONS

1. Who originally owned the property?
2. How was the property originally used?
3. How did the owners feel about handling radium?
4. What was disposed of on the site?
5. At what point did the government step in and cause the site's evacuation?
6. Will T&E be liable under CERCLA?
7. Is Safety Light liable under CERCLA?
8. What is the basis of this lawsuit?
9. What made the disposal an abnormally dangerous activity?
10. What does the court say about the potential of a "parade of horribles" as a result of its decision?

CONSIDER 20.5

Michael and Lauri Maddy own property located next to Vulcan Materials, Inc., a chemical-processing plant. The Maddys have brought suit alleging that the discharge from the plant is a trespass because their lungs and those of their animals have been damaged by chemicals. Is this a correct theory for their suit? Are there alternative theories? *Maddy v. Vulcan Materials Co.*, 737 F. Supp. 1528 (Kan. 1990)

Group Suits—The Effect of Environmentalists

Private suits have had the most effect in terms of obtaining compliance with environmental regulations or abating existing nuisances affecting environmental quality. The reason for their success may be the ultimate outcome of the litigation—possible business shutdowns and, at the least, significant damages and costs.

In some cases, environmental groups that have the organizational structure and funding bring these suits. In some cases, the environmental groups are formed to protest one specific action, such as Citizens Against the Squaw Peak Parkway. Other groups are national organizations that take on environmental issues and litigation in all parts of the country. Examples of these national groups include the Sierra Club, the Environmental Defense Fund, Inc., the National Resources Defense Council, and the League of Conservation Voters. Some environmental groups represent business interests in environmental issues, as does the Mountain States Legal Foundation, which becomes involved in presenting business issues when private organizations and individuals bring environmental suits.

These groups have been successful in bringing private damage and injunctive relief suits, and in forcing agencies to promulgate regulations required under the federal laws.

Cautions and Conclusions

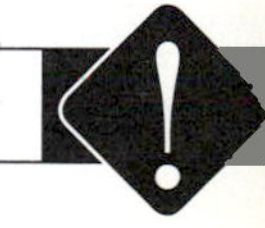

The implications of environmental laws on real property transactions are tremendous. Anyone seeking to purchase property for industrial use must be familiar with the air quality standards and release permit requirements in the area to determine if industrial use is possible, and if it is possible, if it will be more costly because of environmental constraints. Due diligence is required before property is sold. That due diligence includes a look at the property as well as at how it has been used. Property owners must also be diligent in voluntary audits and disclosure to the EPA to minimize liability. There are government and private mechanisms for enforcement of environmental laws, including citizen suits under both statutory and common law.

Key Terms

acid rain, 569
Air Pollution Control Act, 567
Air Quality Act, 567
Asbestos Hazard Emergency Response Act (AHERA), 581
Asset Conservation, Lender Liability, and Deposit Insurance Protection Act of 1996, 573
best available treatment (BAT), 571
best conventional treatment (BCT), 571
brownfields, 576
bubble concept, 568
Clean Air Act, 568
Clean Air Act Amendments of 1990, 569
Clean Water Act, 571
Community-Right-to-Know substance, 581
Comprehensive Environmental Response, Compensation, and Liability Act (CERCLA), 572
conventional pollutants, 571
Council on Environmental Quality (CEQ), 586
effluent guidelines, 571

Emissions Offset Policy, 568
Endangered Species Act, 581
environmental impact statement (EIS), 578
Environmental Protection Agency (EPA), 568
Federal Environmental Pesticide Control Act, 580
federal implementation plan (FIP), 569
Federal Water Pollution Control Act of 1972, 571
Federal Water Pollution Control Administration (FWPCA), 570
Hazardous Substance Response Trust Fund, 573
Incentives for Self-Policing, Disclosure, Correction, and Prevention of Violations, 577
maximum achievable control technology (MACT), 569
National Environmental Policy Act (NEPA) of 1969, 578
National Pollution Discharge Elimination System (NPDES), 571
Noise Control Act of 1972, 580
Nonattainment area, 568
nonconventional pollutants, 571
nuisance, 588
Occupational Safety and Health Administration (OSHA), 580
Oil Pollution Act (OPA), 572
point sources, 571
prevention of significant deterioration (PSD) areas, 568
Resource Conservation and Recovery Act of 1976 (RCRA), 572
Resource Recovery Act, 572
Rivers and Harbors Act of 1899, 571
Safe Drinking Water Act, 572
Solid Waste Disposal Act, 572
Superfund, 573
Superfund Amendment and Reauthorization Act, 573
Surface Mining and Reclamation Act of 1977, 580
state implementation plans (SIPs), 568
toxic pollutants, 581
Toxic Substances Control Act (TOSCA), 572
Water Quality Act, 570

Chapter Problems

1. In 1976, Swainsboro Print Works (SPW), a cloth-printing facility, entered into a "factoring" agreement with Fleet Factors Corporation (Fleet) in which Fleet agreed to advance funds against the assignment of SPW's accounts receivable. As collateral for these advances, Fleet obtained a security interest in SPW's textile facility and all of its equipment, inventory, and fixtures.

In August 1979, SPW filed for bankruptcy under Chapter 11 (the corporate-reorganization chapter). The factoring agreement continued until early 1981 when Fleet ceased advancing funds because SPW's debt to Fleet exceeded Fleet's estimate of the value of SPW's accounts receivable. On February 27, 1981, SPW ceased operations and began to liquidate its inventory. Fleet continued to collect the accounts receivable assigned to it under Chapter 11. In December 1981, SPW was adjudicated a bankrupt under Chapter 7, and the bankruptcy trustee assumed title and control of SPW's facility.

In May 1982, Fleet foreclosed on its security interest in some of SPW's inventory and equipment and contracted with Baldwin Industrial Liquidators (Baldwin) to conduct an auction of the collateral. Baldwin sold the material "as is" and "in place" on June 22, 1982, with buyers assuming the responsibility for removal of the materials.

On August 31, 1982, Fleet contracted with Nix Riggers (Nix) to remove the unsold equipment in consideration for leaving the premises "broom clean." Nix had performed its work in the facility by the end of December 1983.

On January 20, 1984, the Environmental Protection Agency (EPA) inspected the facility and found 700 55-gallon drums containing toxic chemicals and 44 truck-loads of material containing asbestos. The EPA incurred costs of $400,000 in cleaning up the SPW facility. On July 7, 1987, the facility was conveyed to Emanuel County, Georgia, at a foreclosure sale from SPW's failure to pay state and county taxes.

The government sued Fleet and the two principal officers and stockholders of SPW to recover the costs of cleaning up the hazardous waste.

Can Fleet be held liable under CERCLA? *United States v. Fleet Factors Corp.*, 901 F.2d 1550 (11th Cir. 1990)

2. A group of landowners situated near the Sanders Lead Company brought suit to recover for damages to their agricultural property from accumulations of lead particulates and sulfur oxide deposits released in Sanders's production process. The landowners' property had increased in value because of its commercial potential in being close to the plant. Sanders employs most of the town residents in its operations. What common law and statutory rights do the landowners have, and what relief can be obtained? *Borland v. Sanders Lead Co., Inc.*, 369 So.2d 523 (Ala. 1979)

3. Reynolds Metal has been held to the same technological standards in its pollution control for can manufacturing plants as those applied to aluminum manufacturers. Reynolds claims the processes are different and that the technology is not yet available for can manufacturing. Does Reynolds have a point? *Reynolds Metals Co. v. EPA*, 760 F.2d 549 (D.C. 1985)

4. The Mitchells lived in a residential section of Beverly Hills, Michigan, and sought to enjoin the operation of a nearby piggery. The pigs were fed in an open field, and any garbage not eaten by the pigs was plowed under by tractors. The odors from the operation, particularly in the spring and summer, were such that the use and enjoyment of the Mitchells' property was impaired. The Mitchells filed suit for an injunction and/or damages. Who will win? Are any federal statutory violations involved? *Mitchell v. Hines*, 9 N.W.2d 547 (Mich. 1943)

5. Kelley Technical Coatings is an industrial paint manufacturing company which operates two plants in Louisville, Kentucky. Arthur Sumner was the Vice President in charge of manufacturing operations for Kelley. Sumner oversaw the manufacturing process at both plants, including the storage and disposal of hazardous wastes. He was also responsible for environmental regulatory compliance, and submitted the necessary paperwork to the state environmental authorities to register Kelley as a generator of hazardous waste.

Kelley generated hazardous wastes in its manufacturing process, including spent solvents, such as toluene, ethyl benzene, xylene, and methyl ethyl ketone; excess and unusable paint, paint resins, and other paint ingredients which contained, among other things, toxic heavy metals such as chromium, lead, cadmium, and nickel; and paint sludge. Kelley accumulated hundreds of drums of these waste materials and stored them in drums behind one of its plants. Kelley never applied for a permit to store or dispose of its hazardous wastes on-site.

In July 1992 when the Kentucky Department of Environmental Protection inspected the Kelley plants, there were between 600 and 1,000 drums behind one of the plants. The drums had been stored on-site for more than 90 days, and in some cases for many years. Some of the drums had rusted and were leaking on the ground.

Between 1986 and 1989, Sumner had arranged for a licensed hazardous waste disposal company to remove and dispose of some of the drums containing hazardous wastes. From late 1989 to July 1992, however, no drums of hazardous waste were shipped off-site. Instead, in an effort to save money, Kelley contracted with a hazardous waste disposal company to come on-site and drain the liquids from the drums. After the bulk of the hazardous wastes were drained off, employees were directed to pour off any rainwater that had collected into the drums onto the ground and to consolidate the remaining residue into one drum. The consolidation process resulted in the spilling of hazardous substances onto the ground.

Both Kelley and Sumner were convicted under the RCRA. They appealed their convictions on the grounds that they did not have the *mens rea* required for conviction under the RCRA statute. Are they correct? Are they criminally responsible? *U.S. v. Kelley Technical Coatings, Inc.*, 157 F.3d 432 (C.A. 6 1998)

6. Albert J. Hubenthal leased approximately 55 acres of property in Winona County, Minnesota, to start a worm-farming operation. Shortly thereafter, he began to collect large amounts of material including waste paper, cardboard, used tires, scrap wood, scrap metal, leather, and other building materials that he contends were essential to the worm-farming operation.

The county attorney filed suit seeking to compel Hubenthal to clean up the property on the grounds that it was a public nuisance. After a hearing, the lower court enjoined Hubenthal from storing solid-waste material that could be a "source of filth and sickness" and from maintaining a junkyard. The order gave Hubenthal 30 days to clean up, which he failed to do. Two months after the order was issued, county officials took three days to remove the materials accumulated from Hubenthal's farm. Hubenthal filed suit for trespass and violation of his due process rights. Is it a nuisance? Can the government clean it up? *Hubenthal v. County of Winona*, 751 F.2d 243 (8th Cir. 1984)

7. From July 7, 1944, to December 16, 1980, Herschel and Nellie McLeod owned a 117-acre piece of land in the town of California, Maryland, in St. Mary's County (referred to as the California Maryland Drum site or CMD site). During this period of ownership, Maryland Bank & Trust (MB&T) loaned money to the McLeods for the operation of his two businesses: Greater St. Mary's Disposal, Inc., and Waldorf Sanitation of St. Mary's, Inc., which were both trash and garbage businesses. The record indicates that MB&T was aware of the nature of the businesses, but it is unclear when it acquired its awareness.

During 1972 to 1973, the McLeods permitted the dumping of hazardous wastes on their property, including lead, chromium, mercury, zinc, and ethylbenzene.

In 1980, the McLeods' son, Mark, obtained a loan from MB&T and purchased the 117 acres from his parents. Mark failed to make payments, and MB&T instituted foreclosure proceedings in 1981 and bought the property at a sale in May 1982.

The EPA discovered the hazardous waste problems and conducted a cleanup of the site at a cost of $551,713.50. The EPA then demanded payment from MB&T. When payment was refused, the EPA brought suit to collect the cost of the cleanup. Can EPA collect from MB&T? *United States v. Maryland Bank & Trust Co.*, 632 F. Supp. 573 (D. Md. 1986)

8. Frezzo Brothers, Incorporated, is a Pennsylvania firm engaged in mushroom farming at a location near Avondale. To produce their mushrooms, Guido and James Frezzo (the two family members responsible for the operation of the business) used a growing medium that consisted of fermented hay and horse manure. White Clay Creek, which flowed alongside of the Frezzo operation, was considerably polluted, and upon analysis the pollutants were found to consist mainly of horse manure. There had been no rain in the area, and the Environmental Protection Agency charged the Frezzos and their corporation with willfully discharging manure into the stream. The Frezzos claim the right to use the stream as riparians, and the United States government claims environmental regulations will control over common law rights. Would discharging manure into a stream be a violation of any environmental laws? *United States v. Frezzo Brothers, Inc.*, 602 F.2d 1123 (3d Cir. 1979)

9. First Capital Life Insurance Company made a loan of $7,300,000 to Schneider, Inc., in 1986. The loan was secured by a mortgage on real property located in Allegheny County, Pennsylvania. Schneider failed to make payments in 1988, and in 1989 First Capital declared the loan in default. First Capital then sent representatives to the property to conduct an environmental inspection. Schneider employees refused to grant access to the property. There was no provision in the mortgage regarding such inspections upon default. Combining your knowledge from Chapter 15 on financing and this chapter on environmental liability issues, determine whether First Capital should be permitted access to the property prior to foreclosure. *First Capital Life Insurance Co. v. Schneider, Inc.*, 608 A.2d 1082 (Pa. 1992)

10. One hundred-and-forty-three residents of the Barnegat Pines Development area in Lacey Township, Ocean County, New Jersey, brought suit against Exxon Corporation and Richard E. and Susan M. Ritchie, who did business operating a gasoline station known as Lacey Exxon. The residents brought suit in nuisance, trespass, and under various environmental laws alleging that gasoline from Rule's service station, which had operated between 1959 and 1975 as a Texaco Station, had seeped into the groundwater and contaminated their wells.

The residents had an expert witness, Albert D. Young, a consultant in petroleum distribution and a retired Exxon employee, who had 35 years of experience in overseeing, viewing, and evaluating the distribution, storage, and retail sale of gasoline. Young testified that the complaint of suspected gasoline contamination of wells in the present case was typical of the kind of situation he had frequently investigated. According to Young, the service station probably spilled gasoline "more frequently than not" between 1959 and 1975 and the spilled gasoline would have seeped to the groundwater. Young's opinion was based on his knowledge that such discharges were routine occurrences in probably all 200,000 service stations ever in existence.

Also, after considering the results of soil gas studies showing the presence of petroleum vapors in the soil of the old tank field at the station, Young found it more probable than not that spills would have occurred during deliveries in the pre-1975 period because when tank sizes failed to keep pace with truck capacities, overfills were routine at all stations. Such spills could have gone undetected by the station owner.

The jury returned a verdict of no liability in favor of both the Rtichies and Exxon. Was the jury' verdict correct? What case law could the appellate court apply in making its decision? *Bahrle v. Exxon Corp.*,652 A.2d 178 (N.J. Super. 1995)

For research activities related to this chapter, go to our text companion website at www.thomsonedu.com/westbuslaw/jennings.

Legal Issues in Land and Economic Development

CHAPTER 21

Plans get you into things, but you got to work your way out.

Will Rogers

If a builder builds a house for a man and does not make its construction firm, and the house which he has built collapses and causes the death of the owner of the house, the builder shall be put to death.

Hammurabi's Code

Real estate planning and development are not easy tasks. In fact, real estate development requires knowledge from the other 21 chapters of this book, along with an understanding of some new areas of law. From interaction with zoning and planning commissions to negotiations with lenders for financing to bids with contractors, a developer faces law at every turn in the complex maze of real estate development.

This chapter covers the stages of real estate development and the laws that apply and affect those stages of development. From construction law to syndication requirements to zoning and planning constraints, development requires constant interaction and compliance with the law. Figure 21.1 (on page 600) provides a flowchart look at the process of land development.

Land Acquisition

Market Analysis

Because real estate investments have been so profitable in the past few years, the idea of doing a market analysis on buying and developing land seems redundant. Before acquiring land or deciding on the type of subdivision, a developer should know the economic status and physical needs of those in the area. The purpose of such

Figure 21.1 Steps in Land Development

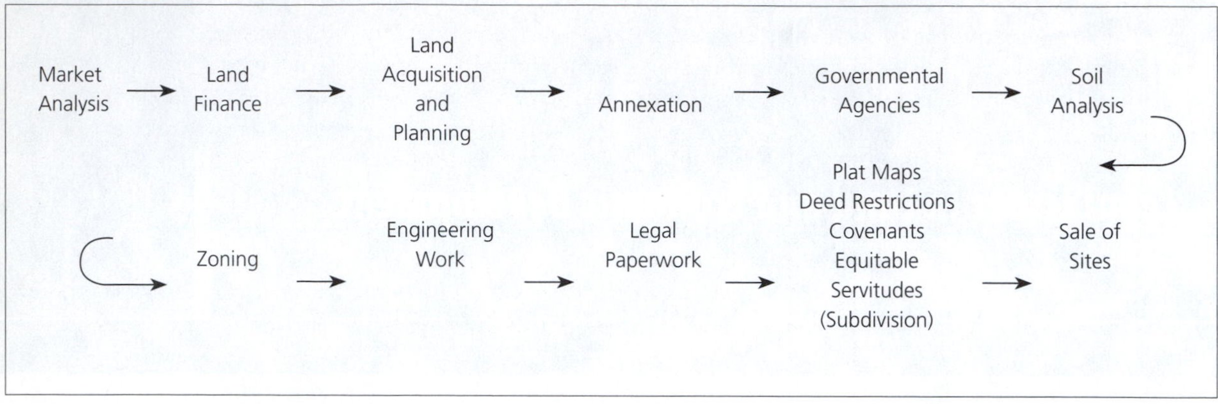

preliminary study is to determine what housing will sell. For example, areas with a concentration of families need subdivisions with larger, single-family homes. In that same area, townhouses and condominiums might not sell. In college towns, on the other hand, smaller housing units sell because investors and students need that type of unit for rental properties or temporary residences.

Governmental Analysis

Developers must work closely with governmental agencies at all steps of their project.

Annexation

In some cases, no land parcels that are large enough for subdivision are located within city limits. However, the developer will have a difficult time selling properties in the subdivision if the city emergency and utility services are not available. One alternative is to have a private corporation furnish these services, but a better and more frequently used alternative is parcel annexation by the city.

The process of **annexation** is similar to a change in zoning and follows the same process that any change in zoning would require. The public hearing required allows objections, feedback, and questions (see Chapter 19).

Interstate Land Sales

If a developer is selling unimproved lots, the Interstate Land Sales Full Disclosure Act (ILSFDA; 15 U.S.C. §1701 *et seq.*) will apply. HUD requires statements of record and property reports (see Chapter 14).

Federal Loan Approvals for Sales

If the developer is selling single or multiunit housing units, Federal Housing Administration (FHA) and Veterans Administration (VA) financing for buyers helps increase sales. The FHA and VA must approve the subdivision before buyers can obtain this government-backed financing.

The Cost of Development—Impact Fees

In recent years, rapid growth has found cities and counties unable to maintain the pace or fund the cost of creating the government infrastructure for new developments. As a result, local governments have been requiring developers to bear some of these costs, such as the cost of new schools and additional fire and police personnel.

Often called **impact fees,** these special assessments cover the costs of expanded government services required because of new subdivisions.

Impact fees have not set well with developers and have been a continuing basis for judicial challenge each time cities and counties implement a new type of fee. For example, impact fees for constructing schools seem to be fairly well sanctioned by the courts, but development fees for expansion of roads and highways still create judicial controversy. Developers use several theories to challenge impact fees, including the city or town's lack of statutory authority as well as the constitutionality of a tax assessed without proper process. The cases are split in terms of both authority and constitutionality, with many towns and cities going back to the drawing board, as it were, to find a way to impose the fees to cover the additional costs of expansive growth.[1] The following case, the most recent available decision on impact fees, resulted from Mississippi towns imposing impact fees in the post-Katrina redevelopment effort as a means of rebuilding the schools, parks, fire and police departments, and all other services necessary as towns and cities rebuilt themselves following this hurricane of the century.

Mayor and Bd. of Aldermen, City of Ocean Springs v. Homebuilders Ass'n of Mississippi, Inc.

932 So.2d 44 (Miss. 2006)

FACTS

The Mayor and Board of Aldermen of the city of Ocean Springs, Mississippi ("City"), adopted a Comprehensive Plan, which included separate impact fee ordinances which authorized the assessment, collection, and expenditure of "development impact fees" for various municipal improvements, services, equipment, and vehicles.

The Home Builders Association of Mississippi, Inc. (appellees), appeared at three public hearings conducted by the City regarding impact fees. Representatives of the Home Builders repeatedly commented on and protested each of the ordinances, to no avail, as the ordinances were approved by the City. The impact fees were to be paid in addition to any and all other applicable land-use, zoning, planning, adequate public facilities, platting, or other related fees, requirements, standards, and conditions imposed by the City. The following list shows the impact fees assessed:

(1) Development Impact Fee Procedures Ordinance
(2) General Municipal Facilities Development Impact Fee Ordinance
(3) Fire Facilities Development Impact Fee Ordinance
(4) Park and Recreation Facilities Development Impact Fee Ordinance
(5) Police Facilities Development Impact Fee Ordinance
(6) Major Roadways Development Impact Fee Ordinance
(7) Water Facilities Development Impact Fee Ordinance

The Home Builders filed suit challenging the impact fees and the Circuit Court held the impact fees to be a void taxing measure. The City appealed the decision.

JUDICIAL OPINION

Randolph, Justice. The State of Mississippi does not have a specific constitutional provision or statute regarding implementation of development impact fees, nor can authority be found in the common law. This truth has been implicitly, if not explicitly, recognized by the Executive and Legislative branches of state government, and the City. The "Development Impact Fee Report" prepared for the City in 2002, stated, "[W]e believe that the Impact Fee Program reflects the city's needs [and] will be entirely consistent with the *proposed Mississippi*

1. For decisions that recognize impact fees as valid, see *Caparco v. Town of Danville*, 886 A.2d 1045 (N.H. 2005); *McCarthy v. City of Leawood*, 894 P.2d 836 (Kan. 1995); *Idaho Bldg. Contractors Ass'n v. City of Coeur d'Alene*, 890 P.2d 326 (Idaho 1995) (valid as a tax, but city had no authority for impact fees); *City of Dunedin v. Contractors and Builders Ass'n of Pinellas County*, 312 So.2d 763 (Fla. App. 1975) (but Florida is all over the maps on these impact fees, depending upon the county and the nature of the fees, with some struck down, e.g., *Broward County v. Janis Development Corp.*, 311 So. 2d 371 (Fla. App. 1975)). For cases in which impact fees were held invalid, see *Cranberry Tp. v. Builders Ass'n of Metropolitan Pittsburgh*, 621 A.2d 563 (Pa. 1993); *Country Joe, Inc. v. City of Eagan*, 560 N.W.2d 681 (Minn. 1997); and *New Jersey Builders Ass'n v. Mayor and Tp. Committee of Bernards Tp.*, Somerset County, 108 N.J. 223, 528 A.2d 555 (1987).

development impact fee enabling legislation...." (emphasis added). To date, the Mississippi legislature has not adopted a statute authorizing development impact fees or enabling legislation to authorize a city to adopt and implement impact fees.

There are twenty-seven (27) states which have adopted development impact fee statutes, although five of the states' statutes related exclusively to roads.

Article IV, Section 80 of the Mississippi Constitution declares, "[p]rovision shall be made by general laws to prevent the abuse by cities, towns, and other municipal corporations of their powers of assessment, taxation, borrowing money, and contracting debts." Appellees argue this provision of the Mississippi Constitution prohibits assessments or taxation, unless there is specific statutory authority allowing the City to do so. In *Adams v. Kuykendall*, 83 Miss. 571, 35 So. 830, 835 (1904), this Court stated, "[w]e hold the taxing power of the sovereign is vested solely in the State and its relinquishment is never to be inferred."

The Circuit Court found no express grant of authority under the Municipal Planning statutes. We agree. Under the Municipal Planning Statutes, Miss.Code Ann. Section 17-1-1, *et seq.*, there are no provisions which grant authority to adopt impact fees or other revenue raising mechanisms to implement the City's Comprehensive Plan.

The City further urges the authority to impose impact fees exists under Miss.Code Ann. Section 21-17-5, commonly known as the Home Rule Statute. The City relies on the language of Section 21-17-5(1), "[e]xcept as otherwise provided in subsection (2) of this section, the powers granted to governing authorities of municipalities in this section are complete without the existence of or reference to any specific authority granted in any other statute or law of the state of Mississippi" as its authority, and does not require a specific legislative mandate.

The City relies on the Home Rule Statute and argues the foregoing cases grant authority to impose impact fees. In part, we agree. [w]e find that Home Rule authority grants municipalities authority to impose *fees,* as long as the imposition is not inconsistent with legislative mandate or the Mississippi Constitution, and is a fee, as opposed to a tax, as discussed *infra.*

We conclude there is no constitutional basis, legislative enactment, or common law doctrine, which empowers cities to adopt and impose development impact fees.

The Circuit Court held, "[t]he fact that the City labeled this exaction 'fee' rather than 'tax' is not important; the purpose of the enactment governs over terminology." The City argues that because the impact fees were reasonably related to the infrastructure needs created by new development and the fees were earmarked and deposited into a special fund, the impact fees meet the criteria for fees. Appellees successfully argued before the Circuit Court that the City was utilizing the fees for general municipal purposes and as a revenue-raising mechanism, therefore they were a tax.

[t]he United States Court of Appeals for the Fifth Circuit was called upon to address the distinction between a tax and a fee in *Home Builders Ass'n of Miss. v. City of Madison, Miss.*, 143 F.3d 1006, 1011 (5th Cir.1998), and held:

> *Workable distinctions emerge from the relevant case law, however: the classic tax sustains the essential flow of revenue to the government, while the classic fee is linked to some regulatory scheme. The classic tax is imposed by a state or municipal legislature, while the classic fee is imposed by an agency upon those it regulates. The classic tax is designed to provide benefit for the entire community, while the classic fee is designed to raise money to help defray an agency's regulatory expenses.*

The State of Mississippi has adopted similar distinctions stating, "[t]he chief distinction is that a tax is an exaction for public purposes while a fee relates to an individual privilege or benefit to the payer." Miss. Att'y Gen. Op. 1996–0425 (1996)

Aside from claiming authority from the Home Rule Statute and general zoning and planning powers, the City asserts it may impose impact fees as necessary regulatory fees, under its police power.

The fees at issue do not qualify as regulatory in nature. These fees cannot be said to cover "administrative expenses" incurred by the City. In order to obtain a building permit, these fees must be paid; however, the fees are not based on the administrative expense the City incurs in issuing the building permit.

Further, to be regulatory in nature, there must be a specific benefit conferred on the payer of the fee. The Circuit Court found the City's impact fees did not provide any special benefit to the parties paying the fees. The City submits, "[b]enefit is guaranteed by earmarking impact fee revenue in a separate fund from the general fund and restricting the use of impact fee revenue to new infrastructure that will benefit new development." The parties agree the fees were deposited into a separate account from the City's general municipal fund. However, to be determined is whether the developers upon whom the impact fees were imposed were receiving the benefit or if the benefit of the fees was being received by the municipality as a whole.

Section 5 of the Procedures Ordinance, states the purpose and intent of the impact fees "is to promote the health, safety, and general welfare of the residents of the City."

The learned trial judge observed, "[t]his is little, if any, assurance that such funds provide a special benefit to the class upon whom the burden is imposed. Simply opening a special account earmarked for particular city services or facilities is insufficient to provide a 'special' benefit to those utilizing the service or facility."

In conjunction with the City's Procedures Ordinance, the six Ordinances were adopted for general municipal purposes, fire department purposes, park and recreation purposes, police department purposes, major roadways and water facility purposes. At a 2002 public hearing, Bruce Peshoff, the principal in the design of the City's impact fees, stated the "first round" of impact fees were being developed for fire, parks and for *general municipal services.*

The public services identified in the Ordinances have traditionally been funded by tax revenues. The City is responsible for general municipal services that benefit the City as a whole.

[T]he ordinances... raise money for... traditional, general municipal services and facilities normally funded by tax revenues raised by legislatively authorized schemes. If the rationale of the City were sufficient to impliedly vest municipalities with revenue-raising authority by implication, there would cease to be a need for exercising the taxing power of the State. A municipality could classify any exaction as a "fee" for the provision of services or facilities and evade the Constitutional and Legislative limitations placed upon governing authorities in regard to taxation.

Because the fee has no relation to the expenses of the city in approving subdivision plats or building permits, it cannot be justified as an incident of the exercise of its police powers.

Impact fees are not per se illegal; however, the authority to implement the fees rests with the Legislature.

"The county and city are not authorized to impose taxes without direct authorization from the Legislature. Even under home rule provisions... the city and county are explicitly barred from levying taxes other than those authorized by statute." Miss. Att'y Gen. Op. 1989–124 (1989). In *City of Jackson v.Freeman-Howie, Inc.*, 239 Miss. 84, 121 So.2d 120, 123 (1960) we held, "[a] city derives its existence and powers by its charter from the State, and can perform the acts for which it has authority thereunder except such as may be in conflict with the Constitution."

Courts cannot fault the logic or the foresight that induces the municipality to consider the long term impact of permitted development on municipal resources and public facilities. However, in the absence of legislative intent, municipalities cannot depart from traditionally authorized methods of financing public facilities so as to allocate the costs of substantial public projects among new developments on the basis of their anticipated impact.

While sound argument may be made, especially in the aftermath of Hurricane Katrina [that] the City is in need of the added revenue impact fees would bring, the ability to assess such fees is a decision for the citizens of this state, either through a constitutional amendment or legislative action.

Because these fees constitute a tax, the municipality must have enabling legislation in order to levy and collect this tax. The municipality has been given no such authority and in imposing such fees has stepped outside of its authority.

Affirmed.

CASE QUESTIONS

1. Describe what the fees will be used for and how their use is important in the case.
2. What must exist before impact fees can be valid?
3. What is the difference between a regulatory fee and a tax? Why is this distinction important to the court?

CONSIDER 21.1

In 2003, the City of Lincoln, Nebraska (the City), enacted an ordinance conditioning the issuance of a building permit for new residential development on the payment of "impact fees," intended to offset the expenses associated with providing municipal services to the new development. The "Impact Fee Ordinance" (the Ordinance) provided

any person who applies for a building permit for a development or who applies for any other permit for a development where a building permit is not required, or who seeks to engage in a development for which no permit is required, shall pay a water system impact fee, water distribution impact fee, wastewater impact fee, arterial street impact fee, and neighborhood park and trail impact fee unless the type of development described in the permit or to be engaged in is specifically exempted, waived or subsidized by this ordinance, or unless the type of development described in the permit or to be engaged in is not located in an impact fee benefit district for the above-described impact fees.

CONSIDER 21.1
(continued)

The Home Builders Association of Lincoln has filed suit challenging the authority of Lincoln to impose such fees. Determine what the court should do and why. Be sure to base your answer on what you learned from the Mississippi law analysis. *Home Builders Ass'n of Lincoln v. City of Lincoln*, 711 N.W.2d 871 (Neb. 2006).

Use Restrictions

Chapter 2 covered use restrictions in fee simple defeasible grants. The following case illustrates that, in revitalization projects, a grantor's restriction on land use controls developers as well as the government in working jointly with developers.

White v. Metropolitan Dade County

563 So.2d 117 (Fla. 1990)

FACTS

In 1940, several members of the Matheson family deeded three tracts of land located on the northern portion of Key Biscayne to Dade County. The 680 acres came to be known as Crandon Park. In the recorded deeds, the grantors expressly provided:

This conveyance is made upon the express condition that the lands hereby conveyed shall be perpetually used and maintained for public park purposes only; and in case the use of said land for park purposes shall be abandoned, then and in that event the said grantor, his heirs, grantees or assigns, shall be entitled upon their request to have the said lands reconveyed to them.

Since the time of the original grant, several amendatory deeds have been issued by the grantors to allow ancillary uses such as the construction of public roads, public utilities, and a firehouse. However, the grantors did refuse to allow the building of a cable satellite dish.

In 1986, the Dade County Board of County Commissioners entered into an agreement with Arvida International Championships, Inc. (Arvida), and the International Players Championship, Inc. (IPC), to construct a permanent tennis complex on the property. The complex consisted of 15 tennis courts, service roads, utilities, and landscaping and took up 28 acres. The agreement with Arvida and IPC provided that for two weeks each year the complex would become the site of the Lipton International Players Championship Tennis Tournament (Lipton tournament).

In February 1987, the first Lipton tournament was held before approximately 213,000 people. A permanent clubhouse was then erected, with plans calling for a 12,000 seat stadium. The facilities are closed to the public for periods of time before and after the Lipton tournament (three weeks before and one week after) for site preparation and dismantling. When additional parking space became necessary, the grantors' heirs refused to give consent for more parking, and a suit resulted seeking an injunction against the Lipton tournament on the grounds that the deed restriction was violated and the master plan for Dade County was violated because the park was designated as an "environmentally sensitive parkland." The trial court found for Dade County, and the grantors' heirs and environmental groups (appellants) appealed.

JUDICIAL OPINION

Gersten, Judge. Appellant/heirs first contend that the construction of the tennis complex violates the deed restriction. As previously stated, the deed provides that the "lands hereby conveyed shall be perpetually used and maintained for public park purposes only."

"In construing restrictive covenants the question is primarily one of intention and the fundamental rule is that the intention of the parties as shown by the agreement governs, being determined by a fair interpretation of the entire text of the covenant." Similarly, "the terms of dedications of land for park purposes where the lands are conveyed by private individuals are to be construed more strictly than is the case where the lands are acquired by the public body by purchase or condemnation."

Appellant/heirs argue that it was the intent of the Matheson family to limit the use of Crandon Park to passive activities such as picnicking, swimming, and the like. We glean no such intention from the language of the deed. Further, the Florida Supreme Court has adopted a very broad definition for what a "park" encompasses. The court has stated:

[A] park is considered not only as ornamental but also as a place for recreation and amusement. Changes in the concepts of parks have continued and the trend is certainly toward expanding and enlarging the facilities for amusement and recreation found therein.

The court further explained that the permissible uses for a public park include:

[T]ennis courts, playground and dancing facilities, skating, a swimming pool and bathhouse, horseshoe pitching, walking, horseback riding, athletic sports and other outdoor exercises... golfing and baseball... parking facilities... provided always that a substantial portion of the park area remains in grass, trees, shrubs and flowers, with seats and tables for picnicking, for the use by and enjoyment of the public.

We conclude that the construction of the tennis complex did not violate the "public park purposes only" provision of the deed restriction.

Appellant/heirs next argue that turning the tennis complex over to a commercial operator violates the deed restriction. We do not agree. Florida courts have consistently ruled that commercial benefit does not defeat a park's purposes.

Finally, appellant/heirs contend that the operation of the Lipton tournament violates the deed restriction because it deprives the public of the use and enjoyment of Crandon Park, including the use and enjoyment of tennis facilities. We are persuaded by this argument and rule that the holding of the Lipton tournament violates the deed restriction because it virtually bars the public uses of Crandon Park during the tournament, and does bar public use of the tennis complex, for extended periods of time.

In ruling that the holding of the Lipton tournament violates the deed restriction, we note that a distinction must be made between "park purposes" and "public purposes." Assuming *arguendo* that the Lipton tournament is an economic success which brings innumerable benefits to Dade County and its citizens, such an undeniable public purpose is not consistent with a deed restriction mandating the narrower "public park purposes only."

In addition, the word "only" in the deed restriction at issue further buttresses our ruling that the operation of the Lipton tournament, as presently constituted, violates the restriction.

Dade County contends that the tennis complex is consistent with the "public park purposes" restriction provided for in the deed. In support, Dade County argues that the complex is open to the public when the tournament is not being held, the site of the tennis complex utilizes less than 5 percent of Crandon Park, and that a valid park purpose is served by "spectating." Dade County also points to the benefits derived by Dade County from having the Lipton tournament in Dade County.

Here, the public, in fact, is deprived from using these tennis facilities for a period of three to four weeks during the Tournament Period. Further, under the contract as to the 1987 tournament, Arvida had the right to exclude the public for as long as five months.

Dade County argues that the use of the property as a tennis complex is better than its previous use as a dump. While we agree that a tennis complex in a public park, is better than a dump in a public park, we note that the County's previous use of the site as a dump, was also in violation of the deed restriction. We do not congratulate Dade County for shifting from one impermissible use to another.

Finally, Dade County argues, and we agree, that it is well settled that "equity abhors a forfeiture," that "such restrictions are not favored in law if they have the effect of destroying an estate," and that they "will be construed strictly and will be most strongly construed against the grantor."

Appellants/heirs, however, clearly represented to the court and the trial court that they were not seeking a reversal. What appellant/heirs want is a declaratory judgement that the present use of the park is in violation of the deed restriction and an injunction to prevent any further erosion of the "public park purposes only" deed restriction.

We therefore declare Dade County to be in violation of the deed restriction. We reverse the trial court order as to the deed restriction, and remand for entry of an order enjoining Dade County from permitting the Lipton tournament to proceed as it is presently held. Our ruling does not prevent Dade County from using the tennis complex for tennis tournaments. It merely seeks to insure that in holding such tournaments, public access to the rest of Crandon Park is not infringed; and use of the tennis complex is not denied to the public for unreasonable periods of time.

We reverse the trial court order on this point and remand for entry of an order enjoining any further development at the site.

CASE QUESTIONS

1. What type of land interest was created with the grant to Dade County?

2. How does the court interpret the "park only" requirement?

3. Of what significance is the fact that the public cannot use the courts before, during, and after the tournament?

4. Did Dade County violate other restrictions apart from the deed restrictions?

5. Do the heirs of the grantors want the land returned to them?

6. Must the complex be removed because of environmental concerns?

Governmental Approval

Zoning

Even property that is already designated for residential zoning may need to be changed for its density. Some cities limit the number of housing units per acre, and if the developer is planning a condominium development or single-family dwellings on minuscule lots, the density restrictions may need to be waived. (See Chapter 18 for a discussion of obtaining zoning variances.)

ETHICAL ISSUE

Suppose that a member of the city council who is scheduled to vote on a particular zoning application is the beneficiary of a family trust that owns property in the area near where the proposed project will be built. The effect of the project going forward will be a substantial increase in value of the surrounding properties. Should the city council member participate in the discussions and vote on the zoning for the proposed project? What issues do you see in such a scenario?

Protests of Residents Exercising Rights

Developers not only deal with cities and government agencies, they must work with various interest and watchdog groups that exist to preserve parks, historic buildings, beachfront and coastal zones, and, generally speaking, the environment. Their support may be necessary for approval by the governmental bodies.

Because of these third-party groups and their political power, many developers have found that presenting a more extensive **master-planned community**, reached through negotiations with agencies and third-party groups, allows for faster processing. Developers now propose larger-scale projects that are actually community development as opposed to subdivision creation; this larger-scale and integrative approach is sometimes referred to as a **planned unit development (PUD)**. The community plan envisions parks, commercial and office facilities, and a completely preplanned layout. To obtain approval for the concept, the developer may be required to guarantee the use of the land in a certain way and thus may present a full package of covenants that will govern the community. For example, the developer may agree that certain areas will remain as parks for the planned community, or that only single-family residences will be constructed in certain areas of the community.

The Uniform Planned Community Act has been adopted in several states. The primary purpose of this act is to help establish structures, policies, and procedures that recognize the powerful private lawmaking bodies that exist within these communities and their fundamental impact on property rights and property owners. Increasing litigation involving homeowners and homeowners' associations has resulted in increasing legislation to cover the various issues and procedures in planned communities. (See Chapter 11 for more information on HOAs.)

Land Finance

Financing a real estate development is often not as simple as going to the bank and obtaining a mortgage loan. A developer may have to be more creative and bring together a pool of investors to finance the project. These investors will want something more than interest as a return on their funds; they will want to join in on the profits made from the development project. **Real estate syndication** is a generic term for the process of investor ownership of real estate projects. Real estate syndication allows developers to acquire nontraditional funding for a project through groups of individual investors. Syndication can be something as simple as pooling funds to buy an apartment complex or as complex as the development of raw land into a planned community or commercial complex. The following sections cover the forms of and laws that apply to the various forms of syndications.

The Basics of Real Estate Syndication

The primary party in a real estate syndication is the entrepreneur or syndicator. Those who invest in the syndicate are referred to as *unit purchasers*. The form of the syndicate may be a partnership, a corporation, a limited liability company (LLC), or a real estate investment trust (REIT).

Syndication Forms–General Partnerships

A **general partnership** is a form of doing business that can be used for syndication so that all the profits and losses flow through to the individual partners. Their personal assets are all subject to the creditors of the partnership. Governed by the **Uniform Partnership Act (UPA)**, this law has been adopted in 49 states so that partnership structures are fairly clear for purposes of national syndication.

The Internal Revenue Code (IRC) recognized partnerships as an aggregate of the partners only and permits each partner to report his or her share of the partnership's income, gains, and losses. In a real estate investment, this attribute of partnership taxation enables the partners or unit owners to enjoy the full benefit of deductions for depreciation.

As just discussed, there are no tax consequences to the partnership upon the contribution. However, the basis issue for the partnership remains. The basis of the property is, very simply, the cost of the property plus what has been put into the property. For purposes of a real estate partnership, the basis of contributed property is the partner's basis. Thus, if A, B, and C form the ABC partnership and A contributes a piece of property with a basis of $300,000, the partnership basis is $300,000 (26 U.S.C. §723).

The contributing partner has no tax consequences upon contribution of the property to the partnership, but will have tax consequences if the partnership interest is transferred or if the partnership terminates and the partner is paid the value of his or her interest. At that time, the partner may have to recognize income.

Practical Tip

A checklist for those interested in getting into syndication:

1. *Check the current market value of the properties involved.*
2. *Check current leases, rental fees, payment histories, and terms.*
3. *Check the property and syndicator's expenses.*
4. *Perform a cash flow analysis.*
5. *If there are vacancies, why? How does the market look?*
6. *Check title, taxes, assessment, public records.*
7. *Check on the tax implications.*
8. *Check the zoning.*
9. *Check for environmental issues, liability, and targets.*
10. *Check terms of underlying loan agreements, mortgages, deeds of trust, and other contracts.*
11. *Determine whether state and federal securities laws apply to the syndication.*
12. *Check the background and experience of the syndicator(s).*
13. *Review the paperwork for the syndication structure and, if applicable, of the syndicator.*
14. *Are sales people licensed real estate agents? Are they licensed securities dealers?*
15. *Verify brokerage fees and other commissions for sales of interest in the syndication.*

Syndication Forms–Limited Partnerships

A **limited partnership** is a form of doing business and syndication governed by the **Uniform Limited Partnership Act (ULPA)** and the **Revised Uniform Limited Partnership Act (RULPA)**.

A limited partnership is a partnership with a slight variation in the liability of those involved. There are two types of partners in a limited partnership: there must be at least one **general partner** and one **limited partner**. General partners have the same liability as all partners in a general partnership—full and complete personal liability for all partnership obligations and losses. Limited partners' liability is limited to the amount of their capital contributions. Their personal assets are not placed at the risk of the limited partnership's success. The most they can lose is the amount of their investment.

A limited partnership is a statutory creature. Unlike a general partnership that can be formed with an agreement or **articles of partnership**, a limited partnership must be created formally with a public filing of the document of creation, often called the **articles of limited partnership**. The articles must be filed with a public office, generally the secretary of state in the state where the limited partnership is created and will do business.

The principal advantages of a limited partnership is that limited partners have only limited liability and the income and losses, just as with a general partnership, flow through to the individual partners' income tax returns. If the limited partners comply with the rules for limited liability, their liability is limited to the amount of their capital contribution.

In many limited partnerships, the general partner contributes an undeveloped piece of property, and the limited partners furnish the money for its development. Limited partners are known in lay terms as silent partners and must not create the impression that they are involved in firm management and so fully liable as general partner/managers are.

The following case involves an issue of a limited partner involved in the management of a business.

American National Ins. Co. v. Gilroy, Sims & Associates, Ltd.

874 F. Supp. 971 (E.D. Mo. 1995)

FACTS

Gilroy, Sims & Associates, Ltd. (Gilroy, Sims), was a limited partnership engaged in real estate development whose original general partners were Richard Gilroy and William Sims. Thomas Green and John Murphy, Jr., were listed as limited partners along with certain other individuals on the certificate of limited partnership. Green and Murphy took an active role in the day-to-day operations of the real estate developed by the limited partnership. Financing was obtained to construct the venture's building in St. Louis in 1968, and a mortgage was payable to American National Insurance Co. over 27 years. In 1976, the partnership executed a Restated Agreement, and Green and Murphy became general partners of Gilroy, Sims, agreeing to "unlimited liability for the debts of the partnership." In the fall of 1990, the partnership stopped making mortgage payments. After foreclosure by American National, a deficiency of $1,437,840 was outstanding. Green and Murphy believed that as limited partners when the debt was incurred in 1968, they were absolved from any personal liability beyond the assets of the firm. They moved for summary judgment.

JUDICIAL OPINION

Gunn, D. J. With respect to defendants Green and Murphy's motion for summary judgment for the remaining deficiency, the Court finds that defendants are liable for the remaining deficiency pursuant to the terms of the Restated Agreement.

Even though the Restated Agreement signed by Green and Murphy provides that "the partners shall have unlimited liability for the debts of the partnership," Green and Murphy contend that as incoming partners they are liable for prior debts only to the extent of partnership property and are absolved of personal liability under §17 of the Uniform Partnership Act. An incoming partner, however, may by agreement bind himself to personal liability for past debts. See *Resolution Trust Corp. v. Teem Partnership*, 835 F. Supp. 563, 570 (D. Colo. 1993) (some jurisdictions interpreting parallel statutes have held that UPA §17 does not apply to incoming partner who expressly assumes pre-existing obligation).

The dispositive issue before the Court is whether Green and Murphy assumed personal liability for the pre-existing debts and, if so, to what extent. In executing the restated agreement, defendants failed to limit the debts or time period of the debts for which they assumed unlimited liability, but instead assumed liability as general partners for all of the debts of the partnership in section 10. Defendants expressly adopted the partnership obligation incurred prior to their execution of the Restated Agreement by their words as well as their actions. Moreover, section 5 of the Restated Agreement describing the duration of the partnership specifically provides that the partnership commenced on November 1, 1968.

Under Missouri law, limited partners are not liable as general partners if they do not take part in the control of the day-to-day business operations of the partnership. *First Wisconsin Nat'l Bank v. Towboat Partners, Ltd.*, 630 F. Supp. 171, 176 (E.D. Mo. 1986) (limited partners not liable if only possible control was over expenditure of funds from extended line of credit agreed to by limited partners under restructuring agreement to keep partnership afloat). Although Green and Murphy's limited partner status would ordinarily limit their potential liability to creditors, their active roles in taking part in the control of the business subjected them to potential general partner liability.

Judgment against Green and Murphy.

CASE QUESTIONS

1. Were the incoming general partners, Green and Murphy, personally liable for the preexisting partnership obligations in this case?
2. Under what circumstances may limited partners be subjected to general partner liability?
3. Were Green and Murphy subject to unlimited personal liability as general partners for the indebtedness that arose while they were limited partners?

Syndication Forms–Corporations

Nature and Creation

The corporation form of syndication has the advantages of limited liability and unlimited duration. Partnerships are subject to dissolution when a partner withdraws, goes bankrupt, or dies. Limited partnerships have the same problems with regard to their general partners, but corporations can go on in perpetuity regardless of the investors' status.

State laws on corporation are not as uniform as those on partnerships and limited partnerships. However, the **Model Business Corporation Act (MBCA)** and **Revised Model Business Corporation Act (RMBCA)** are adopted in about one-third of the states. Many other states have portions of these model acts or use them as models for their own laws.

A corporation is also a statutory creature and must be created formally by public filing of a document known as the **articles of incorporation**. These articles must be published, and once formed, a corporation must file annual reports and keep separate books and records for the corporate transactions, even when there is just a single shareholder. A corporation is known as a fictitious person, with all the rights of an individual (except taking the Fifth Amendment). The owners or shareholders own a percentage of this entity, but that entity has a legal existence that allows it to take and hold title to real property, obtain a loan to purchase property, and give a mortage on that property to secure the corporate debt under that loan.

One benefit of partnership structure that is lost when investors form a "C" corporation is the ability of the investors to directly deduct losses from their income. However, the IRC does permit corporations to elect **Subchapter S** or **S corporation** status. With an S corporation, the shareholders have the protection of limited liability and the benefit of direct deduction of losses. This direct deduction of losses is critical in real estate corporations because of the depreciation deductions for real property.

Subchapter S structure is limited to certain types of corporations, and the Subchapter S election must be made before the taxable year ends and and filed with the IRS. There are limits on the number of shareholders, classes of stock, and income sources for S corporations.

Syndication Forms–Limited Liability Companies (LLC)

Nature and Creation

A relatively new business structure that is popular in real estate syndication is the **limited liability company**, or **LLC**. Now permitted in all states and the District of Columbia, this form of business organization is a business entity that offers the limited liability of a corporation but permits the tax advantages of a partnership. The IRS permits the flow-through handling of LLC income and losses in the same manner as those of partnerships, limited partnerships, and S corporations. The owners of an LLC are called members, and the members or owners then report their portion of the income or losses on their individual tax returns.

An LLC is also a statutory creature, complete with filing requirements, with most states mandating the use of the words "limited liability company" or the letters "LLC" or "LC" following the company's name.

The members manage their LLC through an operating agreement. An operating agreement would be equivalent to the bylaws of a corporation or a partnership agreement. The members can specify that they will manage the LLC together, or they can delegate that responsibility to a managing member, called a manager. However, all the LLC members enjoy limited liability. The owners, managers, and members of an LLC do not have personal liability for the debts of the LLC itself.

LLCs offer the best features of all business forms when the owners wish to enjoy the tax benefits of flow-through income and losses. In real estate investments, the flow-through aspect is often a critical feature for investors provided their liability exposure is limited to their investment. With an LLC, real estate investors can enjoy flow-through benefits, limited liability, and a voice in management without losing that protection.

Syndication Forms–Limited Liability Partnerships (LLP)

The newest form of business structure is the **limited liability partnership** or **LLP**. LLP is a partnership with unique statutory protection for all its members. Not all states have LLP statutes, but those that do have strict formal requirements for the creation of an LLP, yet another statutory creature. If the LLP formation requirements are not met, the owners have just a general partnership with full personal liability for all the partners. If the LLP is formed correctly, all partners have limited liability, with no personal liability exposure except to the extent of the capital contribution. The LLP has the flow-through characteristic for income, with losses and profits flowing through to the partners. All partners or a designated partner can manage without risking personal liability exposure.

Syndication Forms–Investment Trusts

Nature and Creation

Real estate investment trusts (REITs) and **mortgage investment trusts (MITs)** are legislative creatures that permit small investors access to the returns a diversified portfolio of real estate can provide. Instead of being a limited partner or a shareholder, the investor owns a beneficial interest in a trust. The idea for this form of real estate syndication originated in Massachusetts more than a century ago, and remains popular today because of the tax benefits this form of investment provides for investors as well as the access to capital its provides for real estate developers.

The modern-day REIT took hold in 1960, when the IRC was amended to allow the tax benefits of a Massachusetts-type trust (26 U.S.C. §§856–858 and §4981). With clarity on the tax implications of these investments, REITs and MITs have had explosive growth. REIT offerings were at $39 billion in 2004, an increase from $24 billion in 2003. There are now 200 REITs in the public securities market (see discussion below) with a total market valuation of $310 billion.[2]

A REIT is set up as any other trust is with a trust agreement or declaration of trust. As discussed in Chapter 15, a trust separates legal and equitable title. In a REIT, the trustee holds legal title to the property to be developed and is also responsible for the management of the properties in the trust, which is really a portfolio of real estate investments. Each investor, as a beneficiary, holds equitable title to the property, or at least a percentage of those properties. A **trust certificate** given to each beneficiary reflects the level and amount of the investor's ownship. Investors are not involved in the management of the properties or the portfolio; they allow the trustee to handle the real estate investments.

REIT portfolios vary significantly. **Equity trusts** own real estate and have rental income as their primary source of income. Depreciation benefits for investors (discussed in Chapter 22) are great for equity trust investors. **Mortgage trusts** hold investments in mortgages on real property. Many commercial banks and insurance companies have created mortgage trusts, with the primary source of income being the interest earned on the owned mortgages. Some trusts are **mixed trusts**; they own both property and mortgages and have rental and interest income. In recent years, trusts have been used as methods for financing individual projects, as when a corporation creates a **specialty trust** for the purpose of expanding its operations. For example, a national restaurant chain could create a trust for the purpose of constructing new restaurants.

REIT owners/beneficiaries are not personally liable for the obligations of the trust; their liability is limited to the trust assets. Beneficiaries vote for the management of the trust in that they elect the trustees. The trustees owe a fiduciary duty to the beneficiaries and the trust, and must act with the best interests of the trust and its beneficiaries as a priority.

If a trust qualifies for REIT treatment, then the REIT is taxed only on undistributed income and gains. If the income or gains are distributed to the beneficiaries, there are no taxes to the trust. REITs avoid the double taxation of corporations. The beneficiaries are taxed as individuals on the current or accumulated income; however, they are not entitled to the benefit of individual deduction of trust losses. To qualify as a REIT for purposes of these tax benefits, the REIT must have predominantly passive income from real property. REITs must follow the 75/95 rule. Seventy-five percent of a REIT's gross income must consist of income from the following sources: (a) rents from real property; (b) interest from mortgage loans; (c) gain from the disposition of real property or mortgage loans (other than inventory); (d) dividends from or gains from disposition of shares in other REITs; (e) abatements and refunds of real property taxes; (f) income from foreclosure property; (g) commitment fees received as consideration for entering into agreements to make mortgage loans or to purchase or lease real property; and (h) income from qualifying temporary investments of new capital. Second, at least 95 percent of the REIT's gross income must consist

2. Michelle Napoli, *Mall Shopping*, Institutional Investor, March 2005, at 149. Cristina Arumi/Jonathan Ivinson, *Europe Debates Real Estate Investment Trusts, International Tax Review*, March 2005, at 21.

of the following: (1) income that satisfies the 75 percent income test; (2) dividends; (3) interest; and (4) gains from the disposition of stock or securities.[3] If a REIT falls short on these specific IRS requirements, then the REIT is taxed as a corporation (26 U.S.C. §4981).

Figure 21.2 provides a chart comparison of the various forms of real estate syndication.

Securities Issues in Finance and Syndication

While general partnerships do not involve any sales of securities because the general partners all have debt, work, and contribution responsibilities, limited partnership interests, interests in REITs, share ownership in corporations, and interests in LLCs have been included as forms of securities for the purposes of the application of federal securities laws. Unless exempted, all sales of securities must be registered with both state and federal governments. When registration is required for the sale of interests in whatever form of syndication chosen, syndication becomes more expensive because of the complicated paperwork involved in the registration process. Some real estate syndications are small and structured to fit exemptions from the complicated and costly federal securities registration. However, many REITs are structured as publicy-traded securities so that investors can buy and sell their REIT interests on national exchanges, an attractive flexibility that brings wider pools of capital to real estate development projects. For example, many of the malls around the country are owned by REITs.

Exemptions from Registration Under Securities Act of 1933

Intrastate Offering Exemption The **intrastate offering exemption** exists because the Commerce Clause prohibits the federal government from regulating purely intrastate matters. To qualify for the intrastate exemption, the investors (offerees) and issuer must all be residents of the same state. (If there is one out-of-state offeree, the exemption will not apply.) Further, the issuer must meet the following requirements:

1. Eighty percent of its assets must be located in the state.
2. Eighty percent of its income must be earned from operations within the state.
3. Eighty percent of the proceeds from the sale must be used on operations within the state.

Small Offering Exemption–Regulation A Although the **small offering exemption (Regulation A)** is not a true exemption, it is a shortcut method of registration. The lengthy, complicated processes of full registration are simplified in that only a short-form registration statement is filed. Regulation A applies to issues of $5 million or less during any 12-month period.

Small Offering Exemption–Regulation D **Regulation D** is the product of the Securities Exchange Commission (SEC) evaluation of the impact of its rules on the ability of small businesses to raise capital. It was designed to simplify and clarify existing exemptions, expand the availability of exemptions, and achieve uniformity between state and federal exemptions. These small offering exemptions have been popular in structuring real estate developments. Regulation D creates a three-tiered exemption structure that permits sales without registration.

3. This explanation comes from Jack H. McCall, "A Primer on Real Estate Trusts: The Legal Basics of REITS," 2 Transactions: Tenn. J. Bus. L. 1(2001).

Figure 21.2 Forms of Real Estate Syndication

	General Partnership	Limited Partnership	Limited Liability Company (LLC)	Limited Liability Partnership (LLP)	Corporations*	S Corporations or Subchapter S Corporations
Creation	No formality required.	File a certificate of limited partnership with appropriate state office.	File articles of organization with appropriate agency.	Registration of LLP filed with state government.	File articles of incorporation with appropriate agency.	File articles of incorporation with appropriate agency.
Liability	Unlimited liability of each partner for firm debts.	General partners: unlimited liability for firm debts. Limited partners: no liability beyond loss of investment.	All members are liable for LLC debts to the extent of their capital contributions and equity in firm. No personal liability beyond such.	No liability for partners beyond their contributions and equity in firm, except unlimited personal liability for their wrongful acts and those of persons whom they supervise.	Limited liability except: watered shares corporate veil pierced.	Limited liability except: watered shares or when corporate veil pierced.
Management	All partners according to their partnership agreement or the UPA or RUPA.	General partners according to their partnership agreement or the ULPA or the RULPA. Limited partners excluded.	By members of of firm, who may delegate authority to managers.	All partners according to their partnership agreement or state law.	Officers and board	Officers and board
Dissolution	As set forth in the partnership agreement for the UPA or RUPA.	As set forth in the partnership agreement or the ULPA or RULPA.	As set forth in LLC statute or articles of organization.	As set forth in partnership agreement by state law.	Major corporate transaction (Vote).	Major corporate transaction (Vote).
Control/Transfer	Can transfer interest, but not partner status.	More easily transferred.	No admission without consent of majority.	No admission without consent of majority.	Shares (with reasonable restrictions) are easily transferred.	Restrictions on transfer to comply with S Corporation IRS regulations.
Taxes	Partner taxes profits and losses or individual return (flow-through).	Same as partnership (flow-through).	Flow-through treatment.	Flow-through treatment.	Corporation pays taxes; shareholders pay taxes on dividends.	Shareholders pay taxes; take losses; flow-through.

*S or Subchapter S Corporations formed under state law; tax status election (Small Business Job Protection Act of 1996).

Rule 502 places a number of limitations on the means an issuer can use in offering securities. Some exempt securities cannot be sold through general advertising or through seminars initiated through advertising. Further, all the securities sold must be subject to restrictions to prevent the immediate rollover of the securities involved in these exempt transactions.

The three tiers of Regulation D exemptions are as follows:

- The **Rule 504 exemption** applies to offerings of up to $1 million (within any 12-month period). This type of issue is used by sellers of securities who are raising a small amount of money and wish to sell shares or interest to small investors. Sales of stock to directors, officers, and employees are not counted in the total aggregate offering limitation of $1 million.
- The **Rule 505 exemption** covers sales of up to $5 million (in some cases the amount can rise to $7.5 million with state registration), provided there are no more than 35 nonaccredited investors. If the issue is sold to both accredited and nonaccredited investors, the issuer must give all buyers a prospectus.
- The **Rule 506 exemption** has no dollar limitation, but the number and type of investors are limited. There can be any number of **accredited investors**,[4] but the number of nonaccredited investors is limited to 35. There must be restrictions on the resale of the shares.

CONSIDER 21.2

A, a promoter, has put together a real estate limited partnership for the purpose of constructing a shopping center. A has a great deal of experience in commercial development but no financing for the project. His plan is to raise money by selling $10 million of limited partnership interests at a cost of $10,000 each. A does not want to be limited to in-state investors for the sale of the interests. Will A have to register the sale with the SEC?

Figure 21.3 is a summary of the complex security issues in real estate syndication.

State Laws on Securities

All states have some form of law governing the sale of securities. The types of registrations required and the available exemptions vary from state to state. In some states, copies of the federal registration information may be filed with the state for purposes of state registration; when SEC approval is obtained, the state will give its approval. In merit-review states, the securities and the partnership are actually reviewed to determine the quality of the offering.

CONSIDER 21.3

Francine Weiss and a number of other Maryland residents invested in the BJV real estate syndication. After she and the others lost most of their investment, they sued the principals in the syndication. During the course of the lawsuit they discovered that the property interests they purchased were at prices two to two and one-half times their actual market value. The BJV principals claim that the prices charged were to permit Francine and the other investors a great tax break by allowing them more to depreciate. How could Francine and the others have avoided the loss of their investment? *Weiss v. Lehman*, 713 F. Supp. 489 (D.D.C. 1989)

4. Accredited investors are those who meet mandatory standards for income and accounts.

Figure 21.3 1933 Act Exemptions

Name	Size Limitation	Offeree/Buyer Limitation	Resale Limitation	Public Offering	Filing Required	Time
Intrastate exemption. 15 U.C.C. §77(c)(a)(11)	No	Buyers must be residents of state of incorporation: 80% requirements	Yes, stock must transfer restrictions for 9 months	Yes, in state	Yes (14 days)	None
Small offering exemption, 15 U.C.C. §77D. Regulation A	$5,000,000 (issuers/12-month period)	Short-form registration required	No	Yes	Yes (short form)	12-month period
Rule 504—small offering Regulation D	$1,000,000 or less (in 12-month period)	None, unlimited, accredited and non-alike	No	Yes	Yes (within 15 days of first sale)	12-month period
Rule 505, Regulation D	$5,000,000 $7,500,000 (state)	No more than 35, excluding accredited	Some—2-year holding period	No (audited financials for nonaccredited)	Yes (within 15 days of first sale)	12-month period
Rule 506, Regulation D	No	Unlimited accredited and 35 non-sophisticated investors	Yes, stock restrictions	No	Yes (within 15 days of first sale)	2 years

Land Improvement and Construction

The development, once financed, moves to the physical work of construction.

Over the past decade, community atmosphere has become important in developments. For example, the Lincoln Institute of Land Policy estimates that there are 4,000,000 residents in 30,000 gated communities. These communities have the appeal not just of safety, but of uniformity and thoughtful planning in the design of the community.

Legal Paperwork for Development and Construction

The developer must provide a subdivision or plat map with easements, roads, and lots clearly indicated. The plat map, which has been recorded, will be used as a reference point for descriptions of all lots to be sold in the subdivision. (See Chapter 7 for more detail on plat maps and their importance in legal descriptions.)

In addition to the plat map, the developer will record restrictions or **protective covenants** for the subdivision. These covenants, or **deed restrictions**, cover the following issues:

1. Minimum square footage requirements for all dwelling units constructed within the subdivision
2. Restrictions on in-home business operations
3. Restrictions on the types of animals that may be kept on the lots
4. Restrictions on dividing lots and selling smaller portions of them

5. Restrictions on the types of structures that may be erected in addition to the dwelling units
6. Restrictions on use so that nuisances do not occur

Deed restrictions are based on the common law concept of covenants. At common law, covenants were restrictions placed in the deed from the grantor to the grantee. In addition to the requirement that the covenant be in the deed, the covenant had to meet the following requirements to be enforceable:

1. The covenant had to *touch and concern* the land.
2. The grantor and grantee had to intend that the covenant be a permanent restriction on the land.
3. There has to be privity between the grantor who created the covenant and the grantee

The problem with these common law requirements was the privity requirement. There is privity in the initial sale by the developer to the first buyer but privity ended once the first buyer transfers the property. This problem is solved with a clause in the deed that transfers title subject to all the restrictions that have been recorded for the subdivision. Most deed restrictions (covenants) are now subject to statutory requirements if they are to be valid. For example, most states now require that the developer have buyers sign statements that they have received a copy of the deed restrictions and that they understand that their use of the property is subject to those restrictions. Title companies cannot close on subsequent transfers of the property unless and until buyers receive a copy of the deed restrictions and also sign off on them. In many areas buyers are given a notebook with the deed restrictions that is sent via certified mail so that the developer can prove receipt by the buyer of the deed restrictions.

Even without the statutory deed restriction delivery requirements, the pattern of development can be binding. If the covenants and restrictions are visible by looking at a subdivision or area, courts will uphold them. For example, a buyer who sees the same roofing material in a subdivision is required to honor that restriction. An obvious scheme of development is binding on buyers. To protect those who already own homes in the subdivision, the common law doctrine of **equitable servitudes** exists. An equitable servitude is a restriction on land use that exists because of the nature of the subdivision or area. Under this doctrine, buyers of land within a partially developed subdivision are required to use the land purchased in a manner consistent with the plan of development in existence at the time of their purchase. The basis for the doctrine of equitable servitude is notice; a party who purchases land in an area where a common scheme of development is obvious is bound to abide by the development scheme.

In addition, a developer who pulls out of a subdivision prior to its completion may face the issue of misrepresentation because the existing property owners purchased under the assumption that the subdivision would be completed with certain forms of construction. Both the doctrine of equitable servitudes and the remedy of misrepresentation serve to protect homeowners from declines in property values in the event a developer decides not to complete a subdivision and sells the lots to others.

Some experts see a shift from governmental control of land use through zoning to private control through the use of covenants and deed restrictions. These new structures are called residential community associations, common interest communities, residential private government, and gated communities. Whatever the name, these areas, created by developers in the initial recorded documents for the development of the community, are self-contained units of private law governance, created and sustained through covenants.

The following case deals with an issue of the enforceability of covenants.

CAPPELLO V. CIRESI

691 A.2d 42 (Conn. Supre. 1996)

FACTS

Vincent and Irene Cappello (plaintiffs) own property in a subdivision in Fairfield, Connecticut, known as Lakeview Acres. All the lots are subject to a restriction created in 1943 that prohibits the use of the lots for anything other than single-family dwellings. The lots are all delineated on a map recorded in the land records of the town of Fairfield on September 16, 1943. The language in the recorded documents provides: "Such restrictions constitute negative easements which may be enforced by any grantee against any other grantee, each parcel becoming both a dominant and servient parcel."

The Cappellos' property consists of lots one and two and the southern portions of lots five and six as delineated on map number 1,251. The parcels are contiguous and, together, constitute a rectangular-shaped parcel with 275 feet of frontage on the Boston Post Road and 111 feet of frontage on Hulls Highway, which intersects with the Boston Post Road. Lot one is a corner lot fronting on both the Boston Post Road and Hulls Highway and is improved with a single-family house. The southern portions of lots five and six front on the Boston Post Road and contain no improvements.

Anthony Ciresi and others (defendants) are the owners of the other property within the subdivision. Their lots front on Arbor Drive, Arbor Terrace, and Hulls Highway. Three of the defendants testified: Charles McDonald, Ernest Sapp, and Edward Byrne. McDonald relied on the long-term protection provided by the covenants when he purchased his home 41 years ago. Sapp believed the covenants would protect the neighborhood when he purchased his home six years ago. Byrne was aware of the covenants when he purchased his home in 1986 and believed that they would keep the area as a single-family neighborhood.

Lakeview Acres is a mature development consisting of single-family residences that have been improved over the years. No lots are being used for anything other than residential purposes. The rear lot lines of eight of the original lots abut the Boston Post Road. The Cappellos own one of the abutting lots (lot one) and the abutting portion of two other lots (lots five and six). Since 1943, the Boston Post Road has undergone a dramatic change. Today, the property along the Boston Post Road from the Fairfield-Bridgeport border to the Fairfield-Westport border is used mostly for commercial purposes and is in a designed commercial district zone. Clearly, the best and highest use of the appellees' property would be commercial development. This use would be consistent with the uses along the Boston Post Road but inconsistent with the present use of the lots within Lakeview Acres.

The Cappellos filed suit seeking relief from the restrictions on the use of their land.

JUDICIAL OPINION

Thim, Judge. The second ground on which the plaintiffs seek relief requires this court to determine whether there has been such a change in the area as to defeat the objects and purposes of the restrictive covenants so that they are no longer effective. The plaintiffs claim that the commercial development along the Boston Post Road since 1943 is a sufficient change to warrant the removal of the restrictions. The defendants, on the other hand, contend that the change is not sufficient because Lakeview Acres is still a residential area. The plaintiffs focus on the changes outside the subdivision. The defendants focus on the subdivision.

"In the majority of states, changes outside the limits of the tract, even though they do impinge on the border lots, do not justify any relaxation of enforcement of the restrictions within the tract, so long as such enforcement remains beneficial to most of the property in the tract."

The character of Lakeview Acres as a residential area has not been affected by the commercial development along the Boston Post Road outside the subdivision. The changes have not defeated the objects and purposes of the restrictive covenants. Lakeview Acres is entirely a residential area. "The fact that the [plaintiffs'] property would be of more value if the restriction were removed is of no consequence.... The [plaintiffs] purchased the land with full knowledge that the... tract was subject to the restriction; [they] got everything [they] bargained for, and presumably took the restriction into consideration when [they] agreed on the price [they] paid...."

The plaintiffs have not shown such a change in the restricted area as would justify this court's declaring the restrictions on the plaintiffs' land invalid.

This court finds the restrictive covenants to be valid burdens on the plaintiffs' property. The restrictions may be enforced by any defendant. Judgment shall enter for the defendants.

CASE QUESTIONS

1. Why do the Cappellos want the restrictions lifted?
2. Why do the other landowners wish the restrictions to remain?
3. Can the restrictions be enforced?
4. What advice on restrictive covenants could you offer to a potential buyer looking in a residential neighborhood?

CONSIDER 21.4

Shalimar Estates is a residential land development consisting of 134 acres in Tempe, Arizona. The development consists of a golf course and adjacent residential lots. The golf course is an integral part of the development, and the lots were sold to buyers with the sales representations that there would always be a golf course and that their homes would always overlook a golf course. There were, however, no deed restrictions on the use of the golf course property. The original developer sold the property, and the developers planned to eliminate the golf course to maximize the property value. The homeowners have brought suit on the basis of the representations made to them. Can they win? *Shalimar Association v. D.O.C. Enterprises, Ltd.*, 688 P.2d 682 (Ariz. 1984)

Construction Stage

Terminology and Parties

Understanding the names and roles of the parties in the construction project is helpful in determining rights and obligations, summarized in the list that follows:

1. The **owner** owns the land on which the building is being constructed.
2. The **construction lender** finances the project during the construction period.
3. The **permanent lender** or **lender** carries the mortgage on the property once construction is completed. (The permanent lender pays the construction lender's loan once construction is complete.)
4. The **general contractor** or **prime contractor** or **builder** is responsible for the coordination of the construction.
5. The **architect** may work with the general contractor or owner in making sure the building is constructed properly.
6. The **subcontractors** (usually a large group) perform individual projects for the construction. Subcontractors are responsible for separate jobs such as the electrical system, the heating and cooling system, and the roof.
7. The **suppliers** (a form of subcontractor) do no actual construction work but are usually a large group consisting of all businesses that supply materials for use in the construction project.
8. The **surety** or **sureties** stand as **guarantors** for either payment or performance according to the terms of the owner's contract or the contracts of subcontractors and suppliers.
9. The **insurer** for the owner, the contractor, or any other party stands liable in the event of destruction of the project during its course.
10. The **governmental supervisor** is the party who must be consulted or who must inspect as the project progresses.

Assurance in Construction—Bonds

One of the procedures an owner or developer can use to lessen the chances that a construction project will come to a disastrous end is to require certain types of bonds by the contractor. Three types of bonds are involved in construction projects. The first is the **bid bond**, which is a guaranty by a bonding company that a contractor will actually complete the contract at the bid price. If the contractor does not perform according to the terms of the bid and at the bid price, the contractor is liable for damages to the owner. However, these damage claims are of little comfort if the contractor has not performed because it is out of business or has filed for bankruptcy. The bonding company or surety will be liable to the owner when these financial collapses occur.

A **performance bond** is a guaranty by a bonding company that a project will be completed. If a contractor stops work on a project, the performance bond company is required to pay whatever is necessary to get the project completed. This amount, sometimes referred to as the **penal sum**, is usually equal to the contract price. Under a performance bond, the bonding company usually has the option of completing the construction itself or hiring another company to do the project.

The final form of bond, the **payment bond**, is one that offers insurance that the subcontractors will be paid. Under this type of bond, the bonding company agrees to pay subcontractors if the general contractor does not pay their claims. This type of bond serves as a means for preventing liens on the property by subcontractors. Many bonding companies issue a combination performance and payment bond. This combination bond usually gives the owner less protection because amounts paid to subcontractors will reduce the obligation amount for performance.

Practical Tip

On checking the background of general contractors:

- *Check whether the contractor has the technical capacity, workforce, and equipment necessary to do the job.*
- *Obtain a list of previously completed and ongoing projects.*
- *Check on previous jobs and experience levels.*
- *Contact other developers who have used the contractor for references. Rely on public documents to obtain names other than those references offered by the contractor.*
- *Check whether the contractor has enough office and support staff to complete the job.*
- *Obtain a list of subcontractors and contact them about the contractor's job-management skills.*
- *Verify payment of subcontractors from previous jobs.*
- *Verify the contractor's reputation and integrity. Discussions with occupants of projects completed by contractor can reveal information about the quality of work.*
- *Review financial statements, talk with bankers, and insist on bonds.*

The cost of all these bonds can be substantial. Many owners and developers forego these bonds with the idea of keeping the premium that would be required to cover the costs associated with a breach or default by the contractor. There is reduced cost, but also increased risk.

Formation of Construction Contracts

The formation of construction contracts is nearly standardized procedure. The owner sends out a **bid notice**, which is an invitation for offers. General contractors then have the opportunity to bid on the project. Before bidding, general contractors notify subcontractors to invite offers for subcontract work.

The subcontractors' submission of bids to the general contractor for their portion of the work is an offer. The general contractor's submission of a bid with the incorporated subcontractors' bids to the owner is an offer. When the owner reviews the bids, makes a decision, and notifies the chosen general contractor, there is a contract between the owner and the general contractor.

Much of the bidding, particularly between subcontractors and general contractors, is done orally as a matter of practice. Although industry practice allows and encourages such oral commitments, one party may find itself at the mercy of the other party's denial

Figure 21.4 Legal Relationships in the Bidding Process

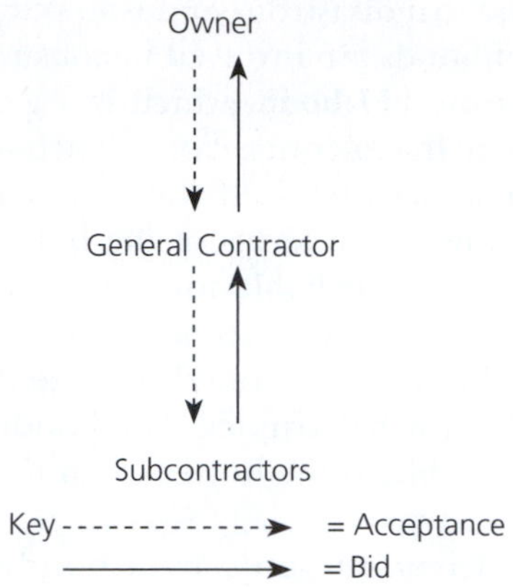

Owner

General Contractor

Subcontractors

Key - - - - - - - - - - - - -➤ = Acceptance

———————➤ = Bid

of a conversation or contradiction of a figure or term. A good practice is to require written verification of terms so that there is some basis for the general contractor's bid for the project. Figure 21.4 summarizes the flow of legal events in the formation stage of the construction contract.

With this layered offer structure, there is a period of danger for the general contractor. It is possible for the owner to notify the general contractor of acceptance of the bid and have the general contractor bound to perform before the general contractor has had the chance to accept the offers of the subcontractors on which the bid was based. Since the subcontractors can revoke their offers at any time prior to acceptance, they could in this case revoke their offers after the general contractor is contractually bound to-perform.

To avoid this problem, the general contractor has several alternatives. First, in the invitation for bids the general contractor could specify that once submitted, a bid is irrevocable. Second, the general contractor could make acceptance automatic upon the owner's acceptance of the general contractor's bid. Finally, the courts have used the doctrine of promissory estoppel to require subcontractors to perform according to their bids once the general contractor has relied upon the bids. Reliance occurs once the general contractor uses the subcontractors' bids in the bid to the owner/developer.

CONSIDER 21.5

Gordon, a general contractor, was submitting bids to the city's port authority to construct a bridge in the city. Coronis submitted a bid to Gordon as subcontractor for the structural steel work. Gordon incorporated the Coronis bid in his bid to the port authority. After the city had accepted Gordon's bid, but before Gordon notified Coronis, Coronis revoked its bid and refused to perform. Gordon had to hire another subcontractor, Elizabeth Iron Works, to do the steel work at an additional cost of $53,000. Gordon has sued Coronis to recover the $53,000. What is the result? *E. A. Coronis Assoc. v. M. Gordon Constr. Co.*, 216 A.2d 246 (Supp. Ct. N. J. 1966)

Payment and Payment Assurances in Construction Contracts

Because of the large number of parties involved and the need for money to flow down from its source to the general contractor, subcontractors, and suppliers, payment of the parties is a major issue in the construction contract and in construction litigation.

Indeed, the payment problem is the basis for the mechanic's lien system (see Chapter 6).

General contractors are entitled to payment as their work is completed and may stop performance if payment is not made, so work stoppage is a means of security for them. General contractors usually have the benefit of a three-party arrangement, whereby the funds are held by a third party (examples of third parties used are lenders, architects, escrow companies, attorneys, trustees, and banks) and released upon the architect's certification of adequate completion. With the three-party system, the general contractors know the funds exist—it is simply a matter of performance to have them released.

Owners can also use the three-party system to ensure performance by the general contractor. Most standard contracts permit withholding a certain amount of the contract amount to cover defective work, late performance, or the general contractor's failure to pay subcontractors and suppliers. The withheld amount is typically 10 percent of the contract price and also 10 percent of each installment made during the construction period.

General contractors can also protect themselves against the subcontractors for the owner's nonpayment through the use of a **flow-down clause**. Under a flow-down clause, the general contractor is not required to pay the subcontractors until the owner has paid the general contractor.

Contract Price

Usually, the price in a construction contract is fixed and covers the entire project. Other forms of pricing include **unit pricing**, in which the contract is broken down into units. For example, excavation could be one unit in a project. Framing could be another unit. The overhead costs for the project would be divided among the units according to the amount of time or cost involved in each unit. The unit system makes the payment division easier. Another form of pricing that leaves many variables and can create problems is the **cost-plus formula**, in which the general contractor recovers whatever the cost of construction is along with a predetermined percentage or amount for profit. The difficulty with the cost-plus system is determining which costs are reimbursable as project costs and which are the general contractor's cost of doing business: personnel salaries, equipment, and other overhead items.

After the price or price formula is determined and construction begins, two possible problem areas may affect the price paid for the project by the owner: changed circumstances and work-order changes.

Changed Circumstances. The general contractor's bid on a project is based on assumptions about the project location, soil content, weather analysis, and other variable factors. If significant, unanticipated changes occur in those assumptions, the general contractor's costs will increase. With these cost increases, the issue arises of whether the price of completion will also increase. A clause in standard form contracts provides for price increases when (1) there are concealed conditions below the surface of the ground or concealed conditions in any existing structure at variance with those conditions indicated by contract; and (2) there are unknown physical conditions of an unusual nature at the site, differing materially from those ordinarily encountered and generally recognized as part of the work provided for in the contract. Other conditions that are considered unusual and unknown are unseasonal or unusually bad weather conditions, labor problems, and material shortages. Even without a changed-circumstances provision in the contract, the contractor is entitled to obtain an increased price if costs are greater because of misrepresentation of conditions by the owner in the bid information, the negotiations, or the contract.

Change Orders. The second type of situation in which a contractor may increase the project price is through a **change order**. Because of circumstances or preferences, the owner may wish to change plans and specifications that represent additional costs to the contractor.

A change order may be necessary for several reasons. The change may be needed simply because the owner or developer sees the project as it progresses and perceives that it does not look the same as it did in conception or on paper. Zoning changes may have been approved after the time the contract is negotiated but before construction begins or before a building permit has been issued for the plans that now violate the zoning laws. In the case of shopping centers, a change may be necessary to keep an anchor tenant or attract another tenant. There may be facilities missing. For example, with the passage of the Americans with Disabilities Act in 1990, many businesses now must comply by providing access for employees with disabilities, changes that are more easily made during construction than after construction is complete. The lender may also require a change in the construction for better utilization of the project. Also, the contractor may discover during the course of construction that additional work is necessary and will want authorization for the work so that additional compensation can be paid. A typical change-order clause will provide as follows:

A change order is a written order to the contractor that is signed by the owner and the architect, issued after execution of the contract, authorizing a change in the contract sum or contract time. The contract sum and contract time may be altered by change order only.

The owner, without invalidating the contract, may order changes in the work within the general scope of the contract, the contract sum and the contract time being adjusted accordingly.

The contractor, provided he receives a written order signed by the owner, shall promptly proceed with the work involved.

The following case deals with the issue of oral change orders.

Hoth v. White

799 P.2d 213 (Utah 1990)

FACTS

Amy and Karl White (defendants) contacted Polar Bear Homes to inquire about having it build the Whites' new custom house. Charles R. Team (d/b/a Team Realty) was involved in these discussions. On August 26, 1986, the Whites met with Dean R. Morgan (d/b/a Polar Bear Homes) and Charles Team (appellants) and contracted to have Polar Bear build a custom, energy-efficient house according to plans drafted by Amy White and given to Morgan. Construction was to be completed by December 10, 1986, and the Whites were to supply construction financing of $40,000.

Morgan subcontracted with Michael and Jeffrey Hoth (d/b/a Hoth Brothers/plaintiffs) to frame the house for $6,000. Morgan provided the Hoths with the plans but not the specifications (they were listed on a separate sheet).

The Hoths began framing the house during the first week in October 1986 but did not complete their work until February 12, 1987, two months after the entire house was to have been completed. Many problems arose during construction that required changes to be made in the framing. Some of the required changes resulted from the improper pouring of the foundation, some from the Hoths' ignorance of some of the specifications, some because the plans were incomplete or unclear, and some because Amy White changed her mind as to what she wanted. Amy White was present on the job site nearly every day and interacted frequently with the Hoths. Although the Hoths substantially completed framing the house, they did not completely finish the job, making it necessary for the Whites to hire other subcontractors to come in and complete the work.

During the months of October and November 1986, the Whites made progress payments on the construction but were not provided with any accounting of the funds spent. By January 1987, the Whites had already provided appellants with $43,000. Soon after January 3, 1987, Morgan acknowledged at least a $10,000 overrun on the contract price and asked the Whites to pay half of that.

The Whites deferred making a decision on this request until the house was completed.

The Whites refused to give Morgan any more money and began paying the construction bills directly as well as directly hiring subcontractors to complete the building, thus bypassing Morgan. Morgan testified that he felt he had lost all control of the project and had been taken off the job. The Whites, however, stated that they consistently requested him to return to the job and assume his responsibilities, especially with the numerous structural problems present. They concluded that they had to take over because the construction was substantially behind schedule, and Morgan was not paying the bills or otherwise doing his job.

On March 16, 1987, at Morgan's suggestion, the Hoths filed a mechanic's lien on the house, claiming the unpaid balance of $2,500 plus an additional $1,410 for extra work and material supplied by them beyond the scope of the initial subcontract. Their total claim was $3,910.

In September 1987, the Hoths filed this action to foreclose on their mechanic's lien. On September 25, 1987, the Whites answered and counterclaimed for substandard work, disputing the amount and character of the "extra" items that the Hoths had determined were not within the scope of the original subcontract.

The trial court found that the Whites were liable to pay the Hoths the remaining $2,500 balance on the original contract plus $1,009 of the "extras," less an offset of $516 for the costs the Whites had been required to pay to other subcontractors to finish the framing. It also ordered the Whites to pay the Hoths $1,000 in attorney fees, plus court costs to be determined from the record, for a net judgment of $3,993 plus costs. It then ordered the Hoths to indemnify the Whites in the amount of $2,993 and costs, plus pay $1,000 to the Whites for attorney fees.

The Hoths appealed.

JUDICIAL OPINION

Garff, Judge. The trial court found that either the Whites or appellants ordered certain extras, that some of the "extras" came about as a result of lack of detail in the plans, and that the Hoths were entitled to compensation for them in the amount of $1,009. It also found that, although the Hoths had substantially completed the contract, they had failed to complete a portion of it, requiring the Whites to obtain labor from other sources at a cost of $516, which the court offset against the Hoths' compensation.

As the trial court found, the record indicates that a substantial number of the extras came about as a result of requests by Amy White, although several were requested by Morgan. Viewing the evidence in the light most favorable to the findings, the record suggests that many of the changes requested by the Whites were made to bring the residence into conformance with the specifications, which the Whites gave to Morgan but were not transmitted by Morgan to the Hoths, and because mistakes were made in pouring the foundation which resulted in problems which the extras were designed to correct.

Relevant contract terms provide that "[t]he amount of the purchase price may be increased if additional costs are incurred for extras as described hereafter. Buyer agrees to pay for the cost of all such extras as agreed to in a written change order as part of the purchasing price of the property," and "[n]o changes shall be made to the Plans and Specifications or the purchase price except as agreed to in a written change order signed by Buyer and Contractor which sets forth the change to be made and the amount of adjustment in the purchase price required by said change." The contract thus clearly provides that unless there is a written change order signed by the parties for each extra, the purchase price is not to be increased and the buyer, therefore, is not responsible for paying for the extra. It is undisputed that the parties signed no such written change orders.

We find that the trial court did not err in requiring appellants to pay that portion of the extras not paid for by the Whites.

Affirmed.

CASE QUESTIONS

1. Diagram the relationship of the parties.
2. Why were there so many changes for the Hoths?
3. Did the contract address change orders?
4. Was anything in writing with respect to the change orders?
5. Who is liable to the Hoths?
6. Who is ultimately liable for the changes?

Substantial Performance by Contractor

Construction contracts present the unique problem of how to determine when the contractor has performed well enough to satisfy the terms of the contract. Because of the nature of construction, perfection is not possible and variations between plans or specifications may be required as problems with soil, weather, and other elements arise during construction. Contractors enjoy the slack afforded by the doctrine of **substantial performance**, which provides that a contractor may recover for completed projects in spite of variations between the plans and the actual finished product.

> ***Practical Tip***
>
> *Change-order procedures should be placed in the construction contract and followed. Variation from the process will result in the adoption of that process as the parties' agreed-upon means of procedure. Further, confusion and error result when others believe the change-order process remains the same as in the written agreement. Often the time saved by not following the process results in greater expense and litigation later.*

The following questions are the test for substantial performance:

1. Is the construction for practical purposes just as good?

2. Was the minor breach by the contractor nonmalicious?

3. Can the owner be compensated for the substitution or error made by the contractor?

An example of substantial performance is when the wrong color scheme or cabinet work is installed in a home or office. The owner may not be as happy, but the error meets the three criteria, and the contractor will be paid the contract price less an adjustment for the owner to be compensated or have the work redone.

Substantial performance does not excuse a contractor for errors in construction and poor workmanship.

In home construction, the contractor is required for one year (in most states) to repair or replace faulty construction problems under the implied warranty (see Chapter 14).

Compliance with Building Codes

One of the critical requirements for adequate performance by a contractor is that the structure comply with state and local building codes. Building codes may restrict building height, ceiling height, window placement, fire sprinkler systems, exits, lighting, and materials. Contractors must be familiar with building codes and will be liable for their failure to meet the codes.

Compliance with the Americans with Disabilities Act

Both in the new construction of buildings and under the retrofit requirements of the Fair Housing Act (see Chapter 19), the issue of access and usability for those with disabilities is now a critical part of construction. Buildings constructed after 1988 must have access and accommodations for those with disabilities. The Americans with Disabilities Act **(ADA)** required all existing buildings to be accessible and that facilities accommodate those with disabilities.

The following case deals with the construction requirements imposed on businesses under the ADA.

PINNOCK V. INTERNATIONAL HOUSE OF PANCAKES FRANCHISEE

844 F. Supp. 574 (S.D. Cal. 1993); *cert. den.* 512 U.S. 1228 (1994)

FACTS

Theodore A. Pinnock, an attorney, is unable to walk and uses a wheelchair. Pinnock dined at Majid Zahedi's (defendant) restaurant, a franchise of the International House of Pancakes, on June 21, 1992. When Pinnock went to use the restroom in the restaurant, he discovered the door to the men's room was too narrow to allow his wheelchair to pass through. Pinnock was forced to remove himself from his wheelchair and crawl into the restroom. Pinnock filed suit for violation of ADA, the California Unruh Civil Rights Act, and intentional infliction of emotional distress. Zahedi filed a motion for summary judgment.

JUDICIAL OPINION

Rhoades, District Judge. Zahedi argues that Congress does not have constitutional authority to regulate his facility, asserting that title III of the ADA exceeds the powers granted Congress by the U.S. Constitution. Congress enacted title III pursuant to Article I, Section 8, of the United States Constitution, which grants Congress the power to "regulate Commerce...among the several States" and to enact all laws necessary and proper to this end.

As the Supreme Court recognized in the context of racial discrimination, the restaurant industry unquestionably affects interstate commerce in a substantial way.

Even aside from its membership in an interstate industry, Zahedi's restaurant demonstrates characteristics which place it squarely in the category of interstate commerce. It is a franchise of a large, international, publicly traded corporation ("IHOP Corp."), organized under Delaware law. IHOP Corp. had total retail sales of $479 million in 1992, operates 547 franchises in thirty-five states, Canada, and Japan, and employs 16,000 persons. Furthermore, Zahedi's restaurant is located directly across the street from State Highway 163, and within two miles of two interstate highways. There are three hotels within walking distance, and three motels within one and one-half miles of the restaurant. The courts have found these facts to be indicia of a business operating in interstate commerce.

Congressional enactment of title III of the ADA was well within Congress' power to regulate interstate commerce under the Commerce Clause.

Zahedi argues that many of the terms used in section 12182(b)(2) of title III are unconstitutionally vague and are therefore in violation of the Due Process Clause of the Fifth Amendment. Statutes which fail to adequately specify the actions or conduct necessary to conform with the law pose problems for which the Supreme Court has expressed serious concern.

Title III of the ADA is a civil statute regulating commercial conduct. As such, Zahedi can successfully sustain its challenge only if he can prove that the enactment specifies "no standard of conduct...at all."

Title III requires existing places of public accommodation to remove architectural barriers to access, where such removal is "readily achievable." The term is defined in the statute as "easily accomplishable and able to be carried out without much difficulty or expense." The statute enumerates four factors to consider when determining whether a modification is readily achievable, and the legislative history lists examples of the types of changes Congress believes are readily achievable. These include specific examples for small stores and restaurants such as rearranging tables and chairs and installing small ramps and grab bars in restrooms.

In addition, the federal regulation further elucidates the term "readily achievable" by adding other factors. These include the overall financial resources of the parent corporation and safety requirements. The regulation lists 21 examples of barrier removal likely to be "readily achievable" in many circumstances, such as installing ramps and repositioning shelves and telephones.

Finally, the preamble to the regulation provides further explanation and notes that use of a more specific standard would contravene the goals of the ADA:

the Department has declined to establish in the final rule any kind of numerical formula for determining whether an action is readily achievable. It would be difficult to devise a specific ceiling on compliance costs that would take into account the vast diversity of enterprises covered by the ADA's public accommodation requirements and the economic situation that any particular entity would find itself in at any moment.

Title III provides that where barrier removal is not readily achievable, a covered entity must make its goods or services available through "alternative methods if such methods are readily achievable." The legislative history, the regulation itself, and the preamble all provide specific examples of appropriate alternatives to barrier removal. These include providing curb service or home delivery, coming to the door of the facility to handle transactions, serving beverages at a table for persons with disabilities where a bar is inaccessible, providing assistance to retrieve items from inaccessible shelves, and relocating services and activities to accessible locations.

Illustrations of the term "reasonable modifications" are provided in the title III regulation and its preamble. For example, stores in which all of the checkout aisles are not accessible are required to ensure that an adequate number of accessible checkout aisles are left open at all times. Likewise, facilities that do not permit entry to animals would be required to modify such policies as they apply to service animals accompanying disabled individuals.

The terms "reasonable modifications" and "fundamental alteration" are therefore not unconstitutionally vague.

Title III requires covered entities to afford their goods and services to an individual with a disability "in the most integrated setting appropriate to the needs of the individual." One example provides that

it would be a violation of this provision to require persons with mental disabilities to eat in the back room of a restaurant or to refuse to allow a person with a disability to full use of a health spa because of stereotypes about the person's ability to participate.

Zahedi challenges the ADA on the grounds that it is retroactive legislation and therefore violates the Due Process Clause of the Fifth Amendment.

The relevant inquiry is whether the legislation imposes liability or penalty for conduct occurring prior to the effective date of the statute. The ADA provided an 18-month notice period in which businesses could comply with the Act's requirements, and no liability was imposed prior to the end of that period. Small businesses were given an even lengthier notice period. Pinnock's complaint was not filed until September 9, 1992, nearly two years after the ADA was passed on July 26, 1990. The requirements of the title III do not subject Zahedi to retroactive legislation.

Zahedi contends that the expenditure of funds necessary to make the restrooms in his facility accessible to individuals in wheelchairs, if required under the ADA, would constitute a taking of private property "for public use, without just compensation" in violation of the Fifth Amendment's Due Process Clause. In *Lucas v. South Carolina Coastal Council*, 505 U.S. 1003, 112 S.Ct. 2886, 120 L.Ed.2d 798 (1992), the Supreme Court delineated three situations in which a governmental restraint is considered a taking, therefore requiring compensation. These three situations are: 1) When the regulation compels a permanent physical invasion of the property; 2) When the regulation denies an owner all economically beneficial or productive use of its land; 3) When the regulation in question does not substantially advance a legitimate governmental objective. If either of the first two situations occur, the regulation will be considered a taking regardless of whether the action achieves an important public benefit or has only minimal impact on the owner. The expenditure of funds required by title III does not constitute a taking under the Fifth Amendment as defined in Lucas.

A cornerstone of the law of takings is that if a regulation has the effect of establishing a permanent physical occupation, it will be a taking. *Loretto v. Teleprompter Manhattan CATV*, 458 U.S. 419, 430, 102 S.Ct. 3164, 3173, 73 L.Ed.2d 868 (1982).

Zahedi argues that the remodeling required under the ADA may result in the loss of as many as 20 seating places in his restaurant. Zahedi cites *Loretto* in support of his argument that a regulation which requires a restaurant to widen restrooms and thereby restricts the use of part of his property, violates the Fifth Amendment. Zahedi, however, provides an inaccurate recitation of *Loretto*. The Supreme Court's analysis in *Loretto* rests on the finding that a regulation which gives an outside entity the right to physically intrude upon the property is actually the granting of an easement without compensation, which can constitute a taking. This case, however, does not involve the granting of Zahedi's property to another party for its own exclusive use and profit. Rather, the ADA merely proscribes Zahedi's use of part of his own property and it therefore could be likened to a zoning regulation. Since the ADA merely regulates the use of property and does not give anyone physical occupation of Zahedi's property, it is not within the Supreme Court's first category of takings.

The remodeling which Zahedi claims is required under the ADA regulations could result in the loss of approximately 20 seating places in his restaurant. The mere loss of approximately 20 seating places surely will not deny Zahedi all economically viable use of his property.

The Court must also consider whether the requirements of the statute frustrate the property owner's reasonable investment-backed expectations. As discussed above, the ADA was specifically drafted to avoid the imposition of economic hardship upon the operators of public accommodations, particularly those running smaller operations. A showing of frustration of investment-backed expectation is a very difficult one to make, and the impact of the ADA's barrier removal requirements pales in comparison to many of the regulations which the Supreme Court has upheld.

Regulations have been upheld even where they resulted in a complete restriction upon a specific individual's future exploitation of the property for profit.

Zahedi argues that the ADA constitutes a "national building code" which trespasses the regulatory area reserved to the states by the Tenth Amendment.

Title III's statutory scheme does not displace local building codes. It is a federal civil rights act that sets forth accessibility standards that places of public accommodation and commercial facilities must follow. Departures from the ADA Standards are expressly permitted where "alternative designs and technologies used will provide substantially equivalent or greater access to and usability of the facility." State and local building codes remain in effect to be enforced by state officials. State officials are not required to adopt or enforce the ADA Standards for Accessible Design.

Having carefully considered each of Zahedi's constitutional challenges, it is clear that none of these challenges can prevail. Zahedi's motion for summary judgment is denied.

CASE QUESTIONS

1. What violation of ADA does Pinnock allege occurred?

2. List the constitutional arguments Zahedi made in challenging the application of the ADA to his property.

3. Is Zahedi's restaurant involved in interstate commerce? Why?

4. Does the ADA constitute a taking of property that must be compensated?

5. Is the ADA unconstitutionally vague?

6. Is the ADA retroactive?

Cautions and Conclusions

Real estate development is a complex process that involves all areas of real estate law. The three steps in development are land acquisition, land finance, and land improvement and construction. In all three steps, there are individual rights and governmental regulations. In land acquisition, developers must consider the zoning laws, the planning components of local governments, impact fees, and the rights and interests of those affected by the proposed development. In land finance, the developer must consider the sources of funds available and how best to structure the financing in terms of tax, liability, and management issues. At times, a developer's choice for financing may also involve the sale of securities and require compliance with federal and state laws on the sale of securities. In land improvement and construction, the developer must be aware of private land-use restrictions such as covenants and create a plan consistent with those restrictions. In addition, the entire body of construction law with its protections for payment and performance comes into play as buildings are constructed.

Developers must work their ways through a complex process for the creation of a successful project. One key to success is to carefully review and follow all the laws affecting everything from securities sales to construction bonds. Good developers work with policy setters, law makers, neighbors, contractors, and regulators to be certain that their project is not just successful but in compliance with the law and well received by members of the community.

Key Terms

Chapter Problems

1. A wishes to put together a syndicate for the purpose of purchasing and operating two apartment complexes. A feels she can best sell the syndicate interests if the investors are able to directly deduct the depreciation losses that will result from the first three years of operation. What form of syndication will allow A's investors to take such deductions?

2. Burr, a general contractor, was bidding on a plant project for General Motors. Burr had two bids from electrical subcontractors. One was from Corbin-Dykes, and the other from White Sands. White Sands agreed to do the project for $4,000 less than Corbin-Dykes's bid if it could do the work in conjunction with another project it had in the area. Burr used Corbin-Dykes's bid and was awarded the project. However, Burr contracted with White Sands because it could do the work in the same amount of time at $4,000 less. Corbin-Dykes brought suit on the grounds of promissory estoppel and sought to force Burr to pay them. What was the result? *Corbin-Dykes Electric Co. v. Burr*, 500 P.2d 632 (Ariz. App. 1972)

3. Gough agreed to put up the trusses on a Kinney Shoe Store that Chuckrow was building as general contractor. Gough put up the trusses, but later that day, 30 of the 32 erected trusses fell down. Gough put them back up and demanded additional compensation. Chuckrow refused, saying that the trusses fell down because of Gough's poor workmanship. Gough maintained that they fell down because of faulty plans and specifications. What was the result? *Robert Chuckrow Construction Co. v. Gough*, 159 S.E.2d 469 (Ga. App. 1968)

4. In 1948 the Phipps family devised real property to Palm Beach County. The deed provided in part that the conveyed premises were to be used only as a "public park and public bathing beach and recreational area...and for no other purpose." Although the 1948 deed did not contain a reverter clause, it did provide that this recreational use restriction "runs with the land in perpetuity and upon any breach or threatened breach thereof, the Grantor, its successors or assigns, or any person being a resident of Palm Beach County, Florida, may bring any appropriate action therefor."

Nine years later, in October 1957, Palm Beach County conveyed the property to the Town of Palm Beach. This 1957 deed did not reiterate the specific restrictive public recreation language of the 1948 deed, but instead provided that the conveyance was "subject to easements, covenants, limitations, reservations and restrictions of record."

At the time of the 1948 conveyance, a caretaker's shack existed on the property. In 1964, the shack was expanded to a fire station complex and then expanded again in 1979. The Town now seeks to replace the old fire station with a new one on a different site within the same property. The new proposed fire station will constitute approximately 1.7 percent of the approximately 714,000 square feet of the property.

In an effort to prevent construction of this new fire station, Anthony Martin, a resident of Palm Beach County, sued the Town seeking enforcement of the 1948 deed restriction. Can Martin enforce the deed restriction and prevent construction of the firehouse? *Martin v. Town of Palm Beach*, 643 So.2d 112 (Fla. App. 1994)

5. Jesse and Michele Knight were interested in buying a lot in a subdivision in the Manor Estates. They went to the sales office and talked with Mr. David Goates. They explained that they were interested in buying a lot and building a home with a basement apartment that they could then rent out for income purposes. Goates was unclear about whether the apartment would be permitted, but stated that he had friends who had such apartments even when the deed restrictions prohibited them.

The Knights purchased a lot and built their home with the basement apartment, which they then rented. There was a deed restriction prohibiting such use in the subdivision. The Knights claim Goates is guilty of misrepresentation, and they did not know about the recorded restrictions. Will the Knights be permitted to rent their basement? *Secor v. Knight*, 716 P.2d 790 (Ut. 1986)

6. Century Homes has been involved in a subdivision development of luxury homes for three years. The market for these large, expensive homes is no longer active, and Century is selling the remaining lots to builders who will be building small, inexpensive homes. Prior to Century's sales of the lots, the smallest home in the subdivision was 2,500 square feet. One builder is planning a 1,500-square-foot home. The existing home owners wish to know if they have any protections. What is the result?

7. George D. Warner and other property owners in Terry Cove Subdivision, Unit One, a subdivision in Orange Beach, Alabama, filed suit against Orange Beach Marina, Inc., seeking an interpretation of restrictive covenants applicable to the Terry Cove Subdivision, Unit One. A proposed use involved the further subdivision of the lots for the development of a high-quality condominium project that would include 40 single-family residential units arranged in a circular fashion around a private yacht basin or marina with a yacht club, health club, tennis courts, and guardhouse.

The restrictive covenant read as follows:

1. Nothing but a single [family] private dwelling or residence of not less than 900 sq. ft. living area designed for occupancy of families shall be erected on any lot in these units of said subdivision with the exception of those lots or tracts that shall be designated by the said Dot-Dot Corporation [the developer of the subdivision and original fee owner of the subdivision property] shall be the sole authority to designate any area for commercial venture.

2. No residence of any kind of what is commonly known as "boxed," "pilings," or "sheet metal" construction shall be built on said tract unless the same shall be covered over upon all the outside walls with lumber, weatherboard, brick, stone or other materials with the exception of wet or dry marinas on locations as designated by the said Dot-Dot Corporation.

The Trial Court found that the proposed development by Orange Beach violated the restrictive covenants, and that the restrictive covenants could not be amended without the consent of the Terry Cove property owners. Can the restrictive covenants be ignored? *Orange Beach Marina, Inc. v. Warner*, 500 So.2d 1068 (Ala. 1986)

8. Culver City required Robert Ehrlich, a developer, to pay $280,000 in land-use change impact fees and $33,220 in lieu of meeting the art requirement of all new developments in exchange for approval of Ehrlich's proposed 30-unit town-home development. Ehrlich says the fees do not advance a legitimate public purpose. Can Culver City extract the fees? *Ehrlich v. City of Culver City*, 19 Cal. Rptr. 2d 468 (1993)

9. James Broward was developing a project in Palm Beach County, Florida. The project was one for 65 luxury condominiums. When the construction contract was awarded to Warren Construction, Inc., each condominium was to have a balcony. When construction was nearly 50 percent completed, the planning commission withdrew its approval for the balconies on the condominium and ruled that the building must have a flat face. The planning commission found that balconies tend to become storage places for occupants and take on a look that is not pleasing aesthetically. Broward wishes to know his rights and whether the timing of the withdrawal of approval is legal. Offer Mr. Broward some advice. Suppose Mr. Broward decides to go ahead and remove the balcony from the construction plans. He calls to notify the foreman at Warren Construction. Is this oral notification sufficient? What if there are additional costs in changing the building from having balconies to being flat-faced? Can Warren demand more money for the changes?

10. The city of North Las Vegas (respondent/cross appellant) adopted an ordinance requiring payment of a fee when an applicant applied for a city building permit. The fee proceeds were earmarked for the funding of fire protection and emergency medical services within the city. Southern Nevada Homebuilders Association (SNHBA) filed a complaint asserting that the ordinance was invalid. SNHBA then filed a motion for summary judgment on the grounds that the city's special building permit fees constituted an unlawful tax that substantially benefited those who were not subject to the payment of such fees. The district court granted summary judgment and the city appealed. Should the city prevail? Provide the backdrop on impact fees as part of your answer. *Southern Nevada Homebuilders Association, Inc. v. City of North Las Vegas*, 913 P.2d 1276 (Nev. 1996)

For research activities related to this chapter, go to our text companion website at www.thomsonedu.com/westbuslaw/jennings.

Tax Aspects of Real Estate Ownership and Transfer

CHAPTER 22

Taxes are what we pay for a civilized society.

Oliver Wendell Holmes, Jr.

The power of taxing people and their property is essential to the very existence of government.

James Madison

There are three different types of taxes affecting land ownership and transfer. Property tax is an annual assessment based on the value of the property. Real estate ownership and property transfer can provide tax breaks, such as a deduction for the mortgage interest paid on a residence. Finally, estate, gift, or inheritance taxes (or all three) are paid when property is transferred after the death of its owner (see Chapter 17). The purpose of this chapter is to give a general overview of the taxes that affect and involve real estate ownership and transfer. This chapter answers the following questions: What is property tax? How is the amount of property tax determined? What happens if property taxes are not paid? Can the amount of the property tax be contested? What effects on income does the sale of property have? Can owning property offer income tax deductions and credits? Are there any exemptions for gains made from the sale of property?

Property Taxes

Property taxes have been documented from as early as 596 B.C., when the city of Athens levied a tax on the property owners who lived in that city. Roman taxes applied to both real and personal property. During the reign of England's Henry II, there was a 10 percent tax rate on all "rents and movable properties." In 1697,

England levied its first "land tax." When the colonists arrived in North America, they brought poll, property, and faculty (income earning capacity) taxes with them.

The purpose of levying the various forms of taxes was to support the government. Property taxes in the United States currently account for 85 percent of the tax revenues of local governments and finance about half of all local government expenditures. As property tax rates have increased, the issue of valuation has become a critical one for landowners. Property taxes are a sure thing: there is always property to tax even when there is no income, and nonpayment has the remedies of a lien or sale of the property (discussed later in the chapter).

Property tax rates are an emotional issue that often brings out ballot initiatives that limit rates or amount of valuation or taxation. California, with its Proposition 13, was the first state to undertake property tax reform through the ballot box. These citizen initiatives on tax limitations are frequent and constitutionally valid. Because of high property values during the period from 2004 through 2006, assessed values for homes rose dramatically. With the declining of values in 2007, new taxpayer initiatives that demanded legislative changes and reduction in assessed values percolated up around the country.[1] In the following U.S. Supreme Court case, a new home buyer challenged Proposition 13 because of its resulting effect on her costs of home ownership.

NORDLINGER V. HAHN

505 U.S. 1 (1992)

FACTS

Stephanie Nordlinger lived in a rented apartment in Los Angeles, never owning any real property until 1988, when she purchased her first home in the Baldwin Hills neighborhood of Los Angeles County for $170,000.

In early 1989, Nordlinger (petitioner) received an assessed value notice for her property from the Los Angeles County Tax Assessor (Hahn/respondent) that reassessed the home upward to $170,100. The new assessed value resulted in a tax increase of $453.60, or a 36 percent increase to $1,701.00. Nordlinger later learned from talking with her neighbors that she was paying five times more in taxes than some of her neighbors who had owned their homes since 1975. For example, an identical house one block away from Nordlinger's had an assessed valuation of $35,820 and a resulting annual tax of $358.20.

This disparity resulted because of the voter passage of California's Proposition 13 (Title XIIIA), a tax-limiting proposal. The maximum amount that any pre-1976 home owner's assessed value could be increased per year was 2 percent. The amount of the assessed value adjustment was limited to per-year inflation, but the maximum was 2 percent. Thus, a pre-1976 owner of a $2.1 million Malibu home paid only a few dollars more than Nordlinger for property taxes. Nordlinger paid her taxes under protest and filed suit against the assessor on the grounds that her tax was unconstitutional. The trial court dismissed the complaint and the court of appeals affirmed. The California Supreme Court was rejecting all such tax challenges, and Nordlinger appealed to the United States Supreme Court.

JUDICIAL OPINION

Blackmun, Justice. The Equal Protection Clause of the Fourteenth Amendment, §1, commands that no State shall "deny to any person within its jurisdiction the equal protection of the laws." Of course, most laws differentiate in some fashion between classes of persons. The Equal Protection Clause does not forbid classifications. It simply keeps governmental decision-makers from treating differently persons who are in all relevant respects alike.

As a general rule, "legislatures are presumed to have acted within their constitutional power despite the fact that in practice their laws result in some inequality."

Accordingly, this Court's cases are clear that, unless a classification warrants some form of heightened review because it jeopardizes exercise of a fundamental right or categorizes on the basis of an inherently suspect

1. Jeff D. Opdyke, "Homeowners Wage a Tax Rebellion," *Wall Street Journal*, April 28, 2007, p. B1.

characteristic, the Equal Protection Clause requires only that the classification rationally further a legitimate state interest.

As between newer and older owners, Article XIIIA does not discriminate with respect to either the tax rate or the annual rate of adjustment in assessments. Newer and older owners alike benefit in both the short and long run from the protections of a 1% tax rate ceiling and no more than a 2% increase in assessment value per year. New and old owners are treated differently with respect to one factor only—the basis on which their property is initially assessed. Petitioner's true complaint is that the State has denied her—a new owner—the benefit of the same assessment value that her neighbors—older owners—enjoy.

We have no difficulty in ascertaining at least two rational or reasonable considerations of difference or policy that justify denying petitioner the benefits of her neighbors' lower assessments. First, the States have a legitimate interest in local neighborhood preservation, continuity, and stability—*Euclid v. Ambler Realty Co.*, 272 U.S. 365, 47 S.Ct. 114, 71 L.Ed. 303 (1926). The State therefore legitimately can decide to structure its tax system to discourage rapid turnover in ownership of homes and businesses, for example, in order to inhibit displacement of lower income families by the forces of gentrification or of established, "mom-and-pop" businesses by newer chain operations. By permitting older owners to pay progressively less in taxes than new owners of comparable property, the Article XIIIA assessment scheme rationally furthers this interest.

Second, the State legitimately can conclude that a new owner at the time of acquiring his property does not have the same reliance interest warranting protection against higher taxes as does an existing owner. The State may deny a new owner at the point of purchase the right to "lock in" to the same assessed value as is enjoyed by an existing owner of comparable property, because an existing owner rationally may be thought to have vested expectations in his property or home that are more deserving of protection than the anticipatory expectations of a new owner at the point of purchase. A new owner has full information about the scope of future tax liability before acquiring the property, and if he thinks the future tax burden is too demanding, he can decide not to complete the purchase at all. By contrast, the existing owner, already saddled with his purchase, does not have the option of deciding not to buy his home if taxes become prohibitively high. To meet his tax obligations, he might be forced to sell his home or to divert his income away from the purchase of food, clothing, and other necessities. In short, the State may decide that it is worse to have owned and lost, than never to have owned at all.

Petitioner and *amici** argue with some appeal that Article XIIIA frustrates the "American dream" of home ownership for many younger and poorer California families. They argue that Article XIIIA places start-up businesses that depend on ownership of property at a severe disadvantage in competing with established businesses. They argue that Article XIIIA dampens demand for and construction of new housing and buildings. And they argue that Article XIIIA constricts local tax revenues at the expense of public education and vital services.

Time and again, however, this Court has made clear in the rational-basis context that the "Constitution presumes that, absent some reason to infer antipathy, even improvident decisions will eventually be rectified by the democratic process and that judicial intervention is generally unwarranted no matter how unwisely we may think a political branch has acted" [footnote omitted]. *Vance v. Bradley*, 440 U.S. 93, 97, 99 S.Ct. 939, 942–943, 59 L.Ed.2d 171 (1979). Certainly, California's grand experiment appears to vest benefits in a broad, powerful, and entrenched segment of society, and, as the Court of Appeal surmised, ordinary democratic processes may be unlikely to prompt its reconsideration or repeal. Yet many wise and well-intentioned laws suffer from the same malady. Article XIIIA is not palpably arbitrary, and we must decline petitioner's request to upset the will of the people of California.

Affirmed.

CASE QUESTIONS

1. When did Nordlinger buy her property and for how much?
2. When was the property reassessed?
3. Discuss and compare Nordlinger's property taxes with those in her neighborhood and other California areas.
4. What two reasons does the Court give as a rational basis for the difference in treatment of home owners?
5. How does the Court respond to Nordlinger's point about the American dream?
6. Does the Court uphold California's property tax scheme?

*Friends of the court; interested parties filing briefs.

Assessment

A tax **assessment** estimates the value of land for the purposes of taxation. The amount of tax is calculated on an assessment rate, such as $10 per $1,000 valuation. This ratio is called a millage rate; one mill equals 1/10th percentage of the assessed value, and the assessed value of property for tax purposes is generally 35–50 percent of the property's market value. Property owners pay at the same rate but in different amounts depending on the assessed value of their property. For example, if the tax rate is $10 per $1,000 of valuation and a property is valued at $300,000, then the tax would be $3,000. However, someone with property valued at only $100,000 would pay property tax of $1000.

Real property taxes are *ad valorem* taxes because the amount of tax increases with the property value. Property taxes are not based on the ability to pay or on the amount of government services received. *Ad valorem* taxes are constitutional so long as the uniform rate structure is applied.

Each taxing entity has a tax **assessor** or other official prepare a list of all properties and owners, a list known as a **property tax roll**. Once the list is completed, the assessor (who is usually an elected official) determines valuations for all properties on the list (see discussion in the next section).

In some states, only fee holders are subject to the *ad valorem* **tax** on real property, whereas other states tax leasehold interests as well as some form of real-property interests. Because of statutory limitations on tax rates, some local governments have become creative in collecting new revenues. For example, some states now collect transfer fees as a property tax when title to property changes hands. These additional taxes, beyond the traditional *ad valorem* property taxes, are constitutional so long as the system is uniform across all transfers, with the transfer tax determined according to a formula. *C. R. Campbell Construction Co. v. City of Charleston*, 481 S.E.2d 437 (S.C. 1997).

Methods of Valuation for Assessment

The assessment of property involves a great deal of discretion, and assessors are never without criticism. In some states, in 2007, challenges to assessed values rose 30 to 70 percent over 2006 levels because of increasing values in homes and, then, sudden declines. However, assessed values tend to be lower than market values, and average national assessment figures for properties are at about 30 percent of market value.

The timing of an assessment can affect the assessment figure. In many areas, assessments are not done on an annual basis but biennially or as infrequently as every three or four years. In some cases, raw land is being assessed, but a subdivision or some other type of development is imminent because of surrounding property usage. Some assessments will value the property as if it were capable of being in use at the time (the highest and best-use concept) and will, of course, cause a higher tax on the property. Sometimes, this type of future value assessment serves to force development because the owner of raw land cannot afford the assessed value tax.

There are three different approaches for valuation of property. The **market approach** bases the value of the property on an analysis and correlation of actual transaction prices. The assessor examines sales and purchases of property similar to the one being assessed.

Under the **income approach**, the value of the land is based upon prospective income that the land produces. In using this approach, the assessor can examine net income, net operating income, gross or net rental income, and gross or net cash flow. In this category, assessors often determine the highest and best use of the property as the basis for valuation, such as its potential use as a casino vs. a country club, with the later capable of generating much higher revenues. *Snider v. Casino Aztar/Aztar Missouri Gaming Corp.,* 156 S.W.3d 341 (Mo. 2005).

The third, known as the **cost approach**, is based on what it would cost to replace the buildings on the property. The assessor examines information such as the total replacement cost of the building and then subtracts out factors such as deterioration of the premises and whether the facility is obsolete.

> ***Practical Tip***
>
> *Changes and limitations in property taxes have taken effect all around the country. When a listing agreement or property owner provides information on current taxes, be sure to check the valuation rates and procedures to be certain you know the full tax costs associated with the property.*

Under any of the formulas, the task of assessment is complex, with room for disagreement about the numbers used and the projections in those formulas where some estimating is involved. Lawyers who specialize in assessment appeals assist clients in appealing the value assessed to their properties.

The following case deals with one of the more complex valuation issues that confront appraisers today, one that deals with property transfer rights such as air rights and other components of land ownership. (Refer to Chapter 3 for a discussion of the extent of land interests and the components that could be transferred as land rights without surrendering all rights in the property.)

Mitsui Fudosan (U.S.A.), Inc. v. County of Los Angeles

268 Cal. Rptr. 356 (1990)

FACTS

The County of Los Angeles adopted a redevelopment plan for the Central Business District Redevelopment Project. The plan limited Mitsui Fudosan (U.S.A.), Inc. (Mitsui), to a maximum floor area ratio of six square feet of building area to one square foot of parcel area. However, Mitsui could exceed that level through transfer of other unused floor area ratios from other parcels within the project area. Making use of these so-called transfer development rights (TDRs), Mitsui, in 1983, purchased from several adjacent landowners at a cost of $8,209,000 sufficient TDRs to permit it to construct an additional 490,338 square feet of building area, more than doubling the density originally permitted.

Beginning in the 1984–85 tax year, the county assessor increased Mitsui's base assessment by $8,209,000 to reflect the value of the TDR transactions. This resulted in increased taxes of $266,821.10 for the 1984–86 tax years. Mitsui paid the taxes under protest and appealed to the county appeals board. The appeals board labeled the issue a legal question and summarily denied the application. The trial court granted Mitsui's motion for summary judgment and ordered a refund. The county appealed.

JUDICIAL OPINION

Gates, Associate Justice. For purposes of taxation "this '[p]roperty' includes all matters and things, real, personal, and mixed, capable of private ownership." (§103.) "Real estate" or "real property," in turn, encompasses "[t]he possession of, claim to, ownership of, or right to the possession of land." (§104, subd. (a).)

The word "land" is not specifically defined by the Revenue and Taxation Code or related property tax regulations. However, no purpose would be served by attempting to force relatively recent three-dimensional land use concepts such as TDRs into one of the cubicles reserved for traditional interests in real property. Virtually since its inception it has been the law of this state that "[t]he sort of property in land which is taxable under our laws is not limited to the title in fee".

Whether or not TDRs are actually embodied within the definition of air rights, which already have been classified under the heading "land," or represent something entirely separate, they are appropriately viewed as one of the fractional interests in the complex bundle of rights arising from the ownership of land. As the density in urban areas increases, diminishing the number of sites available for new construction, the ability to exploit air space in various ways to achieve vertical expansion becomes essential. Property rights which evolve as a means of furthering such goals are properly subject to taxation.

The transactions in the instant case bear all the hallmarks of a transfer of real property. The owners of the donor parcels received valuation consideration, over eight million dollars, in fact, in return for divesting themselves of a portion of their own property interests, interests which are now possessed and owned by Mitsui.

In addition, in conjunction with the conveyances escrows were opened, escrow instructions and purchase and sale agreements were executed, title reports and insurance issued, property surveys were obtained and covenants restricting development were recorded against the donor parcels.

We find unpersuasive Mitsui's suggestion that it merely purchased some type of "zoning variance." As the County quite correctly observes, "[i]n a typical situation of rezoning, an owner does not negotiate with nearby property owners for the acquisition of property rights. A change in zoning does not entail title reports, sales contracts, brokerage commissions, etc." The mere fact that future zoning changes might diminish the value of a TDR is essentially irrelevant since the same fate could befall any property purchased for purposes of development.

The transactions here under review were intended to, and did, involve the transfer of a most significant present, beneficial property interest. The terms of that transfer, as well as the price paid by Mitsui, amply supports an inference that the entire fee interest in the TDRs was transferred. In the absence of substantial and convincing evidence to the contrary, the assessor was entitled to rely upon the purchase price for purposes of determining their full cash value.

The judgment is reversed.

CASE QUESTIONS

1. What additional assessment was made against Mitsui?
2. What are TDRs?
3. Are TDRs property? Why or why not? Explain their characteristics.
4. What is the significance of increasing urbanization?
5. Is the additional assessment upheld?

CONSIDER 22.1

The Villard Houses, located in Manhattan, and leased by the Archdiocese from the royal Brunei family of Borneo, are known as a fine evocation of the Italian Renaissance. In 1974, the Archdiocese leased the airspace above the Villard Houses to Harry Helmsley, who, with the help of his wife, Leona, built the Palace Hotel around these brownstones and architectural wonders. However, the 99-year-lease held by the Archdiocese expired in 2001. With the hotel in the airspace, the Brunei family and the Archdiocese battled for control. The Helmsleys bowed out by selling the hotel to one of the princes in the Brunei family for $202 million. The Archdiocese has offered to rent the airspace to the prince for $9 million because it has factored in the value of the Villard Houses. The prince is willing to pay $4.5 million for the airspace because he maintains that the value of the Villard Houses should not be included in his airspace.[2] How should property taxes be allocated on these land interests? Should the value as a whole be assessed against both owners?

CONSIDER 22.2

Apply the various valuation methods to determine what should be used in determining the value of the properties.

a. Total Petroleum had operated a refinery, and while the assessor was appraising it, Total Petroleum was in the process of disassembling the plant because of environmental concerns. The assessor valued the land without the refinery buildings, but valued the property at nearly the same amount as with the refinery buildings. Total Petroleum argues that the assessor should take into account the environmental cleanup issues. What valuation method would be best for Total Petroleum? *In the Matter of Equalization Appeals of Total Petroleum*, 16 P.3d 981 (Kan. App. 2000)
b. J. C. Penney's was one of four anchor tenants in a Ridgedale, Minnesota, shopping center. The parties argued over which valuation was appropriate: comparable values of retail stores from around the country or value based on the revenue stream per square foot. The income approach produces a lower value. Which should the court use? *J. C. Penney Properties, Inc. v. County of Hennepin*, 2000 WL 1862657 (Minn. Tax Ct. 2000) (only Westlaw cite available)

2. Charles V. Bagli, "The Church, the Royals and Rent at the Palace," *New York Times*, December 29, 2000, A19.

CONSIDER 22.2

(continued)

c. What if land is blessed with timber, but the landowner has sold the timber to another? Should the value of the timber be included before the third party can harvest it? *City of Hillsborough v. Hughes, 538 S.E.2d 586 (N.C. App. 2000)*

Environmental Issues and Assessment

EPA mandates on cleanups (see Chapter 20) have resulted in questions about the valuation of polluted property. Hazardous waste on the property and a government mandate for cleanup have some effect on the value of the property. The following case addresses this issue.

Matter of Commerce Holding Corp. v. Board of Assessors of the Town of Babylon

673 N.E.2d 127 (N. Y. App. 1996)

FACTS

Commerce Holding Corporation owns a parcel of industrial property in the town of Babylon in Suffolk County. The property, purchased by Commerce in 1984, consists of 2.7 acres of land improved with a one-story industrial building that is presently divided into 37 rental units. A former tenant on the property performed metal-plating operations on the premises and discharged wastewater containing copper, lead, cadmium, zinc, and other metals into on-site leaching pools, ultimately resulting in severe subsurface contamination.

As a result of the contamination, the property was designated as a Superfund site in 1986, making the owner strictly liable for its cleanup. In 1988, Commerce entered into a consent decree with the EPA to remediate the site.

From 1986 to 1991, assessors for the Town valued Commerce's property at between $1.5 million and $2.6 million each year. Commerce filed timely challenges to each yearly assessment on the grounds of excessive valuation. The lower court held that the value of the property has declined because of environmental issues, and the Town appealed.

JUDICIAL OPINION

Ciparick, Justice. In a hearing before Supreme Court, real estate experts for both Commerce and the Town primarily used the income capitalization method to determine the value of the property as if unaffected by contamination, and then subtracted a cost to cure from that value. Specifically, Commerce's expert valued the property by using an income capitalization approach, with a sales approach for the land only, and then subtracted from the property's value in each year the total remaining cost to cure all the contamination. The outstanding cost to cure was calculated in 1991 dollars, trended back to account for inflation in each of the prior years, and reduced by any sums actually spent on remediation that particular year. By contrast, the Town's expert valued the property in an uncontaminated state based on comparable sales data "blended" with an income capitalization approach, and then subtracted from the property's value only the amount actually expended by Commerce in the year the costs were incurred.

The cardinal principle of property valuation for tax purposes, set forth in the State Constitution, is that property "[a]ssessments shall in no case exceed full value". As this Court has stated, the "ultimate purpose of valuation...is to arrive at a fair and realistic value of the property involved".

The concept of "full value" is typically equated with market value, or what "a seller under no compulsion to sell and a buyer under no compulsion to buy" would agree to as the subject property's price. In view of this market-oriented definition of full value, the assessment of property value for tax purposes must take into account any factor affecting a property's marketability (accord, RPTL 302[1] ["The taxable status of real property...shall be determined annually according to its condition"]). It follows that when environmental contamination is shown to depress a property's value, the contamination must be considered in property tax assessment.

The Town nevertheless asks this Court to adopt a per se rule barring any assessment reduction for environmental contamination. Otherwise, the Town contends, polluters would succeed in shifting the cost of environmental cleanup to the innocent taxpaying public in contravention of the public policy of imposing remediation costs on polluting property owners and their successors in title.

Whatever the merits of the Town's argument, the "full value" requirement is a constitutional mandate that cannot be swept aside in favor of the asserted environmental policy. As the State Board of Equalization and Assessment has recognized, the public policy "argument, while possessing superficial appeal, runs afoul of the requirement found in…New York's Constitution, that real property may not be assessed at more than its full (fair market) value". The high courts of Massachusetts and New Jersey have ruled likewise, concluding that statutory and constitutional full value requirements cannot be subordinated to environmental policy concerns.

Thus, in response to the Town's contention that assessment reductions for environmental contamination will encourage landowners to delay remediating their property, this policy argument cannot eviscerate the constitutional directive. Moreover, the Town's concern appears to be overstated; whatever tax benefit Commerce might obtain by deferring implementation of remedial measures pales in comparison to Commerce's potential liability for failure to take appropriate remedial action, including severe penalties under CERCLA (see, 42 USC §9607[c][3]) and $2,000 in daily penalties for noncompliance with the consent order.

We also reject the Town's argument that because Commerce, by consent order, has agreed to pay the cleanup costs even if it sells the property, the property's market value would be unaffected by the presence of contamination. This contention is belied by the reality that a purchaser of the site, on notice of the environmental contamination, nevertheless would be liable for the cleanup costs under CERCLA. Moreover, that Commerce has agreed to remediate the property does not resolve the question of whether, and to what extent, the contamination in fact affects the value of the land. As Commerce's expert opined, a buyer of the property would have demanded an abatement in the purchase price to account for the contamination notwithstanding the existence of the consent order. Whether a property owner's agreement to pay the cleanup costs would affect the property's value in a given case is a factual matter for the assessment board, but it cannot be said, as a matter of law, that the existence of the consent order in this case precluded an assessment reduction.

While it is not possible to prescribe any one method to assess the effects of environmental contamination, there are certain factors that should be considered. These include the property's status as a Superfund site, the extent of the contamination, the estimated cleanup costs, the present use of the property, the ability to obtain financing and indemnification in connection with the purchase of the property, potential liability to third parties, and the stigma remaining after cleanup.

Against this backdrop, we cannot say that the methodology here employed was erroneous as a matter of law. The valuation of Commerce's property was accomplished by the use of the income capitalization approach to determine the value in an uncontaminated state of this income-producing property, combined with a downward environmental adjustment in the amount of outstanding cleanup costs. While cognizant of the potential of this valuation method to overstate the effects of environmental contamination, we nevertheless conclude that cleanup costs are an acceptable, if imperfect, surrogate to quantify environmental damage and provide a sound measure of the reduced amount a buyer would be willing to pay for the contaminated property.

The Town next argues that even if the entire remaining cost to cure was properly deducted in connection with each yearly assessment, this amount should have been discounted to its present value. However, Commerce's expert testified that the estimated cleanup costs were present value estimates, which he described as the present financial impact of the cleanup on the property's value. The Town failed to introduce any controverting evidence and its challenge is thus precluded.

In conclusion, we hold that based on the record in this case, the reviewing court properly considered the effects of environmental contamination in assessing the value of Commerce's property and applied an acceptable valuation technique.

Affirmed.

CASE QUESTIONS

1. What happened to the property to cause it to be designated as a Superfund site?
2. Why was the problem with the Superfund designation not considered in valuation?
3. Did the Superfund designation affect market value?
4. How will the land be valued for purposes of taxation?
5. Do you agree with the court's decision? What public policy implications follow from it?

In *RJE Corp. v. Northville Industries Corp.*, 198 F. Supp.2d 249 (E.D.N.Y., 2002), the court clarified the inclusion of environmental issues in the valuation process by limiting their inclusion to one-time capital types of expenditures for cleanup. Values of property cannot be reduced by the ongoing maintenance costs that all landowners and property owners experience.

CONSIDER 22.3

What if the environmental damage is caused negligently or intentionally by the owner? Must the property be valued in light of the damage that has occurred given the owner's role? *Reliable Electronic Finishing Co. v. Board of Assessors of Canton*, 573 N.E.2d 959 (Mass. 1991)

ETHICAL ISSUE

Do you think landowners who have been responsible for dumping toxic substances on a property should be able to reduce the value of their property, at least temporarily, for purposes of taxes? Do you see potential for abuse?

Exemptions from Assessment and Tax

All states have some land exempt from assessment and tax. Federal properties are exempt unless the federal government consents to taxation. Some states that have large amounts of federal lands receive a percentage of profits from mineral operations on the land, but these receipts are not the equivalent of a property tax yield. State and local government property is also generally exempt from assessment and taxation. Examples include governmental buildings, parks, and preserves. Most states provide tax exemptions for properties held by nonprofit and charitable institutions. Definitions of exempt organizations vary from state to state.

> **Practical Tip**
>
> *Some states have used their property tax structure to attract new business to the state. For example, businesses may be given a 5- or 10-year exemption from payment of tax or they may be taxed at a lower rate. This type of favorable treatment can affect decisions made by companies on the placement of plants or storage facilities.*

Objections to Assessed Value

The due process clause requires that property owners have the opportunity to object to or protest assessed values of their properties. Due process requires several basic steps:

1. Property owners must be notified of the assessed value of their property.
2. Property owners must be given a reasonable amount of time after assessment to gather information and prepare a protest.
3. Property owners must have a procedure for filing a protest and must be given instructions about the how's and when's of such a filing.
4. The local governmental body must provide a hearing forum: an administrative body or some form of judicial review for the property owners' presentation of protests.
5. Property owners have the burden of proof, during the hearing, to show the overvaluation of the property.

No tax can be constitutionally imposed or made final until the property owner has had the opportunity to object. Once the hearing has been held and an adverse decision rendered, the property owner must pay the taxes but may seek judicial review and challenge the assessment and tax in court.

CONSIDER 22.4

In 1996, Lawrence C. Kuperman paid $185,000 to purchase a 50-acre parcel located in the De Luz area of Fallbrook, California. Angie Fedele, a real estate appraiser in the Assessor's office, valued the property in 1993 at $300,000 when it changed ownership. By 1996, the value of the property was $313,076. Fedele initially believed Kuperman's $185,000 purchase price "look[ed] low." However, after considering declines in the real

CONSIDER 22.4
(continued)

estate market from 1993 to 1996, information about the property contained in the "Multiple Listing Service," comparable sales, and evidence showing the parcel possibly had unexploded military ordnance from Camp Pendleton, she determined the purchase price was within the range of market value for the property.

In September 2002, Kuperman filed an application with the Assessor for a reduction in the base year value of his property on the assessment rolls because he had discovered in August 2001 that San Diego Gas & Electric Company (SDG & E) had an easement over his land. This easement had been recorded in 1972 but had not been disclosed on the exceptions to the title insurance policy issued when Kuperman purchased the property in 1996. At the time he made his application to the Assessor, the enrolled value of the real property on the Assessor's roll was $198,447. Kuperman believed the real property should be valued at $38,242.

The Assessor denied Kuperman's application. Kuperman appealed to the Board. The Board denied his appeal because it was untimely filed. State statute limits the right of appeal to four years after the base year value.

Kuperman filed suit to have the Board's decision set aside. The court found Kuperman's application was untimely. Kupperman appealed claiming that his due process rights were violated. Discuss the time limitation and whether Kupperman should be permitted his appeal. *Kuperman v. Assessment Appeals Bd. No. 1*, 40 Cal.Rptr.3d 703 (Cal. App. 2006).

Collection of Taxes

Accompanying the assessment notice is the total amount of tax due and the date the tax is due. Most states provide a period during which the tax may be paid, along with a grace period. In the case of residential properties subject to a mortgage or deed of trust, the mortgagee or trustee or an assigned servicing agent generally pays the taxes for the property owner through monthly withholdings included in mortgage payments and disclosed in the loan agreement.

Tax Liens

Because property tax is not a personal obligation but a property obligation, the nonpayment of the tax allows a lien on the property. Once the tax is not paid, the enforcement agency can execute and file a lien upon the property. Each state's statutes must provide procedures for translating nonpayment of property taxes into a lien. In some states, nonpayment results in an automatic lien on the property without any filing or recording. In these states, title cannot be cleared or insured until the tax records are checked to be sure there are no property tax delinquencies.

The effect of a **tax lien**, in most states, is to make all other liens and mortgages inferior and to give the tax lien first priority for payment. The tax lien may be removed only by payment of the tax due plus any delinquencies and statutory penalties that accrue due to nonpayment. (See Chapter 6 for a discussion of other liens.)

Tax Sales

The authority to foreclose on a lien or sell property to pay delinquent taxes must also be provided for in the statutory process and authority. The key factor in the **tax sale** of real property is due process. Before a tax sale can be valid, property owners must be notified and allowed an opportunity to respond.

Due process does not require judicial proceedings prior to the tax sale. Although the procedures for tax sales vary from state to state, they usually begin with notice, delivery of notice to the property owner, and the publication of notice of sale.

When the sale is held, anyone may bid, because the sale must be a public one. The proceeds from the sale are applied first to satisfy the taxes due, interest accrued during nonpayment, any applicable penalties, and the costs of the sale. After those amounts have been satisfied, payment goes according to priorities of the secured parties. (See Chapters 5, 6, 13, and 15 for a complete discussion of priorities.)

In most states, the tax sale is not a final resolution of the property owner's rights, for the delinquent property owner usually has a right of redemption. This right may be exercised in two ways, but whichever method a state follows, the purchase of property at a tax sale does not result in full and complete title. The rights obtained by a buyer at a tax sale are subject to the property owner's right of redemption.

Under one method of redemption, the buyer is given a deed to the property, but the deed conveys only defeasible title. At any time during the statutory redemption period, the title of the buyer can be defeated if the property owner is able to pay all amounts due in taxes, interest, penalties, and costs. Once the statutory period expires, the defeasible title becomes full fee simple title. The statutory period varies from state to state from six months to six years.

Under the other method of redemption, the buyer at a tax sale is given only a certificate of sale, which is simply evidence of the purchase. Once the redemption period has expired, the buyer is given a deed to the property.

Under either method, the deed given is called a **tax deed** and is issued by the appropriate tax agency or official in the jurisdiction. The tax deed, like a sheriff's deed, has no warranties either express or implied; the buyer's title is only as good as the agency's or official's compliance with the requirements for a valid tax sale. If there is noncompliance, the buyer runs the risk of having the sale set aside by a property owner who has been denied due process. The following U.S. Supreme Court decision deals with an owner's appeal of a tax sale and whether the notice given met due process standards.

JONES V. FLOWERS

547 U.S. 220 (2005)

FACTS

Gary Jones (petitioner) purchased his home in Little Rock, Arkansas, in 1967. Gary and his wife spent 26 blessed years of bliss in the home, but, in 1993, they called it quits. Gary moved out of their North Bryan Street home, but his wife[3] remained there. Southern gentleman and court orders being what they are, Jones continued making the mortgage payments on the home until 1997, when the 30-year mortgage on the property was paid off, and Jones owned the property free and clear of that long-term obligation that had been used to secure the house. Jones assumed that his obligations on the marriage and home were fulfilled, so the taxes went unpaid.

By 2000, the Commissioner of State Lands in Arkansas was trying to notify Jones of his delinquency and his right of redemption. The letter indicated that if Jones did not remedy the delinquency, the property would be sold on April 17, 2002. Pursuant to statutory procedures, the Commissioner sent a certified letter to Jones at the North Bryan Street address. No one was home to sign for the Commissioner's letter, and no one appeared at the post office to claim it. The letter was returned to the Commissioner as "unclaimed."

Two weeks prior to the noticed date of sale, the Commissioner published a notice of sale of the North Bryan Street house, but there were no takers in this

[3] The missus is never named in the court opinion, being referred to only as "his wife."

public offer.[4] The Commissioner then undertook the process of a private sale via bid. Enter Linda Flowers, who submitted her bid for $21,042.15.[5] The Commissioner tried the notice mailing once again at the North Bryan Street address and, once again, the post office returned the letter "unclaimed."

When the 30-day post-redemption period expired, Ms. Flowers served an unlawful detainer notice on the North Bryan Street occupants, one of whom was Jones's daughter, who managed to get the notice to Jones, and all in just a few days.

Jones then filed suit against the Commissioner challenging the sale on the grounds of a lack of adequate notice. Flowers and the Commissioner moved for summary judgment, contending that the notice provisions of the Arkansas statute satisfied the state constitutional requirements. The trial court granted summary judgment for Flowers, and the state and the Arkansas Supreme Court affirmed. The U.S. Supreme Court granted *certiorari* because of conflicts in the circuits on the requirements of notice on property sales.

JUDICIAL OPINION

Roberts, Chief Justice. Due process does not require that a property owner receive actual notice before the government may take his property. Rather, we have stated that due process requires the government to provide "notice reasonably calculated, under all the circumstances, to apprise interested parties of the pendency of the action and afford them an opportunity to present their objections."

We do not think that a person who actually desired to inform a real property owner of an impending tax sale of a house he owns would do nothing when a certified letter sent to the owner is returned unclaimed. If the Commissioner prepared a stack of letters to mail to delinquent taxpayers, handed them to the postman, and then watched as the departing postman accidentally dropped the letters down a storm drain, one would certainly expect the Commissioner's office to prepare a new stack of letters and send them again. No one "desirous of actually informing" the owners would simply shrug his shoulders as the letters disappeared and say "I tried." Failure to follow up would be unreasonable, despite the fact that the letters were reasonably calculated to reach their intended recipients when delivered to the postman.

By the same token, when a letter is returned by the post office, the sender will ordinarily attempt to resend it, if it is practicable to do so.... This is especially true when, as here, the subject matter of the letter concerns such an important and irreversible prospect as the loss of a house. Although the State may have made a reasonable calculation of how to reach Jones, it had good reason to suspect when the notice was returned that Jones was "no better off than if the notice had never been sent."

It is certainly true, as the Commissioner and Solicitor General contend, that the failure of notice in a specific case does not establish the inadequacy of the attempted notice; in that sense, the constitutionality of a particular procedure for notice is assessed *ex ante*, rather than *post hoc*. But if a feature of the State's chosen procedure is that it promptly provides additional information to the government about the effectiveness of notice, it does not contravene the *ex ante* principle to consider what the government does with that information in assessing the adequacy of the chosen procedure. After all, the State knew *ex ante* that it would promptly learn whether its effort to effect notice through certified mail had succeeded. It would not be inconsistent with the approach the Court has taken in notice cases to ask, with respect to a procedure under which telephone calls were placed to owners, what the State did when no one answered. Asking what the State does when a notice letter is returned unclaimed is not substantively different.

We think there were several reasonable steps the State could have taken. What steps are reasonable in response to new information depends upon what the new information reveals. The return of the certified letter marked "unclaimed" meant either that Jones still lived at 717 North Bryan Street, but was not home when the postman called and did not retrieve the letter at the post office, or that Jones no longer resided at that address. One reasonable step primarily addressed to the former possibility would be for the State to resend the notice by regular mail, so that a signature was not required. The Commissioner says that use of certified mail makes actual notice more likely, because requiring the recipient's signature protects against misdelivery. But that is only true, of course, when someone is home to sign for the letter, or to inform the mail carrier that he has arrived at the wrong address. Otherwise, "[c]ertified mail is dispatched and handled in transit as ordinary mail," United States Postal Service, Domestic Mail Manual §503.3.2.1 (Mar. 16, 2006), and the use of certified mail might make actual notice less likely in some cases—the letter cannot be left like regular mail to be examined at the end of the day, and it can only be retrieved from the post office for a specified period of time. Following up with regular mail might also increase the chances of actual notice to Jones if—as it turned out—he had moved. Even occupants who ignored certified mail notice slips addressed to the owner (if any had been left) might scrawl the owner's new address

4. The notice was published in the state's largest circulation newspaper, the *Arkansas Democrat Gazette*.

5. To add insult to divorce and other injuries, the property was valued at $80,000 at the time of the Flowers deal.

on the notice packet and leave it for the postman to retrieve, or notify Jones directly.

Other reasonable followup measures, directed at the possibility that Jones had moved as well as that he had simply not retrieved the certified letter, would have been to post notice on the front door, or to address otherwise undeliverable mail to "occupant." Most States that explicitly outline additional procedures in their tax sale statutes require just such steps. Either approach would increase the likelihood that the owner would be notified that he was about to lose his property, given the failure of a letter deliverable only to the owner in person. That is clear in the case of an owner who still resided at the premises. It is also true in the case of an owner who has moved: Occupants who might disregard a certified mail slip not addressed to them are less likely to ignore posted notice, and a letter addressed to them (even as "occupant") might be opened and read. In either case, there is a significant chance the occupants will alert the owner, if only because a change in ownership could well affect their own occupancy. In fact, Jones first learned of the State's effort to sell his house when he was alerted by one of the occupants—his daughter—after she was served with an unlawful detainer notice.

Jones believes that the Commissioner should have searched for his new address in the Little Rock phonebook and other government records such as income tax rolls. We do not believe the government was required to go this far. As the Commissioner points out, the return of Jones' mail marked "unclaimed" did not necessarily mean that 717 North Bryan Street was an incorrect address; it merely informed the Commissioner that no one appeared to sign for the mail before the designated date on which it would be returned to the sender. An open-ended search for a new address—especially when the State obligates the taxpayer to keep his address updated with the tax collector,—imposes burdens on the State significantly greater than the several relatively easy options outlined above.

We hold that when mailed notice of a tax sale is returned unclaimed, the State must take additional reasonable steps to attempt to provide notice to the property owner before selling his property, if it is practicable to do so. Under the circumstances presented here, additional reasonable steps were available to the State. We therefore reverse the judgment of the Arkansas Supreme Court.

DISSENTING OPINION

Thomas, Scalia, and Kennedy, Justices. Arkansas' attempts to contact petitioner by certified mail at his "record address," without more, satisfy due process.

[w] have refused to evaluate the reasonableness of a particular method of notice by comparing it to alternative methods that are identified after the fact.... Its rejection of Arkansas' selected method of notice—a method this court has repeatedly concluded is constitutionally sufficient—is based upon information that was unavailable when notice was sent. Indeed, the Court's proposed notice methods—regular mail, posting and addressing mail to "occupant," ante—are entirely the product of *post hoc* considerations, including the discovery that members of the petitioner's family continued to live in the house.

The Court's proposed methods, aside from being constitutionally unnecessary, are also burdensome, impractical, and no more likely to effect notice than the methods actually employed by the State.

In Arkansas, approximately 18,000 parcels of delinquent real estate are certified annually. Under the Court's rule, the State will bear the burden of locating thousands of delinquent property owners. These administrative burdens are not compelled by the Due Process Clause. Here, Arkansas has determined that its law requiring property owners to maintain a current address with the state taxing authority, in conjunction with its authorization to send property notices to the record address, is an efficient and fair way to administer its tax collection system. The Court's decision today forecloses such a reasonable system and burdens the State with inefficiencies caused by delinquent taxpayers.

Moreover, the Court's proposed methods are no more reasonably calculated to achieve notice than the methods employed by the State here. Regular mail is hardly foolproof; indeed, it is arguably less effective than certified mail. Certified mail is tracked, delivery attempts are recorded, actual delivery is logged, and notices are posted to alert someone at the residence that certified mail is being held at a local post office. By creating a record, these features give parties grounds for defending or challenging notice. By contrast, regular mail is untraceable; there is no record of either delivery or receipt. Had the State used regular mail, petitioner would presumably argue that it should have sent notice by certified mail because it creates a paper trail.

Interestingly, the Court stops short of saddling the State with the other steps that petitioner argues a State should take any time the interested party fails to claim letters mailed to his record address, namely searching state tax records, the phone-book, the Internet, department of motor vehicle records, or voting rolls, contacting his employer, or employing debt collectors. Here, the Court reasons that because of the context—the fact that the letter was returned merely "unclaimed" and petitioner had a duty to maintain a current address—the State is not required to go as far as petitioner urges. Though the methods proposed by petitioner are severely flawed (for instance, the commonality of his surname "Jones" calls into question the fruitfulness of Internet and phone-book searches), there is no principled basis for the Court's conclusion that petitioner's other proposed methods would "impos[e] burdens on the State significantly greater than the several relatively easy options outlined [by the Court]."

If 'title to property should not depend on factual vagaries,' then it certainly cannot turn on 'wrinkles' caused by a property owner's failure to be a prudent ward of his interests. The meaning of the Constitution should not turn on the antics of tax evaders and scofflaws. Nor is the self-created conundrum in which petitioner finds himself a legitimate ground for imposing additional constitutional obligations on the State.

CASE QUESTIONS

1. What is the significance of an *ex ante* evaluation of due process?
2. What additional steps will Arkansas need to take to meet the standards of this decision?
3. What is the dissent's concern with the majority's decision?

CONSIDER 22.5

Indiana's tax sale statute requires that the notice of sale be sent to the property owners' "last known address." The Auditor of Marshall County sent Urbano and Irma Elizondo a notice of sale, which was returned by the post office for an incorrect address. However, the auditor had access to the Elizondos' current address through public records. No follow-up mailing was made. When the Elizondos protested the sale, the statute of limitations had expired. They claim they were denied due process because they did not receive the notice. Are they correct? *Elizondo v. Read,* 556 N.E.2d 959 (Ind. 1990)

Income Tax and Real Property

Although income tax is a personal tax and is tied not to ownership of property but to earning of income, real estate ownership and transfer does affect the net income of an individual.

Home Interest Deduction

The **Internal Revenue Code (IRC)** permits home mortgage interest as a personal deduction, along with the mortgage interest from one other residence that the taxpayer uses as a second home under IRC definitions. The IRC also allows taxes paid on those properties as a personal deduction. The amount of debt that qualifies for the interest deduction is limited. Current rules break residential interest into two categories: **acquisition indebtedness** and **home equity indebtedness**. The maximum acquisition indebtedness that can qualify for deductible interest is $1,000,000 ($500,000 for married persons who file separately) (26 U.S.C. §163(1)). The maximum home equity indebtedness is $100,000 ($50,000 for marrieds who file separately). Any interest paid in excess of these amounts is considered personal interest and is subject to the phaseout rules of the now completely undeductible credit card and other loan interest.

Because of economic changes, many homeowners have been refinancing their residences at lower rates but were also taking advantage of the low-cost funds by pulling out their equity in the home in addition to refinancing the original mortgage. The amount of interest that is deductible in a refinancing is the amount the taxpayer paid plus any improvements. If the taxpayer takes out more equity than the basis in the house, the interest attributable to that portion of the loan is not deductible as home mortgage interest. For example, homeowner A bought her home for $170,000 and has landscaped and added a pool at a cost of $22,000. The market value of her home is $300,000, but she can refinance only $192,000 (the basis, which is the cost plus improvements) to have the full amount of the loan interest be deductible. If she borrows more, she will be required to break out the deductible interest from the nondeductible interest.

An original home loan interest is deductible only to the extent of the fair market value of the home. These interest deduction limitations were designed to prevent manipulation of the real estate tax benefits. For example, this provision prevents someone from borrowing more than the home's value in order to have deductible interest, such as buying a home for $280,000 and financing $300,000.

Installment Sales

The IRC limits the use of the installment sales method of reporting income from property sales. Although the restrictions on installment sales do not apply to personal residence sales (hence wrap-around mortgage remains a popular means of financing), they do apply to business sales. The deferral of gains is the tax benefit in installment sales and that deferral is still available for installment sales of personal use (residence) property.

Sales of Property and Basis

The key figures for determining whether there is taxable income (gain) when real property is transferred are **basis** and sale price. The basis in a home is the cost if it was purchased or the cost of construction if it was rebuilt, plus additions, improvements, special assessments paid for local improvements, and costs of repair of casualty damage.

For commercial properties, the basis is, again, the cost in terms of price paid or construction costs, plus improvements, but less the **depreciation** taken over the life of the property. Depreciation is a business expense for wear and tear on the building, and it is subtracted from the value of the property for purposes of determining the property's basis.

To determine the gain on a property sale, the expenses of the sale and the basis are taken from the selling price to arrive at the figure. An example using numbers follows:

Gain Realized Calculation

Selling price of property	*$297,000*
Less Selling Expenses	*–3,000*
Amount realized	*$294,000*
Basis of Property	
Cost	*$275,000*
Depreciation	*10,000*
Improvements	*2,000*
Adjusted basis	*$287,000*
Gain realized	*$ 7,000*

Residential Property Sales, Basis, and Exclusions

The basis for residential property is computed in the same way just discussed. However, depreciation is not available for homeowners and the computation of gains for residential property is very different from commercial property or property held for investment. If a taxpayer sells a principal residence and buys a replacement within the time restrictrions of the IRC, the gain from the sale of the old principal residence is recognized only if the adjusted sales price of the old residence exceeds the cost of the new residence. The adjusted price is the price less the cost of the residence and any fix-up costs expended. Also, there is a limited exclusion from gross income for gains on the sale of a residence by someone who is 55 or older (3 IRC §1034(b)(1) IRC §121). The effect of this capital gains tax break is to allow upgrading in homes by residential purchasers, with one break on a sale without a replacement residence as these lifetime homeowners, perhaps, prepare for retirement.

Depreciation Issues in Real Estate

Property depreciation can be computed using the straight-line method (the value of the property is divided by the number of years it will be used and it is then depreciated at that rate for each of those years); the sum-of-the-years digits method (the number of years of property use are added together and then used as a denominator in a fraction applied each year); or the double-declining balance method (more depreciation is taken in the early years and declines as the property ages). However, the IRC requires the **Maximum Accelerated Cost Recovery System (MACRS)** method for real estate if the real property was placed into use after 1986.

Under MACRS, real estate is depreciated over a 3, 5, 7, 10, 15, 20, 27.5, 31.5,or 39-year period. The amount of time for the depreciation is controlled by the type of real estate, and all categories are spelled out under the tax code. These classifications for depreciation do have some public-policy purposes. For example, properties used for solar, geothermal, or wind energy production can be depreciated as five-year properties. Furniture and appliances in rental properties can also be depreciated over a five-year period. Apartment buildings are subject to a period of 27.5 years, while farm buildings have the 20-year depreciation life. The tax code also contains depreciation tables that provide the annual depreciation figure for property values at given year rates.

Property Exchanges

Investment properties can be exchanged in a process named after the IRC provision that governs it, the 1031 exchange. An exchange of like-kind property (commercial for commercial or residential for residential) results in a gain only if cash or other property is actually received by the taxpayer. For example, suppose that Taxpayer A owns a cabin that is worth $420,000, but that was purchased for $63,000 about 15 years earlier. Taxpayer A wants to upgrade and build a newer cabin, at a cost of $435,000. If Taxpayer A sells the first cabin, closes on the new cabin within 180 days of selling that cabin, and if the money is transferred from the the first cabin escrow directly to the new cabin escrow, then Taxpayer A owes no capital gains tax on the gain made in the sale of the first cabin (the $420,000 less the cost of $63,000 plus any improvements made to that cabin). And, Taxpayer A's basis is now the price of the new cabin, a stepped-up basis gained through the exchange.

Capital Gains

When real property is sold, the money made above basis and costs is known as a **capital gain** if the seller has owned the property for "more than 12 months."[6] In 1997, Congress established a cap of 20 percent on the amount of tax on capital gains.[7] Capital gains (at the federal level) remain at 15 percent through 2008 and then increase to the 20 percent level. Capital losses in sales of real property can be used to offset capital gains. Capital gains transactions require professional tax advice.

Low Income Housing Credit

The IRC provides tax credits for **low income housing**. These tax credits provide incentives for developers to construct, for example, apartment complexes that will accept Section 8 (low income voucher program) tenants. These Section 8 credits, as they are often called, can be claimed annually for a 10-year period and can generate one of the few remaining significant tax savings in owning real estate. Qualifying for the credit requires that rent in such projects be set according to formulas established by the federal government, which factor in standards of living and income in the area where the project is located. HUD sets rents by the market rates. In other words, strict rent controls apply when this credit is available to low income housing developers. Further, the credit is not available to owners with buildings that are in violation of local health, safety, and building codes. The credit can be used to offset passive income and can be carried forward to future years. In addition to federal tax credits, state and local governments also provide tax benefits for developers who construct low income housing.

Real Estate Investment, Passive Income, and Deductions

The depreciation deductions for real property can be substantial. Prior to tax reform in 1986, many real estate investors were taking their large depreciation deductions from their real property investments and deducting them from their other income. The result was that many taxpayers showed little income, no income, or, in many cases, paper losses because of the extensive depreciation deductions.

This rather large loophole in the tax code was closed when the IRC was amended to make a distinction between passive and active income and losses. **Active income** exists when the taxpayer "materially participates" in the business, as in those situations where the taxpayer earns a wage from the business or owns the business as a sole proprietor. **Passive income** results from partnership earnings from real estate investments. Indeed, the federal tax laws include a presumption that all income from real estate partnerships is passive. Since most real estate investments are in the form of limited partnerships, the extra benefit for real estate investors of being able to use their real estate losses to offset other income is not available. The losses, often called **suspended or passive losses**, may be carried forward indefinitely but cannot be used to reduce other income. For example, a loss on a real estate investment could not be taken against the active salary income of the individual investor.

At-Risk Rule

Real estate investment activities are subject to the **at-risk rules**. Real estate investors are at risk for only those borrowed funds for which they have personal liability. The

6 There was a wrinkle during 1997 and 1998 that required an 18-month holding period, but the 12-month period was restored by the IRS Restructuring and Reform Act of 1998.

7 That rate is 10 percent for those in the 15 percent bracket. A special lower rate of 18 percent applies (for those in higher tax brackets) to transactions after December 31, 2000, if the asset sold was held for more than 5 years.

amount a taxpayer has at risk is the initial capital contribution plus any borrowed amounts as long as the taxpayer has personal liability for repayment or has pledged property that is not used in the activity as collateral for the loan. Even these two tests will not put the taxpayer at risk if the lender is also involved in the activity in some way other than as a creditor. Again, interest losses cannot be taken in real estate syndications when the syndicating entity or partnership was the lender for the operating partnership. Investors are not really at risk when the syndicator is the lender.

If the taxpayer is not at risk, the losses must be taken from that activity and not from other income. Again, the losses can be carried forward indefinitely.

Cautions and Conclusions

A practical note for the discussion on property taxes is to verify taxes and do a title search to determine whether there are any tax liens on the property. Looking into assessment and valuation provides insight into the value of the property as well as into the tax costs of ownership.

Buyers and sellers should always investigate the tax consequences of their real estate transactions before entering into contracts. In some cases, the sale may be structured to maximize benefits. In the case of property ownership, checking for all possible deductions provides for a greater return on the property investment.

Those who own property should monitor assessment and watch for notices on valuation as well as any delinquency. Following the tax activity on your property is an important part of maintaining ownership and preventing liens.

No property transaction is complete without a tax-effect investigation—both on the property and on the income of the parties involved.

Key Terms

acquisition indebtedness, 640
active income, 643
ad valorem tax, 630
assessment, 630
assessor, 630
at-risk rules, 643
basis, 641
capital gains, 643
cost approach, 631
depreciation, 641
home equity indebtedness, 640
income approach, 630
Internal Revenue Code (IRC), 640
low income housing, 643
market approach, 630
Maximum Accelerated Cost Recovery System (MACRS), 642
passive income, 643
Passive or suspended loss, 643
property tax roll, 630
suspended losses, 643
tax deed, 637
tax lien, 636
tax sale, 636

Chapter Problems

1. Galena Oaks Corporation constructed apartment units for the purpose of renting them. Because of a factory shutdown in the area, most of the tenants left and the apartments were difficult to rent. Galena sold the units and treated the gain as a capital gain. The IRS claims the gain is ordinary income. What is the result?

2. Otis and Ethel Wade are considering purchasing a second home in the Catskills. The home will be an A-frame cabin, and they plan to spend six to ten weeks plus five to six weekends there per year. Currently, the Wades own a home in New Rochelle and have paid off ten years of their 30-year mortgage. They wish to finance the purchase of the cabin but are concerned that the interest may no longer be deductible. Offer Otis and Ethel an explanation of the deductibility of interest payments on second homes.

3. Myron and Glenda Warren are interested in refinancing their home. The home has been appraised at $250,000. They bought it for $150,000 and added a pool for $20,000. Their landscaping cost $17,500, and drapes and flooring cost $8,000. The lender will refinance up to 80 percent of the appraised value. The Warrens want to be certain the full amount of their loan is deductible. How much can they finance and still have fully deductible interest?

4. Roberta Hathaway is a limited partner in a partnership that runs a shopping center. The center had a loss of $600,000 during its first year because tenants were hard to find. Roberta's share of the loss is $50,000. She will have personal income of $62,000. Can she take the loss? If so, how much?

5. Suppose that Hathaway was a limited partner in a HUD low income housing development. Would the result be different?

6. Will the general partner/operating partner in the shopping center be able to deduct his $200,000 portion of the loss? What additional information would you need?

7. The owner of a 24-unit motel converted it to 20 condominiums. The assessor increased the value of the property because he maintained that the income potential had increased. Can the assessor use a different valuation than previously used on the property, i.e., the market value method? *Lincoln Assessor v. Jones*, 15 Or. Tax Ct. 28, 2000 WL 1863496.

8. Glenda Johnson purchased her home in 1987 for $145,000. In 1990, she added a swimming pool that cost $20,000. Her landscaping cost her $2,800, and her draperies and shutters were $3,100. In 2003, Glenda decided to sell her home because she had found a larger home in a better neighborhood. She was able to sell her house for $293,000. What will she owe in taxes on this sale? Can you compute her basis?

9. Cecos International, Inc., was the owner and operator of a former hazardous waste facility now subject to an EPA cleanup and litigation regarding liability. Cecos has proposed deducting the cost of the cleanup from the valuation, which would render the property valueless. The assessor has proposed simply a reduction in fair market value. Which method should be followed? *Vogelgesang v. Cecos International, Inc.*, 1993 Ohio App. Lexis 1478 (Ohio App. March 15, 1993); *Inmar Associates v. Borough of Carlstadt*, 549 A.2d 38 (N.J. 1988)

10. Dade County's property appraisal adjustments board assessed the value of the property of the Bath Club, which brought a trial court action challenging the assessments. The trial court refused to reduce the assessments, and the Bath Club appealed on several grounds, one of which was that the board's authority to appoint special masters to take testimony and make recommendations denied procedural due process since taxpayers could not appear and offer testimony. Are the taxpayers correct? *Bath Club, Inc. v. Dade County*, 394 So.2d 110 (Fla. 1981)

For research activities related to this chapter, go to our text companion website at www.thomsonedu.com/westbuslaw/jennings.

APPENDIX A: THE UNITED STATES CONSTITUTION

Article I

Section 1

All legislative Powers herein granted shall be vested in a Congress of the United States, which shall consist of a Senate and House of Representatives.

Section 2

The House of Representatives shall be composed of Members chosen every second Year by the People of the several States, and the Electors in each State shall have the Qualifications requisite for Electors of the most numerous Branch of the State Legislature.

No Person shall be a Representative who shall not have attained to the Age of twenty five Years, and been seven Years a Citizen of the United States, and who shall not, when elected, be an Inhabitant of that State in which he shall be chosen.

Representatives and direct Taxes shall be apportioned among the several States which may be included within this Union, according to their respective Numbers, which shall be determined by adding to the whole Number of free Persons, including those bound to Service for a Term of Years, and excluding Indians not taxed, three fifths of all other Persons. The actual Enumeration shall be made within three Years after the first Meeting of the Congress of the United States, and within every subsequent Term of ten Years, in which Manner as they shall by Law direct. The Number of Representatives shall not exceed one for every thirty Thousand, but each State shall have at Least one Representative; and until such enumeration shall be made, the State of New Hampshire shall be entitled to choose three, Massachusetts eight, Rhode Island and Providence Plantations one, Connecticut five, New York six, New Jersey four, Pennsylvania eight, Delaware one, Maryland six, Virginia ten, North Carolina five, South Carolina five, and Georgia three.

When vacancies happen in the Representation from any State, the Executive Authority thereof shall issue Writs of Election to fill such Vacancies.

The House of Representatives shall chuse their Speaker and other Officers; and shall have the sole Power of Impeachment.

Section 3

The Senate of the United States shall be composed of two Senators from each State, chosen by the Legislature thereof, for six Years; and each Senator shall have one Vote.

Immediately after they shall be assembled in Consequence of the first Election, they shall be divided as equally as may be into three Classes. The Seats of the Senators of the first Class shall be vacated at the Expiration of the second Year, of the second Class at the Expiration of the fourth Year, and of the third Class at the Expiration of the sixth Year, so that one third may be chosen every second Year; and if Vacancies happen by Resignation, or otherwise, during the Recess of the Legislature of any State, the Executive thereof may make temporary Appointments until the next Meeting of the Legislature, which shall then fill such Vacancies.

No Person shall be a Senator who shall not have attained to the Age of thirty Years, and been nine Years a Citizen of the United States, and who shall not, when elected, be an Inhabitant of that State for which he shall be chosen.

The Vice President of the United States shall be President of the Senate, but shall have no Vote, unless they be equally divided.

The Senate shall chuse their other Officers, and also a President pro tempore, in the Absence of the Vice President, or when he shall exercise the Office of President of the United States.

The Senate shall have the sole Power to try all Impeachments. When sitting for that Purpose, they shall be on Oath or Affirmation. When the President of the United States is tried the Chief Justice shall preside: And no Person shall be convicted without the Concurrence of two thirds of the Members present.

Judgment in Cases of Impeachment shall not extend further than to removal from Office, and disqualification to hold and enjoy any Office of honor, Trust or Profit under the United States: but the Party convicted shall nevertheless be liable and subject to Indictment, Trial, Judgment and Punishment, according to Law.

Section 4

The Times, Places and Manner of holding Elections for Senators and Representatives, shall be prescribed in each State by the Legislature thereof; but the Congress may at any time by Law make or alter such Regulations, except as to the Places of chusing Senators.

The Congress shall assemble at Least once in every Year, and such Meeting shall be on the first Monday in December, unless they shall by Law appoint a different Day.

Section 5

Each House shall be the Judge of the Elections, Returns and Qualifications of its own Members, and a Majority of each shall constitute a Quorum to do Business; but a smaller Number may adjourn from day to day, and may be authorized to compel the Attendance of absent Members, in such Manner, and under such Penalties as each House may provide.

Each House may determine the Rules in its Proceedings, punish its Members for disorderly Behaviour, and, with the Concurrence of two thirds, expel a Member.

Each House shall keep a Journal of its Proceedings, and from time to time publish the same, excepting such Parts as may in their Judgment require Secrecy; and the Yeas and Nays of the Members of either House on any question shall, at the Desire of one fifth of those Present, be entered on the Journal.

Neither House, during the Session of Congress, shall, without the Consent of the other, adjourn for more than three days, nor to any other Place than that in which the two Houses shall be sitting.

Section 6

The Senators and Representatives shall receive a Compensation for their Services, to be ascertained by Law, and paid out of the Treasury of the United States. They shall in all Cases, except Treason, Felony and Breach of the Peace, be privileged from Arrest during their Attendance at the Session of their respective Houses, and in going to and returning from the same; and for any Speech or Debate in either House, they shall not be questioned in any other Place.

No Senator or Representative shall, during the Time for which he was elected, be appointed to any civil Office under the Authority of the United States, which shall have been created, or the Emoluments whereof shall have been encreased during such time; and no Person holding any Office under the United States, shall be a Member of either House during his Continuance in Office.

Section 7

All Bills for raising Revenue shall originate in the House of Representatives; but the Senate may propose or concur with amendments as on other Bills.

Every Bill which shall have passed the House of Representatives and the Senate, shall, before it become a Law, be presented to the President of the United States; If he approve he shall sign it, but if not he shall return it, with his Objections to that House in which it shall have originated, who shall enter the Objections at large on their Journal, and proceed to reconsider it. If after such Reconsideration two thirds of that House shall agree to pass the Bill, it shall be sent, together with the Objections, to the other House, by which it shall like wise be reconsidered, and if approved by two thirds of that House, it shall become a Law. But in all such Cases the Votes of both Houses shall be determined by Yeas and Nays, and the names of the Persons voting for and against the Bill shall be entered on the Journal of each House respectively. If any Bill shall not be returned by the President within ten Days (Sundays excepted) after it shall have been presented to him, the Same shall be a Law, in like Manner as if he had signed it, unless the Congress by their Adjournment prevent its Return, in which Case it shall not be a Law.

Every Order, Resolution, or Vote to which the Concurrence of the Senate and House of Representatives may be necessary (except on a question of Adjournment) shall be presented to the President of the United States; and before the Same shall take Effect, shall be approved by him, or being disapproved by him, shall be repassed by two thirds of the Senate and House of Representatives, according to the Rules and Limitations prescribed in the Case of a Bill.

Section 8

The Congress shall have Power To lay and collect Taxes, Duties, Imposts and Excises, to pay the Debts and provide for the common Defense and general Welfare of the United States; but all Duties, Imposts and Excises shall be uniform throughout the United States;

To borrow Money on the credit of the United States;

To regulate Commerce with foreign Nations, and among the several States, and with the Indian Tribes;

To establish an uniform Rule of Naturalization, and uniform Laws on the subject of Bankruptcies throughout the United States;

To coin Money, regulate the Value thereof, and of foreign Coin, and fix the Standard of Weights and Measures;

To provide for the Punishment of counterfeiting the Securities and current Coin of the United States;

To establish Post Offices and post Roads;

To promote the Progress of Science and useful Arts, by securing for limited Times to Authors and Inventors the exclusive Right to their respective Writings and Discoveries;

To constitute Tribunals inferior to the supreme Court;

To define and punish Piracies and Felonies committed on the high Seas, and Offenses against the Law of Nations;

To declare War, grant Letters of Marque and Reprisal, and make Rules concerning Captures on Land and Water;

To raise and support Armies, but no Appropriation of Money to that Use shall be for a longer Term than two Years;

To provide and maintain a Navy;

To make Rules for the Government and Regulation of the land and naval Forces;

To provide for calling forth the Militia to execute the Laws of the Union, suppress Insurrections and repel Invasions;

To provide for organizing, arming, and disciplining, the Militia, and for governing such Part of them as may be employed in the Service of the United States, reserving to the States respectively, the Appointment of the Officers, and the Authority of training the Militia according to the discipline prescribed by Congress;

To exercise exclusive Legislation in all Cases whatsoever, over such District (not exceeding ten Miles square) as may, by Cession of particular States, and the Acceptance of Congress, become the Seat of the Government of the United States, and to exercise like Authority over all Places purchased by the Consent of the Legislature of the State in which the Same shall be, for the Erection of Forts, Magazines, Arsenals, dock-Yards, and other needful Buildings;—And

To make all Laws which shall be necessary and proper for carrying into Execution the foregoing Powers, and all other Powers vested by this Constitution in the Government of the United States, or in any Department or Officer thereof.

Section 9

The Migration or Importation of such Persons as any of the States now existing shall think proper to admit, shall not be prohibited by the Congress prior to the Year one thousand eight hundred and eight, but a Tax or duty may be imposed on such Importation, not exceeding ten dollars for each Person.

The Privilege of the Writ of Habeas Corpus shall not be suspended, unless when in Cases of Rebellion or Invasion the public Safety may require it.

No Bill of Attainder or ex post facto Law shall be passed.

No Capitation, or other direct, Tax shall be laid, unless in Proportion to the Census or Enumeration herein before directed to be taken.

No Tax or Duty shall be laid on Articles exported from any State.

No Preference shall be given to any Regulation of Commerce or Revenue to the Ports of one State over those of another; nor shall Vessels bound to, or from, one State, be obliged to enter, clear or pay Duties in another.

No Money shall be drawn from the Treasury, but in Consequence of Appropriations made by Law; and a regular Statement and Account of the Receipts and Expenditures of all public Money shall be published from time to time.

No Title of Nobility shall be granted by the United States: And no Person holding any Office of Profit or Trust under them, shall, without the Consent of the Congress, accept of any present, Emolument, Office, or Title, of any kind whatever, from any King, Prince or foreign State.

Section 10

No State shall enter into any Treaty, Alliance, or Confederation; grant Letters of Marque and Reprisal; coin Money; emit Bills of Credit; make any Thing but gold and silver Coin a Tender in Payment of Debts; pass any Bill of Attainder, ex post facto Law or law impairing the Obligation of Contracts, or grant any Title of Nobility.

No State shall, without the Consent of the Congress, lay any Imposts or Duties on Imports or Exports, except what may be absolutely necessary for executing its inspection Laws: and the net Produce of all Duties and Imposts, laid by any State on Imports or Exports, shall be for the Use of the Treasury of the United States; and all such Laws shall be subject to the Revision and Control of the Congress.

No State shall, without the Consent of Congress, lay any Duty on Tonnage, keep Troops, or Ships of War in time of Peace, enter into any Agreement or Compact with another State, or with a foreign Power, or engage in War, unless actually invaded, or in such imminent Danger as will not admit of delay.

Article II

Section 1

The executive Power shall be vested in a President of the United States of America. He shall hold his Office during the Term of four Years, and, together with the Vice President, chosen for the same Term, be elected, as follows:

Each State shall appoint, in such Manner as the Legislature thereof may direct, a Number of Electors, equal to the whole Number of Senators and Representatives to which the State may be entitled in the Congress: but no Senator or Representative, or Person holding an Office of Trust or Profit under the United States, shall be appointed an Elector.

The Electors shall meet in their respective States, and vote by Ballot for two Persons, of whom one at least shall not be an Inhabitant of the same State with themselves. And they shall make a List of all the Persons voted for, and of the Number of Votes for each; which List they shall sign and certify, and transmit sealed to the Seat of the Government of the United States, directed to the President of the Senate. The President of the Senate shall, in the Presence of the Senate and House of Representatives, open all the Certificates, and the Votes shall then be counted. The Person having the greatest Number of Votes shall be the President, if such Number be a Majority of the whole Number of Electors appointed; and if there be more than one who have such Majority, and have an equal Number of Votes, then the House of Representatives shall immediately chuse by Ballot one of them for President; and if no Person have a Majority, then from the five highest on the List the said House shall in like Manner chuse the President. But in chusing the President, the Votes shall be taken by States, the Representation from each State having one Vote; a quorum for this Purpose shall consist of a Member or Members from two thirds of the States, and a Majority of all the States shall be necessary to a Choice. In every Case, after the Choice of the President, the Person having the greatest Number of Votes of the Electors shall be the Vice President. But if there should remain two or more who have equal Votes, the Senate shall chuse from them by Ballot the Vice President.

The Congress may determine the Time of chusing the Electors, and the Day on which they shall give their Votes; which Day shall be the same throughout the United States.

No Person except a natural born Citizen, or a Citizen of the United States, at the time of the Adoption of this Constitution, shall be eligible to the Office of President; neither shall any Person be eligible to that Office who shall not have attained to the Age of thirty-five Years, and been fourteen years a Resident within the United States.

In Case of the Removal of the President from Office, or of his Death, Resignation, or Inability to discharge the Powers and Duties of the said Office, the Same shall devolve on the Vice President, and the Congress may by Law provide for the Case of Removal, Death, Resignation, or Inability, both of the President and Vice President, declaring what Officer shall then act as President, and such Officer shall act accordingly, until the Disability be removed, or a President shall be elected.

The President shall, at stated Times, receive for his Services, a Compensation, which shall neither be encreased nor diminished during the Period for which he shall have been elected, and he shall not receive within that Period any other Emolument from the United States, or any of them.

Before he enter on the Execution of his Office, he shall take the following Oath or Affirmation:—"I do solemnly swear (or affirm) that I will faithfully execute the Office of President of the United States, and will to the best of my Ability, preserve, protect, and defend the Constitution of the United States."

Section 2

The President shall be Commander in Chief of the Army and Navy of the United States, and of the Militia of the several States, when called into the actual Service of the United States; he may require the Opinion, in writing, of the principal Officer in each of the executive Departments, upon any Subject relating to the Duties of their respective Offices, and he shall have Power to grant Reprieves and Pardons for Offenses against the United States, except in Cases of Impeachment.

He shall have Power, by and with the Advice and Consent of the Senate, to make Treaties, provided two thirds of the Senators present concur; and he shall nominate, and by and with the Advice and Consent of the Senate, shall appoint Ambassadors, other public Ministers and Consuls, Judges of the supreme Court, and all other Officers of the United States, whose Appointments are not herein otherwise provided for, and which shall be established by Law: but the Congress may by Law vest the Appointment of such inferior Officers, as they think proper, in the President alone, in the Courts of Law, or in the Heads of Departments.

The President shall have Power to fill up all Vacancies that may happen during the Recess of the Senate, by granting Commissions which shall expire at the End of their next Session.

Section 3

He shall from time to time give to the Congress Information of the State of the Union, and recommend to their Consideration such Measures as he shall judge necessary and expedient; he may, on extraordinary Occasions, convene both Houses, or either of them, and in Case of Disagreement between them, with Respect to the Time of Adjournment, he may adjourn them to such Time as he shall think proper; he shall receive Ambassadors and other public Ministers; he shall take Care that the Laws be faithfully executed, and shall Commission all the Officers of the United States.

Section 4

The President, Vice President and all Civil Officers of the United States, shall be removed from Office on Impeachment for, and Conviction of, Treason, Bribery, or other high Crimes and Misdemeanors.

Article III

Section 1

The judicial Power of the United States, shall be vested in one supreme Court, and in such inferior Courts as the Congress may from time to time ordain and establish. The Judges, both of the supreme and inferior Courts, shall hold their Offices during good Behaviour, and shall, at stated Times, receive for their Services, a Compensation, which shall not be diminished during their Continuance in Office.

Section 2

The judicial Power shall extend to all Cases, in Law and Equity, arising under this Constitution, the Laws of the United States, and Treaties made, or which shall be made, under their Authority;—to all Cases affecting Ambassadors, other public Ministers and Consuls;—to all Cases of admiralty and maritime Jurisdiction;—to Controversies to which the United States shall be a Party;—to Controversies between two or more States;—between a State and Citizens of another State;—between Citizens of different States,—between Citizens of the same State claiming Lands under Grants of different States, and between a State, or the Citizens thereof, and foreign States, Citizens or Subjects.

In all Cases affecting Ambassadors, other public Ministers and Consuls, and those in which a State shall be Party, the Supreme Court shall have original Jurisdiction. In all the other Cases before mentioned, the supreme Court shall have appellate Jurisdiction, both as to Law and Fact, with such Exceptions, and under such Regulations as the Congress shall make.

The Trial of all Crimes, except in Cases of Impeachment, shall be by Jury; and such Trial shall be held in the State where the said Crimes shall have been committed; but when not committed within any State, the Trial shall be at such Place or Places as the Congress may by Law have directed.

Section 3

Treason against the United States, shall consist only in levying War against them, or in adhering to their Enemies, giving them Aid and Comfort. No Person shall be convicted of Treason unless on the Testimony of two Witnesses to the same overt Act, or on Confession in open Court.

The Congress shall have Power to declare the Punishment of Treason, but no Attainder of Treason shall work Corruption of Blood, or Forfeiture except during the Life of the Person attainted.

Article IV

Section 1

Full Faith and Credit shall be given in each State to the public Arts, Records, and judicial Proceedings of every other State. And the Congress may by general Laws prescribe the Manner in which such Acts, Records and Proceedings shall be proved, and the Effect thereof.

Section 2

The Citizens of each State shall be entitled to all Privileges and Immunities of Citizens in the several States.

A Person charged in any State with Treason, Felony, or other Crime, who shall flee from Justice, and be found in another State, shall on Demand of the executive Authority of the State from which he fled, be delivered up, to be removed to the State having Jurisdiction of the Crime.

No Person held to Service or Labour in one State, under the Laws thereof, escaping into another, shall, in Consequence of any Law or Regulation therein, be discharged from such Service or Labour, but shall be delivered up on Claim of the Party to whom such Service or Labour may be due.

Section 3

New States may be admitted by the Congress into this Union; but no new State shall be formed or erected within the Jurisdiction of any other State; nor any State be formed by the Junction of two or more States, or Parts of States, without the Consent of the Legislatures of the States concerned as well as of the Congress.

The Congress shall have Power to dispose of and make all needful Rules and Regulations respecting the Territory or other Property belonging to the United States; and nothing in this Constitution shall be so construed as to Prejudice any Claims of the United States, or of any particular State.

Section 4

The United States shall guarantee to every State in this Union a Republican Form of Government, and shall protect each of them against Invasion; and on Application of the Legislature, or of the Executive (when the Legislature cannot be convened) against domestic Violence.

Article V

The Congress, whenever two thirds of both Houses shall deem it necessary, shall propose Amendments to this Constitution, or, on the Application of the Legislatures of two thirds of the several States, shall call a Convention for proposing Amendments, which, in either Case, shall be valid to all Intents and Purposes, as Part of this Constitution, when ratified by the Legislatures of three fourths of the several States, or by Conventions in three fourths thereof, as the one or the other Mode of Ratification may be proposed by the Congress; Provided that no Amendment which may be made prior to the Year One thousand eight hundred and eight shall in any Manner affect the first and fourth Clauses in the Ninth Section of the first Article; and that no State, without its Consent, shall be deprived of its equal Suffrage in the Senate.

Article VI

All Debts contracted and Engagements entered into, before the Adoption of this Constitution, shall be as valid against the United States under this Constitution, as under the Confederation.

This Constitution, and the Laws of the United States which shall be made in Pursuance thereof; and all Treaties made, or which shall be made, under the Authority of the United States, shall be the supreme Law of the Land; and the judges in every State shall be bound thereby, any Thing in the Constitution or Laws of any State to the Contrary notwithstanding.

The Senators and Representatives before mentioned, and the Members of the several State Legislatures, and all executive and judicial Officers, both of the United States and of the several States, shall be bound by Oath or Affirmation, to support this Constitution; but no religious Test shall ever be required as a Qualification to any Office or public Trust under the United States.

Article VII

The Ratification of the Conventions of nine States, shall be sufficient for the Establishment of this Constitution between the States so ratifying the Same.

Amendment I (1791)

Congress shall make no law respecting an establishment of religion, or prohibiting the free exercise thereof; or abridging the freedom of speech, or of the press; or the right of the people peaceably to assemble, and to petition the Government for a redress of grievances.

Amendment II (1791)

A well regulated Militia, being necessary to the security of a free State, the right of the people to keep and bear Arms, shall not be infringed.

Amendment III (1791)

No Soldier shall, in time of peace be quartered in any house, without the consent of the Owner, nor in time of war, but in a manner to be prescribed by law.

Amendment IV (1791)

The right of the people to be secure in their persons, houses, papers, and effects, against unreasonable searches and seizures, shall not be violated, and no Warrants shall issue, but upon probable cause, supported by Oath or affirmation, and particularly describing the place to be searched, and the persons or things to be seized.

Amendment V (1791)

No person shall be held to answer for a capital or otherwise infamous crime, unless on a presentment or indictment of a Grand Jury, except in cases arising in the land or naval forces, or in the Militia, when in actual service in time of War or public danger; nor shall any person be subject for the same offense to be twice put in jeopardy of life or limb; nor shall be compelled in any criminal case to be a witness against himself, nor be deprived of life, liberty, or property, without due process of law; nor shall private property be taken for public use, with out just compensation.

Amendment VI (1791)

In all criminal prosecutions, the accused shall enjoy the right to a speedy and public trial, by an impartial jury of the State and district wherein the crime shall have been committed, which district shall have been previously ascertained by law, and to be informed of the nature and cause of the accusation; to be confronted with the witnesses against him; to have compulsory process for obtaining Witnesses in his favor, and to have the Assistance of Counsel for his defense.

Amendment VII (1791)

In Suits at common law, where the value in controversy shall exceed twenty dollars, the right of trial by jury shall be preserved, and no fact tried by a jury, shall be otherwise reexamined in any Court of the United States, than according to the rules of the common law.

Amendment VIII (1791)

Excessive bail shall not be required nor excessive fines imposed, nor cruel and unusual punishments inflicted.

Amendment IX (1791)

The enumeration in the Constitution, of certain rights, shall not be construed to deny or disparage others retained by the people.

Amendment X (1791)

The powers not delegated to the United States by the Constitution, nor prohibited by it to the States, are reserved to the States respectively, or to the people.

Amendment XI (1798)

The Judicial power of the United States shall not be construed to extend to any suit in law or equity, commenced or prosecuted against one of the United States by Citizens of another State, or by Citizens or Subjects of any Foreign State.

Amendment XII (1804)

The Electors shall meet in their respective states and vote by ballot for President and Vice President, one of whom, at least, shall not be an inhabitant of the same state with themselves; they shall name in their ballots the person voted for as President, and in distinct ballots the person voted for as Vice-President, and they shall make distinct lists of all persons voted for as President, and of all persons voted for as Vice-President, and of the number of votes for each, which lists they shall sign and certify, and transmit sealed to the seat of the government of the United States, directed to the President of the Senate;—The President of the Senate shall, in the presence of the Senate and House of Representatives, open all the certificates and the votes shall then be counted;—The person having the greatest number of votes for President, shall be the President, if such number be a majority of the whole number of Electors appointed; and if no person have such majority, then from the persons having the highest numbers not exceeding three on the list of those voted for as President, the House of Representatives shall choose immediately, by ballot, the President. But in choosing the President, the votes shall be taken by states, the representation from each state having one vote; a quorum for this purpose shall consist of a member or members from two-thirds of the states, and a majority of all the states shall be necessary to a choice. And if the House of Representatives shall not choose a President whenever the right of choice shall devolve upon them, before the fourth day of March next following, then the Vice-President shall act as President, as in the case of the death or other constitutional disability of the President—The person having the greatest number of votes as Vice-President, shall be the Vice-President, if such number be a majority of the whole number of Electors appointed, and if no person have a majority, then from the two highest numbers on the list, the Senate shall choose the Vice-President; a quorum for the purpose shall consist of two-thirds of the whole numbers of Senators, and a majority of the whole number shall be necessary to a choice. But no person constitutionally ineligible to the office of President shall be eligible to that of Vice President of the United States.

Amendment XIII (1865)

Section 1

Neither slavery nor involuntary servitude, except as a punishment for crime whereof the party shall have been duly convicted, shall exist within the United States, or any place subject to their jurisdiction.

Section 2

Congress shall have power to enforce this article by appropriate legislation.

Amendment XIV (1868)

Section 1

All persons born or naturalized in the United States and subject to the jurisdiction thereof, are citizens of the United States and of the State wherein they reside. No State shall make or enforce any law which shall abridge the privileges or immunities of citizens of the United States; nor shall any State deprive any person of life, liberty, or property, without due process of law; nor deny to any person within its jurisdiction the equal protection of the laws.

Section 2

Representatives shall be apportioned among the several States according to their respective numbers, counting the whole number of persons in each State, excluding Indians not taxed. But when the right to vote at any election for the choice of electors for President and Vice President of the United States, Representatives in Congress, the Executive and Judicial officers of a State, or the members of the Legislature thereof, is denied to any of the male inhabitants of such State, being twenty-one years of age, and citizens of the United States, or in any way abridged, except for participation in rebellion, or other crime, the basis of representation therein shall be reduced in the proportion which the number of such male citizens shall bear to the whole number of male citizens twenty-one years of age in such State.

Section 3

No person shall be a Senator or Representative in Congress, or elector of President and Vice President, or hold any office, civil or military, under the United States, or under any State, who, having previously taken an oath, as a member of Congress, or as an officer of the United States, or as a member of any State legislature, or as an executive or judicial officer of any State, to support the Constitution of the United States, shall have engaged in insurrection or rebellion against the same, or given aid or comfort to the enemies thereof. But Congress may by a vote of two-thirds of each House, remove such disability.

Section 4

The validity of the public debt of the United States, authorized by law, including debts incurred for payment of pensions and bounties for services in suppressing insurrection or rebellion, shall not be questioned. But neither the United States nor any State shall assume or pay any debt or obligation incurred in aid of insurrection or rebellion against the United States, or any claim for the loss or emancipation of any slave; but all such debts, obligations and claims shall be held illegal and void.

Section 5

The Congress shall have power to enforce, by appropriate legislation, the provisions of this article.

Amendment XV (1870)

Section 1
The right of citizens of the United States to vote shall not be denied or abridged by the United States or by any State on account of race, color, or previous condition of servitude.

Section 2
The Congress shall have power to enforce this article by appropriate legislation.

Amendment XVI (1913)

The Congress shall have power to lay and collect taxes on incomes, from whatever source derived, without apportionment among the several States, and without regard to any census or enumeration.

Amendment XVII (1913)

The Senate of the United States shall be composed of two Senators from each State, elected by the people thereof, for six years; and each Senator shall have one vote. The electors in each State shall have the qualifications requisite for electors of the most numerous branch of the State legislatures.

When vacancies happen in the representation of any State in the Senate, the executive authority of such State shall issue writs of election to fill such vacancies: *Provided,* That the legislature of any State may empower the executive thereof to make temporary appointments until the people fill the vacancies by election as the legislature may direct.

This amendment shall not be so construed as to affect the election or term of any Senator chosen before it becomes valid as part of the Constitution.

Amendment XVIII (1919)

Section 1
After one year from the ratification of this article the manufacture, sale, or transportation of intoxicating liquors within, the importation thereof into, or the exportation thereof from the United States and all territory subject to the jurisdiction thereof for beverage purposes is hereby prohibited.

Section 2
The Congress and the several States shall have concurrent power to enforce this article by appropriate legislation.

Section 3
This article shall be inoperative unless it shall have been ratified as an amendment to the Constitution by the legislatures of the several States, as provided in the Constitution, within seven years from the date of the submission hereof to the States by the Congress.

Amendment XIX (1920)

The right of citizens of the United States to vote shall not be denied or abridged by the United States or by any State on account of sex.

Congress shall have power to enforce this article by appropriate legislation.

Amendment XX (1933)

Section 1
The terms of the President and Vice President shall end at noon on the 20th day of January, and the terms of Senators and Representatives at noon on the 3d day of January, of the years in which such terms would have ended if this article had not been ratified; and the terms of their successors shall then begin.

Section 2
The Congress shall assemble at least once in every year, and such meeting shall begin at noon on the 3d day of January, unless they shall by law appoint a different day.

Section 3
If, at the time fixed for the beginning of the term of the President, the President elect shall have died, the Vice President elect shall become President. If a President shall not have been chosen before the time fixed for the beginning of his term, or if the President elect shall have failed to qualify, then the Vice President elect shall act as President until a President shall have qualified; and the Congress may by law provide for the case wherein neither a President elect nor a Vice President elect shall have qualified, declaring who shall then act as President, or the manner in which one who is to act shall be selected, and such person shall act accordingly until a President or Vice President shall have qualified.

Section 4
The Congress may by law provide for the case of the death of any of the persons from whom the House of Representatives may choose a President whenever the right of choice shall have devolved upon them, and for the case of the death of any of the

persons from whom the Senate may choose a Vice President whenever the right of choice shall have devolved upon them.

Section 5
Sections 1 and 2 shall take effect on the 15th day of October following the ratification of this article.

Section 6
This article shall be inoperative unless it shall have been ratified as an amendment to the Constitution by the legislatures of three fourths of the several States within seven years from the date of its submission.

Amendment XXI (1933)

Section 1
The eighteenth article of amendment to the Constitution of the United States is hereby repealed.

Section 2
The transportation or importation into any State, Territory, or possession of the United States for delivery or use therein of intoxicating liquors, in violation of the laws thereof, is hereby prohibited.

Section 3
This article shall be inoperative unless it shall have been ratified as an amendment to the Constitution by conventions in the several States, as provided in the Constitution, within seven years from the date of the submission hereof to the States by the Congress.

Amendment XXII (1951)

Section 1
No person shall be elected to the office of the President more than twice, and no person, who has held the office of President, or acted as President, for more than two years of a term to which some other person was elected President shall be elected to the Office of the President more than once. But this Article shall not apply to any person holding the office of President when this Article was proposed by the Congress, and shall not prevent any person who may be holding the office of President, or acting as President, during the term within which this Article becomes operative from holding the Office of President or acting as President during the remainder of such term.

Section 2
This article shall be inoperative unless it shall have been ratified as an amendment to the Constitution by the legislatures of three fourths of the several States within seven years from the date of its submission to the States by the Congress.

Amendment XXIII (1961)

Section 1
The District constituting the seat of Government of the United States shall appoint in such manner as the Congress may direct:

A number of electors of President and Vice President equal to the whole number of Senators and Representatives in Congress to which the District would be entitled if it were a State, but in no event more than the least populous State; they shall be in addition to those appointed by the States, but they shall be considered, for the purposes of the election of President and Vice President, to be electors appointed by a State; and they shall meet in the District and perform such duties as provided by the twelfth article of amendment.

Section 2
The Congress shall have power to enforce this article by appropriate legislation.

Amendment XXIV (1964)

Section 1
The right of citizens of the United States to vote in any primary or other election for President or Vice President, for electors for President or Vice President, or for Senator or Representative in Congress, shall not be denied or abridged by the United States or any State by reason of failure to pay any poll tax or other tax.

Section 2
The Congress shall have power to enforce this article by appropriate legislation.

Amendment XXV (1967)

Section 1
In case of the removal of the President from office or of his death or resignation, the Vice President shall become President.

Section 2

Whenever there is a vacancy in the office of the Vice President, the President shall nominate a Vice President who shall take office upon confirmation by a majority vote of both Houses of Congress.

Section 3

Whenever the President transmits to the President pro tempore of the Senate and the Speaker of the House of Representatives his written declaration that he is unable to discharge the powers and duties of his office, and until he transmits to them a written declaration to the contrary, such powers and duties shall be discharged by the Vice President as Acting President.

Section 4

Whenever the Vice President and a majority of either the principal officers of the executive departments or of such other body as Congress may by law provide, transmit to the President pro tempore of the Senate and the Speaker of the House of Representatives their written declaration that the President is unable to discharge the powers and duties of his office, the Vice President shall immediately assume the powers and duties of the office as Acting President.

Thereafter, when the President transmits to the President pro tempore of the Senate and the Speaker of the House of Representatives his written declaration that no inability exists, he shall resume the powers and duties of his Office unless the Vice President and a majority of either the principal officers of the executive department or of such other body as Congress may by law provide, transmit within four days to the President pro tempore of the Senate and the Speaker of the House of Representatives their written declaration that the President is unable to discharge the powers and duties of his office. Thereupon Congress shall decide the issue, assembling within forty-eight hours for that purpose if not in session. If the Congress, within twenty-one days after receipt of the latter written declaration, or, if Congress is not in session, within twenty-one days after Congress is required to assemble, determines by two-thirds vote of both Houses that the President is unable to discharge the powers and duties of his office, the Vice President shall continue to discharge the same as Acting President; otherwise, the President shall resume the powers and duties of his office.

Amendment XXVI (1971)

Section 1

The right of citizens of the United States, who are eighteen years of age or older, to vote shall not be denied or abridged by the United States or by any State on account of age.

Section 2

The Congress shall have power to enforce this article by appropriate legislation.

Amendment XXVII (1992)

No law varying the compensation for services of the Senators and Representatives shall take effect until an election of representatives shall have intervened.

APPENDIX B: THE SHERMAN ACT

15 U.S.C. § 1 ET SEQ. (EXCERPTS)

SEC. 1.—TRUSTS, ETC., IN RESTRAINT OF TRADE ILLEGAL; PENALTY

Every contract, combination in the form of trust or otherwise, or conspiracy, in restraint of trade or commerce among the several States, or with foreign nations, is declared to be illegal. Every person who shall make any contract or engage in any combination or conspiracy hereby declared to be illegal shall be deemed guilty of a felony, and, on conviction thereof, shall be punished by fine not exceeding $10,000,000 if a corporation, or, if any other person, $350,000, or by imprisonment not exceeding three years, or by both said punishments, in the discretion of the court.

SEC. 2.—MONOPOLIZING TRADE A FELONY; PENALTY

Every person who shall monopolize, or attempt to monopolize, or combine or conspire with any other person or persons, to monopolize any part of the trade or commerce among the several States, or with foreign nations, shall be deemed guilty of a felony, and, on conviction thereof, shall be punished by fine not exceeding $10,000,000 if a corporation, or, if any other person, $350,000, or by imprisonment not exceeding three years, or by both said punishments, in the discretion of the court.

APPENDIX C: THE FAIR HOUSING ACT

42 U.S.C. S 3601 ET SEQ. (EXCERPTS)

Sec. 3601.—Declaration of policy

It is the policy of the United States to provide, within constitutional limitations, for fair housing throughout the United States.

Sec. 3602.—Definitions

As used in this subchapter—

(a) "Family" includes a single individual.

(b) "Person" includes one or more individuals, corporations, partnerships, associations, labor organizations, legal representatives, mutual companies, joint-stock companies, trusts, unincorporated organizations, trustees, trustees in cases under title 11, receivers, and fiduciaries.

(c) "To rent" includes to lease, to sublease, to let and otherwise to grant for a consideration the right to occupy premises not owned by the occupant.

(d) "Discriminatory housing practice" means an act that is unlawful under section 3604, 3605, 3606, or 3617 of this title.

(e) "Handicap" means, with respect to a person—

- **(1)** a physical or mental impairment which substantially limits one or more of such person's major life activities,
- **(2)** a record of having such an impairment, or
- **(3)** being regarded as having such an impairment, but such term does not include current, illegal use of or addiction to a controlled substance (as defined in section 802 of title 21).

(f) "Aggrieved person" includes any person who—

- **(1)** claims to have been injured by a discriminatory housing practice; or
- **(2)** believes that such person will be injured by a discriminatory housing practice that is about to occur.

(g) "Familial status" means one or more individuals (who have not attained the age of 18 years) being domiciled with—

- **(1)** a parent or another person having legal custody of such individual or individuals; or
- **(2)** the designee of such parent or other person having such custody, with the written permission of such parent or other person.

The protections afforded against discrimination on the basis of familial status shall apply to any person who is pregnant or is in the process of securing legal custody of any individual who has not attained the age of 18 years.

Sec. 3603.—Effective dates of certain prohibitions

(a) Application to certain described dwellings

Subject to the provisions of subsection (b) of this section and section 3607 of this title, the prohibitions against discrimination in the sale or rental of housing set forth in section 3604 of this title shall apply:

- **(1)** Upon enactment of this subchapter, to—
  - **(A)** dwellings owned or operated by the Federal Government;
  - **(B)** dwellings provided in whole or in part with the aid of loans, advances, grants, or contributions made by the Federal Government, under agreements entered into after November 20, 1962, unless payment due thereon has been made in full prior to April 11, 1968;
  - **(C)** dwellings provided in whole or in part by loans insured, guaranteed, or otherwise secured by the credit of the Federal Government, under agreements entered into after November 20, 1962, unless payment thereon has been made in full prior to April 11, 1968: Provided, That nothing contained in subparagraphs (B) and (C) of this subsection shall be applicable to dwellings solely by virtue of the fact that they are subject to mortgages held by an FDIC or FSLIC institution; and
  - **(D)** dwellings provided by the development or the redevelopment of real property purchased, rented, or otherwise

obtained from a State or local public agency receiving Federal financial assistance for slum clearance or urban renewal with respect to such real property under loan or grant contracts entered into after November 20, 1962.

(2) After December 31, 1968, to all dwellings covered by paragraph (1) and to all other dwellings except as exempted by subsection (b) of this section.

(b) Exemptions

Nothing in section 3604 of this title (other than subsection (c)) shall apply to—

(1) any single-family house sold or rented by an owner:

Provided, That such private individual owner does not own more than three such single-family houses at any one time: Provided further, That in the case of the sale of any such single-family house by a private individual owner not residing in such house at the time of such sale or who was not the most recent resident of such house prior to such sale, the exemption granted by this subsection shall apply only with respect to one such sale within any twenty-four month period: Provided further, That such bona fide private individual owner does not own any interest in, nor is there owned or reserved on his behalf, under any express or voluntary agreement, title to or any right to all or a portion of the proceeds from the sale or rental of, more than three such single-family houses at any one time: Provided further, That after December 31, 1969, the sale or rental of any such single-family house shall be excepted from the application of this subchapter only if such house is sold or rented

(A) without the use in any manner of the sales or rental facilities or the sales or rental services of any real estate broker, agent, or salesman, or of such facilities or services of any person in the business of selling or renting dwellings, or of any employee or agent of any such broker, agent, salesman, or person and

(B) without the publication, posting or mailing, after notice, of any advertisement or written notice in violation of section 3604(c) of this title; but nothing in this proviso shall prohibit the use of attorneys, escrow agents, abstractors, title companies, and other such professional assistance as necessary to perfect or transfer the title, or

(2) rooms or units in dwellings containing living quarters occupied or intended to be occupied by no more than four families living independently of each other, if the owner actually maintains and occupies one of such living quarters as his residence.

(c) Business of selling or renting dwellings defined

SEC. 3604.—DISCRIMINATION IN THE SALE OR RENTAL OF HOUSING AND OTHER PROHIBITED PRACTICES

As made applicable by section 3603 of this title and except as exempted by sections 3603(b) and 3607 of this title, it shall be unlawful—

(a) To refuse to sell or rent after the making of a bona fide offer, or to refuse to negotiate for the sale or rental of, or otherwise make unavailable or deny, a dwelling to any person because of race, color, religion, sex, familial status, or national origin.

(b) To discriminate against any person in the terms, conditions, or privileges of sale or rental of a dwelling, or in the provision of services or facilities in connection therewith, because of race, color, religion, sex, familial status, or national origin.

(c) To make, print, or publish, or cause to be made, printed, or published any notice, statement, or advertisement, with respect to the sale or rental of a dwelling that indicates any preference, limitation, or discrimination based on race, color, religion, sex, handicap, familial status, or national origin, or an intention to make any such preference, limitation, or discrimination.

(d) To represent to any person because of race, color, religion, sex, handicap, familial status, or national origin that any dwelling is not available for inspection, sale, or rental when such dwelling is in fact so available.

(e) For profit, to induce or attempt to induce any person to sell or rent any dwelling by representations regarding the entry or prospective entry into the neighborhood of a person or persons of a particular race, color, religion, sex, handicap, familial status, or national origin.

(f) **(1)** To discriminate in the sale or rental, or to otherwise make unavailable or deny, a dwelling to any buyer or renter because of a handicap of—

(A) that buyer or renter, [1]

(B) a person residing in or intending to reside in that dwelling after it is so sold, rented, or made available; or

(C) any person associated with that buyer or renter.

(2) To discriminate against any person in the terms, conditions, or privileges of sale or rental of a dwelling, or in the provision of services or facilities in connection with such dwelling, because of a handicap of—

(A) that person; or

(B) a person residing in or intending to reside in that dwelling after it is so sold, rented, or made available; or

(C) any person associated with that person.

(3) For purposes of this subsection, discrimination includes—

(A) a refusal to permit, at the expense of the handicapped person, reasonable modifications of existing premises occupied or to be occupied by such person if such modifications may be necessary to afford such person full enjoyment of the premises except that, in the case of a rental, the landlord may where it is reasonable to do so condition permission for a modification on the renter agreeing to restore the interior of the premises to the condition that existed before the modification, reasonable wear and tear excepted. [2]

(B) a refusal to make reasonable accommodations in rules, policies, practices, or services, when such accommodations may be necessary to afford such person equal opportunity to use and enjoy a dwelling; or

(C) in connection with the design and construction of covered multifamily dwellings for first occupancy after the date that is 30 months after September 13, 1988, a failure to design and construct those dwellings in such a manner that—

(i) the public use and common use portions of such dwellings are readily accessible to and usable by handicapped persons;

(ii) all the doors designed to allow passage into and within all premises within such dwellings are sufficiently wide to allow passage by handicapped persons in wheelchairs; and

(iii) all premises within such dwellings contain the following features of adaptive design:

(I) an accessible route into and through the dwelling;

(II) light switches, electrical outlets, thermostats, and other environmental controls in accessible locations;

(III) reinforcements in bathroom walls to allow later installation of grab bars; and

(IV) usable kitchens and bathrooms such that an individual in a wheelchair can maneuver about the space.

(4) Compliance with the appropriate requirements of the American National Standard for buildings and facilities providing accessibility and usability for physically handicapped people (commonly cited as "ANSI A117.1") suffices to satisfy the requirements of paragraph (3)(C)(iii).

(5) **(A)** If a State or unit of general local government has incorporated into its laws the requirements set forth in paragraph (3)(C), compliance with such laws shall be deemed to satisfy the requirements of that paragraph.

Sec. 3605.—Discrimination in Residential Real Estate-Related Transactions

(a) In general

It shall be unlawful for any person or other entity whose business includes engaging in residential real estate-related transactions to discriminate against any person in making available such a transaction, or in the terms or conditions of such a transaction, because of race, color, religion, sex, handicap, familial status, or national origin.

(b) "Residential real estate-related transaction" defined

As used in this section, the term "residential real estate-related transaction" means any of the following:

(1) The making or purchasing of loans or providing other financial assistance—
   (A) for purchasing, constructing, improving, repairing, or maintaining a dwelling; or
   (B) secured by residential real estate.

(2) The selling, brokering, or appraising of residential real property.

(c) Appraisal exemption

Nothing in this subchapter prohibits a person engaged in the business of furnishing appraisals of real property to take into consideration factors other than race, color, religion, national origin, sex, handicap, or familial status.

Sec. 3606.—Discrimination in the provision of brokerage services

After December 31, 1968, it shall be unlawful to deny any person access to or membership or participation in any multiple-listing service, real estate brokers' organization or other service, organization, or facility relating to the business of selling or renting dwellings, or to discriminate against him in the terms or conditions of such access, membership, or participation, on account of race, color, religion, sex, handicap, familial status, or national origin.

Sec. 3607.—Religious organization or private club exemption

(a) Nothing in this subchapter shall prohibit a religious organization, association, or society, or any nonprofit institution or organization operated, supervised or controlled by or in conjunction with a religious organization, association, or society, from limiting the sale, rental or occupancy of dwellings which it owns or operates for other than a commercial purpose to persons of the same religion, or from giving preference to such persons, unless membership in such religion is restricted on account of race, color, or national origin. Nor shall anything in this subchapter prohibit a private club not in fact open to the public, which as an incident to its primary purpose or purposes provides lodgings which it owns or operates for other than a commercial purpose, from limiting the rental or occupancy of such lodgings to its members or from giving preference to its members.

Sec. 3613.—Enforcement by private persons

(a) Civil action

(1) **(A)** An aggrieved person may commence a civil action in an appropriate United States district court or State court not later than 2 years after the occurrence or the termination of an alleged discriminatory housing practice, or the breach of a conciliation agreement entered into under this subchapter, whichever occurs last, to obtain appropriate relief with respect to such discriminatory housing practice or breach.

(b) Appointment of attorney by court

Upon application by a person alleging a discriminatory housing practice or a person against whom such a practice is alleged, the court may—

(1) appoint an attorney for such person; or

(2) authorize the commencement or continuation of a civil action under subsection (a) of this section without the payment of fees, costs, or security, if in the opinion of the court such person is financially unable to bear the costs of such action.

(c) Relief which may be granted

(1) In a civil action under subsection (a) of this section, if the court finds that a discriminatory housing practice has occurred or is about to occur, the court may award to the plaintiff actual and punitive damages, and subject to subsection (d) of this section, may grant as relief, as the court deems appropriate, any permanent or temporary injunction, temporary restraining order, or other order (including an order enjoining the defendant from engaging in such practice or ordering such affirmative action as may be appropriate).

(2) In a civil action under subsection (a) of this section, the court, in its discretion, may allow the prevailing party, other than the United States, a reasonable attorney's fee and costs. The United States shall be liable for such fees and costs to the same extent as a private person.

APPENDIX D: INTERSTATE LAND SALES FULL DISCLOSURE ACT (ILSFDA)

15 U.S.C. S 1701 ET SEQ. (EXCERPTS)

Sec. 1701.–Definitions

For the purposes of this chapter, the term—

(3) "subdivision" means any land which is located in any State or in a foreign country and is divided or is proposed to be divided into lots, whether contiguous or not, for the purpose of sale or lease as part of a common promotional plan;

(4) "common promotional plan" means a plan, undertaken by a single developer or a group of developers acting in concert, to offer lots for sale or lease; where such land is offered for sale by such a developer or group of developers acting in concert, and such land is contiguous or is known, designated, or advertised as a common unit or by a common name, such land shall be presumed, without regard to the number of lots covered by each individual offering, as being offered for sale or lease as part of a common promotional plan;

(5) "developer" means any person who, directly or indirectly, sells or leases, or offers to sell or lease, or advertises for sale or lease any lots in a subdivision;

(6) "agent" means any person who represents, or acts for or on behalf of, a developer in selling or leasing, or offering to sell or lease, any lot or lots in a subdivision; but shall not include an attorney at law whose representation of another person consists solely of rendering legal services;

(10) "purchaser" means an actual or prospective purchaser or lessee of any lot in a subdivision; and

(11) "offer" includes any inducement, solicitation, or attempt to encourage a person to acquire a lot in a subdivision.

Sec. 1702.–Exemptions

(a) Sale or lease of lots generally

Unless the method of disposition is adopted for the purpose of evasion of this chapter, the provisions of this chapter shall not apply to—

(1) the sale or lease of lots in a subdivision containing less than twenty-five lots;

(2) the sale or lease of any improved land on which there is a residential, commercial, condominium, or industrial building, or the sale or lease of land under a contract obligating the seller or lessor to erect such a building thereon within a period of two years.

Sec. 1703.–Requirements respecting sale or lease of lots

(a) Prohibited activities

It shall be unlawful for any developer or agent, directly or indirectly, to make use of any means or instruments of transportation or communication in interstate commerce, or of the mails—

(1) with respect to the sale or lease of any lot not exempt under section 1702 of this title—

(A) to sell or lease any lot unless a statement of record with respect to such lot is in effect in accordance with section 1706 of this title;

(B) to sell or lease any lot unless a printed property report, meeting the requirements of section 1707 of this title, has been furnished to the purchaser or lessee in advance of the signing of any contract or agreement by such purchaser or lessee;

(C) to sell or lease any lot where any part of the statement of record or the property report contained an untrue statement of a material fact or omitted to state a material fact required to be stated therein pursuant to sections 1704 through 1707 of this title or any regulations thereunder; or

(D) to display or deliver to prospective purchasers or lessees advertising and promotional material which is inconsistent with information required to be disclosed in the property report; or

(2) with respect to the sale or lease, or offer to sell or lease, any lot not exempt under section 1702(a) of this title—

(A) to employ any device, scheme, or artifice to defraud;

(B) to obtain money or property by means of any untrue statement of a material fact, or any omission to state a material fact necessary in order to make the statements made (in light of the circumstances in which they were made and within the context of the overall offer and sale or lease) not misleading, with respect to any information pertinent to the lot or subdivision;

(C) to engage in any transaction, practice, or course of business which operates or would operate as a fraud or deceit upon a purchaser; or

(D) to represent that roads, sewers, water, gas, or electric service, or recreational amenities will be provided or completed by the developer without stipulating in the contract of sale or lease that such services or amenities will be provided or completed.

(b) Revocation of nonexempt contract or agreement at option of purchaser or lessee; time limit.

Any contract or agreement for the sale or lease of a lot not exempt under section 1702 of this title may be revoked at the option of the purchaser or lessee until midnight of the seventh day following the signing of such contract or agreement or until such later time as may be required pursuant to applicable State laws, and such contract or agreement shall clearly provide this right.

(c) Revocation of contract or agreement at option of purchaser or lessee where required property report not supplied

In the case of any contract or agreement for the sale or lease of a lot for which a property report is required by this chapter and the property report has not been given to the purchaser or lessee in advance of his or her signing such contract or agreement, such contract or agreement may be revoked at the option of the purchaser or lessee within two years from the date of such signing, and such contract or agreement shall clearly provide this right.

(e) Repayment of purchaser or lessee upon revocation of all money paid under contract or agreement to seller or lessor

If a contract or agreement is revoked pursuant to subsection (b), (c), or (d) of this section, if the purchaser or lessee tenders to the seller or lessor (or successor thereof) an instrument conveying his or her rights and interests in the lot, and if the rights and interests and the lot are in a condition which is substantially similar to the condition in which they were conveyed or purported to be conveyed to the purchaser or lessee, such purchaser or lessee shall be entitled to all money paid by him or her under such contract or agreement.

Sec. 1704.—Registration of subdivisions

Filing of statement of record

A subdivision may be registered by filing with the Secretary a statement of record, meeting the requirements of this chapter and such rules and regulations as may be prescribed by the Secretary in furtherance of the provisions of this chapter. A statement of record shall be deemed effective only as to the lots specified therein.

Sec. 1705.—Information required in statement of record

The statement of record shall contain the information and be accompanied by the documents specified hereinafter in this section—

(1) the name and address of each person having an interest in the lots in the subdivision to be covered by the statement of record and the extent of such interest;

(2) a legal description of, and a statement of the total area included in, the subdivision and a statement of the topography thereof, together with a map showing the division proposed and the dimensions of the lots to be covered by the statement of record and their relation to existing streets and roads;

(3) a statement of the condition of the title to the land comprising the subdivision, including all encumbrances and deed restrictions and covenants applicable thereto;

(4) a statement of the general terms and conditions, including the range of selling prices or rents at which it is proposed to dispose of the lots in the subdivision;

(5) a statement of the present condition of access to the subdivision, the existence of any unusual conditions relating to noise or safety which affect the subdivision and are known to the developer, the availability of sewage disposal facilities and other public utilities (including water, electricity, gas, and telephone facilities) in the subdivision, the proximity in miles of the subdivision to nearby municipalities, and the nature of any improvements to be installed by the developer and his estimated schedule for completion;

(6) in the case of any subdivision or portion thereof against which there exists a blanket encumbrance, a statement of the consequences for an individual purchaser of a failure, by the person or persons bound, to fulfill obligations under the instrument or instruments creating such encumbrance and the steps, if any, taken to protect the purchaser in such eventuality;

(7) **(A)** copy of its articles of incorporation, with all amendments thereto, if the developer is a corporation;

(B) copies of all instruments by which the trust is created or declared, if the developer is a trust;

(C) copies of its articles of partnership or association and all other papers pertaining to its organization, if the developer is a partnership, unincorporated association, joint stock company, or any other form of organization; and

(D) if the purported holder of legal title is a person other than developer, copies of the above documents for such person;

(8) copies of the deed or other instrument establishing title to the subdivision in the developer or other person and copies of any instrument creating a lien or encumbrance upon the title of developer or other person or copies of the opinion or opinions of counsel in respect to the title to the subdivision in the developer or other person or copies of the title insurance policy guaranteeing such title;

(9) copies of all forms of conveyance to be used in selling or leasing lots to purchasers;

(10) copies of instruments creating easements or other restrictions;

(11) such certified and uncertified financial statements of the developer as the Secretary may require; and

(12) such other information and such other documents and certifications as the Secretary may require as being reasonably necessary or appropriate for the protection of purchasers.

Sec. 1707.—Property report

(a) Contents of report

A property report relating to the lots in a subdivision shall contain such of the information contained in the statement of record, and any amendments thereto, as the Secretary may deem necessary, but need not include the documents referred to in paragraphs (7) to (11), inclusive, of section 1705 of this title. A property report shall also contain such other information as the Secretary may by rules or regulations require as being necessary or appropriate in the public interest or for the protection of purchasers.

(b) Promotional use

The property report shall not be used for any promotional purposes before the statement of record becomes effective and then only if it is used in its entirety. No person may advertise or represent that the Secretary approves or recommends the subdivision or the sale or lease of lots therein. No portion of the property report shall be underscored, italicized, or printed in larger or bolder type than the balance of the statement unless the Secretary requires or permits it.

Sec. 1709.—Civil liabilities

(a) Violations; relief recoverable

A purchaser or lessee may bring an action at law or in equity against a developer or agent if the sale or lease was made in violation of section 1703(a) of this title. In a suit authorized by this subsection, the court may order damages, specific performance, or such other relief as the court deems fair, just, and equitable. In determining such relief the court may take into account, but not be limited to, the following factors: the contract price of the lot or leasehold; the amount the purchaser or lessee actually paid; the cost of any improvements to the lot; the fair market value of the lot or leasehold at the time relief is determined; and the fair market value of the lot or leasehold at the time such lot was purchased or leased.

(b) Enforcement of rights by purchaser or lessee

A purchaser or lessee may bring an action at law or in equity against the seller or lessor (or successor thereof) to enforce any right under subsection (b), (c), (d), or (e) of section 1703 of this title.

Sec. 1717.-Penalties for violations

Any person who willfully violates any of the provisions of this chapter, or the rules and regulations prescribed pursuant thereto, or any person who willfully, in a statement of record filed under, or in a property report issued pursuant to, this chapter, makes any untrue statement of a material fact or omits to state any material fact required to be stated therein, shall upon conviction be fined not more than $10,000 or imprisoned not more than five years, or both.

Sec. 1717a.–Civil money penalties

(a) In general

(1) Authority

Whenever any person knowingly and materially violates any of the provisions of this chapter or any rule, regulation, or order issued under this chapter, the Secretary may impose a civil money penalty on such person in accordance with the provisions of this section. The penalty shall be in addition to any other available civil remedy or any available criminal penalty, and may be imposed whether or not the Secretary imposes other administrative sanctions.

(2) Amount of penalty

The amount of the penalty, as determined by the Secretary, may not exceed $1,000 for each violation, except that the maximum penalty for all violations by a particular person during any 1-year period shall not exceed $1,000,000. Each violation of this chapter, or any rule, regulation, or order issued under this chapter, shall constitute a separate violation with respect to each sale or lease or offer to sell or lease. In the case of a continuing violation, as determined by the Secretary, each day shall constitute a separate violation.

APPENDIX E: TRUTH-IN-LENDING ACT

15 U.S.C. S 1601 ET SEQ. (EXCERPTS)

Sec. 1637a.—Disclosure requirements for open end consumer credit plans secured by consumer's principal dwelling

(a) Application disclosures

In the case of any open end consumer credit plan which provides for any extension of credit which is secured by the consumer's principal dwelling, the creditor shall make the following disclosures in accordance with subsection (b) of this section:

(1) Fixed annual percentage rate

Each annual percentage rate imposed in connection with extensions of credit under the plan and a statement that such rate does not include costs other than interest.

(2) Variable percentage rate

In the case of a plan which provides for variable rates of interest on credit extended under the plan—

(A) a description of the manner in which such rate will be computed and a statement that such rate does not include costs other than interest;

(B) a description of the manner in which any changes in the annual percentage rate will be made, including—

(i) any negative amortization and interest rate carryover;

(ii) the timing of any such changes;

(iii) any index or margin to which such changes in the rate are related; and

(iv) a source of information about any such index;

(C) if an initial annual percentage rate is offered which is not based on an index—

(i) a statement of such rate and the period of time such initial rate will be in effect; and

(ii) a statement that such rate does not include costs other than interest;

(D) a statement that the consumer should ask about the current index value and interest rate;

(E) a statement of the maximum amount by which the annual percentage rate may change in any 1-year period or a statement that no such limit exists;

(F) a statement of the maximum annual percentage rate that may be imposed at any time under the plan;

(G) subject to subsection (b)(3) of this section, a table, based on a $10,000 extension of credit, showing how the annual percentage rate and the minimum periodic payment amount under each repayment option of the plan would have been affected during the preceding 15-year period by changes in any index used to compute such rate;

(3) Other fees imposed by the creditor

An itemization of any fees imposed by the creditor in connection with the availability or use of credit under such plan, including annual fees, application fees, transaction fees, and closing costs (including costs commonly described as "points"), and the time when such fees are payable.

(4) Rights of creditor with respect to extensions of credit

A statement that—

(A) under certain conditions, the creditor may terminate any account under the plan and require immediate repayment of any outstanding balance, prohibit any additional extension of credit to the account, or reduce the credit limit applicable to the account; and

(B) the consumer may receive, upon request, more specific information about the conditions under which the creditor may take any action described in subparagraph (A).

(5) Repayment options and minimum periodic payments

The repayment options under the plan, including—

(A) if applicable, any differences in repayment options with regard to—

(i) any period during which additional extensions of credit may be obtained; and

(ii) any period during which repayment is required to be made and no additional extensions of credit may be obtained;

(B) the length of any repayment period, including any differences in the length of any repayment period with regard to the periods described in clauses (i) and (ii) of subparagraph (A); and

(C) an explanation of how the amount of any minimum monthly or periodic payment will be determined under each such option, including any differences in the determination of any such amount with regard to the periods described in clauses (i) and (ii) of subparagraph (A).

(6) Example of minimum payments and maximum repayment period

An example, based on a $10,000 outstanding balance and the interest rate (other than a rate not based on the index under the plan) which is, or was recently, in effect under such plan, showing the minimum monthly or periodic payment, and the time it would take to repay the entire $10,000 if the consumer paid only the minimum periodic payments and obtained no additional extensions of credit.

(7) Statement concerning balloon payments

If, under any repayment option of the plan, the payment of not more than the minimum periodic payments required under such option over the length of the repayment period—

(A) would not repay any of the principal balance; or

(B) would repay less than the outstanding balance by the end of such period, as the case may be, a statement of such fact, including an explicit statement that at the end of such repayment period a balloon payment (as defined in section 1665b(f) of this title) would result which would be required to be paid in full at that time.

(b) Time and form of disclosures

(1) Time of disclosure

(A) In general

The disclosures required under subsection (a) of this section with respect to any open end consumer credit plan which provides for any extension of credit which is secured by the consumer's principal dwelling and the pamphlet required under subsection (e) of this section shall be provided to any consumer at the time the creditor distributes an application to establish an account under such plan to such consumer.

(B) Telephone, publications, and third party applications

In the case of telephone applications, applications contained in magazines or other publications, or applications provided by a third party, the disclosures required under subsection (a) of this section and the pamphlet required under subsection (e) of this section shall be provided by the creditor before the end of the 3-day period beginning on the date the creditor receives a completed application from a consumer.

(2) Form

(A) In general

Except as provided in paragraph (1)(B), the disclosures required under subsection (a) of this section shall be provided on or with any application to establish an account under an open end consumer credit plan which provides for any extension of credit which is secured by the consumer's principal dwelling.

(B) Segregation of required disclosures from other information

The disclosures required under subsection (a) of this section shall be conspicuously segregated from all other terms, data, or additional information provided in connection with the application, either by grouping the disclosures separately on the application form or by providing the disclosures on a separate form, in accordance with regulations of the Board.

(C) Precedence of certain information

The disclosures required by paragraphs (5), (6), and (7) of subsection (a) of this section shall precede all of the other required disclosures.

(D) Special provision relating to variable interest rate information

Whether or not the disclosures required under subsection (a) of this section are provided on the application form, the variable rate information described in subsection (a)(2) of this section may be provided separately from the other information required to be disclosed.

SEC. 1647.—HOME EQUITY PLANS

(a) Index requirement

In the case of extensions of credit under an open end consumer credit plan which are subject to a variable rate and are secured by a consumer's principal dwelling, the index or other rate of interest to which changes in the annual percentage rate are related shall be based on an index or rate of interest which is publicly available and is not under the control of the creditor.

(b) Grounds for acceleration of outstanding balance.

A creditor may not unilaterally terminate any account under an open end consumer credit plan under which extensions of credit are secured by a consumer's principal dwelling and require the immediate repayment of any outstanding balance at such time, except in the case of—

(1) fraud or material misrepresentation on the part of the consumer in connection with the account;

(2) failure by the consumer to meet the repayment terms of the agreement for any outstanding balance; or

(3) any other action or failure to act by the consumer which adversely affects the creditor's security for the account or any right of the creditor in such security.

This subsection does not apply to reverse mortgage transactions.

APPENDIX F: REAL ESTATE SETTLEMENT PROCEDURES ACT

12 U.S.C. S 2601 ET SEQ. (EXCERPTS)

SEC. 2601.—CONGRESSIONAL FINDINGS AND PURPOSE

(a) The Congress finds that significant reforms in the real estate settlement process are needed to insure that consumers throughout the Nation are provided with greater and more timely information on the nature and costs of the settlement process and are protected from unnecessarily high settlement charges caused by certain abusive practices that have developed in some areas of the country. The Congress also finds that it has been over two years since the Secretary of Housing and Urban Development and the Administrator of Veterans' Affairs submitted their joint report to the Congress on "Mortgage Settlement Costs" and that the time has come for the recommendations for Federal legislative action made in that report to be implemented.

(b) It is the purpose of this chapter to effect certain changes in the settlement process for residential real estate that will result—

- **(1)** in more effective advance disclosure to home buyers and sellers of settlement costs;
- **(2)** in the elimination of kickbacks or referral fees that tend to increase unnecessarily the costs of certain settlement services;
- **(3)** in a reduction in the amounts home buyers are required to place in escrow accounts established to insure the payment of real estate taxes and insurance; and
- **(4)** in significant reform and modernization of local recordkeeping of land title information.

SEC. 2602.—DEFINITIONS

For purposes of this chapter—

the term "federally related mortgage loan" includes any loan (other than temporary financing such as a construction loan) which—

(A) is secured by a first or subordinate lien on residential real property (including in dividual units of condominiums and cooperatives) designed principally for the occupancy of from one to four families, including any such secured loan, the proceeds of which are used to prepay or pay off an existing loan secured by the same property; and

(B) **(i)** is made in whole or in part by any lender the deposits or accounts of which are insured by any agency of the Federal Government, or is made in whole or in part by any lender which is regulated by any agency of the Federal Government, or

(ii) is made in whole or in part, or insured, guaranteed, supplemented, or assisted in any way, by the Secretary or any other officer or agency of the Federal Government or under or in connection with a housing or urban development program administered by the Secretary or a housing or related program administered by any other such officer or agency; or

(iii) is intended to be sold by the originating lender to the Federal National Mortgage Association, the Government National Mortgage Association, the Federal Home Loan Mortgage Corporation, or a financial institution from which it is to be purchased by the Federal Home Loan Mortgage Corporation; or

(iv) is made in whole or in part by any "creditor", as defined in section 1602(f) of title 15, who makes or invests in residential real estate loans aggregating more than $1,000,000 per year, except that for the purpose of this chapter, the term "creditor" does not include any agency or instrumentality of any State.

Sec. 2603.—Uniform settlement statement

(a) The Secretary, in consultation with the Administrator of Veteran's Affairs, the Federal Deposit Insurance Corporation, and the Director of the Office of Thrift Supervision, shall develop and prescribe a standard form for the statement of settlement costs which shall be used (with such variations as may be necessary to reflect differences in legal and administrative requirements or practices in different areas of the country) as the standard real estate settlement form in all transactions in the United States which involve federally related mortgage loans. Such form shall conspicuously and clearly itemize all charges imposed upon the borrower and all charges imposed upon the seller in connection with the settlement and shall indicate whether any title insurance premium included in such charges covers or insures the lender's interest in the property, the borrower's interest, or both. The Secretary may, by regulation, permit the deletion from the form prescribed under this section of items which are not, under local laws or customs, applicable in any locality, except that such regulation shall require that the numerical code prescribed by the Secretary be retained in forms to be used in all localities. Nothing in this section may be construed to require that that part of the standard form which relates to the borrower's transaction be furnished to the seller, or to require that that part of the standard form which relates to the seller be furnished to the borrower.

(b) The form prescribed under this section shall be completed and made available for inspection by the borrower at or before settlement by the person conducting the settlement, except that

- **(1)** the Secretary may exempt from the requirements of this section settlements occurring in localities where the final settlement statement is not customarily provided at or before the date of settlement, or settlements where such requirements are impractical and
- **(2)** the borrower may, in accordance with regulations of the Secretary, waive his right to have the form made available at such time. Upon the request of the borrower to inspect the form prescribed under this section during the business day immediately preceding the day of settlement, the person who will conduct the settlement shall permit the borrower to inspect those items which are known to such person during such preceding day.

Sec. 2604.—Special information booklets

(a) Distribution by Secretary to lenders to help borrowers

The Secretary shall prepare and distribute booklets to help persons borrowing money to finance the purchase of residential real estate better to understand the nature and costs of real estate settlement services. The Secretary shall distribute such booklets to all lenders which make federally related mortgage loans.

(b) Form and detail; cost elements, standard settlement form, escrow accounts, selection of persons for settlement services; consideration of differences in settlement procedures

Each booklet shall be in such form and detail as the Secretary shall prescribe and, in addition to such other information as the Secretary may provide, shall include in clear and concise language—

- **(1)** a description and explanation of the nature and purpose of each cost incident to a real estate settlement;
- **(2)** an explanation and sample of the standard real estate settlement form developed and prescribed under section 2603 of this title;
- **(3)** a description and explanation of the nature and purpose of escrow accounts when used in connection with loans secured by residential real estate;
- **(4)** an explanation of the choices available to buyers of residential real estate in selecting persons to provide necessary services incident to a real estate settlement; and
- **(5)** an explanation of the unfair practices and unreasonable or unnecessary charges to be avoided by the prospective buyer with respect to a real estate settlement.

Such booklets shall take into consideration differences in real estate settlement procedures which may exist among the several States and territories of the United States and among separate political subdivisions within the same State and territory.

(c) Estimate of charges

Each lender shall include with the booklet a good faith estimate of the amount or range of charges for specific settlement services the borrower is likely to incur in connection with the settlement as prescribed by the Secretary.

(d) Distribution by lenders to loan applicants at time of receipt or preparation of applications

Each lender referred to in subsection (a) of this section shall provide the booklet described in such subsection to each person from whom it receives or for whom it prepares a written application to borrow money to finance the purchase of residential real estate. Such booklet shall be provided by delivering it or placing it in the mail not later than 3 business days after the lender receives the application, but no booklet need be provided if the lender denies the application for credit before the end of the 3-day period.

(e) Printing and distribution by lenders of booklets approved by Secretary

Booklets may be printed and distributed by lenders if their form and content are approved by the Secretary as meeting the requirements of subsection (b) of this section.

Sec. 2607.—Prohibition against kickbacks and unearned fees

(a) Business referrals

No person shall give and no person shall accept any fee, kickback, or thing of value pursuant to any agreement or understanding, oral or otherwise, that business incident to or a part of a real estate settlement service involving a federally related mortgage loan shall be referred to any person.

(b) Splitting charges

No person shall give and no person shall accept any portion, split, or percentage of any charge made or received for the rendering of a real estate settlement service in connection with a transaction involving a federally related mortgage loan other than for services actually performed.

(c) Fees, salaries, compensation, or other payments

Nothing in this section shall be construed as prohibiting

(1) the payment of a fee

(A) to attorneys at law for services actually rendered or

(B) by a title company to its duly appointed agent for services actually performed in the issuance of a policy of title insurance or

(C) by a lender to its duly appointed agent for services actually performed in the making of a loan,

(2) the payment to any person of a bona fide salary or compensation or other payment for goods or facilities actually furnished or for services actually performed,

(3) payments pursuant to cooperative brokerage and referral arrangements or agreements between real estate agents and brokers.

(d) Penalties for violations; joint and several liability; treble damages; actions for injunction by Secretary and by State officials; costs and attorney fees; construction of State laws

(1) Any person or persons who violate the provisions of this section shall be fined not more than $10,000 or imprisoned for not more than one year, or both.

(2) Any person or persons who violate the prohibitions or limitations of this section shall be jointly and severally liable to the person or persons charged for the settlement service involved in the violation in an amount equal to three times the amount of any charge paid for such settlement service.

(3) No person or persons shall be liable for a violation of the provisions of subsection (c)(4)(A) of this section if such person or persons proves by a preponderance of the evidence that such violation was not intentional and resulted from a bona fide error notwithstanding maintenance of procedures that are reasonably adapted to avoid such error.

(4) The Secretary, the Attorney General of any State, or the insurance commissioner of any State may bring an action to enjoin violations of this section.

(5) In any private action brought pursuant to this subsection, the court may award to the prevailing party the court costs of the action together with reasonable attorneys fees.

(6) No provision of State law or regulation that imposes more stringent limitations on affiliated business arrangements shall be construed as being inconsistent with this section.

Sec. 2608.—Title companies; liability of seller

(a) No seller of property that will be purchased with the assistance of a federally related mortgage loan shall require directly or indirectly, as a condition to selling the property, that title insurance covering the property be purchased by the buyer from any particular title company.

(b) Any seller who violates the provisions of subsection (a) of this section shall be liable to the buyer in an amount equal to three times all charges made for such title insurance.

Sec. 2609.—Limitation on requirement of advance deposits in escrow accounts

In general

A lender, in connection with a federally related mortgage loan, may not require the borrower or prospective borrower—

(1) to deposit in any escrow account which may be established in connection with such loan for the purpose of assuring payment of taxes, insurance premiums, or other charges with respect to the property, in connection with the settlement, an aggregate sum (for such purpose) in excess of a sum that will be sufficient to pay such taxes, insurance premiums and other charges attributable to the period beginning on the last date on which each such charge would have been paid under the normal lending practice of the lender and local custom, provided that the selection of each such date constitutes prudent lending practice, and ending on the due date of its first full installment payment under the mortgage, plus one-sixth of the estimated total amount of such taxes, insurance premiums and other charges to be paid on dates, as provided above, during the ensuing twelve-month period; or

(2) to deposit in any such escrow account in any month beginning with the first full installment payment under the mortgage a sum (for the purpose of assuring payment of taxes, insurance premiums and other charges with respect to the property) in excess of the sum of

(A) one-twelfth of the total amount of the estimated taxes, insurance premiums and other charges which are reasonably anticipated to be paid on dates during the ensuing twelve months which dates are in accordance with the normal lending practice of the lender and local custom, provided that the selection of each such date constitutes prudent lending practice, plus

(B) such amount as is necessary to maintain an additional balance in such escrow account not to exceed one-sixth of the estimated total amount of such taxes, insurance premiums and other charges to be paid on dates, as provided above, during the ensuing twelve-month period: Provided, however, That in the event the lender determines there will be or is a deficiency he shall not be prohibited from requiring additional monthly deposits in such escrow account to avoid or eliminate such deficiency.

(2) Annual statement

(A) In general

Any servicer that has established or continued an escrow account in connection with a federally related mortgage loan shall submit to the borrower for which the escrow account has been established or continued a statement clearly itemizing, for each period described in subparagraph (B) (during which the servicer services the escrow account), the amount of the borrower's current monthly payment, the portion of the monthly payment being placed in the escrow account, the total amount paid into the escrow account during the period, the total amount paid out of the escrow account during the period for taxes, insurance premiums, and other charges (as separately identified), and the balance in the escrow account at the conclusion of the period.

(B) Time of submission

The statement required under subparagraph (A) shall be submitted to the borrower not less than once for each 12-month period, the first such period beginning on the first January

1st that occurs after November 28, 1990, and shall be submitted not more than 30 days after the conclusion of each such 1-year period.

(d) Penalties

(1) In general

In the case of each failure to submit a statement to a borrower as required under subsection (c) of this section, the Secretary shall assess to the lender or escrow servicer failing to submit the statement a civil penalty of $50 for each such failure, but the total amount imposed on such lender or escrow servicer for all such failures during any 12-month period referred to in subsection (b) [1] of this section may not exceed $100,000.

(2) Intentional violations

If any failure to which paragraph (1) applies is due to intentional disregard of the requirement to submit the statement, then, with respect to such failure—

(A) the penalty imposed under paragraph (1) shall be $100; and

(B) in the case of any penalty determined under subparagraph (A), the $100,000 limitation under paragraph (1) shall not apply.

GLOSSARY

A

Abstract of title A concise statement of the substance of documents or facts appearing on the public land records that affect the title to a particular tract.

Abstractor's certificate A summary by the abstractors of what was and was not examined in the title review.

Acceleration clause Provision in note, mortgage, or deed of trust that provides for the acceleration of the due date of the loan; generally results in the full amount of the loan being due upon default such as nonpayment.

Acceptance Action of offeree in agreeing to terms of an offer that results in a binding contract.

Accredited investor Under federal securities law, an investor who meets certain financial standards and can qualify for purchases of certain types of securities exempt from registration.

Acid rain An environmental hazard that results from sulfur dioxide pollution from factories and coal-fired utility plants; the pollution is carried long distances and appears in rain and snow in areas far removed from the pollution sources.

Acknowledgment Notary signature and seal; appears on deeds and some contracts as well as on wills.

Acquisition indebtedness For tax purposes, determination of qualified residential interest; the amount of debt entered into for purchase of a primary or secondary residence.

Act Statute enacted by a legislative body.

Action for dispossession Court proceeding by landlord to have tenant removed from property; generally brought for nonpayment of rent or destruction of landlord's premises.

Active income For income tax purposes, income earned as wages or other forms of compensation for work/services performed.

Ad valorem tax Tax based on value that increases as value increases. Property taxes are *ad valorem* taxes.

Ademption In testate distribution, the failure of a gift if the property is no longer owned by the testator at the time of death.

Adjustable rate mortgage (ARM) A type of mortgage with a rate that changes according to some interest-rate index.

Administrator Male party responsible for the probate of an intestate estate.

Administratrix Female party responsible for the probate of an intestate estate; antiquated.

Advancement Common law doctrine that subtracts amounts of inter vivos gifts from an heir's share of decedent's estate (still followed in some states).

Adverse possession Method of acquiring title to land by openly taking possession of and using another's property for a certain period of time.

Advertisement Under Regulation Z, public disclosure of credit terms.

Aesthetic zoning Zoning that regulates the appearance of property and exists for beautification purposes or architectural uniformity.

Affirmative easement An easement that involves the use of another's property; e.g., a right of access.

After-acquired property clause Mortgage, note, or security interest provision that provides that the security for the loan includes the existing property and any property added after the note; mortgage security interest is attached to newly acquired property.

Agent One who acts on another's behalf. In real estate, the agent is the party who works to bring the buyers and sellers of real estate together in exchange for payment (generally a commission).

Air lot That portion of the airspace from 23 feet above the earth's surface to the heavens.

Air Pollution Control Act The original federal act relating to air pollution; provided for studies but did little to control air pollution (1955).

Air Quality Act 1967 federal act that provided HEW with the authority to oversee state air pollution control plans and implementation.

Air rights Property ownership rights in the air above the surface.

All-adult covenant Deed restriction that limits residency in a particular area to certain ages andprohibits residency of children less than a certain age.

Americans with Disabilities Act (ADA) 1990 federal law prohibiting discrimination on the basis of disability and requiring reasonable accommodation by employers and landowners.

Anaconda mortgage Mortgage covering all debt owed by the mortgagor to the mortgagee.

Anchor tenant The tenant in a shopping center that leases the largest space and will draw the greatest amount of traffic; e.g., grocery store in a plaza or a major department store in a mall.

Annexation Taking in an area of land as part of a governmental unit (city, town, or county). Many subdivisions are annexed before they are developed.

Antenuptial agreements Premarital contracts in which the spouses-to-be waive their interests in each other's properties that will be accumulated during the course of the marriage.

Architect Participant in the construction process; may oversee quality of subcontractors' work and issue lien waivers.

Article 9 Section of the Uniform Commercial Code that governs security interests in personal property and fixtures.

Articles of incorporation Document used to create a corporation.

Articles of limited partnership The limited partnership agreement.

Articles of partnership Document used to create a partnership.

As is Clause in contract that waives any warranty-protection.

Asbestos Hazard Emergency Response Act (AHERA) Federal law that mandates inspection of facilities receiving federal funds to determine presence of asbestos and asbestos fibers.

Assessment Process whereby a tax amount is assigned to a parcel of real estate on the basis of the value of the parcel.

Assessor Public official responsible for the valuation and assessment of real property and the subsequent collection of taxes.

Asset Conservation, Lender Liability and Deposit Insurance Protection Act Federal law that clarifies the liability of lenders on real property pledged as security for a loan.

Assignment Process of transferring contract rights to another; e.g., assignment of a mortgage or lease.

Assumption Process whereby a buyer of real property agrees to assume responsibility for payments on an existing mortgage on the property.

At-risk rules Under the Internal Revenue Code, a restriction on taking losses that requires those taking the loss to have funds at the risk of the operation of the business.

Attached home A form of multiunit housing; it generally has common walls with other homes.

B

Balloon payment Provision in a mortgage or mortgage note that calls for the payment of a large lump sum at the end of the mortgage period.

Balloon payment clause Clause in mortgage that requires a large payment at one time to satisfy the debt obligation.

Baselines In the United States Government Survey, the major east-west guide lines.

Basis Property owner's cost of property; used for computing gain or loss on the sale of property.

Bequest A gift of personal property by will.

Best available treatment (BAT) The highest standard the EPA can impose for the control of water pollution.

Best conventional treatment (BCT) A standard for water pollution control that requires a firm to follow the best commonly used treatment methods; a standard that is lower than best available treatment.

Bid bond Guarantor of bid submitted on construction project that guarantees bidder will do work at price bid.

Bid notice Call for bids on a project by a contractor.

Blockbusting Illegal racial discrimination practice wherein real estate brokers attempt (by encouraging listings and sales in a neighborhood) to change the racial composition of a neighborhood.

Board of adjustment Governmental entity (usually at city or county level) that is responsible for approving variances and adjustments.

Bona fide purchaser (BFP) Good faith purchaser.

Bounds See Metes and bounds.

Broker Party who is licensed to handle property listings.

Brownfield Land sites that are undeveloped due to contamination and/or designation as a Superfund site.

Brundage clause Provision in a mortgage that calls for the mortgagor to pay all taxes on the property.

Bubble concept EPA concept of examining all air pollutants in an area as if they came from a single source; this concept is used in making a decision regarding the possibility of a new plant in the area.

Builder See General contractor.

Business judgment rule Standard for imposing liability on directors of corporation; they must give time and thought to decisions.

Bylaws In multiunit housing, the document governing the details of operation; voting rights of members, meetings, notices, etc.

C

Capital gains The amount of a net gain made on the sale of property; carries a special lower tax rate.

Caption The legal description in an abstract.

Case precedent Doctrine of stare decisis; examining prior decisions to reach decisions in present cases.

Cash-to-mortgage sale Sale of real property in which the buyer pays the difference between the sales price and the mortgage balance and then takes over the mortgage (assumption).

Centerline rule Rule that provides landowners adjoining streams and rivers ownership of the land beneath these waters to the centerline of the river or stream.

Change order In construction contracts, a change in work, design, or materials.

Citation Legal shorthand referring to cases, statutes, regulations, and ordinances.

Cite See Citation.

Clean Air Act One of the original air pollution statutes that gave HEW authority to monitor interstate pollution problems.

Clean Air Act Amendments of 1990 First major revisions to Clean Air Act with coverage of acid rain and vehicle emissions and provision of new deadlines for SIPs.

Clean Water Act Major federal statute on water pollution that gave the federal government authority and control.

Cleaning deposit The amount in a lease that a tenant is required to pay prior to commencement of the lease to cover the cleaning of the premises when the tenant has gone; under URLTA, the lease must state if this deposit is nonrefundable.

Code of Federal Regulations (CFR) Compilation of regulations of federal agencies.

Codicil An addendum to a will.

Column lots Portion of air rights from the surface of the Earth to 23 feet above the surface.

Commercial mortgage Mortgage on nonresidential property.

Common area maintenance (CAM) Fee charged to tenant in commercial leases to pay costs of maintenance of sidewalks in shopping and other commercial centers; fee is often a pro rata share of expenses based on that paid in other commercial projects.

Common law Uncodified law found in cases or in the history of real property.

Community property Method of married persons' co-ownership of property; limited to certain states.

Community property with right of survivorship Relatively new form of marital property ownership that has a couple owning the property subject to their marital interests while alive with automatic vesting in surviving spouse upon death of one spouse

Community Reinvestment Act (CRA) Federal law establishing record-keeping requirements for lenders' investments in inner-city areas.

Community-Right-to-Know substance Federal disclosure law requiring notification of presence of toxic substance on property, including items such as asbestos.

Comprehensive Environmental Response, Compensation, and Liability Act (CERCLA) The Superfund; program for private payment by polluting industries for cleanup of toxic waste.

Condition precedent In a contract, a requirement before the contract can be performed; e.g., delivering marketable title or qualifying for financing.

Condominium Form of multiunit housing in which the owner owns the area between the walls and ceiling.

Consent statutes Statutes that permit the attachment of a lien if the property owner consented to the work done by the lienor even though there was no direct contract with the owner.

Conservation easement A negative easement given by a property owner that provides that the property will not be used in such a way as to destroy a historic site on the property.

Consideration The detriment given by each party to the contract; e.g., the land conveyed by the seller and the money paid by the buyer.

Construction lender Party serving as financier for a project during construction.

Constructive delivery Delivery other than direct delivery to the person; delivering by precluding access by all others.

Constructive eviction Process whereby a tenant is forced to leave leased premises because the premises are in a state of disrepair and uninhabitable.

Consumer Price Index (CPI) adjustment clause Clause that allows for rent increases when the CPI changes.

Contingent remainder Future interest that follows a life estate and that is not certain to follow or has unknown takers.

Contract for deed Another name for an installment contract; financing transaction in which seller carries the buyer and holds onto title until the buyer has paid in full.

Contract statutes With references to liens, statutes that require lienors to have a direct contractual agreement with property owners to be able to place lien on property on which work was performed.

Contractual lien Liens that arise because of a contractual agreement between the lienor and the owner of the liened property.

Conventional mortgage Mortgage not insured by a government agency.

Conventional pollutant One of the categories of water pollutants of the EPA; subject to the least amount of restriction and regulation.

Conversion restrictions Laws that regulate the conversion of leased premises into multiunit houses to afford protection for the existing tenants.

Cooperative Form of multiunit housing in which a corporation owns the property and owners of the shares in the corporation live in each of the units.

Co-ownership Label given to ownership of property by more than one person.

Cost approach Tax appraisal method that bases value of the property on its original cost plus costs of improvement.

Cost-plus formula In construction, a method of pricing in which the contractor charges all costs plus a profit margin.

Council on Environmental Quality (CEQ) Established in 1966 by the National Environment Protection Act as part of the executive branch of government and given the responsibility of formulating national policies on the quality of the environment and making recommendations to lawmakers based on its policies.

Counteroffer Offer made in response to offeror by the offeree; can occur by a change in the offeror's terms.

Covenant Promise in a deed that affects or limits the use of the conveyed property.

Cumulative classification Zoning system that permits higher uses in lower-use areas; e.g., residential uses in commercially zoned areas.

Curtesy rights Right of husband to a life estate in all real property owned by his wife during their marriage provided they had children.

D

Declaration of condominium Master deed for condominium project; the document recorded to reflect the units involved on the real property. See also Declaration of horizontal property regime and covenants.

Declaration of covenants, conditions, and restrictions (CCRs) The restrictions and limitations on the use and construction of land.

Declaration of horizontal property regime and covenants Another name for the declaration of condominium; multiunit housing is often referred to as horizontal housing regimes; the master deed recorded to reflect the existence of the multiunit housing and the location and number of units on the property.

Deed Instrument used to convey title to real property.

Deed in lieu of foreclosure Process of borrower/property owner/mortgagor surrendering title to property to prevent lender's foreclosure.

Deed of bargain and sale A deed with warranty protection limited to the time of the grantor's ownership; see special warranty deed.

Deed of trust Security interest in real property in which title is held by a trustee until the borrower and occupant of the land repays the beneficiary (lender) the amount of the loan.

Deed restrictions Provisions usually recorded for subdivisions; the CCRs; restrictions of the use, development, and construction of the premises.

Default Failure to comply with mortgage or promissory note requirements; generally a failure to pay or obtain insurance.

Deficiency judgment Judgment against the mortgagor or borrower after foreclosure sale, requiring payment of the amount due on the loan that was not obtained through sale of the mortgaged property.

Delivery Requirement for gifts and transfers of property by deed that mandates some form of actual or constructive possession by the grantee.

Department of Housing and Urban Development (HUD) Federal agency responsible for regulation of interstate land sales and other federal acts affecting real property.

Depreciation Wear and tear on property; can be deducted each year and used to offset income earned on income-producing property; greatly limited under Tax Reform Act.

Designated agency Agency relationship in which seller names agent to act on his/her behalf in closing transaction.

Devise Gift of real property by will.

Devisee Recipient of real property gift by will.

Disinheritance Process of leaving an heir out of a will; not giving anything to someone who would ordinarily receive a share of the estate if there were an intestate distribution.

Doctrine of Ancient Lights Theory that originated in England that provides right to light if so used for 20 years or more; this prescriptive form of rights is no longer followed in the United States.

Doctrine of Correlative Rights Term in oil and gas law that limits recovery of oil and gas in situations where others' rights or deposits would be destroyed.

Doctrine of Emblements In landlord/tenant relationship, the right of the tenant to remove crops from the leased premises even after the lease expires if the tenant is responsible for their production.

Doctrine of Worthier Title Theory that gives a grantee the full fee simple title when the grant is made "to grantee with remainder to the heirs of the grantee;" the two estates are merged into a fee simple estate for the grantee.

Dominant estate A property owner who holds an appurtenant easement in another's property; the land enjoying the benefit of an easement through another's property.

Dominant tenement See Dominant estate.

Donee Recipient of a gift.

Donor One who makes a gift.

Dower rights Rights of widow in husband's estate; not applicable in all states.

Dual agency Agency relationship in which broker represents both the buyer and the seller.

Due-on-sale clause Clause in mortgage or mortgage note that requires full payment of the loan when the property is sold; in effect, a prohibition on assumptions.

E

Earnest money Deposit given by buyer on signing a contract for the purchase of property.

Easement Right to use another's property for access, light, and so on.

Easement appurtenant Easement that benefits a particular tract of land; generally an access easement or right of way.

Easement by express grant Easement given in a deed by the original landowner to provide a means of access for the purchaser of one part of the land.

Easement by express reservation Easement reserved in a deed by the original landowner to provide a means of access across a purchaser's land.

Easement by implication Easement that arises based on need because of previous use of the property in the same manner when the property was owned in a single tract.

Easement by necessity Easement given by circumstances that require it; the property is inaccessible or unusable without it.

Easement in gross An easement that does not benefit a particular tract of land; e.g., utility easements that run through all parcels of land in an area.

Effluent guidelines EPA standards for release of materials into waterways.

Emblements With regard to leases, the right of the tenant to harvest growing crops even after the lease has terminated if the tenant was responsible for growing the crops.

Eminent domain Process of governmental entity taking title to private property for public purposes.

Emissions Offset Policy EPA policy of requiring a reduction of other pollution sources in the area to allow the operation of a new plant and source of emissions.

Endangered Species Act (ESA) Federal law that affords protection for habitats of species designated as endangered; requires biological evaluation of impact of development and projects on species population.

Environmental contingency clause Provision in contract that provides buyer with the right to rescind the contract if environmental hazards that cannot be cleared arise during the course of a due diligence search.

Environmental impact statement (EIS) Report required to be filed when a governmental agency is taking action that will have an effect on the environment; e.g., construction of a dam by the Army Corps of Engineers.

Environmental Protection Agency (EPA) Governmental agency responsible for the enforcement of environmental laws.

Equal Credit Opportunity Act (ECOA) Federal law prohibiting discrimination in credit decisions.

Equal Protection clause Part of the Fifth and Fourteenth Amendments to the Constitution; requires that laws apply equally to all.

Equitable liens Liens created as a result of a mortgage arrangement; also referred to as contractual liens.

Equitable relief Court remedies that require parties to perform certain acts or specifically perform a contract.

Equitable servitude Restriction on land use arising because an area has a common scheme or development that puts buyers on notice that particular uses and construction are required or prohibited.

Equity participation financing Creative financing technique in which the lender will share in the appreciation of the property and will be entitled to a portion of the equity on sale of the mortgaged property.

Equity trust Method of syndication in which investors have an interest in the equity in real estate and will earn an investment through equity appreciation.

Errors and omissions insurance Professional liability insurance for brokers and agents.

Escalation clause Clause generally in a lease, providing for increasing rent.

Escheat Process whereby property of a decedent is given to the state because no heirs are available.

Escrow Process whereby details of property transfer, payments, and deed conveyance are handled by a third party.

Escrow instructions Contract between buyer, seller, and escrow agent for the closing of escrow on a property transfer.

Exclusionary zoning Zoning that prohibits certain types of businesses, activities, or housing in certain areas.

Exclusive agency listing Listing agreement that requires the seller to pay the commission to the broker only if the listing broker sells the property; the seller may sell the property independently and not be required to pay a commission.

Exclusive right (or listing) to sell Listing that requires the seller to pay the broker-agent a commission regardless of who obtains a buyer for the property.

Executor Male party responsible for the probate of a decedent's estate pursuant to the decedent's will.

Executory interest Future interest that is not a remainder and not an interest in the grantor.

Executrix Female party responsible for the probate of a decedent's estate pursuant to the decedent's will.

F

Federal Consumer Credit Protection Act Federal law requiring disclosures, billing practices, and rights in consumer credit transactions.

Federal Deposit Insurance Corporation (FDIC) Federal agency that regulates savings and loan institutions.

Federal Environmental Pesticide Control Act Federal law regulating the manufacture, containment, labeling, transportation, and use of pesticides.

Federal Home Loan Bank Board (FHLBB) Federal agency that regulates VA/FHA loans and lending practices.

Federal implementation plan (FIP) Part of the 1990 amendments to the Clean Air Act that requires the imposition of federal standards in the event states fail to meet deadlines and requirements for their SIPs.

Federal National Mortgage Association (FNMA) (or Fannie Mae) Government corporation that purchases mortgages on the market.

Federal Savings and Loan Insurance Corporation (FSLIC) Federal agency charged with the supervision and insuring of banks and other financial institutions.

Federal Water Pollution Control Act of 1972 Federal law that was the first anti—water pollution law with enforcement and details.

Federal Water Pollution Control Administration (FWPCA) Originally the agency responsible for developing and enforcing water pollution control; merged into EPA in 1975.

Fee An inheritable interest in land.

Fee interest In oil and gas ownership, owner owns both the surface and subsurface rights.

Fee simple Highest land interest; full title; right to convey or transfer by will or mortgage without restriction.

Fee simple absolute Another term for a fee simple.

Fee simple defeasible A fee simple estate that can be lost by violation of a condition or use restriction placed in the transfer by the grantor.

Fee simple determinable Full title to land so long as certain conduct is avoided; e.g., "To A so long as the premises are never used for a bar."

Fee simple subject to a condition subsequent Full title provided that there is compliance with a condition; e.g., "To A upon the condition that the property is used for school purposes."

Fee tail Full title restricted in its passage to direct descendants of the owner.

FHA Federal agency that provides a market for lower-rate consumer home mortgages and governs the terms and conditions for those loans if the lender desires to sell loans through FHA.

Fifth Amendment Provision in United States Constitution that provides guarantee of due process.

Financial Institutions Reform Recovery and Enforcement Act (FIRREA) Federal law that followed the savings and loan debacle; implements controls on bank lending practices on real estate, including appraisals.

Financing statement Document filed to protect a security interest; must contain information about the parties and a description of the collateral.

Fixed rent In shopping center and commercial leases, rental standard of paying net rent (after utility costs or other fees specific in lease).

Fixtures Personal property that becomes attached to and is so closely associated with real property that it becomes a part of the real property.

Flow-down clause Clause in a construction contract that does not require the general contractor to pay subcontractors and suppliers until the owner has paid the general contractor.

Forcible detainer Action by landlord for rent; requires tenant to pay or be evicted by court order.

Foreclosure Process of selling mortgaged property to satisfy the debt owed by the defaulting mortgagor.

Foreclosure by advertisement (notice of sale) Creditor's remedy of sale by providing public notice; used in deeds of trust.

Forfeiture Loss of rights; in a contract for deed, the loss of all interest in the property for nonpayment.

Fourteenth Amendment Application of due process rights to the states (including the Equal Protection Clause), which requires uniform application of laws and nondiscrimination; applied in cases in which land conveyances attempt to include racial restrictions.

Freehold An interest in land is uncertain or unlimited in duration.

Fructus industriales Vegetation that grows on property as result of work of owner or tenant; i.e., crops.

Fructus naturales Vegetation that grows naturally on property; not the result of efforts of the owner or tenant.

FWPCA See Federal Water Pollution Control Administration (FWPCA).

G

Garden homes Form of multiunit housing; usually a townhome that includes a small enclosed yard or patio.

General contractor In a construction project, the party responsible for the construction; can hire subcontractors and suppliers but bears ultimate responsibility; has direct contractual relationship with owner, construction lender, or both.

General partner Investor with full personal liability for partnership debt.

General partnership Voluntary association of two or more persons as co-owners in a business for profit.

General plan Development plan and zoning areas as developed by city or county; provides zoning designations for all areas within the municipality or county.

Geothermal energy Form of energy that is the result of naturally formed pockets of hot steam; can be a mineral right.

Good-faith purchaser Buyer who buys property with no knowledge (constructive or actual) of any title defects, liens, or other problems other than those specifically disclosed by the seller; also called *bfp* or *bona fide* purchaser.

Government National Mortgage Association (GNMA) (or Ginnie Mae Government) Agency that insures loans sold on the market.

Grantor/grantee index system Method of recordkeeping for land transactions; all transactions are recorded under the name of both the grantor and grantee to permit title to be traced according to the transfers among parties.

Grid The 24-mile square created between each guide meridian and parallel in the United States Government survey.

Gross rent Flat rent in commercial lease; no percentage of profits.

Guaranteed Mortgage Package (GMP) Proposed HUD reforms to RESPA disclosures that would require upfront commitment on closing costs and loan rents; whether the proposals are pro-consumer or detrimental in terms of increased costs is debatable.

Guarantors Parties who agree to stand liable if a debtor defaults.

Guide meridians Vertical lines placed every 24 miles on the United States Government Survey; intersect with parallels to create 24-miles squares used for describing land parcels.

H

Habendum clause Clause in deed indicating the type of land interest being conveyed; in mineral lease, a clause that establishes the length of the lease,the grounds for termination, and drilling delay penalties.

Hazardous Substance Response Trust Fund Fund created under federal environmental laws; known as the Superfund for use in cleanup of toxic waste.

Hold zoning Interim zoning adopted prior to the time of the finalized general plan.

Holographic will Will entirely in the handwriting of the testator and signed by the testator (valid in some states).

Home equity indebtedness Consumer debt secured by residence of debtor; includes mortgage, other loans, and lines of credit.

Home Mortgage Disclosure Act Federal law mandating disclosure on consumer loans for second mortgages on residential property.

Homestead exemption Debtor protection that entitles the debtor to a certain amount in real property that is exempt from attachment by creditors.

Horizontal property acts or regimes Multiunit housing laws that govern forms of housing such as condominiums, cooperatives, and townhouses.

I

Impact fees Fees paid by developers for schools and other public facilities needed because of additional population developer brings in with project.

Implied warranty of habitability Implied warranty given by contractors of new homes to buyers; between landlord and tenant, the landlord's guaranty that the premises are fit for habitation and, if not, will be put into that condition.

Incentives for Self-Policing, Disclosure, Correction, and Prevention of Violations EPA guidelines for company's voluntary audit for and disclosure of environmental violations.

Income approach Tax appraisal method that bases value of the property on the income generated by the property.

Installment land contract A contract for deed; method of selling property in which the seller serves as the financier for the buyer and the purchase; seller holds onto title until there has been payment in full under an installment payment plan.

Insurer Party who indemnifies for loss.

Integration SEC practice of combining back-to-back exempt offerings with result being offerer is in noncompliance with restrictions for exemption.

Intensity zoning Zoning laws that control the number of structures or degree of occupancy in a given area.

Inter vivos During the life of; while alive; e.g., an inter vivos gift.

Interest Acceleration clause Clause in note that increases interest in the event of a default.

Interim zoning Hold zoning; temporary zoning before general plan is developed.

Intermediary Another name for a statutory broker.

Internal Revenue Code (IRC) Federal law governing income taxation.

Interstate Land Sales Full Disclosure Act (ILSFDA) Federal law regulating the sale of property across state lines; requires advance filing of sales materials, mandatory disclosure of certain information, and prohibitions on promises about the land's future development.

Intestate Death without a will.

Intestate succession Statutory method for distributing the property of those who die without a will (intestate).

Intrastate offering exemption Under the 1933 Securities Act, an exemption from SEC registration requirements for certain securities offered in one state by a corporation primarily operating in that state.

Invitee Party who has a specific invitation to enter another's property or is a member of the public in a public place.

Involuntary lien Lien that does not result from a contractual arrangement; e.g., a tax lien or a judicial lien.

J

Joint tenancy Method of co-ownership that gives title to the property to the last survivor.

Joint will Will made in conjunction with another's will; requires distribution of property in a certain way regardless of who dies first.

Judicial deed Deed given by court after litigation of rights in the subject property.

Judicial foreclosure Foreclosure accomplished by filing a petition with the proper court; not a power of sale.

Judicial lien Lien on property that is the result of a judgment; lien to collect a court judgment.

Just compensation In eminent domain, the requirement that landowners whose property is taken for public purposes be adequately paid for the loss of that property.

L

Lapse In probate of a will, what happens when beneficiary dies prior to testator; the gift ends.

Laughing heir statute Statute that limits the degree of relationship of relatives who can inherit property from an intestate; causes property to escheat to the state before a remote relative would inherit an intestate's estate.

Lease-purchase Financing method that permits potential buyers to lease property for a period with an option to buy.

Legacy Gift of money by will.

Legatee Beneficiary/donee of gift of money by will.

Lender See Permanent lender.

Lender liability Doctrine that makes lenders liable for the lack of timely approval or withdrawal of an approval for financing already issued.

License Revocable right to enter another's property.

Licensee Party who enters another's land with express or implied permission; i.e., a social guest.

Lien Interest in real property that serves as security for repayment of a debt.

Lien theory One theory of mortgages that gives the mortgagor title to the property and the mortgagee a lien on the property as security for debt repayment.

Lienee Person whose property is subject to a lien.

Lienor Party who places a lien on real property.

Life estate Interest in land that lasts for the life of the grantee.

Life estate *pur autre vie* Life estate that lasts for the length of some measuring life other than that of the grantee.

Life tenants Those who hold a life estate in property.

Limited agent Agent whose authority is limited in time or scope.

Limited Liability Company (LLC) Business entity that is a cross between a corporation and a partnership.

Limited Liability Partnership (LLP) Business entity that has limited liability for all partners (except for professional negligence of each).

Limited partner Investor in limited partnership whose maximum liability is his capital investment.

Limited partnership A partnership with at least one general partner in which limited partners can purchase interest and be liable only to the extent of their interests and not risk personal liability.

Liquidated damages Damages that are specified in formula or in amount in the written and signed agreement of the parties; must be reasonable.

Lis pendens "Suit or action pending;" document recorded with the land records to indicate a suit involving the land is pending; filed in mortgage foreclosures and quiet title actions.

Listing agreement Contract between a broker and landowner for the broker's services in helping to sell the owner's property.

Livery of seisin English ceremony for passage of title; involved a physical transfer of a clod of earth between grantor and grantee.

Living trust Trust created by settlor who is alive.

Living will Term for authorization to take testator off life-support equipment recognized in many states but must use appropriate or required language and be formally executed.

Long-term land contract See Contract for deed.

Low income housing Under Tax Reform Act of 1986, special housing category affording investors special tax treatment.

M

Market approach Tax appraisal method that bases value of the property on prices of similar properties.

Marketable title Form of title generally required to be delivered in the sale of property; property is free from liens and there are no defects in title other than those noted or agreed to.

Master deed In a condominium development, the document recorded to reflect the location of the project and the individual units.

Master mortgage Single mortgage document recorded for all loans and referenced to save recording fees.

Master plan General plan for zoning.

Master-planned community Large development project that involves construction of all facilities as well as housing.

Materials lien Lien on property for the amount due for materials furnished to the owner or to others performing work on the land.

Maximum Accelerated Cost Recovery System (MACRS) Under federal tax law, a method of depreciation.

Maximum Achievable Control Technology (MACT) Term under Clean Air Act Amendments of 1990; establishes standards for pollution control on utilities and other targeted industries for scrubbers and other antipollution devices.

Mechanic's liens Liens placed on real property to secure amount due to those who performed work or supplied materials for improvements or other projects on the land.

Metes See Metes and bounds.

Metes and bounds Method of land description that begins with a permanent object and then through distances and directions describes the parcel of land.

Mineral interest Ownership right to minerals on property; could also be a lease.

Mineral rights Subsurface rights in property; the rights to mine minerals; also known as mineral interest.

Mineral servitude Easement across the surface of the land for access to the land.

Misrepresentation Giving incorrect or misleading information to a party in contract negotiations or failing to disclose relevant information; inaccurate information that would affect the buying or selling decision.

Mixed trust Real estate investment trust that owns both property and mortgages.

Model Business Corporation Act (MBCA) Uniform law on corporations adopted in approximately one-third of the states.

Model Real Estate Cooperative Act Model act on co-ops.

Model Real Estate Time-Share Act Model act on time-share real property interests.

Monetary relief Form of remedy for contract or trespass which awards money damages for breach.

Mortgage Lien Lien on real property used to secure a debt.

Mortgage broker Agent who matches borrowers with mortgage companies.

Mortgage investment trusts (MITs) Real estate syndication method that provides investment opportunity in pool of mortgages.

Mortgage trust Real estate syndication trust that invests in real estate mortgages.

Mortgagee Lender or party who holds the mortgage lien.

Mortgagor Borrower or party occupying land that is mortgaged.

Multiple listing A listing that appears on more than one broker's inventory of homes.

Multiple listing service (MLS) A specific multiple listing service that is nationwide and to which most brokers subscribe.

Mutual will Wills of parties that are reciprocal in their distribution; usually based on a contract to make a will; generally enforceable.

N

National Association of Realtors (NAR) Professional organization of brokers and agents; has standards for admission and maintenance of membership.

National Environmental Policy Act (NEPA) 1969 Act that requires federal agencies to do an EIS before they approve a project.

National Pollution Discharge Elimination System (NPDES) Permit system that requires EPA approval for water discharges.

Negative easement An easement that prohibits a property owner from doing something that affects the property of another; e.g., a solar easement is a negative easement.

Net listing Type of listing that allows the broker to collect as a commission any amount received that is above the figure set as the seller's net take on the sale of the property.

Net-net-net See Triple net.

No deal, no commission clause Provision in listing agreement that requires a sale of property to close before any commission is due and owing to the broker.

Noise Control Act of 1972 Environmental statute regulating noise levels, disclosure requirements, and precautions.

Nonagent broker Broker who sells property via multi-listing but is not the listing broker.

Nonattainment area In environmental regulation, those areas that have not reached acceptable levels of pollution; highly regulated.

Nonconforming use In zoned areas, a use that does not comply with the area's zoning but that existed prior to the time the zoning was effective.

Nonconventional pollutant Second in line in terms of water pollution dangers; EPA can require higher pretreatment standards for nonconventional pollutants.

Noncumulative classification Method of zoning in which use in a particular area is limited to the zoned use; e.g., industrial zones cannot include residential buildings and apartment areas cannot include single-family dwellings.

Nonfreehold estates Type of land interest that is certain and definite in duration, such as a lease for a period of time.

Nonownership states Method for oil and gas ownership that disallows ownership of oil and gas until they have been captured through drilling.

Notice statute Form of recording statute that gives later bona fide purchasers priority in the case of multiple purchases if the previous purchasers fail to give notice by recording their transactions.

Novation Original parties to a contract and a new third party agree to substitute the third party for the performance of the agreement.

Nuisance Use of property so as to interfere with another's use and enjoyment of property; e.g., bad smells and loud noises.

Nuncupative will Oral will; not valid in all states.

O

Occupational Safety and Health Administration (OSHA) Federal agency responsible for assuring safety in the workplace.

Offer Initial communication in contract formation that, if accepted, results in the formation of a contract.

Office of Thrift Supervision Federal agency charged with oversight of savings and loans.

Oil and gas interest Form of ownership in which a portion of a mineral interest is assigned.

Oil Pollution Act (OPA) Federal law that requires companies to bear the cost of clean-up for an oil spill and also imposes civil and criminal penalties for certain types of spills.

Open listing Listing that pays a commission to whichever broker or salesperson sells the property; permits the owner to list with more than one broker and be liable for only one commission.

Operating expenses In commercial leases, the costs of running the property; variable and defined by lease.

Option Right (which has been paid for) to purchase property during a certain period of time.

Ordinances Laws passed on a local level of country, state, or city governments.

Ownership states Method for oil and gas ownership right determination that states mineral rights can be lost only if someone first captures the oil and gas by drilling.

Owners' associations Corporations or other organized entities that have private laws that control the architecture, use, and modification of property within a subdivision or multiple-unit housing development.

P

Paid outside closing (POC) Costs not paid through escrow or closing.

Parallels Horizontal guidelines in the United States Government Survey.

Passive income Income from investments for income tax purposes.

Passive loss Loss resulting from passive activity; under the Tax Reform Act, there are limitations on taking passive losses, i.e., passive losses can be taken only from passive income and not from wages and other income as many taxpayers had done in the past to maximize the benefits of real estate ownership.

Patio home Form of multiunit housing that generally includes a closed-in yard or patio area.

Patriot Act Federal law with many provisions designed to curb terrorist activities; impacts real estate transactions because of disclosure requirements imposed on escrow agents regarding transfer of title and deposits of cash; imposes new disclosure and signature requirements for buyers and sellers.

Payment bond In construction, a bond on the general contractor to ensure payment to subcontractors and suppliers; i.e., if the general contractor does not pay, the surety will pay.

Penal sum Sum bonding company must pay to have project completed if contractor fails to perform.

Per capita Method of allocation of intestate property among heirs; basic principle is that each heir gets an equal share.

Per Stirpes Method of distributing property to heirs whereby those closer in relation to the decedent get greater shares.

Percentage rent Rent for commercial properties expressed as a percentage of net or gross income.

Perfection Process of gaining priority on an Article 9 security interest; requires a filing of a financing statement to give public notice of the creditor's interest.

Performance bond Bond on general contractor that guarantees performance; if the general contractor does not perform, the surety will provide performance or payment for damages resulting from noncompletion of the work.

Periodic tenancy Temporary possessory interest in land that runs on a period-to-period basis such as a month-to-month lease.

Permanent lender Once construction is complete, the lender who will carry the permanent financing on the project; pays the construction lender and assumes priority.

Personal representative Party responsible for the probate of a will under the Uniform Probate Code; formerly referred to as an executor.

Planned unit development (PUD) Subdivision that includes a development of a full community.

Plat map Method of land description that relies on a recorded map of a subdivision, with each deed making reference to the map and the particular lot being transferred.

Point source Discharge point where water leaves land and runs into streams, rivers, and so on.

Possibility of reverter Future interest in the grantor that follows a fee simple determinable.

Posthumous heirs Heirs born after the death of the decedent.

Power of sale In a deed-of-trust financing arrangement, the right of the trustee to sell the property on default by the trustor-borrower.

Power of termination Future interest in the grantor that follows a fee simple subject to a condition subsequent.

Premarital agreements Contracts that serve to waive marital property rights of the spouses; must be voluntary and carefully drafted.

Premises The words of conveyance in a deed; e.g., "do hereby grant and convey."

Prenuptial agreements Agreements in advance of marriage that alter statutory marital property rights.

Prepayment penalty clause Clause in mortgage or promissory note that requires the mortgagor to pay an additional charge for paying off the loan early.

Prescription Process of acquiring an easement through adverse use of the easement over a required period of time.

Pretermitted A testator's child conceived prior to testator's death but born after testator dies.

Prevention of significant deterioration (PSD) areas Part of 1977 Clean Air Act amendments establishing emission standards for clean areas to prevent pollution.

Prime contractor General contractor on a project.

Prime meridians The key vertical lines in the United States Government Survey.

Principal meridians See Prime meridians.

Prior Appropriation Doctrine Water allocation policy of first to use the water gets the rights to that water.

Private law Laws between individual parties; e.g., landlord's rules and regulations or the terms of acontract.

Probate Process of collecting the assets of a decedent; paying the decedent's debts, determining the decedent's heirs, and distributing property to the heirs.

Procuring cause of the sale standard Standard of determining commission among brokers under an open listing agreement.

Profit Rights of removal in another's property; shorthand for profit a prendre.

Profit a prendre Right to enter another's land for the purpose of removing soil, water, minerals, or another resource.

Promissory note Two-party debt instrument that,in real estate, is generally secured by a mortgage or deed of trust or some other interest in real estate.

Property report Summary of facts about undeveloped land required to be given to purchasers (part of ILSFDA).

Property tax roll Assessor's formal records of parcels of land; the valuation and assessment.

Proprietary lease Interest of cooperative owner in a dwelling unit.

Prorated Allocation of prepaid insurance, taxes, and rent; generally done at close of escrow between buyer and seller.

Prorationing rules Rules that limit oil and gas production at the well site.

Protective covenants In development, covenants regarding nature and/or use of structures.

Psychological disclosure statutes Statutes that require disclosure of events on property that create psychological reactions in buyers and affect market value; e.g., the fact that a home has been the site of a murder or that those who lived there were infected with the AIDS virus; some statutory limitations apply.

Purchase money mortgage A mortgage used to secure a debt for the funds used to buy the mortgaged property.

Purchase money security interest (PMSI) Under Article 9 of the UCC, a security interest given to a lender who financed the purchase of the property that is the collateral.

Pure race statute Recording priority statute that awards title (in the event of multiple conveyances) to the first purchaser to record.

Q

Quasi-easement A right-of-way as it existed when there was unity of ownership in a parcel of land.

Quiet title action Court action brought to determine the true owner of a piece of land.

Quitclaim deed Deed that serves to transfer title if the grantor has any such title; there are no guarantees that the grantor has any title or good title.

R

Race/notice system State recording statutes that award title to the first bona fide purchaser to record his or her title when there are conflicting claims of ownership in the property.

Range In the United States Government Survey, the lines placed vertically every six miles between the guide meridians.

Real estate investment trust (REIT) Form of real estate syndication in which investors hold trust interests and enjoy profits of trust's real estate holdings.

Real Estate Settlement Procedures Act (RESPA) Federal statute regulating disclosure of closing costs in advance and prohibiting kickbacks for referring customers to title companies.

Real estate syndication Group investment in real estate in the forms of trusts, partnerships, and corporations.

Realtor Trademark/name used by the National Association of Realtors (NAR) to refer to one of its members.

Recording Process of placing a deed or other document on the public records to give notice of a transaction or interest in the land.

Recreational lease In multiunit housing, a lease that runs for a short period of time during each year; sometimes called time sharing.

Redlining Practice of targeting certain areas or neighborhood as high-risk areas for loans or insurance or requiring lower valuation.

Refinancing Negotiating a new loan for real estate; generally done to obtain a lower rate or in the case of a sale, to allow a buyer to be able to purchase a property.

Regulation D Under the 1933 Securities Act, an SEC regulation that provides three different small offering exemptions from registration according to limitations on size of the offering or the number of investors; includes Rules 504, 505, and 506.

Regulation Z (Truth-in-Lending Act) The Federal Reserve Board's regulations on disclosures in all types of credit transactions.

Remainder Future interest in someone other than the grantor; a remainder follows a life estate.

Rent controls Statutory maximums for rents on residential property.

Repair and deduct A tenant's right to repair leased premises when the landlord fails to do so and to deduct the cost of the repairs from his or her rent.

Rescission Right to treat a contract as if it never existed; rescind contract rights; generally appropriate in cases of fraud and misrepresentation.

Residential mortgage transactions Mortgages for the purchase of property to be used primarily as a residence for the buyer.

Resolution Trust Corporation (RTC) Defunct federal agency that handled savings and loan cleanup.

Resource Conservation and Recovery Act of 1976 (RCRA) Federal law regulating hazardous waste and garbage that requires record keeping and controls amounts of garbage.

Resource Recovery Act Part of the federal environmental statutory scheme on the clean-up of property contaminated with toxic substances.

Reverse mortgage A form of mortgage that enables retired individuals to draw the equity from their homes in the form of a monthly payment. No payments or finance charges are due on the loan underlying the mortgage until the owner dies.

Reversion Future interest in grantor that results after life estate terminates and no remainder interest was given.

Revised Model Business Corporation Act (RMBCA) Model act on corporations; adopted in about one-third of states.

Revised Uniform Limited Partnership Act (RULPA) New uniform law updating ULPA.

Right of entry Future interest in grantor that results when the grantee fails to honor the condition placed on the grant of a fee simple subject to a condition subsequent.

Riparian Doctrine In water rights, governs the landowner who adjoins water; a theory that entitles all riparians to use of their water; does not allow one riparian to use all of the water.

Rivers and Harbors Act of 1899 A federal statute that attempted to regulate dumping in rivers and harbors; a predecessor to today's environmental statutes; still used.

Royalty interest Interest landowner retains upon leasing of oil well.

Rules 504–506 exemptions Regulation D; the rules of the SEC on small-offering exemptions in securities sales.

Rule Against Perpetuities Rule that prohibits the control of estates from the grave; provides a duration cap on contingent remainders and executory interests.

Rule in Dumpor's Case English rule that provides that if a landlord consents to one assignment of the lease by the tenant, the landlord consents to all subsequent assignments; most statutes have abolished by statute the effects of this rule.

Rule in Shelley's Case Common law rule that merges future and present interests in A when grant is "To A for life, remainder to A's heirs"; has been abolished in many states.

Rule of Capture In mineral rights, a first-in-time-is-first-in-right philosophy in which the first to take subsurface minerals has title regardless of property boundary lines.

Rule of reason In easements, the standard followed in making decisions regarding the expansion of easement use; in antitrust, a standard for determining non per se violations.

S

Safe Drinking Water Act 1986 amendment to Clean Water Act that establishes minimum standards for drinking water purity; states must adopt federal minimums or their own higher standards.

Satisfaction of mortgage Payment of full loan amount by mortgagor.

Saving clause Provision for alternative distribution of property being willed away can be a defense to the Rule Against Perpetuities.

Section In the United States Government Survey, one-mile squares in townships.

Securities Act of 1933 Federal law governing the initial sale of securities on the public markets.

Securities and Exchange Commission (SEC) The federal agency responsible for overseeing and policing the sales of securities on the primary and secondary markets.

Security agreement Under Article 9, the contract that gives the creditor a lien in the personal property or fixture; makes it the collateral for the loan.

Security deposit In the lease, the amount of money prepaid by the tenant to secure performance of the lease and often provides the amount of liquidated damages if the tenant does not perform.

Security interest Creditor's right in collateral under Article 9; the lien on the personal property or fixture.

Self-help Remedy for tenants with premises in disrepair; the right to repair defects on the property and then seek reimbursement.

Self-proving will A will that is acknowledged or notarized and thereby enjoys presumption of validity.

Servient estate Land through which an easement runs or that is subject to the easement.

Servient tenement Land through which an easement runs or that is subject to the easement.

Shared-appreciation mortgages Method of creative financing in which the lender charges a lower interest rate in exchange for the right to a return of a portion of the equity, including the increased value, of the home.

Sheriff's deed Form of title given to a buyer at a mortgage foreclosure sale; carries no warranties.

Sick building syndrome Conditions in building that cause respiratory and other ailments in occupants; causes vary from lack of ventilation to use of various materials; EPA and OSHA have developed guidelines and standards for ventilation and remediation.

Small offering exemption Exception to SEC registration requirements based on limited amount of the offering or limited numbers of purchasers.

Social issue zoning Use of zoning to control influences in the community; e.g., the prohibition of adult theaters near residential districts.

Solar easement law A negative easement that prevents the servient estate from doing anything that would block the sunlight access of the dominant estate.

Soldiers and Sailors Relief Act Federal law that provides time restrictions on foreclosures involving those in active military service.

Solid Waste Disposal Act Initial federal act on waste disposal that provided states with money for research on solid- waste disposal.

Special permit Exception to zoning uses provided by a board of adjustment.

Special warranty deed Deed that provides warranty of title only for the period during which the grantor owned the property; see bargain and sale deed.

Specialty trust A trust created for a specific purpose; e.g., a corporate trust created to expand the firm's real estate holdings.

Specific happenings increase provisions In commercial leases; provisions that result in increase in rental fees.

Specific performance Equitable remedy that requires a party to a contract to perform the contract promise or promises.

Squatters's rights A lay term for adverse possession or prescription.

Standard State Zoning Enabling Act Standard act adopted by most jurisdictions to govern the development and enforcement of a zoning plan.

State implementation plans (SIP) All state and local laws and ordinances that make up the state's air pollution control plan.

Statement of record Under ILSFDA, the disclosure document filed with HUD before any sales of underdeveloped land can occur.

Statute of Frauds Statute dictating what types of contracts must be in writing to be enforceable.

Statutory broker Term used in some states to describe a broker who represents both buyer and seller; special disclosures required to serve in this capacity.

Statutory lien Right in land created by statute as a means of ensuring payment for work, materials, or other obligations.

Statutory right of redemption Specified period of time after foreclosure sale for buyer to redeem property by paying full amount of debt, interest, and costs associated with foreclosure.

Steering Form of racial discrimination in which brokers or salespeople direct interested purchasers away from and toward certain neighborhoods to control racial composition.

Stop notice statutes Statute that allows subcontractors and materials suppliers to record a document and/or give service or notice of their rights to payment to the owner or general so that disputed payment issues are resolved before there is double payment or end of funding.

Straight term mortgage Mortgage with fixed interest rate for a set number of years.

Strawman transaction Transaction that is artificial and nonpermanent; generally used to satisfy the unities required for creating a joint tenancy.

Subchapter S corporation A special form of corporation under the IRC that allows the protection of limited liability but direct flow-through of profits and losses.

Subcontractor A worker hired by the general contractor on a project to complete certain portions of the project.

Subdivision trust Form of financing in which seller and buyer are trust beneficiaries, and a third party acts as trustee. Seller and buyer will share in the profits of land development after the seller has paid for the property.

Subject to sale A transfer of real property in which the buyer takes the property subject to an existing mortgage but does not agree to assume responsibility for the mortgage payments.

Sublease Arrangement in which a tenant leases rental property to another, and the tenant becomes landlord to the subtenant.

Subordinate mortgage Mortgage with a lesser priority than a preexisting mortgage.

Substantial performance Construction doctrine that requires good faith completion of a project but not necessarily perfection.

Superfund The fund created by the federal government to sponsor cleanup of toxic waste disposal sites.

Superfund Amendment and Reauthorization Act Federal law establishing cleanup funding, policies, and liability for toxic wastes.

Surety One who stands as a guarantor for an obligation, as in a payment or performance bond.

Surface Mining and Reclamation Act of 1977 Federal law that regulates surface mining and the required cleanup afterwards.

Suspended losses For tax purposes, losses that exceed passive income and are carried forward to future years' passive income.

T

Taking Term used to describe the government action of taking private property for permanent public purposes.

Taking Issues Under Fifth Amendment, constitutional protections in eminent domain.

Tax deed Form of title given in the event property is sold to satisfy taxes; carries no warranties.

Tax lien Lien placed on property for amount of unpaid taxes.

Tax Reform Act (TRA) Federal law (1986) that substantially changed real estate income tax issues.

Tax sale Foreclosure sale on property for nonpayment of taxes.

Telecommunications Act of 1996 Federal law that includes regulation of local zoning for location of cellular phone towers; section of this federal law was passed to limit the local resistance to placement of the towers because the local objections were impeding the progress of the cellular network.

Tenancy at sufferance Tenancy wherein the tenant is on the property of the landlord but has no right to be and may be evicted at any time.

Tenancy at will Tenancy wherein the tenant remains as long as both parties agree; either party may terminate at any time and without notice.

Tenancy by the entirety Method of co-ownership that is a joint tenancy between husband and wife.

Tenancy for years Tenancy for a stated period of time.

Tenancy in common Simplest form of co-ownership; unless otherwise stated, the presumed method of ownership for multiple landowners.

Tenancy in partnership Form of co-ownership in which the parties are partners; similar to joint tenancy in that the partners have a right of survivorship.

Testamentary Disposition by will.

Testamentary capacity The requisite mental capacity needed to make a valid will; a person's need to understand who his or her relatives are and how the property will be distributed by his or her will.

Time-sharing Form of multiunit housing in which owners own the unit for a limited period of time during each year.

Title insurance Insurance that pays damages to the buyer of property in the event certain title defects arise.

Title theory Theory of mortgage law that puts title in the mortgagee and possession in the mortgagor.

Torrens system System for recording land titles designed to prevent the selling of the same parcel of land to more than one person.

Tortious Interference with expectation of inheritance new tort that allows recovery if potential beneficiary can demonstrate that another deprived him or her of her inheritance.

Townhouse Form of multiunit housing in which the owner owns the area in the unit and also owns the land on which the unit is located.

Township Term in the United States Government Survey for the six-mile squares formed between the guide meridians and the parallels.

Toxic pollutant EPA classification for the worst form of water pollutants.

Toxic Substances Control Act (TOSCA) Federal law regulating the manufacture, labeling, and distribution of toxic substances.

Tract index system Form of land record that keeps history of title through identification of transactions with the particular tract.

Trade fixture Personal property that is attached to real property but is used in the operation of a business; remains the tenant's property a misnomer in that it is personal property.

Transaction broker Broker used for a sale but not listing broker.

Transfer development rights In areas in which building heights are limited, the right to sell air rights for purposes of business expansion and construction; i.e., a company not using all of its height expansion allowance can transfer the right to build in the air space to another company.

Transfer disclosure statement (TDS) In some states a form that provides information about the residential property being transferred: length of ownership; date of construction; construction and improvements, etc.

Trapping statutes Another name for stop notice statutes.

Trespass Invasion of the property of another by a person or object.

Trespassers One who is on the property of another without permission.

Triggering language In credit advertisements, language describing credit terms that will require full and complete disclosure of all credit terms under Regulation Z.

Triple net Form of commercial lease rental formula; tenant pays taxes, insurance, and maintenance and fixed rent above these amounts.

Trust certificate In a real estate trust, the evidence of ownership given to each trust holder.

Truth-in-Lending Act Name given to federal statutes and regulations concerning credit terms and their disclosure.

U

Undue influence The use of a confidential relationship to gain benefits under a will or contract.

Uniform Commercial Code (UCC) Uniform statute adopted in most states that governs commercial transactions; Article 9 deals with security interests in fixtures.

Uniform Common Interest Ownership Act Uniform law on multiple ownership issues.

Uniform Condominium Act (UCA) Uniform law adopted in some states governing ownership, rights, and obligations in condominium interests.

Uniform Land Transactions Act (ULTA) Uniform act with provisions governing land contracts.

Uniform Limited Partnership Act (ULPA) Uniform act governing formation, operation, and dissolution of limited partnerships.

Uniform Marital Property Act Uniform law that provides for ownership of property by married persons and means of division of property in the event of divorce or death.

Uniform Marketable Title Act Uniform law on what is required to deliver marketable title in sale.

Uniform Partnership Act (UPA) Uniform statute adopted in most states governing the creation, operation, and dissolution of partnerships.

Uniform Premarital Agreement Act Uniform law adopted in some states that governs the drafting and execution of premarital agreements.

Uniform Probate Code (UPC) Uniform law adopted in about one-third of the states governing the distribution of intestate property, the making of wills and probate, and administration of estates.

Uniform Residential Landlord Tenant Act (URLTA) Uniform law governing residential leases.

Uniform Rights of the Terminally Ill Act Proposed uniform law on the rights of the terminally ill to refuse treatment; would establish rules for electing refusal of treatment.

Uniform Settlement Statement (USS) Under RESPA, the required form for showing how money was paid and distributed at close of escrow.

Uniform Simultaneous Death Act (USDA) Uniform law designed to allow direct distribution to heirs next in line when husband and wife die simultaneously (or within five days of each other).

Unit pricing Means of costing in construction that divides contract into units for prices and payment.

United States Code (U.S.C.) Compilation of all federal laws.

United States Constitution Framework for federal government.

United States Government Survey National survey of land.

Unities In co-ownership, the presence of requirements on creation; i.e., the interests must have been created at the same time, with the same title and interest, and with equal possession rights.

Usury Charging interest rates in excess of the statutorily allowed maximums.

V

VA Veteran's Administration.

Vacation license Form of time-sharing interest ownership.

Variances Approved uses of land outside the scope of an area's zoning.

Vested remainder A remainder that will automatically take effect when the life estate ends.

Vested remainder subject to complete divestment A remainder that can be completely lost if the terms of vesting are not met; not automatic on termination of the life estate.

Vested remainder subject to partial divestment A remainder that can be partially lost as other remaindermen develop, i.e., more children are born during the life estate.

Voluntary lien A lien created because of a contract as opposed to a tax lien, which is involuntary.

W

Waiver agreement In liens, a document that waives the right of a supplier or laborer to lien the property; generally given in exchange for payment.

Warranty deed Deed that conveys title and carries warranties that the title is good, the transfer is proper, and there are no liens and encumbrances other than the ones noted.

Water Quality Act One of the predecessors to today's federal water pollution control statutory scheme.

Water rights System of priority for water use.

Wetlands Protected areas near water; formerly known as swamps.

Will Legal document that transfers property rights from testator to named beneficiaries.

Workout In commercial real estate loans, the process of adjusting loan repayment because of borrower's financial difficulties.

Z

Zoning Process of regulating land use by designating areas of a community for certain uses.

Zoning commission Governmental agency responsible for developing the zoning plan.

CASE INDEX

Note: Page numbers in *italics* refer to illustrations.
Page numbers followed by "n" indicate footnotes.

A

B

C

D

E

F

G

Q

R

S

SUBJECT INDEX

Note: Page numbers in *italics* refer to illustrations. Page numbers followed by an "n" indicate footnotes.

A

B

C

E

G

H

I

J

K

L

T

U